The Founders' Constitution

The Founders' Constitution

Edited by
Philip B. Kurland
and
Ralph Lerner

VOLUME FOUR

Article 2, Section 2,

through Article 7

Liberty Fund

This book is published by Liberty Fund, Inc., a foundation established to encourage study of the ideal of a society of free and responsible individuals.

The cuneiform inscription that serves as our logo and as the design motif for our endpapers is the earliest-known written appearance of the word "freedom" (*amagi*), or "liberty." It is taken from a clay document written about 2300 B.C. in the Sumerian city-state of Lagash.

Philip B. Kurland was the William R. Kenan, Jr., Distinguished Service Professor in the College and professor in the Law School, University of Chicago.

Ralph Lerner is the Benjamin Franklin Professor in the College and professor in the Committee on Social Thought, University of Chicago.

Library of Congress Cataloging-in-Publication Data

The Founders' Constitution / edited by Philip B. Kurland and Ralph Lerner.
  p.   cm.
  Originally published: Chicago: University of Chicago Press, 1987.
  Includes bibliographical references and index.
  Contents: v. 1. Major themes—v. 2. Preamble through Article 1, Section 8, Clause 4—v. 3. Article 1, Section 8, Clause 5, through Article 2, Section 1—v. 4. Article 2, Section 2, through Article 7—v. 5. Amendments I–XII.
  ISBN 0-86597-279-6 (set: pbk.: alk. paper)—ISBN 0-86597-302-4 (v. 1: pbk.: alk. paper)—ISBN 0-86597-303-2 (v. 2: pbk.: alk. paper)
  1. Constitutional history—United States—Sources. I. Kurland, Philip B. II. Lerner, Ralph.

KF4502 .F68 2000
342.73′029—dc21   99-052811

ISBN 0-86597-304-0 (v. 3 pbk.: alk. paper)
ISBN 0-86597-305-9 (v. 4 pbk.: alk. paper)
ISBN 0-86597-306-7 (v. 5 pbk.: alk. paper)

Liberty Fund, Inc.
11301 North Meridian Street
Carmel, IN 46032

Cover design by Erin Kirk New, Watkinsville, Georgia

Printed and bound by Sheridan Books, Chelsea, Michigan

To Joshua and Jesse

Contents

Note on References

References to documents follow a consistent pattern both in the cross-references (in the detailed tables of contents) and in the indexes. Where a document in volume 1 is being cited, reference is to chapter and document numbers: thus, for example, ch. 15, no. 23. Where the document is to be found in one of the subsequent volumes, which are organized by Constitutional article, section, and clause, or by amendment, reference is in this mode: 1.8.8, no. 12; or, Amend. I (religion), no. 66. Each document heading consists of its serial number in that particular chapter; an author and title (or letter writer and addressee, or speaker and forum); date of publication, writing, or speaking; and, where not given in the first part of the heading, an identification of the source of the text being reprinted. These sources are presented in short-title form, the author of the source volume being presumed (unless otherwise noted) to be the first proper name mentioned in the document heading. Thus, for example, in the case of a letter from Alexander Hamilton to Governor George Clinton, "Papers 1:425–28" would be understood to refer to the edition fully described under "Hamilton, Papers" in the list of short titles found at the back of each volume.

A somewhat different form has been followed in the case of the proceedings of the Constitutional Convention that met in Philadelphia from late May to mid-September of 1787. As might be expected, we have included many extracts from the various records kept by the participants while they were deliberating over the shape and character of a new charter of government. For any particular chapter or unit, those extracts have been grouped as a single document, titled "Records of the Federal Convention," and placed undated in that chapter's proper time slot. The bracketed note that precedes each segment within that selection of the "Records" lists the volume and opening page numbers in the printed source (Max Farrand's edition), the name of the participant whose notes are here being reproduced (overwhelmingly Madison, but also Mason, Yates, others, and the Convention's official Journal), and the month and day of 1787 when the reported transaction took place.

Article 2, Section 2, Clause 1

The President shall be Commander in Chief of the Army and Navy of the United States, and of the Militia of the several States, when called into the actual Service of the United States; he may require the Opinion, in writing, of the principal Officer in each of the executive Departments, upon any Subject relating to the Duties of their respective Offices, and he shall have Power to grant Reprieves and Pardons for Offenses against the United States, except in Cases of Impeachment.

1

Records of the Federal Convention

[*1:66; Madison, 1 June*]

Mr. Madison thought it would be proper, before a choice shd. be made between a unity and a plurality in the Executive, to fix the extent of the Executive authority; that as certain powers were in their nature Executive, and must be given to that departmt. whether administered by one or more persons, a definition of their extent would assist the judgment in determining how far they might be safely entrusted to a single officer. He accordingly moved that so much of the clause before the Committee as related to the powers of the Executive shd. be struck out & that after the words "that a national Executive ought to be instituted" there be inserted the words following viz, "with power to carry into effect. the national laws. to appoint to offices in cases not otherwise provided for, and to execute such other powers not Legislative nor Judiciary in their nature as may from time to time be delegated by the national Legislature". The words "not legislative nor judiciary in their nature" were added to the proposed amendment in consequence of a suggestion by Genl Pinkney that improper powers might otherwise be delegated,

Mr. Wilson seconded this motion

Mr. Pinkney moved to amend the amendment by striking out the last member of it; viz. "and to execute such other powers not Legislative nor Judiciary in their nature as may from time to time be delegated." He said they were unnecessary, the object of them being included in the "power to carry into effect the national laws".

Mr. Randolph seconded the motion.

Mr. Madison did not know that the words were absolutely necessary, or even the preceding words. "to appoint to offices" &c. the whole being perhaps included in the first member of the proposition. He did not however see any inconveniency in retaining them, and cases might happen in which they might serve to prevent doubts and misconstructions.

In consequence of the motion of Mr. Pinkney, the question on Mr. Madison's motion was divided; and the words objected to by Mr. Pinkney struck out; by the votes of Connecticut. N. Y. N. J. Pena. Del. N. C. & Geo: agst. Mass. Virga. & S. Carolina the preceding part of the motion being first agreed to: Connecticut divided, all the other States in the affirmative.

[1:113; Mason, 4 June]

We have not yet been able to define the powers of the Executive, and however moderately some gentlemen may talk or think upon the subject, I believe there is a general tendency to a strong Executive, and I am inclined to think a strong Executive necessary. If strong and extensive powers are vested in the Executive, and that executive consists only of one person, the government will of course degenerate (for I will call it degeneracy) into a monarchy—a government so contrary to the genius of the people that they will reject even the appearance of it.

[4:15; Mason, 4 June]

It is not yet determined how the Executive is to be regulated whether it is to act solely from its own Judgment, or with the Advice of others whether there is, or is not to be a Council annexed to it; and if a Council, how far their Advice shall operate in controuling the Judgment of the supreme magistracy—If there is no Council of State, and the executive power be vested in a single Person; what are the Provisions for its proper Operation, upon casual Disability by sickness, or otherwise.—These are Subjects which must come under our Consideration; and perhaps some of the most important Objections would be obviated by placing the executive Power in the hands of three, instead of one Person.

There is also to be a Council of Revision; invested, in a great Measure, with a Power of Negative upon the Laws; and an Idea has been suggested, either within or without doors, that this Council should be formed of the principal

Officers of the State,—I presume of the members of the Treasury Board, the Board of War, the Navy Board, and the Department for foreign Affairs: it is unnecessary, if not improper, to examine this part of the Subject now, but I will venture to hazard an Opinion, when it comes to be thoroughly investigated, that we can hardly find worse Materials out of which to create a Council of Revision; or more improper or unsafe Hands, in which to place the Power of a Negative upon our Laws.—It is proposed, I think, Sir, in the Plan upon your Table, that this Council of Revision shall be formed out of the Members of the Judiciary Departments joined with the Executive; and I am inclined to think, when the Subject shall be taken up, it may be demonstrated, that this will be the wisest and safest mode of constituting this important Council of Revision.—But the foederal inferior Courts of Justice must, I presume, be fixed in the several respective States, and consequently most of them at a great Distance from the Seat of the foederal Government: the almost continual Operation of the Council of Revision upon the Acts of the national Parliament, and upon their Negative of the Acts of the several State legislatures, will require that this Council should be easily and speedily convened; and consequently, that only the Judges of the Supreme foederal Court, fixed near the Seat of Government, can be Members of it; their Number will be small: by placing the Executive Power in three Persons, instead of one, we shall not only increase the Number of the Council of Revision (which I have endeavoured to show will want increasing), but by giving to each of the three a Vote in the Council of Revision, we shall increase the Strength of the Executive, in that particular Circumstance, in which it will most want Strength—in the Power of defending itself against the Encroachments of the Legislature.—These, I must acknowledge, are with me, weighty Considerations for vesting the Executive rather in three than in one Person.

[1:244; Madison, 15 June]

4. Resd. . . . that the Executives besides their general authority to execute the federal acts ought to appoint all federal officers not otherwise provided for, & to direct all military operations; provided that none of the persons composing the federal Executive shall on any occasion take command of any troops, so as personally to conduct any enterprise as General, or in other capacity.

[1:292; Madison, 18 June]

IV. The supreme Executive authority of the United States to be vested in a Governour to be elected to serve during good behaviour—the election to be made by Electors chosen by the people in the Election Districts aforesaid— The authorities & functions of the Executive to be as follows: to have a negative on all laws about to be passed, and the execution of all laws passed, to have the direction of war when authorized or begun; to have with the advice and approbation of the Senate the power of making all treaties; to have the sole appointment of the heads or chief officers of the departments of Finance, War and Foreign Affairs; to have the nomination of all other officers (Ambassadors to foreign Nations included) subject to the approbation or rejection of the Senate; to have the power of pardoning all offences except Treason; which he shall not pardon without the approbation of the Senate.

[2:135, 145, 146, 157, 171; *Committee of Detail*]

—In the Presidt. the executive Authority of the U.S. shall be vested.—His Powers and Duties—He shall have a Right to advise with the Heads of the different Departments at his Council

· · · · ·

5. His powers shall be
  1. to carry into execution the national laws.
  2. to (command and superintend the militia,) to be Commander in Chief of the Land & Naval Forces of the Union & of the Militia of the sevl. states
  (3. to direct their discipline)
  (4. to direct the executives of the states to call them or any part for the support of the national government.)*

· · · · ·

The power of pardoning vested in the Executive (which) his pardon shall not however, be pleadable to an Impeachmt.*

· · · · ·

That the Executive direct all military Operations
. . . the Executive shall be authorised to enforce and compel Obedience by calling forth the Powers of the United States. . . .

There shall be a President, in which the Ex. Authority of the U.S. shall be vested. It shall be his Duty to inform the Legislature of the Condition of U. S. so far as may respect his Department—to recommend Matters to their Consideration—to correspond with the Executives of the several States—to attend to the Execution of the Laws of the U. S.—to transact Affairs with the Officers of Government, civil and military—to expedite all such Measures as may be resolved on by the Legislature—to inspect the Departments of foreign Affairs—War—Treasury—Admiralty—to reside where the Legislature shall sit—to commission all Officers, and keep the Great Seal of U. S.—He shall, by Virtue of his Office, be Commander in chief of the Land Forces of U. S. and Admiral of their Navy—He shall have Power to convene the Legislature on extraordinary Occasions—to prorogue them, provided such Prorogation shall not exceed   Days in the space of any —He may suspend Officers, civil and military

· · · · ·

He shall have power to grant Reprieves and Pardons; but his Pardon shall not be pleadable in Bar of an Impeachment. He shall be Commander in Chief of the Army and Navy of the United States, and of the Militia of the Several States.

[2:328; *Madison, 18 Aug.*]

Mr. Elseworth observed that a Council had not yet been provided for the President. He conceived there ought to

*[EDITORS' NOTE.—Words in parentheses were crossed out in the original.]

be one. His proposition was that it should be composed of the President of the Senate– the Chief-Justice, and the Ministers as they might be estabd. for the departments of foreign & domestic affairs, war finance, and marine, who should advise but not conclude the President.

Mr Pinkney wished the proposition to lie over, as notice had been given for a like purpose by Mr. Govr. Morris who was not then on the floor. His own idea was that the President shd. be authorized to call for advice or not as he might chuse. Give him an able Council and it will thwart him; a weak one and he will shelter himself under their sanction.

Mr Gerry was agst. letting the heads of the departments, particularly of finance have any thing to do in business connected with legislation. He mentioned the Chief Justice also as particularly exceptionable. These men will also be so taken up with other matters as to neglect their own proper duties.

Mr. Dickenson urged that the great appointments should be made by the Legislature, in which case they might properly be consulted by the Executive—but not if made by the Executive himself—This subject by general Consent lay over; & the House proceeded to the clause "To raise armies".

[2:342; *Madison, 20 Aug.*]

Mr. Govr. Morris 2ded. by Mr. Pinkney submitted the following propositions which were in like manner referred to the Committee of Detail.

"To assist the President in conducting the Public affairs there shall be a Council of State composed of the following officers—1. The Chief Justice of the Supreme Court, who shall from time to time recommend such alterations of and additions to the laws of the U. S. as may in his opinion be necessary to the due administration of Justice, and such as may promote useful learning and inculcate sound morality throughout the Union: He shall be President of the Council in the absence of the President

· · · · ·

The President may from time to time submit any matter to the discussion of the Council of State, and he may require the written opinions of any one or more of the members: But he shall in all cases exercise his own judgment, and either Conform to such opinions or not as he may think proper; and every officer abovementioned shall be responsible for his opinion on the affairs relating to his particular Department.

[2:367; *Journal, 22 Aug.*]

after the 2nd section of the 10th article insert the following as a 3rd section.

"The President of the United States shall have a Privy-Council which shall consist of the President of the Senate, the Speaker of the House of representatives, the Chief-Justice of the Supreme-Court, and the principal Officer in the respective departments of foreign affairs, domestic-affairs, War, Marine, and Finance, as such departments of office shall from time to time be established—whose duty it shall be to advise him in matters respecting the execution of his Office, which he shall think proper to lay before them: But their advice shall not conclude him, nor affect his responsibility for the measures which he shall adopt"

[2:411; *Journal, 25 Aug.*]

It was moved and seconded to insert the words "except in cases of impeachment" after the word "pardons" 2 sect. 10 article

which passed in the affirmative

On the question to agree to the following clause

"but his pardon shall not be pleadable in bar"

it passed in the negative [Ayes—4; noes—6.]

[2:419; *Madison, 25 Aug.*]

Mr. Sherman moved to amend the "power to grant reprieves & pardon" so as to read "to grant reprieves until the ensuing session of the Senate, and pardons with consent of the Senate."

On the question

N—H— no. Mas. no. Ct. ay— Pa no Md. no. Va. no. N. C. no. S. C. no. Geo. no. [Ayes—1; noes—8.]

"except in cases of impeachment" inserted nem: con: after "pardon"

On the question to agree to—"but his pardon shall not be pleadable in bar"

N.H. ay—Mas—no. Ct. no— Pa. no— Del. no. Md. ay. Va. no. N— C— ay— S. C. ay— Geo. no. [Ayes—4; noes—6.]

[2:426; *Madison, 27 Aug.*]

Mr. Govr. Morris. The question of a Council was considered in the Committee, where it was judged that the Presidt. by persuading his Council—to concur in his wrong measures, would acquire their protection for them—

Mr. Wilson approved of a Council, in preference to making the Senate a party to appointmts.

Mr. Dickinson was for a Council. It wd. be a singular thing if the measures of the Executive were not to undergo some previous discussion before the President

Mr Madison was in favor of the instruction to the Committee proposed by Col. Mason.

The motion of Mr. Mason was negatived. Maryd. ay. S. C. ay. Geo. ay—N. H. no. Mas. no. Ct: no. N. J. no Pa. no. Del. no. Va. no. N C no. [Ayes—3; noes—8.]

On the question, "authorizing the President to call for the opinions of the Heads of Departments, in writing": it passed in the affirmative, N. H. only being no. The clause was then unanimously agreed to.

[2:564; *Madison, 10 Sept.*]

Mr. Randolph moved to refer to the Committee also a motion relating to pardons in cases of Treason—which was agreed to nem: con:

[2:575, 599; *Committee of Style*]

He shall have power to grant reprieves and pardons except in cases of impeachment. He shall be Commander in Chief of the Army and Navy of the United States, and of the Militia of the several States when called into the actual service of the United States; and may require the opinion

in writing of the principal officer in each of the executive departments upon any subject relating to the duties of their respective offices.

. . . . .

Art X. sect. 2. being resumed,

Mr. L. Martin moved to insert the words "after conviction" after the words "reprieves and pardons"

Mr. Wilson objected that pardon before conviction might be necessary in order to obtain the testimony of accomplices. He stated the case of forgeries in which this might particularly happen.—Mr. L. Martin withdrew his motion.

Mr. Sherman moved to amend the clause giving the Executive the command of the Militia, so as to read "and of the Militia of the several States, *when called into the actual service of the U— S—*" and on the Question

N—H. ay. Mas. abst. Ct. ay. N—J. abst Pa ay. Del. no. Md ay. Va. ay. N— C. abst. S. C— no. Geo— ay, [Ayes—6; noes—2; absent—3.]

[2:499; *Madison, 4 Sept.*]

(8) After the words "into the service of the U S." in sect. 2. art: 10. add "and may require the opinion in writing of the principal Officer in each of the Executive Departments, upon any subject relating to the duties of their respective offices."

[2:533; *Journal, 7 Sept.*]

It was moved and seconded to postpone the consideration of the 4 sect. of the report in order to take up the following.

That it be an instruction to the Committee of the States to prepare a clause or clauses for establishing an Executive Council, as a Council of State, for the President of the United States, to consist of six Members, two of which from the Eastern, two from the middle, and two from the southern States with a rotation and duration of office similar to that of the Senate; such Council to be appointed by the Legislature or by the Senate.

On the question to postpone

it passed in the negative [Ayes—3; noes—8.]

[To agree to the last question Ayes—11; noes—0.]

[2:541; *Madison, 7 Sept.*]

"and may require the opinion in writing of the principal officer in each of the Executive Departments, upon any subject relating to the duties of their respective offices." being before the House

Col: Mason said that in rejecting a Council to the President we were about to try an experiment on which the most despotic Governments had never ventured—The Grand Signor himself had his Divan. He moved to postpone the consideration of the clause in order to take up the following

"That it be an instruction to the Committee of the States to prepare a clause or clauses for establishing an Executive Council, as a Council of State for the President of the U. States, to consist of six members, two of which from the Eastern, two from the middle, and two from the Southern

States, with a Rotation and duration of office similar to those of the Senate; such Council to be appointed by the Legislature or by the Senate".

Doctor Franklin 2ded. the motion. We seemed he said too much to fear cabals in appointments by a number, and to have too much confidence in those of single persons. Experience shewed that caprice, the intrigues of favorites & mistresses, &c were nevertheless the means most prevalent in monarchies. among instances of abuse in such modes of appointment, he mentioned the many bad Governors appointed in G. B. for the Colonies. He thought a Council would not only be a check on a bad President but be a relief to a good one.

Sect. 2. The president shall be commander in chief of the army and navy of the United States, and of the militia of the several States: he may require the opinion, in writing, of the principal officer in each of the executive departments, upon any subject relating to the duties of their respective offices, when called into the actual service of the United States, and he shall have power to grant reprieves and pardons for offences against the United States, except in cases of impeachment.

[2:626; Madison, 15 Sept.]

Art. II. sect. 2. "he shall have power to grant reprieves and pardons for offences against the U.S. &c"

Mr Randolph moved to "except cases of treason". The prerogative of pardon in these cases was too great a trust. The President may himself be guilty. The Traytors may be his own instruments.

Col: Mason supported the motion.

Mr Govr Morris had rather there should be no pardon for treason, than let the power devolve on the Legislature.

Mr Wilson. Pardon is necessary for cases of treason, and is best placed in the hands of the Executive. If he be himself a party to the guilt he can be impeached and prosecuted.

Mr. King thought it would be inconsistent with the Constitutional separation of the Executive & Legislative powers to let the prerogative be exercised by the latter—A Legislative body is utterly unfit for the purpose. They are governed too much by the passions of the moment. In Massachusetts, one assembly would have hung all the insurgents in that State: the next was equally disposed to pardon them all. He suggested the expedient of requiring the concurrence of the Senate in Acts of Pardon.

Mr. Madison admitted the force of objections to the Legislature, but the pardon of treasons was so peculiarly improper for the President that he should acquiesce in the transfer of it to the former, rather than leave it altogether in the hands of the latter. He would prefer to either an association of the Senate as a Council of advice, with the President.

Mr Randolph could not admit the Senate into a share of the Power. the great danger to liberty lay in a combination between the President & that body—

Col: Mason. The Senate has already too much power— There can be no danger of too much lenity in legislative pardons, as the Senate must con concur, & the President moreover can require ⅔ of both Houses

On the motion of Mr. Randolph

N. H.no—Mas. no—Ct. divd. N— J— no. Pa. no—Del. no. Md no—Va ay—N—C. no—S. C. no. Geo—ay. [Ayes—2; noes—8; divided—1.]

[2:638; Mason, 15 Sept.]

The President of the United States has no Constitutional Council, a thing unknown in any safe and regular government. He will therefore be unsupported by proper information and advice, and will generally be directed by minions and favorites; or he will become a tool to the Senate— or a Council of State will grow out of the principal officers of the great departments; the worst and most dangerous of all ingredients for such a Council in a free country; for they may be induced to join in any dangerous or oppressive measures, to shelter themselves, and prevent an inquiry into their own misconduct in office. Whereas, had a constitutional council been formed (as was proposed) of six members, viz.: two from the Eastern, two from the Middle, and two from the Southern States, to be appointed by vote of the States in the House of Representatives, with the same duration and rotation of office as the Senate, the executive would always have had safe and proper information and advice; the president of such a council might have acted as Vice-President of the United States *pro tempore*, upon any vacancy or disability of the chief magistrate; and long continued sessions of the Senate, would in a great measure have been prevented. From this fatal defect has arisen the improper power of the Senate in the appointment of public officers, and the alarming dependence and connection between that branch of the legislature and the supreme Executive.

Hence also sprung that unnecessary and dangerous officer the Vice-President, who for want of other employment is made president of the Senate, thereby dangerously blending the executive and legislative powers, besides always giving to some one of the States an unnecessary and unjust preeminence over the others.

The President of the United States has the unrestrained power of granting pardons for treason, which may be sometimes exercised to screen from punishment those whom he had secretly instigated to commit the crime, and thereby prevent a discovery of his own guilt.

5

COMMANDER IN CHIEF

2

WILLIAM BLACKSTONE, COMMENTARIES 1:254
1765

II. The king is considered, in the next place, as the generalissimo, or the first in military command, within the kingdom. The great end of society is to protect the weakness of individuals by the united strength of the community: and the principle use of government is to direct that united strength in the best and most effectual manner, to answer the end proposed. Monarchical government is allowed to be the fittest of any for this purpose: it follows therefore, from the very end of it's institution, that in a monarchy the military power must be trusted in the hands of the prince.

3

A GEORGIAN
15 Nov. 1787
Storing 5.9.10

Art. 2, sect. 2. If the president should at any time be incompetent for military command in war, etc. (for he cannot be prevented from taking the chief command when it is his right) and should choose to take the command notwithstanding, what ill consequences may not result? for we know there are many wise and good men, and very fit for civil rulers, but are quite unfit for the command of armies and navies. Would it not be better said, "That the president, with the advice of both Houses of Congress, shall be commander in chief, etc. etc. etc." By this clause, ought we not to look into the troubles in Holland, and see how the Stadtholder (laying aside his hereditary claims) behaved, contrary to the positive orders of the States General, his masters, during our late glorious revolution? and has he not accumulated powers destructive to their commonwealth, and which are now the sole cause of their present troubles? and should we not avoid the like by making the president ineligible to the office as many years as you allow him to hold it? and that he only be commander in chief, and nominate and appoint all officers, civil and military, by and with the advice of the senate, etc. only? Therefore I would advise the clause, *"But the Congress may by law vest the appointment of such inferior officers as they think proper in the president alone,"* etc. be struck out.

4

LUTHER MARTIN, GENUINE INFORMATION
1788
Storing 2.4.85

Objections were made to that part of this article, by which the President is appointed commander in chief of the army and navy of the United States, and of the militia of the several States, and it was wished to be so far restrained, that he should not command in person; but this could not be obtained. The power given to the President of granting reprieves and pardons, was also thought extremely dangerous, and as such opposed—The President thereby has the power of pardoning those who are guilty of treason, as well as of other offences; it was said that no treason was so likely to take place as that in which the President himself might be engaged—The attempt to assume to himself powers not given by the constitution, and establish himself in regal authority; in which attempt a provision is made for him to secure from punishment the creatures of his ambition, the associates and abettors of his treasonable practices, by granting them pardons should they be defeated in their attempts to subvert the constitution.

5

ALEXANDER HAMILTON, FEDERALIST, NO. 74, 500
25 Mar. 1788

The President of the United States is to be "Commander in Chief of the army and navy of the United States, and of the militia of the several States *when called into the actual service* of the United States." The propriety of this provision is so evident in itself; and it is at the same time so consonant to the precedents of the State constitutions in general, that little need be said to explain or enforce it. Even those of them, which have in other respects coupled the Chief Magistrate with a Council, have for the most part concentred the military authority in him alone. Of all the cares or concerns of government, the direction of war most peculiarly demands those qualities which distinguish the exercise of power by a single hand. The direction of war implies the direction of the common strength; and the power of directing and employing the common strength, forms an usual and essential part in the definition of the executive authority.

6

DEBATE IN VIRGINIA RATIFYING CONVENTION
18 June 1788
Elliot 3:496–98

Mr. GEORGE MASON, animadverting on the magnitude of the powers of the President, was alarmed at the additional power of commanding the army in person. He admitted the propriety of his being commander-in-chief, so far as to give orders and have a general superintendency; but he thought it would be dangerous to let him command in person, without any restraint, as he might make a bad use of it. He was, then, clearly of opinion that the consent of a majority of both houses of Congress should be required before he could take the command in person. If at any time it should be necessary that he should take the personal command, either on account of his superior abilities or other cause, then Congress would agree to it; and all dangers would be obviated by requiring their consent. He called to gentlemen's recollection the extent of what the late commander-in-chief might have done, from his great abilities, and the strong attachment of both officers and soldiers towards him, if, instead of being disinterested, he had been an ambitious man. So disinterested and amiable a character as General Washington might never command again. The possibility of danger ought to be guarded against. Although he did not disapprove of the President's consultation with the principle executive officers, yet he objected to the want of an executive council, which he conceived to be necessary to any regular free government. There being none such, he apprehended a council would arise out of the Senate, which, for want of real responsibility, he thought dangerous. You will please, says he, to recollect that removal from office, and future disqualification to hold any office, are the only consequences of conviction on impeachment. Now, I conceive that the President ought not to have the power of pardoning, because he may frequently pardon crimes which were advised by himself. It may happen, at some future day, that he will establish a monarchy, and destroy the republic. If he has the power of granting pardons before indictment, or conviction, may he not stop inquiry and prevent detection? The case of treason ought, at least, to be excepted. This is a weighty objection with me.

Mr. LEE reminded his honorable friend that it did not follow, of necessity, that the President should command in person; that he was to command as a civil officer, and might only take the command when he was a man of military talents, and the public safety required it. He thought the power of pardoning, as delineated in the Constitution, could be nowhere so well placed as in the President. It was so in the government of New York, and had been found safe and convenient.

Mr. MASON replied, that he did not mean that the President was of necessity to command, but he might if he pleased; and if he was an ambitious man, he might make a dangerous use of it.

Mr. GEORGE NICHOLAS hoped the committee would not advert to this; that the army and navy were to be raised by Congress, and not by the President. It was on the same footing with our state government; for the governor, with the council, was to imbody the militia, but, when actually imbodied, they were under the sole command of the governor. The instance adduced was not similar. General Washington was not a President. As to possible danger, any commander might attempt to pervert what was intended for the common defence of the community to its destruction. The President, at the end of four years, was to relinquish all his offices. But if any other person was to have the command, the time would not be limited.

Mr. MASON answered, that it did not resemble the state Constitution, because the governor did not possess such extensive powers as the President, and had no influence over the navy. The liberty of the people had been destroyed by those who were military commanders only. The danger here was greater by the junction of great civil powers to the command of the army and fleet. Although Congress are to raise the army, said he, no security arises from that; for, in time of war, they must and ought to raise an army, which will be numerous, or otherwise, according to the nature of the war, and then the President is to command without any control.

7

DEBATE IN NORTH CAROLINA RATIFYING CONVENTION
28 July 1788
Elliot 4:107–8, 114–15

Mr. IREDELL. Mr. Chairman, I was in hopes that some other gentleman would have spoken to this clause. It conveys very important powers, and ought not to be passed by. I beg leave, in as few words as possible, to speak my sentiments upon it. I believe most of the governors of the different states have powers similar to those of the President. In almost every country, the executive has the command of the military forces. From the nature of the thing, the command of armies ought to be delegated to one person only. The secrecy, despatch, and decision, which are necessary in military operations, can only be expected from one person. The President, therefore, is to command the military forces of the United States, and this power I think a proper one; at the same time it will be found to be sufficiently guarded. A very material difference may be observed between this power, and the authority of the king of Great Britain under similar circumstances. The king of Great Britain is not only the commander-in-chief of the land and naval forces, but has power, in time of war, to raise fleets and armies. He has also authority to declare war. The President has not the power of declaring war by his own authority, nor that of raising fleets and armies. These powers are vested in other hands. The power of declaring war is expressly given to Congress, that is, to the two branches of the legislature—the Senate, composed of representatives of the state legislatures, the House of Representatives, deputed by the people at large. They have also expressly delegated to them the powers of raising and supporting armies, and of providing and maintaining a navy.

With regard to the militia, it must be observed, that though he has the command of them when called into the actual service of the United States, yet he has not the power of calling them out. The power of calling them out is vested in Congress, for the purpose of executing the laws of the Union. When the militia are called out for any purpose, some person must command them; and who so proper as that person who has the best evidence of his possessing the general confidence of the people? I trust, therefore, that the power of commanding the militia, when called forth into the actual service of the United States, will not be objected to.

. . . . .

Mr. MILLER acknowledged that the explanation of this clause by the member from Edenton had obviated some objections which he had to it; but still he could not entirely approve of it. He could not see the necessity of vesting this power in the President. He thought that his influence would be too great in the country, and particularly over the military, by being the commander-in-chief of the army, navy, and militia. He thought he could too easily abuse such extensive powers, and was of opinion that Congress ought to have power to direct the motions of the army. He considered it as a defect in the Constitution, that it was not expressly provided that Congress should have the direction of the motions of the army.

Mr. SPAIGHT answered, that it was true that the command of the army and navy was given to the President; but that Congress, who had the power of raising armies, could certainly prevent any abuse of that authority in the President—that they alone had the means of supporting armies, and that the President was impeachable if he in any manner abused his trust. He was surprised that any objection should be made to giving the command of the army to one man; that it was well known that the direction of an army could not be properly exercised by a numerous body of men; that Congress had, in the last war, given the exclusive command of the army to the commander-in-chief, and that if they had not done so, perhaps the independence of America would not have been established.

8

HOUSE OF REPRESENTATIVES, PROTECTION OF TRADE
22 June 1797
Annals 7:363–66

Mr. BROOKS did not apprehend any danger from leaving it in the power of the President to make use of the frigates as he pleased.

Mr. GALLATIN said, that after having determined that the three frigates should be got ready for sea, it became necessary to say upon what business they should be employed. There might be different opinions on the subject, but it was necessary to define the object. If not, they had reason to apprehend, from his Speech, that the President would employ them as convoys. The difficulties attending such an employ had been shown when the subject of galleys was under consideration; they were so many that the peace of the country would be greatly endangered by such an employment of the frigates. The danger was greatly increased by the disputed article of our treaty with France, which the President would be under the necessity of enforcing.

In ordinary times he said, the principle of the gentleman from New Jersey was a good one. If we had frigates in service, they were not from day to day to say how they should be employed; but, under our present circumstances, he thought the object ought to be defined, and that they ought to depart from the maxim laid down by that gentleman.

Mr. SEWALL was in favor of striking out the clause. If the President were to be limited at all he should have no objection to limit him with respect to convoys, from the incompetency of three vessels to that end; but these frigates were to be considered as the public force, as the navy of the United States. It was true, it was a small one; but it was such as Congress had thought proper to raise, and put in the power of the President. And why should this power be limited? It seemed as if they supposed, from his natural disposition, or from some other cause, he would abuse it, by employing the vessels contrary to law, and thereby involve the country in war.

The Constitution, Mr. S. said, had defined him to be commander-in-chief of the navy, and having a navy the command of course devolved upon him. If those vessels were but for a particular purpose, they might designate their object, but they were begun in 1794, and the act gave the President authority to "equip and employ these vessels." If at that period, when, in the opinion of many gentlemen, there was a greater prospect of war than at present, no object was pointed out for the vessels, he did not see why any should now be pointed out. With respect to the disputed articles in the French Treaty, they had already expressed an opinion of the President, which, he doubted not, would have its effect.

Mr. WILLIAMS thought that, having given the President

a discretionary power, in the first section of the bill, they ought not now to take it from him; because, if he did not see occasion to man the frigates, he would never do it; but if he did see occasion for manning them, they ought not to take from him the power of employing them as he pleased. He was, therefore, in favor of the motion of the gentleman from New Jersey.

Mr. GILES asked whether to ascertain the object upon which these vessels should be employed was a Legislative or an Executive act? It was certainly legislative. They ought to say to the President—Here is the force, and there is the object. It was said they had already given an opinion to the President, with respect to the disputed articles in the French Treaty; he now wished a law to be passed in conformity to that opinion.

He said, they were often charged with a want of confidence in the present President. He was free to own he had not much confidence in the President. His Speech, at the opening of the session, had destroyed all his confidence; but, however high their opinion might be of the Executive, they ought not to lodge improper powers in his hands.

Mr. HARPER was in favor of the motion. He wished to provide force, and not to direct the use of it; he believed this was the object for which they were called together. He was willing to leave the use of this force to the President, because he could employ it in a manner only applicable to peace; to employ it otherwise would be a breach of his power. He, therefore, could not repel any violation of our rights by force, except previously authorized by Congress.

The gentleman from Virginia, Mr. Harper said, need not to have told them that he had no confidence in the present Executive. He might have said in no Executive; for it was well known he never missed going out of the way to say rude things of the late President; but he did not believe this was the best way of discharging their duty. He believed the public cared little what his opinion of the President was; he thought they ought to do their duty and leave the President to do his. Mr. H. denied that they had the right to direct the public force. If we were at war with Great Britain, they should have no right to say to the President, attack Canada or the Islands. The use of this force must be left to the President; if he abuses it, upon his own head would lie the responsibility, and not upon them.

Mr. S. SMITH had not made up his mind on the subject. If the power of the employing the frigates was wholly left with the President, though he had not the power of declaring war, yet he might so employ them as to lead to war, particularly with respect to the French Treaty articles. On the other hand, it seemed to be a poor employment for these frigates, after all the expense which they had cost, to keep them within the jurisdiction of the United States. They could not cruise there, indeed, without danger of running on the shoals. Understanding, as he did, that by voting for the striking out of this clause, he should not be precluded from voting for the amendment of the gentleman from Virginia; if he should conclude to do so, he should vote for striking out the section in question.

Mr. MACON proposed a clause similar in effect to that proposed by the gentleman from Virginia to be inserted in place of one struck out, but the Chairman declared it not in order.

Mr. DAYTON said, that those gentlemen who were not prepared to vote for retaining the eleventh section, must be prepared to say these frigates shall be employed as convoys. It was to avoid this, that he had moved to strike it out. He again expressed his wish that the direction of this force might be left with the President.

Mr. GILES declared his intention of voting for striking out the section, and to risk the insertion of another afterwards.

The question for striking out was carried without a division.

Mr. GILES then moved to insert the section before proposed by Mr. MACON, to confine the use of our frigates to the protection of our coasts, and commerce within the jurisdiction of the United States.

Mr. OTIS did not think that the object of the mover of this amendment would be obtained by it, since he believed vessels would be as much exposed to danger within as without the jurisdiction of the United States. He trusted they should leave this business to the President; for whatever personal objections gentlemen might have to him, (because he was not the man of their choice,) he believed the people at large would be willing he should have this power. Indeed, he thought whatever it might display of candor in gentlemen to say they had no confidence in the first officer of Government, it had very little of discretion in it. It was to destroy one of the objects of the session, which was to show to the world that we are not a divided people.

Mr. O. did not say that Congress had not a right to designate the object of this force; but he believed it would not be convenient; for, said he, suppose either of the Barbary States were to declare war against us. (and they all knew there was no certain reliance upon their observance of treaties,) should not the President have a right to send those vessels into the Mediterranean? Or, suppose we wanted to send an Ambassador to a foreign country, or despatches to our Minister residing there, shall we, said he, limit his power in this respect?

It seemed to be the object of gentlemen, Mr. O. said, to hang a dead weight upon every measure, to prevent any thing effectual from being done, that an idea might go abroad that the President had called them together unnecessarily. If gentlemen could succeed in this, the people might adopt their opinion, and believe that the President was unworthy of their good opinion.

He thought, when all the world was in arms, and we did not know how soon we might be involved in the calamity, it behooved us to be upon our guard, and to give the President such powers as should enable him to take proper measures of defence against any attack that might be made upon us.

Mr. MACON thought every thing which had been introduced about confidence or the want of it, in the President, was extremely irrelevant and improper. For gentlemen to charge others with a want of confidence in the President, because they happened to disagree in opinion, was extraordinary conduct. His reason for proposing the present amendment, was to prevent these vessels being sent to the Mediterranean or the West Indies. He read an extract from the law of 1794, to show that the object of the frigates was there designated to be against the Algerines. His object was now, that they should be employed on the coast, and no where else. If a provision of this kind was not agreed to, they knew, from his Speech, upon what business the President would employ them. He had given his opinion to the House with candor, and he wished the House to be equally explicit.

Mr. GALLATIN observed, it seemed to be the opinion of the gentleman from Massachusetts, that if they defined the object upon which these vessels were to be employed, they should be chargeable with disrespect to the President. We have, or we have not a right, said Mr. G., to define the object. If we have not the right, we ought not to exercise it; but if we had the right, there could be no disrespect shown to the President, by an exercise of that right. It might be improper, but could not be disrespectful. If once such an argument as this were admitted, it would be introduced on every occasion when it would have weight. Indeed, the gentleman saw that such an assertion was likely to have its weight on this question, and therefore introduced it. He wished to know whether the clause from the Senate did not define the object? and if so, whether that body could be charged with wanting respect for the President?

The object of the frigates had never been defined, for a good reason; because they were never ordered to be manned till now. The gentleman from South Carolina had said they were not to be used for any hostile purposes whatever. He wished to know how they were then to be employed? He thought they would be somewhat expensive packet boats, to carry despatches abroad. He knew only of two purposes for which they could be used, that is, to be held in readiness in case of war, and in the mean time to be employed in some purpose or other, which he thought should be defined, and not left in doubt. He therefore hoped the amendment would be agreed to.

Mr. DANA said, admitting that they had a right to define the object of this armament, it was no reason why they should insist upon exercising it. He agreed that they had a right. He had no objection to leaving the business to the President, except that, if the vessels were employed in convoying our commerce, he should have wished to have shared the responsibility with him. He denied that the danger which had been predicted could arise from the disputed articles in the French Treaty, as the President had a right to give such instructions to the commanders on that subject, as he saw proper.

Mr. W. SMITH thought the proposition vague, since it did not say the vessels should not be used in any other way. Gentlemen were begging the question, when they said, that if the business were left with the President, the consequence would be that the vessels would be employed as a convoy, since he did not believe they were equal to that object. It was his wish that the hands of the President should not be tied.

9

ST. GEORGE TUCKER,
BLACKSTONE'S COMMENTARIES
1:App. 329–31
1803

1. The first is, That he shall be commander in chief of the army and navy of the United States, and of the militia of the several states, when called into the service of the United States. A power similar to that of the king of England, and of the stadtholder of Holland, before the late revolution; yet qualified, by some important restrictions, which I believe were not to be found in either of those governments. As, first; he cannot make rules for the regulation and government of the army and navy, himself, but they must be governed according to regulations established by congress. But notwithstanding this provision in the constitution, the act of 5 Cong. c. 74, authorised the president to make and establish such rules for training and disciplining the corps of volunteers, authorised to be raised by that act, as should be thought necessary to prepare them for actual service. . . . Secondly; the president of the United States hath not an unqualified right to appoint what officers he pleases; but such appointment (if there be no provision to the contrary made by law) must be made with the advice and consent of the senate: a restriction, perhaps of little importance, whilst the right of nomination, in all cases, and the right of filling up vacancies during the recess of the senate, remain uncontrollably in his power; to which may be added, the authority given him by the act for raising a provisional army, (and perhaps some others) to appoint such officers as he may think proper in the recess of the senate; "the appointment of field officers to be submitted to the advice and consent of the senate, at their next subsequent meeting;" leaving the appointment of all officers of inferior rank to the discretion of the president, alone. The stadtholder of Holland derived his power and influence in great measure from a similar authority. . . . A third and infinitely more important check, than either of the former, so long as elections continue as frequent, as at present, is, that no appropriation for the support of an army can be made for a longer term than two years, the period for which congress is chosen. This puts it in the power of the people, by changing the representatives, to give an effectual check to the power of the executive at the end of that period. . . . In England, the power of raising armies, *ad libitum*, is vested in the king, though he is said to be dependent upon the parliament for their support; a supply bill, which is always limited to one year, passes accordingly, every session. Should it be refused, (a case which I believe has not happened for more than a century), a dissolution would pave the way, immediately, for a more complying parliament. Fourthly; the militia of the several states, though subject to his command when called into actual service, can only be called into service by the authority of congress, and must be gov-

erned according to law: the states, moreover, have the right of appointing the officers, and training the militia, according to the discipline prescribed by congress, reserved to them by the constitution. But we have seen in what manner this very important clause has been evaded, by at acts of 5 Cong. c. 64 and 74, authorising the president to accept companies of volunteers, and to appoint their officers, &c. A precedent, which if it be drawn into authority and practice in future, may be regarded as superceding every part of the constitution, which reserves to the states any effectual authority over their militia.

10

LITTLE V. BAREME
2 Cranch 170 (1804)

(See 1.8.11, no. 13)

11

JAMES MONROE TO CHAIRMAN OF SENATE MILITARY COMMITTEE
Feb. 1815

Writings 5:308–18

(See 1.8.15, no. 18)

12

JOSEPH STORY, COMMENTARIES ON THE CONSTITUTION 3:§§ 1485–86
1833

---

§ 1485. The command and application of the public force, to execute the laws, to maintain peace, and to resist foreign invasion, are powers so obviously of an executive nature, and require the exercise of qualities so peculiarly adapted to this department, that a well-organized government can scarcely exist, when they are taken away from it. Of all the cases and concerns of government, the direction of war most peculiarly demands those qualities, which distinguish the exercise of power by a single hand. Unity of plan, promptitude, activity, and decision, are indispensable to success; and these can scarcely exist, except when a single magistrate is entrusted exclusively with the power. Even the coupling of the authority of an executive council with him, in the exercise of such powers enfeebles the system, divides the responsibility, and not unfrequently defeats every energetic measure. Timidity, indecision, obstinacy, and pride of opinion, must mingle in all such

councils, and infuse a torpor and sluggishness, destructive of all military operations. Indeed, there would seem to be little reason to enforce the propriety of giving this power to the executive department, (whatever may be its actual organization,) since it is in exact coincidence with the provisions of our state constitutions; and therefore seems to be universally deemed safe, if not vital to the system.

§ 1486. Yet the clause did not wholly escape animadversion in the state conventions. The propriety of admitting the president to be commander-in-chief, so far as to give orders, and have a general superintendency, was admitted. But it was urged, that it would be dangerous to let him command in person without any restraint, as he might make a bad use of it. The consent of both houses of congress ought, therefore, to be required, before he should take the actual command. The answer then given was, that though the president might, there was no necessity, that he should, take the command in person; and there was no probability, that he would do so, except in extraordinary emergencies, and when he was possessed of superior military talents. But if his assuming the actual command depended upon the assent of congress what was to be done, when an invasion, or insurrection took place during the recess of congress? Besides, the very power of restraint might be so employed as to cripple the executive department, when filled by a man of extraordinary military genius. The power of the president, too, might well be deemed safe; since he could not, of himself, declare war, raise armies, or call forth the militia, or appropriate money for the purpose; for these powers all belonged to congress. In Great Britain, the king is not only commander-in-chief of the army, and navy, and militia, but he can declare war; and, in time of war, can raise armies and navies, and call forth the militia of his own mere will. So, that (to use the words of Mr. Justice Blackstone) the sole supreme government and command of the militia within all his majesty's realms and dominions, and of all forces by sea and land, and of all forts and places of strength, ever was and is the undoubted right of his majesty; and both houses or either house of parliament cannot, nor ought to pretend to the same. The only power of check by parliament is, the refusal of supplies; and this is found to be abundantly sufficient to protect the nation against any war against the sense of the nation, or any serious abuse of the power in modern times.

OPINIONS IN WRITING

13

JAMES IREDELL, NORTH CAROLINA
RATIFYING CONVENTION
28 July 1788
Elliot 4:108–10

The next part, which says "that he may require the opinion in writing of the principal officers," is, in some degree, substituted for a council. He is only to consult them if he thinks proper. Their opinion is to be given him in writing. By this means he will be aided by their intelligence; and the necessity of their opinions being in writing, will render them more cautious in giving them, and make them responsible should they give advice manifestly improper. This does not diminish the responsibility of the President himself.

They might otherwise have colluded, and opinions have been given too much under his influence.

It has been the opinion of many gentlemen, that the President should have a council. This opinion, probably, has been derived from the example in England. It would be very proper for every gentleman to consider attentively whether that example ought to be imitated by us. Although it be a respectable example, yet, in my opinion, very satisfactory reasons can be assigned for a departure from it in this Constitution.

It was very difficult, immediately on our separation from Great Britain, to disengage ourselves entirely from ideas of government we had been used to. We had been accustomed to a council under the old government, and took it for granted we ought to have one under the new. But examples ought not to be implicitly followed; and the reasons which prevail in Great Britain for a council do not apply equally to us. In that country, the executive authority is vested in a magistrate who holds it by birthright. He has great powers and prerogatives, and it is a constitutional maxim, *that he can do no wrong.* We have experienced that he can do wrong, yet no man can say so in his own country. There are no courts to try him for any high crimes; nor is there any constitutional method of depriving him of his throne. If he loses it, it must be by a general resistance of his people, contrary to *forms* of law, as at the revolution which took place about a hundred years ago. It is, therefore, of the utmost moment in that country, that whoever is the instrument of any act of government should be personally responsible for it, since the king is not; and, for the same reason, that no act of government should be exercised but by the instrumentality of some

person who can be accountable for it. Every thing, therefore, that the king does, must be by some *advice,* and the adviser of course answerable. Under our Constitution we are much happier.

No man has an authority to injure another with impunity. No man is better than his fellow-citizens, nor can pretend to any superiority over the meanest man in the country. If the President does a single act by which the people are prejudiced, he is punishable himself, and no other man merely to screen him. If he commits any misdemeanor in office, he is impeachable, removable from office, and incapacitated to hold any office of honor, trust, or profit. If he commits any crime, he is punishable by the laws of his country, and in capital cases may be deprived of his life. This being the case, there is not the same reason here for having a council which exists in England. It is, however, much to be desired, that a man who has such extensive and important business to perform should have the means of some assistance to enable him to discharge his arduous employment. The advice of the principal executive officers, which he can at all times command, will, in my opinion, answer this valuable purpose. He can at no time want advice, if he desires it, as the principal officers will always be on the spot. Those officers, from their abilities and experience, will probably be able to give as good, if not better, advice than any counsellors would do; and the solemnity of the advice in writing, which must be preserved, would be a great check upon them.

Besides these considerations, it was difficult for the Convention to prepare a council that would be unexceptionable. That jealousy which naturally exists between the different states enhanced this difficulty. If a few counsellors were to be chosen from the Northern, Southern, or Middle States, or from a few states only, undue preference might be given to those particular states from which they should come. If, to avoid this difficulty, one counsellor should be sent from each state, this would require great expense, which is a consideration, at this time, of much moment, especially as it is probable that, by the method proposed, the President may be equally well advised without any expense at all.

We ought also to consider that, had he a council by whose advice he was bound to act, his responsibility, in all such cases, must be destroyed. You surely would not oblige him to follow their advice, and punish him for obeying it. If called upon on any occasion of dislike, it would be natural for him to say, "You know my council are men of integrity and ability: I could not act against their opinions, though I confess my own was contrary to theirs." This, sir, would be pernicious. In such a situation, he might easily combine with his council, and it might be impossible to fix a fact upon him. It would be difficult often to know whether the President or counsellors were most to blame.

A thousand plausible excuses might be made, which would escape detection. But the method proposed in the Constitution creates no such embarrassment. It is plain and open. And the President will personally have the credit of good, or the censure of bad measures; since, though he may ask advice, he is to use his own judgment in following or rejecting it. For all these reasons, I am clearly of opinion that the clause is better as it stands than if the President were to have a council. I think every good that can be derived from the institution of a council may be expected from the advice of these officers, without its being liable to the disadvantages to which it appears to me, the institution of a council would be.

14

THOMAS JEFFERSON TO WALTER JONES
5 Mar. 1810
Writings 11:137–38

I received duly your favor of the 19th ultimo, and I salute you with all ancient and recent recollections of friendship. I have learned, with real sorrow, that circumstances have arisen among our executive counsellors, which have rendered foes those who once were friends. To themselves it will be a source of infinite pain and vexation, and therefore chiefly I lament it, for I have a sincere esteem for both parties. To the President it will be really inconvenient; but to the nation I do not know that it can do serious injury, unless we were to believe the newspapers, which pretend that Mr. Gallatin will go out. That indeed would be a day of mourning for the United States; but I hope that the position of both gentlemen may be made so easy as to give no cause for either to withdraw. The ordinary business of every day is done by consultation between the President and the Head of the department alone to which it belongs. For measures of importance or difficulty, a consultation is held with the Heads of departments, either assembled, or by taking their opinions separately in conversation or in writing. The latter is most strictly in the spirit of the constitution. Because the President, on weighing the advice of all, is left free to make up an opinion for himself. In this way they are not brought together, and it is not necessarily known to any what opinion the others have given. This was General Washington's practice for the first two or three years of his administration, till the affairs of France and England threatened to embroil us, and rendered consideration and discussion desirable. In these discussions, Hamilton and myself were daily pitted in the cabinet like two cocks. We were then but four in number, and, according to the majority, which of course was three to one, the President decided. The pain was for Hamilton and myself, but the public experienced no inconvenience. I practised this last method, because the harmony was so cordial among us all, that we never failed, by

a contribution of mutual views on the subject, to form an opinion acceptable to the whole. I think there never was one instance to the contrary, in any case of consequence. Yet this does, in fact, transform the executive into a directory, and I hold the other method to be more constitutional. It is better calculated too to prevent collision and irritation, and to cure it, or at least suppress its effects when it has already taken place. It is the obvious and sufficient remedy in the present case, and will doubtless be resorted to.

15

WILLIAM WIRT, OFFICE OF ATTORNEY GENERAL
12 June 1818
1 Ops. Atty. Gen. 211

The commission of Attorney General authorizes and empowers him to execute the duties of that office *according to law;* and the law which creates this office prescribes its duties in the following terms: *"Whose duty it shall be* to prosecute and conduct all suits in the Supreme Court, in which the United States shall be concerned, and to give his advice and opinions upon questions of law, *when required by the President of the United States, or when requested by the heads of any of the departments, touching any matters that may concern their departments."* Under this law, which is the only one upon the subject, I do not think myself authorized to give an *official opinion* in any case, except on the call of the President, or some one of the heads of departments; and I should consider myself as transcending the limits of my commission in a very unjustifiable manner, in attempting to attach the weight of *my office* to any opinion not authorized by the law which prescribes my duties. You will, I trust, excuse me, therefore, in declining to give the *official* opinion which you request; and which I assure you I do, not from any want of respect to you, but purely from a sense of official duty, and my respect for the law which prescribes that duty.

If you think the matter of sufficient consequence to make an *official* opinion from me desirable, you will, perhaps, have it in your power to give your application such a direction, through the Navy Department, or that of War, as to justify me in expressing the opinion *officially*, which I have every *personal* disposition to give.

16

WILLIAM WIRT, DUTIES OF THE
ATTORNEY GENERAL
3 Feb. 1820
1 Ops. Atty. Gen. 335

Sir: The order of the House of Representatives of the United States, of the 28th January last, "that the petition of Joseph Wheaton, and the accompanying documents, together with the report of the Committee of Claims, of the 6th January instant, thereon, be referred to the Attorney General of the United States, and that he be requested to report his opinion thereupon to this House," was handed me by Major Wheaton (the petitioner) this evening, together with the documents which are now returned.

The duties of Attorney General's office are specified by our laws, and are confined to the following heads:

1. "To prosecute and conduct all suits in the Supreme Court in which the United States shall be concerned."

2. "To give his advice and opinion upon questions of law, when required by the President of the United States, or when requested by the heads of any of the departments, touching any matters that may concern their departments."

3. "To discharge the duties of a commissioner of the sinking fund."

The Attorney General is sworn to discharge the duties of his office *according to law.* To be instrumental in enlarging the sphere of his official duties beyond that which is prescribed by law, would, in my opinion, be a violation of this oath. Under this impression I have, with great care, perused all the documents which have been handed to me in this case, for the purpose of ascertaining whether the order with which I have been honored from the House of Representatives falls under either head of my official duties; and it appears to me that it does not. A reference to the law will show, I think, that this is indisputably clear.

I had the honor to intimate this impression in the case of Major Thomas, referred to me officially by the House of Representatives, in the session of 1818–'19, in the hope that if it was thought advisable to connect the Attorney General with the House of Representatives in that character of legal counsellor which he holds by the existing law towards the President and heads of departments, a provision would be made by law for that purpose.

No such provision having been made, and believing, as I do, that in a government purely of laws it would be incalculably dangerous to permit an officer to act, under color of his office, beyond the pale of the law, I trust I shall be excused from making any official report on the order with which the House has honored me. It is true that in this case I should have the sanction of the House for the measure; and it is not less true that my respect for the House impels me strongly to obey the order. The precedent, however, would not be the less dangerous, on account of the purity of motives in which it originated. The maxim is as old, at least, as republican Rome, that *omnia mala exempla ex bonis orta sunt:* on this ground I hope to be excused by the House of Representatives for declining their request. And I assure you, sir, that it gives me more pain to be thus obliged to decline it, than it would give me trouble to make the report; but in a conflict between my wishes and my sense of duty, there ought to be no question which I should obey. I may be wrong in my view of the subject. The order may be sanctioned by former precedents; but my predecessors in office have left nothing for my guidance; and I am constrained, therefore, to act on my own construction of the law as it stands.

REPRIEVES AND PARDONS

17

WILLIAM BLACKSTONE, COMMENTARIES
4:397–402
1769

This is indeed one of the great advantages of monarchy in general, above any other form of government; that there is a magistrate, who has it in his power to extend mercy, wherever he thinks it is deserved: holding a court of equity in his own breast, to soften the rigour of the general law, in such criminal cases as merit an exemption from punishment. Pardons (according to some theorists) should be excluded in a perfect legislation, where punishments are mild but certain: for that the clemency of the prince seems a tacit disapprobation of the laws. But the exclusion of pardons must necessarily introduce a very dangerous power in the judge or jury, that of construing the criminal law by the spirit instead of the letter; or else it must be holden, what no man will seriously avow, that the situation and circumstances of the offender (though they alter not the essence of the crime) ought to make no distinction in the punishment. In democracies, however, this power of pardon can never subsist; for there nothing higher is acknowleged than the magistrate who administers the laws: and it would be impolitic for the power of judging and of pardoning to center in one and the same person. This (as the president Montesquieu observes) would oblige him very often to contradict himself, to make and to unmake his decisions: it would tend to confound all ideas of right among the mass of the people; as they would find it difficult to tell, whether a prisoner were discharged by his innocence, or obtained a pardon through favour. In Holland therefore, if there be no stadtholder, there is no power of pardoning lodged in any other member of the state. But in monarchies the king acts in a superior sphere; and, though he regulates the whole government as the first mover, yet he does not appear in any of the disagreeable or invidious parts of it. Whenever the nation see him personally engaged, it is only in works of legislature, magnificence, or compassion. To him therefore the people look up as the fountain of nothing but bounty and grace; and these repeated acts of goodness, coming immediately from his own hand, endear the sovereign to his subjects, and contribute more than any thing to root in their hearts that filial affection, and personal loyalty, which are the sure establishment of a prince.

Under this head, of pardons, let us briefly consider, 1. The *object* of pardon: 2. The *manner* of pardoning: 3. The method of *allowing* a pardon: 4. The *effect* of such pardon, when allowed.

1. And, first, the king may pardon all offences merely against the crown, or the public; excepting, 1. That, to preserve the liberty of the subject, the committing any man to prison out of the realm, is by the *habeas corpus* act, 31 Car. II. c. 2. made a *praemunire*, unpardonable even by the king. Nor, 2. Can the king pardon, where private justice is principally concerned in the prosecution of offenders: *"non potest rex gratiam facere cum injuria et damno aliorum."* Therefore in appeals of all kinds (which are the suit, not of the king, but of the party injured) the prosecutor may release, but the king cannot pardon. Neither can he pardon a common nuisance, while it remains unredressed, or so as to prevent an abatement of it; though afterwards he may remit the fine: because, though the prosecution is vested in the king to avoid multiplicity of suits, yet (during it's continuance) this offence favours more of the nature of a *private* injury to each individual in the neighbourhood, than of a *public* wrong. Neither, lastly, can the king pardon an offence against a popular or penal statute, after information brought: for thereby the informer hath acquired a private property in his part of the penalty.

There is also a restriction of a peculiar nature, that affects the prerogative of pardoning, in case of parliamentary impeachments; *viz.* that the king's pardon cannot be *pleaded* to any such impeachment, so as to impede the inquiry, and stop the prosecution of great and notorious offenders. Therefore when, in the reign of Charles the second, the earl of Danby was impeached by the house of commons of high treason and other misdemesnors, and pleaded the king's pardon in bar of the same, the commons alleged, "that there was no precedent, that ever any pardon was granted to any person impeached by the commons of high treason, or other high crimes, *depending the impeachment;*" and therefore resolved, "that the pardon so pleaded was illegal and void, and ought not to be allowed *in bar* of the impeachment of the commons of England:" for which resolution they assigned this reason to the house of lords, "that the setting up a pardon to be a *bar* of an impeachment defeats the whole use and effect of impeach-

ments: for should this point be admitted, or stand doubted, it would totally discourage the exhibiting any for the future; whereby the chief institution for the preservation of the government would be destroyed." Soon after the revolution, the commons renewed the same claim, and voted, "that a pardon is not *pleadable in bar* of an impeachment." And, at length, it was enacted by the act of settlement, 12 & 13 W. III. c. 2. "that no pardon under the great seal of England shall be *pleadable* to an impeachment by the commons in parliament." But, after the impeachment has been solemnly heard and determined, it is not understood that the king's royal grace is farther restrained or abridged: for, after the impeachment and attainder of the six rebel lords in 1715, three of them were from time to time reprieved by the crown, and at length received the benefit of the king's most gracious pardon.

2. As to the *manner* of pardoning: it is a general rule, that, wherever it may reasonably be presumed the king is deceived, the pardon is void. Therefore any suppression of truth, or suggestion of falshood, in a charter of pardon, will vitiate the whole; for the king was misinformed. General words have also a very imperfect effect in pardons. A pardon of all felonies will not pardon a conviction or attainder of felony; (for it is presumed the king knew not of those proceedings) but the conviction or attainder must be particularly mentioned: and a pardon of felonies will not include piracy; for that is no felony punishable at the common law. It is also enacted by statute 13 Ric. II. st. 2. c. 1. that no pardon for treason, murder, or rape, shall be allowed, unless the offence be particularly specified therein; and particularly in murder it shall be expressed, whether it was committed by lying in wait, assault, or malice prepense. Upon which sir Edward Coke observes, that it was not the intention of the parliament that the king should ever pardon murder under these aggravations; and therefore they prudently laid the pardon under these restrictions, because they did not conceive it possible that the king would ever excuse an offence by name, which was attended with such high aggravations. And it is remarkable enough, that there is no precedent of a pardon in the register for any other homicide, than that which happens *se defendendo* or *per infortunium:* to which two species the king's pardon was expressly confined by the statutes 2 Edw. III. c. 2. and 14 Edw. III. c. 15. which declare that no pardon of homicide shall be granted, but only where the king may do it *by the oath of his crown;* that is to say, where a man slayeth another in his own defence, or by misfortune. But the statute of Richard the second, beforementioned, enlarges by implication the royal power; provided the king is not deceived in the intended object of his mercy. And therefore pardons of murder were always granted with a *non obstante* of the statute of King Richard, till the time of the revolution; when, the doctrine of *non obstante*'s ceasing, it was doubted whether murder could be pardoned generally: but it was determined by the court of king's bench, that the king may pardon on an indictment of murder, as well as a subject may discharge an appeal. Under these and a few other restrictions, it is a general rule, that a pardon shall be taken most beneficially *for* the subject, and most strongly *against* the king.

A pardon may also be *conditional:* that is, the king may extend his mercy upon what terms he pleases; and may annex to his bounty a condition either precedent or subsequent, on the performance whereof the validity of the pardon will depend: and this by the common law. Which prerogative is daily exerted in the pardon of felons, on condition of transportation to some foreign country (usually to some of his majesty's colonies and plantations in America) for life, or for a term of years; such transportation or banishment being allowable and warranted by the *habeas corpus* act, 31 Car. II. c. 2. §. 14. and rendered more easy and effectual by statute 8 Geo. III. c. 15.

3. With regard to the manner of *allowing* pardons; we may observe, that a pardon by act of parliament is more beneficial than by the king's charter: for a man is not bound to plead it, but the court must *ex officio* take notice of it; neither can he lose the benefit of it by his own *laches* or negligence, as he may of the king's charter of pardon. The king's charter of pardon must be specially pleaded, and that at a proper time: for if a man is indicted, and has a pardon in his pocket, and afterwards puts himself upon his trial by pleading the general issue, he has waived the benefit of such pardon. But, if a man avails himself thereof as soon as by course of law he may, a pardon may either be pleaded upon arraignment, or in arrest of judgment, or in the present stage of proceedings, in bar of execution. Antiently, by statute 10 Edw. III. c. 2. no pardon of felony could be allowed, unless the party found sureties for the good behaviour before the sheriff and coroners of the county. But that statute is repealed by the statute 5 & 6 W. & M. c. 13. which, instead thereof, gives the judges of the court a discretionary power to bind the criminal, pleading such pardon, to his good behaviour, with two sureties, for any term not exceeding seven years.

4. Lastly, the *effect* of such pardon by the king, is to make the offender a new man; to acquit him of all corporal penalties and forfeitures annexed to that offence for which he obtains his pardon; and not so much to restore his former, as to give him a new, credit and capacity. But nothing can restore or purify the blood when once corrupted, if the pardon be not allowed till after attainder, but the high and transcendent power of parliament. Yet if a person attainted receives the king's pardon, and afterwards hath a son, that son may be heir to his father; because the father, being made a new man, might transmit new inheritable blood: though, had he been born before the pardon, he could never have inherited at all.

18

GEORGIA CONSTITUTION OF 1777, ART. 19
Thorpe 2:781

ART. XIX. The governor shall, with the advice of the executive council, exercise the executive powers of govern-

ment, according to the laws of this State and the constitution thereof, save only in the case of pardons and remission of fines, which he shall in no instance grant; but he may reprieve a criminal, or suspend a fine, until the meeting of the assembly, who may determine therein as they shall judge fit.

19

MASSACHUSETTS CONSTITUTION OF 1780, PT. 2, CH. 2, SEC. 1, ART. 8
Thorpe 3:1901–2

VIII. The power of pardoning offences, except such as persons may be convicted of before the senate by an impeachment of the house, shall be in the governor, by and with the advice of council; but no charter of pardon, granted by the governor, with advice of the council before conviction, shall avail the party pleading the same, notwithstanding any general or particular expressions contained therein, descriptive of the offence or offences intended to be pardoned.

20

ALEXANDER HAMILTON, FEDERALIST, NO. 74, 500–503
25 Mar. 1788

He is also to be authorised "to grant reprieves and pardons for offences against the United States *except in cases of impeachment.*" Humanity and good policy conspire to dictate, that the benign prerogative of pardoning should be as little as possible fettered or embarrassed. The criminal code of every country partakes so much of necessary severity, that without an easy access to exceptions in favor of unfortunate guilt, justice would wear a countenance too sanguinary and cruel. As the sense of responsibility is always strongest in proportion as it is undivided, it may be inferred that a single man would be most ready to attend to the force of those motives, which might plead for a mitigation of the rigor of the law, and least apt to yield to considerations, which were calculated to shelter a fit object of its vengeance. The reflection, that the fate of a fellow creature depended on his *sole fiat*, would naturally inspire scrupulousness and caution: The dread of being accused of weakness or connivance would beget equal circumspection, though of a different kind. On the other hand, as men generally derive confidence from their numbers, they might often encourage each other in an act of obduracy and might be less sensible to the apprehension of suspicion or censure for an injudicious or affected clemency. On these accounts, one man appears to be a more eligible dispenser of the mercy of the government than a body of men.

The expediency of vesting the power of pardoning in the President has, if I mistake not, been only contested in relation to the crime of treason. This, it has been urged, ought to have depended upon the assent of one or both of the branches of the legislative body. I shall not deny that there are strong reasons to be assigned for requiring in this particular the concurrence of that body or of a part of it. As treason is a crime levelled at the immediate being of the society, when the laws have once ascertained the guilt of the offender, there seems a fitness in refering the expediency of an act of mercy towards him to the judgment of the Legislature. And this ought the rather to be the case, as the supposition of the connivance of the Chief Magistrate ought not to be entirely excluded. But there are also strong objections to such a plan. It is not to be doubted that a single man of prudence and good sense, is better fitted, in delicate conjunctures, to balance the motives, which may plead for and against the remission of the punishment, than any numerous body whatever. It deserves particular attention, that treason will often be connected with seditions, which embrace a large proportion of the community; as lately happened in Massachusetts. In every such case, we might expect to see the representation of the people tainted with the same spirit, which had given birth to the offense. And when parties were pretty equally matched, the secret sympathy of the friends and favorers of the condemned person, availing itself of the good nature and weakness of others, might frequently bestow impunity where the terror of an example was necessary. On the other hand, when the sedition had proceeded from causes which had inflamed the resentments of the major party, they might often be found obstinate and inexorable, when policy demanded a conduct of forbearance and clemency. But the principal arguments for reposing the power of pardoning in this case in the Chief Magistrate is this—In seasons of insurrection or rebellion, there are often critical moments, when a well timed offer of pardon to the insurgents or rebels may restore the tranquility of the commonwealth; and which, if suffered to pass unimproved, it may never be possible afterwards to recall. The dilatory process of convening the Legislature, or one of its branches, for the purpose of obtaining its sanction to the measure, would frequently be the occasion of letting slip the golden opportunity. The loss of a week, a day, an hour, may sometimes be fatal. If it should be observed that a discretionary power with a view to such contingencies might be occasionally conferred upon the President; it may be answered in the first place, that it is questionable whether, in a limited constitution, that power could be delegated by law; and in the second place, that it would generally be impolitic before-hand to take any step which might hold out the prospect of impunity. A proceeding of this kind, out of the usual course, would be likely to be construed into an argument of timidity or of weakness, and would have a tendency to embolden guilt.

21

GILBERT LIVINGSTON, PROPOSED AMENDMENT, NEW YORK RATIFYING CONVENTION
4 July 1788
Elliot 2:408

Sec. 2. Clause 1, respecting the *powers of the President,*—

"*Resolved,* as the opinion of this committee, that the President of the United States should never command the army, militia, or navy of the United States, in person, without the consent of the Congress; and that he should not have the power to grant pardons for treason, without the consent of the Congress; but that, in cases where persons are convicted of treason, he should have authority to grant reprieves, until their cases can be laid before the Congress."

22

JAMES IREDELL, NORTH CAROLINA RATIFYING CONVENTION
28 July 1788
Elliot 4:110–14

Another power that he has is to grant pardons, except in cases of impeachment. I believe it is the sense of a great part of America, that this power should be exercised by their governors. It is in several states on the same footing that it is here. It is the genius of a republican government that the laws should be rigidly executed, without the influence of favor or ill-will—that, when a man commits a crime, however powerful he or his friends may be, yet he should be punished for it; and, on the other hand, though he should be universally hated by his country, his real guilt alone, as to the particular charge, is to operate against him. This strict and scrupulous observance of justice is proper in all governments; but it is particularly indispensable in a republican one, because, in such a government, the law is superior to every man, and no man is superior to another. But, though this general principle be unquestionable, surely there is no gentleman in the committee who is not aware that there ought to be exceptions to it; because there may be many instances where, though a man offends against the letter of the law, yet peculiar circumstances in his case may entitle him to mercy. It is impossible for any general law to foresee and provide for all possible cases that may arise; and therefore an inflexible adherence to it, in every instance, might frequently be the cause of very great injustice. For this reason, such a power ought to exist somewhere; and where could it be more properly vested, than in a man who had received such strong proofs of his possessing the highest confidence of the people? This power, however, only refers to offences against the United States, and not against particular states. Another reason for the President possessing this authority, is this: it is often necessary to convict a man by means of his accomplices. We have sufficient experience of that in this country. A criminal would often go unpunished, were not this method to be pursued against him. In my opinion, till an accomplice's own danger is removed, his evidence ought to be regarded with great diffidence. If, in civil causes of property, a witness must be entirely disinterested, how much more proper is it he should be so in cases of life and death! This power is naturally vested in the President, because it is his duty to watch over the public safety; and as that may frequently require the evidence of accomplices to bring great offenders to justice, he ought to be intrusted with the most effectual means of procuring it.

I beg leave further to observe, that, for another reason, I think there is a propriety in leaving this power to the general discretion of the executive magistrate, rather than to fetter it in any manner which has been proposed. It may happen that many men, upon plausible pretences, may be seduced into very dangerous measures against their country. They may aim, by an insurrection, to redress imaginary grievances, at the same time believing, upon false suggestions, that their exertions are necessary to save their country from destruction. Upon cool reflection, however, they possibly are convinced of their error, and clearly see through the treachery and villainy of their leaders. In this situation, if the President possessed the power of pardoning, they probably would throw themselves on the equity of the government, and the whole body be peaceably broken up. Thus, at a critical moment, the President might, perhaps, prevent a civil war. But if there was no authority to pardon, in that delicate exigency, what would be the consequence? The principle of self-preservation would prevent their parting. Would it not be natural for them to say, "We shall be punished if we disband. Were we sure of mercy, we would peaceably part. But we know not that there is any chance of this. We may as well meet one kind of death as another. We may as well die in the field as at the gallows." I therefore submit to the committee if this power be not highly necessary for such a purpose.

We have seen a happy instance of the good effect of such an exercise of mercy in the state of Massachusetts, where, very lately, there was so formidable an insurrection. I believe a great majority of the insurgents were drawn into it by false artifices. They at length saw their error, and were willing to disband. Government, by a wise exercise of lenity, after having shown its power, generally granted a pardon; and the whole party were dispersed. There is now as much peace in that country as in any state in the Union.

A particular instance which occurs to me shows the utility of this power very strongly. Suppose we were involved in war. It would be then necessary to know the designs of the enemy. This kind of knowledge cannot always be procured but by means of spies—a set of wretches whom all nations despise, but whom all employ; and, as they would

assuredly be used against us, a principle of self-defence would urge and justify the use of them on our part. Suppose, therefore, the President could prevail upon a man of some importance to go over to the enemy, in order to give him secret information of his measures. He goes off privately to the enemy. He feigns resentment against his country for some ill usage, either real or pretended, and is received, possibly, into favor and confidence. The people would not know the purpose for which he was employed. In the mean time, he secretly informs the President of the enemy's designs, and by this means, perhaps, those designs are counteracted, and the country saved from destruction. After his business is executed, he returns into his own country, where the people, not knowing he had rendered tham any service, are naturally exasperated against him for his supposed treason. I would ask any gentleman whether the President ought not to have the power of pardoning this man. Suppose the concurrence of the Senate, or any other body, was necessary; would this obnoxious person be properly safe? We know in every country there is a strong prejudice against the executive authority. If a prejudice of this kind, on such an occasion, prevailed against the President, the President might be suspected of being influenced by corrupt motives, and the application in favor of this man be rejected. Such a thing might very possibly happen when the prejudices of party were strong; and therefore no man, so clearly entitled as in the case I have supposed, ought to have his life exposed to so hazardous a contingency.

The power of impeachment is given by this Constitution, to bring great offenders to punishment. It is calculated to bring them to punishment for crime which it is not easy to describe, but which every one must be convinced is a high crime and misdemeanor against the government. This power is lodged in those who represent the great body of the people, because the occasion for its exercise will arise from acts of great injury to the community, and the objects of it may be such as cannot be easily reached by an ordinary tribunal. The trial belongs to the Senate, lest an inferior tribunal should be too much awed by so powerful an accuser. After trial thus solemnly conducted, it is not probable that it would happen once in a thousand times, that a man actually convicted would be entitled to mercy; and if the President had the power of pardoning in such a case, this great check upon high officers of state would lose much of its influence. It seems, therefore, proper that the general power of pardoning should be abridged in this particular instance. The punishment annexed to this conviction on impeachment can only be removal from office, and disqualification to hold any place of honor, trust, or profit. But the person convicted is further liable to a trial at common law, and may receive such common-law punishment as belongs to a description of such offences, if it be punishable by that law. I hope, for the reasons I have stated, that the whole of this clause will be approved by the committee. The regulations altogether, in my opinion, are as wisely contrived as they could be. It is impossible for imperfect beings to form a perfect system. If the present one may be productive of possible inconveniences, we are not to reject it for that reason, but inquire whether any other system could be devised which would be attended with fewer inconveniences, in proportion to the advantages resulting. But we ought to be exceedingly attentive in examining, and still more cautious in deciding, lest we should condemn what may be worthy of applause, or approve of what may be exceptionable. I hope that, in the explanation of this clause, I have not improperly taken up the time of the committee.

23

JAMES WILSON, EXECUTIVE DEPARTMENT, LECTURES ON LAW
1791
Works 2:442–44

He has power to grant reprieves and pardons for offences against the United States, except in cases of impeachment.

To prevent crimes, is the noblest end and aim of criminal jurisprudence. To punish them, is one of the means necessary for the accomplishment of this noble end and aim.

The certainty of punishments is of the greatest importance, in order to constitute them fit preventives of crimes. This certainty is best obtained by accuracy in the publick police, by vigilance and activity in the executive officers of justice, by a prompt and certain communication of intelligence, by a proper distribution of rewards for the discovery and apprehension of criminals, and, when they are apprehended, by an undeviating and inflexible strictness in carrying the laws against them into sure and full execution.

All this will be readily allowed. What should we then think of a power, given by the constitution or the laws, to dispense with accuracy in the public police, and with vigilance, vigour, and activity in the search and seizure of offenders? Such a power, it must be admitted, would seem somewhat extraordinary.

What, it will next be asked, should we think of a power, given by the constitution or the laws, to dispense with their execution upon criminals, after they have been apprehended, tried, convicted, and condemned? In other words—can the power to pardon be admissible into any well regulated government? Shall a power be given to insult the laws, to protect crimes, to indemnify, and, by indemnifying, to encourage criminals?

From this, or from a similar view of things, many writers, and some of them very respectable as well as humane, have been induced to conclude, that, in a government of laws, the power of pardoning should be altogether unknown.

Would you prevent crimes? says the Marquis of Beccaria: let the laws be clear and simple: let the entire force of the nation be united in their defence: let them, and them only, be feared. The fear of the laws is salutary: but the fear of man is a fruitful and a fatal source of crimes. Happy the nation, in which pardons will be considered as

dangerous! Clemency is a virtue which belongs to the legislator, and not to the executor of the laws; a virtue, which should shine in the code, and not in private judgment. The prince, in pardoning, gives up the publick security in favour of an individual: and, by his ill judged benevolence, proclaims an act of impunity.

With regard, says Rousseau, to the prerogative of granting pardon to criminals, condemned by the laws of their country, and sentenced by the judges, it belongs only to that power, which is superiour both to the judges and the laws—the sovereign authority. Not that it is very clear, that even the supreme power is vested with such a right, or that the circumstances, in which it might be exerted, are frequent or determinate. In a well governed state, there are but few executions; not because many are pardoned; but because there are few criminals. Under the Roman republick, neither the senate nor the consuls ever attempted to grant pardons: even the people never did this, although they sometimes recalled their own sentence.

In Persia, when the king has condemned a person, it is no longer lawful to mention his name, or to intercede in his favour. Though his majesty were drunk and beside himself; yet the decree must be executed; otherwise he would contradict himself; and the law admits of no contradiction.

"Extremes, in nature, equal ends produce;" so in politicks, as it would seem.

The more general opinion, however, is, that in a state, there ought to be a power of pardoning offences. The exclusion of pardons, says Sir William Blackstone, must necessarily introduce a very dangerous power in the judge or jury, that of construing the criminal law by the spirit instead of the letter; or else it must be holden, what no man will seriously avow, that the situation and circumstances of the offender (though they alter not the essence of the crime) ought to make no distinction in the punishment.

I cannot, upon this occasion, enter into the discussion of the great point suggested and decided, in a very few words, by the learned Author of the Commentaries—that judges and juries have no power of construing the criminal law by the spirit instead of the letter. But I cannot, upon any occasion, suffer it to pass under my notice, without entering my caveat against implicit submission to this decision. I well know the humane rule, that, in the construction of a penal law, neither judge nor jury can extend it to facts equally criminal to those specified in the letter, if they are not contained in the letter. But I profess myself totally ignorant of any rule—I think it would be an inhuman one—that the letter of a penal law may be carried beyond the spirit of it; and it may certainly be carried by the letter beyond the spirit, if judges and juries are prohibited, in construing it, from considering the spirit as well as the letter. But to return to our present subject.

The most general opinion, as we have already observed, and, we may add, the best opinion, is, that, in every state, there ought to be a power to pardon offences. In the mildest systems, of which human societies are capable, there will still exist a necessity of this discretionary power, the proper exercise of which may arise from the possible circumstances of every conviction. Citizens, even condemned citizens, may be unfortunate in a higher degree, than that, in which they are criminal. When the cry of the nation rises in their favour; when the judges themselves, descending from their seats, and laying aside the formidable sword of justice, come to supplicate in behalf of the person, whom they have been obliged to condemn; in such a situation, clemency is a virtue; it becomes a duty.

But where ought this most amiable prerogative to be placed? Is it compatible with the nature of every species of government? With regard to both these questions, different opinions are entertained.

With regard to the last, the learned Author of the Commentaries on the laws of England declares his unqualified sentiment—"In democracies, this power of pardon can never subsist; for there nothing higher is acknowledged than the magistrate, who administers the laws: and it would be impolitick for the power of judging and of pardoning to centre in one and the same person. This would oblige him (as the President Montesquieu observes) very often to contradict himself, to make and unmake his decisions: it would tend to confound all ideas of right among the mass of the people; as they would find it difficult to tell, whether a prisoner were discharged by his innocence, or obtained a pardon through favour. In Holland, therefore, if there be no stadtholder, there is no power of pardoning lodged in any other member of the state.

"But in monarchies, the king acts in a superiour sphere; and though he regulates the whole government as the first mover, yet he does not appear in any of the disagreeable or invidious parts of it. Whenever the nation see him personally engaged, it is only in works of legislature, magnificence, or compassion."

Let us observe, by the way, the mighty difference between the person described by Selden, as the first magistrate among the Saxons, and him described by Sir William Blackstone, as the monarch of England since that period. The former was set in regular motion by the laws: the latter is the first mover, who regulates the whole government.

Let me also repeat here, what has been mentioned in another place. One of the most enlightened writers on English jurisprudence imagines, that the power of pardoning is a power incommunicable to the democratical species of government. For the western world new and rich discoveries in jurisprudence have been reserved. We have found, that this species of government—the best and the purest of all—that, in which the supreme power remains with the people—is capable of being formed, arranged, proportioned, and organized in such a manner, as to exclude the inconveniences, and to secure the advantages of all the others.

Why, according to Sir William Blackstone, can the power to pardon never subsist in a democracy? Because, says he, there, nothing higher is acknowledged, than the magistrate, who administers the laws. By pursuing the principle of democracy to its true source, we have discovered, that the law is higher than the magistrate, who administers it; that the constitution is higher than both; and that the supreme power, remaining with the people, is higher than all the three. With perfect consistency, there-

fore, the power of pardoning may subsist in our democratical governments: with perfect propriety, we think, it is vested in the president of the United States.

24

GEORGE WASHINGTON, PROCLAMATION OF 10 JULY 1795
Richardson 1:181

Whereas the commissioners appointed by the President of the United States to confer with the citizens in the western counties of Pennsylvania during the late insurrection which prevailed therein, by their act and agreement bearing date the 2d day of September last, in pursuance of the powers in them vested, did promise and engage that, if assurances of submission to the laws of the United States should be bona fide given by the citizens resident in the fourth survey of Pennsylvania, in the manner and within the time in the said act and agreement specified, a general pardon should be granted on the 10th day of July then next ensuing of all treasons and other indictable offenses against the United States committed within the said survey before the 22d day of August last, excluding therefrom, nevertheless, every person who should refuse or neglect to subscribe such assurance and engagement in manner aforesaid, or who should after such subscription violate the same, or willfully obstruct or attempt to obstruct the execution of the acts for raising a revenue on distilled spirits and stills, or be aiding or abetting therein; and

Whereas I have since thought proper to extend the said pardon to all persons guilty of the said treasons, misprisions of treasons, or otherwise concerned in the late insurrection within the survey aforesaid who have not since been indicted or convicted thereof, or of any other offense against the United States:

Therefore be it known that I, George Washington, President of the said United States, have granted, and by these presents do grant, a full, free, and entire pardon to all persons (excepting as is hereinafter excepted) of all treasons, misprisions of treason, and other indictable offenses against the United States committed within the fourth survey of Pennsylvania before the said 22d day of August last past, excepting and excluding therefrom, nevertheless, every person who refused or neglected to give and subscribe the said assurances in the manner aforesaid (or having subscribed hath violated the same) and now standeth indicted or convicted of any treason, misprision of treason, or other offense against the said United States, hereby remitting and releasing unto all persons, except as before excepted, all penalties incurred, or supposed to be incurred, for or on account of the premises.

25

ST. GEORGE TUCKER,
BLACKSTONE'S COMMENTARIES
1:APP. 331–32
1803

The power of granting pardons, says judge Blackstone, is the most amiable prerogative of a king of England; and is one of the great advantages of monarchy, above any other form of government: in democracies, he adds, this power of pardon can never subsist. It is happy for the people of America that many speculative notions concerning the disadvantages and imperfections of democratic forms of government, have been found to be practically false. In all the democratic states of North America, the power of pardoning is regularly vested (as in the federal government of the United States) in the supreme executive magistrate; and this flower of monarchical prerogative has been found to flourish in a perfect republican soil, not less than in it's native climate. The president of the United States is not, like a governor of Virginia, constrained to act by advice of a council, but the power of pardoning is left entirely to the dictates of his own bosom. The cases in which it has been exercised, manifest the propriety of the existence of such a power in every state, whatever be the form of it's government. In cases of impeachment, as the prosecution is carried on by the representatives of the people, and the judgment can only extend to removal from, and disqualification to hold or enjoy any office under the United States, in future, the constitution has wisely provided, that the same person in whom the right of nomination to office is vested, shall not have the power to remove that disqualification, which the guilt of the offender has brought upon himself. In England, no pardon can be pleaded in bar of an impeachment; but the king may pardon after conviction upon an impeachment. He can not by an exercise of his prerogative avert the disgrace of a conviction; but he can avert it's effects, and restore the offender to his credit.

26

WILLIAM WIRT, PARDONS
30 Mar. 1820
1 Ops. Atty. Gen. 341

The power of pardon, as given by the constitution, is the power of absolute and entire pardon. On the principle, however, that the greater power includes the less, I am of opinion that the power of pardoning absolutely includes the power of pardoning conditionally. There is, however, great danger lest a conditional pardon should operate as an absolute one, from the difficulty of enforcing the condition, or, in case of a breach of it, resorting to the original sentence of condemnation; which difficulty arises from the limited powers of the national government. For example: you could not pardon on a condition to be enforced by the officers of a State government—as, for instance, working at the wheelbarrow in the streets of Baltimore, under the superintendence of the town officers—because you have no political connexion with these officers, and, consequently, no control over them. But suppose a pardon granted on a condition to be executed by officers of the federal government—as, for example, to work on a public fortification—and suppose this condition violated, by running away; where is the power of arrest, in these circumstances, given by any law of the United States? And suppose the arrest could be made; where is the clause in any of our judiciary acts that authorizes a court to proceed in such a state of things? And, without some positive legislative regulation on the subject, I know that some of our federal judges would not feel themselves at liberty to proceed *de novo* on the original case. It is true, the King of England grants such conditional pardons by the common law; but the same common law has provided the mode of proceeding for a breach of the condition on the part of the culprit. We have no common law here, however; and hence arises the difficulty.

I understand from Judge Duvall that convicts have been pardoned by the President of the United States on condition of joining the navy of the United States: evidence of which, if it be so, may, I presume, be found in the Department of State. This is a safe and practicable condition; for although in case of desertion the original sentence of condemnation could not be resorted to, yet the new offence of desertion leads to the same catastrophe. If a condition can be devised whose execution would be certain, I have no doubt that the President may pardon on such condition. All conditions precedent would be of this character; *e. g.*, pardon to a military officer under sentence of death, on the previous condition of resigning his commission.

On the second question, whether pardon can precede condemnation, I am of the opinion that the President may, if he chooses, grant such pardon. There is nothing in the terms in which the power of pardon is granted which requires that it shall be preceded by a sentence of conviction on the verdict of a jury. There is nothing in the force of the term *pardon* which implies a previous condemnation. A pardon pre-supposes an offence, and nothing more. If the party confesses his guilt, every degree of certainty as to the fact of the perpetration of the offence is gained that a trial could gain; because, if he were arraigned and pleaded guilty, no jury would be empannelled, and no evidence would be heard in the case, but judgment would be entered on his own plea. But where a pardon is granted on the voluntary confession of one who has not been indicted, the confession should be in writing, and the pardon founded on the specific offence confessed; in other words, it should be a special pardon, so as not to protect the party against a prosecution for any more aggravated offence than he has thought proper to confess. And it is proper to suggest, further, that it would be much safer, as a general rule, to require a previous trial and condemnation; because all previous pardons must be granted on *ex parte* representations, by which the President may be deceived; whereas, on a full trial on the plea of not guilty, the court and jury will never fail to recommend to mercy, if there be any ground for such recommendation; and the President will thus be placed on a sure footing. The latter course, too, so far as I am informed, is more consonant with the general practice both of the State and federal governments, and is least exposed to discontent and censure, of which there is always danger from the adoption of a new, although a legal course.

27

WILLIAM RAWLE, A VIEW OF THE CONSTITUTION
OF THE UNITED STATES 174–78
1829 (2d ed.)

A power to grant reprieves and pardons is expressly given to the president.

That punishments should in all cases be strictly appropriate to the offence and certain in their execution, is indeed the perfection of criminal law, but the fallibility of human judgment would render an inflexible rule to this effect, too severe for human nature. An act may fall within the purview of the law and justly subject the party to conviction; yet there may be alleviating circumstances, which induce even those who deliver the verdict or pronounce the judgment, to feel repugnance at its being executed: but it would tend to overthrow the barriers of law, if the tribunal which is to decide on the guilt or innocence of the accused, were permitted to intermix other considerations. At first view, benevolent minds would not object to the admission of these principles in favour of the accused, on his trial, but the general interests of society have a stronger claim on the humanity of feelings justly regulated, than the particular case of the individual. The general interest requires that the administration of justice should not be diverted from its settled course, by an erroneous assumption of power and an irregular distribution of justice. If the law is plain, the duty of the tribunal is to conform to it, because the law is as compulsory on the tribunal as on the offender.

But the condition of society would be miserable if the severity of the law could in no form be mitigated, and if those considerations which ought not to operate on a jury or a judge could have no influence elsewhere.

Independently of other views, we may instance the case of treason against the state. Public policy may require that the offenders, though convicted, should be forgiven: severity may increase the opposition of that part of the community which was engaged in the combination; mercy may produce conciliation and submission; but if the guilt is proved, no such considerations can be admitted into the deliberations of the court. It is therefore expedient and

wise, to deposit in some other part of the government, the power of granting pardons; a power, which notwithstanding the strange assertions of Blackstone and Montesquieu, is not inconsistent with the nature of a democratic government. The most illustrious minds are sometimes seduced from plain and obvious truths by the illusions of theory, and when we are told that the power of pardon can *never subsist* in democracies, because nothing higher is acknowledged than the magistrate who administers the law, and because it would confound all ideas of right among the mass of the people, as they would find it difficult to tell whether a prisoner was discharged by his innocence, or obtained a pardon through favour, we must at once perceive that the position is fallacious, by being too general.

The inconvenience suggested in the latter member of it, corresponds indeed with what has been already observed, if confined to the judicial tribunal that originally acts on the case, but the first part of it indicates a want of acquaintance with the subdivisions of authority compatible with the purest democracy. It is the office of the judge to convict the guilty; the execution of the sentence is the duty of the executive authority, the time and place of execution are no part of the judgment of the court. It is true, that during a vacancy in the office of president, which as has been seen, is carefully provided against, there would be no power to grant a pardon, but the moment the office is again filled, the power would be revived.

The power to grant pardons extends to all cases, except impeachments. Some considerations on the subject of impeachments will be presented hereafter; at present, it may not be improper to observe, that not only in the Constitution of the United States, but in those of almost every state in the Union, we find the English doctrine of impeachments introduced, but the difference in respect to granting pardons to the persons impeached is not preserved.

Impeachments are generally efforts of the people of that country through their representatives in the house of commons, to obtain redress before a distinct and independent tribunal, for the mal-practices of the great officers of the crown. No pardon previously granted, can shelter the accused from a full inquiry, and thus his misconduct, if substantiated, is developed and exposed to the nation, but after the impeachment has been solemnly heard and determined, it is not understood that the royal grace is further restrained or abridged.

With us, no pardon can be granted either before or after the impeachment; and perhaps, if this mode of trial is retained at all, it is right that the sentence of a guarded and august tribunal, which, as we shall find, is exceedingly limited in the extent of its punishments, should be excepted from the general power of the president to defeat the effect of the condemnation.

In respect to another jurisdiction, it may be doubted whether he possesses the power to pardon.

It seems to result from the principle on which the power to punish contempts of either house of the legislature is founded, that the executive authority cannot interpose, in any shape, between them and the offender. The main object is to preserve the purity and independence of the legislature, for the benefit of the people. It acts, therefore, on its own power, without reference to, or dependence upon, any other. If the executive authority could, by granting a pardon, or, in any other mode, protect those who insidiously or violently interrupted or defeated their operations, the legislature, which is the superior body, would be so far dependent on the good will of the executive. And it would be only, as it were, by the permission of the latter, that it exercised a jurisdiction of so much importance to the people's rights. The Constitution is as silent in respect to the right of granting pardons in such cases, as it is in respect to the creation of the jurisdiction itself. One arises by implication; the other is excluded by implication.

In all other than these two cases, the power is general and unqualified. It may be exercised as well before as after a trial, and it extends alike to the highest and the smallest offences. The remission of fines, penalties, and forfeitures, under the revenue laws, is included in it, and in this shape it is frequently exercised: but although it may relieve the party from the necessity of paying money into the treasury, the president cannot, after the money has reached the treasury, compel the restitution of it.

The Constitution no where expressly describes any mode of punishment: it empowers congress in four enumerated cases to provide the punishment. They are treason, piracy, offences against the law of nations, and counterfeiting the securities and current coin of the United States. The power of congress to inflict punishment in other cases is derived from implication only, but it is necessary to carry the Constitution into effect, and is embraced in the general provision to pass all laws which may be necessary and proper. The pardoning power is as extensive as the punishing power, and applies as well to punishments imposed by virtue of laws under this implied authority, as to those where it is expressed. The only exceptions are the two cases we have already mentioned, in one of which the power of pardoning is expressly withheld—and in the other it is incompatible with the peculiar nature of the jurisdiction.

In the exercise of the "benign perogative of pardoning," as it has been justly termed, the president stands alone. The Constitution imposes no restraint upon him by requiring him to consult others. As the sense of responsibility is always strong in proportion as it is undivided, a single man will be most ready to attend to the force of those motives, which ought to plead for a mitigation of the rigour of the law, and less inclined to yield to considerations calculated to shelter proper subjects from its punishment. On the other hand; as men generally derive confidence from their number, they might often encourage each other in acts of obduracy, and be less sensible to apprehensions of censure for an injudicious or an affected clemency.

In addition to this objection, there would be a great inconvenience in imposing on the president the necessity of consulting a body, which, whether already a permanent part of the government as the senate, or specially created for the purpose, it might be difficult to convene on occasions when perhaps an immediate decision would be highly expedient.

28

JOHN MACPHERSON BERRIEN,
PARDONS BEFORE CONVICTION
12 Oct. 1829
2 Ops. Atty. Gen. 275

Sir: I have carefully examined the memorial of Abel S. Dungan, and the accompanying documents, (which are herewith returned;) and I have now the honor to state to you such reflections as have occurred to me on the perusal.

A variety of considerations seem to me to render it inexpedient, generally, to interpose the pardoning power previously to trial. It is not denied, however, that cases may exist in which such an interposition would be proper; and it is admitted that the case presented, on the evidence furnished by the memorialist, is a strong one. The application seems to me, however, to be premature; for the reasons which I will proceed to state.

At the May term of the circuit court of the United States for the district of Maryland, in the current year, an indictment was found against the memorialist for murder, on the testimony of three witnesses. The next session of that court will be held in December; and, alleging that he cannot safely proceed to trial in the absence of witnesses whom he states to be important, and that the United States will probably be unprepared for trial from a similar cause, the memorialist asks from the President, in consideration of the difficulty of obtaining a trial at any certain time, that he will examine the evidence submitted, and grant a *nolle prosequi*. As a further inducement to this, he alleges that the absent witnesses are seafaring men, whose return is uncertain; and that he is himself prevented by the pendency of this prosecution from embarking on any voyage, and thereby from earning a subsistence for his family.

These suggestions will be entitled to consideration, if, at the next term of the court, a trial cannot be had, but, as that will speedily occur, it seems to me that it would be improper, by any previous interposition of the pardoning power, to anticipate the state of things which may then exist. In the mean time, I would respectfully recommend that the memorial and accompanying documents be laid before the district attorney of Maryland, and that he be instructed to communicate any information in his possession relating to this case, which may, in his opinion, be assistant to the Executive of the United States in deciding on this application.

29

UNITED STATES v. WILSON
7 Pet. 150 (1833)

[Marshall, C.J.:] In this case the grand jury had found an indictment against the prisoner for robbing the mail, to which he had pleaded not guilty. Afterwards, he withdrew this plea, and pleaded guilty. On a motion by the district attorney, at a subsequent day, for judgment, the court suggested the propriety of inquiring as to the effect of a certain pardon, understood to have been granted by the president of the United States to the defendant, since the conviction on this indictment, alleged to relate to a conviction on another indictment, and that the motion was adjourned till the next day. On the succeeding day the counsel for the prisoner appeared in court, and on his behalf waived and declined any advantage or protection which might be supposed to arise from the pardon referred to; and thereupon the following points were made by the district attorney:

1. That the pardon referred to is expressly restricted to the sentence of death passed upon the defendant under another conviction, and as expressly reserves from its operation the conviction now before the court.

2. That the prisoner can, under this conviction, derive no advantage from the pardon without bringing the same judicially before the court.

The prisoner being asked by the court whether he had any thing to say why sentence should not be pronounced for the crime whereof he stood convicted in this particular case, and whether he wished in any manner to avail himself of the pardon referred to, answered that he had nothing to say, and that he did not wish in any manner to avail himself, in order to avoid the sentence in this particular case, of the pardon referred to.

The judges were thereupon divided in opinion on both points made by the district attorney, and ordered them to be certified to this court.

A certiorari was afterwards awarded to bring up the record of the case in which judgment of death had been pronounced against the prisoner. The indictment charges a robbery of the mail, and putting the life of the driver in jeopardy. The robbery charged in each indictment is on the same day, at the same place and on the same carrier.

We do not think that this record is admissible, since no direct reference is made to it in the points adjourned by the circuit court: and without its aid we cannot readily comprehend the questions submitted to us.

If this difficulty be removed, another is presented by the terms in which the first point is stated on the record. The attorney argued, first, that the pardon referred to is expressly restricted to the sentence of death passed upon the defendant under another conviction, and as expressly reserves from its operation the conviction now before the court. Upon this point the judges were opposed in opinion. Whether they were opposed on the fact, or on the inference drawn from it by the attorney; and what that inference was, the record does not explicitly inform us. If the question on which the judges doubted was, whether such a pardon ought to restrain the court from pronouncing judgment in the case before them, which was expressly excluded from it; the first inquiry is, whether the robbery charged in the one indictment is the same with that charged in the other. This is neither expressly affirmed nor denied. If the convictions be for different robberies, no question of law can arise on the effect which the pardon of the one may have on the proceedings for the others.

If the statement on the record be sufficient to inform this court, judicially, that the robberies are the same, we are not told on what point of law the judges were divided. The only inference we can draw from the statement is, that it was doubted whether the terms of the pardon could restrain the court from pronouncing the judgment of law on the conviction before them. The prisoner was convicted of robbing the mail, and putting the life of the carrier in jeopardy, for which the punishment is death. He had also been convicted on an indictment for the same robbery, as we now suppose, without putting life in jeopardy, for which the punishment is fine and imprisonment; and the question supposed to be submitted is, whether a pardon of the greater offence, excluding the less, necessarily comprehends the less, against its own express terms.

We should feel not much difficulty on this statement of the question, but it is unnecessary to discuss or decide it.

Whether the pardon reached the less offence or not, the first indictment comprehended both the robbery and the putting life in jeopardy, and the conviction and judgment pronounced upon it extended to both. After the judgment no subsequent prosecution could be maintained for the same offence, or for any part of it, provided the former conviction was pleaded. Whether it could avail without being pleaded, or in any manner relied on by the prisoner, is substantially the same question with that presented in the second point, which is, "that the prisoner can, under this conviction, derive no advantage from the pardon, without bringing the same judicially before the court by plea, motion or otherwise."

The constitution gives to the president, in general terms, "the power to grant reprieves and pardons for offences against the United States."

As this power had been exercised from time immemorial by the executive of that nation whose language is our language, and to whose judicial institutions ours bear a close resemblance; we adopt their principles respecting the operation and effect of a pardon, and look into their books for the rules prescribing the manner in which it is to be used by the person who would avail himself of it.

A pardon is an act of grace, proceeding from the power entrusted with the execution of the laws, which exempts the individual, on whom it is bestowed, from the punishment the law inflicts for a crime he has committed. It is the private, though official act of the executive magistrate, delivered to the individual for whose benefit it is intended, and not communicated officially to the court. It is a constituent part of the judicial system, that the judge sees only with judicial eyes, and knows nothing respecting any particular case, of which he is not informed judicially. A private deed, not communicated to him, whatever may be its character, whether a pardon or release, is totally unknown and cannot be acted on. The looseness which would be introduced into judicial proceedings, would prove fatal to the great principles of justice, if the judge might notice and act upon facts not brought regularly into the cause. Such a proceeding, in ordinary cases, would subvert the best established principles, and overturn those rules which have been settled by the wisdom of ages.

Is there any thing peculiar in a pardon which ought to distinguish it in this respect from other facts?

We know of no legal principle which will sustain such a distinction.

A pardon is a deed, to the validity of which delivery is essential, and delivery is not complete without acceptance. It may then be rejected by the person to whom it is tendered; and if it be rejected, we have discovered no power in a court to force it on him.

It may be supposed that no being condemned to death would reject a pardon; but the rule must be the same in capital cases and in misdemeanours. A pardon may be conditional; and the condition may be more objectionable than the punishment inflicted by the judgment.

The pardon may possibly apply to a different person or a different crime. It may be absolute or conditional. It may be controverted by the prosecutor, and must be expounded by the court. These circumstances combine to show that this, like any other deed, ought to be brought "judicially before the court by plea, motion or otherwise."

The decisions on this point conform to these principles. Hawkins, b. 2, ch. 37, sect. 59, says, "but it is certain that a man may waive the benefit of a pardon under the great seal, as where one who hath such a pardon doth not plead it, but takes the general issue, after which he shall not resort to the pardon." In sect. 67, he says, "an exception is made of a pardon after plea."

Notwithstanding this general assertion, a court would undoubtedly at this day permit a pardon to be used after the general issue. Still, where the benefit is to be obtained through the agency of the court, it must be brought regularly to the notice of that tribunal.

Hawkins says, sec. 64, "it will be error to allow a man the benefit of such a pardon unless it be pleaded." In sect. 65, he says, "he who pleads such a pardon must produce it *sub fide sigilli*, though it be a plea in bar, because it is presumed to be in his custody, and the property of it belongs to him."

Comyn, in his Digest, tit. Pardon, letter H, says, "if a man has a charter of pardon from the king, he ought to plead it in bar of the indictment; and if he pleads not guilty he waives his pardon." The same law is laid down in Bacon's Abridgment, title Pardon; and is confirmed by the cases these authors quote.

We have met with only one case which might seem to question it. Jenkins, page 169, case 62, says, "if the king pardons a felon, and it is shown to the court, and yet the felon pleads guilty, and waives the pardon, he shall not be hanged; for it is the king's will that he shall not, and the king has an interest in the life of his subject. The books to the contrary are to be understood where the charter of pardon is not shown to the court."

This vague dictum supposes the pardon to be shown to the court. The waiver spoken of is probably that implied waiver which arises from pleading the general issue: and the case may be considered as determining nothing more than that the prisoner may avail himself of the pardon by showing it to the court, even after waiving it by pleading the general issue. If this be, and it most probably is the fair and sound construction of this case, it is reconciled with all the other decisions, so far as respects the present inquiry.

Blackstone, in his 4th vol. p. 337, says, "a pardon may be pleaded in bar." In p. 376, he says, "it may also be pleaded in arrest of judgment." In p. 401, he says, "a pardon by act of parliament is more beneficial than by the king's charter; for a man is not bound to plead it, but the court must, *ex officio*, take notice of it; neither can he lose the benefit of it by his own laches or negligence, as he may of the king's charter of pardon. The king's charter of pardon must be specially pleaded, and that at a proper time; for if a man is indicted and has a pardon in his pocket, and afterwards puts himself upon his trial by pleading the general issue, he has waived the benefit of such pardon. But if a man avails himself thereof, as by course of law he may, a pardon may either be pleaded on arraignment, or in arrest of judgment, or, in the present stage of proceedings, in bar of execution."

The reason why a court must ex officio take notice of a pardon by act of parliament, is that it is considered as a public law; having the same effect on the case as if the general law punishing the offence had been repealed or annulled.

This court is of opinion that the pardon in the proceedings mentioned, not having been brought judicially before the court by plea, motion or otherwise, cannot be noticed by the judges.

30

JOSEPH STORY, COMMENTARIES ON THE
CONSTITUTION 3:§§ 1488–98
1833

§ 1488. The next power is, "to grant reprieves and pardons." It has been said by the marquis Beccaria, that the power of pardon does not exist under a perfect administration of the laws; and that the admission of the power is a tacit acknowledgment of the infirmity of the course of justice. But if this be a defect at all, it arises from the infirmity of human nature generally; and in this view, is no more objectionable, than any other power of government; for every such power, in some sort, arises from human infirmity. But if it be meant, that it is an imperfection in human legislation to admit the power of pardon in any case, the proposition may well be denied, and some proof, at least, be required of its sober reality. The common argument is, that where punishments are mild, they ought to be certain; and that the clemency of the chief magistrate is a tacit disapprobation of the laws. But surely no man in his senses will contend, that any system of laws can provide for every possible shade of guilt, a proportionate degree of punishment. The most, that ever has been, and ever can be done, is to provide for the punishment of crimes by some general rules, and within some general limitations. The total exclusion of all power of pardon would necessarily introduce a very dangerous power in judges and juries, of following the spirit, rather than the letter of the laws; or, out of humanity, of suffering real offenders wholly to escape punishment; or else, it must be holden, (what no man will seriously avow,) that the situation and circumstances of the offender, though they alter not the essence of the offence, ought to make no distinction in the punishment. There are not only various gradations of guilt in the commission of the same crime, which are not susceptible of any previous enumeration and definition; but the proofs must, in many cases, be imperfect in their own nature, not only as to the actual commission of the offence, but also, as to the aggravating or mitigating circumstances. In many cases, convictions must be founded upon presumpions and probabilities. Would it not be at once unjust and unreasonable to exclude all means of mitigating punishment, when subsequent inquiries should demonstrate, that the accusation was wholly unfounded, or the crime greatly diminished in point of atrocity and aggravation, from what the evidence at the trial seemed to establish? A power to pardon seems, indeed, indispensable under the most correct administration of the law by human tribunals; since, otherwise, men would sometimes fall a prey to the vindictiveness of accusers, the inaccuracy of testimony, and the fallibility of jurors and courts. Besides; the law may be broken, and yet the offender be placed in such circumstances, that he will stand, in a great measure, and perhaps wholly, excused in moral and general justice, though not in the strictness of the law. What then is to be done? Is he to be acquitted against the law; or convicted, and to suffer punishment infinitely beyond his deserts? If an arbitrary power is to be given to meet such cases, where can it be so properly lodged, as in the executive department?

§ 1489. Mr. Justice Blackstone says, that "in democracies, this power of pardon can never subsist; for, there, nothing higher is acknowledged, than the magistrate, who administers the laws; and it would be impolitic for the power of judging, and of pardoning to center in one and the same person. This (as the president Montesquieu, observes) would oblige him very often to contradict himself, to make and unmake his decisions. It would tend to confound all ideas of right among the mass of the people, as they would find it difficult to tell, whether a prisoner was discharged by his innocence, or obtained a pardon through favour." And hence, he deduces the superiority of a monarchical government; because in monarchies, the king acts in a superior sphere; and may, therefore, safely be trusted with the power of pardon, and it becomes a source of personal loyalty and affection.

§ 1490. But, surely, this reasoning is extremely forced and artificial. In the first place, there is [no] more difficulty or absurdity in a democracy, than in a monarchy, in such cases, if the power of judging and pardoning be in the same hands; as if the monarch be at once the judge, and the person, who pardons. And Montesquieu's reasoning is in fact addressed to this very case of a monarch, who is at once the judge, and dispenser of pardons. In the next place, there is no inconsistency in a democracy any more, than in a monarchy, in entrusting one magistrate with a power to try the cause, and another with a power to pardon. The one power is not incidental to, but in contrast with the other. Nor, if both powers were lodged in the same magistrate, would there be any danger of their being necessarily confounded; for they may be required to be acted upon separately, and at different times, so as to be known as distinct prerogatives. But, in point of fact, no such reasoning has the slightest application to the American governments, or, indeed, to any others, where there is a separation of the general departments of government, legislative, judicial, and executive, and the powers of each are administered by distinct persons. What difficulty is there in the people delegating the judicial power to one body of magistrates, and the power of pardon to another, in a republic any more, than there is in the king's delegating the judicial power to magistrates, and reserving the pardoning power to himself, in a monarchy? In truth, the learned author, in his extreme desire to recommend a kingly form of government, seems on this, as on many other occasions, to have been misled into the most loose and inconclusive statements. There is not a single state in the Union, in which there is not by its constitution a power of pardon lodged in some one department of government, distinct from the judicial. And the power of remitting penalties is in some cases, even in England, entrusted to judicial officers.

§ 1491. So far from the power of pardon being incompatible with the fundamental principles of a republic, it may be boldly asserted to be peculiarly appropriate, and safe in all free states; because the power can there be guarded by a just responsibility for its exercise. Little room will be left for favouritism, personal caprice, or personal resentment. If the power should ever be abused, it would be far less likely to occur in opposition, than in obedience to the will of the people. The danger is not, that in republics the victims of the law will too often escape punishment by a pardon; but that the power will not be sufficiently exerted in cases, where public feeling accompanies the prosecution, and assigns the ultimate doom to persons, who have been convicted upon slender testimony, or popular suspicions.

§ 1492. The power to pardon, then, being a fit one to be entrusted to all governments, humanity and sound policy dictate, that this benign prerogative should be, as little as possible, fettered, or embarrassed. The criminal code of every country partakes so much of necessary severity, that, without an easy access to exceptions in favour of unfortunate guilt, justice would assume an aspect too sanguinary and cruel. The only question is, in what department of the government it can be most safely lodged; and that must principally refer to the executive, or legislative department. The reasoning in favour of vesting it in the executive department may be thus stated. A sense of responsibility is always strongest in proportion, as it is undivided. A single person would, therefore, be most ready to attend to the force of those motives, which might plead for a mitigation of the rigour of the law; and the least apt to yield to considerations, which were calculated to shelter a fit object of its vengeance. The consciousness, that the life, or happiness of an offender was exclusively within his discretion, would inspire scrupulousness and caution; and the dread of being accused of weakness, or connivance, would beget circumspection of a different sort. On the other hand, as men generally derive confidence from numbers, a large assembly might naturally encourage each other in acts of obduracy, as no one would feel much apprehension of public censure. A public body, too, ordinarily engaged in other duties, would be little apt to sift cases of this sort thoroughly to the bottom, and would be disposed to yield to the solicitations, or be guided by the prejudices of a few; and thus shelter their own acts of yielding too much, or too little, under the common apology of ignorance, or confidence. A single magistrate would be compelled to search, and act upon his own responsibility; and therefore would be at once a more enlightened dispenser of mercy, and a more firm administrator of public justice.

§ 1493. There are probably few persons now, who would not consider the power of pardon in ordinary cases, as best deposited with the president. But the expediency of vesting it in him in any cases, and especially in cases of treason, was doubted at the time of adopting the constitution; and it was then urged, that it ought at least in cases of treason to be vested in one, or both branches of the legislature. That there are strong reasons, which may be assigned in favour of vesting the power in congress in cases of treason, need not be denied. As treason is a crime levelled at the immediate existence of society, when the laws have once ascertained the guilt of the offender, there would seem to be a fitness in referring the expediency of an act of mercy towards him to the judgment of the legislature. But there are strong reasons also against it. Even in such cases a single magistrate, of prudence and sound sense, would be better fitted, than a numerous assembly, in such delicate conjunctures, to weigh the motives for and against the remission of the punishment, and to ascertain all the facts without undue influence. The responsibility would be more felt, and more direct. Treason, too, is a crime, that will often be connected with seditions, embracing a large portion of a particular community; and might under such circumstances, and especially where parties were nearly poised, find friends and favourites, as well as enemies and opponents, in the councils of the nation. So, that the chance of an impartial judgment might be less probable in such bodies, than in a single person at the head of the nation.

§ 1494. A still more satisfactory reason is, that the legislature is not always in session; and that their proceedings must be necessarily slow, and are generally not completed, until after long delays. The inexpediency of deferring the execution of any criminal sentence, until a long and indefinite time after a conviction, is felt in all communities. It destroys one of the best effects of punishment, that, which arises from a prompt and certain administration of justice following close upon the offence. If the legislature is invested with the authority to pardon, it is obviously indispensable, that no sentence can be properly executed, at least in capital cases, until they have had time to act. And a mere postponement of the subject from session to session would be naturally sought by all those, who favoured the convict, and yet doubted the success of his application. In many cases delay would be equivalent to a pardon, as to its influence upon public opinion, either in weakening the detestation of the crime, or encouraging the commission of it. But the principal argument for reposing the power of pardon in the executive magistrate in cases of treason is, that in seasons of insurrection, or rebellion, there are critical moments, when a well-timed offer of pardon to the insurgents, or rebels, may restore the tranquillity of the Commonwealth; and if these are suffered to pass unimproved, it may be impossible afterwards to interpose with the same success. The dilatory process of convening the legislature, or one of the branches, for the purpose of sanctioning such a measure, would frequently be the loss of the golden opportunity. The loss of a week, of a day, or even of an hour may sometimes prove fatal. If a discretionary power were confided to the president to act in such emergencies, it would greatly diminish the importance of the restriction. And it would generally be impolitic to hold out, either by the constitution or by law, a prospect of impunity by confiding the exercise of the power to the executive in special cases; since it might be construed into an argument of timidity or weakness, and thus have a tendency to embolden guilt. In point of fact, the power has always been found safe in the hands of the state executives in treason, as well as in other cases; and there can be no practical reason, why it should not be equally safe with the executive of the Union.

§ 1495. There is an exception to the power of pardon, that it shall not extend to cases of impeachment, which takes from the president every temptation to abuse it in cases of political and official offences by persons in the public service. The power of impeachment will generally be applied to persons holding high offices under the government; and it is of great consequence, that the president should not have the power of preventing a thorough investigation of their conduct, or of securing them against the disgrace of a public conviction by impeachment, if they should deserve it. The constitution has, therefore, wisely interposed this check upon his power, so that he cannot, by any corrupt coalition with favourites, or dependents in high offices, screen them from punishment.

§ 1496. In England (from which this exception was probably borrowed) no pardon can be pleaded in bar of an impeachment. But the king may, after conviction upon an impeachment pardon the offender. His prerogative, therefore, cannot prevent the disgrace of a conviction; but it may avert its effects, and restore the offender to his credit. The president possesses no such power in any case of impeachment; and, as the judgment upon a conviction extends no farther, than to a removal from office, and disqualification to hold office, there is not the same reason for its exercise after conviction, as there is in England; since (as we have seen) the judgment there, so that it does not exceed what is allowed by law, lies wholly in the breast of the house of lords, as to its nature and extent, and may, in many cases, not only reach the life, but the whole fortune of the offender.

§ 1497. It would seem to result from the principle, on which the power of each branch of the legislature to punish for contempts is founded, that the executive authority cannot interpose between them and the offender. The main object is to secure a purity, independence, and ability of the legislature adequate to the discharge of all their duties. If they can be overawed by force, or corrupted by largesses, or interrupted in their proceedings by violence, without the means of self-protection, it is obvious, that they will soon be found incapable of legislating with wisdom or independence. If the executive should possess the power of pardoning any such offender, they would be wholly dependent upon his good will and pleasure for the exercise of their own powers. Thus, in effect, the rights of the people entrusted to them would be placed in perpetual jeopardy. The constitution is silent in respect to the right of granting pardons in such cases, as it is in respect to the jurisdiction to punish for contempts. The latter arises by implication; and to make it effectual the former is excluded by implication.

§ 1498. Subject to these exceptions, (and perhaps there may be others of a like nature standing on special grounds,) the power of pardon is general and unqualified, reaching from the highest to the lowest offences. The power of remission of fines, penalties, and forfeitures is also included in it; and may in the last resort be exercised by the executive, although it is in many cases by our laws confided to the treasury department. No law can abridge the constitutional powers of the executive department, or interrupt its right to interpose by pardon in such cases.

SEE ALSO:

Commander in Chief

Generally 1.8.15; 1.8.16
Indiana Constitution of 1816, art. 4, sec. 7, Thorpe 2:1063
James Kent, Commentaries 1:264 (1826)
William Rawle, A View of the Constitution of the United States 151–61 (2d ed. 1829)

Reprieves and Pardons

Generally 2.4; 3.3
Luther Martin, Genuine Information, 1788, Storing 2.4.85
James Iredell, Marcus, Answers to Mr. Mason's Objections to the New Constitution, 8 Jan. 1788, Pamphlets 350–54
Pierce Butler to Weedon Butler, 5 May 1788, Farrand 3:302
George Washington, Seventh Annual Address, 8 Dec. 1795, Richardson 1:184
Charles Lee, Assurance of Pardon, 18 Nov. 1797, 1 Ops. Atty. Gen. 77
John Adams, Proclamation of Amnesty, 21 May 1800, 9 Fed. Cas. 945, no. 5,127
People v. *James*, 2 Caines 57 (N.Y. 1804)
William Wirt, Power of the President to Mitigate Sentence of Death, 4 Jan. 1820, 1 Ops. Atty. Gen. 327
William Wirt, Pardon of Piratical Murderer, 9 May 1820, 1 Ops. Atty. Gen. 359
State v. *Fuller*, 1 McCord 178 (S.C. 1821)
William Wirt, Conditional Pardons, 16 Aug. 1821, 1 Ops. Atty. Gen. 482
James Kent, Commentaries 1:265–66 (1826)
State v. *Smith*, 1 Bailey 283 (S.C. 1829)
John Macpherson Berrien, Pardons and Remissions of Forfeitures, 17 Mar. 1830, 2 Ops. Atty. Gen. 329
State v. *Addington*, 2 Bailey 516 (S.C.1831)

Article 2, Section 2, Clauses 2 and 3

He shall have Power, by and with the Advice and Consent of the Senate, to make Treaties, provided two thirds of the Senators present concur; and he shall nominate, and by and with the Advice and Consent of the Senate, shall appoint Ambassadors, other public Ministers and Consuls, Judges of the supreme Court, and all other Officers of the United States, whose Appointments are not herein otherwise provided for, and which shall be established by Law: but the Congress may by Law vest the Appointment of such inferior Officers, as they think proper, in the President alone, in the Courts of Law, or in the Heads of Departments.

The President shall have Power to fill up all Vacancies that may happen during the Recess of the Senate, by granting Commissions which shall expire at the End of their next Session.

1. Records of the Federal Convention

Foreign Affairs

2. William Blackstone, Commentaries (1765)
3. James Wilson, Pennsylvania Ratifying Convention, 11 Dec. 1787
4. James Iredell, Marcus, Answers to Mr. Mason's Objections to the New Constitution, 1788
5. Federal Farmer, no. 11, 10 Jan. 1788
6. Debate in South Carolina House of Representatives, 16–17 Jan. 1788
7. James Madison, Federalist, no. 42, 22 Jan. 1788
8. John Jay, Federalist, no. 64, 5 Mar. 1788
9. Alexander Hamilton, Federalist, no. 75, 26 Mar. 1788
10. Debate in Virginia Ratifying Convention, 18–19 June 1788
11. Debate in North Carolina Ratifying Convention, 24, 28 July 1788
12. George Washington to Senate Committee on Treaties and Nominations, 10 Aug. 1789
13. *United States* v. *Ravara,* 27 Fed. Cas. 713, no. 16,122 (C.C.D.Pa. 1793), in 3.2.1, no. 36
14. Alexander Hamilton, Pacificus, no. 1, 29 June 1793
15. James Madison, Letters of Helvidius, nos. 1–4, 24 Aug.–14 Sept. 1793
16. Thomas Jefferson to Edmond Charles Genet, 22 Nov. 1793
17. Senate, Presentation of the Colors of France, 6 Jan. 1796
18. Alexander Hamilton to George Washington, 7 Mar. 1796, in vol. 1, ch. 10, no. 19
19. Alexander Hamilton to William Loughton Smith, 10 Mar. 1796, in vol. 1, ch. 10, no. 20
20. George Washington to House of Representatives, 30 Mar. 1796
21. George Washington to Alexander Hamilton, 31 Mar. 1796
22. James Madison, The Jay Treaty, House of Representatives, 6 Apr. 1796
23. An Act to Declare the Treaties Heretofore Concluded with France, No Longer Obligatory on the United States, 1 Stat. 578 (1798)
24. St. George Tucker, Blackstone's Commentaries (1803)
25. Thomas Jefferson, Proposed Amendment to the Constitution, July 1803
26. Thomas Jefferson to William Dunbar, 17 July 1803
27. Thomas Jefferson to Wilson Cary Nicholas, 7 Sept. 1803
28. Thomas Jefferson to James Madison, 14 July 1804
29. Senate, Committee on Foreign Relations, Reports, 15 Feb. 1816
30. Rufus King, African Slave Trade, Senate, 12 Jan. 1818
31. James Kent, Commentaries (1826)
32. William Rawle, A View of the Constitution of the United States (2d ed. 1829)
33. *United States* v. *Benner,* 24 Fed. Cas. 1084, no. 14,568 (C.C.E.D.Pa. 1830)
34. Joseph Story, Commentaries on the Constitution (1833)

Appointment and Removal

35. William Blackstone, Commentaries (1765)
36. Luther Martin, Genuine Information, 1788
37. Federal Farmer, no. 13, 14 Jan. 1788, in 1.6.2, no. 4
38. Federal Farmer, no. 14, 17 Jan. 1788
39. Alexander Hamilton, Federalist, no. 76, 1 Apr. 1788
40. Alexander Hamilton, Federalist, no. 77, 2 Apr. 1788
41. Debate in North Carolina Ratifying Convention, 28 July 1788
42. House of Representatives, Treasury Department, 29 June 1789
43. James Madison to Thomas Jefferson, 30 June 1789
44. John Adams, Notes of a Debate in the Senate, 15 July 1789
45. John Adams to Roger Sherman, [20?] July 1789
46. Roger Sherman to John Adams, July 1789
47. Samuel Adams to Richard Henry Lee, 29 Aug. 1789
48. Thomas Jefferson, Opinion on Powers of the Senate respecting Diplomatic Appointments, 24 Apr. 1790
49. James Wilson, Government, Lectures on Law, 1791
50. George Mason to James Monroe, 30 Jan. 1792
51. *Marbury* v. *Madison,* 1 Cranch 137 (1803), in 3.2.1, no. 47
52. St. George Tucker, Blackstone's Commentaries (1803)
53. James Madison to Senate of United States, June 1813
54. James Monroe to James Madison, 10 May 1822
55. *United States* v. *Maurice,* 2 Marshall's C.C. 96 (C.C.D.Va. 1823)
56. William Rawle, A View of the Constitution of the United States (2d ed. 1829)
57. John Macpherson Berrien, Commissions Granted during Recess of Senate, 16 Apr. 1830
58. Joseph Story, Commentaries on the Constitution (1833)

1

RECORDS OF THE FEDERAL CONVENTION

[1:21; Journal, 29 May]

7. Resd. that a National Executive be instituted . . . to enjoy the Executive rights vested in Congress by the Confederation.

. . . . .

9. Resd. that a National Judiciary be established . . . to be chosen by the National Legislature. . . .

[1:63; Journal, 1 June]

It was then moved, by Mr. Madison, seconded by Mr. Wilson, after the word instituted to add the words

"with power to carry into execution the national laws,—to appoint to offices in cases not otherwise provided for;"

[1:66; Madison, 1 June]

Mr. Madison thought it would be proper, before a choice shd. be made between a unity and a plurality in the Executive, to fix the extent of the Executive authority; that as certain powers were in their nature Executive, and must be given to that departmt. whether administered by one or more persons, a definition of their extent would assist the judgment in determining how far they might be safely entrusted to a single officer. He accordingly moved that so much of the clause before the Committee as related to the powers of the Executive shd. be struck out & that after the words "that a national Executive ought to be instituted" there be inserted the words following viz, "with power to carry into effect. the national laws. to appoint to offices in cases not otherwise provided for, and to execute such other powers "not Legislative nor Judiciary in their nature." as may from time to time be delegated by the national Legislature". The words "not legislative nor judiciary in their nature" were added to the proposed amendment in consequence of a suggestion by Genl Pinkney that improper powers might otherwise be delegated,

Mr. Wilson seconded this motion

Mr. Pinkney moved to amend the amendment by striking out the last member of it; viz. "and to execute such other powers not Legislative nor Judiciary in their nature as may from time to time be delegated." He said they were unnecessary, the object of them being included in the "power to carry into effect the national laws".

Mr. Randolph seconded the motion.

Mr. Madison did not know that the words were absolutely necessary, or even the preceding words. "to appoint to offices" &c. the whole being perhaps included in the first member of the proposition. He did not however see any inconveniency in retaining them, and cases might happen in which they might serve to prevent doubts and misconstructions.

In consequence of the motion of Mr. Pinkney, the question on Mr. Madison's motion was divided; and the words objected to by Mr. Pinkney struck out; by the votes of Connecticut. N. Y. N. J. Pena. Del. N. C. & Geo: agst. Mass. Virga. & S. Carolina the preceding part of the motion being first agreed to: Connecticut divided, all the other States in the affirmative.

[1:116; Journal, 5 June]

It was then moved and seconded to strike out the words "the national legislature" so as to read

to be appointed by.

On the question to strike out

it passed in the affirmative [Ayes—8; noes—2.]

Notice was given by Mr. Wilson that he should at a future day move for a reconsideration of that clause which respects "inferior tribunals"

Mr C. Pinckney gave notice that when the clause which respects the appointment of the Judiciary came before the Committee he should move to restore the words

"the national legislature"

[1:119; Madison, 5 June]

The Clause—"that the national Judiciary be chosen by the National Legislature", being under consideration.

Mr. Wilson opposed the appointmt of Judges by the national Legisl: Experience shewed the impropriety of such appointmts. by numerous bodies. Intrigue, partiality, and concealment were the necessary consequences. A principal reason for unity in the Executive was that officers might be appointed by a single, responsible person.

Mr. Rutlidge was by no means disposed to grant so great a power to any single person. The people will think we are leaning too much towards Monarchy. He was against establishing any national tribunal except a single supreme one. The State Tribunals are most proper to decide in all cases in the first instance.

Docr. Franklin observed that two modes of chusing the Judges had been mentioned, to wit, by the Legislature and by the Executive. He wished such other modes to be suggested as might occur to other gentlemen; it being a point of great moment. He would mention one which he had understood was practiced in Scotland. He then in a brief and entertaining manner related a Scotch mode, in which the nomination proceeded from the Lawyers, who always selected the ablest of the profession in order to get rid of him, and share his practice among themselves. It was here he said the interest of the electors to make the best choice, which should always be made the case if possible.

Mr. Madison disliked the election of the Judges by the Legislature or any numerous body. Besides, the danger of intrigue and partiality, many of the members were not judges of the requisite qualifications. The Legislative talents which were very different from those of a Judge, commonly recommended men to the favor of Legislative Assemblies. It was known too that the accidental circumstances of presence and absence, of being a member or not a member, had a very undue influence on the appointment. On the other hand He was not satisfied with referring the appointment to the Executive. He rather inclined to give it to the Senatorial branch, as numerous eno' to be confided in—as not so numerous as to be governed by the motives of the other branch; and as being sufficiently stable and independent to follow their deliberate judgments. He hinted this only and moved that the *appointment by the Legislature* might be struck out, & and a blank left to be hereafter filled on maturer reflection. Mr. Wilson seconds it. On the question for striking out. Massts. ay. Cont. no. N. Y. ay. N. J. ay. Pena. ay. Del. ay. Md. ay. Va. ay. N. C. ay. S. C. no. Geo. ay. [Ayes—9; noes—2.]

Mr. Wilson gave notice that he should at a future day move for a reconsideration of that clause which respects "inferior tribunals"

Mr. Pinkney gave notice that when the clause respecting the appointment of the Judiciary should again come before the Committee, he should move to restore the "appointment by the national Legislature"

[1:224; *Journal, 13 June*]

It was moved by Mr Pinckney seconded by Mr Sherman to insert after the words "One supreme Tribunal" "the Judges of which to be appointed by the second branch of the national Legislature.

. . . . .

[Executive] to appoint to offices in cases not otherwise provided for.

[1:232; *Madison, 13 June*]

Mr. Pinkney & Mr. Sherman moved to insert after the words "one supreme tribunal" the words "the Judges of which to be appointed by the national Legislature"

Mr. Madison, objected to an appt. by the whole Legislature. Many of them were incompetent Judges of the requisite qualifications. They were too much influenced by their partialities. The candidate who was present, who had displayed a talent for business in the legislative field, who had perhaps assisted ignorant members in business of their own, or of their Constituents, or used other winning means, would without any of the essential qualifications for an expositor of the laws prevail over a competitor not having these recommendations but possessed of every necessary accomplishment. He proposed that the appointment should be made by the Senate, which as a less numerous & more select body, would be more competent judges, and which was sufficiently numerous to justify such a confidence in them.

Mr. Sharman & Mr. Pinkney withdrew their motion, and the appt. by the Senate was agd. to nem. con.

[1:292; *Madison, 18 June*]

IV. The supreme Executive authority of the United States . . . to have the sole appointment of the heads or chief officers of the departments of Finance, War and Foreign Affairs; to have the nomination of all other officers (Ambassadors to foreign Nations included) subject to the approbation or rejection of the Senate;

[1:300; *Yates, 18 June*]

[Hamilton plan] . . . The executive to have the power of negativing all laws—to make war or peace, with the advice of the senate—to make treaties with their advice, but to have the sole direction of all military operations, and to send ambassadors and appoint all military officers, and to pardon all offenders, treason excepted, unless by advice of the senate. On his death or removal, the president of the senate to officiate, with the same powers, until another is elected. Supreme judicial officers to be appointed by the executive and the senate. The legisature to appoint courts in each state, so as to make the state governments unnecessary to it.

[2:23; *Journal, 17 July*]

On the question to agree to the following clause namely

"to appoint to offices in cases not otherwise provided for"

it passed unanimously in the affirmative

[2:41; *Madison, 18 July*]

"The Judges of which to be appointd. by the 2d. branch of the Natl. Legislature."

Mr. Ghorum, wd. prefer an appointment by the 2d branch to an appointmt. by the whole Legislature; but he thought even that branch too numerous, and too little personally responsible, to ensure a good choice. He suggested that the Judges be appointed by the Execuve. with the advice & consent of the 2d branch, in the mode prescribed by the constitution of Masts. This mode had been long practised in that country, & was found to answer perfectly well.

Mr. Wilson, still wd. prefer an an appointmt. by the Executive; but if that could not be attained, wd. prefer in the next place, the mode suggested by Mr. Ghorum. He thought it his duty however to move in the first instance "that the Judges be appointed by the Executive." Mr. Govr. Morris 2ded. the motion.

Mr. L. Martin was strenuous for an appt. by the 2d. branch. Being taken from all the States it wd. be best informed of characters & most capable of making a fit choice.

Mr. Sherman concurred in the observations of Mr. Martin, adding that the Judges ought to be diffused, which would be more likely to be attended to by the 2d. branch, than by the Executive.

Mr Mason. The mode of appointing the Judges may depend in some degree on the mode of trying impeachments, of the Executive. If the Judges were to form a tribunal for that purpose, they surely ought not to be appointed by the Executive. There were insuperable objections besides agst. referring the appointment to the Executive. He mentioned as one, that as the seat of Govt. must be in some one State, and the Executive would remain in office for a considerable time, for 4, 5, or 6 years at least he would insensibly form local & personal attachments within the particular State that would deprive equal merit elsewhere, of an equal chance of promotion.

Mr. Ghorum. As the Executive will be responsible in point of character at least, for a judicious and faithful discharge of his trust, he will be careful to look through all the States for proper characters.—The Senators will be as likely to form their attachments at the seat of Govt where they reside, as the Executive. If they can not get the man of the particular State to which they may respectively belong, they will be indifferent to the rest. Public bodies feel no personal responsibly and give full play to intrigue & cabal. Rh. Island is a full illustration of the insensibility to character produced by a participation of numbers, in dishonorable measures, and of the length to which a public body may carry wickedness & cabal.

Mr. Govr. Morris supposed it would be improper for an impeachmt. of the Executive to be tried before the Judges. The latter would in such case be drawn into intrigues with the Legislature and an impartial trial would be frustrated. As they wd. be much about the seat of Govt they might even be previously consulted & arrangements might be made for a prosecution of the Executive. He thought therefore that no argument could be drawn from the probability of such a plan of impeachments agst. the motion before the House.

Mr. Madison, suggested that the Judges might be appointed by the Executives with the concurrence of ⅓ at least of the 2d. branch. This would unite the advantage of responsibility in the Executive with the security afforded in the 2d. branch agst. any incautious or corrupt nomination by the Executive.

Mr. Sherman, was clearly for an election by the Senate. It would be composed of men nearly equal to the Executive, and would of course have on the whole more wisdom. They would bring into their deliberations a more diffusive knowledge of characters. It would be less easy for candidates to intrigue with them, than with the Executive Magistrate. For these reasons he thought there would be a better security for a proper choice in the Senate than in the Executive.

Mr. Randolph. It is true that when the appt. of the Judges was vested in the 2d. branch an equality of votes had not been given to it. Yet he had rather leave the appointmt. there than give it to the Executive. He thought the advantage of personal responsibility might be gained in the Senate by requiring the respective votes of the members to be entered on the Journal. He thought too that the hope of receiving appts. would be more diffusive if they depended on the Senate, the members of which wd. be diffusively known, than if they depended on a single man who could not be personally known to a very great extent; and consequently that opposition to the System, would be so far weakened

Mr. Bedford thought there were solid reasons agst. leaving the appointment to the Executive. He must trust more to information than the Senate. It would put it in his power to gain over the larger States, by gratifying them with a preference of their Citizens. The responsibility of the Executive so much talked of was chimerical. He could not be punished for mistakes.

Mr. Ghorum remarked that the Senate could have no better information than the Executive They must like him, trust to information from the members belonging to the particular State where the Candidate resided. The Executive would certainly be more answerable for a good appointment, as the whole blame of a bad one would fall on him alone. He did not mean that he would be answerable under any other penalty than that of public censure, which with honorable minds was a sufficient one.

On the question for referring the appointment of the Judges to the Executive, instead of the 2d. branch

Mas. ay. Cont. no. Pa. ay. Del. no. Md. no Va. no. N. C. no. S. C. no—Geo. absent. [Ayes—2; noes—6; absent—1.]

Mr. Ghorum moved "that the Judges be nominated and appointed by the Executive, by & with the advice & consent of the 2d branch & every such nomination shall be made at least   days prior to such appointment". This mode he said had been ratified by the experience of 140 years in Massachusstts. If the appt. should be left to either branch of the Legislature, it will be a mere piece of jobbing.

Mr. Govr. Morris 2ded. & supported the motion.

Mr. Sherman thought it less objectionable than an absolute appointment by the Executive; but disliked it as too much fettering the Senate.

Question on Mr. Ghorum's motion

Mas. ay. Con. no. Pa. ay. Del. no. Md. ay. Va. ay. N. C. no. S. C. no. Geo. absent. [Ayes—4; noes—4; absent—1.]

Mr. Madison moved that the Judges should be nominated by the Executive, & such nomination should become an appointment if not disagreed to within   days by ⅔ of the 2d. branch. Mr. Govr. Morris 2ded. the motion. By common consent the consideration of it was postponed till tomorrow.

[2:80; Madison, 21 July]

The motion made by Mr. Madison July 18. & then postponed, "that the Judges shd. be nominated by the Executive & such nominations become appointments unless disagreed to by ⅔ of the 2d. branch of the Legislature," was now resumed.

Mr. Madison stated as his reasons for the motion. 1 that it secured the responsibility of the Executive who would in general be more capable & likely to select fit characters than the Legislature, or even the 2d. b. of it, who might hide their selfish motives under the number concerned in the appointment- 2 that in case of any flagrant partiality or error, in the nomination, it might be fairly presumed that ⅔ of the 2d. branch would join in putting a negative on it. 3. that as the 2d. b. was very differently constituted when the appointment of the Judges was formerly referred to it, and was now to be composed of equal votes from all the States, the principle of compromise which had prevailed in other instances required in this that their shd. be a concurrence of two authorities, in one of which the people, in the other the states, should be represented. The Executive Magistrate wd be considered as a national officer, acting for and equally sympathising with every part of the U. States. If the 2d. branch alone should have this power, the Judges might be appointed by a minority of the people, tho' by a majority, of the States, which could not be justified on any principle as their proceedings were to relate to the people, rather than to the States: and as it would moreover throw the appointments entirely into the hands of ye Nthern States, a perpetual ground of jealousy & discontent would be furnished to the Southern States.

Mr. Pinkney was for placing the appointmt. in the 2d. b. exclusively. The Executive will possess neither the requisite knowledge of characters, nor confidence of the people for so high a trust.

Mr. Randolph wd. have preferred the mode of appointmt. proposed formerly by Mr Ghorum, as adopted in the Constitution of Massts. but thought the motion depending so great an improvement of the clause as it stands, that he anxiously wished it success. He laid great stress on the responsibility of the Executive as a security for fit appointments. Appointments by the Legislatures have generally resulted from cabal, from personal regard, or some other consideration than a title derived from the proper qualifications. The same inconveniencies will proportionally prevail if the appointments be be referred to either branch of the Legislature or to any other authority administered by a number of individuals.

Mr. Elseworth would prefer a negative in the Executive on a nomination by the 2d. branch, the negative to be overruled by a concurrence of ⅔ of the 2d. b. to the mode proposed by the motion; but preferred an absolute appointment by the 2d. branch to either. The Executive will be regarded by the people with a jealous eye. Every power for augmenting unnecessarily his influence will be disliked. As he will be stationary it was not to be supposed he could have a better knowledge of characters. He will be more open to caresses & intrigues than the Senate. The right to supersede his nomination will be ideal only. A nomination under such circumstances will be equivalent to an appointment.

Mr. Govr. Morris supported the motion. 1. The States in their corporate capacity will frequently have an interest staked on the determination of the Judges. As in the Senate the States are to vote the Judges ought not to be appointed by the Senate. Next to the impropriety of being Judge in one's own cause, is the appointment of the Judge. 2. It had been said the Executive would be uninformed of characters. The reverse was ye truth. The Senate will be so. They must take the character of candidates from the flattering pictures drawn by their friends. The Executive in the necessary intercourse with every part of the U. S. required by the nature of his administration, will or may have the best possible information. 3. It had been said that a jealousy would be entertained of the Executive. If the Executive can be safely trusted with the command of the army, there can not surely be any reasonable ground of Jealousy in the present case. He added that if the Objections agst. an appointment of the Executive by the Legislature, had the weight that had been allowed there must be some weight in the objection to an appointment of the Judges by the Legislature or by any part of it.

Mr. Gerry. The appointment of the Judges like every other part of the Constitution shd. be so modeled as to give satisfaction both to the people and to the States. The mode under consideration will give satisfaction to neither. He could not conceive that the Executive could be as well informed of characters throughout the Union, as the Senate. It appeared to him also a strong objection that ⅔ of the Senate were required to reject a nomination of the Executive. The Senate would be constituted in the same manner as Congress. And the appointments of Congress have been generally good.

Mr. Madison observed that he was not anxious that ⅔ should be necessary to disagree to a nomination. He had given this form to his motion chiefly to vary it the more clearly from one which had just been rejected. He was content to obviate the objection last made, and accordingly so varied the motion as to let a majority reject.

Col. Mason found it his duty to differ from his colleagues in their opinions & reasonings on this subject. Notwithstanding the form of the proposition by which the appointment seemed to be divided between the Executive & Senate, the appointment was substantially vested in the former alone. The false complaisance which usually prevails in such cases will prevent a disagreement to the first nominations. He considered the appointment by the Executive as a dangerous prerogative. It might even give him an influence over the Judiciary department itself. He did not think the difference of interest between the Northern and Southern States could be properly brought into this argument. It would operate & require some precautions in the case of regulating navigation, commerce & imposts; but he could not see that it had any connection with the Judiciary department.

On the question, the motion now being "that the executive should nominate, & such nominations should become appointments unless disagreed to by the Senate"

Mas. ay. Ct. no. Pa. ay. Del. no. Md. no. Va. ay. N. C. no. S. C no. Geo. no. [Ayes—3; noes—6.]

On question for agreeing to the clause as it stands by which the Judges are to be appointed by 2d. branch

Mas. no. Ct. ay. Pa. no. Del. ay. Md. ay. Va. no. N. C. ay. S. C. ay. Geo. ay. [Ayes—6; noes—3.]

[2:121; Madison, 26 July]

—to appoint to offices in cases not otherwise provided for—to be removeable on impeachment & conviction of mal-practice or neglect of duty—to receive a fixt compensation for the devotion of his time to the public service, to be paid out of the Natl. Treasury"—it passed in the affirmative.

N. H. ay. Mas. not on floor. Ct. ay. N. J. ay. Pa. no. Del. no. Md. no. Va. divd. Mr. Blair & Col. Mason ay. Genl. Washington & Mr Madison no. Mr. Randolph happened to be out of the House. N–C–ay. S. C. ay. Geo. ay. [Ayes—6; noes—3; divided—1; absent—1.]

[2:132, 136, 143, 155, 169; Committee of Detail]

Resolved That a national Executive be instituted to consist of a single Person—to be chosen for the Term of six Years—with Power to carry into Execution the national Laws—to appoint to Offices in Cases not otherwise provided for— . . .

Resolved That a national Judiciary be established to consist of one Supreme Tribunal—the Judges of which shall be appointed by the second Branch of the national Legislature—

. . . . .

15. S. & H. D. in C. ass. shall institute Offices and appoint Officers for the Departments of for. Affairs, War, Treasury and Admiralty—

. . . . .

(3. the lawful territory To make treaties of commerce
(qu: as to senate)   Under the foregoing restrictions)
4. (To make treaties of peace or alliance
(qu: as to senate)   under the foregoing restrictions, and
                    without the surrender of territory
                        for an equivalent,
                and in no case, unless a superior title.) . . .
3. The powers destined for the senate peculiarly, are
        1. To make treaties of commerce
        2. to make Treaties of peace & Alliance
        3. to appoint the judiciary
        4. to send Embassadors
4. The executive . . .
        5. to appoint to offices not otherwise provided
            for. by the constitution . . .
5. The Judiciary
        1. shall consist of one supreme tribunal
        2. the judges whereof shall be appointed by the
            senate*

. . . . .

The Senate (shall be empowered) *of the United States shall have Power* to make Treaties of (Peace, of Alliance, and of Commerce,) to send Ambassadors, and to appoint the Judges of the Supreme national Court*

. . . . .

11.

The Senate of the United States shall have Power to make Treaties; to send Ambassadors; and to appoint the Judges of the Supreme (national) Court. . . .

12.

He shall commission all the Officers of the United States and (shall) appoint (Officers in all Cases) (such of them whose appts.) them in all cases not otherwise provided for by this Constitution. . . .

14.

The Judges of the Supreme (National) Court shall (be chosen by the Senate by Ballott). (They shall) hold their Offices during good Behaviour.*

[2:183; *Madison, 6 August*]

Sect 1. The Senate of the United States shall have power to make treaties, and to appoint Ambassadors, and Judges of the supreme Court.

. . . . .

he shall commision all the officers of the United States; and shall appoint officers in all cases not otherwise provided for by this Constitution.

[2:297; *Madison, 15 Aug.*]

Mr. Mercer should hereafter be agst. returning to a reconsideration of this section. He contended, (alluding to Mr. Mason's observations) that the Senate ought not to have the power of treaties. This power belonged to the Executive department; adding that Treaties would not be final so as to alter the laws of the land, till ratified by legislative authority. This was the case of Treaties in Great Britain; particularly the late Treaty of Commerce with France.

Col. Mason. did not say that a Treaty would repeal a law; but that the Senate by means of treaty might alienate

*[EDITORS' NOTE.—Words in parentheses were crossed out in the original.]

territory &c. without legislative sanction. The cessions of the British Islands in W— Indies by Treaty alone were an example— If Spain should possess herself of Georgia therefore the Senate might by treaty dismember the Union. He wished the motion to be decided now, that the friends of it might know how to conduct themselves.

[2:319; *Madison, 17 Aug.*]

Mr Butler moved to give the Legislature power of peace, as they were to have that of war.

Mr Gerry 2ds him. 8 Senators may possibly exercise the power if vested in that body, and 14 if all should be present; and may consequently give up part of the U. States. The Senate are more liable to be corrupted by an Enemy than the whole Legislature.

On the motion for adding "and peace" after "war"

N. H. no. Mas. no. Ct. no. Pa. no. Del. no. Md. no. Va no. N. C. no S. C no. Geo. no. [Ayes—0; noes—10.]

[2:389; *Madison, 23 Aug.*]

Art: IX being next for consideration,

Mr Govr Morris argued agst. the appointment of officers by the Senate. He considered the body as too numerous for the purpose; as subject to cabal; and as devoid of responsibility.—If Judges were to be tried by the Senate according to a late report of a Committee it was particularly wrong to let the Senate have the filling of vacancies which its own decrees were to create.

. . . . .

Art IX. sect. 1. being resumed, to wit "The Senate of the U. S. shall have power to make treaties, and to appoint Ambassadors, and Judges of the Supreme Court."

Mr. Madison observed that the Senate represented the States alone, and that for this as well as other obvious reasons it was proper that the President should be an agent in Treaties.

Mr. Govr. Morris did not know that he should agree to refer the making of Treaties to the Senate at all, but for the present wd. move to add as an amendment to the section, after "Treaties"—"but no Treaty shall be binding on the U. S. which is not ratified by a law."

Mr Madison suggested the inconvenience of requiring a legal *ratification* of treaties of alliance for the purposes of war &c &c

Mr. Ghorum. Many other disadvantages must be experienced if treaties of peace and all negociations are to be previously ratified—and if not previously, the Ministers would be at a loss how to proceed— What would be the case in G. Britain if the King were to proceed in this maner? American Ministers must go abroad not instructed by the same Authority (as will be the case with other Ministers) which is to ratify their proceedings.

Mr. Govr. Morris. As to treaties of alliance, they will oblige foreign powers to send their Ministers here, the very thing we should wish for. Such treaties could not be otherwise made, if his amendment shd. succeed. In general he was not solicitous to multiply & facilitate Treaties. He wished none to be made with G. Britain, till she should be at war. Then a good bargain might be made with her. So with other foreign powers. The more difficulty in making treaties, the more value will be set on them.

Mr. Wilson. In the most important Treaties, the King of G. Britain being obliged to resort to Parliament for the execution of them, is under the same fetters as the amendment of Mr. Morris will impose on the Senate. It was refused yesterday to permit even the Legislature to lay duties on exports. Under the clause, without the amendment, the Senate alone can make a Treaty, requiring all the Rice of S. Carolina to be sent to some one particular port.

Mr. Dickinson concurred in the amendment, as most safe and proper, tho' he was sensible it was unfavorable to the little States; wch would otherwise have an *equal* share in making Treaties.

Docr. Johnson thought there was something of solecism in saying that the acts of a Minister with plenipotentiary powers from one Body, should depend for ratification on another Body. The Example of the King of G. B. was not parallel. Full & compleat power was vested in him—If the Parliament should fail to provide the necessary means of execution, the Treaty would be violated.

Mr. Ghorum in answer to Mr. Govr Morris, said that negociations on the spot were not to be desired by us, especially if the whole Legislature is to have any thing to do with Treaties. It will be generally influenced by two or three men, who will be corrupted by the Ambassadors here. In such a Government as ours, it is necessary to guard against the Government itself being seduced.

Mr. Randolph observing that almost every Speaker had made objections to the clause as it stood, moved in order to a further consideration of the subject, that the Motion of Mr. Govr. Morris should be postponed, and on this question It was lost the States being equally divided.

Massts. no. Cont. no. N. J.—ay—Pena. ay. Del. ay. Md. ay. Va. ay—N. C. no. S. C. no—Geo. no. [Ayes—5; noes—5.]

On Mr. Govr. Morris Motion

Masts. no. Cont no. N. J. no. Pa. ay—Del. no—Md. no. Va. no. N. C divd S. C. no. Geo—no. [Ayes—1; noes—8; divided—1.]

The several clauses of Sect: 1. art IX, were then separately postponed after inserting "and other public Ministers" next after "Ambassadors."

Mr. Madison hinted for consideration, whether a distinction might not be made between different sorts of Treaties—Allowing the President & Senate to make Treaties eventual and of Alliance for limited terms—and requiring the concurrence of the whole Legislature in other Treaties.

The 1st Sect. art IX. was finally referred nem: con: to the committee of Five,

[2:395; McHenry, 23 Aug.]

The IX article being taken up, It was motioned that no treaty should be binding till it received the sanction of the legislature.

It was said that a minister could not then be instructed by the Senate who were to appoint him, or if instructed there could be no certainty that the house of representatives would agree to confirm what he might agree to under these instructions.

To this it was answered that all treaties which contravene a law of England or require a law to give them operation or effect are inconclusive till agreed to by the legislature of Great Britain.

Except in such cases the power of the King without the concurrence of the parliament conclusive.

Mr. Maddison. the Kings power over treaties final and original except in granting subsidies or dismembering the empire. These required parliamentary acts.

Commieed.

[2:405; Madison, 24 Aug.]

Mr. Sherman objected to the sentence "and shall appoint officers in all cases not otherwise provided for by this Constitution". He admitted it to be proper that many officers in the Executive Department should be so appointed—but contended that many ought not, as general officers in the Army in time of peace &c. Herein lay the corruption in G. Britain. If the Executive can model the army, he may set up an absolute Government; taking advantage of the close of a war and an army commanded by his creatures. James 2d. was not obeyed by his officers because they had been appointed by his predecessors not by himself. He moved to insert "or by law" after the word "Constitution".

On Motion of Mr Madison "officers" was struck out and "to offices" inserted, in order to obviate doubts that he might appoint officers without a previous creation of the offices by the Legislature.

On the question for inserting "or by law as moved by Mr. Sherman

N. H. no. Mas. no. Ct. ay. N. J. no. Pena. no. Del. no. Md. no. Va. no. N. C. absent. S. C. no. Geo. no. [Ayes—1; noes—9; absent—1.]

Mr. Dickinson moved to strike out the words "and shall appoint to offices in all cases not otherwise provided for by this Constitution" and insert—"and shall appoint to all offices established by this Constitution, except in cases herein otherwise provided for, and to all offices which may hereafter be created by law."

Mr Randolph observed that the power of appointments was a formidable one both in the Executive & Legislative hands—and suggested whether the Legislature should not be left at liberty to refer appointments in some cases, to some State Authority.

Mr. Dickenson's motion, it passed in the affirmative

N. H. no. Mas—no—Ct ay—N—J.—ay. Pa. ay—Del. no. Md ay. Va. ay—N—C. abst. S. C no Geo—ay [Ayes—6; noes—4; absent—1.]

Mr. Dickinson then moved to annex to his last amendment "except where by law the appointment shall be vested in the Legislatures or Executives of the several States". Mr. Randolph 2ded. the motion

Mr. Wilson—If this be agreed to it will soon be a standing instruction from the State Legislatures to pass no law creating offices, unless the appts be referred to them.

Mr. Sherman objected to "Legislatures" in the motion, which was struck out by consent of the movers.

Mr. Govr. Morris—This would be putting it in the

power of the States to say, "You shall be viceroys but we will be viceroys over you"—

The motion was negatived without a Count of the States—

[2:418; Madison, 25 Aug.]

On The question now taken on Mr. Dickinson motion of yesterday, allowing appointments to offices, to be referred by the Genl. Legislature to the Executives of the several States" as a farther amendment to sect. 2. art. X., the votes were

N. H. no Mas. no. Ct ay. Pa. no—Del no. Md divided—Va. ay—N—C—no—S. C. no. Geo. ay—[Ayes—3; noes—6; divided—1.]

In amendment of the same section, "other public Ministers" were inserted after "ambassadors".

Mr. Govr Morris moved to strike out of the section—"and may correspond with the supreme Executives of the several States" as unnecessary and implying that he could not correspond with others. Mr. Broome 2ded. him.

On the question

N. H. ay. Mas. ay. Ct. ay. Pa. ay. Del. ay. Md. no. Va. ay. N. C. ay—S. C. ay. Geo—ay. [Ayes—9; noes—1.]

[2:420; McHenry, 25 Aug.]

The clause in the 2 sect. X article, "he shall commission all the officers of the U. S. and shall appoint officers in all cases not otherwise provided for by this constitution, was moved to be amended by adding, except where by law the Executive of the several States shall have the power—Amendment negatives. Maryland divided—D. C. and J. against Martin and myself affirm.

[4:57; Mason, 31 Aug.]

The power of making Treaties & appg. ambasrs. &c to be in ye. Senate with the concurrence of ye. Council of St: or vice versa

The appointmt. to all offices estabd. by the legisl: to be in the Executive with ye. concurrence of ye. Senate

[2:495; Journal, 4 Sept.]

Sect. 4. The President by and with the advice and consent of the Senate, shall have power to make treaties: and he shall nominate and by and with the advice and consent of the Senate shall appoint Ambassadors and other public Ministers, Judges of the supreme Court, and all other officers of the U. S. whose appointments are not otherwise herein provided for. But no Treaty except Treaties of Peace shall be made without the consent of two thirds of the Members present

[2:538; Madison, 7 Sept.]

The Section 4.—to wit, "The President by & with the advice and consent of the Senate shall have power to make Treaties &c"

Mr. Wilson moved to add, after the word "Senate" the words, "and House of Representatives". As treaties he said are to have the operation of laws, they ought to have the sanction of laws also. The circumstance of secrecy in the business of treaties formed the only objection; but this he

thought, so far as it was inconsistent with obtaining the Legislative sanction, was outweighed by the necessity of the latter.

Mr. Sherman thought the only question that could be made was whether the power could be safely trusted to the Senate. He thought it could; and that the necessity of secrecy in the case of treaties forbade a reference of them to the whole Legislature.

Mr Fitzsimmons 2ded. the motion of Mr Wilson, & on the question

N. H. no. Mas. no. Ct. no. N. J. no. Pa ay. Del. no. Md. no Va. no. N. C. no. S. C. no. Geo. no. [Ayes—1; noes—10.]

The first sentence as to making treaties, was then Agreed to: nem: con:

—"He shall nominate &c Appoint ambassadors &c."

Mr. Wilson objected to the mode of appointing, as blending a branch of the Legislature with the Executive. Good laws are of no effect without a good Executive; and there can be no good Executive without a responsible appointment of officers to execute. Responsibility is in a manner destroyed by such an agency of the Senate—He would prefer the Council proposed by Col: Mason, Provided its advice should not be made obligatory on the President.

Mr. Pinkney was against joining the Senate in these appointments, except in the instances of Ambassadors who he thought ought not to be appointed by the President

Mr. Govr. Morris said that as the President was to nominate, there would be responsibility, and as the Senate was to concur, there would be security. As Congress now make appointments there is no responsibility.

Mr Gerry—The idea of responsibility in the nomination to offices is chimerical—The President can not know all characters, and can therefore always plead ignorance.

Mr King. As the idea of a Council proposed by Col. Mason has been supported by Mr. Wilson, he would remark that most of the inconveniencies charged on the Senate are incident to a Council of Advice. He differed from those who thought the Senate would sit constantly. He did not suppose it was meant that all the minute officers were to be appointed by the Senate, or any other original source, but by the higher officers of the departments to which they belong. He was of opinion also that the people would be alarmed at an unnecessary creation of New Corps which must increase the expence as well as influence of the Government.

On the question on these words in the clause viz—"He shall nominate & by & with the advice and consent of the Senate, shall appoint ambassadors, and other public ministers (and Consuls) Judges of the supreme Court" Agreed to: nem: con: the insertion of "(and consuls" having first taken place.

On the question on the following words "And all other officers of U. S—"

N. H.—ay—Mas ay. Ct ay. N—J—ay. Pa. no. Del. ay. Md. ay. Va ay. N—C. ay. S—C. no. Geo. ay. [Ayes—9; noes—2.]

On motion of Mr. Spaight—"that the President shall have power to fill up all vacancies that may happen during the recess of the Senate by granting Commissions which shall expire at the end of the next Session of the Senate" It was agreed to nem: con:

Section 4. "The President by and with the advice and consent of the Senate shall have power to make Treaties"—"*But no treaty shall be made without the consent of two thirds of the members present*"—this last being before the House.

Mr Wilson thought it objectionable to require the concurrence of ⅔ which puts it in the power of a minority to controul the will of a majority.

Mr. King concurred in the objection; remarking that as the Executive was here joined in the business, there was a check which did not exist in Congress where The concurrence of ⅔ was required.

Mr. Madison moved to insert after the word "treaty" the words "except treaties of peace" allowing these to be made with less difficulty than other treaties—It was agreed to nem: con:

Mr. Madison then moved to authorize a concurrence of two thirds of the Senate to make treaties of peace, without the concurrence of the President".—The President he said would necessarily derive so much power and importance from a state of war that he might be tempted, if authorized, to impede a treaty of peace. Mr. Butler 2ded. the motion

Mr Gorham thought the precaution unnecessary as the means of carrying on the war would not be in the hands of the President, but of the Legislature.

Mr. Govr Morris thought the power of the President in this case harmless; and that no peace ought to be made without the concurrence of the President, who was the general Guardian of the National interests.

Mr. Butler was strenuous for the motion, as a necessary security against ambitious & corrupt Presidents. He mentioned the late perfidious policy of the Statholder in Holland; and the artifices of the Duke of Marlbro' to prolong the war of which he had the management.

Mr. Gerry was of opinion that in treaties of peace a greater rather than less proportion of votes was necessary, than in other treaties. In Treaties of peace the dearest interests will be at stake, as the fisheries, territory &c. In treaties of peace also there is more danger to the extremities of the Continent, of being sacrificed, than on any other occasions.

Mr. Williamson thought that Treaties of peace should be guarded at least by requiring the same concurrence as in other Treaties.

On the motion of Mr. Madison & Mr. Butler

N. H. no. Mas. no. Ct. no. N. J. no. Pa. no. Del—no. Md. ay—Va no—N. C. no. S. C. ay. Geo. ay. [Ayes—3; noes—8.]

On the part of the clause concerning treaties amended by the exception as to Treaties of peace.

N. H. ay. Mas. ay. Ct. ay. N. J. no. Pa. no. Del. ay. Md. ay. Va. ay. N—C. ay. S—C. ay—Geo. no. [Ayes—8; noes—3.]

[*4:58; Madison, 7 Sept.*]

[Memorandum]

But no Treaty (of peace) shall be made without the concurrence of the House of Representatives, by which the territorial boundaries of the U. S. may be contracted, or by which the common rights of *navigation* or *fishery* recognized to the U. States by the late treaty of peace, or accruing to them by virtue of the laws of nations may be abridged

7 September 1787

The subject was then debated, but the motion does not appear to have been made.

[*2:547; Madison, 8 Sept.*]

Mr. King moved to strike out the "exception of Treaties of peace" from the general clause requiring two thirds of the Senate for making Treaties

Mr. Wilson wished the requisition of two thirds to be struck out altogether. If the majority cannot be trusted, it was a proof, as observed by Mr. Ghorum, that we were not fit for one Society.

A reconsideration of the whole clause was agreed to.

Mr. Govr. Morris was agst. striking out the "exception of Treaties of peace" If two thirds of the Senate should be required for peace, the Legislature will be unwilling to make war for that reason, on account of the Fisheries or the Mississippi, the two great objects of the Union. Besides, if a Majority of the Senate be for peace, and are not allowed to make it, they will be apt to effect their purpose in the more disagreeable mode, of negativing the supplies for the war.

Mr. Williamson remarked that Treaties are to be made in the branch of the Govt. where there may be a majority of the States without a majority of the people, Eight men may be a majority of a quorum, & should not have the power to decide the conditions of peace. There would be no danger, that the exposed States, as S. Carolina or Georgia, would urge an improper war for the Western Territory.

Mr. Wilson If two thirds are necessary to make peace, the minority may perpetuate war, against the sense of the majority.

Mr. Gerry enlarged on the danger of putting the essential rights of the Union in the hands of so small a number as a majority of the Senate, representing perhaps, not one fifth of the people. The Senate will be corrupted by foreign influence.

Mr. Sherman was agst leaving the rights, established by the Treaty of Peace, to the Senate, & moved to annex a "proviso that no such rights shd be ceded without the sanction of the Legislature.

Mr Govr. Morris seconded the ideas of Mr Sherman.

Mr. Madison observed that it had been too easy in the present Congress to make Treaties altho' nine States were required for the purpose.

On the question for striking "except Treaties of peace"

N. H. ay. Mas. ay. Ct. ay. N. J. no. Pa. ay. Del. no. Md. no—Va. ay. N. C.—ay. S. C. ay. Geo—ay [Ayes—8; noes—3.]

Mr. Wilson & Mr Dayton move to strike out the clause requiring two thirds of the Senate for making Treaties.—on which,

N. H no—Mas—no—Ct. divd. N—J. no. Pa. no Del. ay. Md. no. Va. no. N. C. no S. C. no. Geo. no. [Ayes—1; noes—9; divided—1.]

Mr Rutlidge & Mr. Gerry moved that "no Treaty be made without the consent of ⅔ of all the members of the Senate"—according to the example in the present Congs

Mr. Ghorum. There is a difference in the case, as the President's consent will also be necessary in the new Govt.

On the question

N—H. no—Mass no—(Mr. Gerry ay) Ct. no. N. J—no. Pa. no. Del. no. Md. no. Va. no. N. C. ay. S. C. ay. Geo. ay. [Ayes—3; noes—8.]

Mr. Sherman movd, that "no Treaty be made without a Majority of the whole number of the Senate—Mr. Gerry seconded him.

Mr. Williamson. This will be less security than ⅔ as now required.

Mr Sherman—It will be less embarrassing.

On the question, it passed in the negative.

N. H. no. Mas. ay. Ct. ay. N. J. no. Pa. no. Del. ay. Md. no. Va. no. N—C—no. S. C. ay. Geo. ay. [Ayes—5; noes—6.]

Mr. Madison movd. that a Quorum of the Senate consist of ⅔ of all the members.

Mr. Govr. Morris—This will put it in the power of one man to break up a Quorum.

Mr. Madison, This may happen to any Quorum.

On the Question it passed in the negative

N. H. no. Mas. no. Ct. no. N. J. no. Pa. no—Del. no—Md. ay. Va. ay. N. C. ay. S. C. ay. Geo. ay. [Ayes—5; noes—6.]

Mr. Williamson & Mr Gerry movd. "that no Treaty shd. be made witht previous notice to the members, & a reasonable time for their attending."

On the Question

All the States no, except N—C—S. C. & Geo. ay.

On a question on clause of the Report of the Come. of Eleven relating to Treaties by ⅔ of the Senate. All the States were ay—except Pa N. J. & Geo. no.

Mr. Gerry movd. that no officer shall be appd but to offices created by the Constitution or by law."—This was rejected as unnecessary by six no's and five ays;

The Ayes. Mas. Ct. N. J. N. C. Geo.—Noes—N. H. Pa.: Del. Md Va. S. C. [Ayes—5; noes—6.]

[2:574, 599; Committee of Style]

Sect. 4. The President by and with the advice and consent of the Senate, shall have power to make treaties: and he shall nominate and by and with the advice and consent of the Senate shall appoint Ambassadors, other public Ministers and Consuls, Judges of the supreme Court, and all other officers of the U. S. whose appointments are not otherwise herein provided for. But no Treaty shall be made without the consent of two thirds of the Members present.

. . . . .

(a) He shall have power, by and with the advice and consent of the senate, to make treaties, provided two-thirds of the senators present concur; and he shall nominate, and by and with the advice and consent of the senate, shall appoint ambassadors, other public ministers and consuls, judges of the supreme court, and all other officers of the United States, whose appointments are not herein otherwise provided for.

[2:627; Madison, 15 Sept.]

Art II. sect. 2. (paragraph 2) To the end of this, Mr Governr. Morris moved to annex "but the Congress may by law vest the appointment of such inferior Officers as they think proper, in the President alone, in the Courts of law, or in the heads of Departments." Mr Sherman 2ded. the motion

Mr. Madison. It does not go far enough if it be necessary at all—Superior Officers below Heads of Departments ought in some cases to have the appointment of the lesser offices.

Mr Govr Morris There is no necessity. Blank Commissions can be sent—

On the motion

N. H. ay. Mas—no—Ct ay. N. J. ay. Pa. ay. Del. no. Md. divd Va no. N. C. ay—S C no. Geo—no—[Ayes—5; noes—5; divided—1.]

The motion being lost by the equal division of votes, It was urged that it be put a second time, some such provision being too necessary, to be omitted. and on a second question it was agreed to nem. con.

. . . . .

Art: II. Sect. 2. After "Officers of the U. S. whose appointments are not otherwise provided for," were added the words "and which shall be established by law".

[2:639; Mason, 15 Sept.]

By declaring all treaties supreme laws of the land, the Executive and the Senate have, in many cases, an exclusive power of legislation; which might have been avoided by proper distinctions with respect to treaties, and requiring the assent of the House of Representatives, where it could be done with safety.

FOREIGN AFFAIRS

2

WILLIAM BLACKSTONE, COMMENTARIES
1:245–47, 249
1765

With regard to foreign concerns, the king is the delegate or representative of his people. It is impossible that the individuals of a state, in their collective capacity, can transact the affairs of that state with another community equally numerous as themselves. Unanimity must be wanting to their measures, and strength to the execution of their counsels. In the king therefore, as in a center, all the rays of his people are united, and form by that union a consistency, splendor, and power, that make him feared and respected by foreign potentates; who would scruple to enter into any engagements, that must afterwards be revised and ratified by a popular assembly. What is done by the royal authority, with regard to foreign powers, is the act of the whole nation: what is done without the king's concurrence is the act only of private men. And so far is this point carried by our law, that it hath been held, that should all the subjects of England make war with a king in league with the king of England, without the royal assent, such war is no breach of the league. And, by the statute 2 Hen. V. c. 6. any subject committing acts of hostility upon any nation in league with the king, was declared to be guilty of high treason: and, though that act was repealed by the statute 20 Hen. VI. c. 11. so far as relates to the making this offence high treason, yet still it remains a very great offence against the law of nations, and punishable by our laws, either capitally or otherwise, according to the circumstances of the case.

I. The king therefore, considered as the representative of his people, has the sole power of sending embassadors to foreign states, and receiving embassadors at home. This may lead us into a short enquiry, how far the municipal laws of England intermeddle with or protect the rights of these messengers from one potentate to another, whom we call embassadors.

The rights, the powers, the duties, and the privileges of embassadors are determined by the law of nature and nations, and not by any municipal constitutions. For, as they represent the persons of their respective masters, who owe no subjection to any laws but those of their own country, their actions are not subject to the control of the private law of that state, wherein they are appointed to reside. He that is subject to the coercion of laws is necessarily dependent on that power by whom those laws were made: but an embassador ought to be independent of every power, except that by which he is sent; and of consequence ought not to be subject to the mere municipal laws of that nation, wherein he is to exercise his functions. If he grossly offends, or makes an ill use of his character, he may be sent home and accused before his master; who is bound either to do justice upon him, or avow himself the accomplice of his crimes. But there is great dispute among the writers on the laws of nations, whether this exemption of embassadors extends to all crimes, as well natural as positive; or whether it only extends to such as are *mala prohibita,* as coining, and not to those that are *mala in se,* as murder. Our law seems to have formerly taken in the restriction, as well as the general exemption. For it has been held, both by our common lawyers and civilians, that an embassador is privileged by the law of nature and nations; and yet, if he commits any offence against the law of reason and nature, he shall lose his privilege: and that therefore, if an embassador conspires the death of the king in whose land he is, he may be condemned and executed for treason; but if he commits any other species of treason, it is otherwise, and he must be sent to his own kingdom. And these positions seem to be built upon good appearance of reason. For since, as we have formerly shewn, all municipal laws act in subordination to the primary law of nature, and, where they annex a punishment to natural crimes, are only declaratory of and auxiliary to that law; therefore to this natural, universal rule of justice embassadors, as well as other men, are subject in all countries; and of consequence it is reasonable that wherever they transgress it, there they shall be liable to make atonement. But, however these principles might formerly obtain, the general practice of Europe seems now to have adopted the sentiments of the learned Grotius, that the security of embassadors is of more importance than the punishment of a particular crime. And therefore few, if any, examples have happened within a century past, where an embassador has been punished for any offence, however atrocious in it's nature.

. . . . .

II. It is also the king's prerogative to make treaties, leagues, and alliances with foreign states and princes. For it is by the law of nations essential to the goodness of a league, that it be made by the sovereign power; and then it is binding upon the whole community: and in England the sovereign power, *quoad hoc,* is vested in the person of the king. Whatever contracts therefore he engages in, no other power in the kingdom can legally delay, resist, or annul. And yet, lest this plenitude of authority should be abused to the detriment of the public, the constitution (as was hinted before) hath here interposed a check, by the means of parliamentary impeachment, for the punishment of such ministers as advise or conclude any treaty, which shall afterwards be judged to derogate from the honour and interest of the nation.

3

JAMES WILSON, PENNSYLVANIA RATIFYING CONVENTION
11 Dec. 1787
Elliot 2:505–7

We are told that the share which the Senate have in making treaties is exceptionable; but here they are also under a check, by a constituent part of the government, and nearly the immediate representative of the people—I mean the President of the United States. They can make no treaty without his concurrence. The same observation applies in the appointment of officers. Every officer must be nominated solely and exclusively by the President.

Much has been said on the subject of treaties; and this power is denominated a blending of the legislative and executive powers in the Senate. It is but justice to represent the favorable, as well as unfavorable, side of a question, and from thence determine whether the objectionable parts are of a sufficient weight to induce a rejection of this Constitution.

There is no doubt, sir, but, under this Constitution, treaties will become the supreme law of the land; nor is there any doubt but the Senate and President possess the power of making them. But though the treaties are to have the force of laws, they are in some important respects very different from other acts of legislation. In making laws, our own consent alone is necessary. In forming treaties, the concurrence of another power becomes necessary. Treaties, sir, are truly contracts, or compacts, between the different states, nations, or princes, who find it convenient or necessary to enter into them. Some gentlemen are of opinion that the power of making treaties should have been placed in the legislature at large; there are, however, reasons that operate with great force on the other side. Treaties are frequently (especially in time of war) of such a nature, that it would be extremely improper to publish them, or even commit the secret of their negotiation to any great number of persons. For my part, I am not an advocate for secrecy in transactions relating to the public; not generally even in forming treaties, because I think that the history of the diplomatic corps will evince, even in that great department of politics, the truth of an old adage, that "honesty is the best policy," and this is the conduct of the most able negotiators; yet sometimes secrecy may be necessary, and therefore it becomes an argument against committing the knowledge of these transactions to too many persons. But in their nature treaties originate differently from laws. They are made by equal parties, and each side has half of the bargain to make; they will be made between us and powers at the distance of three thousand miles. A long series of negotiation will frequently precede them; and can it be the opinion of these gentlemen that the legislature should be in session during this whole time?

It well deserves to be remarked, that, though the House of Representatives possess no active part in making treaties, yet their legislative authority will be found to have strong restraining influences upon both President and Senate. In England, if the king and his ministers find themselves, during their negotiation, to be embarrassed because an existing law is not repealed, or a new law is not enacted, they give notice to the legislature of their situation, and inform them that it will be necessary, before the treaty can operate, that some law be repealed, or some be made. And will not the same thing take place here? Shall less prudence, less caution, less moderation, take place among those who negotiate treaties for the United States, than among those who negotiate them for the other nations of the earth? And let it be attended to, that, even in the making of treaties, the states are immediately represented, and the people mediately represented; two of the constituent parts of government must concur in making them. Neither the President nor the Senate, solely, can complete a treaty; they are checks upon each other, and are so balanced as to produce security to the people.

4

JAMES IREDELL, MARCUS, ANSWERS TO MR. MASON'S OBJECTIONS TO THE NEW CONSTITUTION
1788
Pamphlets 355–56

VII. Objection.

"By declaring all treaties the supreme law of the land, the Executive and the Senate have, in many cases, an exclusive power of legislation; which might have been avoided by proper distinctions with respect to treaties, and requiring the assent of the House of Representatives, where it could be done with safety."

Answer.

Did not Congress very lately unanimously resolve, in adopting the very sensible letter of Mr. Jay, that a treaty when once made pursuant to the sovereign authority, *ex vi termini* became immediately the law of the land? It seems to result unavoidably from the nature of the thing, that when the constitutional right to make treaties is exercised, the treaty so made should be binding upon those who delegated authority for that purpose. If it was not, what foreign power would trust us? And if this right was restricted by any such fine checks as Mr. Mason has in his imagination, but has not thought proper to disclose, a critical occasion might arise, when for want of a little rational confidence in our own government we might be obliged to submit to a master in an enemy. Mr. Mason wishes the

House of Representatives to have some share in this business, but he is immediately sensible of the impropriety of it, and adds "where it can be done with safety." And how is it to be known whether it can be done with safety or not, but during the pendency of a negotiation? Must not the President and Senate judge whether it can be done with safety or not? If they are of opinion it is unsafe, and the House of Representatives of course not consulted, what becomes of this boasted check, since, if it amounts to no more than that the President and Senate may consult the House of Representatives if they please, they may do this as well without such a provision as with it. Nothing would be more easy than to assign plausible reasons, after the negotiation was over, to show that a communication was unsafe, and therefore surely a precaution that could be so easily eluded, if it was not impolitic to the greatest degree, must be thought trifling indeed. It is also to be observed, that this authority, so obnoxious in the new Constitution (which is unfortunate in having little power to please some persons, either as containing new things or old), is vested indefinitely and without restriction in our present Congress, who are a body constituted in the same manner as the Senate is to be, but there is this material difference in the two cases, that we shall have an additional check, under the new system of a President of high personal character chosen by the immediate body of the people.

5

FEDERAL FARMER, NO. 11
10 Jan. 1788
Storing 2.8.147

By the art. 2. sect. 2. treaties must be made with the advice and consent of the senate, and two-thirds of those present must concur: also, with consent of the senate, almost all federal officers, civil and military, must be appointed. As to treaties I have my doubts; but as to the appointments of officers, I think we may clearly shew the senate to be a very improper body indeed to have any thing to do with them. I am not perfectly satisfied, that the senate, a branch of the legislature, and court for trying impeachments, ought to have a controuling power in making all treaties; yet, I confess, I do not discern how a restraint upon the president in this important business, can be better or more safely lodged: a power to make and conclude all treaties is too important to be vested in him alone, or in him and an executive council, only sufficiently numerous for other purpose, and the house of representatives is too numerous to be concerned in treaties of peace and of alliance. This power is now lodged in congress, to be exercised by the consent of nine states. The federal senate, like the delegations in the present congress, will represent the states,

and the consent of two-thirds of that senate will bear some similitude to the consent of nine states. It is probable the United States will not make more than one treaty, on an average, in two or three years, and this power may always be exercised with great deliberation: perhaps the senate is sufficiently numerous to be trusted with this power, sufficiently small to proceed with secrecy, and sufficiently permanent to exercise this power with proper consistency and due deliberation. To lodge this power in a less respectable and less numerous body might not be safe; we must place great confidence in the hands that hold it, and we deceive ourselves if we give it under an idea, that we can impeach, to any valuable purpose, the man or men who may abuse it.

On a fair construction of the constitution, I think the legislature has a proper controul over the president and senate in settling commercial treaties. By art. 1. sect. [8]. the legislature will have power to regulate commerce with foreign nations, &c. By art. 2. sect. 2. the president, with the advice and consent of two-thirds of the senate, may make treaties. These clauses must be considered together, and we ought never to make one part of the same instrument contradict another, if it can be avoided by any reasonable construction. By the first recited clause, the legislature has the power, that is, as I understand it, the sole power to regulate commerce with foreign nations, or to make all the rules and regulations respecting trade and commerce between our citizens and foreigners: by the second recited clause, the president and senate have power generally to make treaties.—There are several kinds of treaties—as treaties of commerce, of peace, of alliance, &c. I think the words to "make treaties," may be consistently construed, and yet so as it shall be left to the legislature to confirm commercial treaties; they are in their nature and operation very distinct from treaties of peace and of alliance; the latter generally require secrecy, it is but very seldom they interfere with the laws and internal police of the country; to make them is properly the exercise of executive powers, and the constitution authorises the president and senate to make treaties, and gives the legislature no power, directly or indirectly, respecting these treaties of peace and alliance. As to treaties of commerce, they do not generally require secrecy, they almost always involve in them legislative powers, interfere with the laws and internal police of the country, and operate immediately on persons and property, especially in the commercial towns: (they have in Great-Britain usually been confirmed by parliament;) they consist of rules and regulations respecting commerce; and to regulate commerce, or to make regulations respecting commerce, the federal legislature, by the constitution, has the power. I do not see that any commercial regulations can be made in treaties, that will not infringe upon this power in the legislature: therefore, I infer, that the true construction is, that the president and senate shall make treaties; but all commercial treaties shall be subject to be confirmed by the legislature. This construction will render the clauses consistent, and make the powers of the president and senate, respecting treaties, much less exceptionable.

6

DEBATE IN SOUTH CAROLINA HOUSE OF REPRESENTATIVES
16–17 Jan. 1788
Elliot 4:267–68, 269–70, 271, 277–81

[*16 Jan.*]

Hon. JOHN RUTLEDGE (one of the delegates of the Federal Convention) thought the gentleman mistaken both as to law and fact; for every treaty was law paramount, and must operate. [Read part of the 9th article of Confederation.] In England, treaties are not necessarily ratified, as was proved when the British Parliament took up the last treaty of peace. A vote of disapprobation dispossessed Lord Shelburne, the minister, of his place; the Commons only addressed the king for having concluded a peace; yet this treaty is binding in our courts and in England. In that country, American citizens can recover debts due to them under the treaty; and in this, but for the treaty, what violences would have taken place! What security had violent tories, stealers of horses, and a number of lawless men, but a law that we passed for recognizing the treaty? There might have been some offenders punished; but if they had obtained a writ of *habeas corpus,* no doubt they would have been relieved. There was an obvious difference between treaties of peace and those of commerce, because commercial treaties frequently clashed with the laws upon that subject; so that it was necessary to be ratified in Parliament. As a proof that our present Articles of Confederation were paramount, it was there expressed that France should enjoy certain privileges. Now, supposing any law had passed taking those privileges away, would not the treaty be a sufficient bar to any local or municipal laws? What sort of power is that which leaves individuals in full power to reject or approve? Suppose a treaty was unexpectedly concluded between two nations at war; could individual subjects ravage and plunder under letters of marque and reprisal? Certainly not. The treaty concluded, even secretly, would be a sufficient bar to the establishment. Pray, what solid reasons could be urged to support gentlemen's fears that our new governors would wish to promote measures injurious to their native land? Was it not more reasonable that, if every state in the Union had a negative voice, a single state might be tampered with, and defeat every good intention? Adverting to the objection relative to the instalment law being done away, he asked, supposing a person gave security conformable to that law, whether, judging from precedent, the judges would permit any further proceedings contrary to it. He scouted the idea that only ten members would ever be left to manage the business of the Senate; yet, even if so, our delegates might be part of that ten, and consequently our interest secured.

. . . . .

Mr. PRINGLE: . . . All the gentleman's objections may be comprised in the following compass: By the article, the President, with ten senators, if only ten attend, may make treaties to bind all the states—that the treaties have the force of, and indeed are paramount to, the laws of the land—therefore, the President and Senate have a legislative power; and then he gives scope to a great deal of declamation on the vast danger of their having such legislative power, and particularly that they might have a treaty which might thus repeal the instalment law. This is a greater power, he says, than the king of France has; the king of Great Britain has his ratified by Parliament—the treaties of the French king must be registered. But he conceived the gentleman was mistaken as to those treaties made by these monarchs. The king of France registers his edicts on some occasions, to facilitate the execution, but not his treaties. The king of Great Britain's treaties are discussed by Parliament, not for ratification, but to discover whether the ministers deserve censure or approbation. The making of treaties is justly a part of their prerogative: it properly belongs to the executive part of government, because they must be conducted with despatch and secrecy not to be expected in larger assemblies. No such dangers as the gentleman apprehends can ensue from vesting it with the President and Senate. Although the treaties they make may have the force of laws when made, they have not, therefore, legislative power. It would be dangerous, indeed, to trust them with the power of making laws to affect the rights of individuals; for this might tend to the oppression of individuals, who could not obtain redress. All the evils would, in that case, flow from blending the legislative, executive, and judicial powers. This would violate the soundest principles of policy and government. It is not with regard to the power of making treaties as of legislation in general. The treaties will affect all the individuals equally of all the states. If the President and Senate make such as violate the fundamental laws, and subvert the Constitution, or tend to the destruction of the happiness and liberty of the states, the evils, equally oppressing all, will be removed as soon as felt, as those who are oppressed have the power and means of redress. Such treaties, not being made with good faith, and on the broad basis of reciprocal interest and convenience, but by treachery and a betraying of trust, and by exceeding the powers with which the makers were intrusted, ought to be annulled. No nations would keep treaties thus made. Indeed, it is too much the practice for them to make mutual interest and convenience the rule of observation, or period of duration. As for the danger of repealing the instalment law, the gentleman has forgot that one article ordains that there shall be no retrospective law. The President and Senate will, therefore, hardly ever make a treaty that would be of this kind. After other arguments to obviate the objections of the honorable gentleman, Mr. Speaker concluded with saying, that it was not necessary for him to urge what further occurred to him, as he saw several of the honorable members of the Convention preparing, whose duty it more particularly was, and who were more able to confute the honorable gentleman in opposition.

Dr. DAVID RAMSAY asked if the gentleman meant us ever to have any treaties at all. If not superior to local laws, who will trust them? Would not the question naturally be,

"Did you mean, when you made treaties, to fulfil them?" Establish once such a doctrine, and where will you find ambassadors? If gentlemen had been in the situation of receiving similar information with himself, they would have heard letters read from our ambassadors abroad, in which loud complaints were made that America had become faithless and dishonest. Was it not full time that such conduct as this should be amended?

. . . . .

Hon. RAWLINS LOWNDES desired gentlemen to consider that his antagonists were mostly gentlemen of the law, who were capable of giving ingenious explanations to such points as they wished to have adopted. He explained his opinion relative to treaties to be, that no treaty concluded contrary to the express laws of the land could be valid. The king of England, when he concluded one, did not think himself warranted to go further than to promise that he would endeavor to induce his Parliament to sanction it. The security of a republic is jealousy; for its ruin may be expected from unsuspecting security. Let us not, therefore, receive this proffered system with implicit confidence, as carrying with it the stamp of superior perfection; rather let us compare what we already possess with what we are offered for it. We are now under the government of a most excellent constitution, one that had stood the test of time, and carried us through difficulties generally supposed to be insurmountable; one that had raised us high in the eyes of all nations, and given to us the enviable blessings of liberty and independence; a constitution sent like a blessing from Heaven; yet we are impatient to change it for another, that vested power in a few men to pull down that fabric, which we had raised at the expense of our blood. Charters ought to be considered as sacred things. In England, an attempt was made to alter the charter of the East India Company; but they invoked heaven and earth in their cause; moved lords, nay, even the king, in their behalf, and thus averted the ruin with which they were threatened.

[17 Jan.]

Gen. CHARLES COTESWORTH PINCKNEY observed, that the honorable gentleman (Mr. Lowndes) who opposed the new Constitution had asserted that treaties made under the old Confederation were not deemed paramount to the laws of the land, and that treaties made by the king of Great Britain required the ratification of Parliament to render them valid. The honorable gentleman is surely mistaken in his assertion. His honorable friend (Chancellor Rutledge) had clearly shown that, by the 6th, 9th, and 13th Articles of the old Confederation, Congress have a power to make treaties, and each state is pledged to observe them; and it appears, from the debates of the English Parliament, that the House of Commons did not ratify, but actually censure, the peace made by the king of Great Britain with America; yet the very members who censured it acknowledged it was binding on the nation. [Here the general read extracts from the parliamentary debates of the 17th and 21st of February, 1784.] Indeed, the doctrine that the king of Great Britain may make a treaty with a foreign state, which shall irrevocably bind his subjects, is asserted by the best writers on the laws and constitution of England—particularly by Judge Blackstone, who, in the first book of his Commentaries, (ch. 7, p. 257,) declares "that it is the king's prerogative to make treaties, leagues, and alliances, with foreign states and princes, and that no other power in the kingdom can legally delay, resist, or annul them." If treaties entered into by Congress are not to be held in the same sacred light in America, what foreign nation will have any confidence in us? Shall we not be stigmatized as a faithless, unworthy people, if each member of the Union may, with impunity, violate the engagements entered into by the federal government? Who will confide in us? Who will treat with us if our practice should be conformable to this doctrine? Have we not been deceiving all nations, by holding forth to the world, in the 9th Article of the old Confederation, that Congress may make treaties, if we, at the same time, entertain this improper tenet, that each state may violate them? I contend that the article in the new Constitution, which says that treaties shall be paramount to the laws of the land, is only declaratory of what treaties were, in fact, under the old compact. They were as much the law of the land under that Confederation, as they are under this Constitution; and we shall be unworthy to be ranked among civilized nations if we do not consider treaties in this view. Vattel, one of the best writers on the law of nations, says, "There would be no more security, no longer any commerce between mankind, did they not believe themselves obliged to preserve their faith, and to keep their word. Nations, and their conductors, ought, then, to keep their promises and their treaties inviolable. This great truth is acknowledged by all nations. Nothing adds so great a glory to a prince and the nation he governs, as the reputation of an inviolable fidelity to his engagements. By this, and their bravery, the Swiss have rendered themselves respectable throughout Europe. This national greatness of soul is the source of immortal glory; upon it is founded the confidence of nations, and it thus becomes a certain instrument of power and splendor." Surely this doctrine is right; it speaks to the heart, it impresses itself on the feelings of mankind, and convinces us that the tranquillity, happiness, and prosperity, of the human race, depend on inviolably preserving the faith of treaties.

Burlamaqui, another writer of great reputation on political law, says "that treaties are obligatory on the subjects of the powers who enter into treaties; they are obligatory as conventions between the contracting powers; but they have the force of law with respect to their subjects." These are his very words: *"Ils ont force de loi a l'égard des sujets, considérés comme tels;* and it is very manifest," continues he, "that two sovereigns, who enter into a treaty, impose, by such treaty, an obligation on their subjects to conform to it, and in no manner to contravene it." It is remarkable that the words made use of by Burlamaqui establish the doctrine, recognized by the Constitution, that treaties shall be considered as the law of the land; and happy will it be for America if they shall be always so considered: we shall then avoid the disputes, the tumults, the frequent wars, we must inevitably be engaged in, if we violate treaties. By our treaty with France, we declare she shall have all the privileges, in matters of commerce, with the most favored nation. Suppose a particular state should think proper to grant a particular privilege to Holland, which she refuses to France; would not this be a violation of the treaty with France? It certainly would; and we in this state would be answerable for the consequences attending such violation by another state; for we do not enter into treaties as separate states, but as united states; and all the members of the Union are answerable for the breach of a treaty by any one of them. South Carolina, therefore, considering its situation, and the valuable produce it has to export, is particularly interested in maintaining the sacredness of treaties, and the good faith with which they should be observed by every member of the Union. But the honorable gentleman complains that the power of making treaties is vested in the President and Senate, and thinks it is not placed so safely with them as with the Congress under the old Confederation. Let us examine this objection. By the old Confederation, each state had an equal vote in Congress, and no treaty could be made without the assent of the delegates from nine states. By the present Constitution, each state sends two members to the Senate, who vote *per capita;* and the President has power, with advice and consent of the Senate, to make treaties, provided two thirds of the Senate present concur. This inconvenience attended the old method: it was frequently difficult to obtain a representation from nine states; and if only nine states were present, they must all concur in making a treaty. A single member would frequently prevent the business from being concluded; and if he absented himself, Congress had no power to compel his attendance. This actually happened when a treaty of importance was about to be concluded with the Indians; and several states, being satisfied, at particular junctures, that the nine states present would not concur in sentiments on the subject of a treaty, were indifferent whether their members attended or not. But now that the senators vote individually, and not by states, each state will be anxious to keep a full representation in the Senate; and the Senate has now power to compel the attendance of its own members. We shall thus have no delay, and business will be conducted in a fuller representation of the states than it hitherto has been. All the members of the Convention, who had served in Congress, were so sensible of the advantage attending this mode of voting, that the measure was adopted unanimously. For my own part, I think it infinitely preferable to the old method. So much for the manner of voting.

Now let us consider whether the power of making treaties is not as securely placed as it was before. It was formerly vested in Congress, who were a body constituted by the legislatures of the different states in equal proportions. At present, it is vested in a President, who is chosen by the people of America, and in a Senate, whose members are chosen by the state legislatures, each legislature choosing two members. Surely there is greater security in vesting this power as the present Constitution has vested it, than in any other body. Would the gentleman vest it in the President alone? If he would, his assertion that the power we have granted was as dangerous as the power vested by

Parliament in the proclamations of Henry VIII., might have been, perhaps, warranted. Would he vest it in the House of Representatives? Can secrecy be expected in sixty-five members? The idea is absurd. Besides, their sessions will probably last only two or three months in the year; therefore, on that account, they would be a very unfit body for negotiation whereas the Senate, from the smallness of its numbers, from the equality of power which each state has in it, from the length of time for which its members are elected, from the long sessions they may have without any great inconveniency to themselves or constituents, joined with the president, who is the federal head of the United States, form together a body in whom can be best and most safely vested the diplomatic power of the Union.

7

JAMES MADISON, FEDERALIST, NO. 42,
279–80
22 Jan. 1788

The powers to make treaties and to send and receive Ambassadors, speak their own propriety. Both of them are comprized in the articles of confederation; with this difference only, that the former is disembarrassed by the plan of the Convention of an exception, under which treaties might be substantially frustrated by regulations of the States; and that a power of appointing and receiving "other public Ministers and Consuls," is expressly and very properly added to the former provision concerning Ambassadors. The term Ambassador, if taken strictly, as seems to be required by the second of the articles of confederation, comprehends the highest grade only of public Ministers; and excludes the grades which the United States will be most likely to prefer where foreign embassies may be necessary. And under no latitude of construction will the term comprehend Consuls. Yet it has been found expedient, and has been the practice of Congress to employ the inferior grades of public Ministers; and to send and receive Consuls. It is true that where treaties of commerce stipulate for the mutual appointment of Consuls, whose functions are connected with commerce, the admission of foreign Consuls may fall within the power of making commercial treaties; and that where no such treaties exist, the mission of American Consuls into foreign countries, may *perhaps* be covered under the authority given by the 9th article of the Confederation, to appoint all such civil officers as may be necessary for managing the general affairs of the United States. But the admission of Consuls into the United States, where no previous treaty has stipulated it, seems to have been no where provided for. A supply of the omission is one of the lesser instances in which the Convention have improved on the model before them. But the most minute provisions become important when they tend to obviate the necessity or the pretext for gradual and unobserved usurpations of power; a list of the cases in which Congress have been betrayed, or forced by the defects of the confederation into violations of their chartered authorities, would not a little surprize those who have paid no attention to the subject; and would be no inconsiderable argument in favor of the new Constitution, which seems to have provided no less studiously for the lesser, than the more obvious and striking defects of the old.

8

JOHN JAY, FEDERALIST, NO. 64,
432–38
5 Mar. 1788

It is a just and not a new observation, that enemies to particular persons and opponents to particular measures, seldom confine their censures to such things only in either, as are worthy of blame. Unless on this principle it is difficult to explain the motives of their conduct, who condemn the proposed constitution in the aggregate, and treat with severity some of the most unexceptionable articles in it.

The 2d. section gives power to the president *"by and with the advice and consent of the senate to make treaties* PROVIDED TWO THIRDS OF THE SENATORS PRESENT CONCUR."

The power of making treaties is an important one, especially as it relates to war, peace and commerce; and it should not be delegated but in such mode, and with such precautions, as will afford the highest security, that it will be exercised by men the best qualified for the purpose, and in the manner most conducive to the public good. The convention appears to have been attentive to both these points—they have directed the president to be chosen by select bodies of electors to be deputed by the people for that express purpose; and they have committed the appointment of senators to the state legislatures. This mode has in such cases, vastly the advantage of elections by the people in their collective capacity, where the activity of party zeal taking advantage of the supineness, the ignorance, and the hopes and fears of the unwary and interested, often places men in office by the votes of a small proportion of the electors.

As the select assemblies for choosing the president, as well as the state legislatures who appoint the senators will in general be composed of the most enlightened and respectable citizens, there is reason to presume that their attention and their votes will be directed to those men only who have become the most distinguished by their abilities and virtue, and in whom the people perceive just grounds for confidence. The constitution manifests very particular attention to this object. By excluding men under thirty five from the first office, and those under thirty from the second, it confines the electors to men of whom the people have had time to form a judgment, and with respect to whom they will not be liable to be deceived by those brilliant appearances of genius and patriotism, which like transient meteors sometimes mislead as well as dazzle. If the observation be well founded, that wise kings will always be served by able ministers, it is fair to argue that as an assembly of select electors possess in a greater degree than kings, the means of extensive and accurate information relative to men and characters, so will their appointments bear at least equal marks of discretion and discernment. The inference which naturally results from these considerations is this, that the president and senators so chosen will always be of the number of those who best understand our national interests, whether considered in relation to the several states or to foreign nations, who are best able to promote those interests, and whose reputation for integrity inspires and merits confidence. With such men the power of making treaties may be safely lodged.

Although the absolute necessity of system in the conduct of any business, is universally known and acknowledged, yet the high importance of it in national affairs has not yet become sufficiently impressed on the public mind. They who wish to commit the power under consideration to a popular assembly, composed of members constantly coming and going in quick succession, seem not to recollect that such a body must necessarily be inadequate to the attainment of those great objects, which require to be steadily contemplated in all their relations and circumstances, and which can only be approached and achieved by measures, which not only talents, but also exact information and often much time are necessary to concert and to execute. It was wise therefore in the convention to provide not only that the power of making treaties should be committed to able and honest men, but also that they should continue in place a sufficient time to become perfectly acquainted with our national concerns, and to form and introduce a system for the management of them. The duration prescribed is such as will give them an opportunity of greatly extending their political informations and of rendering their accumulating experience more and more beneficial to their country. Nor has the convention discovered less prudence in providing for the frequent elections of senators in such a way, as to obviate the inconvenience of periodically transferring those great affairs entirely to new men, for by leaving a considerable residue of the old ones in place, uniformity and order, as well as a constant succession of official information, will be preserved.

There are few who will not admit that the affairs of trade and navigation should be regulated by a system cautiously formed and steadily pursued; and that both our treaties and our laws should correspond with, and be made to promote it. It is of much consequence that this correspondence and conformity be carefully maintained, and they who assent to the truth of this position, will see and confess that it is well provided for by making the concurrence of the senate necessary both to treaties and to laws.

It seldom happens in the negociation of treaties of whatever nature, but that perfect *secrecy* and immediate *dispatch* are sometimes requisite. There are cases where the most useful intelligence may be obtained, if the persons possessing it can be relieved from apprehensions of discovery. Those apprehensions will operate on those persons whether they are actuated by mercenary or friendly motives, and there doubtless are many of both descriptions, who would rely on the secrecy of the president, but who would not confide in that of the senate, and still less in that of a large popular assembly. The convention have done well therefore in so disposing of the power of making treaties, that although the president must in forming them act by the advice and consent of the senate, yet he will be able to manage the business of intelligence in such manner as prudence may suggest.

They who have turned their attention to the affairs of men, must have perceived that there are tides in them. Tides, very irregular in their duration, strength and direction, and seldom found to run twice exactly in the same manner or measure. To discern and to profit by these tides in national affairs, is the business of those who preside over them, and they who have had much experience on this head inform us, that there frequently are occasions when days, nay even when hours are precious. The loss of a battle, the death of a Prince, the removal of a minister, or other circumstances intervening to change the present posture and aspect of affairs, may turn the most favorable tide into a course opposite to our wishes. As in the field, so in the cabinet, there are moments to be seized as they pass, and they who preside in either, should be left in capacity to improve them. So often and so essentially have we heretofore suffered from the want of secrecy and dispatch, that the Constitution would have been inexcusably defective if no attention had been paid to those objects. Those matters which in negociations usually require the most secrecy and the most dispatch, are those preparatory and auxiliary measures which are not otherwise important in a national view, than as they tend to facilitate the attainment of the objects of the negociation. For these the president will find no difficulty to provide, and should any circumstance occur which requires the advice and consent of the senate, he may at any time convene them. Thus we see that the constitution provides that our negociations for treaties shall have every advantage which can be derived from talents, information, integrity, and deliberate investigations on the one hand, and from secrecy and dispatch on the other.

But to this plan as to most others that have ever appeared, objections are contrived and urged.

Some are displeased with it, not on account of any errors or defects in it, but because as the treaties when made are to have the force of laws, they should be made only by men invested with legislative authority. These gentlemen seem not to consider that the judgments of our courts, and the commissions constitutionally given by our governor, are as valid and as binding on all persons whom they concern, as the laws passed by our legislature are. All constitutional acts of power, whether in the executive or in the judicial departments, have as much legal validity and obligation as if they proceeded from the Legislature, and therefore whatever name be given to the power of making treaties, or however obligatory they may be when made, certain it is that the people may with much propriety commit the power to a distinct body from the legislature, the executive or judicial. It surely does not follow that because

they have given the power of making laws to the Legislature, that therefore they should likewise give them power to do every other act of sovereignty by which the citizens are to be bound and affected.

Others, though content that treaties should be made in the mode proposed, are averse to their being the *supreme* laws of the land. They insist and profess to believe, that treaties, like acts of assembly, should be repealable at pleasure. This idea seems to be new and peculiar to this country, but new errors as well as new truths often appear. These gentlemen would do well to reflect that a treaty is only another name for a bargain; and that it would be impossible to find a nation who would make any bargain with us, which should be binding on them *absolutely,* but on us only so long and so far as we may think proper to be bound by it. They who make laws may without doubt amend or repeal them, and it will not be disputed that they who make treaties may alter or cancel them; but still let us not forget that treaties are made not by only one of the contracting parties, but by both, and consequently that as the consent of both was essential to their formation at first, so must it ever afterwards be to alter or cancel them. The proposed Constitution therefore has not in the least extended the obligation of treaties. They are just as binding, and just as far beyond the lawful reach of legislative acts now, as they will be at any future period, or under any form of government.

However useful jealousy may be in republics, yet when, like Bile in the natural, it abounds too much in the body politic; the eyes of both become very liable to be deceived by the delusive appearances which that malady casts on surrounding objects. From this cause probably proceed the fears and apprehensions of some, that the President and Senate may make treaties without an equal eye to the interests of all the States. Others suspect that the two-thirds will oppress the remaining third, and ask whether those gentlemen are made sufficiently responsible for their conduct—whether if they act corruptly they can be punished; and if they make disadvantageous treaties, how are we to get rid of those treaties?

As all the States are equally represented in the senate, and by men the most able and the most willing to promote the interests of their constituents, they will all have an equal degree of influence in that body, especially while they continue to be careful in appointing proper persons, and to insist on their punctual attendance. In proportion as the United States assume a national form, and a national character, so will the good of the whole be more and more an object of attention; and the government must be a weak one indeed, if it should forget that the good of the whole can only be promoted by advancing the good of each of the parts or members which compose the whole. It will not be in the power of the president and senate to make any treaties, by which they and their families and estates will not be equally bound and affected with the rest of the community; and having no private interest distinct from that of the nation, they will be under no temptations to neglect the latter.

As to corruption, the case is not supposable, he must either have been very unfortunate in his intercourse with the world, or possess a heart very susceptible of such impressions, who can think it probable that the president and two-thirds of the senate will ever be capable of such unworthy conduct. The idea is too gross and too invidious to be entertained. But in such a case, if it should ever happen, the treaty so obtained from us would, like all other fraudulent contracts, be null and void by the laws of nations.

With respect to their responsibility, it is difficult to conceive how it could be encreased. Every consideration that can influence the human mind, such as honor, oaths, reputation, conscience, the love of country, and family affections and attachments, afford security for their fidelity. In short, as the constitution has taken the utmost care that they shall be men of talents and integrity, we have reason to be persuaded that the treaties they make will be as advantageous as all circumstances considered could be made; and so far as the fear of punishment and disgrace can operate, that motive to good behavior is amply afforded by the article on the subject of impeachments.

9

ALEXANDER HAMILTON, FEDERALIST, NO. 75,
503–9
26 Mar. 1788

The president is to have power "by and with the advice and consent of the senate, to make treaties, provided two-thirds of the senators present concur." Though this provision has been assailed on different grounds, with no small degree of vehemence, I scruple not to declare my firm persuasion, that it is one of the best digested and most unexceptionable parts of the plan. One ground of objection is, the trite topic of the intermixture of powers; some contending that the president ought alone to possess the power of making treaties; and others, that it ought to have been exclusively deposited in the senate. Another source of objection is derived from the small number of persons by whom a treaty may be made: Of those who espouse this objection, a part are of opinion that the house of representatives ought to have been associated in the business, while another part seem to think that nothing more was necessary than to have substituted two-thirds of *all* the members of the senate to two-thirds of the members *present*. As I flatter myself the observations made in a preceding number, upon this part of the plan, must have sufficed to place it to a discerning eye in a very favourable light, I shall here content myself with offering only some supplementary remarks, principally with a view to the objections which have been just stated.

With regard to the intermixture of powers, I shall rely upon the explanations already given, in other places of the true sense of the rule, upon which that objection is founded; and shall take it for granted, as an inference from them, that the union of the executive with the senate, in the article of treaties, is no infringement of that rule. I venture to add that the particular nature of the power of making treaties indicates a peculiar propriety in that union. Though several writers on the subject of government place that power in the class of executive authorities, yet this is evidently an arbitrary disposition: For if we attend carefully to its operation, it will be found to partake more of the legislative than of the executive character, though it does not seem strictly to fall within the definition of either of them. The essence of the legislative authority is to enact laws, or in other words to prescribe rules for the regulation of the society. While the execution of the laws and the employment of the common strength, either for this purpose or for the common defence, seem to comprise all the functions of the executive magistrate. The power of making treaties is plainly neither the one nor the other. It relates neither to the execution of the subsisting laws, nor to the enaction of new ones, and still less to an exertion of the common strength. Its objects are CONTRACTS with foreign nations, which have the force of law, but derive it from the obligations of good faith. They are not rules prescribed by the sovereign to the subject, but agreements between sovereign and sovereign. The power in question seems therefore to form a distinct department, and to belong properly neither to the legislative nor to the executive. The qualities elsewhere detailed, as indispensable in the management of foreign negotiations, point out the executive as the most fit agent in those transactions; while the vast importance of the trust, and the operation of treaties as laws, plead strongly for the participation of the whole or a part of the legislative body in the office of making them.

However proper or safe it may be in governments where the executive magistrate is an hereditary monarch, to commit to him the entire power of making treaties, it would be utterly unsafe and improper to entrust that power to an elective magistrate of four years duration. It has been remarked upon another occasion, and the remark is unquestionably just, that an hereditary monarch, though often the oppressor of his people, has personally too much at stake in the government to be in any material danger of being corrupted by foreign powers. But a man raised from the station of a private citizen to the rank of chief magistrate, possessed of but a moderate or slender fortune, and looking forward to a period not very remote, when he may probably be obliged to return to the station from which he was taken, might sometimes be under temptations to sacrifice his duty to his interest, which it would require superlative virtue to withstand. An avaricious man might be tempted to betray the interests of the state to the acquisition of wealth. An ambitious man might make his own aggrandizement, by the aid of a foreign power, the price of his treachery to his constituents. The history of human conduct does not warrant that exalted opinion of human virtue which would make it wise in a nation to commit interests of so delicate and momentous a kind as those which concern its intercourse with the rest of the world to the sole disposal of a magistrate, created and circumstanced, as would be a president of the United States.

To have entrusted the power of making treaties to the

senate alone, would have been to relinquish the benefits of the constitutional agency of the president, in the conduct of foreign negotiations. It is true, that the senate would in that case have the option of employing him in this capacity; but they would also have the option of letting it alone; and pique or cabal might induce the latter rather than the former. Besides this, the ministerial servant of the senate could not be expected to enjoy the confidence and respect of foreign powers in the same degree with the constitutional representative of the nation; and of course would not be able to act with an equal degree of weight or efficacy. While the union would from this cause lose a considerable advantage in the management of its external concerns, the people would lose the additional security, which would result from the co-operation of the executive. Though it would be imprudent to confide in him solely so important a trust; yet it cannot be doubted, that his participation in it would materially add to the safety of the society. It must indeed be clear to a demonstration, that the joint possession of the power in question by the president and senate would afford a greater prospect of security, than the separate possession of it by either of them. And whoever has maturely weighed the circumstances, which must concur in the appointment of a president will be satisfied, that the office will always bid fair to be filled by men of such characters as to render their concurrence in the formation of treaties peculiarly desirable, as well on the score of wisdom as on that of integrity.

The remarks made in a former number, which has been alluded to in an other part of this paper, will apply with conclusive force against the admission of the house of representatives to a share in the formation of treaties. The fluctuating, and taking its future increase into the account, the multitudinous composition of that body, forbid us to expect in it those qualities which are essential to the proper execution of such a trust. Accurate and comprehensive knowledge of foreign politics; a steady and systematic adherence to the same views; a nice and uniform sensibility to national character, decision, *secrecy* and dispatch; are incompatible with the genius of a body so variable and so numerous. The very complication of the business by introducing a necessity of the concurrence of so many different bodies, would of itself afford a solid objection. The greater frequency of the calls upon the house of representatives, and the greater length of time which it would often be necessary to keep them together when convened, to obtain their sanction in the progressive stages of a treaty, would be source of so great inconvenience and expence, as alone ought to condemn the project.

The only objection which remains to be canvassed is that which would substitute the proportion of two thirds of all the members composing the senatorial body to that of two thirds of the members *present*. It has been shewn under the second head of our inquiries that all provisions which require more than the majority of any body to its resolutions have a direct tendency to embarrass the operations of the government and an indirect one to subject the sense of the majority to that of the minority. This consideration seems sufficient to determine our opinion, that the convention have gone as far in the endeavour to secure the advantage

of numbers in the formation of treaties as could have been reconciled either with the activity of the public councils or with a reasonable regard to the major sense of the community. If two thirds of the whole number of members had been required, it would in many cases from the non attendance of a part amount in practice to a necessity of unanimity. And the history of every political establishment in which this principle has prevailed is a history of impotence, perplexity and disorder. Proofs of this position might be adduced from the examples of the Roman tribuneship, the Polish diet and the states general of the Netherlands; did not an example at home render foreign precedents unnecessary.

To require a fixed proportion of the whole body would not in all probability contribute to the advantages of a numerous agency, better than merely to require a proportion of the attending members. The former by making a determinate number at all times requisite to a resolution diminishes the motives to punctual attendance. The latter by making the capacity of the body to depend on a *proportion* which may be varied by the absence or presence of a single member, has the contrary effect. And as, by promoting punctuality, it tends to keep the body complete, there is great likelihood that its resolutions would generally be dictated by as great a number in this case as in the other; while there would be much fewer occasions of delay. It ought not to be forgotten that under the existing confederation two members *may* and usually *do* represent a state; whence it happens that Congress, who now are solely invested with *all the powers* of the union, rarely consists of a greater number of persons than would compose the intended senate. If we add to this, that as the members vote by states, and that where there is only a single member present from a state, his vote is lost, it will justify a supposition that the active voices in the senate, where the members are to vote individually, would rarely fall short in number of the active voices in the existing Congress. When in addition to these considerations we take into view the cooperation of the president, we shall not hesitate to infer that the people of America would have greater security against an improper use of the power of making treaties, under the new constitution, than they now enjoy under the confederation. And when we proceed still one step further, and look forward to the probable augmentation of the senate, by the erection of new states, we shall not only perceive ample ground of confidence in the sufficiency of the numbers, to whose agency that power will be entrusted; but we shall probably led to conclude that a body more numerous than the senate would be likely to become, would be very little fit for the proper discharge of the trust.

10

DEBATE IN VIRGINIA RATIFYING CONVENTION
18–19 June 1788
Elliot 3:499–515

[*18 June*]

Mr. GEORGE MASON thought this a most dangerous clause, as thereby five states might make a treaty; ten senators—the representatives of five states—being two thirds of a quorum. These ten might come from the five smallest states. By the Confederation, nine states were necessary to concur in a treaty. This secured justice and moderation. His principal fear, however, was not that five, but that seven, states—a bare majority—would make treaties to bind the Union.

Mr. GEORGE NICHOLAS, in answer to Mr. Mason, insisted that we were on a safer footing in this Constitution than in the Confederation. The possibility of five states making treaties was founded on a supposition of the non-attendance of the senators from the other states. This non-attendance, he observed, might be reciprocated. It was presumable that, on such important occasions, they would attend from all the states, and then there must be a concurrence of nine states. The approbation of the President, who had no local views, being elected by no particular state, but the people at large, was an additional security.

Mr. MASON differed widely from the gentleman. He conceived that the contiguity of some states, and remoteness of others, would prevent that reciprocity which he had mentioned. Some states were near the seat of government; others far from it; for instance, Georgia was eight or nine hundred miles from it. Suppose, says he, a partial treaty is made by the President, and is to be ratified by the Senate. They do not always sit. Who is to convene them? The President. Is it presumable that he would call distant states to make the ratification, or those states whose interest he knew to be injured by the treaty he had proposed? This, I conceive, will have a contrary effect from what the gentleman says.

A desultory conversation took place.

Mr. NICHOLAS asked if it was presumable that the President, who depended on the people for his political existence, would sacrifice the interest of the eight largest states, to accommodate the five smallest. The gentleman had said once that the Senate would be always sitting, and yet five states were now to effect the business, because the rest were away.

Mr. LEE compared the possibility of non-attendance of the senators to that in our state legislature. It consisted of one hundred and seventy members: a majority of these was forty-four, which were competent to pass any law. He demanded if all our laws were bad because forty-four might pass them. The case was similar. Although two thirds of the senators present could form a treaty, it was not presumable it could often happen that there should be

but a bare quorum present on so important an occasion, when the consequence of non-attendance was so well known.

Mr. MADISON thought it astonishing that gentlemen should think that a treaty could be got up with surprise, or that foreign nations should be solicitous to get a treaty only ratified by the senators of a few states. Were the President to commit any thing so atrocious as to summon only a few states, he would be impeached and convicted, as a majority of the states would be affected by his misdemeanor.

Mr. HENRY begged gentlemen to consider the condition this country would be in if two thirds of a quorum should be empowered to make a treaty: they might relinquish and alienate territorial rights, and our most valuable commercial advantages. In short, if any thing should be left us, it would be because the President and senators were pleased to admit it. The power of making treaties, by this Constitution, ill-guarded as it is, extended farther than it did in any country in the world. Treaties were to have more force here than in any part of Christendom; for he defied any gentleman to show any thing so extensive in any strong, energetic government in Europe. Treaties rest, says he, on the laws and usages of nations. To say that they are municipal is, to me, a doctrine totally novel. To make them paramount to the Constitution and laws of the states, is unprecedented. I would give them the same force and obligation they have in Great Britain, or any other country in Europe. Gentlemen are going on in a fatal career; but I hope they will stop before they concede this power unguarded and unaltered.

Mr. MADISON, instead of being alarmed, had no doubt but the Constitution would increase, rather than decrease, the security of territorial rights and commercial advantages, as it would augment the strength and respectability of the country. The honorable gentleman, says he, has said we are making great innovations in extending the force of treaties. Are not treaties the law of the land in England? I will refer you to a book which is in every man's hand—Blackstone's Commentaries. It will inform you that the treaties made by the king are to be the supreme law of the land. If they are to have any efficacy, they must be the law of the land: they are so in every country. He thinks that, by the power of making treaties, the empire may be dismembered in time of peace. The king of Great Britain has the power of making peace, but he has no power of dismembering the empire, or alienating any part of it. Nay, the king of France has no right of alienating part of his dominions to any power whatsoever. The power of making treaties does not involve a right of dismembering the Union.

Mr. HENRY asked how the power of the king of Great Britain, with respect to dismembering the empire, would stand, if the constitution had declared that treaties would be effectual, notwithstanding any thing in the constitution or laws of the country. He would confess his error, if the gentleman could prove that the power of the king of Great Britain, and that of Congress, in making treaties, were similar.

Mr. MADISON conceived that, as far as the king of Great

Britain had a constitutional power of making a treaty, such a treaty was binding. He did not say that his power was unlimited. One exception was, that he could not dismember the empire.

Mr. GRAYSON, after discriminating the difference of what was called the law of nations in different countries, and its different operations, said he was exceedingly alarmed about this clause. His apprehensions were increased from what he had seen. He went over the grounds which had been before developed, of the dangers to which the right of navigating the Mississippi would be exposed, if two thirds of the senators present had a right to make a treaty to bind the Union. Seven states had already discovered a determined resolution of yielding it to Spain. There was every reason, in his opinion, to believe they would avail themselves of the power as soon as it was given them. The prevention of emigrations to the westward, and consequent superiority of the southern power and influence, would be a powerful motive to impel them to relinquish that river. He warmly expatiated on the utility of that navigation, and the impolicy of surrendering it up. The consent of the President he considered as a trivial check, if, indeed, it was any; for the election would be so managed that he would always come from a particular place, and he would pursue the interest of such place. Gentlemen had said that the senators would attend from all the states. This, says he, is impracticable, if they be not nailed to the floor. If the senators of the Southern States be gone but one hour, a treaty may be made by the rest, yielding that inestimable right. This paper will be called the law of nations in America; it will be the Great Charter of America; it will be paramount to every thing. After having once consented to it, we cannot recede from it. Such is my repugnance to the alienation of a right which I esteem so important to the happiness of my country, that I would object to this Constitution if it contained no other defect.

Mr. NICHOLAS, in answer to the observations of the gentleman last up, on the law of nations, said he thought it was dictated by no particular nation; that there was no such thing as a particular law of nations, but that the law of nations was permanent and general. It was superior to any act or law of any nation; it implied the consent of all, and was mutually binding on all, being acquiesced in for the common benefit of all. Gentlemen recurred to their favorite business again—their scuffle for Kentucky votes. He compared the king of England's power to make treaties to that given by this clause. He insisted they resembled each other. If a treaty was to be the supreme law of the land here, it was so in England. The power was as unlimited in England as it was here. Let gentlemen, says he, show me that the king can go so far, and no farther, and I will show them a like limitation in America. But, say they, the President has no check. The worthy member says the weight of power ought to be in this part of the continent, because the number of inhabitants will be greater here. If so, every freeholder having a right to vote for the President, by the interposition of electors, will attend to his interests. This is a sufficient check.

Mr. HENRY. Mr. Chairman, gentlemen say that the king of Great Britain has the same right of making treaties that our President has here. I will have no objection to this, if you make your president a king. But I will adduce a difference between an American treaty and an English treaty. Recollect the case of the Russian ambassador: he was arrested contrary to the rights of his master. The Russian emperor demanded the man, at whose instance his ambassador was arrested, to be given up to him, to be put to instant death. What did the queen say? She wrote him that that was something paramount to what she could do; that it exceeded her power to comply with his demand, because it was contrary to the constitution and laws. But how is it here? Treaties are binding, notwithstanding our laws and constitutions. Let us illustrate this fatal instance. Suppose the case of the Russian ambassador to happen here. The President can settle it by a treaty, and have the man arrested, and punished according to the Russian manner. The constitutions of these states may be most flagrantly violated without remedy. And still will gentlemen compare the two cases? So great was the anxiety of Queen Anne, that she wrote a letter to the Russian prince with her own hand, apologizing for her inability to comply with his demands. The Parliament was consulted, and a law made to prevent such arrests for the future. I say again that, if you consent to this power, you depend on the justice and equity of those in power. We may be told that we shall find ample refuge in the law of nations. When you yourselves have your necks so low that the President may dispose of your rights as he pleases, the law of nations cannot be applied to relieve you. Sure I am, if treaties are made infringing our liberties, it will be too late to say that our constitutional rights are violated. We are in contact with two powers—Great Britain and Spain. They may claim our most valuable territories, and treaties may be made to yield them. It is easy on our part to define our unalienable rights, and expressly secure them, so as to prevent future claims and disputes. Suppose you be arraigned as offenders and violators of a treaty made by this government. Will you have that fair trial which offenders are entitled to in your own government? Will you plead a right to appeal to the trial by jury? You will have no right to appeal to your own Constitution. You must appeal to your Continental Constitution. A treaty may be made giving away your rights, and inflicting unusual punishments on its violators. It is contended that, if the king of Great Britain makes a treaty within the line of his prerogative, it is the law of the land. I agree that this is proper, and, if I could see the same checks in that paper which I see in the British government, I would consent to it. Can the English monarch make a treaty which shall subvert the common law of England, and the constitution? Dare he make a treaty that shall violate Magna Charta, or the bill of rights? Dare he do any thing derogatory to the honor, or subversive of the great privileges, of his people? No, sir. If he did, it would be nugatory, and the attempt would endanger his existence.

The king of France calls his Parliament to give him power to make what regulations, with regard to treaties, they may think conducive to the interest of the nation. In the time of Henry IV., a treaty with Sigismund, king of Poland, was ratified by the Parliament. You have not even as much security as that. You prostrate your rights to the President and Senate. This power is therefore dangerous and destructive.

Gov. RANDOLPH. Mr. Chairman, I conceive that neither the life nor property of any citizen, nor the particular right of any state, can be affected by a treaty. The lives and properties of European subjects are not affected by treaties, which are binding on the aggregate community in its political, social capacity.

The honorable gentleman says that, if you place treaties on the same footing here as they are in England, he will consent to the power, because the king is restrained in making treaties. Will not the President and Senate be restrained? Being creatures of that Constitution, can they destroy it? Can any particular body, instituted for a particular purpose, destroy the existence of the society for whose benefit it is created? It is said there is no limitation of treaties. I defy the wisdom of that gentleman to show how they ought to be limited. When the Constitution marks out the powers to be exercised by particular departments, I say no innovation can take place. An honorable gentlemen says that this is the Great Charter of America. If so, will not the last clause of the 4th article of the Constitution secure against dismemberment? It provides that "nothing in this Constitution shall be so construed as to prejudice any claims of the United States, or of any particular state." And if this did not constitute security, it follows, from the nature of civil association, that no particular part shall sacrifice the whole.

[19 June]

Mr. GRAYSON, after recapitulating the dangers of losing the Mississippi, if the power of making treaties, as delineated in the Constitution, were granted, insisted, most strenuously, that the clause which the honorable gentleman had cited as a security against a dismemberment of the empire was no real security; because it related solely to the back lands claimed by the United States and different states. This clause was inserted for the purpose of enabling Congress to dispose of, and make all needful rules and regulations respecting, the territory, or other property, belonging to the United States, and to ascertain clearly that the claims of particular states, respecting territory, should not be prejudiced by the alteration of government, but be on the same footing as before; that it could not be construed to be a limitation of the power of making treaties. Its sole intention was to obviate all the doubts and disputes which existed, under the Confederation, concerning the western territory and other places in controversy in the United States. He defended his former position with respect to a particular law of nations. I insist, says he, that the law of nations is founded on particular laws of different nations. I have mentioned some instances: I will mention some more. It is the part of the laws of several Oriental nations to receive no ambassadors, and to burn their prisoners. It is a custom with the grand seignior to receive, but not to send ambassadors. It is a particular custom with him, in time of war with Russia, to put the Russian ambassador in the Seven Towers. But the worthy member said that it was odd there should be a particular law of nations.

I beg leave to tell him that the United States are entering into a particular law of nations now. I do not deny the existence of a general law of nations; but I contend that, in different nations, there are certain laws or customs, regulating their conduct towards other nations, which are as permanently and immutably observed as the general law of nations. Of course there was a law of nations incident to the Confederation. Any person may renounce a right secured to him by any particular law or custom of a nation. If Congress have no right, by the law of nations, to give away a part of the empire, yet, by this compact, they may give it up. I look on that compact to be a part of the law of nations. The treaty of Munster formed a great part of the law of nations. How is the Scheldt given up? By that treaty, though contrary to the law of nations. Cannot Congress give the Mississippi also by treaty, though such cession would deprive us of a right to which, by the law of nations, we are inalienably and indefeasibly entitled? I lay it down as a principle that nations can, as well as individuals, renounce any particular right. Nations who inhabit on the sources of rivers have a right to navigate them, and go down, as well as the waters themselves.

Mr. GEORGE NICHOLAS again drew a parallel between the power of the king of Great Britain and that of Congress, with respect to making treaties. He contended that they were on the same foundation, and that every possible security which existed in the one instance was to be found in the other. To prove that there was no constitutional limit to the king's power of making treaties, and that treaties, when once by him made, were the supreme law of the land, he quoted the following lines in Blackstone's Commentaries, vol. i. page 257: "It is also the king's prerogative to make treaties, leagues, and alliances, with foreign states and princes; for it is, by the law of nations, essential to the goodness of a league, that it be made by the sovereign power; and then it is binding upon the whole community; and in England the sovereign power, *quoad hoc*, is vested in the person of the king. Whatever contracts, therefore, he engages in, no other power in the kingdom can legally delay, resist, or annul." A further proof, says Mr. Nicholas, that there is no limitation in this respect, is afforded by what he adds: "And yet, lest this plenitude of authority should be abused, to the detriment of the public, the constitution has interposed a check, by the means of parliamentary impeachment, for the punishment of such ministers as, from criminal motives, advise or conclude any treaty which shall afterwards be judged to derogate from the honor and interest of the nation." How does this apply to this Constitution? The President and Senate have the same power of making treaties; and when made, they are to have the same force and validity. They are to be the supreme law of the land here. This book shows us they are so in England.

Have we not seen, in America, that treaties were violated, though they are, in all countries, considered as the supreme law of the land? Was it not, therefore, necessary to declare, in explicit terms, that they should be so here? How, then, is this Constitution on a different footing from the government of Britain? The worthy member says, that they can make a treaty relinquishing our rights, and inflicting punishments; because all treaties are declared paramount to the constitutions and laws of the states. An attentive consideration of this will show the committee that they can do no such thing. The provision of the 6th article is, that this Constitution, and the laws of the United States which shall be made in pursuance thereof, and all the treaties made, or which shall be made, under the authority of the United States, shall be the supreme law of the land. They can, by this, make no treaty which shall be repugnant to the spirit of the Constitution, or inconsistent with the delegated powers. The treaties they make must be under the authority of the United States, to be within their province. It is sufficiently secured, because it only declares that, in pursuance of the powers given, they shall be the supreme law of the land, notwithstanding any thing in the constitution or laws of particular states.

The fact which he has adduced from the English history respecting the Russian ambassador, does not apply to this part of the Constitution. The arrest of that ambassador was an offence against the law of nations. There was no tribunal to punish it before. An act was therefore made to prevent such offences for the future; appointing a court to try offenders against it, and pointing out their punishment. That act acknowledges the arrest to have been a violation of the law of nations, and that it was a defect in their laws that no remedy had been provided against such violations before. I think it must appear, to the satisfaction of the committee, that this power is similar to what it is in England.

Mr. GEORGE MASON. Mr. Chairman, it is true that this is one of the greatest acts of sovereignty, and therefore ought to be most strongly guarded. The cession of such a power, without such checks and guards, cannot be justified: yet I acknowledge such a power must rest somewhere. It is so in all governments. If, in the course of an unsuccessful war, we should be compelled to give up part of our territories, or undergo subjugation if the general government could not make a treaty to give up such a part for the preservation of the residue, the government itself, and consequently the rights of the people, must fall. Such a power must, therefore, rest somewhere. For my own part, I never heard it denied that such a power must be vested in the government. Our complaint is, that it is not sufficiently guarded, and that it requires much more solemnity and caution than are delineated in that system. It is more guarded in England. Will any gentleman undertake to say that the king, by his prerogative, can dismember the British empire? Could the king give Portsmouth to France? He could not do this without an express act of Parliament—without the consent of the legislature in all its branches. There are other things which the king cannot do, which may be done by the President and Senate in this case. Could the king, by his prerogative, enable foreign subjects to purchase lands, and have an hereditary indefeasible title? This would require an express act of Parliament.

Though the king can make treaties, yet he cannot make a treaty contrary to the constitution of his country. Where did their constitution originate? It is founded on a number of maxims, which, by long time, are rendered sacred and inviolable. Where are there such maxims in the American Constitution? In that country, which we formerly called our mother country, they have had, for many centuries, certain fundamental maxims, which have secured their persons and properties, and prevented a dismemberment of their country. The common law, sir, has prevented the power of the crown from destroying the immunities of the people. We are placed in a still better condition—in a more favorable situation than perhaps any people ever were before. We have it in our power to secure our liberties and happiness on the most unshaken, firm, and permanent basis. We can establish what government we please. But by that paper we are consolidating the United States into one great government, and trusting to constructive security. You will find no such thing in the English government. The common law of England is not the common law of these states. I conceive, therefore, that there is nothing in that Constitution to hinder a dismemberment of the empire.

Will any gentleman say that they may not make a treaty, whereby the subjects of France, England, and other powers, may buy what lands they please in this country? This would violate those principles which we have received from the mother country. The indiscriminate admission of all foreigners to the first rights of citizenship, without any permanent security for their attachment to the country, is repugnant to every principle of prudence and good policy. The President and Senate can make any treaty whatsoever. We wish not to refuse, but to guard, this power, as it is done in England. The empire there cannot be dismembered without the consent of the national Parliament. We wish an express and explicit declaration, in that paper, that the power which can make other treaties cannot, without the consent of the national Parliament—the national legislature—dismember the empire. The Senate alone ought not to have this power; much less ought a few states to have it. No treaty to dismember the empire ought to be made without the consent of three fourths of the legislature in all its branches. Nor ought such a treaty to be made but in case of the most urgent and unavoidable necessity. When such necessity exists, there is no doubt but there will be a general and uniform vote of the Continental Parliament.

Mr. CORBIN largely expatiated on the propriety of vesting this power in the general government, in the manner proposed by the plan of the Convention. He also contended that the empire could not be dismembered without the consent of the part dismembered. To obviate the force of the observations made by an honorable gentleman respecting the relinquishment of the Scheldt, he adduced the late complaints and efforts of the emperor of Germany respecting that river. He insisted that no part of the Constitution was less exceptionable than this. If, says he, there be any sound part in this Constitution, it is in this clause. The representatives are excluded from interposing in making treaties, because large popular assemblies are very improper to transact such business, from the impossibility of their acting with sufficient secrecy, despatch, and decision, which can only be found in small bodies, and because such numerous bodies are ever subject to factions and party animosities. It would be dangerous to give this power to the President alone, as the concession of such power to one individual is repugnant to republican principles. It is, therefore, given to the President and the Senate (who represent the states in their individual capacities) conjointly. In this it differs from every government we know. It steers with admirable dexterity between the two extremes, neither leaving it to the executive, as in most other governments, nor to the legislative, which would too much retard such negotiation.

The honorable gentleman said that treaties are not the supreme law of the land in England. My honorable friend proved the contrary by the Commentaries of Blackstone. Let me confirm it by a circumstance fresh in the memory of every body. When the treaty was made by us with England, it was disapproved of by the English Parliament, and the administration was turned out: yet the treaty was good. Does not this prove that it was binding on the nation, and that the king has such a power? What other proof do gentlemen wish? In England, it is a maxim that the king can do no wrong, yet they have sufficient responsibility, as the ministry can do wrong; for if they advise him to make a treaty derogatory to the honor and interest of the nation, they do it at the risk of their heads. If the king were to make such a treaty himself, contrary to the advice of his ministry, an honest or prudent minister would resign. The President of the United States is responsible in person himself, as well as the senators.

But, say gentlemen, all treaties made under this Constitution are to be the supreme law of nations; that is, in their way of construction, paramount to the constitution itself, and the laws of Congress. It is as clear as that two and two make four, that the treaties made are to be binding on the states only. Is it not necessary that they should be binding on the states? Fatal experience has proved that treaties would never be complied with, if their observance depended on the will of the states; and the consequences would be constant war. For if any one state could counteract any treaty, how could the United States avoid hostility with foreign nations? Do not gentlemen see the infinite dangers that would result from it, if a small part of the community could drag the whole confederacy into war?

The honorable gentleman on the other side tells us that this doctrine is not founded, because, in England, it is declared that the consent of Parliament is necessary. Had the honorable gentleman used his usual discernment and penetration, he would see the difference between a commercial treaty and other treaties. A commercial treaty must be submitted to the consideration of Parliament, because such treaties will render it necessary to alter some laws, add new clauses to some, and repeal others. If this be not done, the treaty is void, *quoad hoc.* The Mississippi cannot be dismembered but in two ways—by a common treaty, or a commercial treaty. If the interest of Congress will lead them to yield it by the first, the law of nations would justify the people of Kentucky to resist, and the cession would be nugatory. It cannot, then, be surrendered by a common treaty. Can it be done by a commercial treaty? If it should, the consent of the House of Representatives would be req-

uisite, because of the correspondent alterations that must be made in the laws.

[Here Mr. Corbin illustrated his position by reading the last clause of the treaty with France, which gives certain commercial privileges to the subjects of France; to give full effect to which, certain correspondent alterations were necessary in the commercial regulations.]

This, continues he, secures legislative interference. Some of the most extraordinary calculations that ever were made have been adduced to prove that the navigation of the Mississippi is on a worse ground than it was before. We are told that five states can make a treaty. This is on a supposition that the senators from the other states will be absent, which is wild and extravagant. On this ground, three states can prevent it; and if Kentucky become a state, two other states, with it, can prevent the making such a treaty. I wish not to assert, but to prove. Suppose there be fourteen members, and the members from Kentucky be of the number. Two thirds, which are ten, are necessary to make a treaty. Three members, together with the two members from Kentucky, will be sufficient to prevent its being made. But suppose all the other states to be present, (which is the fair conclusion, for it is fair to conclude that men will be attentive to their own interest;) what would be the consequence? There would be twenty-eight; two thirds of which are nineteen, which is one member more than the senators of nine states; so that, in such a case, ten states must concur in the treaty; whereas, by the old Confederation, only nine states were necessary. I defy any man to confute this doctrine. The argument of gentlemen is therefore disingenuous. I am more forcibly led to this conclusion when I hear gentlemen go to barbarous nations to adduce proofs of the requisites of a social government.

Mr. HENRY. Mr. Chairman, this great national concern is handled in a manner quite new to me. When arguments are used which are calculated in their nature to mislead men,—when I reflect on the subject, I dread that our rights are about to be given away, though I may possibly be mistaken. I said yesterday, and not without thinking much on the subject, that my mind would be at ease were we on the same grounds, in this respect, as the English are. Gentlemen think that Great Britain was adduced by me, in this instance, unfortunately for myself, because the learned Judge Blackstone says that treaties are binding on the nation, and the king can make treaties. That learned judge says there is one thing which operates as a guard. That thing we have not in this paper—it is responsibility. He tells you that the minister who will sacrifice the interest of the nation is subject to parliamentary impeachment. This has been ever found to be effectual. But I beg gentlemen to consider the American impeachment. What is it? It is a mere sham—a mere farce. When they do any thing derogatory to the honor or interest of their country, they are to try themselves. Is it so in England? The history of that country shows that they have blocks and gibbets. The violators of the public interest have been tried justly and impartially, and perished by those necessary instruments of justice. Can there be any security where offenders mutually try one another? I hope gentlemen will consider the necessity of amendment in this clause.

We are told that the state rights are preserved. Suppose the state right to territory be preserved; I ask and demand, How do the rights of persons stand, when they have power to make any treaty, and that treaty is paramount to constitutions, laws, and every thing? When a person shall be treated in the most horrid manner, and most cruelly and inhumanly tortured, will the security of territorial rights grant him redress? Suppose an unusual punishment in consequence of an arrest similar to that of the Russian ambassador; can it be said to be contrary to the state rights?

I might go on in this discrimination; but it is too obvious that the security of territory is no security of individual safety. I ask, How are the state rights, individual rights, and national rights, secured? Not as in England; for the authority quoted from Blackstone would, if stated right, prove, in a thousand instances, that, if the king of England attempted to take away the rights of individuals, the law would stand against him. The acts of Parliament would stand in his way. The bill and declaration of rights would be against him. The common law is fortified by the bill of rights. The rights of the people cannot be destroyed, even by the paramount operation of the law of nations, as the case of the Russian ambassador evinces. If you look for a similar security in the paper on your table, you look in vain. That paper is defective without such a declaration of rights. It is unbounded without such restrictions. If the Constitution be paramount, how are the constitutions and laws of the states to stand? Their operation will be totally controlled by it; for it is paramount to every thing, unless you can show some guard against it. The rights of persons are exposed as it stands now.

The calculation of the honorable gentleman (Mr. Corbin) was wrong. I am sure he spoke from the best of his recollection, when he referred to our treaty of peace with Great Britain, and said that it was binding on the nation, though disapproved of by Parliament. Did not an act of Parliament pass, acknowledging the independence of America? If the king of England wished to dismember the empire, would he dare to attempt it without the advice of Parliament? The most hardy minister would not dare to advise him to attempt it without a previous consultation of Parliament. No cession of territory is binding on the nation unless it be fortified by an act of Parliament. Will it be so in your American government? No. They will tell you that they are omnipotent as to this point.

We are so used to speak of enormity of powers, that we are familiarized with it. To me this power appears still destructive; for they can make any treaty. If Congress forbears to exercise it, you may thank them; but they may exercise it if they please, and as they please. They have a right, from the paramount power given them, to do so. Will the gentleman say that this power is paramount to the state laws only? Is it not paramount to the Constitution and every thing? Can any thing be paramount to what is paramount? Will not the laws of Congress be binding on Congress, as well as on any particular state? Will they not

be bound by their own acts? The worthy gentleman must see the impropriety of his assertion. To render this safe, I conceive we must adopt my honorable friend's amendment. The component part of this supreme power are the President, senators, and House of Representatives. The latter is the most material part. They ought to interpose in the formation of treaties. When their consent is necessary, there will be a certainty of attending to the public interests.

Mr. Henry then contended that there was real responsibility in the British government, and sufficient security arising from the common law, declaration of rights, &c.; whereas, in this government, there was no barrier to stop their mad career. He hoped to obtain the amendments which his honorable friend had proposed.

Mr. MADISON. Mr. Chairman, I am persuaded that, when this power comes to be thoroughly and candidly viewed, it will be found right and proper. As to its extent, perhaps it will be satisfactory to the committee that the power is, precisely, in the new Constitution as it is in the Confederation. In the existing confederacy, Congress are authorized indefinitely to make treaties. Many of the states have recognized the treaties of Congress to be the supreme law of the land. Acts have passed, within a year, declaring this to be the case. I have seen many of them. Does it follow, because this power is given to Congress, that it is absolute and unlimited? I do not conceive that power is given to the President and Senate to dismember the empire, or to alienate any great, essential right. I do not think the whole legislative authority have this power. The exercise of the power must be consistent with the object of the delegation.

One objection against the amendment proposed is this, that, by implication, it would give power to the legislative authority to dismember the empire—a power that ought not to be given, but by the necessity that would force assent from every man. I think it rests on the safest foundation as it is. The object of treaties is the regulation of intercourse with foreign nations, and is external. I do not think it possible to enumerate all the cases in which such external regulations would be necessary. Would it be right to define all the cases in which Congress could exercise this authority? The definition might, and probably would, be defective. They might be restrained, by such a definition, from exercising the authority where it would be essential to the interest and safety of the community. It is most safe, therefore, to leave it to be exercised as contingencies may arise.

It is to be presumed that, in transactions with foreign countries, those who regulate them will feel the whole force of national attachment to their country. The contrast being between their own nation and a foreign nation, is it not presumable they will, as far as possible, advance the interest of their own country? Would it not be considered as a dangerous principle in the British government were the king to have the same power in internal regulations as he has in the external business of treaties? Yet as, among other reasons, it is natural to suppose he will prefer the interest of his own to that of another country, it is thought proper to give him this external power of making treaties.

This distinction is well worth the consideration of gentlemen. I think the argument of the gentleman who restrained the supremacy of these to the laws of particular states, and not to Congress, is rational. Here the supremacy of a treaty is contrasted with the supremacy of the laws of the states. It cannot be otherwise supreme. If it does not supersede their existing laws, as far as they contravene its operation, it cannot be of any effect. To counteract it by the supremacy of the state laws, would bring on the Union the just charge of national perfidy, and involve us in war.

Suppose the king of Great Britain should make a treaty with France, where he had a constitutional right; if the treaty should require an internal regulation, and the Parliament should make a law to that effect, that law would be binding on the one, though not on the other nation. Suppose there should be a violation of right by the exercise of this power by the President and Senate; if there was apparent merit in it, it would be binding on the people; for where there is a power for any particular purpose, it must supersede what may oppose it, or else it can be no power. For instance, where there is a power of declaring war, that power, as to declaring war, supersedes every thing. This would be an unfortunate case, should it happen; but should it happen, there is a remedy; and there being a remedy, they will be restrained against abuses.

11

DEBATE IN NORTH CAROLINA RATIFYING CONVENTION
24, 28 July 1788
Elliot 4:27–28, 115–34

[*24 July*]

Mr. LENOIR. Mr. Chairman, I have a greater objection on this ground than that which has just been mentioned. I mean, sir, the legislative power given to the President himself. It may be admired by some, but not by me. He, sir, with the Senate, is to make treaties, which are to be the supreme law of the land. This is a legislative power given to the President, and implies a contradiction to that part which says that all legislative power is vested in the two houses.

Mr. SPAIGHT answered, that it was thought better to put that power into the hands of the senators as representatives of the states—that thereby the interest of every state was equally attended to in the formation of treaties—but that it was not considered as a legislative act at all.

Mr. IREDELL. Mr. Chairman, this is an objection against the inaccuracy of the sentence. I humbly conceive it will appear accurate on a due attention. After a bill is passed by both houses, it is to be shown to the President. Within a certain time, he is to return it. If he disapproves of it, he is to state his objections in writing; and it depends on Congress afterwards to say whether it shall be a law or not.

Now, sir, I humbly apprehend that, whether a law passes by a bare majority, or by two thirds, (which are required to concur after he shall have stated objections,) what gives active operation to it is, the will of the senators and representatives. The President has no power of legislation. If he does not object, the law passes by a bare majority; and if he objects, it passes by two thirds. His power extends only to cause it to be reconsidered, which secures a greater probability of its being good. As to his power with respect to treaties, I shall offer my sentiments on it when we come properly to it.

Mr. MACLAINE intimated, that if any gentleman was out of order, it was the gentleman from Wilkes (Mr. Lenoir)—that treaties were the supreme law of the land in all countries, for the most obvious reasons—that laws, or legislative acts, operated upon individuals, but that treaties acted upon states—that, unless they were the supreme law of the land, they could have no validity at all—that the President did not act in this case as a legislator, but rather in his executive capacity.

Mr. LENOIR replied that he wished to be conformable to the rules of the house; but he still thought the President was possessed of legislative powers, while he could make treaties, joined with the Senate.

Mr. IREDELL. Mr. Chairman, I think the gentleman is in order. When treaties are made, they become as valid as legislative acts. I apprehend that every act of the government, legislative, executive, or judicial, if in pursuance of a constitutional power, is the law of the land. These different acts become the acts of the state by the instrumentality of its officers. When, for instance, the governor of this state grants a pardon, it becomes the law of the land, and is valid. Every thing is the law of the land, let it come from what power it will, provided it be consistent with the Constitution.

Mr. LENOIR answered, that that comparison did not hold.

Mr. IREDELL continued. If the governor grants a pardon, it becomes a law of the land. Why? Because he has power to grant pardons by the Constitution. Suppose this Constitution is adopted, and a treaty made; that treaty is the law of the land. Why? Because the Constitution grants the power of making treaties.

[*28 July*]

Mr. PORTER. Mr. Chairman, there is a power vested in the Senate and President to make treaties, which shall be the supreme law of the land. Which among us can call them to account? I always thought that there could be no proper exercise of power without the suffrage of the people; yet the House of Representatives has no power to intermeddle with treaties. The President and seven senators, as nearly as I can remember, can make a treaty which will be of great advantage to the Northern States, and equal injury to the Southern States. They might give up the rivers and territory of the Southern States. Yet, in the preamble of the Constitution, they say *all the people* have done it. I should be glad to know what power there is of calling the President and Senate to account.

Mr. SPAIGHT answered that, under the Confederation,

two thirds of the states might make treaties; that, if the senators from all the states attended when a treaty was about to be made, two thirds of the states would have a voice in its formation. He added, that he would be glad to ask the gentleman what mode there was of calling the present Congress to account.

Mr. PORTER repeated his objection. He hoped that gentlemen would not impose on the house; that the President could make treaties with two thirds of the senate; that the President, in that case, voted rather in a legislative than in an executive capacity, which he thought impolitic.

Gov. JOHNSTON. Mr. Chairman, in my opinion, if there be any difference between this Constitution and the Confederation, with respect to treaties, the Constitution is more safe than the Confederation. We know that two members from each state have a right, by the Confederation, to give the vote of that state, and two thirds of the states have a right also to make treaties. By this Constitution, two thirds of the senators cannot make treaties without the concurrence of the President. Here is, then, an additional guard. The calculation that seven or eight senators, with the President, can make treaties, is totally erroneous. Fourteen is a quorum; two thirds of which are ten. It is upon the improbable supposition that they will not attend, that the objection is founded that ten men, with the President, can make treaties. Can it be reasonably supposed that they will not attend when the most important business is agitated—when the interests of their respective states are most immediately affected?

. . . . .

Mr. SPENCER. Mr. Chairman, I rise to declare my disapprobation of this, likewise. It is an essential article in our Constitution, that the legislative, the executive, and the supreme judicial powers, of government, ought to be forever separate and distinct from each other. The Senate, in the proposed government of the United States, are possessed of the legislative authority in conjunction with the House of Representatives. They are likewise possessed of the sole power of trying all impeachments, which, not being restrained to the officers of the United States, may be intended to include all the officers of the several states in the Union. And by this clause they possess the chief of the executive power; they are, in effect, to form treaties, which are to be the law of the land; and they have obviously, in effect, the appointment of all the officers of the United States. The President may nominate, but they have a negative upon his nomination, till he has exhausted the number of those he wishes to be appointed. He will be obliged, finally, to acquiesce in the appointment of those whom the Senate shall nominate, or else no appointment will take place. Hence it is easy to perceive that the President, in order to do any business, or to answer any purpose in this department of his office, and to keep himself out of perpetual hot water, will be under a necessity to form a connection with that powerful body, and be contented to put himself at the head of the leading members who compose it. I do not expect, at this day, that the outline and organization of this proposed government will be materially altered. But I cannot but be of opinion that the government would have been infinitely better and more secure, if the

President had been provided with a standing council, composed of one member from each of the states, the duration of whose office might have been the same as that of the President's office, or for any other period that might have been thought more proper; for it can hardly be supposed, if two senators can be sent from each state, who are fit to give counsel to the President, that one such cannot be found in each state qualified for that purpose. Upon this plan, one half the expense of the Senate, as a standing council to the President in the recess of Congress, would evidently be saved; each state would have equal weight in this council, as it has now in the Senate. And what renders this plan the more eligible is, that two very important consequences would result from it, which cannot result from the present plan. The first is, that the whole executive department, being separate and distinct from that of the legislative and judicial, would be amenable to the justice of the land: the President and his council, or either or any of them, might be impeached, tried, and condemned, for any misdemeanor in office. Whereas, on the present plan proposed, the Senate, who are to advise the President, and who, in effect, are possessed of the chief executive powers, let their conduct be what it will, are not amenable to the public justice of their country: if they may be impeached, there is no tribunal invested with jurisdiction to try them. It is true that the proposed Constitution provides that, when the President is tried, the chief justice shall preside. But I take this to be very little more than a farce. What can the Senate try him for? For doing that which they have advised him to do, and which, without their advice, he would not have done. Except what he may do in a military capacity—when, I presume, he will be entitled to be tried by a court martial of general officers—he can do nothing in the executive department without the advice of the Senate, unless it be to grant pardons, and adjourn the two Houses of Congress to some day to which they cannot agree to adjourn themselves—probably to some term that may be convenient to the leading members of the Senate.

I cannot conceive, therefore, that the President can ever be tried by the Senate with any effect, or to any purpose for any misdemeanor in his office, unless it should extend to high treason, or unless they should wish to fix the odium of any measure on him, in order to exculpate themselves; the latter of which I cannot suppose will ever happen.

Another important consequence of the plan I wish had taken place is that, the office of the President being thereby unconnected with that of the legislative, as well as the judicial, he would have that independence which is necessary to form the intended check upon the acts passed by the legislature before they obtain the sanction of laws. But, on the present plan, from the necessary connection of the President's office with that of the Senate, I have little ground to hope that his firmness will long prevail against the overbearing power and influence of the Senate, so far as to answer the purpose of any considerable check upon the acts they may think proper to pass in conjunction with the House of Representatives; for he will soon find that, unless he inclines to compound with them, they can easily hinder and control him in the principal articles of his office. But, if nothing else could be said in favor of the plan of a standing council to the President, independent of the Senate, the dividing the power of the latter would be sufficient to recommend it; it being of the utmost importance towards the security of the government, and the liberties of the citizens under it. For I think it must be obvious to every unprejudiced mind, that the combining in the Senate the power of legislation, with a controlling share in the appointment of all the officers of the United States, (except those chosen by the people,) and the power of trying all impeachments that may be found against such officers, invests the Senate at once with such an enormity of power, and with such an overbearing and uncontrollable influence, as is incompatible with every idea of safety to the liberties of a free country, and is calculated to swallow up all other powers, and to render that body a despotic aristocracy.

Mr. PORTER recommended the most serious consideration when they were about to give away power; that they were not only about to give away power to legislate or make laws of a supreme nature, and to make treaties, which might sacrifice the most valuable interests of the community, but to give a power to the general government to drag the inhabitants to any part of the world as long as they pleased; that they ought not to put it in the power of any man, or any set of men, to do so; and that the representation was defective, being not a substantial, immediate representation. He observed that, as treaties were the supreme law of the land, the House of Representatives ought to have a vote in making them, as well as in passing them.

Mr. J. M'DOWALL. Mr. Chairman: permit me, sir, to make a few observations, to show how improper it is to place so much power in so few men, without any responsibility whatever. Let us consider what number of them is necessary to transact the most important business. Two thirds of the members present, with the President, can make a treaty. Fourteen of them are a quorum, two thirds of which are ten. These ten may make treaties and alliances. They may involve us in any difficulties, and dispose of us in any manner, they please. Nay, eight is a majority of a quorum, and can do every thing but make treaties. How unsafe are we, when we have no power of bringing those to an account! It is absurd to try them before their own body. Our lives and property are in the hands of eight or nine men. Will these gentlemen intrust their rights in this manner?

Mr. DAVIE. Mr. Chairman, although treaties are mere conventional acts between the contracting parties, yet, by the law of nations, they are the supreme law of the land to their respective citizens or subjects. All civilized nations have concurred in considering them as paramount to an ordinary act of legislation. This concurrence is founded on the reciprocal convenience and solid advantages arising from it. A due observance of treaties makes nations more friendly to each other, and is the only means of rendering less frequent those mutual hostilities which tend to depopulate and ruin contending nations. It extends and facilitates that commercial intercourse, which, founded on the

universal protection of private property, has, in a measure, made the world one nation.

The power of making treaties has, in all countries and governments, been placed in the executive departments. This has not only been grounded on the necessity and reason arising from that degree of secrecy, design, and despatch, which is always necessary in negotiations between nations, but to prevent their being impeded, or carried into effect, by the violence, animosity, and heat of parties, which too often infect numerous bodies. Both of these reasons preponderated in the foundation of this part of the system. It is true, sir, that the late treaty between the United States and Great Britain has not, in some of the states, been held as the supreme law of the land. Even in this state, an act of Assembly passed to declare its validity. But no doubt that treaty was the supreme law of the land without the sanction of the Assembly; because, by the Confederation, Congress had power to make treaties. It was one of those original rights of sovereignty which were vested in them; and it was not the deficiency of constitutional authority in Congress to make treaties that produced the necessity of a law to declare their validity; but it was owing to the entire imbecility of the Confederation.

On the principle of the propriety of vesting this power in the executive department, it would seem that the whole power of making treaties ought to be left to the President, who, being elected by the people of the United States at large, will have their general interest at heart. But that jealousy of executive power which has shown itself so strongly in all the American governments, would not admit this improvement. Interest, sir, has a most powerful influence over the human mind, and is the basis on which all the transactions of mankind are built. It was mentioned before that the extreme jealousy of the little states, and between the commercial states and the non-importing states, produced the necessity of giving an equality of suffrage to the Senate. The same causes made it indispensable to give to the senators, as representatives of states, the power of making, or rather ratifying, treaties. Although it militates against every idea of just proportion that the little state of Rhode Island should have the same suffrage with Virginia, or the great commonwealth of Massachusetts, yet the small states would not consent to confederate without an equal voice in the formation of treaties. Without the equality, they apprehended that their interest would be neglected or sacrificed in negotiations. This difficulty could not be got over. It arose from the unalterable nature of things. Every man was convinced of the inflexibility of the little states in this point. It therefore became necessary to give them an absolute equality in making treaties.

The learned gentleman on my right, (Mr. Spencer,) after saying that this was an enormous power, and that blending the different branches of government was dangerous, said, that such accumulated powers were inadmissible, and contrary to all the maxims of writers. It is true, the great Montesquieu, and several other writers, have laid it down as a maxim not to be departed from, that the legislative, executive, and judicial powers should be separate and distinct. But the idea that these gentlemen had in view has been misconceived or misrepresented. An absolute and complete separation is not meant by them. It is impossible to form a government upon these principles. Those states who had made an absolute separation of these three powers their leading principle, have been obliged to depart from it. It is a principle, in fact, which is not to be found in any of the state governments. In the government of New York, the executive and judiciary have a negative similar to that of the President of the United States. This is a junction of all the three powers, and has been attended with the most happy effects. In this state, and most of the others, the executive and judicial powers are dependent on the legislature. Has not the legislature of this state the power of appointing the judges? Is it not in their power also to fix their compensation? What independence can there be in persons who are obliged to be obsequious and cringing for their office and salary? Are not our judges dependent on the legislature for every morsel they eat? It is not difficult to discern what effect this may have on human nature. The meaning of this maxim I take to be this—that the whole legislative, executive, and judicial powers should not be exclusively blended in any one particular instance. The Senate try impeachments. This is their only judicial cognizance. As to the ordinary objects of a judiciary—such as the decision of controversies, the trial of criminals, &c.—the judiciary is perfectly separate and distinct from the legislative and executive branches. The House of Lords, in England, have great judicial powers; yet this is not considered as a blemish in their constitution. Why? Because they have not the whole legislative power. Montesquieu, at the same time that he laid down this maxim, was writing in praise of the British government. At the very time he recommended this distinction of powers, he passed the highest eulogium on a constitution wherein they were all partially blended. So that the meaning of the maxim, as laid down by him and other writers, must be, that these three branches must not be entirely blended in one body. And this system before you comes up to the maxim more completely than the favorite government of Montesquieu. The gentleman from Anson has said that the Senate destroys the independence of the President, because they must confirm the nomination of officers. The necessity of their interfering in the appointment of officers resulted from the same reason which produced the equality of suffrage. In other countries, the executive or chief magistrate, alone, nominates and appoints officers. The small states would not agree that the House of Representatives should have a voice in the appointment to offices; and the extreme jealousy of all the states would not give it to the President alone. In my opinion, it is more proper as it is than it would be in either of those cases. The interest of each state will be equally attended to in appointments, and the choice will be more judicious by the junction of the Senate to the President. Except in the appointments of officers, and making of treaties, he is not joined with them in any instance. He is perfectly independent of them in his election. It is impossible for human ingenuity to devise any mode of election better calculated to exclude undue influence. He is chosen by the electors appointed by the people. He

is elected on the same day in every state, so that there can be no possible combination between the electors. The affections of the people can be the only influence to procure his election. If he makes a judicious nomination, is it to be presumed that the Senate will not concur in it? Is it to be supposed the legislatures will choose the most depraved men in the states to represent them in Congress? Should he nominate unworthy characters, can it be reasonably concluded that they will confirm it? He then says that the senators will have influence to get themselves reëlected; nay, that they will be perpetually elected.

I have very little apprehension on this ground. I take it for granted that the man who is once a senator will very probably be out for the next six years. Legislative influence changes. Other persons rise, who have particular connections to advance them to office. If the senators stay six years out of the state governments, their influence will be greatly diminished. It will be impossible for the most influential character to get himself reëlected after being out of the country so long. There will be an entire change in six years. Such futile objections, I fear, proceed from an aversion to any general system. The same learned gentleman says that it would be better, were a council, consisting of one from every state, substituted to the Senate. Another gentleman has objected to the smallness of this number. This shows the impossibility of satisfying all men's minds. I beg this committee to place these two objections together, and see their glaring inconsistency. If there were thirteen counsellors, in the manner he proposes, it would destroy the responsibility of the President. He must have acted also with a majority of them. A majority of them is seven, which would be a quorum. A majority of these would be four, and every act to which the concurrence of the Senate and the President is necessary could be decided by these four. Nay, less than a majority—even one—would suffice to enable them to do the most important acts. This, sir, would be the effect of this council. The dearest interests of the community would be trusted to two men. Had this been the case, the loudest clamors would have been raised, with justice, against the Constitution, and these gentlemen would have loaded their own proposition with the most virulent abuse.

On a due consideration of this clause, it appears that this power could not have been lodged as safely any where else as where it is. The honorable gentleman (Mr. M'Dowall) has spoken of a consolidation in this government. That is a very strange inconsistency, when he points out, at the same time, the necessity of lodging the power of making treaties with the representatives, where the idea of a consolidation can alone exist; and when he objects to placing it in the Senate, where the federal principle is completely preserved. As the Senate represents the sovereignty of the states, whatever might affect the states in their political capacity ought to be left to them. This is the certain means of preventing a consolidation. How extremely absurd is it to call that disposition of power a consolidation of the states, which must to all eternity prevent it! I have only to add the principle upon which the General Convention went—that the power of making treaties could nowhere be so safely lodged as in the President and Senate; and the extreme jealousy subsisting between some of the states would not admit of it elsewhere. If any man will examine the operation of that jealousy, in his own breast, as a citizen of North Carolina, he will soon feel the inflexibility that results from it, and perhaps be induced to acknowledge the propriety of this arrangement.

Mr. M'DOWALL declared, that he was of the same opinion as before, and that he believed the observations which the gentleman had made, on the apparent inconsistency of his remarks, would have very little weight with the committee; that giving such extensive powers to so few men in the Senate was extremely dangerous; and that he was not the more reconciled to it from its being brought about by the inflexibility of the small, pitiful states to the north. He supposed that eight members in the Senate from those states, with the President, might do the most important acts.

Mr. SPAIGHT. Mr. Chairman, the gentleman objects to the smallness of the number, and to their want of responsibility. He argues as if the senators were never to attend, and as if the northern senators were to attend more regularly than those from the south. Nothing can be more unreasonable than to suppose that they will be absent on the most important occasions. What responsibility is there in the present Congress that is not in the Senate? What responsibility is there in our state legislature? The senators are as responsible as the members of our legislature. It is to be observed, that though the senators are not impeachable, yet the President is. He may be impeached and punished for giving his consent to a treaty, whereby the interest of the community is manifestly sacrificed.

Mr. SPENCER. Mr. Chairman, the worthy gentleman from Halifax has endeavored to obviate my objections against the want of responsibility in the President and senators, and against the extent of their power. He has not removed my objections. It is totally out of their power to show any degree of responsibility. The executive is tried by his advisers. The reasons I urged are so cogent and strong with me, that I cannot approve of this clause. I can see nothing of any weight against them. [Here Mr. Spencer spoke so low that he could not distinctly be heard.] I would not give the President and senators power to make treaties, because it destroys their responsibility. If a bad treaty be made, and he impeached for it, the Senate will not pronounce sentence against him, because they advised him to make it. If they had legislative power only, it would be unexceptionable; but when they have the appointment of officers, and such extensive executive powers, it gives them such weight as is inadmissible. Notwithstanding what gentlemen have said in defence of the clause, the influence of the Senate still remains equally formidable to me. The President can do nothing unless they concur with him. In order to obtain their concurrence, he will compromise with them. Had there been such a council as I mentioned, to advise him, the Senate would not have had such dangerous influence, and the responsibility of the President would have been secured. This seems obviously clear to be the case.

Mr. PORTER. Mr. Chairman, I only rise to make one ob-

servation on what the gentleman has said. He told us, that if the Senate were not amenable, the President was. I beg leave to ask the gentleman if it be not inconsistent that they should punish the President, whom they advised themselves to do what he is impeached for. My objection still remains. I cannot find it in the least obviated.

Mr. BLOODWORTH desired to be informed whether treaties were not to be submitted to the Parliament in Great Britain before they were valid.

Mr. IREDELL. Mr. Chairman, the objections to this clause deserve great consideration. I believe it will be easy to obviate the objections against it, and that it will be found to have been necessary, for the reasons stated by the gentleman from Halifax, to vest this power in some body composed of representatives of states, where their voices should be equal; for in this case the sovereignty of the states is particularly concerned, and the great caution of giving the states an equality of suffrage in making treaties, was for the express purpose of taking care of that sovereignty, and attending to their interests, as political bodies, in foreign negotiations. It is objected to as improper, because, if the President or Senate should abuse their trust, there is not sufficient responsibility, since he can only be tried by the Senate, by whose advice he acted; and the Senate cannot be tried at all. I beg leave to observe that, when any man is impeached, it must be for an error of the heart, and not of the head. God forbid that a man, in any country in the world, should be liable to be punished for want of judgment. This is not the case here. As to errors of the heart, there is sufficient responsibility. Should these be committed, there is a ready way to bring him to punishment. This is a responsibility which answers every purpose that could be desired by a people jealous of their liberty. I presume that, if the President, with the advice of the Senate, should make a treaty with a foreign power, and that treaty should be deemed unwise, or against the interest of the country, yet if nothing could be objected against it but the difference of opinion between them and their constituents, they could not justly be obnoxious to punishment. If they were punishable for exercising their own judgment, and not that of their constituents, no man who regarded his reputation would accept the office either of a senator or President. Whatever mistake a man may make, he ought not to be punished for it, nor his posterity rendered infamous. But if a man be a villain, and wilfully abuse his trust, he is to be held up as a public offender, and ignominiously punished. A public officer ought not to act from a principle of fear. Were he punishable for want of judgment, he would be continually in dread; but when he knows that nothing but real guilt can disgrace him, he may do his duty firmly, if he be an honest man; and if he be not, a just fear of disgrace may, perhaps, as to the public, have nearly the effect of an intrinsic principle of virtue. According to these principles, I suppose the only instances, in which the President would be liable to impeachment, would be where he had received a bribe, or had acted from some corrupt motive or other. If the President had received a bribe, without the privity or knowledge of the Senate, from a foreign power, and, under the influence of that bribe, had address enough with the Senate, by artifices and misrepresentations, to seduce their consent to a pernicious treaty,—if it appeared afterwards that this was the case, would not that Senate be as competent to try him as any other persons whatsoever? Would they not exclaim against his villany? Would they not feel a particular resentment against him, for being made the instrument of his treacherous purposes? In this situation, if any objection could be made against the Senate as a proper tribunal, it might more properly be made by the President himself, lest their resentment should operate too strongly, rather than by the public, on the ground of a supposed partiality. The President must certainly be punishable for giving false information to the Senate. He is to regulate all intercourse with foreign powers, and it is his duty to impart to the Senate every material intelligence he receives. If it should appear that he has not given them full information, but has concealed important intelligence which he ought to have communicated, and by that means induced them to enter into measures injurious to their country, and which they would not have consented to had the true state of things been disclosed to them,—in this case, I ask whether, upon an impeachment for a misdemeanor upon such an account, the Senate would probably favor him. With respect to the impeachability of the Senate, that is a matter of doubt.

There have been no instances of impeachment for legislative misdemeanors; and we shall find, upon examination, that the inconveniences resulting from such impeachments would more than preponderate the advantages. There is no greater honor in the world than being the representative of a free people. There is no trust on which the happiness of the people has a greater dependence. Yet who ever heard of impeaching a member of the legislature for any legislative misconduct? It would be a great check on the public business, if a member of the Assembly was liable to punishment for his conduct as such. Unfortunately, it is the case, not only in other countries, but even in this, that division and differences in opinion will continually arise. On many questions there will be two or more parties. These often judge with little charity of each other, and attribute every opposition to their own system to an ill motive. We know this very well from experience; but, in my opinion, this constant suspicion is frequently unjust. I believe, in general, both parties really think themselves right, and that the majority of each commonly act with equal innocence of intention. But, with the usual want of charity in these cases, how dangerous would it be to make a member of the legislature liable to impeachment! A mere difference of opinion might be interpreted, by the malignity of party, into a deliberate, wicked action.

It therefore appears to me at least very doubtful whether it would be proper to render the Senate impeachable at all; especially as, in the branches of executive government, where their concurrence is required, the President is the primary agent, and plainly responsible, and they, in fact, are but a council to validate proper, or restrain improper, conduct in him; but if a senator is impeachable, it could only be for corruption, or some other wicked motive, in which case, surely those senators who

had acted from upright motives would be competent to try him. Suppose there had been such a council as was proposed, consisting of thirteen, one from each state, to assist the President in making treaties, &c.; more general alarm would have been excited, and stronger opposition made to this Constitution, than even at present. The power of the President would have appeared more formidable, and the states would have lost one half of their security; since, instead of two representatives, which each has now for those purposes, they would have had but one. A gentleman from New Hanover has asked whether it is not the practice, in Great Britain, to submit treaties to Parliament, before they are esteemed as valid. The king has the sole authority, by the laws of that country, to make treaties. After treaties are made, they are frequently discussed in the two houses, where, of late years, the most important measures of government have been narrowly examined. It is usual to move for an address of approbation; and such has been the complaisance of Parliament for a long time, that this seldom hath been withheld. Sometimes they pass an act in conformity to the treaty made; but this, I believe, is not for the mere purpose of confirmation, but to make alterations in a particular system, which the change of circumstances requires. The constitutional power of making treaties is vested in the crown; and the power with whom a treaty is made considers it as binding, without any act of Parliament, unless an alteration by such is provided for in the treaty itself, which I believe is sometimes the case. When the treaty of peace was made in 1763, it contained stipulations for the surrender of some islands to the French. The islands were given up, I believe, without any act of Parliament. The power of making treaties is very important, and must be vested somewhere, in order to counteract the dangerous designs of other countries, and to be able to terminate a war when it is begun. Were it known that our government was weak, two or more European powers might combine against us. Would it not be politic to have some power in this country, to obviate this danger by a treaty? If this power was injudiciously limited, the nations where the power was possessed without restriction would have greatly the advantage of us in negotiation; and every one must know, according to modern policy, of what moment an advantage in negotiation is. The honorable member from Anson said that the accumulation of all the different branches of power in the Senate would be dangerous. The experience of other countries shows that this fear is without foundation. What is the Senate of Great Britain opposed to the House of Commons, although it be composed of an hereditary nobility, of vast fortunes, and entirely independent of the people? Their weight is far inferior to that of the Commons. Here is a strong instance of the accumulation of powers of the different branches of government without producing any inconvenience. That Senate, sir, is a separate branch of the legislature, is the great constitutional council of the crown, and decides on lives and fortunes in impeachments, besides being the ultimate tribunal for trying controversies respecting private rights. Would it not appear that all these things should render them more formidable than the other house? Yet the Commons have generally been able to carry every thing before them. The circumstance of their representing the great body of the people, alone gives them great weight. This weight has great authority added to it, by their possessing the right (a right given to the people's representatives in Congress) of exclusively originating money bills. The authority over money will do every thing. A government cannot be supported without money. Our representatives may at any time compel the Senate to agree to a reasonable measure, by withholding supplies till the measure is consented to. There was a great debate, in the Convention, whether the Senate should have an equal power of originating money bills. It was strongly insisted, by some, that they should; but at length a majority thought it unadvisable, and the clause was passed as it now stands. I have reason to believe that our representatives had a great share in establishing this excellent regulation, and in my opinion they deserve the public thanks for it. It has been objected that this power must necessarily injure the people, inasmuch as a bare majority of the Senate might alone be assembled, and eight would be sufficient for a decision. This is on a supposition that many of the senators would neglect attending. It is to be hoped that the gentlemen who will be honored with seats in Congress will faithfully execute their trust, as well in attending as in every other part of their duty. An objection of this sort will go against all government whatever. Possible abuse, and neglect of attendance, are objections which may be urged against any government which the wisdom of man is able to construct. When it is known of how much importance attendance is, no senator would dare to incur the universal resentment of his fellow-citizens by grossly absenting himself from his duty. Do gentlemen mean that it ought to have been provided, by the Constitution, that the whole body should attend before particular business was done? Then it would be in the power of a few men, by neglecting to attend, to obstruct the public business, and possibly bring on the destruction of their country. If this power be improperly vested, it is incumbent on gentlemen to tell us in what body it could be more safely and properly lodged.

I believe, on a serious consideration, it will be found that it was necessary, for the reasons mentioned by the gentleman from Halifax, to vest the power in the Senate, or in some other body representing equally the sovereignty of the states, and that the power, as given in the Constitution, is not likely to be attended with the evils which some gentlemen apprehend. The only real security of liberty, in any country, is the jealousy and circumspection of the people themselves. Let them be watchful over their rulers. Should they find a combination against their liberties, and all other methods appear insufficient to preserve them, they have, thank God, an ultimate remedy. That power which created the government can destroy it. Should the government, on trial, be found to want amendments, those amendments can be made in a regular method, in a mode prescribed by the Constitution itself. Massachusetts, South Carolina, New Hampshire, and Virginia, have all proposed amendments; but they all concurred in the necessity of an immediate adoption. A constitutional mode of altering the Constitution itself is, perhaps, what has never been known among mankind before. We have this security, in addition to the natural watchfulness of the people, which I hope will never be found wanting. The objections I have answered deserved all possible attention; and for my part, I shall always respect that jealousy which arises from the love of public liberty.

Mr. SPENCER. Mr. Chairman, I think that no argument can be used to show that this power is proper. If the whole legislative body—if the House of Representatives do not interfere in making treaties, I think they ought at least to have the sanction of the whole Senate. The worthy gentleman last up has mentioned two cases wherein he supposes that impeachments will be fairly tried by the senators. He supposes a case where the President had been guilty of corruption, and by that means had brought over and got the sanction of two thirds of the senators; and that, if it should be afterwards found that he brought them over by artifices, they would be a proper body to try him. As they will be ready to throw the odium off their own shoulders on him, they may pronounce sentence against him. He mentions another case, where, if a majority was obtained by bribing some of the senators, those who were innocent might try those who were guilty. I think that these cases will happen but rarely in comparison to other cases, where the senators may advise the President to deviate from his duty, and where a majority of them may be guilty. And should they be tried by their own body when thus guilty, does not every body see the impropriety of it? It is universally disgraceful, odious, and contemptible, to have a trial where the judges are accessory to the misdemeanor of the accused. Whether the accusation against him be true or not, if afraid for themselves, they will endeavor to throw the odium upon him. There is an extreme difference between the case of trying this officer and that of trying their own members. They are so different, that I consider they will always acquit their own members; and if they condemn the President, it will be to exonerate themselves. It appears to me that the powers are too extensive, and not sufficiently guarded. I do not wish that an aristocracy should be instituted. An aristocracy may arise out of this government, though the members be not hereditary. I would therefore wish that every guard should be placed, in order to prevent it. I wish gentlemen would reflect that the powers of the Senate are so great in their legislative and judicial capacities, that, when added to their executive powers, particularly their interference in the appointment of all officers in the continent, they will render their power so enormous as to enable them to destroy our rights and privileges. This, sir, ought to be strictly guarded against.

Mr. IREDELL. Mr. Chairman, the honorable gentleman must be mistaken. He suggests that an aristocracy will arise out of this government. Is there any thing like an aristocracy in this government? This insinuation is uncandidly calculated to alarm and catch prejudices. In this government there is not the least symptom of an aristocracy, which is, where the government is in a select body of men entirely independent of the people; as, for instance, an hereditary nobility, or a senate for life, filling up vacancies by their own authority. Will any member of this government hold his station by any such tenure? Will not all authority flow, in every instance, directly or indirectly from the people? It is contended, by that gentleman, that the addition of the power of making treaties to their other powers, will make the Senate dangerous; that they would be even dangerous to the representatives of the people. The gentleman has not proved this in theory. Whence will he adduce an example to prove it? What passes in England directly disproves his assertion. In that country, the representatives of the people are chosen under undue influence; frequently by direct bribery and corruption. They are elected for seven years, and many of the members hold offices under the crown—some during pleasure, others for life. They are also not a genuine representation of the people, but, from a change of circumstances, a mere shadow of it. Yet, under these disadvantages, they having the sole power of originating money bills, it has been found that the power of the king and lords is much less considerable than theirs. The high prerogatives of the king, and the great power and wealth of the lords, have been more than once mentioned in the course of the debates. If, under such circumstances, such representatives,—mere shadows of representatives,—by having the power of the purse, and the sacred name of the people, to rely upon, are an overmatch for the king and lords, who have such great hereditary qualifications, we may safely conclude that our own representatives, who will be a genuine representation of the people, and having equally the right of originating money bills, will, at least, be a match for the Senate, possessing qualifications so inferior to those of the House of Lords in England.

It seems to be forgotten that the Senate is placed there for a very valuable purpose—as a guard against any attempt of consolidation. The members of the Convention were as much averse to consolidation as any gentleman on this floor; but without this institution, (I mean the Senate, where the suffrages of the states are equal,) the danger would be greater. There ought to be some power given to the Senate to counteract the influence of the people by their biennial representation in the other house, in order to preserve completely the sovereignty of the states. If the people, through the medium of their representatives, possessed a share in making treaties and appointing officers, would there not be a greater balance of power in the House of Representatives than such a government ought to possess? It is true that it would be very improper if the Senate had authority to prevent the House of Representatives from protecting the people. It would be equally so if the House of Representatives were able to prevent the Senate from protecting the sovereignty of the states. It is probable that either house would have sufficient authority to prevent much mischief. As to the suggestion of a tendency to aristocracy, it is totally groundless. I disdain every principle of aristocracy. There is not a shadow of an aristocratical principle in this government. The President is only chosen for four years—liable to be impeached—and dependent on the people at large for his reëlection. Can this mode of appointment be said to have an aristocratical principle in it? The Senate is chosen by the legislatures. Let us consider the example of other states, with respect to the construction of their Senate. In this point, most of

them differ; though they almost all concur in this, that the term of election for senators is longer than that for representatives. The reason of this is, to introduce stability into the laws, and to prevent that mutability which would result from annual elections of both branches. In New York, they are chosen for three years; in Virginia, they are chosen for four years; and in Maryland, they are chosen for five years. In this Constitution, although they are chosen for six years, one third go out every second year, (a method pursued in some of the state constitutions,) which at the same time secures stability to the laws, and a due dependence on the state legislatures. Will any man say that there are any aristocratical principles in a body who have no power independent of the people, and whereof one third of the members are chosen, every second year, by a wise and select body of electors? I hope, therefore, that it will not be considered that there are any aristocratical principles in this government, and that it will be given up as a point not to be contended for. The gentleman contends that a council ought to be instituted in this case. One objection ought to be compared with another. It has been objected against the Constitution that it will be productive of great expense. Had there been a council, it would have been objected that it was calculated for creating new offices, and increasing the means of undue influence. Though he approves of a council, others would not.

12

GEORGE WASHINGTON TO SENATE COMMITTEE ON TREATIES AND NOMINATIONS
10 Aug. 1789
Writings 30:377–79

The President has the "power by and with the advice and consent of the Senate, to make treaties and to appoint Officers."

The Senate when these powers are exercised, is evidently a Council only to the President, however [necessary] its concurrence may be to his Acts. It seems incident to this relation between them, that not only the *time* but the *place* and manner of consultation should be with the President. It is probable that the place may vary. The indisposition or inclination of the President may require, that the Senate should be summoned to the President's House. Whenever the Government shall have buildings of its own, an executive Chamber will no doubt be provided, where the Senate will generally attend the President. It is not impossible that the place may be made to depend in some degree on the nature of the business. In the appointment to offices, the agency of the Senate is purely executive, and they may be summoned to the President. In treaties, the agency is perhaps as much of a legislative nature and the business may possibly be referred to their deliberations in their legislative chamber. The occasion for this distinction will be lessened, if not destroyed, when a chamber shall be appropriated for the joint business of the President and the Senate.

The *manner* of consultation may also vary. The indisposition of the President may supersede the mere question of conveniency. The inclination or ideas of different Presidents may be different. The opinions both of President and Senators as to the proper manner may be changed by experience. In some kinds of business it may be found best for the President to make his propositions orally and in person, in others by written message. On some occasions it may be most convenient that the President should attend the deliberations and decisions on his propositions; on others that he should not; or that he should not attend the whole of the time. In other cases again, as in Treaties of a complicated nature, it may happen that he will send his propositions in writing and consult the Senate in person after time shall have been allowed for consideration. Many other varieties may be suggested as to the *mode*, by practice.

If these remarks be just, it would seem not amiss, that the Senate should accommodate their rules to the uncertainty of the particular mode and place that may be preferred; providing for the reception of either oral [or] written propositions, and for giving their consent and advice in either the *presence* or *absence* of the President, leaving him free to use the mode and place that may be found most eligible and accordant with other business which may be before him at the time.

13

UNITED STATES V. RAVARA
27 Fed. Cas. 713, no. 16,122 (C.C.D.Pa. 1793)

(See 3.2.1, no. 36)

14

ALEXANDER HAMILTON, PACIFICUS, NO. 1
29 June 1793
Papers 15:33–43

As attempts are making very dangerous to the peace, and it is to be feared not very friendly to the constitution of the UStates—it becomes the duty of those who wish well to both to endeavour to prevent their success.

The objections which have been raised against the Proclamation of Neutrality lately issued by the President have been urged in a spirit of acrimony and invective, which demonstrates, that more was in view than merely a free discussion of an important public measure; that the discussion covers a design of weakening the confidence of the People in the author of the measure; in order to remove or lessen a powerful obstacle to the success of an opposi-

tion to the Government, which however it may change its form, according to circumstances, seems still to be adhered to and pursued with persevering Industry.

This Reflection adds to the motives connected with the measure itself to recommend endeavours by proper explanations to place it in a just light. Such explanations at least cannot but be satisfactory to those who may not have leisure or opportunity for pursuing themselves an investigation of the subject, and who may wish to perceive that the policy of the Government is not inconsistent with its obligations or its honor.

The objections in question fall under three heads—
1 That the Proclamation was without authority
2 That it was contrary to our treaties with France
3 That it was contrary to the gratitude, which is due from this to that country; for the succours rendered us in our own Revolution.
4 That it was out of time & unnecessary.

In order to judge of the solidity of the first of these objection[s], it is necessary to examine what is the nature and design of a proclamation of neutrality.

The true nature & design of such an act is—to *make known* to the powers at War and to the Citizens of the Country, whose Government does the Act that such country is in the condition of a Nation at Peace with the belligerent parties, and under no obligations of Treaty, to become an *associate in the war* with either of them; that this being its situation its intention is to observe a conduct conformable with it and to perform towards each the duties of neutrality; and as a consequence of this state of things, to give warning to all within its jurisdiction to abstain from acts that shall contravene those duties, under the penalties which the laws of the land (of which the law of Nations is a part) annexes to acts of contravention.

This, and no more, is conceived to be the true import of a Proclamation of Neutrality.

It does not imply, that the Nation which makes the declaration will forbear to perform to any of the warring Powers any stipulations in Treaties which can be performed without rendering it an *associate* or *party* in the War. It therefore does not imply in our case, that the UStates will not make those distinctions, between the present belligerent powers, which are stipulated in the 17th and 22d articles of our Treaty with France; because these distinctions are not incompatible with a state of neutrality; they will in no shape render the UStates an *associate* or *party* in the War. This must be evident, when it is considered, that even to furnish *determinate* succours, of a certain number of Ships or troops, to a Power at War, in consequence of *antecedent treaties having no particular reference to the existing war*, is not inconsistent with neutrality; a position well established by the doctrines of Writers and the practice of Nations.

But no special aids, succours or favors having relation to war, not positively and precisely stipulated by some Treaty of the above description, can be afforded to either party, without a breach of neutrality.

In stating that the Proclamation of Neutrality does not imply the non performance of any stipulations of Treaties which are not of a nature to make the Nation an associate or party in the war, it is conceded that an execution of the clause of Guarantee contained in the 11th article of our Treaty of Alliance with France would be contrary to the sense and spirit of the Proclamation; because it would engage us with our whole force as an *associate* or *auxiliary* in the War; it would be much more than the case of a definite limited succour, previously ascertained.

It follows that the Proclamation is virtually a manifestation of the sense of the Government that the UStates are, *under the circumstances of the case, not bound* to execute the clause of Guarantee.

If this be a just view of the true force and import of the Proclamation, it will remain to see whether the President in issuing it acted within his proper sphere, or stepped beyond the bounds of his constitutional authority and duty.

It will not be disputed that the management of the affairs of this country with foreign nations is confided to the Government of the UStates.

It can as little be disputed, that a Proclamation of Neutrality, where a Nation is at liberty to keep out of a War in which other Nations are engaged and means so to do, is a *usual* and a *proper* measure. *Its main object and effect are to prevent the Nation being immediately responsible for acts done by its citizens, without the privity or connivance of the Government, in contravention of the principles of neutrality.*

An object this of the greatest importance to a Country whose true interest lies in the preservation of peace.

The inquiry then is—what department of the Government of the UStates is the proper one to make a declaration of Neutrality in the cases in which the engagements of the Nation permit and its interests require such a declaration.

A correct and well informed mind will discern at once that it can belong neither to the Legislative nor Judicial Department and of course must belong to the Executive.

The Legislative Department is not the *organ* of intercourse between the UStates and foreign Nations. It is charged neither with *making* nor *interpreting* Treaties. It is therefore not naturally that Organ of the Government which is to pronounce the existing condition of the Nation, with regard to foreign Powers, or to admonish the Citizens of their obligations and duties as founded upon that condition of things. Still less is it charged with enforcing the execution and observance of these obligations and those duties.

It is equally obvious that the act in question is foreign to the Judiciary Department of the Government. The province of that Department is to decide litigations in particular cases. It is indeed charged with the interpretation of treaties; but it exercises this function only in the litigated cases; that is where contending parties bring before it a specific controversy. It has no concern with pronouncing upon the external political relations of Treaties between Government and Government. This position is too plain to need being insisted upon.

It must then of necessity belong to the Executive Department to exercise the function in Question—when a proper case for the exercise of it occurs.

It appears to be connected with that department in var-

ious capacities, as the *organ* of intercourse between the Nation and foreign Nations—as the interpreter of the National Treaties in those cases in which the Judiciary is not competent, that is in the cases between Government and Government—as that Power, which is charged with the Execution of the Laws, of which Treaties form a part—as that Power which is charged with the command and application of the Public Force.

This view of the subject is so natural and obvious—so analogous to general theory and practice—that no doubt can be entertained of its justness, unless such doubt can be deduced from particular provisions of the Constitution of the UStates.

Let us see then if cause for such doubt is to be found in that constitution.

The second Article of the Constitution of the UStates, section 1st, establishes this general Proposition, That "The EXECUTIVE POWER shall be vested in a President of the United States of America."

The same article in a succeeding Section proceeds to designate particular cases of Executive Power. It declares among other things that the President shall be Commander in Chief of the army and navy of the UStates and of the Militia of the several states when called into the actual service of the UStates, that he shall have power by and with the advice of the senate to make treaties; that it shall be his duty to receive ambassadors and other public Ministers and to take care that the laws be faithfully executed.

It would not consist with the rules of sound construction to consider this enumeration of particular authorities as derogating from the more comprehensive grant contained in the general clause, further than as it may be coupled with express restrictions or qualifications; as in regard to the cooperation of the Senate in the appointment of Officers and the making of treaties; which are qualifications of the general executive powers of appointing officers and making treaties: Because the difficulty of a complete and perfect specification of all the cases of Executive authority would naturally dictate the use of general terms—and would render it improbable that a specification of certain particulars was design[e]d as a substitute for those terms, when antecedently used. The different mode of expression employed in the constitution in regard to the two powers the Legislative and the Executive serves to confirm this inference. In the article which grants the legislative powers of the Govern. the expressions are—"*All Legislative powers herein granted shall be vested in a Congress of the UStates;*" in that which grants the Executive Power the expressions are, as already quoted "The EXECUTIVE POWER shall be vested in a President of the UStates of America."

The enumeration ought rather therefore to be considered as intended by way of greater caution, to specify and regulate the principal articles implied in the definition of Executive Power; leaving the rest to flow from the general grant of that power, interpreted in conformity to other parts of the constitution and to the principles of free government.

The general doctrine then of our constitution is, that the EXECUTIVE POWER of the Nation is vested in the President;

subject only to the *exceptions* and *qu[a]lifications* which are expressed in the instrument.

Two of these have been already noticed—the participation of the Senate in the appointment of Officers and the making of Treaties. A third remains to be mentioned the right of the Legislature "to declare war and grant letters of marque and reprisal."

With these exceptions the EXECUTIVE POWER of the Union is completely lodged in the President. This mode of construing the Constitution has indeed been recognized by Congress in formal acts, upon full consideration and debate. The power of removal from office is an important instance.

And since upon general principles for reasons already given, the issuing of a proclamation of neutrality is merely an Executive Act; since also the general Executive Power of the Union is vested in the President, the conclusion is, that the step, which has been taken by him, is liable to no just exception on the score of authority.

It may be observed that this Inference would be just if the power of declaring war had not been vested in the Legislature, but that this power naturally includes the right of judging whether the Nation is under obligations to make war or not.

The answer to this is, that however true it may be, that the right of the Legislature to declare war includes the right of judging whether the Nation be under obligations to make War or not—it will not follow that the Executive is in any case excluded from a similar right of Judgment, in the execution of its own functions.

If the Legislature have a right to make war on the one hand—it is on the other the duty of the Executive to preserve Peace till war is declared; and in fulfilling that duty, it must necessarily possess a right of judging what is the nature of the obligations which the treaties of the Country impose on the Government; and when in pursuance of this right it has concluded that there is nothing in them inconsistent with a *state* of neutrality, it becomes both its province and its duty to enforce the laws incident to that state of the Nation. The Executive is charged with the execution of all laws, the laws of Nations as well as the Municipal law, which recognises and adopts those laws. It is consequently bound, by faithfully executing the laws of neutrality, when that is the state of the Nation, to avoid giving a cause of war to foreign Powers.

This is the direct and proper end of the proclamation of neutrality. It declares to the UStates their situation with regard to the Powers at war and makes known to the Community that the laws incident to that situation will be enforced. In doing this, it conforms to an established usage of Nations, the operation of which as before remarked is to obviate a responsibility on the part of the whole Society, for secret and unknown violations of the rights of any of the warring parties by its citizens.

Those who object to the proclamation will readily admit that it is the right and duty of the Executive to judge of, or to interpret, those articles of our treaties which give to France particular privileges, in order to the enforcement of those privileges: But the necessary consequence of this is, that the Executive must judge what are the proper bounds of those privileges—what rights are given to other nations by our treaties with them—what rights the law of Nature and Nations gives and our treaties permit, in respect to those Nations with whom we have no treaties; in fine what are the reciprocal rights and obligations of the United States & of all & each of the powers at War.

The right of the Executive to receive ambassadors and other public Ministers may serve to illustrate the relative duties of the Executive and Legislative Departments. This right includes that of judging, in the case of a Revolution of Government in a foreign Country, whether the new rulers are competent organs of the National Will and ought to be recognised or not: And where a treaty antecedently exists between the UStates and such nation that right involves the power of giving operation or not to such treaty. For until the new Government is *acknowleged*, the treaties between the nations, as far at least as regards *public* rights, are of course suspended.

This power of determining virtually in the case supposed upon the operation of national Treaties as a consequence, of the power to receive ambassadors and other public Ministers, is an important instance of the right of the Executive to decide the obligations of the Nation with regard to foreign Nations. To apply it to the case of France, if there had been a Treaty of alliance *offensive* and defensive between the UStates and that Country, the unqualified acknowlegement of the new Government would have put the UStates in a condition to become an associate in the War in which France was engaged—and would have laid the Legislature under an obligation, if required, and there was otherwise no valid excuse, of exercising its power of declaring war.

This serves as an example of the right of the Executive, in certain cases, to determine the condition of the Nation, though it may consequentially affect the proper or improper exercise of the Power of the Legislature to declare war. The Executive indeed cannot control the exercise of that power—further than by the exer[c]ise of its general right of objecting to all acts of the Legislature; liable to being overruled by two thirds of both houses of Congress. The Legislature is free to perform its own duties according to its own sense of them—though the Executive in the exercise of its constitutional powers, may establish an antecedent state of things which ought to weigh in the legislative decisions. From the division of the Executive Power there results, in reference to it, a *concurrent* authority, in the distributed cases.

Hence in the case stated, though treaties can only be made by the President and Senate, their activity may be continued or suspended by the President alone.

No objection has been made to the Presidents having acknowleged the Republic of France, by the Reception of its Minister, without having consulted the Senate; though that body is connected with him in the making of Treaties, and though the consequence of his act of reception is to give operation to the Treaties heretofore made with that Country: But he is censured for having declared the UStates to be in a state of peace & neutrality, with regard to the Powers at War; because the right of *changing* that state & *declaring war* belongs to the Legislature.

It deserves to be remarked, that as the participation of the senate in the making of Treaties and the power of the Legislature to declare war are exceptions out of the general "Executive Power" vested in the President, they are to be construed strictly—and ought to be extended no further than is essential to their execution.

While therefore the Legislature can alone declare war, can alone actually transfer the nation from a state of Peace to a state of War—it belongs to the "Executive Power," to do whatever else the laws of Nations cooperating with the Treaties of the Country enjoin, in the intercourse of the UStates with foreign Powers.

In this distribution of powers the wisdom of our constitution is manifested. It is the province and duty of the Executive to preserve to the Nation the blessings of peace. The Legislature alone can interrupt those blessings, by placing the Nation in a state of War.

But though it has been thought adviseable to vindicate the authority of the Executive on this broad and comprehensive ground—it was not absolutely necessary to do so. That clause of the constitution which makes it his duty to "take care that the laws be faithfully executed" might alone have been relied upon, and this simple process of argument pursued.

The President is the constitutional EXECUTOR of the laws. Our Treaties and the laws of Nations form a part of the law of the land. He who is to execute the laws must first judge for himself of their meaning. In order to the observance of that conduct, which the laws of nations combined with our treaties prescribed to this country, in reference to the present War in Europe, it was necessary for the President to judge for himself whether there was any thing in our treaties incompatible with an adherence to neutrality. Having judged that there was not, he had a right, and if in his opinion the interests of the Nation required it, it was his duty, as Executor of the laws, to proclaim the neutrality of the Nation, to exhort all persons to observe it, and to warn them of the penalties which would attend its non observance.

The Proclamation has been represented as enacting some new law. This is a view of it entirely erroneous. It only proclaims a *fact* with regard to the *existing state* of the Nation, informs the citizens of what the laws previously established require of them in that state, & warns them that these laws will be put in execution against the Infractors of them.

15

JAMES MADISON, LETTERS OF
HELVIDIUS, NOS. 1–4
24 Aug.–14 Sept. 1793
Writings 6:138–77

No. I.

Several pieces with the signature of PACIFICUS were lately published, which have been read with singular pleasure and applause, by the foreigners and degenerate citizens among us, who hate our republican government, and the French revolution; whilst the publication seems to have been too little regarded, or too much despised by the steady friends to both.

Had the doctrines inculcated by the writer, with the natural consequences from them, been nakedly presented to the public, this treatment might have been proper. Their true character would then have struck every eye, and been rejected by the feelings of every heart. But they offer themselves to the reader in the dress of an elaborate dissertation; they are mingled with a few truths that may serve them as a passport to credulity; and they are introduced with professions of anxiety for the preservation of peace, for the welfare of the government, and for the respect due to the present head of the executive, that may prove a snare to patriotism.

In these disguises they have appeared to claim the attention I propose to bestow on them: with a view to show, from the publication itself, that under colour of vindicating an important public act, of a chief magistrate who enjoys the confidence and love of his country, principles are advanced which strike at the vitals of its constitution, as well as at its honour and true interest.

As it is not improbable that attempts may be made to apply insinuations, which are seldom spared when particular purposes are to be answered, to the author of the ensuing observations, it may not be improper to premise, that he is a friend to the constitution, that he wishes for the preservation of peace, and that the present chief magistrate has not a fellow-citizen, who is penetrated with deeper respect for his merits, or feels a purer solicitude for his glory.

This declaration is made with no view of courting a more favourable ear to what may be said than it deserves. The sole purpose of it is, to obviate imputations which might weaken the impressions of truth; and which are the more likely to be resorted to, in proportion as solid and fair arguments may be wanting.

The substance of the first piece, sifted from its inconsistencies and its vague expressions, may be thrown into the following propositions:

That the powers of declaring war and making treaties are, in their nature, executive powers:

That being particularly vested by the constitution in other departments, they are to be considered as exceptions out of the general grant to the executive department:

That being, as exceptions, to be construed strictly, the powers not strictly within them, remain with the executive:

That the executive consequently, as the organ of intercourse with foreign nations, and the interpreter and executor of treaties, and the law of nations, is authorized to expound all articles of treaties, those involving questions of war and peace, as well as others;—to judge of the obligations of the United States to make war or not, under any *casus foederis* or eventual operation of the contract, relating to war; and to pronounce the state of things resulting from the obligations of the United States, as understood by the executive:

That in particular the executive had authority to judge, whether in the case of the mutual guaranty between the United States and France, the former were bound by it to engage in the war:

That the executive has, in pursuance of that authority, decided that the United States are not bound:—And

That its proclamation of the 22nd of April last, is to be taken as the effect and expression of that decision.

The basis of the reasoning is, we perceive, the extraordinary doctrine, that the powers of making war, and treaties, are in their nature executive; and therefore comprehended in the general grant of executive power, where not especially and strictly excepted out of the grant.

Let us examine this doctrine: and that we may avoid the possibility of mistaking the writer, it shall be laid down in his own words; a precaution the more necessary, as scarce any thing else could outweigh the improbability, that so extravagant a tenet should be hazarded at so early a day, in the face of the public.

His words are—"Two of these [exceptions and qualifications to the executive powers] have been already noticed—the participation of the senate in the *appointment of officers,* and the *making of treaties.* A *third* remains to be mentioned—the right of the legislature to *declare war, and grant letters of marque and reprisal.*"

Again—"It deserves to be remarked, that as the participation of the senate in the *making of treaties,* and the power of the legislature to *declare war,* ~~are~~ *exceptions* out of the general *executive power,* vested in the president; they are to be construed *strictly,* and ought to be extended no further than is *essential* to their execution."

If there be any countenance to these positions, it must be found either, first, in the writers of authority on public law; or, 2d, in the quality and operation of the powers to make war and treaties; or, 3d, in the constitution of the United States.

1. It would be of little use to enter far into the first source of information, not only because our own reason and our own constitution, are the best guides; but because a just analysis and discrimination of the powers of government, according to their executive, legislative, and judiciary qualities, are not to be expected in the works of the most received jurists, who wrote before a critical attention was paid to those objects, and with their eyes too much on monarchical governments, where all powers are confounded in the sovereignty of the prince. It will be found, however, I believe, that all of them, particularly Wolsius,

Burlemaqui, and Vatel, speak of the powers to declare war, to conclude peace, and to form alliances, as among the highest acts of the sovereignty; of which the legislative power must at least be an integral and preeminent part.

Writers, such as Locke, and Montesquieu, who have discussed more the principles of liberty and the structure of government, lie under the same disadvantage, of having written before these subjects were illuminated by the events and discussions which distinguish a very recent period. Both of them, too, are evidently warped by a regard to the particular government of England, to which one of them owed allegiance[1]; and the other professed an admiration bordering on idolatry. Montesquieu, however, has rather distinguished himself by enforcing the reasons and the importance of avoiding a confusion of the several powers of government, than by enumerating and defining the powers which belong to each particular class. And Locke, notwithstanding the early date of his work on civil government, and the example of his own government before his eyes, admits that the particular powers in question, which, after some of the writers on public law he calls *federative,* are really *distinct* from the *executive,* though almost always united with it, and *hardly to be separated into distinct hands.* Had he not lived under a monarchy, in which these powers were united; or had he written by the lamp which truth now presents to lawgivers, the last observation would probably never have dropped from his pen. But let us quit a field of research which is more likely to perplex than to decide, and bring the question to other tests of which it will be more easy to judge.

2. If we consult, for a moment, the nature and operation of the two powers to declare war and to make treaties, it will be impossible not to see, that they can never fall within a proper definition of executive powers. The natural province of the executive magistrate is to execute laws, as that of the legislature is to make laws. All his acts, therefore, properly executive, must presuppose the existence of the laws to be executed. A treaty is not an execution of laws: it does not presuppose the existence of laws. It is, on the contrary, to have itself the force of a *law,* and to be carried into *execution,* like all *other laws,* by the *executive magistrate.* To say then that the power of making treaties, which are confessedly laws, belongs naturally to the department which is to execute laws, is to say, that the executive department naturally includes a legislative power. In theory this is an absurdity—in practice a tyranny.

The power to declare war is subject to similar reasoning. A declaration that there shall be war, is not an execution of laws: it does not suppose pre-existing laws to be executed: it is not, in any respect, an act merely executive. It is, on the contrary, one of the most deliberate acts that can be performed; and when performed, has the effect of *repealing* all the *laws* operating in a state of peace, so far as they are inconsistent with a state of war; and of *enacting,* as a *rule for the executive, a new code* adapted to the relation between the society and its foreign enemy. In like manner, a conclusion of peace *annuls* all the *laws* peculiar to a state

---

[1] The chapter on prerogative shows, how much the reason of the philosopher was clouded by the royalism of the Englishman.

of war, and *revives* the general *laws* incident to a state of peace.

These remarks will be strengthened by adding, that treaties, particularly treaties of peace, have sometimes the effect of changing not only the external laws of the society, but operate also on the internal code, which is purely municipal, and to which the legislative authority of the country is of itself competent and complete.

From this view of the subject it must be evident, that although the executive may be a convenient organ of preliminary communications with foreign governments, on the subjects of treaty or war; and the proper agent for carrying into execution the final determinations of the competent authority; yet it can have no pretensions, from the nature of the powers in question compared with the nature of the executive trust, to that essential agency which gives validity to such determinations.

It must be further evident, that if these powers be not in their nature purely legislative, they partake so much more of that, than of any other quality, that under a constitution leaving them to result to their most natural department, the legislature would be without a rival in its claim.

Another important inference to be noted is, that the powers of making war and treaty being substantially of a legislative, not an executive nature, the rule of interpreting exceptions strictly must narrow, instead of enlarging, executive pretensions on those subjects.

3. It remains to be inquired, whether there be any thing in the constitution itself, which shows, that the powers of making war and peace are considered as of an executive nature, and as comprehended within a general grant of executive power.

It will not be pretended, that this appears from any *direct* position to be found in the instrument.

If it were *deducible* from any particular expressions, it may be presumed, that the publication would have saved us the trouble of the research.

Does the doctrine, then, result from the actual distribution of powers among the several branches of the government? or from any fair analogy between the powers of war and treaty, and the enumerated powers vested in the executive alone?

Let us examine:

In the general distribution of powers, we find that of declaring war expressly vested in the congress, where every other legislative power is declared to be vested; and without any other qualification than what is common to every other legislative act. The constitutional idea of this power would seem then clearly to be, that it is of a legislative and not an executive nature.

This conclusion becomes irresistible, when it is recollected, that the constitution cannot be supposed to have placed either any power legislative in its nature, entirely among executive powers, or any power executive in its nature, entirely among legislative powers, without charging the constitution, with that kind of intermixture and consolidation of different powers, which would violate a fundamental principle in the organization of free governments. If it were not unnecessary to enlarge on this topic

here, it could be shown, that the constitution was originally vindicated, and has been constantly expounded, with a disavowal of any such intermixture.

The power of treaties is vested jointly in the president and in the senate, which is a branch of the legislature. From this arrangement merely, there can be no inference that would necessarily exclude the power from the executive class: since the senate is joined with the president in another power, that of appointing to offices, which, as far as relate to executive offices at least, is considered as of an executive nature. Yet on the other hand, there are sufficient indications that the power of treaties is regarded by the constitution as materially different from mere executive power, and as having more affinity to the legislative than to the executive character.

One circumstance indicating this, is the constitutional regulation under which the senate give their consent in the case of treaties. In all other cases, the consent of the body is expressed by a majority of voices. In this particular case, a concurrence of two-thirds at least is made necessary, as a substitute or compensation for the other branch of the legislature, which, on certain occasions, could not be conveniently a party to the transaction.

But the conclusive circumstance is, that treaties, when formed according to the constitutional mode, are confessedly to have force and operation of *laws*, and are to be a rule for the courts in controversies between man and man, as much as any *other laws*. They are even emphatically declared by the constitution to be "the supreme law of the land."

So far the argument from the constitution is precisely in opposition to the doctrine. As little will be gained in its favour from a comparison of the two powers, with those particularly vested in the president alone.

As there are but few, it will be most satisfactory to review them one by one.

"The president shall be commander in chief of the army and navy of the United States, and of the militia when called into the actual service of the United States."

There can be no relation worth examining between this power and the general power of making treaties. And instead of being analogous to the power of declaring war, it affords a striking illustration of the incompatibility of the two powers in the same hands. Those who are to *conduct a war* cannot in the nature of things, be proper or safe judges, whether *a war ought* to be *commenced, continued,* or *concluded.* They are barred from the latter functions by a great principle in free government, analogous to that which separates the sword from the purse, or the power of executing from the power of enacting laws.

"He may require the opinion in writing of the principal officers in each of the executive departments upon any subject relating to the duties of their respective offices; and he shall have power to grant reprieves and pardons for offences against the United States, except in case of impeachment." These powers can have nothing to do with the subject.

"The president shall have power to fill up vacancies that may happen during the recess of the Senate, by granting commissions which shall expire at the end of the next session." The same remark is applicable to this power, as also to that of "receiving ambassadors, other public ministers, and consuls." The particular use attempted to be made of this last power will be considered in another place.

"He shall take care that the laws shall be faithfully executed, and shall commission all officers of the United States." To see the laws faithfully executed constitutes the essence of the executive authority. But what relation has it to the power of making treaties and war, that is, of determining what the *laws shall be* with regard to other nations? No other certainly than what subsists between the powers of executing and enacting laws; no other, consequently, than what forbids a coalition of the powers in the same department.

I pass over the few other specified functions assigned to the president, such as that of convening the legislature, &c., &c., which cannot be drawn into the present question.

It may be proper however to take notice of the power of removal from office, which appears to have been adjudged to the president by the laws establishing the executive departments; and which the writer has endeavoured to press into his service. To justify any favourable inference from this case, it must be shown, that the powers of war and treaties are of a kindred nature to the power of removal, or at least are equally within a grant of executive power. Nothing of this sort has been attempted, nor probably will be attempted. Nothing can in truth be clearer, than that no analogy, or shade of analogy, can be traced between a power in the supreme officer responsible for the faithful execution of the laws, to displace a subaltern officer employed in the execution of the laws; and a power to make treaties and to declare war, such as these have been found to be in their nature, their operation, and their consequences.

Thus it appears that by whatever standard we try this doctrine, it must be condemned as no less vicious in theory than it would be dangerous in practice. It is countenanced neither by the writers on law; nor by the nature of the powers themselves; nor by any general arrangements, or particular expressions, or plausible analogies, to be found in the constitution.

Whence then can the writer have borrowed it?

There is but one answer to this question.

The power of making treaties and the power of declaring war, are *royal prerogatives* in the *British government*, and are accordingly treated as *executive prerogatives* by *British commentators*.

We shall be the more confirmed in the necessity of this solution of the problem, by looking back to the area of the constitution, and satisfying ourselves that the writer could not have been misled by the doctrines maintained by our own commentators on our own government. That I may not ramble beyond prescribed limits, I shall content myself with an extract from a work which entered into a systematic explanation and defence of the constitution; and to which there has frequently been ascribed some influence in conciliating the public assent to the government in the form proposed. Three circumstances conspire in giving weight to this cotemporary exposition. It was made at a time when no application to *persons or measures* could bias:

the opinion given was not transiently mentioned, but formally and critically elucidated: it related to a point in the constitution which must consequently have been viewed as of importance in the public mind. The passage relates to the power of making treaties; that of declaring war, being arranged with such obvious propriety among the legislative powers, as to be passed over without particular discussion.

"Though several writers on the subject of government place that power [*of making treaties*] in the class of *executive authorities*, yet this is *evidently* an *arbitrary disposition*. For if we attend *carefully* to its operation, it will be found to partake *more* of the *legislative* than of the *executive* character, though it does not seem strictly to fall within the definition of either of them. The essence of the legislative authority, is to enact laws; or, in other words, to prescribe rules for the regulation of the society: while the execution of the laws and the employment of the common strength, either for this purpose, or for the common defence, seem to comprise *all* the functions of the *executive magistrate*. The power of making treaties is *plainly* neither the one nor the other. It relates neither to the execution of the subsisting laws, nor to the enaction of new ones, and still less to an exertion of the common strength. Its objects are contracts with foreign nations, which have the *force of law*, but derive it from the obligations of good faith. They are not rules prescribed by the sovereign to the subject, but agreements between sovereign and sovereign. The power in question seems therefore to form a distinct department, and to belong properly neither to the legislative nor to the executive. The qualities elsewhere detailed as indispensable in the management of foreign *negotiations*, point out the executive as the most fit agent in those transactions; whilst the vast importance of the trust, and the operation of treaties *as laws*, plead strongly for the participation of the whole or a part of the *legislative body*, in the office of making them."—*Federalist*, p. 418.[1]

It will not fail to be remarked on this commentary, that whatever doubts may be started as to the correctness of its reasoning against the legislative nature of the power to make treaties; it is *clear, consistent*, and *confident*, in deciding that the power is *plainly* and *evidently* not an *executive power*.

No. II.

The doctrine which has been examined is pregnant with inferences and consequences against which no ramparts in the constitution could defend the public liberty or scarcely the forms of republican government. Were it once established that the powers of war and treaty are in their nature executive; that so far as they are not by strict construction transferred to the legislature, they actually belong to the executive; that of course all powers not less executive in their nature than those powers, if not granted to the legislature, may be claimed by the executive; if granted, are to be taken *strictly*, with a residuary right in the executive; or, as will hereafter appear, perhaps claimed as a concur-

[1] No. 75, written by Mr. Hamilton.

rent right by the executive; and no citizen could any longer guess at the character of the government under which he lives; the most penetrating jurist would be unable to scan the extent of constructive prerogative.

Leaving however to the leisure of the reader deductions which the author, having omitted, might not choose to own, I proceed to the examination of one, with which that liberty cannot be taken.

"However true it may be, (says he,) that the right of the legislature to declare war *includes the right of judging*, whether the legislature be under obligations to make war or not, it will not follow that the executive is *in any case* excluded from a *similar right* of judging in the execution of its own functions."

A material error of the writer, in this application of his doctrine, lies in his shrinking from its regular consequences. Had he stuck to his principle in its full extent, and reasoned from it without restraint, he would only have had to defend himself against his opponents. By yielding the great point, that the right to declare war, *though to be taken strictly*, includes the right to judge, whether the nation be under obligation to make war or not, he is compelled to defend his argument, not only against others, but against himself also. Observe, how he struggles in his own toils.

He had before admitted, that the right to declare war is vested in the legislature. He here admits, that the right to declare war includes the right to judge, whether the United States be obliged to declare war or not. Can the inference be avoided, that the executive, instead of having a similar right to judge, is as much excluded from the right to judge as from the right to declare?

If the right to declare war be an exception out of the general grant to the executive power, every thing included in the right must be included in the exception; and, being included in the exception, is excluded from the grant.

He cannot disentangle himself by considering the right of the executive to judge as *concurrent* with that of the legislature: for if the executive have a concurrent right to judge, and the right to judge be included in (it is in fact the very essence of) the right to declare, he must go on and say, that the executive has a concurrent right also to declare. And then, what will he do with his other admission, that the power to declare is an exception out of the executive power?

Perhaps an attempt may be made to creep out of the difficulty through the words, "in the execution of its functions." Here, again, he must equally fail.

Whatever difficulties may arise in defining the executive authority in particular cases, there can be none in deciding on an authority clearly placed by the constitution in another department. In this case, the constitution has decided what shall not be deemed an executive authority; though it may not have clearly decided in every case what shall be so deemed. The declaring of war is expressly made a legislative function. The judging of the obligations to make war, is admitted to be included as a legislative function. Whenever, then, a question occurs, whether war shall be declared, or whether public stipulations require it,

the question necessarily belongs to the department to which those functions belong—and no other department can be *in the execution of its proper functions*, if it should undertake to decide such a question.

There can be no refuge against this conclusion, but in the pretext of a *concurrent* right in both departments to judge of the obligations to declare war; and this must be intended by the writer, when he says, "It will not follow, that the executive is excluded *in any case* from a *similar right* of judging," &c.

As this is the ground on which the ultimate defence is to be made, and which must either be maintained, or the works erected on it demolished; it will be proper to give its strength a fair trial.

It has been seen, that the idea of a *concurrent* right is at variance with other ideas, advanced or admitted by the writer. Laying aside, for the present, that consideration, it seems impossible to avoid concluding, that if the executive, as such, has a concurrent right with the legislature to judge of obligations to declare war, and the right to judge be essentially included in the right to declare, it must have the same concurrent right to declare, as it has to judge; and, by another analogy, the same right to judge of other causes of war, as of the particular cause found in a public stipulation. So that whenever the executive, *in the course of its functions*, shall meet with these cases, it must either infer an equal authority in all, or acknowledge its want of authority in any.

If any doubt can remain, or rather if any doubt could ever have arisen, which side of the alternative ought to be embraced, it can be with those only who overlook or reject some of the most obvious and essential truths in political science.

The power to judge of the causes of war, as involved in the power to declare war, is expressly vested, where all other legislative powers are vested, that is, in the congress of the United States. It is consequently determined by the constitution to be a *legislative power*. Now, omitting the inquiry here, in what respects a compound power may be partly legislative, and partly executive, and accordingly vested *partly* in the one, and *partly* in the other department, or *jointly* in both; a remark used on another occasion is equally conclusive on this, that the same power cannot belong, *in the whole* to *both* departments, or be properly so vested as to operate *separately* in *each*. Still more evident is it, that the same *specific function or act*, cannot possibly belong to the *two* departments, and be *separately* exerciseable by *each*.

Legislative power may be *concurrently* vested in different legislative bodies. Executive powers may be concurrently vested in different executive magistrates. In legislative acts the executive may have a participation, as in the qualified negative on the laws. In executive acts, the legislature, or at least a branch of it, may participate, as in the appointment to offices. Arrangements of this sort are familiar in theory, as well as in practice. But an independent exercise of an *executive act* by the legislature *alone*, or of a *legislative* act by the executive *alone*, one or other of which must happen in every case where the same act is exerciseable by each, and the latter of which would happen in the case urged by the writer, is contrary to one of the first and best maxims of a well-organized government, and ought never to be founded in a forced construction, much less in opposition to a fair one. Instances, it is true, may be discovered among ourselves, where this maxim has not been faithfully pursued; but being generally acknowledged to be errors, they confirm, rather than impeach the truth and value of the maxim.

It may happen also, that different independent departments, the legislative and executive, for example, may, in the exercise of their functions, interpret the constitution differently, and thence lay claim to the same power. This difference of opinion is an inconvenience not entirely to be avoided. It results from what may be called, if it be thought fit, a *concurrent* right to expound the constitution. But this *species* of concurrence is obviously and radically different from that in question. The former supposes the constitution to have given the power to one department only; and the doubt to be, to which it has been given. The latter supposes it to belong to both; and that it may be exercised by either or both, according to the course of exigencies.

A concurrent authority in two independent departments, to perform the same function with respect to the same thing, would be as awkward in practice, as it is unnatural in theory.

If the legislature and executive have both a right to judge of the obligations to make war or not, it must sometimes happen, though not at present, that they will judge differently. The executive may proceed to consider the question to-day; may determine that the United States are not bound to take part in a war, and, *in the execution of its functions,* proclaim that determination to all the world. To-morrow, the legislature may follow in the consideration of the same subject; may determine that the obligations impose war on the United States, and, *in the execution of its functions* enter into a *constitutional declaration,* expressly contradicting the *constitutional proclamation.*

In what light does this present the constitution to the people who established it? In what light would it present to the world a nation, thus speaking, through two different organs, equally constitutional and authentic, two opposite languages, on the same subject, and under the same existing circumstances?

But it is not with the legislative rights alone that this doctrine interferes. The rights of the judiciary may be equally invaded. For it is clear that if a right declared by the constitution to be legislative, and actually vested by it in the legislature, leaves, notwithstanding, a similar right in the executive, whenever a case for exercising it occurs, *in the course of its functions;* a right declared to be judiciary and vested in that department may, on the same principle, be assumed and exercised by the executive *in the course of its functions;* and it is evident that occasions and pretexts for the latter interference may be as frequent as for the former. So again the judiciary department may find equal occasions in the execution of *its* functions, for usurping the authorities of the executive; and the legislature for stepping into the jurisdiction of both. And thus all the powers of government, of which a partition is so carefully made

among the several branches, would be thrown into absolute hotchpot, and exposed to a general scramble.

It is time however for the writer himself to be heard, in defence of his text. His comment is in the words following:

"If the legislature have a right to make war on the one hand, it is, on the other, the duty of the executive to preserve peace, till war is declared; and in fulfilling that duty, it must necessarily possess a right of judging what is the nature of the obligations which the treaties of the country impose on the government; and when, in pursuance of this right, it has concluded that there is nothing inconsistent with a state of neutrality, it becomes both its province and its duty to enforce the laws incident to that state of the nation. The executive is charged with the execution of all laws, the laws of nations, as well as the municipal law which recognises and adopts those laws. It is consequently bound, by faithfully executing the laws of neutrality, when that is the state of the nation, to avoid giving a cause of war to foreign powers."

To do full justice to this masterpiece of logic, the reader must have the patience to follow it step by step.

If the legislature have a right to make war on the one hand, it is, on the other, the duty of the executive to preserve peace till war is declared.

It will be observed that here is an explicit and peremptory assertion, that it is the *duty* of the executive *to preserve peace* till *war is declared.*

And in fulfilling that duty it must necessarily possess a right of judging what is the nature of the obligations which the treaties of the country impose on the government; That is to say, in fulfilling *the duty to preserve peace,* it must necessarily possess the right to judge whether *peace ought to be preserved;* in other words, *whether its duty should be performed.* Can words express a flatter contradiction? It is self-evident that the *duty* in this case is so far from *necessarily implying the right,* that it *necessarily excludes it.*

And when in pursuance of this right it has concluded that there is nothing in them (obligations) inconsistent with a state of neutrality, IT BECOMES both its province and its duty to enforce the laws incident to that state of the nation.

And what if it should conclude that there is something inconsistent? Is it or is it not the province and duty of the executive to enforce the same laws? Say it is, you destroy the right to judge. Say it is not, you cancel the duty to preserve peace, till war is declared.

Take this sentence in connexion with the preceding, and the contradictions are multiplied. Take it by itself, and it makes the right to judge and conclude, whether war be obligatory, absolute and operative; and the duty to preserve peace subordinate and conditional.

It will have been remarked by the attentive reader, that the term *peace* in the first clause has been silently exchanged in the present one for the term *neutrality.* Nothing however is gained by shifting the terms. Neutrality means peace, with an allusion to the circumstances of other nations being at war. The term has no reference to the existence or nonexistence of treaties or alliances between the nation at peace and the nations at war. The laws incident to a state of neutrality, are the laws incident to a state of peace, with such circumstantial modifications only as are required by the new relation of the nations at war: until war therefore be duly authorized by the United States, they are as *actually* neutral when other nations are at war, as they are at peace (if such a distinction in the terms is to be kept up) when other nations are not at war. The existence of *eventual* engagements which can only take effect on the declaration of the legislature, cannot, without that declaration, change the *actual* state of the country, any more in the eye of the executive than in the eye of the judiciary department. The laws to be the guide of both, remain the same to each, and the same to both.

Nor would more be gained by allowing the writer to define, than to shift the term neutrality. For suppose, if you please, the existence of obligations to join in war to be inconsistent with neutrality, the question returns upon him, what laws are to be enforced by the executive, until effect shall be given to those obligations by the declaration of the legislature? Are they to be the laws incident to those obligations, that is, incident to war? However strongly the doctrines or deductions of the writer may tend to this point, it will not be avowed. Are the laws to be enforced by the executive, then, in such a state of things, to be the *same* as if no such obligations existed? Admit this, which you must admit, if you reject the other alternative, and the argument lands precisely where it embarked—in the position, that it is the absolute duty of the executive in *all* cases to preserve peace till war is declared, not that it is *"to become the province and duty of the executive"* after it has concluded that there is nothing in those obligations inconsistent with a state of peace and neutrality. The right to judge and conclude therefore, so solemnly maintained in the text, is lost in the comment.

We shall see, whether it can be reinstated by what follows.

The executive is charged with the execution of all laws, the laws of nations as well as the municipal law which recognises and adopts those laws. It is consequently bound, by faithfully executing the laws of neutrality when that is the state of the nation, to avoid giving cause of war to foreign powers.

The first sentence is a truth, but nothing to the point in question. The last is *partly true* in its proper meaning, but *totally untrue* in the meaning of the writer. That the executive is bound faithfully to execute the laws of neutrality, whilst those laws continue unaltered by the competent authority, is true; but not for the reason here given, to wit, to avoid giving cause of war to foreign powers. It is bound to the faithful execution of these as of all other laws internal and external, by the nature of its trust and the sanction of its oath, even if turbulent citizens should consider its so doing as a cause of war at home, or unfriendly nations should consider its so doing as a cause of war abroad. The duty of the executive to preserve external peace, can no more suspend the force of external laws, than its duty to preserve internal peace can suspend the force of municipal laws.

It is certain that a faithful execution of the laws of neutrality may tend as much in some cases, to incur war from one quarter, as in others to avoid war from other quarters. The executive must nevertheless execute the laws of neutrality whilst in force, and leave it to the legislature to de-

cide, whether they ought to be altered or not. The executive has no other discretion than to convene and give information to the legislature on occasions that may demand it; and whilst this discretion is duly exercised, the trust of the executive is satisfied, and that department is not responsible for the consequences. It could not be made responsible for them without vesting it with the legislative as well as with the executive trust.

These remarks are obvious and conclusive, on the supposition that the expression "laws of neutrality" means simply what the words import, and what alone they can mean, to give force or colour to the inference of the writer from his own premises. As the inference itself however, in its proper meaning, does not approach towards his avowed object, which is to work out a prerogative for the executive to judge, in common with the legislature, whether there be cause of war or not in a public obligation, it is to be presumed that "in faithfully executing the laws of neutrality," an exercise of that prerogative was meant to be included. On this supposition the inference, as will have been seen, does not result from his own premises, and has been already so amply discussed, and, it is conceived, so clearly disproved, that not a word more can be necessary on this branch of his argument.

No. III.

In order to give colour to a right in the executive to exercise the legislative power of judging, whether there be a cause of war in a public stipulation—two other arguments are subjoined by the writer to that last examined.

The first is simply this: "It is the right and duty of the executive to judge of and interpret those articles of our treaties which give to France particular privileges, *in order to the enforcement of those privileges:*" from which it is stated, as a necessary consequence, that the executive has certain other rights, among which is the right in question.

This argument is answered by a very obvious distinction. The first right is essential to the execution of the treaty, *as a law in operation,* and interferes with no right vested in another department. The second, viz., the right in question, is not essential to the execution of the treaty, or any other law: on the contrary, the article to which the right is applied cannot, as has been shown, from the very nature of it, be *in operation* as a law, without a previous declaration of the legislature; and all the laws to be *enforced* by the executive remain, in the mean time, precisely the same, whatever be the disposition or judgment of the executive. This second right would also interfere with a right acknowledged to be in the legislative department.

If nothing else could suggest this distinction to the writer, he ought to have been reminded of it by his own words, "in order to the enforcement of those privileges"— Was it in order to the *enforcement* of the article of guaranty, that the right is ascribed to the executive?

The other of the two arguments reduces itself into the following form: the executive has the right to receive public ministers; this right includes the right of deciding, in the case of a revolution, whether the new government, sending the minister, ought to be recognised, or not; and this, again, the right to give or refuse operation to preexisting treaties.

The power of the legislature to declare war, and judge of the causes for declaring it, is one of the most express and explicit parts of the constitution. To endeavour to abridge or *affect* it by strained inferences, and by hypothetical or singular occurrences, naturally warns the reader of some lurking fallacy.

The words of the constitution are, "He (the president) shall receive ambassadors, other public ministers, and consuls." I shall not undertake to examine, what would be the precise extent and effect of this function in various cases which fancy may suggest, or which time may produce. It will be more proper to observe, in general, and every candid reader will second the observation, that little, if any thing, more was intended by the clause, than to provide for a particular mode of communication, *almost* grown into a right among modern nations; by pointing out the department of the government, most proper for the ceremony of admitting public ministers, of examining their credentials, and of authenticating their title to the privileges annexed to their character by the law of nations. This being the apparent design of the constitution, it would be highly improper to magnify the function into an important prerogative, even where no rights of other departments could be affected by it.

To show that the view here given of the clause is not a new construction, invented or strained for a particular occasion—I will take the liberty of recurring to the cotemporary work already quoted, which contains the obvious and original gloss put on this part of the constitution by its friends and advocates.

"The president is also to be authorized to receive ambassadors and other public ministers. This, though it has been a rich theme of declamation, is more a matter of *dignity* than of *authority*. It is a circumstance, that will be *without consequence* in the administration of the government, and it is far more convenient that it should be arranged in this manner, than that there should be a necessity for convening the legislature or one of its branches upon every arrival of a foreign minister, though it were merely to take the place of a departed predecessor." *Fed.*, p. 389.[1]

Had it been foretold in the year 1788, when this work was published, that before the end of the year 1793, a writer, assuming the merit of being a friend to the constitution, would appear, and gravely maintain, that this function, which was to be *without consequence* in the administration of the government, might have the consequence of deciding on the validity of revolutions in favour of liberty, "of putting the United States in a condition to become an associate in war"—nay, "of laying the *legislature* under an *obligation* of *declaring* war," what would have been thought and said of so visionary a prophet?

The moderate opponents of the constitution would probably have disowned his extravagance. By the advocates of the constitution, his prediction must have been treated as "an experiment on public credulity, dictated either by a deliberate intention to deceive, or by the over-

_____
[1]No. 69, written by Mr. Hamilton.

flowings of a zeal too intemperate to be ingenuous."

But how does it follow from the function to receive ambassadors and other public ministers, that so consequential a prerogative may be exercised by the executive? When a foreign minister presents himself, two questions immediately arise: Are his credentials from the existing and acting government of his country? Are they properly authenticated? These questions belong of necessity to the executive; but they involve no cognizance of the question, whether those exercising the government have the right along with the possession. This belongs to the nation, and to the nation alone, on whom the government operates. The questions before the executive are merely questions of fact; and the executive would have precisely the same right, or rather be under the same necessity of deciding them, if its function was simply to receive *without any discretion to reject* public ministers. It is evident, therefore, that if the executive has a right to reject a public minister, it must be founded on some other consideration than a change in the government, or the newness of the government; and consequently a right to refuse to acknowledge a new government cannot be implied by the right to refuse a public minister.

It is not denied that there may be cases in which a respect to the general principles of liberty, the essential rights of the people, or the overruling sentiments of humanity, might require a government, whether new or old, to be treated as an illegitimate despotism. Such are in fact discussed and admitted by the most approved authorities. But they are great and extraordinary cases, by no means submitted to so limited an organ of the national will as the executive of the United States; and certainly not to be brought by any torture of words, within the right to receive ambassadors.

That the authority of the executive does not extend to a question, whether an *existing* government ought to be recognised or not, will still more clearly appear from an examination of the next inference of the writer, to wit: that the executive has a right to give or refuse activity and operation to preexisting treaties.

If there be a principle that ought not to be questioned within the United States, it is, that every nation has a right to abolish an old government and establish a new one. This principle is not only recorded in every public archive, written in every American heart, and sealed with the blood of a host of American martyrs; but is the only lawful tenure by which the United States hold their existence as a nation.

It is a principle incorporated with the above, that governments are established for the national good, and are organs of the national will.

From these two principles results a third, that treaties formed by the government, are treaties of the nation, unless otherwise expressed in the treaties.

Another consequence is, that a nation, by exercising the right of changing the organ of its will, can neither disengage itself from the obligations, nor forfeit the benefits of its treaties. This is a truth of vast importance, and happily rests with sufficient firmness, on its own authority. To silence or prevent cavil, I insert, however, the following extracts: "Since then such a treaty (a treaty not *personal* to the sovereign) directly relates to the body of the state, it subsists though the form of the republic happens to be changed, and though it should be even transformed into a monarchy—for the state and the nation are always the same, whatever changes are made in the form of the government—and the treaty concluded with the nation, remains in force as long as the nation exists."—Vatel, B. II, § 85. "It follows that as a treaty, notwithstanding the change of a democratic government into a monarchy, continues in force with the new king, in like manner, if a *monarchy* becomes a *republic*, the treaty made with the king does not expire on that account, unless it was manifestly personal."—Burlam, part iv., c. ix., § 16, ¶ 6.

As a change of government then makes no change in the obligations or rights of the party to a treaty, it is clear that the executive can have no more right to suspend or prevent the operation of a treaty, on account of the change, than to suspend or prevent the operation, where no such change has happened. Nor can it have any more right to suspend the operation of a treaty in force as a law, than to suspend the operation of any other law.

The logic employed by the writer on this occasion, will be best understood by accommodating to it the language of a proclamation, founded on the prerogative and policy of suspending the treaty with France.

Whereas a treaty was concluded on the ———— day of ———— between the United States and the French nation, through the kingly government, which was then the organ of its will: and whereas the said nation hath since exercised its right (nowise abridged by the said treaty) of changing the organ of its will, by abolishing the said kingly government, as inconsistent with the rights and happiness of the people, and establishing a republican in lieu thereof, as most favourable to the public happiness, and best suited to the genius of a people become sensible of their rights and ashamed of their chains: and whereas, by the constitution of the United States, the executive is authorized to receive ambassadors, other public ministers, and consuls: and whereas a public minister, duly appointed and commissioned by the new republic of France, hath arrived and presented himself to the executive, in order to be received in his proper character, now be it known, that by virtue of the said right vested in the executive to receive ambassadors, other public ministers and consuls, and of the rights included therein, the executive hath refused to receive the said minister from the said republic, and hath thereby caused the activity and operation of all treaties with the French nation, *hitherto in force as supreme laws of the land*, to be suspended until the executive, by taking off the said suspension, shall revive the same: of which all persons concerned are to take notice at their peril.

The writer, as if beginning to feel that he was grasping at more than he could hold, endeavours all of a sudden to squeeze his doctrine into a smaller size, and a less vulnerable shape. The reader shall see the operation in his own words.

"And where *a treaty* antecedently exists between the United States and such nation, [a nation whose government has undergone a revolution,] that right [the right of judging, whether the new rulers ought to be recognised or not] involves the power of giving operation or not to *such treaty. For* until the new government is acknowledged, the treaties between the nations *as far at least* as regards *public rights,* are *of course* suspended."

This qualification of the suspending power, though reluctantly and inexplicitly made, was prudent, for two reasons: first, because it is pretty evident that *private rights,* whether of judiciary or executive cognizance, may be carried into effect without the agency of the foreign government: and therefore would not be suspended, of course, by a rejection of that agency: secondly, because the judiciary, being an independent department, and acting under an oath to pursue the law of treaties as the supreme law of the land, might not readily follow the executive example; and a *right* in *one expositor* of treaties, to consider them as *not in force,* whilst it would be the *duty* of *another expositor* to consider them as *in force,* would be a phenomenon not so easy to be explained. Indeed, as the doctrine stands qualified, it leaves the executive the right of suspending the law of treaties in relation to rights of one description, without exempting it from the duty of enforcing it in relation to rights of another description.

But the writer is embarked in so unsound an argument, that he does not save the rest of his inference by this sacrifice of one half of it. It is not true, that *all public rights* are of course suspended by a refusal to acknowledge the government, or even by a suspension of the government. And in the next place, the right in question does not follow from the necessary suspension of public rights, in consequence of a refusal to acknowledge the government.

Public rights are of two sorts: those which require the agency of government; those which may be carried into effect without that agency.

As public rights are the rights of the nation, not of the government, it is clear, that wherever they can be made good to the nation, without the office of government, they are not suspended by the want of an acknowledged government, or even by the want of an existing government; and that there are important rights of this description, will be illustrated by the following case.

Suppose, that after the conclusion of the treaty of alliance between the United States and France, a party of the enemy had surprised and put to death every member of congress; that the occasion had been used by the people of America for changing the old confederacy into such a government as now exists, and that in the progress of this revolution, an interregnum had happened: suppose further, that during this interval, the states of South Carolina and Georgia, or any other parts of the United States, had been attacked, and been put into evident and imminent danger of being irrecoverably lost, without the interposition of the French arms; is it not manifest, that as the treaty is the treaty of the United States, not of their government, the people of the United States could not forfeit their right to the guaranty of their territory by the accidental suspension of their government; and that any attempt, on the part of France, to evade the obligations of the treaty, by pleading the suspension of government, or by refusing to acknowledge it, would justly have been received with universal indignation, as an ignominious perfidy?

With respect to public rights that cannot take effect in favour of a nation without the agency of its government, it is admitted that they are suspended of course where there is no government in existence, and also by a refusal to acknowledge an existing government. But no inference in favour of a *right* to suspend the operation of treaties, can be drawn from either case. Where the existence of the government is suspended, it is a case of necessity; it would be a case happening without the act of the executive, and consequently could prove nothing for or against the right. In the other case, to wit, of a refusal by the executive to recognise an *existing government,* however certain it may be, that a suspension of some of the public rights might ensue; yet it is equally certain, that the refusal would be without right or authority; and that no right or authority could be implied or produced by the unauthorized act. If a right to do whatever might bear an analogy to the necessary consequence of what was done without right, could be inferred from the analogy, there would be no other limit to power than the limit to its ingenuity.

It is no answer to say that it may be doubtful, whether a government does or does not exist; or doubtful which may be the existing and acting government. The case stated by the writer is, that there are existing rulers; that there is an acting government; but that they are *new* rulers; and that it is a *new* government. The full reply, however, is to repeat what has been already observed; that questions of this sort are mere questions of fact; that as such only, they belong to the executive, that they would equally belong to the executive, if it was tied down to the reception of public ministers, without any discretion to receive or reject them; that where the fact appears to be, that no government exists, the consequential suspension is independent of the executive; that where the fact appears to be, that the government does exist, the executive must be governed by the fact, and can have no right or discretion, on account of the date or form of the government, to refuse to acknowledge it, either by rejecting its public ministers, or by any other step taken on that account. If it does refuse on that account, the refusal is a wrongful act, and can neither prove nor illustrate a rightful power.

I have spent more time on this part of the discussion than may appear to some, to have been requisite. But it was considered as a proper opportunity for presenting some important ideas, connected with the general subject, and it may be of use in showing how very superficially, as well as erroneously, the writer has treated it.

In other respects, so particular an investigation was less necessary. For allowing it to be, as contended, that a suspension of treaties might happen from a *consequential* operation of a right to receive public ministers, which is an *express right* vested by the constitution; it could be no proof, that the same or a *similar* effect could be produced by the *direct* operation of a *constructive power.*

Hence the embarrassments and gross contradictions of the writer in defining, and applying his ultimate inference from the operation of the executive power with regard to public ministers.

At first it exhibits an "important instance of the right of the executive to decide the obligation of the nation with regard to foreign nations."

Rising from that, it confers on the executive, a right "to put the United States in a condition to become an associate in war."

And at its full height, it authorizes the executive "to lay the legislature under *an obligation* of declaring war."

From this towering prerogative, it suddenly brings down the executive to the right of "*consequentially affecting* the proper or improper exercise of the power of the legislature to declare war."

And then, by a caprice as unexpected as it is sudden, it espouses the cause of the legislature; rescues it from the executive right "to lay it under an *obligation* of declaring war;" and asserts it to be "free to perform its *own* duties according to its *own* sense of them," without any other control than what it is liable to, in every other legislative act.

The point at which it finally seems to rest, is, that "the executive, in the exercise of its *constitutional powers,* may establish an antecedent state of things, which ought to *weigh* in the *legislative decisions;*" a prerogative which will import a great deal, or nothing, according to the handle by which you take it; and which at the same time, you can take by no handle that does not clash with some inference preceding.

If "by weighing in the legislative decisions" be meant having *an influence* on the *expediency* of this or that decision, in the *opinion* of the legislature; this is no more than what every antecedent state of things ought to have, from whatever cause proceeding; whether from the use or abuse of constitutional powers, or from the exercise of constitutional or assumed powers. In this sense, the power to establish an antecedent state of things is not contested. But then it is of no use to the writer, and is also in direct contradiction to the inference, that the executive may "lay the *legislature* under an *obligation* to decide in favour of *war.*"

If the meaning be as is implied by the force of the terms "constitutional powers," that the antecedent state of things produced by the executive, ought to have a *constitutional weight* with the legislature; or, in plainer words, imposes a *constitutional obligation* on the *legislative decisions;* the writer will not only have to combat the arguments by which such a prerogative has been disproved; but to reconcile it with his last concession, that "the legislature is *free* to perform its duties according to its *own* sense of them." He must show that the legislature is, at the same time *constitutionally free* to pursue its *own judgment,* and *constitutionally bound* by the *judgment of the executive.*

No. IV.

The last papers completed the view proposed to be taken of the arguments in support of the new and aspiring doctrine, which ascribes to the executive the prerogative of judging and deciding, whether there be causes of war or not in the obligations of treaties; notwithstanding the express provision in the constitution, by which the legislature is made the organ of the national will, on questions, whether there be or be not a cause for declaring war. If the answer to these arguments has imparted the conviction which dictated it, the reader will have pronounced that they are generally superficial, abounding in contradictions, never in the least degree conclusive to the main point, and not unfrequently conclusive against the writer himself: whilst the doctrine—that the powers of treaty and war, are in their nature executive powers, which forms the basis of those arguments, is as indefensible and as dangerous as the particular doctrine to which they are applied.

But it is not to be forgotten that these doctrines, though ever so clearly disproved, or ever so weakly defended, remain before the public a striking monument of the principles and views which are entertained and propagated in the community.

It is also to be remembered, that however the consequences flowing from such premises, may be disavowed at this time, or by this individual, we are to regard it as morally certain, that in proportion as the doctrines make their way into the creed of the government, and the acquiescence of the public, every power that can be deduced from them, will be deduced, and exercised sooner or later by those who may have an interest in so doing. The character of human nature gives this salutary warning to every sober and reflecting mind. And the history of government in all its forms and in every period of time, ratifies the danger. A people, therefore, who are so happy as to possess the inestimable blessing of a free and defined constitution cannot be too watchful against the introduction, nor too critical in tracing the consequences, of new principles and new constructions, that may remove the landmarks of power.

Should the prerogative which has been examined, be allowed, in its most limited sense, to usurp the public countenance, the interval would probably be very short, before it would be heard from some quarter or other, that the prerogative either amounts to nothing, or means a right to judge and conclude that the obligations of treaty impose war, as well as that they permit peace; that it is fair reasoning to say, that if the prerogative exists at all, an operative rather than an *inert* character ought to be given to it.

In support of this conclusion, there would be enough to echo, "that the prerogative in this active sense, is connected with the executive in various capacities—as the organ of intercourse between the nation and foreign nations—as the interpreter of national treaties" (a violation of which may be a cause of war)—"as that power which is charged with the execution of the laws, of which treaties make a part—as that power, which is charged with *the command and application of the public force.*"

With additional force, it might be said, that the executive is as much the *executor* as the *interpreter* of treaties; that if by virtue of the *first* character, it is to judge of the *obligations* of treaties, it is, by virtue of the *second*, equally authorised to carry those obligations into *effect*. Should there occur, for example, a *casus foederis*, claiming a military co-operation of the United States, and a military force should happen to be under the command of the executive, it must have the same right, as *executor of public treaties*, to *employ*

the public force, as it has in quality of *interpreter of public treaties* to decide, whether it ought to be *employed*.

The case of a treaty of peace would be an auxiliary to comments of this sort: it is a condition annexed to every treaty, that an infraction even of an important article, on one side, extinguishes the obligations on the other: and the immediate consequence of a dissolution of a treaty of peace is a restoration of a state of war. If the executive is "to decide on the obligation of the nation with regard to foreign nations"—"to pronounce the *existing condition* (in the sense annexed by the writer) of the nation with regard to them; and to admonish the citizens of their obligations and duties, as founded upon *that condition* of things"—"to judge what are the *reciprocal rights* and obligations of the United States, and of all and each of the powers at war;"—add, that if the executive, moreover, possesses all powers relating to war, *not strictly* within the power to *declare war*, which any pupil of political casuistry could distinguish from a mere *relapse* into a war that *had been declared:* with this store of materials, and the example given of the use to be made of them, would it be difficult to fabricate a power in the executive to plunge the nation into war, whenever a treaty of peace might happen to be infringed?

But if any difficulty should arise, there is another mode chalked out, by which the end might clearly be brought about, even without the violation of the treaty of peace; especially if the other party should happen to change its government at the crisis. The executive could *suspend* the treaty of peace *by refusing to receive an ambassador* from the *new* government; and the state of war *emerges of course*.

This is a sample of the use to which the extraordinary publication we are reviewing might be turned. Some of the inferences could not be repelled at all. And the least regular of them must go smoothly down with those who had swallowed the gross sophistry which wrapped up the original dose.

Every just view that can be taken of this subject, admonishes the public of the necessity of a rigid adherence to the simple, the received, and the fundamental doctrine of the constitution, that the power to declare war, including the power of judging of the causes of war, is *fully* and *exclusively* vested in the legislature; that the executive has no right, in any case, to decide the question, whether there is or is not cause for declaring war; that the right of convening and informing congress, whenever such a question seems to call for a decision, is all the right which the constitution has deemed requisite or proper; and that for such, more than for any other contingency, this right was specially given to the executive.

In no part of the constitution is more wisdom to be found, than in the clause which confides the question of war or peace to the legislature, and not to the executive department. Beside the objection to such a mixture to heterogeneous powers, the trust and the temptation would be too great for any one man; not such as nature may offer as the prodigy of many centuries, but such as may be expected in the ordinary successions of magistracy. War is in fact the true nurse of executive aggrandizement. In war, a physical force is to be created; and it is the executive will, which is to direct it. In war, the public treasures are to be unlocked; and it is the executive hand which is to dispense them. In war, the honours and emoluments of office are to be multiplied; and it is the executive patronage under which they are to be enjoyed. It is in war, finally, that laurels are to be gathered; and it is the executive brow they are to encircle. The strongest passions and most dangerous weaknesses of the human breast; ambition, avarice, vanity, the honourable or venial love of fame, are all in conspiracy against the desire and duty of peace.

Hence it has grown into an axiom that the executive is the department of power most distinguished by its propensity to war: hence it is the practice of all states, in proportion as they are free, to disarm this propensity of its influence.

As the best praise then that can be pronounced on an executive magistrate, is, that he is the friend of peace; a praise that rises in its value, as there may be a known capacity to shine in war: so it must be one of the most sacred duties of a free people, to mark the first omen in the society, of principles that may stimulate the hopes of other magistrates of another propensity, to intrude into questions on which its gratification depends. If a free people be a wise people also, they will not forget that the danger of surprise can never be so great, as when the advocates for the prerogative of war can sheathe it in a symbol of peace.

The constitution has manifested a similar prudence in refusing to the executive the *sole* power of making peace. The trust in this instance also, would be too great for the wisdom, and the temptations too strong for the virtue, of a single citizen. The principle reasons on which the constitution proceeded in its regulation of the power of treaties, including treaties of peace, are so aptly furnished by the work already quoted more than once, that I shall borrow another comment from that source.

"However proper or safe it may be in a government where the executive magistrate is an hereditary monarch, to commit to him the entire power of making treaties, it would be utterly unsafe and improper to entrust that power to an elective magistrate of four years' duration. It has been remarked upon another occasion, and the remark is unquestionably just, that an hereditary monarch, though often the oppressor of his people, has personally too much at stake in the government to be in any material danger of being corrupted by foreign powers: but that a man raised from the station of a private citizen to the rank of chief magistrate, possessed of but a moderate or slender fortune, and looking forward to a period not very remote, when he may probably be obliged to return to the station from which he was taken, might sometimes be under temptations to sacrifice his duty to his intererst, which it would require superlative virtue to withstand. An avaricious man might be tempted to betray the interests of the state to the acquisition of wealth. An ambitious man might make his own aggrandizement, by the aid of a foreign power, the price of his treachery to his constituents. The history of human conduct does not warrant that exalted opinion of human virtue, which would make it wise in a nation to commit interests of so delicate and momentous a kind, as *those which concern its intercourse* with the rest of the

world, to the *sole* disposal of a magistrate created and circumstanced as would be a president of the United States." p. 418.[1]

I shall conclude this paper and this branch of the subject, with two reflections, which naturally arise from this view of the constitution.

The first is, that as the personal interest of an hereditary monarch in the government, is the *only* security against the temptation incident to the commitment of the delicate and momentous interests of the nation, which concern its intercourse with the rest of the world, to the disposal of a single magistrate, it is a plain consequence, that every addition that may be made to the *sole* agency and influence of the executive, in the intercourse of the nation with foreign nations, is an increase of the dangerous temptation to which an *elective and temporary* magistrate is exposed; and an *argument* and *advance* towards the security afforded by the personal interests of an *hereditary* magistrate.

Secondly, as the constitution has not permitted the executive *singly* to conclude or judge that peace ought to be made, it might be inferred from that circumstance alone, that it never meant to give it authority, *singly*, to judge and conclude that war ought not to be made. The trust would be precisely similar and equivalent in the two cases. The right to say that war ought not to go on, would be no greater than the right to say that war ought not to begin. Every danger of error or corruption, incident to such a prerogative in one case, is incident to it in the other. If the constitution therefore has deemed it unsafe or improper in the one case, it must be deemed equally so in the other case.

[1]*Federalist*, No. 75, written by Mr. Hamilton.

16

THOMAS JEFFERSON TO EDMOND CHARLES GENET
22 Nov. 1793
Works 8:73–74

In my letter of October 2, I took the liberty of noticing to you, that the commission of consul to M. Dannery ought to have been addressed to the President of the United States. He being the only channel of communication between this country and foreign nations, it is from him alone that foreign nations or their agents are to learn what is or has been the will of the nation; and whatever he communicates as such, they have a right, and are bound to consider as the expression of the nation, and no foreign agent can be allowed to question it, to interpose between him and any other branch of Government, under the pretext of either's transgressing their functions, nor to make himself the umpire and final judge between them. I am, therefore, sir, not authorized to enter into any discussions with you on the meaning of our constitution in any part of it, or to prove to you, that it has ascribed to him alone the admission or interdiction of foreign agents. I inform you of the fact by authority from the President. I had observed to you that we were persuaded, that, in the case of the consul Dannery, the error in the address had proceeded from no intention in the Executive Council of France to question the functions of the President, and therefore no difficulty was made in issuing the commission. We are still under the same persuasion. But in your letter of the 14th instant, you *personally* question the authority of the President, and, in consequence of that, have not addressed to him the commissions of Messrs. Pennevert and Chervi, making a point of this formality on your part; it becomes necessary to make a point of it on ours also; and I am therefore charged to return you those commissions, and to inform you that, bound to enforce respect to the order of things established by our constitution, the President will issue no exequatur to any consul or vice consul, not directed to him in the usual form, after the party from whom it comes, has been apprized that such should be the address.

17

SENATE, PRESENTATION OF THE COLORS OF FRANCE
6 Jan. 1796
Annals 5:32–33, 35, 36

Mr. ELLSWORTH next combated the resolution as originally offered as unconstitutional. Nothing, he contended, could be found in the Constitution to authorize either branch of the Legislature to keep up any kind of correspondence with a foreign nation. To Congress were given the powers of legislation and the right of declaring war. If authority beyond this is assumed, however trifling the encroachment at first, where will it stop? It might be said, that this was a mere matter of ceremony and form, and, therefore, could do no harm. A correspondence with foreign nations was a business of difficulty and delicacy—the peace and tranquility of a country may hinge on it. Shall the Senate, because they may think it in one case trifling, or conceive the power ought to be placed in them, assume it? If it was not specially delegated by the Constitution, the Senate might, perhaps, but it is positively placed in the hands of the Executive. The people who sent us here, (said Mr. E.,) placed their confidence in the PRESIDENT in matters of this nature, and it does not belong to the Senate to assume it.

So forcibly, he said, were both Houses impressed with the impropriety of the Legislature corresponding with any foreign Power, that, when it was announced to them that the unfortunate Louis XVI. had accepted the Constitution of '89, the communication was sent back to the PRESIDENT, with a request that he would answer it on their behalf, with congratulations and best wishes.

But even this, he considered, they had not strictly a right to do. It was only saving appearances. Neither branch had a right to dictate to the PRESIDENT what he should answer.

The Constitution left the whole business in his breast. It was wrong to place him in the dilemma of disobliging the Legislature or sacrificing his own discretion. But if such practices had inadvertently been followed, it was full time to recede from them.

He recapitulated, in a few words, and concluded, by observing, that should the motion for striking out prevail, members would still be in order to amend the resolution, if they chose, by adding to the warmth of expression it already contained.

Mr. BUTLER considered the situation into which the member up before him seemed desirous that the Senate should be placed, as highly degrading; they were to be deprived of the right of expressing their own sentiments, they were to have no voice, no will, no opinion of their own, but such as it would please the Executive to express for them.

The only fault he found in the resolve was, that it was not full and expressive enough. He observed, that it appeared the studied desire of one part of the House to cut off all communication between the people of the United States and the people of the French Republic. Their representatives are now told, that they can have no will, no voice, but through the Executive. Their constituents never intended that they should be placed in this ridiculous point of view, and he declared he never could sit under it silently.

He turned to the Journals of the Senate to show that in the proceedings in the case of the answer to the communication from Robespierre and others, there was a considerable division in the Senate, and the mode adopted was by a majority only; but did not meet the sense of the Senate very generally.

Upon the presentation of the flag to the PRESIDENT, the Minister particularly observes, that it is for the people of the United States. The PRESIDENT in his answer, speaks of himself and his own feelings. He read part of his answer—"Born in a land of Liberty," &c. He does intimate, he observed, in a cursory manner, that he trusts he speaks the sentiments of his fellow-citizens: but does not attempt to make any professions of either branch of the Legislature, thinking, no doubt, that when the subject came before them, they would speak for themselves.

Suppose, he asked, that the expression of friendship contained in the PRESIDENT's Address on the occasion, fell short of the feelings of the Senate, would they, he asked, adopt the expressions for their own? For his own part, he declared, he could not leave it to others to speak his sentiments, but chose to reserve that right to himself. Even if no communication had been received from the French Republic, no token of attachment, the present period in their affairs, the establishment of a new Government, would warrant an address of congratulation. There could be no impropriety in it, unless there were objections to drawing nigher to the Republic. Besides, the address of the Committee of Safety, was certainly intended for the Legislature, being directed to the Representatives, unless it could be denied that the Senate were Representatives of the people of the United States.

There was nothing in the Constitution, he contended,

that could prevent the Legislature from expressing their sentiments: it was not an Executive act, but a mere complimentary answer to a complimentary presentation. If this right was denied them, where would the principle stop, the Senate might be made in time mere automata. It was as proper, he contended, for the Senate to express an opinion on the occasion as for the PRESIDENT or House of Representatives.

He concluded by observing, that the resolution as offered, said as little as could be said on the occasion, and he never could consent to the striking out, which would cause it to be entered only on the Journal, and would be an indirect slight of the French Republic, as the sentiments of the Senate would not be communicated to them.

Mr. TAZEWELL was happy to find no difference in the Senate as to the substance of the resolution. As the form, however, had been made matter of debate, some importance had been given to it which its intrinsic consequence perhaps did not deserve, and it became the Senate to weigh well their decision. It certainly, he said, could not be unknown to the Senate, that unfavorable impressions had traveled abroad respecting their feelings. . . .

. . . . .

Mr. BURR was against striking out. The National Convention, he observed, might, when they received the answer to their first communication, have said, as is now said on the floor of the Senate, that the correspondence there ended, and that it was not necessary to make us a reply; but they acted differently, and he hoped the Senate would acknowledge the receipt of their pledge of friendship. Indeed, he said, he could not see that any great harm would arise in the two branches of the Legislature interchanging even once a year a letter of friendship and good will with the Republic. It was objected that the present resolution was no answer to the letter. A few lines would make it so, and they might easily be added. The omission did not prove, as had been asserted by one member, that it was impossible to answer it. That it was not impossible was testified by the proceedings of the other branch. He did not intend to slight the dignity of the Senate, however, he said, by quoting the proceedings of the other House as a binding rule of proceeding for this; but their proceedings certainly proved the possibility of making an answer; and besides, there was full as much propriety in looking for precedents in their conduct, as in the proceedings of a British Parliament. Each, however, in their place might deserve weight though not implicit reliance.

He advocated the rights of the Senate to answer for themselves, and the propriety of acknowledging the receipt of the Colors, which were not sent to the Executive exclusively.

He concluded by citing the Senate's own precedents in analogous cases, and he hoped, that it would not be insisted that the practice of two or three successive years deserved to be laid to the charge of inadvertency.

. . . . .

Whereupon, it was

Resolved, unanimously, that the PRESIDENT be informed the Senate have received, with the purest pleasure, the evidences of the continued friendship of the French Repub-

lic, which accompanied his Message of the 4th inst.

That the Senate unite with him in all the feelings expressed to the Minister of France on the presentation of the Colors of his nation, and devoutly wish that this symbol of the triumphs and enfranchisement of that great people, given as a pledge of faithful friendship, and placed among the evidences and memorials of the freedom and independence of the United States, may contribute to cherish and perpetuate the sincere affection by which the two Republics are so happily united.

Ordered, That the Secretary lay this resolution before the PRESIDENT OF THE UNITED STATES.

18

ALEXANDER HAMILTON TO GEORGE WASHINGTON
7 Mar. 1796
Papers 20:68–69

(See vol. 1, ch. 10, no. 19)

19

ALEXANDER HAMILTON TO
WILLIAM LOUGHTON SMITH
10 Mar. 1796
Papers 20:72–73

(See vol. 1, ch. 10, no. 20)

20

GEORGE WASHINGTON TO HOUSE OF
REPRESENTATIVES
30 Mar. 1796
Writings 35:2–4

Gentlemen of the House of Representatives: With the utmost attention I have considered your resolution of the 24th. instant, requesting me to lay before your House, a copy of the instructions to the Minister of the United States who negotiated the Treaty with the King of Great Britain, together with the correspondence and other documents relative to that Treaty, excepting such of the said papers as any existing negotiation may render improper to be disclosed.

In deliberating upon this subject, it was impossible for me to lose sight of the principle which some have avowed in its discussion; or to avoid extending my views to the consequences which must flow from the admission of that principle.

I trust that no part of my conduct has ever indicated a disposition to withhold any information which the Constitution has enjoined upon the President as a duty to give, or which could be required of him by either House of Congress as a right; And with truth I affirm, that it has been, as it will continue to be, while I have the honor to preside in the Government, my constant endeavour to harmonize with the other branches thereof; so far as the trust delegated to me by the People of the United States, and my sense of the obligation it imposes to "preserve, protect and defend the Constitution" will permit.

The nature of foreign negotiations requires caution; and their success must often depend on secrecy: and even when brought to a conclusion, a full disclosure of all the measures, demands, or eventual concessions, which may have been proposed or contemplated, would be extremely impolitic: for this might have a pernicious influence on future negotiations; or produce immediate inconveniences, perhaps danger and mischief, in relation to other powers. The necessity of such caution and secrecy was one cogent reason for vesting the power of making Treaties in the President, with the advice and consent of the Senate, the principle on which that body was formed confining it to a small number of Members.

To admit then a right in the House of Representatives to demand, and to have as a matter of course, all the Papers respecting a negotiation with a foreign power, would be to establish a dangerous precedent.

It does not occur that the inspection of the papers asked for, can be relative to any purpose under the cognizance of the House of Representatives, except that of an impeachment, which the resolution has not expressed. I repeat, that I have no disposition to withhold any information which the duty of my station will permit, or the public good shall require to be disclosed: and in fact, all the Papers affecting the negotiation with Great Britain were laid before the Senate, when the Treaty itself was communicated for their consideration and advice.

The course which the debate has taken, on the resolution of the House, leads to some observations on the mode of making treaties under the Constitution of the United States.

Having been a member of the General Convention, and knowing the principles on which the Constitution was formed, I have ever entertained but one opinion on this subject; and from the first establishment of the Government to this moment, my conduct has exemplified that opinion, that the power of making treaties is exclusively vested in the President, by and with the advice and consent of the Senate, provided two thirds of the Senators present concur, and that every treaty so made, and promulgated, thenceforward became the Law of the land. It is thus that the treaty making power has been understood by foreign Nations: and in all the treaties made with them, *we* have declared, and *they* have believed, that when ratified by the President with the advice and consent of the Senate, they became obligatory. In this construction of the Constitution every House of Representatives has heretofore acquiesced; and until the present time, not a doubt or suspicion has appeared to my knowledge that this construction was not the true one. Nay, they have more than acquiesced: for till now, without controverting the obligation of such treaties, they have made all the requisite provisions for carrying them into effect.

There is also reason to believe that this construction agrees with the opinions entertained by the State Conventions, when they were deliberating on the Constitution; especially by those who objected to it, because there was not required, in *commercial treaties,* the consent of two thirds of the whole number of the members of the Senate, instead of two thirds of the Senators present; and because in treaties respecting territorial and certain other rights and claims, the concurrence of three fourths of the whole number of the members of both houses respectively, was not made necessary.

21

GEORGE WASHINGTON TO ALEXANDER HAMILTON
31 March 1796
Writings 35:6–8

My dear Sir: I do not know how to thank you sufficiently, for the trouble you have taken to dilate on the request of the House of Representatives for the Papers relative to the British Treaty; or how to apologize for the trouble (much greater than I had any idea of giving) which you have taken to shew the impropriety of that request.

From the first moment, and from the fullest conviction in my own mind, I had resolved to *resist the principle* wch. was evidently intended to be established by the call of the House of Representatives; and only deliberated on the manner, in which this could be done, with the least bad consequences.

To effect this, three modes presented themselves to me: 1. a denial of the Papers in toto, assigning concise, but cogent reasons for that denial; 2. to grant them in whole; or 3. in part; accompanied with a pointed protest against the right of the House to controul Treaties, or to call for Papers without specifying their object; and against the compliance being drawn into precedent.

I had as little hesitation in deciding that the first was the most tenable ground, but from the peculiar circumstances of *this case* It merited consideration, if the *principle* could be saved, whether facility in the provisions might not result from a compliance. An attentive examination however of the Papers and the subject, soon convinced me that to furnish *all* the Papers would be highly improper; and that a *partial* deliver of them would leave the door open for as much calumny as the entire refusal, perhaps more so, as it might, and I have no doubt would be said, that all such as were essential to the purposes of the house, were withheld.

Under these impressions, I proceeded, with the heads of Departments and the Attorney General, to collect materials; and to prepare an answer, subject however to revision, and alteration, according to circumstances. This answer was ready on Monday, and proposed to be sent in on Tuesday but it was delayed until I should receive what was expected; not doing it definitively on that day, the delivery of my answer was further postponed till the next; notwithstanding the anxious solicitude which was visible in all quarters, to learn the result of Executive decision.

Finding that the draft I had prepared, embraced most, if not all the principles which were detailed in the Paper I received yesterday; though not the reasonings. That it would take considerable time to copy the latter, and above all, having understood that if the Papers were refused a fresh demand, with strictures might be expected; I sent in the answer wch. was ready; reserving the other as a source for reasoning if my information proves true.

22

JAMES MADISON, THE JAY TREATY, HOUSE OF REPRESENTATIVES
6 Apr. 1796
Writings 6:263–79

Mr. MADISON rose, and spoke as follows: When the Message was first proposed to be committed, the proposition had been treated by some gentlemen not only with levity but with ridicule. He persuaded himself that the subject would appear in a very different light to the Committee; and he hoped that it would be discussed on both sides without either levity, intemperance, or illiberality.

If there were any question which could make a serious appeal to the dispassionate judgment, it must be one which respected the meaning of the Constitution; and if any Constitutional question could make the appeal with peculiar solemnity, it must be in a case like the present, where two of the constituted authorities interpreted differently the extent of their respective powers.

It was a consolation, however, of which every member would be sensible, to reflect on the happy difference of our situation, on such occurrences, from that of Governments in which the constituent members possessed independent and hereditary prerogatives. In such Governments, the parties having a personal interest in their public stations, and not being amenable to the national will, disputes concerning the limits of their respective authorities might be productive of the most fatal consequences. With us, on the contrary, although disputes of that kind are always to be regretted, there were three most precious resources against the evil tendency of them. In the first place, the responsibility which every department feels to the public will, under the forms of the Constitution, may be expected to prevent the excesses incident to conflicts between rival and irresponsible authorities. In the next place, if the difference cannot be adjusted by friendly conference and mutual concession, the sense of the constituent body, brought into the Government through the ordinary elective channels, may supply a remedy. And if this resource should fail, there remains, in the third and last place, that provident article in the Constitution itself, by which an avenue is always open to the sovereignty of the people, for explanations or amendments, as they might be found indispensable.

If, in the present instance, it was to be particularly regretted that the existing difference of opinion had arisen, every motive to the regret was a motive to calmness, to candor, and the most respectful delicacy towards the other constituted authority. On the other hand, the duty which the House of Representatives must feel to themselves and to their constituents required that they should examine the subject with accuracy, as well as with candor, and decide on it with firmness, as well as with moderation.

In this temper, he should proceed to make some observations on the Message before the Committee, and on the reasons contained in it.

The Message related to two points: First. The application made for the papers. Secondly. The Constitutional rights of Congress, and of the House of Representatives, on the subject of Treaties.

On the first point, he observed, that the right of the House to apply for any information they might want, had been admitted by a number in the minority, who had opposed the exercise of the right in this particular case. He thought it clear that the House must have a right, in all cases, to ask for information which might assist their deliberations on the subjects submitted to them by the Constitution; being responsible, nevertheless, for the propriety of the measure. He was as ready to admit that the Executive had a right, under a due responsibility, also, to withhold information, when of a nature that did not permit a disclosure of it at the time. And if the refusal of the President had been founded simply on a representation, that the state of the business within his department, and the contents of the papers asked for, required it, although he might have regretted the refusal, he should have been little disposed to criticise it. But the Message had contested what appeared to him a clear and important right of the House; and stated reasons for refusing the papers, which, with all the respect he could feel for the Executive, he could not regard as satisfactory or proper.

One of the reasons was, that it did not occur to the Executive that the papers could be relative to any purpose under the cognizance, and in the contemplation of the House. The other was, that the purpose for which they were wanted was not expressed in the resolution of the House.

With respect to the first, it implied that the Executive was not only to judge of the proper objects and functions of the Executive department, but, also, of the objects and functions of the House. He was not only to decide how far the Executive trust would permit a disclosure of information, but how far the Legislative trust could derive advantage from it. It belonged, he said, to each department to judge for itself. If the Executive conceived that, in relation to his own department, papers could not be safely communicated, he might, on that ground, refuse them, because he was the competent though a responsible judge within his own department. If the papers could be communicated without injury to the objects of his department, he ought not to refuse them as irrelative to the objects of the House of Representatives; because the House was, in such cases, the only proper judge of its own objects.

The other reason of refusal was, that the use which the House meant to make of the papers was not expressed in the resolution.

As far as he could recollect, no precedent could be found in the records of the House, or elsewhere, in which the particular object in calling for information was expressed in the call. It was not only contrary to right to require this, but it would often be improper in the House to express the object. In the particular case of an impeachment referred to in the Message, it might be evidently improper to state that to be the object of information which might possibly lead to it, because it would involve the preposterous idea of first determining to impeach, and then inquiring whether an impeachment ought to take place. Even the holding out an impeachment as a contemplated or contingent result of the information called for, might be extremely disagreeable in practice, as it might inflict a temporary pain on an individual, whom an investigation of facts might prove to be innocent and perhaps meritorious.

From this view of the subject he could not forbear wishing that, if the papers were to be refused, other reasons had been assigned for it. He thought the resolutions offered by the gentleman from North Carolina, one of which related to this subject, ought to stand on the Journal along with the Message which had been entered there. Both the resolutions were penned with moderation and propriety. They went no farther than to assert the rights of the House; they courted no reply; and it ought not to be supposed they could give any offence.

The second object to which the measure related, was the Constitutional power of the House on the subject of Treaties.

Here, again, he hoped it may be allowable to wish that it had not been deemed necessary to take up, in so solemn a manner, a great Constitutional question, which was not contained in the resolution presented by the House, which had been incidental only to the discussion of that resolution, and which could only have been brought into view through the unauthentic medium of the newspapers. This, however, would well account for the misconception which had taken place in the doctrine maintained by the majority in the late question. It had been understood by the Executive, that the House asserted its assent to be necessary to the validity of Treaties. This was not the doctrine maintained by them. It was, he believed, fairly laid down in the resolution proposed, which limited the power of the House over Treaties, to cases where Treaties embraced Legislative subjects, submitted by the Constitution to the power of the House.

Mr. M. did not mean to go into the general merits of this question, as discussed when the former resolution was before the Committee. The Message did not request it, having drawn none of its reasoning from the text of the Constitution. It had merely affirmed that the power of making Treaties is exclusively vested by the Constitution in the President, by and with the advice and consent of the Senate. Nothing more was necessary on this point than to observe, that the Constitution had as expressly and exclusively vested in Congress the power of making laws, as it had vested in the President and Senate the power of making Treaties.

He proceeded to review the several topics on which the Message relied. First. The intention of the body which framed the Constitution. Secondly. The opinions of the State Conventions who adopted it. Thirdly. The peculiar rights and interests of the smaller States. Fourthly. The manner in which the Constitution had been understood by the Executive and the foreign nations, with which Treaties had been formed. Fifthly. The acquiescence and acts of the House on former occasions.

1. When the members on the floor, who were members of the General Convention, particularly a member from Georgia and himself, were called on in a former debate for the sense of that body on the Constitutional question, it was a matter of some surprise, which was much increased by the peculiar stress laid on the information expected. He acknowledged his surprise, also, at seeing the Message of the Executive appealing to the same proceedings in the General Convention, as a clue to the meaning of the Constitution.

It had been his purpose, during the late debate, to make some observations on what had fallen from the gentlemen from Connecticut and Maryland, if the sudden termination of the debate had not cut him off from the opportunity. He should have reminded them that this was the ninth year since the convention executed their trust, and that he had not a single note in this place to assist his memory. He should have remarked, that neither himself nor the other members who had belonged to the Federal Convention, could be under any particular obligation to rise in answer to a few gentlemen, with information, not merely of their own ideas at that period, but of the intention of the whole body; many members of which, too, had probably never entered into the discussions of the subject. He might have further remarked, that there would not be much delicacy in the undertaking, as it appeared that a sense had been put on the Constitution by some who were members of the Convention, different from that which must have been entertained by others, who had concurred in ratifying the Treaty.

After taking notice of the doctrine of Judge Wilson, who was a member of the Federal Convention, as quoted by Mr. Gallatin from the Pennsylvania debates, he proceeded to mention that three gentlemen, who had been members of the Convention, were parties to the proceedings in Charleston, South Carolina, which, among other objections to the Treaty, represented it as violating the Constitution. That the very respectable citizen who presided at the meeting in Wilmington, whose resolutions made a similar complaint, had also been a distinguished member of the body that formed the Constitution.

It would have been proper for him, also, to have recollected what had, on a former occasion, happened to himself during a debate in the House of Representatives. When the bill for establishing a National Bank was under consideration, he had opposed it, as not warranted by the Constitution, and incidentally remarked, that his impression might be stronger, as he remembered that, in the Convention, a motion was made and negatived, for giving Congress a power to grant charters of incorporation. This slight reference to the Convention, he said, was animadverted on by several, in the course of the debate, and particularly by a gentleman from Massachusetts, who had himself been a member of the Convention, and whose remarks were not unworthy the attention of the Committee. Here Mr. M. read a paragraph from Mr. Gerry's speech, from the Gazette of the United States, page 814, protesting, in strong terms, against arguments drawn from that source.

Mr. M. said, he did not believe a single instance could be cited in which the sense of the Convention had been required or admitted as material in any Constitutional question. In the case of the Bank, the Committee had seen how a glance at that authority had been treated in this House. When the question on the suability of the States was depending in the Supreme Court, he asked, whether it had ever been understood that the members of the Bench, who had been members of the Convention, were called on for the meaning of the Convention on that very important point, although no Constitutional question would be presumed more susceptible of elucidation from that source.

He then adverted to that part of the Message which contained an extract from the Journal of the Convention, showing that a proposition "that no Treaty should be binding on the United States, which was not ratified by law," was explicitly rejected. He allowed this to be much more precise than any evidence drawn from the debates in the Convention, or resting on the memory of individuals. But, admitting the case to be as stated, of which he had no doubt, although he had no recollection of it, and admitting the record of the Convention to be the oracle that ought to decide the true meaning of the Constitution, what did this abstract vote amount to? Did it condemn the doctrine of the majority? So far from it, that, as he understood their doctrine, they must have voted as the Convention did; for they do not contend that no Treaty shall be operative without a law to sanction it; on the contrary, they admit that some Treaties will operate without this sanction; and that it is no further applicable in any case than where Legislative objects are embraced by Treaties. The term "ratify" also deserved some attention; for, although of loose signification in general, it had a technical meaning different from the agency claimed by the House on the subject of Treaties.

But, after all, whatever veneration might be entertained for the body of men who formed our Constitution, the sense of that body could never be regarded as the oracular guide in expounding the Constitution. As the instrument came from them it was nothing more than the draft of a plan, nothing but a dead letter, until life and validity were breathed into it by the voice of the people, speaking through the several State Conventions. If we were to look, therefore, for the meaning of the instrument beyond the face of the instrument, we must look for it, not in the General Convention, which proposed, but in the State Conventions, which accepted and ratified the Constitution. To these also the Message had referred, and it would be proper to follow it.

2. The debates of the Conventions in three States (Pennsylvania, Virginia, and North Carolina) had been before introduced into the discussion of this subject, and were believed the only publications of the sort which contained any lights with respect to it. He would not fatigue the Committee with a repetition of the passages then read to them. He would only appeal to the Committee to decide whether it did not appear, from a candid and collected view of the debates in those Conventions, and particularly in that of Virginia, that the Treaty-making power was a limited power; and that the powers in our Constitution, on this subject bore an analogy to the powers on the same subject in the Government of Great Britain. He wished, as little as any member could to extend the analogies between the two Governments; but it was clear that the constituent parts of two Governments might be perfectly heterogeneous, and yet the powers be similar.

At once to illustrate his meaning, and give a brief reply to some arguments on the other side, which had heretofore been urged with ingenuity and learning, he would mention, as an example, the power of pardoning offences. This power was vested in the President; it was a prerogative also of the British King. And, in order to ascertain the extent of the technical term "pardon," in our Constitution, it would not be irregular to search into the meaning and exercise of the power in Great Britain. Yet, where is the general analogy between an hereditary Sovereign, not accountable for his conduct, and a Magistrate like the President of the United States, elected for four years, with limited powers, and liable to impeachment for the abuse of them?

In referring to the debates of the State Conventions as published, he wished not to be understood as putting entire confidence in the accuracy of them. Even those of Virginia, which had been probably taken down by the most skilful hand, (whose merit he wished by no means to disparage,) contained internal evidence in abundance of chasms and misconceptions of what was said.

The amendments proposed by the several Conventions were better authority, and would be found, on a general view, to favor the sense of the Constitution which had prevailed in this House. But even here it would not be reasonable to expect a perfect precision and system in all their votes and proceedings. The agitations of the public mind on that occasion, with the hurry and compromise which generally prevailed in settling the amendments to be proposed, would at once explain and apologize for the several apparent inconsistencies which might be discovered.

He would not undertake to say that the particular amendment referred to in the Message, by which two states require that "no Commercial Treaty should be ratified without the consent of two-thirds of the whole number of Senators, and that no Territorial rights, &c. should be ceded without the consent of three-fourths of the members of both Houses," was digested with an accurate attention to the whole subject. On the other hand, it was no proof that those particular Conventions, in annexing these guards to the Treaty power, understood it as different from that espoused by the majority of the House. They might consider Congress as having the power contended for over Treaties stipulating on Legislative subjects, and still very consistently wish for the amendment they proposed. They might not consider the Territorial-rights and other objects for which they required the concurrence of three-fourths of the members of both Houses as coming within any of the enumerated powers of Congress, and, therefore, as not protected by that control over Treaties. And although they might be sensible that Commercial Treaties were under that control, yet, as they would always come before Congress with great weight after they had passed through the regular forms and sanctions of the Treaty department, it might be deemed of real importance that the authority should be better guarded which was to give that weight to them.

He asked, whether it might not happen, even in the progress of a Treaty through the Treaty department, that each succeeding sanction might be given, more on account of preceding sanctions than of any positive approbation? And no one could doubt, therefore, that a Treaty which had received all these sanctions would be controlled with great reluctance by the Legislature, and, consequently, that it might be desirable to strengthen the barriers against making improper Treaties, rather than trust too much to the Legislative control over carrying them into effect.

But, said Mr. M., it will be proper to attend to other amendments proposed by the ratifying Conventions, which may throw light on their opinions and intentions on the subject in question. He then read from the Declaration of Rights proposed by Virginia to be prefixed to the Constitution, the seventh article, which is as follows:

"That all power of suspending laws, or the execution of laws, by any authority, without the consent of the Representatives of the people in the Legislature, is injurious to their rights, and ought not to be exercised."

The Convention of North Carolina, as he showed, had laid down the same principle in the same words. And it was to be observed that, in both Conventions, the article was under the head of a Declaration of Rights, "asserting and securing from encroachment the essential and inalienable rights of the people," according to the language of the Virginia Convention; and "asserting and securing from encroachment the great principles of civil and religious liberty, and the inalienable rights of the people," as expressed by the Convention of North Carolina. It must follow that these two Conventions considered it as a fundamental, inviolable, and universal principle in a free Government, that no power could supersede a law without the consent of the Representatives of the people in the Legislature.

In the Maryland Convention also, it was among the amendments proposed, though he believed not decided on, "that no power of suspending laws, or the execution of laws, unless derived from the Legislature, ought to be exercised or allowed."

The Convention of North Carolina had further explained themselves on this point, by their twenty-third amendment proposed to the Constitution, in the following words: "That no Treaties which shall be directly opposed to the existing laws of the United States in Congress assembled, shall be valid until such laws shall be repealed or made conformable to such Treaty; nor shall any Treaty be valid which is contradictory to the Constitution of the United States."

The latter part of the amendment was an evidence that the amendment was intended to ascertain rather than to alter the meaning of the Constitution; as it could not be supposed to have been the real intention of the Constitution that a Treaty contrary to it should be valid.

He proceeded to read the following amendments accompanying the ratification of State Conventions:

The New York Convention had proposed "that no standing army or regular troops shall be raised or kept up in time of peace without the consent of two-thirds of the Senators and Representatives in each House."

"That no money be borrowed on the credit of the United States, without the assent of two-thirds of the Senators and Representatives in each House."

The New Hampshire Convention had proposed "that no standing army shall be kept up in time of peace, unless with the consent of three-quarters of the members of each branch of Congress." In the Maryland Convention a proposition was made in the same words.

The Virginia Convention had proposed "that no navigation law, or law regulating commerce, shall be passed without the consent of two-thirds of the members present in both Houses."

"That no standing army or regular troops shall be raised or kept up in time of peace, without the consent of two-thirds of the members present in both Houses."

"That no soldier shall be enlisted for any longer term than four years, except in time of war, and then for no longer term than the continuance of the war."

The Convention of North Carolina had proposed the same three amendments in the same words.

On a review of these proceedings, may not, said he, the question be fairly asked, whether it ought to be supposed that the several Conventions who showed so much jealousy with respect to the powers of commerce, of the sword, and of the purse, as to require, for the exercise of them, in some cases two-thirds, in others three-fourths of both branches of the Legislature, could have understood that, by the Treaty clauses in the Constitution, they had given to the President and Senate, without any control whatever from the House of Representatives, an absolute and unlimited power over all those great objects?

3. It was with great reluctance, he said, that he should touch on the third topic—the alleged interest of the smaller States in the present question. He was the more unwilling to enter into this delicate part of the discussion, as he happened to be from a State which was in one of the extremes in point of size. He should limit himself, therefore, to two observations. The first was, that if the spirit of amity and mutual concession from which the Constitution resulted was to be consulted on expounding it, that construction ought to be favored which would preserve the mutual control between the Senate and House of Repre-

sentatives, rather than that which gave powers to the Senate not controllable by, and paramount over those of the House of Representatives, whilst the House of Representatives could in no instance exercise their powers without the participation and control of the Senate. The second observation was, that, whatever jealousy might unhappily have prevailed between the smaller and larger States, as they had most weight in one or the other branch of Government, it was a fact, for which he appealed to the Journals of the old Congress, from its birth to its dissolution, and to those of the Congress under the present Government, that in no instance would it appear, from the yeas and nays, that a question had been decided by a division of the votes according to the size of the States. He considered this truth as affording the most pleasing and consoling reflection, and as one that ought to have the most conciliating and happy influence on the temper of all the States.

4. A fourth argument in the Message was drawn from the manner by which the Treaty power had been understood by both parties in the negotiations with foreign Powers. "In all the Treaties made, *we* have declared and *they* have believed," &c. By *we*, he remarked, was to be understood the Executive alone, who had made the declaration, and in no respect the House of Representatives. It was certainly to be regretted, as had often been expressed, that different branches of the Government should disagree in the construction of their powers; but when this could not be avoided, each branch must judge for itself; and the judgment of the Executive could in this case be no more an authority overruling the judgment of the House than the judgment of the House could be an authority overruling that of the Executive. It was also to be regretted that any foreign nation should at any time proceed under a misconception of the meaning of our Constitution. But no principle was better established in the Laws of Nations, as well as in common reason, than that one nation is not to be the interpreter of the Constitution of another. Each nation must adjust the forms and operations of its own Government, and all others are bound to understand them accordingly. It had before been remarked, and it would be proper to repeat it here, that of all nations Great Britain would be the least likely to object to this principle, because the construction given to our Government was particularly exemplified in her own.

5. In the fifth and last place, he had to take notice of the suggestion, that every House of Representatives had concurred in the construction of the Treaty power, now maintained by the Executive; from which it followed that the House could not now consistently act under a different construction. On this point, it might be sufficient to remark, that this was the first instance in which a foreign Treaty had been made since the establishment of the Constitution; and that this was the first time the Treaty-making power had come under formal and accurate discussion. Precedents, therefore, would readily be perceived to lose much of their weight. But whether the precedents found in the proceedings preparatory to the Algerine Treaty, or in the provisions relative to the Indian Treaties, were inconsistent with the right which had been contended for in behalf of the House, he should leave to be decided by the Committee. A view of these precedents had been pretty fully presented to them by a gentleman from New York [Mr. Livingston] with all the observations which the subject seemed to require.

On the whole, it appeared that the rights of the House on the two great Constitutional points had been denied by a high authority in the Message before the Committee. This Message was entered on the Journals of the House. If nothing was entered in opposition thereto, it would be inferred that the reasons in the Message had changed the opinion of the House, and that their claims on those great points were relinquished. It was proper, therefore, that the questions, brought fairly before the Committee in the propositions of the gentleman [Mr. Blount] from North Carolina, should be examined and formally decided. If the reasoning of the Message should be deemed satisfactory, it would be the duty of this branch of the Government to reject the propositions, and thus accede to the doctrines asserted by the Executive. If, on the other hand, this reasoning should not be satisfactory, it would be equally the duty of the House, in some such firm, but very decent terms, as are proposed, to enter their opinions on record. In either way, the meaning of the Constitution would be established, as far as depends on the vote of the House of Representatives.

23

An Act to Declare the Treaties Heretofore Concluded with France, No Longer Obligatory on the United States
1 Stat. 578 (1798)

Whereas the treaties concluded between the United States and France have been repeatedly violated on the part of the French government; and the just claims of the United States for reparation of the injuries so committed have been refused, and their attempts to negotiate an amicable adjustment of all complaints between the two nations, have been repelled with indignity: And whereas, under authority of the French government, there is yet pursued against the United States, a system of predatory violence, infracting the said treaties, and hostile to the rights of a free and independent nation:

Be it enacted by the Senate and House of Representatives of the United States of America in Congress assembled, That the United States are of right freed and exonerated from the stipulations of the treaties, and of the consular convention, heretofore concluded between the United States and France; and that the same shall not henceforth be regarded as legally obligatory on the government or citizens of the United States.

Approved, July 7, 1798.

24

ST. GEORGE TUCKER,
BLACKSTONE'S COMMENTARIES
1:APP. 332–36, 338–40
1803

Treaties, as defined by Puffendorf, are certain agreements made by sovereigns, between one another, of great use both in war, and peace; of these, there are two kinds; the one such as reinforce the observance of what by the law of nature we were before obliged to; as the mutual exercise of civility, and humanity, or the prevention of injuries on either side; the second, such as add some new engagement to the duties of natural law; or at least determine what was before too general and indefinite in the same, to some thing particular, and precise. Of those which add some new engagement to those duties which natural law imposes upon all nations, the most usual relate to, or in their operation may affect, the sovereignty of the state; the unity of its parts, it's territory, or other property; it's commerce with foreign nations, and *vice versa;* the mutual privileges and immunities of the citizens, or subjects of the contracting powers, or the mutual aid of the contracting nations, in case of an attack, or hostility, from any other quarter. To all these objects, if there be nothing in the fundamental laws of the state which contradicts it, the power of making treaties extends, and is vested in the conductors of states, according to the opinion of Vattel.

In our constitution, there is no restriction as to the subjects of treaties, unless perhaps the guarantee of a republican form of government, and of protection from invasion, contained in the fourth article, may be construed to impose such a restriction, in behalf of the several states, against the dismemberment of the federal republic. But whether this restriction may extend to prevent the alienation, by cession, of the western territory, not being a part of any state, may be somewhat more doubtful. The act of cession from Virginia militates, expressly, against such an alienation of that part of the western territory which was ceded by this state. Nevertheless, it is said to have been in contemplation soon after the establishment of the federal government, to cede the right of pre-emption to the lands in that territory to the Indians, who were then supposed to be in treaty for the same with the crown of Great Britain. The president, who had not authorised any such article, and who is said to have disapproved of it, in submitting the treaty to the consideration of the senate, called their attention particularly to that part of it; in consequence of which it was rejected, though warmly supported in the senate, as has been said. If the power of making such a dismemberment be questionable at any rate, it is much more so, when it is recollected, that the constitution seems to have vested congress, collectively, and not any one or two branches of it only, with the power to dispose of that territory. The effect of this extraordinary treaty, if it had been ratified by the senate and the president, may

easily be conceived. Great Britain, at that time not a little disposed to enmity towards the United States, would no doubt have insisted upon such an acquisition of territory, made under the faith of a treaty between the United States and the Indians; and thus the United States might either have been deprived of their territory by an unconstitutional treaty, or involved in a war for it's preservation, by the proceedings of a body, whose authority does not extend to a final decision upon a question, whether war be necessary and expedient. This shews the collision which may possibly arise between the several branches of the congress, in consequence of this modification of the treaty-making power. For, being entrusted to a branch of the congress only, without the possibility of control or check by the other branch, so far as respects the conclusion and ratification of any treaty whatsoever, it may well happen, at some time or other, that the president and senate may overstep the limits of their just authority, and the house of representatives be so tenacious of their own constitutional rights, as not to yield to the obligations imposed upon them by a treaty, the terms of which they do not approve.

But the senate, in matters of treaty, are not only without control, they may be said also to be without even the least shadow of responsibility in the individuals who compose that body. In England, says judge Blackstone, lest this plenitude of authority should be abused to the detriment of the public, the constitution hath interposed a check by means of parliamentary impeachment, for the punishment of such members as from criminal motives advise or conclude any treaty, which shall afterwards be judged to derogate from the honour and interest of the nation. But where shall we find this responsibility in our constitution? Does it arise from the power of impeachment vested in the house of representatives by the constitution? It has been solemnly decided, that a senator is not a civil officer of the United States, and therefore not liable to impeachment. Even were it otherwise, the power of impeachment would, in the case we are now speaking of, be nugatory, as will presently appear. . . . Does it consist then in the power of impeaching the ambassador, by whom it was concluded, or the president, by whom it has been ratified, both of whom are unquestionably impeachable, I presume? The ambassador is appointed by the president, with the advice and consent of the senate: it may be presumed that his instructions have been submitted to and approved by them, though a different practice is said to have been established. If the treaty be ratified, and the minister be impeached for concluding it, because it is derogatory to the honour, the interest, or perhaps to the sovereignty and independence of the nation, who are to be his judges? The senate by whom it has been approved and ratified. If the president be impeached for giving improper instructions to the ambassador, and for ratifying the treaty concluded by him pursuant to his instructions. who are to be his judges? The senate, to whom the treaty has been submitted, by whom it has been approved, and by whose advice it has been ratified. The constitution requires, that a majority of two-thirds of the senate, at least, must advise the conclusion of a treaty, before it can be ratified by the president; it likewise requires that a majority of two-thirds at least must concur in the judgment in case of conviction. A quorum for the trial upon an impeachment, consequently cannot possibly be formed, without calling in some of those senators to be judges, who had either actually advised or dissented from the ratification of the treaty. Can such judges be deemed impartial? If they can, from which class shall they be chosen; from those who proposed the rejection of the treaty, or from those who advised its final ratification? Sophistry itself might be puzzled by the dilemma.

. . . . .

But, to return to the treaty-making-power; it appears to be somewhat extraordinary, that that branch of the federal government, who are by the constitution required to concur, in a declaration of war, before any such declaration can be made, should be wholly precluded from voting at all, upon a question of peace. . . . They are judges of the causes of war; of the existence of those causes; of the resources, and ability of the states to prosecute and support a war; of the expediency of applying those resources to the obtaining redress, or satisfaction for the injury received; in short, of every possible circumstance that can induce the nation to incur the hazard, or expence of a war: and yet, if through timidity, venality, or corruption, the president, and two thirds of a majority of the senate can be prevailed upon to relinquish the prosecution of the war, and conclude a treaty, the house of representatives have not power to prevent, or retard the measure; although it should appear to them, that the object for which the war hath been undertaken, hath not been attained, and that it was neither relinquished from necessity, or inability to prosecute it, with effect.

These objections are not intended, to extend to the agency which the president and senate may have, in the formation of a treaty; nor to the principle that treaties with foreign nations should be regarded as a part of the supreme law of the land. . . . The honour and peace of the nation certainly require that it's compacts should be duly observed, and carried into effect with perfect good faith. And though it may be the result of sound discretion to confide the formation of a treaty, in the first instance, to the president and senate, only; yet the safety of the nation seems to require that the final ratification of any compact, which is to form a part of the supreme law of the land, should, as well as other laws of the federal government, depend upon the concurrent approbation of every branch of the congress, before they acquire such a sanction as to become irrevocable, without the consent of a foreign nation; or without hazarding an imputation against the honour and faith of the nation, in the performance of it's contracts.

It may not be improper here to add something on the subject of that part of the constitution, which declares that treaties made by the president and senate shall be a part of the supreme law of the land: acts of congress made pursuant to the powers delegated by the constitution are to be regarded in the same light. What then is the effect of a treaty made by the president and senate, some of the articles of which may contain stipulations on legislative objects, or such as are expressly vested in congress by the

constitution, until congress shall make a law carrying them into effect? Is congress bound to carry such stipulations into effect, whether they approve or disapprove of them? Have they no negative, no discretion upon the subject? The answer seems to be, that it is in some respects, an inchoate act. It is the law of the land, and binding upon the nation in all it's parts, except so far as relates to those stipulations. It's final fate, in case of refusal on the part of congress, to carry those stipulations into effect, would depend on the will of the other nation. If they were satisfied that the treaty should subsist, although some of the original conditions should not be fulfilled on our part, the whole, except those stipulations embracing legislative objects, might remain a treaty. But if the other nation chose not to be bound, they would be at liberty to say so, and the treaty would be defeated. And this construction seems to be consonant with that resolution, of the house of representatives, wherein they declare, "That when a treaty stipulates regulations on any of the subjects submitted by the constitution to the power of congress, it must depend for it's execution, as to such stipulations, on a law or laws to be passed by congress; and it is the constitutional right and duty of the house of representatives, in all such cases, to deliberate on the expediency, or inexpediency, of carrying such treaty into effect, and to determine and act thereon, as in their judgment, may be most conducive to the public good. . . . A contrary construction would render the power of the president and senate paramount to that of the whole congress, even upon those subjects upon which every branch of congress is, by the constitution, required to deliberate. Let it be supposed, for example, that the president and senate should stipulate by treaty with any foreign nation, that in case of war between that nation and any other, the United States should immediately declare war against that nation: Can it be supposed that such a treaty would be so far the law of the land, as to take from the house of representatives their constitutional right to deliberate on the expediency or inexpediency of such a declaration of war, and to determine and act thereon, according to their own judgment?

25

THOMAS JEFFERSON, PROPOSED AMENDMENT TO THE CONSTITUTION
July 1803
Works 10:3–8

Louisiana, as ceded by France to the U S. is made a part of the U S. Its white inhabitants shall be citizens, and stand, as to their rights & obligations, on the same footing with other citizens of the U S. in analogous situations. Save only that as to the portion thereof lying North of an East & West line drawn through the mouth of Arkansa river, no new State shall be established, nor any grants of land made, other than to Indians in exchange for equivalent portions of land occupied by them, until authorised by further subsequent amendment to the Constitution shall be made for these purposes.

Florida also, whenever it may be rightfully obtained, shall become a part of the U S. Its white inhabitants shall thereupon be Citizens & shall stand, as to their rights & obligations, on the same footing with other citizens of the U S. in analogous situations.

26

THOMAS JEFFERSON TO WILLIAM DUNBAR
17 July 1803
Works 10:19

Before you receive this, you will have heard, through the channel of the public papers, of the cession of Louisiana by France to the United States. The terms as stated in the *National Intelligencer*, are accurate. That the treaty may be ratified in time, I have found it necessary to convene Congress on the 17th of October; and it is very important for the happiness of the country that they should possess all the information which can be obtained respecting it, that they make the best arrangement practicable for its good government. It is the most necessary, because, they will be obliged to ask from the People an amendment of the Constitution, authorizing their receiving the province into the Union, and providing for its government; and the limitations of power which shall be given by that amendment, will be unalterable but by the same authority.

27

THOMAS JEFFERSON TO WILSON CARY NICHOLAS
7 Sept. 1803
Works 10:10

I am aware of the force of the observations you make on the power given by the Constn to Congress, to admit new States into the Union, without restraining the subject to the territory then constituting the U S. But when I consider that the limits of the U S are precisely fixed by the treaty of 1783, that the Constitution expressly declares itself to be made for the U S, I cannot help believing the intention was to permit Congress to admit into the Union new States, which should be formed out of the territory for which, & under whose authority alone, they were then acting. I do not believe it was meant that they might receive England, Ireland, Holland, &c. into it, which would be the case on your construction. When an instrument admits two constructions, the one safe, the other dangerous, the one precise, the other indefinite, I prefer that which is

safe & precise. I had rather ask an enlargement of power from the nation, where it is found necessary, than to assume it by a construction which would make our powers boundless.

28

THOMAS JEFFERSON TO JAMES MADISON
14 July 1804
Works 10:91–92

The inclosed reclamations of Girod & Chote against the claims of Bapstropp to a monopoly of the Indian commerce supposed to be under the protection of the 3d article of the Louisiana Convention, as well as some other claims to abusive grants, will probably force us to meet that question. The article has been worded with remarkable caution on the part of our negociators. It is that the inhabitants shall be admitted as soon as possible, according to the principles of our Constn., to the enjoyment of all the rights of citizens, and, *in the mean time, en* attendant, shall be maintained in their liberty, property & religion. That is that they shall continue under the protection of the treaty, until the principles of our constitution can be extended to them, when the protection of the treaty is to cease, and that of our own principles to take it's place. But as this could not be done at once, it has been provided to be as soon as our rules will admit. Accordingly Congress has begun by extending about 20. particular laws by their titles, to Louisiana. Among these is the act concerning intercourse with the Indians, which establishes a system of commerce with them admitting no monopoly. That class of rights therefore are now taken from under the treaty & placed under the principles of our laws. I imagine it will be necessary to express an opinion to Govr. Claiborne on this subject, after you shall have made up one.

29

SENATE, COMMITTEE ON FOREIGN RELATIONS
15 Feb. 1816
Reports 8:24

The President is the constitutional representative of the United States with regard to foreign nations. He manages our concerns with foreign nations and must necessarily be most competent to determine when, how, and upon what subjects negotiation may be urged with the greatest prospect of success. For his conduct he is responsible to the Constitution. The committee consider this responsibility the surest pledge for the faithful discharge of his duty. They think the interference of the Senate in the direction of foreign negotiations calculated to diminish that responsibility and thereby to impair the best security for the national safety. The nature of transactions with foreign nations, moreover, requires caution and unity of design, and their success frequently depends on secrecy and dispatch.

30

RUFUS KING, AFRICAN SLAVE TRADE, SENATE
12 Jan. 1818
Annals 31:106–7

Without adverting to the several branches of the executive power, for the purpose of distinguishing the cases in which it is exclusively vested in the President, from those in which it is vested in him jointly with the Senate, it will suffice on this occasion to observe that, in respect to foreign affairs, the President has no exclusive binding power, except that of receiving the Ambassadors and other foreign Ministers, which, as it involves the decision of the competence of the power which sends them, may be an act of this character; to the validity of all other definitive proceedings in the management of the foreign affairs, the Constitutional advice and consent of the Senate are indispensable.

In these concerns the Senate are the Constitutional and the only responsible counsellors of the President. And in this capacity the Senate may, and ought to, look into and watch over every branch of the foreign affairs of the nation; they may, therefore, at any time call for full and exact information respecting the foreign affairs, and express their opinion and advice to the President respecting the same, when, and under whatever other circumstances, they may think such advice expedient.

There is a peculiar jealousy manifested in the Constitution concerning the power which shall manage the foreign affairs, and make treaties with foreign nations. Hence the provision which requires the consent of two-thirds of the Senators to confirm any compact with a foreign nation that shall bind the United States; thus putting it in the power of a minority of the Senators, or States to control the President and a majority of the Senate: a check on the Executive power to be found in no other case.

To make a treaty includes all the proceedings by which it is made; and the advice and consent of the Senate being necessary in the making of treaties, must necessarily be so, touching the measures employed in making the same. The Constitution does not say that treaties shall be concluded, but that they shall be made, by and with the advice and consent of the Senate: none therefore can be made without such advice and consent; and the objections against the agency of the Senate in making treaties, or in advising the President to make the same, cannot be sustained, but by giving to the Constitution an interpretation different from its obvious and most salutary meaning.

To support the objection, this gloss must be given to the Constitution, "that the President shall make treaties, and by and with the advice and consent of the Senate ratify the same." That this is, or could have been intended to be the interpretation of the Constitution, one observation will disprove. If the President alone has power to make a treaty, and the same be made pursuant to the powers and instructions given to his Minister, its ratification follows as a matter of course, and to refuse the same would be a violation of good faith; to call in the Senate to deliberate, to advise, and to consent to an act which it would be binding on them to approve and ratify, will, it is presumed, be deemed too trivial to satisfy the extraordinary provision of the Constitution, that has been cited.

31

JAMES KENT, COMMENTARIES 1:154–68
1826

The object of war is peace, and it is the duty of every belligerent power to make war fulfil its end with the least possible mischief, and to accelerate, by all fair and reasonable means, a just and honourable peace. The same power which has the right to declare and carry on war, would seem naturally to be the proper power to make and conclude a treaty of peace; but the disposition of this power will depend upon the local constitution of every nation; and it sometimes happens, that the power of making peace is committed to a body of men who have not the power to make war. In Sweden, after the death of Charles XII. the king could declare war without the consent of the national Diet, but he made peace in conjunction with the Senate. So, by the constitution of the United States, the President, by and with the advice and consent of two thirds of the Senate, may make peace, but it is reserved to Congress to declare war. This provision in our constitution is well adapted (as will be shown more fully hereafter) to unite in the negotiation and conclusion of treaties, the advantage of talents, experience, stability, and a comprehensive knowledge of national interests, with the requisite secrecy and despatch.

Treaties of peace, when made by the competent power, are obligatory upon the whole nation. If the treaty requires the payment of money to carry it into effect, and the money cannot be raised but by an act of the legislature, the treaty is morally obligatory upon the legislature to pass the law, and to refuse it would be a breach of public faith. The department of the government that is intrusted by the constitution with the treaty making power, is competent to bind the national faith in its discretion; for the power to make treaties of peace must be coextensive with all the exigencies of the nation, and necessarily involves in it that portion of the national sovereignty which has the exclusive direction of all diplomatic negotiations and contracts with foreign powers. All treaties made by that power become of absolute efficacy, because they are the supreme law of the land.

There can be no doubt that the power competent to bind the nation by treaty, may alienate the public domain and property by treaty. If a nation has conferred upon its executive department, without reserve, the right of treating and contracting with other states, it is considered as having invested it with all the power necessary to make a valid contract. That department is the organ of the nation, and the alienations by it are valid, because they are done by the reputed will of the nation. The fundamental laws of a state may withhold from the executive department the power of alienating what belongs to the state, but if there be no express provision of that kind, the inference is, that it has confided to the department charged with the power of making treaties, a discretion commensurate with all the great interests, and wants, and necessities of the nation. A power to make treaties of peace necessarily implies a power to decide the terms on which they shall be made, and foreign states could not deal safely with the government upon any other presumption. The power that is intrusted generally and largely with authority to make valid treaties of peace, can, of course, bind the nation by alienation of part of its territory, and this is equally the case whether that territory be already in the occupation of the enemy, or remains in the possession of the nation, and whether the property be public or private. In the case of the schooner *Peggy*, the Supreme Court of the United States admitted, that individual rights acquired by war, and vested rights of the citizens, might be sacrificed by treaty for national purposes. So, in the case of *Ware* v. *Hylton*, it was said to be a clear principle of national law, that private rights might be sacrificed by treaty to secure the public safety, though the government would be bound to make compensation and indemnity to the individuals whose rights had thus been surrendered. The power to alienate, and the duty to make compensation, are both laid down by Grotius in equally explicit terms.

A treaty of peace is valid and binding on the nation, if made with the present ruling power of the nation, or the government *de facto*. Other nations have no right to interfere with the domestic affairs of any particular nation, or to examine and judge of the title of the party in possession of the supreme authority. They are to look only to the fact of possession. And it is an acknowledged rule of international law, that the principal party in whose name the war is made, cannot justly make peace without including those defensive allies in the pacification who have afforded assistance, though they may not have acted as principals; for it would be faithless and cruel for the principal in the war to leave his weaker ally to the full force of the enemy's resentment. The ally is, however, to be no farther a party to the stipulations and obligations of the treaty, than he has been willing to consent. All that the principal can require, is, that his ally be considered as restored to a state of peace. Every alliance in which all the parties are principals in the war, obliges the allies to treat in concert, though each one makes a separate treaty of peace for himself.

The effect of a treaty of peace is to put an end to the war, and to abolish the subject of it. Peace relates to the war which it terminates. It is an agreement to waive all discussion concerning the respective rights of the parties, and to bury in oblivion all the original causes of the war. It forbids the revival of the same war, by taking arms for the cause which at first kindled it, though it is no objection to any subsequent pretensions to the same thing, on other foundations. After peace, the revival of grievances arising before the war is not to be encouraged, for treaties of peace are intended to put an end to such complaints; and if grievances then existing are not brought forward at the time when peace is concluded, it is to be presumed that it is not intended to bring them forward at any future time. Peace leaves the contracting parties without any right of committing hostility for the very cause which kindled the war, or for what has passed in the course of it. It is, therefore, no longer permitted to take up arms again for the same cause. But this will not preclude the right to complain and resist, if the same grievances which kindled the war be renewed and repeated, for that would furnish a new injury and a new cause of war equally just with the former war. If an abstract right be in question between the parties, the right, for instance, to impress at sea one's own subjects, from the merchant vessels of the other, and the parties make peace without taking any notice of the question, it follows, of course, that all past grievances, damages, and injury, arising under such claim, are thrown into oblivion, by the amnesty which every treaty implies; but the claim itself is not thereby settled, either one way or the other. It remains open for future discussion, because the treaty wanted an express concession or renunciation of the claim itself.

A treaty of peace leaves every thing in the state in which it finds it, if there be no express stipulation on the subject. If nothing be said in a treaty of peace about the conquered country or places, they remain with the possessor, and his title cannot afterwards be called in question. During war, the conqueror has only a usufructuary right to the territory he has subdued, and the latent right and title of the former sovereign continues, until a treaty of peace, by its silence, or by its express stipulation, shall have extinguished his title for ever.

The peace does not affect rights which had no relation to the war. Debts existing prior to the war, and injuries committed prior to the war, but which made no part of the reasons for undertaking it, remain entire, and the remedies are revived. There are certain cases in which even debts contracted, or injuries committed, between two subjects of the belligerent powers, during the war, are the ground of a valid claim. This would be the case if the debt between them was contracted, or the injury was committed, in a neutral country.

A treaty of peace binds the contracting parties from the moment of its conclusion. But, like a truce, it cannot affect the subjects of the nation with guilt, by reason of acts of hostility subsequent to the date of the treaty, provided they were committed before the treaty was known. All that can be required in such cases is, that the government make immediate restitution of things captured after the cessation of hostilities; and to guard against inconvenience from the want of due knowledge of the treaty, it is usual to fix the periods at which hostilities are to cease at different places, and for the restitution of property taken afterwards.

But though individuals are not deemed criminal for continuing hostilities after the date of the peace, so long as they are ignorant of it, a more difficult question to determine is, whether they are responsible, *civiliter*, in such cases. Grotius says, they are not liable to answer in damages, but it is the duty of the government to restore what has been captured and not destroyed. In the case of the American ship *Mentor*, which was taken and destroyed, off Delaware bay, by British ships of war, in 1783, after the cessation of hostilities, but before that fact had come to the knowledge of either of the parties, the point was much discussed; and it was held, that the injured party could not pass over the person from whom the alleged injury had been received, and fix it on the commander of the English squadron on that station, who was totally ignorant of the whole transaction, and at the distance of thirty leagues from the place where it passed. There was no instance in the annals of the prize courts, of such a remote and consequential responsibility, in such a case. The actual wrongdoer is the person to answer in judgment, and to him the responsibility (if any) is attached. He may have other persons responsible over to him, but the injured party could look only to him. The better opinion was, that though such an act be done through ignorance of the cessation of hostilities, yet mere ignorance of that fact would not protect the officer from civil responsibility in a prize court; and that, if he acted through ignorance, his own government must protect him and save him harmless. When a place or country is exempted from hostility by articles of peace, it is the duty of the government to use due diligence to give its subjects notice of the fact, and the government ought, in justice, to indemnify its subjects, who act in ignorance of the peace. And yet it would seem, from that case, that the American owner was denied redress in the British admiralty, not only against the admiral of the fleet on that station, but against the immediate author of the injury. Sir William Scott denied the relief against the admiral; and ten years before that time, relief had equally been denied by his predecessor, against the person who did the injury. If that decision was erroneous, an appeal ought to have been prosecuted. We have then the decision of the English High Court of Admiralty, denying any relief in such a case, and an opinion of Sir William Scott, many years afterwards, that the original wrong-doer was liable. The opinions cannot otherwise be reconciled, than upon the ground that the prize courts have a large and equitable discretion, in allowing or withholding relief, according to the special circumstances of the individual case; and that there is no fixed or inflexible general rule on the subject.

If a time be fixed by the treaty for hostilities to cease in a given place, and a capture be previously made, but with knowledge of the peace, it has been a question among the writers on public law, whether the captured property should be restored. The better, and the more reasonable opinion, is, that the capture would be null, though made before the day limited, provided the captor was previously informed of the peace; for, as Emerigon observes, since constructive knowledge of the peace, after the time limited

in the different parts of the world, renders the capture void, much more ought actual knowledge of the peace to produce that effect.

Another question arose subsequent to the treaty of Ghent of 1814, in one of the British vice-admiralty courts, on the validity of a recapture by a British ship of war, of a British vessel captured by an American privateer. The capture made by the American cruiser was valid, being made before the period fixed for the cessation of hostilities, and in ignorance of the fact; but the prize had not been carried into port and condemned, and while at sea she was recaptured by the British cruiser after the period fixed for the cessation of hostilities, but without knowledge of the peace. It was decided, that the possession of the vessel by the American privateer was a lawful possession, and that the British cruiser could not, after the peace, lawfully use force to divest this lawful possession. The restoration of peace put an end, from the time limited, to all force, and then the general principle applied, that things acquired in war remain, as to title and possession, precisely as they stood when the peace took place. The *uti possidetis* is the basis of every treaty of peace, unless it be otherwise agreed. Peace gives a final and perfect title to captures without condemnation, and as it forbids all force, it destroys all hopes of recovery as much as if the vessel was carried *infra praesidia*, and condemned. A similar doctrine was held in the case of the schooner *Sophie*, and the treaty of peace had the effect of quieting all titles of possession arising from the war, and of putting an end to the claim of all former proprietors, to things of which possession was acquired by right of war.

If nothing be said to the contrary, things stipulated to be restored are to be returned in the condition they were taken; but this does not relate to alterations which have been the natural consequence of time, and of the operations of war. A fortress or a town is to be restored in that condition it was when taken, as far as it shall still be in the condition when the peace is made. There is no obligation to repair, as well as restore, a dismantled fortress, or a ravaged territory. The peace extinguishes all claim for damages done in war, or arising from the operations of war. Things are to be restored in the condition the peace found them; and to dismantle a fortification, or to waste a country, after the conclusion of the peace, and previous to the surrender, would be an act of perfidy.

Treaties of every kind, when made by the competent authority, are as obligatory upon nations, as private contracts are binding upon individuals; and they are to receive a fair and liberal interpretation, and to be kept with the most scrupulous good faith. Their meaning is to be ascertained by the same rules of construction and course of reasoning which we apply to the interpretation of private contracts. If a treaty should in fact be violated by one of the contracting parties, either by proceedings incompatible with the particular nature of the treaty, or by an intentional breach of any of its articles, it rests alone with the injured party to pronounce it broken. The treaty, in such a case, is not absolutely void, but voidable, at the election of the injured party. If he chooses not to come to a rupture, the treaty remains obligatory. He may waive or remit the infraction committed, or he may demand a just satisfaction.

There is a very material and important distinction made by the writers on public law, between a new war for some new cause, and a breach of a treaty of peace. In the former case, the rights acquired by the treaty subsist, notwithstanding the new war; but, in the latter case, they are annulled by the breach of the treaty of peace, on which they are founded. A new war may interrupt the exercise of the rights acquired by the former treaty, and, like other rights, they may be wrested from the party by the force of arms. But then they become newly acquired rights, and partake of the operation and result of the new war. To re-commence a war, by breach of the articles of a treaty of peace, is deemed much more odious than to provoke a war by some new demand and aggression, for the latter is simply injustice, but, in the former case, the party is guilty both of perfidy and injustice. The violation of any one article of a treaty, is a violation of the whole treaty; for all the articles are dependent on each other, and one is to be deemed a condition of the other, and a violation of any single article overthrows the whole treaty, if the injured party elects so to consider it. This may, however, be prevented by an express provision, that if one article be broken, the others shall, nevertheless, continue in full force. We have a strong instance in our own history of the annihilation of treaties by the act of the injured party. In 1798, the Congress of the United States declared that the treaties with France were no longer obligatory on the United States, as they had been repeatedly violated on the part of the French government, and all just claims for reparation refused.

As a general rule, the obligations of treaties are dissipated by hostility. But if a treaty contains any stipulations which contemplate a state of future war, and make provision for such an exigency, they preserve their force and obligation when the rupture takes place. All those duties of which the exercise is not necessarily suspended by the war, subsist in their full force. The obligation of keeping faith is so far from ceasing in time of war, that its efficacy becomes increased, from the increased necessity of it. What would become of prisoners of war, and the terms of capitulation of garrisons and towns, if the word of an enemy was not to be relied on? The faith of promises and treaties which have reference to a state of war, is to be held as sacred in war as in peace, and among enemies as among friends. All the writers on public law admit this position, and they have never failed to recommend the duty and the observance of good faith, by the most powerful motives, and the most pathetic and eloquent appeals which could be addressed to the reason and to the moral sense of nations. The 10th article of the treaty between the United States and Great Britain, in 1794, may be mentioned as an instance of a stipulation made for war. It provided, that debts due from individuals of the one nation to those of the other, and the shares or moneys which they might have in the public funds, or in public or private banks, should never, in any event of war, be sequestered or confiscated. There can be no doubt that the obligation of that article was not impaired by the war of 1812, but remained throughout that war, and continues to this day, binding

upon the two nations, and will continue so until they mutually agree to rescind the article; for it is a principle of universal jurisprudence, that a compact cannot be rescinded by one party only, if the other party does not consent to rescind it, and does no act to destroy it. In the case of *The Society for Propagating the Gospel* v. *New-Haven*, the Supreme Court of the United States would not admit the doctrine that treaties became extinguished *ipso facto* by war, unless revived by an express or implied renewal on the return of peace. Such a doctrine is not universally true. Where treaties contemplate a permanent arrangement of national rights, or which, by their terms, are meant to provide for the event of an intervening war, it would be against every principle of just interpretation to hold them extinguished by the event of war. They revive at peace, unless waived, or new and repugnant stipulations be made.

With respect to the cession of places or territories by a treaty of peace, though the treaty operates from the making of it, it is a principle of public law, that the national character of the place agreed to be surrendered by treaty, continues as it was under the character of the ceding country, until it be actually transferred. Full sovereignty cannot be held to have passed by the mere words of the treaty, without actual delivery. To complete the right of property, the right to the thing, and the possession of the thing, must be united. This is a necessary principle in the law of property in all systems of jurisprudence. There must be both the *jus in rem*, and the *jus in re*, according to the distinction of the civilians, and which Barbeyrac says they borrowed from the canon law. This general law of property applies to the right of territory no less than to other rights. The practice of nations has been conformable to this principle, and the conventional law of nations is full of instances of this kind, and several of them were stated by Sir Wm. Scott in the opinion which he gave in the case of the *Fama*.

The release of a territory from the dominion and sovereignty of the country, if that cession be the result of coercion or conquest, does not impose any obligation upon the government to indemnify those who may suffer a loss of property by the cession. The annals of our own state furnish a strong illustration of this position. The territory composing the state of Vermont belonged to this state, and it separated from it, and erected itself into an independent state, without the consent, and against the will, of the government of this state. The latter continued for many years to object to the separation, and to discover the strongest disposition to reclaim by force the allegiance of the inhabitants of that state. But they were unable to do it; and it was the case of a revolution effected by force, analogous to that which was then in action between this country and Great Britain. And when this state found itself under the necessity of acknowledging the independence of Vermont, a question arose before our legislature, whether they were bound in duty to make compensation to individual citizens whose property would be sacrificed by the event, because their titles to land lying within the jurisdiction of Vermont, and derived from New-York, would be disregarded by the government of that state. The claimants were heard at the bar of the House of Assembly, by counsel, in 1787, and it was contended on their behalf, that the state was bound, upon the principles of the social compact, to protect and defend the rights and property of all its members, and that, whenever it became necessary, upon grounds of public expediency and policy, to withdraw the protection of government from the property of any of its citizens, without actually making the utmost efforts to reclaim the jurisdiction of the country, the state was bound to make compensation for the loss. In answer to this argument, it was stated, that the independence of Vermont was an act of force beyond the power of this state to control, and equivalent to a conquest of that territory, and the state had not the competent ability to recover, by force of arms, their sovereignty over it, and it would have been folly and ruin to have attempted it. All pacific means had been tried without success, and as the state was compelled to yield to a case of necessity, it had discharged its duty, and it was not required, upon any of the doctrines of public law, or principles of political or moral obligation, to indemnify the sufferers. The cases in which compensation had been made for losses consequent upon revolutions in government, were peculiar and gratuitous, and rested entirely on benevolence, and were given from motives of policy, or as a reward for extraordinary acts of loyalty and exertion. No government can be supposed to be able, consistently with the welfare of the whole community, and it is, therefore, not required, to assume the burthen of losses produced by conquest, or the violent dismemberment of the state. It would be incompatible with the fundamental principles of the social compact.

This was the doctrine which prevailed in the legislature of this state; and when the act of July 14th, 1789, was passed, authorizing commissioners to declare the consent of the state to the independence of Vermont, it was expressly declared, that the act was not to be construed to give any person claiming lands in Vermont, under title from this state, any right to any compensation whatsoever from New-York.

32

WILLIAM RAWLE, A VIEW OF THE CONSTITUTION OF THE UNITED STATES 195–96
1829 (2d ed.)

The power of receiving foreign ambassadors, carries with it among other things, the right of judging in the case of a revolution in a foreign country, whether the new rulers ought to be recognised. The legislature indeed possesses a superior power, and may declare its dissent from the executive recognition or refusal, but until that sense is declared, the act of the executive is binding. The judicial power can take no notice of a new government, till one or the other of those two departments has acted on it. Circumstances may render the decision of great importance to the interests and peace of the country. A precipitate acknowledgement of the independence of part of a foreign nation, separating itself from its former head, may provoke the resentment of the latter: a refusal to do so, may disgust the former, and prevent the attainment of amity and commerce with them, if they succeed. The principles on which the separation takes place must also be taken into consideration, and if they are conformable to those which led to our own independence, and appear likely to be preserved, a strong impulse will arise in favour of a recognition; because it may be for our national interest, which the president is bound pre-eminently to consult, to promote the dissemination and establishment, at least in our own neighbourhood, of those principles which form the strongest foundations of good government.

But the most accurate and authentic information should be procured of the actual state and prospect of success of such newly erected states, for it would not be justifiable in the president to involve the country in difficulties, merely in support of an abstract principle, if there was not a reasonable prospect of perseverance and success on the part of those who have embarked in the enterprise. The caution of President Monroe in sending commissioners to South America, for the purpose of making inquiries on the spot, in preference to a reliance on vague rumours and partial representations, was highly commendable.

The power of congress on this subject cannot be controlled; they may, if they think proper, acknowledge a small and helpless community, though with a certainty of drawing a war upon our country; but greater circumspection is required from the president, who, not having the constitutional power to declare war, ought ever to abstain from a measure likely to produce it.

Among other incidents arising from foreign relations, it may be noticed that congress, which cannot conveniently be always in session, may devolve on the president, duties that at first view seem to belong only to themselves. It has been decided, that a power given to the president to revive an act relating to foreign intercourse, when certain measures, having a described effect should take place on the part of two foreign nations, was perfectly constitutional. The law thus rendered him the responsible judge of that effect.

33

UNITED STATES V. BENNER
24 Fed. Cas. 1084, no. 14,568 (C.C.E.D.Pa. 1830)

BALDWIN, Circuit Justice (charging jury). By the constitution of the United States, the power of receiving ambassadors and other public ministers, is vested in the president of the United States; this power is plenary and supreme, with which no other department of the government can interfere, and when exercised by the president, carries with it all the sanction which the constitution can give to an act done by its authority. In the reception of ambassadors and ministers, the president is the government, he judges of the mode of reception, and by the act of reception, the person so received, becomes at once clothed with all the immunities which the law of nations and the United States, attach to the diplomatic character.

The evidence of the reception of Mr. Brandis in this character, is the certificate from the secretary of the state which has been read. By the law organizing the department of state, it is the special duty of this officer, to perform all such duties as shall be entrusted to him by the president, to conduct the business of the department in such manner as he shall order and instruct, also to take an oath for the faithful performance of his duties. He is denominated in the law, "the secretary of foreign affairs;" his appropriate duties are, correspondence and communication with foreign ministers under the orders of the president; he has the custody of all the papers and archives of the department in relation to the concerns of the United States with foreign nations. Whatever act then is done by that department must be taken to be done by the orders or instructions of the president; the certificate of the secretary under the seal, oath, and responsibility of office, must also be taken as full evidence of the act certified. The president acts in that department through the secretary, the one directs, the other performs the duties assigned; the law makes that department with all its officers, the agent of the executive branch of the government, so that a certificate under its seal by the secretary is full evidence, that what has been done by the department has been done by it in that capacity. If the law imposed on that department any duties upon subjects over which the president had no control, or none exclusive of the other branches of the government, a certificate from its chief officer would not be evidence that it was done by the president; but as it can act on no subject unless under his orders, its acts must be taken to be his, especially as to the reception of ministers, as to which congress has no power to enjoin any duties on the department, or its officers.

You will therefore consider Mr. Brandis as having been recognised by the president in the character of an attaché to the legation of Denmark in the United States; and that such recognition is, per se, an authorization and reception of him, within the meaning of the act of congress, for we cannot presume, that the president would recognise a minister, without receiving him. In the case of U. S. v. Liddle [Case No. 15,598], it was held by this court, that a certificate from the secretary of state, that a chargé d'affaires of Spain, had introduced a person to the president as an attaché and secretary to that legation, was evidence of his reception as such. U. S. v. Liddle [supra]; U. S. v. Ortega [Case No. 15,971]. Such recognition invests him with the immunities of a minister, in whatever form it may be done, and no court or jury can require any other evidence of a reception: we instruct you then as a matter of law, that at the time of the alleged arrest, Mr. Brandis was a minister of Denmark in the character stated in the certificate.

The only remaining question is, whether he was arrested, imprisoned, or violence offered to his person by the defendant. An arrest is the taking, seizing or detaining the person of another, touching or putting hands upon him in the execution of process, or any act indicating an intention to arrest. Imprisonment is the detention of another against his will, depriving him of the power of locomotion: if you believe the witnesses, the evidence fully establishes these charges in the indictment. Whether Mr. Brandis submitted or consented to the arrest is not material. The privileges of a foreign minister are not personal, nor is their violation punished as an injury to himself, the immunity from arrest is the privilege of the sovereign who sends him, the injury is done to him, in the person of his representative. The laws of nations protect the minister, that he may not be obstructed in the business of his mission, his person is as inviolable as his sovereign, within whose territory he is presumed to reside.

Hence the laws of the country to which he is sent, can no more be enforced against him, than in the country from whence he came; being considered as in the territory of his own sovereign, no other has any jurisdiction over him. The consent of the sovereign to the violation of the rights and privileges which belong to himself, either in person or in his representative, are equally necessary, whether the minister resides in a foreign country or his own. The general law of all nations, as well as the municipal laws of each, exempt ministers from all jurisdiction or control over their persons, so long as their representative character is recognised by the government which sends or receives them; if they exercise the functions of ministers, or retain that character, their exemptions attach to their office whether they claim them or not. There is no principle of national law, or any word in the act of congress, which justifies the arrest of a minister who waives the privileges of the diplomatic character, you will therefore dismiss all considerations of this kind from your minds. But though the person of a minister is inviolable, yet he is not exempted from the law of self defence; if he unlawfully assaults another, the attack may be repelled by as much force as will prevent its continuance or repetition. The counsel for the defendant has endeavoured to bring his case within this principle, by evidence that he received a blow from Mr. Brandis; were the fact so, however, it would be no justification of the arrest on process, which is not a right of self defence.

It is objected to this prosecution, that the defendant was not an officer within the meaning of the law; but this objection cannot avail him, the warrant was directed "to the constable of ——— ward," the defendant assumed and acted in that character in the execution of the warrant, and must be considered as one de facto estopped by his acts from denying it.

It is next contended that it must be proved that the defendant knew Mr. Brandis to be a minister at the time of the arrest; the law does not make knowledge an ingredient in the offence, the case meets fully the definition of the offence prohibited by the act of congress, which, as a general rule, is all that is requisite to find a verdict of guilty; this objection has been overruled by this court in other cases,— U. S. v. Liddle [supra]; U. S. v. Ortega [supra],—and, we think, very properly.

. . . . .

HOPKINSON, District Judge. The defendant was put upon his trial upon an indictment containing six counts. The first charged, that he did imprison one Louis Brandis, he being public minister, to wit, the secretary of the legation from his majesty the king of Denmark, near the United States of America. The second, that he did imprison the said Louis Brandis, he being a public minister, to wit, an attaché to the legation of his majesty the king of Denmark, near the United States. The third sets forth that a certain writ was sued forth and prosecuted by one George Wilson, from one John Binns, an alderman of the city of Philadelphia, whereby the person of the said Louis Brandis, a public minister, the secretary of the legation of his majesty the king of Denmark, authorized and received as such by the president of the United States, was arrested; and that the defendant, Peter R. Benner, being an officer, to wit, a constable of the city of Philadelphia, did execute the said writ and thereby arrest the person of the said Louis Brandis. The fourth is the same with the third, except that Louis Brandis is styled an attaché of the legation of his majesty the king of Denmark. The fifth charges, that the defendant did offer violence to the person of the said Louis Brandis, a public minister, to wit, the secretary of the legation of his majesty the king of Denmark. And the sixth is the same with the fifth, except that Louis Brandis is styled an attaché to the legation. After a full hearing upon all the facts and law of the case, it was given to the jury under a charge from the court, in which the evidence was reviewed, and the questions of law distinctly answered. The jury returned with a verdict of conviction on the second count of the indictment, and of acquittal as to all the others. The counsel of the defendant has filed certain reasons in arrest of the judgment on this conviction; and other reasons for a new trial. Both motions have been elaborately argued, and are now to be decided.

The reasons in arrest of judgment are two: (1) That the only count on which the verdict is given against the accused does not describe him as an officer; does not charge him with having executed process, nor state any offence against any act of congress or law of the United States. (2) That the said count does not state that a public minister of any foreign power or state, authorized and received as such by the president of the United States, was imprisoned, or was or might have been arrested or imprisoned.

The act of congress upon which this indictment is framed provides, in its different sections, for different classes of cases, and the counts of the indictment are made to meet the different provisions of these sections. The twenty-fifth section enacts, that if any writ or process shall be sued forth or prosecuted in any of the courts of the United States, or of a particular state, whereby the person of any ambassador or other public minister of any foreign prince or state, authorized and received as such by the president of the United States, may be arrested or imprisoned, &c., such writ or process shall be adjudged to be utterly null and void. The twenty-sixth section enacts that in case any person or persons shall sue forth or prosecute any such writ or process, such person or persons, and all attorneys or solicitors prosecuting or soliciting in such case, and all officers executing any such writ or process,

being thereof convicted, &c. The twenty-seventh section enacts, that if any person shall violate any safe conduct, or passport duly obtained, and issued under the authority of the United States, or shall strike, wound, imprison, &c., by offering violence to the person of an ambassador or other public minister, such person, &c. The twenty-fifth and twenty-sixth sections afford protection and redress for public ministers, authorized and received as such by the president of the United States and against arrest and imprisonment under and by virtue of any writ or process sued forth and prosecuted in any court of the United States, or of a particular state, or by any judge or justice therein, and all the counts in this indictment intended to charge an offence in violation of these sections, do state that Louis Brandis was a public minister, authorized and received as such by the president of the United States; that a writ was sued forth against him from an alderman of the city of Philadelphia, and that the defendant, being an officer, did execute the said writ, and thereby arrest the person of the said Louis Brandis; upon these counts the defendant is acquitted by the verdict of the jury. The twenty-seventh section of the act is intended to cover other cases not described in the preceding sections, and makes it penal for any person to imprison the person of a public minister, although he may not be authorized and received as such by the president of the United States, and although the person who thus offers violence to his person, be not an officer, and does it not by virtue of any writ or process from any court, judge or justice. The count on which the defendant has been convicted, charges the offence punishable under this section of the act, and the offence is described in the indictment as it is described in the act; which does not require that the defendant should be an officer having executed process, nor that the public minister, who was imprisoned, should have been authorized and received as such by the president of the United States.

The reasons for a new trial will now be considered. The second count on which the defendant has been convicted, relates to the same transaction, and the same public minister as the first, of which he is acquitted, and differs from it only in describing the minister as an attaché to the legation of Denmark, and the first calls him the secretary of the legation; but it was the clear right of the jury, and so it was given them in charge, to find a general verdict of guilty, leaving it to the court to apply it to the counts in the indictment, or to select for themselves the count on which they would render the verdict, as in their opinion the evidence might warrant. If the count were bad in itself, such a verdict could not be maintained; but it is no objection to it, that it is substantially the same with another count on which the defendant has been acquitted, for the different counts of an indictment always relate to the same transaction, describing it in different ways, or with different circumstances, that the jury may apply their verdict to all or either of them, as the evidence shall warrant; or if the verdict be generally guilty, the application of it is made by the court. No injury or injustice is done to the defendant, who is put but once on his trial for the same offence. The jury, in this case, have not selected the count for their verdict of conviction to which the evidence most particularly applies; but this was for them to judge of, and is no cause of complaint on the part of the defendant; it cannot affect his punishment, and is clearly maintained by the evidence.

It is our opinion that the reasons filed in arrest of judgment are not maintained, and it is ordered that the motion be overruled.

34

JOSEPH STORY, COMMENTARIES ON THE CONSTITUTION 3:§§ 1517, 1559–64
1833

§ 1517. Some doubts appear to have been entertained in the early stages of the government, as to the correct exposition of the constitution in regard to the agency of the senate in the formation of treaties. The question was, whether the agency of the senate was admissible previous to the negotiation, so as to advise on the instructions to be given to the ministers; or was limited to the exercise of the power of advice and consent, after the treaty was formed; or whether the president possessed an option to adopt one mode, or the other, as his judgment might direct. The practical exposition assumed on the first occasion, which seems to have occurred in President Washington's administration, was, that the option belonged to the executive to adopt either mode, and the senate might advise before, as well as after, the formation of a treaty. Since that period, the senate have been rarely, if ever, consulted, until after a treaty has been completed, and laid before them for ratification. When so laid before the senate, that body is in the habit of deliberating upon it, as, indeed, it does on all *executive* business, in secret, and with closed doors. The senate may wholly reject the treaty, or advise and consent to a ratification of part of the articles, rejecting others, or recommend additional or explanatory articles. In the event of a partial ratification, the treaty does not become the law of the land, until the president and the foreign sovereign have each assented to the modifications proposed by the senate. But, although the president may ask the advice and consent of the senate to a treaty, he is not absolutely bound by it; for he may, after it is given, still constitutionally refuse to ratify it. Such an occurrence will probably be rare, because the president will scarcely incline to lay a treaty before the senate, which he is not disposed to ratify.

. . . . .

§ 1559. The next power is to receive ambassadors and other public ministers. This has been already incidentally touched. A similar power existed under the confederation; but it was confined to receiving "ambassadors," which word, in a strict sense, (as has been already stated,) comprehends the highest grade only of ministers, and not those of an inferior character. The policy of the United States would ordinarily prefer the employment of the in-

ferior grades; and therefore the description is properly enlarged, so as to include all classes of ministers. Why the receiving of consuls was not also expressly mentioned, as the appointment of them is in the preceding clause, is not easily to be accounted for, especially as the defect of the confederation on this head was fully understood. The power, however, may be fairly inferred from other parts of the constitution; and indeed seems a general incident to the executive authority. It has constantly been exercised without objection; and foreign consuls have never been allowed to discharge any functions of office, until they have received the exequatur of the president. Consuls, indeed, are not diplomatic functionaries, or political representatives of a foreign nation; but are treated in the character of mere commercial agents.

§ 1560. The power to receive ambassadors and ministers is always an important, and sometimes a very delicate function; since it constitutes the only accredited medium, through which negotiations and friendly relations are ordinarily carried on with foreign powers. A government may in its discretion lawfully refuse to receive an ambassador, or other minister, without its affording any just cause of war. But it would generally be deemed an unfriendly act, and might provoke hostilities, unless accompanied by conciliatory explanations. A refusal is sometimes made on the ground of the bad character of the minister, or his former offensive conduct, or of the special subject of the embassy not being proper, or convenient for discussion. This, however, is rarely done. But a much more delicate occasion is, when a civil war breaks out in a nation, and two nations are formed, or two parties in the same nation, each claiming the sovereignty of the whole, and the contest remains as yet undecided, *flagrante bello*. In such a case a neutral nation may very properly withhold its recognition of the supremacy of either party, or of the existence of two independent nations; and on that account refuse to receive an ambassador from either. It is obvious, that in such cases the simple acknowledgment of the minister of either party, or nation, might be deemed taking part against the other; and thus as affording a strong countenance, or opposition, to rebellion and civil dismemberment. On this account, nations, placed in such a predicament, have not hesitated sometimes to declare war against neutrals, as interposing in the war; and have made them the victims of their vengeance, when they have been anxious to assume a neutral position. The exercise of this prerogative of acknowledging new nations, or ministers, is, therefore, under such circumstances, an executive function of great delicacy, which requires the utmost caution and deliberation. If the executive receives an ambassador, or other minister, as the representative of a new nation, or of a party in a civil war in an old nation, it is an acknowledgment of the sovereign authority *de facto* of such new nation, or party. If such recognition is made, it is conclusive upon the nation, unless indeed it can be reversed by an act of congress repudiating it. If, on the other hand, such recognition has been refused by the executive, it is said, that congress may, notwithstanding, solemnly acknowledge the sovereignty of the nation, or party. These, however, are propositions, which have hitherto remained, as abstract statements, under the constitution; and, therefore, can be propounded, not as absolutely true, but as still open to discussion, if they should ever arise in the course of our foreign diplomacy. The constitution has expressly invested the executive with power to receive ambassadors, and other ministers. It has not expressly invested congress with the power, either to repudiate, or acknowledge them. At all events, in the case of a revolution, or dismemberment of a nation, the judiciary cannot take notice of any new government, or sovereignty, until it has been duly recognised by some other department of the government, to whom the power is constitutionally confided.

§ 1561. That a power, so extensive in its reach over our foreign relations, could not be properly conferred on any other, than the executive department, will admit of little doubt. That it should be exclusively confided to that department, without any participation of the senate in the functions, (that body being conjointly entrusted with the treaty-making power,) is not so obvious. Probably the circumstance, that in all foreign governments the power was exclusively confided to the executive department, and the utter impracticability of keeping the senate constantly in session, and the suddenness of the emergencies, which might require the action of the government, conduced to the establishment of the authority in its present form. It is not, indeed, a power likely to be abused; though it is pregnant with consequences, often involving the question of peace and war. And, in our own short experience, the revolutions in France, and the revolutions in South America, have already placed us in situations, to feel its critical character, and the necessity of having, at the head of the government, an executive of sober judgment, enlightened views, and firm and exalted patriotism.

§ 1562. As incidents to the power to receive ambassadors and foreign ministers, the president is understood to possess the power to refuse them, and to dismiss those who, having been received, become obnoxious to censure, or unfit to be allowed the privilege, by their improper conduct, or by political events. While, however, they are permitted to remain, as public functionaries, they are entitled to all the immunities and rights, which the law of nations has provided at once for their dignity, their independence, and their inviolability.

§ 1563. There are other incidental powers, belonging to the executive department, which are necessarily implied from the nature of the functions, which are confided to it. Among these, must necessarily be included the power to perform them, without any obstruction or impediment whatsoever. The president cannot, therefore, be liable to arrest, imprisonment, or detention, while he is in the discharge of the duties of his office; and for this purpose his person must be deemed, in civil cases at least, to possess an official inviolability. In the exercise of his political powers he is to use his own discretion, and is accountable only to his country, and to his own conscience. His decision, in relation to these powers, is subject to no control; and his discretion, when exercised, is conclusive. But he has no authority to control other officers of the government, in relation to the duties imposed upon them by law, in cases not touching his political powers.

§ 1564. In the year 1793, president Washington thought it his duty to issue a proclamation, forbidding the citizens of the United States to take any part in the hostilities, then existing between Great Britain and France; warning them against carrying goods, contraband of war; and enjoining upon them an entire abstinence from all acts, inconsistent with the duties of neutrality. This proclamation had the unanimous approbation of his cabinet. Being, however, at variance with the popular passions and prejudices of the day, this exercise of incidental authority was assailed with uncommon vehemence, and was denied to be constitutional. It seems wholly unnecessary now to review the grounds of the controversy, since the deliberate sense of the nation has gone along with the exercise of the power, as one properly belonging to the executive duties. If the President is bound to see to the execution of the laws, and treaties of the United States; and if the duties of neutrality, when the nation has not assumed a belligerent attitude, are by the law of nations obligatory upon it, it seems difficult to perceive any solid objection to a proclamation, stating the facts, and admonishing the citizens of their own duties and responsibilities.

APPOINTMENT AND REMOVAL

35

WILLIAM BLACKSTONE, *Commentaries* 1:262
1765

From the same principle also arises the prerogative of erecting and disposing of offices: for honours and offices are in their nature convertible and synonymous. All offices under the crown carry in the eye of the law an honour along with them; because they imply a superiority of parts and abilities, being supposed to be always filled with those that are most able to execute them. And, on the other hand, all honours in their original had duties or offices annexed to them: an earl, *comes,* was the conservator or governor of a county; and a knight, *miles,* was bound to attend the king in his wars. For the same reason therefore that honours are in the disposal of the king, offices ought to be so likewise; and as the king may create new titles, so may he create new offices: but with this restriction, that he cannot create new offices with new fees annexed to them, nor annex new fees to old offices; for this would be a tax upon the subject, which cannot be imposed but by act of parliament. Wherefore, in 13 Hen. IV, a new office being created by the king's letters patent for measuring cloths, with a new fee for the same, the letters patent were, on account of the new fee, revoked and declared void in parliament.

36

LUTHER MARTIN, GENUINE INFORMATION
1788

Storing 2.4.86

To that part of this article also, which gives the President a right to *nominate,* and with the consent of the senate to appoint all the officers, civil and military, of the United States, there were considerable opposition—it was said that the person who *nominates,* will always in reality *appoint,* and that this was giving the President a power and influence, which together with the other powers, bestowed upon him, would place him above all restraint or controul. In fine, it was urged, that the President as here constituted, was a KING, in every thing but the name; that though he was to be chosen for a limited time, yet at the expiration of that time if he is not re-elected, it will depend entirely upon his own moderation whether he will resign that authority with which he has once been invested—that from his having the appointment of all the variety of officers in every part of the civil department for the union, who will be very numerous—in them and their connexions, relations, friends and dependants, he will have a formidable host devoted to his interest, and ready to support his ambitious views. That the army and navy, which may be encreased without restraint as to numbers, the officers of which, from the highest to the lowest, are all to be appointed by him, and dependant on his will and pleasure, and commanded by him in person, will, of course, be subservient to his wishes, and ready to execute his commands; in addition to which, the militia also are entirely subjected to his orders—That these circumstances, combined together, will enable him, when he pleases, to become a *King* in *name,* as well as in *substance,* and establish himself in office not only for his own life, but even if he chooses, to have that authority perpetuated to his family.

37

FEDERAL FARMER, NO. 13
14 Jan. 1788

Storing 2.8.169–70

(See 1.6.2, no. 4)

38

FEDERAL FARMER, NO. 14
17 Jan. 1788

Storing 2.8.173–76

To continue the subject of appointments:—Officers, in the fifth place, may be appointed by the heads of departments or courts of law. Art. 2. sect. 2. respecting appointments, goes on—"But congress may by law vest the appointment of such inferior officers as they think proper in the president alone, in the courts of law, or in the heads of departments." The probability is, as the constitution now stands, that the senate, a branch of the legislature, will be tenacious of the power of appointment, and much too sparingly part with a share of it to the courts of law, and heads of departments. Here again the impropriety appears of the senate's having, generally, a share in the appointment of officers. We may fairly presume, that the judges, and principal officers in the departments, will be able well informed men in their respective branches of business; that they will, from experience, be best informed as to proper persons to fill inferior offices in them; that they will feel themselves responsible for the execution of their several branches of business, and for the conduct of the officers they may appoint therein.—From these, and other considerations, I think we may infer, that impartial and judicious appointments of subordinate officers will, generally, be made by the courts of law, and the heads of departments. This power of distributing appointments, as circumstances may require, into several hands, in a well formed disinterested legislature, might be of essential service, not only in promoting beneficial appointments, but, also, in preserving the balance in government: a feeble executive may be strengthened and supported by placing in its hands more numerous appointments; an executive too influential may be reduced within proper bounds, by placing many of the inferior appointments in the courts of law, and heads of departments; nor is there much danger that the executive will be wantonly weakened or strengthened by the legislature, by thus shifting the appointments of inferior officers, since all must be done by legislative acts, which cannot be passed without the consent of the executive, or the consent of two-thirds of both branches—a good legislature will use this power to preserve the balance and perpetuate the government. Here again we are brought to our ultimatum:—is the legislature so constructed as to deserve our confidence?

6. Officers may be appointed by the state governments. By art. I. sect. 8. the respective states are authorised exclusively to appoint the militia-officers. This not only lodges the appointments in proper places, but it also tends to distribute and lodge in different executive hands the powers of appointing to offices, so dangerous when collected into the hands of one or a few men.

It is a good general rule, that the legislative, executive, and judicial powers, ought to be kept distinct; but this, like other general rules, has its exceptions; and without these exceptions we cannot form a good government, and properly balance its parts, and we can determine only from reason, experience, and a critical inspection of the parts of the government, how far it is proper to intermix those powers. Appointment, I believe, in all mixed governments, have been assigned to different hands—some are made by the executive, some by the legislature, some by the judges and some by the people. It has been thought adviseable by the wisest nations, that the legislature should so far exercise executive and judicial powers as to appoint some officers, judge of the elections of its members, and impeach and try officers for misconduct—that the executive should have a partial share in legislation—that judges should appoint some subordinate officers, and regulate so far as to establish rules for their own proceedings. Where the members of the government, as the house, the senate, the executive, and judiciary, are strong and complete, each in itself, the balance is naturally produced, each party may take the powers congenial to it, and we have less need to be anxious about checks, and the subdivision of powers.

If after making the deductions, already alluded to, from the general power to appoint federal officers the residuum shall be thought to be too large and unsafe, and to place an undue influence in the hands of the president and council, a further deduction may be made, with many advantages, and, perhaps, with but a few inconveniencies; and that is, by giving the appointment of a few great officers to the legislature—as of the commissioners of the treasury—of the comptroller, treasurer, master coiner, and some of the principal officers in the money department—of the sheriffs or marshalls of the United States—of states attorneys, secretary of the home department, and secretary at war, perhaps, of the judges of the supreme court—of major-generals and admirals. The appointments of these officers, who may be at the heads of the great departments of business, in carrying into execution the national system, involve in them a variety of considerations; they will not often occur, and the power to make them ought to remain in safe hands. Officers of the above description are appointed by the legislatures in some of the states, and in some not. We may, I believe, presume that the federal legislature will possess sufficient knowledge and discernment to make judicious appointments; however, as these appointments by the legislature tend to increase a mixture of power, to lessen the advantages of impeachments and responsibility, I would by no means contend for them any further than it may be necessary for reducing the power of the executive within the bounds of safety. To determine with propriety how extensive power the executive ought to possess relative to appointments, we must also examine the forms of it, and its others powers; and these forms and other powers I shall now proceed briefly to examine.

39

ALEXANDER HAMILTON, FEDERALIST, NO. 76, 509–15
1 Apr. 1788

The President is "to *nominate* and by and with the advice and consent of the Senate to appoint Ambassadors, other public Ministers and Consuls, Judges of the Supreme Court, and all other officers of the United States, whose appointments are not otherwise provided for in the Constitution. But the Congress may by law vest the appointment of such inferior officers as they think proper in the President alone, or in the Courts of law, or in the heads of departments. The President shall have power to fill up *all vacancies* which may happen *during the recess of the Senate,* by granting commissions which shall *expire* at the end of their next session."

It has been observed in a former paper, "that the true test of a good government is its aptitude and tendency to produce a good administration." If the justness of this observation be admitted, the mode of appointing the officers of the United States contained in the foregoing clauses, must when examined be allowed to be entitled to particular commendation. It is not easy to conceive a plan better calculated than this, to produce a judicious choice of men for filling the offices of the Union; and it will not need proof, that on this point must essentially depend the character of its administration.

It will be agreed on all hands, that the power of appointment in ordinary cases ought to be modified in one of three ways. It ought either to be vested in a single man— or in a *select* assembly of a moderate number—or in a single man with the concurrence of such an assembly. The exercise of it by the people at large, will be readily admitted to be impracticable; as, waving every other consideration it would leave them little time to do any thing else. When therefore mention is made in the subsequent reasonings of an assembly or body of men, what is said must be understood to relate to a select body or assembly of the description already given. The people collectively from their number and from their dispersed situation cannot be regulated in their movements by that systematic spirit of cabal and intrigue, which will be urged as the chief objections to reposing the power in question in a body of men.

Those who have themselves reflected upon the subject, or who have attended to the observations made in other parts of these papers, in relation to the appointment of the President, will I presume agree to the position that there would always be great probability of having the place supplied by a man of abilities, at least respectable. Premising this, I proceed to lay it down as a rule, that one man of discernment is better fitted to analise and estimate the peculiar qualities adapted to particular offices, than a body of men of equal, or perhaps even of superior discernment.

The sole and undivided responsibility of one man will naturally beget a livelier sense of duty and a more exact regard to reputation. He will on this account feel himself under stronger obligations, and more interested to investigate with care the qualities requisite to the stations to be filled, and to prefer with impartiality the persons who may have the fairest pretentions to them. He will have *fewer* personal attachments to gratify than a body of men, who may each be supposed to have an equal number, and will be so much the less liable to be misled by the sentiments of friendship and of affection. A single well directed man by a single understanding, cannot be distracted and warped by that diversity of views, feelings and interests, which frequently distract and warp the resolutions of a collective body. There is nothing so apt to agitate the passions of mankind as personal considerations, whether they relate to ourselves or to others, who are to be the objects of our choice or preference. Hence, in every exercise of the power of appointing to offices by an assembly of men, we must expect to see a full display of all the private and party likings and dislikes, partialities and antipathies, attachments and animosities, which are felt by those who compose the assembly. The choice which may at any time happen to be made under such circumstances will of course be the result either of a victory gained by one party over the other, or of a compromise between the parties. In either case, the intrinsic merit of the candidate will be too often out of sight. In the first, the qualifications best adapted to uniting the suffrages of the party will be more considered than those which fit the person for the station. In the last the coalition will commonly turn upon some interested equivalent—"Give us the man we wish for this office, and you shall have the one you wish for that." This will be the usual condition of the bargain. And it will rarely happen that the advancement of the public service will be the primary object either of party victories or of party negociations.

The truth of the principles here advanced seems to have been felt by the most intelligent of those who have found fault with the provision made in this respect by the Convention. They contend that the President ought solely to have been authorized to make the appointments under the Fœderal Government. But it is easy to shew that every advantage to be expected from such an arrangement would in substance be derived from the power of *nomination,* which is proposed to be conferred upon him; while several disadvantages which might attend the absolute power of appointment in the hands of that officer, would be avoided. In the act of nomination his judgment alone would be exercised; and as it would be his sole duty to point out the man, who with the approbation of the Senate should fill an office, his responsibility would be as complete as if he were to make the final appointment. There can in this view be no difference between nominating and appointing. The same motives which would influence a proper discharge of his duty in one case would exist in the other. And as no man could be appointed, but upon his

previous nomination, every man who might be appointed would be in fact his choice.

But might not his nomination be overruled? I grant it might, yet this could only be to make place for another nomination by himself. The person ultimately appointed must be the object of his preference, though perhaps not in the first degree. It is also not very probable that his nomination would often be overruled. The Senate could not be tempted by the preference they might feel to another to reject the one proposed; because they could not assure themselves that the person they might wish would be brought forward by a second or by any subsequent nomination. They could not even be certain that a future nomination would present a candidate in any degree more acceptable to them: And as their dissent might cast a kind of stigma upon the individual rejected; and might have the appearance of a reflection upon the judgment of the chief magistrate; it is not likely that their sanction would often be refused, where there were not special and strong reasons for the refusal.

To what purpose then require the co-operation of the Senate? I answer that the necessity of their concurrence would have a powerful, though in general a silent operation. It would be an excellent check upon a spirit of favoritism in the President, and would tend greatly to preventing the appointment of unfit characters from State prejudice, from family connection, from personal attachment, or from a view to popularity. And, in addition to this, it would be an efficacious source of stability in the administration.

It will readily be comprehended, that a man, who had himself the sole disposition of offices, would be governed much more by his private inclinations and interests, than when he was bound to submit the propriety of his choice to the discussion and determination of a different and independent body; and that body an entire branch of the Legislature. The possibility of rejection would be a strong motive to care in proposing. The danger to his own reputation, and, in the case of an elective magistrate, to his political existence, from betraying a spirit of favoritism, or an unbecoming pursuit of popularity, to the observation of a body, whose opinion would have great weight in forming that of the public, could not fail to operate as a barrier to the one and to the other. He would be both ashamed and afraid to bring forward for the most distinguished or lucrative stations, candidates who had no other merit, than that of coming from the same State to which he particularly belonged, or of being in some way or other personally allied to him, or of possessing the necessary insignificance and pliancy to render them the obsequious instruments of his pleasure.

To this reasoning, it has been objected, that the President by the influence of the power of nomination may secure the compliance of the Senate to his views. The supposition of universal venality in human nature is little less an error in political reasoning than the supposition of universal rectitude. The institution of delegated power implies that there is a portion of virtue and honor among mankind, which may be a reasonable foundation of confidence. And experience justifies the theory: It has been found to exist in the most corrupt periods of the most corrupt governments. The venality of the British House of Commons has been long a topic of accusation against that body, in the country to which they belong, as well as in this; and it cannot be doubted that the charge is to a considerable extent well founded. But it is as little to be doubted that there is always a large proportion of the body, which consists of independent and public spirited men, who have an influential weight in the councils of the nation. Hence it is (the present reign not excepted) that the sense of that body is often seen to controul the inclinations of the monarch, both with regard to men and to measures. Though it might therefore be allowable to suppose, that the executive might occasionally influence some individuals in the Senate; yet the supposition that he could in general purchase the integrity of the whole body would be forced and improbable. A man disposed to view human nature as it is, without either flattering its virtues or exaggerating its vices, will see sufficient ground of confidence in the probity of the Senate, to rest satisfied not only that it will be impracticable to the Executive to corrupt or seduce a majority of its members; but that the necessity of its co-operation in the business of appointments will be a considerable and salutary restraint upon the conduct of that magistrate. Nor is the integrity of the Senate the only reliance. The constitution has provided some important guards against the danger of executive influence upon the legislative body: It declares that "No Senator, or representative shall, during the time *for which he was elected*, be appointed to any civil office under the United States, which shall have been created, or the emoluments whereof shall have been encreased during such time; and no person holding any office under the United States shall be a member of either house during his continuance in office."

40

ALEXANDER HAMILTON, FEDERALIST, NO. 77,
515–19
2 Apr. 1788

It has been mentioned as one of the advantages to be expected from the co-operation of the senate, in the business of appointments, that it would contribute to the stability of the administration. The consent of that body would be necessary to displace as well as to appoint. A change of the chief magistrate therefore would not occasion so violent or so general a revolution in the officers of the government, as might be expected if he were the sole disposer of offices. Where a man in any station had given satisfactory evidence of his fitness for it, a new president would be restrained from attempting a change, in favour of a person more agreeable to him, by the apprehension that the discountenance of the senate might frustrate the attempt, and bring some degree of discredit upon himself. Those who can best estimate the value of a steady administration will be most disposed to prize a provision, which connects the official existence of public men with the approbation or disapprobation of that body, which from the greater permanency of its own composition, will in all probability be less subject to inconstancy, than any other member of the government.

To this union of the senate with the president, in the article of appointments, it has in some cases been objected, that it would serve to give the president an undue influence over the senate; and in others, that it would have an opposite tendency; a strong proof that neither suggestion is true.

To state the first in its proper form is to refute it. It amounts to this—The president would have an improper *influence over* the senate; because the senate would have the power of *restraining* him. This is an absurdity in terms. It cannot admit of a doubt that the intire power of appointment would enable him much more effectually to establish a dangerous empire over that body, than a mere power of nomination subject to their controul.

Let us take a view of the converse of the proposition—"The senate would influence the executive." As I have had occasion to remark in several other instances, the indistinctness of the objection forbids a precise answer. In what manner is this influence to be exerted? In relation to what objects? The power of influencing a person, in the sense in which it is here used, must imply a power of conferring a benefit upon him. How could the senate confer a benefit upon the president by the manner of employing their right of negative upon his nominations? If it be said they might sometimes gratify him by an acquiescence in a favorite choice, when public motives might dictate a different conduct; I answer that the instances in which the president could be personally interested in the result, would be too few to admit of his being materially affected by the compliances of the senate. The POWER which can *originate* the disposition of honors and emoluments, is more likely to attract than to be attracted by the POWER which can merely obstruct their course. If by influencing the president be meant *restraining* him, this is precisely what must have been intended. And it has been shewn that the restraint would be salutary, at the same time that it would not be such as to destroy a single advantage to be looked for from the uncontrouled agency of that magistrate. The right of nomination would produce all the good of that of appointment and would be in a great measure avoid its ills.

Upon a comparison of the plan for the appointment of the officers of the proposed government with that which is established by the constitution of this state a decided preference must be given to the former. In that plan the power of nomination is unequivocally vested in the executive. And as there would be a necessity for submitting each nomination to the judgement of an entire branch of the legislature, the circumstances attending an appointment, from the mode of conducting it, would naturally become matters of notoriety; and the public would be at no loss to determine what part had been performed by the different actors. The blame of a bad nomination would fall upon the president singly and absolutely. The censure of rejecting a good one would lie entirely at the door of the senate; aggravated by the consideration of their having counteracted the good intentions of the executive. If an ill appointment should be made the executive for nominating and the senate for approving would participate though in different degrees in the opprobrium and disgrace.

The reverse of all this characterises the manner of appointment in this state. The council of appointment consists of from three to five persons, of whom the governor is always one. This small body, shut up in a private apartment, impenetrable to the public eye, proceed to the execution of the trust committed to them. It is known that the governor claims the right of nomination, upon the strength of some ambiguous expressions in the constitution; but it is not known to what extent, or in what manner he exercises it; nor upon what occasions he is contradicted or opposed. The censure of a bad appointment, on account of the uncertainty of its author, and for want of a determinate object, has neither poignancy nor duration. And while an unbounded field for cabal and intrigue lies open, all idea of responsibility is lost. The most that the public can know is, that the governor claims the right of nomination: That *two* out of the considerable number of *four* men can too often be managed without much difficulty: That if some of the members of a particular council should happen to be of an uncomplying character, it is frequently not impossible to get rid of their opposition, by regulating the times of meeting in such a manner as to render their attendance inconvenient: And that, from whatever cause it may proceed, a great number of very improper appointments are from time to time made. Whether a governor of this state avails himself of the ascendant he must necessarily have, in this delicate and important part of the administration, to prefer to offices men who are best qualified for them: Or whether he prostitutes that advantage to the advancement of persons, whose chief merit is their implicit devotion to his will, and to the support of a despicable and dangerous system of personal influence, are questions which unfortunately for the community can only be the subjects of speculation and conjecture.

Every mere council of appointment, however constituted, will be a conclave, in which cabal and intrigue will have their full scope. Their number, without an unwarrantable increase of expence, cannot be large enough to preclude a facility of combination. And as each member will have his friends and connections to provide for, the desire of mutual gratification will beget a scandalous bartering of votes and bargaining for places. The private attachments of one man might easily be satisfied; but to satisfy the private attachments of a dozen, or of twenty men, would occasion a monopoly of all the principal employments of the government, in a few families, and would lead more directly to an aristocracy or an oligarchy, than any measure that could be contrived. If to avoid an accumulation of offices, there was to be a frequent change in the persons, who were to compose the council, this would involve the mischiefs of a mutable administration in their full extent. Such a council would also be more liable to executive influence than the senate, because they would be fewer in number, and would act less immediately under

the public inspection. Such a council in fine as a substitute for the plan of the convention, would be productive of an increase of expence, a multiplication of the evils which spring from favouritism and intrigue in the distribution of the public honors, a decrease of stability in the administration of the government, and a diminution of the security against an undue influence of the executive. And yet such a council has been warmly contended for as an essential amendment in the proposed constitution.

I could not with propriety conclude my observations on the subject of appointments, without taking notice of a scheme, for which there has appeared some, though but a few advocates; I mean that of uniting the house of representatives in the power of making them. I shall however do little more than mention it, as I cannot imagine that it is likely to gain the countenance of any considerable part of the community. A body so fluctuating, and at the same time so numerous, can never be deemed proper for the exercise of that power. Its unfitness will appear manifest to all, when it is recollected that in half a century it may consist of three or four hundred persons. All the advantages of the stability, both of the executive and of the senate, would be defeated by this union; and infinite delays and embarrassments would be occasioned. The example of most of the states in their local constitutions, encourages us to reprobate the idea.

41

Debate in North Carolina Ratifying Convention
28 July 1788
Elliot 4:134, 135–36

Mr. Iredell: As to offices, the Senate has no other influence but a restraint on improper appointments. The President proposes such a man for such an office. The Senate has to consider upon it. If they think him improper, the President must nominate another, whose appointment ultimately again depends upon the Senate. Suppose a man nominated by the President; with what face would any senator object to him without a good reason? There must be some decorum in every public body. He would not say, "I do not choose this man, because a friend of mine wants the office." Were he to object to the nomination of the President, without assigning any reason, his conduct would be reprobated, and still might not answer his purpose. Were an office to be vacant, for which a hundred men on the continent were equally well qualified, there would be a hundred chances to one whether his friend would be nominated to it. This, in effect, is but a restriction on the President. The power of the Senate would be more likely to be abused were it vested in a council of thirteen, of which there would be one from each state. One man could be more easily influenced than two. We have therefore a double security. I am firmly of opinion that, if you take all the powers of the President and Senate together, the vast influence of the representatives of the people will preponderate against them in every case where the public good is really concerned.

. . . . .

Mr. MACLAINE. It has been objected to this part, that the power of appointing officers was something like a monarchical power. Congress are not to be sitting at all times; they will only sit from time to time, as the public business may render it necessary. Therefore the executive ought to make temporary appointments, as well as receive ambassadors and other public ministers. This power can be vested nowhere but in the executive, because he is perpetually acting for the public; for, though the Senate is to advise him in the appointment of officers, &c., yet, during the recess, the President must do this business, or else it will be neglected; and such neglect may occasion public inconveniences. But there is an objection made to another part, that has not yet been read. His power of adjourning both houses, when they disagree, has been by some people construed to extend to any length of time. If gentlemen look at another part of the Constitution, they will find that there is a positive injunction, that the Congress must meet at *least once* in every year; so that he cannot, were he so inclined, prevent their meeting within a year. One of the best provisions contained in it is, that he shall commission all officers of the United States, and shall take care that the laws be faithfully executed. If he takes care to see the laws faithfully executed, it will be more than is done in any government on the continent; for I will venture to say that our government, and those of the other states, are, with respect to the execution of the laws, in many respects mere ciphers.

42

HOUSE OF REPRESENTATIVES, TREASURY DEPARTMENT
29 June 1789
Annals 1:611–14

Mr. MADISON observed, that the committee had gone through the bill without making any provision respecting the tenure by which the Comptroller is to hold his office. He thought it was a point worthy of consideration, and would, therefore, submit a few observations upon it.

It will be necessary, said he, to consider the nature of this office, to enable us to come to a right decision on the subject; in analyzing its properties, we shall easily discover they are not purely of an executive nature. It seems to me that they partake of a judiciary quality as well as executive; perhaps the latter obtains in the greatest degree. The principal duty seems to be deciding upon the lawfulness and justice of the claims and accounts subsisting between the United States and particular citizens: this partakes strongly of the judicial character, and there may be strong

reasons why an officer of this kind should not hold his office at the pleasure of the executive branch of the Government. I am inclined to think that we ought to consider him something in the light of an arbitrator between the public and individuals, and that he ought to hold his office by such a tenure as will make him responsible to the public generally; then again it may be thought, on the other side, that some persons ought to be authorized on behalf of the individual, with the usual liberty of referring to a third person, in case of disagreement, which may throw some embarrassment in the way of the first idea.

Whatever, Mr. Chairman, may be my opinion with respect to the tenure by which an executive officer may hold his office according to the meaning of the constitution, I am very well satisfied, that a modification by the Legislature may take place in such as partake of the judicial qualities, and that the legislative power is sufficient to establish this office on such a footing as to answer the purposes for which it is prescribed.

With this view he would move a proposition, to be inserted in the bill; it was that the Comptroller should hold his office during ——— years, unless sooner removed by the President: he will always be dependent upon the Legislature, by reason of the power of impeachment; but he might be made still more so, when the House took up the Salary bill. He would have the person re-appointable at the expiration of the term, unless he was disqualified by a conviction on an impeachment before the Senate; by this means the Comptroller would be dependent upon the President, because he can be removed by him; he will be dependent upon the Senate, because they must consent to his election for every term of years; and he will be dependent upon this House, through the means of impeachment, and the power we shall reserve over his salary; by which means we shall effectually secure the dependence of this officer upon the Government. But making him thus thoroughly dependent, would make it necessary to secure his impartiality, with respect to the individual. This might be effected by giving any person, who conceived himself aggrieved, a right to petition the Supreme Court for redress, and they should be empowered to do right therein; this will enable the individual to carry his claim before an independent tribunal.

A provision of this kind exists in two of the United States at this time, and is found to answer a very good purpose. He mentioned this, that gentlemen might not think it altogether novel. The committee, he hoped, would take a little time to examine the idea.

Mr. STONE thought it necessary to have time allowed the committee for considering the proposition; it was perfectly novel to him, and he dared to say the same of many other members; but, at the first view, he thought he saw several objections to it. As the Comptroller was an inferior officer, his appointment might be vested in the President by the Legislature; but, according to the determination which had already taken place, it did not necessarily follow that he should have the power of dismissal; and before it was given, its propriety ought to be apparent. He did not know whether the office should be held during good behavior, as the gentleman proposed; for if it was intended to be held during a term of years, and then the officer to be re-appointed, if he had not been convicted on impeachment, it would be tantamount to holding it during all the time he behaved well. But he thought all officers, except the judges, should hold their offices during pleasure. He also thought it unnecessary to consider the Comptroller as a judge, and give, by an express clause in the bill, a right to the complainant to appeal from his decision. He considered this as the right of every man, upon the principles of common law, therefore securing it by the statute would be a work of supererogation.

Mr. SMITH, of South Carolina, approved the idea of having the Comptroller appointed for a limited time, but thought during that time he ought to be independent of the Executive, in order that he might not be influenced by that branch of the Government in his decisions.

Mr. SEDGWICK did not rise to oppose the measure, but to suggest some doubts of its effects. The first was, as mentioned by the gentleman from Maryland, (Mr. STONE,) that the officer would hold his office by the firm tenure of good behavior, inasmuch as he was to be reappointed at the expiration of the first term, and so on.

Mr. MADISON begged the gentlemen would excuse him for this interruption, but he suspected he was misapprehended; he said the officer should be re-appointable at the expiration of the term—not re-appointed.

Mr. SEDGWICK acknowledged he had misunderstood the gentleman; but, as he had now explained himself, he did not see that the proposition came up to the intention he had expressed: so far from making him independent, as a judge ought to be, it subjected him to more subordination than any other officer.

He also conceived that a majority of the House had decided that all officers concerned in executive business should depend upon the will of the President for their continuance in office; and with good reason, for they were the eyes and arms of the principal Magistrate, the instruments of execution. Now the office of Comptroller seemed to bear a strong affinity to this branch of the Government. He is to provide for the regular and punctual payment of all moneys which may be collected, and to direct prosecutions for delinquencies; he is to preserve the public accounts, to countersign warrants, and to report to the Secretary. These are important executive duties, and the man who has to perform them ought, he thought, to be dependent upon the President.

He did not mean, by what he said, to give a decided opinion, but merely to suggest for consideration some doubts which had arisen in his mind since the subject was introduced.

Mr. BENSON did not like the object of the motion, because it was, in some measure, setting afloat the question which had already been carried.

He wished there might be some certainty in knowing what was the tenure of offices; he thought they were well fixed now, if nothing more was done with the question. The judges hold theirs during good behavior, as established by the constitution; all others, during pleasure. He was afraid that the present motion would lead to a different construction from the one lately adopted; by devices of this kind, he apprehended the Legislature might overthrow the executive power; he would therefore vote against it, if it were not withdrawn.

Mr. MADISON did not wish a decision on the subject, further than gentlemen were prepared.

When I was up before, said he, I endeavored to show that the nature of this office differed from the others upon which the House had decided; and, consequently, that a modification might take place, without interfering with the former distinction; so that it cannot be said we depart from the spirit of the constitution.

Several arguments were adduced to show the Executive Magistrate had constitutionally a right to remove subordinate officers at pleasure. Among others it was urged, with some force, that these officers were merely to assist him in the performance of duties, which, from the nature of man, he could not execute without them, although he had an unquestionable right to do them if he were able; but I question very much whether he can or ought to have any interference in the settling and adjusting the legal claims of individuals against the United States. The necessary examination and decision in such cases partake too much of the judicial capacity to be blended with the executive. I do not say the office is either executive or judicial; I think it rather distinct from both, though it partakes of each, and therefore some modification, accommodated to those circumstances, ought to take place. I would, therefore, make the officer responsible to every part of the Government.

Surely the Legislature have the right to limit the salary of any officer; if they have this, and the power of establishing offices at discretion, it can never be said that, by limiting the tenure of an office, we devise schemes for the overthrow of the executive department.

If gentlemen will consult the true spirit and scope of the constitution, they will perhaps find my propositions not so obnoxious.

43

JAMES MADISON TO THOMAS JEFFERSON
30 June 1789
Papers 12:270–72

The other bills depending relate to the collection of the Impost, and the establishment of a war, foreign, and Treasury Department. The bills on the two first of these departments have passed the House of Representatives, and are before the Senate. They gave birth to a very interesting constitutional question—by what authority removals from office were to be made. The Constitution being silent on the point, it was left to construction. Four opinions were advanced: 1. That no removal could be made but by way of impeachment. To this it was objected that it gave to every officer, down to tide waiters and tax gatherers, the tenure of good behavior. 2. That it devolved on the Legislature, to be disposed of as might be proper. To this it was objected that the legislature might then dispose of it to be exercised by themselves, or even by the House of Representatives. 3. That it was incident to the power of appointment, and therefore belonged to the President and Senate. To this it was said that the Senate, being a *Legislative* body, could not be considered in an *Executive* light farther than was expressly declared; that such a construction would transfer the trust of seeing the laws duly executed from the President, the most responsible, to the Senate, the least responsible branch of the Government; that officers would intrench themselves behind a party in the Senate, bid defiance to the President, and introduce anarchy and discord into the Executive Department; that the Senate were to be Judges in case of impeachment, and ought not, therefore, to be previously called on for a summary opinion on questions of removal; that in their Legislative character they ought to be kept as cool and unbiased as possible, as the constitutional check on the passions and parties of the other House, and should, for that reason also, be as little concerned as possible in those *personal* matters, which are the great source of factious animosities. 4. That the Executive power being generally vested in the President, and the Executive function of removal not expressly taken away, it remained with the President. To this was objected the rule of construction on which the third opinion rested, and the danger of creating too much weight in the Executive scale. After very long debates the 4th opinion prevailed, as most consonant to the text of the Constitution, to the policy of mixing the Legislative and Executive Departments as little as possible, and to the requisite responsibility and harmony in the Executive Department. What the decision of the Senate will be cannot yet be even conjectured. As soon as the bills are passed, Mr. Jay and General Knox will of course have their commissions renewed.

The bill relating to the Treasury Department is still before the House of Representatives. The Board will be discontinued, but the business will be so arranged as to make the comptroller and other officers checks on the Head of the Department. It is not clear who this will be. The members of Congress are disqualified. Hamilton is most talked of.

The Senate have in hand a bill for the Judiciary Department. It is found a pretty arduous task, and will probably be long on its way through the two Houses.

44

JOHN ADAMS, NOTES OF A DEBATE IN THE SENATE
15 July 1789
Works 3:408–12

Power of Removal.

July 15. *Carroll.* The executive power is commensurate with the legislative and judicial powers.

The rule of construction of treaties, statutes, and deeds.

The same power which creates must annihilate. This is true where the power is simple, but when compound, not.

If a minister is suspected to betray secrets to an enemy, the Senate not sitting, cannot the President displace nor suspend?

The States-General of France demanded that offices should be during good behavior.

It is improbable that a bad president should be chosen—but may not bad senators be chosen?

Is there a due balance of power between the executive and legislative, either in the General Government or State governments?

Montesquieu. English liberty will be lost when the legislative shall be more corrupt than the executive. Have we not been witnesses of corrupt acts of legislatures, making depredations? Rhode Island yet perseveres.

Ellsworth. We are sworn to support the Constitution.

There is an explicit grant of power to the President, which contains the power of removal. The executive power is granted; not the executive powers hereinafter enumerated and explained.

The President, not the Senate, appoint; they only consent and advise.

The Senate is not an executive council; has no executive power.

The grant to the President express, not by implication.

Butler. This power of removal would be unhinging the equilibrium of power in the Constitution.

The Stadtholder withheld the fleet from going out, to the annoyance of the enemies of the nation.

In treaties, all powers not expressly given, are reserved.

Treaties to be gone over, clause by clause, by the President and Senate together, and modelled.

The other branches are imbecile; disgust and alarm; the President not sovereign; the United States sovereign, or people or Congress sovereign.

The House of Representatives would not be induced to depart, so well satisfied of the grounds.

Ellsworth. The powers of this Constitution are all vested; parted from the people, from the States, and vested, not in Congress, but in the President.

The word sovereignty is introduced without determinate ideas. Power in the last resort. In this sense the sovereign executive is in the President.

The United States will be parties to a thousand suits. Shall process issue in their name versus or for themselves?

The President, it is said, may be put to jail for debt.

Lee. United States merely figurative, meaning the people.

Grayson. The President is not above the law; an absurdity to admit this idea into our government. Not improbable that the President may be sued. Christina II. of Sweden committed murder. France excused her. The jurors of our lord the President, present that the President committed murder. A monarchy by a side wind. You make him *vindex injuriarum.* The people will not like "the jurors of our lord, the President," nor "the peace of our lord, the President," nor his dignity; his crown will be left out. Do not wish to make the Constitution a more unnatural, monstrous production, than it is. The British Court is a three-legged stool; if one leg is longer than another, the stool will not stand.

Unpalatable; the removal of officers not palatable. We should not risk any thing for nothing. Come forward like men, and reason openly, and the people will hear more quietly than if you attempt side winds. This measure will do no good, and will disgust.

Lee. The danger to liberty greater from the disunited opinions and jarring plans of many, than from the energetic operations of one. Marius, Sylla, Caesar, Cromwell trampled on liberty with armies.

The power of pardon; of adjourning the legislature.

Power of revision sufficient to defend himself. He would be supported by the people.

Patronage gives great influence. The interference more nominal than real.

The greater part of power of making treaties in the President.

The greatest power is in the President; the less in the Senate.

Cannot see responsibility in the President or the great officers of State.

A masked battery of constructive powers would complete the destruction of liberty.

Can the executive lay embargoes, establish fairs, tolls, &c?

The federal government is limited; the legislative power of it is limited; and, therefore, the executive and judicial must be limited.

The executive not punishable but by universal convulsion, as Charles I.

The legislative in England not so corrupt as the executive.

There is no responsibility in the President or ministry.

Blackstone. The liberties of England owing to juries. The greatness of England owing to the genius of that people.

The Crown of England can do what it pleases, nearly.

There is no balance in America to such an executive as that in England.

Does the executive arm mean a standing army?

Willing to make a law that the President, if he sees gross misconduct, may suspend *pro tempore.*

Patterson. Laments that we are obliged to discuss this question; of great importance and much difficulty.

The executive coextensive with the legislative. Had the clause stood alone, would not there have been a devolution of all executive power?

Exceptions are to be construed strictly. This is an invariable rule.

Grayson. The President has not a continental interest, but is a citizen of a particular State. A. K. of E. otherwise; K. of E. counteracted by a large, powerful, rich, and hereditary aristocracy. Hyperion to a satyr.

Where there are not intermediate powers, an alteration of the government must be to despotism.

Powers ought not to be inconsiderately given to the executive without proper balances.

Triennial and septennial parliaments made by corruption of the executive.

Bowstring. General Lally. Brutus's power to put his sons to death.

The power creating shall have that of uncreating. The minister is to hold at pleasure of the appointer.

If it is in the Constitution, why insert it in the law? brought in by a side wind, inferentially.

There will be every endeavor to increase the consolidatory powers; to weaken the Senate, and strengthen the President.

No evil in the Senate's participating with the President in removal.

Read. The President is to take care that the laws be faithfully executed. He is responsible. How can he do his duty or be responsible, if he cannot remove his instruments?

It is not an equal sharing of the power of appointment between the President and Senate. The Senate are only a check to prevent impositions on the President.

The minister an agent, a deputy to the great executive.

Difficult to bring great characters to punishment or trial. Power of suspension.

Johnson. Gentlemen convince themselves that it is best the President should have the power, and then study for arguments.

Exceptions. Not a grant. Vested in the President would be void for uncertainty. Executive power is uncertain. Powers are moral, mechanical, material. Which of these powers? what executive power? The land; the money; conveys nothing. What land? what money?

Unumquodque dissolvitur eodem modo quo ligatur.

Meddles not with the question of expediency.

The executive wants power by its duration and its want of a negative, and power to balance. *Federalist.*

Ellsworth. What is the difference between a grant and a partition?

Izard. Cujus est instituere, ejus est abrogare.

45

JOHN ADAMS TO ROGER SHERMAN
[20?] July 1789
Works 6:432–36

There is another sense and another degree in which the executive is blended with the legislature, which is liable to great and just objection; which excites alarms, jealousies, and apprehensions, in a very great degree. I mean, 1st, the negative of the senate upon appointments to office; 2d. the negative of the senate upon treaties; and 3d. the negative of the two houses upon war. I shall confine myself, at present, to the first. The negative of the senate upon appointments is liable to the following objections:—

1. It takes away, or, at least, it lessens the responsibility of the executive. Our constitution obliges me to say, that it lessens the responsibility of the president. The blame of an injudicious, weak, or wicked appointment, is shared so much between him and the senate, that his part of it will

be too small. Who can censure him, without censuring the senate, and the legislatures who appoint them? All their friends will be interested to vindicate the president, in order to screen them from censure. Besides, if an impeachment against an officer is brought before them, are they not interested to acquit him, lest some part of the odium of his guilt should fall upon them, who advised to his appointment?

2. It turns the minds and attention of the people to the senate, a branch of the legislature, in executive matters. It interests another branch of the legislature in the management of the executive. It divides the people between the executive and the senate; whereas, all the people ought to be united to watch the executive, to oppose its encroachments, and resist its ambition. Senators and representatives, and their constituents, in short, the aristocratical and democratical divisions of society ought to be united on all occasions to oppose the executive or the monarchical branch, when it attempts to overleap its limits. But how can this union be effected, when the aristocratical branch has pledged its reputation to the executive, by consenting to an appointment?

3. It has a natural tendency to excite ambition in the senate. An active, ardent spirit, who is rich and able, and has a great reputation and influence, will be solicited by candidates for office. Not to introduce the idea of bribery, because, though it certainly would force itself in, in other countries, and will probably here, when we grow populous and rich, it is not yet to be dreaded, I hope, ambition must come in already. A senator of great influence will be naturally ambitious and desirous of increasing his influence. Will he not be under a temptation to use his influence with the president as well as his brother senators, to appoint persons to office in the several states, who will exert themselves in elections, to get out his enemies or opposers, both in senate and house of representatives, and to get in his friends, perhaps his instruments? Suppose a senator to aim at the treasury office for himself, his brother, father, or son. Suppose him to aim at the president's chair, or vice-president's, at the next election, or at the office of war, foreign, or domestic affairs. Will he not naturally be tempted to make use of his whole patronage, his whole influence, in advising to appointments, both with president and senators, to get such persons nominated as will exert themselves in elections of president, vice-president, senators, and house of representatives, to increase his interest and promote his views? In this point of view, I am very apprehensive that this defect in our constitution will have an unhappy tendency to introduce corruption of the grossest kinds, both of ambition and avarice, into all our elections, and this will be the worst of poisons to our constitution. It will not only destroy the present form of government, but render it almost impossible to substitute in its place any free government, even a better limited-monarchy, or any other than a despotism or a simple monarchy.

4. To avoid the evil under the last head, it will be in danger of dividing the continent into two or three nations, a case that presents no prospect but of perpetual war.

5. This negative on appointments is in danger of involving the senate in reproach, censure, obloquy, and suspicion, without doing any good. Will the senate use their negative or not? If not, why should they have it? Many will censure them for not using it; many will ridicule them, and call them servile, &c. If they do use it, the very first instance of it will expose the senators to the resentment of not only the disappointed candidate and all his friends, but of the president and all his friends, and these will be most of the officers of government, through the nation.

6. We shall very soon have parties formed; a court and country party, and these parties will have names given them. One party in the house of representatives will support the president and his measures and ministers; the other will oppose them. A similar party will be in the senate; these parties will study with all their arts, perhaps with intrigue, perhaps with corruption, at every election to increase their own friends and diminish their opposers. Suppose such parties formed in the senate, and then consider what factious divisions we shall have there upon every nomination.

7. The senate have not time. The convention and Indian treaties.

You are of opinion "that the concurrence of the senate in the appointments to office, will strengthen the hands of the executive, and secure the confidence of the people, much better than a select council, and will be less expensive."

But in every one of these ideas, I have the misfortune to differ from you.

It will weaken the hands of the executive, by lessening the obligation, gratitude, and attachment of the candidate to the president, by dividing his attachment between the executive and legislative, which are natural enemies. Officers of government, instead of having a single eye and undivided attachment to the executive branch, as they ought to have, consistent with law and the constitution, will be constantly tempted to be factious with their factious patrons in the senate. The president's own officers, in a thousand instances, will oppose his just and constitutional exertions, and screen themselves under the wings of their patrons and party in the legislature. Nor will it secure the confidence of the people. The people will have more confidence in the executive, in executive matters, than in the senate. The people will be constantly jealous of factious schemes in the senators to unduly influence the executive, to serve each other's private views. The people will also be jealous that the influence of the senate will be employed to conceal, connive at, and defend guilt in executive officers, instead of being a guard and watch upon them, and a terror to them. A council, selected by the president himself, at his pleasure, from among the senators, representatives, and nation at large, would be purely responsible. In that case, the senate would be a terror to privy counsellors; its honor would never be pledged to support any measure or instrument of the executive beyond justice, law, and the constitution. Nor would a privy council be more expensive. The whole senate must now deliberate on every appointment, and if they ever find time for it, you will find that a great deal of time will be required and consumed in this service. Then, the president might have a constant executive council; now, he has none.

I said, under the seventh head, that the senate would not have time. You will find that the whole business of this government will be infinitely delayed by this negative of the senate on treaties and appointments. Indian treaties and consular conventions have been already waiting for months, and the senate have not been able to find a moment of time to attend to them; and this evil must constantly increase. So that the senate must be constantly sitting, and must be paid as long as they sit. . . .

But I have tired your patience. Is there any truth in these broken hints and crude surmises, or not? To me they appear well founded and very important.

46

ROGER SHERMAN TO JOHN ADAMS
July 1789
Adams Works 6:440–42

I received your letter of the twentieth instant. I had in mine, of the same date, communicated to you my ideas on that part of the constitution, limiting the president's power of negativing the acts of the legislature; and just hinted some thoughts on the propriety of the provision made for the appointment to offices, which I esteem to be a power nearly as important as legislation.

If that was vested in the president alone, he might, were it not for his periodical election by the people, render himself despotic. It was a saying of one of the kings of England, that while the king could appoint the bishops and judges, he might have what religion and law he pleased.

It appears to me the senate is the most important branch in the government, for aiding and supporting the executive, securing the rights of the individual states, the government of the United States, and the liberties of the people. The executive magistrate is to execute the laws. The senate, being a branch of the legislature, will naturally incline to have them duly executed, and, therefore, will advise to such appointments as will best attain that end. From the knowledge of the people in the several states, they can give the best information as to who are qualified for office; and though they will, as you justly observe, in some degree lessen his responsibility, yet their advice may enable him to make such judicious appointments, as to render responsibility less necessary. The senators being eligible by the legislatures of the several states, and dependent on them for reëlection, will be vigilant in supporting their rights against infringement by the legislature or executive of the United States; and the government of the Union being federal, and instituted by the several states for the advancement of their interests, they may be considered as so many pillars to support it, and, by the exercise of the state governments, peace and good order may be preserved in places most remote from the seat of the federal government, as well as at the centre. And the municipal and federal rights of the people at large will be regarded by the senate, they being elected by the immediate representatives of the people, and their rights will be best secured by a due execution of the laws. What temptation can the senate be under to partiality in the trial of officers of whom they had a voice in the appointment? Can they be disposed to favor a person who has violated his trust and their confidence?

The other evils you mention, that may result from this power, appear to me but barely possible. The senators will doubtless be in general some of the most respectable citizens in the states for wisdom and probity, superior to mean and unworthy conduct, and instead of undue influence, to procure appointments for themselves or their friends, they will consider that a fair and upright conduct will have the best tendency to preserve the confidence of the people and of the states. They will be disposed to be diffident in recommending their friends and kindred, lest they should be suspected of partiality; and the other members will feel the same kind of reluctance, lest they should be thought unduly to favor a person, because related to a member of their body; so that their friends and relations would not stand so good a chance for appointment to offices, according to their merit, as others.

The senate is a convenient body to advise the president, from the smallness of its numbers. And I think the laws would be better framed and more duly administered, if the executive and judiciary officers were in general members of the legislature, in case there should be no interference as to the time of attending to their several duties. This I have learned by experience in the government in which I live, and by observation of others differently constituted. I see no principles in our constitution that have any tendency to aristocracy, which, if I understand the term, is a government by nobles, independent of the people, which cannot take place, in either respect, without a total subversion of the constitution. As both branches of Congress are eligible from the citizens at large, and wealth is not a requisite qualification, both will commonly be composed of members of similar circumstances in life. And I see no reason why the several branches of the government should not maintain the most perfect harmony, their powers being all directed to one end, the advancement of the public good.

If the president alone was vested with the power of appointing all officers, and was left to select a council for himself, he would be liable to be deceived by flatterers and pretenders to patriotism, who would have no motive but their own emolument. They would wish to extend the powers of the executive to increase their own importance; and, however upright he might be in his intentions, there would be great danger of his being misled, even to the subversion of the constitution, or, at least, to introduce such evils as to interrupt the harmony of the government, and deprive him of the confidence of the people.

But I have said enough upon these speculative points, which nothing but experience can reduce to a certainty.

47

SAMUEL ADAMS TO RICHARD HENRY LEE
29 Aug. 1789
Writings 4:335–36

The Power of removing federal Officers at the Pleasure of the President is to be found the Constitution or it is not. If it is, What Need was there of an Act or Decision of Congress to authorize it? But if it is not, could Congress give so important a Power? What have the United States been contending for? Liberty. This is the great Object of their State Governments, and has not the federal Constitution the same Object in View? If therefore a Doubt arises respecting the Exercise of any Power, no Construction, I conceive, should militate with the main Design, or Object of the Charter. If there is a total Silence in the Constitution, is it not natural to conclude that an Officer holding during Pleasure is removable by the same Power which appointed him, whether vested in a single Person, or a joint Number? I am sensible, it is said, that a single Person, being amenable for his Exercise of Power will use the utmost Circumspection. This may be true, but may not this Idea be carried too far in Practice? May not some Powers vested in a single Man give him such Weight and Influence as to render any Restraint from his feeling himself amenable of little, or no Effect. If this Power lodged in the Discretion of a single Person will afford a greater Security against Corruption because of his Amenability, why should not the Power of appointing as well as removing Officers be given to him? In the one Case the gracious Hand may be held forth, in the other, the threatning Rod; and both may be used for improper Purposes. In England, "the King can do no wrong" is a Maxim. His Ministers are made accountable for him; and how often have corrupt Ministers and Councellors been brought to the Block for Follies and Crimes committed by their Royal Masters who can do no Wrong? And it may also be asked, how often such Ministers and Councellors have found Means to get themselves screened from Punishment through the Influence of their Masters, by procuring Parliamentary Sanctions to such Crimes and Follies? But in the Removal of Officers the President has not a Constitutional Council. He must therefore be solely accountable.

48

THOMAS JEFFERSON, OPINION ON POWERS OF THE SENATE RESPECTING DIPLOMATIC APPOINTMENTS
24 Apr. 1790
Papers 16:378–80

The Constitution having declared that the President "shall *nominate,* and by and with the advice and consent of the Senate, shall *appoint* ambassadors other public ministers and consuls" the President desires my opinion Whether the Senate has a right to negative the *grade* he may think it expedient to use in a foreign mission, as well as the *persons* to be appointed?

I think the Senate has no right to negative the *grade.*

The Constitution has divided the powers of government into three branches, Legislative, Executive and Judiciary, lodging each with a distinct magistracy. The Legislative it has given completely to the Senate and House of representatives: it has declared that "the Executive powers shall be vested in the President," submitting only special articles of it to a negative by the Senate; and it has vested the Judiciary power in the courts of justice, with certain exceptions also in favor of the Senate.

The transaction of business with foreign nations is Executive altogether. It belongs then to the head of that department, *except* as to such portions of it as are specially submitted to the Senate. *Exceptions* are to be construed strictly. The Constitution itself indeed has taken care to circumscribe this one within very strict limits: for it gives the *nomination* of the foreign Agent to the President, the *appointment* to him and the Senate jointly, the *commissioning* to the President. This analysis calls our attention to the strict import of each term. To *nominate* must be to *propose:* *appointment* seems that act of the will which constitutes or makes the Agent: and the *Commission* is the public evidence of it. But there are still other acts previous to these, not specially enumerated in the Constitution; to wit 1. the destination of a mission to the particular country where the public service calls for it: and 2. the character, or grade to be employed in it. The natural order of all these is 1. destination. 2. grade. 3. nomination. 4. appointment. 5. commission. If *appointment* does not comprehend the neighboring acts of *nomination,* or *commission,* (and the constitution says it shall not, by giving them exclusively to the President) still less can it pretend to comprehend those previous and more remote of *destination* and *grade.* The Constitution, analysing the three last, shews they do not comprehend the two first. The 4th. is the only one it submits to the Senate, shaping it into a right to say that "A. or B. is unfit to be appointed." Now this cannot comprehend a right to say that "A. or B. is indeed fit to be appointed, but the grade fixed on is not the fit one to employ," or "our connections with the country of his destination are not such as to call for any mission." The Senate is not supposed by the Constitution to be acquainted with the concerns of the Executive department. It was not intended that these should be communicated to them; nor can they therefore be qualified to judge of the necessity which calls for a mission to any particular place, or of the particular grade, more or less marked, which special and secret circumstances may call for. All this is left to the President. They are only to see that no unfit person be employed.

It may be objected that the Senate may, by continual negatives on the *person*, do what amounts to a negative on the *grade;* and so indirectly defeat this right of the President. But this would be a breach of trust, an abuse of the power confided to the Senate, of which that body cannot be supposed capable. So the President has a power to convoke the legislature; and the Senate might defeat that power by refusing to come. This equally amounts to a negative on the power of convoking. Yet nobody will say they possess such a negative, or would be capable of usurping it by such oblique means. If the Constitution had meant to give the Senate a negative on the grade or destination, as well as the person, it would have said so in direct terms, and not left it to be effected by a sidewind. It could never mean to give them the *use* of one power thro the *abuse* of another.

49

James Wilson, Government, Lectures on Law
1791
Works 1:294–95

The appointment to offices is an important part of the executive authority. Much of the ease, much of the reputation, much of the energy, and much of the safety of the nation depends on judicious and impartial appointments. But are impartiality and fine discernment likely to predominate in a numerous executive body? In proportion to their own number, will be the number of their friends, favourites, and dependents. An office is to be filled. A person nearly connected, by some of the foregoing ties, with one of those who are to vote in filling it, is named as a candidate. His patron is under no necessity to take any part, particularly responsible, in his appointment. He may appear even cold and indifferent on the occasion. But he possesses an advantage, the value of which is well understood in bodies of this kind. Every member, who gives, on his account, a vote for his friend, will expect the return of a similar favour on the first convenient opportunity. In this manner, a reciprocal intercourse of partiality, of interestedness, of favouritism, perhaps of venality, is established; and, in no particular instance, is there a practicability of tracing the poison to its source. Ignorant, vicious, and prostituted characters are introduced into office; and some of those, who voted, and procured others to vote for them, are the first and loudest in expressing their astonishment, that the door of admission was ever opened to

men of their infamous description. The suffering people are thus wounded and buffeted, like Homer's Ajax, in the dark; and have not even the melancholy satisfaction of knowing by whom the blows are given. Those who possess talents and virtues, which would reflect honour on office, will be reluctant to appear as candidates for appointments. If they should be brought into view; what weight will virtue, merit, and talents for office have, in a balance held and poized by partiality, intrigue, and chicane?

The person who nominates or makes appointments to offices, should be known. His own office, his own character, his own fortune should be responsible. He should be alike unfettered and unsheltered by counsellors. No constitutional stalking horse should be provided for him to conceal his turnings and windings, when they are too dark and too crooked to be exposed to publick view. Instead of the dishonourable intercourse, which I have already mentioned, an intercourse of a very different kind should be established—an intercourse of integrity and discernment on the part of the magistrate who appoints, and of gratitude and confidence on the part of the people, who will receive the benefit from his appointments. Appointments made and sanctioned in this highly respectable manner, will, like a fragrant and beneficent atmosphere, diffuse sweetness and gladness around those, to whom they are given. Modest merit will be beckoned to, in order to encourage her to come forward. Bare-faced impudence and unprincipled intrigue will receive repulse and disappointment, deservedly their portion.

If a contrary conduct should unfortunately be observed—and, unfortunately, a contrary conduct will be sometimes observed—it will be known by the citizens, whose conduct it is: and, if they are not seized with the only distemper incurable in a free government—the distemper of being wanting to themselves—they will, at the next general election, take effectual care, that the person, who has once shamefully abused their generous and unsuspecting confidence, shall not have it in his power to insult and injure them a second time, by the repetition of such an ungrateful return.

50

George Mason to James Monroe
30 Jan. 1792
Papers 3:1254–56

I see by a late Paper, that Gr. Morris is appointed our Minister, to the Court of France; so that, I suppose, the Opposition in the Senate has been outvoted.

I don't think a more injudicious Appointment cou'd have been made. In the present Situation of France, to appoint a Man of his known monarchical Principles has rather the Appearance of Insult, than of Compliment, or Congratulation. And altho' Mr. Morris's Political Creed may not be known generally in France, it must be well known to Mr. de la Fayette, the most influential Character in the Nation. What a Man seems to value himself upon, and glory in, can't long remain a Secret, in a public Character. "Coercion by G——d" is his favourite Maxim in government. And in his place, as a Member of the federal Convention in Philadelphia, I heard him express the following sentiment. "We must have a Monarch sooner or later" (tho' I think his word was a *Despot*) "and the sooner we take him, while we are able to make a Bargain with him, the better." Is this a Man to represent the United States of America, in a Country, which has just reformed an arbitrary Monarchy into a free government? Such a Character, perhaps, wou'd not have been displeasing at the Court of Petersburg, or Berlin; but is surely very ill suited to that of Paris.

The Question lately agitated in the Senate is a most important one. I am decidedly of opinion, that the Words of the Constitution "He shall nominate, and by & with the Advice and Consent of the Senate, appoint Ambassadors" &c. give the Senate the Power of interfering in every part of the Subject, except the Right of nominating. There is some thing remarkable in the Arangement of the Words "He shall nominate." This gives to the President *alone* the Right of *Nomination*. And if the Senate were to refuse their Approbation of the person nominated (which the subsequent Part of the Clause puts in their Power) they wou'd have no Right to nominate another Person; the Right of Nomination being complete in the President. "And by and with the Advice & Consent of the Senate appoint Ambassadors" &c. The Word *"Advice"* here clearly relates in the Judgment of the Senate on the Expediency or Inexpediency of the Measure, or Appointment; and the Word *"Consent"* to their Approbation or Disapprobation of the Person nominated; otherwise the word *Advice* has no Meaning at all—and it is a well known Rule of Construction, that no Clause or Expression shall be deemed superfluous, or nugatory, which is capable of a fair and rational Meaning. The Nomination, of Course, brings the Subject fully under the Consideration of the Senate; who have then a Right to decide upon it's Propriety or Impropriety. The peculiar Character or Predicament of the Senate in the Constitution of the General Government, is a strong Confirmation of this Construction.

The Senate are not the immediate Representatives of the people at large, nor elected by them. They are elected by the Legislatures of the different States, and they represent respectively, the Sovereignty of the separate States, in the general Union. Upon no other Principle can the Equality of Representation, in the larger and smaller States be justified. The Senate act in a diplomatic, as well as a legislative Character; and it is in the former Capacity that they give advice to the President; and partake of some Executive Powers. The Constitution therefore wisely & Properly directs, the Ambassadors &c. shall not be appointed, but with the Advice & Approbation of the States, which form the Union, thro' their Organ, or Representative, the Senate. I wish this important Subject to be fairly discussed, upon it's merits, and decided upon, in the Infancy of the new Government and in the presidentcy of General Washington; who, I am sure, is strongly attach'd

to the Rights & Liberty of our country; but we are not sure, that this will be the Case with his Successors.

51

MARBURY V. MADISON
1 Cranch 137 (1803)

(See 3.2.1, no. 47)

52

ST. GEORGE TUCKER,
BLACKSTONE'S COMMENTARIES
1:APP. 342–43
1803

The act of 5 Cong. c. 153, authorised the president to make appointments to fill any vacancies in the army and navy which may have happened during that session of the senate. And this without any reservation of the right of the senate to approve, or reject, at a succeeding session. This was among the manifold acts of that period for encreasing the power of the president, far beyond the limits assigned by the constitution; limits already sufficiently large for every beneficial purpose. The right of nomination to office in all cases where the senate are to be consulted upon the appointment, being the undoubted privilege of the president under the constitution, should he persist in the nomination of a person to office after the senate have rejected him, there is no constitutional control over him, by which he may be compelled to nominate any other person. The office then may be kept vacant through this disagreement between them. But if it should have happened that the office became vacant during the recess of the senate, and the vacancy were filled by a commission which should expire, not at the meeting of the senate, but at the end of their session, then, in case such a disagreement between the president and senate, if the president should persist in his opinion, and make no other nomination, the person appointed by him during the recess of the senate would continue to hold his commission, until the end of their session: so that the vacancy would happen a second time during the recess of the senate, and the president consequently, would have the sole right of appointing a second time; and the person whom the senate have rejected, may be instantly replaced by a new commission. And thus it is evidently in the power of the president to continue any person in office, whom he shall once have appointed in the recess of the senate, as long as he may think proper. A circumstance which renders the power of nomination, and of filling up vacancies during the recess of the senate, too great, to require any further extention. Even the control of elections loses it's force, in great measure, in such cases:

the influence of a president, and the activity and zeal of his partizans encreasing in proportion to the number of offices which he has power to fill, and to the measure of obligation which the persons preferred by his favour, may suppose they owe to him, for the distinction.

Perhaps these inconveniencies might have been avoided, if the constitution had required more than one person to have been put in nomination by the president for those offices, where the concurrence of the senate is required to complete the appointment, or, that in case of disagreement between the president and senate, two thirds of the latter might appoint, without a previous nomination by the president, in case he should decline any further nomination, after the first had been rejected.

53

JAMES MADISON TO SENATE OF UNITED STATES
June 1813

Writings 8:250–51

I have recd. from the Committee appointed by the resolution of the Senate of the [14] day of [June] a copy of that resolution, which authorizes the Committee to confer with the P. on the subject of the nomination made by him of a Min: Plenipo. to Sweden.

Conceiving it to be my duty to decline the proposed conference with the Committee, & it being uncertain when it may be convenient to explain to the Committee & thro' them, to the Senate, the grounds of my so doing, I think it proper to address the explanation directly to the Senate.

Without entering into a general review of the relations, in which the constitution has placed the several departments of the Govt. to each other, it will suffice to remark

That the Executive & Senate in the cases of appointments to Office & of Treaties, are to be considered as independent of and co-ordinate with each other. If they agree the appointments or treaties are made. If the Senate disagree they fail. If the Senate wish information previous to their final decision, the practice, keeping in view the constitutional relations of the Senate & the Executive has been either to request the Executive to furnish it, or to refer the subject to a committee of their body to communicate either formally or informally with the head of the proper Department.

The appointment of a Committee of the Senate to confer immediately with the Executive himself appears to lose sight of the co-ordinate relation between the Executive & the Senate which the Constitution has established, & which ought therefore to be maintained.

The relation between the Senate & House of Representatives in whom legislative power is concurrently vested, is sufficiently analogous to illustrate that between the Executive & senate in making appointments & treaties. The two houses are in like manner independent of & co-ordinate with each other; and the invariable practice of each in ap-

pointing Committees of conference & consultation is to commission them to confer not with the co-ordinate Body itself, but with a Committee of that Body. And although both branches of the Legislature may be too numerous to hold conveniently a conference with committees were they to be appointed by either to confer with the entire Body of the other, it may be fairly presumed that if the whole number of either branch were not too large for the purpose, the objection to such a conference, being agst. the principle, as derogating from the co-ordinate relations of the two Houses, would retain all its force.

I add only that I am entirely persuaded of the purity of the intentions of the Senate, in the course they have pursued on this occasion, & with which my view of the subject makes it my duty not to accord; & that they will be cheerfully furnished with all the suitable information in possession of the Executive, in any mode deemed consistent with the principles of the Constitution, and the settled practice under it.

54

JAMES MONROE TO JAMES MADISON
10 May 1822

Writings 6:285–86

Your view of the Constitution, as to the powers of the Executive in the appointment of public Ministers, is in strict accord with my own, and is, as I understand, supported by numerous precedents, under successive administrations. A foreign mission is not an office, in the sense of the Constitution, which authorizes the President to fill vacancies in the recess of the Senate. It is not an office created by law, nor subject to the rules applicable to such offices. It exists only when an appointment is made, and terminates when it ceases, whether by the recall, death, or resignation of the Minister. It exists in the contemplation of the Constitution, with every power, and may be filled with any, or terminated with either, as circumstances may require, according to the judgment of the Executive. If an appointment can be made by the Executive, in the recess of the Senate, to a court at which we have been represented, to fill a vacancy created by the death or resignation of the Minister, I am of opinion that it may be made to a court at which we have never been represented. A different Constitution would embarrass the government much in its movements, and be productive of great mischief. I will search for the precedents which you have mentioned, as it is probable that I may have occasion for them.

55

UNITED STATES V. MAURICE
2 Marshall's C.C. 96 (C.C.D.Va. 1823)

MARSHALL, J.: . . . The Constitution, art. 2, sec. 2, declares, that the President "shall nominate, and, by and with the advice and consent of the Senate, shall appoint ambassadors, &c.," "and all other officers of the United States, whose appointments are not herein otherwise provided for, and which shall be established by law."

I feel no diminution of reverence for the framers of this sacred instrument, when I say that some ambiguity of expression has found its way into this clause. If the relative *"which,"* refers to the word "appointments," that word is referred to in a sense rather different from that in which it had been used. It is used to signify the act of placing a man in office, and referred to as signifying the office itself. Considering this relative as referring to the word "offices," which word, if not expressed, must be understood, it is not perfectly clear whether the words "which" offices "shall be established by law," are to be construed as ordaining, that all offices of the United States shall be established by law, or merely as limiting the previous general words to such offices as shall be established by law. Understood in the first sense, this clause makes a general provision, that the President shall nominate, and by and with the consent of the Senate, appoint to all offices of the United States, with such exceptions only as are made in the Constitution; and that all offices (with the same exceptions) shall be established by law. Understood in the last sense, this general provision comprehends those offices only which might be established by law, leaving it in the power of the executive, or of those who might be entrusted with the execution of the laws, to create in all laws of legislative omission, such offices as might be deemed necessary for their execution, and afterwards to fill those offices.

I do not know whether this question has ever occurred to the legislative or executive of the United States, nor how it may have been decided. In this ignorance of the course which may have been pursued by the government, I shall adopt the first interpretation, because I think it accords best with the general spirit of the Constitution, which seems to have arranged the creation of office among legislative powers, and because, too, this construction is, I think, sustained by the subsequent words of the same clause, and by the third clause of the same section.

The sentence which follows, and forms an exception to the general provision which had been made, authorizes Congress "by law to vest the appointment of such inferior officers as they think proper, in the President alone, in the courts of law, or in the heads of departments." This sentence, I think, indicates an opinion in the framers of the Constitution, that they had provided for all cases of offices.

The third section empowers the President "to fill up all vacancies that may happen during the recess of the Senate, by granting commissions which shall expire at the end of their next session."

This power is not confined to vacancies which may happen in offices created by law. If the convention supposed that the President might create an office, and fill it originally without the consent of the Senate, that consent would not be required for filling up a vacancy in the same office.

The Constitution then is understood to declare, that all offices of the United States, except in cases where the Constitution itself may otherwise provide, shall be established by law.

Has the office of agent of fortifications been established by law?

From the year 1794 to the year 1808, Congress passed several acts, empowering the President to erect fortifications, and appropriating large sums of money to enable him to carry these acts into execution. No system for their execution has ever been organized by law. The legislature seems to have left this subject to the discretion of the executive. The President was, consequently, at liberty to employ any means which the Constitution and laws of the United States placed under his control. He might, it is presumed, employ detachments from the army, or he might execute the work by contract, in all the various forms which contracts can assume. Might he organize a corps, consisting of labourers, managers, paymasters, providers &c., with distinct departments of duty, prescribed and defined by the executive, and with such fixed compensation as might be annexed to the various parts of the service? If this mode of executing the law be consistent with the Constitution, there is nothing in the law itself to restrain the president from adopting it. But the general language of the law must be limited by the Constitution, and must be construed to empower the President to employ those means only which are constitutional. According to the construction given in this opinion to the second section of the second article of that instrument, it directs that all offices of the United States shall be established by law: and I do not think that the mere direction that a thing shall be done, without prescribing the mode of doing it, can be fairly construed into the establishment of an office for the purpose, if the object can be effected without one. It is not necessary, or even a fair inference from such an act, that Congress intended it should be executed through the medium of offices, since there are other ample means by which it may be executed, and since the practice of the government has been for the legislature, wherever this mode of executing an act was intended, to organize a system by law, and either to create the several laws expressly, or to authorize the President in terms, to employ such persons as he might think proper, for the performance of particular services.

If, then, the agent of fortifications be an officer of the United States, in the sense in which that term is used in the Constitution, his office ought to be established by law, and cannot be considered as having been established by the acts empowering the President, generally, to cause fortifications to be constructed.

Is the agent of fortifications an officer of the United

States? An office is defined to be "a public charge or employment," and he who performs the duties of the office, is an officer. If employed on the part of the United States, he is an officer of the United States. Although an office is "an employment," it does not follow that every employment is an office. A man may certainly be employed under a contract, express or implied, to do an act, or perform a service, without becoming an officer. But if a duty be a continuing one, which is defined by rules prescribed by the government, and not by contract, which an individual is appointed by government to perform, who enters on the duties appertaining to his station, without any contract defining them, if those duties continue, though the person be changed; it seems very difficult to distinguish such a charge or employment from an office, or the person who performs the duties from an officer.

. . . . .

The fifth plea is, that James Maurice was never legally appointed, but was, on the 1st day of August, 1818, appointed by the secretary of war, agent of fortifications for Norfolk, Hampton Roads, and the lower part of the Chesapeake Bay, without any provisions of law whatever, authorizing and empowering him to make such appointment, and directly contrary to an act entitled, an act &c., passed the 3d of March, 1809.

To this plea there is a demurrer.

The first question arising on this demurrer, respects the validity of this appointment, made by the secretary of war. It is too clear, I think, for controversy, that appointments to office can be made by heads of department, in those cases only which Congress has authorized by law; and I know of no law which has authorized the secretary of war to make this appointment. There is certainly no statute which directly and expressly confers the power; and the army regulations, which are exhibited as having been adopted by Congress, in the act of the 2d of March, 1821, declares that agents shall be appointed, but not that they shall be appointed by the secretary of war. If this mode of appointment formed a part of the regulations previous to the revision of September, 1816, that is a fact which might or might not be noticed if averred in the pleadings. The Court is not informed of its existence by this demurrer. It must therefore be supposed not to exist, and James Maurice cannot be considered as a regularly appointed agent of fortifications.

. . . . .

Without entering on the inquiry respecting the limits which may circumscribe the capacity of the United States to contract, I venture to say that it is co-extensive with the duties and powers of government. Every contract which subserves to the performance of a duty, may be rightfully made.

The Constitution, which has vested the whole legislative powers of the Union in Congress, has declared that the President "shall take care that the laws be faithfully executed." The manner in which a law shall be executed does not always form a part of it; a power, not limited or regulated by the words of the acts, has been given by the legislature to the executive, to construct fortifications; and large sums of money have been appropriated to the object.

It is not and cannot be denied, that these laws might have been carried into execution by means of contract; yet, there is no act of Congress, expressly authorizing the executive to make any contract in the case. It is useless, and would be tedious, to multiply examples, but many might be given to illustrate the truth of the proposition. It follows, as a necessary consequence, that the duty, and of course the right, to make contracts may flow from an act of Congress, which does not in terms prescribe this duty; the proposition then is true, that there is a power to contract in every case where it is necessary to the execution of a public duty.

56

WILLIAM RAWLE, A VIEW OF THE CONSTITUTION OF THE UNITED STATES 162–67
1829 (2d ed.)

In addition to the power over the army, navy, and militia, already noticed, the president has a qualified power of appointing the executive and judicial officers. The former of these are held during his pleasure; the latter during good behaviour. In respect to both, the commissions are granted by the president, but they specify that it is by and with the advice and consent of the senate. It was deemed expedient that the approbation of the senate should be given, unless a vacancy happened during its recess, in which case commissions are granted which expire at the end of the next session.

It may, however, be questioned, whether this restraint on the power of the president fully corresponds with the confidence which is otherwise reposed in him, and whether it does not in some degree affect the responsibility to public opinion which would accompany an unlimited power of appointments.

If it were left entirely to himself to select such agents as he might deem qualified for public duties, he would of course be scrupulous in his choice; but if a senate, either actuated by party motives, or for want of information of the fitness of the individual, rejects the nomination, not only may the public interests suffer in the immediate case, but the president be impelled to inadequate substitutions. It is true, that the converse of this proposition may also be admitted. Improper nominations, proceeding from personal or party influence, may be properly rejected by a virtuous and inflexible senate; but in the latter case, if it ever should be our misfortune to have a man so actuated, in possession of this high office, we may see him immediately after the rising of the senate, dismiss the incumbent, or in case of their rejecting one nomination, withholding another, and availing himself of the power to appoint during the recess. It would, therefore, appear upon the whole, that with the possibility of an evasion which would render the constitutional provision so entirely nugatory, it would have been more beneficial to have left this power in the president without restraint, and the more so, as the consent of the senate is not required for the dismission of the officer.

It would be improper to pass over the construction given by the senate to the power of appointing during their recess. It has been held by that venerable body, that if new offices are created by congress, the president cannot, after the adjournment of the senate, make appointments to fill them. The vacancies do not *happen* during the recess of the senate.

The text is not very explicit as to the officers whose appointments require the consent of the senate: it enumerates *ambassadors, other public ministers, and consuls, judges of the supreme court, and all other officers of the United States, whose appointments are not therein otherwise provided for, and which shall be established by law; but the congress may by law vest the appointment of such inferior officers as they think proper in the president alone, in the courts of law, or in the heads of departments.* The term "inferior" is somewhat vague, and it is perhaps left to congress to determine how to apply it; if they do not otherwise direct, the consent of the senate is necessary under the qualifications described.

A proper selection and appointment of subordinate officers, is one of the strongest marks of a powerful mind. It is a duty of the president to acquire, as far as possible, an intimate knowledge of the capacities and characters of his fellow citizens; to disregard the importunities of friends; the hints or menaces of enemies; the bias of party, and the hope of popularity. The latter is sometimes the refuge of feeble-minded men, but its gleam is transient if it is obtained by a dereliction of honest duty and sound discretion. Popular favour is best secured by carefully ascertaining and strictly pursuing the true interests of the people. The president himself is elected on the supposition that he is the most capable citizen to understand and promote those interests, and in every appointment he ought to consider himself as executing a public trust of the same nature.

Neither should the fear of giving offence to the public, or pain to the individual, deter him from the immediate exercise of his power of removal on proof of incapacity or infidelity in the subordinate officer. The public, uninformed of the necessity, may be surprised, and at first dissatisfied; but public approbation ultimately accompanies the fearless and upright discharge of duty. On the other hand, hasty and capricious dismissions from office are equally reprehensible. Although the officer may be dependent on the pleasure of the president, a sound discretion is expected to regulate that pleasure. The motives to attain a degree of excellence in the knowledge and performance of official duties are greatly abated, if the tenure is rendered altogether uncertain; and if he who by industry, capacity, and fidelity, has proved himself a useful servant of the public, is causelessly removed, the public will have much reason to complain.

A mode of proceeding is interwoven with the military organization of great benefit to the sound constitution of the army. Although the president is unquestionably authorized to deprive any military officer of his commission at pleasure, yet the established practice is, to allow the individual, whose conduct has given dissatisfaction, an opportunity of explaining and vindicating it, by means of a regular tribunal, before he is dismissed, suspended, or even reproved. The same usage prevails in the navy. Thus a sort of tenure during good behavour is produced, the effect of which, with men of integrity, is eminently useful. In the diversified employments of civil life, no similar institution could be systematically adopted, and a full analogy, therefore, cannot exist; but if we sometimes see in the revolutions of party, as well in other countries as in this, whole hosts of meritorious officers suddenly swept away, and their places filled by men without superior qualifications, we may regret that the principle is lost sight of, and that no remedy can be applied.

Four executive departments have been created by congress at different times. The department of state—of the treasury—of war—and of the navy—over each of which a *principal officer*, denominated the secretary, presides. Through one of these organs, the directions of the president are communicated, in all matters relative to their respective departments. But it has been decided that the president is not confined in his executive functions to the use of a particular department. Thus in a case where it was objected that an order from the secretary of state ought not to be considered as an act of the president; it was held that reference must be had to this department for the official acts of the president, which are not more immediately connected with duties of some other department, but, nevertheless, the president, for the more easy and expeditious discharge of his executive duties, may direct some other department to make known the measures which he may think proper to take. They are equally his acts, whether they emanate from the department of state, or any other department. His immediate mandate to an inferior officer is in no case necessary.

All commissions to officers issue from, and are signed by the president. When the president has nominated, the senate approved, and the commission is signed, the appointment is complete. If the officer be removable at the pleasure of the president, the commission may be arrested by him, if it is in the office of the secretary of state, but, if it is an office during good behaviour, the appointment is not revocable, and, after it has received the approbation of the senate, cannot be annulled.

Delivery is not essential to the validity of a commission, nor is it affected by detention after it has been signed by the president, if the officer is not removable at pleasure. If in such case, the secretary of state being possessed of the commission, should refuse to deliver it, the judicial officer may nevertheless lawfully exercise his functions, and will be entitled to his legal compensations.

Sickness, absence, or death, might delay the executing a commission, and the public interests in some cases, (as for instance the judge of a district court,) suffer great injury during the vacancy of the office. The commission is not the exclusive evidence of the appointment.

The appointments made, and commissions issued during the recess of the senate, are in force only till the end of the ensuing session. When their advice and consent are given, it is to be considered not as a confirmation of the preceding appointment made during the recess, but strictly as a new one; a new official oath must be taken; and if it is an office in which security is required, a new security must be given.

57

JOHN MACPHERSON BERRIEN, COMMISSIONS GRANTED DURING RECESS OF SENATE
16 Apr. 1830
2 Ops. Atty. Gen. 336

SIR: I have the honor to acknowledge the receipt of your communication of yesterday, asking my opinion—

Whether the rejection, by the Senate, of the nomination of Mr. Isaac Hill to the office of Second Comptroller of the Treasury, has vacated the commission granted on the Executive appointment to that office, made during the late recess of the Senate?

Or whether a commission, issued under an executive appointment, continues until the end of the succeeding session of Congress, or until another commission shall be issued on a nomination approved by the Senate?

Mr. Hill was appointed, during the last recess of the Senate, to fill a vacancy occurring during the recess. That appointment was made in pursuance of the third clause of the second section of the constitution, which declares that "the President shall have power to fill all vacancies that may happen during the recess of the Senate, by granting commissions which shall expire at the end of their next session." The commission issued to Mr. Hill was, I presume, in conformity with these provisions. It was then a grant of the office to the end of the next session of Congress succeeding its date; subject intermediately, as all such offices are, to the pleasure of the President.

Under the preceding clause of the same section of the constitution, the President is authorized to nominate, and, by and with the advice and consent of the Senate, to appoint all officers of the United States whose appointments are not otherwise provided for in the constitution, and which shall be established by law—with the provision, which is inapplicable to the present inquiry, that Congress may vest the appointment of such inferior officers as they may think proper in the President alone, in the courts of law, or in the heads of departments.

In the exercise of the power thus conferred upon the President, Mr. Isaac Hill was, during the present session of Congress, nominated by him to the Senate, and the nomination has been rejected by that body. I apprehend that the commission granted to Mr. Hill, in the recess, remains untouched by this nomination, and the rejection of it.

The limitation, which is affixed to it by the constitution, is, the end of the present session of Congress, unless it be sooner determined by the pleasure of the President. To this, the decision of the Supreme Court in the case of the

United States vs. Kirkpatrick has superadded another limitation. That court has, in that case, decided that the acceptance of a commission, issued after the confirmation by the Senate of an executive appointment made during the recess, on a nomination to that body of the same individual, is a virtual superseding and surrender of the commission granted on the original appointment; so that, by force of that decision, if Mr. Hill's nomination had been confirmed, and a new commission had issued under an appointment made in conformity to the advice and consent of the Senate, after the acceptance by him of such new commission, that which he originally held would have been virtually superseded, and would not have continued until the end of the present session of Congress; but this would be the result of the concurring acts of the President and the officer: of the former, in the new appointment consequent to the advice and consent of the Senate; of the latter, in the acceptance of the commission issued under such new appointment.

In the case under consideration, whether the commission of Mr. Hill shall continue until the end of the present session of Congress, or be sooner determined, seems to me to depend on the pleasure of the President. He certainly has the power, by and with the advice and consent of the Senate, to determine it by a new appointment, to take effect immediately. But this power is derived from his right of removal. If he abstains from the exercise of that power—if he delays the nomination until the last day of the session, or nominates immediately, specifying that the appointment is to take effect at the end of the present session—in either case, Mr. Hill's commission, undetermined by any act of the executive will, is left to expire, by its own constitutional limitation, at the end of the present session of Congress.

The following proceedings, which have been adverted to among others, seem to conform to this view of the subject:

On the 5th of March, 1799, Mr. Adams, then President, appointed Eugene Brenan an inspector of the revenue; on the 4th of the following December, he nominated that individual to the Senate, for the same office; on the 10th of that month, the nomination was rejected by that body; and, on the 12th of the same month, he made a new nomination in the following terms: "I nominate Julius Nicolls, jr., of South Carolina, to be inspector of survey number three in that State, in place of Eugene Brenan, whose commission will expire at the end of the present session of the Senate;" and on the 13th, the Senate advised and consented to that nomination.

On the 17th January, 1814, Mr. Madison nominated to the Senate, as principal assessor for the twenty-eighth collection district of New York, Homer R. Phelps, who had been appointed to that office during the recess. On the 24th of that month, the nomination was rejected by the Senate; and on the 31st, the President nominated sundry assessors, and, among the rest, "Asahel E. Paine for the twenty-eighth collection district of New York, in room of Homer R. Phelps;" which nomination was confirmed on the 2d of February.

In the first of these cases, Mr. Adams left the officer to enjoy the benefit of the commission granted during the recess, until the end of the then current session of Congress, although his commission was rejected in the early part of that session. In the second, Mr. Madison, conforming to the opinion of the Senate, as expressed in their vote of rejection, determined the executive appointment by appointing a new officer in the room of the person so appointed.

In the first, the President forbore to exercise the power of removal, but left the executive commission, granted during the recess, to expire by its own limitation. The executive commission granted in the second case was determined by the exercise of that power.

Upon the whole, I am of opinion that the commission granted during the recess to Mr. Hill will continue until the end of the present session of Congress, unless it be sooner determined by his resignation, or by the pleasure of the President.

58

JOSEPH STORY, COMMENTARIES ON THE
CONSTITUTION 3:§§ 1519–26, 1528–33,
1535–40, 1548, 1550–53
1833

§ 1519. Under the confederation, an exclusive power was given to congress of "sending and receiving ambassadors." The term "ambassador," strictly construed, (as would seem to be required by the second article of that instrument,) comprehends the highest grade only of public ministers; and excludes those grades, which the United States would be most likely to prefer, whenever foreign embassies may be necessary. But under no latitude of construction could the term, "ambassadors," comprehend consuls. Yet it was found necessary by congress to employ the inferior grades of ministers, and to send and receive consuls. It is true, that the mutual appointment of consuls might have been provided for by treaty; and where no treaty existed, congress might perhaps have had the authority under the ninth article of the confederation, which conferred a general authority to appoint officers managing the general affairs of the United States. But the admission of foreign consuls into the United States, when not stipulated for by treaty, was no where provided for. The whole subject was full of embarrassment and constitutional doubts; and the provision in the constitution, extending the appointment to other public ministers and consuls, as well as to ambassadors, is a decided improvement upon the confederation.

§ 1520. In the first draft of the constitution, the power was given to the president to appoint officers in all cases, not otherwise provided for by the constitution; and the advice and consent of the senate was not required. But in the same draft, the power to appoint ambassadors and judges of the Supreme Court was given to the senate. The advice and consent of the senate, and the appointment by the president of ambassadors, and ministers, consuls, and

judges of the Supreme Court, was afterwards reported by a committee, as an amendment, and was unanimously adopted.

§ 1521. The mode of appointment to office, pointed out by the constitution, seems entitled to peculiar commendation. There are several ways, in which in ordinary cases the power may be vested. It may be confided to congress; or to one branch of the legislature; or to the executive alone; or to the executive in concurrence with any selected branch. The exercise of it by the people at large will readily be admitted by all considerate statesmen, to be impracticable, and therefore need not be examined. The suggestions, already made upon the treaty-making power, and the inconveniences of vesting it in congress, apply with great force to that of vesting the power of appointment to office in the same body. It would enable candidates for office to introduce all sorts of cabals, intrigues, and coalitions into congress; and not only distract their attention from their proper legislative duties; but probably in a very high degree influence all legislative measures. A new source of division and corruption would thus be infused into the public councils, stimulated by private interests, and pressed by personal solicitations. What would be to be done, in case the senate and house should disagree in an appointment? Are they to vote in convention, or as distinct bodies? There would be practical difficulties attending both courses; and experience has not justified the belief, that either would conduce either to good appointments, or to due responsibility.

§ 1522. The same reasoning would apply to vesting the power exclusively in either branch of the legislature. It would make the patronage of the government subservient to private interests, and bring into suspicion the motives and conduct of members of the appointing body. There would be great danger, that the elections at the polls might be materially influenced by this power, to confer, or to withhold favours of this sort.

§ 1523. Those, who are accustomed to profound reflection upon the human character and human experience, will readily adopt the opinion, that one man of discernment is better fitted to analyze and estimate the peculiar qualities, adapted to particular offices, than any body of men of equal, or even of superior discernment. His sole and undivided responsibility will naturally beget a livelier sense of duty, and a more exact regard to reputation. He will inquire with more earnestness, and decide with more impartiality. He will have fewer personal attachments to gratify, than a body of men; and will be less liable to be misled by his private friendships and affections; or, at all events, his conduct will be more open to scrutiny, and less liable to be misunderstood. If he ventures upon a system of favoritism, he will not escape censure, and can scarcely avoid public detection and disgrace. But in a public body appointments will be materially influenced by party attachments and dislikes; by private animosities, and antipathies, and partialities; and will be generally founded in compromises, having little to do with the merit of candidates, and much to do with the selfish interests of individuals and cabals. They will be too much governed by local, or sectional, or party arrangements. A president, chosen from the nation at large, may well be presumed to possess high intelligence, integrity, and sense of character. He will be compelled to consult public opinion in the most important appointments; and must be interested to vindicate the propriety of his appointments by selections from those, whose qualifications are unquestioned, and unquestionable. If he should act otherwise, and surrender the public patronage into the hands of profligate men, or low adventurers, it will be impossible for him long to retain public favour. Nothing, no, not even the whole influence of party, could long screen him from the just indignation of the people. Though slow, the ultimate award of popular opinion would stamp upon his conduct its merited infamy. No president, however weak, or credulous, (if such a person could ever under any conjuncture of circumstances obtain the office,) would fail to perceive, or to act upon admonitions of this sort. At all events, he would be less likely to disregard them, than a large body of men, who would share the responsibility, and encourage each other in the division of the patronage of the government.

§ 1524. But, though these general considerations might easily reconcile us to the choice of vesting the power of appointment exclusively in the president, in preference to the senate, or house of representatives alone; the patronage of the government, and the appointments to office are too important to the public welfare, not to induce great hesitation in vesting them exclusively in the president. The power may be abused; and, assuredly, it will be abused, except in the hands of an executive of great firmness, independence, integrity, and public spirit. It should never be forgotten, that in a republican government offices are established, and are to be filled, not to gratify private interests and private attachments; not as a means of corrupt influence, or individual profit; not for cringing favourites, or court sycophants; but for purposes of the highest public good; to give dignity, strength, purity, and energy to the administration of the laws. It would not, therefore, be a wise course to omit any precaution, which, at the same time, that it should give to the president a power over the appointments of those, who are in conjunction with himself to execute the laws, should also interpose a salutary check upon its abuse, acting by way of preventive, as well as of remedy.

§ 1525. Happily, this difficult task has been achieved by the constitution. The president is to nominate, and thereby has the sole power to select for office; but his nomination cannot confer office, unless approved by a majority of the senate. His responsibility and theirs is thus complete, and distinct. He can never be compelled to yield to their appointment of a man unfit for office; and, on the other hand, they may withhold their advice and consent from any candidate, who in their judgment does not possess due qualifications for office. Thus, no serious abuse of the power can take place without the co-operation of two co-ordinate branches, of the government, acting in distinct spheres; and, if there should be any improper concession on either side, it is obvious, that from the structure and changes, incident to each department, the evil cannot long endure, and will be remedied, as it should be, by the elective franchise. The consciousness of this check will make the president more circumspect, and deliberate in his nominations for office. He will feel, that, in case of a disagreement of opinion with the senate, his principal vindication must depend upon the unexceptionable character of his nomination. And in case of a rejection, the most, that can be said, is, that he had not his first choice. He will still have a wide range of selection; and his responsibility to present another candidate, entirely qualified for the office, will be complete and unquestionable.

§ 1526. Nor is it to be expected, that the senate will ordinarily fail of ratifying the appointment of a suitable person for the office. Independent of the desire, which such a body may naturally be presumed to feel, of having offices suitably filled, (when they cannot make the appointment themselves,) there will be a responsibility to public opinion for a rejection, which will overcome all common private wishes. Cases, indeed, may be imagined, in which the senate from party motives, from a spirit of opposition, and even from motives of a more private nature, may reject a nomination absolutely unexceptionable. But such occurrences will be rare. The more common error, (if there shall be any) will be too great a facility to yield to the executive wishes, as a means of personal, or popular favour. A president will rarely want means, if he shall choose to use them, to induce some members of such a body to aid his nominations; since a correspondent influence may be fairly presumed to exist, to gratify such persons in other recommendations for office, and thus to make them indirectly the dispensers of local patronage. It will be, principally, with regard to high officers, such as ambassadors, judges, heads of departments, and other appointments of great public importance, that the senate will interpose to prevent an unsuitable choice. Their own dignity, and sense of character, their duty to their country, and their very title to office will be materially dependent upon a firm discharge of their duty on such occasions.

· · · · ·

§ 1528. It was objected by some persons, at the time of the adoption of the constitution, that this union of the executive with the senate in appointments would give the president an undue influence over the senate. This argument is manifestly untenable, since it supposes, that an undue influence *over* the senate is to be acquired by the power of the latter to *restrain* him. Even, if the argument were well founded, the influence of the president over the senate would be still more increased, by giving him the exclusive power of appointment; for then he would be wholly beyond restraint. The opposite ground was assumed by other persons, who thought the influence of the senate over the president would by this means become dangerous, if not irresistible. There is more plausibility in this suggestion; but it proceeds upon unsatisfactory reasoning. It is certain, that the senate cannot, by their refusal to confirm the nominations of the president, prevent him from the proper discharge of his duty. The most, that can be suggested, is, that they may induce him to yield to their favourites, instead of his own, by resisting his nominations. But if this should happen in a few rare instances, it is obvious, that his means of influence would ordinarily form a counter check. The power, which can originate the disposal of honours and emoluments, is more likely to attract, than to be attracted by the power, which can merely obstruct their course. But in truth, in every system of government there are possible dangers, and real difficulties; and to provide for the suppression of all influence of one department, in regard to another, would be as visionary, as to provide, that human passions and feelings should never influence public measures. The most, that can be done, is to provide checks, and public responsibility. The plan of the constitution seems as nearly perfect for this purpose, as any one can be; and indeed it has been less censured, than any other important delegation of power in that instrument.

§ 1529. The other part of the clause, while it leaves to the president the appointment to all offices, not otherwise provided for, enables congress to vest the appointment of such inferior officers, as they may think proper, in the president, in the courts of law, or in the heads of departments. The propriety of this discretionary power in congress, to some extent, cannot well be questioned. If any discretion should be allowed, its limits could hardly admit of being exactly defined; and it might fairly be left to congress to act according to the lights of experience. It is difficult to foresee, or to provide for all the combinations of circumstances, which might vary the right to appoint in such cases. In one age the appointment might be most proper in the president; and in another age, in a department.

§ 1530. In the practical course of the government, there does not seem to have been any exact line drawn, who are, and who are not, to be deemed *inferior* officers in the sense of the constitution, whose appointment does not necessarily require the concurrence of the senate. In many cases of appointments, congress have required the concurrence of the senate, where, perhaps, it might not be easy to say, that it was required by the constitution. The power of congress has been exerted to a great extent, under this clause, in favour of the executive department. The president is by law invested, either solely, or with the senate, with the appointment of all military and naval officers, and of the most important civil officers, and especially of those connected with the administration of justice, the collection of the revenue, and the supplies and expenditures of the nation. The courts of the Union possess the narrow prerogative of appointing their own clerk, and reporter, without any farther patronage. The heads of department are, in like manner, generally entitled to the appointment of the clerks in their respective offices. But the great anomaly in the system is the enormous patronage of the postmaster general, who is invested with the sole and exclusive authority to appoint, and remove all deputy post-masters; and whose power and influence have thus, by slow degrees, accumulated, until it is, perhaps, not too much to say, that it rivals, if it does not exceed, in value and extent, that of the president himself. How long a power so vast, and so accumulating, shall remain without any check on the part of any other branch of the government, is a question for statesmen, and not for jurists. But it cannot be disguised, that it will be idle to impose constitutional restraints upon high executive appointments, if this power,

which pervades every village of the republic, and exerts an irresistible, though silent, influence in the direct shape of office, or in the no less inviting form of lucrative contracts, is suffered to remain without scrutiny or rebuke. It furnishes no argument against the interposition of a check, which shall require the advice and consent of the senate to appointments, that the power has not hitherto been abused. In its own nature, the post-office establishment is susceptible of abuse to such an alarming degree; the whole correspondence of the country is so completely submitted to the fidelity and integrity of the agents, who conduct it; and the means of making it subservient to mere state policy are so abundant, that the only surprise is, that it has not already awakened the public jealousy, and been placed under more effectual control. It may be said, without the slightest disparagement of any officer, who has presided over it, that if ever the people are to be corrupted, or their liberties are to be prostrated, this establishment will furnish the most facile means, and be the earliest employed to accomplish such a purpose.

§ 1531. It is observable, that the constitution makes no mention of any power of removal by the executive of any officers whatsoever. As, however, the tenure of office of no officers, except those in the judicial department, is, by the constitution, provided to be during good behaviour, it follows by irresistible inference, that all others must hold their offices during pleasure, unless congress shall have given some other duration to their office. As far as congress constitutionally possess the power to regulate, and delegate the appointment of "inferior officers," so far they may prescribe the term of office, the manner in which, and the persons by whom, the removal, as well as the appointment to office, shall be made. But two questions naturally occur upon this subject. The first is, to whom, in the absence of all such legislation, does the power of removal belong; to the appointing power, or to the executive; to the president and senate, who have concurred in the appointment, or to the president alone? The next is, if the power of removal belongs to the executive, in regard to any appointments confided by the constitution to him; whether congress can give any duration of office in such cases, not subject to the exercise of this power of removal? Hitherto the latter has remained a merely speculative question, as all our legislation, giving a limited duration to office, recognises the executive power of removal, as in full force.

§ 1532. The other is a vastly important practical question; and, in an early stage of the government, underwent a most elaborate discussion. The language of the constitution is, that the president "shall nominate, and, by and with the advice and consent of the senate, appoint," &c. The power to nominate does not naturally, or necessarily include the power to remove; and if the power to appoint does include it, then the latter belongs conjointly to the executive and the senate. In short, under such circumstances, the removal takes place in virtue of the new appointment, by mere operation of law. It results, and is not separable, from the appointment itself.

§ 1533. This was the doctrine maintained with great earnestness by the Federalist; and it had a most material tendency to quiet the just alarms of the overwhelming influence, and arbitrary exercise of this prerogative of the executive, which might prove fatal to the personal independence, and freedom of opinion of public officers, as well as to the public liberties of the country. Indeed, it is utterly impossible not to feel, that, if this unlimited power of removal does exist, it may be made, in the hands of a bold and designing man, of high ambition, and feeble principles, an instrument of the worst oppression, and most vindictive vengeance. Even in monarchies, while the councils of state are subject to perpetual fluctuations and changes, the ordinary officers of the government are permitted to remain in the silent possession of their offices, undisturbed by the policy, or the passions of the favourites of the court. But in a republic, where freedom of opinion and action are guaranteed by the very first principles of the government, if a successful party may first elevate their candidate to office, and then make him the instrument of their resentments, or their mercenary bargains; if men may be made spies upon the actions of their neighbours, to displace them from office; or if fawning sycophants upon the popular leader of the day may gain his patronage, to the exclusion of worthier and abler men, it is most manifest, that elections will be corrupted at their very source; and those, who seek office, will have every motive to delude, and deceive the people. It was not, therefore, without reason, that, in the animated discussions already alluded to, it was urged, that the power of removal was incident to the power of appointment. That it would be a most unjustifiable construction of the constitution, and of its implied powers, to hold otherwise. That such a prerogative in the executive was in its own nature monarchical and arbitrary; and eminently dangerous to the best interests, as well as the liberties, of the country. It would convert all the officers of the country into the mere tools and creatures of the president. A dependence, so servile on one individual, would deter men of high and honourable minds from engaging in the public service. And if, contrary to expectation, such men should be brought into office, they would be reduced to the necessity of sacrificing every principle of independence to the will of the chief magistrate, or of exposing themselves to the disgrace of being removed from office, and that too at a time, when it might no longer be in their power to engage in other pursuits.

. . . . .

§ 1535. On the other hand, those, who after the adoption of the constitution held the doctrine, (for before that period it never appears to have been avowed by any of its friends, although it was urged by its opponents, as a reason for rejecting it,) that the power of removal belonged to the president, argued, that it resulted from the nature of the power, and the convenience, and even necessity of its exercise. It was clearly in its nature a part of the executive power, and was indispensable for a due execution of the laws, and a regular administration of the public affairs. What would become of the public interests, if during the recess of the senate the president could not remove an unfaithful public officer? If he could not displace a corrupt ambassador, or head of department, or other officer engaged in the finances, or expenditures of the government? If the executive, to prevent a non-execution of the laws, or a non-performance of his own proper functions, had a right to suspend an unworthy officer from office, this power was in no respect distinguishable from a power of removal. In fact, it is an exercise, though in a more moderated form, of the same power. Besides; it was argued, that the danger, that a president would remove good men from office was wholly imaginary. It was not by the splendour attached to the character of a particular president like Washington, that such an opinion was to be maintained. It was founded on the structure of the office. The man, in whose favour a majority of the people of the United States would unite, to elect him to such an office, had every probability at least in favour of his principles. He must be presumed to possess integrity, independence, and high talents. It would be impossible, that he should abuse the patronage of the government, or his power of removal, to the base purposes of gratifying a party, or of ministering to his own resentments, or of displacing upright and excellent officers for a mere difference of opinion. The public odium, which would inevitably attach to such conduct, would be a perfect security against it. And, in truth, removals made from such motives, or with a view to bestow the offices upon dependents, or favourites, would be an impeachable offence. One of the most distinguished framers of the constitution on that occasion, after having expressed his opinion decidedly in favour of the existence of the power of removal in the executive, added: "In the first place he will be impeachable by this house before the senate for such an act of mal-administration; for I contend, that the wanton removal of meritorious officers would subject him to impeachment, and removal from his high trust."

§ 1536. After a most animated discussion, the vote finally taken in the house of representatives was affirmative of the power of removal in the president, without any co-operation of the senate, by the vote of thirty-four members against twenty. In the senate the clause in the bill, affirming the power, was carried by the casting vote of the vice-president.

§ 1537. That the final decision of this question so made was greatly influenced by the exalted character of the president, then in office, was asserted at the time, and has always been believed. Yet the doctrine was opposed, as well as supported, by the highest talents and patriotism of the country. The public, however, acquiesced in this decision; and it constitutes, perhaps, the most extraordinary case in the history of the government of a power, conferred by implication on the executive by the assent of a bare majority of congress, which has not been questioned on many other occasions. Even the most jealous advocates of state rights seem to have slumbered over this vast reach of authority; and have left it untouched, as the neutral ground of controversy, in which they desired to reap no harvest, and from which they retired without leaving any protestations of title or contest. Nor is this general acquiescence and silence without a satisfactory explanation. Until a very recent period, the power had been exercised in few cases, and generally in such, as led to their own vindication. During the administration of President Washington few removals were made, and none without cause; few were made in that of the first President Adams. In that of President Jefferson the circle was greatly enlarged; but yet it was kept within narrow bounds, and with an express disclaimer of the right to remove for differences of opinion, or otherwise, than for some clear public good. In the administrations of the subsequent presidents, Madison, Monroe, and J. Q. Adams, a general moderation and forebearance were exercised with the approbation of the country, and without disturbing the harmony of the system. Since the induction into office of President Jackson, an opposite course has been pursued; and a system of removals and new appointments to office has been pursued so extensively, that it has reached a very large proportion of all the offices of honour and profit in the civil departments of the country. This is matter of fact; and beyond the statement of the fact it is not the intention of the Commentator to proceed. This extraordinary change of system has awakened general attention, and brought back the whole controversy, with regard to the executive power of removal, to a severe scrutiny. Many of the most eminent statesmen in the country have expressed a deliberate opinion, that it is utterly indefensible, and that the only sound interpretation of the constitution is that avowed upon its adoption; that is to say, that the power of removal belongs to the appointing power.

§ 1538. Whether the predictions of the original advocates of the executive power, or those of the opposers of it, are likely, in the future progress of the government, to be realized, must be left to the sober judgment of the community, and to the impartial award of time. If there has been any aberration from the true constitutional exposition of the power of removal, (which the reader must decide for himself,) it will be difficult, and perhaps impracticable, after forty years' experience, to recall the practice to the correct theory. But at all events, it will be a consolation to those, who love the Union, and honour a devotion to the patriotic discharge of duty, that in regard to "inferior officers," (which appellation probably includes ninety-nine out of a hundred of the lucrative offices in the government,) the remedy for any permanent abuse is still within the power of congress, by the simple expedient of requiring the consent of the senate to removals in such cases.

§ 1539. Another point of great practical importance is, when the appointment of any officer is to be deemed complete. It will be seen in a succeeding clause, that the president is to "commission all the officers of the United States." In regard to officers, who are removable at the will of the executive, the point is unimportant, since they may be displaced, and their commission arrested at any moment. But if the officer is not so removable, the time, when the appointment is complete, becomes of very deep interest.

§ 1540. This subject was very elaborately discussed in the celebrated case of *Marbury* v. *Madison*.

. . . . .

§ 1548. Another question, growing out of appointments, is, at what time the appointee is to be deemed in office,

whether from the time of his acceptance of the office, or his complying with the preliminary requisitions, (such, as taking the oath of office, giving bond for the faithful discharge of his duties, &c.) or his actual entry upon the duties of his office. This question may become of great practical importance in cases of removals from office, and also in cases, where by law officers are appointed for a limited term. It frequently happens, that no formal removal from office is made by the president, except by nominating another person to the senate, in place of the person removed, and without any notice to him. In such a case, is the actual incumbent in office *de facto* removed immediately upon the nomination of a new officer? If so, then all his subsequent acts in the office are void, though he may have no notice of the nomination, and may, from the delay to give such notice, go on for a month to perform its functions. Is the removal to be deemed complete only, when the nomination has been confirmed? Or, when notice is actually given to the incumbent? Or, when the appointee has accepted the office? Hitherto this point does not seem to have received any judicial decision, and therefore must be treated as open to controversy. If the decision should be, that in such cases the nomination without notice creates a removal *de facto*, as well as *de jure*, it is obvious, that the public, as well as private individuals, may become sufferers by unintentional and innocent violations of law. A collector, for instance, may receive duties, may grant clearances to vessels, and may perform other functions of the office for months after such a nomination, without the slightest suspicion of any want of legal authority. Upon one occasion it was said by the Supreme Court, that "when a person appointed to any office (under the United States) refuses to accept that office, the successor is nominated in the place of the person, who has declined to accept, and not in the place of the person, who had been previously in office, and had created the original vacancy." From this remark, it would seem to be the opinion of the court, that the office is completely filled in every case of vacancy, as soon as the appointment is complete; independently of the acceptance of the appointee. If so, it would seem to follow, that the removal must, at all events, be complete, as soon as a new appointment is made.

. . . . .

§ 1550. This clause [2.2.3] was not in the first draft of the constitution; but was afterwards inserted by an amendment, apparently without objection. One of the most extraordinary instances of a perverse intention to misrepresent, and thereby to render odious the constitution, was in the objection, solemnly urged against this clause, that it authorized the president to fill vacancies in the senate itself, occurring during the recess; a power, which, in another clause of the constitution, was expressly confided to the state executive. It is wholly unnecessary, however, now to dwell upon this preposterous suggestion, since it does not admit of a doubt, that the power given to the president is applicable solely to appointments to offices under the United States, provided for by the constitution and laws of the Union. It is only another proof of the gross exaggerations, and unfounded alarms, which were constantly resorted to for the purpose of defeating a system, which could scarcely fail of general approbation, if it was fairly understood.

§ 1551. The propriety of this grant is so obvious, that it can require no elucidation. There was but one of two courses to be adopted; either, that the senate should be perpetually in session, in order to provide for the appointment of officers; or, that the president should be authorized to make temporary appointments during the recess, which should expire, when the senate should have had an opportunity to act on the subject. The former course would have been at once burthensome to the senate, and expensive to the public. The latter combines convenience, promptitude of action, and general security.

§ 1552. The appointments so made, by the very language of the constitution, expire at the next session of the senate; and the commissions given by him have the same duration. When the senate is assembled, if the president nominates the same officer to the office, this is to all intents and purposes a new nomination to office; and, if approved by the senate, the appointment is a new appointment, and not a mere continuation of the old appointment. So that, if a bond for fidelity in office has been given under the first appointment and commission, it does not apply to any acts done under the new appointment and commission.

§ 1553. The language of the clause is, that the president shall have power to fill up *vacancies,* that may happen during the recess of the senate. In 1813, President Madison appointed and commissioned ministers to negotiate the treaty of peace of Ghent during the recess of the senate; and a question was made, whether he had a constitutional authority so to do, there being no *vacancy* of any existing office; but this being the creation of a new office. The senate, at their next session, are said to have entered a protest against such an exercise of power by the executive. On a subsequent occasion, (April 20, 1822,) the senate seem distinctly to have held, that the president could not create the office of minister, and make appointments to such an office during the recess, without the consent of the senate. By "vacancies" they understood to be meant vacancies occurring from death, resignation, promotion, or removal. The word "happen" had relation to some casualty, not provided for by law. If the senate are in session, when offices are created by law, which have not as yet been filled, and nominations are not then made to them by the president, he cannot appoint to such offices during the recess of the senate, because the vacancy does not happen during the recess of the senate. In many instances, where offices are created by law, special power is on this very account given to the president to fill them during the recess; and it was then said, that in no other instances had the president filled such vacant offices without the special authority of law.

SEE ALSO:

Generally 2.4; 3.1.1; 4.3.1; 5; 6.2

Foreign Affairs

Luther Martin, Maryland House of Delegates, 29 Nov. 1787, Farrand 3:158

Hugh Williamson to James Madison, 2 June 1788, Farrand 3:306–7

Dawson, Virginia Ratifying Convention, 24 June 1788, Elliot 3:609–10

George Washington to Le Comte de Moustier, 25 May 1789, Writings 30:333–35

Roger Sherman, House of Representatives, 18 June 1789, Annals 1:537–38

House of Representatives, Indian Treaties, 11 Aug. 1789, Annals 1:690–98

House of Representatives, On Foreign Intercourse, 19, 26–27 Jan. 1790, Annals 1:1062–66, 1081–87, 1088–92

James Monroe to Thomas Jefferson, 27 June 1793, Writings 1:261–62

Alexander Hamilton, Pacificus, nos. 2–7, July 1793, Papers 15:55–63, 65–69, 82–86, 90–95, 100–106, 130–35

Alexander Hamilton, The Defence, nos. 26–28, Jan. 1796, Papers 20:3–10, 13–22, 22–34

House of Representatives, American Seamen, 1 Mar. 1796, Annals 5:395–96

Alexander Hamilton to Rufus King, 16 Mar. 1796, Papers 20:76–77

Alexander Hamilton to George Washington, 24 Mar. 1796, Papers 20:81–82

Alexander Hamilton to George Washington, 28 Mar. 1796, Papers 20:83–85

Alexander Hamilton to George Washington, 29 Mar. 1796, Papers 20:85–103

House of Representatives, Treaty with Great Britain, 2 Mar.–7 Apr. 1796, Annals 5:426–783

Robert Goodloe Harper, 10 Apr. 1796, Cunningham 1:50–52

James Madison to James Monroe, 18 Apr. 1796, Letters 2:96–97

Philip van Cortlandt, 20 May 1796, Cunningham 1:58–60

St. George Tucker, Blackstone's Commentaries 1:App. 341–42 (1803)

House of Representatives, Commerce with Great Britain, 9–10, 12 Jan. 1816, Annals 29:530–32, 567–71, 612–16, 631–33, 648–50

The Divine Pastora, 4 Wheat. 52 (1819)

James Kent, Commentaries 1:266–69, 270 (1826)

John Macpherson Berrien, Public Ministers, 3 Nov. 1829, 2 Ops. Atty. Gen. 290

William Rawle, A View of the Constitution of the United States 63–76 (2d ed. 1829)

John Macpherson Berrien, Authority and Jurisdiction of Consuls, 8 Sept. 1830, 2 Ops. Atty. Gen. 378

Worcester v. Georgia, 6 Pet. 515 (1832)

United States v. Percheman, 7 Pet. 51 (1833)

Appointment and Removal

Edmund Randolph to Speaker of (Va.) House of Delegates, 10 Oct. 1787, Farrand 3:127

James Madison to Thomas Jefferson, 24 Oct. 1787, Papers 10:209

Alexander Hamilton, Federalist, no. 67, 11 Mar. 1788, 452–57

James Monroe, Observations upon the Proposed New Federal Government, Feb. 1789, Writings 1:382–83

House of Representatives, Creation of Department of Foreign Affairs, 19, 21 May, 16–19, 22 June 1789, Annals 1:368–83, 396–97, 455–585

John Adams, Diary, 15 July 1789, Works 3:408

Roger Sherman to John Adams, 20 July 1789, Adams Works 6:439

House of Representatives, Additional Appropriations, 3 July 1797, Annals 7:435–39

William Findley, House of Representatives, 23 Jan. 1798, Annals 7:905

House of Representatives, Foreign Intercourse, 1–2 Mar. 1798, Annals 7:1118–23, 1167–76

Senate, Executive Appointments, 31 Mar., 2 Apr. 1814, Annals 26:649–705, 707–20

Gouverneur Morris to W.H. Wells, 24 Feb. 1815, Farrand 3:421

William Wirt, Duty of President as to Register of Wills, 15 June 1818, 1 Ops. Atty. Gen. 212

James Monroe, Message to the Senate, 13 Apr. 1822, Richardson 2:132–36

William Wirt, Executive Authority to Fill Vacancies, 22 Oct. 1823, 1 Ops. Atty. Gen. 631

United States v. Kirkpatrick, 9 Wheat. 720 (1824)

John Macpherson Berrien, Navy Agents—Appointment during Recess, 2 Apr. 1830, 2 Ops. Atty. Gen. 333

Roger Taney, Power of President to Fill Vacancies, 19 July 1832, 2 Ops. Atty. Gen. 525–30

Article 2, Section 3

He shall from time to time give to the Congress Information of the State of the Union, and recommend to their Consideration such Measures as he shall judge necessary and expedient; he may, on extraordinary Occasions, convene both Houses, or either of them, and in Case of Disagreement between them, with Respect to the Time of Adjournment, he may adjourn them to such Time as he shall think proper; he shall receive Ambassadors and other public Ministers; he shall take Care that the Laws be faithfully executed, and shall Commission all the Officers of the United States.

1

BILL OF RIGHTS, SECS. 1 AND 2
1 W. & M., 2d sess., c. 2, 16 Dec. 1689

1. That the pretended power of suspending of laws, or the execution of laws, by regal authority, without consent of parliament, is illegal.

2. That the pretended power of dispensing with laws, or the execution of laws, by regal authority, as it hath been assumed and exercised of late, is illegal.

2

VIRGINIA DECLARATION OF
RIGHTS, SEC. 7
12 June 1776

7. That all power of suspending laws, or the execution of laws, by any authority without consent of the representatives of the people, is injurious to their rights, and ought not to be exercised.

3

DELAWARE DECLARATION OF RIGHTS AND FUNDAMENTAL RULES, SEC. 7
11 Sept. 1776
Sources 338

7. That no Power of suspending Laws, or the Execution of Laws, ought to be exercised unless by the Legislature.

4

VERMONT CONSTITUTION OF 1786, CH. 1, ART. 17
Thorpe 6:3753

XVII. The power of suspending laws, or the execution of laws, ought never to be exercised, but by the Legislature, or by authority derived from it, to be exercised in such particular cases only as the Legislature shall expressly provide for.

5

RECORDS OF THE FEDERAL CONVENTION

[1:21; Madison, 29 May]
7. Resd. that a National Executive be instituted; . . . and that besides a general authority to execute the National laws, it ought to enjoy the Executive rights vested in Congress by the Confederation.

[1:63; Journal, 1 June]
It was then moved, by Mr. Madison, seconded by Mr Wilson, after the word instituted to add the words
"with power to carry into execution the national laws,—" . . .
and on a division of the amendment the following clauses were agreed to—namely
"with power to carry into execution the national laws"; . . .

[1:66; Madison, 1 June]
[Wilson:] The only powers he conceived strictly Executive were those of executing the laws, and appointing officers, not appertaining to and appointed by the Legislature.

. . . . .

Mr. Madison thought it would be proper, before a choice shd. be made between a unity and a plurality in the Executive, to fix the extent of the Executive authority; that as certain powers were in their nature Executive, and must be given to that departmt. whether administered by one or more persons, a definition of their extent would assist the judgment in determining how far they might be safely entrusted to a single officer. He accordingly moved that so much of the clause before the Committee as related to the powers of the Executive shd. be struck out & that after the words "that a national Executive ought to be instituted" there be inserted the words following viz, "with power to carry into effect. the national laws. to appoint to offices in cases not otherwise provided for, and to execute such other powers not Legislative nor Judiciary in their nature as may from time to time be delegated by the national Legislature". The words "not legislative nor judiciary in their nature" were added to the proposed amendment in consequence of a suggestion by Genl Pinkney that improper powers might otherwise be delegated,
Mr. Wilson seconded this motion
Mr. Pinkney moved to amend the amendment by striking out the last member of it; viz. "and to execute such other powers not Legislative nor Judiciary in their nature as may from time to time be delegated." He said they were unnecessary, the object of them being included in the "power to carry into effect the national laws".
Mr. Randolph seconded the motion.
Mr. Madison did not know that the words were absolutely necessary, or even the preceding words. "to appoint to offices &c. the whole being perhaps included in the first member of the proposition. He did not however see any inconveniency in retaining them, and cases might happen in which they might serve to prevent doubts and misconstructions.
In consequence of the motion of Mr. Pinkney, the question on Mr. Madison's motion was divided; and the words objected to by Mr. Pinkney struck out; by the votes of Connecticut. N. Y. N. J. Pena. Del. N. C. & Geo: agst. Mass. Virga. & S. Carolina the preceding part of the motion being first agreed to: Connecticut divided, all the other States in the affirmative.

[2:23; Journal, 17 July]
On the question to agree to the following clause namely "with power to carry into effect the national laws"
it passed unanimously in ye affirmative

[2:145, 158, 171; Committee of Detail, IV, VII, IX]
The executive Governor of the united People & States of America. . . .
  5. His powers shall be
    1. to carry into execution the national laws. . . .
    5. to appoint to offices not otherwise provided for by the constitution
      shall propose to the Legisle. from Time to Time by Speech or Messg such Meas as concern this Union. . . .

10. *receiving embassadors* 11. *commissioning offi-*
cers
12. *convene legislature.* . . .

. . . . .

There shall be a President, in which the Ex. Authority
of the U. S. shall be vested. It shall be his Duty to inform
the Legislature of the Condition of U. S. so far as may
respect his Department—to recommend Matters to their
Consideration—to correspond with the Executives of the
several States—to attend to the Execution of the Laws of
the U. S.—to transact Affairs with the Officers of Government, civil and military—to expedite all such Measures as
may be resolved on by the Legislature—to inspect the Departments of foreign Affairs—War—Treasury—Admiralty—to reside where the Legislature shall sit—to commission all Officers, and keep the Great Seal of U. S.—He
shall, by Virtue of his Office, be Commander in chief of
the Land Forces of U. S. and Admiral of their Navy—He
shall have Power to convene the Legislature on extraordinary Occasions—to prorogue them, provided such Prorogation shall not exceed   Days in the space of any
—He may suspend Officers, civil and military

. . . . .

He shall from Time to Time give information to the
Legislature of the State of the (Nation to the Legislature)
Union; he may recommend (Matters) such measures as he
shall judge nesy. & expedt. to their Consideration, and
(he) may convene them on extraordinary Occasions & in
Case of a disagreemt between the 2 Houses with regard to
the Time of Adj. he may adjourn them to such Time as
he shall think proper. (He shall take Care to the best of
his Ability, that the Laws) It shall be his duty to provide
for the due & faithful exec—of the Laws of the United
States (be faithfully executed) to the best of his ability. He
shall commission all the Officers of the United States and
(shall) appoint (Officers in all Cases) (such of them whose
appts.) them in all cases not otherwise provided for by this
Constitution. He shall receive Ambassadors, and shall correspond with the (Governours and other) Supreme Executives (Officers) of the several States.*

[2:404; Madison, 24 Aug.]

Sect. 2. Art: X being taken up. the word information
was transposed & inserted after "Legislature"

On motion of Mr Govr Morris, "he may" was struck out,
& "and" inserted before "recommend" in the clause 2d.
sect—2d art: X. in order to make it the *duty* of the President to recommend, & thence prevent umbrage or cavil at
his doing it—

[2:411; Journal, 25 Aug.]

It was moved and seconded to add the words
"and other public Ministers" after the word "Ambassadors" 2 sect. 10 article
which passed in the affirmative. [Ayes—10; noes—0.]
It was moved and seconded to strike the words "and may
correspond with the supreme executives of the several

*[EDITORS' NOTE.—Words in parentheses were crossed out in
the original.]

States" out of ye 2 sect. 10 article
which passed in the affirmative [Ayes—9; noes—1.]

[2:418; Madison, 25 Aug.]

On The question now taken on Mr. Dickinson motion
of yesterday, allowing appointments to offices, to be referred by the Genl. Legislature to the Executives of the
several States" as a farther amendment to sect. 2. art. X.,
the votes were

N. H. no Mas. no. Ct ay. Pa. no—Del. no. Md divided—
Va. ay— N— C— no— S. C. no. Geo. ay— [Ayes—3;
noes—6; divided—1.]

In amendment of the same section, "other public Ministers" were inserted after "ambassadors".

Mr. Govr Morris moved to strike out of the section—
"and may correspond with the supreme Executives of the
several States" as unnecessary and implying that he could
not correspond with others. Mr. Broome 2ded. him.

On the question

N. H. ay. Mas. ay. Ct. ay. Pa. ay. Del. ay. Md. no. Va. ay.
N. C. ay— S. C. ay. Geo— ay. [Ayes—9; noes—1.]

"Shall receive ambassadors & other public Ministers".
agreed, to nem. con.

[2:547; Journal, 8 Sept.]

It was moved and seconded to amend the 3rd clause of
the 2nd sect. 10 article to read
"He may convene both or either of the Houses on extraordinary occasions"
which passed in the affirmative [Ayes—7; noes—4.]

[2:553; Madison, 8 Sept.]

Mr. McHenry observed that the President had not yet
been any where authorized to convene the Senate, and
moved to amend Art X. sect. 2. by striking out the words
"He may convene them (the Legislature) on extraordinary
occasions" & insert "He may convene both or either of the
Houses on extraordinary occasions"—This he added
would also provide for the case of the Senate being in Session at the time of convening the Legislature.

Mr. Wilson said he should vote agst the motion because
it implied that the senate might be in Session, when the
Legislature was not, which he thought improper.

On the question

N. H. ay— Mas. no. Ct. ay. N. J. ay. Pa. no. Del— ay.
Md. ay. Va. no— N. C. ay. S. C. no. Geo. ay. [Ayes—7;
noes—4.]

[2:574, 600; Committee of Style]

Sect. 2. He shall, from time to time, give to the Legislature information of the State of the Union: and recommend to their consideration such measures as he shall
judge necessary, and expedient: he may convene both or
either of the Houses on extraordinary occasions, and in
case of disagreement between the two Houses, with regard
to the time of adjournment, he may adjourn them to such
time as he shall think proper: he shall take care that the
laws of the United States be duly and faithfully executed:
he shall commission all the officers of the United States;

and shall appoint to all offices established by this constitution except in cases herein otherwise provided for, and to all offices which may hereafter be created by law. He shall receive Ambassadors, other public Ministers and Consuls. He shall have power to grant reprieves and pardons except in cases of impeachment.

. . . . .

Sect. 3. He shall from time to time give to the Congress information of the state of the union, and recommend to their consideration such measures as he shall judge necessary and expedient: he may, on extraordinary occasions, convene both houses, or either of them, and in case of disagreement between them, with respect to the time of adjournment, he may adjourn them to such time as he shall think proper: he shall receive ambassadors and other public ministers: he shall take care that the laws be faithfully executed, and shall commission all the officers of the United States.

6

WILLIAM SYMMES TO CAPT. PETER OSGOOD
15 Nov. 1787
Storing 4.5.2

11. "The President shall take care that the law be faithfully executed."

That there must be an Executive power, independent of the legislature, appears to have been generally agreed among the fabricators of modern constitutions. But I believe it has not until now been supposed essential that this power should be vested in a single person. The execution of the law requires as much prudence as any other department, and the pardoning or refusing to pardon offences, is a very delicate matter. Yet he has no council or assistant, no restraint.

But was ever a commission so *brief*, so *general*, as this of our President? Can we exactly say how far a faithful execution of the laws may extend? or what may be called or comprehended in a faithful execution? If the President be guilty of a misdemeanor, will he not take care to have this excuse? And should it turn against him, may he not plead a mistake! or is he bound to understand the laws, or their operation? Should a Federal law happen to be as generally expressed as the President's authority; must he not interpret the Act! For in many cases he must execute the laws independent of any judicial decision. And should the legislature direct the mode of executing the laws, or any particular law, is he obliged to comply, if he does not think it will amount to a faithful execution? For to suppose that the legislature can make laws to affect the office of President, is to destroy his independence, and in this case to supersede the very constitution. Is there no instance in which he may reject the sense of the legislature, and establish his own, and so far, would he not be to all intents and purposes absolute?

7

ST. GEORGE TUCKER,
BLACKSTONE'S COMMENTARIES
1: APP. 344, 345–47
1803

As from the nature of the executive office it possesses more immediately the sources, and means of information than the other departments of government; and as it is indispensably necessary to wise deliberations and mature decisions, that they should be founded upon the correct knowledge of facts, and not upon presumptions, which are often false, and always unsatisfactory; the constitution has made it the duty of the supreme executive functionary, to lay before the federal legislature, a state of such facts as may be necessary to assist their deliberations on the several subjects confided to them by the constitution. And as any inconveniencies resulting from new laws, or for the want of adequate laws upon any subject, more immediately occur to those who are entrusted with the administration of the government, than to others, less immediately concerned therein; it is likewise provided, that the first magistrate of the union should recommend to the consideration of congress such measures as he shall judge necessary, and proper. But this power of recommending any subject to the consideration of congress, carries no obligation with it. It stands precisely on the same footing, as a message from the king of England to parliament; proposing a subject for deliberation, not pointing out the mode of doing the thing which it recommends. This is considered by De Lolme, as one of the favourable peculiarities of the English constitution, uniting the advantages of originating laws in select assemblies, with the freedom of the legislature, as vested in the representatives of the people. In France, under the present constitution, all laws originate with the executive department: than which, there can not exist a stronger characteristic of a despotic government.

. . . . .

The obligation of oaths upon the consciences of ambitious men has always been very slight, as the general history of mankind but too clearly evinces. Among the Romans, indeed, they were held in great sanctity during the purer ages of the republic, but began to be disregarded as the nation approached to a state of debasement, that fitted them for slavery. Among christian princes, they seem only to have been calculated for the worst, instead of the best purposes: monarchs having long exercised, and seeming to claim, not less than the successors of St. Peter, a kind of dispensing power on this subject, in all cases affecting themselves. A due sense of religion must not only be wanting in such cases, but the moral character of the man must be wholly debased, and corrupted. Whilst these remain unsullied, in the United States, oaths may operate in support of the constitution they have adopted, but no longer. After that period an oath of office will serve merely to designate its duties, and not to secure the faithful performance of them; or, to restrain those who are disposed to violate them.

The right of issuing proclamations is one of the prerogatives of the crown of England. No such power being expressly given by the federal constitution, it was doubted, upon a particular occasion, whether the president possessed any such authority under it: Both houses of congress appear to have recognized the power as one that may be constitutionally exercised by him. Independent of such authority, we might perhaps be justified, in concluding that the obligation upon the president to take care that the laws be faithfully executed, drew after it this power, as a necessary incident thereto. The commencement or determination of laws is frequently made to depend upon events, of which the executive may be presumed to receive and communicate the first authentic information: the notification of such facts seems therefore to be the peculiar province and duty of that department. If the nation be in a state of war with another nation, acts of hostility are justifiable, on the part of our citizens towards theirs; if a truce be concluded; such acts are no longer to be permitted. The fact that such a truce has been made, must be announced by the competent authority; and the law arising from the promulgation of this fact, according to the rules of war and peace, among civilized nations, is such, as to give to the proclamation the apparent effect of a new law to the people. But this is not really the case; it is the established law of nations which operates upon the fact disclosed by the proclamation, viz. That a truce has been concluded between the two nations, who were before at war. But if a proclamation should enjoin any thing to be done, which neither the law of nations, nor any previous act of the legislature, nor any treaty or compact should have made a duty, such injunction would not only be merely void, but an infringment of the constitution. Proclamations are then only binding, when they reinforce the observance of a duty, enjoined by law, but connected with some particular fact, which it may be the duty of the executive to make known.

8

THOMAS JEFFERSON TO JOHN B. COLVIN
20 Sept. 1810
Works 11:146

The question you propose, whether circumstances do not sometimes occur, which make it a duty in officers of high trust, to assume authorities beyond the law, is easy of solution in principle, but sometimes embarrassing in practice. A strict observance of the written laws is doubtless *one* of the high duties of a good citizen, but it is not *the highest*. The laws of necessity, of self-preservation, of saving our country when in danger, are of higher obligation. To lose our country by a scrupulous adherence to written law,

would be to lose the law itself, with life, liberty, property and all those who are enjoying them with us; thus absurdly sacrificing the end to the means. When, in the battle of Germantown, General Washington's army was annoyed from Chew's house, he did not hesitate to plant his cannon against it, although the property of a citizen. When he besieged Yorktown, he leveled the suburbs, feeling that the laws of property must be postponed to the safety of the nation. While the army was before York, the Governor of Virginia took horses, carriages, provisions and even men by force, to enable that army to stay together till it could master the public enemy; and he was justified. A ship at sea in distress for provisions, meets another having abundance, yet refusing a supply; the law of self-preservation authorizes the distressed to take a supply by force. In all these cases, the unwritten laws of necessity, of self-preservation, and of the public safety, control the written laws of *meum* and *tuum*. Further to exemplify the principle, I will state an hypothetical case. Suppose it had been made known to the Executive of the Union in the autumn of 1805, that we might have the Floridas for a reasonable sum, that that sum had not indeed been so appropriated by law, but that Congress were to meet within three weeks, and might appropriate it on the first or second day of their session. Ought he, for so great an advantage to his country, to have risked himself by transcending the law and making the purchase? The public advantage offered, in this supposed case, was indeed immense; but a reverence for law, and the probability that the advantage might still be *legally* accomplished by a delay of only three weeks, were powerful reasons against hazarding the act. But suppose it foreseen that a John Randolph would find means to protract the proceeding on it by Congress, until the ensuing spring, by which time new circumstances would change the mind of the other party. Ought the Executive, in that case, and with that foreknowledge, to have secured the good to his country, and to have trusted to their justice for the transgression of the law? I think he ought, and that the act would have been approved. After the affair of the Chesapeake, we thought war a very possible result. Our magazines were illy provided with some necessary articles, nor had any appropriations been made for their purchase. We ventured, however, to provide them, and to place our country in safety; and stating the case to Congress, they sanctioned the act.

To proceed to the conspiracy of Burr, and particularly to General Wilkinson's situation in New Orleans. In judging this case, we are bound to consider the state of the information, correct and incorrect, which he then possessed. He expected Burr and his band from above, a British fleet from below, and he knew there was a formidable conspiracy within the city. Under these circumstances, was he justifiable, 1st, in seizing notorious conspirators? On this there can be but two opinions; one, of the guilty and their accomplices; the other, that of all honest men. 2d. In sending them to the seat of government, when the written law gave them a right to trial in the territory? The danger of their rescue, of their continuing their machinations, the tardiness and weakness of the law, apathy of the judges, active patronage of the whole tribe of lawyers, unknown disposition of the juries, an hourly expectation of the enemy, salvation of the city, and of the Union itself, which would have been convulsed to its centre, had that conspiracy succeeded; all these constituted a law of necessity and self-preservation, and rendered the *salus populi* supreme over the written law. The officer who is called to act on this superior ground, does indeed risk himself on the justice of the controlling powers of the constitution, and his station makes it his duty to incur that risk. But those controlling powers, and his fellow citizens generally, are bound to judge according to the circumstances under which he acted. They are not to transfer the information of this place or moment to the time and place of his action; but to put themselves into his situation. We knew here that there never was danger of a British fleet from below, and that Burr's band was crushed before it reached the Mississippi. But General Wilkinson's information was very different, and he could act on no other.

From these examples and principles you may see what I think on the question proposed. They do not go to the case of persons charged with petty duties, where consequences are trifling, and time allowed for a legal course, nor to authorize them to take such cases out of the written law. In these, the example of overleaping the law is of greater evil than a strict adherence to its imperfect provisions. It is incumbent on those only who accept of great charges, to risk themselves on great occasions, when the safety of the nation, or some of its very high interests are at stake. An officer is bound to obey orders; yet he would be a bad one who should do it in cases for which they were not intended, and which involved the most important consequences. The line of discrimination between cases may be difficult; but the good officer is bound to draw it at his own peril, and throw himself on the justice of his country and the rectitude of his motives.

9

WILLIAM RAWLE, A VIEW OF THE CONSTITUTION
OF THE UNITED STATES 34–35,
147–50, 171–73
1829 (2d ed.)

The legislative body possesses with us a great advantage over that of those countries where it may be adjourned or dissolved at the pleasure of the executive authority. It is self-moving and self-dependent. Although it may be convened by the executive, it cannot be adjourned or dissolved by it. The time of its assembling is fixed by the Constitution, until which, unless a law has been passed appointing an earlier day, or the president on extraordinary occasions has thought proper to convene it, the *action* of the legislature cannot commence; but if in their opinion the public good shall require it, they may continue uninterruptedly in session, until the termination of the period for which the members of the house of representatives are elected, and they may fix as early a time for the meeting of the next congress as they think proper. A similar principle prevails in all the state constitutions, and it is only where it exists, that a legislature is truly independent. It is as inconsistent with sound principles for the executive to suspend, at its pleasure, the action of the legislature, as for the latter to undertake to deprive the executive of its constitutional functions.

But without a constitutional limit on its duration, it must be conceded, that a power in the legislature to protract its own continuance, would be dangerous. Blackstone attributes the misfortunes of Charles I. to his having unadvisedly passed an act to continue the parliament, then in being, till such time as it should please to dissolve itself, and this is one of the many proofs that the much praised constitution of that country wants the character of certainty. No act of congress could prolong the continuance of the legislature beyond the term fixed by the Constitution.

. . . . .

In the formation of a republic there is perhaps no part more difficult than the right constitution of the executive authority. The three qualities of promptness, vigour, and responsibility, ought to be combined in it. In the two other branches, more deliberation is necessary. Whether to make laws or to expound them, the motions should, in general, be slow and cautious. The acts of either, when constitutionally consummate, are obligatory on those whose duty it is to enforce them. The office of executing a law, excludes the right to judge of it, and of course does not require that the executive power should concur in opinion on its utility. When the meaning and intention of the legislature are ascertained, and the law itself is constitutional, delay in the execution of it is culpable. The public, which may blame the legislator, requires of the executive officer to carry it into effect, because to subvert the order of government, is one of the greatest evils that can befal it. Every individual is bound to obey the law, however objectionable it may appear to him: the executive power is bound not only to obey, but to execute it. To hesitate, to delay, perhaps to lose the proper moment of action, would approach to entire disobedience. A prompt submission to the law, and an immediate preparation to enforce it, are therefore absolutely necessary in relation to the authority from which the law has emanated. But we must also consider this quality in respect to its effect. The operation of a law, whenever the time of acting upon it has arrived, should be immediate and decisive. The law is a power of which the force and existence should never be unfelt or forgotten. Like the pillar which led the Israelites through the wilderness, it should always be in sight. The commonwealth in which its pre-eminence is not constantly present to the mind, is in danger. But the sensation of its continued presence, and uncontrollable power, will be greatly weakened, if time is suffered to elapse without necessity, after its action ought to take place.

On general political principles therefore, as delay is reprehensible, promptness is a duty, the non-performance of which may enable transgressors to escape. For this reason, it is both wise and humane that the execution of laws should be speedy; that is, that no unreasonable interval should be allowed between the violation of the law and the adoption of such measures are may be necessary to enforce it.

For this purpose the executive must also be endowed with sufficient energy. It has been justly said that a feeble executive implies a feeble execution of the government. A feeble execution is but another phrase for a bad execution; and a government ill executed, whatever it may be in theory, must in practice, be a bad government. It is in fact only by the execution of the Constitution and the laws, that the true value of either is known. If they are left as dead letters, they confer no benefit, and avert no evil. Principles without practice are like the intentions of an individual without acts. An energy of action, duly proportioned to the exigencies that arise, must be seated in the executive power. The proportion of the power to the occasions that are expected to require its use, should be as exact as possible. If it falls short, the evils we have already adverted to will ensue; if it exceeds them, the liberty of the people is endangered. It is difficult to adopt general expressions exactly descriptive of the proper extent and limitation of this power. Perhaps those we find in the Constitution are as competent as any that could be applied. "The president *shall take care that the laws shall be faithfully executed.*" The simplicity of the language accords with the general character of the instrument. It declares what is his duty, and it gives him no power beyond it. The Constitution, treaties, and acts of congress, are declared to be the supreme law of the land. He is bound to enforce them; if he attempts to carry his power further, he violates the Constitution.

But although an exact specification of the manner in which the executive power shall be exercised, is not, and could not be introduced into the Constitution, although it would be at once unnecessary and impossible to define all the modes in which it may be executed, yet the auxiliary means are not wholly omitted, and will be noticed after we have considered the composition of the executive.

In some republics, the fear of evil from a single head, has led to the creation of councils and other subdivisions of the executive power, and the consequent imbecility and distractions of those governments have probably contributed to lead most of the nations of Europe to the preference given to monarchies. It was falsely conceived that to vest the executive power in a single person, was inconsistent with the nature of a republic, or it was supposed that a republic so constituted could not long retain its freedom, against the ambitious views, and alarming domination of a single magistrate. But in America, neither the fervour of republican principles, nor the odium of monarchy, then in hostile array against us, overpowered the calm and deliberate exercise of a sound judgment in this respect, and in every state but one, the unity of the executive power was adopted as a principle. Pennsylvania alone, whose original constitution has since been altered by the people, created an executive council, formed of a member from each county, and we have heretofore noticed its feebleness and inefficiency on a distressing occasion.

The experience of nearly half a century in respect to these state governments; the experience of upwards of a third of a century in respect to the United States government, evince that under proper regulations no abuse of such powers is to be feared. Limited and restrained as the president is, creature of the people, and subject to the law, with all power to do right, he possesses none to do wrong; his general responsibility by being undivided, is complete, his liability to impeachment, by accusers, in whose appointment he has no share, before a court which he does not create, both emanating from the same source to which he owes his own existence; his term of office exactly limited, his official power entirely gone the moment that of his successor commences, or the moment when the senate shall pass on him a sentence of deprivation of office; his only safety consists in doing what is right; his speedy and certain destitution would follow a contrary conduct.

. . . . .

It is the duty of the president from time to time to give congress *information of the state of the union;* but although this alone is expressly mentioned in the Constitution, his communications naturally embrace a wider scope than internal affairs. Under the expression, *he is to receive ambassadors,* the president is charged with all transactions between the United States and foreign nations, and he is, therefore, the regular channel through which the legislature becomes informed of the political situation of the United States in its foreign, as well as its domestic relations; yet it has been always understood that he is not required to communicate more than, in his apprehension, may be consistent with the public interests. Either house may at any time apply to him for information; and, in the regular course of government, can apply only to him, where the matter inquired of, is principally under his superintendence and direction, although they frequently exercise the right to call upon the chief officers of executive departments, on matters peculiarly appertaining to them, and in like manner occasionally refer to the attorney general of the United States on subjects appropriate to his office. The applications directly to the president, are generally accompanied with a qualification evincing a correct sense of the obligation on his part to avoid or suspend disclosures, by which the public interest, that both are bound to keep in view, might be affected.

Such disclosures the legislature in general expressly disclaims. In recurrence to our history, it must be obvious, that these official communications are chargeable with being rather more full and liberal than is common in other countries. In support of the practice it has been said, that in republics there ought to be few or no secrets; an illusory opinion, founded on ideal conceptions, and at variance with the useful practice of mankind. If all the transactions of a cabinet, whether in respect to internal or external business, were regularly exhibited to the public eye, its own operations would be impeded; the public mind be perplexed, and improper advantages would sometimes be taken. Foreign powers, pursuing as they invariably do, a different course themselves, would justly object to such proceeding.

The president is also required to recommend to *their consideration such measures as he may deem expedient.* This is an obligation not to be dispensed with. Exercising his office during the recess of the legislature, the members of which, when they return to the mass of citizens, are disengaged from the obligatory inspection of public affairs; supplied by his high functions with the best means of discovering the public exigencies, and promoting the public good, he would not be guiltless to his constituents if he failed to exhibit on the first opportunity, his own impressions of what it would be useful to do, with his information of what had been done. He will then have discharged his duty, and it will rest with the legislature to act according to their wisdom and discretion. These communications were formerly made in person at the opening of the session, and written messages were subsequently sent when necessary, but the whole is now done in writing. It was formerly the practice to return answers, which as a mere matter of ceremony is now disused. The course pursued at present is to refer the message to a committee, who commonly report an analysis of it, and the parts on which it appears necessary to act, are referred to other committees to prepare them for the deliberations of the whole.

10

JOSEPH STORY, COMMENTARIES ON THE
CONSTITUTION 2:§ 892; 3:§§ 1555–57
1833

§ 892. On the day appointed for the assembling of a new congress, the members of each house meet in their separate apartments. The house of representatives then proceed to the choice of a speaker and clerk, and any one member is authorized then to administer the oath of office to the speaker, who then administers the like oath to the other members, and to the clerk. The like oath is administered by any member of the senate, to the president of the senate, who then administers a like oath to all the members, and the secretary of the senate; and this proceeding is had, when, and as often as a new president of the senate, or member, or secretary, is chosen. As soon as these preliminaries are gone through, and a quorum of each house is present, notice is given thereof to the president, who signifies his intention to address them. This was formerly done by way of speech; but is now done by a written message, transmitted to each house, containing a general exposition of the affairs of the nation, and a recommendation of such measures, as the president may deem fit for the consideration of congress. When the habit was for the president to make a speech, it was in the presence of both houses, and a written answer was prepared by each house, which, when accepted, was presented by a committee. At present, no answer whatsoever is given to the contents of the message. And this change of proceeding has been thought, by many statesmen, to be a change for the worse, since the answer of each house enabled each

party in the legislature to express its own views, as to the matters in the speech, and to propose, by way of amendment to the answer, whatever was deemed more correct and more expressive of public sentiment, than was contained in either. The consequence was, that the whole policy and conduct of the administration came under solemn review; and it was animadverted on, or defended, with equal zeal and independence, according to the different views of the speakers in the debate; and the final vote showed the exact state of public opinion on all leading measures. By the present practice of messages, this facile and concentrated opportunity of attack or defence is completely taken away; and the attack or defence of the administration is perpetually renewed at distant intervals, as an incidental topic in all other discussions, to which it often bears very slight, and perhaps no relation. The result is, that a great deal of time is lost in collateral debates, and that the administration is driven to defend itself, in detail, on every leading motion, or measure of the session.

. . . . .

§ 1555. The first part, relative to the president's giving information and recommending measures to congress, is so consonant with the structure of the executive departments of the colonial and state governments, with the usages and practice of other free governments, with the general convenience of congress, and with a due share of responsibility on the part of the executive, that it may well be presumed to be above all real objection. From the nature and duties of the executive department, he must possess more extensive sources of information, as well in regard to domestic as foreign affairs, than can belong to congress. The true workings of the laws; the defects in the nature or arrangements of the general systems of trade, finance, and justice; and the military, naval, and civil establishments of the Union, are more readily seen, and more constantly under the view of the executive, than they can possibly be of any other department. There is great wisdom, therefore, in not merely allowing, but in requiring, the president to lay before congress all facts and information, which may assist their deliberations; and in enabling him at once to point out the evil, and to suggest the remedy. He is thus justly made responsible, not merely for a due administration of the existing systems, but for due diligence and examination into the means of improving them.

§ 1556. The power to convene congress on extraordinary occasions is indispensable to the proper operations, and even safety of the government. Occasions may occur in the recess of congress, requiring the government to take vigorous measures to repel foreign aggressions, depredations, and direct hostilities; to provide adequate means to mitigate, or overcome unexpected calamities; to suppress insurrections; and to provide for innumerable other important exigencies, arising out of the intercourse and revolutions among nations.

§ 1557. The power to adjourn congress in cases of disagreement is equally indispensable; since it is the only peaceable way of terminating a controversy, which can lead to nothing but distraction in the public councils.

SEE ALSO:

Generally 2.2.2
House of Representatives, Case of Jonathan Robbins,
27 Feb., 3–5, 7–8, 10 Mar. 1800, Annals 10:558–78, 583–87,
588–94, 596–619, 621

William Wirt, Power of President to Discontinue Suit,
27 July 1827, 2 Ops. Atty. Gen. 53
Roger B. Taney, The Jewels of the Princess of Orange,
28 Dec. 1831, 7 Jan. 1832, 2 Ops. Atty. Gen. 482, 496

Article 3, Section 1

The judicial Power of the United States, shall be vested in one supreme Court, and in such inferior Courts as the Congress may from time to time ordain and establish. The Judges, both of the supreme and inferior Courts, shall hold their Offices during good Behaviour, and shall, at stated Times, receive for their Services, a Compensation, which shall not be diminished during their Continuance in Office.

1. William Blackstone, Commentaries (1765, 1768)
2. Declaration of Independence, 4 July 1776
3. Delaware Declaration of Rights and Fundamental Rules, sec. 22, 11 Sept. 1776
4. Virginia Constitution of 1776
5. Maryland Constitution of 1776, art. 40
6. Massachusetts Constitution of 1780, ch. 3, arts. 1, 2
7. Records of the Federal Convention
8. Debate in Pennsylvania Ratifying Convention, 4, 11 Dec. 1787
9. Federal Farmer, no. 15, 18 Jan. 1788
10. Brutus, no. 15, 20 Mar. 1788
11. Alexander Hamilton, Federalist, no. 78, 28 May 1788
12. Alexander Hamilton, Federalist, no. 79, 28 May 1788
13. House of Representatives, The Judiciary, 29, 31 Aug. 1789
14. John Jay, Draft of Letter from Justices of the Supreme Court to George Washington, 15 Sept. 1790
15. James Wilson, Government, Lectures on Law, 1791
16. John Jay et al., Letters on Reorganization of the Supreme Court, 1792
17. Kentucky Constitution of 1799, art. 4, sec. 3
18. John Jay to John Adams, 2 Jan. 1801
19. *Respublica* v. *Passmore*, 3 Yeates 441 (Pa. 1802)
20. Alexander Hamilton, The Examination, no. 6, 2 Jan. 1802
21. Senate, Judiciary System, Jan. 1802
22. Alexander Hamilton, The Examination, no. 12, 23 Feb. 1802
23. Alexander Hamilton, The Examination, no. 13, 27 Feb. 1802
24. An Act to Repeal Certain Acts respecting the Organization of the Courts, 2 Stat. 132 (1802)
25. Alexander Hamilton, The Examination, no. 16, 19 Mar. 1802
26. St. George Tucker, Blackstone's Commentaries (1803)
27. *Stuart* v. *Laird*, 1 Cranch 299 (1803)
28. William Cranch, Preface, 1 Cranch iii (1804)
29. An Act concerning Contempts of Court, 3 Apr. 1809, 5 Laws of Pa. 55 (1812)
30. *Yates* v. *Lansing*, 5 Johns. R. 282 (N.Y. 1810)
31. House of Representatives, Removal of Judges, 31 Jan. 1811
32. *Dupy* v. *Wickwise*, 1 Chip. 237 (Vt. 1814)
33. *United States* v. *Jacobson*, 26 Fed. Cas. 567, no. 15,461 (C.C.D.N.Y. 1817)
34. Edward Livingston, System of Penal Laws (1824)
35. William Rawle, A View of the Constitution of the United States (2d ed. 1829)
36. An Act Declaratory of the Law concerning Contempts of Court, 4 Stat. 487 (1831)
37. *Livingston* v. *Moore*, 7 Pet. 469 (1833)
38. Joseph Story, Commentaries on the Constitution (1833)
39. *Ex parte Poulson*, 19 Fed. Cas. 1205, no. 11,350 (C.C.E.D.Pa. 1835)

1

WILLIAM BLACKSTONE, COMMENTARIES
1:259–60; 3:23–24
1765, 1768

In this distinct and separate existence of the judicial power, in a peculiar body of men, nominated indeed, but not removeable at pleasure, by the crown, consists one main preservative of the public liberty; which cannot subsist long in any state, unless the administration of common justice be in some degree separated both from the legislative and also from the executive power. Were it joined with the legislative, the life, liberty, and property, of the subject would be in the hands of arbitrary judges, whose decisions would be then regulated only by their own opinions, and not by any fundamental principles of law; which, though legislators may depart from, yet judges are bound to observe. Were it joined with the executive, this union might soon be an overballance for the legislative. For which reason, by the statute of 16 Car. I. c. 10. which abolished the court of star chamber, effectual care is taken to remove all judicial power out of the hands of the king's privy council; who, as then was evident from recent instances, might soon be inclined to pronounce that for law, which was most agreeable to the prince or his officers. Nothing therefore is more to be avoided, in a free constitution, than uniting the provinces of a judge and a minister of state. And indeed, that the absolute power, claimed and exercised in a neighbouring nation, is more tolerable than that of the eastern empires, is in great measure owing to their having vested the judicial power in their parliaments, a body separate and distinct from both the legislative and executive: and, if ever that nation recovers it's former liberty, it will owe it to the efforts of those assemblies. In Turkey, where every thing is centered in the sultan or his ministers, despotic power is in it's meridian, and wears a more dreadful aspect.

. . . . .

A court is defined to be a place wherein justice is judicially administred. And, as by our excellent constitution the sole executive power of the laws is vested in the person of the king, it will follow that all courts of justice, which are the medium by which he administers the laws, are derived from the power of the crown. For whether created by act of parliament, letters patent, or prescription, (the only methods of erecting a new court of judicature) the kings consent in the two former is expressly, and in the latter impliedly, given. In all these courts the king is supposed in contemplation of law to be always present; but as that is in fact impossible, he is there represented by his judges, whose power is only an emanation of the royal prerogative.

For the more speedy, universal, and impartial administration of justice between subject and subject, the law hath appointed a prodigious variety of courts, some with a more limited, others with a more extensive jurisdiction; some constituted to enquire only, others to hear and determine; some to determine in the first instance, others upon appeal and by way of review. All these in their turns will be taken notice of in their respective places: and I shall therefore here only mention one distinction, that runs throughout them all; *viz.* that some of them are courts *of record*, others *not of record*. A court of record is that where the acts and judicial proceedings are enrolled in parchment for a perpetual memorial and testimony: which rolls are called the records of the court, and are of such high and supereminent authority, that their truth is not to be called in question. For it is a settled rule and maxim that nothing shall be averred against a record, nor shall any plea, or even proof, be admitted to the contrary. And if the existence of a record be denied, it shall be tried by nothing but itself; that is, upon bare inspection whether there be any any such record or no; else there would be no end of disputes. But if there appear any mistake of the clerk in making up such record, the court will direct him to amend it. All courts of record are the king's courts, in right of his crown and royal dignity, and therefore no other court hath authority to fine or imprison. . . .

2

DECLARATION OF INDEPENDENCE
4 July 1776

—He has obstructed the Administration of Justice, by refusing his Assent to Laws for establishing Judiciary powers.—He has made Judges dependent on his Will alone, for the tenure of their offices, and the amount and payment of their salaries.

3

DELAWARE DECLARATION OF RIGHTS AND
FUNDAMENTAL RULES, SEC. 22
11 Sept. 1776
Sources 340

22. That the Independency and Uprightness of Judges are essential to the impartial Administration of Justice, and a great Security to the Rights and Liberties of the People.

4

VIRGINIA CONSTITUTION OF 1776
Thorpe 7:3817–18

The two Houses of Assembly shall, by joint ballot, appoint Judges of the Supreme Court of Appeals, and General Court, Judges in Chancery, Judges of Admiralty, Secretary, and the Attorney-General, to be commissioned by the Governor, and continue in office during good behaviour. In case of death, incapacity, or resignation, the Governor, with the advice of the Privy Council, shall appoint persons to succeed in office, to be approved or displaced by both Houses. These officers shall have fixed and adequate salaries, and, together with all others, holding lucrative offices, and all ministers of the gospel, of every denomination, be incapable of being elected members of either House of Assembly or the Privy Council.

The Governor, with the advice of the Privy Council, shall appoint Justices of the Peace for the counties; and in case of vacancies, or a necessity of increasing the number hereafter, such appointments to be made upon the recommendation of the respective County Courts. The present acting Secretary in Virginia, and Clerks of all the County Courts, shall continue in office. In case of vacancies, either by death, incapacity, or resignation, a Secretary shall be appointed, as before directed; and the Clerks, by the respective Courts. The present and future Clerks shall hold their offices during good behaviour, to be judged of, and determined in the General Court. The Sheriffs and Coroners shall be nominated by the respective Courts, approved by the Governor, with the advice of the Privy Council, and commissioned by the Governor. The Justices shall appoint Constables; and all fees of the aforesaid officers be regulated by law.

5

MARYLAND CONSTITUTION OF 1776, ART. 40
Thorpe 3:1697

XL. That the Chancellor, all Judges, the Attorney-General, Clerks of the General Court, the Clerks of the County Courts, the Registers of the Land Office, and the Registers of Wills, shall hold their commissions during good behaviour, removable only for misbehaviour, on conviction in a Court of law.

6

MASSACHUSETTS CONSTITUTION OF 1780, CH. 3, ARTS. 1, 2
Thorpe 3:1905

ARTICLE I. The tenure, that all commission officers shall by law have in their offices, shall be expressed in their respective commissions. All judicial officers, duly appointed, commissioned, and sworn, shall hold their offices during good behavior, excepting such concerning whom there is different provision made in this constitution: provided, nevertheless, the governor, with consent of the council, may remove them upon the address of both houses of the legislature.

II. Each branch of the legislature, as well as the governor and council, shall have authority to require the opinions of the justices of the supreme judicial court, upon important questions of law, and upon solemn occasions.

7

RECORDS OF THE FEDERAL CONVENTION

[1:21; Madison, 29 May]

9. Resd. that a National Judiciary be established to consist of one or more supreme tribunals, and of inferior tribunals to be chosen by the National Legislature, to hold their offices during good behaviour; and to receive punctually at stated times fixed compensation for their services, in which no increase or diminution shall be made so as to affect the persons actually in office at the time of such increase or diminution. that the jurisdiction of the inferior tribunals shall be to hear & determine in the first instance, and of the supreme tribunal to hear and determine in the dernier resort, all piracies & felonies on the high seas, captures from an enemy; cases in which foreigners or citizens of other States applying to such jurisdictions may be interested, or which respect the collection of the National revenue; impeachments of any National officers, and questions which may involve the national peace and harmony.

[1:95; Journal, 4 June]

It was then moved and seconded to proceed to the consideration of the 9th resolution submitted by Mr Randolph

When on motion to agree to the first clause namely

"resolved that a national judiciary be established"

it passed in the affirmative

It was then moved and seconded to add these words to the first clause of the ninth resolution namely "to consist of One supreme tribunal, and of one or more inferior tribunals.

and on the question to agree to the same.

it passed in the affirmative.

[1:115; Journal, 5 June]

It was moved and seconded to proceed to the further considn of the 9th resolution, submitted by Mr. Randolph.

It was then moved and seconded to amend the last clause by striking out the words "One or more" so as to read "and of inferior to tribunals"

and on the question to strike out

it passed in the affirmative

It was then moved and seconded to strike out the words "the national legislature" so as to read

to be appointed by.

On the question to strike out

it passed in the affirmative [Ayes—8; noes—2.]

Notice was given by Mr. Wilson that he should at a future day move for a reconsideration of that clause which respects "inferior tribunals"

Mr. C. Pinckney gave notice that when the clause which respects the appointment of the Judiciary came before the Committee he should move to restore the words

"the national legislature"

It was then moved and seconded to agree to the following part of the 9th resolution namely.

"To hold their offices during good behaviour and to receive punctually, at stated times, a fixed compensation for their services, in which no encrease or diminution shall be made, so as to affect the persons actually in office at the time of such encrease or diminution"

and on the question to agree to the same

it passed in the affirmative

It was then moved and seconded to postpone the remaining clause of the 9th resolution

and on the question to postpone

it passed in the affirmative

. . . . .

It was moved by Mr Rutledge seconded by Mr. Sherman

To strike out the following words in the 9th resolution submitted by Mr Randolph namely

"and of inferior tribunals"

And on the question to strike out

it passed in the affirmative [Ayes—5; noes—4; divided—2.]

[1:124; Madison, 5 June]

Mr. Rutledge havg. obtained a rule for reconsideration of the clause for establishing *inferior* tribunals under the national authority, now moved that that part of the clause in propos. 9. should be expunged: arguing that the State Tribunals might and ought to be left in all cases to decide in the first instance the right of appeal to the supreme national tribunal being sufficient to secure the national rights & uniformity of Judgmts: that it was making an unnecessary encroachment on the jurisdiction of the States, and creating unnecessary obstacles to their adoption of the new system.—Mr. Sherman 2ded. the motion.

Mr. Madison observed that unless inferior tribunals

were dispersed throughout the Republic with *final* jurisdiction in *many* cases, appeals would be multiplied to a most oppressive degree; that besides, an appeal would not in many cases be a remedy. What was to be done after improper Verdicts in State tribunals obtained under the biassed directions of a dependent Judge, or the local prejudices of an undirected jury? To remand the cause for a new trial would answer no purpose. To order a new trial at the supreme bar would oblige the parties to bring up their witnesses, tho' ever so distant from the seat of the Court. An effective Judiciary establishment commensurate to the legislative authority, was essential. A Government without a proper Executive & Judiciary would be the mere trunk of a body without arms or legs to act or move.

Mr. Wilson opposed the motion on like grounds. he said the admiralty jurisdiction ought to be given wholly to the national Government, as it related to cases not within the jurisdiction of particular states, & to a scene in which controversies with foreigners would be most likely to happen.

Mr. Sherman was in favor of the motion. He dwelt chiefly on the supposed expensiveness of having a new set of Courts, when the existing State Courts would answer the same purpose.

Mr. Dickinson contended strongly that if there was to be a National Legislature, there ought to be a national Judiciary, and that the former ought to have authority to institute the latter.

On the question for Mr. Rutledge's motion to strike out "inferior tribunals"

Massts. divided, Cont. ay. N. Y. divd. N. J. ay. Pa. no. Del. no. Md. no. Va. no. N. C. ay. S. C. ay. Geo ay [Ayes—5; noes—4; divided—2.]

Mr. Wilson & Mr. Madison then moved, in pursuance of the idea expressed above by Mr. Dickinson, to add to Resol: 9. the words following "that the National Legislature be empowered to institute inferior tribunals". They observed that there was a distinction between establishing such tribunals absolutely, and giving a discretion to the Legislature to establish or not establish them. They repeated the necessity of some such provision.

Mr. Butler. The people will not bear such innovations. The States will revolt at such encroachments. Supposing such an establishment to be useful, we must not venture on it. We must follow the example of Solon who gave the Athenians not the best Govt. he could devise; but the best they wd. receive.

Mr. King remarked as to the comparative expence that the establishment of inferior tribunals wd. cost infinitely less than the appeals that would be prevented by them.

On this question as moved by Mr. W. and Mr. M.

Mass. ay. Ct. no. N. Y. divd. N. J. ay. Pa. ay. Del. ay. Md. ay. Va. ay. N. C. ay. S. C. no. Geo. ay. [Ayes—8; noes—2; divided—1.]

[1:126; Yates, 5 June]

The 9th resolve, *That a national judicial be established to consist of one supreme tribunal, and of inferior tribunals, to hold their offices during good behaviour, and no augmentation or diminution in the stipends during the time of holding their offices.*

Agreed to.

Mr. Wilson moved *that the judicial be appointed by the executive,* instead of *the national legislature.*

Mr Madison opposed the motion, and inclined to think that the executive ought by no means to make the appointments, but rather that branch of the legislature called the senatorial; and moves that the words, *of the appointment of the legislature,* be expunged.

. . . . .

Question on the 9th resolve to strike out the words, *and of inferior tribunals.*

Carried by 5 states against 4—2 states divided, of which last number New-York was one.

Mr. Wilson then moved, *that the national legislature shall have the authority to appoint inferior tribunals,* be added to the resolve.

Carried by 7 states against 3. New-York divided. (N. B. Mr. Lansing from New-York was prevented by sickness from attending this day.)

[1:127; King, 5 June]

Rutledge proposes to have a supreme Tribunal to be appointed by the Genl. Govt. but no subordinate Tribunals—except those already in the several States—Wilson agt. it—Dickerson—agt. Wilson the State and Genl. Tribunals will interfere—we want a National Judicial—let it be entire and originate from the Genl. Govt.
Madison proposes to vest the Genl. Govt. with authority to erect an Independent Judicial, coextensive wt. ye. Nation—
5 A.   4 No.   2 divd.

[1:128; Pierce, 5 June]

Mr. Rutledge was of opinion that it would be right to make the adjudications of the State Judges, appealable to the national Judicial.

Mr. Madison was for appointing the Judges by the Senate.

Mr. Hamilton suggested the idea of the Executive's appointing or nominating the Judges to the Senate which should have the right of rejecting or approving.

[1:226; Journal, 13 June]

Resolved that a national Judiciary be established to consist of
One supreme tribunal
To hold their Offices during good behaviour; and to receive punctually, at stated times, a fixed compensation for their services; in which no encrease or diminution shall be made, so as to affect the persons actually in Office at the time of such encrease or diminution.
Resolved that the national Legislature be empowered to appoint inferior Tribunals.

. . . . .

11 Resolved. that a national Judiciary be established to consist of
One supreme Tribunal
The Judges of which to be appointed by the second Branch of the National Legislature.
to hold their offices during good behaviour
to receive, punctually, at stated times, a fixed

compensation for their services: in which no encrease or diminution shall be made so as to affect the persons actually in office at the time of such encrease or diminution
12 Resolved. That the national Legislature be empowered to appoint

inferior Tribunals

[1:238; Yates, 13 June]

It was further agreed, that the judiciary be paid out of the national treasury.

[1:244; Madison, 15 June]

5. Resd. that a federal Judiciary be established to consist of a supreme Tribunal the Judges of which to be appointed by the Executive, & to hold their offices during good behaviour, to receive punctually at stated times a fixed compensation for their services in which no increase or diminution shall be made, so as to affect the persons actually in office at the time of such increase or diminution;

[2:37; Journal, 18 July]

On the question to agree to the following clause of the 11th resolution namely
"That a national Judiciary be established"
it passed unanimously in the affirmative
On the question to agree to the following clause of the 11th resolution namely
"To consist of One supreme Tribunal
it passed unanimously in the affirmative
It was moved and seconded to strike out the words
"second branch of the national Legislature" and to insert the words "national executive" in the 11. resolution
which passed in the negative. [Ayes—2; noes—6.]

[2:41; Madison, 18 July]

Resol. 11. "that a Natl. Judiciary be estabd. to consist of one supreme tribunal." agd. to nem. con.

"The Judges of which to be appointd. by the 2d. branch of the Natl. Legislature."

Mr. Ghorum, wd. prefer an appointment by the 2d branch to an appointmt. by the whole Legislature; but he thought even that branch too numerous, and too little personally responsible, to ensure a good choice. He suggested that the Judges be appointed by the Execuve. with the advice & consent of the 2d branch, in the mode prescribed by the constitution of Masts. This mode had been long practised in that country, & was found to answer perfectly well.

Mr. Wilson, still wd. prefer an an appointmt. by the Executive; but if that could not be attained, wd. prefer in the next place, the mode suggested by Mr. Ghorum. He thought it his duty however to move in the first instance "that the Judges be appointed by the Executive." Mr. Govr. Morris 2ded. the motion.

Mr. L. Martin was strenuous for an appt. by the 2d. branch. Being taken from all the States it wd. be best informed of characters & most capable of making a fit choice.

Mr. Sherman concurred in the observations of Mr. Martin, adding that the Judges ought to be diffused, which would be more likely to be attended to by the 2d. branch, than by the Executive.

Mr. Mason. The mode of appointing the Judges may depend in some degree on the mode of trying impeachments, of the Executive. If the Judges were to form a tribunal for that purpose, they surely ought not to be appointed by the Executive. There were insuperable objections besides agst. referring the appointment to the Executive. He mentioned as one, that as the seat of Govt. must be in some one State, and the Executive would remain in office for a considerable time, for 4, 5, or 6 years at least he would insensibly form local & personal attachments within the particular State that would deprive equal merit elsewhere, of an equal chance of promotion.

Mr. Ghorum. As the Executive will be responsible in point of character at least, for a judicious and faithful discharge of his trust, he will be careful to look through all the States for proper characters.—The Senators will be as likely to form their attachments at the seat of Govt where they reside, as the Executive. If they can not get the man of the particular State to which they may respectively belong, they will be indifferent to the rest. Public bodies feel no personal responsibly and give full play to intrigue & cabal. Rh. Island is a full illustration of the insensibility to character produced by a participation of numbers, in dishonorable measures, and of the length to which a public body may carry wickedness & cabal.

Mr. Govr. Morris supposed it would be improper for an impeachmt. of the Executive to be tried before the Judges. The latter would in such case be drawn into intrigues with the Legislature and an impartial trial would be frustrated. As they wd. be much about the seat of Govt they might even be previously consulted & arrangements might be made for a prosecution of the Executive. He thought therefore that no argument could be drawn from the probability of such a plan of impeachments agst. the motion before the House.

Mr. Madison, suggested that the Judges might be appointed by the Executives with the concurrence of ⅓ at least of the 2d. branch. This would unite the advantage of responsibility in the Executive with the security afforded in the 2d. branch agst. any incautious or corrupt nomination by the Executive.

Mr. Sherman, was clearly for an election by the Senate. It would be composed of men nearly equal to the Executive, and would of course have on the whole more wisdom. They would bring into their deliberations a more diffusive knowledge of characters. It would be less easy for candidates to intrigue with them, than with the Executive Magistrate. For these reasons he thought there would be a better security for a proper choice in the Senate than in the Executive.

Mr. Randolph. It is true that when the appt. of the Judges was vested in the 2d. branch an equality of votes had not been given to it. Yet he had rather leave the appointmt. there than give it to the Executive. He thought the advantage of personal responsibility might be gained in the Senate by requiring the respective votes of the

members to be entered on the Journal. He thought too that the hope of receiving appts. would be more diffusive if they depended on the Senate, the members of which wd. be diffusively known, than if they depended on a single man who could not be personally known to a very great extent; and consequently that opposition to the System, would be so far weakened.

Mr. Bedford thought there were solid reasons agst. leaving the appointment to the Executive. He must trust more to information than the Senate. It would put it in his power to gain over the larger States, by gratifying them with a preference of their Citizens. The responsibility of the Executive so much talked of was chimerical. He could not be punished for mistakes.

Mr. Ghorum remarked that the Senate could have no better information than the Executive. They must like him, trust to information from the members belonging to the particular State where the Candidate resided. The Executive would certainly be more answerable for a good appointment, as the whole blame of a bad one would fall on him alone. He did not mean that he would be answerable under any other penalty than that of public censure, which with honorable minds was a sufficient one.

On the question for referring the appointment of the Judges to the Executive, instead of the 2d. branch

Mas. ay. Cont. no. Pa. ay. Del. no. Md. no Va. no. N. C. no. S. C. no—Geo. absent. [Ayes—2; noes—6; absent—1.]

Mr. Ghorum moved "that the Judges be nominated and appointed by the Executive, by & with the advice & consent of the 2d branch & every such nomination shall be made at least ____ days prior to such appointment". This mode he said had been ratified by the experience of 140 years in Massachussts. If the appt. should be left to either branch of the Legislature, it will be a mere piece of jobbing.

Mr. Govr. Morris 2ded. & supported the motion.

Mr. Sherman thought it less objectionable than an absolute appointment by the Executive; but disliked it as too much fettering the Senate.

Question on Mr. Ghorum's motion

Mas. ay. Con. no. Pa ay. Del. no. Md. ay. Va. ay. N. C. no. S. C. no. Geo. absent. [Ayes—4; noes—4; absent—1.]

Mr. Madison moved that the Judges should be nominated by the Executive, & such nomination should become an appointment if not disagreed to within ____ days by ⅔ of the 2d. branch. Mr. Govr. Morris 2ded. the motion. By common consent the consideration of it was postponed till tomorrow.

"To hold their offices during good behaviour" & "to receive fixed salaries" agreed to nem: con:

"In which (salaries of Judges) no increase or diminution shall be made, so as to affect the persons at the time in office."

Mr. Govr. Morris moved to strike out "or increase". He thought the Legislature ought to be at liberty to increase salaries as circumstances might require, and that this would not create any improper dependence in the Judges.

Docr. Franklin was in favor of the motion, Money may not only become plentier, but the business of the department may increase as the Country becomes more populous.

Mr. Madison. The dependence will be less if the *increase alone* should be permitted, but it will be improper even so far to permit a dependence Whenever an increase is wished by the Judges, or may be in agitation in the legislature, an undue complaisance in the former may be felt towards the latter. If at such a crisis there should be in Court suits to which leading members of the Legislature may be parties, the Judges will be in a situation which ought not to suffered, if it can be prevented. The variations in the value of money, may be guarded agst. by taking for a standard wheat or some other thing of permanent value. The increase of business will be provided for by an increase of the number who are to do it. An increase of salaries may be easily so contrived as not to effect persons in office.

Mr. Govr. Morris. The value of money may not only alter but the State of Society may alter. In this event the same quantity of wheat, the same value would not be the same compensation. The Amount of salaries must always be regulated by the manners & the style of living in a Country. The increase of business can not be provided for in the supreme tribunal in the way that has been mentioned. All the business of a certain description whether more or less must be done in that single tribunal—Additional labor alone in the Judges can provide for additional business. Additional compensation therefore ought not to be prohibited.

On the question for striking out "or increase"

Mas. ay. Cont. ay. Pa. ay. Del. ay. Md. ay. Va. no. N. C. no. S. C. ay. Geo. absent [Ayes—6; noes—2; absent—1.] The whole clause as amended was then agreed to nem: con:

12. Resol: "that Natl. Legislature be empowered to appoint inferior tribunals"

Mr. Butler could see no necessity for such tribunals. The State Tribunals might do the business.

Mr. L. Martin concurred. They will create jealousies & oppositions in the State tribunals, with the jurisdiction of which they will interfere.

Mr. Ghorum. There are in the States already federal Courts with jurisdiction for trial of piracies &c. committed on the Seas. no complaints have been made by the States or the Courts of the States. Inferior tribunals are essential to render the authority of the Natl. Legislature effectual

Mr. Randolph observed that the Courts of the States can not be trusted with the administration of the National laws. The objects of jurisdiction are such as will often place the General & local policy at variance.

Mr. Govr. Morris urged also the necessity of such a provision

Mr. Sherman was willing to give the power to the Legislature but wished them to make use of the State Tribunals whenever it could be done. with safety to the general interest.

Col. Mason thought many circumstances might arise not now to be foreseen, which might render such a power absolutely necessary.

On question for agreeing to 12. Resol: empowering the

National Legislature to appoint "inferior tribunals". Agd. to nem. con.

[2:116; *Journal, 26 July*]

It was moved and seconded to agree to the following Resolution namely.

Resolved That it be an instruction to the Committee to whom were referred the proceedings of the Convention for the establishment of a national government, to receive a clause or clauses, requiring certain qualifications of landed property and citizenship in the United States for the Executive, the Judiciary, and the Members of both branches of the Legislature of the United States; and for disqualifying all such persons as are indebted to, or have unsettled accounts with the United States from being Members of either Branch of the national Legislature.

It was moved and seconded to strike out the word "landed"

    it passed in the affirmative [Ayes—10; noes—1.]

On the question to agree to the clause respecting the qualification as amended

    it passed in the affirmative [Ayes—8; noes—3.]

It was moved and seconded to add the words "and Pensioners of the Government of the United States" to the clause of disqualification

    which passed in the negative. [Ayes—3; noes—7; divided—1.]

It was moved and seconded to strike out the following words, namely

"or have unsettled accounts with"

    which passed in the affirmative. [Ayes—9; noes—2.]

On the question to agree to the clause of disqualification as amended

    it passed in the negative [Ayes—2; noes—9.]

[2:132, 146, 172; *Committee of Detail, I, IV, IX*]

    Resolved That a national Judiciary be established to consist of one Supreme Tribunal—the Judges of which shall be appointed by the second Branch of the national Legislature—to hold their Offices during good Behaviour—to receive punctually at stated Times a fixed Compensation for their Services, in which no Diminution shall be made so as to affect the Persons actually in Office at the Time of such Diminution

    . . . . .

5. The Judiciary
   1. shall consist of one supreme tribunal
   2. the judges whereof shall be appointed by the senate
   3. and of such inferior tribunals, as the legislature may (appoint) establish
  (4. the judges of which shall be also appointed by the senate—)
   5. all the judges shall hold their offices during good behaviour;
   6. and shall receive punctually,
      at stated times
      a (fixed) compensation for their services,
      to be settled by the legislature

in which no diminution shall be made, so as to affect the persons actually in office at the time of such diminution.

and shall swear fidelity to the union.*

. . . . .

14.

The Judicial Power of the United States shall be vested in one Supreme (National) Court, and in such (other) inferior Courts as shall, from Time to Time, be constituted by the Legislature of the United States.

The Judges of the Supreme (National) Court shall (be chosen by the Senate by Ballott). (They shall) hold their Offices during good Behaviour. They shall, at stated Times, receive for their Services, a Compensation, which shall not be diminished during their Continuance in Office.*

[2:186; Madison, 6 Aug.]

XI

Sect. 1. The Judicial Power of the United States shall be vested in one Supreme Court, and in such inferior Courts as shall, when necessary, from time to time, be constituted by the Legislature of the United States.

Sect. 2. The Judges of the Supreme Court, and of the Inferior Courts, shall hold their offices during good behaviour. They shall, at stated times, receive for their services, a compensation, which shall not be diminished during their continuance in office.

[2:335; Journal, 20 Aug.]

No person holding the Office of President of the United States—a Judge of their supreme Court—Secretary for the Department of foreign affairs—of Finance—of Marine—of War—or of

shall be capable of holding at the same time any other office of trust or emolument under the United States, or an individual State.

[2:341; Madison, 20 Aug.]

"Each branch of the Legislature, as well as the Supreme Executive shall have authority to require the opinions of the supreme Judicial Court upon important questions of law, and upon solemn occasions"

[2:423; Journal, 27 Aug.]

On the question to agree to the 1st sect. 11 article as amended.

it passed in the affirmative. [Ayes—6; noes—2.]

It was moved and seconded to add the following clause after the word "behaviour" 2 section. 11 article

"Provided that they may be removed by the Executive on the application by the Senate and House of representatives"

which passed in the negative [Ayes—1; noes—7.]

On the question to agree to the 2nd section of the 11 article as reported

it passed in the affirmative

It was moved and seconded to insert the words

*[EDITORS' NOTE — Words in parentheses were crossed out in the original.]

"encreased or" before the word "diminished" in the 2nd section 11th article.

which passed in the negative. [Ayes—1; noes—5; divided—1.]

It was moved and seconded to add the following words to the 2nd section 11 article

"nor encreased by any act of the Legislature, which shall operate before the expiration of three years after the passing thereof."

which passed in the negative [Ayes—2; noes—5.]

[2:428; Madison, 27 Aug.]

Art: XI being taken up.

Docr. Johnson suggested that the judicial power ought to extend to equity as well as law—and moved to insert the words "both in law and equity" after the words "U. S." in the 1st line of sect. 1.

Mr. Read objected to vesting these powers in the same Court—

On the question

N. H. ay. Mas. absent Ct ay. N. J. abst P. ay—Del. no. Md no. Virga. ay. N—C—abst. S. C. ay. Geo. ay. [Ayes—6; noes—2; absent—3.]

On the question to agree to Sect. 1. art. XI. as amended N—H—ay—Mas. abst. Ct. ay—Pa ay—N—J—abst Del. no. Md. no. Va. ay. N—C—abst S. C. ay Geo. ay. [Ayes—6; noes—2; absent—3.]

Mr. Dickinson moved as an amendment to sect. 2—art XI after the words "good behavior" the words "provided that they may be removed by the Executive on the application by the Senate and House of Representatives."

Mr. Gerry 2ded. the motion

Mr Govr. Morris thought it a contradiction in terms to say that the Judges should hold their offices during good behavior, and yet be removeable without a trial. Besides it was fundamentally wrong to subject Judges to so arbitrary an authority.

Mr. Sherman saw no contradiction or impropriety if this were made part of the Constitutional regulation of the Judiciary establishment. He observed that a like provision was contained in the British Statutes.

Mr. Rutlidge: If the supreme Court is to judge between the U. S. and particular States, this alone is an insuperable objection to the motion.

Mr. Wilson considered such a provision in the British Government as less dangerous than here, the House of Lords & House of Commons being less likely to concur on the same occasions. Chief Justice Holt, he remarked, had *successively* offended by his independent conduct, both houses of Parliament. Had this happened at the same time, he would have been ousted. The Judges would be in a bad situation if made to depend on every gust of faction which might prevail in the two branches of our Govt

Mr. Randolph opposed the motion as weakening too much the independence of the Judges.

Mr Dickinson was not apprehensive that the Legislature composed of different branches constructed on such different principles, would improperly unite for the purpose of displacing a Judge—

On the question for agreeing to Mr. Dickinson's Motion
N. H. no. Mas. abst Ct. ay. N. J. abst Pa. no. Del. no. Md no. Va. no N. C. abst. S—C—no—Geo—no. [Ayes—1; noes—7; absent—3.]

On the question on Sect. 2 art: XI as reported. Del. & Maryd. only no—

Mr. Madison & Mr. McHenry moved to reinstate the words "increased or" before the word "diminished" in the 2d. Sect: art XI.

Mr. Govr. Morris opposed it for reasons urged by him on a former occasion—

Col: Mason contended strenuously for the motion. There was no weight he said in the argument drawn from changes in the value of the metals, because this might be provided for by an increase of salaries so made as not to affect persons in office, and this was the only argument on which much stress seemed to have been laid.

Genl. Pinkney. The importance of the Judiciary will require men of the first talents: large salaries will therefore be necessary, larger than the U.S. can allow in the first instance. He was not satisfied with the expedient mentioned by Col: Mason. He did not think it would have a good effect or a good appearance, for new Judges to come in with higher salaries than the old ones.

Mr Govr Morris said the expedient might be evaded & therefore amounted to nothing. Judges might resign, & then be re-appointed to increased salaries.

On the question
N. H. no—Ct no. Pa no. Del. no—Md. divd Va ay—S. C. no—Geo. abst. also Masts—N. J. & N—C— [Ayes—1; noes—5; divided—1; absent—4.]

Mr. Randolph & Mr. Madison then moved to add the following words to sect 2. art XI. "nor increased by any Act of the Legislature which shall operate before the expiration of three years after the passing thereof "

On this question
N. H. no. Ct. no—Pa. no. Del. no. Md ay—Va ay—S. C. no. Geo—abst also Mas. N. J. & N. C. [Ayes—2; noes—5; absent—4.]

[2:575, 600; Committee of Style]

Sect. 1. The Judicial Power of the United States both in law and equity shall be vested in one Supreme Court, and in such Inferior Courts as shall, when necessary, from time to time, be constituted by the Legislature of the United States.

Sect. 2. The Judges of the Supreme Court, and of the Inferior courts, shall hold their offices during good behaviour. They shall, at stated times, receive for their services, a compensation, which shall not be diminished during their continuance in office.

. . . . .

Sect. 1. The judicial power of the United States, both in law and equity, shall be vested in one supreme court, and in such inferior courts as the Congress may from time to time ordain and establish. The judges, both of the supreme and inferior courts, shall hold their offices during good behaviour, and shall, at stated times, receive for their services, a compensation, which shall not be diminished during their continuance in office.

[2:638; Mason, 15 Sept.]

The Judiciary of the United States is so constructed and extended, as to absorb and destroy the judiciaries of the several States; thereby rendering law as tedious, intricate and expensive, and justice as unattainable, by a great part of the community, as in England, and enabling the rich to oppress and ruin the poor.

8

DEBATE IN PENNSYLVANIA RATIFYING CONVENTION
4, 11 Dec. 1787
Elliot 2:480–81, 514, 539

[James Wilson:] Sir, it has often been a matter of surprise, and frequently complained of even in Pennsylvania, that the *independence of the judges* is not properly secured. The servile dependence of the judges, in some of the states that have neglected to make proper provision on this subject, endangers the liberty and property of the citizen; and I apprehend that, whenever it has happened that the appointment has been for a less period than during good behaviour, this object has not been sufficiently secured; for if, every five or seven years, the judges are obliged to make court for their appointment to office, they cannot be styled independent. This is not the case with regard to those appointed under the general government; for the judges here shall hold their offices during good behavior. I hope no further objections will be taken against this part of the Constitution, the consequence of which will be, that private property, so far as it comes before their courts, and personal liberty, so far as it is not forfeited by crimes, will be guarded with firmness and watchfulness.

It may appear too professional to descend into observations of this kind; but I believe that public happiness, personal liberty, and private property, depend essentially upon the able and upright determinations of independent judges.

Permit me to make one more remark on the subject of the judicial department. Its objects are extended *beyond* the bounds or power of every particular state, and therefore must be proper objects of the general government. I do not recollect any instance where a case can come before the judiciary of the United States, that could possibly be determined by a particular state, except one—which is, where citizens of the same state claim lands under the grant of different states; and in that instance, the power of the two states necessarily comes in competition; wherefore there would be great impropriety in having it determined by either.

. . . . .

I now proceed to the judicial department; and here, Mr. President, I meet an objection, I confess, I had not expected; and it seems it did not occur to the honorable gentleman (Mr. Findley) who made it until a few days ago.

He alleges that the judges, under this Constitution, are not rendered sufficiently independent, because they may hold other offices; and though they may be independent as judges, yet their other office may depend upon the legislature. I confess, sir, this objection appears to me to be a little wire-drawn. In the first place, the legislature can appoint to no office; therefore, the dependence could not be on them for the office, but rather on the President and Senate; but then these cannot add the salary, because no money can be appropriated but in consequence of a law of the United States. No sinecure can be bestowed on any judge but by the concurrence of the whole legislature and the President; and I do not think this an event that will probably happen.

It is true that there is a provision made in the Constitution of Pennsylvania, that the judges shall not be allowed to hold any other office whatsoever; and I believe they are expressly forbidden to sit in Congress; but this, sir, is not introduced as a principle into this Constitution. There are many states in the Union, whose constitutions do not limit the usefulness of their best men, or exclude them from rendering those services to their country for which they are found eminently qualified. New York, far from restricting their chancellor, or judges of the Supreme Court, from a seat in Congress, expressly provide for sending them there on extraordinary occasions. In Connecticut, the judges are not precluded from enjoying other offices. Judges from many states have sat in Congress. Now, it is not to be expected that eleven or twelve states are to change their sentiments and practice, on this subject, to accommodate themselves to Pennsylvania.

. . . . .

[Thomas McKean:] The next objection is against the judicial department. "The judicial power shall be vested in one Supreme Court." An objection is made that the compensation for the services of the judges shall not be *diminished* during their continuance in office; and this is contrasted with the compensation of the President, which is to be neither *increased* nor *diminished* during the period for which he shall be elected. But that of the judges may be increased, and the judge may hold other offices of a lucrative nature, and his judgment be thereby warped.

Do gentlemen not see the reason why this difference is made? Do they not see that the President is appointed but for four years, whilst the judges may continue for life, if they shall so long behave themselves well? In the first case, little alteration can happen in the value of money; but in the course of a man's life, a very great one may take place from the discovery of silver and gold mines, and the great influx of those metals; in which case an increase of salary may be requisite. A security that their compensation shall not be lessened, nor they have to look up to every session for salary, will certainly tend to make those officers more easy and independent.

"The judges may hold other offices of a lucrative nature." This part of the objection reminds me of the scheme that was fallen upon, in Pennsylvania, to prevent any person from taking up large tracts of land. A law was passed restricting the purchaser to a tract not exceeding three hundred acres; but all the difference it made was, that the land was taken up by several patents, instead of one, and the wealthy could procure, if they chose it, three thousand acres. What though the judges could hold no other office, might they not have brothers, children, and other relations, whom they might wish to see placed in the offices forbidden to themselves? I see no apprehensions that may be entertained on this account.

9

FEDERAL FARMER, NO. 15
18 Jan. 1788
Storing 2.8.188

In examining the federal judiciary, there appears to be some things very extraordinary and very peculiar. The judges or their friends may seize every opportunity to raise the judges salaries; but by the constitution they cannot be diminished. I am sensible how important it is that judges shall always have adequate and certain support; I am against their depending upon annual or periodical grants, because these may be withheld, or rendered too small by the dissent or narrowness of any one branch of the legislature; but there is a material distinction betweeen periodical grants, and salaries held under permanent and standing laws: the former at stated periods cease, and must be renewed by the consent of all and every part of the legislature; the latter continue of course, and never will cease or be lowered, unless all parts of the legislature agree to do it. A man has as permanent an interest in his salary fixed by a standing law, so long as he may remain in office, as in any property he may possess; for the laws regulating the tenure of all property, are always liable to be altered by the legislature. The same judge may frequently be in office thirty or forty years; there may often be times, as in cases of war, or very high prices, when his salary may reasonably be increased one half or more; in a few years money may become scarce again, and prices fall, and his salary, with equal reason and propriety be decreased and lowered: not to suffer this to be done by consent of all the branches of the legislature, is, I believe, quite a novelty in the affairs of government. It is true, by a very forced and unnatural construction, the constitution of Massachusetts, by the governor and minority in the legislature, was made to speak this kind of language. Another circumstance ought to be considered; the mines which have been discovered are gradually exhausted, and the precious metals are continually wasting: hence the probability is, that money, the nominal representative of property, will gradually grow scarcer hereafter, and afford just reasons for gradually lowering salaries. The value of money depends altogether upon the quality of it in circulation, which may be also decreased, as well as encreased, from a great variety of causes.

10

BRUTUS, NO. 15
20 Mar. 1788
Storing 2.9.189–92

I do not object to the judges holding their commissions during good behaviour. I suppose it a proper provision provided they were made properly responsible. But I say, this system has followed the English government in this, while it has departed from almost every other principle of their jurisprudence, under the idea, of rendering the judges independent; which, in the British constitution, means no more than that they hold their places during good behavior, and have fixed salaries, they have made the judges *independent,* in the fullest sense of the word. There is no power above them, to controul any of their decisions. There is no authority that can remove them, and they cannot be controuled by the laws of the legislature. In short, they are independent of the people, of the legislature, and of every power under heaven. Men placed in this situation will generally soon feel themselves independent of heaven itself. Before I proceed to illustrate the truth of these assertions, I beg liberty to make one remark—Though in my opinion the judges ought to hold their offices during good behaviour, yet I think it is clear, that the reasons in favour of this establishment of the judges in England, do by no means apply to this country.

The great reason assigned, why the judges in Britain ought to be commissioned during good behavior, is this, that they may be placed in a situation, not to be influenced by the crown, to give such decisions, as would tend to increase its powers and prerogatives. While the judges held their places at the will and pleasure of the king, on whom they depended not only for their offices, but also for their salaries, they were subject to every undue influence. If the crown wished to carry a favorite point, to accomplish which the aid of the courts of law was necessary, the pleasure of the king would be signified to the judges. And it required the spirit of a martyr, for the judges to determine contrary to the king's will.—They were absolutely dependent upon him both for their offices and livings. The king, holding his office during life, and transmitting it to his posterity as an inheritance, has much stronger inducements to increase the prerogatives of his office than those who hold their offices for stated periods, or even for life. Hence the English nation gained a great point, in favour of liberty. When they obtained the appointment of the judges, during good behaviour, they got from the crown a concession, which deprived it of one of the most powerful engines with which it might enlarge the boundaries of the royal prerogative and encroach on the liberties of the people. But these reasons do not apply to this country, we have no hereditary monarch; those who appoint the judges do not hold their offices for life, nor do they descend to their children. The same arguments, therefore,

which will conclude in favor of the tenor of the judge's offices for good behaviour, lose a considerable part of their weight when applied to the state and condition of America. But much less can it be shewn, that the nature of our government requires that the courts should be placed beyond all account more independent, so much so as to be above controul.

I have said that the judges under this system will be *independent* in the strict sense of the word: To prove this I will shew—That there is no power above them that can controul their decisions, or correct their errors. There is no authority that can remove them from office for any errors or want of capacity, or lower their salaries, and in many cases their power is superior to that of the legislature.

1st. There is no power above them that can correct their errors or controul their decisions—The adjudications of this court are final and irreversible, for there is no court above them to which appeals can lie, either in error or on the merits.—In this respect it differs from the courts in England, for there the house of lords is the highest court, to whom appeals, in error, are carried from the highest of the courts of law.

2d. They cannot be removed from office or suffer a diminution of their salaries, for any error in judgement or want of capacity.

It is expressly declared by the constitution,—"That they shall at stated times receive a compensation for their services which shall not be diminished during their continuance in office."

11

ALEXANDER HAMILTON, FEDERALIST, NO. 78,
521–30
28 May 1788

In unfolding the defects of the existing confederation, the utility and necessity of a federal judicature have been clearly pointed out. It is the less necessary to recapitulate the considerations there urged; as the propriety of the institution in the abstract is not disputed: The only questions which have been raised being relative to the manner of constituting it, and to its extent. To these points therefore our observations shall be confined.

The manner of constituting it seems to embrace these several objects—1st. The mode of appointing the judges. 2d. The tenure by which they are to hold their places. 3d. The partition of the judiciary authority between different courts, and their relations to each other.

First. As to the mode of appointing the judges: This is the same with that of appointing the officers of the union in general, and has been so fully discussed in the two last numbers, that nothing can be said here which would not be useless repetition.

Second. As to the tenure by which the judges are to hold

their places: This chiefly concerns their duration in office; the provisions for their support; and the precautions for their responsibility.

According to the plan of the convention, all the judges who may be appointed by the United States are to hold their offices *during good behaviour,* which is conformable to the most approved of the state constitutions; and among the rest, to that of this state. Its propriety having been drawn into question by the adversaries of that plan, is no light symptom of the rage for objection which disorders their imaginations and judgments. The standard of good behaviour for the continuance in office of the judicial magistracy is certainly one of the most valuable of the modern improvements in the practice of government. In a monarchy it is an excellent barrier to the despotism of the prince: In a republic it is a no less excellent barrier to the encroachments and oppressions of the representative body. And it is the best expedient which can be devised in any government, to secure a steady, upright and impartial administration of the laws.

Whoever attentively considers the different departments of power must perceive, that in a government in which they are separated from each other, the judiciary, from the nature of its functions, will always be the least danger-ous to the political rights of the constitution; because it will be least in a capacity to annoy or injure them. The execu-tive not only dispenses the honors, but holds the sword of the community. The legislature not only commands the purse, but prescribes the rules by which the duties and rights of every citizen are to be regulated. The judiciary on the contrary has no influence over either the sword or the purse, no direction either of the strength or of the wealth of the society, and can take no active resolution whatever. It may truly be said to have neither Force nor Will, but merely judgment; and must ultimately depend upon the aid of the executive arm even for the efficacy of its judgments.

This simple view of the matter suggests several impor-tant consequences. It proves incontestibly that the judi-ciary is beyond comparison the weakest of the three de-partments of power;* that it can never attack with success either of the other two; and that all possible care is requi-site to enable it to defend itself against their attacks. It equally proves, that though individual oppression may now and then proceed from the courts of justice, the gen-eral liberty of the people can never be endangered from that quarter: I mean, so long as the judiciary remains truly distinct from both the legislative and executive. For I agree that "there is no liberty, if the power of judging be not separated from the legislative and executive powers." And it proves, in the last place, that as liberty can have nothing to fear from the judiciary alone, but would have every thing to fear from its union with either of the other departments; that as all the effects of such an union must ensue from a dependence of the former on the latter, not-withstanding a nominal and apparent separation; that as

*The celebrated Montesquieu speaking of them says, "of the three powers above mentioned, the JUDICIARY is next to nothing." Spirit of Laws, vol. 1, page 186.

from the natural feebleness of the judiciary, it is in contin-ual jeopardy of being overpowered, awed or influenced by its coordinate branches; and that as nothing can contribute so much to its firmness and independence, as permanency in office, this quality may therefore be justly regarded as an indispensable ingredient in its constitution; and in a great measure as the citadel of the public justice and the public security.

The complete independence of the courts of justice is peculiarly essential in a limited constitution. By a limited constitution I understand one which contains certain spec-ified exceptions to the legislative authority; such for in-stance as that it shall pass no bills of attainder, no *ex post facto* laws, and the like. Limitations of this kind can be pre-served in practice no other way than through the medium of the courts of justice; whose duty it must be to declare all acts contrary to the manifest tenor of the constitution void. Without this, all the reservations of particular rights or privileges would amount to nothing.

Some perplexity respecting the right of the courts to pronounce legislative acts void, because contrary to the constitution, has arisen from an imagination that the doc-trine would imply a superiority of the judiciary to the leg-islative power. It is urged that the authority which can de-clare the acts of another void, must necessarily be superior to the one whose acts may be declared void. As this doc-trine is of great importance in all the American constitu-tions, a brief discussion of the grounds on which it rests cannot be unacceptable.

There is no position which depends on clearer princi-ples, than that every act of a delegated authority, contrary to the tenor of the commission under which it is exercised, is void. No legislative act therefore contrary to the consti-tution can be valid. To deny this would be to affirm that the deputy is greater than his principal; that the servant is above his master; that the representatives of the people are superior to the people themselves; that men acting by virtue of powers may do not only what their powers do not authorise, but what they forbid.

If it be said that the legislative body are themselves the constitutional judges of their own powers, and that the construction they put upon them is conclusive upon the other departments, it may be answered, that this cannot be the natural presumption, where it is not to be collected from any particular provisions in the constitution. It is not otherwise to be supposed that the constitution could in-tend to enable the representatives of the people to substi-tute their *will* to that of their constituents. It is far more rational to suppose that the courts were designed to be an intermediate body between the people and the legislature, in order, among other things, to keep the latter within the limits assigned to their authority. The interpretation of the laws is the proper and peculiar province of the courts. A constitution is in fact, and must be, regarded by the judges as a fundamental law. It therefore belongs to them to as-certain its meaning as well as the meaning of any particu-lar act proceeding from the legislative body. If there should happen to be an irreconcileable variance between the two, that which has the superior obligation and validity ought of course to be preferred; or in other words, the constitution ought to be preferred to the statute, the intention of the people to the intention of their agents.

Nor does this conclusion by any means suppose a superiority of the judicial to the legislative power. It only supposes that the power of the people is superior to both; and that where the will of the legislature declared in its statutes, stands in opposition to that of the people declared in the constitution, the judges ought to be governed by the latter, rather than the former. They ought to regulate their decisions by the fundamental laws, rather than by those which are not fundamental.

This exercise of judicial discretion in determining between two contradictory laws, is exemplified in a familiar instance. It not uncommonly happens, that there are two statutes existing at one time, clashing in whole or in part with each other, and neither of them containing any repealing clause or expression. In such a case, it is the province of the courts to liquidate and fix their meaning and operation: So far as they can by any fair construction be reconciled to each other; reason and law conspire to dictate that this should be done. Where this is impracticable, it becomes a matter of necessity to give effect to one, in exclusion of the other. The rule which has obtained in the courts for determining their relative validity is that the last in order of time shall be preferred to the first. But this is mere rule of construction, not derived from any positive law, but from the nature and reason of the thing. It is a rule not enjoined upon the courts by legislative provision, but adopted by themselves, as consonant to truth and propriety, for the direction of their conduct as interpreters of the law. They thought it reasonable, that between the interfering acts of an *equal* authority, that which was the last indication of its will, should have the preference.

But in regard to the interfering acts of a superior and subordinate authority, of an original and derivative power, the nature and reason of the thing indicate the converse of that rule as proper to be followed. They teach us that the prior act of a superior ought to be preferred to the subsequent act of an inferior and subordinate authority; and that, accordingly, whenever a particular statute contravenes the constitution, it will be the duty of the judicial tribunals to adhere to the latter, and disregard the former.

It can be of no weight to say, that the courts on the pretence of a repugnancy, may substitute their own pleasure to the constitutional intentions of the legislature. This might as well happen in the case of two contradictory statutes; or it might as well happen in every adjudication upon any single statute. The courts must declare the sense of the law; and if they should be disposed to exercise WILL instead of JUDGMENT, the consequence would equally be the substitution of their pleasure to that of the legislative body. The observation, if it proved any thing, would prove that there ought to be no judges distinct from that body.

If then the courts of justice are to be considered as the bulwarks of a limited constitution against legislative encroachments, this consideration will afford a strong argument for the permanent tenure of judicial offices, since nothing will contribute so much as this to that independent spirit in the judges, which must be essential to the faithful performance of so arduous a duty.

This independence of the judges is equally requisite to guard the constitution and the rights of individuals from the effects of those ill humours which the arts of designing men, or the influence of particular conjunctures, sometimes disseminate among the people themselves, and which, though they speedily give place to better information and more deliberate reflection, have a tendency in the mean time to occasion dangerous innovations in the government, and serious oppressions of the minor party in the community. Though I trust the friends of the proposed constitution will never concur with its enemies* in questioning that fundamental principle of republican government, which admits the right of the people to alter or abolish the established constitution whenever they find it inconsistent with their happiness; yet it is not to be inferred from this principle, that the representatives of the people, whenever a momentary inclination happens to lay hold of a majority of their constituents incompatible with the provisions in the existing constitution, would on that account be justifiable in a violation of those provisions; or that the courts would be under a greater obligation to connive at infractions in this shape, than when they had proceeded wholly from the cabals of the representative body. Until the people have by some solemn and authoritative act annulled or changed the established form, it is binding upon themselves collectively, as well as individually; and no presumption, or even knowledge of their sentiments, can warrant their representatives in a departure from it, prior to such an act. But it is easy to see that it would require an uncommon portion of fortitude in the judges to do their duty as faithful guardians of the constitution, where legislative invasions of it had been instigated by the major voice of the community.

But it is not with a view to infractions of the constitution only that the independence of the judges may be an essential safeguard against the effects of occasional ill humours in the society. These sometimes extend no farther than to the injury of the private rights of particular classes of citizens, by unjust and partial laws. Here also the firmness of the judicial magistracy is of vast importance in mitigating the severity, and confining the operation of such laws. It not only serves to moderate the immediate mischiefs of those which may have been passed, but it operates as a check upon the legislative body in passing them; who, perceiving that obstacles to the success of an iniquitous intention are to be expected from the scruples of the courts, are in a manner compelled by the very motives of the injustice they meditate, to qualify their attempts. This is a circumstance calculated to have more influence upon the character of our governments, than but few may be aware of. The benefits of the integrity and moderation of the judiciary have already been felt in more states than one; and though they may have displeased those whose sinister expectations they may have disappointed, they must have commanded the esteem and applause of all the virtuous and disinterested. Considerate men of every description ought to prize whatever will tend to beget or fortify that

*Vide Protest of the minority of the convention of Pennsylvania, Martin's speech, &c.

143

temper in the courts; as no man can be sure that he may not be tomorrow the victim of a spirit of injustice, by which he may be a gainer to-day. And every man must now feel that the inevitable tendency of such a spirit is to sap the foundations of public and private confidence, and to introduce in its stead, universal distrust and distress.

That inflexible and uniform adherence to the rights of the constitution and of individuals, which we perceive to be indispensable in the courts of justice, can certainly not be expected from judges who hold their offices by a temporary commission. Periodical appointments, however regulated, or by whomsoever made, would in some way or other be fatal to their necessary independence. If the power of making them was committed either to the executive or legislature, there would be danger of an improper complaisance to the branch which possessed it; if to both, there would be an unwillingness to hazard the displeasure of either; if to the people, or to persons chosen by them for the special purpose, there would be too great a disposition to consult popularity, to justify a reliance that nothing would be consulted but the constitution and the laws.

There is yet a further and a weighty reason for the permanency of the judicial offices; which is deducible from the nature of the qualifications they require. It has been frequently remarked with great propriety, that a voluminous code of laws is one of the inconveniences necessarily connected with the advantages of a free government. To avoid an arbitrary discretion in the courts, it is indispensable that they should be bound down by strict rules and precedents, which serve to define and point out their duty in every particular case that comes before them; and it will readily be conceived from the variety of controversies which grow out of the folly and wickedness of mankind, that the records of those precedents must unavoidably swell to a very considerable bulk, and must demand long and laborious study to acquire a competent knowledge of them. Hence it is that there can be but few men in the society, who will have sufficient skill in the laws to qualify them for the stations of judges. And making proper deductions for the ordinary depravity of human nature, the number must be still smaller of those who unite the requisite integrity with the requisite knowledge. These considerations apprise us, that the government can have no great option between fit characters; and that a temporary duration in office, which would naturally discourage such characters from quitting a lucrative line of practice to accept a seat on the bench, would have a tendency to throw the administration of justice into hands less able, and less well qualified to conduct it with utility and dignity. In the present circumstances of this country, and in those in which it is likely to be for a long time to come, the disadvantages on this score would be greater than they may at first sight appear; but it must be confessed that they are far inferior to those which present themselves under the other aspects of the subject.

Upon the whole there can be no room to doubt that the convention acted wisely in copying from the models of those constitutions which have established *good behaviour* as the tenure of their judicial offices in point of duration; and that so far from being blameable on this account, their plan would have been inexcuseably defective if it had wanted this important feature of good government. The experience of Great Britain affords an illustrious comment on the excellence of the institution.

12

ALEXANDER HAMILTON, FEDERALIST, NO. 79, 531–34
28 May 1788

Next to permanency in office, nothing can contribute more to the independence of the judges than a fixed provision for their support. The remark made in relation to the president, is equally applicable here. In the general course of human nature, *a power over a man's subsistence amounts to a power over his will.* And we can never hope to see realised in practice the complete separation of the judicial from the legislative power, in any system, which leaves the former dependent for pecuniary resources on the occasional grants of the latter. The enlightened friends to good government, in every state, have seen cause to lament the want of precise and explicit precautions in the state constitutions on this head. Some of these indeed have declared that *permanent* salaries should be established for the judges; but the experiment has in some instances shewn that such expressions are not sufficiently definite to preclude legislative evasions. Something still more positive and unequivocal has been evinced to be requisite. The plan of the convention accordingly has provided, that the judges of the United States "shall at *stated times* receive for their services a compensation, which shall not be *diminished* during their continuance in office."

This, all circumstances considered, is the most eligible provision that could have been devised. It will readily be understood, that the fluctuations in the value of money, and in the state of society, rendered a fixed rate of compensation in the constitution inadmissible. What might be extravagant to-day, might in half a century become penurious and inadequate. It was therefore necessary to leave it to the discretion of the legislature to vary its provisions in conformity to the variations in circumstances; yet under such restrictions as to put it out of the power of that body to change the condition of the individual for the worse. A man may then be sure of the ground upon which he stands, and can never be deterred from his duty by the apprehension of being placed in a less eligible situation. The clause which has been quoted combines both advantages. The salaries of judicial offices may from time to time be altered, as occasion shall require, yet so as never to lessen the allowance with which any particular judge comes into office, in respect to him. It will be observed that a difference has been made by the convention between the compensation of the president and of the judges. That of the former can neither be increased nor diminished. That of the latter can only not be diminished. This probably arose from the difference in the duration of the respective offices. As the president is to be elected for no more than four years, it can rarely happen that an adequate salary, fixed at the commencement of that period, will not continue to be such to the end of it. But with regard to the judges, who, if they behave properly, will be secured in their places for life, it may well happen, especially in the early stages of the government, that a stipend, which would be very sufficient at their first appointment, would become too small in the progress of their service.

This provision for the support of the judges bears every mark of prudence and efficacy; and it may be safely affirmed that, together with the permanent tenure of their offices, it affords a better prospect of their independence than is discoverable in the constitutions of any of the states, in regard to their own judges.

The precautions for their responsibility are comprised in the article respecting impeachments. They are liable to be impeached for mal-conduct by the house of representatives, and tried by the senate, and if convicted, may be dismissed from office and disqualified for holding any other. This is the only provision on the point, which is consistent with the necessary independence of the judicial character, and is the only one which we find in our own constitution in respect to our own judges.

The want of a provision for removing the judges on account of inability, has been a subject of complaint. But all considerate men will be sensible that such a provision would either not be practiced upon, or would be more liable to abuse than calculated to answer any good purpose. The mensuration of the faculties of the mind has, I believe, no place in the catalogue of known arts. An attempt to fix the boundary between the regions of ability and inability, would much oftener give scope to personal and party attachments and enmities, than advance the interests of justice, or the public good. The result, except in the case of insanity, must for the most part be arbitrary; and insanity without any formal or express provision, may be safely pronounced to be a virtual disqualification.

The constitution of New-York, to avoid investigations that must forever be vague and dangerous, has taken a particular age as the criterion of inability. No man can be a judge beyond sixty. I believe there are few at present, who do not disapprove of this provision. There is no station in relation to which it is less proper than to that of a judge. The deliberating and comparing faculties generally preserve their strength much beyond that period, in men who survive it; and when in addition to this circumstance, we consider how few there are who outlive the season of intellectual vigour, and how improbable it is that any considerable proportion of the bench, whether more or less numerous, should be in such a situation at the same time, we shall be ready to conclude that limitations of this sort have little to recommend them. In a republic, where fortunes are not affluent, and pensions not expedient, the dismission of men from stations in which they have served their country long and usefully, on which they depend for subsistence, and from which it will be too late to resort to any other occupation for a livelihood, ought to have some better apology to humanity, than is to be found in the imaginary danger of a superannuated bench.

13

HOUSE OF REPRESENTATIVES, THE JUDICIARY
29, 31 Aug. 1789
Annals 1:796–830

[*29 Aug.*]

MR. LIVERMORE. . . . He wished Congress to establish State Courts of Admiralty, and reject this system, because it would be attended with great inconvenience and expense. The salaries of thirteen district judges, and the necessary buildings for their accommodation, is no inconsiderable saving to a people oppressed so severely by the burthens of the late war. But an objection, in my mind, of greater weight is, that you establish two jurisdictions in the same place. The bill proposes that the State courts shall have concurrent jurisdiction with the district courts. Now under these two establishments debtors may be worried and distressed more than is necessary for the plain and simple administration of justice. A debtor may be in the custody of a State officer, or he may be committed to prison; at the same time there comes an officer from the continental court, what is to be done with the unfortunate person? Is the man to be divided, that one half may appear in one court, the other in another? Can you force the prison, and take him into other custody? or can you compel him to attend a court on the return of the writ, if he is not in your power? If this can be done, your system will furnish opportunities for collusion. A person may be in confinement for an actual debt sued in the State courts, when the marshal of the district shall wrest him out of the hands of the sheriff for a fictitious debt, intended to operate as a rescue. Perhaps gentlemen may think the same jail will answer for both; but you cannot have two keepers of the same jail, and one will refuse to obey a foreign authority. If these objections could be obviated, I should think more favorably of the bill. But, for my part, I cannot see how it is possible. We have supported the Union for thirteen or fourteen years without such courts, from which I infer that they are not necessary, or we should have discovered the inconvenience of being without them; yet I believe Congress have always had ample justice done in all their claims; at least, as I said before, I never heard any complaint, except the case of an appeal on a capture. Now, if we have a Supreme Court, to which appeals can be carried, and an Admiralty Court for deciding cases of a maritime nature, our system will be useful and complete. Why should we suppose that the administration of justice will not be continued with its wonted impartiality? Suppose a merchant gives a bond to pay one hundred dollars duty, cannot that bond be recovered as well and speedily in the State courts as in any continental court whatever? But admitting the judges may be partial, will not the same jury be employed? The jurors must come from the vicinage, and in all probability the district judges will be composed of gentlemen who preside on the benches of the State courts. Now, in this case, it is the same to the Government, to foreigners, and to citizens. But if a distinction is necessary, it can only be with respect to maritime affairs, dependent on the law of nations; and for this reason we mean to make a provision by instituting Courts of Admiralty. If justice cannot be had here, there will be an appeal to the federal Supreme Court, which is all that can be required. Now, with respect to the expense of establishing these latter courts, it will not be a fiftieth part as much as the proposed institution, and its advantage and convenience will be a thousand times as great. The whole bill turns upon striking out this clause. If it is done, I intend to move one for the establishment of Courts of Admiralty, with some regulations respecting appeals.

Mr. SMITH, (of South Carolina.)—As much will depend on the determination of this question, it is necessary it should be well considered by all the committee. It will not be easy to alter the system when once established. The judges are to hold their commissions during good behavior, and after they are appointed, they are only removable by impeachment; consequently this system must be a permanent one. The committee will not, therefore, determine that there shall be district courts until they have reflected seriously on the consequences attending their vote.

After this point is settled, the next which occurs is the extent of jurisdiction to be annexed to this court. This question is as important as the former; for it will be no less difficult than improper to enlarge or curtail the jurisdiction of a court already established.

With respect to the first point, it seems generally conceded that there ought to be a district court of some sort. The constitution, indeed, recognises such a court, because it speaks of "such inferior courts as the Congress shall establish;" and because it gives to the Supreme Court only appellate jurisdiction in most cases of a federal nature. But some gentlemen are of opinion that the district court should be altogether confined to admiralty causes; while others deem it expedient that it should be entrusted with a more enlarged jurisdiction; and should, in addition to admiralty causes, take cognizance of all causes of seizure on land, all breaches of impost laws, of offences committed on the high seas, and causes in which foreigners or citizens of other States are parties. The committee are now to decide between these two opinions. After mature reflection, I am inclined to favor the latter. What are the objections advanced against it? A gentleman from New Hampshire has observed, that such an establishment will be unnecessary, expensive, and disagreeable to our constituents. Justice, he observed, could be as well administered in the State as in the district courts; and should the State courts betray any symptoms of partiality, their adjudications would be subject to revision in the federal Supreme Court, which, in his opinion, afforded sufficient security. If the State courts are to take cognizance of those causes which, by the constitution, are declared to belong to the judicial courts of the United States, an appeal must lie in every case to the latter, otherwise the judicial authority of the Union might be altogether eluded. To deny such an appeal, would be to frustrate the most important objects of the Federal Government, and would obstruct its opera-

tions. The necessity of uniformity in the decision of the federal courts is obvious; to assimilate the principles of national decisions, and collect them, as it were, into one focus, appeals from all the State courts to the Supreme Court would be indispensable. It is, however, much to be apprehended that this constant control of the Supreme Federal Court over the adjudication of the State courts, would dissatisfy the people, and weaken the importance and authority of the State judges. Nay, more, it would lessen their respectability in the eyes of the people, even in causes which properly appertain to the State jurisdictions; because the people, being accustomed to see their decrees overhauled and annulled by a superior tribunal, would soon learn to form an irreverent opinion of their importance and abilities. It appears, therefore, expedient to separate, as much as possible, the State from the federal jurisdiction, to draw a broad line of distinction, to assign clearly to each its precise limits, and to prevent a clashing or interference between them. The expense is suggested as an objection to this system. It is admitted by the gentleman who makes it, that it is proper to have District Courts of Admiralty. These courts must, of necessity, have jurisdiction of offences committed on the high seas. Now the establishment of such a court will induce nearly all the expense that will be requisite; the extension of the system to the length I have stated will occasion a very trifling increase of the expense; and if, after due consideration, it should be found that the latter plan would be more conducive to the happiness and welfare of our constituents than the other, a small increase of the expense ought to be no impediment to the attainment of so valuable an object.

There can be no reason why our constituents should be displeased with the arrangement; the district judge will be elected from among the citizens of the State where he is to exercise his functions, and will feel every inducement to promote the happiness and protect the liberties of his fellow-citizens. He will be more independent than the State judges, holding his commission during good behavior, and not influenced by the fear of a diminution of his salary. Trial by jury will be secured in all cases wherein it is provided in the State courts. Should the district judge be under any bias, it is reasonable to suppose it would be rather in favor of his fellow-citizens, than in favor of foreigners, or the United States. By restricting the State courts to few causes of federal jurisdiction, the number of appeals will be diminished, because every cause tried in those courts will, for the reasons before mentioned, be subject to appeal; whereas the jurisdiction of the district court will be final in many cases. Inasmuch, therefore, as those appeals are grievous to the citizens, which lie from a court within their own State to the Supreme Court at the seat of Government, and at a great distance, they will consequently be benefited by an exemption from them. In the bill, as sent from the Senate, the jurisdiction of the district courts is not so extensive as to occasion any just alarm; it is, in my opinion, rather too confined, and does not embrace objects enough. It would be difficult to take from that court any of its jurisdiction without materially injuring the whole judicial system, except the clause relating to consuls and vice-consuls, which appears to me to be improperly annexed to the district court, and which I shall move to strike out, when we come to that part of the bill. But to what objects do the district courts extend? To admiralty causes and trials for piracy committed on the high seas. Gentlemen have conceded that the district courts shall have jurisdiction of these cases—to offences against the United States.

It is very proper that a court in the United States should try offences committed against the United States. Every nation upon earth punishes by its own courts offences against its own laws. To seizures on land for breaches of the revenue laws, this power will not be censured; it would be *felo de se* to trust the collection of the revenue of the United States to the State judicatures. The disinclination of the judges to carry the law into effect, their disapprobation of a certain duty, the rules of the court, or other obvious causes, might delay or frustrate the collection of the revenue, and embarrass the National Government. From this view it appears that the district court is not clothed with any authority of which the State courts are stripped, but is barely provided with that authority which arises out of the establishment of a National Government, and which is indispensably necessary for its support. Can the State courts at this moment take cognizance of offences committed on the high seas? If they do, it is under an act of Congress, giving them jurisdiction; and, in such cases, the Judge of the Admiralty is associated with two common law Judges; this tribunal becomes then a federal court for the particular occasion, because it is established by Congress. The State courts have no jurisdiction of causes arising from a national impost law, because no such law heretofore existed. Where, then, is the ground of uneasiness suggested by gentlemen? The foregoing observations must persuade them that their alarms have been premature. But it is said that there must be court-houses, judges, marshals, clerks, constables, jails, and gibbets; that these establishments will occasion a heavy and unnecessary burthen, and have a tendency to create disgust in the people.

I readily agree with the gentleman, that there are in every community some individuals who will see, with pain, every new institution in the shape of a constable, jail, or gibbet, and who think that law and courts are an abridgment of their liberty; but I should be very sorry to concur with him that this is a prevailing opinion. I think better of our constituents, and am persuaded they are sensible that those institutions are necessary for the protection of their lives and property; and grow out of the very nature of a federal Government. Care, indeed, should be taken to prevent their being grievous and oppressive; but as long as knaves and rogues exist in the world, and monsters under the form of men, preying upon the innocent, so long will courts and all their concomitants be wanted to redress the wrongs of the latter, and repress the depredations of the former. But let me ask the gentleman whether a Court of Admiralty and a court for the trial of offences on the high seas, which he agrees ought to be established, will not require all these institutions, viz. court-houses, clerks, sheriffs, &c.? There can be no doubt of it. The extension of the jurisdiction of the district court, as far as I think it

necessary, will not occasion any one article of expense, or any one institution that will not be necessary on the gentleman's plan. To suppose that there will be a clashing of jurisdiction between the State and district courts on all occasions, by having a double set of officers, is to suppose the States will take a pleasure in thwarting the Federal Government; it is a supposition not warranted by our fellow-citizens, who, finding that these establishments were created for their benefit and protection, will rather promote than obstruct them; it is a supposition equally opposed to the power of direct taxation, and to the establishment of State and county courts which exist in the several States, and are productive of no such inconvenience. These several courts will have their limits defined, and will move within their respective orbits without any danger of deviation. Besides, I am not persuaded that there will be a necessity for having separate court-houses and jails; those already provided in the several States will be made use of by the district courts. I remember when the court for the trial of piracy, under the authority of Congress, was held at Charleston, the judges sat in the court-house; the prisoners were confined in the jail, were under the custody of the constable, and were executed by the orders of the sheriff of the district of Charleston. All these were State institutions, and yet the court was a federal court.

There is another important consideration; that is, how far the constitution stands in the way of this motion. It is declared by that instrument that the judicial power of the United States shall be vested in one supreme, and in such inferior courts as Congress shall from time to time establish. Here is no discretion, then, in Congress to vest the judicial power of the United States in any other tribunal than in the Supreme Court and the inferior courts of the United States. It is further declared that the judicial power of the United States shall extend to all cases of a particular description. How is that power to be administered? Undoubtedly by the tribunals of the United States; if the judicial power of the United States extends to those specified cases, it follows indisputably that the tribunals of the United States must likewise extend to them. What is the object of the motion? To assign the jurisdiction of some of these very cases to the State courts, to judges, who, in many instances, hold their places for a limited period; whereas, the constitution, for the greater security of the citizen, and to insure the independence of the federal judges, has expressly declared that they shall hold their commissions during good behavior. To judges who are exposed every year to a diminution of salary by the State Legislatures; whereas, the constitution, to remove from the federal judges all dependence on the Legislative or Executive, has protected them from any diminution of their compensation. Whether the expediency or the unconstitutionality of the motion be considered, there are more than sufficient reasons to oppose it. The district court is necessary, if we intend to adhere to the constitution, and to carry the Government into effect. At the same time, I shall cheerfully assist in organizing this court in that mode, which will prevent its being grievous or oppressive, and will render it conducive to the protection and happiness of our constituents.

Mr. JACKSON said he conceived this to be the most important business that had as yet come before the House. It was what he had long considered, and had with difficulty decided, but upon mature consideration was impressed with the same sentiments as the gentleman from New Hampshire. It must be admitted that a society was formed before the rules that governed that society; and consequently the laws and rules were formed merely for the use of that society. In fact, the convenience of the people is, or ought to be, the first principle of every Government; and the people are entitled to expect it. Our present constitution has set out with this declaration, "We the people," in its preamble, and therefore, in the system before us, every attention of the Legislature ought to be drawn to this point. He apprehended, he said, that the system before them was not framed or calculated for that purpose, but appeared to be rather intended to destroy some of the most valuable and important privileges of the citizens. He did not wish to diminish the powers in the Federal Judiciary, which might be thought necessary, and commensurate to the carrying the Government fully into execution; but he considered the system as unnecessary, vexatious, and expensive, and calculated to destroy the harmony and confidence of the people.

The motion has been objected to by the gentleman from South Carolina, for striking out the clause, for several reasons; the first I shall notice is, "that in several of the States the judges are limited in their appointments; that inferior jurisdictions are required by the constitution; and that the State judges are not vested with permanent salaries." Those arguments, he observed, fell to the ground on referring to the constitution; the constitution, he said, did not absolutely require inferior jurisdictions; it says that "the judicial power of the United States shall be vested in one Supreme Court, and in such inferior courts as Congress may, from time to time, ordain and establish." The word "may" is not positive, and it remains with Congress to determine what inferior jurisdictions may be necessary, and what they will ordain and establish; for if they choose or think that no inferior jurisdictions are necessary, there is no obligation to establish them. It then remains with the Legislature of the Union to examine the necessity or expediency of those courts only. On the subject of expediency, he said, for his part, he could not see it, and was of opinion that the State courts would answer every judiciary purpose.

The gentleman from South Carolina has again advanced "that if district and circuit courts are not adopted, the harmony of the States and of the people will be at stake, and that the system will be more vexatious by a series of appeals." He did not agree with that doctrine. He was persuaded that the harmony of the people, their liberties and properties, would be more secure under the legal paths of their ancestors; under their modes of trial, and known methods of decision. They have hitherto been accustomed to receive justice at their own doors in a simple form. The system before the House has a round of courts appellate from one to the other; and the poor man that is engaged with a rich opponent will be harassed in the most cruel manner; and although the sum be limited for appeals, yet the poor individual may have a legal right to a sum superior to that limitation, (say above a certain amount of dollars,) and not possess fortune sufficient to carry on his lawsuit; he must sink under the oppression of his richer neighbor. He was clearly of opinion that the people would much rather have but one appeal, which, he conceived, would answer every purpose; he meant from the State courts immediately to the Supreme Court of the continent. An Admiralty court of jurisdiction he would grant might be necessary for the trial of maritime affairs, and matters relative to the revenue; to which object he would cheerfully enlarge it; and thought for the present it would be far more eligible. The gentleman has likewise advanced that the expense would be as great without as with the inferior jurisdiction. He would beg leave to differ from him, and declared that it would be in the proportion of three to one; for although the clerk and marshal of the district courts are the officers proposed for the circuit courts, yet there would arise a train of inferior officers, consequently attendant on those officers and courts, exclusive of jurors, witnesses, &c. He has likewise advanced, that it would be necessary to prevent confusion; the line of distinction would be much easier preserved in the present state of the department, for many of the reasons pointed out by the gentleman from New Hampshire, exclusive of the difficulty of making new rules. But we are told, he said, it is necessary that every Government should have the power of executing its own laws. This argument would likewise fail, when we find that the constitution, treaties, and laws of the United States are, by the constitution itself, made the supreme laws of the land. Are not the judges of the different States bound by oath to support that supreme law? Will they not recollect those oaths, and be liable to punishment by your act, which has obliged them to take that oath, if they do not respect it as such? Assuredly they will; it is part of the compact formed with the States. But does there not remain the appellate jurisdiction of the Supreme Court to control them, and bring them to their reason? Can they not reverse or confirm the State decrees, as they may find them right or wrong? Consequently, this last argument falls to the ground.

That the system is vexatious can be easily proved, and is too obvious. An offender is dragged from his house, friends, and connexions, to a distant spot, where he is deprived of every advantage of former character, of relations and acquaintance; the right of trial by a jury of the vicinage is done away, and perhaps he is carried to a place where popular clamor might for the moment decide against him; or, if allowed a trial by vicinage, or his neighbors, it is equally vexatious to drag him two or three hundred miles from his home, with evidences to try and give testimony at a distant place; every thing is to be dreaded from it. This, he observed, was contrary to our wonted customs, and we need but revert to the history of Britain, after the conquest, to view what struggles that nation made against innovations of this nature. The monkish clergy joined with the kings to oppress the people, to establish civil law, and get the legal power into their own hands; the people took the alarm, and with the nobility contested the point, which was never finally settled until the great charter of John, which it was one of the causes of producing, and that fixed the ecclesiastical bounds. He would ask if our modes of trial must not be as dear to our fellow-citizens as theirs were to them, and if the same commotions may not be reasonably expected? He feared they would be found so. Is it proper we should be so suspicious of the State judges? He could not, he said, for his part, consider human nature so depraved, as to suppose that, with an oath to observe the supreme law of the land, the State judges would not obey it. In his opinion, it became us, as a wise Legislature, to take up and execute the least exceptionable and milder mode first. There was no requisition, no necessity from the constitution. If, on experiment, it should be found (and the House generally admits our laws are at present experimental) that sufficient attention is not paid, and that our Government requires for its existence a more energetic mode, he pledged himself to agree to any inferior jurisdictions that may be thought necessary for that purpose; but he never could consent to oppress his fellow-citizens without being taught by absolute necessity arising from experience.

Mr. BENSON said, if the House decided in favor of the present question, it would involve a total abandonment of the judicial power, excepting those cases the honorable gentlemen mean to provide for, namely, the Courts of Admiralty and Supreme Courts. The honorable gentleman had observed that difficulties would arise out of the proposed establishment; but these difficulties or embarrassments are not to be charged to the House, they grow out of the constitution itself. The gentlemen suppose that two sovereign and independent authorities can never be exercised over the same territory; but this is not the business of the committee; they could not get rid of these difficulties by retrenching their powers; they must carry the constitution into effect. The gentleman has stated a case, in supposing that process shall issue from the State and continental courts, and both be served upon the defendant at the same time, and then asks what is to be done. Is the man to be divided? Now, in return, he would ask the same question; is the United States to abandon all its powers and jurisdiction, because the exercise of it may be attended with some inconvenience? As well might we ask individual States to abandon theirs, because there is some clashing with the Federal Judiciary. He apprehended that neither were to be abandoned, but that they should endeavor to administer both with as little inconvenience to either as was practicable.

It is not left to the election of the Legislature of the United States whether we adopt or not a judicial system like the one before us; the words in the constitution are plain and full, and must be carried into operation. He would not undertake to say that it was the best system that could be formed; but it had its advantages over some in which the honorable gentleman from New Hampshire (Mr. LIVERMORE) had said that justice was well administered; he thought there was more reliance on judges who were appointed during good behavior, than on others appointed from session to session, and ever dependent on the will of the State Legislatures.

He left it to experience to show whether the Judiciaries would interfere or not; some gentlemen had predicted they would; it was possible that they might, and he did not know but that the interference would be of such a delicate nature, as to compel the United States to relinquish her portion; or, on the other hand, the States individually might consent that the judicial power should be solely exercised by the Union. But all this was wide of the question; the House had nothing more to do than to perform their duty, and carry the constitution into full operation.

Mr. SEDGWICK said, the gentleman would find as many difficulties growing out of the substitute as those he apprehended from the plan on the table. He had asked what will be done with the prisoners if they are taken at the same time in consequence of processes from the national and State courts? I answer by asking him, what will be done with the prisoners if they are taken at the same time by a process from the Admiralty and State courts? The other difficulties he had apprehended were well replied to by the honorable gentleman from South Carolina; and I shall only remark, that we are so circumstanced that two distinct independent powers of judicial proceedings must exist; at least I do not see how we shall get rid of the difficulty, if it is one, until there shall be a change in the constitution.

I did not suppose it was a question at this day, whether this Government is to exercise all the powers of a Government or not. I did conceive, sir, that such an idea could exist in the mind of any gentleman; yet what is the object of the present motion? Sir, it goes to divest the Government of one of its most essential branches; if this is destroyed, your constitution is but the shadow of a Government.

Is it not essential that a Government possess within itself the power necessary to carry its laws into execution? But the honorable gentleman proposes to leave this business to a foreign authority, totally independent of this Legislature, whether our ordinances shall have efficacy or not. Would this be prudent, even if it were in our power? Suppose a State Government was inimical to the Federal Government, and its judges were attached to the same local policy, they might refuse or neglect to attend to the national business; they might be corrupt, and in either case the public might sustain an essential injury. And where would be your redress? Shall we apply to the State Legislatures that patronize them? Can we impeach or have them tried? If we can, how is the trial to be had; before a tribunal established by the State? Can we expect in this way to bring them to justice? Surely no gentleman supposes we can. These are not chimerical suppositions; they are founded in nature, and such as may be expected; indeed, facts have already occurred to prove to us how dangerous it would be to make the State Legislatures the sole guardians of the national faith and honor. Already have the United States been hurled down by those arms from a pinnacle of glory to the lowest state of degradation. The United States, after a glorious and successful struggle, in which they displayed a valor and patriotism astonishing the old world, secured their independence! and a single concession was the price of an honorable peace. The discharge of *bona fide* debts due from the citizens of America to the subjects of Britain was all that Britain required. Now, is it not obvious to every man, that this honorable stipulation ought by all means to be considered the supreme law of the land? Yet, what was the event? State after State, Legislature after Legislature, made laws and regulations in positive opposition to the treaty; and the State Judiciaries could not, or did not, decide contrary to their State ordinances. What have been the consequences of these proceedings? It ill becomes me at this time, when we hope to wipe off every ignominious stain, to recapitulate the evils it has drawn down upon the nation. But I hope they are sufficiently notorious to put us on our guard against trusting essential powers out of our hands, contrary to our duty, and contrary to the wishes of the people.

When we are certain that the Government cannot be organized without establishing its judicial tribunals; when we fear for its existence, (at least its existing with reputation and dignity,) unless we provide for the due execution of national laws and national treaties; shall we forego them because gentlemen apprehend some small difficulties from interfering process? Sir, it has been already demonstrated that the interference will be trifling, if any; it will be too small to authorize us to blast the expected benefits arising from a complete and efficient system of government.

Mr. AMES said, the remarks made by gentlemen on the importance of this question would be of some utility in deciding it. The judicial power is, in fact, highly important to the Government and to the people; to the Government, because by this means its laws are peaceably carried into execution. We know, by experience, what a wretched system that is which is divested of this power. We see the difference between a treaty which independent nations make, and which cannot be enforced without war, and a law which is the will of the society. A refractory individual is made to feel the weight of the whole community. A Government that may make but cannot enforce laws, cannot last long, nor do much good. By the power, too, the people are gainers. The administration of justice is the very performance of the social bargain on the part of Government. It is the reward of their toils; the equivalent for what they grant. They have to plant, to water, to manure the tree, and this the fruit of it. The argument, therefore, *a priori*, is strong against the motion; for while it weakens the Government, it defrauds the people. We live in a time of innovation; but until miracles shall become more common than ordinary events, and surprise us less than the usual course of nature, he should think it a wonderful felicity of invention to propose the expedient of hiring out our judicial power, and employing courts not amenable to our laws, instead of instituting them ourselves as the constitution requires. We might with as great propriety negotiate and assign over our legislative as our judicial power; and it would not be more strange to get the laws made for this body, than after their passage to get them interpreted and executed by those whom we do not appoint, and cannot control. The field of debate is wide; the time for consideration had been so ample, and that remaining for debate so short, that he would not enter fully into it. The gentleman from South Carolina (Mr. SMITH) had very ably proved the expediency of the mo-

tion. He would confine himself, he said, to another point; and if it could be established, it would narrow the discussion.

The branches of the judicial power of the United States are the admiralty jurisdiction, the criminal jurisdiction, cognizance of certain common law cases, and of such as may be given by the statutes of Congress. The constitution, and the laws made in pursuance of it, are the supreme laws of the land. They prescribe a rule of action for individuals. If it is disputed whether an act done is right or wrong, reference must be had to this rule; and whether the action is compared with the rule of action in a State or Federal court, it is equally out of the power of the judges, to say that right is wrong, or that wrong is right. If a man is restrained of his liberty, and for that sues the officer of the General Government in a State court, the defendant shows that he was a marshal, and served a precept according to the law of the United States; then he must be cleared, otherwise the law of the United States would not be the law of the land. But there is a substantial difference between the jurisdiction of the courts and the rules of decision.

In the latter case the court has only to inquire into facts and the rules of action prescribed to individuals. In the former they do not inquire how, but what they may try. The jurisdiction of the court is the depositum of a truth. The supreme power in a State is the fountain of justice. Such streams are derived from this fountain to the courts as the Legislature may positively enact. The judges, as servants to the public, can do that only for which they are employed. The constitution had provided how this trust should be designated. The judges must be named by their Christian and sirnames, commissioned during good behavior, and have salaries. Causes of exclusive federal cognizance cannot be tried otherwise, nor can the judicial power of the United States be otherwise exercised. The State courts were not supposed to be deprived by the constitution of the jurisdiction that they exercised before, over many causes that may be tried now in the national courts. The suitors would have their choice of courts. But who shall try a crime against a law of the United States, or a new created action? Here jurisdiction is made *de novo*. A trust is to be exercised, and this can be done only by persons appointed as judges in the manner before mentioned. The will of the society is expressed and is disobeyed; and who shall interpret and enforce that will but the persons invested with authority from the same society? The State judges are to judge according to the law of the State, and the common law. The law of the United States is a rule to them, but no authority for them. It controlled their decisions, but could not enlarge their powers. Suppose an action was brought on a statute, declaring a forfeiture equal to the whole of the goods against him whoever shall unlade without a permit; before the law was made, no court had jurisdiction. Could a State court sustain such an action? They might as properly assume admiralty jurisdiction, or sustain actions for forfeitures of the British revenue acts. He did not mean any disrespect to the State courts. In some of the States, he knew the judges were highly worthy of trust; that they were safeguards to Government, and ornaments to human nature. But whence should they get the power of trying the supposed action? The States under whom they act, and to whom they are amenable, never had such power to give, and this Government never gave them any. Individuals may be commanded, but are we authorized to require the servants of the States to serve us? It was not only true, he said, that they could not decide this cause, if a provision was neglected to be made, by creating proper tribunals for the decision, but they would not be authorized to do it, even if an act was passed declaring that they should be vested with power; for they must be individually commissioned and salaried to have it constitutionally, and then they would not have it as the State judges. If we may empower one State court, suppose the Supreme Court, we may empower all or any, even the justices of the peace. This will appear more monstrous if we consider the trial of crimes. A statute creates an offence. Shall any justice of the peace be directed to summon a jury to try for treason or piracy? It was true the Government would not direct a thing so wickedly absurd to be done; but who will believe Government may lawfully do it? It would be tedious to pursue this, or even the ideas connected with it, very far. The nature of the subject rendered it difficult to be even perspicuous without being prolix. His wish was to establish this conclusion, that offences against statutes of the United States, and actions, the cognizance whereof is created *de novo*, are exclusively of federal jurisdiction; that no persons should act as judges to try them, except such as may be commissioned agreeably to the constitution; that for the trial of such offences and causes, tribunals must be created. These, with the admiralty jurisdiction, which it is agreed must be provided for, constitute the principal powers of the districts courts. If judges must be paid, they might as well be employed. The remnants of jurisdiction, which may be taken away, are scarcely worth transferring to the State courts, and may as well be exercised by our own.

The question being now called for from several parts of the House,

Mr. STONE said, he hoped the question would not be determined on the discussion it already had. He thought, although gentlemen might have made up their minds on the subject, a very full communication of the principles upon which they acted in this momentous business ought to take place before the question was decided; for to him it appeared of the greatest importance that they should act rightly, and it should be known they acted on right principles. It is admitted, said he, on all hands, to be a work of extreme difficulty; one gentleman has said that it is so difficult, we cannot correct it. But surely we ought to exercise a little patience in the examination; perhaps, on a minute inquiry, we may hear of some road by which we may avoid these difficulties, and amply recompense ourselves, our constituents, and our posterity, for the expense of our time. I confess, for my own part, I wish more information than I have yet received, in order to reconcile me to the bill. I was so unfortunate on a former and memorable occasion as to differ from the majority of this House; perhaps this question may turn upon a similar principle, and

renew that pain which it gives me to oppose what I find to be the voice of my country. I therefore most earnestly wish to be convinced that my ideas are founded on misconception, in order to go with the majority; but if I should be left in the minority, whether from not having my difficulties removed, or because they are insuperable, I shall ever cheerfully submit to the judgment of the House; and on this occasion I am ready to assent to every power necessary to the due administration of the Government. But I declare, in my mind, this is a system founded on principles distinct and separate from the general principles upon which the constitution was framed. It appears to me that the present Government originated in *necessity*, and it ought not to be carried farther than *necessity* will justify.

I believe the scheme of the present Government was considered by those who framed it as dangerous to the liberties of America; if they had not considered it in this point of view, they would not have guarded it in the manner they have done. They supposed that it had a natural tendency to destroy the State Governments; or, on the other hand, they supposed that the State Governments had a tendency to abridge the powers of the General Government; therefore it was necessary to guard against either taking place, and this was to be done properly by establishing a Judiciary for the United States. This Judiciary was likewise absolutely necessary, because a great many purposes of the Union could not be accomplished by the States, from the principle of their government, and could not be executed from a defect in their power. But all these, I presume, are involved in the jurisdiction of the Supreme Federal Court. I apprehend in every thing else the State courts might have had complete and adequate jurisdiction; the State courts could not determine between State and State, because their judgment would be ineffectual; they could never carry it into execution. But I apprehend in all other cases the States could execute that authority which is reposed in the United States. Yet I do not doubt but the caution might be necessary for securing to the General Government, in reserve, those very powers, because such abuses may happen in the State courts, as to render it necessary for the due administration of justice, that the national jurisdiction be carried over such States. But what I am not satisfied of is, whether it is *now* essential that we proceed to make such establishments. I cannot conceive it to be *now* essential; because the business may be done without, and it is not commanded by the constitution; if it is commanded by the constitution, we have no power to restrain or modify it. If it is the right of an alien or foreigner to sue or be sued only in the courts of the United States, then they have a right to that jurisdiction complete, and then Congress must institute courts for taking exclusive cognizance of all cases pointed out in the constitution; but this would be contrary to the principle of the bill, which proposes to establish the inferior courts with concurrent jurisdiction with the State courts.

By the constitution, Congress has a right to establish such inferior courts as they from time to time shall think necessary. If I understand the force of the words "from time to time," it is that Congress may establish such courts when they think proper. I take it they have used another precaution; and this construction is guarded by another clause in the constitution, where it is provided that the constitution itself, and all laws made in pursuance thereof, as well as treaties, shall be the supreme law of the land, and the judges in every State are to be bound thereby; any thing in the State laws or constitutions to the contrary notwithstanding. Now can gentlemen be afraid that the State courts will not decide according to the supreme law? If they are, it is in the discretion of Congress to refuse them the opportunity; but the bill gives them a concurrent jurisdiction, and shows that these dangers are not really apprehended; if they give them concurrent jurisdiction, they have the power of giving them complete; and they may delay from time to time the institution of national courts, until they suppose or have experienced the inadequacy of the State courts to the objects granted by the constitution to the participation of the Judiciary of the United States. If, sir, the State judges are bound to take cognizance of the laws of the United States, and are sworn to support the General Government, the system before us must have originated from a source different from that from which the Government itself derived its existence. Yet, I admit, sir, that there is a *necessity* for instituting Admiralty courts, though it is not because I consider the power of the State inadequate to that object; but because those courts are not instituted in all of them, and it is proper that there should be a maritime jurisdiction within the bounds of every State to determine cases arising within the same. It depends not upon the principle, but on the fact, that I admit it to be *necessary* for Congress to organize an admiralty system; for I take it, that were admiralty courts established in the different States, and were you to make laws that affected admiralty cases, they would be as much obliged to determine by your laws as if you had instituted the courts yourselves. If, then, the State courts have the power, your system is not necessary, unless they will not execute that power; it must therefore depend on your suspicion of their want of judgment or integrity. I declare I can contemplate a time, with great pain, when one of those cases may happen; but I believe the time is not yet arrived, and we ought not to adopt a system which presupposes it.

I know it is of great importance to have the decisions of the courts conformable; and I believe also it is of no inconsiderable importance to the Government, to have it operate as well on individuals as on States. It would be, if liked by the people, one of the strongest chains by which the Union is bound; one of the strongest cements for making this constitution firm and compact. But I would not have the measure adopted at a time, and on a principle, which must have a direct contrary tendency. If we establish federal courts, on the principle that the State courts are not able or willing to do their duty, we establish rivals. But if we honestly conduct upon the principle of the constitution—*necessity*, we may expect some good to result from the exercise of our powers, and prevent any clashing of jurisdiction; but to act on other principles must introduce confusion. Every body knows with what phlegmatic and cool determination, with what disregard of surrounding objects, courts maintain their separate jurisdictions. If we search the history of courts with which we are well acquainted, we shall find, that though they did not absolutely proceed to bloodshed, yet they put the whole community in commotion with the clashing of their jurisdictions; yet in that country the citizen and the community have a remedy. I fancy it is not so in this; I believe, instead of being found what the gentleman from South Carolina has termed them, planets rolling in their orbits, on the immutable principles of order, so as not to interfere with each other, they will be felt in concussion, and their violence will violate the harmony with which gentlemen please their imagination. The clew of separate jurisdiction will twine into such a state of perplexity, as to render it impossible for human wisdom to disentangle it without injury.

The gentlemen have mentioned jails and different processes; they might have traced it down to an execution, and shown us what might have been the consequence. Suppose an alien has a right to a man's property, and a citizen the same, they lay their executions at the same time, the jurisdictions do not know each other, they take no cognizance of each other's proceedings, the land is taken by the State court, and the possessor turned out; if it is taken by the officer of the Continental court, the possessor is turned out also, and an action is brought to determine again who has a right to the property; the State court says the citizen, and the continental court the alien: What is to be done? Here is no tribunal to determine between them; it can only be determined by the sword. Gentlemen ought to examine this part of the subject more fully before they decide it.

Mr. BURKE declared it to be a singular innovation on the privileges of the citizens, and such as they would never submit to; for they never had an idea that by this revolution they were to be put in a worse situation than they were in under the former Government. He said when their State districts courts would be sitting, the Federal courts would be engaged at the same time, and he asked whether the people could ever consider such an accumulation of courts of justice calculated to promote their interest; it would harass them with extreme duty, as witnesses, jurors, &c. and leave them at the mercy of the Judges as to fines, when they should be engaged at another court. With respect to the time of the court sitting, it might be made at a most inconvenient time of the year, and the place might be at the most distant part of the State, where a man might be dragged three or four hundred miles from his home, and tried by men who know nothing of him, or he of them; he was sure, under the circumstances, the freemen of America could never submit to it.

Mr. MADISON said, that all these points might be secured in the bill, when they came to the part that related thereto.

Mr. LAWRENCE expressed himself against the motion for striking out, because he conceived that it was essential to carry this part of the constitution into effect, and that the courts had better be established now than hereafter.

Mr. MADISON said, it would not be doubted that some Judiciary system was necessary to accomplish the objects of the Government, and that it ought to be commensurate with the other branches of the Government. Under the late confederation, it could scarcely be said, that there was any real Legislative power, there was no Executive branch, and the Judicial was so confined as to be of little consequence; in the new constitution a regular system is provided; the Legislative power is made effective for its objects; the Executive is co-extensive with the Legislative, and it is equally proper that this should be the case with the Judiciary. If the latter be concurrent with the State jurisdictions, it does not follow that it will for that reason be impracticable. It is admitted, that a concurrence exists in some cases between the Legislative authorities of the Federal and State Governments; and it may be safely affirmed that there is more, both of novelty and difficulty in that arrangement, than there will be in the other.

To make the State courts federal courts, is liable to insuperable objections, not to repeat that the moment that is done, they will, from the highest down to the county courts, hold their tenures during good behavior, by virtue of the constitution. It may be remarked, that, in another point of view, it would violate the constitution by usurping a prerogative of the Supreme Executive of the United States. It would be making appointments which are expressly vested in that department, not indeed by *nomination,* but by *description,* which would amount to the same thing. But laying these difficulties aside, a review of the constitution of the courts in many States will satisfy us that they cannot be trusted with the execution of the Federal laws. In some of the States it is true they might, and would be safe and proper organs of such a jurisdiction; but in others they are so dependent on State Legislatures, that to make the Federal laws dependent on them, would throw us back into all the embarrassments which characterized our former situation. In Connecticut the Judges are appointed annually by the Legislature, and the Legislature is itself the last resort in civil cases.

In Rhode-Island, which we hope soon to see united with the other States, the case is at least as bad. In Georgia, even under their former constitution, the Judges are triennially appointed, and in a manner by no means unexceptionable. In Pennsylvania they hold their places for seven years only. Their tenures leave a dependence, particularly for the last year or two of the term, which forbid a reliance on Judges who feel it. With respect to their salaries, there are few States, if any, in which the Judges stand on independent ground. On the whole, he said, he did not see how it could be made compatible with the constitution, or safe to the Federal interests, to make a transfer of the Federal jurisdiction to the State courts, as contended for by the gentlemen who oppose the clause in question.

Mr. BURKE said, he had turned himself about to find some way to extricate himself from this measure; but which ever way he turned, the constitution still stared him in the face, and he confessed he saw no way to avoid the evil. He made this candid confession, to let them know why he should be a silent spectator of the progress of the bill; and he had not the most distant hope that the opposition would succeed. If any substitute could be devised that was not contrary to the constitution, it should have his support, but he absolutely despaired of finding any. He was, however, satisfied that the people would feel its inconvenience, and express their dislike to a Judicial system which rendered them insecure in their liberties and property; a system that must be regarded with jealousy and distrust.

Mr. JACKSON.—Sir, the importance of the question induces me to trouble the committee so far as to answer one of the arguments made use of in the opposition, and which I think necessary to do away the impressions they have made, should be answered. The gentleman from Massachusetts (Mr. SEDGWICK) has carried the nation to the highest pinnacle of glory, and in a moment hurled it down to the lowest pitch; and has laid the loss of national faith, credit, and honor to the want of an energetic Judiciary. Every good citizen will, with him, deplore the abject state we have been brought to; but, sir, does this argument hold good here? I am of opinion it is evident it does not. Under the old form of Government, Congress had no compelling Judiciary; no power of reversing the decrees of the State Judges; but it is contended that they have, or ought to have more under the present system. It is allowed, sir, that Congress shall have the power, in its fullest extent, to correct, reverse, or affirm, any decree of a State court; and assuredly the Supreme Court will exercise this power. How then can our national faith or honor be injured by striking out the clause in future? It must be obvious to the gentleman himself, that his fears are groundless; for the Supreme Court will interfere and keep the State Judiciaries within their bounds: That authority will tell them, thus far ye shall go, and no further; and will bring them back when they exceed their bounds, to the principles of their institution.

Another gentleman from Massachusetts (Mr. AMES) has advanced a position I cannot agree with. He has said, that the State courts will not, nor cannot, take cognizance of laws of the Union, as it would be taking up matters out of the bounds of their jurisdiction, and interfering with what was not left to them. Sir, I answer that gentleman with the words of the constitution, "This constitution, and the laws of the United States made in pursuance thereof, and all treaties, &c. shall be the supreme law of the land." This surpasses in power any State laws; the Judges are bound to notice them as the supreme law, and I call upon the gentleman to know, as a professional man, if a criminal was tried for a capital offence under a State law, and could justify himself under the laws of the Union, if the State Judges could condemn him? Sir, they would forfeit their oaths if he was not acquitted; this, however, he has admitted in his argument in some measure. If there was no jurisdiction, neither could they notice the law. I acknowledge that the gentleman has used many specious arguments, but as they rest chiefly on this ground, I think they are done away.

The gentleman from Virginia (Mr. MADISON) has advanced, that, by leaving this power in the hands of the State Judiciaries, or by joining their concurrent authority, you establish them as inferior jurisdictions. If the gentleman will turn to the eleventh and twenty-fifth sections, he will find those positions established, and what fell from the gentleman from Massachusetts concerning jurisdiction is likewise answered. The State courts, by the former, are acknowledged to have concurrent jurisdiction in a large extent, where the United States and an alien are the party, or between citizens of one State and those of another. And if the jurisdiction is acknowledged in some points, it must be supposed to be so in the fullest extent. By the twenty-fifth, sir, they are again fully established; and therefore they are now, by the present system, in every light as fully, agreeably to the gentleman's argument, inferior jurisdictions, as they possibly could be by the principles of the gentleman from New Hampshire. And here, sir, I will advert to the general arguments, used by the gentlemen in opposition, of the necessity of power to enforce the laws of the Union, and support the national existence and honor. Sir, I am opposed in some degree to this clause. For the extent of its power, even supposing the District and Circuit courts abolished, swallows up every shadow of a State Judiciary. Gentlemen, therefore, have no reason to complain of the want of Federal Judiciary power, for the clause declares, "That a final judgment or decree in any suit, in the highest court of law or equity of a State in which the decision of the suit could be had, where the validity of a treaty is drawn in question, or statute thereof, or an authority exercised under the United States; and the decision is against their validity; or where is drawn in question the validity of a statute, or an authority exercised under any State on the ground of their being repugnant to the constitution, treaties, or laws of the United States, and the decision is in favor of such their validity; or where is drawn in question the construction of any clause of the constitution, or of a treaty or statute, or of a commission, held under the United States, and the decision is against the title, right, privilege or exemption specially set up, or claimed by either party under such clause, of the said constitution, treaty, statute, or commission, may be re-examined and reversed, or affirmed in the Supreme Court of the United States." Sir, in my opinion, and I am convinced experience will prove it, that there will not, neither can there be any suit or action brought in any of the State courts, but may, under this clause, be reversed or affirmed by being brought within the cognizance of the Supreme Court. But should there be some exceptions for the present, yet sir, the precedent is so forcible, for it goes so far as even to admit of constructions on some of the articles, that by some means or other those articles will in time be totally lost. Sir, let us look at the Court of Exchequer in England; revenue trials at first engrossed its whole attention; from a series of fiction there is now no personal action but from construction may be brought within their cognizance. It is only a suggestion, and very seldom true, that a plaintiff is a king's debtor, and that the action is well grounded: yet there they have counter checks, and another resort; here the Supreme Court is final. Sir, the gentleman from South Carolina (Mr. BURKE) was right in declaring a resident on Lake Erie might be dragged to New York for trial, or one on the Oconee to Savannah. Nay, sir, I know not how far in time a man might not be dragged; perhaps from the Oconee to be tried in North Carolina; for one part of the bill, without specifying the spot, declares, that the Circuit courts shall have power to hold special sessions for the trial of criminal causes at their discretion. On these considerations, I hope the House will

not adopt the present system, until the milder one is tried. It is calculated to foment and harass the people, without answering any essential purpose.

Mr. SHERMAN said, it was admitted, on all hands, that a Judiciary system was necessary, even upon condition that the Legislature had a discretion in the business; and it required but little attention to discover that the plan proposed by the Senate was better than what gentlemen proposed to substitute, inasmuch as it was more complete, and not more expensive. There would be a uniformity of decision under the former; while the latter would render the construction of the law vague, if not various. It would less disturb the harmony of the States; and of consequence be more agreeable to the people. He hoped the committee would reject the motion for striking out the clause.

Mr. SMITH, of South Carolina, observed, that all the difficulties and inconveniences which the gentlemen have started as arising from the establishment of a District court arise from the Government itself. All the objections made to this court apply equally against having any National Judicature. Indeed if they had any weight, they would as forcibly apply to the very institution which the gentlemen patronize, viz: a court of admiralty and piracy. If there is to be this perpetual clashing of jurisdictions between the Federal and State courts, this eternal jarring between their respective officers, will not these embarrassments exist under any Judicial system that the ingenuity of man can devise? Will they not take place under the establishment proposed by the other side? And will the mere alteration of the court from a district, to a court of admiralty and piracy, remedy this evil? But these objections come too late, a National Government is established. The Judicial power is a component part of this Government, and must be commensurate to it. If we have a Government pervading the Union, we must have a Judicial power of similar magnitude; we must establish courts in different parts of the Union. The only question is, which is the plan best calculated to answer the great object we all have in view, the carrying the Judicial powers into operation with the least inconvenience to the citizens. This double system of jurisprudence is unavoidable; it is as much a part of the constitution as the double system of Legislation; each State has a Legislative power, both operating on the same persons, and in many cases on the same objects; it is infinitely more difficult to mark with precision the limits of the Legislative than the Judicial power; no one, however, disputed the propriety of vesting Congress with a Legislative power over the Union, and yet that power is perhaps more liable to abuse than the Judicial. It has, indeed, been contended, in some of the State conventions, that Congress ought not to be entrusted with direct taxation; and it is remarkable that the same obstacles were urged against that power which is now suggested against this institution. It was then said that Federal and State taxes could not operate at the same time without confusion; it was then facetiously asked, whether the Congressional and State collector, who had seized a horse for the payment of taxes, were to divide him between them; it is now asked, with equal pleasantry, whether the marshal of the district, and the sheriff of the State court, who have taken the same debtor in execution, are to cut him in halves? It was then answered, that if the State collector seized the horse first, he will have the first satisfaction; it was also shown that there are frequently in the same State, state taxes, county taxes, and corporation taxes, and that these never occasioned any clashing or confusion; it may now be answered, that there are at present, in some of the States, state courts, county courts, and corporation courts; and that these are found convenient, and unaccompanied with the clashing so much apprehended. They keep within their particular spheres, and have their limits ascertained. But in answer to one supposition, allow me to state another; suppose a state sheriff and a county sheriff should seize the same debtor, would he be parcelled out between them? Would not the execution that was first served take effect? Is not this the practice at present, and will it not be so under this system? It is very easy for gentlemen, in the warmth of their imaginations, to suppose a variety of cases, and raise a multiplicity of objections against any system of jurisprudence whatever. They will all be more or less liable to some objections on the score of inconvenience, but they are submitted to by good citizens, who are sensible that they are the surest means of protecting their property, reputations, and lives. After all that has been said, it does not appear that we differ so widely as was at first imagined; for the gentlemen who advocate the motion, concede the necessity of some inferior Federal court in each State. What then do gentlemen object to? If it is the name of the court, that may be altered; if it is the frequency of holding them, it will be very easy to amend the clause in that respect; but they move to strike out the clause altogether, when it is granted on all hands that there must be such a court. The objection to the extent of jurisdiction is premature, and ought to be reserved for the clause which ascertains the jurisdiction; if, upon an investigation of that clause, it should appear that it ought to be restricted, that would be the seasonable time for moving to strike out the exceptionable part; but really at present gentlemen are making objections to one clause which, from their own concessions, apply altogether to another. As to several other observations that relate to the time of holding the courts, and the mode of drawing jurors, it is unnecessary to reply fully to them at present, because it would be improper to run into a discussion of the detail, while the question is on the principle of the system. He was no less opposed to the time of holding the courts, and the mode of drawing jurors, provided by the bill, than the gentleman was from whom the objection came, and would add his endeavors with his to effect an alteration in these points; but this is not the proper time, we are now on the principle, whether there shall be a District court: the same answer will apply to the objection that the juries and witnesses will be unnecessarily harassed; every care will be taken to accommodate these courts to the convenience of the citizens of each State.

Several other difficulties have been urged, as growing out of this plan of jurisdiction; a candid discussion will remove and obviate them. It has been said, that the bill provides a number of appeals from the State to the Supreme Court, through the District and Circuit courts, and that the suitors may be persecuted with appeals carried on from one court to another, through four different courts. An attentive examination of the bill is a sufficient answer to this objection. There is no appeal from the State to the District courts; and only a power of removal in certain cases of a Federal jurisdiction, from the State to the Circuit court; neither is there any appeal of fact from the District to the Circuit courts, but in admiralty cases; and these cannot be afterwards carried up to the Supreme Court, but when the value exceeds two thousand dollars.

It has been said, that, under the idea of vicinage, a man may be dragged far from his friends to trial, from Georgia to North Carolina; but it must be remembered that there is a constitutional provision that the criminal shall be tried in the State where the offence is committed, and the bill is conformable to the constitution in this respect. It has been observed that the constitution is no bar to vesting the State courts with Federal powers, for the words, "such inferior courts as Congress shall, from time to time, establish," imply that Congess may not institute them; and if they are not instituted, these powers must of course remain with the State courts. In reply to this argument, it is to be observed, that the words, "such inferior courts," &c. apply to the number and quality of the inferior Federal courts, and not to the possibility of excluding them altogether; it is a latitude of expression empowering Congress to institute such a number of inferior courts, of such particular construction, and at such particular places, as shall be found expedient; in short, in the words of the constitution, Congress may establish such inferior courts as may appear requisite. But that Congress must establish some inferior courts is beyond a doubt; in the first place, the constitution declares that the Judicial power of the United States shall be vested in a supreme and in inferior courts. The words, "shall be vested," have great energy, they are words of command; they leave no discretion to Congress to parcel out the Judicial powers of the Union to State judicatures, where a discretionary power is left to Congress by the constitution; the word "may" is employed where a discretion is left; the word "shall" is the appropriate term; this distinction is cautiously observed. Again, the Supreme Court, in two cases only, has original jurisdiction; in all others it has appellate jurisdiction; but where is the appeal to come from? Certainly not from the State courts; it must come from a Federal tribunal. There is another argument that appears conclusive; the constitution provides that the Judges of the Supreme and inferior courts, shall hold their commissions during good behavior, and shall receive salaries not capable of diminution; and it further provides, that the Judicial power of the Union shall be vested in a supreme and inferior courts; that is, in supreme and inferior courts, whose Judges shall receive their commissions during good behavior, and possess salaries not liable to diminution.

Does not, then, the constitution, in the plainest and most unequivocal language, preclude us from allotting any part of the Judicial authority of the Union to the State judicature? The bill, it is said, is then unconstitutional, for it recognizes the authority of the Federal court to overturn the decisions of the State courts, when those decisions are repugnant to the laws or constitution of the United States.

This is no recognition of any such authority; it is a necessary provision to guard the rights of the Union against the invasion of the States. If a State court should usurp the jurisdiction of Federal causes, and by its adjudications attempt to strip the Federal Government of its constitutional rights, it is necessary that the National tribunal shall possess the power of protecting those rights from such invasion. The committee have been told that this multiplicity of courts, and of appeals, will distress the citizens; and the number of appeals in Great Britain has been alluded to. He had always heard, he said, that there was no country in the world, where justice was better administered than in that country; to its excellent and impartial administration, the property, freedom, and civil rights of its citizens have been attributed. Were appeals too much restrained in this country, he questioned much whether a great clamor would not be raised against such a restriction. The citizens of a free country, when they lose their cause in one court, like to try their chance in another. This is a privilege they consider themselves justly entitled to; and if a litigious man harasses his adversary by vexatious appeals, he is sufficiently punished by having the costs to pay. By limiting appeals to the Supreme Court to sums above one thousand dollars, as is proposed, the poor will be protected from being harassed by appeals to the Supreme Court.

There was one more observation that required an answer; it was said that the juries shall be so drawn as to occasion the smallest inconvenience to the citizens. After having very maturely considered the subject, and attentively examined the bill in all its modifications, and heard all that had been alleged on this occasion, he was perfectly convinced, that whatever defects might be discovered in other parts of the bill, the adoption of this motion would tend to the rejection of every system of national jurisprudence.

Mr. MADISON said, that he was inclined to amend every part of the bill, so as to remove gentlemen's jealousy, provided it could be done consistently with the constitution.

Mr. GERRY was sorry to hear the honorable gentleman from South Carolina (Mr. BURKE) renounce his intention of opposing the system any further; he thought gentlemen ought not to be tired out like a jury.

Mr. BURKE said, he was not tired with the discussion, but was satisfied that the opposition must be unsuccessful.

[*31 Aug.*]

Mr. LIVERMORE thought this law would entirely change the form of Government of the United States.

Several observations have been made on this clause; it is said to be the axis on which the whole turns; some of the objections he had thrown out have been attempted to be answered; among others, the great expense. By expense he did not mean the salaries of Judges; this would, however, be greater than the whole expense of the Judiciary throughout the United States; but he referred to the general expenses which must be borne by the people at large for jails, court-houses, &c.; borne without repining, as the people receive compensation in personal security and public justice; but if all these were doubled throughout, it would be justly considered as intolerable. Another bur-

then, he said, was the rapidity of the course of prosecution in these courts, by which debtors would be obliged very suddenly to pay their debts at a great disadvantage. Something like this occasioned the insurrection in the Commonwealth of Massachusetts. In other States, similar modes of rapidity in the collection of debts have produced conventions. This had been the case to the northward, and, he had been informed, had been the same to the southward.

This new fangled system would eventually swallow up the State courts, as those who were in favor of this rapid mode of receiving debts, would have recourse to them. He then adverted to the clashing circumstances that must arise in the administration of justice, by these independent courts having similar powers. Gentlemen, said he, may be very facetious respecting dividing the body; but these are serious difficulties; the instances mentioned by the gentleman from South Carolina do not apply, the officer here is the same; the same sheriff has the precepts committed to him; and the execution does not clash; the same gaol answers for both.

He did not think that the difficulties had been answered by any of the examples brought for the purpose.

As to the instance of the trial for piracy in the State of South Carolina, that was a particular case, that could not be otherwise provided for; but these so rarely happen, that no precedent could be drawn from them to render it necessary to establish these perpetual courts.

He then referred to the clause, and offered a substitute, and said he thought, upon the whole, that the suggestion thrown out by an honorable gentleman from South Carolina (Mr. BURKE) that there should be no district courts, is better than any substitute.

It may be proper here to refer to the constitution; he then read the clause upon the subject. The Federal court is to have original jurisdiction only in certain specified cases; in all other it is to have only appellate jurisdiction; it is argued from this, that there are to be inferior Federal courts, from which these appeals are to be made. If the constitution had taken from State courts all cognizance of Federal causes, something might be said; but this is not the case. The State courts are allowed jurisdiction in these cases.

It has been objected that bonds taken by the Judges of the Supreme Court cannot be sued in the State courts. He did not see why this could not be done; similar processes have been usual among us in times past, and there has been no difficulty.

Admiralty courts should have cognizance of all maritime matters, and cases of seizures should also be committed to their decision. He hoped, therefore, that the clause would be disagreed to, or struck out, and that the bill might be rejected, that a short concise system might be adopted.

Mr. VINING said, he conceived that the institution of general and independent tribunals were essential to the fair and impartial administration of the laws of the United States. That the power of making laws, of executing them, and a judicial administration of such laws, is in its nature inseparable and indivisible, if not, "justice might be said to be lame as well as blind among us." The only plausible argument which has been urged against this clause, is the expense; it is true that expense must in some degree be necessarily incurred, but it will chiefly consist with the organization of your courts, and the erection of such buildings as may be essential, such as court-houses, gaols, and offices, as the gentleman has mentioned; and what at all events do such expenses amount to? They are the price that is paid for the fair and equal administration of your laws; from your amazingly increasing system of Government, causes must necessarily multiply in a proportionably extensive ratio; these causes must be tried somewhere, and whether it is in a State court, or Federal judicature, can, in the article of expense, make but little difference to the parties; it is only (for the sake of more impartial justice) transferring the business from one tribunal to another.

The gentleman has told us, that the people do not like courts; that they have been opposed and prevented by violence; nay, by an insurrection in Massachusetts. Surely this operates as a powerful reason to prove that there should be a general, independent, and energetic jurisdiction; otherwise if either of the State Judges should be so inclined, or a few sons of faction so assembled, they could ever frustrate the objects of justice; and, besides, from the different periods fixed by the constitution of the United States, and the different constitutions of the several States, with respect to the continuance of the Judges in office, it is equally impossible and inconsistent to make a general, uniform establishment, so as to accommodate them to your Government.

He wished, he said, to see justice so equally distributed, as that every citizen of the United States should be fairly dealt by, and so impartially administered, that every subject or citizen of the world, whether foreigner or alien, friend or foe, should be alike satisfied; by this means, the doors of justice would be thrown wide open, emigration would be encouraged from all countries into your own, and, in short, the United States of America would be made not only an asylum of liberty, but a sanctuary of justice. The faith of treaties would be preserved inviolate; our extensive funding system would have its intended operation; our navigation, impost, and revenue laws would be executed so as to insure their many advantages, whilst the combined effect would establish the public and private credit of the Union.

Mr. STONE.—I am mistaken if the whole subject has yet come before us in its full extent, and I think it ought to be thoroughly investigated before it is decided upon. I declare myself, Mr. Chairman, much pleased with the discussion, and am gratified with the different points of view in which it has been placed; but I conceive there is a variety of considerations arising out of the subject which have not yet been touched upon. I have seriously reflected, sir, on the subject, and have endeavored to give the arguments all the weight they deserve; I think, before we enter into a view of the convenience of the system, it will be right to consider the constitutional ground on which we stand.

Gentlemen, in their arguments, have expressly or impliedly declared, that the constitution, in this respect, is imperative, that it commands the organization of inferior courts; if this doctrine is true, let us see where it will carry us. It is conceded on all hands, that the establishment of

these courts is immutable. If the command of the constitution is imperative, we must carry it through all its branches; but if it is not true, we may model it so as to suit the convenience of the persent time. It appears from the words of the constitution, that Congress may, from time to time, ordain and establish inferior courts, such as they think proper: Now, if this is a command for us to establish inferior courts, if we cannot model or restrain their jurisdictions, the words which give us the power from time to time so to do, are vain and nugatory. Do the words from time to time leave any thing to our discretion? Or must we establish in our own minds a given length of time to gratify its meaning? Are we to compare it with the case of a census, and confine it to a subsequent term of ten years? If you establish inferior courts upon this principle, you have expended your whole power upon the subject for that length of time, and cannot interfere until the term arrives which you have fixed in your own mind for the power to return. But the words ordain and establish will not only go to the appointment of Judges of inferior courts, but they comprehend every thing which relates to them; we have good authority for this opinion, because one branch of the Legislature has expressly laid it down in the bill before us; they have modified the tribunal; they have restrained its jurisdiction; they have directed appeals only to be had in certain cases; they have connected the State courts with the District courts in some cases; this shows that, in their opinion, the articles of the constitution gave them a latitude. It is not said in that instrument, that you shall exercise the judicial power over all those cases, but that the judicial power shall extend to those cases. If it had been the idea of the convention that its Judiciary should extend so as positively to have taken in all these cases, they would so have declared it, and been explicit; but they have given you a power to extend your jurisdiction to them, but have not compelled you to that extension. Several gentlemen have mistaken this idea, and that on very different ground. The gentleman from Virginia has compared the exercise of the Judiciary to that of the Executive and Legislative powers, and seems from his arguments to infer, that if you do not extend the Judiciary power so as to take in all those cases which are specified in the constitution, that you will leave the Judiciary defective. The gentleman from New York seems to think it will be an abandonment of our Judicial power altogether: to what does the Legislative power of this Government extend? To a variety of cases which are not yet put in action; for instance, the Legislative power extends to excises and direct taxes. If you conceive the Judiciary incomplete, because you have not strained it to its utmost extension, cannot you see, from the same principle, that the Legislative power is not complete unless you extend it as far as you have the power? Do you divest yourself of the power by not exercising it? Certainly not. Suppose you were to lay as heavy a land-tax as the people could bear, (and this is in our power by the terms of the constitution;) and suppose the people were to ask you why you had done so, when there was no absolute necessity for it, would you answer that the constitution has given us the power, therefore we must exercise it? Certainly not. The constitution has given us power to admit that a suit in certain cases shall be brought for six-pence; this we may authorize to be done in an inferior court, from the District court it is carried to the Circuit court, and may be brought up into the Supreme Court. This power, I say, we have by the constitution; would it be proper to exercise it? But these circumstances would certainly follow from a construction that the constitution was imperative, and that you must establish inferior tribunals on the terms of the constitution. I understood it to be said, by the gentleman from New York, and decided, that the establishment of inferior courts would draw the whole Judiciary power along with them. If the clause in the constitution commands that inferior courts be established, what are their powers? They will claim all the jurisdiction to which it is declared the Judicial power shall extend, it is the right the constitution has given them after you have established the courts; any modification, therefore, or restriction of their power, would be a nullity; hence it appears to me, if the gentleman's principle is right, that part of your bill which restricts their cognizance to a particular sum is a nullity.

I apprehend that the gentlemen who support this bill have differed widely from the body that passed it, in supposing two things; first, that whatever Continental jurisdiction is exercised, that it follows they are Continental courts, and must have Continental salaries, and hold their offices during good behavior; if this is the case, the Senate have done one of two things, they have either relinquished all the penalties due to Government for a non-compliance of the laws under one hundred dollars, by the 9th section of the bill; or they have established the doctrine which gentlemen on this side contend for. By this section they have given to the State courts jurisdiction in cases of an inferior magnitude; now the very moment any suit is brought by the United States, under one hundred dollars, before a State court, such court becomes a Continental court. I say they must run into this absurdity, or relinquish all suits under one hundred dollars. But if this is not the case; if they do not relinquish this sum, (and the Senate did not suppose this was ever to be given up,) they did what appears, upon the gentleman's principles, strange indeed: they leave Continental courts to be established by their bringing suits, or foreigners bringing suits into the State courts; and in this way they divest the President of his power of appointing judges of inferior courts. This appears to my mind a strange mode of reasoning.

A gentleman has said that it would be impracticable to admit the Judges of the several States to take cognizance of the laws of the United States, because they are laws *de novo*: this I think is the idea. I apprehend that Judges, when they have undertaken their duty, must be considered in two respects—as citizens and as judges. Now as men, they are to submit to the modification of the constitution as it respects them as citizens; and as Judges, they are to consider their relation as such to the constitution, and are to administer justice agreeably to that constitution; as Judges they may divest themselves of this relation; they may resign, but if they continue to act as judges, they are enjoined to obey the constitution of the United States, and laws established under it: now Judges know that it is in the power of the United States to change the State constitutions, and they must conform in every respect. A Judge binds himself not only to act upon the laws which have already passed, but to obey all that may hereafter pass. If it is admitted that the Judges cannot take cognizance of the laws *de novo*, you annihilate the Judicial capacity at a blow; they cannot notice the adoption of the Federal constitution or any law passed after appointment. I can hardly bring myself seriously to consider the subject in this reverse point of view. Gentlemen will be convinced, I hope, that I take all the pains I possibly can to understand and discuss the arguments made use of; they will admit that if my principles are right; Congress may establish the Courts on what terms they may think proper.

It will perhaps be well to consider what the State courts can do, and consider what they are not competent to, and the reason we should not trust them. It appears to me that there is nothing but what the State courts are competent to but certain cases which are specially designated; in cases where a State is a party, they ought not to decide, because they could not execute their judgment; they would be competent to all admiralty cases, but for the fact I mentioned before, that admiralty courts are not established in all the States. I take it to be true that all the judicial powers not taken away by the constitution from the States remain to them, and I take them to be complete republics, to have sovereign power, conformable to their nature; therefore, if the constitution of the United States had not interfered in the subject, even of treason against the Union, the States, I apprehend, except in a few instances, could not have taken notice of it, because I do not know any kind of treason against the United States but is also treason against a particular State. If a man raises an army in the body of a State, unauthorized by the State, is it not rebellion against the State? Suppose it to be done in this State, and they tell you it is not the State of New York they mean to oppose, it is the General Government, pray is not this treason against the State of New York, as a member of the Union? Is not a piracy committed against the United States committed against a particular State? If it had its sovereign authority unimpaired, would any gentlemen contend that they had not power to try for piracy? I apprehend they would not. If a bond is given to the United States, or a penalty accrues under the supreme law of the land, or if a debt is due to a foreigner, may it not be sued in any part of the Union? I believe there is little doubt but this might be properly done—the Senate, by this bill, have given us this construction: foreigners may sue and be sued in all the States. This has already been done; do gentlemen now contend, that these suits shall be exclusively in the Continental courts? If they do, it would be an infringement of the private contracts, it would be an *ex post facto* law. The citizen might suppose, when he contracted his debt, that he might bring his suit in a State court; if you exclude him from this privilege, you destroy the right he had; a right, notwithstanding all that may be affirmed of the wisdom, honesty, and expedition of the courts of the United States, yet to him it may appear ten to one better to be secured in his rights in State courts. I think the inconvenience which will attend these courts has been explained; but certainly it has not been fully considered how far the inconveniences heretofore sustained may be compared to the inconveniences which may hereafter happen; perhaps there are no instances in point. Gentlemen are mistaken, who suppose that because there are many tribunals in the State they are necessarily exposed to the same difficulties as will arise from the establishment of Federal and State courts. I will state a case: A man is taken in Maryland by a writ from the county court, to which he gives bail. If he is taken by writ from the general court, he must also give bail, or go to prison. But if he is unable on the first writ to give bail and goes to prison, then the sheriff returns to the general court that he has taken him, and he is in gaol. This is a good return, as well in civil as in criminal process; as well upon mesne process as in executions; and if either of the courts required his appearance in court, an *habeas corpus* may be granted; by which he will be brought into court, and remanded, if proper. Here is no danger of defeating rights, nor acquiring inconvenience, because the same gaol will be made use of, and the same sheriff will hold, and always be liable for his prisoner. As the courts are connected they will *ex officio* take notice of, and admit the proceedings of, each other.

But in different tribunals, not connected, mischiefs may happen. Will a sheriff be justifiable in delivering up his prisoner to the marshal, or will it be a proper return by the marshal that the prisoner is kept by the State sheriff. If the first position is true, you ought to show that the marshal is liable to the State creditor for an escape, and you ought also to show that the marshal will return his prisoner to the State jail. If the second, you ought to show that the sheriff is justifiable in detaining a man after the cause for which he was committed to his custody ceased. An execution against the property depends upon the same principles; because the priority avoids all difficulty. If all the property is taken by the prior execution, the return of that fact is a proper return. But property is bound by the time of judgment in some cases, and the time of execution is put into the sheriff's hands in others. Now there is no difference where the same sheriff receives all. But suppose there is a different time of rendering judgment, and of receiving execution, and both are levied at the same time either upon body or goods. The rules of the courts are different; there will be different determinations in each, and perhaps each justifying their own affirmation. Even they may clash as to a matter of right. Suppose goods are stolen, and a prosecution is set on foot in the Federal court as of goods belonging to the United States, and at the same time an indictment is laid in the State court, for stealing goods, as for the goods of A: there is a conviction in each; the goods are to be returned to the owner. Now the courts in their several capacities justify their officers; and they proceed severally to seize goods or body; and failing in strength, the *posse comitatus* is raised on both sides; murder may be the consequence; and if it should, each court justifying the act of its officers, and condemning the others, all the officers in the different courts must be hanged for acting legally.

These are the inconveniences which result from a system of this kind, and why are these inconveniences to be encountered? Is it because such a system will be popular? I cannot conceive it warrantable upon this ground; it seems to me to be laid upon a principle directly opposite to that of being agreeable to the people. Will it be agreeable to the Judges? That cannot be, because it is intended to correct the vices of the State Judiciaries. Will it be considered as necessary by the State Legislature? Gentlemen have agreed, that it will not be agreeable to the State Legislatures, and we find in general, the sentiments of the people expressed by the Legislatures: from these circumstances, I conceive that this system cannot, in its nature, be agreeable to the State Governments, or to the people. I do not think this, then, the proper time to establish these courts; it is a measure on which the affection and attachment of the people to the constitution will be risked; it is best to defer the business till the necessity of these courts shall become apparent. I could therefore wish, that the power should be reserved for the occasion, and that nothing should be done the present session but what is absolutely necessary, lest by extending these matters too far, we should give the people a disposition to curtail our authority; they might then not confine themselves to an alteration in the Judicial department alone, they might extend it so far as to injure the Executive and Legislative, if not to the total change or destruction of the whole system of Government. I am, sir, for this Government moving as silently as death, that the people should not perceive the least alteration for the worse in their situation; the exercise of this power will certainly be the most odious that can be exercised, for mankind do not generally view courts of justice with a favorable eye, they are intended to correct the vices of the community, and consequently are disagreeable to human nature. It was well observed, and I concur in the opinion, that of all the wheels in Government, the Judicial is the most disagreeable.

Mr. GERRY.—The gentlemen who support the motion for striking out the clause, urge that this system will interfere with the State Judiciaries, that it will occasion a double set of officers, separate prisons and court-houses, and in general that the expenses will increase to a degree heretofore unknown, and consequently render the establishment obnoxious to the community. These objections are of such weight, as to have made deep impression on my mind. But what do gentlemen propose? Do they believe that these disadvantages can be remedied by Congress? I think they cannot; they result from the constitution itself, and therefore must be borne until the constitution is altered, or until the several States shall modify their courts of judicature so as to comport with our system.

Gentlemen have said, that the Federal Judiciary will be disagreeable to the citizens of the United States. These it should be recollected were divided into two classes; the one was for an unconditional ratification of the present constitution; the other was against such a measure. There appeared to be a majority of the first description, and we must suppose they understood what would be the operation of the system of Government they adopted with such avidity; if they did not, they entrusted the decision to conventions of men whom they supposed did. We must admit that they knew their business, and saw it would be for the benefit of their constituents, or we must suppose they were weak or wicked men to adopt a constitution without understanding it: this last supposition being inadmissible, I take it, then, their observations only refer to that part of our fellow-citizens who were against the unconditional ratification. Now I believe with them, that this part of the community, at least, will be uneasy under the operation of such a Judicial system. But how can it be remedied? The motion of the honorable gentleman from New Hampshire extends to prevent the establishment of inferior tribunals, except for the trial of admiralty causes; what, then, is to be done with all the other cases of which the Supreme Court has only appellate jurisdiction? You cannot make Federal courts of the State courts, because the constitution is an insuperable bar; besides, the laws and constitutions of some States expressly prohibit the State Judges from administering, or taking cognizance of foreign matters. New Hampshire requires all her civil officers to be appointed by the Legislature, and for what length of time they shall determine; now this is contrary to the indispensable tenure required by the constitution of the United States. All Judicial officers in Massachusetts must be appointed by the Governor, with the advice of council, and may be removed by the same power, upon the address of both Houses of the Legislature. There is another provision in the same constitution, incompatible with the terms of the Judicial capacity under Congress. "All writs issuing out of the clerk's office, in any of the courts of law, shall be in the name of the commonwealth of Massachusetts, &c." The constitution of Maryland establishes their Judges on the tenure of good behavior; but they may be removed for misbehavior, on conviction in a court of law. The Judges of the Federal court are to be removed only by impeachment and conviction before Congress. I suppose the same, or similar difficulties exist in every State, and therefore the State courts would be improper tribunals to administer the laws of the United States, while the present constitution remains, or while they are not established by the individual States, upon the terms required in this constitution.

We are to administer this constitution, and therefore we are bound to establish these courts, let what will be the consequence. Gentlemen say they are willing to establish Courts of Admiralty; but what is to become of the other cases to which the continental jurisdiction is extended by the constitution? When we have established the courts as they propose, have fixed the salaries, and the Supreme Executive has appointed the Judges, they will be independent, and no power can remove them; they will be beyond the reach of the Executive or Legislative powers of this Government; they will be unassailable by the State Legislatures; nothing can affect them but the united voice of America, and that only by a change of Government. They will, in this elevated and independent situation attend to their duty—their honor and every sacred tie oblige them. Will they not attend to the constitution as well as your laws? The constitution will undoubtedly be their first rule; and so far as your laws conform to that, they will attend to them, but no further. Would they then be confined by your laws within a less jurisdiction than they were authorized to take by the constitution? You must admit them to

be inferior courts; and the constitution positively says, that the Judicial powers of the United States shall be so vested. They would then inquire what were the Judicial powers of the Union, and undertake the exercise thereof, notwithstanding any Legislative declaration to the contrary; consequently their system would be a nullity, at least, which attempted to restrict the jurisdiction of inferior courts.

It has been said, that much inconvenience will result from the clashing of jurisdiction. Perhaps this is but ideal; if, however, it should be found to be the case, the General Government must remove the obstacles. They are authorized to suppress any system injurious to the administration of this constitution, by the clause granting to Congress the power of making all laws necessary and proper for carrying into execution the powers of the constitution, or any department thereof. It is without a desire to increase the difficulties of the proposed arrangements, that I make these observations, for I am desirous of promoting the unity of the two Governments, and this, I apprehend, can be done only by drawing a line between the two Judicial powers.

Mr. JACKSON.—I would not rise again, but from the great anxiety I feel to have this business well understood and determined. I am not for doing away the whole of the Judiciary power, but so ameliorating it as to make it agreeable and consistent. My heart, sir, is federal; and I would do as much as any member on this floor, on any, and on every occasion, to promote the interests and welfare of the Union. But in the present important question, I conceive the liberties of my fellow-citizens too deeply involved to suffer me to risk such a precious stake, though to secure the efficiency of a National Government.

It has been said in this debate, that the State Judges would be partial, and that there were no means of dragging them to justice. Shall I peremptorily tell the gentlemen who hold this opinion, that there is a constitutional power in existence to call them to account. Need I add that the Supreme Federal Court will have the right to annul these partial adjudications? Thus, then, all these arguments fall to the ground, on the slightest recollection.

Will gentlemen contend that it is for the convenience and security of the people that these inferior courts should be established? I believe this sentiment may be successfully controverted. The accurate Marquis Beccaria points out a danger which it behooves us to guard against. In every society, says he, there is an effort continually tending to confer on one part the height of power and happiness, and to reduce the other to the extreme of weakness and misery. The intent of good laws is to oppose this effort, and diffuse their influence universally and equally. But men generally abandon the care of their most important concerns, to the uncertain prudence and discretion of those whose interest it is to reject the best and wisest institutions; and it is not till they have been led into a thousand mistakes in matters the most essential to their lives and liberties, and are weary of suffering, that they can be induced to apply a remedy to the evils with which they are oppressed. It is then they begin to conceive and acknowledge the most palpable truths which, from their simplicity, commonly escape vulgar minds, incapable of analyzing objects, accustomed to receive impressions without distinction, and to be determined rather by the opinions of others than by the result of their own examination.

This celebrated writer pursues the principle still further, and confines what we urge on our side against an unnecessary establishment of inferior courts. He asserts, with the great Montesquieu, that every punishment which does not arise from absolute necessity is tyrannical; a proposition which may be made more general thus, every act of authority of one man over another for which there is not an absolute necessity is tyrannical. It is upon this, then, that the sovereign's right to punish crimes is founded; that is, upon the necessity of defending the public liberty entrusted to his care, from the usurpation of individuals; and punishments are just, in proportion as the liberty preserved by the sovereign is sacred and valuable.

He now wished the House to consider whether there was a necessity for the present establishment; and if it should appear, as he thought had been plainly shown, that no such necessity existed, it would be a tyranny which the people of this country never would be content to bear.

14

JOHN JAY, DRAFT OF LETTER FROM JUSTICES OF
THE SUPREME COURT TO GEORGE WASHINGTON
15 Sept. 1790
Iredell Life 2:293–96

Sir:—We, the Chief Justice and Associate Justices of the Supreme Court of the United States, in Pursuance of the Letter which you did us the Honor to write on the 3rd of April last, take the liberty of submitting to your consideration the following remarks on the "Act to establish the Judicial Courts of the United States."

It would doubtless have been singular, if a system so new and untried, and which was necessarily formed more on principles of Theory and probable Expediency, than former experience, had in practice, been found entirely free from defects.

The particular and continued attention which our official duties called upon us to pay to this Act, has produced reflections, which, at the time it was made and passed, did not, probably, occur in their full extent either to us or others.

On comparing this Act with the Constitution, we perceive deviations, which in our opinions are important.

The 1st Section of the 3rd Article of the Constitution declares that "the Judicial Power of the United States shall be vested in one *Supreme* Court, and in such inferior Courts, as the Congress may from time to time ordain and establish."

The 2d Section enumerates the cases to which the Judicial Power shall extend. It gives to the Supreme Court original jurisdiction in only *two* cases, but in all others vests it with *appellate* jurisdiction, and that with such exceptions,

and under such regulations as the Congress shall make.

It has long and very universally been deemed essential to the due administration of Justice, that some national Court or Council should be instituted or authorized to examine the acts of the ordinary tribunals, and, ultimately, to affirm or reverse their judgments and decrees: it being important that these tribunals should be confined to the limits of their respective Jurisdictions, and that they should uniformly interpret and apply the Law in the same sense and manner.

The appellate Jurisdiction of the Supreme Court enables it to confine inferior Courts to their proper limits, to correct their involuntary errors, and, in general, to provide that Justice be administered accurately, impartially, and uniformly.

These controlling Powers were unavoidably great and extensive; and of such a nature as to render their being combined with other Judicial Powers, in the same persons, unadvisable.

To the natural as well as legal incompatibility of *ultimate* appellate jurisdiction, with original jurisdiction, we ascribe the exclusion of the Supreme Court from the latter, except in two cases.

Had it not been for this exclusion, the unalterable everbinding decisions of this important Court, would not have been secured against the influence of those predilections for individual opinions, and of those reluctances to relinquish sentiments publicly, though, perhaps, too hastily given, which insensibly and not unfrequently infuse into the minds of the most upright men some degree of partiality for their official and public acts.

Without such exclusion no Court, possessing the *last* resort of justice, would have acquired and preserved that public confidence which is really necessary to render the wisest institutions useful. A celebrated writer justly observes that "next to doing right, the great object in the administration of public justice should be to give public satisfaction."

Had the Constitution permitted the Supreme Court to sit in judgment, and finally to decide on the acts and errors, done and committed by its own members, as judges of inferior and subordinate Courts, much room would have been left for men, on certain occasions, to suspect, that an unwillingness to be thought and found in the wrong had produced an improper adherence to it; or that mutual interest had generated mutual civilities and tendernesses injurious to right.

If room had been left for such suspicions, there would have been reason to apprehend, that the public confidence would diminish almost in proportion to the number of cases in which the Supreme Court might *affirm* the acts of any of its members.

Appeals are seldom made but in doubtful cases, and in which there is, at least, much appearance of reason on both sides: in such cases, therefore, not only the losing party, but others, not immediately interested, would, sometimes, be led to doubt whether the affirmance was entirely owing to the mere preponderance of right.

These, we presume, were among the reasons which induced the Convention to confine the Supreme Court, and consequently its judges, to appellate Jurisdiction. We say, "consequently its judges," because the reasons for the one apply to the other.

We are aware of the distinction between a Court and its Judges, and are far from thinking it illegal or unconstitutional, however it may be inexpedient, to employ them for other purposes, provided the latter purposes be consistent and compatible with the former. But from this distinction it cannot, in our opinion, be inferred, that the Judges of the Supreme Court may also be Judges of inferior and *subordinate* Courts, and be at the same time both the *controllers* and the *controlled*.

The application of these remarks is obvious. The Circuit Courts established by the act are Courts inferior and subordinate to the Supreme Court. They are vested with original jurisdiction in the cases from which the Supreme Court is excluded, and, to us, it would appear very singular, if the Constitution was capable of being so construed, as to exclude the Court, but yet admit the Judges of the Court. We, for our parts, consider the Constitution as plainly opposed to the appointment of the same persons to both offices, nor have we any doubts of their legal incompatibility.

Bacon in his abridgment says, that "offices are said to be incompatible and inconsistent, so as to be executed by one person, when, from the multiplicity of business in them, they cannot be executed with care and ability, or when, their being *subordinate* and interfering with each other, it induces a presumption they cannot be executed with impartiality and honesty—and this my Lord Coke says is of that importance, that if all offices, civil, ecclesiastical, &c., were only executed each by a different person, it would be for the good of the Commonwealth, and advancement of justice, and preferment of serving men."—"If a Forester by patent *for his life,* is made Justice in Eyre of the same Forest, *hac vice* the Forestership is become *void;* for these offices are incompatible, because the Forester is *under the correction* of the Justice in Eyre, and he cannot *judge himself.* Upon a mandamus to restore one to the place of Town Clerk; it was returned, that he was elected Mayor and sworn, and therefore they chose another Town Clerk, and the Court were strong of opinion that the offices were incompatible, because of the *subordination*—a Coroner made a Sheriff, ceases to be a Coroner—so a Parson made a Bishop, and a Judge of the Common Pleas made a Judge of the King's Bench, &c."

Other authorities on this point might be added, but the reasons on which they rest seem to us to require little elucidation or support.

There is in the Act another deviation from the Constitution, which we think it incumbent on us to mention.

The 2d Section of the 2d Article of the Constitution declares that the President "shall nominate, and by and with the advice and consent of the Senate shall appoint Judges of the Supreme Court, and *all* other officers of the United States, whose appointments are not *therein* otherwise provided for."

The Constitution not having otherwise provided for the appointment of the Judges of the Inferior Courts, we conceive that the appointment of some of them, viz., of the Circuit Courts, by an Act of the Legislature, is a departure from the Constitution and an exercise of Powers, which constitutionally and exclusively belong to the President and Senate.

We should proceed, Sir, to take notice of certain defects in the Act relative to Expediency, which we think merit the consideration of the Congress; but, as these are doubtless among the objects of the late reference made by the House of Representatives to the Attorney-General, we think it most proper to forbear making any remarks on the subject at present.

15

JAMES WILSON, GOVERNMENT, LECTURES ON LAW 1791
Works 1:296–97

The third great division of the powers of government is the judicial authority. It is sometimes considered as a branch of the executive power; but inaccurately. When the decisions of courts of justice are made, they must, it is true, be executed; but the power of executing them is ministerial, not judicial. The judicial authority consists in applying, according to the principles of right and justice, the constitution and laws to facts and transactions in cases, in which the manner or principles of this application are disputed by the parties interested in them.

The very existence of a dispute is presumptive evidence, that the application is not altogether without intricacy or difficulty. When intricacy or difficulty takes place in the application, it cannot be properly made without the possession of skill in the science of jurisprudence, and the most unbiassed behaviour in the exercise of that skill. Clear heads, therefore, and honest hearts are essential to good judges.

As all controversies in the community respecting life, liberty, reputation, and property, must be influenced by their judgments; and as their judgments ought to be calculated not only to do justice, but also to give general satisfaction, to inspire general confidence, and to take even from disappointed suiters—for in every cause disappointment must fall on one side—the slightest pretence of complaint; they ought to be placed in such a situation, as not only to be, but likewise to appear superiour to every extrinsick circumstance, which can be supposed to have the smallest operation upon their understandings or their inclinations. In their salaries, and in their offices, they ought to be completely independent: in other words, they should be removed from the most distant apprehension of being affected, in their judicial character and capacity, by any thing, except their own behaviour and its consequences.

"We are," says a very sensible writer on political subjects, "to look upon all the vast apparatus of government as having ultimately no other object or purpose, but the distribution of justice. All men are sensible of the necessity of justice to maintain peace and order; and all men are sensible of the necessity of peace and order for the maintenance of society." "The pure, and wise, and equal administration of the laws," says Mr. Paley, "forms the first end and blessing of social union." But how can society be maintained—how can a state expect to enjoy peace and order, unless the administration of justice is able and impartial? Can such an administration be expected, unless the judges can maintain dignified and independent characters? Can dignity and independence be expected from judges, who are liable to be tossed about by every veering gale of politicks, and who can be secured from destruction, only by dexterously swimming along with every successive tide of party? Is there not reason to fear, that in such a situation, the decisions of courts would cease to be the voice of law and justice, and would become the echo of faction and violence?

16

JOHN JAY ET AL., LETTERS ON REORGANIZATION OF THE SUPREME COURT
1792
Annals 3:1317–22

Gentlemen of the Senate, and of the House of Representatives:

I lay before you a copy of a Letter and representation from the Chief Justice and Associate Judges of the Supreme Court of the United States, stating the difficulties and inconveniences which attend the discharge of their duties, according to the present Judiciary system.

A copy of a Letter from the Judges attending the Circuit Court of the United States for the North Carolina district, in June last, containing their observations on an act passed during the last session of Congress, entitled "An act to provide for the settlement of the claims of widows and orphans barred by the limitations heretofore established, and to regulate the claims to invalid pensions."

GEO. WASHINGTON.

UNITED STATES, *Nov. 7, 1792.*

PHILADELPHIA, *Aug. 9, 1792.*

Sir: Your official connexion with the Legislature, and the consideration that applications from us to them cannot be made in any manner so respectful to Government as through the President, induce us to request your attention to the enclosed representation, and that you will be pleased to lay it before the Congress.

We really, sir, find the burdens laid upon us so excessive that we cannot forbear representing them in strong and explicit terms.

On extraordinary occasions we shall always be ready, as good citizens, to make extraordinary exertions; but while

our country enjoys prosperity, and nothing occurs to require or justify such severities, we cannot reconcile ourselves to the idea of existing in exile from our families, and of being subjected to a kind of life on which we cannot reflect without experiencing sensations and emotions more easy to conceive than proper for us to express.

With the most perfect respect, esteem, and attachment, we have the honor to be, sir, your most obedient and most humble servants,

JOHN JAY,
WILLIAM CUSHING,
JAMES WILSON,
JOHN BLAIR,
JAMES IREDELL,
THOMAS JOHNSON.

The PRESIDENT OF THE UNITED STATES.

The Chief Justice and the Associate Judges of the Supreme Court respectfully represent to the Congress of the United States:

That when the present judicial arrangements took place, it appeared to be a general and well-founded opinion, that the act then passed was to be considered rather as introducing a temporary expedient than a permanent system, and that it would be revised as soon as a period of greater leisure should arrive. The subject was new, and was rendered intricate and embarrassing by local as well as other difficulties; and there was reason to presume that others, not at that time apparent, would be discovered by experience. The ensuing sessions of Congress were so occupied by other affairs of great and pressing importance, that the Judges thought it improper to interrupt the attention of Congress by any application on the subject. That, as it would not become them to suggest what alterations or system ought in their opinion to be formed and adopted, they omit making any remarks on that head; but they feel most sensibly the necessity which presses them to represent—

That the task of holding twenty-seven Circuit Courts a year, in the different States, from New Hampshire to Georgia, besides two sessions of the Supreme Court at Philadelphia, in the two most severe seasons of the year, is a task which, considering the extent of the United States, and the small number of Judges, is too burdensome. That to require of the Judges to pass the greater part of their days on the road, and at inns, and a distance from their families, is a requisition which, in their opinion, should not be made unless in cases of necessity. That some of the present Judges do not enjoy health and strength of body sufficient to enable them to undergo the toilsome journeys through different climates and seasons, which they are called upon to undertake; nor is it probable that any set of Judges, however robust, would be able to support, and punctually execute, such severe duties for any length of time. That the distinction made between the Supreme Court and its Judges, and appointing the same men finally to correct in one capacity the errors which they themselves may have committed in another, is a distinction unfriendly to impartial justice, and to that confidence in the Supreme

Court which it is so essential to the public interest should be reposed in it. The Judges decline minute details, and purposely omit many considerations, which they are persuaded will occur whenever the subject is attentively discussed and considered. They most earnestly request that it may meet with early attention, and that the system may be so modified as that they may be relieved from their present painful and improper situation.

JOHN JAY,
WILLIAM CUSHING,
JAMES WILSON,
JOHN BLAIR,
JAMES IREDELL,
THOMAS JOHNSON.

NEWBERN, NORTH CAROLINA, *June* 8, 1792.

Sir: We, the Judges now attending at the Circuit Court of the United States for the district of North Carolina, conceive it our duty to lay before you some important observations which have occurred to us in the consideration of an act of Congress lately passed, entitled "An act to provide for the settlement of claims of widows and orphans barred by the limitations heretofore established, and to regulate the claims to invalid pensions."

We beg leave to premise, that it is as much an inclination as it is our duty to receive with all possible respect every act of the Legislature, and that we never can find ourselves in a more painful situation than to be obliged to object to the execution of any, more especially to the execution of one founded on the purest principles of humanity and justice, which the act in question undoubtedly is. But, however lamentable a difference in opinion really may be, or with whatever difficulty we may have formed an opinion, we are under the indispensable necessity of acting according to the best dictates of our own judgment, after duly weighing every consideration that can occur to us, which we have done on the present occasion. The extreme importance of the case, and our desire of being explicit beyond the danger of being misunderstood, will, we hope, justify us in stating our observations in a systematic manner. We, therefore, sir, submit to you the following:

1. That the Legislative, Executive, and Judicial Departments are each formed in a separate and independent manner, and that the ultimate basis of each is the Constitution only, within the limits of which each Department can alone justify any act of authority.

2. That the Legislature, among other important powers, unquestionably possess that of establishing Courts in such a manner as to their wisdom shall appear best, limited by the terms of the Constitution only; and to whatever extent that power may be exercised, or however severe the duty they may think proper to require, the Judges, when appointed in virtue of any such establishment, owe implicit and unreserved obedience to it.

3. That, at the same time, such Courts cannot be warranted, as we conceive, by virtue of that part of the Constitution delegating Judicial power for the exercise of which any act of the Legislature is provided, in exercising (even under the authority of another act) any power not in its nature Judicial, or, if Judicial, not provided for upon the terms the Constitution requires.

4. That whatever doubt may be suggested, whether the power in question is properly of a Judicial nature, yet inasmuch as the decision of the Court is not made final, but may be at least suspended in its operation by the Secretary of War, if he shall have cause to suspect imposition or mistake, this subjects the decision of the Court to a mode of revision which we consider to be unwarranted by the Constitution; for, though Congress may certainly establish, in instances not yet provided for, Courts of appellate jurisdiction, yet such Courts must consist of Judges appointed in the manner the Constitution requires, and holding their offices by no other tenure than that of their good behaviour, by which tenure the office of Secretary of War is not held; and we beg leave to add, with all due deference, that no decision of any Court of the United States can, under any circumstances, in our opinion, agreeably to the Constitution, be liable to a reversion, or even suspension, by the Legislature itself, in whom no Judicial power of any kind appears to be vested but the important one relative to impeachments.

These, sir, are our reasons for being of opinion, as we are at present, that this Circuit Court cannot be justified in the execution of that part of the act which requires it to examine, and report an opinion on the unfortunate cases of officers and soldiers disabled in the service of the United States. The part of the act requiring the Court to sit five days for the purpose of receiving applications from such persons, we shall deem it our duty to comply with; for, whether in our opinion such purpose can or cannot be answered, it is, as we conceive, our indispensable duty to keep open any Court of which we have the honor to be Judges, as long as Congress shall direct.

The high respect we entertain for the Legislature, our feelings as men for persons whose situation requires the earliest as well as the most effectual relief, and our sincere desire to promote, whether officially or otherwise, the just and benevolent views of Congress so conspicuous on the present as well as on many other occasions, have induced us to reflect whether we could be justified in acting under this act personally in the character of Commissioners during the session of a Court; and could we be satisfied that we had authority to do so, we would cheerfully devote such part of our time as might be necessary for the performance of the service. But we confess we have great doubts on this head. The power appears to be given to the Court only, and not to the Judges of it; and as the Secretary of War has not a discretion in all instances, but only in those where he has cause to suspect imposition or mistake, to withhold a person recommended by the Court from being named on the pension list, it would be necessary for us to be well persuaded we possessed such an authority before we exercised a power which might be a means of drawing money out of the public Treasury, as effectually as an express appropriation by law. We do not mean, however, to preclude ourselves from a very deliberate consideration whether we can be warranted in executing the purposes of the act in that manner, in case an application should be made.

No application has yet been made to the Court, or to ourselves individually, and, therefore, we have had some doubts as to the propriety of giving an opinion in a case which has not yet come regularly and judicially before us. None can be more sensible than we are of the necessity of Judges being, in general, extremely cautious in not intimating an opinion in any case extra-judicially, because we well know how liable the best minds are, notwithstanding their utmost care, to a bias which may arise from a preconceived opinion, even unguardedly, much more deliberately given. But in the present instance, as many unfortunate and meritorious individuals, whom Congress have justly thought proper objects of immediate relief, may suffer very great distress even by a short delay, and may be utterly ruined by a long one, we determined at all events to make our sentiments known as early as possible, considering this as a case which must be deemed an exception to the general rule upon every principle of humanity and justice; resolving, however, that so far as we are concerned individually, in case an application should be made, we will most attentively hear it; and if we can be convinced this opinion is a wrong one, we shall not hesitate to act accordingly, being as far from the weakness of supposing that there is any reproach in having committed an error, to which the greatest and best men are sometimes liable, as we should be from so low a sense of duty as to think it would not be the highest and most deserved reproach that could be bestowed on any men (much more on Judges) that they were capable, from any motive, of persevering against conviction in apparently maintaining an opinion which they really thought to be erroneous.

We take the liberty to request, sir, that you will be pleased to lay this Letter before the Legislature of the United States at their next session, and have the honor to be, with the highest respect, sir, your most obedient and most faithful servants,

JAMES IREDELL,
One of the Associate Justices of the
Supreme Court of the United States.
JNO. SITGREAVES,
Judge of the United States
for the North Carolina District.
The PRESIDENT OF THE UNITED STATES.

17

KENTUCKY CONSTITUTION OF 1799,
ART. 4, SEC. 3
Thorpe 3:1284

SEC. 3. The judges, both of the supreme and inferior courts, shall hold their offices during good behavior; but

for any reasonable cause, which shall not be sufficient ground of impeachment, the governor shall remove any of them on the address of two-thirds of each house of the general assembly: *Provided, however,* That the cause or causes for which such removal may be required shall be stated at length in such address, and on the journal of each house. They shall at stated times receive for their services an adequate compensation to be fixed by law.

18

JOHN JAY TO JOHN ADAMS
2 Jan. 1801
Correspondence 4:285

Such was the temper of the times, that the Act to establish the Judicial Courts of the United States was in some respects more accommodated to certain prejudices and sensibilities, than to the great and obvious principles of sound policy. Expectations were nevertheless entertained that it would be amended as the public mind became more composed and better informed; but those expectations have not been realized, nor have we hitherto seen convincing indications of a disposition in Congress to realize them. On the contrary, the efforts repeatedly made to place the judicial department on a proper footing have proved fruitless.

I left the bench perfectly convinced that under a system so defective it would not obtain the energy, weight, and dignity which are essential to its affording due support to the national government, nor acquire the public confidence and respect which, as the last resort of the justice of the nation, it should possess. Hence I am induced to doubt both the propriety and the expediency of my returning to the bench under the present system; especially as it would give some countenance to the neglect and indifference with which the opinions and remonstrances of the judges on this important subject have been treated.

19

RESPUBLICA V. PASSMORE
3 Yeates 441 (Pa. 1802)

SHIPPEN, C. J. However libellous the publication complained of may be, we have no cognizance of it in this summary mode, unless it be a contempt of the court. 2 Atky. 469. But we are unanimously of opinion, that in point of law it is such a contempt, and readily concur with Lord HARDWICKE, that "there cannot be any thing of greater consequence than to keep the streams of justice clear and pure, that parties may proceed with safety, both to themselves and their characters." Ib. 471. If the minds of the public can be prejudiced by such improper publications, before a cause is heard, justice cannot be administered. The defendant has set at nought the advice we gave him when we ordered the attachment. He has made no atonement whatever to the person whom he has so deeply injured, and he can only blame himself for the consequences.

The judgment of the court is, that the defendant pay a fine of 50 dollars to the commonwealth, and be imprisoned in the debtor's apartment for the space of 30 days; and afterwards, until the fine and costs are paid.

20

ALEXANDER HAMILTON, THE EXAMINATION, NO. 6
2 Jan. 1802
Papers 25:484–89

In answer to the observations in the last number it may perhaps be said that the Message meant nothing more than to condemn the recent *multiplication* of Federal Courts, and to bring them back to their original organization: considering it as adequate to all the purposes of the Constitution; to all the ends of justice and policy.

Towards forming a right judgment on this subject, it may be useful to those who are not familiar with the subject, to state briefly what was the former and what is the present establishment.

The former consisted of one Supreme Court with six judges, who, twice a year made the tour of the United States, distributed into three circuits, for the trial of causes arising in the respective districts of each circuit; and of fifteen District Courts, each having a single judge. The present consists of one Supreme Court with the like number of judges, to be reduced on the first vacancy happening, to five; of six Circuit Courts, having three distinct judges each, excepting one circuit which has only a single Circuit judge; and of twenty-two District Courts with a judge for each as before: In both plans the Supreme Court is to hold two terms at the seat of government, and the Circuit Courts to be holden twice a year in each district. The material difference in the two plans, as it respects the organs by which they are executed is reducible to the creation of twenty-three additional Judges; sixteen for the six Circuits Courts, seven for the superadded District Courts, and the addition of the necessary clerks, marshals, and subordinate officers of seven Courts. This shews at a single view that the difference of expence as applied to the United States is of trifling consideration.

But here an enquiry naturally presents itself; why was the latter plan substituted to the former and more economical one? The solution is easy and satisfactory. The first was inadequate to its object, and incapable of being carried into execution. The extent of the United States is manifestly too large for the due attendance of the six Judges in the Circuit Courts. The immense journies they were obliged to perform, kept them from their families for several successive months in every year; this rendered the office a grievous burden, and had a strong tendency to banish or exclude men of the best talents and characters, from these important stations. It is known to have been no light inducement with one Chief Justice, whose health was delicate, to quit that office for another attended with less bodily fatigue; and it is well understood that other important members of the Supreme Court were prepared to resign their situations, if there had not been some alteration of the kind which has taken place. It was also no uncommon circumstance for temporary interruptions in the health of particular judges, of whom only one was attached to a Circuit, to occasion a failure in the sessions of the Courts, to the no small disappointment, vexation and loss of the suitor. At any rate the necessity of visiting, within a given time, the numerous parts of an extensive circuit, unavoidably rendered the sessions of each Court so short, that where suits were in any degree multiplied, or intricate, there was not time to get through the business with due deliberation. Besides all this, the incessant fatigues of the judges of the Supreme Court, and their long and frequent absences from home, prevented that continued attention to their studies, which even the most learned will confess to be necessary for those, entrusted in the last resort with questions frequently novel, always of magnitude, affecting not only the property of individuals, but the rights of foreign nations, and the constitution of the country.

For these reasons it became necessary either to renounce the Circuit Courts, or to constitute them differently: the latter was preferred. The United States were divided into six Circuits, with a proper number of Judges to preside over each. No man of discernment will pretend that the number of circuits is too great. Surely three states forming an area of territory equal to that possessed by some of the first powers of Europe, must afford a quantity of business fully sufficient to employ three Judges on a Circuit, twice a year, and certainly not less than this will suffice for the dispatch of business, whether the number of causes be small or great. The inconsiderable addition made to the number of the District Courts will hardly excite criticism, and does not, therefore, claim a particular discussion, nor will their necessity be generally questioned. They are almost continually occupied with revenue, and admiralty causes; besides the great employment collaterally given to the Judges, in the execution of the Bankrupt Act, which probably must encrease instead of being diminished.

Perhaps it may be contended, that the Circuit Courts ought to be abolished altogether, and the business for which they are designed, left to the State Courts, with a right of appeal to the Supreme Court of the United States. Indeed, it is probable that this was the true design of the intimation in the Message. *A disposition to magnify the importance of the particular States, in derogation from that of the United States,* is a feature in that communication, not to be mistaken. But to such a scheme there are insuperable objections. The right of appeal is by no means equal to the right of applying, in the first instance, to a Tribunal agreeable to the suitor. The *desideratum* is to have impartial justice, at a moderate expence, administered "promptly and without delay;" not to be obliged to seek it through the long and tedious and expensive process of an appeal. It is true, that in causes of sufficient magnitude, an appeal ought to be open; which includes the possibility of going through that process: but when the Courts of original jurisdiction are so constituted as not only to deserve but to inspire confidence, appeals, from the inevitable inconvenience attached to them, are exceptions to the general rule of redress; where the contrary is the situation, they become the general rule itself. Appeals then multiplied to a pernicious extent; while the difficulties to which they are liable, operate in numerous instances as a preventative of justice, because they fall with most weight on the least wealthy suitor. It is to be remembered, that the cases in which the Federal Courts would be preferred, are those, where there would exist some distrust of the State Courts; and this distrust would be a fruitful source of appeals. To say that there could be no good cause for this distrust, and that the danger of it is imaginary, is to be wiser than experience, and wiser than the constitution. The first officer of the Government, when speaking in his official capacity, has no right to attempt to be thus wise. His duty exacts of him that he should respectfully acquiesce in the spirit and ideas of that instrument under which he is appointed.

The detail would be invidious, perhaps injurious; else it would be easy to shew, that however great the confidence to which the tribunals in some of the States are entitled, there is just cause for suspicion as to those of others; and that in respect to a still greater number, it would be inexpedient to delegate to them the care of interests which are specially and properly confided to the Government of the United States.

The plan of using the State Courts as substitutes for the Circuit Courts of the Union, is objectionable in another view. The citizens of the United States have a right to expect from those who administer our Government, the effacious enjoyment of those privileges as suitors for which the Constitution has provided. To *turn them round,* therefore, from the enjoyment of those privileges, in originating their causes to the eventual and dilatory resource of an appeal, is in a great degree to defeat the object contemplated. This is a consideration of much real weight, especially to the merchants in our Commercial States.

In the investigation of our subject, it is not to be forgotten, that the right to employ the agency of the State Courts for executing the laws of the Union, is liable to question, and has, in fact, been seriously questioned. This circumstance renders it the more indispensible, that the permanent organization of the Federal Judiciary should be adapted to the prompt and vigorous execution of those laws.

The right of Congress to discontinue judges, once appointed, by the abrogation of the Courts for which they were appointed, especially as it relates to their emoluments, offers matter for a very nice discussion, but which shall now be but superficially touched.

On the one head it is not easy to maintain that Congress cannot abolish Courts, which having been once instituted, are found in practice to be inconvenient and unnecessary:

On the other, if it may be done, so as to include the annihilation of existing Judges, it is evident that the measure may be used to defeat that clause of the Constitution which renders the duration and emoluments of the judicial office coextensive with the good behavior of the officer; an object essential to the independence of the Judges, the security of the citizen and the preservation of the government.

As a medium which may reconcile opposite ideas and obviate opposite inconveniences, it would perhaps, be the best and safest practical const[r]uction to say, that though Congress may abolish the Courts, yet shall the actual Judges retain their character and their emoluments, with the authorities of office, so far as they can be exercised elsewhere than in the courts. For this construction a precedent exists in the last arrangement of the Judiciary. Though the number of Judges of the Supreme Court is reduced from six to five, yet the actual reduction is wisely deferred to the *happening of a vacancy.* The expence of continuing the salaries of the existing incumbent, cannot prudently, be put in competition with the advantage of guarding from invasion, one of the most precious provisions in the Constitution. Nor ought it to be without its weight, that this modification will best comport with good faith on the part of Government, towards those who had been invited to accept offices, not to be held by an uncertain tenure, but during *good behavior.*

Weighing maturely all the very important and very delicate considerations, which appertain to the subject, would a wise or prudent statesman hazard the consequences of immediately unmaking at one session, Courts and Judges which had only been called in into being at the one preceding? Delectable indeed must be the work of disorganization to a mind which can thus rashly advance in its prosecution! Infatuated must that people be, who do not open their eyes to projects so intemperate—so mischievous! Who does not see what is the ultimate object? *"Delenda est Carthago"*—ill-fated Constitution, which Americans had fondly hoped would continue for ages, the guardian of public liberty, the source of national prosperity!

21

SENATE, JUDICIARY SYSTEM
Jan. 1802
*Annals 11:25–28, 33, 38–40, 48–49, 85–86,
119–20, 139–42*

[*8 Jan.*]

[Mr. BRECKENRIDGE:] The document before us shows that, at the passage of this act, the existing courts, not only from their number, but from the suits depending before them, were fully competent to a speedy decision of those suits. It shows, that on the 15th day of June last, there were depending in all the circuit courts, (that of Maryland only excepted, whose docket we have not been furnished with,) one thousand five hundred and thirty-nine suits. It shows that eight thousand two hundred and seventy-six suits of every description have come before those courts, in ten years and upwards. From this it appears, that the annual average amount of suits has been about eight hundred.

But sundry contingent things have conspired to swell the circuit court dockets. In Maryland, Virginia, and in all the Southern and Southwestern States, a great number of suits have been brought by British creditors; this species of controversy is nearly at an end.

In Pennsylvania, the docket has been swelled by prosecutions in consequence of the Western insurrection, by the disturbances in Bucks and Northampton counties; and by the sedition act. These I find amount in that State to two hundred and forty suits.

In Kentucky, non-resident land claimants have gone into the federal court from a temporary convenience: because, until within a year or two past, there existed no court of general jurisdiction co-extensive with the whole State. I find, too, that of the six hundred and odd suits which have been commenced there, one hundred and ninety-six of them have been prosecutions under the laws of the United States.

In most of the States there have been prosecutions under the sedition act. This source of litigation is, I trust, forever dried up. And, lastly, in *all* the States a number of suits have arisen under the excise law; which source of controversy will, I hope, before this session terminates, be also dried up.

But this same document discloses another important fact; which is, that notwithstanding all these untoward and temporary sources of federal adjudication, the suits in those courts are *decreasing;* for, from the dockets exhibited (except Kentucky and Tennessee, whose suits are summed up in the aggregate) it appears, that in 1799 there were one thousand two hundred and seventy-four, and in 1800 there were six hundred and eighty-seven suits commenced; showing a decrease of five hundred and eighty-seven suits.

Could it be necessary then to *increase* courts when suits were *decreasing?* Could it be necessary to multiply judges, when their duties were diminishing? And will I not be justified, therefore, in affirming, that the law was unnecessary, and that Congress acted under a mistaken impression, when they multiplied courts and judges at a time when litigation was actually decreasing?

But, sir, the decrease of business goes a small way in fixing my opinion on this subject. I am inclined to think, that so far from there having been a necessity at this time for an increase of courts and judges, that the time never will arrive when America will stand in need of thirty-eight federal judges. Look, sir, at your Constitution, and see the judicial power there consigned to federal courts, and seriously ask yourself, can there be fairly extracted from those powers subjects of litigation sufficient for six supreme and thirty-two inferior court judges? To me it appears impossible.

The judicial powers given to the federal courts were never intended by the Constitution to embrace, exclusively, subjects of litigation, which could, with propriety, be left with the State courts. Their jurisdiction was intended principally to extend to great national and foreign concerns. Except cases arising under the laws of the United States, I do not at present recollect but three or four kinds in which their power extends to subjects of litigation, in which private persons only are concerned. And can it be possible, that with a jurisdiction embracing so small a portion of private litigation, in a great part of which the State courts might, and ought to participate, that we can stand in need of thirty-eight judges, and expend in judiciary regulations the annual sum of $137,000?

No other country, whose regulations I have any knowledge of, furnishes an example of a system so prodigal and extensive. In England, whose courts are the boast, and said to be the security of the rights of the nation, every man knows there are but twelve judges and three principal courts. These courts embrace, in their original or appellate jurisdiction, almost the whole circle of human concerns.

The King's Bench and Common Pleas, which consist of four judges each, entertain all the common law suits of 40s. and upwards, originating among nine millions of the most commercial people in the world. They moreover revise the proceedings of not only all the petty courts of record in the Kingdom, even down to the courts of pie-poudre, but also of the Court of King's Bench in Ireland; and these supreme courts, after centuries of experiment, are found to be fully competent to *all* the business of the Kingdom.

I will now inquire into the power of Congress to put down these additional courts and judges.

First, as to the courts, Congress are empowered by the Constitution "from time to time, to ordain and establish inferior courts." The act now under consideration, is a legislative construction of this clause in the Constitution, that Congress may abolish as well as create these judicial officers; because it does expressly, in the twenty-seventh section of the act, abolish the then existing inferior courts, for the purpose of making way for the present. This construction, I contend, is correct; but it is equally pertinent to my object, whether it be or be not. If it be correct, then the present inferior courts may be abolished as constitutionally as the last; if it be not, then the law for abolishing the former courts, and establishing the present, was unconstitutional, and consequently repealable.

But independent of this legislative construction, on which I do not found my opinion, nor mean to rely my argument, there is little doubt indeed, in my mind, as to the power of Congress on this law. The first section of the third article vests the judicial power of the United States in one Supreme Court and such inferior courts as Congress may, from time to time, ordain and establish. By this clause Congress *may*, from time to time, establish inferior courts; but it is clearly a discretionary power, and they *may not* establish them. The language of the Constitution is very different when regulations are not left discretional. For example, "The trial," says the Constitution, "of all crimes (except in cases of impeachment) shall be by jury: representatives and direct taxes shall be apportioned according to numbers. All revenue bills shall originate in the

House of Representatives," &c. It would, therefore, in my opinion, be a perversion, not only of language, but of intellect, to say, that although Congress may, from time to time, establish inferior courts, yet, when established, that they shall not be abolished by a subsequent Congress possessing equal powers. It would be a paradox in legislation.

2d. As to the judges. The Judiciary department is so constructed as to be sufficiently secured against the improper influence of either the Executive or Legislative departments. The courts are organized and established by the Legislature, and the Executive creates the judges. Being thus organized, the Constitution affords the proper checks to secure their honesty and independence in office. It declares they shall not be removed from office during good behaviour; nor their salaries diminished during their continuance in office. From this it results, that a judge, after his appointment, is totally out of the power of the President, and his salary secured against legislative diminution, during his continuance in office. The first of these checks, which protects a judge in his office during good behaviour, applies to the President only, who would otherwise have possessed the power of removing him, like all other officers, at pleasure; and the other check, forbidding a diminution of their salaries, applies to the Legislature only. They are two separate and distinct checks, furnished by the Constitution against two distinct departments of the Government; and they are the only ones which are or ought to have been furnished on the subject.

But because the Constitution declares that a judge shall hold his office during good behaviour, can it be tortured to mean, that he shall hold his office after it is abolished? Can it mean, that his tenure should be limited by behaving well in an office which did not exist? Can it mean that an office may exist, although its duties are extinct? Can it mean, in short, that the shadow, to wit, the judge, can remain, when the substance, to wit, the office, is removed? It must have intended all these absurdities, or it must admit a construction which will avoid them.

The construction obviously is, that a judge should hold an existing office, so long as he did his duty in that office; and not that he should hold an office that did not exist, and perform duties not provided by law. Had the construction which I contend against been contemplated by those who framed the Constitution, it would have been necessary to have declared, explicitly, that the judges should hold their offices and their salaries during good behaviour.

Such a construction is not only irreconcileable with reason and propriety, but is repugnant to the principles of the Constitution. It is a principle of our Constitution, as well as of common honesty, that no man shall receive public money but in consideration of public services. Sinecure offices, therefore, are not permitted by our laws or Constitution. By this construction, complete sinecure offices will be created; hosts of Constitutional pensioners will be settled on us, and we cannot calculate how long. This is really creating a new species of public debt, not like any other of our debts; we cannot discharge the principal at any fixed time.

. . . . .

The opinion of Mr. MASON, therefore, was, that this Legislature have no right to repeal the judiciary law; for such an act would be in direct violation of the Constitution.

The Constitution says: "The judicial power of the United States shall be vested in one Supreme Court, and in such inferior courts as the Congress may, from time to time, ordain and establish. The judges, both of the Supreme and inferior courts, shall hold their offices during good behaviour, and shall, at stated times, receive for their services, a compensation, which shall not be diminished during their continuance in office."

Thus it says, "the judges *shall hold* their offices during good behaviour." How can this direction of the Constitution be complied with, if the Legislature shall, from session to session, repeal the law under which the office is held, and *remove the office?* He did not conceive that any words, which human ingenuity could devise, could more completely get over the remarks that had been made by the gentleman from Kentucky. But that gentleman says, that this provision of the Constitution applies exclusively to the President. He considers it as made to supersede the powers of the President to remove the judges. But could this have been the contemplation of the framers of the Constitution, when even the right of the President to remove officers at pleasure, was a matter of great doubt, and had divided in opinion our most enlightened citizens. Not that he stated this circumstance because he had doubts. He thought the President ought to have the right; but it did not emanate from the Constitution; was not expressly found in the Constitution, but sprang from Legislative construction.

Besides, if Congress have the right to repeal the whole of the law, they must possess the right to repeal a section of it. If so, they may repeal the law so far as it applies to a particular district, and thus get rid of an obnoxious judge. They may remove his office from him. Would it not be absurd still to say, that the removed judge held his office during good behaviour?

The Constitution says: "The judges shall, at stated times, receive for their services, a compensation, which shall not be diminished during their continuance in office." Why this provision? Why guard against the power to deprive the judges of their pay in a diminution of it, and not provide against what was more important, their existence?

Mr. MASON knew that a Legislative body was occasionally subject to the dominance of violent passions; he knew that they might pass unconstitutional laws; and that the judges, sworn to support the Constitution, would refuse to carry them into effect; and he knew that the Legislature might contend for the execution of their statutes: Hence the necessity of placing the judges above the influence of these passions; and for these reasons the Constitution had put them out of the power of the Legislature.

. . . . .

[Mr. MORRIS:] Gentlemen say, recur to the ancient system. What is the ancient system? Six judges of the Supreme Court to ride the circuit of America twice a year, and sit twice a year at the seat of Government. Without inquiring into the accuracy of a statement made by the gentleman respecting the courts of England, in which, I apprehend, he will find himself deceived, let me ask what would be the effects of the old system here? Cast an eye over the extent of our country, and a moment's consideration will show that the First Magistrate, in selecting a character for the bench, must seek less the learning of a judge than the agility of a post-boy. Can it be possible that men advanced in years, (for such alone can have the maturity of judgment fitting for the office;) that men educated in the closet—men who, from their habits of life, must have more strength of mind than of body; is it, I say, possible that such men can be running from one end of the continent to the other? Or, if they could, can they find time to hear and decide causes? I have been told by men of eminence on the bench, that they could not hold their offices under the old arrangement.

What is the present system? You have added to the old judges seven district and sixteen circuit judges. What will be the effect of the desired repeal? Will it not be a declaration to the remaining judges that they hold their offices subject to your will and pleasure? And what will be the result of this? It will be, that the check established by the Constitution, wished for by the people, and necessary in every contemplation of common sense, is destroyed. It had been said, and truly, too, that Governments are made to provide against the follies and vices of men. For to suppose that Governments rest upon reason is a pitiful solecism. If mankind were reasonable, they would want no Government. Hence, checks are required in the distribution of power among those who are to exercise it for the benefit of the people. Did the people of America vest all powers in the Legislature? No; they had vested in the judges a check intended to be efficient—a check of the first necessity, to prevent an invasion of the Constitution by unconstitutional laws—a check which might prevent any faction from intimidating or annihilating the tribunals themselves.

On this ground, said Mr. MORRIS, I stand to arrest the victory meditated over the Constitution of my country; a victory meditated by those who wish to prostrate that Constitution for the furtherance of their own ambitious views. Not of him who had recommended this measure, nor of those who now urge it; for, on his uprightness and their uprightness, I have the fullest reliance; but of those in the back-ground who have further and higher objects. These troops that protect the outworks are to be first dismissed. Those posts which present the strongest barriers are first to be taken, and then the Constitution becomes an easy prey.

Let us then, secondly, consider whether we have constitutionally a power to repeal this law. [Here Mr. MORRIS quoted the third article and first section of the Constitution.] I have heard a verbal criticism about the words *shall* and *may*, which appeared the more unnecessary to me, as the same word, *shall*, is applied to both members of the section. For it says "the judicial power, &c. *shall* be vested in one Supreme Court and such inferior courts as the Congress *may*, from time to time, ordain and establish." The Legislature, therefore, had, without doubt, the right of determining, in the first instance, what inferior courts

should be established; but when established, the words are imperative, a part of the judicial power shall vest in them. And "the judges shall hold their offices during good behaviour." They shall receive a compensation which shall not be diminished during their continuance in office. Therefore, whether the remarks be applied to the tenure of office, or the quantum of compensation, the Constitution is equally imperative. After this exposition, gentlemen are welcome to any advantage to be derived from the criticism on *shall* and *may*.

But another criticism, which, but for its serious effects, I would call pleasant, has been made: the amount of which is, you shall not take the man from the office, but you may take the office from the man; you shall not drown him, but you may sink his boat under him; you shall not put him to death, but you may take away his life. The Constitution secures to a judge his office, says he shall hold it, that is, it shall not be taken from him during good behaviour; the Legislature shall not diminish, though their bounty may increase, his salary; the Constitution provides perfectly for the inviolability of his tenure; but yet we may destroy the office which we cannot take away, as if the destruction of the office would not as effectually deprive him of it as the grant to another person. It is admitted that no power derived from the Constitution can deprive him of the office, and yet it is contended that by repeal of the law that office may be destroyed. Is not this absurd? It had been said, that whatever one Legislature can do another can undo; because no Legislature can bind its successor, and therefore that whatever we make we can destroy. This I deny, on the ground of reason, and on that of the Constitution. What! can a man destroy his own children? Can you annul your own compacts? Can you annihilate the national debt? When you have by law created a political existence, can you, by repealing the law, dissolve the corporation you had made? When, by your laws, you give to an individual any right whatever, can you, by a subsequent law, rightfully take it away? No. When you make a compact you are bound by it. When you make a promise you must perform it. Establish the contrary doctrine, and what follows? The whim of the moment becomes the law of the land; your country will be looked upon as a den of robbers; every honest man will fly your shores. Who will trust you, when you are the first to violate your own contracts? The position, therefore, that the Legislature may rightfully repeal every law made by a preceding Legislature, when tested by reason, is untrue; and it is equally untrue when compared with the precepts of the Constitution; for, what does the Constitution say? "You shall make no *ex post facto* law." Is not this an *ex post facto* law?

Gentlemen say the system of the last session is mere theory. For argument sake, it shall be granted; and what then is the language of reason? Try it; put it to the test of experience. What respect can the people have for a Legislature that, without reflection, meets but to undo the acts of its predecessors? Is it prudent, is it decent, even if the law were unwise, thus to commit our reputation and theirs? Is it not highly dangerous to call upon the people to decide which of us are fools, for one of us must be?

And what would be the effect on the injured man who

seeks redress in a court of justice, and whom, by this repeal, you shall have deprived of his right? You have saved him a miserable cent, and you have perhaps utterly ruined him.

But the honorable mover of the resolution has told us not only what is, but what is to be. He has told us not only that suits have decreased, but that they will decrease, and, relying on this preconception, informs us that the internal taxes will be repealed; and grounds the expediency of repealing the judiciary law, on the annihilation of these taxes. Thus, taking for granted the nonexistence of a law that yet exists, he infers from its destruction, and the consequent cessation of suits under it, the inutility of the judicial establishment. And when he has carried his present point, and broken down the judiciary system, he will tell us, perhaps, that we may as well repeal the internal taxes, because we have no judges to enforce the collection of them.

But what will be the effect of these repeals, and of all these dismissions from office? I impeach not the motives of gentlemen who advocate this measure. In my heart I believe them to be upright. But they see not the consequences. We are told the States want, and ought to have, more power. We are told that they are the legitimate sources from which the citizen is to derive protection. Their judges are, I suppose, to enforce our laws. Judges appointed by State authority, supported by State salary, and looking for promotion to State influence, or dependent upon State party. There are some honorable gentlemen now present, who sat in the Convention which formed this Constitution. I appeal to their recollection, if they have not seen the time when the fate of America was suspended by a hair? my life for it, if another convention be assembled, they will part without doing anything. Never, in the flow of time, was there a moment so propitious, as that in which the Convention assembled. The States had been convinced, by melancholy experience, how inadequate they were to the management of our national concerns. The passions of the people were lulled to sleep; State pride slumbered; the Constitution was promulgated; and then it awoke, and opposition was formed; but it was in vain. The people of America bound the States down by this compact.

[12 Jan.]

[Mr. JACKSON, of Georgia:] But I will forbear making any further remarks of this kind, and go into an examination of the Constitutional grounds.

[Mr. J. here quoted the third article, first section of the Constitution.]

Here then, said he, are two tribunals. First, the Supreme Court, the creature of the Constitution, the creature of the people; the other, the inferior jurisdictions, the creature of the Legislature. And notwithstanding the play of gentlemen upon the words shall and may, they are in meaning essentially different. The word *shall*, applied to the Supreme Court, is imperative and commanding, while the word *may*, applied to the inferior courts, is discretionary, and leaves to the Legislature a volition to act, or not to act, as it sees fit.

Again, why are the peculiar and exclusive powers of the Supreme Court designated in the following section of the Constitution, but because the Constitution considered that tribunal as absolutely established; while it viewed the inferior tribunals as dependent upon the will of the Legislature? And that this was the case was evident from the conduct of the Supreme Court on the pension act, which that court had some time since declared unconstitutional; and which declaration, he was convinced, would not have been hazarded by an inferior tribunal.

But does this conclusion rest on judicial power alone? Is it no where else found under other heads of Constitutional power? Yes, sir, under the Legislative head of power, which is the first grant of power made by the Constitution. For by the eighth section of the first article of the Constitution, after enumerating the power of laying taxes, &c., it is declared in the ninth division thereof, "to extend to constitute tribunals inferior to the Supreme Court." Here, then, is a Legislative power given expressly to that body, without restriction or application to any other branch of the National Government. Let those lawyers who hear me decide on the construction of all grants or deeds, if two grants be made in the same deed to two different powers or persons, if the first does not exclusively vest?

Is there a single argument that can be assigned to oppose this construction of the Constitution? Do not the observations of gentlemen, who insist upon the permanent tenure of the Judicial office, place the creature above its creator, man above his God, the model above its mechanic? A good mechanic, when he constructs a machine, tries it; and if it does not succeed, he either mends it or throws it away. Is there not the same necessity for acting in the same way with the inferior tribunals of the Judiciary, which is no other than the machine of the Legislature?

But, upon the principles of gentlemen, the law which creates a judge cannot be touched. The moment it is passed, it exists to the end of time. What is the implication of this doctrine? To alter or amend what may greatly require alteration or amendment, it is necessary to return to the creator, and to inquire what this creator is. My principle is, that the creator is the people themselves; that very people of the United States whom the gentleman from New York had declared ourselves to be the guardians of, to save the people themselves from their greatest enemies; and to save whom from destroying themselves he had invoked this House. Good God! is it possible that I have heard such a sentiment in this body? Rather should I have expected to have heard it sounded from the despots of Turkey, or the deserts of Siberia, than to have heard it uttered by an enlightened legislator of a free country, and on this floor.

But, said Mr. J., let us examine how we are to get at the creator. If the honorable gentleman will put us into the way of doing this with effect, I will abandon all my arguments for this motion. Look to the Constitution, and see how it is to be amended. It can only be amended on the recommendation of two-thirds of both Houses, or, on the application of two-thirds of the States, a convention shall be called, who are to propose amendments, afterwards to be ratified by three-fourths of the States.

There is required first, then, two-thirds of both Houses of Congress. Can this two-thirds be found now, or is there any probability of its being found for twenty years to come, who will concur in making the necessary alterations in the Judiciary system that are now, or may hereafter, be required? On this subject there are as many opinions as there are persons on this floor. I have indeed never found two persons precisely agree. How, then, can we expect three-fourths of the Legislatures of the several States to agree when we cannot agree among ourselves. There is, in fact, no amendment which could reach the case, and exhibit to view all the requisite and necessary regulations for such an extent of country. Such an attempt must form a volume, a Constitution by itself, and after all fall short of the object.

I am clearly, therefore, of opinion that if the power to alter the Judiciary system vests not here, it vests no where. It follows, from the ideas of gentlemen, that we must submit to all the evils of the present system, though it should exhibit all the horrors of the Inquisition.

[14 Jan.]

[Mr. MORRIS:] The honorable member from Virginia [Mr. Mason] has repeated the distinction before taken between the supreme and the inferior tribunals; he has insisted on the distinction between the words *shall* and *may;* has inferred from that distinction, that the judges of the inferior courts are subjects of Legislative discretion; and has contended that the word *may* includes all power respecting the subject to which it is applied, consequently to raise up and to put down, to create and to destroy. I must entreat your patience, sir, while I go more into this subject than I ever supposed would be necessary. By the article so often quoted, it is declared, "that the judicial power of the United States *shall* be vested in one Supreme Court, and in such inferior courts as the Congress *may* from time to time establish." I beg leave to call your attention to what I have already said of these inferior courts. That the original jurisdiction of various subjects being given exclusively to them, it became the bounden duty of Congress to establish such courts. I will not repeat the argument already used on that subject. But I will ask those who urge the distinction between the Supreme Court and the inferior tribunals, whether a law was not previously necessary before the Supreme Court could be organized. They reply, that the Constitution says, there *shall* be a Supreme Court, and therefore the Congress are commanded to organize it, while the rest is left to their discretion. This, sir, is not the fact. The Constitution says, the judicial power shall be vested in one Supreme Court, and in inferior courts. The Legislature can therefore only organize one Supreme Court, but they may establish as many inferior courts as they shall think proper. The designation made of them by the Constitution is, such inferior courts as the Congress may from time to time ordain and establish. But why, say gentlemen, fix precisely one Supreme Court, and leave the rest to Legislative discretion? The answer is simple: It results from the nature of things from the existent and probable state of our country. There was no difficulty in deciding that one and only one Supreme Court would be

proper or necessary, to which should lie appeals from inferior tribunals. Not so as to these. The United States were advancing in rapid progression. Their population of three millions was soon to become five, then ten, afterwards twenty millions. This was well known, as far as the future can become an object of human comprehension. In this increase of numbers, with a still greater increase of wealth, with the extension of our commerce and the progress of the arts, it was evident that although a great many tribunals would become necessary, it was impossible to determine either on the precise number or the most convenient form. The Convention did not pretend to this prescience; but had they possessed it, would it have been proper to have established, then, all the tribunals necessary for all future times?

[18 Jan.]

[Mr. WHITE, of Delaware:] In a preceding part of this Constitution, power is given to Congress to constitute tribunals inferior to the Supreme Court; by the act to which the resolution on your table refers, they did so, and in pursuance of that act, the President of the United States issued commissions to certain gentlemen as judges, they accepted of those commissions, and at the moment of their becoming judges, the Constitution attached to their offices, and guaranteed to them, the same independence and permanency as judges of the Supreme Court, for it makes no distinction. "Judges both of the supreme and inferior courts shall hold their offices during good behaviour." On the acceptance of their commissions, a complete contract was formed between them and the Government; the Constitution told them that the tenure of their offices should be their own good behaviour; the law told them that, for their services, they should receive a certain sum annually; these were the terms, sir, that tempted them to leave their other pursuits in life, and carry into execution this contract; and it is a contract that no power on earth can dissolve but by first altering this Constitution in the manner it directs, or by violating it; and any law attempting its dissolution, operates retrospectively, is an *ex post facto* law, and in that respect, too, unconstitutional.

But, sir, in order to place beyond a question forever the entire independence of the judiciary, the Convention went still further, and in this same section, nay, in this same sentence, for they followed the thing closely up, they declared that these judges, viz., of the supreme and inferior courts "shall, at stated times, receive for their services a compensation which shall not be diminished during their continuance in office." And under the words of this Constitution, we have just the same power to diminish their salaries whilst they continue in office, as we have to remove them from their offices and strip them of all salary; they hold their offices during good behaviour, and the full amount of their salaries whilst in office by the same strength and power of language; for can it be said, sir, that the words "shall not" are more prohibitory than the word "shall" is mandatory? Certainly not. These latter words apply especially to Congress; they must have been introduced for the express purpose of fixing and marking the bounds of Legislative authority towards the judiciary. And it would seem as if the wise framers of this instrument had feared not, sir, that Congress would ever presume themselves authorized absolutely to remove any judges from their offices without cause, as is contemplated in that resolution, for such an idea could never have entered their minds, after they had the moment before expressly declared, in so many words, that the judges, both of the supreme and inferior courts, should hold their offices during good behaviour, but that the aspiring pride and ambition of Legislative power, in some unhappy moment of intemperance or party warmth, might attempt to impair the independence of the judiciary in another way, by assuming a discretionary power over the salaries of the judges, and thus, rendering them dependent upon Legislative pleasure for a precarious support, make them servile and corrupt.

Gentlemen acknowledge that the judges of the Supreme Court are out of their reach, (thank Heaven that they happen to think so, or they, too, would accompany their brethren;) but, say they, the judges of the inferior courts are creatures of our own, and we can do with them as we please. Let me admit, sir, for argument sake, the positive meaning of the Constitution to the contrary notwithstanding, that these words, "the judges, both of the supreme and inferior courts, shall hold their offices during good behaviour," are equivocal. What reasons can gentlemen have to believe, upon what possible grounds can they presume, that the makers of this Constitution did not intend to place the judges of the inferior courts upon the same independent footing as those of the superior courts? Do they not belong to the same great department of your Government; intended to be kept separate and distinct from the other two great departments? Is not their independence equally important to the faithful administration of justice? Certainly, sir, and if possible more so, for it is to them the people, in most instances, must first apply for justice, and a vast proportion of the most important business that passes through their hands, is never carried into the Supreme Court.

. . . . .

[Mr. JOHN EWING COLHOUN, of South Carolina:] On the first point, the most important, as well as the most proper question, is, have we power, under the federal Constitution, to repeal the late act of Congress, so far as it respects the office and salary of the judges appointed under that act? If, by the letter and express words of the Constitution, we have not the power, then farther reasoning on the subject would be unnecessary, and arguments drawn from expediency or inexpediency would be useless and irrelevant to the question.

I am not, sir, disposed to advocate the late Judiciary system in all its modifications, as I think it imperfect, and not adequate to the purposes intended, and that it is not such an arrangement of the Judiciary as ought to have been adopted. But, as it has got into existence, and is in operation, and the judges appointed under the act, commissioned agreeably to the Constitution, during good behaviour, the ground is now changed; and although, previous to the adoption of the act, opposition to the inexpediency of the measure would have been right, would have been

proper; yet now, under existing circumstances, as the law has passed, and the Constitution has attached to the office of the judges appointed under it, durability of office, coextensive with good behaviour, to amend would be proper, but to repeal the act, at least so far as it respects the judges, would be unconstitutional; for I am of opinion, that as soon as their appointments were completed, and their commissions during good behaviour received, that then their offices as judges were completely beyond the reach of Legislative power; and that therefore the present resolution, in its operations, so far as it respects the office of the judges, is unconstitutional, and ought not to be agreed to.

Permit me here, sir, to define the legal rule of explaining a deed, a law, or Constitutional point, and then to apply the part of the Constitution in question to that rule. The rule of law is to make such an exposition of the section or clause under consideration, as will comport with its plain meaning when the words are taken in their common and usual acceptation, agreeably to the English language. If the clause is composed of dubious and uncertain expressions, that will admit of different meanings, or if several parts of the instrument seem to contradict, or be repugnant to each other, then the rule is, to make such a construction, if possible, as will be consistent with reason, and agreeable to the intention and purview of the whole instrument taken together. I think I am correct on the rule of law. Let us now examine the parts of the Constitution connected with the present subject, and apply to them the rules of law. Amongst the detailed powers of the Legislature, under the eighth section of the first article of the Constitution, we find the following, to wit: "to constitute tribunals inferior to the Supreme Court."

If this was the only clause giving them power to establish the inferior courts, I would readily grant that the Legislature could make the law, and at pleasure repeal it, and that the judges, as to the tenure of their office under the act, would be at the will of the Legislature, the existence of the law determining the office of the judge, precisely in the same manner and on the same footing as of the Secretary of State, the Secretary of the Treasury, and the Secretary of the Navy. But the subject is more fully expressed and explained under the proper head, in the first section of the third article of the Constitution, where it says: "The judicial power of the United States shall be vested in one Supreme Court, and in such inferior courts as Congress may, from time to time, ordain and establish. The judges, both of the supreme and inferior courts, shall hold their offices during good behaviour; and shall, at stated times, receive for their services a compensation which shall not be diminished during their continuance in office."

Here the intention of the Constitution is explicit, and cannot be doubted; plainer words and a more clear constructed sentence cannot be penned. "The judges, both of the supreme and inferior courts, shall hold their offices during good behaviour." We all fully and at once understand what is good behaviour in a judge, the oath he takes and the very nature of his office show it; to act with justice, integrity, ability and honor, and to administer justice speedily and impartially, is good behaviour; if he acts contrary, it would be misbehaviour, and the Constitution in that case has given a remedy by impeachment. If the clause, therefore, admits a certain, clear, and consistent construction, and no other part of the Constitution contains any article contradictory to it, which I contend is the case, the construction given by the gentlemen on the other side, being by implication only, and that against the plain and express words of the clause, will not be warranted by the principles of law; for if the Constitution is paramount to an act of the Legislature, then to hold an office during good behaviour, and during the pleasure of the Legislature, are synonymous terms; it must be so, or the act would be repugnant to the Constitution. The Constitution, on the face of it, appears to have been drawn with precision and correctness, nothing superfluous, nothing deficient. Had the Convention intended the construction now insisted for by the favorers of the resolution, to wit: that the judges of the inferior courts held their offices, not during good behaviour, but at the will of the Legislature, an explanatory clause after the words "good behaviour," would have been necessary and should have been inserted, to this effect: "Provided always, that the judges of such inferior courts shall hold their offices *only* during the existence of the law under which they may be appointed." By the clearness with which every part of the Constitution has been penned, it is right, it is fair, by analogy of reasoning, to say, that as no such provision is inserted, no such supposed construction was intended, and that therefore the plain letter and spirit of the Constitution must prevail. But, if possible, to make the matter more clear and conclusive, I beg indulgence, whilst I state three collateral arguments which greatly strengthen and enforce the construction which I advocate of that part of the Constitution. The first is, that all enlightened statesmen, at least since the American Revolution, with concurrent testimony, agree, that the Judiciary ought to be kept separate from, and independent of the Legislative and Executive powers; that without this check and control, there could be no true and rational liberty. Secondly, that the framers of the Constitution, who were themselves amongst the best informed and most distinguished citizens of the Union, intended to keep them distinct and separate, as the three great divisions and supporting pillars of the Constitution; this appears from the distinct position they assigned each on the face of that instrument. And thirdly, by the latter part of the first section of the third article, the Legislature have no power to lessen a judge's salary, even to the amount of one cent. This restriction must refer to the Legislature, as they alone have control over the funds of the Government; for the rule of law is, "that is certain, which can be rendered certain." If, therefore, this clause restrains the Legislature from even diminishing the salary of the judge, *a fortiori*, it prevents the removal from the office itself, as the words composing the whole clause are equally plain and expressive. Thus it appears, at least to me, by the plain and obvious construction of the words of the Constitution, confirmed and explained by the makers of it, that all the judges have a right to hold their offices during good behaviour, and that the Legislature, as a creature of that Constitution, cannot by any Legislative act, remove

them. The gentlemen who advocate the resolution, in support of the measure, say, that Virginia, Maryland, and the last Congress, afford examples of the Legislature abolishing courts, and removing from office judges who, under a Constitution, held their appointments as in the present case, during good behaviour. Let us examine the facts, and see if they apply. Virginia had a general court, with common law jurisdiction, which extended throughout the State, a court of chancery, with equitable jurisdiction, equally extensive, and a court of admiralty; the judges of these three courts constituted the court of appeals. About the year 1787, the Legislature of that State found it necessary to establish circuit courts, and in the law enacted, that "the judges of the court of appeals should be the circuit court judges." This law the judges refused to execute as unconstitutional, and said, "they considered themselves as forming one of the three pillars on which the great fabric of government was erected, and that, when this pillar was endangered, a resignation would subject them to the reproach of deserting their stations, and betraying the sacred interests of society, entrusted with them; that the propriety and necessity of the independence of the judges, is evident in reason and the nature of their office, and that this applies more forcibly to exclude a dependence on the Legislature, a branch of whom, in case of impeachment, is itself a party." This was the opinion formed on the law by the then judges, who were some of the ablest lawyers, and greatest statesmen in the Union. I believe the event was, they protested against the law as unconstitutional, resigned their offices, had the resignation recorded, and afterwards were appointed circuit judges. If this statement is correct, which I presume in substance it is, can it be said, that it affords an example that would justify, or in the smallest degree support the principles of the resolution? In the case of Maryland, I have not had full information, therefore cannot decide. In the case of Tennessee and Kentucky, the district courts were abolished; the judges were not removed from office; but by law continued as circuit court judges, with additional duties and additional salary of five hundred dollars each. They neither vacated their office, nor had to take a new oath or new commissions; therefore, in this case, there was no violation of the Constitution. But, to sum the business up, the case of Virginia is against them; the case of Kentucky and Tennessee, not in point; and Maryland, should it afford an example, is the only and solitary one. But, let us now suppose for argument sake, though the fact is otherwise, that half of the States in the Union passed such laws; if those laws are founded on wrong and unconstitutional ground, should they be a precedent for us? Surely not. If they were founded in error, we ought to correct and not continue the error.

Some gentlemen have said, although we cannot remove the judge from the office, yet we can remove the office from the judge. To me this is a paradox in legislation. Do we mean to act indirectly, what we would not profess to do openly and directly? Are the gentlemen prepared to meet this question in all its consequences? Let me suppose they are, and sketch a law founded on the consequences of their repealing act, and exhibit the case in its real and true light. In framing a law the preamble should state facts, and explain the reasons for passing the act. Suppose, then, we should introduce, instead of their present repealing law, the following, viz: Whereas A, B, C, &c., the sixteen Federal judges appointed under the late act of Congress, although they have been commissioned during good behaviour, and have discharged the duties of the office with integrity, ability, and honor, yet we, the Legislature, in Congress assembled, finding their number to be more than we judge necessary for the administration of justice to the good people of the United States, and deeming the law under which they act not the best possible system that could be adopted, and thinking, also, that the public good requires that the judges of the inferior courts should not hold their offices during good behaviour, but should hold them at the will of the Legislature: Be it therefore enacted, &c., That the said sixteen Federal judges shall be, and they hereby are, removed and discharged from their respective offices as judges, and shall not be entitled to any compensation or salary after the passing of this act. This act and preamble would be in truth only what the repealing act in its effects intended, and will naturally produce.

Are we prepared to vote for a law in this form, with all the true reasons stated on the face of the act, and to wish that publicity should be given to it among our constituents, as an act that completely destroys the independence of their judges?

22

ALEXANDER HAMILTON, THE EXAMINATION, NO. 12
23 Feb. 1802
Papers 25:529–35

From the manner in which the subject was treated in the fifth and sixth numbers of The Examination, it has been doubted, whether the writer did or did not entertain a decided opinion as to the power of Congress to abolish the offices and compensations of Judges, once instituted and appointed pursuant to a law of the United States. In a matter of such high constitutional moment, it is a sacred duty to be explicit. The progress of a bill lately brought into the Senate for repealing the law of the last session, entitled, "An act to provide for the more convenient organization of the courts of the U. States," with the avowed design of superceding the judges, who were appointed under it, has rendered the question far more serious than it was while it rested merely on the obscure suggestion of the Presidential Message. 'Till the experiment had proved the fact, it was hardly to have been imagined, that a majority of either house of Congress, whether from design or error, would have lent its sanction to a glaring violation of our national compact, in that article, which of all others is the most essential to the efficiency and stability of the Government; to the security of property; to the safety and liberty of person. This portentous and frightful phenome-

non has, nevertheless, appeared. It frowns with malignant and deadly aspect upon our constitution. Probably before these remarks shall be read, that Constitution will be no more! It will be numbered among the numerous victims of Democratic phrenzy; and will have given another and an awful lesson to mankind—the prelude perhaps of calamities to this country, at the contemplation of which imagination shudders!

With such a prospect before us, nothing ought to be left unessayed, to open the eyes of thinking men to the destructive projects of those mountebank politicians, who have been too successful in perverting public opinion, and in cheating the people out of their confidence; who are advancing with rapid strides in the work of disorganization—the sure fore-runner of tyranny; and who, if they are not arrested in their mad career, will, ere long, precipitate our nation into all the horrors of anarchy.

It would be vanity to expect to throw much additional light upon a subject which has already exhausted the logic and eloquence of some of the ablest men of our country; yet it often happens, that the same arguments placed in a new attitudes, and accompanied witn illustrations which may have escaped the ardor of a first research, serve both to fortify and to extend conviction. In the hope that this may be the case, the discussion shall be pursued with as much perspicuity and brevity, as can be attained.

The words of the constitution are, "The Judges *both* of the Supreme and Inferior Courts *shall hold their offices during good behaviour*, and shall at stated times receive for their services a compensation which *shall not be diminished during their continuance in office*."

Taking the literal import of the terms as the criterion of their true meaning, it is clear, that the *tenure* or *duration* of the office is limited by no other condition than the *good behaviour* of the incumbent. The words are imperative, simple, and unqualified: "The Judges *shall hold their offices during good behaviour*." Independent therefore of any artificial reasoning to vary the nature and obvious sense of the words, the provision must be understood to vest in the Judge a right to the office, indefeasible but by his own misconduct.

It is consequently the duty of those who deny this right, to shew either that there are certain presumptions of intention deducible from other parts of the constitutional instrument, or certain general principles of constitutional law or policy, which ought to control the literal and substitute a different meaning.

As to presumptions of intention different from the import of the terms, there is not a syllable in the instrument from which they can be inferred; on the contrary, the latter member of the clause cited, affords very strong presumption the other way.

From the injunction, that the compensation of the Judges shall not be diminished, it is manifest, that the Constitution intends to guard the independence of those Officers against the Legislative Department: Because, to this department *alone* would have belonged the power of diminishing their compensations.

When the Constitution is thus careful to tie up the Legislature, from taking away part of the compensation, is it possible to suppose that it can mean to leave that body at full liberty to take away the whole? The affirmative imputes to the Constitution the manifest absurdity of holding to the Legislature this language, "You shall not *weaken* the Independence of the Judicial character, by exercising the power of *lessening* his emolument, but you may *destroy* it altogether, by exercising the greater power of *annihilating* the recompence with the office." No mortal can be so blind as not to see, that by such a construction, the restraint intended to be laid upon the Legislature by the injunction not to lessen the compensations, becomes absolutely nugatory.

In vain is a justification of it sought in that part of the same article which provides that "The Judicial power of the United States shall be vested in one Supreme Court and in such Inferior Courts as the Congress *may* from time to time ordain and establish." The position that a discretionary power to institute Inferior Courts includes virtually a power to abolish them, if true, is nothing to the purpose. The abolition of a court does not necessarily imply that of its Judges. In contemplation of law, the Court and the Judge are distinct things. The Court may have a legal existence, though there may be no Judge to exercise its powers. This may be the case either at the original creation of a Court, previous to the appointment of a Judge, or subsequently by his death, resignation or removal: In the last case, it could not be pretended that the Court had become extinct by the event. In like manner, the office of the Judge may subsist, though the Court in which he is to officiate may be suspended or destroyed. The duties of a Judge, as the office is defined in our Jurisprudence, are two fold—judicial and ministerial. The latter may be performed out of Court, and often without reference to it. As conservator of the peace, which every judge is *ex officio*, many things are done not connected with a judicial controversy, or to speak technically, with a *lis pendens*. This serves to illustrate the idea, that the office is something different from the Court; which is the place or situation for its principal action, yet not altogether essential to its activity. Besides, a Judge is not the less a Judge when out of Court than when in Court. The law does not suppose him to be always in Court, yet it does suppose him to be always in office; in vacation as well as in Term. He has also a property or interest in his office, which entitles him to civil actions and to recompence in damages for injuries that affect him in relation to his office; but he cannot be said to have a property or interest in the Court of which he is a member. All these considerations confirm the hypothesis, that the Court and the Judge are distinct legal entities, and therefore may exist the one independently of the other.

If it be replied, that the office is an incident to the Court, and that the abolition of the principal includes that of the incidents—The answer to this is, that the argument may be well founded as to all subsequent appointments; but not as to those previously made. Though there be no office to be filled in future, it will not follow that one already vested in an individual by a regular appointment and commission, is thereby vacated and divested. Whether this shall or shall not happen must depend on what the Constitution or the law has declared with regard to the *tenure* of the office. Having pronounced that this shall be during good behavior, it will preserve the office, to give effect to that tenure for the benefit of the possessor. To be consistent with itself, it will require and prescribe such a modification and construction of its own acts, as will reconcile its power over the future, with the rights which have been conferred as to the past.

Let it not be said that an office is a mere trust for public benefit, and excludes the idea of a property or a vested interest in the individual. The first part of the proposition is true—the last false. Every office combines the two ingredients of an interest in the possessor, and a trust for the public. Hence it is that the law allows the officer redress by a civil action for an injury in relation to his office, which presupposes property or interest. This interest may be defeasible at the pleasure of the government, or it may have a fixed duration, according to the constitution of the office. The idea of a vested interest holden even by a permanent tenure, so far from being incompatible with the principle that the primary and essential end of every office is the public good, may be conducive to that very end by promoting a diligent, faithful, energetic, and independent execution of the office.

But admitting, as seems to have been admitted by the speakers on both sides the question, that the judge must fall with the court, then the only consequence will be, that Congress cannot abolish a court once established. There is no rule of interpretation better settled than that different provisions in the same instrument, on the same subject, ought to be so construed, as, if possible, to comport with each other, and give a reasonable effect to all.

The provision that "The Judiciary Power shall be vested in one Superior Court and in such inferior courts as the Congress *may* from time to time ordain and establish" is immediately followed by this other provision, "The judges *both* of the Supreme and Inferior Courts shall hold their offices during good behaviour."

The proposition, that a power to do, includes virtually, a power to undo, as applied to a legislative body, is generally but not universally true. All *vested rights* form an exception to the rule. In strict theory, there is no lawful or moral power to divest by a subsequent statute, a right vested in an individual by a prior: And accordingly it is familiar to persons conversant with legal studies, that the repeal of a law does not always work the revocation or divestiture of such rights.

If it be replied, that though a legislature might act immorally and wickedly in abrogating a vested right, yet the legal *validity* of its act for such a purpose could not be disputed; it may be answered that this odious position, in any application of it, is liable to question in every limited Constitution; (that is, in every Constitution which, in its theory, does not suppose the WHOLE POWER of the Nation to be lodged in the legislative body;)—and that it is certainly false in its application to a legislature, the authorities of which are defined by a positive written Constitution, as to every thing which is contrary to the actual provisions of that Constitution. To deny this is to affirm that the *delegated* is paramount to the *constituent* power. It is in fact to affirm there are *no constitutional limits to the Legislative Authority*.

The enquiry then must be, whether the power to abolish Inferior Courts, if implied in that of creating them, is not abridged by the clause which regulates the tenure of Judicial office.

The first thing which occurs in this investigation, is, that the power to abolish is at most, an implied or incidental power, and as such will the more readily yield to any express provision with which it may be inconsistent.

The circumstance of giving to Congress a discretionary power to establish Inferior Courts instead of establishing them specifically in the Constitution, has, with great reason, been ascribed to the impracticability of ascertaining beforehand the number and variety of Courts, which the developement of our national affairs might indicate to be proper; especially in relation to the progress of new settlements, and the creation of new states. This rendered a discretionary power to *institute* Courts indispensable; but it did not alike render indispensable a power to abolish those which were once instituted. It was conceived, that with intelligence, caution, and care, a plan might be pursued in the institution of Courts, which would render abolitions unnecessary. Indeed it is not presumable with regard to establishments of such solemnity and importance, making part of the *organization* of a principal department of the Government, that a fluctuation of plans was anticipated. It is therefore not essential to suppose, that the power to destroy was intended to be included in the power to create: Thus the words "to ordain and establish," may be satisfied by attributing to them only the latter effect.

Consequently when the grant of the power to institute courts, is immediately succeeded by the declaration that the Judges of those Courts shall *hold* their offices during good behaviour; if the exercise of the power to abolish the Courts cannot be reconciled with the actual holding or enjoyment of the office, according to the prescribed tenure, it will follow that the power to abolish is interdicted. The implied or hypothetical power to destroy the office must give way to the express and positive right of holding it during good behaviour. This is agreeable to the soundest rules of construction; the contrary is in subversion of them.

Equally in vain is a justification of the construction adopted by the advocates of the repeal, attempted to be derived from a distinction between the Supreme and Inferior Courts. The argument, that as the former is established by the Constitution, it cannot be annulled by a legislative act, though the latter which must owe their existence to such an act may by the same authority be extinguished, can afford no greater stability to the office of a Judge of the Supreme Court than to that of a Judge of an Inferior Court. The Constitution does indeed establish the Supreme Court; but it is altogether silent as to the number of the Judges. This is as fully left to legislative discretion as the institution of Inferior Courts; and the rule that a power to undo is implied in the power to do, is therefore no less applicable to the reduction of the number of the Judges of the Supreme Court than to the abolition of the Inferior Courts. If the former are not protected by the clause, which fixes the tenure of office, they are no less at the mercy of the legislature than the latter:

And if that clause does protect them, its protection must be equally effectual for the Judges of the Inferior Courts. Its efficacy in either case must be founded on the principle that it operates as a restraint upon the legislative discretion; and if so, there is the like restraint in both cases, because the very same words in the very same sentence define conjunctly the tenure of the offices of the two classes of Judges. No sophistry can elude this conclusion.

It is therefore plain to a demonstration, that the doctrine which affirms the right of Congress to abolish the Judges of the Inferior Courts is absolutely fatal to the independence of the Judiciary department. The observation that so gross an abuse of power as would be implied in the abolition of the Judges of the Supreme Court, ought not to be supposed, can afford no consolation against the extreme danger of the doctrine. The terrible examples before us forbid our placing the least confidence in that delusive observation. Experience, sad experience warns us to dread every extremity—to be prepared for the worst catastrophe that can happen.

23

ALEXANDER HAMILTON, THE EXAMINATION, NO. 13
27 Feb. 1802
Papers 25:539–44

The advocates of the power of Congress to abolish the Judges, endeavor to deduce a presumption of intention favorable to their doctrine, from this argument—The provision concerning the tenure of office (say they) ought to be viewed as a restraint upon the Executive Department, *because,* to this Department belongs the power of removal; in like manner as the provision concerning the diminution of compensations ought to be regarded as a restraint upon the Legislative Department, *because,* to this Department belongs the power of regulating compensations: The different members of the clause ought to be taken distributively in conformity with the distribution of power to the respective Departments.

This is certainly the most specious of the arguments which have been used on that side. It has received several pertinent and forcible answers. But it is believed to be susceptible of one still more direct and satisfactory; which is not recollected to have been yet given.

If, in the theory of the Constitution, there was but one way of *defeating the tenure* of office, and that exclusively appertaining to the Executive Authority, it would be a natural and correct inference that this authority was solely contemplated in a constitutional provision upon the subject. But the fact is clearly otherwise. There are two modes known to the Constitution, in which the tenure of office may be affected—one the abolition of the office; the other the removal of the officer. The first is a legislative act, and operates by removing the office from the person—the last is an Executive act and operates by removing the person from the office. Both equally cause the tenure, enjoyment, or *holding* of the office to cease.

This being the case, the inference which has been drawn, fails. There is no ground for the presumption, that the Constitution, in establishing the tenure of an office, had an exclusive eye to one only of the two modes in which it might be affected. The more rational supposition is, that it intended to reach and exclude both; because, this alone can fulfil the purpose which it appears to have in view: And it ought neither to be understood to aim at less than its language imports, nor to employ inadequate means for accomplishing the end which it professes. Or, the better to elucidate the idea by placing it in another form, it may be said, that since in the nature of things the Legislative, equally with the Executive organ, may by different modes of action affect the tenure of office; when the Constitution undertakes to prescribe what that tenure shall be, it ought to be presumed to intend to guard that which shall have been prescribed against the interference of either department.

In an instrument abounding with examples of restrictions on the Legislative discretion, there is no difficulty in supposing that one was intended in every case in which it may be fairly inferred, either from the words used, or from the object to be effected.

While the reason which has been stated, refers the provision respecting the tenure of judicial office as well to the Executive as to the Legislative department, were it necessary to examine to which, if to either of them, it ought to be deemed most appropriate, there could be no difficulty in selecting the latter, rather than the former. The *tenure* of an office is one of its essential *qualities*. A provision, therefore, which is destined to prescribe or define this quality, may be supposed to have a more peculiar reference to that department which is empowered to constitute the office; either as directory to it in the exercise of its power, or as fixing what otherwise would be left to its discretion.

It is constantly to be recollected that the terms of the provision do not look particularly to either department. They are general, "The Judges shall hold their offices during good behavior." 'Tis not from the terms, therefore, that an exclusive applicability to the Executive Organ can be inferred. On the contrary, they must be narrowed to give them only this effect.

It is different as to the provision concerning compensations. Though equally general in the terms, this can have no relation but to the Legislative department; *because,* as before observed, that Department alone would have had power to diminish the compensations. But this reason for confining that provision to one Department, namely, the power of affecting the compensations, so far from dictating a similar appropriation of the other provision, looks a different way, and requires by analogy that the latter should be applied to both the Departments, each having a power of affecting the tenure of office, in a way peculiar to itself. Nor can it be too often repeated, because it is a consideration of great force, that the design so conspicuous in the former of those two provisions, to secure the

Independence of the Judges against Legislative influence, is a powerful reason for understanding the latter in a sense calculated to advance the same important end, rather than in one which must intirely frustrate it.

A rule of constitutional law opposed to our construction, is attempted to be derived, from the maxim, that the power of legislation is always equal; and that a preceding can never bind or controul a succeeding legislature by its acts, which therefore must always be liable to repeal at the discretion of the successor.

The misapplication, or too extensive application of general maxims or propositions, true in their genuine sense, is one of the most common and fruitful sources of false reasoning. This is strongly exemplified in the present instance. The maxim relied upon, can mean nothing more, than, that as to all those matters which a preceding legislature was free to establish and revoke, a succeeding legislature will be equally free. The latter may do what the former could have done, or it may undo what the former could have undone. But unless it can be maintained, that the power of ordinary legislation is in itself illimitable, incontroulable, incapable of being bound either by its own acts, or by the injunctions or prohibitions of a constitution, it will follow, that the body invested with that power, may bind itself, and may bind its successor; so that neither itself nor its successor can of right revoke acts which may have been once done. To say that a legislature may bind itself, but not its successor, is to affirm, that the latter has not merely an equal, but a greater power than the former, else it could not do what the former was unable to do. Equality of power only will not suffice for the argument. On the other hand, to affirm that a legislature cannot bind itself, is to assert, that there can be no valid pledge of the public faith, that no right can be vested in an individual or collection of individuals, whether of property or of any other description, which may not be resumed at pleasure.

Without doubt a legislature binds itself by all those acts which engage the public faith; which confer on individuals permanent rights; either gratuitously or for valuable consideration; and in all these instances a succeeding one is not less bound. As to a right which may have been conferred by an express provision of the Constitution defining the condition of the enjoyment; or as to an institution or matter in its nature permanent, which the Constitution may have confided to an act of the legislature; its authority terminates with the act that vests the right or makes the establishment. A case, of the first sort, is exemplified in the office of a Judge; of the last, in the creation of a new state, which has been very pertinently mentioned as a decisive instance of power in a legislature to do a thing which being done is irrevocable.

But whatever may be the latitude we assign to the power of a legislature over the acts of a predecessor, it is nothing to the purpose, so long as it shall be admitted that the constitution may bind and controul the legislature. With this admission, the simple inquiry must always be—has or has not the Constitution in the particular instance, bound the legislature? And the solution must be sought in the language, nature, and end of the provision. If these warrant the conclusion that the legislature was intended to be bound, it is perfect nonsense to reply that this cannot be so because a legislature cannot bind itself by its own acts; or because the power of one legislature is equal to that of another. What signifies this proposition, if the Constitution has power to bind the legislature, and has in fact bound it in a given case? Can a general rule disprove the fact of an exception which it is admitted may exist? If so, the argument is always ready, and equally valid to disprove any limitation of the legislative discretion.

Compelled, as they must be, to desist from the use of the argument in the extensive sense in which it has been employed, if its inventors should content themselves with saying, that at least, the principle adduced by them ought to have so much of force, as to make the exception to it depend on an express provision—it may be answered, that in the case under consideration, there is an express provision. No language can be more precise or peremptory than this, "The Judges, *both* of the Supreme and Inferior Courts, shall hold their offices during good behaviour." If this be not an express provision, it is impossible to devise one. But the position, that an express provision is necessary to form an exception, is itself unfounded. Wherever it is clear, whether by a circumstance expressed, or by one so implied as to leave no reasonable doubt, that a limitation of the authority of the legislature was designed by the Constitution, the intention ought to prevail.

A very strong confirmation of the true intent of the provision respecting the tenure of Judicial office results from an argument by analogy. In each of the articles which establishes any branch of the government, the duration of office is a prominent feature. Two years for the House of Representatives, six for the Senate, four for the President and Vice President, are the respective terms of duration; and for the Judges the term of good behaviour is allotted. It is presumable that each was established in the same spirit, as a point material in the organization of the government and of a nature to be properly fundamental. It will not be pretended that the duration of office prescribed as to any other department, is within the reach of Legislative discretion. And why shall that of Judicial Officers form an exception? Why shall the Constitution be supposed less tenacious of securing to this organ of the sovereign power, a fixed duration than to any other? If there be any thing which ought to be supposed to be peculiarly excepted out of the power of the ordinary Legislature, it is emphatically the organization of the several constituent departments of the Government, which in our system are the *Legislative, Executive* and *Judiciary.* Reasons of the most cogent nature recommend that the stability and independence of the last of these three branches should be guarded with particular circumspection and care.

24

AN ACT TO REPEAL CERTAIN ACTS RESPECTING THE ORGANIZATION OF THE COURTS
2 Stat. 132 (1802)

Be it enacted by the Senate and House of Representatives of the United States of America in Congress assembled, That the act of Congress passed on the thirteenth day of February one thousand eight hundred and one, intituled "An act to provide for the more convenient organization of the courts of the United States," from and after the first day of July next, shall be, and is hereby repealed.

SEC. 2. *And be it further enacted,* That the act passed on the third day of March, one thousand eight hundred and one, intituled "An act for altering the times and places of holding certain courts therein mentioned and for other purposes," from and after the said first day of July next, shall be, and is hereby repealed.

SEC. 3. *And be it further enacted,* That all the acts, and parts of acts, which were in force before the passage of the aforesaid two acts, and which by the same were either amended, explained, altered, or repealed, shall be, and hereby are, after the said first day of July next, revived, and in as full and complete force and operation, as if the said two acts had never been made.

SEC. 4. *And be it further enacted,* That all actions, suits, process, pleadings, and other proceedings, of what nature or kind soever, depending or existing in any of the circuit courts of the United States, or in any of the district courts of the United States, acting as circuit courts, or in any of the additional district courts, which were established by the aforesaid act of Congress, passed on the thirteenth day of February, one thousand eight hundred and one, shall be, and hereby are, from and after the said first day of July next, continued over to the circuit courts, and to the district courts, and to the district courts acting as circuit courts respectively, which shall be first thereafter holden in and for the respective circuits and districts, which are revived and established by this act, and to be proceeded in, in the same manner as they would have been, had they originated prior to the passage of the said act, passed on the thirteenth day of February, one thousand eight hundred and one.

SEC. 5. *And be it further enacted,* That all writs and process, which have issued, or may issue before the said first day of July next, returnable to the circuit courts, or to any district court acting as a circuit court, or any additional district court established by the aforesaid act passed the thirteenth day of February, one thousand eight hundred and one, shall be returned to the next circuit court, or district court, or district court acting as a circuit court, re-established by this act: and shall be proceeded on therein, in the same manner as they could, had they been originally returnable to the circuit courts, and district courts acting as circuit courts, hereby revived and established.

APPROVED, March 8, 1802.

25

ALEXANDER HAMILTON, THE EXAMINATION, NO. 16
19 Mar. 1802
Papers 25:564–69

The President, as a politician, is in one sense particularly unfortunate. He furnishes frequent opportunities of arraying him against himself—of combating his opinions at one period by his opinions at another. Without doubt, a wise and good man may, on proper grounds relinquish an opinion which he has once entertained, and the change may even serve as a proof of candour and integrity. But with such a man, especially in matters of high public importance, changes of this sort must be rare. The contrary is always a mark either of a weak and versatile mind, or of an artificial and designing character, which, accommodating its creed, to circumstances, takes up or lays down an article of faith, just as may suit a present convenience.

The question, in agitation, respecting the Judiciary Department, calls up another instance of opposition, between the former ideas of Mr. Jefferson, and his recent conduct. The leading positions which have been advanced as explanatory of the policy of the Constitution, in the structure of the different departments, and as proper to direct the interpretation of the provisions which were contrived to secure the independence and firmness of the Judges, are to be seen in a very emphatical and distinct form in the Notes on Virginia. The passage in which they appear, deserves to be cited at length, as well for its intrinsic merit, as by way of comment upon the true character of its author; presenting an interesting contrast between the maxims, which experience had taught him while Governor of Virginia, and those which now guide him as the official head of a great party in the United States.

It is in these words—

"All the powers of government, legislative, executive and judiciary, result to the legislative body. The concentrating these in the same hands is precisely the definition of despotic government. It will be no alleviation that these powers will be exercised by a plurality of hands, and not by a single one. One hundred and seventy-three despots would surely be as oppressive as one. Let those who doubt it turn their eyes on the Republic of Venice. As little will it avail us that they are chosen by ourselves. An *elective despotism* was not the government we fought for; but one which should not only be founded on free principles, but in which the powers of government should be so divided and balanced among several bodies of magistracy, as that no one could transcend their legal limits, without being effectually *checked* and *restrained* by the others. For this reason that Convention which passed the ordinance of government, laid its foundation on this basis, that the legislative, executive and judiciary departments, should be separate and distinct, so that no person should exercise the powers of more than one of them at the same time. *But no barrier was provided between these several powers.* The judiciary and executive members were left dependent on the legislative for their subsistence in office, and some of them for their continuance in it. If therefore the legislature assumes executive and judiciary powers, no opposition is likely to be made; nor if made can be effectual; because in that case, they may put their proceedings into the form of an act of assembly, which will render them obligatory on the other branches. They have accordingly *in many instances decided rights* which should have been left to *judiciary controversy;* and *the direction of the executive, during the whole time of their session, is becoming habitual and familiar."*

This passage fully recognises these several important truths: that the tendency of our governments is towards a CONCENTRATION of the POWERS of the different departments in the LEGISLATIVE BODY; that such a CONCENTRATION, is precisely the DEFINITION of DESPOTISM, and that an effectual *barrier* between the respective departments ought to exist. It also, by a strong implication, admits that offices during *good behaviour* are independent of the Legislature for their continuance in office. This implication seems to be contained in the following sentence: "The Judiciary and Executive members were left dependent on the Legislature for their subsistence in office, and *some* of them *for their continuance in it."* The word *"some,"* implies that *others* were not left thus dependent; and to what description of officers can the exception be better applied, than to the Judges, the tenure of whose offices was *during good behaviour?*

The sentiments of the President delivered at a *period* when he can be supposed to have been under no improper bias, must be regarded by all those, who respect his judgement, as no light evidence of the truth of the doctrine for which we contend. Let us, however, resume and pursue the subject on its merits, without relying upon the aid of so variable and fallible an authority.

At an early part of the discussion in this Examination, a construction of the Constitution was suggested, to which it may not be amiss to return: It amounts to this, that Congress have power to new-model, or even to abrogate an Inferior Court, but not to abolish the office or emoluments of a Judge of such court previously appointed. In the Congressional debates, some of the speakers against the repealing law, appear to have taken it for granted, that the *abrogation of the court* must draw with it the *abolition of the Judges,* and therefore, have denied in totality, the power of abrogation. In the course of these papers, too, it has been admitted, that if the preservation of the Judges cannot be reconciled with the power to annul the Court, then the existence of this power is rightly denied. But in an affair of such vast magnitude, it is all-important to survey with the utmost caution the ground to be taken, and then to take and maintain it with inflexible fortitude and perseverence. Truth will be most likely to prevail, when the arguments which support it stop at a temperate mean, consistent with practical convenience. Excess is always error. There is hardly any theoretic hypothesis, which, carried to a certain extreme, does not become practically false. In construing a Constitution, it is wise, as far as possible to pursue a course, which will reconcile essential principles with convenient modifications. If guided by this spirit, in the great question which seems destined to decide the fate of our Government, it is believed that the result will accord with the construction, that *Congress have a right to change or abolish Inferior Courts, but not to abolish the actual Judges.*

Towards the support of this construction, it has been shewn in another place, that the Courts and the Judges are distinct legal *entities*, which, in contemplation of law, may exist, independently the one of the other—mutually related, but not inseparable. The act proposed to be repealed exemplifies this idea in practice. It abolishes the District Courts of Tennessee and Kentucky, and transfers their Judges to one of the Circuit Courts. Though the authorities and jurisdiction of those Courts are vested in the Circuit Court, to which the Judges are transferred; yet the *identity of the Courts* ceases. It cannot be maintained that Courts so different in their organization and jurisdiction, are the same; nor could a legislative transfer of the Judges have been constitutional, but upon the hypothesis, that the office of a Judge may survive the Court of which he is a member: a *new appointment* by the Executive, of two additional Judges for the Circuit Court, would otherwise have been necessary.

This precedent in all its points is correct, and exhibits a rational operation of the construction which regards the office of the Judge, as distinct from the Court, as one of the elements or constituent parts of which it is composed: not as a mere incident that must perish with its principal.

It will not be disputed, that the Constitution might have provided *in terms*, and with effect, that an Inferior Court which had been *established by law*, might by law be abolished; nevertheless, that the Judges of such Courts should retain the offices of Judges of the United States, with the emoluments before attached to their offices. The operation of such a provision would be, that when the Court was abolished, all the functions to be executed in that Court, would be suspended, and the Judge could only continue to exert the authorities and perform the duties which might before have been performed, without reference to causes pending in Court; but he would have the capacity to be annexed to another Court, without the intervention of a new appointment, and by that annexation, simply to *renew* the exercise of the authorities and duties which had been suspended.

If this might have been the effect of positive and explicit provision, why may it not likewise be the result of provisions, which, presenting opposite considerations, point to the same conclusion, as a compromise calculated to reconcile those considerations with each other and to unite different objects of public utility? Surely the affirmative infringes no principle of legal construction, transgresses no rule of good sense.

Let us then enquire, whether there are not in this case opposite and conflicting considerations, demanding a compromise of this nature? On the one hand, it is evident that if an inferior court once instituted, though found inconvenient, cannot be abolished, this is to entail upon the community the mischief, be it more or less, of a first error in the administration of the government. On the other hand, it is no less evident, that if the judges hold their offices at the discretion of the legislature, they cease to be a co-ordinate, and become a dependent branch of the government; from which dependence mischiefs infinitely greater are to be expected.

All these mischiefs, the lesser as well as the greater, are avoided by saying, *"Congress may abolish the Courts, but the Judges shall retain their offices with the appurtenant emoluments."* The only remaining inconvenience then, will be one too insignificant to weigh in a national scale, that is, the expence of the compensations of the Incumbents, during their lives. The future and permanent expence will be done away.

But will this construction secure the benefits proposed by the Constitution from the independent tenure of Judicial Office? Substantially it will. The main object is to preserve the judges from being influenced by an apprehension of the loss of the advantages of office. As this loss could not be incurred, that influence would not exist. Their firmness could not be assailed by the danger of being superseded, and perhaps *consigned to want.* Let it be added, that when it was understood not to be in the power of the Legislature to deprive the Judges of their offices and emoluments, it would be a great restraint upon the factious motives, which might induce the abolition of a court. This would be much less likely to happen unless for genuine reasons of public utility; and of course there would be a much better prospect of the stability of Judiciary establishments.

26

St. George Tucker,
Blackstone's Commentaries
1:App. 350–61; 4:App. 23–30
1803

III. The constitution and powers of the judiciary department of the federal government have been equally the subject of applause and censure; of confidence and jealousy. The unexceptionable mode of appointing the judges, and their constitutional independence of every other branch of the government merit an eulogium, which all would have concurred in bestowing on this part of the constitution of the United States, had not the powers of that department been extended to objects which might hazard the tranquility of the union in attempting to secure it. No one doubted the necessity and propriety of a federal judiciary, where an ultimate decision might be had upon such questions as might arise under the law of nations, and eventually embroil the American nation with other sovereign powers: nor was it doubted that such a tribunal was necessary to decide such differences as might possibly arise between the several members of the confederacy, or between parties claiming lands under grants from different states. But the objects of the federal jurisdiction were originally far more numerous; extending to "all cases in law and equity arising under the constitution, the laws of the United States, and treaties made, or to be made, under their authority; to all cases affecting ambassadors, other public ministers and consuls; to all cases of admiralty and maritime jurisdiction; to controversies to which the United States shall be a party; and between two or more states; *between a state and citizens of another state;* between citizens of different states; between citizens of the same state claiming lands under grants of different states; and *between a state,* or the citizens thereof, and foreign states, *citizens or subjects.*" "These objects," a writer on the subject remarks, "are so numerous, and the shades of distinction between civil causes are oftentimes so slight, that it is more than probable the state judicatories will be wholly superceded; for in contests about jurisdiction, the federal court, as the most powerful, will ever prevail." This conclusion will not appear to be ill-founded, if we advert to the ingenious fictions which have been from time to time adopted in the courts of Great Britain, in order to countenance the claim of jurisdiction. But more solid objections seemed to arise from the want of a sufficient security for the liberty of the citizen in criminal prosecutions: the defect of an adequate provision for the trial by jury in civil cases; and the burthens and mischiefs which might arise from the re-examination of facts, upon an appeal. These objections, however, seem to be completely removed by the amendments proposed by the first congress, and since ratified, and made a part of the constitution. Another important objection has been likewise in some degree obviated, by the act of 1 Cong. 1 Sess. c. 20. §. 11, which declares, that no district or circuit court shall have cognizance of any suit upon a promissory note, or other *chose* in action in favour of an assignee, except in cases of foreign bills of exchange, unless a suit might have been prosecuted in such court if no assignment had been made: it is, however, to be wished, that this provison had formed a part of the amendments to the constitution, which were proposed at the same session, since the objection, upon constitutional grounds, still remains: more especially, as a very serious attempt was made during the last session of the sixth congress to repeal this legislative provision. But the grand objection, that the states were made subject to the action of an individual, still remained for several years, notwithstanding the concurring dissent of several states at the time of accepting the constitution. Nor was it till after several of the states had actually been sued in the federal courts, that the third congress proposed an amendment, which declares, "that the judicial power of the United States shall not be construed to extend to any suit in law or equity commenced or prosecuted against one of the United States, by the citizens of another state, or by the citizens or subjects of a foreign state." This amendment having been duly ratified now forms a part of the federal constitution. It is well calculated to secure the peace of the confederacy from the dangers which the former power might have produced, had any compulsory method been adopted for carrying into effect the judgment of a federal court against a state, at the suit of an individual. But whilst the propriety of the amendment is acknowledged, candor requires a further acknowledgment, that in order to render the judicial power completely efficacious, both in the federal and in the state governments, some mode ought to be provided, by which a pecuniary right, established by the judicial sentence of a court against a state, or against the government of the United States, may be enforced. It is believed, that instances might be adduced, where, although such rights have been judicially established, the claimants have not received any benefit from the judgment in their favour, because the legislature have neglected (perhaps willfully) to provide a fund, or make the necessary appropriation required by the constitution, for the discharge of the debt. In this instance, the constitutions both of the federal and state governments seem to stand in need of reform. For what avails it, that an impartial tribunal have decided, that a debt is due from the public to an individual, if those who hold the purse-strings of the government, may nevertheless refuse the payment of a just debt?

But whatever objection may be made to the extent of the judicial power of the federal government; in other respects, as it is now organized, and limited by the constitution itself, by the amendments before mentioned, and by the act referred to, it seems worthy of every encomium, that has ever been pronounced upon the judiciary of Great Britain, to which it's constitution is in no respect inferior; being, indeed, in all respects assimilated to it, with the addition of a constitutional, instead of a legal independence, only. Whatever then has been said by Baron Montesquieu, De Lolme, or Judge Blackstone, or any other writer, on the security derived to the subject from the independence of the judiciary of Great Britain, will apply at least as forcibly to that of the United States. We may go still further. In England the judiciary may be overwhelmed by a combination between the executive and the legislature. In America (according to the true theory of our constitution,) it is rendered absolutely independent of, and superior to the attempts of both, to control, or crush it: First, by the tenure of office, which is during good behaviour; these words (by a long train of decisions in England, even as far back as the reign of Edward the third) in all commissions and grants, public or private, importing an office, or estate, for the life of the grantee, determinable only by his death, or breach of good behaviour. Secondly, by the independence of the judges, in respect to their salaries, which cannot be diminished. Thirdly, by the letter of the constitution which defines and limits the powers of the several co-ordinate branches of the government; and the spirit of it, which forbids any attempt on the part of either to subvert the constitutional independence of the others. Lastly, by that uncontrollable authority in all cases of litigation, criminal or civil, which, from the very nature of things is exclusively vested in this department, and extends to every supposable case which can affect the life, liberty, or property of the citizens of America under the authority of the federal constitution, and laws, except in the case of an impeachment.

The American constitutions appear to be the first in which this absolute independence of the judiciary has formed one of the fundamental principles of the government. Doctor Rutherforth considers the judiciary as a branch only, of the executive authority; and such, in strictness, perhaps, it is in other countries, it's province being to advise the executive, rather than to act independently of it: thus when Titius demands a debt, or a parcel of land of Sempronius, the judgment of the court is, it's advice to the executive, to whom the execution of the laws appertains, to levy the debt for the plaintiff, or put him in possession of the lands which he claims, or to dismiss his demand as unjust and ill founded. So also if Titius be accused of treason, murder, or other crime, and be thereof convicted, the judgment of the court, is it's advice in what manner he shall be punished according to law; which advice is to be carried into effect by the executive officer. Or if he be acquitted, the judgment of the court is it's advice that he be discharged from his confinement, and from further prosecution. In this sense it is, that the judges of the courts of law in England are reckoned among the number of the king's councils, they being his advisers in all cases where the subject matter is of a legal nature. But in the United States of America, the judicial power is a distinct, separate, independent, and *co-ordinate* branch of the government; expressly recognised as such in our state bill of rights, and constitution, and demonstrably so, likewise, by the federal constitution, from which the courts of the United States derive all their powers, in like manner as the legislative and executive departments derive theirs. The obligation which the constitution imposes upon the judiciary department to support the constitution of the United States, would be nugatory, if it were dependent upon either of the other branches of the government, or in any manner subject to their control, since such control might operate to the destruction, instead of the support, of the constitution. Nor can it escape observation, that to require such an oath on the part of the judges, on the one hand, and yet suppose them bound by acts of the legislature, which may violate the constitution which they have sworn to support, carries with it such a degree of impiety, as well as absurdity, as no man who pays any regard to the obligations of an oath can be supposed either to contend for, or to defend.

This absolute independence of the judiciary, both of the executive and the legislative departments, which I contend is to be found, both in the letter, and spirit of our constitutions, is not less necessary to the liberty and security of the citizen, and his property, in a republican government, than in a monarchy: if in the latter, the will of the prince may be considered as likely to influence the conduct of judges created occasionally, and holding their offices only during his pleasure, more especially in cases where a criminal prosecution may be carried on by his orders, and supported by his influence; in a republic, on the other hand,

the violence and malignity of party spirit, as well in the legislature, as in the executive, requires not less the intervention of a calm, temperate, upright, and independent judiciary, to prevent that violence and malignity from exerting itself "to crush in dust and ashes" all opponents to it's tyrannical administration, or ambitious projects. Such an independence can never be perfectly attained, but by a *constitutional tenure of office*, equally independent of the frowns and smiles of the other branches of the government. Judges ought not only to be incapable of holding any other office at the same time, but even of appointment to any but a judicial office. For the hope of favour is always more alluring, and generally more dangerous, than the fear of offending. In England, according to the principles of the common law, a judge cannot hold any other office; and according to the practice there for more than a century, no instance can, I believe, be shewn, where a judge has been appointed to any other than a judicial office, unless it be the honorary post of privy counsellor, to which no emolument is attached. And even this honorary distinction is seldom conferred but upon the chief justice of the king's bench, if I have been rightly informed*. To this cause, not less than to the tenure of their offices *during good behaviour*, may we ascribe that pre-eminent integrity, which amidst surrounding corruption, beams with genuine lustre from the English courts of judicature, as from the sun through surrounding clouds, and mists. To emulate both their wisdom and integrity is an ambition worthy of the greatest characters in any country.

If we consider the nature of the judicial authority, and the manner in which it operates, we shall discover that it cannot, of itself, oppress any individual; for the executive authority must lend it's aid in every instance where oppression can ensue from it's decisions: whilst on the contrary, it's decisions in favour of the citizen are carried into instantaneous effect, by delivering him from the custody and restraint of the executive officer, the moment that an acquittal is pronounced. And herein consists one

---

*Much is it to be regretted that a similar conduct towards the judges of the courts of the United States, has not prevailed in the federal government. Already have we seen two chief justices of the United States, whose duties cannot, certainly, be performed in foreign parts, appointed envoys to distant nations, and still holding their offices in the supreme court of the federal government; offices altogether incompatible, yet held at the same time in manifest violation of every constitutional principle. For surely nothing is more incompatible with the nature of the federal government, than to suppose an office of such high trust and responsibility to have been intended as a *sine cure;* much less that it could have been intended as the means of extending executive influence, or of shielding the president against the effect of an impeachment. For what could more effectually strengthen the hands of an usurping president, than the power of sending into an honourable exile, the very officer whom the constitution expressly requires to preside at his trial, in case of his impeachment? To preserve the lustre of judicial purity, perfectly unsullied, it seems necessary, by an express amendment of the constitution, to disqualify the federal judges from appointment to any other than a judicial office; since such appointments have a natural tendency to excite hopes, and secure compliance, from the prospect or expectation of additional emolument, accumulated honours, or greater pre-eminence of station.

of the great excellencies of our constitution: that no individual can be oppressed whilst this branch of the government remains independent, and uncorrupted; it being a necessary check upon the encroachments, or usurpations of power, by either of the other. Thus, if the legislature should pass a law dangerous to the liberties of the people, the judiciary are bound to pronounce, not only whether the party accused hath been guilty of any violation of it, but whether such a law be permitted by the constitution. If, for example, a law be passed by congress, prohibiting the free exercise of religion, according to the dictates, or persuasions of a man's own conscience; or abridging the freedom of speech, or of the press; or the right of the people to assemble peaceably, or to keep and bear arms; it would, in any of these cases, be the province of the judiciary to pronounce whether any such act were constitutional, or not; and if not, to acquit the accused from any penalty which might be annexed to the breach of such unconstitutional act. If an individual be persecuted by the executive authority, (as if any alien, the subject of a nation with whom the United States were at that time at peace, had been imprisoned by order of the president under the authority of the alien act, 5 Cong. c. 75) it is then the province of the judiciary to decide whether there be any law that authorises the proceedings against him, and if there be none, to acquit him, not only of the present, but of all future prosecutions for the same cause: or if there be, then to examine it's validity under the constitution, as before-mentioned. The power of pardon, which is vested in the executive, in it's turn, constitutes a proper check upon the too great rigor, or abuse of power in the judiciary department. On this circumstance, however, no great stress ought to be laid; since in criminal prosecutions, the executive is in the eye of the law, always plaintiff; and where the prosecution is carried on by it's direction, the purity of the judiciary is the only security for the rights of the citizen. The judiciary, therefore, is that department of the government to whom the protection of the rights of the individual is by the constitution especially confided, interposing it's shield between him and the sword of usurped authority, the darts of oppression, and the shafts of faction and violence. Let us see in what manner this protection, is thus confided to the judiciary department by the constitution.

1. First, then; the judicial power of the United States extends to all cases in law and equity, arising under the constitution, the laws of the United States, and treaties made by their authority. 2. No person shall be deprived of life, liberty, or property, (and these are the objects of all rights) without due process of law; which is the peculiar province of the judiciary to furnish him with. 3. No person shall be held to answer for any crime, unless on presentment or indictment of a grand jury, except in cases arising in the land or naval forces, or in the militia, when in actual service, in time of war or public danger. . . . 4. In criminal cases the accused shall have a speedy and public trial, by an impartial jury of the state and district, where the crime shall be committed. 5. He shall be informed of the nature and cause of his accusation. 6. He shall be confronted by the witnesses against him; and 7,

Shall have compulsory process for obtaining witnesses in his favour.* 8. He shall not be compelled to be a witness against himself. 9. He shall not be subject, for the same offence, to be twice put in jeopardy of life or limb. 10. He shall have the aid of counsel for his defence. 11. His person, house, papers, and effects, shall be free from search or seizure, except upon warrants issued upon probable cause, supported by oath or affirmation, and particularly describing the place to be searched, and the person, or things to be seized. 12. Excessive bail shall not be required of him. 13. The benefit of the writ of *habeas corpus* shall not be denied him, unless in case of actual invasion, or rebellion, the public safety (of which congress are to judge, and suspend the benefit accordingly) may require the suspension of that privilege generally, and not in his particular case, only. 14. Excessive fines shall not be imposed, nor unusual punishments inflicted on him. 15. His private property shall not be taken for the public use without just compensation. 16. He shall not be convicted upon any charge of treason, unless on the testimony of two witnesses, at least, to the same overt act, or on confession in open court. In all these respects, the constitution, by a positive injunction, prescribes the duty of the judiciary department; extending it's powers, on the one hand, so far as to arrest the hand of oppression from any other quarter; and on the other prescribing limits to it's authority, which if violated would be good cause of impeachment, and of removal from office. Thus if the privilege of the writ of *habeas corpus* should be suspended by congress, when there was neither an invasion, nor rebellion in the United States, it would be the duty of the judiciary, nevertheless, to grant the writ, because the act of suspension in that case, being contrary to the express terms of the constitution, would be void. On the other hand, if the benefit of the writ of *habeas corpus*, should be granted to any person, contrary to the provisions of an act for suspending it, during the time of an invasion or rebellion, this would be a good ground for impeaching a judge who should conduct himself in that manner. So, if a judge were to instruct a jury upon the trial of a person for treason, that he might be convicted upon the testimony of a single witness, if such instruction were advisedly, and corruptly given, (and not the mere effect of mistake and misapprehension) it would furnish a good ground for impeachment, and removal of such judge from his office. And any other gross misconduct of a judge in the execution of his office may be punished in like manner.

That absolute independence of the judiciary, for which we contend is not, then, incompatible with the strictest responsibility; (for a judge is no more exempt from it than any other servant of the people, according to the true

---

*On the trial of Mr. Thomas Cooper, in the federal circuit court in Pennsylvania, for a libel against the president of the United States, under the sedition law, it is said, that Mr. Cooper applied to the court for a subpoena to summon the president as a witness in his behalf, and that the court refused to grant one. Upon what principle the application was refused, (notwithstanding this article) I have never been able to obtain satisfactory information. The case was certainly delicate, and might have been perplexing.

principles of the constitution;) but such an independence of the other *co-ordinate* branches of the government as seems absolutely necessary to secure to them the free exercise of their constitutional functions, without the hope of pleasing, or the fear of offending. And, as from the natural feebleness of the judiciary it is in continual jeopardy of being overpowered, awed, or influenced by it's co-ordinate branches, who have the custody of the purse and sword of the confederacy; and as nothing can contribute so much to it's firmness and independence as permanancy in office, this quality therefore may be justly regarded as an indispensable ingredient in it's constitution; and in great measure as the citadel of the public justice and the public security. Nor was it imagined that there was more than one opinion, upon this subject, in the United States, until a recent event proved the contrary. It was supposed that there could not be a doubt that those tribunals in which justice is to be dispensed according to the constitution and laws of the confederacy; in which life, liberty and property are to be decided upon; in which questions might arise as to the constitutional powers of the executive, or the constitutional obligation of an act of the legislature; and in the decision of which the judges might find themselves constrained by duty, and by their oaths, to pronounce against the authority of either, should be stable and permanent; and not dependent upon the will of the executive or legislature, or both, for their existence. That without this degree of permanence, the tenure of office during good behaviour, could not secure to that department the necessary firmness to meet unshaken every question, and to decide as justice and the constitution should dictate without regard to consequences. These considerations induced an opinion which it was presumed was general, if not universal, that the power vested in congress to erect from time to time, tribunals inferior to the supreme court, did not authorise them, at pleasure, to demolish them. Being built upon the rock of the constitution, their foundations were supposed to partake of it's permanency, and to be equally incapable of being shaken by the other branches of the government. But a different construction of the constitution has lately prevailed; it has been determined that a power to ordain and establish from time to time, carries with it a discretionary power to discontinue, or demolish. That although the tenure of office be, *during good behaviour,* this does not prevent the separation of the office from the officer, by putting down the office; but only secures to the officer his station, upon the terms of good behaviour, so long as the office itself remains. . . . Painful indeed is the remark, that this interpretation seems calculated to subvert one of the fundamental pillars of free governments, and to have laid the foundation of one of the most dangerous political schisms that has ever happened in the United States of America.

. . . . .

By the constitution of the United States, it is declared, that the judicial power of the United States shall be vested in one supreme court, and in such inferior courts as congress may, from time to time, ordain and establish; the judges of which shall hold their office during good behaviour, and receive a salary which shall not be diminished during their continuance in office. The judicial power extends to all cases in law and equity arising under the constitution, the laws of the United States, and treaties made under their authority: to all cases affecting ambassadors, other public ministers, and consuls; to all cases of admiralty and maritime jurisdiction; to controversies to which the United States shall be a party; to those between two or more states; between citizens of different states; between citizens of the same state claiming lands under grants of different states; and between a state and foreign states. In the original frame of the constitution, the judicial power was still more extensive; but an amendment has been proposed and ratified, by which it is declared that the judicial power of the United States shall not be construed to extend to any suit in law or equity, commenced or prosecuted against one of the United States, by citizens of another state, or by citizens or subjects of any foreign state. Amendments to the constitution of the United States, Art. 13.

The judicial courts of the United states, as organized by the act of 1 Cong. 1 Sess. c. 20, consisted, first, of a district court in each state, and in that part of Massachusetts which is called the province of Maine, a single judge being appointed for each district, who was by law required to reside within the same; these courts held four sessions in every year. Secondly, of a circuit court; which held two sessions annually in each district, and consisted of two judges of the supreme court who alternately rode the circuits, together with the judge of the district court, or any two of them. But for the convenience of the judges of the supreme court, on whom the duty was founded to fall very hard, a subsequent act required the attendance of one of them only at each circuit court: and, thirdly, of a supreme court, consisting of a chief justice, and five associate justices, which held two sessions annually at the seat of government.

During the second session of the sixth congress a very extensive alteration in the system was proposed, and carried into effect by an act passed on the thirteenth day of February 1801, which, among other provisions, divided the United States into twenty-two districts. The districts were again classed into six circuits, in each of which, (except the sixth, comprehending the districts of East Tenessee, West Tenessee, Kentucky and Ohio,) three judges, to be called circuit judges, one of whom was to be commissioned as chief judge, were authorised to be appointed, with an annual salary of two thousand dollars, each. In the the sixth circuit, one circuit judge only was to be appointed, who together with the district judges of Kentucky and Tenessee was authorised to hold the circuit courts for that circuit; and whenever the office of district judge, in those districts, respectively, should become vacant, such vacancies were to be supplied by the appointment of two additional judges, for that circuit.

The appointments authorised by this act were made by the president for the time being, altho' not more than twenty days remained of the period for which he was elected, after passing the act, which had been carried thro' congress by small majorities, after a strenuous opposition. As soon as the question had been taken and carried in the house of representatives, a member gave notice, which was laid upon the table, that at the next session he should move for a repeal of the act. Some unpopular appointments of judges, made by the president were not calculated to reconcile the opponents of the act to its passage. The question whether a succeeding congress could repeal the law, and by so doing remove the newly appointed judges from office, soon became a popular topic of discussion, in many parts of the United States. And while many who disapproved the law, were satisfied that it could not constitutionally be repealed, so as to affect the judges who held commissions under it, others either doubted, or declared themselves convinced of the constitutionalty, as well as expediency and sound policy of such a measure. Accordingly, very soon after the commencement of the first session of the seventh congress, a motion was made in the senate for the repeal of the act.

The debate was conducted with great ability in both houses successively, during a considerable portion of the session; the several speakers both in favour of the repeal, and against it, displaying a scope of talents and ingenuity in their arguments, which shewed them equally prepared to maintain their opposite opinions. The bill passed the senate by a small majority only; but the majority in favour of the repeal was much greater in the house of representatives. It received the president's assent on the eighth day of March, 1802, and it's passage, as it respects the construction of the constitution of the United States, and of that principle (supposed to be a fundamental one,) which appeared both to require and to have secured the absolute independence of the judiciary department, may be deemed one of the most important events which have taken place in congress since the adoption of the constitution. The act of the 13th Feb. 1801, 6 Cong. 2 Sess. 4. As also, another passed the third day of March, 1801, for altering the times and places of holding certain courts, 6 Cong. 2 Sess. c. 32, were totally repealed, and all acts, and parts of acts, which were in force before the passage thereof, and which by the same were either amended, explained, altered, or repealed, are thereby revived, and declared to be in as full and complete force as if those two acts had never been made. And by a subsequent act of the same session, the districts of the United States (excepting the districts of Maine, Kentucky, and Tenessee,) are formed into six circuits, of which the districts of New Hampshire, Massachusetts, and Rhode Island, constitute the first; Connecticut, New York, and Vermont the second; New Jersey and Pennsylvania the third; Maryland and Delaware the fourth; Virginia and N. Carolina the fifth; and S. Carolina and Georgia the sixth. The chief justice of the U. States, and the several associate justices of the supreme court, are assigned to these courts respectively; and together with the district judges respectively, are to hold two circuit courts annually, in each district, but if only one of them shall attend, the circuit court may be held by the judge so attending. And on every appointment hereafter made of a chief justice or associate justice of the supreme court, the judges shall allot themselves among the several courts, as they shall think fit and such allotment shall be entered upon record. And, if no allotment be made, the president may make the allotment; which he seems authorised to do in the first instance after making any appointment; and the allotment made in either case is binding until another is made.

The district courts of the United States have, exclusively of the courts of the several states, cognizance of all crimes and offences which shall be cognizable under the authority of the United States committed within their respective districts, or upon the high seas, where no other punishment is to be inflicted than whipping, not exceeding thirty stripes, a fine not exceeding one hundred dollars, or a term of imprisonment not exceeding six months: as also exclusive cognizance of all civil causes of admiralty and maritime jurisdiction, and of all captures made within the waters of the United States, or within a marine league of the coasts or shores thereof; of all seizures made under the laws of impost, navigation or trade of the United States, where the seizures are made on waters navigable from the sea, by vessels of ten tons burthen, within their respective districts, as well as upon the high seas: saving to the suitors in all cases the right of a common law remedy where the common law is competent to give it; and also exclusive cognizance of all seizures made on the land or other waters than those before mentioned, and of all suits for penalties and forfeitures incurred under the laws of the United States (except in cases of penalties incurred by breach of the laws imposing duties on wine licences, spirits distilled, or goods sold at auction, where the distance is more than fifty miles from the plase of holding a federal district court, which are also cognizable by the state courts as also cognizance concurrent, with the state courts of all causes where an alien sues for a tort only, in violation of the law of nations, or of any treaty of the United States; and of all suits at common law where the United States sue, and the matter in dispute amounts, exclusive of costs, to one hundred dollars. They have also jurisdiction, (exclusively of the state courts) of all suits against consuls or vice-consuls, except for offences above the description above mentioned. A writ of error lies from the circuit courts of the United States to these courts, where the matter in dispute is more than fifty dollars exclusive of costs. The district courts for Virginia are now held alternately at Richmond and at Norfolk, on the third Tuesday in December, March, June and September, yearly, in addition to which, the district judge hath power to hold special courts at either of those places, or at any other place in the district, as the nature of the business may require.

The circuit courts of the United States, hold two sessions every year in each district: that for Virginia, was formerly held alternately at Williamsburg and Charlottesville, but is now stationary at Richmond, and sits on the twenty-second days of May and November, yearly. The present chief justice of the United States is allotted to this circuit, and that of North-Carolina. The circuit courts now consist of one judge of the supreme court of the United States, according to the allotment made by the act of 7 Cong. 1 Sess. c. 31, and the district judge of the district in which the court is held; but if one of the judges only attend, he may hold the court as was before mentioned. In addition to the stated sessions of these courts, the judges have power to appoint and hold special sessions for the trial of criminals, at any other time and place within the district as convenience may require. These courts have original cognizance concurrent with the state courts, in all suits at common law or in equity, where the matter in dispute exceeds, exclusive of costs, the value of five hundred dollars; and the United States are plaintiffs, or an alien is a party; or the suit is between a citizen of the state where the suit is brought, and a citizen of another state. They have also exclusive cognizance of all crimes and offences cognizable, under the authority of the United States, except where the laws of the United States may otherwise direct, and concurrent jurisdiction with the district courts of the United States, of the crimes and offences cognizable therein. But no person can be arrested in one district, for trial in another, in any civil action, and no civil suit can be brought therein, against an inhabitant of the United States, unless he be an inhabitant of the district, or found therein at the time of serving the writ; nor can these courts take cognizance of any suit, brought by an assignee of a promisory note, or other chose in action, unless a suit might have been prosecuted therein if no assignment had been made, except in cases of foreign bills of exchange. Suits cognizable in these courts, if commenced in a state court against an alien, or a citizen of another state, or if the title of lands be concerned, and the value of the matter in dispute exceeds five hundred dollars, may on certain conditions be removed therein for trial. A writ of error in the nature of an appeal, where the matter in dispute exceeds two thousand dollars, lies from the supreme court of the United States to these courts.

In all cases removed, by appeal or writ of error, from the district courts to the circuit courts, judgment shall be rendered in conformity to the opinion of the judges of the supreme court, presiding at the circuit courts. And in case of disagreement in opinion between the judges presiding in the circuit courts, in any other case, the point upon which the disagreement shall happen, shall, during the same term, upon request of either party, be stated under the direction of the judges, and certified under the seal of the court to the supreme court at their next session, and shall be there finally decided, and the decision shall be remitted to the circuit court and there entered of record, and have effect according to the nature of the judgment or order of the supreme court. But the cause may still proceed in the circuit court, if, in the opinion of the court, further proceedings can be had, without prejudice to the merits. It is further provided that imprisonments shall not be allowed, nor punishment in any case inflicted, where the judges of the circuit court are divided in opinion upon the question touching such punishment or imprisonment.

The supreme court of the United States has jurisdiction exclusively, in all such suits or proceedings against ambassadors or other public ministers, or their domestics, or domestic servants, as a court of law can exercise consistently with the law of nations; and original, but not exclusive, jurisdiction, of all suits brought by ambassadors or other public ministers, or in which a consul or vice consul shall be a party. This court hath likewise power to issue writs of prohibition to the district courts, when proceeding as courts of admiralty and maritime jurisdiction, and writs of mandamus to any courts appointed or persons holding office under the United States. A writ of error lies from this court to the highest court of law or equity of a state, in which a decision in the suit can be had. In any suit where the validity of a treaty, or a statute of, or an authority exercised under, the United States is called in question, on the ground of their being repugnant to the constitution, treaties, or laws of the United States, and the decision is in favor of their validity; or where the construction of any clause in the constitution, or of a treaty, or statute of, or commission held under, the United States is drawn in question, and the decision is against the right, title, privity, or exemption set up, or claimed by either party under the same. But no other error can be assigned but such as immediately respects the above-mentioned questions.

All the courts of the United States have power to issue writs of *scire facias, habeas corpus,* and all other writs not especially provided for, which may be necessary for the exercise of their respective jurisdictions, and agreeable to the principles and usages of law. The judges both of the supreme and district courts, have likewise power to issue writs of *habeas corpus,* where the prisoner is in custody under, or by colour of the authority of, the United States.

The supreme court is hereafter to be holden at Washington, the present seat of government of the United States, on the first Monday in February annually, by any four of the justices thereof; but one or more may make any orders touching any suit preparatory to the trial or decision thereof; and if four justices do not attend within ten days, the court shall be continued over to the next stated session. It is moreover made the duty of the associate justice resident within the fourth circuit, to attend at the city of Washington on the first Monday in August annually, and he is authorised to make any orders touching any suit depending in the supreme court preparatory to the trial or decision thereof: and all writs and process may be returnable to the first Monday in August, as well as to the session to be held in February; and all actions, pleas and other proceedings in any cause civil or criminal shall be continued over to the ensuing February session: so that there is now but one session of the supreme court in every year, for hearing and deciding causes therein depending, the session in August being merely preparatory.

27

STUART V. LAIRD
1 Cranch 299 (1803)

PATERSON, J. (Judge Cushing being absent on account of ill health), delivered the opinion of the court.—On an action instituted by John Laird against Hugh Stuart, a judgment was entered in a court for the fourth circuit, in the eastern district of Virginia, in December term 1801. On this judgment, an execution was issued, returnable to April term 1802, in the same court. In the term of December 1802, John Laird obtained judgment at a court for the fifth circuit, in the Virginia district, against Hugh Stuart and Charles L. Carter, upon their bond for the forthcoming and delivery of certain property therein mentioned, which had been levied upon by virtue of the above execution against the said Hugh Stuart.

Two reasons have been assigned by counsel for reversing the judgment on the forthcoming bond: 1. That as the bond was given for the delivery of property levied on by virtue of an execution issuing out of, and returnable to, a court for the fourth circuit, no other court could legally proceed upon the said bond. This is true, if there be no statutable provision to direct and authorize such proceeding. Congress have constitutional authority to establish, from time to time, such inferior tribunals as they may think proper; and to transfer a cause from one such tribunal to another. In this last particular, there are no words in the constitution to prohibit or restrain the exercise of legislative power. The present is a case of this kind. It is nothing more than the removal of the suit brought by Stuart against Laird, from the court of the fourth circuit to the court of the fifth circuit, which is authorized to proceed upon and carry it into full effect. This is apparent from the 9th section of the act entitled, "An act to amend the judicial system of the United States," passed the 29th of April 1802. The forthcoming bond is an appendage to the cause, or rather a component part of the proceedings.

2d. Another reason for reversal is, that the judges of the supreme court have no right to sit as circuit judges, not being appointed as such, or, in other words, that they ought to have distinct commissions for that purpose. To this objection, which is of recent date, it is sufficient to observe, that practice, and acquiescence under it, for a period of several years, commencing with the organization of the judicial system, affords an irresistible answer, and has indeed fixed the construction. It is a contemporary interpretation of the most forcible nature. This practical exposition is too strong and obstinate to be shaken or controlled. Of course, the question is at rest, and ought not now to be disturbed.

28

WILLIAM CRANCH, PREFACE
1 Cranch iii (1804)

Much of that *uncertainty of the law*, which is so frequently, and perhaps so justly, the subject of complaint in this country, may be attributed to the want of American reports.

Many of the causes, which are the subject of litigation in our courts, arise upon circumstances peculiar to our situation and laws, and little information can be derived from English authorities to lead to a correct decision.

Uniformity, in such cases, can not be expected where the judicial authority is shared among such a vast number of independent tribunals, unless the decisions of the various courts are made known to each other. Even in the same court, analogy of judgment can not be maintained if its adjudications are suffered to be forgotten. It is therefore much to be regretted that so few of the gentlemen of the bar have been willing to undertake the task of reporting.

In a government which is emphatically stiled a government of laws, the least possible range ought to be left for the discretion of the judge. Whatever tends to render the laws certain, equally tends to limit that discretion; and perhaps nothing conduces more to that object than the publication of reports. Every case decided is a check upon the judge. He can not decide a similar case differently, without strong reasons, which, for his own justification, he will wish to make public. The avenues to corruption are thus obstructed, and the sources of litigation closed.

One of the effects, expected from the establishment of a national judiciary, was the uniformity of judicial decision; an attempt, therefore, to report the cases decided by the Supreme Court of the United States, can not need an apology; and perhaps none can be given for the inadequate manner in which that attempt has been executed. It has been the endeavor of the Reporter to give a faithful summary of the arguments of counsel. To do them complete justice he acknowledges himself incompetent. In no instance, perhaps, has he given the words in which the ideas were conveyed, as his attention was almost entirely occupied in collecting the point of the argument. He may have omitted ideas deemed important, and added others supposed to be impertinent; but in no case has he intentionally diminished the weight of the argument. It may possibly be alleged that he has introduced into the reports of some of the cases more of the *record* than was necessary. If he has erred in this, he has been led into the error by observing that many of the cases in the books are rendered useless by the want of a sufficient statement of the case as it appeared upon the record; and he imagined it would be a less fault to insert too much, than to omit any thing material.

He has been relieved from much anxiety, as well as responsibility, by the practice which the court has adopted of reducing their opinion to writing, in all cases of difficulty or importance; and he tenders his tribute of acknowledgement for the readiness with which he was permitted to take copies of those opinions.

He is indebted to Mr. Caldwell, for his notes of the cases which were decided prior to February term 1803, without the assistance of which he would have been unable to report them, as his own notes of those cases, not having been taken with that view, were very imperfect.

He also feels his obligation to those gentlemen of the bar, whose politeness has prompted a ready communication of their notes, which have enabled him more correctly to report their arguments.

Should an apology be deemed necessary for the liberty he has taken in his notes to some of the cases reported, that apology exists in a wish candidly to investigate the truth. In doing this in a respectful manner, he does not feel conscious of giving cause of offence to liberal and candid minds.

If the fate of the present volume should not prove him totally inadequate to the task he has undertaken, it is his intention to report the cases of succeeding terms.

29

AN ACT CONCERNING CONTEMPTS OF COURT
3 Apr. 1809
5 Laws of Pa. 55 (1812)

Sect. I. *Be it enacted by the Senate and House of Representatives of the Commonwealth of Pennsylvania, in General Assembly met, and it is hereby enacted by the authority of the same,* That from and after the passing of this act, the power of the judges of the several courts of this commonwealth to issue attachments and inflict summary punishments for contempts of court shall be restricted to the following cases, *that is to say,* To the official misconduct of the officers of such courts respectively, to the negligence or disobedience of officers, parties, jurors, or witnesses against the lawful process of the court, to the misbehavior of any person in the presence of the court, obstructing the administration of justice.

Sect. II. *And be it further enacted by the authority aforesaid,* That from and after the passing of this act, all publications out of court respecting the conduct of the judges, officers of the court, jurors, witnesses, parties or any of them, of, in and concerning any cause pending before any court of this commonwealth, shall not be construed into a contempt of the said court, so as to render the author, printer, publisher, or either of them, liable to attachment and summary punishment for the same [.]; *but if such publication shall improperly tend to bias the minds of the public, the court, the officers, jurors, witnesses or any of them, on a question pending before the court, any person feeling himself aggrieved by such publication, shall be at liberty either to proceed by indictment, or to bring an action at law against the author, printer, publisher or either of them, and recover thereupon such damages as a jury may think fit to award.*

Sect. III. *And be it further enacted by the authority aforesaid, That the punishment of imprisonment in the first instance shall extend only to such contempts as are committed in open court; and all other contempts shall be punished by fine only: Provided always, That the sheriff or other proper officer, may take into custody, confine or commit to jail, any person fined for a contempt, until such fine is discharged or paid; but if he shall be unable to pay such fine, such person may be committed to prison by the court for any time not exceeding three months.*

Sect. IV. *And be it further enacted by the authority aforesaid, That notwithstanding any thing in this act contained, the said courts shall have power respectively to make rules upon any sheriff or coroner for the return of any writ or writs for the payment of money received on any execution or process, and for the production of the body after a return of cepi corpus to an execution, or in default thereof for the payment of the debt and costs, and also to compel obedience to the said rules or any of them by attachment.*

And the said courts shall have the same powers against former sheriffs and coroners: Provided, That complaint and application is made for that purpose within one year after the termination of their said offices respectively.

Sect. V. *And be it further enacted by the authority aforesaid, That this act shall be and continue in force for and during the term of two years from the passing thereof, and from thence unto the end of the next session of the legislature.*

30

YATES V. LANSING
5 Johns. R. 282 (N.Y. 1810)

KENT, Ch. J. The record before the court presents the case of a civil suit, brought against the chancellor of this state, for an act done by him in his judicial capacity, while sitting in the court of chancery. The pleadings admit that the defendant did, as chancellor, and not otherwise, at a court of chancery, held on the 15th of *September*, 1808, order the plaintiff, after he had been discharged upon *habeas corpus*, by one of the judges of this court, to be recommitted for the contempt and malpractice for which he had been originally imprisoned, and that the action is brought for such reimprisonment, and to recover the penalty mentioned in the 5th section of the *habeas corpus* act.

The counsel who appeared for the plaintiff at the last term, (and who was the same counsel that argued the case upon the *habeas corpus* at the last *February* term,) declined to argue this case, but would not consent that judgment should pass against the plaintiff by default, and pressed the court for a decision during the term, and accompanied his motion with an intimation that he intended to carry the cause, by writ of error, into the court for the correction of errors. This fact must be my apology for bestowing more time upon the case, than the doctrine which it involves, might seem to require. We have given it a deliberate attention, and in the opinion of the court, the action cannot be sustained upon any principle of law, justice or public policy.

The words of the statute upon which the suit is brought, are, "that no person who shall be set at large upon any *habeas corpus*, shall be again imprisoned for the same offence, unless by the legal order or process of the court wherein he is bound by recognisance to appear, or other court having jurisdiction of the cause; and if any person shall knowingly, contrary to this act, recommit or imprison, or cause to be recommitted or imprisoned for the same offence, any person so set at large, he shall forfeit to the party grieved, 1,250 dollars." There appear to be several strong reasons why this section in the statute cannot support the action.

The order of the court of chancery was legal, inasmuch as the previous discharge of the plaintiff was not in a case authorized by the statute, and was null and void in law. This was the decision of the court at the last *August* term, and it will be unnecessary to review that point, or repeat what was then said. According to the judgment of the court, there cannot be a pretext for this suit, even if the defendant was otherwise liable for an undue exercise, or misapplication of the powers of his court.

But the point which I purpose now principally to consider is, whether there be any foundation in law for the suit, admitting that the defendant was mistaken in supposing that the discharge of the plaintiff under the *habeas corpus*, was unduly made. The statute allows the party so discharged, to be again imprisoned for the same offence, provided it be by the legal order or process of the court wherein he is bound by recognisance to appear, *or other court having jurisdiction of the cause.* Any court which has jurisdiction of the subject matter, may reimprison, notwithstanding the discharge. To state a plain case; if a person committed at a court of *oyer and terminer*, or sessions of the peace, of a felony, and imprisoned in the state prison, be discharged by a judge on *habeas corpus*, on the ground that the court had no authority to commit, or that the order of commitment was invalid, would any one doubt that the court might cause the convict to be further reimprisoned either upon the same warrant, if it judged it sufficient, or by awarding a new and better one? The statute never intended such a destruction of principle, as to entrust to a judge in vacation, the power to control the judgment, or check the jurisdiction of a court of record.

Our system of appellate jurisprudence is built upon a sounder foundation, and instead of entrusting to the *fiat* of a single judge, to correct the errors of any court of justice, it has provided the constitutional process by appeal, or a writ of error. It is sufficient that the court which commits, has jurisdiction of the cause of commitment; and as the cause in the present case was an alleged malpractice and contempt, the court of chancery most undoubtedly had jurisdiction over the subject matter. It is decisive on the point, that the court considered the act of which it complained, to be a contempt and malpractice, by being an unauthorized interference with the practice of the court. Every court judges exclusively for itself, of its own contempts; no other court, and much less a single judge out of court, can undertake to judge on the question. The plaintiff was recommitted, to use the language of the order, for "contempt and malpractice;" and whether the court of chancery was right or wrong in considering that the plaintiff's conduct amounted to a contempt, and whether it took the proper steps to ascertain the contempt, is perfectly immaterial as to the point of jurisdiction. It had authority to punish contempts. It must judge what are contempts. Practising as solicitor, without leave, and practising in another's name, and practising in another's name without his knowledge, are all misdemeanors, and contempts of the court. These are undeniable propositions.

On the ground which the court took, then, it certainly had jurisdiction of the subject matter. The case of *Howell*, the recorder of *London*, is to this purpose. He presided at a court of *oyer and terminer*, and fined and imprisoned a juror, for bringing in a wrong verdict. In a suit against him for this act, the whole court of C. B. declared that the *oyer and terminer* had jurisdiction of the cause, because it

had power to punish a misdemeanor in a juror; though in the case before the court, the recorder had made an erroneous judgment in considering the act of the juror as amounting to a misdemeanor, when in fact it was no misdemeanor. (*Hammond* v. *Howell*, 2 *Mod.* 218.)

To be prepared to give a sound construction to the statute giving the penalty in question, we ought to bear in mind the uniform and solemn language of the common law, as to the responsibility of judges, by private suit, for their judicial decisions. "We shall never know," says Lord *Coke*, "the true reason of the interpretation of the statutes, if we know not what the law was before the making of them." Where courts of special and limited jurisdiction exceed their powers, the whole proceeding is *coram non judice*, and all concerned in such void proceedings are held to be liable in trespass. (Case of the *Marshalsea*, 10 *Co.* 68. *Terry* v. *Huntington*, Hardres, 480.) But I believe this doctrine has never been carried so far as to justify a suit against the members of the superior courts of general jurisdiction, for any act done by them in a judicial capacity. There is no such case or decision which I have met with, and I find the doctrine to be decidedly otherwise. In *Miller* v. *Seeve*, (2 *Black. Rep.* 1141.) Lord Ch. J. *De Grey* said, that the judges of the king's superior courts of general jurisdiction were not liable to answer personally for their errors in judgment. The protection as to them was absolute and universal; with respect to the inferior courts, it was only while they act within their jurisdiction. The penalty sought for in the present suit, was, I think, very clearly imposed upon individuals only, acting ministerially or extrajudicially out of court. The words of the statute do not apply to the act of a court done of record; and we ought to require a positive application of the penalty to such a case, before we can in decency presume that the statute intended so far to humble and degrade the judicial department, as to render the judges responsible in a civil suit for their judicial acts.

The doctrine which holds a judge exempt from a civil suit or indictment, for any act done, or omitted to be done by him, sitting as judge, has a deep root in the common law. It is to be found in the earliest judicial records, and it has been steadily maintained by an undisturbed current of decisions in the *English* courts, amidst every change of policy, and through every revolution of their government. A short view of the cases will teach us to admire the wisdom of our forefathers, and to revere a principle on which rests the independence of the administration of justice. *Juvat accedere fontes atque haurire.*

Serjeant *Hawkins* (b. 1. c. 7. p. 6.) lays down this general rule, as the result of his inquiries on the subject; "That the law has freed the judges of all courts of record from all prosecutions whatsoever, except in the parliament, for any thing done by them openly in such courts as judges. For," he adds, "the authority of government cannot be maintained, unless the greatest credit be given to those who are so highly entrusted with the administration of public justice, and that if they should be exposed to the prosecution of those whose partiality to their own causes would induce them to think themselves injured, it would be impossible for them to keep up in the people that veneration of their persons, and submission to their judgments, without which it is impossible to execute the laws with vigour and success."

We meet with the principle here stated as early as the *Book of Assize*, 27 *Ed.* III. pl. 18. The case there was, that A. was indicted, for that being a judge of *oyer and terminer*, certain persons were indicted before him of trespass, and he had entered upon the record that they were indicted of felony, and judgment was demanded, if he should answer for falsifying the record, since he was a judge by commission; and all the judges were of opinion that the presentment was void. And at this same early period we find this wise protection extended equally to grand jurors. In 21 *Ed.* III. *Hil.* pl. 16. a writ of conspiracy was sued in K. B. and the question was, whether it be a good plea to the action, that the defendants were indictors in the case complained of, and it was held to be a good plea. In 9 *Hen.* VI. 60. pl. 9. an action upon the case was brought against A. for fraud, in executing the office of escheator, and *Babington*, J. said, and so it was agreed, that such a suit would not lie against a judge of record. So in 9 *Ed.* IV. 3. pl. 10. it was held by *Littleton*, J. and not denied, that an action of assault and battery would not lie against a justice of the peace, for what he did as a judge of record; and the same principle was afterwards more solemnly advanced by all the judges, in 21 *Ed.* IV. 67. pl. 49. They are concurred in opinion, that for what a justice of the peace, did *in the sessions*, he was not amenable.

These cases, and many more opinions of the like effect, which could be gleaned from the *Year Books*, conclusively show, that judges of all courts of record, from the highest to the lowest, and even jurors, who are judges of fact, were always exempted from prosecution, by action or indictment, for what they did in their judicial character. It did not escape the discernment of the early sages of the law, that the principle requisite to secure a free, vigorous and independent administration of justice, applied to render jurors, as well as judges, inviolable; and I fully acquiesce in the opinion of Lord Ch. J. *Wilmot*, that trials by jury will be buried in the same grave with the authority of the courts who are to preside over them. But I proceed to show that in subsequent periods of the *English* law, the doctrine was equally asserted and enforced. *Staunford*, in his *Pleas of the Crown*, which was first published in 1567, says, (p. 173.) that no prosecution for conspiracy lies against grand jurors, for it shall not be intended, that what they did, by virtue of their oaths, was false and malicious; and that the same law applied to a justice of the peace, for he shall not be punished as a conspirator, for what he does in open sessions as a justice. In the case of *Floyd and Barker*, (12 *Co.* 23.) the subject underwent a solemn consideration by Lord *Coke*, and all the judges; and their resolution was, that no grand juror was responsible for finding an indictment, and that no judge, who tries and gives judgment in a criminal case, or does any act in court, was to be questioned for it, either at the suit of the party, or of the king. And it was observed, "that if the judges of the realm who have the administration of justice, were to be drawn in question, except it be before the king himself, it would tend to the slander of justice, and those who are the

most sincere would not be free from continual calumniations." In *Aire* v. *Sedgwick*, (2 *Roll. Rep.* 199.) *Noy*, J. laid down the same uncontradicted rule, that no action lay against a judge for any thing which he did as judge. But the case of *Hammond* v. *Howell*, (1 *Mod.* 184. 2 *Mod.* 218.) deserves our particular notice, as being peculiarly weighty on the point before us. This is the case to which I have already alluded for another purpose. The defendant was recorder of *London*, and, as one of the judges of *oyer and terminer*, had fined and imprisoned the plaintiff, because he had brought in a verdict, as a petit juror, contrary to the direction of the court and the evidence. If ever a case was calculated to awaken sensibility, and to try the strength of the principle, this must have been one. It arose some time after the decision in *Bushell's* case, in which it was agreed by all the judges, that a juror was not finable for his verdict. The act of the defendant was admitted to have been illegal, and no doubt it struck the whole court as a high-handed and arbitrary measure. The counsel for the plaintiff admitted the weight of the objection, that an action would not lie against a judge of record for what he did, *quatenus* a judge; and he endeavoured to except this case from the general principle, by contending, that what the defendant did, was not warranted by his commission, and that, therefore, he did not act as judge. But the court did not yield to such miserable sophistry; for they held, that the bringing of the action was a greater offence than the imprisonment of the plaintiff, for it was a bold attempt both against the government and justice in general. They said that no authority, or semblance of an authority, had been urged for an action against a judge of record, for doing any thing as judge; that this was never before imagined, and no action would lie against a judge, for a wrongful commitment, any more than for an erroneous judgment; that though the defendant acted erroneously, he acted judicially, and if what he did was corrupt, complaint might be made to the king, and if erroneous, it might be reversed.

The case of *Groenvelt* v. *Burnwell*, (12 *Mod.* 386. 1 *Salk.* 306, 1 *Ld. Raym.* 454.) arose long after the passing of the *habeas corpus* act, and the unanimous opinion of the court of K. B. was given by Sir *John Holt*, whose name has always been held in reverence by *English* freemen; for he was a sound judge and an inflexible patriot, who manifested, on every occasion, a generous and distinguished zeal for the liberties of the people. He went at large into the cases in support of the doctrine, and showed to every one's entire satisfaction, that judges were not liable to an action by the party, for what they did as judges; that no averment was admissible that a judge of record had acted against his duty; that if even a justice of the peace should record that, upon his view, as a force which was no force, he could not be drawn in question, for it is a judicial act; that, in like manner, jurors were not responsible for their verdicts, because they were judges of fact; and he added, in this emphatical language, "that it would expose the justice of the nation, and no man would execute the office of judge, upon peril of being arraigned, by action or indictment, for every judgment he pronounces." In the very modern cases of *Miller* v. *Searl and others*, (2 *Black. Rep.*

1145.) and of *Moslyn* v. *Fabrigas*, (*Cowp.* 172.) *De Grey*, Ch. J. in the one, and Lord *Mansfield* in the other case, explicitly and emphatically declare the same doctrine. Indeed, I am persuaded that the discussion of the question, even under this 5th section of the *habeas corpus* act, would not now be endured in any court in *Westminster Hall*.

I shall close this review of the cases with noticing one arising in an *American* court. The case I allude to is that of *Phelps* v. *Sill*, lately decided in the supreme court of *Connecticut*. (1 *Day's Cases in Error*, 315.) From the characters composing that court, I think the decision entitled to great consideration. That was a suit against a judge of probates for omitting to take security from a guardian, and the court held that the action would not lie. They said that "it was a settled principle, that a judge is not to be questioned in a civil suit for doing, or for neglecting or refusing to do a particular official act, in the exercise of judicial power. That a regard to this maxim was essential to the administration of justice. If by any mistake in the exercise of his office, a judge should injure an individual, hard would be his condition, if he were to be responsible for damages. The rules and principles, which govern the exercise of judicial power, are not, in all cases, obvious; they are often complex, and appear under different aspects to different persons. No man would accept the office of judge, if his estate were to answer for every error in judgment, or if his time and property were to be wasted in litigations with every man whom his decisions might offend."

After this recognition of the principle, I may confidently appeal to every sound and intelligent lawyer, whether it could *possibly* have been the meaning of the *habeas corpus* act to make the chancellor, or any other judge of any other court of record responsible in a civil suit, for a heavy penalty, for an action done of record by him, while sitting in his court of justice? Ought such a sacred principle of the common law, as the one we have been considering, to be subverted, without an express declaration to that effect? Does such a construction appear ever to have been entertained in any book, or by any individual, from the time of the statute of *Charles* II. until the bringing of the present suit? Our act is but a transcript from the *English* statute, and Serjeant *Hawkins* (b. 2. c. 15. § 24.) expressly excludes every such construction. "The *habeas corpus* act," he observes, "makes the judges liable to an action at the suit of the party, *in one case only, viz.* in refusing to award a *habeas corpus*, and seems to leave it to their discretion in all other cases, to pursue the directions of the act, in the same manner as they ought to execute all other laws, without making them subject to the action of the party, or to any other express penalty or forfeiture." The penalty to which the chancellor and judges are liable, is mentioned in the fourth section of the act; and that is given against them by name, and only for their refusal, *in the vacation time*, to allow a writ of *habeas corpus*, when duly applied for. The chancellor and judges may refuse such a writ, at their discretion, if applied for in term time, and the penalty will not attach. It is only when they refuse, in a mere ministerial capacity, to allow a writ, that they are made responsible. The allowance of a writ in vacation, is not a judicial act. It is merely analogous to the case stated in *Green* v. *The*

Hundred of B. (1 *Leon.* 323.) where it was held, that an action on the case lay against a justice of the peace, for refusing to take the oath of the party robbed, because, in such case he did not act as a judge, but as a particular minister appointed by the statute of *Eliz.* to take examinations. The *habeas corpus* act does not, then, in any of its provisions, violate, or even touch the principle, that no suit lies for a judicial act. Though the judge is bound under a penalty, to allow the writ, yet when the prisoner is brought before him he is to discharge, bail, or remand him, as he shall be advised; and no action or penalty is given for what he shall then do or refuse to do.

Judicial exercise of power is imposed upon the courts. They *must* decide and act according to their judgment, and therefore the law will protect them. The chancellor, in the case of the plaintiff, was bound in duty to imprison and reimprison him, if he considered his conduct, as amounting to a contempt of his court. The obligations of his office left him no volition. He was as much bound to punish a contempt committed in his court, as he was bound in any other case to exercise his power. He may possibly have erred in judgment, in calling an act a contempt which did not amount to one, and in regarding a discharge as null, when it was binding. This court may have erred in the same way; still it was but error of judgment, for which neither the chancellor, nor the judges of this court, are or can be responsible in a civil suit. Such responsibility would be an anomaly in jurisprudence. No statute could have intended such atrocious oppression and injustice. The penalty is given only for the voluntary and wilful acts of individuals, acting in a private or ministerial capacity. It is a mulct, and given by way of punishment. *The person* who forfeits it, must *"knowingly, contrary to the act,"* reimprison, or cause the party to be reimprisoned. There must be the *scienter*, or intentional violation of the statute; and this can never be imputed to the judicial proceedings of a court. It would be an impeachable offence, which can never be averred or shown but under the process of impeachment.

No man can foresee the disastrous consequences of a precedent in favour of such a suit. Whenever we subject the established courts of the land to the degradation of private prosecution, we subdue their independence, and destroy their authority. Instead of being venerable before the public, they become contemptible; and we thereby embolden the licentious to trample upon every thing sacred in society, and to overturn those institutions which have hitherto been deemed the best guardians of civil liberty.

I am, therefore, of opinion that judgment ought to be entered for the defendant.

THOMPSON, J, and VAN NESS, J. concurred.

YATES, J. was absent.

SPENCER, J. The decision of the court, at the last *August* term, in the matter of *John V. N. Yates*, entitles the defendant to judgment on the demurrer. A majority of this court held that the recommitment of the plaintiff, after he had been set at large on *habeas corpus*, was a legal and justifiable act.

I have not thought it necessary to examine the other point in the cause, with a view to deliver an opinion on it; but I have so far considered it, as to be unable to subscribe to several positions in the opinion just delivered; I must, therefore, be considered as giving no opinion on that point.

Judgment for the defendant.

31

HOUSE OF REPRESENTATIVES, REMOVAL OF JUDGES
31 Jan. 1811
Annals 22:857

Mr. WRIGHT called for the consideration of the resolution submitted by him on Wednesday last, in the following words:

Resolved, by the Senate and House of Representatives of the United States of America, in Congress assembled, two-thirds of both Houses concurring, That the following section be submitted to the Legislatures of the several States; which, when ratified by the Legislatures of three-fourths of the States, shall be valid and binding as a part of the Constitution of the United States:

"The Judges of the Supreme Court and inferior courts, may be removed from office by the joint address of the Senate and House of Representatives of the United States."

Mr. W. wished it considered barely with a view to a reference to a Committee of the Whole, and to make it the order of the day for some distant day.

The House refused to consider the resolution; 53 to 38.

32

DUPY V. WICKWISE
1 Chip. 237 (Vt. 1814)

By the Court. If the plaintiff be entitled to read the deposition in this case, he is not entitled to read it by virtue of the act of the legislature. The act is most clearly unconstitutional and void. It is an attempt of the legislature to make a judicial decision in a particular case; but the constitution of this State, prohibits the legislature from the exercise of any judicial powers. The act is also retrospective in its operation, is rather in the nature of a legislative sentence, order or decree, than of a law. Besides, if the deposition was not legally taken in this case, it is a mere voluntary affidavit. And, the person making such a voluntary affidavit, does not subject himself to the pains and penalties of perjury, for any false swearing in such affidavit; it is not taken, therefore, under that security to which the person, against whom it is to be read, is entitled; nor can any *ex pos facto* law give that security. Suppose this deposition to have been false, in some material fact, and

that Morse were not dead, but gone to some parts unknown, and, by virtue of this act his deposition read, and a verdict obtained against the defendant, and Morse should return; could he be convicted of perjury, for swearing falsely in giving the deposition? Certainly not. Even if the legislature should have specially provided, that the deponent should be liable to all the pains and penalties of wilful and corrupt perjury, for false swearing; such *ex pos facto* provision would have been void, as being against the constitution of this State, the constitution of the United States, and even against the laws of nature. The deposition, therefore cannot be admitted on the authority of the act of the legislature.

But, the Court on consideration are of opinion that the deposition is legally taken. It seems to have been settled that the person suing in such case may bring the action in his own name only. In England, the writ may be brought *qui tam,* and the declaration be in the name of the person prosecuting only—and, that there is no necessity that the writ or declaration should express the *qui tam.* The person prosecuting may well be considered as the sole plaintiff.

33

UNITED STATES V. JACOBSON
26 Fed. Cas. 567, no. 15,461 (C.C.D.N.Y. 1817)

On the other ground of objection relating to the jurisdiction, the judge said that his private opinion was decidedly in favor of the objection. The act of congress directing the justices of the supreme court of the United States to hold circuit courts was unconstitutional, and not binding on the judges. The supreme court was created by the constitution, and its powers and duties were therein defined. The legislature, therefore, could neither add to the one nor to the other. This precaution was highly proper, as it respected the appellate court of the federal judiciary. If, besides the duties prescribed for it by the constitution, the legislature were at liberty to add to them such others, not only in their own court but in courts with which they had no connection, there would be an end of that independence which should ever exist between co-ordinate branches of the same government; and so long as such power shall continue to be exercised, and be acquiesced in, the supreme court will be kept in a state of dependence on the legislature, which could never have been contemplated by those who framed the constitution. It is a fact that the labor of holding circuit courts has become much more burdensome to the judges of the supreme court than the discharge of their regular, appropriate, and constitutional functions in the court for which they are commissioned. It may be added, for so the fact is, that the business of the supreme court is much impeded by the attention of the judges to their circuit duties, to the very great inconvenience and heavy expense of the suitors therein. Congress have a right to ordain and establish, from time to time, such inferior courts as they may think fit; but they have no power to commission the judges of such courts, nor to appoint any judge by law. If they thought proper, therefore, that a circuit court should consist of a district and another judge, such other judge should have been appointed, as well as the district judge, on the nomination of the president, and by and with the consent of the senate. He should have been commissioned during good behavior, and have received a compensation for his services. But no commissions have ever been granted to the justices of the supreme court constituting them judges of the circuit court, nor have they taken any oath of office as such; and instead of receiving a compensation for these heavy and expensive duties, their salaries as justices of the supreme court have been greatly diminished by them. The inconvenience of the system as it respects the administration of justice may also tend to show that the constitution in this respect has not been pursued. It could never have been intended that the judges of a court, whose principal duties are of an appellate nature, should ever form a constituent part of those inferior tribunals whose decisions they were to revise. The disadvantages of such a system in practice can hardly be estimated, except by those who have had some experience in them. It is certainly desirable that judges of an appellate court should form no opinion in an inferior tribunal; and when sitting separately on questions which are to come before them in a court of appeals, or otherwise, the benefit of consultation, so important to a suitor, and of a judgment resulting from such consultation, without any previous bias, will be in a great measure lost. So very inconsistent are these duties that if the president had been left, as he ought to have been, to nominate and commission a judge of the circuit court, it would hardly have occurred to him to offer such commission to a judge of the supreme court; and if he had, and it had been accepted, such judge must certainly have resigned the one which he before held.

It will be seen, also, by the constitution, that the judges of the supreme court have not only a very limited original jurisdiction, but little or none of a criminal nature; and yet the most extensive criminal cognizance, extending even to the capital offenses, is given to them as members of the circuit courts. Now, if congress cannot extend the original jurisdiction of the supreme court beyond the bounds limited by the constitution, and so that court has decided, it is not seen how they can extend the jurisdiction of the several judges of that court to cases over which the court itself has neither original nor appellate jurisdiction; or how, because the constitution and their commissions have made them judges of the supreme court, congress can, without their consent, make them judges of an inferior court. One thing is certain, that if congress can make them discharge the duties of one inferior court, they can throw into their hands the business of every inferior tribunal that may be established; and, indeed, it is not long since that a bill passed both houses of congress assigning, in certain cases, the duties of the district courts to the judges of the supreme court. The president, Mr. Madison, returned the bill with objections, and it did not pass. These objections are not now before me, but as far as they are recollected,

they would apply as well to the act under consideration as to the one for which they were made. But it is unnecessary to pursue this inquiry further: for although this be my own opinion, which I have thought it my duty to express, it will be remembered that this question came before the supreme court in 1803, when the judges, waiving any opinion on the constitutionality of this act, were pleased to consider the practice of a few years under it as precluding all argument on the subject. Whether, if the question shall ever come before that court, it will consider such acquiescence as putting at rest this great constitutional question I cannot say, as it has never received a decision on its merits. It is not yet too late, in my opinion, to review the one which has taken place; but until that be done in its proper place, this court is bound by it, and must suppose, whatever its opinion may be, that it has a right to hold jurisdiction of this case, and to pronounce judgment on the present verdict.

34

 EDWARD LIVINGSTON, SYSTEM OF PENAL LAWS,
TIT. 5, C. 11, 51–52
1824

Art.   . If any one shall, during the session of any Court of Justice, in the presence of the court, by words or by making a clamour or noise, wilfully obstruct the proceedings of such court, or shall refuse to obey any legal order of such court made for the maintenance of order, or to preserve regularity of proceedings in court, it shall be lawful for the said court to cause the offender to be removed by the proper officer of justice from the building in which the sessions of such court are held; and if such offender shall persevere in returning to and disturbing said court, it shall also be lawful for them to cause him to be imprisoned during the time the court shall be in session during the same day; and the party offending against this article is guilty of a misdemeanor, and shall be punished by fine not exceeding twenty dollars, and by imprisonment not exceeding three days.

Art.   . If any person shall, either verbally in court, or in any pleading or other writing addressed to the judges in any cause pending in any court of justice, use any indecorous, contemptuous or insulting expressions, to or of the court or the judges thereof, with intent to insult the said court or any of the said judges, he shall be punished by simple imprisonment not more than fifteen days, and by fine not exceeding fifty dollars; and the fact of the intent, with which the words were used, and also whether they were indecorous, contemptuous, and insulting, shall be decided by the jury, who shall try the cause. The said punishment shall be doubled on a second conviction for an offence under this article; and for a third, the party shall in addition to the said punishment, if an attorney or counsellor, be suspended for not less than one nor more than four years from practicing in the said court as attorney or counsellor at law, or as attorney in fact.

Art.   . If any one shall obstruct the proceedings of a court of justice by violence, or threats of violence, offered either to the judges, jurors, witnesses, parties or attorneys or counsellors, he shall be fined in a sum not less than one hundred and not exceeding five hundred dollars, and by imprisonment, in close custody, not less than ten days nor more than six months; and if the offender be an attorney or counsellor at law, he shall be suspended from practicing in such court for not less than one nor more than three years, either as attorney or counsellor at law, or as attorney in fact.

Art.   . Courts of justice have no power to inflict any punishment for offences committed against their authority, other than those specially provided for by this code and the code of procedure. All proceedings for offences, heretofore denominated contempts, are abolished. All offences created by this chapter, shall be tried on indictment, or information in the usual form.

35

WILLIAM RAWLE, A VIEW OF THE CONSTITUTION
OF THE UNITED STATES 199–201, 274–80
1829 (2d ed.)

No form of government is complete unless it be accompanied with a judicial power.

To make laws and to execute them are the two great operations of government; but they cannot be fully and correctly executed unless there is somewhere resident a power to expound and apply them. This power is auxiliary to the executive authority, and in some degree partakes of its nature. But it is also required at times to control the executive, and what it decides to be unlawful, the executive cannot perform. It may also in some degree be said to participate in the legislative power. Its construction of the acts of the legislature is received as binding and conclusive, although it does not prevent the legislature from repairing its own defects, or clearing up its own ambiguities by subsequent laws, operating on subsequent cases. A high function also appertains to the judiciary in the exclusive right to expound the Constitution, and thereby to test the validity of all the acts of the legislature.

To the people at large, therefore, this institution is peculiarly valuable, and ought to be eminently cherished by them. On its firm and independent structure they repose with safety, while they perceive in it a faculty which is only set in motion when applied to, but which when thus brought into action, proceeds with competent power if required, to correct the error or subdue the oppression of both or either of the two other branches. A Constitution in which there was an omission to provide an adequate judiciary could not be successfully carried into effect; and if instead of being separate and independent, this power

were either blended with the other two, or those who administer it were dependent on the will and pleasure of others, its lustre would be tarnished and its utility destroyed.

The Constitution of the United States, therefore, required a judicial power, not as an adjunct, but as a necessary component part. The extraordinary complications of the authority of the United States with that of the several states, which seem at first view to throw so many difficulties in the way, fully prove its necessity. The state tribunals are no part of the government of the United States. To render the government of the United States dependent on them, would be a solecism almost as great as to leave out an executive power entirely, and to call on the states alone to enforce the laws of the Union. But it is not inconsistent with this principle that the United States may, whenever it is found expedient, elect to make use of a state tribunal to the same extent as any foreign power may, if it thinks proper to institute suits in the courts of other countries, which is in civil cases only.

The judicial power is general or limited, according to the scope and objects of the government. In a word, it must be fully and exactly commensurate with that of the legislature. It cannot by any terms of language, be made to exceed the legislative power, for such excess would be inconsistent with its nature. If by express words it should, on the other hand, be restrained so as to embrace only a part of the subjects of legislation, it would impair the integrity of the whole system. The protection which it was intended to afford, in regard to the other branches of government, being confined to parts of their conduct, instead of embracing the whole, would produce the incongruous mixture of a theoretic, general power with partial debility and impotence. If general terms are used in describing it, there is no difficulty in defining its proper extent.

In the Constitution of the United States we perceive, not the express creation of a judicial power, but the recognition of it as a necessary part of the government, in which light it was justly considered and has been universally accepted. Its power extends to the great selected objects already noticed, and it is the duty of those who have to administer it, to carry it to that full extent, but never to exceed it. Experience has already shown that from a wise and temperate administration, the apprehension of inconvenience from serious collisions between the state judicatures and those of the United States was unfounded. It must be confessed that the merits of our Constitution have received ample support from the prudence and judgment with which it has been administered, and in no respect has a sounder discretion been exhibited than in the judicatory. If any objection could be sustained to the procedures of the judges of the supreme and circuit courts, it would be that of excessive caution, arising from a systematic anxiety not to exceed their jurisdiction. And it is a strong argument in favour of an elective government, that those men in whom the power of appointment is vested by the choice of the people, have, in regard to these judicial officers, exercised it with so much caution, judgment, and success.

.   .   .   .   .

From these general views of the judicial power, we collect that it is in the nature of a principle incorporated for useful purposes into the Constitution, vested in various agents, some of whom derive their authority from the United States, and some from the states, and holding their offices, as will appear by reference to those constitutions, on various tenures, but all possessing the right of deciding on the validity of a law.

If this power is in itself inordinate, if it is not consistent with the true interests of the people, it might have been excluded from, or carefully qualified in, the Constitution; but it has been established by the people on full deliberation; and a few additional reflections on its nature and utility may be admitted.

In the first place, we may observe, that a judicial power with such extensive attributes, is probably peculiar to this country. Where there is not a fixed and settled constitution, whether written or unwritten, which cannot be altered by the legislature, the judiciary has no power to declare a law unconstitutional. In such countries, the people are at the mercy of the legislature. The appeals which they may make to their constitutions are disregarded if they cannot be enforced, and the constitution possesses merely a nominal value. It tends indeed to excite discontents, by exhibiting rights that cannot be enjoyed, and promising restraints on government that may be broken with impunity.

The Constitution of the United States was not framed, in this respect, on ground new to us. The principle had been previously inserted in all the state constitutions then formed. It has been preserved in all those since established, and none of the alterations which we have heretofore noticed, have been extended to this point.

We may then inquire, in what mode or form of language it could have been excluded from the Constitution, and what would have been the effect of such exclusion. Being in itself a necessary incident to a regular and complete government, its existence is implied from the mere fact of creating such a government; if it is intended that it should not be commensurate with all the powers and obligations of the government, or that it should not form any part of it whatever, express terms of qualification or exclusion would certainly be required.

Now it would be difficult to reconcile the minds of freemen, to whom was submitted the consideration of a scheme of government, professing to contain those principles by which a future legislature and executive were to be regulated, to any declarations that a subversion or abandonment of those principles, by either branch, and particularly by the legislature, should be liable to no resistance or control. The judicial power potentially existed before any laws were passed; it could not be without an object; that object is at first the Constitution. As the legislature proceeds to act, the judicial power follows their proceedings. It is a corrective imposed by the Constitution on their acts. The legislature are not deceived or misled. Nothing indicates that they alone are to decide on the constitutionality of their own acts, or that the people who may be injured by such acts, are unprovided with any other defence than open resistance to them. But without an adequate power in the judiciary to the effect required, the people would either be driven to such resistance; obliged to wait till they could obtain redress through the exercise of their elective powers; or be compelled to patient submission.

The rights of the people are better secured by the general undefined judicial power, necessarily inferred from the general language of the Constitution itself, pre-existing in their own state constitutions, and never surrendered to the United States. In the last mentioned aspect, it would appear surprising that those who were most apprehensive of the self-increasing power of the general government, did not perceive the bulwark of their safety. The courts and the judges of every state possess, as before observed, the right to decide on the constitutionality of a law of their own state and of the United States. The principle itself, and not the mere tribunal, constitutes the public security. That such decisions are subject to the appellate jurisdiction heretofore spoken of, forms no objection to their usefulness. The object of this jurisdiction is to produce uniformity. Instead of reducing, it enhances the value, while it proves the universal bearing of the principle itself.

In the *organization* of this power thus salutary, thus necessary, is found the only difficulty. To render it wholly independent of the people, is objected to by many: to affect its necessary independence by the modes of creating and appointing its ministers, is liable to equal objections. In the first case, arbitrary and despotic proceedings are apprehended. It is supposed to be the natural disposition of man, when placed above control, to abuse his power, or, if no corrupt motives produce this consequence, there sometimes are found a laxity, a carelessness, a want of sufficient exertion and deliberate judgment in the exercise of it. On the other hand, if instead of availing himself of his own knowledge and capacity, the judge submits to be governed by the opinions of others; if he allows the desire to retain his office, the fear of giving offence, or the love of popularity, to form any part of the ingredients of his judgment, an equal violation of his trust is apparent. It is therefore not without anxiety that the patriotic mind endeavours so to regulate the organization of this all essential power, that it shall be safely steered between the two extremes.

In all governments retaining a semblance of the preservation of popular rights, it is believed that the structure of the judicial power ought to be founded on its independence. The tenure of office is therefore generally *during good behaviour*. But in some of our state governments, judges are appointed for a term of years. In some, the appointments are made by the executive, in some by the legislative power. The mode of appointment is of little consequence as to the principle, if, when it has been made, the magistrate is independent of the further favour of the appointing power. The more important question is the condition and duration of the appointment. The condition of good behaviour necessarily accompanies all judicial appointments, for whatever term they may be granted. There are none during pleasure in this country, although the case is otherwise as to some high judicial stations in England. Cases of misbehaviour are therefore to be provided against. Honest errors in judgment do not amount to misbehaviour. The court of the last resort is to correct all those which take place in the previous tribunals. If this court shall itself be deemed to have committed an error, there can be no redress, because from the nature of things, there must be some point at which to stop: and it is better that an individual should sustain an injury, than that the whole system should be thrown into disorder.

This last resort may be differently constituted, but there must be some final mode of deciding.

On some occasions of dissatisfaction with the decisions of the supreme court, different modes of revising even their decisions have been suggested. The last of these known to the author has been to convert the senate into the final court of error and appeal.

Of their competency in a practical view, no doubt can be entertained, but of the benefit which the public would derive by their unavoidable suspension of legislative business, with other high functions devolved on them, while their time was occupied in the trial of causes, there would be much room for doubt.

But, however this ultimate tribunal may be constituted, it is still to be the last resort; and, since human infallibility can no where be found, it may also pronounce erroneous judgments for which there would be no redress.

In all these institutions we must therefore recognise the imperfection of man, and content ourselves with the intention to act rightly, although the decision, in the apprehension of many, may be wrong.

In some states, a power is given to the executive authority on the application of a certain proportion of the legislature to remove a judge from office. Reasons will occur both for and against such a provision. If a judge should be incapacitated by infirmity or age, or be otherwise, without any fault of his own, prevented from performing his duties, he would not be a proper subject for removal by impeachment; yet, where duties cannot be performed, the officer should not be continued. The incapacity should, however, be established in the specific case, and to lay down a general rule, that on the attainment of a certain age, the judge shall no longer be admitted to act, may withdraw from the service of the public a person capable of being highly useful to them. In New York the commission expires at the age of sixty years; in Connecticut at seventy years; and thus their constitutions seem to intend to impose laws on nature itself, or to drive from their own service men in whom may still reside the most useful faculties, improved by time and experience. The Constitution of the United States abstains from this error.

But the power of removal intended, in those states where it is found, to be exercised in cases of actual and not implied incapacity, may in practice be carried further, and if the representatives of the people hold the opinion that the proceedings of a judge are contrary to the public interests, an application for his removal may be made to the governor. If, for instance, he has decided that one of their laws is unconstitutional, and they retain a different opinion, or if his constructions of, and proceedings under a law not objectionable in itself, differ from their own views of the same subject, dissatisfaction with his conduct which may be very honestly felt, may occasion an address for his removal, not as a mode of avoiding or reversing his decisions, for that could not be the effect, but as an example to others, and perhaps in some degree, it might be calculated for a punishment to himself.

Now, laying aside all party considerations which sometimes *may* operate, perhaps unconsciously, with the best men, we must inquire into the principle on which such removal would be founded, and we shall find it to be that of setting up the judgment of the people through their representatives to correct the judgment of the judicial power.

If the Constitution of the particular state fairly admits of this construction, it is the will of the people, and must be obeyed. It is a control reserved to themselves over the general character of the judicial power, and to that extent impairs its absolute independence. In the absence of corrupt motives, which might justify an impeachment, it is the only mode of rectifying a course of erroneous judgments tending to produce public injury. But it is liable to the objection that those who thus undertake to decide, are seldom so well qualified for the task as those whose peculiar studies and occupation may be considered as having enabled them to judge. Another objection is, that removal in this manner being in every sense an evil, a fear of displeasing the legislature may always hover over the mind of the judge, and prevent his being the impartial and inflexible mediator between the legislature and the people, which the people intended he should be.

The advantages and disadvantages of the whole subject must have been duly considered by the framers of our Constitution, and the people at large have confirmed the result of their judgment.

There is, however, one power vested in the legislature, of which they cannot be deprived. They are authorized "from time to time" to ordain and establish tribunals inferior to the supreme court, and such courts they may at any time abolish. Thus, as before noticed, the act of 1801, establishing certain circuit courts was repealed in 1802, and the commissions granted to the judges were consequently avoided.

To this instance we may be permitted to refer, for the purpose of showing the high independence of all party considerations, that appertains to the character of a judge. The supreme court, which affirmed a decision by which the validity of the repealing act was established, was at that time composed entirely of men politically adverse to that which, by a sudden revolution, had become the predominant party in the legislature. Yet the decision was unanimously given, one of the judges only being absent on account of ill-health. And such are the true nature and spirit of a judicial institution, that there can be no doubt that the same principle; the same entire repudiation of party spirit, would govern men of all political impressions, when required to act on similar occasions by the Constitution and their country. Party spirit seldom contaminates judicial functions.

On the whole, it seems that with the right to new model all the inferior tribunals, and thereby to vacate the commissions of their judges, and with the power to impeach all judges whatever, a sufficient control is retained over the judiciary power for every useful purpose; that it is a branch of government which the people have the strongest motives to cherish and support, and that if they value and wish to preserve their Constitution, they ought never to surrender the independence of their judges.

36

AN ACT DECLARATORY OF THE LAW CONCERNING CONTEMPTS OF COURT

4 Stat. 487 (1831)

Be it enacted by the Senate and House of Representatives of the United States of America, in Congress assembled, That the power of the several courts of the United States to issue attachments and inflict summary punishments for contempts of court, shall not be construed to extend to any cases except the misbehaviour of any person or persons in the presence of said courts, or so near thereto as to obstruct the administration of justice, the misbehaviour of any of the officers of the said courts in their official transactions, and the disobedience or resistance by any officer of the said courts, party, juror, witness, or any other person or persons, to any lawful writ, process, order, rule, decree, or command of the said courts.

Sect. 2. *And be it further enacted, That if any person or persons shall, corruptly, or by threats or force, endeavour to influence, intimidate, or impede any juror, witness, or officer, in any court of the United States, in the discharge of his duty, or shall, corruptly, or by threats or force, obstruct, or impede, or endeavour to obstruct or impede, the due administration of justice therein, every person or persons, so offending, shall be liable to prosecution therefor, by indictment, and shall, on conviction thereof, be punished, by fine not exceeding five hundred dollars, or by imprisonment, not exceeding three months, or both, according to the nature and aggravation of the offence.*

37

LIVINGSTON V. MOORE

7 Pet. 469 (1833)

JOHNSON, J.: . . . The objection made to the exercise of this power is, that it is one of a judicial character, and could not exist in the legislature of a country having a constitution which distributes the powers of government into legislative, executive and judicial.

I will not pause to examine the question, whether the subjection of property to the payment of judgments, be in fact a matter appertaining essentially to *judicial* power; or whether, after deciding that the debt is due, the judgment action does not cease, and all that follows is the exercise of legislative or executive power; another view of the subject will, in my opinion, dispose of this question.

The power existing in every body politic is an absolute despotism: in constituting a government, the body politic distributes that power as it pleases, and in the quantity it pleases, and imposes what checks it pleases upon its public functionaries. The natural distribution and the necessary distribution to individual security, is into legislative, executive and judicial; but it is obvious that every community may make a perfect or imperfect separation and distribution of these powers at its will. It has pleased Pennsylvania, in her constitution, to make what most jurists would pronounce an imperfect separation of those powers; she has not thought it necessary to make any imperative provision for incorporating the equity jurisdiction in its full latitude into her jurisprudence: and the consequence is, as it ever will be, that so far as her common law courts are incapable of assuming and exercising that branch of jurisdiction, her legislature must often be called upon to pass laws which bear a close affinity to decrees in equity. Of that character are the acts of 1806 and 1807 under consideration. The relations in which the state and John Nicholson's estate stood to each other, presented a clear case for equitable relief; a lien on the one hand, and property to satisfy it on the other, but no common law means of obtaining a sale. Thus circumstanced, is there any thing in the constitution of Pennsylvania to prevent the passing of these laws?

When it is intimated that the separation of the primary powers of government is incomplete under the constitution of Pennsylvania, it may be necessary to submit a few observations explanatory of the idea.

It is true that the separation of common law from equity jurisdiction is peculiar to Great Britian; no other of the states of the old world having adopted it. But it is equally true that in no other of the states of the old world did the trial by jury constitute a part of their jurisprudence, and every practical lawyer knows that to give jurisdiction to a court of equity, or to distinguish a case of equity jurisdiction from one of common law under the British practice, the averment is indispensable that the complainant is remediless at law. When it is said that the separation of common law from equity jurisdiction is peculiar to Great Britain; it must only be understood, that it is there exercised by distinct courts and under distinct forms. For, as an essential branch or exercise of judicial power, it is acknowledged to exist every where: nor is it possible for any one acquainted with its nature and character, and the remedies it affords for the assertion of rights or the punishment of wrongs, to doubt that the power to exercise it, and the means of exercising it, must exist somewhere; or the administration of justice will be embarrassed if not incomplete. To administer it through the ordinary powers or a common law court is impracticable; and hence, wherever there exists no provision in the jurisprudence of a country for its full exercise; the consequence must ever be, that after the common law courts have ingrafted into their practice as much as can be there assumed, the legislature is compelled to exercise the rest; or else leave a large space for the appropriate field of judicial action unoccupied.

A specimen of this will be found in the early legislation of the state of South Carolina, in which, before the establishment of a court of equity, laws are frequently found authorizing administrators or others to sell lands for the payment of debts, and for similar purposes. And it has been admitted in argument, that similar laws are of frequent occurrence in Pennsylvania.

The provisions of the constitution of that state, on the subject of legislative and judicial power, are as follows. Art. 1, sect. 1. "The legislative power of this commonwealth shall be vested in a general assembly, which shall consist of a senate and house of representatives.

Art. 4, sect. 1. "The judicial power of the commonwealth shall be vested in a supreme court, in courts of oyer and terminer and general jail delivery, in a court of common pleas, orphans' court, register's court, and a court of quarter sessions of the peace of each county, in justices of the peace, and in *such other courts* as the legislature may from time to time establish."

Art. 4, sect. 6. "The supreme court and the several courts of common pleas, shall, besides the powers heretofore usually exercised by them, have the powers of a court of chancery so far as relates to the perpetuating of testimony, the obtaining of evidence from places not within the state, and the care of the persons and estates of those who are non compos mentis; and the legislature shall vest in the said courts such other powers to grant relief in equity as *shall be necessary,* and may from time to time enlarge or diminish those powers, or vest them in such other courts as they may judge proper for the due administration of justice."

It is clear from these quotations, that the legislature possess all the legislative power that the body politic could confer, except so far as they are restricted by the instrument itself. It is equally clear that the constitution recognizes the distinction between common law and equity powers, and the existence of equity powers beyond what it has vested in the supreme court. But what provision has it made for the exercise of those powers? No other than this, that the legislature shall vest in the said courts such other powers to grant relief in equity as shall be found necessary. But where is the limitation prescribed to the legislature in judging of the necessity of vesting such powers? They have not thought it necessary to invest their courts with such powers: and if the reason which influenced them in judging it unnecessary was, that they held themselves competent to afford the necessary relief by the exercise of legislative power; where is the restriction in the constitution that controls them in thus extending or applying the powers with which they hold themselves to be constitutionally vested? They are sought in vain.

Again, "they may from time to time enlarge or diminish those powers, or vest them in such other courts as they shall judge proper, for the due administration of justice." Now they have, by the first section of the same article, the power to establish what courts they please; and suppose they thought proper to have vested the whole equity jurisdiction not specifically disposed of, in a board of commissioners, instead of vesting specific powers in such a board,

where is the constitutional provision that inhibits such an act of legislation?

The plaintiffs contend that it is to be found in the bill of rights of that state or in the constitution of the United States.

Both those constitutions contain the provision against the violation of contracts; and the plaintiffs' counsel insists that there were three contracts in existence between the state of Pennsylvania and John Nicholson, two of them express, and one implied.

The first express contract he finds in the acts of 1782 and 1785; which, in giving the lien upon public accounts, declare that they shall be liens "in the same manner as if judgment had been given in the supreme court." This he construes into a contract that they shall be enforced in the same manner as such a judgment, to wit by judicial process; and then finds the violation of the contract, in the acts which provide for the raising of the money to satisfy those liens by the sale of the land, through this board of commissioners. But a single observation we think disposes of this exception; which is, that the lien of a judgment, of a mortgage, or any other lien, is a very different idea from that of the means by which the lien is to be enforced; the one is the right, the other is the remedy; the one constitutes the contract, and the other the remedy afforded by the policy of the country, where it is not provided by the terms of the contract, for enforcing or effecting the execution of it. The first is unchangeable, without a violation of right; the other may be subject to change at the will of the government. And it may be further observed in the present instance, that the reference to a judgment in the supreme court, is clearly descriptive or illustrative of the meaning of the legislature, with reference only to the *binding efficacy* of the lien given on these public accounts.

The second express contract is found by the plaintiffs in the confession of judgment on the 21st March, 1797; and the violation of this, also, is not enforcing it by judicial process.

This is obviously an attempt to give the character of a contract to that which is nothing more than an obligation, or duty, or necessity imposed by the laws of society. The confession of a judgment does indeed create a contract; but it is only on the side of the defendant, who thus acknowledges or assumes upon himself a debt, which may be made the ground of an action. But on the side of the plaintiff, the necessity of resorting to certain means of enforcing that judgment, is not an obligation arising out of contract, but one imposed upon him by the laws of the country.

Again, it may be answered, if there was in fact such a contract imputable to the state, the performance had become impossible by the act of God, and of the party himself, by his death; and by that confusion of his affairs, which prevented every one from assuming the character of his personal representative.

We proceed to the third, or the implied contract; that which is deduced from the original grant of the land to John Nicholson. This sale, it is insisted, is inconsistent with that contract of grant; that it amounts in fact to a resumption of the land: and in connexion with this, the point of inconsistency with the reason and nature of things was argued and commented upon.

The answer which the case here furnishes we think is this: that subjecting the lands of a grantee to the payment of his debts, can never impair or contravene the rights derived to him under his grant, for in the very act, the full effect of the transfer of interest to him is recognized and asserted: because it is his, is the direct and only reason for subjecting it to his debts.

But it is asserted that in this case the community sits in judgment in its own cause, when it affirms the debt to be due for which the land is subjected to sale, and then subjects the land to sale to satisfy its own decision thus rendered.

This view of the acts of the state is clearly not to be sustained by a reference to the facts of the case. As to the judgment of 1797, that is unquestionably a judicial act; and as to the settled accounts, the lien is there created by the act of men who, quoad hoc, were acting in a judicial character; and their decision being subjected to an appeal to the ordinary, or rather the highest of the tribunals of the country, gives to those settlements a decided judicial character: and were it otherwise, how else are the interests of the state to be protected? The body politic has its claims upon the constituted authorities, as well as individuals; and if the plaintiffs' course of reasoning could be permitted to prevail, it would then follow, that provision might be made for collecting the debts of every one else, but those of the state must go unpaid, whenever legislative aid became necessary to both. This would be pushing the reason and nature of things beyond the limits of natural justice.

It is next contended, that the acts of 1806 and 1807 are unconstitutional and void, because contrary to the ninth section of the Pennsylvania bill of rights, which provides, in the words of magna charta, that no one shall be deprived of his property but by the laws of the land.

This exception has already been disposed of by the view that has been taken of the nature and character of those laws. It has been shown that there is nothing in this provision either inconsistent with natural justice or the constitution of the state: there is nothing of an arbitrary character in them.

They are also charged with being contrary to the ninth article of the amendments of the constitution of the United States, and the sixth section of the Pennsylvania bill of rights, securing the trial by jury.

As to the amendments of the constitution of the United States, they must be put out of the case; since it is now settled that those amendments do not extend to the states: and this observation disposes of the next exception, which relies on the seventh article of those amendments. As to the sixth section of the Pennsylvania bill of rights, we can see nothing in these laws on which to fasten the imputation of a violation of the right of trial by jury; since, in creating the lien attached to the settled accounts, the right of an appeal to a jury is secured to the debtor: and as to the inquest given under the execution law, with a view to ascertaining if the rents and profits can discharge the debt in a limited time, as a prelude to the right of selling; we

are well satisfied that there is no more reason for extending the provision of the amendment to that inquest, than there would be to the inquest of a coroner, or any other mere inquest of office. The word *trial*, used in the sixth section, clearly points to a different object; and the distinction between trial by jury and inquest of office, is so familiar to every mind, as to leave no sufficient ground for extending to the latter that inviolability which could have been intended only for the former. The one appertains to a mere remedy for the recovery of money, which may be altered at any time without any danger to private security; the other is justly regarded in every state in the union, as among the most inestimable privileges of a freeman.

38

JOSEPH STORY, COMMENTARIES ON THE
CONSTITUTION 3:§§ 1568–71, 1574–78, 1583–84,
1591, 1593, 1601–21, 1627, 1629–30
1833

---

§ 1568. The importance of the establishment of a judicial department in the national government has been already incidentally discussed under other heads. The want of it constituted one of the vital defects of the confederation. And every government must, in its essence, be unsafe and unfit for a free people, where such a department does not exist, with powers co-extensive with those of the legislative department. Where there is no judicial department to interpret, pronounce, and execute the law, to decide controversies, and to enforce rights, the government must either perish by its own imbecility, or the other departments of government must usurp powers, for the purpose of commanding obedience, to the destruction of liberty. The will of those, who govern, will become, under such circumstances, absolute and despotic; and it is wholly immaterial, whether power is vested in a single tyrant, or in an assembly of tyrants. No remark is better founded in human experience, than that of Montesquieu, that "there is no liberty, if the judiciary power be not separated from the legislative and executive powers." And it is no less true, that personal security and private property rest entirely upon the wisdom, the stability, and the integrity of the courts of justice. If that government can be truly said to be despotic and intolerable, in which the law is vague and uncertain; it cannot but be rendered still more oppressive and more mischievous, when the actual administration of justice is dependent upon caprice, or favour, upon the will of rulers, or the influence of popularity. When power becomes right, it is of little consequence, whether decisions rest upon corruption, or weakness, upon the accidents of chance, or upon deliberate wrong. In every well organized government, therefore, with reference to the security both of public rights and private rights, it is indispensable, that there should be a judicial department to ascertain, and decide rights, to punish crimes, to administer justice, and to protect the innocent from injury and usurpation.

§ 1569. In the national government the power is equally as important, as in the state governments. The laws and treaties, and even the constitution, of the United States, would become a dead letter without it. Indeed, in a complicated government, like ours, where there is an assemblage of republics, combined under a common head, the necessity of some controlling judicial power, to ascertain and enforce the powers of the Union, is, if possible, still more striking. The laws of the whole would otherwise be in continual danger of being contravened by the laws of the parts. The national government would be reduced to a servile dependence upon the states; and the same scenes would be again acted over in solemn mockery, which began in the neglect, and ended in the ruin, of the confederation. Power, without adequate means to enforce it, is like a body in a state of suspended animation. For all practical purposes it is, as if its faculties were extinguished. Even if there were no danger of collision between the laws and powers of the Union, and those of the states, it is utterly impossible, that, without some superintending judiciary establishment, there could be any uniform administration, or interpretation of them. The idea of uniformity of decision by thirteen independent and co-ordinate tribunals (and the number is now advanced to twenty-four) is absolutely visionary, if not absurd. The consequence would necessarily be, that neither the constitution, nor the laws, neither the rights and powers of the Union, nor those of the states, would be the same in any two states. And there would be perpetual fluctuations and changes, growing out of the diversity of judgment, as well as of local institutions, interests, and habits of thought.

§ 1570. Two ends, then, of paramount importance, and fundamental to a free government, are proposed to be attained by the establishment of a national judiciary. The first is a due execution of the powers of the government; and the second is a uniformity in the interpretation and operation of those powers, and of the laws enacted in pursuance of them. The power of interpreting the laws involves necessarily the function to ascertain, whether they are conformable to the constitution, or not; and if not so conformable, to declare them void and inoperative. As the constitution is the supreme law of the land, in a conflict between that and the laws, either of congress, or of the states, it becomes the duty of the judiciary to follow that only, which is of paramount obligation. This results from the very theory of a republican constitution of government; for otherwise the acts of the legislature and executive would in effect become supreme and uncontrollable, notwithstanding any prohibitions or limitations contained in the constitution; and usurpations of the most unequivocal and dangerous character might be assumed, without any remedy within the reach of the citizens. The people would thus be at the mercy of their rulers, in the state and national governments; and an omnipotence would practically exist, like that claimed for the British Parliament. The universal sense of America has decided, that in the last resort the judiciary must decide upon the constitutionality of the acts and laws of the general and state governments, so far as they are capable of being made the subject of judicial controversy. It follows, that, when they are sub-

jected to the cognizance of the judiciary, its judgments must be conclusive; for otherwise they may be disregarded, and the acts of the legislature and executive enjoy a secure and irresistible triumph. To the people at large, therefore, such an institution is peculiarly valuable; and it ought to be eminently cherished by them. On its firm and independent structure they may repose with safety, while they perceive in it a faculty, which is only set in motion, when applied to; but which, when thus brought into action, must proceed with competent power, if required to correct the error, or subdue the oppression of the other branches of the government. Fortunately too for the people, the functions of the judiciary, in deciding on constitutional questions, is not one, which it is at liberty to decline. While it is bound not to take jurisdiction, if it should not, it is equally true, that it must take jurisdiction, if it should. It cannot, as the legislature may, avoid a measure, because it approaches the confines of the constitution. It cannot pass it by, because it is doubtful. With whatever doubt, with whatever difficulties a case may be attended, it must decide it, when it arises in judgment. It has no more right to decline the exercise of a jurisdiction, which is given, than to usurp that, which is not given. The one, or the other would be treason to the constitution.

§ 1571. The framers of the constitution, having these great principles in view, adopted two fundamental rules with entire unanimity; first, that a national judiciary ought to be established; secondly, that the national judiciary ought to possess powers co-extensive with those of the legislative department. Indeed, the latter necessarily flowed from the former, and was treated, and must always be treated, as an axiom of political government. But these provisions alone would not be sufficient to ensure a complete administration of public justice, or to give permanency to the republic. The judiciary must be so organized, as to carry into complete effect all the purposes of its establishment. It must possess wisdom, learning, integrity, independence, and firmness. It must at once possess the power and the means to check usurpation, and enforce execution of its judgments. Mr. Burke has, with singular sagacity and pregnant brevity, stated the doctrine, which every republic should steadily sustain, and conscientiously inculcate. "Whatever," says he, "is supreme in a state ought to have, as much as possible, its judicial authority so constituted, as not only not to depend upon it, but in some sort to balance it. It ought to give security to its justice against its power. It ought to make its judicature, as it were, something exterior to the state." The best manner, in which this is to be accomplished, must mainly depend upon the mode of appointment, the tenure of office, the compensation of the judges, and the jurisdiction confided to the department in its various branches.

· · · · ·

§ 1574. In the convention, which framed the constitution, no diversity of opinion existed, as to the establishment of a supreme tribunal. The proposition was unanimously adopted. In respect to the establishment of inferior tribunals, some diversity of opinion was in the early stages of the proceedings exhibited. A proposition to establish them was at first adopted. This was struck out by the vote of five states against four, two being divided; and a proposition was then adopted, "that the national legislature be empowered to appoint inferior tribunals," by the vote of seven states against three, one being divided; and ultimately this proposition received the unanimous approbation of the convention.

§ 1575. To the establishment of one court of supreme and final jurisdiction, there do not seem to have been any strenuous objections generally insisted on in the state conventions, though many were urged against certain portions of the jurisdiction, proposed by the constitution to be vested in the courts of the United States. The principal question seems to have been of a different nature, whether it ought to be a distinct co-ordinate department, or a branch of the legislature. And here it was remarked by the Federalist, that the same contradiction of opinion was observable among the opponents of the constitution, as in many other cases. Many of those, who objected to the senate, as a court of impeachment, upon the ground of an improper intermixture of legislative and judicial functions, were, at least by implication, advocates for the propriety of vesting the ultimate decision of all causes in the whole, or in a part of the legislative body.

§ 1576. The arguments, or rather suggestions, upon which this scheme was propounded, were to the following effect. The authority of the Supreme Court of the United States, as a separate and independent body, will be superior to that of the legislature. The power of construing the laws according to the spirit of the constitution will enable that court to mould them into whatever shape, it may think proper; especially, as its decisions will not be in any manner subject to the revision and correction of the legislative body. This is as unprecedented, as it is dangerous. In Great Britain the judicial power in the last resort resides in the house of lords, which is a branch of the legislature. And this part of the British government has been imitated in the state constitutions in general. The parliament of Great Britain, and the legislatures of the several states, can at any time rectify by law the exceptionable decisions of their respective courts. But the errors and usurpations of the Supreme Court of the United States will be uncontrollable, and remediless.

§ 1577. The friends of the constitution, in answer to these suggestions, replied, that they were founded in false reasoning, or a misconception of fact. In the first place, there was nothing in the plan, which directly empowered the national courts to construe the laws according to the *spirit* of the constitution, or which gave them any greater latitude in this respect, than what was claimed and exercised by the state courts. The constitution, indeed, ought to be the standard of construction for the laws; and wherever there was an opposition, the laws ought to give place to the constitution. But this doctrine was not deducible from any circumstance peculiar to this part of the constitution, but from the general theory of a limited constitution; and, as far as it was true, it was equally applicable to the state governments.

§ 1578. So far as the objection went to the organization of the Supreme Court, as a distinct and independent department, it admitted of a different answer. It was founded upon the general maxim of requiring a separation of the different departments of government, as most conducive to the preservation of public liberty and private rights. It would not, indeed, absolutely violate that maxim, to allow the ultimate appellate jurisdiction to be vested in one branch of the legislative body. But there were many urgent reasons, why the proposed organization would be preferable. It would secure greater independence, impartiality, and uniformity in the administration of justice.

. . . . .

§ 1583. In regard to the power of constituting inferior courts of the Union, it is evidently calculated to obviate the necessity of having recourse to the Supreme Court in every case of federal cognizance. It enables the national government to institute, or authorize, in each state or district of the United States, a tribunal competent to the determination of all matters of national jurisdiction within its limits. One of two courses only could be open for adoption; either to create inferior courts under the national authority, to reach all cases fit for the national jurisdiction, which either constitutionally, or conveniently, could not be of original cognizance in the Supreme Court; or to confide jurisdiction of the same cases to the state courts, with a right of appeal to the Supreme Court. To the latter course solid objections were thought to apply, which rendered it ineligible and unsatisfactory. In the first place, the judges of the state courts would be wholly irresponsible to the national government for their conduct in the administration of national justice; so, that the national government would, or might be, wholly dependent upon the good will, or sound discretion of the states, in regard to the efficiency, promptitude, and ability, with which the judicial authority of the nation was administered. In the next place, the prevalency of a local, or sectional spirit might be found to disqualify the state tribunals for a suitable discharge of national judicial functions; and the very modes of appointment of some of the state judges might render them improper channels of the judicial authority of the Union. State judges, holding their offices during pleasure, or from year to year, or for other short periods, would, or at least might, be too little independent to be relied upon for an inflexible execution of the national laws. What could be done, where the state itself should happen to be in hostility to the national government, as might well be presumed occasionally to be the case, from local interests, party spirit, or peculiar prejudices, if the state tribunals were to be the sole depositaries of the judicial powers of the Union, in the ordinary administration of criminal, as well as of civil justice? Besides; if the state tribunals were thus entrusted with the ordinary administration of the criminal and civil justice of the Union, there would be a necessity for leaving the door of appeal as widely open, as possible. In proportion to the grounds of confidence in, or distrust of the subordinate tribunals, ought to be the facility or difficulty of appeals. An unrestrained course of appeals would be a source of much private, as well as public inconvenience. It would encourage litigation, and lead to the most oppressive expenses. Nor should it be omitted, that this very course of appeals would naturally lead to great jealousies, irritations, and collisions between the state courts and the Supreme Court, not only from differences of opinions, but from that pride of character, and consciousness of independence, which would be felt by state judges, possessing the confidence of their own state, and irresponsible to the Union.

§ 1584. In considering the first clause of the third section, declaring, that "the judicial power of the United States shall be vested in one Supreme Court, and in such inferior courts, as the congress may from time to time ordain and establish," we are naturally led to the inquiry, whether congress possess any discretion, as to the creation of a Supreme Court and inferior courts, in whom the constitutional jurisdiction is to be vested. This was at one time matter of much discussion; and is vital to the existence of the judicial department. If congress possess any discretion on this subject, it is obvious, that the judiciary, as a co-ordinate department of the government, may, at the will of congress, be annihilated, or stripped of all its important jurisdiction; for, if the discretion exists, no one can say in what manner, or at what time, or under what circumstances it may, or ought to be exercised. The whole argument, upon which such an interpretation has been attempted to be maintained, is, that the language of the constitution, "shall be vested," is not imperative, but simply indicates the future tense. This interpretation has been overruled by the Supreme Court, upon solemn deliberation.

. . . . .

§ 1591. The constitution has wisely established, that there shall be one Supreme Court, with a view to uniformity of decision in all cases whatsoever, belonging to the judicial department, whether they arise at the common law or in equity, or within the admiralty and prize jurisdiction; whether they respect the doctrines of mere municipal law, or constitutional law, or the law of nations. It is obvious, that, if there were independent supreme courts of common law, of equity, and of admiralty, a diversity of judgment might, and almost necessarily would spring up, not only, as to the limits of the jurisdiction of each tribunal; but as to the fundamental doctrines of municipal, constitutional, and public law. The effect of this diversity would be, that a different rule would, or might be promulgated on the most interesting subjects by the several tribunals; and thus the citizens be involved in endless doubts, not only as to their private rights, but as to their public duties. The constitution itself would or might speak a different language according to the tribunal, which was called upon to interpret it; and thus interminable disputes embarrass the administration of justice throughout the whole country. But the same reason did not apply to the inferior tribunals. These were, therefore, left entirely to the discretion of congress, as to their number, their jurisdiction, and their powers. Experience might, and probably would, show good grounds for varying and modifying them from time to time. It would not only have been unwise, but exceedingly inconvenient, to have fixed the arrangement of these courts in the constitution itself; since congress would have been disabled thereby from adapting them from time to time to the exigencies of the country. But, whatever may be the extent, to which the power of congress reaches,

as to the establishment of inferior tribunals, it is clear from what has been already stated, that all the jurisdiction contemplated by the constitution must be vested in some of its courts, either in an original, or an appellate form.

. . . . .

§ 1593. The mode of appointment of the judges has necessarily come under review, in the examination of the structure and powers of the executive department. The president is expressly authorized, by and with the consent of the senate, to appoint the judges of the Supreme Court. The appointment of the judges of the inferior courts, is not expressly provided for; but has either been left to the discretion of congress, or silently belongs to the president, under the clause of the constitution authorizing him to appoint "all other officers of the United States, whose appointments are not herein otherwise provided for." In the convention, a proposition at first prevailed, for the appointment of the judges of the Supreme Court by the senate, by a decided majority. At a later period, however, upon the report of a committee, the appointment of the judges of the Supreme Court, was given to the president, subject to the advice and consent of the senate, by a unanimous vote. The reasons for the change, were doubtless the same as those, which led to the vesting of other high appointments in the executive department.

. . . . .

§ 1601. These remarks will derive additional strength and confirmation, from a nearer survey of the judicial branch of foreign governments, as well as of the several states composing the Union. In England, the king is considered, as the fountain of justice; not indeed as the author, but as the distributer of it; and he possesses the exclusive prerogative of erecting courts of judicature, and appointing the judges. Indeed, in early times, the kings of England often in person heard and decided causes between party and party. But as the constitution of government became more settled, the whole judicial power was delegated to the judges of the several courts of justice; and any attempt, on the part of the king, now to exercise it in person, would be deemed an usurpation. Anciently, the English judges held their offices according to the tenure of their commissions, as prescribed by the crown, which was generally during the pleasure of the crown, as is the tenure of office of the Lord Chancellor, the judges of the courts of admiralty, and others, down to the present day. In the time of Lord Coke, the Barons of the Exchequer held their offices during good behaviour, while the judges of the other courts of common law held them only during pleasure. And it has been said, that, at the time of the restoration of Charles the Second, the commissions of the judges were during good behaviour. Still, however, it was at the pleasure of the crown, to prescribe what tenure of office it might choose, until after the revolution of 1688; and there can be no doubt, that a monarch so profligate as Charles the Second, would avail himself of the prerogative, as often as it suited his political, or other objects.

§ 1602. It is certain, that this power of the crown must have produced an influence upon the administration, dangerous to private rights, and subversive of the public liberties of the subjects. In political accusations, in an especial manner, it must often have produced the most disgraceful compliances with the wishes of the crown; and the most humiliating surrenders of the rights of the accused. The Statute of 13 Will. 3, ch. 2, provided, that the commissions of the judges of the courts of common law should not be as formerly *durante bene placito*, but should be *quam diu bene se gesserint*, and their salaries be ascertained, and established. They were made removeable, however, by the king, upon the address of both houses of parliament; and their offices expired by the demise of the king. Afterwards by a statute enacted in the reign of George the Third, at the earnest recommendation of the king, a noble improvement was made in the law, by which the judges are to hold their offices during good behaviour, notwithstanding any demise of the crown; and their full salaries are secured to them, during the continuance of their commissions. Upon that occasion, the monarch made a declaration, worthy of perpetual remembrance, that "he looked upon the independence and uprightness of the judges, as essential to the impartial administration of justice; as one of the best securities of the rights and liberties of his subjects; and as most conducive to the honour of the crown." Indeed, since the independence of the judges has been secured by this permanent duration of office, the administration of justice has, with a single exception, flowed on in England, with an uninterrupted, and pure, and unstained current. It is due to the enlightened tribunals of that nation to declare, that their learning, integrity, and impartiality, have commanded the reverence and respect, as well of America, as Europe. The judges of the old parliaments of France (the judicial tribunals of that country) were, before the revolution, appointed by the crown; but they held their offices for life; and this tenure of office gave them substantial independence. Appointed by the monarch, they were considered as nearly out of his power. The most determined exertions of that authority against them only showed their radical independence. They composed permanent bodies politic, constituted to resist arbitrary innovation; and from that corporate constitution, and from most of their powers they were well calculated to afford both certainty and stability to the laws. They had been a safe asylum to secure their laws, in all the revolutions of human opinion. They had saved that sacred deposit of the country during the reigns of arbitrary princes, and the struggles of arbitrary factions. They kept alive the memory and record of the constitution. They were the great security to private property, which might be said (when personal liberty had no existence,) to be as well guarded in France, as in any other country.

§ 1603. The importance of a permanent tenure of office, to secure the independence, integrity, and impartiality of judges, was early understood in France. Louis the Eleventh, in 1467, made a memorable declaration, that the judges ought not to be deposed, or deprived of their offices, but for a forfeiture previously adjudged, and judicially declared by a competent tribunal. The same declaration was often confirmed by his successors; and after the first excesses of the French revolution were passed, the same principle obtained a public sanction. And it has now become incorporated, as a fundamental principle, into the present charter of France, that the judges appointed by the crown shall be irremoveable. Other European nations have followed the same example; and it is highly probable, that as the principles of free governments prevail, the necessity of thus establishing the independence of the judiciary will be generally felt, and firmly provided for.

§ 1604. It has sometimes been suggested, that, though in monarchial governments the independence of the judiciary is essential, to guard the rights of the subjects from the injustice and oppression of the crown; yet that the same reasons do not apply to a republic, where the popular will is sufficiently known, and ought always to be obeyed. A little consideration of the subject will satisfy us, that, so far from this being true, the reasons in favour of the independence of the judiciary apply with augmented force to republics; and especially to such as possess a written constitution with defined powers, and limited rights.

§ 1605. In the first place, factions and parties are quite as common, and quite as violent in republics, as in monarchies; and the same safeguards are as indispensable in the one, as in the other, against the encroachments of party spirit, and the tyranny of factions. Laws, however wholesome or necessary, are frequently the objects of temporary aversion, and popular odium, and sometimes of popular resistance. Nothing is more facile in republics, than for demagogues, under artful pretences, to stir up combinations against the regular exercise of authority. Their selfish purposes are too often interrupted by the firmness and independence of upright magistrates, not to make them at all times hostile to a power, which rebukes, and an impartiality, which condemns them. The judiciary, as the weakest point in the constitution, on which to make an attack, is therefore, constantly that, to which they direct their assaults; and a triumph here, aided by any momentary popular encouragement, achieves a lasting victory over the constitution itself. Hence, in republics, those, who are to profit by public commotions, or the prevalence of faction, are always the enemies of a regular and independent administration of justice. They spread all sorts of delusion, in order to mislead the public mind, and excite the public prejudices. They know full well, that, without the aid of the people, their schemes must prove abortive; and they, therefore, employ every art to undermine the public confidence, and to make the people the instruments of subverting their own rights and liberties.

§ 1606. It is obvious, that, under such circumstances, if the tenure of office of the judges is not permanent, they will soon be rendered odious, not because they do wrong; but because they refuse to do wrong; and they will be made to give way to others, who shall become more pliant tools of the leading demagogues of the day. There can be no security for the minority in a free government, except through the judicial department. In a monarchy, the sympathies of the people are naturally enlisted against the meditated oppressions of their ruler; and they screen his victims from his vengeance. His is the cause of one against the community. But, in free governments, where the majority, who obtain power for the moment, are supposed to represent the will of the people, persecution, especially of a political nature, becomes the cause of the community against one. It is the more violent and unrelenting, because it is deemed indispensable to attain power, or to enjoy the fruits of victory. In free governments, therefore, the independence of the judiciary becomes far more important to the security of the rights of the citizens, than in a monarchy; since it is the only barrier against the oppressions of a dominant faction, armed for the moment with power, and abusing the influence, acquired under accidental excitements, to overthrow the institutions and liberties, which have been the deliberate choice of the people.

§ 1607. In the next place, the independence of the judiciary is indispensable to secure the people against the intentional, as well as unintentional, usurpations of the executive and legislative departments. It has been observed with great sagacity, that power is perpetually stealing from the many to the few; and the tendency of the legislative department to absorb all the other powers of the government has always been dwelt upon by statesmen and patriots, as a general truth, confirmed by all human experience. If the judges are appointed at short intervals, either by the legislative, or the executive department, they will naturally, and, indeed, almost necessarily, become mere dependents upon the appointing power. If they have any desire to obtain, or to hold office, they will at all times evince a desire to follow, and obey the will of the predominant power in the state. Justice will be administered with a faultering and feeble hand. It will secure nothing, but its own place, and the approbation of those, who value, because they control it. It will decree, what best suits the opinions of the day; and it will forget, that the precepts of the law rest on eternal foundations. The rulers and the citizens will not stand upon an equal ground in litigations. The favourites of the day will overawe by their power, or seduce by their influence; and thus, the fundamental maxim of a republic, that it is a government of laws, and not of men, will be silently disproved, or openly abandoned.

§ 1608. In the next place, these considerations acquire (as has been already seen) still more cogency and force, when applied to questions of constitutional law. In monarchies, the only practical resistance, which the judiciary can present, is to the usurpations of a single department of the government, unaided, and acting for itself. But, if the executive and legislative departments are combined in any course of measures, obedience to their will becomes a duty, as well as a necessity. Thus, even in the free government of Great Britain, an act of parliament, combining, as it does, the will of the crown, and of the legislature, is absolute and omnipotent. It cannot be lawfully resisted, or disobeyed. The judiciary is bound to carry it into effect at every hazard, even though it should subvert private rights and public liberty. But it is far otherwise in a republic, like our own, with a limited constitution, prescribing at once the powers of the rulers, and the rights of the citizens. This very circumstance would seem conclusively to show, that the independence of the judiciary is absolutely indispensable to preserve the balance of such a constitution. In no other way can there be any practical restraint upon the acts of the government, or any practical enforcement of the rights of the citizens. This subject has been already examined very much at large, and needs only to be touched in this place. No man can deny the necessity of a judiciary to interpret the constitution and laws, and to preserve the citizens against oppression and usurpation in civil and criminal prosecutions. Does it not follow, that, to enable the judiciary to fulfil its functions, it is indispensable, that the judges should not hold their offices at the mere pleasure of those, whose acts they are to check, and, if need be, to declare void? Can it be supposed for a moment, that men holding their offices for the short period of two, or four, or even six years, will be generally found firm enough to resist the will of those, who appoint them, and may remove them?

§ 1609. The argument of those, who contend for a short period of office of the judges, is founded upon the necessity of a conformity to the will of the people. But the argument proceeds upon a fallacy, in supposing, that the will of the rulers, and the will of the people are the same. Now, they not only may be, but often actually are, in direct variance to each other. No man in a republican government can doubt, that the will of the people is, and ought to be, supreme. But it is the deliberate will of the people, evinced by their solemn acts, and not the momentary ebullitions of those, who act for the majority, for a day, or a month, or a year. The constitution is the will, the deliberate will, of the people. They have declared under what circumstances, and in what manner it shall be amended, and altered; and until a change is effected in the manner prescribed, it is declared, that it shall be the supreme law of the land, to which all persons, rulers, as well as citizens, must bow in obedience. When it is constitutionally altered, then and not until then, are the judges at liberty to disregard its original injunctions. When, therefore, the argument is pressed, that the judges ought to be subject to the will of the people, no one doubts the propriety of the doctrine in its true and legitimate sense.

§ 1610. But those, who press the argument, use it in a far broader sense. In their view, the will of the people, as exhibited in the choice of the rulers, is to be followed. If the rulers interpret the constitution differently from the judges, the former are to be obeyed, because they represent the opinions of the people; and therefore, the judges ought to be removable, or appointed for a short period, so as to become subject to the will of the people, as expressed by and through their rulers. But, is it not at once seen, that this is in fact subverting the constitution? Would it not make the constitution an instrument of flexible and changeable interpretation, and not a settled form of government with fixed limitations? Would it not become, instead of a supreme law for ourselves and our posterity, a mere oracle of the powers of the rulers of the day, to which implicit homage is to be paid, and speaking at different times the most opposite commands, and in the most ambiguous voices? In short, is not this an attempt to erect, behind the constitution, a power unknown, and unprovided for by the constitution, and greater than itself? What become of the limitations of the constitution, if the will of the people, thus inofficially promulgated, forms, for the time being, the supreme law, and the supreme exposition of the law? If the constitution defines the powers of the government, and points out the mode of changing them; and yet, the instrument is to expand in the hands of one set of rulers, and to contract in those of another, where is the standard? If the will of the people is to govern in the construction of the powers of the constitution, and that will is to be gathered at every successive election at the polls, and not from their deliberate judgment, and solemn acts in ratifying the constitution, or in amending it, what certainty can there be in those powers? If the constitution is to be expounded, not by its written text, but by the opinions of the rulers for the time being, whose opinions are to prevail, the first, or the last? When, therefore, it is said, that the judges ought to be subjected to the will of the people, and to conform to their interpretation of the constitution, the practical meaning must be, that they should be subjected to the control of the representatives of the people in the executive and legislative departments, and should interpret the constitution, as the latter may, from time to time, deem correct.

§ 1611. But it is obvious, that elections can rarely, if ever, furnish any sufficient proofs, what is deliberately the will of the people, as to any constitutional or legal doctrines. Representatives and rulers must be ordinarily chosen for very different purposes; and, in many instances, their opinions upon constitutional questions must be unknown to their constituents. The only means known to the constitution, by which to ascertain the will of the people upon a constitutional question, is in the shape of an affirmative or negative proposition by way of amendment, offered for their adoption in the mode prescribed by the constitution. The elections in one year may bring one party into power; and in the next year their opponents, embracing opposite doctrines, may succeed; and so alternate success and defeat may perpetually recur in the same districts, and in the same, or different states.

§ 1612. Surely it will not be pretended, that any constitution, adapted to the American people, could ever contemplate the executive and legislative departments of the government, as the ultimate depositaries of the power to interpret the constitution; or as the ultimate representatives of the will of the people, to change it at pleasure. If, then, the judges were appointed for two, or four, or six years, instead of during good behaviour, the only security, which the people would have for a due administration of public justice, and a firm support of the constitution, would be, that being dependent upon the executive for their appointment during their brief period of office, they might, and would represent more fully, for the time being, the constitutional opinion of each successive executive; and thus carry into effect his system of government. Would this be more wise, or more safe, more for the permanence of the constitution, or the preservation of the liberties of the people, than the present system? Would the judiciary, then, be, in fact, an independent co-ordinate department? Would it protect the people against an ambitious or corrupt executive; or restrain the legislature from acts of unconstitutional authority?

§ 1613. The truth is, that, even with the most secure tenure of office, during good behaviour, the danger is not, that the judges will be too firm in resisting public opinion, and in defence of private rights or public liberties; but, that they will be too ready to yield themselves to the passions, and politics, and prejudices of the day. In a monarchy, the judges, in the performance of their duties with uprightness and impartiality, will always have the support of some of the departments of the government, or at least of the people. In republics, they may sometimes find the other departments combined in hostility against the judicial; and even the people, for a while, under the influence of party spirit and turbulent factions, ready to abandon them to their fate. Few men possess the firmness to resist the torrent of popular opinion; or are content to sacrifice present ease and public favour, in order to earn the slow rewards of a conscientious discharge of duty; the sure, but distant, gratitude of the people; and the severe, but enlightened, award of posterity.

§ 1614. If passing from general reasoning, an appeal is made to the lessons of experience, there is every thing to convince us, that the judicial department is safe to a republic, with the tenure of office during good behaviour; and that justice will ordinarily be best administered, where there is most independence. Of the state constitutions, five only out of twenty-four have provided for any other tenure of office, than during good behaviour; and those adopted by the new states admitted into the Union, since the formation of the national government, have, with two or three exceptions only, embraced the same permanent tenure of office. No one can hesitate to declare, that in the states, where the judges hold their offices during good behaviour, justice is administered with wisdom, moderation, and firmness; and that the public confidence has reposed upon the judicial department, in the most critical times, with unabated respect. If the same can be said in regard to other states, where the judges enjoy a less permanent tenure of office, it will not answer the reasoning, unless it can also be shown, that the judges have never been removed for political causes, wholly distinct from their own merit; and yet have often deliberately placed themselves in opposition to the popular opinion.

§ 1615. The considerations above stated lead to the conclusion, that in republics there are, in reality, stronger reasons for an independent tenure of office by the judges, a tenure during good behaviour, than in a monarchy. Indeed, a republic with a limited constitution, and yet without a judiciary sufficiently independent to check usurpation, to protect public liberty, and to enforce private rights, would be as visionary and absurd, as a society organized without any restraints of law. It would become a democracy with unlimited powers, exercising through its rulers a universal despotic sovereignty. The very theory of a balanced republic of restricted powers presupposes some organized means to control, and resist, any excesses of authority. The people may, if they please, submit all power to their rulers for the time being; but, then, the government should receive its true appellation and character. It would be a government of tyrants, elective, it is true, but still tyrants; and it would become the more fierce, vindictive, and sanguinary, because it would perpetually generate factions in its own bosom, who could succeed only by the ruin of their enemies. It would be alternately characterized, as a reign of terror, and a reign of imbecillity. It would be as corrupt, as it would be dangerous. It would form another model of that profligate and bloody democracy, which, at one time, in the French revolution, darkened by its deeds the fortunes of France, and left to mankind the appalling lesson, that virtue, and religion, genius, and learning, the authority of wisdom, and the appeals of innocence, are unheard and unfelt in the frenzy of popular excitement; and, that the worst crimes may be sanctioned, and the most desolating principles inculcated, under the banners, and in the name of liberty. In human governments, there are but two controlling powers; the power of arms, and the power of laws. If the latter are not enforced by a judiciary above all fear, and above all reproach, the former must prevail; and thus lead to the triumph of military over civil institutions. The framers of the constitution, with profound wisdom, laid the corner stone of our national republic in the permanent independence of the judicial establishment. Upon this point their vote was unanimous. They adopted the results of an enlightened experience. They were not seduced by the dreams of human perfection into the belief, that all power might be safely left to the unchecked operation of the private ambition, or personal virtue of rulers. Nor, on the other hand, were they so lost to a just estimate of human concerns, as not to feel, that confidence must be reposed somewhere; if either efficiency, or safety are to be consulted in the plan of government. Having provided amply for the legislative and executive authorities, they established a balance-wheel, which, by its independent structure, should adjust the irregularities, and check the excesses of the occasional movements of the system.

§ 1616. In the convention a proposition was offered to make the judges removeable by the president, upon the application of the senate and house of representatives; but it received the support of a single state only.

§ 1617. This proposition doubtless owed its origin to the clause in the act of parliament, (13 Will. 3 ch. 2,) making it lawful for the king to remove the judges on the address of both houses of parliament, notwithstanding the tenure of their offices during good behaviour, established by the same act. But a moment's reflection will teach us, that there is no just analogy in the cases. The object of the act of parliament was to secure the judges from removal at the mere pleasure of the crown; but not to render them independent of the action of parliament. By the theory of the British constitution, every act of parliament is supreme and omnipotent. It may change the succession to the crown; and even the very fundamentals of the constitution. It would have been absurd, therefore, to have exempted the judges alone from the general jurisdiction of this supreme authority in the realm. The clause was not introduced into the act, for the purpose of conferring the power on parliament, for it could not be taken away, or restricted; but simply to recognize it, as a qualification of the tenure of office; so that the judges should have no right to complain of any breach of an implied contract with them, and the crown should not be deprived of the means to remove an unfit judge, whenever parliament should in their discretion signify their assent. Besides; in England the judges are not, and cannot be, called upon to decide any constitutional questions; and therefore there was no necessity to place them, and indeed there would have been an impropriety in placing them, even if it had been possible, (which it clearly was not) in a situation, in which they would not have been under the control of parliament.

§ 1618. Far different is the situation of the people of the United States. They have chosen to establish a constitution of government, with limited powers and prerogatives, over which neither the executive, nor the legislature, have any power, either of alteration or control. It is to all the departments equally a supreme, fundamental, unchangeable law, which all must obey, and none are at liberty to disregard. The main security, relied on to check any irregular, or unconstitutional measure, either of the executive, or the legislative department, was (as we have seen) the judiciary. To have made the judges, therefore, removable, at the pleasure of the president and congress, would have been a virtual surrender to them of the custody and appointment of the guardians of the constitution. It would have been placing the keys of the citadel in the possession of those, against whose assaults the people were most strenuously endeavouring to guard themselves. It would be holding out a temptation to the president and congress, whenever they were resisted in any of their measures, to secure a perfect irresponsibility by removing those judges from office, who should dare to oppose their will. In short, in every violent political commotion or change, the judges would be removed from office, exactly as the lord chancellor in England now is, in order, that a perfect harmony might be established between the operations of all the departments of government. Such a power would have been a signal proof of a solicitude to erect defences round the constitution, for the sole purpose of surrendering them into the possession of those, whose acts they were intended to guard against. Under such circumstances, it might well have been asked, where could resort be had to redress grievances, or to overthrow usurpations? *Quis custodiet custodes?*

§ 1619. A proposition of a more imposing nature was to authorize a removal of judges for inability to discharge the duties of their offices. But all considerate persons will readily perceive, that such a provision would either not be practised upon, or would be more liable to abuse, than calculated to answer any good purpose. The mensuration of the faculties of the mind has no place in the catalogue of any known art or science. An attempt to fix the boundary between the region of ability and inability would much oftener give rise to personal, or party attachments and hostilities, than advance the interests of justice, or the public good. And instances of absolute imbecility would be too rare to justify the introduction of so dangerous a provision.

§ 1620. In order to avoid investigations of this sort, which must for ever be vague and unsatisfactory, some persons have been disposed to think, that a limitation of age should be assumed as a criterion of inability; so that there should be a constitutional removal from office, when the judge should attain a certain age. Some of the state constitutions have adopted such a limitation. Thus, in New-York, sixty years of age is a disqualification for the office of judge; and in some other states the period is prolonged to seventy. The value of these provisions has never, as yet, been satisfactorily established by the experience of any state. That they have worked mischievously in some cases is matter of public notoriety. . . .

§ 1621. It is observable, that the constitution has declared, that the judges of the inferior courts, as well as of the Supreme Court, of the United States, shall hold their offices during good behaviour. In this respect there is a marked contrast between the English government and our own. In England the tenure is exclusively confined to the judges of the superior courts, and does not (as we have already seen) even embrace all of these. In fact, a great portion of all the civil and criminal business of the whole kingdom is performed by persons delegated, *pro hac vice*, for this purpose under commissions issued periodically for a single circuit. It is true, that it is, and for a long period has been, ordinarily administered by the judges of the courts of King's Bench, Common Pleas, and Exchequer; but it is not so merely *virtute officii*, but under special commissions investing them from time to time with this authority in conjunction with other persons named in the commission. Such are the commissions of oyer and terminer, of assize, of gaol delivery, and of *nisi prius*, under which all civil and criminal trials of matters of fact are had at the circuits, and in the metropolis. By the constitution of the United States all criminal and civil jurisdiction must be exclusively confided to judges holding their office during good behaviour; and though congress may from time to time distribute the jurisdiction among such inferior courts, as it may create from time to time, and withdraw it at their pleasure, it is not competent for them to confer it upon temporary judges, or to confide it by special commission. Even if the English system be well adapted to the wants of the nation, and secure a wise and beneficent administration of justice in the realm, as it doubtless does; still it is obvious, that, in our popular government, it would be quite too great a power, to trust the whole administration of civil and criminal justice to commissioners, appointed at the pleasure of the president. To the constitution of the United States, and to those, who enjoy its advantages, no judges are known, but such, as hold their offices during good behaviour.

. . . . .

§ 1627. It would be a matter of general congratulation, if this language had been completely borne out by the perusal of our juridical annals. But, unfortunately, a measure was adopted in 1802 under the auspices of president Jefferson, which, if its constitutionality can be successfully vindicated, prostrates in the dust the independence of all inferior judges, both as to the tenure of their office, and their compensation for services, and leaves the constitution a miserable and vain delusion. In the year 1801, congress passed an act reorganizing the judiciary, and authorizing the appointment of sixteen new judges, with suitable salaries, to hold the circuit courts of the United States, in the different circuits created by the act. Under this act the circuit judges received their appointments, and performed the duties of their offices, until the year 1802, when the courts, established by the act, were abolished by a general repeal of it by congress, without in the slightest manner providing for the payment of the salaries of the judges, or for any continuation of their offices. The result of this act, therefore, is (so far as it is a precedent,) that, notwithstanding the constitutional tenure of office of the judges of the inferior courts is during good behaviour, congress may, at any time, by a mere act of legislation, deprive them of their offices at pleasure, and with it take away their whole title to their salaries. How this can be reconciled with the terms, or the intent of the constitution, is more, than any ingenuity of argument has ever, as yet, been able to demonstrate. The system fell, because it was unpopular with those, who were then in possession of power; and the victims have hitherto remained without any indemnity from the justice of the government.

. . . . .

§ 1629. It is almost unnecessary to add, that, although the constitution has, with so sedulous a care, endeavoured to guard the judicial department from the overwhelming influence or power of the other co-ordinate departments of the government, it has not conferred upon them any inviolability, or irresponsibility for an abuse of their authority. On the contrary for any corrupt violation or omission of the high trusts confided to the judges, they are liable to be impeached, (as we have already seen,) and upon conviction removed from office. Thus, on the one hand, a pure and independent administration of public justice is amply provided for; and, on the other hand, an urgent responsibility secured for fidelity to the people.

§ 1630. The judges of the inferior courts, spoken of in the constitution, do not include the judges of courts appointed in the territories of the United States under the authority, given to congress, to regulate the territories of the United States. The courts of the territories are not constitutional courts, in which the judicial power conferred by the constitution on the general government, can be deposited. They are legislative courts, created in virtue of the general sovereignty, which exists in the national government over its territories. The jurisdiction, with which they are invested, is not a part of the judicial power, which is defined in the third article of the constitution; but arises from the same general sovereignty. In legislating for them, congress exercises the combined powers of the general, and of a state government. Congress may, therefore, rightfully limit the tenure of office of the judges of the territorial courts, as well as their jurisdiction; and it has been accordingly limited to a short period of years.

39

EX PARTE POULSON
19 Fed. Cas. 1205, no. 11,350 (C.C.E.D.Pa. 1835)

BALDWIN, Circuit Justice (delivering the opinion of the court). The following are the circumstances under which this motion is made: This action was brought to the last October term of this court, and, being regularly at issue, was ordered for trial on the 11th inst., when a jury was sworn, and the trial proceeded. It was resumed on the 12th, when Mr. Ingersoll, counsel for the plaintiff, stated that he had a motion to submit to the court in relation to a publication which had appeared in Poulson's American Daily Advertiser of that morning. Hugh Grimes, being sworn, deposed that he had purchased at the office of Mr. Poulson a paper, produced and identified, containing the offensive publication, taken from a newspaper published at Bangor, in the state of Maine.

From the evidence given on the trial of the cause thus far it is clear that the publication refers directly to the plaintiff, and the cause of action which he has submitted to the court and jury, and in a manner calculated to produce the worst effect upon the administration of justice, as well by the character of the paper in which it appears as the nature of the remarks upon the plaintiff, his cause now trying, and the witnesses who appear in his behalf.

In the present stage of the cause, it would be improper for the court to express any opinion as to the truth or falsehood of the matter contained in the publication. That must be reserved till all the evidence is heard and commented on by counsel, when it will be ascertained what are the facts of the case. These considerations can have no bearing upon the present application against a person who is no party to the suit, and cannot be the subject of comment without running the risk of prejudging the rights of the contending parties. It is, however, not only a duty to them, but to the public, to express the strongest disapprobation of any outdoor interference with the administration of justice. Be it in whatever mode it may, it cannot fail to embarrass or obstruct if not defeat, the regular course of judicial proceedings.

The supreme law of the land has secured to every man a right of appealing to the law for the redress of an injury of which he complains; has appointed tribunals to hear and determine upon their justice, and prescribe the modes of proceeding according to established rules of evidence and principles of law. The laws will have been enacted in vain, courts of justice will become useless, and suitors be deprived of the benefits of resorting to them for redress, if it shall be their common fate to be obliged to encounter the effect of publications of a description now before us on the merits of their cause. It is headed, "Drew, the Counterfeiter." "This notorious fellow" "has had the effrontery to bring a suit," &c., and the language of the article is of a consistent character throughout. It cannot be

too much reprobated, or the evil example too much feared, when it is suffered to appear in a paper highly respectable, conducted by a most estimable member of society. Nor can any friend to the due administration of the law and justice to the suitors in its courts look on the prevalence of such a practice without the deepest regret. Every good citizen should make the case his own, by supposing himself a plaintiff in a suit on trial by a jury, many, if not all, of whom have read a similar allusion to himself and case. He could appreciate the consequences, and decide whether it was such an interference with the cause of justice as to require the interposition of the law for its prevention and punishment. What has been the fate of Mr. Drew may be the fate of all other suitors. Causes on trial in court may be simultaneously tried in the public papers; the one conducted by established rules, evidence received only on oath, and the law applied by a responsible tribunal, the jury bound to listen in court only to the evidence, the counsel, and the law; but out of court, at liberty to hear and read statements, respecting the case, made without regard to either. It would be but one short step more to take, and the jury would be tampered with at pleasure when not in the box, and be liable to be assailed by any person who might please to attempt to benefit or prejudice a suitor. The moral offence, or the pernicious effects, would be but little aggravated if done in open court, or when the jury are deliberating on their verdict. Let it be done there, or in the public papers, it is a violation of the legal and constitutional rights of those who appeal to the law for redress.

From its nature, it is necessary that the means of prevention should be prompt and summary, or the mischief will become consummated by delaying a remedy which must be sought in the usual forms of law. That which is now asked is of this description, and the injury complained of is the most aggravated kind, though the cause of the republication be inadvertence or the unconsciousness of its impropriety. That is no matter of consideration in the present stage of this motion. The first inquiry is into the jurisdiction of this court to issue an attachment for contempt for a publication relating to a suit on trial, or in any way pending before it.

On March 2, 1831 [4 Stat. 487], congress passed "An act declaratory of the law concerning contempt of court," the first section of which enacts: "That the power of the several courts of the United States, to issue attachments, and inflict summary punishment, for contempt of court, shall not be construed to extend to any cases except misbehaviour of any person or persons in the presence of the said courts, or so near thereto as to obstruct the administration of justice, the misbehaviour of any of the officers of the said courts in their official transactions, and the disobedience or resistance by any officer of the said courts, party, juror, witness, or any other person or persons, to any lawful writ, process, order, rule, decree, or command of the said courts." Pamph. Laws 1831, c. 99. The history of this act, the time of its passage, its title and provisions must be considered together, in order to ascertain its meaning and true construction. It was enacted shortly after the acquittal of Judge Peck, of Missouri, on an impeachment preferred against him for issuing an attachment against a member of the bar for making a publication in relation to a suit which had been decided by that judge. On the trial the law of contempt was elaborately examined by the learned managers of the house of representatives and the counsel for the judge. It was not controverted that all courts had power to attach any person who should make a publication concerning a cause during its pendency, and all admitted its illegality when done while the cause was actually on trial. It had too often been exercised to entertain the slightest doubt that the courts had power, both by the common law and the express terms of the judiciary act, § 17 [1 Stat. 83], as declared by the supreme court, to protect their suitors by the process of attachment.

With this distinct knowledge and recognition of the existing law, it cannot be doubted, that the whole subject was within the view of the legislature; nor that they acted most advisedly on the law of contempt, intending to define in what cases the summary power of the courts should be exercised, and to confine it to the specified cases. From the title and phraseology of the act it would seem to have been their intention to declare that it never existed in any other cases than those enumerated. It is "a declaratory act," which is a declaration of what the law "was, is, and shall be hereafter taken" when put into the form usual in statutes, which operate to settle the law retrospectively. These words are not in this law, but there is an expression which is tantamount,—"the power of the several courts, &c., shall not be construed to extend," &c.,—which refers to the past, the present, and the future, as a proviso or limitation to powers of the courts, from whatever source derived, repudiating their summary action as effectually as if they had never been authorized. As this is an inferior court within the provision of the constitution, it is created by the laws, with such powers only as congress has deemed it proper to confer, among which is this: "And to punish by fine or imprisonment, at the discretion of said courts, all contempts of authority in any cause, or hearing before the same." Act 1789 (1 [Story's Laws] 63; [1 Stat. 88.]) The acts of 1831, must be taken to be the declared construction of this and all other laws limiting its operation in the manner prescribed, and, as generally considered, congress is to this court what the constitution is to the supreme court. Their acts must be construed on the same principles, and operate as constitutional amendments, which is to give such construction to the original act as if the jurisdiction had never been given.

The third article of the constitution extends the judicial power to controversies between a state and citizens of other states, a state and foreign states, citizens or subjects. Suits of this description were brought and sustained till the adoption of the eleventh amendment, which declared, that "the judicial powers of the United States shall not be construed to extend" to such cases. This was held by the supreme court to have retrospective effect, annulling all jurisdiction over such cases past, present, and future. [Bingham v. Cabot] 3 Dall. [3 U. S.] 382; [Cohens v. Virginia] 6 Wheat. [19 U. S.] 405, 408; [Osborn v. Bank of U. S.] 9 Wheat. [22 U. S.] 850, 858. The same effect must be given to this act, so as to make it what it evidently in-

tended to be, a prohibition of the exercise of summary jurisdiction over contempts, excepting only such cases as are defined. In its prospective operation its terms are peremptory, admitting of no construction which can bring the present application within the exception without doing violence to its plain meaning.

There can be no doubt of the constitutional power of congress to act upon this subject, as far as respects our courts. It is no invasion of the rights of a suitor to bring or defend a suit, or in any way affect its legal remedy, in the ordinary course of justice. It is in the discretion of the legislative power to confer upon courts a summary jurisdiction to protect their suitors or itself by summary process, or to deny it. It has been thought proper to do the latter, in language too plain to doubt of the meaning of the law, or, if it could be doubted by an ordinary rule of construction, the occasion and circumstances of its enactment would most effectually remove them. It would ill become any court of the United States to make a struggle to retain any summary power, the exercise of which is manifestly contrary to the declared will of the legislative power. It is not like a case where the right of property or personal liberty is intended to be affected by a law, which the court would construe very strictly to save a right granted or secured by any former law. Neither is it proper to arraign the wisdom or justice of a law to which a court is bound to submit, nor to make an effort to move in relation to a matter when there is an insuperable bar to any efficient action.

The law prohibits the issuing of an attachment, except in certain cases, of which the present is not one. It would therefore be not only utterly useless, but place the court in a position beneath contempt, to grant a rule to show cause why an attachment should not issue, when an exhibition of the act of 1831 would show most conclusive cause. The court is disarmed in relation to the press; it can neither protect itself, or its suitors; libels may be published upon either without stint; the merits of a cause depending for trial or judgment may be discussed at pleasure; anything may be said to jurors through the press, the most wilful misrepresentations made of judicial proceedings, and any improper mode of influencing the decisions of causes by out of door influence practiced with impunity. The second section of the same law provided "That if any person or persons shall corruptly, or by threats, or force, endeavor to influence, intimidate or impede any juror, witness or officer in any court of the United States, in the discharge of his duty, or shall corruptly, or by threat, or force, obstruct or impede, or endeavor to obstruct or impede, the due administration of justice therein, every person or persons so offending shall be liable to prosecution therefor, by indictment," &c. This provision is in further confirmation of the view taken of the first section. It is a clear indication of the meaning of the law, that the misbehavior which may still be punished in a summary manner does not refer to those acts which subject a party to an indictment. To construe it otherwise would be to authorize accumulative punishment for the same offence. Taking the two sections in connection, the law admits of only one construction. The first alludes to that kind of misbehavior which is calculated to disturb the order of the court, such as noise, tumultuous or disorderly behavior, either in or so near to it as to prevent its proceeding in the orderly dispatch of its business; not to any attempt to influence, intimidate, or impede a juror, witness, or officer in the discharge of his duty in any other manner whatever. "The obstruction of the administration of justice," in the first section, refers to that kind of behavior which actually disturbs the court in the exercise of its functions while sitting; "the obstructing and impeding the administration of justice," or the endeavor to do so, in the second, refers to some act of corruption, to some force or threat, by which it is done or attempted to be done. The endeavor to influence, intimidate, or impede a witness, juror, or officer in the discharge of his duty is not punishable unless it is done corruptly, by force or threats. If done by any other manner, the law is silent; and, this being a penal section, its provisions must be confined to the special cases to which it extends. [U. S. v. Wiltberger] 5 Wheat. [18 U. S.] 94, 95.

With this limitation on the summary jurisdiction of the court, and the want of any legal provision making it cognizable by indictment, we cannot say that the publication which is the ground of this motion, or any other, is or can be any disturbance of the business of the court. The action of the press is noiseless, producing the same effects, far or near, it matters not. The business of the court is not interrupted. Judges and jurors can perform their functions on the bench and in the box by confining their attention to the law and evidence. Disorder may be repressed in their presence or hearing in a summary manner, but after an adjournment no attachment can be issued for anything done out of court, during the intermission of its actual session. Nor can any publication, which holds out no corrupt motive to influence a juror, witness, or officer, or uses any threats to influence, intimidate, or impede him in his duty, be the subject of an indictment, consistently with this law. The press is free, if not set to work in the presence of the court, or so near as to interrupt its business. The law does not prohibit any endeavor made to influence or intimidate a juror or witness, if corruption, force, or threats are avoided. Papers may be put into their pockets, conversation held with them, newspapers put into their hands, or statements made in relation to any matter in issue while they are actually impanelled. The court may regret and censure the practice, and perhaps admonish the party who thus tampers with a juror or witness, but can neither punish the offence or prevent its repetition. The law has tied their hands. The judges must be passive. It is not for them to be the first to set the example of disobedience to the law, or attempt to evade plain enactments; most especially not by the exercise of a forbidden jurisdiction. These are all the powers with which congress have entrusted the courts of the United States, in insuring the fair administration of the laws, protecting themselves, jurors, witnesses, and officers from any improper interference with their respective duties, either by attachment or indictment.

For the protection of parties, for their security of a fair and impartial trial and decision of their case on the evidence and law which apply to it; to defend them against the efforts of the press or of individuals to excite a prejudice in the minds of a jury, to induce them to find a verdict on out of door statements, or other means of perverting their judgments,—no legal check is interposed. It is left to the discretion of the conductors of public journals, and all others, to take whatever course their sense of public justice requires; to decide what is proper for jurors to hear and see, as guides to their verdict, whether it is the truth or false, the effects of malice, prejudice, or from any excusable motive. Before the passage of the act of 1831 there was an acknowledged power resting in the sound, legal discretion of the court to be exercised with caution, and from its nature attended with the highest responsibility of the judges, which did authorize them, by the process of attachment, to prevent and punish the publication of articles like the one before us; and in this case it would have been the imperious duty of this court to have brought their powers into action by granting this rule, if the legislative power had not taken it away. How far it would have been proper to exercise them would have depended on the cause shown. On the rule, it was a clear, prima facie case for some interference. But as congress has deemed such a power too dangerous to be entrusted to the discretion of judges on a motion, or of a court and jury on an indictment, and have not thought it expedient to give a remedy to a party who has been injured by a publication by authorizing him to bring a suit against the publisher for damages, we have no cognizance of the matter. The means of redress which had before existed have been taken away without the substitution of any other. The law has left the propriety of such publications to the discretion of the editors of public papers, after long experience of the effects of leaving it to the discretion of courts, who assumed high responsibilities in its exercise; while none is imposed on those in whose breasts it now rests. It is the duty of the court to give the law its full operation. It has been enacted deliberately, with full knowledge not only of the course of the common law, the act of 1789, but of the statute law of Pennsylvania on the same subject, passed in 1809, which gives the injured party a double remedy for any injury complained of in a case like this. After taking from the courts of the state the power to punish for contempt, except in certain cases, the law declares that no publications out of court, concerning any cause depending therein, shall be construed into a contempt, &c., "but, if such publication shall improperly tend to bias the minds of the public, the court, the officers, jurors, witnesses, or any of them, on a question pending before the court, every person feeling himself aggrieved by such publication shall be at liberty either to proceed by indictment, or to bring an action at law against the author, printer, publisher, or either of them, and recover thereupon such damages as a jury may think fit to award." 5 Smith, Laws, p. 55.

Thus it appears that, while suitors in the state courts can be protected against publications like this, they are without protection in the federal courts. The legislature of the state deem it both an indictable and an actionable offence. The legislature of the Union deem it neither a contempt of the law, of the court, an offence to the public, or an injury to a party. The rule must be refused, but it is hoped that an appeal to the sense of justice, the magnanimity of the press to abstain from any publication which shall improperly tend to bias the minds of the public, the court, the officers, jurors, or witnesses in any cause while actually under trial before a jury in this court, may not be in vain. Its conductors should remember that suitors stand unarmed and defenseless before them; that the hands of the court are manackled; that the law of 1831 has placed no arbiter between an editor and a party to a trial, whose life, character, liberty, or property may be put in jeopardy by the influence of the press. The law has taken from him a shield, and from the court the sword. Both must be submissive under the inflictions of the press, be they just or unjust. If it is conducted in the spirit of chivalry, and must be employed on cases depending in the courts, let it be on suitors in state courts, who can meet them in the panoply of the law; not on those who are helpless in this. It is neither manly or generous to assail those who can make no resistance, or inflict an injury for which the sufferer is left without a remedy.

SEE ALSO:

Generally 2.5.3; 3.2.1; 6.1; Amend. I (speech)
James Iredell, Instructions to Chowan County Representatives, Sept. 1783, Papers 2:449
Alexander Hamilton, Federalist, no. 22, 14 Dec. 1787
Alexander Hamilton, Federalist, no. 73, 21 Mar. 1788
Debates in New York Ratifying Convention, 2 July 1788, Elliot 2:400
Luther Martin, Genuine Information, 1788, Storing 2.4.89
Cases of the Judges of the Court of Appeals, 4 Call 136 (Va. 1788)

Edward Carrington to James Madison, 3 Aug. 1789, Madison Papers 12:323
An Act to Establish the Judicial Courts of the United States, 1 Stat. 73 (1789)
Pennsylvania Constitution of 1790, art. 5, sec. 2, Thorpe 5:3097
Kentucky Constitution of 1792, art. 5, secs. 1–5, Thorpe 3:1270–71
An Act in Addition to the Act Entitled "An Act to Establish the Judicial Courts of the United States," 1 Stat. 333 (1793)
Senate, The Judiciary, 5 Mar. 1800, Annals 10:97–102
An Act to Provide for the More Convenient Organization of the Courts of the United States, 2 Stat. 89 (1801)
Gouverneur Morris, Senate, 14 Jan. 1802, Life 3:380–401
Alexander Hamilton, The Examination, no. 14, 2 Mar. 1802, Papers 25:546–52
Alexander Hamilton, The Examination, no. 17, 20 Mar. 1802, Papers 25:569–76
John Stanley, 1 May 1802, Cunningham, 1:288–95
House of Representatives, United States Judges, 27 Jan. 1803, Annals 12:427–40
Senate, Memorial of Judges, 3 Feb. 1803, Annals 12:51–78
Thomas Paine, Constitutional Reform, Aug. 1805, Life 10:266–69
Kempe's Lessee v. *Kennedy,* 5 Cranch 173 (1809)
Louisiana Constitution of 1812, art. 4, sec. 5, Thorpe 3:1386–87
Holder v. *James,* 11 Mass. 396 (1814)
William Wirt, The Judiciary and the Executive, 27 July 1824, 1 Ops. Atty. Gen. 681–83, 684–85
Crane v. *Meginnis,* 1 Gill. & Johns. 463 (Md. 1829)
Virginia Constitution of 1830, art. 5, secs. 1-6, Thorpe 7:3827–28
Tennessee Constitution of 1834, art. 6, secs. 6–7, Thorpe 6:3435

Article 3, Section 2, Clause 1

The judicial Power shall extend to all Cases, in Law and Equity, arising under this Constitution, the Laws of the United States, and Treaties made, or which shall be made, under their Authority;—to all Cases affecting Ambassadors, other public Ministers and Consuls;—to all Cases of admiralty and maritime Jurisdiction;—to Controversies to which the United States shall be a Party;—to Controversies between two or more States;—between a State and Citizens of another State;—between Citizens of different States;—between Citizens of the same State claiming Lands under Grants of different States, and between a State, or the Citizens thereof, and foreign States, Citizens or Subjects.

1. *Dr. Bonham's Case,* 8 Co. Rep. 107a, 114a (C.P. 1610), in Amend. V (due process and taking), no. 1
2. *Lord Sackville's Case,* 28 Eng. Rep. 940 (Ch. 1760)
3. William Blackstone, Commentaries (1765, 1768)
4. Thomas Jefferson, Continental Congress, 1775
5. Articles of Confederation, art. 9, ¶¶ 2–3, 1 Mar. 1781

6. *Clinton* v. *The Hannah,* 5 Fed. Cas. 1056, no. 2,898 (Pa.Adm.Ct. 1781)
7. Records of the Federal Convention
8. Federal Farmer, no. 3, 10 Oct. 1787
9. Charles Pinckney, Observations on the Plan of Government, 1787
10. James Madison to George Washington, 18 Oct. 1787

11. James Wilson, Pennsylvania Ratifying Convention, 1, 7 Dec. 1787
12. Timothy Pickering to Charles Tillinghast, 24 Dec. 1787
13. Oliver Ellsworth, Connecticut Ratifying Convention, 7 Jan. 1788
14. James Madison, Federalist, no. 37, 11 Jan. 1788
15. Federal Farmer, no. 15, 18 Jan. 1788
16. Federal Farmer, no. 18, 25 Jan. 1788
17. James Iredell, Marcus, Answers to Mr. Mason's Objections to the New Constitution, 1788
18. Luther Martin, Genuine Information, 1788
19. Brutus, no. 11, 31 Jan. 1788
20. Brutus, no. 12, 7–14 Feb. 1788
21. Brutus, no. 13, 21 Feb. 1788
22. Brutus, no. 15, 20 Mar. 1788
23. Alexander Hamilton, Federalist, no. 80, 28 May 1788
24. Alexander Hamilton, Federalist, no. 81, 28 May 1788
25. Alexander Hamilton, Federalist, no. 82, 28 May 1788
26. John Marshall, Virginia Ratifying Convention, 20 June 1788
27. A Native of Virginia, Observations upon the Proposed Plan of Federal Government, 1788
28. Samuel Johnston, North Carolina Ratifying Convention, 28 July 1788
29. James Madison, Observations on Jefferson's Draft of a Constitution for Virginia, 15 Oct. 1788
30. James Wilson, Comparison of Constitutions, Lectures on Law, 1791
31. *Hayburn's Case*, 2 Dall. 409 (1792)
32. Thomas Jefferson to John Jay, 18 July 1793
33. John Jay to George Washington, 20 July 1793
34. John Jay to George Washington, 8 Aug. 1793
35. *Shedden* v. *Custis*, 21 Fed. Cas. 1218, no. 12,736 (C.C.D.Va. 1793)
36. *United States* v. *Ravara*, 27 Fed. Cas. 713, nos. 16,122, 16,122a (C.C.D.Pa. 1793, 1794)
37. *United States* v. *Yale Todd*, (1794), in *United States* v. *Ferreira*, 13 How. 40 (1851)
38. *Glass* v. *The Sloop Betsey*, 3 Dall. 6 (1794)
39. *Jansen* v. *Vrow Christina Magdalena*, 13 Fed. Cas. 356, no. 7,216 (D.S.C. 1794)
40. *United States* v. *Worrall*, 2 Dall. 384 (C.C.D.Pa. 1798)
41. *Calder* v. *Bull*, 3 Dall. 386 (1798), in 1.10.1, no. 10
42. *Fowler* v. *Lindsey*, 3 Dall. 411 (1799)
43. *Turner* v. *Bank of North America*, 4 Dall. 8 (1799)
44. *Mossman* v. *Higginson*, 4 Dall. 12 (1800)
45. *Cooper* v. *Telfair*, 4 Dall. 14 (1800)
46. House of Representatives, Judiciary Bill, 7 Jan. 1801
47. *Marbury* v. *Madison*, 1 Cranch 137 (1803)
48. St. George Tucker, Blackstone's Commentaries (1803)
49. *Strawbridge* v. *Curtiss*, 3 Cranch 267 (1806)

50. *Bank of the United States* v. *Deveaux*, 5 Cranch 61 (1809)
51. *United States* v. *Peters*, 5 Cranch 115 (1809)
52. *Hodgson & Thompson* v. *Bowerbank*, 5 Cranch 303 (1809)
53. *Owings* v. *Norwood's Lessee*, 5 Cranch 344 (1809)
54. *Brown* v. *Crippin*, 4 Hen. & M. 173 (Va. 1809)
55. *Livingston* v. *Van Ingen*, 15 Fed. Cas. 697, no. 8,420 (C.C.S.D.N.Y. 1811)
56. *United States* v. *Hudson & Goodwin*, 7 Cranch 32 (1812)
57. *McIntire* v. *Wood*, 7 Cranch 504 (1813)
58. *Clarke* v. *Morey*, 10 Johns. R. 70 (N.Y. 1813)
59. *Jackson* v. *Rose*, 2 Va. Cas. 34 (1814)
60. Gouverneur Morris to Timothy Pickering, 22 Dec. 1814
61. An Act to Vest More Effectually in the State Courts and in the District Courts of the United States Jurisdiction in the Cases Therein Mentioned, 3 Stat. 244 (1815)
62. *Town of Pawlet* v. *Clark*, 9 Cranch 292 (1815)
63. *DeLovio* v. *Boit*, 7 Fed. Cas. 418, no. 3,776 (C.C.D.Mass. 1815)
64. *Corporation of New Orleans* v. *Winter*, 1 Wheat. 91 (1816)
65. *Martin* v. *Hunter's Lessee*, 1 Wheat. 304 (1816)
66. *United States* v. *Coolidge*, 1 Wheat. 415 (1816)
67. *Commonwealth* v. *Kosloff*, 5 Serg. & Rawle 545 (Pa. 1816)
68. *Morgan's Heirs* v. *Morgan*, 2 Wheat. 290 (1817)
69. *Wetherbee* v. *Johnson*, 14 Mass. 412 (1817)
70. James Madison to James Monroe, 27 Dec. 1817
71. *United States* v. *Bevans*, 3 Wheat. 336 (1818)
72. *Cooper* v. *Galbraith*, 6 Fed. Cas. 472, no. 3,193 (C.C.D.Pa. 1819)
73. *United States* v. *Schooner Little Charles*, 1 Marshall's C.C. 380 (C.C.D.Va. 1819)
74. *Cohens* v. *Virginia*, 6 Wheat. 264 (1821)
75. *M'Clung* v. *Silliman*, 6 Wheat. 598 (1821)
76. *The Sarah*, 8 Wheat. 391 (1823)
77. James Madison to Thomas Jefferson, 27 June 1823
78. Rufus King to C. Gore, 1 Feb. 1824
79. *Osborn* v. *Bank of the United States*, 9 Wheat. 738 (1824)
80. *Eakins* v. *Raub*, 12 Serg. & Rawle 330 (Pa. 1825)
81. *United States* v. *Ortega*, 11 Wheat. 467 (1826)
82. *American Insurance Co.* v. *Canter*, 1 Pet. 511 (1828), in 1.8.9, no. 5
83. *Picquet* v. *Swan*, 19 Fed. Cas. 609, no. 11,134 (C.C.D.Mass. 1828), in Amend. V (due process and taking), no. 23
84. William Rawle, A View of the Constitution of the United States (2d ed. 1829)
85. James Madison to M. L. Hurlbert, May 1830
86. *Ex parte Crane*, 5 Pet. 190 (1831)
87. Joseph Story, Commentaries on the Constitution (1833)

1

DR. BONHAM'S CASE
8 Co. Rep. 107a, 114a (C.P. 1610)

(See Amend. V [due process and taking], no. 1)

2

LORD SACKVILLE'S CASE
28 Eng. Rep. 940 (Ch. 1760)

*Certificate of the Judges respecting the Court-Martial
proposed to be held upon
Lord GEORGE SACKVILLE.*

TO THE KING'S most excellent MAJESTY.
MAY IT PLEASE YOUR MAJESTY,

In obedience to your Majesty's commands, signified to us by a letter from the Right Honourable the Lord *Keeper,* referring to us the following question, "Whether an officer of the army having been dismissed from his Majesty's service, and having no military employment, is triable by a Court-Martial for a military offence lately committed by him while in actual service and pay as an officer?"

We have taken the same into consideration, and see no ground to doubt of the legality of the jurisdiction of a Court-Martial in the case put by the above question.

But as the matter may several ways be brought, in due course of law, judicially before some of us by any party affected by that method of trial, if he thinks the court has no jurisdiction; or if the court should refuse to proceed, in case the party thinks they have jurisdiction; we shall be ready, without difficulty, to change our opinion, if we see cause, upon objections that may be then laid before us, though none have occurred to us at present which we think sufficient.

All which is humbly submitted to your Majesty's royal wisdom.

Mansfield; J. Willes; T. Parker; T. Denison; M. Foster; S. S. Smythe; Rich. Adams; H. Bathurst; J. E. Wilmot; W. Noel; Rich. Lloyd.

3d of March 1760.—Mr. Justice *Clive* was absent at *York* on the circuit.

Note: A similar consultation took place a few years prior to it in the case of Admiral *Byng,* and another in the reign of *George* 1st, as to the right of the sovereign to the education and marriage of the children of the Prince of *Wales.* The proceedings upon the latter of these are in Lord *Fortescue's* Reports, 401: and more fully in 15 *Howell's* St. Tr. 1195. The former of these works also contains several early precedents, in which this mode of proceeding has

been resorted to, and authorities by which it is justified, p. 386 *et seq.*

Mr. *Hargrave,* however, in a note to his edition of *Co. Lit.* 110 a, n. 129, has, on the great authority of Lord *Coke,* expressed serious doubts as to the propriety of these extra-judicial consultations: and, indeed, many of the precedents given in the books are extremely objectionable. As in the instances mentioned by *Kelynge,* 9 & 10, preparatory to the trial of the regicides, the judges met at the request of the *Attorney-General,* to advise the king not only as to framing the indictments, but in relation to overt acts and evidence, *Fortesc.* 390. So in the case of *Francis Francia,* in 1717, a conference was held among the judges, three of whom who were to try the prisoner, at which the *Attorney* and *Solicitor-General,* who were to conduct the prosecution next day, lent their assistance, *Foster,* 241; *Fortescue,* 390.

Lord *Bacon,* in a letter to *James* 1st, gives a curious account of his management in endeavouring, according to the king's direction, to obtain the opinion of the Judges of the *King's Bench* separately and privately, previous to the trial of Mr. *Peachman,* a minister, indicted for certain treasonable passages in an unpublished sermon, and of Lord *Coke's* honourable reluctance to give the desired answer. *Bacon's* Works, vol. 4, 595; *Kippis,* Bio. Brit. vol. 3, 682.

It appears also not only from the guarded manner in which the present answer is expressed, but, from Lord *Mansfield's* letter to the Lord *Keeper,* in which it was inclosed, and which is here subjoined from the original amongst Lord *Northington's* papers, that the judges felt considerable disinclination to have their opinions called for in this mode. A similar degree of caution was exhibited in a great case which occurred in the reign of Queen *Anne,* in the year 1711. Upon the revival of the Arian heresy by *Whiston,* doubts were entertained whether the convocation could in the first instance proceed against a person for heresy; and the queen, in consequence of an address from the Upper House, took the opinion of the judges. Four of the judges thought that the convocation had no jurisdiction. The remaining eight (who, together with the *Attorney* and *Solicitor-General,* gave their opinions in favour of the jurisdiction, &c.) expressly reserved to themselves a power to change their mind, in case, upon an argument that might be made for a prohibition, they might see cause for it. *Burnet's* Own Times, vol. III. 325, oct. ed.

Letter of Lord MANSFIELD *to the* Lord KEEPER, *enclosing the above Certificate.*

3d *March* 1760.

MY LORD,

I laid his Majesty's commands before the judges. They are exceedingly thankful to his Majesty for his tenderness in not sending any question to them till the necessity of such reference became manifest and urgent. They have considered the point, and they all agree. In general, they are very averse to giving extra-judicial opinions, especially where they affect a particular case; but the circumstances of the trial now depending ease us of difficulties upon this occasion, and we have laid in our claim not to be bound by this answer. Mr. *J. Clive* is now at *York* upon the circuit, so that there was no opportunity to have his concurrence.

I have the honour to be, &c.   MANSFIELD.

3

WILLIAM BLACKSTONE, COMMENTARIES 1:247–48, 3:68–70, 109–11, 429–37
1765, 1768

In respect to civil suits, all the foreign jurists agree, that neither an embassador, nor any of his train or *comites*, can be prosecuted for any debt or contract in the courts of that kingdom wherein he is sent to reside. Yet sir Edward Coke maintains, that, if an embassador makes a contract which is good *jure gentium*, he shall answer for it here. And the truth is, we find no traces in our lawbooks of allowing any privilege to embassadors or their domestics, even in civil suits, previous to the reign of queen Anne; when an embassador from Peter the great, czar of Muscovy, was actually arrested and taken out of his coach in London, in 1708, for debts which he had there contracted. This the czar resented very highly, and demanded (we are told) that the officers who made the arrest should be punished with death. But the queen (to the amazement of that despotic court) directed her minister to inform him, "that the law of England had not yet protected embassadors from the payment of their lawful debts; that therefore the arrest was no offence by the laws; and that she could inflict no punishment upon any, the meanest, of her subjects, unless warranted by the law of the land." To satisfy however the clamours of the foreign ministers (who made it a common cause) as well as to appease the wrath of Peter, a new statute was enacted by parliament, reciting the arrest which had been made, "in contempt of the protection granted by her majesty, contrary to the law of nations, and in prejudice of the rights and privileges, which embassadors and other public ministers have at all times been thereby possessed of, and ought to be kept sacred and inviolable:" wherefore it enacts, that for the future all process whereby the person of any embassador, or of his domestic or domestic servant, may be arrested, or his goods distreined or seised, shall be utterly null and void; and the persons prosecuting, soliciting, or executing such process shall be deemed violaters of the law of nations, and disturbers of the public repose; and shall suffer such penalties and corporal punishment as the lord chancellor and the two chief justices, or any two of them, shall think fit. But it is expressly provided, that no trader, within the description of the bankrupt laws, who shall be in the service of any embassador, shall be privileged or protected by this act; nor shall any one be punished for arresting an embassador's servant, unless his name be registred with the secretary of state, and by him transmitted to the sheriffs of London

and Middlesex. Exceptions, that are strictly conformable to the rights of embassadors, as observed in the most civilized countries. And, in consequence of this statute, thus enforcing the law of nations, these privileges are now usually allowed in the courts of common law.

. . . . .

III. The maritime courts, or such as have power and jurisdiction to determine all maritime injuries, arising upon the seas, or in parts out of the reach of the common law, are only the court of admiralty, and it's courts of appeal. The court of admiralty is held before the lord high admiral of England, or his deputy, who is called the judge of the court. According to sir Henry Spelman, and Lambard, it was first of all erected by king Edward the third. It's proceedings are according to the method of the civil law, like those of the ecclesiastical courts; upon which account it is usually held at the same place with the superior ecclesiastical courts, at doctors' commons in London. It is no court of record, any more than the spiritual courts. From the sentences of the admiralty judge an appeal always lay, in ordinary course, to the king in chancery, as may be collected from statute 25 Hen. VIII. c. 19. which directs the appeal from the arch-bishop's courts to be determined by persons named in the king's commission, "like as in case of appeal from the admiral-court." But this is also expressly declared by statute 8 Eliz. c. 5. which enacts, that upon appeal made to the chancery, the sentence definitive of the delegates appointed by commission shall be final.

Appeals from the vice-admiralty courts in America, and our other plantations and settlements, may be brought before the courts of admiralty in England, as being a branch of the admiral's jurisdiction, though they may also be brought before the king in council. But in case of prize vessels, taken in time of war, in any part of the world, and condemned in any courts of admiralty or vice-admiralty as lawful prize, the appeal lies to certain commissioners of appeals consisting chiefly of the privy council, and not to judges delegates. And this by virtue of divers treaties with foreign nations; by which particular courts are established in all the maritime countries of Europe for the decision of this question, whether lawful prize or not: for this being a question between subjects of different states, it belongs entirely to the law of nations, and not to the municipal laws of either country, to determine it. The original court, to which this question is permitted in England, is the court of admiralty; and the court of appeal is in effect the king's privy council, the members of which are, in consequence of treaties, commissioned under the great seal for this purpose. In 1748, for the more speedy determination of appeals, the judges of the courts of Westminster-hall, though not privy counsellors, were added to the commission then in being. But doubts being conceived concerning the validity of that commission, on account of such addition, the same was confirmed by statute 22 Geo. II. c. 3. with a proviso, that no sentence given under it should be valid, unless a majority of the commissioners present were actually privy counsellors. But this did not, I apprehend, extend to any future commissions: and such an addition became indeed wholly unnecessary in the course of the war which commenced in 1756; since, during the whole of that war, the commission of appeals was regularly attended and all it's decisions conducted by a judge, whose masterly acquaintance with the law of nations was known and revered by every state in Europe.

. . . . .

IV. I am next to consider such injuries as are cognizable by the courts of the common law. And herein I shall for the present only remark, that all possible injuries whatsoever, that did not fall within the cognizance of either the ecclesiastical, military, or maritime tribunals, are for that very reason within the cognizance of the common law courts of justice. For it is a settled and invariable principle in the laws of England, that every right when with-held must have a remedy, and every injury it's proper redress. The definition and explication of these numerous injuries, and their respective legal remedies, will employ our attention for many subsequent chapters. But, before we conclude the present, I shall just mention two species of injuries, which will properly fall now within our immediate consideration; and which are, either when justice is delayed by an inferior court that has proper cognizance of the cause; or, when such inferior court takes upon itself to examine a cause and decide the merits without any legal authority.

1. The first of these injuries, refusal or neglect of justice, is remedied either by writ of *procedendo,* or of *mandamus.* A writ of *procedendo ad judicium,* issues out of the court of chancery, where judges of any court do delay the parties; for that they will not give judgment, either on the one side or on the other, when they ought so to do. In this case a writ of *procedendo* shall be awarded, commanding them in the king's name to proceed to judgment; but without specifying any particular judgment, for that (if erroneous) may be set aside in the course of appeal, or by writ of error or false judgment: and, upon farther neglect or refusal, the judges of the inferior court may be punished for their contempt, by writ of attachment returnable in the king's bench or common pleas.

A writ of *mandamus* is, in general, a command issuing in the king's name from the court of king's bench, and directed to any person, corporation, or inferior court of judicature, within the king's dominions; requiring them to do some *particular* thing therein specified, which appertains to their office and duty, and which the court of king's bench has previously determined, or at least supposes, to be consonant to right and justice. It is a high prerogative writ, of a most extensively remedial nature: and may be issued in some cases where the injured party has also another more tedious method of redress, as in the case of admission or restitution to an office; but it issues in all cases where the party hath a right to have any thing done, and hath no other specific means of compelling it's performance. A *mandamus* therefore lies to compel the admission or restoration of the party applying, to any office or franchise of a public nature whether spiritual or temporal; to academical degrees; to the use of a meetinghouse; &c: it lies for the production, inspection, or delivery, of public books and papers; for the surrender of the *regalia* of a

corporation; to oblige bodies corporate to affix their common seal; to compel the holding of a court; and for an infinite number of other purposes, which it is impossible to recite minutely. But at present we are more particularly to remark, that it issues to the judges of any inferior court, commanding them to do justice according to the powers of their office, whenever the same is delayed. For it is the peculiar business of the court of king's bench, to superintend all other inferior tribunals, and therein to inforce the due exercise of those judicial or ministerial powers, with which the crown or legislature have invested them: and this, not only by restraining their excesses, but also by quickening their negligence, and obviating their denial of justice. A *mandamus* may therefore be had to the courts of the city of London, to enter up judgment; to the spiritual courts to grant an administration, to swear a churchwarden, and the like. This writ is grounded on a suggestion, by the oath of the party injured, of his own right, and the denial of justice below: whereupon, in order more fully to satisfy the court that there is a probable ground for such interposition, a rule is made (except in some general cases, where the probable ground is manifest) directing the party complained of to shew cause why a writ of *mandamus* should not issue: and, if he shews no sufficient cause, the writ itself is issued, at first in the alternative, either to do thus, or signify some reason to the contrary; to which a return, or answer, must be made at a certain day. And, if the inferior judge, or other person to whom the writ is directed, returns or signifies an insufficient reason, then there issues in the second place a *peremptory mandamus,* to do the thing absolutely; to which no other return will be admitted, but a certificate of perfect obedience and due execution of the writ. If the inferior judge or other person makes no return, or fails in his respect and obedience, he is punishable for his contempt by attachment. But, if he, at the first, returns a sufficient cause, although it should be false in fact, the court of king's bench will not try the truth of the fact upon affidavits; but will for the present believe him, and proceed no farther on the *mandamus.* But then the party injured may have an action against him for his false return, and (if found to be false by the jury) shall recover damages equivalent to the injury sustained; together with a *peremptory mandamus* to the defendant to do his duty. Thus much for the injury of neglect or refusal of justice.

2. The other injury, which is that of encroachment of jurisdiction, or calling one *coram non judice,* to answer in a court that has no legal cognizance of the cause, is also a grievance, for which the common law has provided a remedy by the writ of *prohibition.*

. . . . .

Let us next take a brief, but comprehensive, view of the general nature of *equity,* as now understood and practiced in our several courts of judicature. I have formerly touched upon it, but imperfectly: it deserves a more complete explication. Yet, as nothing is hitherto extant, that can give a stranger a tolerable idea of the courts of equity subsisting in England, as distinguished from the courts of law, the compiler of these observations cannot but attempt it with diffidence: they, who know them best, are too much employed to find time to write; and they, who have attended but little in those courts, must be often at a loss for materials.

Equity then, in it's true and genuine meaning, is the soul and spirit of all law: *positive* law is construed, and *rational* law is made, by it. In this, equity is synonymous to justice; in that, to the true sense and sound interpretation of the rule. But the very terms of a court of *equity* and a court of *law,* as contrasted to each other, are apt to confound and mislead us: as if the one judged without equity, and the other was not bound by any law. Whereas every definition or illustration to be met with, which now draws a line between the two jurisdictions, by setting law and equity in opposition to each other, will be found either totally erroneous, or erroneous to a certain degree.

1. Thus in the first place it is said, that it is the business of a court of equity in England to abate the rigour of the common law. But no such power is contended for. Hard was the case of bond-creditors, whose debtor devised away his real estate; rigorous and unjust the rule, which put the devisee in a better condition than the heir: yet a court of equity had no power to interpose. Hard is the common law still subsisting, that land devised, or descending to the heir, shall not be liable to simple contract debts of the ancestor or devisor, although the money was laid out in purchasing the very land; and that the father shall never immediately succeed as heir to the real estate of the son: but a court of equity can give no relief; though in both these instances the artificial reason of the law, arising from feodal principles, has long ago intirely ceased. The like may be observed of the descent of lands to a remote relation of the whole blood, or even their escheat to the lord, in preference to the owner's half-brother; and of the total stop to all justice, by causing the *parol* to *demur,* whenever an infant is sued as heir or is party to a real action. In all such cases of positive law, the courts of equity, as well as the courts of law, must say with Ulpian, *"hoc quidem perquam durum est, sed ita lex scripta est."*

2. It is said, that a court of equity determines according to the spirit of the rule, and not according to the strictness of the letter. But so also does a court of law. Both, for instance, are equally bound, and equally profess, to interpret statutes according to the true intent of the legislature. In general laws all cases cannot be foreseen; or, if foreseen, cannot be expressed: some will arise that will fall within the meaning, though not within the words, of the legislator; and others, which may fall within the letter, may be contrary to his meaning, though not expressly excepted. These cases, thus out of the letter, are often said to be within the equity, of an act of parliament; and so, cases within the letter are frequently out of the equity. Here by *equity* we mean nothing but the sound interpretation of the law; though the words of the law itself may be too general, too special, or otherwise inaccurate or defective. These then are the cases which, as Grotius says, *"lex non exacte definit, sed arbitrio boni viri permittit;"* in order to find out the true sense and meaning of the lawgiver, from every other topic of construction. But there is not a single rule of interpreting laws, whether equitably or strictly, that is not equally used by the judges in the courts both of law

and equity: the construction must in both be the same; or, if they differ, it is only as one court of law may also happen to differ from another. Each endeavours to fix and adopt the true sense of the law in question; neither can enlarge, diminish, or alter, that sense in a single tittle.

3. Again, it hath been said, that *fraud, accident,* and *trust* are the proper and peculiar objects of a court of equity. But every kind of *fraud* is equally cognizable, and equally adverted to, in a court of law: and some frauds are only cognizable there, as fraud in obtaining a devise of lands, which is always sent out of the equity courts to be there determined. Many *accidents* are also supplied in a court of law; as, loss of deeds, mistakes in receipts or accounts, wrong payments, deaths which make it impossible to perform a condition literally, and a multitude of other contingencies: and many cannot be relieved even in a court of equity; as, if by accident a recovery is ill suffered, a devise ill executed, a contingent remainder destroyed, or a power of leasing omitted in a family settlement. A technical *trust* indeed, created by the limitation of a second use, was forced into a court of equity, in the manner formerly mentioned: and this species of trusts, extended by inference and construction, have ever since remained as a kind of *peculium* in those courts. But there are other trusts, which are cognizable in a court of law: as deposits, and all manner of bailments; and especially that implied contract, so highly beneficial and useful, of having undertaken to account for money received to another's use, which is the ground of an action on the case almost as universally remedial as a bill in equity.

4. Once more; it has been said that a court of equity is not bound by rules or precedents, but acts from the opinion of the judge, founded on the circumstances of every particular case. Whereas the system of our courts of equity is a laboured connected system, governed by established rules, and bound down by precedents, from which they do not depart, although the reason of some of them may perhaps be liable to objection. Thus, the refusing a wife her dower in a trust-estate, yet allowing the husband his curtesy: the holding the penalty of a bond to be merely a security for the debt and interest, yet considering it sometimes as the debt itself, so that the interest shall not exceed that penalty: the distinguishing between a mortgage at *five per cent,* with a clause of reduction to *four,* if the interest be regularly paid, and a mortgage at *four per cent,* with a clause of enlargement to *five,* if the payment of the interest be deferred; so that the former shall be deemed a conscientious, the latter an unrighteous, bargain: all these, and other cases that might be instanced, are plainly rules of positive law; supported only by the reverence that is shewn, and generally very properly shewn, to a series of former determinations; that the rule of property may be uniform and steady. Nay, sometimes a precedent is so strictly followed, that a particular judgment, founded upon special circumstances, gives rise to a general rule.

In short, if a court of equity in England did really act, as a very ingenious writer in the other part of the island supposes it (from theory) to do, it would rise above all law, either common or statute, and be a most arbitrary legislator in every particular case. No wonder he is so often mistaken. Grotius, or Puffendorf, or any other of the great masters of jurisprudence, would have been as little able to discover, by their own light, the system of a court of equity in England, as the system of a court of law. Especially, as the notions before-mentioned, of the character, power, and practice of a court of equity, were formerly adopted and propagated (though not with approbation of the thing) by our principal antiquarians and lawyers; Spelman, Coke, Lambard, and Selden, and even the great Bacon himself. But this was in the infancy of our courts of equity, before their jurisdiction was settled, and when the chancellors themselves, partly from their ignorance of law (being frequently bishops or statesmen) partly from ambition and lust of power (encouraged by the arbitrary principles of the age they lived in) but principally from the narrow and unjust decisions of the courts of law, had arrogated to themselves such unlimited authority, as hath totally been disclaimed by their successors for now above a century past. The decrees of a court of equity were then rather in the nature of awards, formed on the sudden *pro re nata*, with more probity of intention than knowledge of the subject; founded on no settled principles, as being never designed, and therefore never used, for precedents. But the systems of jurisprudence, in our courts both of law and equity, are now equally artificial systems, founded in the same principles of justice and positive law; but varied by different usages in the forms and mode of their proceedings: the one being originally derived (though much reformed and improved) from the feodal customs, as they prevailed in different ages in the Saxon and Norman judicatures; the other (but with equal improvements) from the imperial and pontificial formularies, introduced by their clerical chancellors.

The suggestion indeed of every bill, to give jurisdiction to the courts of equity, (copied from those early times) is, that the complainant hath no remedy at the common law. But he, who should from thence conclude, that no case is judged of in equity where there might have been relief at law, and at the same time casts his eye on the extent and variety of the cases in our equity-reports, must think the law a dead letter indeed. The rules of property, rules of evidence, and rules of interpretation, in both courts, are, or should be, exactly the same: both ought to adopt the best, or must cease to be courts of justice. Formerly some causes, which now no longer exist, might occasion a different rule to be followed in one court, from what was afterwards adopted in the other, as founded in the nature and reason of the thing: but, the instant those causes ceased, the measure of substantial justice ought to have been the same in both. Thus the penalty of a bond, originally contrived to evade the absurdity of those monkish constitutions which prohibited taking interest for money, was therefore very pardonably considered as the real debt in the courts of law, when the debtor neglected to perform his agreement for the return of the loan with interest: for the judges could not, as the law then stood, give judgment that the interest should be specifically paid. But when afterwards the taking of interest became legal, as the necessary companion of commerce, nay after the statute of 37 Hen. VIII. c. 9. had declared the debt or loan itself to be

"the just and true intent" for which the obligation was given, their narrow minded successors still adhered wilfully and technically to the letter of the antient precedents, and refused to consider the payment of principal, interest, and costs, as a full satisfaction of the bond. At the same time more liberal men, who sate in the courts of equity, construed the instrument, according to it's "just and true intent," as merely a security for the loan: in which light it was certainly understood by the parties, at least after these determinations; and therefore this construction should have been universally received. So in mortgages, being only a landed as the other is a personal security for the money lent, the payment of principal, interest, and costs ought at any time, before judgment executed, to have saved the forfeiture in a court of law, as well as in a court of equity. And the inconvenience as well as injustice, of putting different constructions in different courts upon one and the same transaction, obliged the parliament at length to interfere, and to direct by the statutes 4 & 5 Ann. c. 16. and 7 Geo. II. c. 20. that, in the cases of bonds and mortgages, what had long been the practice of the courts of equity should also for the future be followed in the courts of law.

Again; neither a court of equity nor of law can vary men's wills or agreements, or (in other words) make wills or agreements for them. Both are to understand them truly, and therefore both of them uniformly. One court ought not to extend, nor the other abridge, a lawful provision deliberately settled by the parties, contrary to it's just intent. A court of equity, no more than a court of law, can relieve against a penalty in the nature of stated damages; as a rent of 5 *l.* an acre for ploughing up antient meadow: nor against a lapse of time, where the time is material to the contract; as in covenants for renewal of leases. Both courts will equitably construe, but neither pretends to control or change, a lawful stipulation or engagement.

The rules of decision are in both courts equally apposite to the subjects of which they take cognizance. Where the subject-matter is such as requires to be determined *secundum aequum et bonum*, as generally upon actions on the case, the judgments of the courts of law are guided by the most liberal equity. In matters of positive right, both courts must submit to and follow those antient and invariable maxims *"quae relicta sunt et tradita."* Both follow the law of nations, and collect it from history and the most approved authors of all countries, where the question is the object of that law: as in case of the privileges of embassadors, hostages, or ransom-bills. In mercantile transactions they follow the marine law, and argue from the usages and authorities received in all maritime countries. Where they exercise a concurrent jurisdiction, they both follow the law of the proper *forum:* in matters originally of ecclesiastical cognizance, they both equally adopt the canon or imperial law, according to the nature of the subject; and, if a question came before either, which was properly the object of a foreign municipal law, they would both receive information what is the rule of the country, and would both decide accordingly.

Such then being the parity of law and reason which governs both species of courts, wherein (it may be asked) does their essential difference consist? It principally consists in the different modes of administring justice in each; in the mode of proof, the mode of trial, and the mode of relief. Upon these, and upon two other accidental grounds of jurisdiction, which were formerly driven into those courts by narrow decisions of the courts of law, *viz.* the true construction of securities for money lent, and the form and effect of a trust or second use; upon these main pillars hath been gradually erected that structure of jurisprudence, which prevails in our courts of equity, and is inwardly bottomed upon the same substantial foundations as the legal system which hath hitherto been delineated in these commentaries; however different they may appear in their outward form, from the different taste of their architects.

4

THOMAS JEFFERSON, CONTINENTAL CONGRESS 1775

Journals 2:132

Parliament has "extended the jurisdiction of courts of admiralty beyond their antient limits thereby depriving us of the inestimable right of trial by jury in cases affecting both life and property and subjecting both to the arbitrary decision of a single and dependent judge."

5

ARTICLES OF CONFEDERATION, ART. 9, ¶¶ 2–3 1 Mar. 1781

The united states in congress assembled shall also be the last resort on appeal in all disputes and differences now subsisting or that hereafter may arise between two or more states concerning boundary, jurisdiction or any other cause whatever; which authority shall always be exercised in the manner following. Whenever the legislative or executive authority or lawful agent of any state in controversy with another shall present a petition to congress stating the matter in question and praying for a hearing, notice thereof shall be given by order of congress to the legislative or executive authority of the other state in controversy, and a day assigned for the appearance of the parties by their lawful agents, who shall then be directed to appoint by joint consent, commissioners or judges to constitute a court for hearing and determining the matter in question: but if they cannot agree, congress shall name three persons out of each of the united states, and from the list of such persons each party shall alternately strike

out one, the petitioners beginning, until the number shall be reduced to thirteen; and from that number not less than seven, nor more than nine names as congress shall direct, shall in the presence of congress be drawn out by lot, and the persons whose names shall be so drawn or any five of them, shall be commissioners or judges, to hear and finally determine the controversy, so always as a major part of the judges who shall hear the cause shall agree in the determination: and if either party shall neglect to attend at the day appointed, without showing reasons, which congress shall judge sufficient, or being present shall refuse to strike, the congress shall proceed to nominate three persons out of each state, and the secretary of congress shall strike in behalf of such party absent or refusing; and the judgment and sentence of the court to be appointed, in the manner before prescribed, shall be final and conclusive; and if any of the parties shall refuse to submit to the authority of such court, or to appear or defend their claim or cause, the court shall nevertheless proceed to pronounce sentence, or judgment, which shall in like manner be final and decisive, the judgment or sentence and other proceedings being in either case transmitted to congress, and lodged among the acts of congress for the security of the parties concerned: provided that every commissioner, before he sits in judgment, shall take an oath to be administered by one of the judges of the supreme or superior court of the state, where the cause shall be tried, "well and truly to hear and determine the matter in question, according to the best of his judgment, without favour, affection or hope of reward:" provided also, that no state shall be deprived of territory for the benefit of the united states.

All controversies concerning the private right of soil claimed under different grants of two or more states, whose jurisdictions as they may respect such lands, and the states which passed such grants are adjusted, the said grants or either of them being at the same time claimed to have originated antecedent to such settlement of jurisdiction, shall on the petition of either party to the congress of the united states, be finally determined as near as may be in the same manner as is before prescribed for deciding disputes respecting territorial jurisdiction between different states.

6

CLINTON v. THE HANNAH

5 Fed. Cas. 1056, no. 2,898 (Pa.Adm.Ct. 1781)

A plea to the jurisdiction of the court was filed in this cause: and the question was, whether a shipwright might sue in the admiralty for his contract wages for building a ship or vessel designed for navigation on the high seas? After long argument, the judge gave his opinion as follows. The authorities which the libellants have urged in favour of the jurisdiction of this court, in the present case, are Croke, 296, and 1 Rolle, 533. All the other authorities adduced having reference to those, except one in 1 Strange, 707. In the first edition of Croke, 296, we find resolutions upon cases of admiralty jurisdiction subscribed by all the judges of both benches, in April, 1632; wherein, amongst other things, it is resolved that a shipwright may sue in the admiralty, provided his suit be against the ship. Rolle, as a faithful abridger, gives the law as it then stood under the authority of these resolutions. In article 19, he mentions the doctrine respecting shipwrights, and cites the case of Tasker v. Gale. And in article 21, he gives the law respecting charter-parties, adding these remarkable words: "As it was declared by the court to have been lately resolved by all the judges of England." So that those resolutions seem to be the only foundation upon which these doctrines rest. And it is very observable, that although Croke records the resolutions as they were subscribed in Hilary term, the eighth of Charles, yet he does not report the case of Tasker v. Gale, although adjudged (according to Rolle) in the ninth of Charles, which must have been but a few months after. Neither hath any other reporter of that period noticed this case. From which it seems probable, that those resolutions, and the judgment in the case of Tasker v. Gale, were not admitted as good law even in that day.

But it is further observable, that when Sir Harbottle Grimestone published Croke's Reports in the year 1657, he prefixed, even to this first edition, a declaration under the title Mantissa, that the resolutions of the judges in February, 1632, were not of authority: and for this reason (according to Comyns) those resolutions were totally omitted in the subsequent editions of that work. Since that time no instance can be found in the books, where either these resolutions, or the case of Tasker v. Gale adjudged thereupon, have been referred to either by the court, or in the pleadings in any adjudged case, except in the case of Wooward v. Bonithan, Sir T. Raymond, p. 3: and there the court declared, that those resolutions had been denied by several judges, and renounced by even some of those who had subscribed them. And of this, Danvers also takes particular notice. Page 271. Therefore the authority of these resolutions seems to have been abolished by general consent. But another case has been referred to as authority in point, viz. 1 Strange, 707. The report is very short, and in these words: "On a motion for a prohibition, it was held, that a carpenter may sue for wages in the admiralty." This report, however, is too slight and solitary to authorize a decision contrary to general established rules. The word "carpenter" doth not precisely indicate a shipwright, but may be applicable to a mariner on board a vessel; and as the cases referred to in the margin of this report, respecting the officers of a ship who sued in the admiralty as mariners, the probability is, that this also was an officer called the "ship's carpenter:" a doubt having arisen whether the subordinate officers of a ship, as well as the master, were not prohibited from suing in the admiralty for wages. If the resolutions of the judges in 1632, and the decision in the case of Tasker v. Gale, were admitted as law, and if the carpenter mentioned in 1 Strange, 707, was the shipwright or builder, how is it possible that the judges so lately as the year 1765, should declare in court, that no

instance could be found where both the contract and service were to be done on land, within the body of a county, that the common law courts ever permitted the admiralty to have jurisdiction? I refer to 2 Wils. 265: and this opinion was given in the case of a pilot suing for services done, indeed within the body of a county, but in a case of a much stronger maritime complexion than the present.

There are several exceptions to the general rules of law respecting admiralty jurisdiction, as ascertained by the statutes: such as suits for mariners' wages, and on hypothecations made by the master in foreign parts, &c. &c. which have been so often contested, and so often allowed, for good and weighty reasons, that they have become confirmed law, and it would be in vain now to oppose the general rule to the general practice. But this does not appear to be the case with respect to shipwrights; neither are the same reasons applicable to them. Their contract is made with persons whom they know, or ought to know; their services are all executed within the body of the county, and mostly on dry land above high water mark; their wages have no reference to a voyage performed, or to be performed; the shipwrights have no interest or concern whatever in the vessel after she is on float, and the merchant hath paid for her; and lastly, the practice of former times doth not justify the admiralty's taking cognizance of their suits. Let the bill be dismissed, as not being within the jurisdiction of the court.

7

RECORDS OF THE FEDERAL CONVENTION

[1:22; Virginia Plan, Madison, 29 May]
. . . that the jurisdiction of the inferior tribunals shall be to hear & determine in the first instance, and of the supreme tribunal to hear and determine in the dernier resort, all piracies & felonies on the high seas, captures from an enemy; cases in which foreigners or citizens of other States applying to such jurisdictions may be interested, or which respect the collection of the National revenue; impeachments of any National officers, and questions which may involve the national peace and harmony.

[1:28; Paterson, 29 May]
2. A natl Judiciary to be elected by the natl. Legr.—To consist of an inferior and superior Tribunal—To determine Piracies, Captures, Disputes between Foreigners and Citizens, and the Citizen of one State and that of another, Revenue-matters, national Officers—

[1:211; Journal, 12 June]
It was moved and seconded to alter the resolution submitted by Mr Randolph, so as to read as follows namely.

"That the jurisdiction of the supreme Tribunal shall be to hear and determine in the dernier resort all piracies, felonies &ca"

It was moved and seconded to postpone the whole of the last clause generally.

It was then moved and seconded to strike out the words "all piracies and felonies on the high seas"

passed in the affirmative

It was moved and seconded to strike out the words "all captures from an enemy"

passed in the affirmative

It was moved and seconded to strike out the words "other States" and to insert the words "two distinct States in the union"

passed in the affirmative

[1:223; Journal, 13 June]

It was moved by Mr Randolph seconded by Mr Madison to adopt the following resolution respecting the national Judiciary namely

"That the jurisdiction of the national Judiciary shall extend to cases which respect the collection of the national revenue, impeachments of any national officers, and questions which involve the national peace and harmony"

passed in the affirmative

. . . . .

13 Resolved. that the jurisdiction of the national Judiciary shall extend to cases which respect the collection of the national revenue: impeachments of any national Officers: and questions which involve the national peace and harmony.

[1:238; Yates, 13 June]

Gov. Randolph observed the difficulty in establishing the powers of the judiciary—the object however at present is to establish this principle, to wit, the security of foreigners where treaties are in their favor, and to preserve the harmony of states and that of the citizens thereof. This being once established, it will be the business of a sub-committee to detail it; and therefore moved to obliterate such parts of the resolve so as only to establish the principle, to wit, *that the jurisdiction of the national judiciary shall extend to all cases of national revenue, impeachment of national officers, and questions which involve the national peace or harmony.* Agreed to unanimously.

[1:243; New Jersey Plan, Madison, 15 June]

. . . provided that all punishments, fines, forfeitures & penalties to be incurred for contravening such acts rules and regulations shall be adjudged by the Common law Judiciarys of the State in which any offence contrary to the true intent & meaning of such Acts rules & regulations shall have been committed or perpetrated, with liberty of commencing in the first instance all suits & prosecutions for that purpose in the superior Common law Judiciary in such State, subject nevertheless, for the correction of all errors, both in law & fact in rendering judgment, to an appeal to the Judiciary of the U. States

. . . . .

. . . that the Judiciary so established shall have authority to hear & determine in the first instance on all impeachments of federal officers, & by way of appeal in the dernier resort in all cases touching the rights of Ambassadors,

in all cases of captures from an enemy, in all cases of piracies & felonies on the high seas, in all cases in which foreigners may be interested, in the construction of any treaty or treaties, or which may arise on any of the Acts for regulation of trade, or the collection of the federal Revenue:

[1:292; Madison, 18 June]

VII. The Supreme Judicial authority to be vested in Judges to hold their offices during good behaviour with adequate and permanent salaries. This Court to have original jurisdiction in all causes of capture, and an appellative jurisdiction in all causes in which the revenues of the general Government or the citizens of foreign nations are concerned.

[1:317; Madison, 19 June]

[Madison]—He observed that the plan of Mr. Pat—son besides omitting a controul over the States as a general defence of the federal prerogatives was particularly defective in two of its provisions. 1. Its ratification was not to be by the people at large, but by the *Legislatures.* It could not therefore render the acts of Congs. in pursuance of their powers even legally *paramount* to the Acts of the States. 2. It gave to the federal tribunal an appellate jurisdiction only—even in the criminal cases enumerated, The necessity of any such provision supposed a danger of undue acquittals in the State tribunals. Of what avail wd. an appellate tribunal be, after an acquttal? Besides in most if not all of the States, the Executives have by their respective *Constitutions* the right of pardg. How could this be taken from them by a *legislative ratification* only?

[2:39; Journal, 18 July]

It was moved and seconded to strike the words "impeachments of national Officers" out of the 13th resolution

which passed unanimously in the affirmative

It was moved and seconded to alter the 13th resolution so as to read as follows namely

That the jurisdiction of the national Judiciary shall extend to cases arising under laws passed by the general Legislature, and to such other questions as involve the National peace and harmony

which passed unanimously in the affirmative

[2:132; Committee of Detail, I]

Resolved That the Jurisdiction of the national Judiciary shall extend to Cases arising under the Laws passed by the general Legislature, and to such other Questions as involve the national Peace and Harmony.

[2:135; Committee of Detail, III]

14. S. & H. D. in C. ass. shall be the last Resort on Appeal in Disputes between two or more States; which Authority shall be exercised in the following Manner &c

15. S. & H. D. in C. ass. shall institute Offices and appoint Officers for the Departments of for. Affairs, War, Treasury and Admiralty——

They shall have the exclusive Power of declaring what shall be Treason & Misp. of Treason agt. U. S.—and of instituting a federal judicial Court, to which an Appeal shall be allowed from the judicial Courts of the several States in all Causes wherein Questions shall arise on the Construction of Treaties made by U. S.—or on the Law of Nations—or on the Regulations of U. S. concerning Trade & Revenue—or wherein U. S. shall be a Party—The Court shall consist of _____ Judges to be appointed during good Behaviour—S. & H. D. in C. ass shall have the exclusive Right of instituting in each State a Court of Admiralty, and appointing the Judges &c of the same for all maritime Causes which may arise therein respectively.

[2:146; Committee of Detail, IV]

7. The jurisdiction of the supreme tribunal shall extend
   1 to all cases, arising under laws passed by the general Legislature
   2. to impeachments of officers, and
   3. to such other cases, as the national legislature may assign, as involving the national peace and harmony,
      in the collection of the revenue in disputes between citizens of different states

in disputes between a State & a Citizen or Citizens of another State
      in disputes between different states; and
      in disputes, in which subjects or citizens of other countries are concerned
   & in Cases of Admiralty Jurisdn

But this supreme jurisdiction shall be appellate only, except in Cases of Impeachmt. & those instances, in which the legislature shall make it original. and the legislature shall organize it

8. The whole or a part of the jurisdiction aforesaid according to the discretion of the legislature may be assigned to the inferior tribunals, as original tribunals.

[2:157; Committee of Detail, VII]

That the Judiciary have authority to hear and determine all Impeachments of foederal Officers; and, by Way of Appeal, in all Cases touching the Rights of Ambassadors—in all Cases of Capture from an Enemy—in all Cases of Piracies and Felonies on the high Seas—in all Cases of Revenue—in all Cases in which Foreigners may be interested in the Construction of any Treaty, or which may arise on any Act for regulating Trade or collecting Revenue or on the Law of Nations, or general commercial or marine Laws

. . . . .

The foederal judicial Court shall try Officers of the U. S. for all Crimes &C in their Offices—

The Legislature of U. S. shall have the exclusive Right of instituting in each State a Court of Admiralty for hearing and determining maritime Causes.

[2:160; Committee of Detail, VIII]

In all Disputes and Controversies now subsisting, or that may hereafter subsist between two or more States, the Senate shall possess the following Powers. Whenever the Legislature, or the Executive Authority, or the lawful Agent of any State in Controversy with another shall by Memorial to the Senate, state the Matter in Question, and apply for a Hearing, Notice of such Memorial and application shall be given by Order of the Senate to the Legislature or the Executive Authority of the other State in Controversy. The Senate shall also assign a Day for the Appearance of the Parties by their Agents before that House. The Agents shall be directed to appoint by joint Consent Commissioners or Judges to constitute a Court for hearing and determining the Matter in Question. But if the Agents cannot agree, the Senate shall name three Persons out of each of the several States, and from the List of such Persons each Party shall alternately strike out one until the Number shall be reduced to thirteen; and from that Number not less than seven, nor more than nine Names, as the Senate shall direct, shall, in their Presence, be drawn out by Lot; and the Persons, whose names shall be so drawn, or any five of them, shall be Commissioners or Judges to hear and finally determine the Controversy; provided a major Part of the Judges, who shall hear the cause agree in the Determination. If either Party shall neglect to attend at the Day assigned, without showing sufficient Reasons for not attending, or, being present, shall refuse to strike, the Senate shall proceed to nominate three Persons out of each State, and the Secretary or Clerk of the Senate shall strike in Behalf of the Party absent or refusing. If any of the Parties shall refuse to submit to the Authority of such Court, or shall not appear to prosecute or defend their Claim or Cause; the Court shall nevertheless proceed to pronounce Judgment. The Judgment shall be final and conclusive. The Proceedings shall be transmitted to the President of the Senate and shall be lodged among the public Records for the security of the Parties concerned. Every Commissioner shall before he sit in Judgment, take an Oath, to be administered by one of the Judges of the Supreme or Superior Court of the State, where the Cause shall be tried, "well and truly to hear and determine the Matter in Question, according to the best of his Judgment, without Favour, Affection or Hope of Reward."

All Controversies concerning Lands claimed under different Grants of two or more States, whose Jurisdictions, as they respect such Lands, shall have been decided or adjusted subsequent to such Grants, shall, on Application to the Senate, be finally determined, as near as may be in the same Manner as is before prescribed for deciding Controversies between different States.

. . . . .

[2:170, 172; Committee of Detail, IX]

In all Disputes and Controversies now subsisting, or that may hereafter subsist between two or more States respecting Jurisdn or Territory, the Senate shall possess the following Powers. Whenever the Legislature, or the Executive Authority, or the lawful Agent of any State, in controversy with another, shall, by Memorial to the Senate, state the Matter in Question, and apply for a Hearing, Notice of such Memorial and Application shall be given, by Order of the Senate, to the Legislature, or the Executive Authority of the other State in Controversy. The Senate shall also assign a Day for the Appearance of the Parties, by their Agents before that House. The Agents shall be directed to appoint, by joint Consent, Commissioners or Judges to constitute a Court for hearing and determining the Matter in Question. But if the Agents cannot agree, the Senate shall name three Persons out of each of the several States; and from the List of such Persons each Party shall alternately strike out one, until the Number shall be reduced to thirteen; and from that Number not less than seven, nor more than nine names, as the Senate shall direct, shall in their Presence, be drawn out by Lot; and the Persons whose Names shall be so drawn, or any five of them shall be Commissioners or Judges to hear and finally determine the Controversy, provided a majority of the Judges, who shall hear the Cause, agree in the Determination. If either Party shall neglect to attend at the Day assigned, without shewing sufficient Reasons for not attending; or being present, shall refuse to strike, the Senate shall proceed to nominate three Persons out of each State, and the Clerk of the Senate shall strike in Behalf of the Party absent or refusing. If any of the Parties shall refuse to submit to the Authority of such Court, or shall not appear to prosecute or defend their Claim or Cause; the Court shall nevertheless proceed to pronounce Judgment. The Judgment shall be final and conclusive. The Proceedings shall be transmitted to the President of the Senate, and shall be lodged among the public Records for the Security of the Parties concerned. Every Commissioner shall, before he sit in Judgment, take an Oath, to be administered by one of the Judges of the Supreme or Superior Court of the State where the Cause shall be tried, "well and truly to hear and determine the Matter in Question according to the best of his Judgment, without Favor, Affection or Hope of Reward."

All controversies concerning Lands claimed under different Grants of two or more States, whose Jurisdictions as they respect such Lands, shall have been decided or adjusted subsequent to such Grants or any of them shall, on Application to the Senate, be finally determined, as near as may be, in the same manner as is before prescribed for deciding Controversies between different States.

. . . . .

The Jurisdiction of the Supreme Court shall extend to all Cases arising under Laws passed by the Legislature of the United States; to all Cases affecting Ambassadors other public Ministers & Consuls, to the Trial of Impeachments of Officers of the United States; to all Cases of Admiralty and Maritime Jurisdiction; to Controversies between States,—except those wh. regard Jurisdn or Territory,—betwn a State and a Citizen or Citizens of another State, between Citizens of different States and between a State or the Citizens thereof and foreign States, Citizens or Subjects. In Cases of Impeachment, Cases affecting Ambassadors other public Ministers & Consuls, and those in which

a State shall be a Party, this Jurisdiction shall be original. In all the other Cases beforementioned, it shall be appellate, with such Exceptions and under such Regulations as the Legislature shall make. The Legislature may assign any part of the Jurisdiction above mentd.,—except the Trial of the Executive—, in the Manner and under the Limitations which it shall think proper to such inferior Courts as it shall constitute from Time to Time.

[2:183, 186; Madison, 6 Aug.]

Sect. 2. In all disputes and controversies now subsisting, or that may hereafter subsist between two or more States, respecting jurisdiction or territory, the Senate shall possess the following powers. Whenever the Legislature, or the Executive authority, or lawful Agent of any State, in controversy with another, shall by memorial to the Senate, state the matter in question, and apply for a hearing; notice of such memorial and application shall be given by order of the Senate, to the Legislature or the Executive authority of the other State in Controversy. The Senate shall also assign a day for the appearance of the parties, by their agents, before the House. The Agents shall be directed to appoint, by joint consent, commissioners or judges to constitute a Court for hearing and determining the matter in question. But if the Agents cannot agree, the Senate shall name three persons out of each of the several States; and from the list of such persons each party shall alternately strike out one, until the number shall be reduced to thirteen; and from that number not less than seven nor more than nine names, as the Senate shall direct, shall in their presence, be drawn out by lot; and the persons whose names shall be so drawn, or any five of them shall be commissioners or Judges to hear and finally determine the controversy; provided a majority of the Judges, who shall hear the cause, agree in the determination. If either party shall neglect to attend at the day assigned, without shewing sufficient reasons for not attending, or being present shall refuse to strike, the Senate shall proceed to nominate three persons out of each State, and the Clerk of the Senate shall strike in behalf of the party absent or refusing. If any of the parties shall refuse to submit to the authority of such Court; or shall not appear to prosecute or defend their claim or cause, the Court shall nevertheless proceed to pronounce judgment. The judgment shall be final and conclusive. The proceedings shall be transmitted to the President of the Senate, and shall be lodged among the public records, for the security of the parties concerned. Every Commissioner shall, before he sit in judgment, take an oath, to be administred by one of the Judges of the Supreme or Superior Court of the State where the cause shall be tried, "well and truly to hear and determine the matter in question according to the best of his judgment, without favor, affection, or hope of reward."

Sect. 3. All controversies concerning lands claimed under different grants of two or more States, whose jurisdictions, as they respect such lands shall have been decided or adjusted subsequent to such grants, or any of them, shall, on application to the Senate, be finally determined, as near as may be, in the same manner as is before prescribed for deciding controversies between different States.

. . . . .

Sect. 3. The Jurisdiction of the Supreme Court shall extend to all cases arising under laws passed by the Legislature of the United States; to all cases affecting Ambassadors, other Public Ministers and Consuls; to the trial of impeachments of Officers of the United States; to all cases of Admiralty and maritime jurisdiction; to controversies between two or more States, (except such as shall regard Territory or Jurisdiction) between a State and Citizens of another State, between Citizens of different States, and between a State or the Citizens thereof and foreign States, citizens or subjects. In cases of impeachment, cases affecting Ambassadors, other Public Ministers and Consuls, and those in which a State shall be party, this jurisdiction shall be original. In all the other cases before mentioned, it shall be appellate, with such exceptions and under such regulations as the Legislature shall make. The Legislature may assign any part of the jurisdiction above mentioned (except the trial of the President of the United States) in the manner, and under the limitations which it shall think proper, to such Inferior Courts, as it shall constitute from time to time.

[2:335; Journal, 20 Aug.]

The jurisdiction of the supreme court shall be extended to all controversies between the United States and an individual State—or the United States and the Citizen of an individual State.

To assist the President in conducting the Public affairs there shall be a Council of State composed of the following Officers. 1. The Chief Justice of the supreme Court, who shall from time to time recommend such alterations of, and additions to, the Laws of the United-States as may in his opinion be necessary to the due administration of Justice, and such as may promote useful learning and inculcate sound morality throughout the Union: He shall be President of the Council in the absence of the President.

[2:342; Madison, 20 Aug.]

"The Jurisdiction of the supreme Court shall be extended to all controversies between the U. S. and an individual State, or the U. S. and the Citizens of an individual State"

These propositions were referred to the Committee of detail without debate or consideration of them, by the House.

Mr. Govr. Morris 2ded. by Mr. Pinkney submitted the following propositions which were in like manner referred to the Committee of Detail.

"To assist the President in conducting the Public affairs there shall be a Council of State composed of the following officers—1. The Chief Justice of the Supreme Court, who shall from time to time recommend such alterations of and additions to the laws of the U. S. as may in his opinion be necessary to the due administration of Justice, and such as may promote useful learning and inculcate sound morality

throughout the Union: He shall be President of the Council in the absence of the President

[2:367; Journal, 22 Aug.]

"The President of the United States shall have a Privy-Council which shall consist of the President of the Senate, the Speaker of the House of representatives, the Chief Justice of the Supreme Court, and the principal Officer in the respective departments of foreign affairs, domestic-affairs, War, Marine, and Finance, as such departments of office shall from time to time be established—whose duty it shall be to advise him in matters respecting the execution of his Office, which he shall think proper to lay before them: But their advice shall not conclude him, nor affect his responsibility for the measures which he shall adopt"

[2:400; Madison, 24 Aug.]

Sect: 2 & 3 of art: IX being taken up,

Mr Rutlidge said this provision for deciding controversies between the States was necessary under the Confederation, but will be rendered unnecessary by the National Judiciary now to be established, and moved to strike it out.

Docr. Johnson 2ded. the Motion

Mr. Sherman concurred: so did Mr Dayton.

Mr. Williamson was for postponing instead of striking out, in order to consider whether this might not be a good provision, in cases where the Judiciary were interested or too closely connected with the parties—

Mr. Ghorum had doubts as to striking out, The Judges might be connected with the States being parties—He was inclined to think the mode proposed in the clause would be more satisfactory than to refer such cases to the Judiciary—

On the Question for postponing the 2d and 3d Section, it passed in the negative

N. H. ay. Masts. no. Cont. no N. J. no. Pena abst. Del. no. Md. no. Va no. N. C. ay S—C no. Geo. ay. [Ayes—3; noes—7; absent—1.]

Mr. Wilson urged the striking out, the Judiciary being a better provision.

On Question for striking out 2 & 3 Sections Art: IX

N. H. ay. Mas: ay. Ct. ay. N. J—ay. Pa. abst. Del—ay. Md. ay. Va ay. N. C. no. S. C. ay—Geo. no. [Ayes—8; noes—2; absent—1.]

[2:422; Journal, 27 Aug.]

It was moved and seconded to insert the words

"both in Law and Equity" after the words "United States"

1 line, 1 sect, 11th article

which passed in the affirmative [Ayes—6; noes—2.]

On the question to agree to the 1st sect. 11 article as amended.

it passed in the affirmative. [Ayes—6; noes—2.]

. . . . .

It was moved and seconded to postpone the following clause "in cases of impeachment"

which passed in the affirmative

It was moved and seconded to insert the words

"the United States or" before the words "a State shall be a party"

which passed in the affirmative

It was moved and seconded to agree to the following amendment.

In all the other cases beforementioned original jurisdiction shall be in the Courts of the several States but with appeal both as to Law and fact to the courts of the United States, with such exceptions and under such regulations, as the Legislatures shall make.

The last motion being withdrawn,

It was moved and seconded to amend the clause to read

"In cases of impeachment, cases affecting Ambassadors, other public Ministers and Consuls, and those in which a State shall be Party, this jurisdiction shall be original In all the other cases before mentioned it shall be appellate both as to law and fact with such exceptions and under such regulations as the Legislature shall make"

which passed in the affirmative

It was moved and seconded to add the following clause to the last amendment.

"But in cases in which the United States shall be a Party the jurisdiction shall be original or appellate as the Legislature may direct"

[To strike out the words "original or" Ayes—6; noes—2.]

which passed in the negative [Ayes—3; noes—5.]

On the question to reconsider the 3rd section 11 article it passed in the affirmative

It was moved and seconded to strike out the words

"The jurisdiction of the Supreme Court" and to insert the words "The Judicial Power"

which passed in the affirmative

It was moved and seconded to strike out the words "this jurisdiction shall be original" and to insert the words "The supreme Court shall have original jurisdiction"

which passed in the affirmative

It was moved and seconded to agree to the following amendment

"In all the other cases before mentioned the judicial power shall be exercised in such manner as the Legislature shall direct"

which passed in the negative [Ayes—2; noes—6.]

It was moved and seconded to strike out the last clause of the 3rd sect. 11 article

which passed in the affirmative [Ayes—8; noes—0.]

It was moved and seconded to insert the words "both in law and equity" before the word "arising" in the first line, 3rd section, 11 article.

which passed in the affirmative.

It was moved and seconded to insert after the words "between citizens of different States" the words "between Citizens of the same State claiming lands under grants of different States

which passed in the affirmative

[2:428; Madison, 27 Aug.]

Mr. Dickinson moved as an amendment to sect. 2—art XI after the words "good behavior" the words "provided that they may be removed by the Executive on the application by the Senate and House of Representatives."

Mr. Gerry 2ded. the motion

Mr Govr. Morris thought it a contradiction in terms to say that the Judges should hold their offices during good behavior, and yet be removeable without a trial. Besides it was fundamentally wrong to subject Judges to so arbitrary an authority.

Mr. Sherman saw no contradiction or impropriety if this were made part of the Constitutional regulation of the Judiciary establishment. He observed that a like provision was contained in the British Statutes.

Mr. Rutlidge: If the supreme Court is to judge between the U. S. and particular States, this alone is an insuperable objection to the motion.

. . . . .

Sect. 3—art. XI. being taken up—the following clause was postponed—viz. "to the trial of impeachments of officers of the U. S." by which the jurisdiction of the supreme Court was extended to such cases.

Mr Madison & Mr. Govr. Morris moved to insert after the word "controversies" the words "to which the U— S— shall be a party"—which was agreed to nem: con:

Docr. Johnson moved to insert the words "this Constitution and the" before the word "laws"

Mr Madison doubted whether it was not going too far to extend the jurisdiction of the Court generally to cases arising Under the Constitution, & whether it ought not to be limited to cases of a Judiciary Nature. The right of expounding the Constitution in cases not of this nature ought not to be given to that Department.

The motion of Docr. Johnson was agreed to nem: con: it being generally supposed that the jurisdiction given was constructively limited to cases of a Judiciary nature—

On motion of Mr Rutlidge, the words "passed by the Legislature" were struck out, and after the words "U. S" were inserted nem. con: the words "and treaties made or which shall be made under their authority"—conformably to a preceding amendment in another place.

The clause "in cases of impeachment", was postponed.

Mr. Govr. Morris wished to know what was meant by the words "In all the cases before mentioned it (jurisdiction) shall be appellate with such exceptions &c," whether it extended to matters of fact as well as law—and to cases of Common law as well as Civil law.

Mr. Wilson. The Committee he believed meant facts as well as law & Common as well as Civil law. The jurisdiction of the federal Court of Appeals had he said been so construed.

Mr. Dickinson moved to add after the word "appellate" the words "both as to law & fact which was agreed to nem: con:

Mr. Madison & Mr. Govr. Morris moved to strike out the beginning of the 3d sect. "The jurisdiction of the supreme Court" & to insert the words "the Judicial power" which was agreed to nem: con:

The following motion was disagreed to, to wit to insert "In all the other cases before mentioned the Judicial power shall be exercised in such manner as the Legislature shall direct" Del. Virga ay

N. H Con. P .M. S. C. G no [Ayes—2; noes—6.]

On a question for striking out the last sentence of sect. 3. "The Legislature may assign &c—"

N. H. ay— Ct ay. Pa ay. Del— ay— Md ay— Va ay— S— C. ay— Geo. ay. [Ayes—8; noes—0.]

Mr. Sherman moved to insert after the words "between Citizens of different States" the words, "between Citizens of the same State claiming lands under grants of different States"—according to the provision in the 9th. art: of the Confederation—which was agreed to nem: con:

[2:432; Mason, 27 Aug.]

The judicial power of the United States shall be vested in one Supreme Court and in such Courts of Admiralty as Congress shall establish in any of the States. And also in Courts of Admiralty to be established in such of the States as Congress shall direct.

The jurisdiction of the supreme courts shall extend to all cases in law and equity arising under this Constitution, the laws of the United States and treaties made or which shall be made under their authority; to all cases affecting ambassadors, other public ministers and consuls; to all cases of admiralty and maritime jurisdiction; to controversies to which the United States shall be a party, to controversies between two or more States; between *citizens of the same State* claiming lands of different States, and between *a State and the citizens thereof* and foreign States, citizens or subjects.

In all cases affecting ambassadors, other public ministers and consuls, and those in which a State shall be a party, and suits between persons claiming lands under grants of different States the Supreme Court shall have original jurisdiction, and in all the other cases before mentioned the Supreme Courts shall have appellate jurisdiction as to law only, except in cases of equity and admiralty and maritime jurisdiction in which last mentioned cases the Supreme Court shall have appellate jurisdiction, both as to law and fact.

In all cases of admiralty and maritime jurisdiction, the Admiralty Courts appointed by Congress shall have original jurisdiction, and an appeal may be made to the Supreme Court of Congress for any sum and in such manner as Congress may by law direct.

In all other cases not otherwise provided for the *Superior* State Courts shall have original jurisdiction, and an appeal may be made to the Supreme federal Court in all cases where the subject in controversy or the decree or judgment of the State court shall be of the value of one thousand dollars and in cases of less value the appeal shall be to the High Court of Appeals, Court of Errors or other Supreme Court of the State where the suit shall be tried.

The trial of all crimes, except in case of impeachment shall be in the Superior Court of that State where the offence shall have been committed in such manner as the Congress shall by law direct except that the trial shall be by a jury. But when the crime shall not have been committed within any one of the United States the trial shall be at such place and in such manner as Congress shall by law direct, except that such trial shall also be by a jury.

[2:437; Madison, 28 Aug.]

Art XI sect. 3. "It was moved to strike out the words "it shall be appellate" & to insert the words "the supreme Court shall have appellate jurisdiction",—in order to prevent uncertainty whether "it" referred to the *supreme Court,* or to the *Judicial power.*

On the question

N. H. ay. Mas. ay. Ct. ay. N. J. abst. Pa. ay. Del. ay. Md. no. Va. ay. N C ay. S. C. ay. Geo. ay. [Ayes—9; noes—1; absent—1.]

[2:458; Journal, 30 Aug.]

Nothing in this Constitution shall be construed to alter the claims of the United States or of the individual States to the western territory but all such claims may be examined into and decided upon by the supreme Court of the United States

It was moved and seconded to postpone the last proposition in order to take up the following.

The Legislature shall have power to dispose of and make all needful rules and regulations respecting the territory or other property belonging to the United States: and nothing in this Constitution contained shall be so construed as to prejudice any claims either of the United States or of any particular State

It was moved and seconded to add the following clause to the last proposition

"But all such claims may be examined into and decided upon by the Supreme Court of the United States"

which passed in the negative [Ayes—2; noes—8.]

[2:576, 600; Committee of Style]

Sect. 3. The Judicial Power shall extend to all cases both in law and equity arising under this Constitution and the laws of the United States, and treaties made or which shall be made under their authority; to all cases affecting Ambassadors, other Public Ministers and Consuls; to all cases of Admiralty and Maritime Jurisdiction; to Controversies to which the United States shall be a party, to controversies between two or more States (except such as shall regard Territory and Jurisdiction) between a State and citizens of another State, between citizens of different States, between citizens of the same State claiming lands under grants of different States, and between a State or the citizens thereof and foreign States, citizens or subjects. In cases affecting Ambassadors, other Public Ministers and Consuls, and those in which a State shall be party, the Supreme Court shall have original jurisdiction. In all other cases beforementioned the Supreme Court shall have appellate jurisdiction both as to law and fact with such exceptions and under such regulations as the Legislature shall make.

. . . . .

Sect. 2. The judicial power shall extend to all cases, both in law and equity, arising under this constitution, the laws of the United States, and treaties made, or which shall be made, under their authority. To all cases affecting ambassadors, other public ministers and consuls. To all cases of admiralty and maritime jurisdiction. To controversies to which the United States shall be a party. To controversies between two or more States; between a state and citizens of another state; between citizens of different States; between citizens of the same state claiming lands under grants of different States, and between a state, or the citizens thereof, and foreign States, citizens or subjects.

In cases affecting ambassadors, other public ministers and consuls, and those in which a state shall be a party, the supreme court shall have original jurisdiction. In all the other cases before mentioned, the supreme court shall have appellate jurisdiction, both as to law and fact, with such exceptions, and under such regulations as the Congress shall make.

8

FEDERAL FARMER, NO. 3
10 Oct. 1787
Storing 2.8.41–43

There are some powers proposed to be lodged in the general government in the judicial department, I think very unnecessarily. I mean powers respecting questions arising upon the internal laws of the respective states. It is proper the federal judiciary should have powers co-extensive with the federal legislature—that is, the power of deciding finally on the laws of the union. By Art. 3. Sect. 2. the powers of the federal judiciary are extended (among other things) to all cases between a state and citizens of another state—between citizens of different states—between a state or the citizens thereof, and foreign states, citizens or subjects. Actions in all these cases, except against a state government, are now brought and finally determined in the law courts of the states respectively; and as there are no words to exclude these courts of their jurisdiction in these cases, they will have concurrent jurisdiction with the inferior federal courts in them; and, therefore, if the new constitution be adopted without any amendment in this respect, all those numerous actions, now brought in the state courts between our citizens and foreigners, between citizens of different states, by state governments against foreigners, and by state governments against citizens of other states, may also be brought in the federal courts; and an appeal will lay in them from the state courts, or federal inferior courts, to the supreme judicial court of the union. In almost all these cases, either party may have the trial by jury in the state courts; excepting paper money and tender laws, which are wisely guarded against in the proposed constitution, justice may be obtained in these courts on reasonable terms; they must be more competent to proper decisions on the laws of their respective states, than the federal courts can possibly be. I do not, in any point of view, see the need of opening a new jurisdiction to these causes—of opening a new scene of expensive law suits—of suffering foreigners, and citizens of different states, to drag each other many hundred miles into the federal courts. It is true, those courts may be so organized by a wise and prudent legislature, as to make the obtaining of justice in them tolerably easy; they may in general be organized on the common law principles of the country: But this benefit is by no means secured by the constitution. . . .

There can be but one supreme court in which the final jurisdiction will centre in all federal causes—except in cases where appeals by law shall not be allowed: The judicial powers of the federal courts extends in law and equity to certain cases: and, therefore, the powers to determine on the law, in equity, and as to the fact, all will concentre in the supreme court:—These powers, which by this constitution are blended in the same hands, the same judges, are in Great-Britain deposited in different hands—to wit, the decision of the law in the law judges, the decision in equity in the chancellor, and the trial of the fact in the jury. It is a very dangerous thing to vest in the same judge power to decide on the law, and also general powers in equity; for if the law restrain him, he is only to step into his shoes of equity, and give what judgment his reason or opinion may dictate; we have no precedents in this country, as yet, to regulate the divisions in equity as in Great Britain; equity, therefore, in the supreme court for many years will be mere discretion. I confess in the constitution of this supreme court, as left by the constitution, I do not see a spark of freedom or a shadow of our own or the British common law.

This court is to have appellate jurisdiction in all the other cases before mentioned: Many sensible men suppose that cases before mentioned respect, as well the criminal cases as the civil ones, mentioned antecedently in the constitution, if so an appeal is allowed in criminal cases—contrary to the usual sense of law. How far it may be proper to admit a foreigner or the citizen of another state to bring actions against state governments, which have failed in performing so many promises made during the war, is doubtful: How far it may be proper so to humble a state, as to oblige it to answer to an individual in a court of law, is worthy of consideration; the states are now subject to no such actions; and this new jurisdiction will subject the states, and many defendants to actions, and processes, which were not in the contemplation of the parties, when the contract was made; all engagements existing between citizens of different states, citizens and foreigners, states and foreigners; and states and citizens of other states were made the parties contemplating the remedies then existing on the laws of the states—and the new remedy proposed to be given in the federal courts, can be founded on no principle whatever.

9

CHARLES PINCKNEY, OBSERVATIONS ON THE PLAN OF GOVERNMENT
1787
Farrand 3:117

The 10th article gives Congress a right to institute all such offices as are necessary for managing the concerns of the Union; of erecting a Federal Judicial Court, for the purposes therein specified; and of appointing Courts of Admiralty for the trial of maritime causes in the States respectively. The institution of a Federal Judicial upon the principles mentioned in this article, has been long wanting. At present there is no Tribunal in the Union capable of taking cognizance of their officers who shall misbehave in any of their departments, or in their ministerial capacities out of the limits of the United States; for this, as well as the trial of questions arising on the law of nations, the construction of treaties, or any of the regulations of Congress in pursuance of their powers, or wherein they may be a party, there ought certainly to be a Judicial, acting under the authority of the Confederacy; for securing whose independence and integrity some adequate provision must be made, not subject to the controul of the Legislature. As the power of deciding finally in cases of Appeal and all Maritime Regulations are to be vested in the United States, the Courts of Admiralty in the several States, which are to be governed altogether by their Regulations, and the Civil Law, ought also to be appointed by them; it will serve as well to secure the uprightness of the Judges, as to preserve an uniformity of proceeding in Maritime Cases, throughout the Union.

10

JAMES MADISON TO GEORGE WASHINGTON
18 Oct. 1787
Papers 10:196–97

I have been this day honoured with your favor of the 10th. instant, under the same cover with which is a copy of Col. Mason's objections to the Work of the Convention. . . . What he means by the dangerous tendency of the Judiciary I am at some loss to comprehend. It never was intended, nor can it be supposed that in ordinary cases the inferior tribunals will not have final jurisdiction in order to prevent the evils of which he complains. The great mass of suits in every State lie between Citizen & Citizen, and relate to matters not of federal cognizance. . . . What can he mean by saying that the Common law is not secured by the new constitution, though it has been adopted by the

State Constitutions. The common law is nothing more than the unwritten law, and is left by all the constitutions equally liable to legislative alterations. I am not sure that any notice is particularly taken of it in the Constitutions of the States. If there is, nothing more is provided than a general declaration that it shall continue along with other branches of law to be in force till legally changed. The constitution of Virga. drawn up by Col Mason himself, is absolutely silent on the subject. An *ordinance* passed during the same Session, declared the Common law as heretofore & all Statutes of prior date to the 4 of James I. to be still the law of the land, merely to obviate pretexts that the separation from G. Britain threw us into a State of nature, and abolished all civil rights and Obligations. Since the Revolution every State has made great inroads & with great propriety in many instances on this *monarchical* code. The "revisal of the laws" by a Committe[e] of wch. Col. Mason was a member, though not an acting one, abounds with such innovations. The abolition of the *right of primogeniture*, which I am sure Col. Mason does not disapprove, falls under this head. What could the Convention have done? If they had in general terms declared the Common law to be in force, they would have broken in upon the legal Code of every State in the most material points: they wd. have done more, they would have brought over from G.B. a thousand heterogeneous & antirepublican doctrines, and even the *ecclesiastical Hierarchy itself*, for that is a part of the Common law. If they had undertaken a discrimination, they must have formed a digest of laws, instead of a Constitution. This objection surely was not brought forward in the Convention, or it wd. have been placed in such a light that a repetition of it out of doors would scarcely have been hazarded. Were it allowed the weight which Col. M. may suppose it deserves, it would remain to be decided whether it be candid to arraign the Convention for omissions which were never suggested to them—or prudent to vindicate the dissent by reasons which either were not previously thought of, or must have been wilfully concealed.

11

JAMES WILSON, PENNSYLVANIA RATIFYING CONVENTION
1, 7 Dec. 1787
Elliot 2:445–46, 489–94

This could not have been the case in a compound legislature; it is therefore proper to have efficient restraints upon the legislative body. These restraints arise from different sources. I will mention some of them. In this Constitution, they will be produced, in a very considerable degree, by a *division of the power* in the legislative body itself. Under this system, they may arise likewise from the interference of those officers who will be introduced into the executive and judicial departments. They may spring also from another source—the election by the people; and finally, under this Constitution, they may proceed from the great and last resort—from the *people* themselves. I say, under this Constitution, the legislature may be restrained, and kept within its prescribed bounds, by the interposition of the judicial department. This I hope, sir, to explain clearly and satisfactorily. I had occasion, on a former day, to state that the power of the Constitution was paramount to the power of the legislature acting under that Constitution; for it is possible that the legislature, when acting in that capacity, may transgress the bounds assigned to it, and an act may pass, in the usual *mode*, notwithstanding that transgression; but when it comes to be discussed before *the judges,*—when they consider its principles, and find it to be incompatible with the superior power of the Constitution,—it is their duty to pronounce it *void;* and judges independent, and not obliged to look to every session for a continuance of their salaries, will behave with intrepidity, and refuse to the act the sanction of judicial authority. In the same manner, the President of the United States could shield himself, and refuse to carry into effect an act that *violates* the Constitution.

. . . . .

The article respecting the judicial department is objected to as going too far, and is supposed to carry a very indefinite meaning. Let us examine this: "The judicial power shall extend to all cases, in law and equity, *arising under this Constitution and the laws of the United States.*" Controversies may certainly arise under this Constitution and the laws of the United States, and is it not proper that there should be judges to decide them? The honorable gentleman from Cumberland (Mr. Whitehill) says that laws may be made inconsistent with the Constitution; and that therefore the powers given to the judges are dangerous. For my part, Mr. President, I think the contrary inference true. If a law should be made inconsistent with those powers vested by this instrument in Congress, the judges, as a consequence of their independence, and the particular powers of government being defined, will declare such law to be null and void; for the power of the Constitution predominates. Any thing, therefore, that shall be enacted by Congress contrary thereto, will not have the force of law.

The judicial power extends to all cases arising under treaties made, or which shall be made, by the United States. I shall not repeat, at this time, what has been said with regard to the power of the states to make treaties; it cannot be controverted, that, when made, they ought to be observed. But it is highly proper that this regulation should be made; for the truth is,—and I am sorry to say it,—that, in order to prevent the payment of British debts, and from other causes, our treaties have been violated, and violated, too, by the express laws of several states in the Union. Pennsylvania—to her honor be it spoken—has hitherto done no act of this kind; but it is acknowledged on all sides, that many states in the Union have infringed the treaty; and it is well known that, when the minister of the United States made a demand of Lord Carmarthen of a surrender of the western posts, he told the minister, with truth and justice, "The treaty under which you claim those possessions has not been performed on your part; until

that is done, those possessions will not be delivered up." This clause, sir, will show the world that we make the faith of treaties a constitutional part of the character of the United States; that we secure its performance no longer nominally, for the judges of the United States will be enabled to carry it into effect, let the legislatures of the different states do what they may.

The power of judges extends to all cases affecting ambassadors, other public ministers, and consuls. I presume very little objection will be offered to this clause; on the contrary, it will be allowed proper and unexceptionable.

This will also be allowed with regard to the following clause: "*all cases of admiralty and maritime jurisdiction.*"

The next is, "*to controversies to which the United States shall be a party.*" Now, I apprehend it is something very incongruous, that, because the United States are a party, it should be urged, as an objection, that their judges ought not to decide, when the universal practice of all nations has, and unavoidably must have, admitted of this power. But, say the gentlemen, the sovereignty of the states is destroyed, if they should be engaged in a controversy with the United States, because a suiter in a court must acknowledge the jurisdiction of that court, and it is not the custom of sovereigns to suffer their names to be made use of in this manner. The answer is plain and easy: the government of each state ought to be subordinate to the government of the United States.

"*To controversies between two or more states.*" This power is vested in the present Congress; but they are unable, as I have already shown, to enforce their decisions. The additional power of carrying their decree into execution, we find, is therefore necessary, and I presume no exception will be taken to it.

"*Between a state and citizens of another state.*" When this power is attended to, it will be found to be a necessary one. Impartiality is the leading feature in this Constitution; it pervades the whole. When a citizen has a controversy with another state, there ought to be a tribunal where both parties may stand on a just and equal footing.

"*Between citizens of different states, and between a state, or the citizens thereof, and foreign states, citizens, or subjects.*" This part of the jurisdiction, I presume, will occasion more doubt than any other part; and, at first view, it may seem exposed to objections well founded and of great weight; but I apprehend this can be the case only at first view. Permit me to observe here, with regard to this power, or any other of the foregoing powers given to the federal court, that they are not exclusively given. In all instances, the parties may commence suits in the courts of the several states. Even the United States may submit to such decision if they think proper. Though the citizens of a state, and the citizens or subjects of foreign states, may sue in the federal court, it does not follow that they must sue. These are the instances in which the jurisdiction of the United States may be exercised; and we have all the reason in the world to believe that it will be exercised impartially; for it would be improper to infer that the judges would abandon their duty, the rather for being independent. Such a sentiment is contrary to experience, and ought not to be hazarded. If the people of the United States are fairly represented, and the President and Senate are wise enough to choose men of abilities and integrity for judges, there can be no apprehension, because, as I mentioned before, the government can have no interest in injuring the citizens.

But when we consider the matter a little further, is it not necessary, if we mean to restore either public or private credit, that foreigners, as well as ourselves, have a just and impartial tribunal to which they may resort? I would ask how a merchant must feel to have his property lie at the mercy of the laws of Rhode Island. I ask, further, How will a creditor feel who has his debts at the mercy of tender laws in other states? It is true that, under this Constitution, these particular iniquities may be restrained in future; but, sir, there are other ways of avoiding payment of debts. There have been instalment acts, and other acts of a similar effect. Such things, sir, destroy the very sources of credit.

Is it not an important object to extend our manufactures and our commerce? This cannot be done, unless a proper security is provided for the regular discharge of contracts. This security cannot be obtained, unless we give the power of deciding upon those contracts to the general government.

I will mention, further, an object that I take to be of particular magnitude, and I conceive these regulations will produce its accomplishment. The object, Mr. President, that I allude to, is *the improvement of our domestic navigation,* the instrument of trade between the several states. Private credit, which fell to decay from the destruction of public credit, by a too inefficient general government, will be restored; and this valuable intercourse among ourselves must give an increase to those useful improvements that will astonish the world. At present, how are we circumstanced! Merchants of eminence will tell you that they cannot trust their property to the laws of the state in which their correspondents live. Their friend may die, and may be succeeded by a representative of a very different character. If there is any particular objection that did not occur to me on this part of the Constitution, gentlemen will mention it; and I hope, when this article is examined, it will be found to contain nothing but what is proper to be annexed to the general government. The next clause, so far as it gives original jurisdiction in cases affecting ambassadors, I apprehend, is perfectly unexceptionable.

It was thought proper to give the citizens of foreign states full opportunity of obtaining justice in the general courts, and this they have by its appellate jurisdiction; therefore, in order to restore credit with those foreign states, that part of the article is necessary. I believe the alteration that will take place in their minds when they learn the operation of this clause, will be a great and important advantage to our country; nor is it any thing but justice: they ought to have the same security against the state laws that may be made, that the citizens have; because regulations ought to be equally just in the one case as in the other. Further, it is necessary in order to preserve peace with foreign nations. Let us suppose the case, that a wicked law is made in some one of the states, enabling a debtor to pay his creditor with the fourth, fifth, or sixth part of the real value of the debt, and this creditor, a foreigner, complains to his prince or sovereign, of the injustice that has been done him. What can that prince or sovereign do? Bound by inclination, as well as duty, to redress the wrong his subject sustains from the hand of perfidy, he cannot apply to the particular guilty state, because he knows that, by the Articles of Confederation, it is declared that no state shall enter into treaties. He must therefore apply to the United States; the United States must be accountable. "My subject has received a flagrant injury: do me justice, or I will do myself justice." If the United States are answerable for the injury, ought they not to possess the means of compelling the faulty state to repair it? They ought; and this is what is done here. For now, if complaint is made in consequence of such injustice, Congress can answer, "Why did not your subject apply to the General Court, where the unequal and partial laws of a particular state would have had no force?"

In two cases the Supreme Court has original jurisdiction—that affecting ambassadors, and when a state shall be a party. It is true it has appellate jurisdiction in more, but it will have it under such restrictions as the Congress shall ordain. I believe that any gentleman, possessed of experience or knowledge on this subject, will agree that it was impossible to go further with any safety or propriety, and that it was best left in the manner in which it now stands.

"In all the other cases before mentioned, the Supreme Court shall have appellate jurisdiction, both as to law and fact." The jurisdiction as to fact may be thought improper; but those possessed of information on this head see that it is necessary. We find it essentially necessary from the ample experience we have had in the courts of admiralty with regard to captures. Those gentlemen who, during the late war, had their vessels retaken, know well what a poor chance they would have had when those vessels were taken in their states and tried by juries, and in what a situation they would have been if the Court of Appeals had not been possessed of authority to reconsider and set aside the verdicts of those juries. Attempts were made by some of the states to destroy this power; but it has been confirmed in every instance.

There are other cases in which it will be necessary; and will not Congress better regulate them, as they rise from time to time, than could have been done by the Convention? Besides, if the regulations shall be attended with inconvenience, the Congress can alter them as soon as discovered. But any thing done in Convention must remain unalterable but by the power of the citizens of the United States at large.

I think these reasons will show that the powers given to the Supreme Court are not only safe, but constitute a wise and valuable part of the system.

12

TIMOTHY PICKERING TO CHARLES TILLINGHAST
24 Dec. 1787
Life 2:359–60, 366–67

He [the Federal Farmer] objects to the powers of the judicial department, saying: "In the Judges of the Supreme Court are lodged the *law,* the equity, and the *fact.*" These powers, he says, in well-balanced governments, are ever kept distinct. Why, Sir, there are no such governments in the world, save the British, and those which have been formed on the British model; that is, the governments of the United States. Except in those governments, a court of equity, distinct from a court of *law,* is unknown. And among the United States, two or three only, I believe, have such distinct courts of equity. In the rest, the courts of law possess also the powers of courts of equity, for the most common and useful purposes. "It is," says the "Federal Farmer," "very dangerous to vest, in the same Judge, power to decide on the law and also general powers in equity; for, if the law restrain him, he is only to step into his shoes of equity, and give what judgment his reason or opinion may dictate." Sir, this is all stuff. Read a few passages in "Blackstone's Commentaries," and you will be convinced of it. "Equity" (says he, Book III., chapter xxvii.), "is the soul and spirit of all law. Positive (or statute) law is construed, and rational law is made, by it. In this, equity is synonymous to justice; in that, to the true sense and sound interpretation of the rule. But the very terms of a court of equity and a court of law, as contrasted to each other, are apt to confound and mislead us; as if the one judged without equity, and the other was not bound by any law. Whereas, every definition or illustration to be met with, which now draws a line between the two jurisdictions, by setting law and equity in opposition to each other, will be found either totally erroneous or erroneous to a certain degree." "Thus, it is said that it is the business of a court of equity in England to abate the rigor of the common law. But no such power is contended for." "It is also said that a court of equity determines, according to the spirit of the rule, and not according to the strictness of the letter. But so also does a court of law. Both, for instance, are equally bound, and equally profess to interpret statutes according to the true intent of the legislature." "There is not a single rule of interpreting laws, whether equitably or strictly, that is not equally used by the Judges in the courts both of law and equity." "Each endeavors to fix and adopt the true sense of the law in question, and neither can enlarge, diminish, or alter that sense in a single tittle." Where then, you will ask, consists the essential difference between the two courts? Take Blackstone's answer: "It principally consists in the different modes of administering justice in each; in the *mode of proof,* the *mode of trial,* and the *mode of relief.*" From him, also, you will learn that an act of Parliament was passed, in the reign of

Edward I. (see "Commentaries," Book III., chapter iv.), making provisions which, by a little liberality in the Judges of the courts of law, "might have effectually answered all the purposes of a court of equity." As our ideas of a court of equity are derived from the English jurisprudence, so, doubtless, the Convention, in declaring that the judicial power shall extend to all cases in *equity* as well as *law,* under the Federal jurisdiction, had, principally, a reference to the *mode* of *administering justice* in cases of equity, agreeably to the practice of the Court of Chancery in England.

. . . . .

There is but one other objection which I have time to notice. That respects the judicial power. The 'Federal Farmer' and other objectors say, the causes between a State and citizens of another State, between citizens of different States, and between a State, or the citizens thereof, and the citizens or subjects of foreign States, should be left, as they now are, to the decision of the particular State courts. The other cases enumerated in the Constitution seem to be admitted as properly cognizable in the *Federal* courts. With respect to all the former, it may be said, generally, that as the local laws of the several States may differ from each other, as particular States may pass laws unjust in their nature, or partially unjust, as they regard foreigners and the citizens of other States, it seems to be a wise provision which puts it in the power of such foreigners and citizens to resort to a court where they may reasonably expect to obtain *impartial* justice. But as the courts of particular States will, in these cases, have a concurrent jurisdiction, so whilst they proceed with reasonable despatch, and support their characters by upright decisions, they will probably be almost exclusively resorted to. But there is a particular and very cogent reason for securing to *foreigners* a trial, either in the first instance or by appeal in a *Federal* court. With respect to *foreigners,* all the States form but *one nation.* This *nation* is responsible for the conduct of all its members towards foreign nations, their citizens, and subjects, and therefore ought to possess the power of doing justice to the latter. Without this power a single State, or one of its citizens, might embroil the whole Union in a foreign war.

The trial by jury, in civil cases, I grant, is not explicitly secured by the Constitution; but we have been told the reason of the omission: and to me it is satisfactory. In many of the civil causes subject to the jurisdiction of the Federal courts, trial by jury would evidently be improper; in others, it was found impracticable in the Convention to fix on the mode of constituting juries. But we may assure ourselves that the first Congress will make provision for introducing it in every case in which it shall be proper and practicable. Recollect that the Congress of 1775 directed jury trials in the cases of captures at sea, and that the inconveniences soon discovered in that mode of trial obliged them to recommend an alteration, and to commit all admiralty causes to the decision of the Judge alone. So if the Convention had positively fixed a trial by jury in all the civil cases in which it is contended that it ought to have been established, it might have been found highly inconvenient in practice, as in the case above stated; but, if fixed by the Constitution, the inconvenience would have had to be endured (whatever mischief might arise from it) until the Constitution itself should be altered.

13

OLIVER ELLSWORTH, CONNECTICUT RATIFYING CONVENTION
7 Jan. 1788
Elliot 2:196

This Constitution defines the extent of the powers of the general government. If the general legislature should at any time overleap their limits, the judicial department is a constitutional check. If the United States go beyond their powers, if they make a law which the Constitution does not authorize, it is void; and the judicial power, the national judges, who to secure their impartiality, are to be made independent, will declare it to be void. On the other hand, if the states go beyond their limits, if they make a law which is a usurpation upon the federal government the law is void; and upright, independent judges will declare it to be so. Still, however, if the United States and the individual states will quarrel, if they want to fight, they may do it, and no frame of government can possibly prevent it.

14

JAMES MADISON, FEDERALIST, NO. 37,
235–37
11 Jan. 1788

The experience of ages, with the continued and combined labors of the most enlightened Legislators and jurists, have been equally unsuccessful in delineating the several objects and limits of different codes of laws and different tribunals of justice. The precise extent of the common law, the statute law, the maritime law, the ecclesiastical law, the law of corporations and other local laws and customs, remain still to be clearly and finally established in Great-Britain, where accuracy in such subjects has been more industriously pursued than in any other part of the world. The jurisdiction of her several courts, general and local, of law, of equity, of admiralty, &c. is not less a source of frequent and intricate discussions, sufficiently denoting the indeterminate limits by which they are respectively circumscribed. All new laws, though penned with the greatest technical skill, and passed on the fullest and most mature deliberation, are considered as more or less obscure and equivocal, until their meaning be liquidated and ascertained by a series of particular discussions and adjudications. Besides the obscurity arising from the complexity of objects, and the imperfection of the human faculties, the medium

through which the conceptions of men are conveyed to each other, adds a fresh embarrassment. The use of words is to express ideas. Perspicuity therefore requires not only that the ideas should be distinctly formed, but that they should be expressed by words distinctly and exclusively appropriated to them. But no language is so copious as to supply words and phrases for every complex idea, or so correct as not to include many equivocally denoting different ideas. Hence, it must happen, that however accurately objects may be discriminated in themselves, and however accurately the discrimination may be considered, the definition of them may be rendered inaccurate by the inaccuracy of the terms in which it is delivered. And this unavoidable inaccuracy must be greater or less, according to the complexity and novelty of the objects defined. When the Almighty himself condescends to address mankind in their own language, his meaning, luminous as it must be, is rendered dim and doubtful, by the cloudy medium through which it is communicated.

15

FEDERAL FARMER, NO. 15
18 Jan. 1788
Storing 2.8.185

The business of the judicial department is, properly speaking, judicial in part, in part executive, done by judges and juries, by certain recording and executive officers, as clerks, sheriffs, etc. they are all properly limbs, or parts, of the judicial courts, and have it in charge, faithfully to decide upon, and execute the laws, in judicial cases, between the public and individuals, between man and man. The recording and executive officers, in this department, may well enough be formed by legislative acts, from time to time: but the offices, the situation, the powers and duties of judges and juries, are too important, as they respect the political system, as well as the administration of justice, not to be fixed on general principles by the constitution. It is true, the laws are made by the legislature; but the judges and juries, in their interpretations, and in directing the execution of them, have a very extensive influence for preserving or destroying liberty, and for changing the nature of the government. It is an observation of an approved writer, that judicial power is of such a nature, that when we have ascertained and fixed its limits, with all the caution and precision we can, it will yet be formidable, somewhat arbitrary and despotic—that is, after all our cares, we must leave a vast deal to the discretion and interpretation—to the wisdom, integrity, and politics of the judges— These men, such is the state even of the best laws, may do wrong, perhaps, in a thousand cases, sometimes with, and sometimes without design, yet it may be impracticable to convict them of misconduct. These considerations shew, how cautious a free people ought to be in forming this, as well as the other branches of their government, especially when connected with other considerations equally deserving of notice and attention. When the legislature makes a bad law, or the first executive magistrates usurp upon the rights of the people, they discover the evil much sooner, than the abuses of power in the judicial department; the proceedings of which are far more intricate, complex, and out of their immediate view. A bad law immediately excites a general alarm; a bad judicial determination, though not less pernicious in its consequences, is immediately felt, probably, by a single individual only, and noticed only by his neighbours, and a few spectators in the court. In this country, we have been always jealous of the legislature, and especially the executive; but not always of the judiciary: but very few men attentively consider the essential parts of it, and its proceedings, as they tend to support or to destroy free government: only a few professional men are in a situation properly to do this; and it is often alledged, that instances have not frequently occurred, in which they have been found very alert watchmen in the cause of liberty, or in the cause of democratic republics. Add to these considerations, that particular circumstances exist at this time to increase our inattention to limiting properly the judicial powers, we may fairly conclude, we are more in danger of sowing the seeds of arbitrary government in this department than in any other. In the unsettled state of things in this country, for several years past, it has been thought, that our popular legislatures have, sometimes, departed from the line of strict justice, while the law courts have shewn a disposition more punctually to keep to it. We are not sufficiently attentive to the circumstances, that the measures of popular legislatures naturally settle down in time, and gradually approach a mild and just medium; while the rigid systems of the law courts naturally become more severe and arbitrary, if not carefully tempered and guarded by the constitution, and by laws, from time to time. It is true, much has been written and said about some of these courts lately, in some of the states; but all has been about their fees, &c. and but very little to the purposes, as to their influence upon the freedom of the government.

16

FEDERAL FARMER, NO. 18
25 Jan. 1788
Storing 2.8.224

As to all federal objects, the union will have complete jurisdiction over them, of course any where, and every where. I still think, that no actions ought to be allowed to be brought in the federal courts, between citizens of different states, at least, unless the cause be of very considerable importance: that no action against a state government, by any citizen or foreigner, ought to be allowed; and no action, in which a foreign subject is party, at least, unless it be of very considerable importance, ought to be instituted in the federal courts—I confess, I can see no reason whatever, for a foreigner, or for citizens of different states, carrying sixpenny causes into the federal courts; I think the state courts will be found by experience, to be bottomed on better principles, and to administer justice better than the federal courts.

17

JAMES IREDELL, MARCUS, ANSWERS TO MR. MASON'S OBJECTIONS TO THE NEW CONSTITUTION
1788
Pamphlets 342–44

IV. Objection.

"The judiciary of the United States is so constructed and extended, as to absorb and destroy the judiciaries of the several States; thereby rendering law as tedious, intricate and expensive and justice as unattainable by a great part of the community, as in England; and enabling the rich to oppress and ruin the poor."

Answer.

Mr. Mason has here asserted, "That the judiciary of the United States is so constructed and extended, as to absorb and destroy the judiciaries of the several States." How is this the case? Are not the State judiciaries left uncontroled as to the affairs of that *State* only? In this, as in all other cases, where there is a wise distribution, power is commensurate to its object. With the mere internal concerns of a State Congress are to have nothing to do: In no case but where the Union is in some measure concerned, are the federal courts to have any jurisdiction. The State judiciary will be a satellite waiting upon its proper planet: That of the Union, like the sun, cherishing and preserving a whole planetary system.

In regard to a possible ill construction of this authority, we must depend upon our future legislature in this case as well as others, in respect to which it is impracticable to define every thing, that it will be provided for so as to occasion as little expense and distress to individuals as can be. *In parting with the coercive authority over the States as States, there must be a coercion allowed as to individuals. The former power no man of common sense can any longer seriously contend for; the latter is the only alternative.* Suppose an objection should be made that the future legislature should not ascertain salaries, because they might divide among themselves and their officers all the revenue of the Union. Will not every man see how irrational it is to expect that any government can exist which is to be fettered in its most necessary operations for fear of abuse?

18

LUTHER MARTIN, GENUINE INFORMATION
1788
Storing 2.4.89–92

By the *third article*, the judicial power of the United States is vested in *one supreme court*, and in such *inferior courts*, as the Congress may from time to time ordain and establish: These courts, and *these only*, will have a right to decide upon the laws of the United States, and all questions arising upon their construction, and in a judicial manner to carry those laws into execution; to which the courts both superior and inferior of the respective States and their judges and other magistrates are rendered incompetent. To the courts of the general government are also *confined* all cases in law or equity, arising under the proposed constitution, and treaties made under the authority of the United States—all cases affecting ambassadors, other public ministers and consuls—all cases of admiralty and maritime jurisdiction—all controversies to which the United States are a party—all controversies between two or more States—between a State and citizens of another State—between citizens of the same State, claiming lands under grants of different States, and between a State or the citizens thereof, and foreign States, citizens, or subjects. Whether therefore, any *laws* or *regulations* of the *Congress*, or *any acts* of *its President* or *other officers* are *contrary to*, or not *warranted by* the constitution, rests *only* with the judges, who are *appointed* by Congress to *determine;* by whose determinations *every State* must be *bound*. Should any question arise between a foreign consul and any of the citizens of the United States, however remote from the seat of empire, it is to be heard before the judiciary of the general government, and in the *first* instance to be heard in the supreme court, however inconvenient to the parties, and however trifling the subject of dispute.

Should the mariners of an American or foreign vessel, while in any American port, have occasion to sue for their wages, or in any other instance a controversy belonging to the admiralty jurisdiction should take place between them and their masters or owners, it is in the courts of the general government the suit must be instituted; and either party may carry it by appeal to its supreme court; the injury to commerce and the oppression to individuals which may thence arise need not be enlarged upon. Should a citizen of Virginia, Pennsylvania, or any other of the United States be indebted to, or have debts due from, a citizen of this State, or any other claim be subsisting on one side or the other, in consequence of commercial or other transactions, it is only in the courts of Congress that either can apply for redress. The case is the same should any claim subsist between citizens of this State and foreigners, merchants, mariners, and others, whether of a commercial or of any other nature, they must be prosecuted in the same courts; and though in the first instance they may be brought in the inferior, yet an appeal may be made to the supreme judiciary, even from the remotest State in the union.

The inquiry concerning, and trial of every offence against, and breach of the laws of Congress, are also *confined* to its courts; the same courts also have the *sole* right to inquire concerning and try every offence, from the lowest to the highest, committed by the citizens of any other State, or of a foreign nation, against the laws of this State within its territory—and in *all these cases* the decision may be ultimately brought before the supreme tribunal, since the *appellate jurisdiction* extends to *criminal* as well as to civil cases.

And in all those cases where the general government has jurisdiction in civil questions, the proposed constitution *not only* makes *no provision for the trial by jury* in the *first* instance, but by its appellate jurisdiction *absolutely takes away that inestimable privilege*, since it expressly declares the supreme court shall have appellate jurisdiction both as to law and *fact*.—Should therefore, a jury be adopted in the *inferior* court, it would only be a *needless expence*, since on an appeal the *determination* of that *jury, even on questions of fact*, however honest and upright, is to be of *no possible effect*—the supreme court is to take up *all questions of fact*—to *examine the evidence relative* thereto—to *decide upon* them in the *same manner* as if they had *never been tried by a jury*—nor is *trial by jury secured in criminal cases:* it is true, that in the first instance, in the inferior court the trial is to be by jury, in this and in this only, is the difference between criminal and civil cases; but, Sir, the *appellate jurisdiction extends*, as I have observed, to cases *criminal* as well as to civil, and on the *appeal* the *court* is to *decide not only* on the law but on the *fact*, if, therefore, *even in criminal* cases the general government is not satisfied with the verdict of the jury, its officer may remove the prosecution to the supreme court, and *there* the *verdict of the jury is to be of no effect*, but the *judges of this court* are to *decide upon the fact* as well as the law, the *same as in civil cases*.

19

BRUTUS, NO. 11
31 Jan. 1788
Storing 2.9.130–38

The nature and extent of the judicial power of the United States, proposed to be granted by this constitution, claims our particular attention.

Much has been said and written upon the subject of this new system on both sides, but I have not met with any writer, who has discussed the judicial powers with any degree of accuracy. And yet it is obvious, that we can form but very imperfect ideas of the manner in which this government will work, or the effect it will have in changing the internal police and mode of distributing justice at present subsisting in the respective states, without a thorough investigation of the powers of the judiciary and of the manner in which they will operate. This government is a complete system, not only for making, but for executing laws. And the courts of law, which will be constituted by it, are not only to decide upon the constitution and the laws made in pursuance of it, but by officers subordinate to them to execute all their decisions. The real effect of this system of government, will therefore be brought home to the feelings of the people, through the medium of the judicial power. It is, moreover, of great importance, to examine with care the nature and extent of the judicial power, because those who are to be vested with it, are to be placed in a situation altogether unprecedented in a free country. They are to be rendered totally independent, both of the people and the legislature, both with respect to their offices and salaries. No errors they may commit can be corrected by any power above them, if any such power there be, nor can they be removed from office for making ever so many erroneous adjudications.

The only causes for which they can be displaced, is, conviction of treason, bribery, and high crimes and misdemeanors.

This part of the plan is so modelled, as to authorise the courts, not only to carry into execution the powers expressly given, but where these are wanting or ambiguously expressed, to supply what is wanting by their own decisions.

That we may be enabled to form a just opinion on this subject, I shall, in considering it,

1st. Examine the nature and extent of the judicial powers—and

2d. Enquire, whether the courts who are to exercise them, are so constituted as to afford reasonable ground of confidence, that they will exercise them for the general good.

With a regard to the nature and extent of the judicial powers, I have to regret my want of capacity to give that full and minute explanation of them that the subject merits. To be able to do this, a man should be possessed of a degree of law knowledge far beyond what I pretend to. A number of hard words and technical phrases are used in this part of the system, about the meaning of which gentlemen learned in the law differ.

Its advocates know how to avail themselves of these phrases. In a number of instances, where objections are made to the powers given to the judicial, they give such an explanation to the technical terms as to avoid them.

Though I am not competent to give a perfect explanation of the powers granted to this department of the government, I shall yet attempt to trace some of the leading features of it, from which I presume it will appear, that they will operate to a total subversion of the state judiciaries, if not, to the legislative authority of the states.

In article 3d, sect. 2d, it is said, "The judicial power shall extend to all cases in law and equity arising under this constitution, the laws of the United States, and treaties made, or which shall be made, under their authority, &c."

The first article to which this power extends, is, all cases in law and equity arising under this constitution.

What latitude of construction this clause should receive,

it is not easy to say. At first view, one would suppose, that it meant no more than this, that the courts under the general government should exercise, not only the powers of courts of law, but also that of courts of equity, in the manner in which those powers are usually exercised in the different states. But this cannot be the meaning, because the next clause authorises the courts to take cognizance of all cases in law and equity arising under the laws of the United States; this last article, I conceive, conveys as much power to the general judicial as any of the state courts possess.

The cases arising under the constitution must be different from those arising under the laws, or else the two clauses mean exactly the same thing.

The cases arising under the constitution must include such, as bring into question its meaning, and will require an explanation of the nature and extent of the powers of the different departments under it.

This article, therefore, vests the judicial with a power to resolve all questions that may arise on any case on the construction of the constitution, either in law or in equity.

1st. They are authorised to determine all questions that may arise upon the meaning of the constitution in law. This article vests the courts with authority to give the constitution a legal construction, or to explain it according to the rules laid down for construing a law.—These rules give a certain degree of latitude of explanation. According to this mode of construction, the courts are to give such meaning to the constitution as comports best with the common, and generally received acceptation of the words in which it is expressed, regarding their ordinary and popular use, rather than their grammatical propriety. Where words are dubious, they will be explained by the context. The end of the clause will be attended to, and the words will be understood, as having a view to it; and the words will not be so understood as to bear no meaning or a very absurd one.

2d. The judicial are not only to decide questions arising upon the meaning of the constitution in law, but also in equity.

By this they are empowered, to explain the constitution according to the reasoning spirit of it, without being confined to the words or letter.

"From this method of interpreting laws (says Blackstone) by the reason of them, arises what we call equity;" which is thus defined by Grotius, "the correction of that, wherein the law, by reason of its universality, is deficient["]; for since in laws all cases cannot be foreseen, or expressed, it is necessary, that when the decrees of the law cannot be applied to particular cases, there should some where be a power vested of defining those circumstances, which had they been foreseen the legislator would have expressed; and these are the cases, which according to Grotius, ["]lex non exacte definit, sed arbitrio boni viri permittet."

The same learned author observes, "That equity, thus depending essentially upon each individual case, there can be no established rules and fixed principles of equity laid down, without destroying its very essence, and reducing it to a positive law."

From these remarks, the authority and business of the

courts of law, under this clause, may be understood.

They will give the sense of every article of the constitution, that may from time to time come before them. And in their decisions they will not confine themselves to any fixed or established rules, but will determine, according to what appears to them, the reason and spirit of the constitution. The opinions of the supreme court, whatever they may be, will have the force of law; because there is no power provided in the constitution, that can correct their errors, or controul their adjudications. From this court there is no appeal. And I conceive the legislature themselves, cannot set aside a judgment of this court, because they are authorised by the constitution to decide in the last resort. The legislature must be controuled by the constitution, and not the constitution by them. They have therefore no more right to set aside any judgment pronounced upon the construction of the constitution, than they have to take from the president, the chief command of the army and navy, and commit it to some other person. The reason is plain; the judicial and executive derive their authority from the same source, that the legislature do theirs; and therefore in all cases, where the constitution does not make the one responsible to, or controulable by the other, they are altogether independent of each other.

20

BRUTUS, NO. 12
7–14 Feb. 1788
Storing 2.9.146–54

First. Let us enquire how the judicial power will effect an extension of the legislative authority.

Perhaps the judicial power will not be able, by direct and positive decrees, ever to direct the legislature, because it is not easy to conceive how a question can be brought before them in a course of legal discussion, in which they can give a decision, declaring, that the legislature have certain powers which they have not exercised, and which, in consequence of the determination of the judges, they will be bound to exercise. But it is easy to see, that in their adjudications they may establish certain principles, which being received by the legislature, will enlarge the sphere of their power beyond all bounds.

It is to be observed, that the supreme court has the power, in the last resort, to determine all questions that may arise in the course of legal discussion, on the meaning and construction of the constitution. This power they will hold under the constitution, and independent of the legislature. The latter can no more deprive the former of this right, than either of them, or both of them together, can take from the president, with the advice of the senate, the power of making treaties, or appointing ambassadors.

In determining these questions, the court must and will assume certain principles, from which they will reason, in forming their decisions. These principles, whatever they may be, when they become fixed, by a course of decisions, will be adopted by the legislature, and will be the rule by which they will explain their own powers. This appears evident from this consideration, that if the legislature pass laws, which, in the judgment of the court, they are not authorised to do by the constitution, the court will not take notice of them; for it will not be denied, that the constitution is the highest or supreme law. And the courts are vested with the supreme and uncontroulable power, to determine, in all cases that come before them, what the constitution means; they cannot, therefore, execute a law, which, in their judgment, opposes the constitution, unless we can suppose they can make a superior law give way to an inferior. The legislature, therefore, will not go over the limits by which the courts may adjudge they are confined. And there is little room to doubt but that they will come up to those bounds, as often as occasion and opportunity may offer, and they may judge it proper to do it. For as on the one hand, they will not readily pass laws which they know the courts will not execute, so on the other, we may be sure they will not scruple to pass such as they know they will give effect, as often as they may judge it proper.

From these observations it appears, that the judgment of the judicial, on the constitution, will become the rule to guide the legislature in their construction of their powers.

What the principles are, which the courts will adopt, it is impossible for us to say; but taking up the powers as I have explained them in my last number, which they will possess under this clause, it is not difficult to see, that they may, and probably will, be very liberal ones.

We have seen, that they will be authorized to give the constitution a construction according to its spirit and reason, and not to confine themselves to its letter.

To discover the spirit of the constitution, it is of the first importance to attend to the principal ends and designs it has in view. These are expressed in the preamble, in the following words, viz. "We, the people of the United States, in order to form a more perfect union, establish justice, insure domestic tranquility, provide for the common defence, promote the general welfare, and secure the blessings of liberty to ourselves and our posterity, do ordain and establish this constitution," &c. If the end of the government is to be learned from these words, which are clearly designed to declare it, it is obvious it has in view every object which is embraced by any government. The preservation of internal peace—the due administration of justice—and to provide for the defence of the community, seems to include all the objects of government; but if they do not, they are certainly comprehended in the words, "to provide for the general welfare." If it be further considered, that this constitution, if it is ratified, will not be a compact entered into by states, in their corporate capacities, but an agreement of the people of the United States, as one great body politic, no doubt can remain, but that the great end of the constitution, if it is to be collected from the preamble, in which its end is declared, is to constitute a government which is to extend to every case for which any government is instituted, whether external or internal. The courts, therefore, will establish this as a principle in expounding the constitution, and will give every part of it such an explanation, as will give latitude to every department under it, to take cognizance of every matter, not only that affects the general and national concerns of the union, but also of such as relate to the administration of private justice, and to regulating the internal and local affairs of the different parts.

Such a rule of exposition is not only consistent with the general spirit of the preamble, but it will stand confirmed by considering more minutely the different clauses of it.

The first object declared to be in view is, "To form a perfect union." It is to be observed, it is not an union of states or bodies corporate; had this been the case the existence of the state governments, might have been secured. But it is a union of the people of the United States considered as one body, who are to ratify this constitution, if it is adopted. Now to make a union of this kind perfect, it is necessary to abolish all inferior governments, and to give the general one compleat legislative, executive and judicial powers to every purpose. The courts therefore will establish it as a rule in explaining the constitution to give it such a construction as will best tend to perfect the union or take from the state governments every power of either making or executing laws. The second object is "to establish justice." This must include not only the idea of instituting the rule of justice, or of making laws which shall be the measure or rule of right, but also of providing for the application of this rule or of administering justice under it. And under this the courts will in their decisions extend the power of the government to all cases they possibly can, or otherwise they will be restricted in doing what appears to be the intent of the constitution they should do, to wit, pass laws and provide for the execution of them, for the general distribution of justice between man and man. Another end declared is "to insure domestic tranquility." This comprehends a provision against all private breaches of the peace, as well as against all public commotions or general insurrections; and to attain the object of this clause fully, the government must exercise the power of passing laws on these subjects, as well as of appointing magistrates with authority to execute them. And the courts will adopt these ideas in their expositions. I might proceed to the other clause, in the preamble, and it would appear by a consideration of all of them separately, as it does by taking them together, that if the spirit of this system is to be known from its declared end and design in the preamble, its spirit is to subvert and abolish all the powers of the state government, and to embrace every object to which any government extends.

As it sets out in the preamble with this declared intention, so it proceeds in the different parts with the same idea. Any person, who will peruse the 8th section with attention, in which most of the powers are enumerated, will perceive that they either expressly or by implication extend to almost every thing about which any legislative power can be employed. But if this equitable mode of construction is applied to this part of the constitution; nothing can stand before it.

This will certainly give the first clause in that article a construction which I confess I think the most natural and grammatical one, to authorise the Congress to do any thing which in their judgment will tend to provide for the general welfare, and this amounts to the same thing as general and unlimited powers of legislation in all cases.

This same manner of explaining the constitution, will fix a meaning, and a very important one too, to the 12th [18th] clause of the same section, which authorises the Congress to make all laws which shall be proper and necessary for carrying into effect the foregoing powers, &c. A voluminous writer in favor of this system, has taken great pains to convince the public, that this clause means nothing: for that the same powers expressed in this, are implied in other parts of the constitution. Perhaps it is so, but still this will undoubtedly be an excellent auxilliary to assist the courts to discover the spirit and reason of the constitution, and when applied to any and every of the other clauses granting power, will operate powerfully in extracting the spirit from them.

I might instance a number of clauses in the constitution, which, if explained in an *equitable* manner, would extend the powers of the government to every case, and reduce the state legislatures to nothing; but, I should draw out my remarks to an undue length, and I presume enough has been said to shew, that the courts have sufficient ground in the exercise of this power, to determine, that the legislature have no bounds set to them by this constitution, by any supposed right the legislatures of the respective states may have, to regulate any of their local concerns.

21

BRUTUS, NO. 13
21 Feb. 1788
Storing 2.9.159–65

The next paragraph extends its authority, to all cases, in law and equity, arising under the laws of the United States. This power, as I understand it, is a proper one. The proper province of the judicial power, in any government, is, as I conceive, to declare what is the law of the land. To explain and enforce those laws, which the supreme power or legislature may pass; but not to declare what the powers of the legislature are. I suppose the cases in equity, under the laws, must be so construed, as to give the supreme court not only a legal, but equitable jurisdiction of cases which may be brought before them, or in other words, so, as to give them, not only the powers which are now exercised by our courts of law, but those also, which are now exercised by our court of chancery. If this be the meaning, I have no other objection to the power, than what arises from the undue extension of the legislative power. For, I conceive that the judicial power should be commensurate with the legislative. Or, in other words, the supreme court should have authority to determine questions arising under the laws of the union.

The next paragraph which gives a power to decide in law and equity, on all cases arising under treaties, is unintelligible to me. I can readily comprehend what is meant by deciding a case under a treaty. For as treaties will be the law of the land, every person who have rights or privileges secured by treaty, will have aid of the courts of law, in recovering them. But I do not understand, what is meant by equity arising under a treaty. I presume every right which can be claimed under a treaty, must be claimed by virtue of some article or clause contained in it, which gives the right in plain and obvious words; or at least, I conceive, that the rules for explaining treaties, are so well ascertained, that there is no need of having recourse to an equitable construction. If under this power, the courts are to explain treaties, according to what they conceive are their spirit, which is nothing less than a power to give them whatever extension they may judge proper, it is a dangerous and improper power. The cases affecting ambassadors, public ministers, and consuls—of admiralty and maritime jurisdiction; controversies to which the United States are a party, and controversies between states, it is proper should be under the cognizance of the courts of the union, because none but the general government, can, or ought to pass laws on their subjects. But, I conceive the clause which extends the power of the judicial to controversies arising between a state and citizens of another state, improper in itself, and will, in its exercise, prove most pernicious and destructive.

It is improper, because it subjects a state to answer in a court of law, to the suit of an individual. This is humiliating and degrading to a government, and, what I believe, the supreme authority of no state ever submitted to.

The states are now subject to no such actions. All contracts entered into by individuals with states, were made upon the faith and credit of the states; and the individuals never had in contemplation any compulsory mode of obliging the government to fulfil its engagements.

The evil consequences that will flow from the exercise of this power, will best appear by tracing it in its operation. The constitution does not direct the mode in which an individual shall commence a suit against a state or the manner in which the judgement of the court shall be carried into execution, but it gives the legislature full power to pass all laws which shall be proper and necessary for the purpose. And they certainly must make provision for these purposes, or otherwise the power of the judicial will be nugatory. For, to what purpose will the power of a judicial be, if they have no mode, in which they can call the parties before them? Or of what use will it be, to call the parties to answer, if after they have given judgement, there is no authority to execute the judgment? We must, therefore, conclude, that the legislature will pass laws which will be effectual in this head. An individual of one state will then have a legal remedy against a state for any demand he may have against a state to which he does not belong. Every state in the union is largely indebted to individuals. For the payment of these debts they have given notes payable to the bearer. At least this is the case in this state. Whenever a citizen of another state becomes possessed of one of these notes, he may commence an action in the supreme court of the general government; and I cannot see any way in which he can be prevented from recovering. It is

easy to see, that when this once happens, the notes of the state will pass rapidly from the hands of citizens of the state to those of other states.

And when the citizens of other states possess them, they may bring suits against the state for them, and by this means, judgments and executions may be obtained against the state for the whole amount of the state debt. It is certain the state, with the utmost exertions it can make, will not be able to discharge the debt she owes, under a considerable number of years, perhaps with the best management, it will require twenty or thirty years to discharge it. This new system will protract the time in which the ability of the state will enable them to pay off their debt, because all the funds of the state will be transferred to the general government, except those which arise from internal taxes.

The situation of the states will be deplorable. By this system, they will surrender to the general government, all the means of raising money, and at the same time, will subject themselves to suits at law, for the recovery of the debts they have contracted in effecting the revolution.

The debts of the individual states will amount to a sum, exceeding the domestic debt of the United States; these will be left upon them, with power in the judicial of the general government, to enforce their payment, while the general government will possess an exclusive command of the most productive funds, from which the states can derive money, and a command of every other source of revenue paramount to the authority of any state.

It may be said that the apprehension that the judicial power will operate in this manner is merely visionary, for that the legislature will never pass laws that will work these effects. Or if they were disposed to do it, they cannot provide for levying an execution on a state, for where will the officer find property whereon to levy?

To this I would reply, if this is a power which will not or cannot be executed, it was useless and unwise to grant it to the judicial. For what purpose is a power given which it is imprudent or impossible to exercise? If it be improper for a government to exercise a power, it is improper they should be vested with it. And it is unwise to authorise a government to do what they cannot effect.

22

BRUTUS, NO. 15
20 Mar. 1788
Storing 2.9.186–89, 193

I said in my last number, that the supreme court under this constitution would be exalted above all other power in the government, and subject to no controul. The business of this paper will be to illustrate this, and to shew the danger that will result from it. I question whether the world ever saw, in any period of it, a court of justice invested with such immense powers, and yet placed in a situation so little responsible. Certain it is, that in England, and in the several states, where we have been taught to believe, the courts of law are put upon the most prudent establishment, they are on a very different footing.

The judges in England, it is true, hold their offices during their good behaviour, but then their determinations are subject to correction by the house of lords; and their power is by no means so extensive as that of the proposed supreme court of the union.—I believe they in no instance assume the authority to set aside an act of parliament under the idea that it is inconsistent with their constitution. They consider themselves bound to decide according to the existing laws of the land, and never undertake to controul them by adjudging that they are inconsistent with the constitution—much less are they vested with the power of giving an *equitable* construction to the constitution.

The judges in England are under the controul of the legislature, for they are bound to determine according to the laws passed by them. But the judges under this constitution will controul the legislature, for the supreme court are authorised in the last resort, to determine what is the extent of the powers of the Congress; they are to give the constitution an explanation, and there is no power above them to set aside their judgment The framers of this constitution appear to have followed that of the British, in rendering the judges independent, by granting them their offices during good behaviour, without following the constitution of England, in instituting a tribunal in which their errors may be corrected; and without adverting to this, that the judicial under this system have a power which is above the legislative, and which indeed transcends any power before given to a judicial by any free government under heaven.

I do not object to the judges holding their commissions during good behaviour. I suppose it a proper provision provided they were made properly responsible. But I say, this system has followed the English government in this, while it has departed from almost every other principle of their jurisprudence, under the idea, of rendering the judges independent; which, in the British constitution, means no more than that they hold their places during good behaviour, and have fixed salaries, they have made the judges *independent*, in the fullest sense of the word. There is no power above them, to controul any of their decisions. There is no authority that can remove them, and they cannot be controuled by the laws of the legislature. In short, they are independent of the people, of the legislature, and of every power under heaven. Men placed in this situation will generally soon feel themselves independent of heaven itself.

. . . . .

3d. The power of this court is in many cases superior to that of the legislature. I have shewed, in a former paper, that this court will be authorised to decide upon the meaning of the constitution, and that, not only according to the natural and ob[vious] meaning of the words, but also according to the spirit and intention of it. In the exercise of this power they will not be subordinate to, but above the legislature. For all the departments of this government will receive their powers, so far as they are expressed in the constitution, from the people immediately, who are the source of power. The legislature can only exercise such powers as are given them by the constitution, they cannot assume any of the rights annexed to the judicial, for this plain reason, that the same authority which vested the legislature with their powers, vested the judicial with theirs—both are derived from the same source, both therefore are equally valid, and the judicial hold their powers independently of the legislature, as the legislature do of the judicial.—The supreme cort then have a right, independent of the legislature, to give a construction to the constitution and every part of it, and there is no power provided in this system to correct their construction or do it away. If, therefore, the legislature pass any laws, inconsistent with the sense the judges put upon the constitution, they will declare it void; and therefore in this respect their power is superior to that of the legislature. In England the judges are not only subject to have their decisions set aside by the house of lords, for error, but in cases where they give an explanation to the laws or constitution of the country, contrary to the sense of the parliament, though the parliament will not set aside the judgement of the court, yet, they have authority, by a new law, to explain a former one, and by this means to prevent a reception of such decisions. But no such power is in the legislature. The judges are supreme—and no law, explanatory of the constitution, will be binding on them.

23

ALEXANDER HAMILTON, FEDERALIST, NO. 80,
534–41
28 May 1788

To judge with accuracy of the proper extent of the federal judicature, it will be necessary to consider in the first place what are its proper objects.

It seems scarcely to admit of controversy that the judiciary authority of the union ought to extend to these several descriptions of causes. 1st. To all those which arise out of the laws of the United States, passed in pursuance of their just and constitutional powers of legislation; 2d. to all those which concern the execution of the provisions expressly contained in the articles of union; 3d. to all those in which the United States are a party; 4th. to all those which involve the PEACE of the CONFEDERACY, whether they relate to the intercourse between the United States and foreign nations, or to that between the States themselves; 5th. to all those which originate on the high seas, and are of admiralty or maritime jurisdiction; and lastly, to all those in which the state tribunals cannot be supposed to be impartial and unbiassed.

The first point depends upon this obvious consideration that there ought always to be a constitutional method of giving efficacy to constitutional provisions. What for instance would avail restrictions on the authority of the state legislatures, without some constitutional mode of enforcing the observance of them? The states, by the plan of the convention are prohibited from doing a variety of things; some of which are incompatible with the interests of the union, and others with the principles of good government. The imposition of duties on imported articles, and the emission of paper money, are specimens of each kind. No man of sense will believe that such prohibitions would be scrupulously regarded, without some effectual power in the government to restrain or correct the infractions of them. This power must either be a direct negative on the state laws, or an authority in the federal courts, to over-rule such as might be in manifest contravention of the articles of union. There is no third course that I can imagine. The latter appears to have been thought by the convention preferable to the former, and I presume will be most agreeable to the states.

As to the second point, it is impossible by any argument or comment to make it clearer than it is in itself. If there are such things as political axioms, the propriety of the judicial power of a government being co-extensive with its legislative, may be ranked among the number. The mere necessity of uniformity in the interpretation of the national laws, decides the question. Thirteen independent courts of final jurisdiction over the same causes, arising upon the same laws, is a hydra in government, from which nothing but contradiction and confusion can proceed.

Still less need be said in regard to the third point. Controversies between the nation and its members or citizens, can only be properly referred to the national tribunals. Any other plan would be contrary to reason, to precedent, and to decorum.

The fourth point rests on this plain proposition, that the peace of the WHOLE ought not to be left at the disposal of a PART. The union will undoubtedly be answerable to foreign powers for the conduct of its members. And the responsibility for an injury ought ever to be accompanied with the faculty of preventing it. As the denial or perversion of justice by the sentences of courts, as well as in any other manner, is with reason classed among the just causes of war, it will follow that the federal judiciary ought to have cognizance of all causes in which the citizens of other countries are concerned. This is not less essential to the preservation of the public faith, than to the security of the public tranquility. A distinction may perhaps be imagined between cases arising upon treaties and the laws of nations, and those which may stand merely on the footing of the municipal law. The former kind may be supposed proper for the federal jurisdiction, the latter for that of the states. But it is at least problematical whether an unjust sentence against a foreigner, where the subject of controversy was wholly relative to the *lex loci*, would not, if unredressed, be an aggression upon his sovereign, as well as one which violated the stipulations in a treaty or the general laws of nations. And a still greater objection to the distinction would result from the immense difficulty, if not impossibility, of a practical discrimination between the cases of one complection and those of the other. So great a proportion of the cases in which foreigners are parties involve national questions, that it is by far most safe and most expedient to refer all those in which they are concerned to the national tribunals.

The power of determining causes between two states, between one state and the citizens of another, and between the citizens of different states, is perhaps not less essential to the peace of the union than that which has been just examined. History gives us a horrid picture of the dissentions and private wars which distracted and desolated Germany prior to the institution of the IMPERIAL CHAMBER by Maximilian, towards the close of the fifteenth century; and informs us at the same time of the vast influence of that institution in appeasing the disorders and establishing the tranquility of the empire. This was a court invested with authority to decide finally all differences between the members of the Germanic body.

A method of terminating territorial disputes between the states, under the authority of the federal head, was not unattended to, even in the imperfect system by which they have been hitherto held together. But there are many other sources, besides interfering claims of boundary, from which bickerings and animosities may spring up among the members of the union. To some of these we have been witnesses in the course of our past experience. It will readily be conjectured that I allude to the fraudulent laws which have been passed in too many of the states. And though the proposed constitution establishes particular guards against the repetition of those instances which have heretofore made their appearance, yet it is warrantable to apprehend that the spirit which produced them will assume new shapes that could not be foreseen, nor specifically provided against. Whatever practices may have a tendency to disturb the harmony between the states, are proper objects of federal superintendence and control.

It may be esteemed the basis of the union, that "the citizens of each state shall be entitled to all the privileges and immunities of citizens of the several states." And if it be a just principle that every government *ought to possess the means of executing its own provisions by its own authority*, it will follow, that in order to the inviolable maintenance of that equality of privileges and immunities to which the citizens of the union will be entitled, the national judiciary ought to preside in all cases in which one state or its citizens are opposed to another state or its citizens. To secure the full effect of so fundamental a provision against all evasion and subterfuge, it is necessary that its construction should be committed to that tribunal, which, having no local attachments, will be likely to be impartial between the different states and their citizens, and which, owing its official existence to the union, will never be likely to feel any bias inauspicious to the principles on which it is founded.

The fifth point will demand little animadversion. The most bigotted idolizers of state authority have not thus far shewn a disposition to deny the national judiciary the cognizance of maritime causes. These so generally depend on the laws of nations, and so commonly affect the rights of foreigners, that they fall within the considerations which are relative to the public peace. The most important part of them are by the present confederation submitted to federal jurisdiction.

The reasonableness of the agency of the national courts in cases in which the state tribunals cannot be supposed to be impartial, speaks for itself. No man ought certainly to be a judge in his own cause, or in any cause in respect to which he has the least interest or bias. This principle has no inconsiderable weight in designating the federal courts as the proper tribunals for the determination of controversies between different states and their citizens. And it ought to have the same operation in regard to some cases between the citizens of the same state. Claims to land under grants of different states, founded upon adverse pretensions of boundary, are of this description. The courts of neither of the granting states could be expected to be unbiassed. The laws may have even prejudged the question, and tied the courts down to decisions in favour of the grants of the state to which they belonged. And even where this had not been done, it would be natural that the judges, as men, should feel a strong predilection to the claims of their own government.

Having thus laid down and discussed the principles which ought to regulate the constitution of the federal judiciary, we will proceed to test, by these principles, the particular powers of which, according to the plan of the convention, it is to be composed. It is to comprehend, "all cases in law and equity arising under the constitution, the laws of the United States, and treaties made, or which shall be made under their authority; to all cases affecting ambassadors, other public ministers and consuls; to all cases of admiralty and maritime jurisdiction; to controversies to which the United States shall be a party; to controversies between two or more states, between a state and citizens of another state, between citizens of different states, between citizens of the same state claiming lands under grants of different states, and between a state or the citizens thereof, and foreign states, citizens and subjects." This constitutes the entire mass of the judicial authority of the union. Let us now review it in detail. It is then to extend,

First. To all cases in law and equity *arising under the constitution* and *the laws of the United States*. This corresponds to the two first classes of causes which have been enumerated as proper for the jurisdiction of the United States. It has been asked what is meant by "cases arising under the constitution," in contradistinction from those "arising under the laws of the United States." The difference has been already explained. All the restrictions upon the authority of the state legislatures, furnish examples of it. They are not, for instance, to emit paper money; but the interdiction results from the constitution, and will have no connection with any law of the United States. Should paper money, notwithstanding, be emitted, the controversies concerning it would be cases arising upon the constitution, and not upon the laws of the United States, in the ordinary signification of the terms. This may serve as a sample of the whole.

It has also been asked, what need of the word "equity"? What equitable causes can grow out of the constitution and laws of the United States? There is hardly a subject of litigation between individuals, which may not involve those ingredients of *fraud, accident, trust* or *hardship*, which

would render the matter an object of equitable, rather than of legal jurisdiction, as the distinction is known and established in several of the states. It is the peculiar province, for instance, of a court of equity to relieve against what are called hard bargains: These are contracts, in which, though there may have been no direct fraud or deceit, sufficient to invalidate them in a court of law; yet there may have been some undue and unconscionable advantage taken of the necessities or misfortunes of one of the parties, which a court of equity would not tolerate. In such cases, where foreigners were concerned on either side, it would be impossible for the federal judicatories to do justice without an equitable, as well as a legal jurisdiction. Agreements to convey lands claimed under the grants of different states, may afford another example of the necessity of an equitable jurisdiction in the federal courts. This reasoning may not be so palpable in those states where the formal and technical distinction between LAW and EQUITY is not maintained as in this state, where it is exemplified by every day's practice.

The judiciary authority of the union is to extend—

Second. To treaties made, or which shall be made under the authority of the United States, and to all cases affecting ambassadors, other public ministers and consuls. These belong to the fourth class of the enumerated cases, as they have an evident connection with the preservation of the national peace.

Third. To cases of admiralty and maritime jurisdiction. These form altogether the fifth of the enumerated classes of causes proper for the cognizance of the national courts.

Fourth. To controversies to which the United States shall be a party. These constitute the third of those classes.

Fifth. To controversies between two or more states, between a state and citizens of another state, between citizens of different states. These belong to the fourth of those classes, and partake in some measure of the nature of the last.

Sixth. To cases between the citizens of the same state, *claiming lands under grants of different states*. These fall within the last class, and *are the only instance in which the proposed constitution directly contemplates the cognizance of disputes between the citizens of the same state*.

Seventh. To cases between a state and the citizens thereof, and foreign states, citizens, or subjects. These have been already explained to belong to the fourth of the enumerated classes, and have been shewn to be in a peculiar manner the proper subjects of the national judicature.

From this review of the particular powers of the federal judiciary, as marked out in the constitution, it appears, that they are all conformable to the principles which ought to have governed the structure of that department, and which were necessary to the perfection of the system. If some partial inconveniencies should appear to be connected with the incorporation of any of them into the plan, it ought to be recollected that the national legislature will have ample authority to make such *exceptions* and to prescribe such regulations as will be calculated to obviate or remove these inconveniencies. The possibility of particular mischiefs can never be viewed by a well-informed mind as a solid objection to a general principle, which is calculated to avoid general mischiefs, and to obtain general advantages.

24

Alexander Hamilton, Federalist, no. 81, 542–52
28 May 1788

That there ought to be one court of supreme and final jurisdiction is a proposition which has not been, and is not likely to be contested. The reasons for it have been assigned in another place, and are too obvious to need repetition. The only question that seems to have been raised concerning it, is whether it ought to be a distinct body, or a branch of the legislature. The same contradiction is observable in regard to this matter, which has been remarked in several other cases. The very men who object to the senate as a court of impeachments, on the ground of an improper intermixture of powers, advocate, by implication at least, the propriety of vesting the ultimate decision of all causes in the whole, or in a part of the legislative body.

The arguments or rather suggestions, upon which this charge is founded, are to this effect: "The authority of the proposed supreme court of the United States, which is to be a separate and independent body, will be superior to that of the legislature. The power of construing the laws, according to the *spirit* of the constitution, will enable that court to mould them into whatever shape it may think proper; especially as its decisions will not be in any manner subject to the revision or correction of the legislative body. This is as unprecedented as it is dangerous. In Britain, the judicial power in the last resort, resides in the house of lords, which is a branch of the legislature; and this part of the British government has been imitated in the state constitutions in general. The parliament of Great-Britain, and the legislatures of the several states, can at any time rectify by law, the exceptionable decisions of their respective courts. But the errors and usurpations of the supreme court of the United States will be uncontrolable and remediless." This, upon examination, will be found to be altogether made up of false reasoning upon misconceived fact.

In the first place, there is not a syllable in the plan under consideration, which *directly* empowers the national courts to construe the laws according to the spirit of the constitution, or which gives them any greater latitude in this respect, than may be claimed by the courts of every state. I admit however, that the constitution ought to be the standard of construction for the laws, and that wherever there is an evident opposition, the laws ought to give place to the constitution. But this doctrine is not deducible from any circumstance peculiar to the plan of the convention; but from the general theory of a limited constitution; and as far as it is true, is equally applicable to most, if not to all the state governments. There can be no objection

therefore, on this account, to the federal judicature, which will not lie against the local judicatures in general, and which will not serve to condemn every constitution that attempts to set bounds to the legislative discretion.

But perhaps the force of the objection may be thought to consist in the particular organization of the proposed supreme court; in its being composed of a distinct body of magistrates, instead of being one of the branches of the legislature, as in the government of Great-Britain and in that of this state. To insist upon this point, the authors of the objection must renounce the meaning they have laboured to annex to the celebrated maxim requiring a separation of the departments of power. It shall nevertheless be conceded to them, agreeably to the interpretation given to that maxim in the course of these papers, that it is not violated by vesting the ultimate power of judging in a *part* of the legislative body. But though this be not an absolute violation of that excellent rule; yet it verges so nearly upon it, as on this account alone to be less eligible than the mode preferred by the convention. From a body which had had even a partial agency in passing bad laws, we could rarely expect a disposition to temper and moderate them in the application. The same spirit, which had operated in making them, would be too apt to operate in interpreting them: Still less could it be expected, that men who had infringed the constitution, in the character of legislators, would be disposed to repair the breach, in the character of judges. Nor is this all: Every reason, which recommends the tenure of good behaviour for judicial offices, militates against placing the judiciary power in the last resort in a body composed of men chosen for a limited period. There is an absurdity in referring the determination of causes in the first instance to judges of permanent standing, and in the last to those of a temporary and mutable constitution. And there is a still greater absurdity in subjecting the decisions of men selected for their knowledge of the laws, acquired by long and laborious study, to the revision and control of men, who for want of the same advantage cannot but be deficient in that knowledge. The members of the legislature will rarely be chosen with a view to those qualifications which fit men for the stations of judges; and as on this account there will be great reason to apprehend all the ill consequences of defective information; so on account of the natural propensity of such bodies to party divisions, there will be no less reason to fear, that the pestilential breath of faction may poison the fountains of justice. The habit of being continually marshalled on opposite sides, will be too apt to stifle the voice both of law and of equity.

These considerations teach us to applaud the wisdom of those states, who have committed the judicial power in the last resort, not to a part of the legislature, but to distinct and independent bodies of men. Contrary to the supposition of those, who have represented the plan of the convention in this respect as novel and unprecedented, it is but a copy of the constitutions of New-Hampshire, Massachusetts, Pennsylvania, Delaware, Maryland, Virginia, North-Carolina, South-Carolina and Georgia; and the preference which has been given to these models is highly to be commended.

It is not true, in the second place, that the parliament of Great Britain, or the legislatures of the particular states, can rectify the exceptionable decisions of their respective courts, in any other sense than might be done by a future legislature of the United States. The theory neither of the British, nor the state constitutions, authorises the revisal of a judicial sentence, by a legislative act. Nor is there any thing in the proposed constitution more than in either of them, by which it is forbidden. In the former as well as in the latter, the impropriety of the thing, on the general principles of law and reason, is the sole obstacle. A legislature without exceeding its province cannot reverse a determination once made, in a particular case; though it may prescribe a new rule for future cases. This is the principle, and it applies in all its consequences, exactly in the same manner and extent, to the state governments, as to the national government, now under consideration. Not the least difference can be pointed out in any view of the subject.

It may in the last place be observed that the supposed danger of judiciary encroachments on the legislative authority, which has been upon many occasions reiterated, is in reality a phantom. Particular misconstructions and contraventions of the will of the legislature may now and then happen; but they can never be so extensive as to amount to an inconvenience, or in any sensible degree to affect the order of the political system. This may be inferred with certainty from the general nature of the judicial power; from the objects to which it relates; from the manner in which it is exercised; from its comparative weakness, and from its total incapacity to support its usurpations by force. And the inference is greatly fortified by the consideration of the important constitutional check, which the power of instituting impeachments, in one part of the legislative body, and of determining upon them in the other, would give to that body upon the members of the judicial department. This is alone a complete security. There never can be danger that the judges, by a series of deliberate usurpations on the authority of the legislature, would hazard the united resentment of the body entrusted with it, while this body was possessed of the means of punishing their presumption by degrading them from their stations. While this ought to remove all apprehensions on the subject, it affords at the same time a cogent argument for constituting the senate a court for the trial of impeachments.

Having now examined, and I trust removed the objections to the distinct and independent organization of the supreme court, I proceed to consider the propriety of the power of constituting inferior courts,* and the relations which will subsist between these and the former.

The power of constituting inferior courts is evidently calculated to obviate the necessity of having recourse to the supreme court, in every case of federal cognizance. It is intended to enable the national government to institute or *authorise* in each state or district of the United States, a tribunal competent to the determination of matters of national jurisdiction within its limits.

But why, it is asked, might not the same purpose have been accomplished by the instrumentality of the state courts? This admits of different answers. Though the fitness and competency of those courts should be allowed in the utmost latitude; yet the substance of the power in question, may still be regarded as a necessary part of the plan, if it were only to empower the national legislature to commit to them the cognizance of causes arising out of the national constitution. To confer the power of determining such causes upon the existing courts of the several states, would perhaps be as much "to constitute tribunals," as to create new courts with the like power. But ought not a more direct and explicit provision to have been made in favour of the state courts? There are, in my opinion, substantial reasons against such a provision: The most discerning cannot foresee how far the prevalency of a local spirit may be found to disqualify the local tribunals for the jurisdiction of national causes; whilst every man may discover that courts constituted like those of some of the states, would be improper channels of the judicial authority of the union. State judges, holding their offices during pleasure, or from year to year, will be too little independent to be relied upon for an inflexible execution of the national laws. And if there was a necessity for confiding the original cognizance of causes arising under those laws to them, there would be a correspondent necessity for leaving the door of appeal as wide as possible. In proportion to the grounds of confidence in, or diffidence of the subordinate tribunals, ought to be the facility or difficulty of appeals. And well satisfied as I am of the propriety of the appellate jurisdiction in the several classes of causes to which it is extended by the plan of the convention, I should consider every thing calculated to give in practice, an *unrestrained course* to appeals as a source of public and private inconvenience.

I am not sure but that it will be found highly expedient and useful to divide the United States into four or five, or half a dozen districts; and to institute a federal court in each district, in lieu of one in every state. The judges of these courts, with the aid of the state judges, may hold circuits for the trial of causes in the several parts of the respective districts. Justice through them may be administered with ease and dispatch; and appeals may be safely circumscribed within a very narrow compass. This plan appears to me at present the most eligible of any that could be adopted, and in order to it, it is necessary that the power of constituting inferior courts should exist in the full extent in which it is to be found in the proposed constitution.

These reasons seem sufficient to satisfy a candid mind, that the want of such a power would have been a great defect in the plan. Let us now examine in what manner the judicial authority is to be distributed between the supreme and the inferior courts of the union.

---

*This power has been absurdly represented as intended to abolish all the county courts in the several states, which are commonly called inferior courts. But the expressions of the constitution are to constitute "tribunals INFERIOR TO THE SUPREME COURT," and the evident design of the provision is to enable the institution of local courts subordinate to the supreme, either in states or larger districts. It is ridiculous to imagine that county courts were in contemplation.

The supreme court is to be invested with original jurisdiction, only "in cases affecting ambassadors, other public ministers and consuls, and those in which A STATE shall be a party." Public ministers of every class, are the immediate representatives of their sovereigns. All questions in which they are concerned, are so directly connected with the public peace, that as well for the preservation of this, as out of respect to the sovereignties they represent, it is both expedient and proper, that such questions should be submitted in the first instance to the highest judicatory of the nation. Though consuls have not in strictness a diplomatic character, yet as they are the public agents of the nations to which they belong, the same observation is in a great measure applicable to them. In cases in which a state might happen to be a party, it would ill suit its dignity to be turned over to an inferior tribunal.

Though it may rather be a digression from the immediate subject of this paper, I shall take occasion to mention here, a supposition which has excited some alarm upon very mistaken grounds: It has been suggested that an assignment of the public securities of one state to the citizens of another, would enable them to prosecute that state in the federal courts for the amount of those securities. A suggestion which the following considerations prove to be without foundation.

It is inherent in the nature of sovereignty, not to be amenable to the suit of an individual *without its consent*. This is the general sense and the general practice of mankind; and the exemption, as one of the attributes of sovereignty, is now enjoyed by the government of every state in the union. Unless therefore, there is a surrender of this immunity in the plan of the convention, it will remain with the states, and the danger intimated must be merely ideal. The circumstances which are necessary to produce an alienation of state sovereignty, were discussed in considering the article of taxation, and need not be repeated here. A recurrence to the principles there established will satisfy us, that there is no colour to pretend that the state governments, would by the adoption of that plan, be divested of the privilege of paying their own debts in their own way, free from every constraint but that which flows from the obligations of good faith. The contracts between a nation and individuals are only binding on the conscience of the sovereign, and have no pretensions to a compulsive force. They confer no right of action independent of the sovereign will. To what purpose would it be to authorise suits against states, for the debts they owe? How could recoveries be enforced? It is evident that it could not be done without waging war against the contracting state; and to ascribe to the federal courts, by mere implication, and in destruction of a pre-existing right of the state governments, a power which would involve such a consequence, would be altogether forced and unwarrantable.

Let us resume the train of our observations; we have seen that the original jurisdiction of the supreme court would be confined to two classes of causes, and those of a nature rarely to occur. In all other causes of federal cognizance, the original jurisdiction would appertain to the inferior tribunals, and the supreme court would have nothing more than an appellate jurisdiction, "with such *ex-*

ceptions, and under such *regulations* as the congress shall make."

The propriety of this appellate jurisdiction has been scarcely called in question in regard to matters of law; but the clamours have been loud against it as applied to matters of fact. Some well intentioned men in this state, deriving their notions from the language and forms which obtain in our courts, have been induced to consider it as an implied supersedure of the trial by jury, in favour of the civil law mode of trial, which prevails in our courts of admiralty, probates and chancery. A technical sense has been affixed to the term "appellate," which in our law parlance is commonly used in reference to appeals in the course of the civil law. But if I am not misinformed, the same meaning would not be given to it in any part of New-England. There an appeal from one jury to another is familiar both in language and practice, and is even a matter of course, until there have been two verdicts on one side. The word "appellate" therefore will not be understood in the same sense in New-England as in New-York, which shews the impropriety of a technical interpretation derived from the jurisprudence of any particular state. The expression taken in the abstract, denotes nothing more than the power of one tribunal to review the proceedings of another, either as to the law or fact, or both. The mode of doing it may depend on ancient custom or legislative provision, (in a new government it must depend on the latter) and may be with or without the aid of a jury, as may be judged adviseable. If therefore the re-examination of a fact, once determined by a jury, should in any case be admitted under the proposed constitution, it may be so regulated as to be done by a second jury, either by remanding the cause to the court below for a second trial of the fact, or by directing an issue immediately out of the supreme court.

But it does not follow that the re-examination of a fact once ascertained by a jury, will be permitted in the supreme court. Why may it not be said, with the strictest propriety, when a writ of error is brought from an inferior to a superior court of law in this state, that the latter has jurisdiction of the fact, as well as the law? It is true it cannot institute a new enquiry concerning the fact, but it takes cognizance of it as it appears upon the record, and pronounces the law arising upon it.* This is jurisdiction of both fact and law, nor is it even possible to separate them. Though the common law courts of this state ascertain disputed facts by a jury, yet they unquestionably have jurisdiction of both fact and law; and accordingly, when the former is agreed in the pleadings, they have no recourse to a jury, but proceed at once to judgment. I contend therefore on this ground, that the expressions, "appellate jurisdiction, both as to law and fact," do not necessarily imply a re-examination in the supreme court of facts decided by juries in the inferior courts.

The following train of ideas may well be imagined to have influenced the convention in relation to this particular provision. The appellate jurisdiction of the supreme

---

*This word is a compound of JUS and DICTIO, juris, dictio, or a speaking or pronouncing of the law.

court (may it have been argued) will extend to causes determinable in different modes, some in the course of the COMMON LAW, and others in the course of the CIVIL LAW. In the former, the revision of the law only, will be, generally speaking, the proper province of the supreme court; in the latter, the re-examination of the fact is agreeable to usage, and in some cases, of which prize causes are an example, might be essential to the preservation of the public peace. It is therefore necessary, that the appellate jurisdiction should, in certain cases, extend in the broadest sense to matters of fact. It will not answer to make an express exception of cases, which shall have been originally tried by a jury, because in the courts of some of the states, *all causes* are tried in this mode;* and such an exception would preclude the revision of matters of fact, as well where it might be proper, as where it might be improper. To avoid all inconveniencies, it will be safest to declare generally, that the supreme court shall possess appellate jurisdiction, both as to law and *fact,* and that this jurisdiction shall be subject to such *exceptions* and regulations as the national legislature may prescribe. This will enable the government to modify it in such a manner as will best answer the ends of public justice and security.

This view of the matter, at any rate puts it out of all doubt that the supposed *abolition* of the trial by jury, by the operation of this provision, is fallacious and untrue. The legislature of the United States would certainly have full power to provide that in appeals to the supreme court there should be no re-examination of facts where they had been tried in the original causes by juries. This would certainly be an authorised exception; but if for the reason already intimated it should be thought too extensive, it might be qualified with a limitation to such causes only as are determinable at common law in that mode of trial.

The amount of the observations hitherto made on the authority of the judicial department is this—that it has been carefully restricted to those causes which are manifestly proper for the cognizance of the national judicature, that in the partition of this authority a very small portion of original jurisdiction has been reserved to the supreme court, and the rest consigned to the subordinate tribunals—that the supreme court will possess an appellate jurisdiction both as to law and fact in all the cases referred to them, but subject to any *exceptions* and *regulations* which may be thought adviseable; that this appellate jurisdiction does in no case *abolish* the trial by jury, and that an ordinary degree of prudence and integrity in the national councils will insure us solid advantages from the establishment of the proposed judiciary, without exposing us to any of the inconveniencies which have been predicted from that source.

*I hold that the states will have concurrent jurisdiction with the subordinate federal judicatories, in many cases of federal cognizance, as will be explained in my next paper.

25

ALEXANDER HAMILTON, FEDERALIST, NO. 82,
553–57
28 May 1788

The erection of a new government, whatever care or wisdom may distinguish the work, cannot fail to originate questions of intricacy and nicety; and these may in a particular manner be expected to flow from the establishment of a constitution founded upon the total or partial incorporation of a number of distinct sovereignties. 'Tis time only that can mature and perfect so compound a system, can liquidate the meaning of all the parts, and can adjust them to each other in a harmonious and consistent WHOLE.

Such questions accordingly have arisen upon the plan proposed by the convention, and particularly concerning the judiciary department. The principal of these respect the situation of the state courts in regard to those causes, which are to be submitted to federal jurisdiction. Is this to be exclusive, or are those courts to possess a concurrent jurisdiction? If the latter, in what relation will they stand to the national tribunals? These are inquiries which we meet with in the mouths of men of sense, and which are certainly intitled to attention.

The principles established in a former paper teach us, that the states will retain all *pre-existing* authorities, which may not be exclusively delegated to the federal head; and that this exclusive delegation can only exist in one of three cases; where an exclusive authority is in express terms granted to the union; or where a particular authority is granted to the union, and the exercise of a like authority is prohibited to the states, or where an authority is granted to the union with which a similar authority in the states would be utterly incompatible. Though these principles may not apply with the same force to the judiciary as to the legislative power; yet I am inclined to think that they are in the main just with respect to the former as well as the latter. And under this impression I shall lay it down as a rule that the state courts will *retain* the jurisdiction they now have, unless it appears to be taken away in one of the enumerated modes.

The only thing in the proposed constitution, which wears the appearance of confining the causes of federal cognizance to the federal courts is contained in this passage—"The JUDICIAL POWER of the United States *shall be vested* in one supreme court, and in *such* inferior courts as the congress shall from time to time ordain and establish." This might either be construed to signify, that the supreme and subordinate courts of the union should alone have the power of deciding those causes, to which their authority is to extend; or simply to denote that the organs of the national judiciary should be one supreme court and as many subordinate courts as congress should think proper to appoint, or in other words, that the United States should exercise the judicial power with which they are to be invested through one supreme tribunal and a certain number of inferior ones to be instituted by them. The first excludes, the last admits the concurrent jurisdiction of the state tribunals: And as the first would amount to an alienation of state power by implication, the last appears to me the most natural and the most defensible construction.

But this doctrine of concurrent jurisdiction is only clearly applicable to those descriptions of causes of which the state courts have previous cognizance. It is not equally evident in relation to cases which may grow out of, and be *peculiar* to the constitution to be established: For not to allow the state courts a right of jurisdiction in such cases can hardly be considered as the abridgement of a pre-existing authority. I mean not therefore to contend that the United States in the course of legislation upon the objects entrusted to their direction may not commit the decision of causes arising upon a particular regulation to the federal courts solely, if such a measure should be deemed expedient; but I hold that the state courts will be divested of no part of their primitive jurisdiction, further than may relate to an appeal; and I am even of opinion, that in every case in which they were not expressly excluded by the future acts of the national legislature, they will of course take cognizance of the causes to which those acts may give birth. This I infer from the nature of judiciary power, and from the general genius of the system. The judiciary power of every government looks beyond its own local or municipal laws, and in civil cases lays hold of all subjects of litigation between parties within its jurisdiction though the causes of dispute are relative to the laws of the most distant part of the globe. Those of Japan not less than of New-York may furnish the objects of legal discussion to our courts. When in addition to this, we consider the state governments and the national governments as they truly are, in the light of kindred systems and as parts of ONE WHOLE, the inference seems to be conclusive that the state courts would have a concurrent jurisdiction in all cases arising under the laws of the union, where it was not expressly prohibited.

Here another question occurs—what relation would subsist between the national and state courts in these instances of concurrent jurisdiction? I answer that an appeal would certainly lie from the latter to the supreme court of the United States. The constitution in direct terms, gives an appellate jurisdiction to the supreme court in all the enumerated cases of federal cognizance, in which it is not to have an original one; without a single expression to confine its operation to the inferior federal courts. The objects of appeal, not the tribunals from which it is to be made, are alone contemplated. From this circumstance and from the reason of the thing it ought to be construed to extend to the state tribunals. Either this must be the case, or the local courts must be excluded from a concurrent jurisdiction in matters of national concern, else the judiciary authority of the union may be eluded at the pleasure of every plaintiff or prosecutor. Neither of these consequences ought without evident necessity to be involved; the latter would be intirely inadmissible, as it would defeat some of the most important and avowed purposes of the proposed government, and would essentially embarrass its

measures. Nor do I perceive any foundation for such a supposition. Agreeably to the remark already made, the national and state systems are to be regarded as ONE WHOLE. The courts of the latter will of course be natural auxiliaries to the execution of the laws of the union, and an appeal from them will as naturally lie to that tribunal, which is destined to unite and assimilate the principles of national justice and the rules of national decisions. The evident aim of the plan of the convention is that all the causes of the specified classes, shall for weighty public reasons receive their original or final determination in the courts of the union. To confine therefore the general expressions giving appellate jurisdiction to the supreme court to appeals from the subordinate federal courts, instead of allowing their extension to the state courts, would be to abridge the latitude of the terms, in subversion of the intent, contrary to every sound rule of interpretation.

But could an appeal be made to lie from the state courts to the subordinate federal judicatories? This is another of the questions which have been raised, and of greater difficulty than the former. The following considerations countenance the affirmative. The plan of the convention in the first place authorises the national legislature "to constitute tribunals inferior to the supreme court." It declares in the next place that, "the JUDICIAL POWER of the United States *shall be vested* in one supreme court and in such inferior courts as congress shall ordain and establish"; and it then proceeds to enumerate the cases to which this judicial power shall extend. It afterwards divides the jurisdiction of the supreme court into original and appellate, but gives no definition of that of the subordinate courts. The only outlines described for them are that they shall be "inferior to the supreme court" and that they shall not exceed the specified limits of the federal judiciary. Whether their authority shall be original or appellate or both is not declared. All this seems to be left to the discretion of the legislature. And this being the case, I perceive at present no impediment to the establishment of an appeal from the state courts to the subordinate national tribunals; and many advantages attending the power of doing it may be imagined. It would diminish the motives to the multiplication of federal courts, and would admit of arrangements calculated to contract the appellate jurisdiction of the supreme court. The state tribunals may then be left with a more entire charge of federal causes; and appeals in most cases in which they may be deemed proper instead of being carried to the supreme court, may be made to lie from the state courts to district courts of the union.

26

JOHN MARSHALL, VIRGINIA RATIFYING CONVENTION
20 June 1788
Papers 1:275–85

This part of the plan before us, is a great improvement on that system from which we are now departing. Here are tribunals appointed for the decision of controversies, which were before, either not at all, or improperly provided for.—That many benefits will result from this to the members of the collective society, every one confesses. Unless its organization be defective, and so constructed as to injure, instead of accommodating the convenience of the people, it merits our approbation. After such a candid and fair discussion by those Gentlemen who support it—after the very able manner in which they have investigated and examined it, I conceived it would be no longer considered as so very defective, and that those who opposed it, would be convinced of the impropriety of some of their objections.—But I perceive they still continue the same opposition. Gentlemen have gone on an idea, that the Federal Courts will not determine the causes which may come before them, with the same fairness and impartiality, with which other Courts decide. What are the reasons of this supposition?—Do they draw them from the manner in which the Judges are chosen, or the tenure of their office?—What is it that makes us trust our Judges?—Their independence in office, and manner of appointment. Are not the Judges of the Federal Court chosen with as much wisdom, as the Judges of the State Governments?—Are they not equally, if not more independent?—If so, shall we not conclude, that they will decide with equal impartiality and candour?—If there be as much wisdom and knowledge in the United States, as in a particular State, shall we conclude that that wisdom and knowledge will not be equally exercised in the selection of the Judges?

The principle on which they object to the Federal jurisdiction, seems to me to be founded on a belief, that there will not be a fair trial had in those Courts. If this Committee will consider it fully, they will find it has no foundation, and that we are as secure there as any where else. What mischief results from some causes being tried there?—Is there not the utmost reason to conclude, that Judges wisely appointed, and independent in their office, will never countenance any unfair trial?—What are the subjects of its jurisdiction? Let us examine them with an expectation that causes will be as candidly tried there, as elsewhere, and then determine. The objection, which was made by the Honorable Member who was first up yesterday (Mr. *Mason*) has been so fully refuted, that it is not worth while to notice it. He objected to Congress having power to create a number of Inferior Courts according to the necessity of public circumstances. I had an apprehension that those Gentlemen who placed no confidence in Congress, would object that there might be no Inferior Courts. I own that

I thought, that those Gentlemen would think there would be no Inferior Courts, as it depended on the will of Congress, but that we should be dragged to the centre of the Union. But I did not conceive, that the power of increasing the number of Courts could be objected to by any Gentleman, as it would remove the inconvenience of being dragged to the centre of the United States. I own that the power of creating a number of Courts, is, in my estimation, so far from being a defect, that it seems necessary to the perfection of this system. After having objected to the number and mode, he objected to the subject matter of their cognizance.—(Here Mr. *Marshall* read the 2d section.)—These, Sir, are the points of Federal jurisdiction to which he objects, with a few exceptions. Let us examine each of them with a supposition, that the same impartiality will be observed there, as in other Courts, and then see if any mischief will result from them.—With respect to its cognizance in all cases arising under the Constitution and the laws of the United States, he says, that the laws of the United States being paramount to the laws of particular States, there is no case but what this will extend to. Has the Government of the United States power to make laws on every subject?—Does he understand it so?—Can they make laws affecting the mode of transferring property, or contracts, or claims between citizens of the same State? Can they go beyond the delegated powers? If they were to make a law not warranted by any of the powers enumerated, it would be considered by the Judges as an infringement of the Constitution which they are to guard:—They would not consider such a law as coming under their jurisdiction.—They would declare it void. It will annihilate the State Courts, says the Honorable Gentleman. Does not every Gentleman here know, that the causes in our Courts are more numerous than they can decide, according to their present construction? Look at the dockets.—You will find them crouded with suits, which the life of man will not see determined. If some of these suits be carried to other Courts, will it be wrong? They will still have business enough. Then there is no danger, that particular subjects, small in proportion, being taken out of the jurisdiction of the State Judiciaries, will render them useless and of no effect. Does the Gentleman think that the State Courts will have no cognizance of cases not mentioned here? Are there any words in this Constitution which excludes the Courts of the States from those cases which they now possess? Does the Gentleman imagine this to be the case? Will any Gentleman believe it? Are not controversies respecting lands claimed under the grants of different States, the only controversies between citizens of the same State, which the Federal Judiciary can take cognizance of? The case is so clear, that to prove it would be an useless waste of time. The State Courts will not lose the jurisdiction of the causes they now decide. They have a concurrence of jurisdiction with the Federal Courts in those cases, in which the latter have cognizance.

How disgraceful is it that the State Courts cannot be trusted, says the Honorable Gentleman! What is the language of the Constitution? Does it take away their jurisdiction? Is it not necessary that the Federal Courts should have cognizance of cases arising under the Constitution, and the laws of the United States? What is the service or purpose of a Judiciary, but to execute the laws in a peaceable orderly manner, without shedding blood, or creating a contest, or availing yourselves of force? If this be the case, where can its jurisdiction be more necessary than here? To what quarter will you look for protection from an infringement on the Constitution, if you will not give the power to the Judiciary? There is no other body that can afford such a protection. But the Honorable Member objects to it, because, he says, that the officers of the Government will be screened from merited punishment by the Federal Judiciary. The Federal Sheriff, says he, will go into a poor man's house, and beat him, or abuse his family, and the Federal Court will protect him. Does any Gentleman believe this? Is it necessary that the officers will commit a trespass on the property or persons of those with whom they are to transact business? Will such great insults on the people of this country be allowable? Were a law made to authorise them, it would be void. The injured man would trust to a tribunal in his neighbourhood. To such a tribunal he would apply for redress, and get it. There is no reason to fear that he would not meet that justice there, which his country will be ever willing to maintain. But on appeal, says the Honorable Gentleman, what chance is there to obtain justice? This is founded on an idea, that they will not be impartial. There is no clause in the Constitution which bars the individual member injured, from applying to the State Courts to give him redress. He says that there is no instance of appeals as to fact in common law cases. The contrary is well known to you, Mr. Chairman, to be the case in this Commonwealth. With respect to mills, roads, and other cases, appeals lye from the Inferior to the Superior Court, as to fact as well as law. Is it a clear case, that there can be no case in common law, in which an appeal as to fact might be proper and necessary? Can you not conceive a case where it would be productive of advantages to the people at large, to submit to that tribunal the final determination, involving facts as well as law? Suppose it should be deemed for the convenience of the citizens, that those things which concerned foreign Ministers, should be tried in the Inferior Courts—If justice would be done, the decision would satisfy all. But if an appeal in matters of fact could not be carried to the Superior Court, then it would result, that such cases could not be tried before the Inferior Courts, for fear of injurious and partial decisions.

But, Sir, where is the necessity of discriminating between the three cases of chancery, admiralty, and common law? Why not leave it to Congress? Will it enlarge their powers? Is it necessary for them wantonly to infringe your rights? Have you any thing to apprehend, when they can in no case abuse their power without rendering themselves hateful to the people at large? When this is the case, something may be left to the Legislature freely chosen by ourselves, from among ourselves, who are to share the burdens imposed upon the community, and who can be changed at our pleasure. Where power may be trusted, and there is no motive to abuse it, it seems to me to be as well to leave it undetermined, as to fix it in the Constitution.

With respect to disputes between a State, and the citizens of another State, its jurisdiction has been decried with unusual vehemence. I hope no Gentleman will think that a State will be called at the bar of the Federal Court. Is there no such case at present? Are there not many cases in which the Legislature of Virginia is a party, and yet the State is not sued? It is not rational to suppose, that the sovereign power shall be dragged before a Court. The intent is, to enable States to recover claims of individuals residing in other States. I contend this construction is warranted by the words. But, say they, there will be partiality in it if a State cannot be defendant—if an individual cannot proceed to obtain judgment against a State, though he may be sued by a State. It is necessary to be so, and cannot be avoided. I see a difficulty in making a State defendant, which does not prevent its being plaintiff. If this be only what cannot be avoided, why object to the system on that account? If an individual has a just claim against any particular State, is it to be presumed, that on application to its Legislature, he will not obtain satisfaction? But how could a State recover any claim from a citizen of another State, without the establishment of these tribunals?

The Honorable Member objects to suits being instituted in the Federal Courts by the citizens of one State, against the citizens of another State. Were I to contend, that this was necessary in all cases, and that the Government without it would be defective, I should not use my own judgment. But are not the objections to it carried too far? Though it may not in general be absolutely necessary, a case may happen, as has been observed, in which a citizen of one State ought to be able to recur to this tribunal, to recover a claim from the citizen of another State. What is the evil which this can produce?—Will he get more than justice there?—The independence of the Judges forbids it. What has he to get?—Justice. Shall we object to this, because a citizen of another State can obtain justice without applying to our State Courts? It may be necessary with respect to the laws and regulations of commerce, which Congress may make. It may be necessary in cases of debt, and some other controversies. In claims for land it is not necessary, but it is not dangerous. In the Court of which State will it be instituted, said the Honorable Gentleman? It will be instituted in the Court of the State where the defendant resides,—where the law can come at him, and no where else. By the laws of which State will it be determined, said he? By the laws of the State where the contract was made. According to those laws, and those only, can it be decided. Is this a novelty?—No—it is a principle in the jurisprudence of this Commonwealth. If a man contracted a debt in the East-Indies, and it was sued for here, the decision must be consonant to the laws of that country.—Suppose a contract made in Maryland, where the annual interest is at six per centum; and a suit instituted for it in Virginia—What interest would be given now, without any Federal aid?—The interest of Maryland most certainly; and if the contract had been made in Virginia, and suit brought in Maryland, the interest of Virginia must be given without doubt.—It is now to be governed by the laws of that State where the contract was made. The laws which governed the contract at its formation, govern it in its decision. To preserve the peace of the Union only, its jurisdiction in this case ought to be recurred to.—Let us consider that when citizens of one State carry on trade in another State, much must be due to the one from the other, as is the case between North-Carolina and Virginia. Would not the refusal of justice to our citizens, from the Courts of North-Carolina, produce disputes between the States? Would the Federal Judiciary swerve from their duty in order to give partial and unjust decisions?

The objection respecting the assignment of a bond to a citizen of another State, has been fully answered. But suppose it were to be tried as he says, what could be given more than was actually due in the case he mentioned? It is *possible*, in our Courts as they now stand, to obtain a judgment for more than justice. But the Court of Chancery grants relief. Would it not be so in the Federal Court? Would not depositions be taken, to prove the payments, and if proved, would not the decision of the Court be accordingly?

He objects in the next place to its jurisdiction in controversies between a State, and a foreign State. Suppose, says he, in such a suit, a foreign State is cast, will she be bound by the decision? If a foreign State brought a suit against the Commonwealth of Virginia, would she not be barred from the claim if the Federal Judiciary thought it unjust? The previous consent of the parties is necessary. And, as the Federal Judiciary will decide, each party will acquiesce. It will be the means of preventing disputes with foreign nations. On an attentive consideration of these Courts, I trust every part will appear satisfactory to the Committee.

The exclusion of trial by jury in this case, he urged to prostrate our rights. Does the word Court only mean the Judges? Does not the determination of a jury, necessarily lead to the judgment of the Court? Is there any thing here which gives the Judges exclusive jurisdiction of matters of fact? What is the object of a jury trial? To inform the Court of the facts. When a Court has cognizance of facts, does it not follow, that they can make enquiry by a jury? It is impossible to be otherwise. I hope that in this country, where impartiality is so much admired, the laws will direct facts to be ascertained by a jury. But, says the Honorable Gentleman, the juries in the ten miles square will be mere tools of parties, with which he would not trust his person or property; which, he says, he would rather leave to the Court. Because the Government may have a district ten miles square, will no man stay there but the tools and officers of the Government?—Will no body else be found there?—Is it so in any other part of the world, where a Government has Legislative power?—Are there none but officers and tools of the Government of Virginia in Richmond?—Will there not be independent merchants, and respectable Gentlemen of fortune, within the ten miles square?—Will there not be worthy farmers and mechanics?—Will not a good jury be found there as well as any where else?—Will the officers of the Government become improper to be on a jury?—What is it to the Government, whether this man or that man succeeds?—It is all one thing. Does the Constitution say, that juries shall consist of officers, or that the Supreme Court shall be held in the ten miles square? It was acknowledged by the Honorable

Member, that it was secure in England. What makes it secure there?—Is it their Constitution?—What part of their Constitution is there, that the Parliament cannot change? —As the preservation of this right is in the hands of Parliament, and it has ever been held sacred by them, will the Government of America be less honest than that of Great Britain? Here a restriction is to be found. The jury is not to be brought out of the State. There is no such restriction in that Government; for the laws of Parliament decide every thing respecting it. Yet Gentlemen tell us, that there is safety there, and nothing here but danger. It seems to me, that the laws of the United States will generally secure trials by a jury of the vicinage, or in such manner as will be most safe and convenient for the people.

But it seems that the right of challenging the jurors, is not secured in this Constitution. Is this done by our own Constitution, or by any provision of the English Government? Is it done by their Magna Charta, or Bill of Rights? This privilege is founded on their laws. If so, why should it be objected to the American Constitution, that it is not inserted in it? If we are secure in Virginia, without mentioning it in our Constitution, why should not this security be found in the Federal Court?

The Honorable Gentleman said much about the quitrents in the Northern Neck. I will refer it to the Honorable Gentleman himself. Has he not acknowledged, that there was no complete title? Was he not satisfied, that the right of the legal representative of the proprietor did not exist at the time he mentioned? If so, it cannot exist now. I will leave it to those Gentlemen who come from that quarter. I trust they will not be intimidated on this account, in voting on this question. A law passed in 1782, which secures this. He says that many poor men may be harrassed and injured by the representative of Lord Fairfax. If he has no right, this cannot be done. If he has this right and comes to Virginia, what laws will his claims be determined by? By those of this State. By what tribunals will they be determined? By our State Courts. Would not the poor man, who was oppressed by an unjust prosecution, be abundantly protected and satisfied by the temper of his neighbours, and would he not find ample justice? What reason has the Honorable Member to apprehend partiality or injustice? He supposes, that if the Judges be Judges of both the Federal and State Courts, they will incline in favour of one Government. If such contests should arise, who could more properly decide them, than those who are to swear to do justice? If we can expect a fair decision any where, may we not expect justice to be done by the Judges of both the Federal and State Governments? But, says the Honorable Member, laws may be executed tyrannically. Where is the independency of your Judges? If a law be executed tyrannically in Virginia, to what can you trust? To your Judiciary. What security have you for justice? Their independence. Will it not be so in the Federal Court?

Gentlemen ask what is meant by law cases, and if they be not distinct from facts. Is there no law arising on cases in equity and admiralty? Look at the acts of Assembly.— Have you not many cases, where law and fact are blended? Does not the jurisdiction in point of law as well as fact, find itself completely satisfied in law and fact? The Honorable Gentleman says, that no law of Congress can make any exception to the Federal appellate jurisdiction of fact as well as law. He has frequently spoken of technical terms, and the meaning of them. What is the meaning of the term *exception*? Does it not mean an alteration and diminution? Congress is empowered to make exceptions to the appellate jurisdiction, as to law and fact, of the Supreme Court.—These exceptions certainly go as far as the Legislature may think proper, for the interest and liberty of the people.—Who can understand this word, *exception*, to extend to one case as well as the other? I am persuaded, that a reconsideration of this case will convince the Gentleman, that he was mistaken. This may go to the cure of the mischief apprehended. Gentlemen must be satisfied, that this power will not be so much abused as they have said.

The Honorable Member says, that he derives no consolation from the wisdom and integrity of the Legislature, because we call them to rectify defects which it is our duty to remove. We ought well to weigh the good and evil before we determine—We ought to be well convinced, that the evil will be really produced before we decide against it. If we be convinced that the good greatly preponderates, though there be small defects in it, shall we give up that which is really good, when we can remove the little mischief it may contain, in the plain easy method pointed out in the system itself?

I was astonished when I heard the Honorable Gentleman say, that he wished the trial by jury to be struck out entirely. Is there no justice to be expected by a jury of our fellow citizens? Will any man prefer to be tried by a Court, when the jury is to be of his countrymen, and probably of his vicinage? We have reason to believe the regulations with respect to juries will be such as shall be satisfactory. Because it does not contain all, does it contain nothing? But I conceive that this Committee will see there is safety in the case, and that there is no mischief to be apprehended.

He states a case, that a man may be carried from a federal to an antifederal corner, (and *vice versa*) where men are ready to destroy him. Is this probable? Is it presumeable that they will make a law to punish men who are of different opinions in politics from themselves? Is it presumeable, that they will do it in one single case, unless it be such a case as must satisfy the people at large? The good opinion of the people at large must be consulted by their Representatives; otherwise mischiefs would be produced, which would shake the Government to its foundation. As it is late, I shall not mention all the Gentleman's argument: But some parts of it are so glaring, that I cannot pass them over in silence. He says that the establishment of these tribunals, and more particularly in their jurisdiction of controversies between citizens of these States, and foreign citizens and subjects, is like a retrospective law. Is there no difference between a tribunal which shall give justice and effect to an existing right, and creating a right that did not exist before? The debt or claim is created by the individual. He has bound himself to comply with it. Does the creation of a new Court amount to a retrospective law?

We are satisfied with the provision made in this country on the subject of trial by jury. Does our Constitution direct trials to be by jury? It is required in our Bill of Rights, which is not a part of the Constitution. Does any security arise from hence? Have you a jury when a judgment is obtained on a replevy bond, or by default? Have you a jury when a motion is made for the Commonwealth, against an individual; or when a motion is made by one joint obligor against another, to recover sums paid as security? Our Courts decide in all these cases, without the intervention of a jury; yet they are all civil cases. The Bill of Rights is merely recommendatory. Were it otherwise, the consequence would be, that many laws which are found convenient, would be unconstitutional. What does the Government before you say? Does it exclude the Legislature from giving a trial by jury in civil cases? If it does not forbid its exclusion, it is on the same footing on which your State Government stands now. The Legislature of Virginia does not give a trial by jury where it is not necessary. But gives it wherever it is thought expedient. The Federal Legislature will do so too, as it is formed on the same principles.

The Honorable Gentleman says, that unjust claims will be made, and the defendant had better pay them than go to the Supreme Court. Can you suppose such a disposition in one of your citizens, as that to oppress another man, he will incur great expences? What will he gain by an unjust demand? Does a claim establish a right? He must bring his witnesses to prove his claim. If he does not bring his witnesses, the expences must fall upon him. Will he go on a calculation that the defendant will not defend it; or cannot produce a witness? Will he incur a great deal of expence, from a dependance on such a chance? Those who know human nature, black as it is, must know, that mankind are too well attached to their interest to run such a risk. I conceive, that this power is absolutely necessary, and not dangerous; that should it be attended by little inconveniences, they will be altered, and that they can have no interest in not altering them. Is there any real danger?—When I compare it to the exercise of the same power in the Government of Virginia, I am persuaded there is not. The Federal Government has no other motive, and has every reason of doing right, which the Members of our State Legislature have. Will a man on the Eastern Shore, be sent to be tried in Kentuckey; or a man from Kentuckey be brought to the Eastern Shore to have his trial? A Government by doing this, would destroy itself. I am convinced, the trial by jury will be regulated in the manner most advantageous to the community.

27

A NATIVE OF VIRGINIA, OBSERVATIONS UPON THE
PROPOSED PLAN OF FEDERAL GOVERNMENT
1788
Monroe Writings 1:384–87

No part of the Constitution seems to have been so little understood, or so purposely misconstrued, as this article. Its enemies have mustered all their forces against the Federal Court; and have loudly sounded the trumpet, for the benevolent purpose of alarming the good people of Virginia, with the fears of *visionary* danger and imaginary oppression. They have told them the Federal Court, like Aron's rod, would swallow up all the judiciary authority of the respective States. That a citizen of Virginia may be forced to Philadelphia for a debt of 5*l.* although it was contracted with a fellow citizen: And, above all, that the trial by jury is not preserved. In a word, it is the Federal Court that is to be made the great instrument of tyranny.

These indeed would be serious objections were they well founded.

It is on all hands admitted, that a Federal Court is necessary, for a variety of purposes, and under a variety of circumstances.

The only question then is, whether the enumeration of the cases assigned to the Federal Court, by this article, is likely to produce oppression? Or if there be any ground to apprehend that Congress will not, by law, provide a remedy for all probable hardships, and render the federal jurisdiction convenient to every part of the United States?

There has been no objection raised to the Federal Court having original jurisdiction, in all cases respecting public Ministers, and where a State may be a party: and these are the only cases wherein it has *original jurisdiction*. In these cases, in controversies between two or more States, and between a State and citizens of another State, and between citizens of the same claiming lands under grants of different States, the present Congress have the right of determining. Here the Judiciary is blended in an eminent degree with the Legislative authority; a strong reason, among many others, for new modeling that unskilfully organized body.

The Convention sensible of this defect, has wisely assigned the cognizance of these and other controversies to a proper tribunal, a Court of Law.

Among these controversies, there is but one possible case where a dispute between two citizens of the same State can be carried, even by appeal, to the Federal Court; and that is, when they claim the same land under grants from different States. As their title is derived through States, this case is precisely within the reason which applies to controversies wherein two States are parties.

Notwithstanding this, we are told that in the most ordinary cases, a citizen of Virginia may be dragged within the appellate jurisdiction of the Federal Court, although the transaction which gave rise to the controversy originated between fellow citizens. This, it is said, may be effected, by assigning a bond, for instance, given by one fellow citizen to another, either to a foreigner or a citizen of another State. To this I answer, that such assignment would not be attended with any such consequence; because it is a principle in law, that the assignee stands in the place of the assignor; and is neither in a better nor a worse condition. It is likewise asserted, that if two citizens of the same State claim lands lying in a different State, that their suit may be carried to the Federal Court for final determination. This assertion is equally groundless. For this being a local action, it must be determined in the State wherein the lands lie.

And I repeat it again, because it cannot be too often repeated, that but one possible case exists, where a controversy between citizens of the same State can be carried into the Federal Court. How then is it possible that the Federal Court can ever swallow up the State jurisdictions, or be converted to the purposes of oppression.

Several reasons occur why the Federal Court should possess an appellate jurisdiction in controversies between foreigners and citizens, and between the citizens of different States. A foreigner should have the privilege of carrying his suit to the Federal Court, as well for the sake of justice, as from political motives. Were he confined to seek redress in the tribunal of that State, wherein he received the injury, he might not obtain it, from the influence of his adversary; and by giving him this additional and certain means of obtaining justice, foreigners will be encouraged to trade with us, to give us credit, and to employ their capitals in our country. These controversies must for the most part arise from commercial transactions, by which the bulk of the people can be seldom effected. The first part of this reasoning equally applies to controversies between citizens of different States. Besides, were the jurisdiction of the Federal Court not coextensive with the government itself, as far as foreigners are concerned, a controversy between individuals might produce a national quarrel, which commencing in reprisals, would probably terminate in war. Suppose a subject of France or Great Britain should complain to the Minister residing at the seat of Congress, that it was impossible to obtain justice in a Court of Law, in Virginia, for instance. The minister represents the matter to his Court. That Court will apply to the Congress, not to the individual State, for redress. Congress replies, "we lament that it is not in our power to remedy the evil; but we have no authority over the jurisprudence of the State." Is it probable that such an answer will be satisfactory to powerful nations? Will they not say "we must take that redress by force which your feeble government denies us? We are under the necessity of seizing American property wherever we can lay our hands upon it, till the just demands of our subjects are satisfied."

Those objectors who are so much alarmed for the trial by jury, seem little acquainted either with the origin or use of that celebrated mode of trial.

I will take leave to inform them, that by our laws a variety of important causes are daily determined without the intervention of a jury, not only in the Court of Chancery, but in those of common law; and that by several of our Acts of Assembly, the General Court has a power of assessing fines as high as 500*l.* for inconsiderable delinquencies, without the intervention of a jury, even to find the fact.

As I have before observed, these causes will be from the nature of things, generally mercantile disputes; must be matters of account, which will be referred to commissioners, as is the practice of all common law Courts in similar cases. Whenever it may be necessary that the facts should be stated, no doubt they will be found by a jury of the State, from whence the cause is carried; and will be made a part of the record.

In criminal cases, the trial by jury is most important. In criminal cases the Constitution has established it unequivocally. But in having only recognized this trial in criminal, it by no means follows that it takes it away in civil cases: And we may fairly presume, that by the law which the Congress will make to compleat the system of the Federal Court, it will be introduced, as far as it shall be found practicable, and applicable to such controversies as from their nature are subjects proper to be determined in that Court.

28

SAMUEL JOHNSTON, NORTH CAROLINA RATIFYING CONVENTION
28 July 1788
Elliot 4:141

Gov. JOHNSTON. Mr. Chairman, the learned member from Anson says that the federal courts have exclusive jurisdiction of all cases in law and equity arising under the Constitution and laws of the United States. The opinion which I have always entertained is, that they will, in these cases, as well as in several others, have concurrent jurisdiction with the state courts, and not exclusive jurisdiction. I see nothing in this Constitution which hinders a man from bringing suit wherever he thinks he can have justice done him. The jurisdiction of these courts is established for some purposes with which the state courts have nothing to do, and the Constitution takes no power from the state courts which they now have. They will have the same business which they have now, and if so, they will have enough to employ their time.

29

JAMES MADISON, OBSERVATIONS ON JEFFERSON'S DRAFT OF A CONSTITUTION FOR VIRGINIA
15 Oct. 1788
Papers 11:293

In the State Constitutions & indeed in the Fedl. one also, no provision is made for the case of a disagreement in expounding them; and as the Courts are generally the last in making their decision, its results to them, by refusing or not refusing to execute a law, to stamp it with its final character. This makes the Judiciary Dept paramount in fact to the Legislature, which was never intended, and can never be proper.

30

JAMES WILSON, COMPARISON OF CONSTITUTIONS, LECTURES ON LAW
1791
Works 1:326–31

In England, the judges of the superiour courts do not now, as they did formerly, hold their commissions and their salaries at the pleasure of the crown; but they still hold them at the pleasure of the parliament: the judicial subsists, and may be blown to annihilation, by the breath of the legislative department. In the United States, the judges stand upon the sure basis of the constitution: the judicial department is independent of the department of legislature. No act of congress can shake their commissions or reduce their salaries. "The judges, both of the supreme and inferiour courts, shall hold their offices during good behaviour, and shall, at stated times, receive for their services a compensation, which shall not be diminished during their continuance in office." It is not lawful for the president of the United States to remove them on the address of the two houses of congress. They may be removed, however, as they ought to be, on conviction of high crimes and misdemeanors.

The judges of the United States stand on a much more independent footing than that on which the judges of England stand, with regard to jurisdiction, as well as with regard to commissions and salaries. In many cases, the jurisdiction of the judges of the United States is ascertained and secured by the constitution: as to these, the power of the judicial is coordinate with that of the legislative department. As to the other cases, by the necessary result of the constitution, the authority of the former is paramount to the authority of the latter.

It will be proper to illustrate, at some length, the nature

and consequences of these important doctrines concerning the judicial department of the United States; and, at the same time, to contrast them with the doctrines held concerning the same department in England. Much useful and practical information may be drawn from this comparative review.

It is entertaining, and it may be very instructive, to trace and examine the opinions of the English courts and lawyers concerning the decision, which may be given, in the judicial department, upon the validity or invalidity of acts of parliament.

In some books we are told plainly, and without any circumlocution or disguise—that an act of parliament against law and reason is, therefore, void—that, in many cases, the common law will control acts of parliament; and sometimes adjudge them to be utterly void: for when an act of parliament is against common right and reason, or repugnant, or impossible to be performed; the common law will control it, and adjudge such act to be void. Some statutes are made against law and right, which those who made them perceiving, would not put them in execution—that an act of parliament made against natural equity, as to make a man judge in his own cause, is void in itself; for *jura naturae immutabilia*, and they are *leges legum*.

My Lord Chief Justice Holt expresses himself, upon this delicate and embarrassing subject, in his usual blunt and decided manner: "It is a very reasonable and true saying, that if an act of parliament should ordain, that the same person should be a party and a judge, or, which is the same thing, judge in his own cause; it would be a void act of parliament; for it is impossible that one should be judge and party; for the judge is to determine between party and party, or between the government and the party; and an act of parliament can do no wrong; though it may do several things, that look pretty odd."

These doctrines and sayings, however reasonable and true they appear to be, have been, nevertheless, deemed too bold; for they are irreconcilable with the lately introduced positions concerning the supreme, absolute, and uncontrollable power of the British parliament. Accordingly, Sir William Blackstone, on the principles of his system, expresses himself in the following manner, remarkably guarded and circumspect, as to the extent of the parliamentary power. "If there arise *out* of acts of parliament, *collaterally*, any absurd consequences, *manifestly* contradictory to common reason; they are, with regard to *those collateral* consequences, void. I lay down the rule with these restrictions; though I know it is generally laid down more largely—that acts of parliament contrary to reason are void. But if the parliament will *positively* enact a thing to be done, which is unreasonable; I know of no power that can control it: and the examples usually alleged in support of this sense of the rule do none of them prove, that, where the *main object* of a statute is unreasonable, the judges are at liberty to reject it: for that were to set the judicial power above that of the legislature, which would be subversive of all government." "No court has power to defeat the intent of the legislature, when couched in such evident and express words, as to leave no doubt concerning its intention."

The successour of Sir William Blackstone in the Vinerian chair walks in his footsteps. "It is certain," he admits, "no human authority can rightfully infringe or abrogate the smallest particle of natural or divine law; yet a British judge, of highly deserved estimation, seems in some measure unguarded in asserting from the bench, that an act of parliament made against natural equity, is void in itself. The principle is infallibly true; the application of it, and the conclusion, dangerous. We must distinguish between right and power; between moral fitness and political authority. We cannot expect that all acts of legislators will be ethically perfect; but if their proceedings are to be decided upon by their subjects, government and subordination cease."

It is very true—we ought to "distinguish between right and power:" but I always apprehended, that the true use of this distinction was, to show that power, in opposition to right, was devested of every title, not that it was clothed with the strongest title, to obedience. Is it really true, that if "the parliament will positively enact an unreasonable thing—a thing manifestly contradictory to common reason—there is no power that can control it?" Is it really true that such a power, vested in the judicial department, would set it above the legislature, and would be subversive of all government? If all this is true; what will the miserable, but unavoidable consequence be? Is it possible, in the nature of things, that all which is positively enacted by parliament can be decreed and enforced by the courts of justice? It will not be pretended. The words in two different laws may be clearly repugnant to one another. The law supposes that, sometimes, this is the case; and accordingly has provided, as we are told in the Commentaries, that, in this case, the later law takes place of the elder. "Leges posteriores, priores contrarias abrogant," we are told, and properly told, is a maxim of universal law, as well as of the English constitutions. Suppose two such repugnant laws to be produced in the same cause, before the same court: what must it do? It must control one, or obey neither. In this last instance, the remedy would be worse than the disease: but there is not the least occasion to have recourse to this desperate remedy. The rule which we have cited from the Commentaries, shows the method that should be followed. In the case supposed, the first law is repealed by the second: the second, therefore, is the only existing law.

Two contradictory laws, we have seen, may flow from the same source: and we have also seen, what, in that case, is to be done. But two contradictory laws may flow likewise from different sources, one superiour to the other: what is to be done in this case?

We are informed, in another part of the Commentaries, that, "on the two foundations of the law of nature, and the law of revelation, all human laws depend; that is to say, no human laws should be suffered to contradict these"—that, if any human law should enjoin us to commit what is prohibited by these, we are bound to transgress that human law, or else we must offend both the natural and the divine. What! are we bound to transgress it?—And are the courts of justice forbidden to reject it? Surely these positions are inconsistent and irreconcilable.

But to avoid the contradiction, shall it be said, that we are bound to suppose every thing, positively and plainly enacted by the legislature, to be, at least, not repugnant to natural or revealed law? This may lead us out of intricate mazes respecting the omnipotence; but, I am afraid, it will lead us into mazes equally intricate and more dangerous concerning the infallibility of parliament. This tenet in the political creed will be found as heterodox as the other.

"I know of no power," says Sir William Blackstone, "which can control the parliament." His meaning is obviously, that he knew no *human* power sufficient for this purpose. But the parliament may, unquestionably, be controlled by natural or revealed law, proceeding from *divine* authority. Is not this authority superiour to any thing that can be enacted by parliament? Is not this superiour authority binding upon the courts of justice? When repugnant commands are delivered by two different authorities, one inferiour and the other superiour; which must be obeyed? When the courts of justice obey the superiour authority, it cannot be said with propriety that they control the inferiour one; they only declare, as it is their duty to declare, that this inferiour one is controlled by the other, which is superiour. They do not repeal the act of parliament: they pronounce it void, because contrary to an overruling law. From that overruling law, they receive the authority to pronounce such a sentence. In this derivative view, their sentence is of obligation paramount to the act of the inferiour legislative power.

In the United States, the legislative authority is subjected to another control, beside that arising from natural and revealed law; it is subjected to the control arising from the constitution. From the constitution, the legislative department, as well as every other part of government, derives its power: by the constitution, the legislative, as well as every other department, must be directed; of the constitution, no alteration by the legislature can be made or authorized. In our system of jurisprudence, these positions appear to be incontrovertible. The constitution is the supreme law of the land: to that supreme law every other power must be inferiour and subordinate.

Now, let us suppose, that the legislature should pass an act, manifestly repugnant to some part of the constitution; and that the operation and validity of both should come regularly in question before a court, forming a portion of the judicial department. In that department, the "judicial power of the United States is vested" by the "people," who "ordained and established" the constitution. The business and the design of the judicial power is, to administer justice according to the law of the land. According to two contradictory rules, justice, in the nature of things, cannot possibly be administered. One of them must, of necessity, give place to the other. Both, according to our supposition, come regularly before the court, for its decision on their operation and validity. It is the right and it is the duty of the court to decide upon them: its decision must be made, for justice must be administered according to the law of the land. When the question occurs—What is the law of the land? it must also decide this question. In what manner is this question to be decided? The answer seems to be a very easy one. The supreme power of the United States has given one rule: a subordinate power in the United States has given a contradictory rule: the former is the law

of the land: as a necessary consequence, the latter is void, and has no operation. In this manner it is the right and it is the duty of a court of justice, under the constitution of the United States, to decide.

This is the necessary result of the distribution of power, made, by the constitution, between the legislative and the judicial departments. The same constitution is the supreme law to both. If that constitution be infringed by one, it is no reason that the infringement should be abetted, though it is a strong reason that it should be discountenanced and declared void by the other.

The effects of this salutary regulation, necessarily resulting from the constitution, are great and illustrious. In consequence of it, the bounds of the legislative power—a power the most apt to overleap its bounds—are not only distinctly marked in the system itself; but effectual and permanent provision is made, that every transgression of those bounds shall be adjudged and rendered vain and fruitless. What a noble guard against legislative despotism!

This regulation is far from throwing any disparagement upon the legislative authority of the United States. It does not confer upon the judicial department a power superiour, in its general nature, to that of the legislature; but it confers upon it, in particular instances, and for particular purposes, the power of declaring and enforcing the superiour power of the constitution—the supreme law of the land.

This regulation, when considered properly, is viewed in a favourable light by the legislature itself. "It has been objected," said a learned member of the house of representatives, in a late debate, "that, by adopting the bill before us, we expose the measure to be considered and defeated by the judiciary of the United States, who may adjudge it to be contrary to the constitution, and therefore void, and not lend their aid to carry it into execution. This gives me no uneasiness. I am so far from controverting this right in the judiciary, that it is my boast and my confidence. It leads me to greater decision on all subjects of a constitutional nature, when I reflect, that, if from inattention, want of precision, or any other defect, I should do wrong, there is a power in the government, which can constitutionally prevent the operation of a wrong measure from affecting my constituents. I am legislating for a nation, and for thousands yet unborn; and it is the glory of the constitution, that there is a remedy for the failures even of the legislature itself."

It has already appeared, that the laws, in England, respecting the independency of the judges, have been construed as confined to those in the superiour courts. In many courts, nay in almost all the courts, which have jurisdiction in criminal, even in capital cases, the judges are still appointed and commissioned occasionally, and at the pleasure of the crown. Those courts, though possessing only a local jurisdiction, and confined to particular districts, are yet of a general nature, and are universally diffused over the kingdom. Such are the courts of oyer and terminer and general gaol delivery. They are held twice in every year in every county of the kingdom, except the four northern ones, in which they are held only once, and London and Middlesex, in which they are held eight times. By their commissions, the judges of those courts have authority to hear and determine all treasons, felonies, and misdemeanors; and to try and deliver every prisoner who shall be in the gaol, when they arrive at the circuit town, whenever indicted, or for whatever crime committed. Sometimes also, upon particular emergencies, the king issues a special or extraordinary commission of oyer and terminer and gaol delivery, confined to those offences which stand in need of immediate inquiry and punishment. Those courts are held before the king's commissioners, among whom are usually—but not necessarily, as it would seem—two judges of the courts at Westminster.

It is somewhat surprising, that, in a nation where the value of liberty and personal security has been so long and so well known, less care has been taken to provide for the independency of the judges in criminal than in civil jurisdiction. Is property of more consequence than life or personal liberty? Is it more likely to become the selected and devoted object of ministerial vengeance or resentment? If peculiar precaution was necessary or proper to ensure the independence of the judges on the crown, one would think it most reasonable to apply that precaution to the independence of those judges, who exercise criminal jurisdiction. Even treason may be tried before judges, named, for the occasion, and during pleasure, by him, who, in law, is supposed to be personally as well as politically offended.

To the constitution of the United States, and to those who enjoy the advantages of that constitution, no judges are known, but such as hold their offices during good behaviour.

31

HAYBURN'S CASE
2 Dall. 409 (1792)

This was a motion for a *mandamus*, to be directed to the circuit court for the district of Pennsylvania, commanding the said court to proceed in a certain petition of William Hayburn, who had applied to be put on the pension list of the United States, as an invalid pensioner. The principal case arose upon the act of congress passed the 23d of March 1792. (1 U. S. Stat. 243.)

The Attorney-General *(Randolph)*, who made the motion for the *mandamus*, having premised that it was done *ex officio*, without an application from any particular person, but with a view to procure the execution of an act of congress, particularly interesting to a meritorious and unfortunate class of citizens, THE COURT declared, that they entertained great doubt upon his right, under such circumstances, and in a case of this kind, to proceed *ex officio;* and directed him to state the principles on which he attempted to support the right. The Attorney-General, accordingly, entered into an elaborate description of the powers and duties of his office:—

But THE COURT being divided in opinion on that question, the motion, made *ex officio*, was not allowed.

The Attorney-General then changed the ground of his interposition, declaring it to be at the instance, and on behalf of Hayburn, a party interested; and he entered into the merits of the case, upon the act of congress, and the refusal of the judges to carry it into effect.

THE COURT observed, that they would hold the motion under advisement, until the next term; but no decision was ever pronounced, as the legislature, at an intermediate session, provided, in another way, for the relief of the pensioners.[a]

[Note]

[a]See an act passed the 28th February 1793 (1 U. S. Stat. 324).—As the reasons assigned by the judges, for declining to execute the first act of Congress, involve a great constitutional question, it will not be thought improper to subjoin them, in illustration of Hayburn's case.

The circuit court for the district of New York (consisting of JAY, Chief Justice, CUSHING, Justice, and DUANE, District Judge) proceeded, on the 5th of April 1791, to take into consideration the act of congress entitled, "An act to provide for the settlement of the claims of widows and orphans barred by the limitations heretofore established, and to regulate the claims to invalid pensions;" and were, thereupon, unanimously, of opinion and agreed,

"That by the constitution of the United States, the government thereof is divided into *three* distinct and independent branches, and that it is the duty of each to abstain from, and to oppose, encroachments on either. That neither the legislative nor the executive branches, can constitutionally assign to the judicial any duties, but such as are properly judicial, and to be performed in a judicial manner.

"That the duties assigned to the circuit, by this act, are not of that description, and that the act itself does not appear to contemplate them as such; inasmuch as it subjects the decisions of these courts, made pursuant to those duties, first to the consideration and suspension of the secretary at war, and then to the revision of the legislature; whereas, by the constitution, neither the secretary at war, nor any other executive officer, nor even the legislature, are authorized to sit as a court of errors on the judicial acts or opinions of this court.

"As, therefore, the business assigned to this court, by the act, is not judicial, nor directed to be performed judicially, the act can only be considered as appointing commissioners for the purposes mentioned in it, by *official* instead of *personal* description. That the judges of this court regard themselves as being the commissioners designated by the act, and therefore, as being at liberty to accept or decline that office. That as the objects of this act are exceedingly benevolent, and do real honor to the humanity and justice of congress; and as the judges desire to manifest, on all proper occasions, and in every proper manner, their high respect for the national legislature, they will execute this act in the capacity of commissioners.

"That as the legislature have a right to extend the session of this court for any term, which they may think proper by law to assign, the term of five days, as directed by this act, ought to be punctually observed. That the judges of this court will, as usual, during the session thereof, adjourn the court from day to day, or other short periods, as circumstances may render proper, and that they will, regularly, between the adjournments, proceed, as commissioners, to execute the business of this act in the same court room, or chamber."

The circuit court for the district of Pennsylvania (consisting of WILSON and BLAIR, Justices, and PETERS, District Judge) made the following representation, in a letter jointly addressed to the president of the United States, on the 18th of April 1792.

"To you it officially belongs to 'take care that the laws' of the United States 'be faithfully executed.' Before you, therefore, we think it our duty to lay the sentiments, which, on a late painful occasion, governed us with regard to an act passed by the legislature of the Union.

"The people of the United States have vested in congress all *legislative* powers granted in the constitution. They have vested in one supreme court, and in such inferior courts as the congress shall establish, 'the *judicial* power of the United States.' It is worthy of remark, that in congress the *whole* legislative power of the United States is not vested. An important part of that power was exercised by the people themselves, when they 'ordained and established the constitution.' This constitution is 'the supreme law of the land.' This supreme law 'all judicial officers of the United States are bound, by oath or affirmation, to support.'

"It is a principle important to freedom, that in government, the *judicial* should be distinct from, and independent of, the legislative department. To this important principle, the people of the United States, in forming their constitution, have manifested the highest regard. They have placed their *judicial* power, not in congress, but in 'courts.' They have ordained that the 'judges of those courts shall hold their offices during good behavior,' and that 'during their continuance in office, their salaries shall not be diminished.'

"Congress have lately passed an act, to regulate, among other things, 'the claims to invalid pensions.' Upon due consideration, we have been unanimously of opinion, that, under this act, the circuit court held for the Pennsylvania district could not proceed

"1st. Because the business directed by this act is not of a judicial nature. It forms no part of the power vested by the constitution in the courts of the United States; the circuit court must, consequently, have proceeded *without* constitutional authority. 2d. Because, if, upon that business, the court had proceeded, its *judgments* (for its *opinions* are its judgments) might, under the same act, have been revised and controlled by the legislature, and by an officer in the executive department. Such revision and control we

deemed radically inconsistent with the independence of that judicial power which is vested in the courts; and consequently, with that important principle which is so strictly observed by the constitution of the United States.

"These, Sir, are the reasons of our conduct. Be assured that, though it became necessary, it was far from being pleasant. To be obliged to act contrary either to the obvious directions of congress, or to a constitutional principle, in our judgment equally obvious, excited feelings in us, we hope never to experience again."

The circuit court for the district of North Carolina (consisting of IREDELL, Justice, and SITGREAVES, District Judge) made the following representation, in a letter jointly addressed to the President of the United States, on the 8th of June 1792.

"We, the judges now attending at the circuit court of the United States for the district of North Carolina, conceive it our duty to lay before you some important observations which have occurred to us in the consideration of an act of congress lately passed, entitled, 'An act to provide for the settlement of the claims of widows and orphans, barred by the limitations heretofore established, and to regulate the claims to invalid pensions.'

"We beg leave to premise, that it is as much our inclination, as it is our duty, to receive with all possible respect every act of the legislature, and that we never can find ourselves in a more painful situation, than to be obliged to object to the execution of any, more especially, to the execution of one founded on the purest principles of humanity and justice, which the act in question undoubtedly is. But, however lamentable a difference in opinion really may be, or with whatever difficulty we may have formed an opinion, we are under the indispensable necessity of acting according to the best dictates of our own judgment, after duly weighing every consideration that can occur to us; which we have done on the present occasion.

"The extreme importance of the case, and our desire of being explicit, beyond the danger of being misunderstood, will, we hope, justify us in stating our observations in a systematic manner. We therefore, Sir, submit to you the following:—

"1. That the legislative, executive and judicial departments are each formed in a separate and independent manner; and that the ultimate basis of each is the constitution only, within the limits of which each department can alone justify any act of authority.

"2. That the legislature, among other important powers, unquestionably possess that of establishing courts in such a manner as to their wisdom shall appear best, limited by the terms of the constitution only; and to whatever extent that power may be exercised, or however severe the duty they may think proper to require, the judges, when appointed in virtue of any such establishment, owe implicit and unreserved obedience to it.

"3. That, at the same time, such courts cannot be warranted, as we conceive, by virtue of that part of the constitution delegating *judicial* power, for the exercise of which any act of the legislature is provided, in exercising (even under the authority of another act) any power not in its nature *judicial*, or, if *judicial*, not provided for upon the terms the constitution requires.

"4. That whatever doubt may be suggested, whether the power in question is properly of a judicial nature, yet, inasmuch as the decision of the court is not made final, but may be at least suspended in its operation, by the secretary at war, if he shall have cause to suspect imposition or mistake; this subjects the decision of the court to a mode of revision, which we consider to be unwarranted by the constitution; for though congress may certainly establish, in instances not yet provided for, courts of appellate jurisdiction, yet such courts must consist of judges appointed in the manner the constitution requires, and holding their offices by no other tenure than that of their good behavior, by which tenure the office of secretary at war is not held. And we beg leave to add, with all due deference, that no decision of any court of the United States can, under any circumstances, in our opinion, agreeable to the constitution, be liable to a revision, or even suspension, by the legislature itself, in whom no judicial power of any kind appears to be vested, but the important one relative to impeachments.

"These, Sir, are our reasons for being of opinion, as we are at present, that this circuit court cannot be justified in the execution of that part of the act, which requires it to examine and report an opinion on the unfortunate cases of officers and soldiers disabled in the service of the United States. The part of the act requiring the court to sit five days, for the purpose of receiving applications from such persons, we shall deem it our duty to comply with; for, whether, in our opinion, such purpose can or cannot be answered, it is, as we conceive, our indispensable duty to keep open any court of which we have the honor to be judges, as long as congress shall direct.

"The high respect we entertain for the legislature, our feelings, as men, for persons whose situation requires the earliest, as well as the most effectual relief, and our sincere desire to promote, whether officially or otherwise, the just and benevolent views of congress, so conspicuous on the present as well as on many other occasions, have induced us to reflect, whether we could be justified in acting, under this act, personally, in the character of commissioners, during the session of a court; and could we be satisfied that we had authority to do so, we would cheerfully devote such part of our time as might be necessary for the performance of the service. But we confess we have great doubts on this head. The power appears to be given to the court only, and not to the judges of it; and as the secretary at war has not a discretion, in all instances, but only in those where he has cause to suspect imposition or mistake, to withhold a person recommended by the court from being named on the pension list, it would be necessary for us to be well persuaded we possessed such an authority, before we exercised a power, which might be a means of drawing money out of the public treasury as effectually as an express appropriation by law. We do not mean, however, to preclude ourselves from a very deliberate consideration, whether we can be warranted in executing the purposes of the act in that manner, in case an application should be made.

"No application has yet been made to the court, or to ourselves individually, and therefore, we have had some doubts as to the propriety of giving an opinion in a case which has not yet come regularly and judicially before us. None can be more sensible than we are of the necessity of judges being, in general, extremely cautious in not intimating an opinion, in any case, extra-judicially, because we well know how liable the best minds are, notwithstanding their utmost care, to a bias, which may arise from a preconceived opinion, even unguardedly, much more, deliberately, given: but in the present instance, as many unfortunate and meritorious individuals, whom congress have justly thought proper objects of immediate relief, may suffer great distress, even by a short delay, and may be utterly ruined, by a long one, we determined, at all events, to make our sentiments known as early as possible, considering this as a case which must be deemed an exception to the general rule, upon every principle of humanity and justice; resolving, however, that so far as we are concerned, individually, in case an application should be made, we will most attentively hear it; and if we can be convinced this opinion is a wrong one, we shall not hesitate to act accordingly, being so far from the weakness of supposing that there is any reproach in having committed an error, to which the greatest and best men are sometimes liable, as we should be, from so low a sense of duty, as we think it would not be the highest and most deserved reproach that could be bestowed on any men (much more on judges) that they were capable, from any motive, of persevering against conviction, in apparently maintaining an opinion, which they really thought to be erroneous."

32

THOMAS JEFFERSON TO JOHN JAY
18 July 1793
Jay Correspondence 3:486–87

The war which has taken place among the powers of Europe produces frequent transactions within our ports and limits, on which questions arise of considerable difficulty, and of greater importance to the peace of the United States. These questions depend for their solution on the construction of our treaties, on the laws of nature and nations, and on the laws of the land, and are often presented under circumstances *which do not give a cognisance of them to the tribunals of the country*. Yet their decision is so little analogous to the ordinary functions of the executive, as to occasion much embarrassment and difficulty to them. The President therefore would be much relieved if he found himself free to refer questions of this description to the opinions of the judges of the Supreme Court of the United States, whose knowledge of the subject would secure us against errors dangerous to the peace of the United States, and their authority insure the respect of all parties. He has therefore asked the attendance of such of the judges as could be collected in time for the occasion, to know, in the first place, their opinion, whether the public may, with propriety, be availed of their *advice on these questions?* And if they may, to present, for their advice, the abstract questions which have already occurred, or may soon occur, from which they will themselves strike out such as any circumstances might, in their opinion, forbid them to pronounce on.

33

JOHN JAY TO GEORGE WASHINGTON
20 July 1793
Correspondence 3:487–88

We have taken into consideration the letter written to us, by your direction, on the 18th inst., by the Secretary of State. The question, "whether the public may, with propriety, be availed of the advice of the judges on the questions alluded to," appears to us to be of much difficulty as well as importance. As it affects the judicial department, we feel a reluctance to decide it without the advice and participation of our absent brethren.

The occasion which induced our being convened is doubtless urgent; of the degree of that urgency we cannot judge, and consequently cannot propose that the answer to this question be postponed until the sitting of the Supreme Court. We are not only disposed, but desirous, to promote the welfare of our country in every way that may consist with our official duties. We are pleased, sir, with every opportunity of manifesting our respect for you, and are solicitous to do whatever may be in our power to render your administration as easy and agreeable to yourself as it is to our country. If circumstances should forbid further delay, we will immediately resume the consideration of the question, and decide it.

34

JOHN JAY TO GEORGE WASHINGTON
8 Aug. 1793
Correspondence 3:488–89

We have considered the previous question stated in a letter written by your direction to us by the Secretary of State on the 18th of last month, [regarding] the lines of separation drawn by the Constitution between the three departments of the government. These being in certain respects checks upon each other, and our being judges of a court in the

last resort, are considerations which afford strong arguments against the propriety of our extra-judicially deciding the questions alluded to, especially as the power given by the Constitution to the President, of calling on the heads of departments for opinions, seems to have been *purposely* as well as expressly united to the *executive* departments.

We exceedingly regret every event that may cause embarrassment to your administration, but we derive consolation from the reflection that your judgment will discern what is right, and that your usual prudence, decision, and firmness will surmount every obstacle to the preservation of the rights, peace, and dignity of the United States.

35

SHEDDEN V. CUSTIS
21 Fed. Cas. 1218, no. 12,736 (C.C.D.Va. 1793)

IREDELL, Circuit Justice. The jurisdiction of the court is limited to particular persons; and, therefore, must be averred. For the difference has been rightly taken by the defendant's counsel, between courts of limited and those of general jurisdiction. In the latter, exceptions to the jurisdiction must be pleaded; but in the former the defendant is not bound to plead it, for the plaintiff must entitle himself to sue there. If the declaration had alleged that the plaintiff was a foreigner, then the defendant must have pleaded the disability, as he would have admitted his capacity to sue. Ability to sue here is a fact which rests more in the knowledge of the plaintiff than of the defendant; and, therefore, the former should show himself capable of suing here. It is not the same with regard to the place of contract, for that the defendant knows as well as the plaintiff; and, therefore, if there be any exceptions on that ground, it being a thing in the knowledge of the defendant, he should plead it for the same reason that the plaintiff must aver his capacity in the other case. It is important that it should appear upon the record that the court had jurisdiction and has only decided on cases within its cognizance.

JAY, Circuit Justice. I at first thought it questionable on the ground of a difference between jurisdiction over the subject-matter and over persons. But on reflection, I do not think the distinction is important. The English practice has been rightly stated by the defendant's counsel, and those rules are more necessary to be observed here than there, on account of a difference of the general and state governments, which should be kept separate, and each left to do the business properly belonging to it. Therefore, this court should not exceed its limits, and try causes not within its jurisdiction. Consequently, the jurisdiction ought to appear, but it does not in this case; and, therefore, I think the judgment should be arrested.

36

UNITED STATES v. RAVARA

27 Fed. Cas. 713, nos. 16,122, 16,122a
(C.C.D.Pa. 1793, 1794)

The defendant, a consul from Genoa, was indicted for a misdemeanor, in sending anonymous and threatening letters to Mr. Hammond, the British minister, Mr. Holland, a citizen of Philadelphia, and several other persons, with a view to extort money.

. . . . .

Before WILSON, and IREDELL, Circuit Justices, and PETERS, District Judge.

WILSON, Circuit Justice. I am of opinion, that although the constitution vests in the supreme court an original jurisdiction, in cases like the present, it does not preclude the legislature from exercising the power of vesting a concurrent jurisdiction, in such inferior courts, as might by law be established. And as the legislature has expressly declared, that the circuit court shall have "exclusive cognizance of all crimes and offences, cognizable under the authority of the United States," I think the indictment ought to be sustained.

IREDELL, Circuit Justice. I do not concur in this opinion, because it appears to me, that for obvious reasons of public policy, the constitution intended to vest an exclusive jurisdiction in the supreme court, upon all questions relating to the public agents of foreign nations. Besides, the context of the judiciary article of the constitution seems fairly to justify the interpretation, that the word "original," means "exclusive," jurisdiction.

PETERS, District Judge. As I agree in the opinion expressed by Judge WILSON, for the reasons which he has assigned, it is unnecessary to enter into any detail.

The motion for quashing the indictment was accordingly rejected, and the defendant pleaded not guilty; but his trial was postponed, by consent, till the next term.

. . . . .

Before JAY, Circuit Justice, and PETERS, District Judge.
THE COURT were of opinion in the charge, that the offence was indictable, and that the defendant was not privileged from prosecution in virtue of his consular appointment. The jury, after a short consultation, pronounced the defendant guilty; but he was afterwards pardoned, on condition (as I have heard) that he surrendered his commission and exequatur.

37

UNITED STATES v. YALE TODD (1794), IN UNITED STATES v. FERREIRA

13 How. 40 (1851)

Note by the Chief Justice, Inserted by Order of the Court.

Since the aforegoing opinion was delivered, the attention of the court has been drawn to the case of the United States *v.* Yale Todd, which arose under the act of 1792, and was decided in the Supreme Court, February 17, 1794. There was no official reporter at that time, and this case has not been printed. It shows the opinion of the court upon a question which was left in doubt by the opinions of the different judges, stated in the note to Hayburn's case. And as the subject is one of much interest, and concerns the nature and extent of judicial power, the substance of the decision in Yale Todd's case is inserted here, in order that it may not be overlooked, if similar questions should hereafter arise.

The 2d, 3d, and 4th sections of the act of 1792, were repealed at the next session of Congress by the act of February 28, 1793. It was these three sections that gave rise to the questions stated in the note to Hayburn's case. The repealing act provided another mode for taking testimony, and deciding upon the validity of claims to the pensions granted by the former law; and by the 3d section it saved all rights to pensions which might be founded "upon any legal adjudication," under the act of 1792, and made it the duty of the Secretary of War, in conjunction with the Attorney-General, to take such measures as might be necessary to obtain an adjudication of the Supreme Court, "on the validity of such rights, claimed under the act aforesaid, by the determination of certain persons styling themselves commissioners."

It appears from this case, that Chief Justice Jay and Justice Cushing acted upon their construction of the act of 1792, immediately after its passage and before it was repealed. And the saving and proviso, in the act of 1793, was manifestly occasioned by the difference of opinion upon that question which existed among the justices, and was introduced for the purpose of having it determined, whether under the act conferring the power upon the Circuit Courts, the judges of those courts when refusing for the reasons assigned by them to acts as courts, could legally act as commissioners out of court. If the decision of the judges, as commissioners, was a legal adjudication, then the party's right to the pension allowed him was saved; otherwise not.

In pursuance of this act of Congress, the case of Yale Todd was brought before the Supreme Court, in an amicable action, and upon a case stated at February Term, 1794.

The case was docketed by consent, the United States being plaintiff and Todd the defendant. The declaration was for one hundred and seventy-two dollars and ninety-one cents, for so much money had and received by the defendant to the use of the United States; to which the defendant pleaded *non assumpsit*.

The case as stated, admitted that on the 3d of May, 1792, the defendant appeared before the Hon. John Jay, William Cushing, and Richard Law, then being judges of the Circuit Court held at New Haven, for the District of Connecticut, then and there sitting, and claiming to be commissioners under the act of 1792, and exhibited the vouchers and testimony to show his right under that law to be placed on the pension list; and that the judges above named, being judges of the Circuit Court, and then and there sitting at New Haven, in and for the Connecticut District, proceeded, as commissioners designated in the said act of Congress, to take the testimony offered by Todd, which is set out at large in the statement, together with their opinion that Todd ought to be placed on the pension list, and paid at the rate of two thirds of his former monthly wages, which they understood to have been eight dollars and one third per month, and the sum of one hundred and fifty dollars for arrears.

The case further admits, that the certificate of their proceedings and opinions, and the testimony they had taken, were afterwards, on the 5th of May, 1792, transmitted to the Secretary of War, and that by means thereof Todd was placed on the pension list, and had received from the United States one hundred and fifty dollars for arrears, and twenty-two dollars and ninety-one cents claimed for his pension aforesaid, said to be due on the 2d of September, 1792.

And the parties agreed that if upon this statement the said judges of the Circuit Court sitting as commissioners, and not as a Circuit Court, had power and authority by virtue of said act so to order and adjudge of and concerning the premises, that then judgment should be given for the defendant, otherwise for the United States, for one hundred and seventy-two dollars and ninety-one cents, and six cents cost.

The case was argued by Bradford, Attorney-General for the United States, and Hillhouse for the defendant; and the judgment of the court was rendered in favor of the United States for the sum above mentioned.

Chief Justice Jay and Justice Cushing, Wilson, Blair, and Paterson, were present at the decision. No opinion was filed stating the grounds of the decision. Nor is any dissent from the judgment entered on the record. It would seem, therefore, to have been unanimous, and that Chief Justice Jay and Justice Cushing became satisfied, on further reflection, that the power given in the act of 1792 to the Circuit Court as a court, could not be construed to give it to the judges out of court as commissioners. It must be admitted that the justice of the claims and the meritorious character of the claimants would appear to have exercised some influence on their judgments in the first instance, and to have led them to give a construction to the law which its language would hardly justify upon the most liberal rules of interpretation.

The result of the opinions expressed by the judges of the Supreme Court of that day in the note to Hayburn's case, and in the case of the United States *v.* Todd, is this:

1. That the power proposed to be conferred on the Circuit Courts of the United States by the act of 1792 was not judicial power within the meaning of the Constitution, and was, therefore, unconstitutional, and could not lawfully be exercised by the courts.

2. That as the act of Congress intended to confer the power on the courts as a judicial function, it could not be construed as an authority to the judges composing the court to exercise the power out of court in the character of commissioners.

3. That money paid under a certificate from persons not authorized by law to give it, might be recovered back by the United States.

The case of Todd was docketed by consent in the Supreme Court; and the court appears to have been of opinion that the act of Congress of 1793, directing the Secretary of War and Attorney-General to take their opinion upon the question, gave them original jurisdiction. In the early days of the Government, the right of Congress to give original jurisdiction to the Supreme Court, in cases not enumerated in the Constitution, was maintained by many jurists, and seems to have been entertained by the learned judges who decided Todd's case. But discussion and more mature examination has settled the question otherwise; and it has long been the established doctrine, and we believe now assented to by all who have examined the subject, that the original jurisdiction of this court is confined to the cases specified in the Constitution, and that Congress cannot enlarge it. In all other cases its power must be appellate.

38

GLASS V. THE SLOOP BETSEY

3 Dall. 6 (1794)

BY THE COURT: The Judges being decidedly of opinion, that every District Court in the *United States*, possesses all the powers of a court of Admiralty, whether considered as an instance, or as a prize court, and that the plea of the aforesaid Appellee, *Pierre Arcade Johannene*, to the jurisdiction of the District Court of *Maryland*, is insufficient: THEREFORE IT IS CONSIDERED by the Supreme Court aforesaid, and now finally decreed and adjudged by the same, that the said plea be, and the same is hereby overruled and dismissed, and that the decree of the said District Court of Maryland, founded thereon, be, and the same is hereby revoked, reversed and annulled.

AND the said Supreme Court being further clearly of opinion, that the District Court of *Maryland* aforesaid, has jurisdiction competent to enquire, and to decide, whether, in the present case, restitution ought to be made to the claimants, or either of them, in whole or in part (that is whether such restitution can be made consistently with the laws of nations and the treaties and laws of the *United States*) THEREFORE IT IS ORDERED AND ADJUDGED that the said District Court of *Maryland* do proceed to determine upon the libel of the said *Alexander S. Glass,* and others, agreeably to law and right, the said plea to the jurisdiction of the said court, notwithstanding.

AND the said Supreme Court being further of opinion, that no foreign power can of right institute, or erect, any court of judicature of any kind, within the jurisdiction of the *United States,* but such only as may be warranted by, and be in pursuance of treaties, IT IS THEREFORE DECREED AND ADJUDGED that the admiralty jurisdiction, which has been exercised in the *United States* by the Consuls of *France,* not being so warranted, is not of right.

39

JANSEN V. VROW CHRISTINA MAGDALENA
13 Fed. Cas. 356, no. 7,216 (D.S.C. 1794)

BEE, District Judge . . . The principal points for the decision of the court appear to be: 1st. Whether this court has any and what jurisdiction relative to matters arising on the high seas. 2dly. Whether the 17th article of the treaty with France restrain such jurisdiction; or whether the act of the 5th of June last controls it. By the third section of the judiciary act of congress [1 Stat. 73] it is declared that there shall be a district court in each district to consist of one judge, who shall hold four sessions annually, and special courts at his discretion. By the ninth section, the powers of the district courts are expressed, 1st, as to criminal, 2d, as to civil causes. The court shall have exclusive original cognizance in all civil causes of admiralty and maritime jurisdiction; and concurrent jurisdiction with the courts of the several states, or the circuit courts of the United States (as the case may be) where an alien sues for a tort only in violation of the law of nations, or a treaty of the United States. By the 2d section of the 3d article of the constitution of the United States, it is declared, that the judicial power of the United States shall extend to all cases arising under the constitution and laws of the United States, and treaties made, or to be made. To all cases affecting ambassadors, other public ministers and consuls, and to all cases of admiralty and maritime jurisdiction. In all cases affecting ambassadors, other public ministers and consuls, and those in which a state shall be a party, the supreme court shall have original jurisdiction; in all other cases, appellate jurisdiction under such regulations as congress shall make. The circuit court has no original jurisdiction; but has appellate jurisdiction in causes of admiralty and maritime jurisdiction; in which the district court alone has original jurisdiction. Redress must be had there, or nowhere. Suitors, however injured, would look in vain to the laws of this country for redress. They would be stopped in limine, and the appellate jurisdiction of the circuit and of the supreme courts would be virtually annihilated; since there would be no terminus à quo, no fixed point from which they might commence their procedure.

In addition to the clauses already recited from the judiciary act, the judges of the supreme court have by their decree in Glass v. The Betsey, 3 Dall. [3 U. S.] 6, decided that the several district courts throughout the United States possess all the powers of courts of admiralty, whether considered as instance or prize courts. That case was elaborately argued, and with great ability. The judges of the supreme court held it under advisement for some days, and then decided it so fully as to leave the jurisdiction of this court no longer doubtful. The question was considered as well with respect to the law of nations, as to the 17th article of the treaty with France; and, was fully set at rest on both grounds. But it is said that the act of congress of June, 1794 [1 Stat. 384], by declaring that the district courts shall take cognizance of complaints, by whomsoever instituted, in cases of captures made within the waters of the United States or within a marine league of the coasts or shores thereof, intended to oust them of all other jurisdiction. But the argument has no sort of force. Glass's Case [supra], had established the jurisdiction of the court in cases of neutral or American property captured on the high seas and brought infra praesidia of our courts. It was there determined that, under such circumstances, the American citizen, or neutral, might institute his suit in the district court, and obtain redress from it. But the act of congress now relied on goes farther, and enacts that, if our jurisdictional limits are violated, restitution shall be made even to a party belligerent who shall complain to the court, and prove his case to come within the provisions of that act. The sixth and seventh articles of the treaty with France assert and recognize the same right. Holland, Prussia, and Sweden have done so by their several treaties with us. No state could maintain its peace or sovereignty, if it were otherwise. I have no hesitation, therefore, in pronouncing that the district court has full jurisdiction upon the present occasion.

40

UNITED STATES V. WORRALL
2 Dall. 384 (C.C.D.Pa. 1798)

CHASE, Justice.—This is an indictment for an offence highly injurious to morals, and deserving the severest punishment; but as it is an indictment at common law, I dismiss, at once, everything that has been said about the constitution and laws of the United States.

In this country, every man sustains a two-fold political capacity; one in relation to the state, and another in relation to the United States. In relation to the state, he is subject to various municipal regulations, founded upon the state constitution and policy, which do not affect him in his relation to the United States: for the constitution of the Union is the source of all the jurisdiction of the national government; so that the departments of the government can never assume any power, that is not expressly granted by that instrument, nor exercise a power in any other manner than is there prescribed. Besides the particular cases, which the 8th section of the 1st article designates, there is a power granted to congress to create, define and punish crimes and offences, whenever they shall deem it necessary and proper by law to do so, for effectuating the objects of the government; and although bribery is not among the crimes and offences specifically mentioned, it is certainly included in this general provision. The question, however, does not arise about the power, but about the exercise of the power:—Whether the courts of the United States can punish a man for any act, before it is declared by a law of the United States to be criminal? Now, it appears to my mind, to be as essential that congress should define the offences to be tried, and apportion the punishments to be inflicted, as that they should erect courts to try the criminal, or to pronounce a sentence on conviction.

It is attempted, however, to supply the silence of the constitution and statutes of the Union, by resorting to the common law, for a definition and punishment of the offence which has been committed: but, in my opinion, the United States, as a federal government, have no common law; and consequently, no indictment can be maintained in their courts, for offences merely at the common law. If, indeed, the United States can be supposed, for a moment, to have a common law, it must, I presume, be that of England; and yet, it is impossible to trace when, or how, the system was adopted or introduced. With respect to the individual states, the difficulty does not occur. When the American colonies were first settled by our ancestors, it was held, as well by the settlers, as by the judges and lawyers of England, that they brought hither, as a birth-right and inheritance, so much of the common law, as was applicable to their local situation, and change of circumstances. But each colony judged for itself, what parts of the common law were applicable to its new condition; and in various modes, by legislative acts, by judicial decisions, or by constant usage, adopted some parts, and rejected others. Hence, he who shall travel through the different states, will soon discover, that the whole of the common law of England has been nowhere introduced; that some states have rejected what others have adopted; and that there is, in short, a great and essential diversity, in the subjects to which the common law is applied, as well as in the extent of its application. The common law, therefore, of one state, is not the common law of another; but the common law of England is the law of each state, so far as each state has adopted it; and it results from that position, connected with the judicial act, that the common law will always apply to suits between citizen and citizen, whether they are instituted in a federal, or state court.

But the question recurs, when and how, have the courts of the United States acquired a common-law jurisdiction, in criminal cases? The United States must possess the common law themselves, before they can communicate it to their judicial agents: Now, the United States did not bring it with them from England; the constitution does not create it; and no act of congress has assumed it. Besides, what is the common law to which we are referred? Is it the common law entire, as it exists in England; or modified as it

exists in some of the states; and of the various modifications, which are we to select, the system of Georgia or New Hampshire, of Pennsylvania or Connecticut?

Upon the whole, it may be a defect in our political institutions, it may be an inconvenience in the administration of justice, that the common-law authority, relating to crimes and punishments, has not been conferred upon the government of the United States, which is a government in other respects also of a limited jurisdiction: but judges cannot remedy political imperfections, nor supply any legislative omission. I will not say, whether the offence is at this time cognisable in a state court. But, certainly, congress might have provided, by law, for the present case, as they have provided for other cases of a similar nature; and yet, if congress had ever declared and defined the offence, without prescribing a punishment, I should still have thought it improper to exercise a discretion upon that part of the subject.

PETERS, Justice.—Whenever a government has been established, I have always supposed, that a power to preserve itself was a necessary, and an inseparable concomitant. But the existence of the federal government would be precarious, it could no longer be called an independent government, if, for the punishment of offences of this nature, tending to obstruct and pervert the administration of its affairs, an appeal must be made to the state tribunals, or the offenders must escape with absolute impunity. The power to punish misdemeanors, is originally and strictly a common-law power; of which, I think, the United States are constitutionally possessed. It might have been exercised by congress, in the form of a legislative act; but it may also, in my opinion, be enforced in a course of judicial proceeding. Whenever an offence aims at the subversion of any federal institution, or at the corruption of its public officers, it is an offence against the well-being of the United States; from its very nature, it is cognisable under their authority; and consequently, it is within the jurisdiction of this court, by virtue of the 11th section of the judicial act.

41

CALDER v. BULL
3 Dall. 386 (1798)

(See 1.10.1, no. 10)

42

FOWLER v. LINDSEY
3 Dall. 411 (1799)

WASHINGTON, Justice.—The first question that occurs from the arguments, on the present occasion, respects the nature of the rights, that are contested in the suits, depending in the circuit court. Without entering into a critical examination of the constitution and laws, in relation to the jurisdiction of the supreme court, I lay down the following as a safe rule: That a case which belongs to the jurisdiction of the supreme court, on account of the interest that a state has in the controversy, must be a case in which a state is either nominally, or substantially, the party. It is not sufficient, that a state may be consequentially affected; for in such case (as where the grants of different states are brought into litigation), the circuit court has clearly a jurisdiction. And this remark furnishes an answer to the suggestions, that have been founded on the remote interest of the state, in making retribution to her grantees, upon the event of an eviction.

It is not contended, that the states are nominally the parties; nor do I think that they can be regarded as substantially the parties to the suits: nay, it appears to me, that they are not even interested or affected. They have a right either to the soil or to the jurisdiction. If they have the right of soil, they may contest it, at any time, in this court, notwithstanding a decision in the present suits; and though they may have parted with the right of soil, still, the right of jurisdiction is unimpaired. A decision, as to the former object, between individual citizens, can never affect the right of the state, as to the latter object: it is *res inter alios acta*. For, suppose the jury in some cases should find in favor of the title under New York; and in others, they should find in favor of the title under Connecticut, how would this decide the right of jurisdiction? And on what principle, can private citizens, in the litigation of their private claims, be competent to investigate, determine and fix the important rights of sovereignty?

The question of jurisdiction remaining, therefore, unaffected by the proceedings in these suits, is there no other mode by which it may be tried? I will not say, that a state could sue at law for such an incorporeal right as that of sovereignty and jurisdiction; but even if a court of law would not afford a remedy, I can see no reason why a remedy should not be obtained in a court of equity. The state of New York might, I think, file a bill against the state of Connecticut, praying to be quieted as to the boundaries of the disputed territory; and this court, in order to effectuate justice, might appoint commissioners to ascertain and report those boundaries. There being no redress at law, would be a sufficient reason for the interposition of the equitable powers of the court; since, it is monstrous, to talk of existing rights, without applying correspondent remedies.

But as it is proposed to remove the suits under consideration from the circuit court into this court, by writs of *certiorari*, I ask, whether it has ever happened, in the course of judicial proceedings, that a *certiorari* has issued from a superior to an inferior court, to remove a cause merely from a defect of jurisdiction? I do not know that such a case could ever occur. If the state is really a party to the suit in the inferior court, a plea to the jurisdiction may be there put in; or, perhaps, without such a plea, this court would reverse the judgment on a writ of error: and if the state is not a party, there is no pretence for the removal.

A *certiorari*, however, can only issue, as original process, to remove a cause, and change the *venue*, when the superior court is satisfied, that a fair and impartial trial will not otherwise be obtained; and it is sometimes used, as auxiliary process, where, for instance, diminution of the record is alleged, on a writ of error: but in such cases, the superior court must have jurisdiction of the controversy. And as it does not appear to me, that this court has exclusive or original jurisdiction of the suits in question, I am of opinion, that the rule must be discharged.

PATERSON, Justice.—The rule to show cause why a *venire* should not be awarded to summon a jury from some district other than that of Connecticut or New York, cannot be supported. It has, indeed, been abandoned. The argument proceeds on the ground of removing the cause into this court, as having exclusive jurisdiction of it, because it is a controversy between states. The constitution of the United States, and the act of congress, although the phraseology be somewhat different, may be construed in perfect conformity with each other. The present is a controversy between individuals, respecting their right or title to a particular tract of land, and cannot be extended to third parties or states. Its decision will not affect the state of Connecticut or New York; because neither of them is before the court, nor is it possible to bring either of them, as a party, before the court, in the present action. The state, as such, is not before us. Besides, if the cause should be removed into this court, it would answer no purpose; for I am not able to discern by what authority we could change the *venue*, or direct a jury to be drawn from another district. As to this particular, there is no devolution of power, either by the constitution or law. The authority must be given—we cannot usurp or take it.

If the point of jurisdiction be raised by the pleadings, the circuit court is competent to its decision; and therefore, the cause cannot be removed into this court previously to such decision. To remove a cause from one court to another, on the allegation of the want of jurisdiction, is a novelty in judicial proceedings. Would not the *certiorari* to remove, be an admission of the jurisdiction below? Neither of the motions is within the letter or spirit of the constitution or law.

How far a suit may, with effect, be instituted in this court, to decide the right of jurisdiction between two states, abstractedly from the right of soil, it is not necessary to determine. The question is a great one; but not before us. I regret the incompetence of this court to give the aid prayed for. No prejudice or passion, whether of a state or personal nature, should insinuate itself in the administration of justice. Jurymen, especially, should be above all prejudice, all passion, and all interest in the matter to be determined. But it is the duty of judges to declare, and not to make the law.

CUSHING, Justice.—These motions are to be determined, rather by the constitution and the laws made under it, than by any remote analogies drawn from English practice.

Both by the constitution and the judicial act, the supreme court has original jurisdiction, where a state is a party. In this case, the state does not appear to be a party, by anything on the record. It is a controversy or suit between private citizens only; an action of ejectment, in which the defendant pleads to the jurisdiction, that the land lies in the state of New York, and issue is taken on that fact. Whether the land lies in New York or Connecticut, does not appear to affect the right or title to the land in question. The right of jurisdiction and the right of soil may depend on very different words, charters and foundations. A decision of that issue can only determine the controversy as between the private citizens, who are parties to the suit, and the event only give the land to the plaintiff or defendant; but could have no controlling influence over the line of jurisdiction; with respect to which, if either state has a contest with the other, or with individuals, the state has its remedy, I suppose, under the constitution and the laws, by proper application, but not in this way; for she is not a party to the suit.

If an individual will put the event of his cause in a plea of this kind, on a fact, which is not essential to his right; I cannot think, it can prejudice the right of jurisdiction appertaining to a state. I agree with the rest of the court, that neither of the motions can be granted.

43

TURNER V. BANK OF NORTH AMERICA
4 Dall. 8 (1799)

ELLSWORTH, *Chief Justice.* The action below was brought by the president and directors of the Bank of *North America,* who are well described to be citizens of *Pennsylvania,* against *Turner* and others, who are well described to be citizens of *North Carolina,* upon a promissory note, made by the defendant, payable to *Biddle* & Co., and which, by assignment, became the property of the plaintiffs. *Biddle* & Co. are no otherwise described, than as "using trade and merchandize in partnership together," at *Philadelphia* or *North Carolina.* And judgment was for the plaintiff.

The error assigned, the only one insisted on, is, that it does not appear from the record, that Biddle & Co. the promisees, or any of them, are citizens of a state other than that of North Carolina, or aliens.

A circuit court, though an *inferior* court, in the language of the constitution, is not so in the language of the common law; nor are its proceedings subject to the scrutiny of those narrow rules, which the caution, or jealousy, of the courts at *Westminster,* long applied to courts of that denomination; but are entitled to as liberal intendments, or presumptions, in favour of their regularity, as those of any supreme court. A circuit court however, is of *limited* jurisdiction; and has cognizance, not of cases generally, but only of a few specially circumstanced, amounting to a small proportion of the cases, which an unlimited jurisdiction would embrace. And the fair presumption is (not as

with regard to a court of general jurisdiction, that a cause is within its jurisdiction unless the contrary appears, but rather) that a cause is without its jurisdiction till the contrary appears. This renders it necessary, in as much as the proceedings of no court can be deemed valid further than its jurisdiction appears, or can be presumed, to set forth upon the record of a circuit court, the facts or circumstances, which give jurisdiction, either expressly, or in such manner as to render them certain by legal intendment. Among those circumstances, it is necessary, where the defendant appears to be a citizen of one state, to show that the plaintiff is a citizen of some other state, or an alien; or if (as in the present case) the suit be upon a promissory note, by an assignee, to show, that the original promissee is so: for, by a special provision of the statute, it is his description, as well as that of the assignee, which effectuates jurisdiction.

But here the description given of the promissee only is, that "he used trade" at Philadelphia or North Carolina; which, taking either place for that where he used trade, contains no averment that he was a citizen of a state, other than that of North Carolina, or an alien; nor any thing which, by legal intendment, can amount to such averment. We must, therefore, say that there is error.

It is exceedingly to be regretted, that exceptions which might be taken in abatement and often cured in a moment, should be reserved to the last stage of a suit, to destroy its fruits.

44

MOSSMAN V. HIGGINSON
4 Dall. 12 (1800)

By the Court: The decisions on this subject, govern the present case; and the eleventh section of the judiciary act can, and must receive a construction, consistent with the constitution. It says, it is true, in general terms, that the circuit court shall have cognizance of suits "where an alien is a party;" but as the legislative power of confering jurisdiction on the federal courts, is in this respect, confined to suits between citizens and foreigners, we must so expound the terms of the law, as to meet the case, "where, indeed, an alien is one party," but a citizen is the other. Neither the constitution, nor the act of congress, regard, on this point, the subject of the suit, but the parties. A description of the parties is therefore indispensable to the exercise of jurisdiction. There is here no such description. . . .

45

COOPER V. TELFAIR

4 Dall. 14 (1800)

Basil Cooper, at present of the island of Jamaica, in the dominions of his Britannic majesty, formerly an inhabitant of the state of Georgia, brought an action in the circuit court of Georgia, to November term 1797, against Edward Telfair, of the district of Georgia, upon a bond for 1000*l.* sterling, equal to $4285.70, dated the 14th of May 1774.

After *oyer* of the bond and condition, the defendant pleaded in bar, 1st, Payment: 2d, "That on the fourth day of May 1782, an act was passed by the legislature of the state of Georgia, entitled 'An act for inflicting penalties on, and confiscating the estate of such persons as are therein declared guilty of treason, and for other purposes therein mentioned,' by which it is, among other things, enacted and declared, 'that all and every the persons, named and included in the said act, are banished from the said state; and that all and singular the estate, real and personal, of each and every of the aforesaid persons, which they held, possessed or were entitled to, in law or equity, on the 19th day of April 1775, and which they have held since, or do hold in possession, or others holding in trust for them, or to which they are, or may be, entitled, in law or equity, or which they may have, hold or be possessed of, in right of others, together with all debts, dues and demands of whatsoever nature, that are or may be owing to the aforesaid persons, or either of them, be confiscated to and for the benefit of this state.' That the said Basil Cooper is expressly named and included in the above in part recited acts; and that he was, on the said 4th day of May 1782, and for a long time before, a citizen of the state of Georgia, and of the United States of America. That the said Basil Cooper, being a citizen, &c., owing allegiance, &c., on the 4th of May 1782, and for a long time before, adhered to the troops of his Britannic majesty, then at open war with the said state of Georgia and United States of America, and did take up arms with the said troops, &c. That the said Basil Cooper hath never since returned within the limits and jurisdiction of the said United States, or either of them. That by virtue of the above-recited act, and also of an act, entitled, 'An act to continue an act to authorize the auditor to liquidate the demands of such persons as have claims against the confiscated estates, and for other purposes therein mentioned,' passed the 13th February 1786: and of another act entitled 'An act to compel the settlement of the public accounts, for inflicting penalties on officers of this state, who may neglect their duty, and for vesting the auditors with certain powers for the more speedy settlement of the accounts of this state, with the United States,' passed the 10th of February 1787; the sum of money mentioned in the condition of the bond, and all interest thereon, have become forfeited and confis-

cated to the state of Georgia; and the right of action attached thereto; and no cause of action hath accrued to the said Basil Cooper to demand and have of the said Edward Telfair, the said sum of money, &c."

To this plea, the plaintiff replied, "that he was never tried, convicted or attainted of the crime of treason alleged against him; and that by the constitution of the state (in force at the time of passing the acts in the said plea set forth, to wit, on the 4th day of May 1782), unanimously agreed to in a convention of the people of this state, on the 5th of February 1777, it is ordained, that—

"Article 1. The legislative, executive and judiciary departments shall be separate and distinct, so that neither exercise the powers properly belonging to the other.

"Article 7. The house of assembly shall have power to make such laws and regulations, as may be conducive to the good order and well-being of the state, provided such laws and regulations be not repugnant to the true intent and meaning of any rule or regulation contained in this constitution.

"Article 39. All matters of breach of the peace, felony, murder and treason against the state, to be tried in the county where the crime was committed, &c.

"Article 60. The principles of the *habeas corpus* act shall be part of this constitution.

"Article 61. The freedom of the press, and the trial by jury, to remain inviolate for ever.

"And that the said recited acts, so far as they can operate to bar the said Basil from maintaining his action, are repugnant to the true intent and meaning of divers rules and regulations contained in the said constitution, and are, as to the action of the said Basil, null and void: without that, &c." The defendant demurred to the replication; and the plaintiff joined in demurrer.

On the 2d of May 1799, the circuit court, composed of ELLSWORTH, Chief Justice, and CLAY, District Judge, decided, that the replication was insufficient; that the plea in bar was sufficient; and that judgment on the demurrer be entered for the defendant. Upon this judgment, the present writ of error was brought, and the following errors ssigned: 1. The general errors. 2. That the plea does not set forth the constitutional power of the legislature of Georgia, to deprive the plaintiff of his rights as a citizen; and on their own authority, to pass sentence of confiscation and banishment. 3. That the judgment decides that the legislature had cognisance of the treason alleged against the plaintiff, and could legally try, convict and banish him; whereas, they had no such power, on constitutional principles. 4. That by the judgment, it appears, the legislature could deprive individuals of their lives and property, without trial by jury, or inquest of office, contrary to the constitution of Georgia. 5. That the judgment gives effect to an act of Georgia, which is an union and usurpation of judicial, as well as legislative powers; which powers the constitution declares should be kept separate.

. . . . .

On the 13th of February 1800, the judges (except the Chief Justice, who had decided the cause in the circuit court) delivered their opinions, *seriatim*, in substance, as follows:

WASHINGTON, Justice.—The constitution of Georgia does not expressly interdict the passing of an act of attainder and confiscation, by the authority of the legislature. Is such an act, then, so repugnant to any constitutional regulation, as to be excepted from the legislative jurisdiction, by a necessary implication? Where an offence is not committed within some county of the state, the constitution makes no provision for a trial, neither as to the place, nor as to the manner. Is such an offence (perhaps, the most dangerous treason) to be considered as beyond the reach of the government, even to forfeit the property of the offender, within its territorial boundary? If the plaintiff in error had shown, that the offence with which he was charged, had been committed in any county of Georgia, he might have raised the question of conflict and collision, between the constitution and the law: but as that fact does not appear, there is no ground on which I could be prepared to say, that the law is void. The presumption, indeed, must always be in favor of the validity of laws, if the contrary is not clearly demonstrated.

CHASE, Justice.—I agree, for the reason which has been assigned, to affirm the judgment. Before the plaintiff in error could claim the benefit of a trial by jury, under the constitution, it was, at least, incumbent upon him to show, that the offence charged was committed in some county of Georgia, in which case alone, the constitution provides for the trial. But even if he had established that fact, I should not have thought the law a violation of the constitution. The general principles contained in the constitution are not to be regarded as rules to fetter and control; but as matter merely declaratory and directory: for even in the constitution itself, we may trace repeated departures from the theoretical doctrine, that the legislative, executive and judicial powers should be kept separate and distinct.

There is, likewise, a material difference between laws passed by the individual states, during the revolution, and laws passed subsequently to the organization of the federal constitution. Few of the revolutionary acts would stand the rigorous tests now applied: and although it is alleged, that all acts of the legislature, in direct opposition to the prohibitions of the constitution, would be void; yet, it still remains a question, where the power resides to declare it void? It is, indeed, a general opinion, it is expressly admitted by all this bar, and some of the judges have, individually, in the circuits, decided, that the supreme court can declare an act of congress to be unconstitutional, and therefore, invalid; but there is no adjudication of the supreme court itself upon the point. I concur, however, in the general sentiment, with reference to the period, when the existing constitution came into operation; but whether the power under the existing constitution, can be employed to invalidate laws previously enacted, is a very different question, turning upon very different principles; and with respect to which, I abstain from giving an opinion; since, on other ground, I am satisfied with the correctness of the judgment of the circuit court.

PATERSON, Justice.—I consider it a sound political proposition, that wherever the legislative power of a government is undefined, it includes the judicial and executive attributes. The legislative power of Georgia, though it is in some respects restricted and qualified, is not defined by the constitution of the state. Had, then, the legislature power to punish its citizens, who had joined the enemy, and could not be punished by the ordinary course of law? It is denied, because it would be an exercise of judicial authority. But the power of confiscation and banishment does not belong to the judicial authority, whose process could not reach the offenders: and yet, it is a power that grows out of the very nature of the social compact, which must reside somewhere, and which is so inherent in the legislature, that it cannot be divested or transferred, without an express provision of the constitution.

The constitutions of several of the other states of the Union, contain the same general principles and restrictions; but it never was imagined, that they applied to a case like the present; and to authorize this court to pronounce any law void, it must be a clear and unequivocal breach of the constitution, not a doubtful and argumentative application.

CUSHING, Justice.—Although I am of opinion, that this court has the same power that a court of the state of Georgia would possess, to declare the law void, I do not think, that the occasion would warrant an exercise of the power. The right to confiscate and banish, in the case of an offending citizen, must belong to every government. It is not within the judicial power, as created and regulated by the constitution of Georgia: and it, naturally, as well as tacitly, belongs to the legislature.

BY THE COURT.—Let the judgment be affirmed, with costs.

46

HOUSE OF REPRESENTATIVES, JUDICIARY BILL
7 Jan. 1801
Annals 10:891–96

Mr. DENNIS . . . As to the expediency of delegating Judicial powers to the State courts, it presented a more difficult inquiry. It was certainly a kind of clumsy affair. Under all other Governments the Judicial authority was at least coextensive with the Legislative; and in many Governments it went beyond it in a decision of cases under the law of nations.

Besides, Mr. D. discerned no way of compelling State Judges to perform their duty; and there appeared to be peculiar hardships in obliging courts and juries, supported by particular counties, to perform Federal duties.

Mr. HARPER had as little doubt of the Constitutionality as he had of the expediency of this delegation of power. At present we are not under the necessity of establishing a

Judicial system as extensive as the powers of Congress. If we were constitutionally obliged to do this, we should be compelled to cover the whole ground, and to institute a great number of new courts. It is true that we cannot enforce on the State courts, as a matter of duty, a performance of the acts we confide to them; but we give them the power, and until they refuse to exercise it, we have no cause to complain. He did not believe this proviso necessary. But as some gentlemen thought it was necessary, he would vote for it.

Mr. BIRD declared himself still of opinion, that the delegation of Judicial power to the State courts was unconstitutional. This is denied by the gentleman from Maryland. The argument he makes use of stands thus: He denies the unconstitutionality of the transfer, because we have practised it; therefore we have the power. Is this correct reasoning? Does the practice of a particular thing demonstrate it to be right?

The extreme difficulty of stretching out Judicial power in federal tribunals, which was alleged, was not a question of right, but of expediency. If it were a question of right, then must the question of right, as superior, supersede the minor question of expediency.

Some gentlemen seemed to think that, as soon as Congress pass a particular law, there exists a right and a duty in the State courts to execute it. But our own practice destroys this idea; for all our laws on the subject actually give power to the State courts; the expression is, "they may have jurisdiction in certain cases."

It had been asked, whether the laws of the United States did not bind the State Judges? He answered that they bound them as citizens but not as Judges. Even the gentleman from South Carolina admits that there is no obligation imposed upon them to act. This furnished a strong argument of the inconsistency of gentlemen, as the Judges were neither bound to execute our laws nor punishable for omitting to execute them. Further, the institution of a Judiciary coextensive with the other branches of the Government, was essential to the due administration of all just plans of civil policy. On the Judiciary depended the fair administration of justice. It was an organ of essential use and necessity. It should be attached to the system of which it formed a part, independently of all other systems. As well might the organ of one human body expect to derive support from the organ of another disconnected body, as the Federal Judiciary expect to gain support from State tribunals. So thought the framers of the Constitution; and a cotemporaneous commentator on it has declared that a Judiciary coextensive with the Legislature is so natural as not to require argument to support it.

Mr. B. then went over the same ground with that taken by him in a former debate.

He concluded by declaring that, until the point was better cleared of Constitutional objections, all arguments of inexpediency were perfectly futile.

Mr. NOTT said, the simple question was, whether the Congress of the United States had or had not the Constitutional right of transferring to the State judicatories the power of trying causes arising under the Constitution or laws of the United States. In discussing this question he should not consider the consequences resulting from the decision, for although the consequences might be as his colleague (Mr. HARPER) had represented, that the Judiciary of the United States must be made coextensive with the State judiciaries, if this power was not admitted, yet if so the Constitution was written, so it must be understood. The Constitution could not be bent as convenience might require. The decision, therefore, must be made by the instrument itself.

The Constitution provided that the Judicial power of the United States should be vested in one Supreme Court and such inferior courts as the Congress might from time to time ordain and establish; and also that they should hold their offices during good behaviour, &c.

Mr. N. said, the clause in the Constitution requiring inferior courts, was equally imperative with that requiring a Supreme Court, with this difference only, that the Supreme Court was limited to one, but the details of the inferior courts were left to Congress. The expression "inferior courts" was a technical expression, as well understood by every lawyer as any in our law books. It meant a court possessed of subordinate powers within the same Judiciary system, and necessarily implied a superior court, capable of controlling an undue exercise of those powers; that the State Legislatures might with as much propriety be called inferior to the Federal Legislature, or the Executive of any State be called a subordinate officer of the President of the United States, as the State courts could be considered inferior courts of the United States.

The words in the Constitution were, "such inferior courts as Congress may ordain and establish;" and it was not sufficient to say that by giving the power to try causes arising under the Constitution,. &c., you, *quo ad hoc*, made them courts of the United States; for there was an essential difference between ordaining and establishing courts and transferring power to courts already ordained and established. The obvious meaning of the Constitution, was that the Judicial power of the United States should be confided to courts established and organized by their own Government. Besides, Mr. N. observed, it was required that the Judges should hold their offices during good behaviour; but this was not the case in the several States; in some, he said, they held their commissions for a limited time; in others during the pleasure of the Legislature, and in others they could not hold them after a certain period of life.

There was another objection, he said, to this mode of appointing officers of the United States. The Constitution has provided that the President should appoint all the officers of the United States not otherwise appointed by the Constitution, except Congress should by law provide otherwise, as mentioned in the same clause of the Constitution. The Judges were not, however, of that description of officers contemplated by the Constitution, the appointment of whom Congress might vest in some other department, and if they were, that power had never yet been exercised by Congress. This, in effect, would be to divest the President of the power given him by the Constitution of appointing all officers, and to exercise it ourselves.

The doctrine he contended for would be further obvious by a reference to the second section of the third article of the Constitution, expressing the cases to which the Judicial power of the United States should extend. . . .

He said there was a marked difference between the words of the Constitution relating to the catalogue of cases enumerated in the first part of that section, and those in the latter part of the same. The word "all" was prefixed to each of the cases first mentioned, down to the words "admiralty and maritime jurisdiction" inclusive, but was omitted in all the subsequent cases. He could see no reason why that word was added in the former part of the section, and omitted in the latter, except it meant that there was no case of the former description to which the Judicial power of the United States should not extend; in fact that the courts of the United States should have exclusive jurisdiction of all those cases, and in the latter their jurisdiction should be concurrent with the State courts.

It was further to be observed, he said, that the first description of cases here enumerated, were such as had received their birth from the Constitution and laws of the United States, and could not have existed previous to the establishment of the Government, or be such as immediately involved the rights and interests of the General Government; but that the latter were such as the individual States might have jurisdiction of, previous to that period. He presumed the State courts were not vested with more power under the present Constitution than they were before, unless given them by the Constitution; nor are they divested of any, unless by the same instrument, or by Congress, in pursuance of the power therein given to them. And he had seen no part of the Constitution that delegated this power to the State courts, or that authorized Congress to do it. It appeared to him that the meaning of the Constitution was to give to the courts of the United States exclusive jurisdiction over cases arising under the Constitution or laws of the United States, and also over all cases immediately affecting the general interests, and to reserve to the individual States the exclusive jurisdiction over their own local concerns; and that in cases involving their own interest and the rights of others, they might have concurrent jurisdiction. It was acknowledged by the gentleman from Delaware (Mr. BAYARD) that Congress had no power to compel the State courts to perform that duty, but that the Judges of the several States were bound to obey all the acts of Congress. Other gentlemen had observed, that this doctrine would go to deny that the stamp act, or any similar act, was binding on the State Judiciaries. On this Mr. N. observed, that the State courts were bound to observe all the Constitutional laws of Congress. When, therefore, Congress passed a law that no instrument of writing for the payment of money should be received in any State court as evidence of such debt, unless the same was upon stamped paper, the Judges were bound to obey it; but if they should pass a law giving power to any county court within the United States, to try persons guilty of treason against the United States, that law would not be obligatory upon them; nevertheless, it would be an act of Congress. Mr. N. said, the distinction was between cases arising under the Constitution and laws of the United States, and those that did not. His idea might be further illustrated by the act above mentioned (the stamp act.) If a person should give a note of hand for a hundred dollars on unstamped paper, with a view of evading that act, he was liable to a penalty; that would of course be a case arising under a law of the United States, and would be exclusively cognizable in the courts of the United States. But an action brought on a note of hand written on stamped paper, is not a case arising under the law of the United States, but arises from the contract itself; and, although no note had been given, the contract would, nevertheless, have existed. The stamp act does not require a contract to be in writing; but if people will have their contracts tested by written evidence, it requires that paper should be stamped.

Mr. N. said, wherever a duty was enjoined by law, the person who was guilty of the non-performance of that duty incurred the penalty annexed, and that penalty could be recovered no other way but by indictment, unless otherwise expressly provided by the law itself. And how would gentlemen frame an indictment in a State court, to embrace a case that had occurred under a law of the United States? It was essential in every indictment, to lay the offence to have been committed against the law of the State, and to conclude against the peace and dignity of the same. But, surely, gentlemen would not contend that an offence against a law of the United States was an offence against the law of an individual State, or against its peace and dignity. The gentleman from Delaware (Mr. BAYARD) had observed that penalties incurred under the revenue laws were not considered as crimes, but were recoverable in actions of debt. But, said Mr. N., merely changing the action or the mode of recovering the penalty cannot alter the nature of the offence, nor the tribunal before whom it is to be tried. It was still a case arising under a law of the United States, and although a debt, it was one in which the defendant not even in contemplation of law had any agency. And to contend that because a penalty is by an act of Congress recoverable by an action of debt, therefore they have a right to transfer these cases to the State courts for adjudication, is to say that Congress may first give themselves the power to delegate it, and then exercise the power that is acquired.

But, said Mr. N., if it is true that Congress have a right to impose this duty on the Judges of the State courts, they must have the right to compel a performance of it. It was incompatible with the idea of sovereignty, to pass laws and not to have the power and the means of carrying them into execution.

Upon the whole, he had seen no part of the Constitution that authorized Congress to delegate such power to the State courts, or that authorized the State courts to execute it, and he should therefore vote against the proposed amendment.

Mr. BAYARD considered the question of the delegation of power altogether misapplied. The proviso moved by the gentleman from Maryland related to the jurisdiction of the State courts, not over offences, but over civil suits, which were brought by the United States for debts arising out of contracts with the individuals indebted to the Government. Now, it would puzzle him to say why the State courts should not decide cases in which the United States were a party, as well as in any other description of cases, when it was known that their jurisdiction extended over all actions for debt.

47

MARBURY v. MADISON
1 Cranch 137 (1803)

OPINION OF THE COURT.—At the last term, on the affidavits then read and filed with the clerk, a rule was granted in this case, requiring the secretary of state to show cause why a *mandamus* should not issue, directing him to deliver to William Marbury his commission as a justice of the peace for the county of Washington, in the district of Columbia.

No cause has been shown, and the present motion is for a *mandamus*. The peculiar delicacy of this case, the novelty of some of its circumstances, and the real difficulty attending the points which occur in it, require a complete exposition of the principles on which the opinion to be given by the court is founded. These principles have been, on the side of the applicant, very ably argued at the bar. In rendering the opinion of the court, there will be some departure in form, though not in substance, from the points stated in that argument.

In the order in which the court has viewed this subject, the following questions have been considered and decided: 1st. Has the applicant a right to the commission he demands? 2d. If he has a right, and that right has been violated, do the laws of his country afford him a remedy? 3d. If they do afford him a remedy, is it a *mandamus* issuing from this court?

The first object of inquiry is—Has the applicant a right to the commission he demands? His right originates in an act of congress passed in February 1801, concerning the district of Columbia. After dividing the district into two counties, the 11th section of this law enacts, "that there shall be appointed in and for each of the said counties, such number of discreet persons to be justices of the peace, as the president of the United States shall, from time to time, think expedient, to continue in office for five years.

It appears, from the affidavits, that, in compliance with this law, a commission for William Marbury, as a justice of peace for the county of Washington, was signed by John Adams, then President of the United States; after which, the seal of the United States was affixed to it; but the commission has never reached the person for whom it was made out. In order to determine whether he is entitled to this commission, it becomes necessary to inquire, whether he has been appointed to the office. For if he has been appointed, the law continues him in office for five years, and he is entitled to the possession of those evidences of office, which, being completed, became his property.

The 2d section of the 2d article of the constitution declares, that "the president shall nominate, and by and with the advice and consent of the senate, shall appoint ambassadors, other public ministers and consuls, and all other officers of the United States, whose appointments are not otherwise provided for." The 3d section declares, that "he shall commission all the officers of the United States."

An act of congress directs the secretary of state to keep the seal of the United States, "to make out and record, and affix the said seal to all civil commissions to officers of the United States, to be appointed by the president, by and with the consent of the senate, or by the president alone; provided, that the said seal shall not be affixed to any commission, before the same shall have been signed by the president of the United States."

These are the clauses of the constitution and laws of the United States, which affect this part of the case. They seem to contemplate three distinct operations: 1st. The nomination: this is the sole act of the president, and is completely voluntary. 2d. The appointment: this is also the act of the president, and is also a voluntary act, though it can only be performed by and with the advice and consent of the senate. 3d. The commission: to grant a commission to a person appointed, might, perhaps, be deemed a duty enjoined by the constitution. "He shall," says that instrument, "commission all the officers of the United States."

1. The acts of appointing to office, and commissioning the person appointed, can scarcely be considered as one and the same; since the power to perform them is given in two separate and distinct sections of the constitution. The distinction between the appointment and the commission, will be rendered more apparent, by adverting to that provision in the second section of the second article of the constitution, which authorizes congress "to vest, by law, the appointment of such inferior officers, as they think proper, in the president alone, in the courts of law, or in the heads of departments;" thus contemplating cases where the law may direct the president to commission an officer appointed by the courts, or by the heads of departments. In such a case, to issue a commission would be apparently a duty distinct from the appointment, the performance of which, perhaps, could not legally be refused.

Although that clause of the constitution which requires the president to commission all the officers of the United States, may never have been applied to officers appointed otherwise than by himself, yet it would be difficult to deny the legislative power to apply it to such cases. Of consequence, the constitutional distinction between the appointment to an office and the commission of an officer who has been appointed, remains the same, as if, in practice, the president had commissioned officers appointed by an authority other than his own. It follows, too, from the existence of this distinction, that if an appointment was to be evidenced by any public act, other than the commission, the performance of such public act would create the officer; and if he was not removable at the will of the president, would either give him a right to his commission, or enable him to perform the duties without it.

These observations are premised, solely for the purpose of rendering more intelligible those which apply more directly to the particular case under consideration.

This is an appointment made by the president, by and with the advice and consent of the senate, and is evidenced by no act but the commission itself. In such a case, therefore, the commission and the appointment seem inseparable; it being almost impossible to show an appointment, otherwise than by providing the existence of a commission; still the commission is not necessarily the appointment, though conclusive evidence of it.

But at what stage, does it amount to this conclusive evidence? The answer to this question seems an obvious one. The appointment being the sole act of the president, must be completely evidenced, when it is shown that he has done everything to be performed by him. Should the commission, instead of being evidence of an appointment, even be considered as constituting the appointment itself; still, it would be made, when the last act to be done by the president was performed, or, at farthest, when the commission was complete.

The last act to be done by the president is the signature of the commission: he has then acted on the advice and consent of the senate to his own nomination. The time for deliberation has then passed: he has decided. His judgment, on the advice and consent of the senate, concurring with his nomination, has been made, and the officer is appointed. This appointment is evidenced by an open unequivocal act; and being the last act required from the person making it, necessarily excludes the idea of its being, so far as respects the appointment, an inchoate and incomplete transaction.

Some point of time must be taken, when the power of the executive over an officer, not removable at his will, must cease. That point of time must be, when the constitutional power of appointment has been exercised. And this power has been exercised, when the last act, required from the person possessing the power, has been performed: this last act is the signature of the commission. This idea seems to have prevailed with the legislature, when the act passed converting the department of foreign affairs into the department of state. By that act, it is enacted, that the secretary of state shall keep the seal of the United States, "and shall make out and record, and shall affix the said seal to all civil commissions to officers of the United States, to be appointed by the president;" "provided, that the said seal shall not be affixed to any commission, before the same shall have been signed by the President of the United States; nor to any other instrument or act, without the special warrant of the president therefor."

The signature is a warrant for affixing the great seal to the commission; and the great seal is only to be affixed to an instrument which is complete. It attests, by an act, supposed to be of public notoriety, the verity of the presidential signature. It is never to be affixed, until the commission is signed, because the signature, which gives force and effect to the commission, is conclusive evidence that the appointment is made.

The commission being signed, the subsequent duty of the secretary of state is prescribed by law, and not to be guided by the will of the president. He is to affix the seal of the United States to the commission, and is to record it.

This is not a proceeding which may be varied, if the judgment of the executive shall suggest one more eligible; but is a precise course accurately marked out by law, and is to be strictly pursued. It is the duty of the secretary of state, to conform to the law, and in this he is an officer of the United States, bound to obey the laws. He acts, in this respect, as has been very properly stated at the bar, under the authority of law, and not by the instructions of the president. It is a ministerial act, which the law enjoins on a particular officer for a particular purpose.

If it should be supposed, that the solemnity of affixing the seal is necessary, not only to the validity of the commission, but even to the completion of an appointment, still, when the seal is affixed, the appointment is made, and the commission is valid. No other solemnity is required by law; no other act is to be performed on the part of government. All that the executive can do, to invest the person with his office, is done; and unless the appointment be then made, the executive cannot make one without the co-operation of others.

After searching anxiously for the principles on which a contrary opinion may be supported, none have been found, which appear of sufficient force to maintain the opposite doctrine. Such as the imagination of the court could suggest, have been very deliberately examined, and after allowing them all the weight which it appears possible to give them, they do not shake the opinion which has been formed. In considering this question, it has been conjectured, that the commission may have been assimilated to a deed, to the validity of which delivery is essential. This idea is founded on the supposition, that the commission is not merely evidence of an appointment, but is itself the actual appointment; a supposition by no means unquestionable. But for the purpose of examining this objection fairly, let it be conceded, that the principle claimed for its support is established.

The appointment being, under the constitution, to be made by the president, personally, the delivery of the deed of appointment, if necessary to its completion, must be made by the president also. It is not necessary, that the delivery should be made personally to the grantee of the office: it never is so made. The law would seem to contemplate, that it should be made to the secretary of the state, since it directs the secretary to affix the seal to the commission, after it shall have been signed by the president. If, then, the act of delivery be necessary to give validity to the commission, it has been delivered, when executed and given to the secretary, for the purpose of being sealed, recorded and transmitted to the party.

But in all cases of letters-patent, certain solemnities are required by law, which solemnities are the evidences of the validity of the instrument: a formal delivery to the person is not among them. In cases of commissions, the sign manual of the president, and the seal of the United States are those solemnities. This objection, therefore, does not touch the case.

It has also occurred as possible, and barely possible, that the transmission of the commission, and the acceptance thereof, might be deemed necessary to complete the right of the plaintiff. The transmission of the commission is a practice, directed by convenience, but not by law. It cannot, therefore, be necessary to constitute the appointment, which must precede it, and which is the mere act of the president. If the executive required that every person appointed to an office should himself take means to procure his commission, the appointment would not be the less valid on that account. The appointment is the sole act of the president; the transmission of the commission is the sole act of the officer to whom that duty is assigned, and may be accelerated or retarded by circumstances which can have no influence on the appointment. A commission is transmitted to a person already appointed; not to a person to be appointed or not, as the letter inclosing the commission should happen to get into the post-office and reach him in safety, or to miscarry.

It may have some tendency to elucidate this point, to inquire, whether the possession of the original commission be indispensably necessary to authorize a person, appointed to any office, to perform the duties of that office. If it was necessary, then a loss of the commission would lose the office. Not only negligence, but accident or fraud, fire or theft, might deprive an individual of his office. In such a case, I presume, it could not be doubted, but that a copy from the record of the office of the secretary of state would be, to every intent and purpose, equal to the original: the act of congress has expressly made it so. To give that copy validity, it would not be necessary to prove that the original had been transmitted and afterwards lost. The copy would be complete evidence that the original had existed, and that the appointment had been made, but not that the original had been transmitted. If, indeed, it should appear, that the original had been mislaid in the office of state, that circumstance would not affect the operation of the copy. When all the requisites have been performed, which authorize a recording officer to record any instrument whatever, and the order for that purpose has been given, the instrument is, in law, considered as recorded, although the manual labor of inserting it in a book kept for that purpose may not have been performed. In the case of commissions, the law orders the secretary of state to record them. When, therefore, they are signed and sealed, the order for their being recorded is given; and whether inserted in the book or not, they are in law recorded.

A copy of this record is declared equal to the original, and the fees to be paid by a person requiring a copy are ascertained by law. Can a keeper of a public record erase therefrom a commission which has been recorded? Or can he refuse a copy thereof to a person demanding it on the terms prescribed by law? Such a copy would, equally with the original, authorize the justice of peace to proceed in the performance of his duty, because it would, equally with the original, attest his appointment.

If the transmission of a commission be not considered as necessary to give validity to an appointment, still less is its acceptance. The appointment is the sole act of the president; the acceptance is the sole act of the officer, and is, in plain common sense, posterior to the appointment. As he may resign, so may he refuse to accept: but neither the one nor the other is capable of rendering the appointment a nonentity.

That this is the understanding of the government, is apparent from the whole tenor of its conduct. A commission bears date, and the salary of the officer commences, from his appointment; not from the transmission or acceptance of his commission. When a person appointed to any office refuses to accept that office, the successor is nominated in the place of the person who has declined to accept, and not in the place of the person who had been previously in office, and had created the original vacancy.

It is, therefore, decidedly the opinion of the court, that when a commission has been signed by the president, the appointment is made; and that the commission is complete, when the seal of the United States has been affixed to it by the secretary of state.

Where an officer is removable at the will of the executive, the circumstance which completes his appointment is of no concern; because the act is at any time revocable; and the commission may be arrested, if still in the office. But when the officer is not removable at the will of the executive, the appointment is not revocable, and cannot be annulled: it has conferred legal rights which cannot be resumed. The discretion of the executive is to be exercised, until the appointment has been made. But having once made the appointment, his power over the office is terminated, in all cases where, by law, the officer is not removable by him. The right to the office is then in the person appointed, and he has the absolute unconditional power of accepting or rejecting it.

Mr. Marbury, then, since his commission was signed by the president, and sealed by the secretary of state, was appointed; and as the law creating the office, gave the officer a right to hold for five years, independent of the executive, the appointment was not revocable, but vested in the officer legal rights, which are protected by the laws of his country. To withhold his commission, therefore, is an act deemed by the court not warranted by law, but violative of a vested legal right.

2. This brings us to the second inquiry; which is: If he has a right, and the right has been violated, do the laws of his country afford him a remedy?

The very essence of civil liberty certainly consists in the right of every individual to claim the protection of the laws, whenever he receives an injury. One of the first duties of government is to afford that protection. In Great Britain, the king himself is sued in the respectful form of a petition, and he never fails to comply with the judgment of his court.

In the 3d vol. of his Commentaries (p. 23), Blackstone states two cases in which a remedy is afforded by mere operation of law. "In all other cases," he says, "it is a general and indisputable rule, that where there is a legal right, there is also a legal remedy by suit, or action at law, whenever that right is invaded." And afterwards (p. 109, of the same vol.), he says, "I am next to consider such injuries as are cognisable by the courts of the common law. And herein I shall, for the present, only remark, that all possible injuries whatsoever, that did not fall within the exclusive cognisance of either the ecclesiastical, military or maritime tribunals, are, for that very reason, within the cognisance of the common-law courts of justice; for it is a settled and invariable principle in the laws of England, that every right, when withheld, must have a remedy, and every injury its proper redress."

The government of the United States has been emphatically termed a government of laws, and not of men. It will certainly cease to deserve this high appellation, if the laws furnish no remedy for the violation of a vested legal right. If this obloquy is to be cast on the jurisprudence of our country, it must arise from the peculiar character of the case.

It behooves us, then, to inquire whether there be in its composition any ingredient which shall exempt it from legal investigation, or exclude the injured party from legal redress. In pursuing this inquiry, the first question which presents itself is, whether this can be arranged with that class of cases which come under the description of *damnum absque injuria;* a loss without an injury. This description of cases never has been considered, and it is believed, never can be considered, as comprehending offices of trust, of honor or of profit. The office of justice of peace in the district of Columbia is such an office; it is, therefore, worthy of the attention and guardianship of the laws. It has received that attention and guardianship: it has been created by special act of congress, and has been secured, so far as the laws can give security, to the person appointed to fill it, for five years. It is not, then, on account of the worthlessness of the thing pursued, that the injured party can be alleged to be without remedy.

Is it in the nature of the transaction? Is the act of delivering or withholding a commission to be considered as a mere political act, belonging to the executive department alone, for the performance of which entire confidence is placed by our constitution in the supreme executive; and for any misconduct respecting which, the injured individual has no remedy? That there may be such cases is not to be questioned; but that every act of duty, to be performed in any of the great departments of government, constitutes such a case, is not to be admitted.

By the act concerning invalids, passed in June 1794 (1 U. S. Stat. 392), the secretary at war is ordered to place on the pension list, all persons whose names are contained in a report previously made by him to congress. If he should refuse to do so, would the wounded veteran be without remedy? Is it to be contended, that where the law, in precise terms, directs the performance of an act, in which an individual is interested, the law is incapable of securing obedience to its mandate? Is it on account of the character of the person against whom the complaint is made? Is it to be contended that the heads of departments are not amenable to the laws of their country? Whatever the practice on particular occasions may be, the theory of this principle will certainly never be maintained. No act of the legislature confers so extraordinary a privilege, nor can it derive countenance from the doctrines of the common law. After stating that personal injury from the king to a subject is presumed to be impossible, Blackstone (vol. 3, p. 255), says, "but injuries to the rights of property can scarcely be committed by the crown, without the intervention of its officers; for whom the law, in matters of right, entertains no respect or delicacy; but furnishes various methods of detecting the errors and misconduct of those agents, by whom the king has been deceived and induced to do a temporary injustice."

By the act passed in 1796, authorizing the sale of the lands above the mouth of Kentucky river (1 U. S. Stat. 464), the purchaser, on paying his purchase-money, becomes completely entitled to the property purchased; and on producing to the secretary of state the receipt of the treasurer, upon a certificate required by the law, the president of the United States is authorized to grant him a patent. It is further enacted, that all patents shall be countersigned by the secretary of state, and recorded in his office. If the secretary of state should choose to withhold this patent; or, the patent being lost, should refuse a copy of it; can it be imagined, that the law furnishes to the injured person no remedy? It is not believed, that any person whatever would attempt to maintain such a proposition.

It follows, then, that the question, whether the legality of an act of the head of a department be examinable in a court of justice or not, must always depend on the nature of that act. If some acts be examinable, and others not, there must be some rule of law to guide the court in the exercise of its jurisdiction. In some instances, there may be difficulty in applying the rule to particular cases; but there cannot, it is believed, be much difficulty in laying down the rule.

By the constitution of the United States, the president is invested with certain important political powers, in the exercise of which he is to use his own discretion, and is accountable only to his country in his political character, and to his own conscience. To aid him in the performance of these duties, he is authorized to appoint certain officers, who act by his authority, and in conformity with his orders. In such cases, their acts are his acts; and whatever opinion may be entertained of the manner in which executive discretion may be used, still there exists, and can exist, no power to control that discretion. The subjects are political: they respect the nation, not individual rights, and being entrusted to the executive, the decision of the executive is conclusive. The application of this remark will be perceived, by adverting to the act of congress for establishing the department of foreign affairs. This officer, as his duties were prescribed by that act, is to conform precisely to the will of the president: he is the mere organ by whom that will is communicated. The acts of such an officer, as an officer, can never be examinable by the courts. But when the legislature proceeds to impose on that officer other duties; when he is directed peremptorily to perform certain acts; when the rights of individuals are dependent on the performance of those acts; he is so far the officer of the law; is amenable to the laws for his conduct; and cannot, at his discretion, sport away the vested rights of others.

The conclusion from this reasoning is, that where the heads of departments are the political or confidential agents of the executive, merely to execute the will of the president, or rather to act in cases in which the executive possesses a constitutional or legal discretion, nothing can be more perfectly clear, than that their acts are only politically examinable. But where a specific duty is assigned by law, and individual rights depend upon the performance of that duty, it seems equally clear, that the individual who considers himself injured, has a right to resort to the laws of his country for a remedy.

If this be the rule, let us inquire, how it applies to the case under the consideration of the court. The power of nominating to the senate, and the power of appointing the person nominated, are political powers, to be exercised by the president, according to his own discretion. When he has made an appointment, he has exercised his whole power, and his discretion has been completely applied to the case. If, by law, the officer be removable at the will of the president, then a new appointment may be immediately made, and the rights of the officer are terminated. But as a fact which has existed, cannot be made never to have existed, the appointment cannot be annihilated; and consequently, if the officer is by law not removable at the will of the president, the rights he has acquired are protected by the law, and are not resumable by the president. They cannot be extinguished by executive authority, and he has the privilege of asserting them in like manner, as if they had been derived from any other source.

The question whether a right has vested or not, is, in its nature, judicial, and must be tried by the judicial authority. If, for example, Mr. Marbury had taken the oaths of a magistrate, and proceeded to act as one; in consequence of which, a suit has been instituted against him, in which his defence had depended on his being a magistrate, the validity of his appointment must have been determined by judicial authority. So, if he conceives that, by virtue of his appointment, he has a legal right either to the commission which has been made out for him, or to a copy of that commission, it is equally a question examinable in a court, and the decision of the court upon it must depend on the opinion entertained of his appointment. That question has been discussed, and the opinion is, that the latest point of time which can be taken as that at which the appointment was complete, and evidenced, was when, after the signature of the president, the seal of the United States was affixed to the commission.

It is, then, the opinion of the Court: 1st. That by signing the commission of Mr. Marbury, the President of the United States appointed him a justice of peace for the county of Washington, in the district of Columbia; and that the seal of the United States, affixed thereto by the secretary of state, is conclusive testimony of the verity of the signature, and of the completion of the appointment; and that the appointment conferred on him a legal right to the office for the space of five years. 2d. That, having this legal title to the office, he has a consequent right to the commission; a refusal to deliver which is a plain violation of that right, for which the laws of his country afford him a remedy.

3. It remains to be inquired whether he is entitled to the remedy for which he applies? This depends on—1st. The nature of the writ applied for; and 2d. The power of this court.

1st. The nature of the writ. Blackstone, in the 3d volume of his Commentaries, page 110, defines a *mandamus* to be "a command issuing in the king's name, from the court of king's bench, and directed to any person, corporation or inferior court of judicature, within the king's dominions, requiring them to do some particular thing therein specified, which appertains to their office and duty, and which the court of king's bench has previously determined, or at least supposes, to be consonant to right and justice."

Lord MANSFIELD, in 3 Burr. 1267, in the case of *The King* v. *Baker et al.*, states, with much precision and explicitness, the cases in which this writ may be used. "Whenever," says that very able judge, "there is a right to execute an office, perform a service, or exercise a franchise (more especially if it be in a matter of public concern, or attended with profit), and a person is kept out of possession, or dispossessed of such right, and has no other specific legal remedy, this court ought to assist by *mandamus*, upon reasons of justice, as the writ expresses, and upon reasons of public policy, to preserve peace, order and good government." In the same case, he says, "this writ ought to be used upon all occasions where the law has established no specific remedy, and where in justice and good government there ought to be one." In addition to the authorities now particularly cited, many others were relied on at the bar, which show how far the practice has conformed to the general doctrines that have been just quoted.

This writ, if awarded, would be directed to an officer of government, and its mandate to him would be, to use the words of Blackstone, "to do a particular thing therein specified, which appertains to his office and duty, and which the court has previously determined, or at least supposes, to be consonant to right and justice." Or, in the words of Lord MANSFIELD, the applicant, in this case, has a right to execute an office of public concern, and is kept out of possession of that right. These circumstances certainly concur in this case.

Still, to render the *mandamus* a proper remedy, the officer to whom it is to be directed, must be one to whom, on legal principles, such writ may be directed; and the person applying for it must be without any other specific and legal remedy.

1. With respect to the officer to whom it would be directed. The intimate political relation subsisting between the president of the United States and the heads of departments, necessarily renders any legal investigation of the acts of one of those high officers peculiarly irksome, as well as delicate; and excites some hesitation with respect to the propriety of entering into such investigation. Impressions are often received, without much reflection or examination, and it is not wonderful, that in such a case as this, the assertion, by an individual, of his legal claims in a court of justice, to which claims it is the duty of that court to attend, should at first view be considered by some, as an attempt to intrude into the cabinet, and to intermeddle with the prerogatives of the executive.

It is scarcely necessary for the court to disclaim all pretensions to such a jurisdiction. An extravagance, so absurd and excessive, could not have been entertained for a moment. The province of the court is, solely, to decide on the rights of individuals, not to inquire how the executive, or executive officers, perform duties in which they have a discretion. Questions in their nature political, or which are, by the constitution and laws, submitted to the executive, can never be made in this court.

But, if this be not such a question; if, so far from being an intrusion into the secrets of the cabinet, it respects a paper which, according to law, is upon record, and to a copy of which the law gives a right, on the payment of ten cents; if it be no intermeddling with a subject over which the executive can be considered as having exercised any control; what is there, in the exalted station of the officer, which shall bar a citizen from asserting, in a court of justice, his legal rights, or shall forbid a court to listen to the claim, or to issue a *mandamus*, directing the performance of a duty, not depending on executive discretion, but on particular acts of congress, and the general principles of law?

If one of the heads of departments commits any illegal act, under color of his office, by which an individual sustains an injury, it cannot be pretended, that his office alone exempts him from being sued in the ordinary mode of proceeding, and being compelled to obey the judgment of the law. How then, can his office exempt him from this particular mode of deciding on the legality of his conduct, if the case be such a case as would, were any other individual the party complained of, authorize the process?

It is not by the office of the person to whom the writ is directed, but the nature of the thing to be done, that the propriety or impropriety of issuing a *mandamus* is to be determined. Where the head of a department acts in a case, in which executive discretion is to be exercised; in which he is the mere organ of executive will; it is again repeated, that any application to a court to control, in any respect, his conduct would be rejected without hesitation. But where he is directed by law to do a certain act, affecting the absolute rights of individuals, in the performance of which he is not placed under the particular direction of the president, and the performance of which the president cannot lawfully forbid, and therefore, is never presumed to have forbidden; as, for example, to record a commission or a patent for land, which has received all the legal solemnities; or to give a copy of such record; in such cases, it is not perceived, on what ground the courts of the country are further excused from the duty of giving judgment that right be done to an injured individual, than if the same services were to be performed by a person not the head of a department.

This opinion seems not now, for the first time, to be taken up in this country. It must be well recollected, that in 1792, an act passed, directing the secretary at war to place on the pension list such disabled officers and soldiers as should be reported to him, by the circuit courts, which act, so far as the duty was imposed on the courts, was deemed unconstitutional; but some of the judges, thinking that the law might be executed by them in the character of commissioners, proceeded to act, and to report in that character. This law being deemed unconstitutional, at the circuits, was repealed, and a different system was established; but the question whether those persons who had been reported by the judges, as commissioners, were entitled, in consequence of that report, to be placed on the pension list, was a legal question, properly determinable in the courts, although the act of placing such persons on the list was to be performed by the head of a department.

That this question might be properly settled, congress passed an act, in February 1793, making it the duty of the secretary of war, in conjunction with the attorney-general, to take such measures as might be necessary to obtain an adjudication of the supreme court of the United States on the validity of any such rights, claimed under the act aforesaid. After the passage of this act, a *mandamus* was moved for, to be directed to the secretary of war, commanding him to place on the pension list, a person stating himself to be on the report of the judges. There is, therefore, much reason to believe, that this mode of trying the legal right of the complainant was deemed, by the head of a department, and by the highest law-officer of the United States, the most proper which could be selected for the purpose. When the subject was brought before the court, the decision was, not that a *mandamus* would not lie to the head of a department, directing him to perform an act, enjoined by law, in the performance of which an individual had a vested interest; but that a *mandamus* ought not to issue in that case; the decision necessarily to be made, if the report of the commissioners did not confer on the applicant a legal right. The judgment, in that case, is understood to have decided the merits of all claims of that description; and the persons, on the report of the commissioners, found it necessary to pursue the mode prescribed by the law, subsequent to that which had been deemed unconstitutional, in order to place themselves on the pension list. The doctrine, therefore, now advanced, is by no means a novel one.

It is true, that the *mandamus*, now moved for, is not for the performance of an act expressly enjoined by statute. It is to deliver a commission; on which subject, the acts of congress are silent. This difference is not considered as affecting the case. It has already been stated, that the applicant has, to that commission, a vested legal right, of which the executive cannot deprive him. He has been appointed to an office, from which he is not removable at the will of the executive; and being so appointed, he has a right to the commission which the secretary has received from the president for his use. The act of congress does not indeed order the secretary of state to send it to him, but it is placed in his hands for the person entitled to it; and cannot be more lawfully withheld by him, than by any other person.

It was at first doubted, whether the action of *detinue* was not a specific legal remedy for the commission which has been withheld from Mr. Marbury; in which case, a *mandamus* would be improper. But this doubt has yielded to the consideration, that the judgment in *detinue* is for the thing itself, *or* its value. The value of a public office, not to be sold, is incapable of being ascertained; and the applicant has a right to the office itself, or to nothing. He will obtain the office by obtaining the commission, or a copy of it, from the record.

This, then, is a plain case for a *mandamus*, either to deliver the commission, or a copy of it from the record; and it only remains to be inquired, whether it can issue from this court?

The act to establish the judicial courts of the United States authorizes the supreme court, "to issue writs of *mandamus*, in cases warranted by the principles and usages of law, to any courts appointed or persons holding office, under the authority of the United States." The secretary of state, being a person holding an office under the authority of the United States, is precisely within the letter of this description; and if this court is not authorized to issue a write of *mandamus* to such an officer, it must be because the law is unconstitutional, and therefore, absolutely incapable of conferring the authority, and assigning the duties which its words purport to confer and assign.

The constitution vests the whole judicial power of the United States in one supreme court, and such inferior courts as congress shall, from time to time, ordain and establish. This power is expressly extended to all cases arising under the laws of the United States; and consequently, in some form, may be exercised over the present case; because the right claimed is given by a law of the United States.

In the distribution of this power, it is declared, that "the supreme court shall have original jurisdiction, in all cases affecting ambassadors, other public ministers and consuls, and those in which a state shall be a party. In all other cases, the supreme court shall have appellate jurisdiction." It has been insisted, at the bar, that as the original grant of jurisdiction to the supreme and inferior courts, is general, and the clause, assigning original jurisdiction to the supreme court, contains no negative or restrictive words, the power remains to the legislature, to assign original jurisdiction to that court, in other cases than those specified in the article which has been recited; provided those cases belong to the judicial power of the United States.

If it had been intended to leave it in the discretion of the legislature, to apportion the judicial power between the supreme and inferior courts, according to the will of that body, it would certainly have been useless to have proceeded further than to have defined the judicial power, and the tribunals in which it should be vested. The subsequent part of the section is mere surplusage—is entirely without meaning, if such is to be the construction. If congress remains at liberty to give this court appellate jurisdiction, where the constitution has declared their jurisdiction shall be original; and original jurisdiction where the constitution has declared it shall be appellate; the distribution of jurisdiction, made in the constitution, is form without substance. Affirmative words are often, in their operation, negative of other objects than those affirmed; and in this case, a negative or exclusive sense must be given to them, or they have no operation at all.

It cannot be presumed, that any clause in the constitution is intended to be without effect; and therefore, such a construction is inadmissible, unless the words require it. If the solicitude of the convention, respecting our peace with foreign powers, induced a provision that the supreme court should take original jurisdiction in cases which might be supposed to affect them; yet the clause would have proceeded no further than to provide for such cases, if no further restriction on the powers of congress had been intended. That they should have appellate jurisdiction in all other cases, with such exceptions as congress might make, is no restriction; unless the words be deemed exclusive of original jurisdiction.

When an instrument organizing, fundamentally, a judicial system, divides it into one supreme, and so many inferior courts as the legislature may ordain and establish; then enumerates its powers, and proceeds so far to distribute them, as to define the jurisdiction of the supreme court, by declaring the cases in which it shall take original jurisdiction, and that in others it shall take appellate jurisdiction, the plain import of the words seems to be, that in one class of cases, its jurisdiction is original, and not appellate; in the other, it is appellate, and not original. If any other construction would render the clause inoperative, that is an additional reason for rejecting such other construction, and for adhering to their obvious meaning. To enable this court, then, to issue a *mandamus*, it must be shown to be an exercise of appellate jurisdiction, or to be necessary to enable them to exercise appellate jurisdiction.

It has been stated at the bar, that the appellate jurisdiction may be exercised in a variety of forms, and that if it be the will of the legislature that a *mandamus* should be used for that purpose, that will must be obeyed. This is true, yet the jurisdiction must be appellate, not original. It is the essential criterion of appellate jurisdiction, that it revises and corrects the proceedings in a cause already instituted, and does not create that cause. Although, therefore, a *mandamus* may be directed to courts, yet to issue such a writ to an officer, for the delivery of a paper, is, in effect, the same as to sustain an original action for that paper, and therefore, seems not to belong to appellate, but to original jurisdiction. Neither is it necessary in such a case as this, to enable the court to exercise its appellate jurisdiction. The authority, therefore, given to the supreme court by the act establishing the judicial courts of the United States, to issue writs of *mandamus* to public officers, appears not to be warranted by the constitution; and it becomes necessary to inquire, whether a jurisdiction so conferred can be exercised.

The question, whether an act, repugnant to the constitution, can become the law of the land, is a question deeply interesting to the United States; but, happily, not of an intricacy proportioned to its interest. It seems only necessary to recognise certain principles, supposed to have been long and well established, to decide it. That the people have an original right to establish, for their future government, such principles as, in their opinion, shall most conduce to their own happiness, is the basis on which the whole American fabric has been erected. The exercise of this original right is a very great exertion; nor can it, nor ought it, to be frequently repeated. The principles, therefore, so established, are deemed fundamental: and as the authority from which they proceed is supreme, and can seldom act, they are designed to be permanent.

This original and supreme will organizes the government, and assigns to different departments their respective powers. It may either stop here, or establish certain limits not to be transcended by those departments. The government of the United States is of the latter description. The powers of the legislature are defined and limited; and that those limits may not be mistaken or forgotten, the constitution is written. To what purpose are powers limited, and to what purpose is that limitation committed to writing, if these limits may, at any time, be passed by those intended to be restrained? The distinction between a government with limited and unlimited powers is abolished, if those limits do not confine the persons on whom they are imposed, and if acts prohibited and acts allowed, are of equal obligation. It is a proposition too plain to be contested, that the constitution controls any legislative act repugnant to it; or that the legislature may alter the constitution by an ordinary act.

Between these alternatives, there is no middle ground. The constitution is either a superior paramount law, unchangeable by ordinary means, or it is on a level with ordinary legislative acts, and, like other acts, is alterable when the legislature shall please to alter it. If the former part of the alternative be true, then a legislative act, contrary to the constitution, is not law: if the latter part be true, then written constitutions are absurd attempts, on the part of the people, to limit a power, in its own nature, illimitable.

Certainly, all those who have framed written constitutions contemplate them as forming the fundamental and paramount law of the nation, and consequently, the theory of every such government must be, that an act of the legislature, repugnant to the constitution, is void. This theory is essentially attached to a written constitution, and is, consequently, to be considered, by this court, as one of the fundamental principles of our society. It is not, therefore, to be lost sight of, in the further consideration of this subject.

If an act of the legislature, repugnant to the constitution, is void, does it, notwithstanding its invalidity, bind the courts, and oblige them to give it effect? Or, in other words, though it be not law, does it constitute a rule as operative as if it was a law? This would be to overthrow, in fact, what was established in theory; and would seem, at first view, an absurdity too gross to be insisted on. It shall, however, receive a more attentive consideration.

It is, emphatically, the province and duty of the judicial department, to say what the law is. Those who apply the rule to particular cases, must of necessity expound and interpret that rule. If two laws conflict with each other, the courts must decide on the operation of each. So, if a law be in opposition to the constitution; if both the law and the constitution apply to a particular case, so that the court must either decide that case, conformable to the law, disregarding the constitution; or conformable to the constitution, disregarding the law; the court must determine which of these conflicting rules governs the case: this is of the very essence of judicial duty. If then, the courts are to regard the constitution, and the constitution is superior to any ordinary act of the legislature, the constitution, and not such ordinary act, must govern the case to which they both apply.

Those, then, who controvert the principle, that the constitution is to be considered, in court, as a paramount law, are reduced to the necessity of maintaining that courts must close their eyes on the constitution, and see only the law. This doctrine would subvert the very foundation of all written constitutions. It would declare that an act which, according to the principles and theory of our government, is entirely void, is yet, in practice, completely obligatory. It would declare, that if the legislature shall do what is expressly forbidden, such act, notwithstanding the express prohibition, is in reality effectual. It would be giving to the legislature a practical and real omnipotence, with the same breath which professes to restrict their powers within narrow limits. It is prescribing limits, and declaring that those limits may be passed at pleasure. That it thus reduces to nothing, what we have deemed the greatest improvement on political institutions, a written constitution, would, of itself, be sufficient, in America, where written constitutions have been viewed with so much reverence, for rejecting the construction. But the peculiar expressions of the constitution of the United States furnish additional arguments in favor of its rejection. The judicial power of the United States is extended to all cases arising under the constitution. Could it be the intention of those who gave this power, to say, that in using it, the constitution should not be looked into? That a case arising under the constitution should be decided, without examining the instrument under which it arises? This is too extravagant to be maintained. In some cases, then, the constitution must be looked into by the judges. And if they can open it at all, what part of it are they forbidden to read or to obey?

There are many other parts of the constitution which serve to illustrate this subject. It is declared, that "no tax or duty shall be laid on articles exported from any state." Suppose, a duty on the export of cotton, of tobacco or of flour; and a suit instituted to recover it. Ought judgment to be rendered in such a case? ought the judges to close their eyes on the constitution, and only see the law?

The constitution declares "that no bill of attainder or *ex post facto* law shall be passed." If, however, such a bill should be passed, and a person should be prosecuted under it; must the court condemn to death those victims whom the constitution endeavors to preserve?

"No person," says the constitution, "shall be convicted of treason, unless on the testimony of two witnesses to the same *overt* act, or on confession in open court." Here, the language of the constitution is addressed especially to the courts. It prescribes, directly for them, a rule of evidence not to be departed from. If the legislature should change that rule, and declare one witness, or a confession out of court, sufficient for conviction, must the constitutional principle yield to the legislative act?

From these, and many other selections which might be made, it is apparent, that the framers of the constitution contemplated that instrument as a rule for the government of courts, as well as of the legislature. Why otherwise does it direct the judges to take an oath to support it? This oath certainly applies in an especial manner, to their conduct in their official character. How immoral to impose it on them, if they were to be used as the instruments, and the knowing instruments, for violating what they swear to support!

The oath of office, too, imposed by the legislature, is

completely demonstrative of the legislative opinion on this subject. It is in these words: "I do solemnly swear, that I will administer justice, without respect to persons, and do equal right to the poor and to the rich; and that I will faithfully and impartially discharge all the duties incumbent on me as ———, according to the best of my abilities and understanding, agreeably to the constitution and laws of the United States." Why does a judge swear to discharge his duties agreeably to the constitution of the United States, if that constitution forms no rule for his government? if it is closed upon him, and cannot be inspected by him? If such be the real state of things, this is worse than solemn mockery. To prescribe, or to take this oath, becomes equally a crime.

It is also not entirely unworthy of observation, that in declaring what shall be the supreme law of the land, the constitution itself is first mentioned; and not the laws of the United States, generally, but those only which shall be made in pursuance of the constitution, have that rank.

Thus, the particular phraseology of the constitution of the United States confirms and strengthens the principle, supposed to be essential to all written constitutions, that a law repugnant to the constitution is void; and that courts, as well as other departments, are bound by that instrument.

48

ST. GEORGE TUCKER,
BLACKSTONE'S COMMENTARIES
1:APP. 151–53, 378–79, 412–13, 416–17,
418–26, 428–33; 5:APP. 3–10
1803

And here it ought to be remembered that no case of *municipal* law can arise under the constitution of the United States, except such as are expressly comprehended in that instrument. For the *municipal* law of one state or nation has no force or obligation in any other nation; and when several states, or nations unite themselves together by a federal compact, each retains its own municipal laws, without admitting or adopting those of any other member of the union, unless there be an article expressly to that effect. The municipal laws of the several American states differ essentially from each other; and as neither is entitled to a preference over the other, on the score of intrinsic superiority, or obligation; and as there is no article in the compact which bestows any such preference upon any, it follows, that the municipal laws of no one state can be resorted to as a general rule for the rest. And as the states, and their respective legislatures are absolutely independent of each other, so neither can any common rule be extracted from their several municipal codes. For, although concurrent laws, or rules may perhaps be met with in their codes, yet it is in the power of their legislatures, respectively to destroy that concurrence at any time, by

enacting an entire new law on the subject; so that it may happen that that which is a concurrent law in all the states to-day may cease to be law in one, or more of them to-morrow. Consequently neither the particular municipal law of any one, or more, of the states, nor the concurrent municipal laws of the whole of them, can be considered as the common rule, or measure of justice in the courts of the federal republic; neither hath the federal government any power to establish such a common rule, generally; no such power being granted by the constitution. And the principle is certainly much stronger, that neither the common nor statute law of any other nation, ought to be a standard for the proceedings of this, unless previously made its own by legislative adoption: which, not being permited by the original compact, by which the government is *created,* any attempt to introduce it, in that or any other mode, would be a manifest breach of the terms of that compact.

Another light in which this subject may be viewed is this. Since each state in becoming a member of a federal republic retains an uncontrolled jurisdiction over all cases of *municipal* law, every grant of jurisdiction to the confederacy, in any such case, is to be considered as special, inasmuch as it derogates from the antecedent rights and jurisdiction of the state making the concession, and therefore ought to be construed strictly, upon the grounds already mentioned. Now, the cases falling under the head of *municipal law,* to which the authority of the federal government extends, are few, definite, and enumerated, and are all carved out of the sovereign authority, and former exclusive, and uncontrollable jurisdiction of the *states* respectively: they ought therefore to receive the strictest construction. Otherwise the gradual and sometimes imperceptible usurpations of power, will end in the total disregard of all its intended limitations.

If it be asked, what would be the consequence in case the federal government should exercise powers not warranted by the constitution, the answer seems to be, that where the act of usurpation may immediately affect an individual, the remedy is to be sought by recourse to that judiciary, to which the cognizance of the case properly belongs. Where it may affect a state, the state legislature, whose rights will be invaded by every such act, will be ready to mark the innovation and sound the alarm to the people: and thereby either effect a change in the federal representation, or procure in the mode prescribed by the constitution, further "declaratory and restrictive clauses", by way of amendment thereto. An instance of which may be cited in the conduct of the Massachusetts legislature: who, as soon as that state was sued in the federal court, by an individual, immediately proposed, and procured an amendment to the constitution, declaring that the judicial power of the United States shall not be construed to extend to any suit brought by an individual against a state.

. . . . .

Having accompanied the commentator, to the fountain head, from whence he deduces the common law of England, it becomes us to trace its progress to our own shores. This, as it respects the commonwealth of Virginia, considered as an independant state, unconnected with any other, might have been regarded as an unnecessary trouble at this day; the convention, by which the constitution of the commonwealth was established, having expressly declared, "That the common law of England, and all statutes, or acts of parliament made in aid of the common law, prior to the fourth year, of James the first, which are of a general nature not local to that kingdom, together with the several acts of the colony then in force, so far as the same may consist with the several ordinances, declarations, and resolutions of the general convention, shall be considered as in full force, until the same shall be altered by the legislative power of the commonwealth." Ordinances of Convention May, 1776, c. 5. Chancellor's Revisal, p. 37.

But some late incidents having given rise to an opinion, that the common law of England, is not only the law of the American States, respectively, according to the mode in which they may, severally have adopted it, but that it is likewise the law of the federal government, a much wider field for investigation is thereby opened; of the importance of which, the general assembly of Virginia, at their session in the winter of 1799, have thus expressed their sentiments, in behalf of themselves, and their constituents.

"It is distressing to reflect, that it ever should have been made a question, whether the constitution of the United States on the whole face, of which, is seen so much labour to enumerate and define the several objects of federal power, could intend to introduce in the lump, in an indirect manner, and by a forced construction of a few phrases, the vast and multifarious jurisdiction involved in the common law; a law filling so many ample volumes; a law overspreading the entire field of legislation; a law that would sap the foundation of the constitution, as a system of limited, and specified powers."

. . . . .

4. How far that portion of the common law and statutes of England, which has been retained by the several states, respectively, has been engrafted upon, or made a part of the constitution of the United States.

It will be remembered, that the object of the several states in the adoption of that instrument, was not the establishment of a general consolidated government, which should swallow up the state sovereignties, and annihilate their several jurisdictions, and powers, as *states;* but a federal government, with powers limited to certain determinate objects; viz. their intercourse and concerns with foreign nations; and with each other, as separate and independent states; and, as members of the same confederacy: leaving the administration of their internal, and domestic concerns, to the absolute and uncontrolable jurisdiction of the states, respectively; except in one or two particular instances, specified, and enumerated in the constitution. And because this principle was supposed not to have been expressed with sufficient precision, and certainty, an amendatory article was proposed, adopted, and ratified; whereby it is expressly declared, that, "the powers not delegated to the United States by the constitution, nor prohibited by it to the states, are reserved to the states respectively, or to the people." This article is, indeed, nothing more than an express recognition of the law of nations; for Vattel informs us, "that several sovereign, and independent states may unite themselves together by a perpetual confederacy, without each in particular ceasing to be a perfect state. They will form together a federal republic: the deliberations in common will offer no violence to the sovereignty of each member, though they may in certain respects put some constraint on the exercise of it, in virtue of voluntary engagements." And with respect to the construction and interpretation of that article, the great Bacon gives us the following rule: "As exception strengthens the force of a law in cases not excepted; so enumeration weakens it, in cases not enumerated." Now, the powers prohibited by the constitution to the states, respectively, are all exceptions to powers, which they before enjoyed; the powers granted to congress, are all enumerations of new powers thereby created: the prohibition on the states, operating, therefore, as an exception, strengthens their claim to all powers not excepted: on the other hand, the grant of powers to the federal government operating only by way of enumeration, weakens it's claim in all cases not enumerated.

These things being premised, I shall take a short survey of the constitution of the United States, with a view to discover, whether that instrument contains any grant of general jurisdiction in common law cases, to the federal government; or prohibits the states from the exercise of such general jurisdiction: except only, in some few cases, particularly enumerated. For without such grant the federal government cannot exercise such a jurisdiction; and without such prohibition, the states, respectively, cannot be abridged of it.

1. The powers delegated to congress, are not all legislative: Many of them have been usually supposed to belong to the executive department; such are,

The power of declaring war; granting letters of marque and reprisal; raising and supporting armies, and navies; and borrowing money; none of which contain, or can be presumed to imply, any grant of general jurisdiction in common law cases. The legislative powers of congress, are also determinate, and enumerated.

. . . . .

15. That congress shall have power to make all laws which shall be *necessary* and *proper* for carrying into execution the foregoing powers, and all other vested by the constitution in the government of the United States, or in any department or officer thereof.

This clause, I apprehend, cannot be construed to enlarge any power before specifically granted; nor to grant any new power, not before specifically enumerated; or granted in some other part of the constitution. On the contrary it seems calculated to restrain the federal government from the exercise of any power, not *necessarily* an *appendage* to, and *consequence* of some power particularly *enumerated*. Acts of congress to be binding, must be made pursuant to the constitution; otherwise they are *not laws,* but a mere *nullity;* or what is worse, *acts of usurpation.* The people are not only not bound by them, but the several departments and officers of the governments, both federal, and state, are *bound by oath to oppose them;* for, being bound by oath to support the constitution, they must violate that oath, whenever they give their sanction, by obedience, or otherwise, to any unconstitutional act of any department of the government.

If the reader can discover in any of the powers before enumerated, that which contains a grant of general jurisdiction in common law cases to the federal government, our enquiry is at an end. And he will render an incomparable act of service to his country, by laying his finger upon that clause, and pointing it out to his fellow-citizens, that they may no longer puzzle themselves, or their agents, about a question of such importance. . . . But, if he can not do this, and is not yet convinced that no such grant is contained in the constitution, I must request him patiently to attend me, whilst we hunt for it in some other part of that instrument.

. . . . .

3. In that article, which relates to the constitution and powers of the judiciary department. It is therein declared,

That the judicial power shall extend to all cases in law and equity, arising under the constitution; the laws of the United States; and treaties made, or which shall be made, under their authority; to all cases affecting ambassadors, other public ministers, and consuls; to all cases of admiralty; to controversies to which the United States shall be a party; to controversies between two, or more states; between citizens of different states; between citizens of the same state, claiming lands under grants from different states; and between a state and foreign states.

Such is the power of the judiciary department, as now limited by the thirteenth article of the amendments to the constitution of the United States. I shall endeavour to analize the whole.

1. The judicial power of the federal government extends to all cases in law and equity arising under the constitution. Now, the powers granted to the federal government, or prohibited to the states, being all enumerated, the cases arising under the *constitution,* can only be such as arise out of some *enumerated* power delegated to the federal government, or prohibited to those of the several states. These general words include what is comprehended in the next clause, viz. Cases arising under the laws of the United States. But as contra-distinguished from that clause, it comprehends some cases afterwards enumerated, e. g. Controversies between two or more states; between a state and foreign states; between citizens of the same state claiming lands under grants of different states; all which may arise under the *constitution,* and not under any law of the U. States. Many other cases might be enumerated, which would fall strictly under this clause, and no other. As, if a citizen of one state should be denied the privileges of a citizen in another; so, if a person held to service or labour in one state, should escape into another and obtain protection there, as a free man; so, if a state should coin money, and declare the same to be a legal tender in payment of debt, the validity of such a tender, if made, would fall within the meaning of this clause. So also, if a state should, without consent of congress, lay any duty upon goods imported, the question as to the validity of such an act, if disputed, would come within the meaning of this clause, and not of any other. . . . In all these cases equitable circumstances may arise, the cognizance of which, as

well as such as were strictly legal, would belong to the federal judiciary, in virtue of this clause.

2. The judicial power of the United States extends to all cases arising under the laws of the United States; . . . now as the subjects upon which congress have the power to legislate, are all specially enumerated, so the judicial authority, under this clause, is limited to the same subjects as congress have power to legislate upon. Thus congress being authorised to pass uniform laws of naturalization, the question whether a person is an alien, or not, falls under this head, provided the party were an alien born. So, also, if a person be accused of counterfeiting the public securities of the United States, this question would be cognizable in the federal courts, under this clause; but if he were accused of any other forgery: of this offence the state courts, and not the federal courts, possess jurisdiction.

3. The power of the federal judiciary extends to cases arising under treaties; as well those already made, as to such as might be made after the adoption of the constitution. . . . Of the former kind were the questions concerning the validity of payments made into the state treasuries by British debtors, during the war; of the latter sort, may be such questions as may hereafter arise under the treaty of 1794, enabling British subjects, though aliens, to hold and inherit lands, within the U. States. . . . In neither of the preceding clauses can we find any thing like a grant of general jurisdiction in common law cases.

4. To all cases affecting ambassadors, other public ministers, and consuls; these cases, although provided for in some countries by statute, where that is not the case, belong to the law of nations, and not to the common law.

5. To all cases of admiralty and maritime jurisdiction; these were never held to be within the jurisdiction of the common law.

6. To *controversies* to which the United States shall be a party. The word *cases* used in the preceding clauses of this article comprehends, generally, I apprehend all cases, whether civil or criminal, which are capable of falling under these heads, respectively, instances of which it might be unnecessary here to repeat: I shall however add to what I have before said, that it comprehends such *criminal* cases as may arise within the precincts of the seat of government, not exceeding ten miles square; or within the precincts of forts, dockyards, magazines, and arsenals, purchased with the consent of the state in which they may be; and finally, treason against the U. States; piracies and felonies committed upon the high seas; and offences against the law of nations; and against the revenue laws of the U.S.

The word controversies, as here used, must be understood merely as relating to such as are of a *civil* nature. It is probably unknown in any other sense, as I do not recollect ever to have heard the expression, *criminal controversy.* As here applied, it seems particularly appropriated to such disputes as might arise between the U. States, and any one or more states, respecting territorial, or fiscal, matters. . . . Or between the U. States and their debtors, contractors, and agents. This construction is confirmed by the application of the word in the ensuing clauses, where it evidently refers to disputes of a *civil* nature only, such for example, as may arise between two or more states; or between citizens of different states; or between a state, and the citizens of another state; none of which can possibly be supposed to relate to such as are of a criminal nature, unless we could suppose it was meant to deprive the states of the power of punishing murder or theft, if committed by a foreigner, or the citizen of another state.

7. The judicial power extends likewise to controversies between two or more states; and between a state, and foreign states. These must be proceeded in, and determined according to the law of nations, and not according to the common law.

8. To controversies between citizens of different states; and between citizens of any state and the subjects or citizens of foreign states. . . . In these cases, the municipal law of the place where the cause of controversy arises, whether that be one of the United States, or Great Britain, France, Spain, Holland, Hamburg, or any other country; or the general law of merchants; or, the general law of nations according to the nature and circumstances of the case, must be the rule of decision, in whatever court the suit may be brought. Thus if a bond be given in Philadelphia, the rate of interest must be settled according to the laws of Pennsylvania. If a bill of exchange be drawn in Virginia, the rate of damages must be settled by the law of that state. If in England, Hamburg, or Cadiz, the custom of merchants in those places, respectively, must govern. If a ransom bill be drawn at sea, the law of nations in that case must be consulted. If the controversy relate to lands, the law of the state where the lands lie must be referred to; unless the lands be claimed under grants from different states; in which case the territorial rights of each state must be inquired into. The same must be done, in the last case which remains to be noticed; viz:

9. Controversies between citizens of the same state claiming lands under grants of different states. None of the cases enumerated in this, and the preceding paragraph can be construed to give general jurisdiction in cases at common law, or such as ordinarily arise between citizens of the same state; under which description, civil suits, in general, (with the exception of the case here supposed) are comprehended; or such as may arise between a state, and its own citizens, or subjects; under which head crimes and misdemeanors are comprehended. This being the only enumerated case, in which the federal courts can take cognizance of any civil controversy between citizens of the same state, it cannot extend to such common law cases, as may arise between them; all such cases being reserved to the jurisdiction of the states, respectively. And on the other hand, as it does not extend to *any case* that may arise between a state and its own citizens or subjects; nor to any case between a state, and foreign citizens or subjects, or the citizens of any other state. . . so every such case, whether civil or criminal, and whether it arise under the law of nations, the common law, or law of the state, belongs exclusively, to the jurisdiction of the states, respectively. And this, as well from the reason of the thing, as from the express declarations contained in the twelfth and thirteenth articles of the amendments to the constitution.

Having thus minutely examined *all* the *enumerated pow-*

ers, which are vested in the federal government, or any of its departments, and not finding any grant of general jurisdiction in cases at common law, we are warranted, under the twelfth article of amendments, in concluding, that *no such jurisdiction* has been *granted;* and consequently, that it remains with the *states, respectively, in all cases not enumerated;* so far, as their several constitutions and legislative acts, may admit the authority and obligation of the common law, or statutes of England, in each state, respectively.

But it has, I believe, been said, that if this general jurisdiction in common law cases has not been granted to the federal government in express terms, yet it is given by *implication*. This admits of several answers:

1. The twelfth article of the amendments was proposed, adopted and ratified, for the express purpose of rebutting, this doctrine of grant by *implication:* since it expressly declares, that the *powers not delegated* to the United States, by the constitution, *nor prohibited* by it to the states, are *reserved* to the states respectively, or to the people. And this I hold to be a full answer to the conceit. . . . But,

2dly. If this were not the case, it would be absurdity in the extreme, to suppose a grant, by *implication,* of general power to the federal government to revive, and enforce such parts of the common law, or statutes of England, as the *states* by their respective constitutions had severally condemned in express terms; and rejected, repealed, and annulled as dangerous, absurd, or incompatible with that system of government which they had, respectively, established.

3dly. This is probably the first instance in which it has been supposed that sovereign and independent states can be abridged of their rights, as sovereign states, by *implication,* only. . . . For, no free nation can be bound by any law but it's own will; and where that will is manifested by any written document, as a convention, league, treaty, compact, or agreement, the nation is bound, only according as that will is expressed *in* the instrument by which it binds itself. And as every nation is bound to preserve itself, or, in other words, it's independence; so no interpretation whereby it's destruction, or that of the state, which is the same thing, may be hazarded, can be admitted in any case where it has not, in the *most express terms*, given it's consent to such an interpretation. Now if this construction were once established, that the federal government possesses general jurisdiction over all cases at common law, what else could be the consequence, but, at one stroke, to annihilate the states altogether; and to repeal and annul their several constitutions, bills of rights, legislative codes, and political institutions in all cases whatsoever. For, what room, or occasion, could there be for a constitution, if the common law of England, be *paramount* thereto; or for a state legislature, if their acts are not laws, but mere nullities; or for courts, if their decisions, founded upon the constitutions and laws of the states, are for that reason null and void?

4thly. If it were admitted, that the federal government, by implication, possesses general jurisdiction over all cases at common law; this construction could not be carried into practice, without annihilating the states, and repealing, and annulling, their several constitutions, bills of rights, and legislative codes: as a few instances will demonstrate.

The constitution of Virginia declares, and the constitutions of the other states agree therewith, that the legislative, executive, and judiciary departments shall be separate and distinct: the common law unites all three in one and the same person.

The constitution of Maryland declares there shall be no forfeiture of any part of the estate of any person for any crime, except murder, or treason against the state; the laws of Virginia have abolished forfeitures in all cases: The doctrine of forfeiture, in case of conviction, or attainder for any crime, is one of the pillars of criminal jurisprudence, by the common law.

The constitution of Pennsylvania declares, that the penal laws as theretofore used in that state, shall be reformed, and punishment made less sanguinary, and more proportionate to crimes. If the common law be revived, this article is a mere nullity. South-Carolina has an article in it's constitution to the same effect.

The same constitution declares, that the printing presses shall be free to every person who undertakes to examine the proceedings of the legislature, or any part of the government. It is contended by some persons in power, that the common law does not permit this freedom to any person.

The constitution of Georgia declares, that no grand-jury shall consist of fewer than eighteen persons; the common law deems sixteen a sufficient number.

The same constitution will not allow of a special verdict in any case: The practice of the common law courts in England for five hundred years past, has been to the contrary.

The constitution of North Carolina, declares, that every foreigner who comes to settle in that state, having first taken an oath of allegiance to the same, may purchase, or by other just means acquire, hold, and transfer land, or other real estate; and after one year's residence shall be deemed a free citizen. The constitution of Pennsylvania, has an article to the same effect. . . . The foreigner is not naturalized immediately upon taking the oath of allegiance; he continues an alien for a year; and if he departs before its expiration, remains an alien: yet he may acquire, hold, and transfer lands: by the common law, an alien can not hold lands.

The constitution of Georgia, prohibits entails; and declares that the real estate of a person dying intestate shall be divided equally among his children: that the widow shall have a child's part, or her dower, at her option. And if there be no children the estate shall be divided among the next of kin. The common law admits of entails; and absolutely rejects the other provisions of this article.

The constitutions and laws of all the states of the union, (except Massachusetts, where there have been judicial decisions to the contrary), admit slavery. The common [law], as understood for many centuries past in England, absolutely rejects slavery. . . . Should a question arise upon that subject in Maryland, Virginia, North Carolina, South Carolina or Georgia, it might be of serious consequence, if the common law were pronounced to be paramount to the laws of the states.

Lastly, The constitutions and laws of all the states, in which the common law and statutes of England have been expressly adopted, in a certain degree, declare that those laws are not to be construed so as to impair any of the rights and privileges contained in their respective constitutions and laws; and further subject them to be repealed, altered, or annulled, by acts of their respective legislatures: the construction contended for, would render the common law *paramount* to those constitutional declarations, and to all legislative acts.

. . . . .

5th. But to return to our subject; there are certain passages in the constitution, and the amendments thereto, not yet noticed, which perhaps may be relied on to establish this doctrine of a grant of general jurisdiction to the federal courts or government, in cases at common law, by *implication:* These are,

1. The privilege of the writ of *habeas corpus* shall not be suspended, unless when in cases of rebellion or invasion, the public safety may require it.

2. The trial of all crimes, except in cases of impeachment, shall be by jury.

3. In suits at common law, the right of trial by jury, shall, (in general) be preserved: and no fact tried by a jury, shall be otherwise re-examined in any court of the United States, than according to the rules of the common law.

In all these passages, we may be told, the common law is evidently referred to as the *law* of the *land*. This is not the case; it is referred to as a known law: and might in strictness have been referred to as the law of the several states, so far as their constitutions and legislative codes, respectively, have admitted or adopted it. Will any man who knows any thing of the laws of England, affirm, that the civil, or Roman imperial law, is the general law of the land in England, because many of it's maxims, and it's course of proceedings, are generally admitted and established in the high court of chancery, which is the highest court of civil jurisdiction, except the parliament, in the kingdom? Or that the canon, or Roman ecclesiastical law, is the general law of the land, because marriages are solemnized according to it's rites; or because simony, which is an ecclesiastical offence, is also made an offence by statute?

But it will be asked, what is meant by suits at common law, the cognizance of which, from this article, appears to belong to the federal courts. The answer is easy; in many of the states, the courts are distinguished by the epithets of common law courts, and courts of equity. In the former, the rules and mode of proceeding in the English courts of common law jurisdiction, have under different modifications been adopted; the latter pursue the course of the civil law. Suits cognizable in these courts, respectively, are consequently denominated, suits at common law, and suits in equity, comprehending under these terms *all* civil suits, except such as are of a maritime nature. . . . The trial by jury being the usual mode of trial in all the states, except in the courts of equity, it was thought expedient to preserve the same mode of trial in the federal courts, as in the state courts. The article gives not a *new* jurisdiction, not before expressly granted, in the third article of the constitution; it merely prescribes a mode of trial.

We may fairly infer from all that has been said that the common law of England stands precisely upon the same footing in the federal government, and courts of the United States, *as such*, as the civil and ecclesiastical laws stand upon in England: That is to say, it's maxims and rules of proceeding are to be adhered to, whenever the written law is silent, in cases of a similar, or analogous nature, the cognizance whereof is by the constitution vested in the federal courts; it may govern and direct the course of proceeding, in such cases, but cannot give jurisdiction in *any case*, where jurisdiction is not expressly given by the constitution. The same may be said of the *civil law;* the rules of proceeding in which, whenever the written law is silent, are to be observed in cases of equity, and of admiralty, and maritime jurisdiction. In short, as the matters cognizable in the federal courts, belong, (as we have before shown, in reviewing the powers of the judiciary department) partly to the law of nations, partly to the common law of England; partly to the civil law; partly to the maritime law, comprehending the laws of Oleron and Rhodes; and partly to the general law and custom of merchants; and partly to the municipal laws of any foreign nation, or of any state in the union, where the cause of action may happen to arise, or where the suit may be instituted; so, the law of nations, the common law of England, the civil law, the law maritime, the law merchant, or the *lex loci*, or law of the foreign nation, or state, in which the cause of aciton may arise, or shall be decided, must in their turn be resorted to as the rule of decision, according to the nature and circumstances of each case, respectively. So that each of these laws may be regarded, so far as they apply to such cases, respectively, as the law of the land. But to infer from hence, that the common law of England is the general law of the United States, is to the full as absurd as to suppose that the laws of Russia, or Germany, are the general law of the land, because in a controversy respecting a contract made in either of those empires, it might be necessary to refer to the laws of either of them, to decide the question between the litigant parties. Nor can I find any more reason for admitting the penal code of England to be in force in the United States, (except so far as the states, respectively may have adopted it, within their several jurisdictions) than for admitting that of the Roman empire, or of Russia, Spain, or any other nation, whatever.

One or two instances, in addition to those already mentioned, may set this matter in a clearer light. If a suit be brought in a federal court upon a bond executed in England, the bond must be actually sealed, because the common law of England requires that every bond, deed, or covenant, should be executed in that manner; and if it be not, it is not a bond, but merely a simple contract; but if the bond be executed in Virginia, where a scroll by way of seal, is by law declared to be as effectual as if the instrument were actually sealed, there the law of the state shall prevail, and turn that contract into a specialty, by which the lands of the obligor may be bound, which in England would only bind his goods and chattels, after his decease. So if a bill of exchange be drawn in Virginia, an action of

debt may be maintained thereupon, in that state; but if it be drawn in any other state, or country, the action I apprehend, must be brought, even in that state upon the custom of merchants. Thus, the *lex loci* may operate not only so as to determine the nature of the contract, but of the remedy. And with respect to the mode of proceeding, in order to a remedy, wherever the constitution and laws of the United States are silent, there, I apprehend, the law of the state, where the suit is brought, ought to be observed as a guide: thus if a suit be brought upon a bond the plaintiff may demand bail, in Virginia, as of course, and an endorsement to that effect will be sufficient to compel the sheriff, who executes the writ, to take bail at his peril. But in England, the plaintiff in that case, must make an affidavit of the sum actually due upon the bond, otherwise the sheriff is not obliged to take bail. So in the same case, if the sheriff neglects to take bail where he ought to do it, the plaintiff may proceed, in Virginia, against the defendant and sheriff, at the same time, and shall have judgment for his debt against both at once, unless special bail be put in; whereas in England, he must bring a special action on the case, against the sheriff, for neglect of his duty, instead of having the remedy which the laws of Virginia furnish him with. So also, if a bond be executed in London, and a suit be brought thereupon, in the state of Virginia, the defendant cannot plead *non est factum*, as is the usual course of pleading in England, unless he verifies his plea by affidavit; without which it cannot be received; and the same course of proceeding, I apprehend, is to be observed in the federal, as in the state courts.

From the whole of the preceding examination, we may deduce the following conclusions:

First . . . . That the common law of England, and every statute of that kingdom, made for the security of the life, liberty, or property of the subject, before the settlement of the British colonies, respectively, so far as the same were applicable to the nature of their situation and circumstances, respectively, were brought over to America, by the first settlers of the colonies, respectively; and remained in full force therein, until repealed, altered, or amended by the legislative authority of the colonies, respectively; or by the constitutional acts of the same, when they became sovereign and independent states.

Secondly . . . . That neither the common law of England, nor the statutes of that kingdom, were, at any period antecedent to the revolution, the general and uniform law of the land in the British colonies, now constituting the United States.

Thirdly . . . . That as the adoption or rejection of the common law and statutes of England, or any part thereof, in one colony, could not have any operation or effect in another colony, possessing a constitutional legislature of it's own; so neither could the adoption or rejection thereof by the constitutional, or legislative act of one sovereign and independent state, have any operation or effect in another sovereign independent state; because every such state hath an exclusive right to be governed by it's own laws only.

Fourthly . . . . Therefore the authority and obligation of the common law and statutes of England, as such in the

American states, must depend solely upon the constitutional or legislative authority of each state, respectively; as contained in their several bills of rights, constitutions, and legislative declarations. . . . . which, being different in different states, and wholly independent of each other, cannot establish any uniform law, or rule of obligation in all the states.

Fifthly . . . . That neither the articles of confederation and perpetual union, nor, the present constitution of the United States, ever did, or do, authorize the federal government, or any department thereof, to declare the common law or statutes of England, or of any other nation, to be the law of the land in the United States, generally, as one nation; nor to legislate upon, or exercise jurisdiction in, any case of municipal law, not delegated to the United States by the constitution.

. . . . .

The complicated system of government in the United States, imposes upon us the necessity of a frequent recurrence to fundamental principles, in order to ascertain to what department of it any particular subject appertains. In no respect is this recurrence more necessary, than in the examination of the nature of crimes and misdemeanours; the cognizance of which, by the *federal* courts, will depend altogether upon the nature and tenor of that instrument, upon which the jusisdiction is founded: in the exposition of which, we have been repeatedly obliged to recur to the nature of the compact, for a due exposition of the text. If for example, the constitution of the United States had been intended for the establishment of a consolidated national government, instead of a federal republic, the same strict interpretation, which is at present necessary, in order to preserve to the states, respectively, whatever rights they had no design to part with, might perhaps, in many instances have been dispensed with.

It has been well observed by one of the judges of the supreme court of the United States, that "in this country every man sustains a twofold political capacity: one in relation to the *state*, and another in relation to the *United States*. In relation to the state, he is subject to various municipal regulations, founded upon the state constitution and policy, which do *not* affect him in his relation to the *United States*: For the constitution of the union is the source of all the jurisdiction of the national government; so that the departments of *that* government, can never assume any power, that is not expressly granted by that instrument, nor exercise a power, in any other manner than is there prescribed." This is, indeed, a short, clear, and comprehensive exposition of the principles of a limited government, founded upon compact between sovereign and independent states.

For it cannot, I presume, be denied, or even doubted, that the constitution of the United States, is the instrument by which the federal government was *created;* its powers defined; their extent limited; the duties of the public functionaries prescribed; and the principles according to which the government is to be administered, delineated;

That the federal government of the United States, is that *portion,* only, of the sovereign power, which, in the opinion of the people of the several states, could be more advantageously administered in common, than by the states respectively;

That the several states at the time of adopting that constitution, being free, sovereign, and independent states, and possessing all the rights, powers, and jurisdictions, incident to civil government, according to their several constitutions; and having expressly stipulated, that the powers not delegated to the United States by the constitution, nor prohibited by it, to the states, are reserved to the states respectively, or to the people; every power which has been carved out of the sovereignty of the states, respectively, must be construed strictly, wherever it may derogate from any power which they possessed antecedently;

And, on the other hand, that all the powers granted to the *federal* government, are either expressly enumerated, and positive; or must be both necessary, and proper to the execution of some enumerated power, which is expressly granted.

If these be the genuine principles of the federal constitution, as, I apprehend they are, then it seems impossible to refuse our full assent to the learned judge's observations on the subject. Adopting them therefore as our guide, let us proceed in our enquiry.

A crime or misdemeanour, as defined by judge Blackstone, "is an act committed, or omitted in violation of a PUBLIC LAW, either forbidding, or commanding it:" from whence it follows, that the cognizance and punishment of all crimes and misdemeanours, belongs exclusively to that body politic, or state to which the right to enact such a public law belongs.

The cognizance of all crimes and misdemeanours committed within the body of any state, therefore, belongs exclusively to the jurisdiction of that state; unless it hath by compact or treaty surrendered its jurisdiction in any particular cases to some other power. And in like manner the cognizance of all crimes and misdemeanours committed on the high seas (where all nations have a common jurisdiction) by citizens of the same state against each other; or, by common pirates, or robbers, against the citizens of any state, belongs to that particular state to whose citizens the injury is offered. And consequently the American states respectively, as soon as they became sovereign, and independent states, were entitled to exclusive jurisdiction in the case of all crimes and misdemeanours, whatsoever, committed within the body of such states, respectively, or upon the high seas, in every case where any other state or nation might claim jurisdiction under similar circumstances.

By the articles of confederation concluded between the states some years after; each state, expressly, "retained its sovereignty, freedom, and independence, and every power, *jurisdiction,* and right, which was not, by that confederation, expressly delegated to the United States in Congress assembled," The ninth article ceded to congress, the sole and exclusive right of making *rules* for the government, and regulation of the land and naval forces of the United States; and of appointing courts for the trial of *piracies* and *felonies committed on the high seas:* so that the states *retained* the exclusive cognizance of all *civil* crimes and misdemeanours, whatsoever, except in the cases therein mentioned. And this exclusive jurisdiction they continued to retain until the adoption of the present constitution.

By the third article of that instrument it is declared, "that the judicial power of the United States, shall extend to all cases arising under the constitution, the laws of the United States, and treaties made, or which shall be made under their authority." The same article defines the offence of treason against the United States, but leaves to Congress the power to declare the punishment, thereof, under certain limitations. Treason against the *United States,* is, therefore, one of those crimes, to which the jurisdiction of the federal courts extends.

The eighth section of the first article, among other things, declares, that congress shall have power to *provide* for the *punishment* of counterfeiting the securities and current coin of the United States; to define and punish piracies, and felonies committed on the high seas, and offences against the law of nations; to exercise exclusive jurisdiction within certain specified limits; and to make all laws, which shall be *necessary* and *proper* for carrying into execution the foregoing powers, and all other powers vested by the constitution in the government of the United States, or in any department or officer thereof.

To apply then, the observations of the learned judge; since neither Congress, nor any other department of the *federal* government, can ever assume any power that is not expressly granted by the constitution, nor exercise it, in any other manner, than is there prescribed, it appears to be essential that congress should define all offences against the United States, except treason; and prescribe the punishment to be inflicted for that and every other offence against the United States, before the federal courts can proceed to try a criminal or to pronounce sentence upon him in case of conviction.

If this be doubted, let us suppose that any person had committed treason against the United States, before the passage of the act of Congress, declaring the punishment of that offence; could the federal courts, or any other, have proceeded to judgment against him for the same, or, if they could, what judgment could they have pronounced? Let us suppose again that congress having defined the offence of piracy, had omitted to declare the punishment; could the federal courts have supplied this omission by pronouncing such a sentence as they might suppose the crime deserved? Again, let us suppose that congress may have omitted altogether to define or to declare the punishment of any other offence committed upon the high seas; will it be contended that the federal courts could in any such case punish the offender, however atrocious his offence regarded in a moral light may appear? In none of these cases (as I apprehend) could the federal courts proceed to punish the delinquent, although in every one of them, the offence may be clearly acknowledged to arise under the constitution of the United States.

If in cases arising upon the high seas, (in all which the federal courts, under the federal constitution and laws, possess a jurisdiction, altogether exclusive of the state courts) it be necessary that an offence be first defined, and the punishment thereof declared by congress; how much more necessary is it, that offences committed within the body of any state should, in the same manner, be first defined, and the punishment thereof declared by a law of the United States, before the courts of the United States can undertake to inquire into or punish it? For the presumption is, that every offence, committed within the body of any state, is an offence against that state only; and, that the state courts have the sole and exclusive cognizance and punishment thereof, unless it be shewn, that the federal constitution, or some act of congress made in pursuance of it, have altogether divested the state courts of jurisdiction over the subject. For although we may readily admit, that besides the particular case of treason and those which the eighth section of the first article designates, there is a power granted to congress to *create* and to define and punish offences, whenever it may be *necessary* and *proper* to do so, in order to carry into execution, the specific powers granted to the federal government, still it appears indispensably necessary, that congress should first *create*, (that is, define and declare the punishment of,) every such offence, before it can have existence as such, against the United States.

It has been attempted, however, to supply the silence of the constitution and statutes of the union, by resorting to the common law for the definition and punishment of offences in such cases. To which, the same judge has given the following clear and emphatic answer. "In my opinion, the *United States* as a *federal government have no common law:* and consequently, no indictment can be maintained in their courts for offences merely at the common law. If indeed the United States can be supposed for a moment to have a common law, it must, I presume, be that of England; and *yet it is impossible to trace, when, or how, the system was adopted, or introduced.* With respect to the individual states, the difficulty does not occur. When the American colonies were first settled by our ancestors, it was held, as well by the settlers as by the judges and lawyers of England, that they brought hither, as a birth right and inheritance, so much of the common law as was applicable to their local situation, and change of circumstances. But each colony judged for itself, what parts of the common law were applicable to its new condition; and in various modes, by legislative acts, by judicial decisions, or by constant usage, adopted some parts and rejected others. Hence, he who shall travel through the different states will soon discover, that the *whole* of the *common law* has been *no where* introduced; that some states have rejected what others have adopted; and that there is, in short, a *great* and *essential diversity* in the *subjects* to which the *common law* is applied, as well as in the *extent* of its application. The common law, therefore, of one state, is not the common law of another; but the common law of England is the law of each state, *so far as each state has adopted it;* and the results from that position connected with the judicial act, that the common law will always apply to suits between citizen and citizen."

"But the question recurs, when and how, *the courts of the United States* acquired a *common law jurisdiction in* CRIMINAL *cases?* The United States must possess the law themselves, before they can communicate it to their judicial agents:

now the *United States* did not bring it with them from England; *the constitution does not create it;* and no act of congress has *assumed it.* Besides, what is the common law to which we are referred? Is it the common law *entire,* as it exists in England; or *modified,* as it exists in some of the states; and, of the various modifications, which are we to select, the system of Georgia or New Hampshire, of Pennsylvania or Connecticut?"

"Upon the whole," he concludes, "it *may* be a defect in our political institutions, it may be an inconvenience in the administration of justice, that the common law authority relating to crimes and punishments, has not been conferred upon the government of the *United States,* which is a government, in other respects also, of a limitted jurisdiction: *but judges cannot remedy political imperfections, or, supply any legislative omission.*"

Unfortunately, perhaps, for the United States, this opinion did not prevail, the court being divided in their judgments. . . . We are, therefore, not only without a precedent: but, what is infinitely more important, a principle, which might have been deemed clear, and well ascertained, is now, in some degree, rendered doubtful. Nevertheless, until a contrary division shall have subverted the apparently solid foundation of that which I have cited, I shall venture to recommend it to the student, as containing the most clear, correct, and convincing, illustration of the principles of the federal constitution.

From what has been said, we may venture to draw the following conclusions.

1. That the cognizance of every crime and misdemeanor, whatsoever, committed within the body of any state, belongs to the courts of that state, in which the offence is committed, *exclusively;* unless it can be shewn that a power over the subject hath been *expressly* granted to the United States, by the federal constitution.

2. That the federal courts possess no jurisdiction, whatsoever, over any crime or misdemeanor, which is an offence by the *common law, only,* and not declared to be such, by the constitution, or some statute of the United States.

3. That although a certain class of offences, may, by the constitution of the United States, be declared to be within the jurisdiciton of the federal courts, yet those courts cannot proceed to take cognizance thereof, unless they be first defined, by the constitution; or by statute; nor to punish them, unless the punishment be likewise *prescribed* by a statute of the *United States.*

49

STRAWBRIDGE V. CURTISS
3 Cranch 267 (1806)

MARSHALL, Ch. J., delivered the opinion of the court.—The court has considered this case, and is of opinion, that the jurisdiction cannot be supported.

The words of the act of congress are, "where an alien is a party, or the suit is between a citizen of a state where the suit is brought, and a citizen of another state." The court understands these expressions to mean, that each distinct interest should be represented by persons, all of whom are entitled to sue, or may be sued, in the federal courts. That is, that where the interest is joint, each of the persons concerned in that interest must be competent to sue, or liable to be sued, in those courts.

But the court does not mean to give an opinion in the case where several parties represent several distinct interests, and some of those parties are, and others are not, competent to sue, or liable to be sued, in the courts of the United States.

50

BANK OF THE UNITED STATES V. DEVEAUX
5 Cranch 61 (1809)

March 15. MARSHALL, *Ch. J.,* delivered the opinion of the court as follows:

Two points have been made in this cause.

1. That a corporation, composed of citizens of one state, may sue a citizen of another state, in the federal courts.

2. That a right to sue in those courts is conferred on this bank by the law which incorporates it.

The last point will be first considered.

The judicial power of the United States, as defined in the constitution, is dependent, 1st. On the nature of the case; and, 2d. On the character of the parties.

By the judicial act, the jurisdiction of the circuit courts is extended to cases where the constitutional right to plead and be impleaded, in the courts of the Union, depends on the character of the parties; but where that right depends on the nature of the case, the circuit courts derive no jurisdiction from that act, except in the single case of a controversy between citizens of the same state, claiming lands under grants from different states.

Unless, then, jurisdiction over this cause has been given to the Circuit Court by some other than the judicial act, the bank of the United States had not a right to sue in that court, upon the principle that the case arises under a law of the United States.

The plaintiffs contend that the incorporating act confers this jurisdiction.

That act creates the corporation, gives it a capacity to make contracts and to acquire property, and enables it "to sue and be sued, plead and be impleaded, answer and be answered, defend and be defended, in courts of record, or any other place whatsoever."

This power, if not incident to a corporation, is conferred by every incorporating act, and is not understood to enlarge the jurisdiction of any particular court, but to give a capacity to the corporation to appear, as a corporation, in any court which would, by law, have cognizance of the cause, if brought by individuals. If jurisdiction is given by this clause to the federal courts, it is equally given to all courts having original jurisdiction, and for all sums however small they may be.

But the 9th article of the 7th section of the act furnishes a conclusive argument against the construction for which the plaintiffs contend. That section subjects the president and directors, in their individual capacity, to the suit of any person aggrieved by their putting into circulation more notes than is permitted by law, and expressly authorizes the bringing of that action in the federal or state courts.

This evinces the opinion of Congress, that the right to sue does not imply a right to sue in the courts of the Union unless it be expressed. This idea is strengthened also by the law respecting patent rights. That law expressly recognizes the right of the patentee to sue in the circuit courts of the United States.

The court, then, is of opinion, that no right is conferred on the bank, by the act of incorporation, to sue in the federal courts.

2. The other point is one of much more difficulty.

The jurisdiction of this court being limited, so far as respects the character of the parties in this particular case, "to controversies between citizens of different states," both parties must be citizens, to come within the description.

That invisible, intangible, and artificial being, that mere legal entity, a corporation aggregate, is certainly not a citizen; and, consequently, cannot sue or be sued in the courts of the United States, unless the rights of the members, in this respect, can be exercised in their corporate name. If the corporation be considered as a mere faculty, and not as a company of individuals, who, in transacting their joint concerns, may use a legal name, they must be excluded from the courts of the Union.

The duties of this court, to exercise jurisdiction where it is conferred, and not to usurp it where it is not conferred, are of equal obligation. The constitution, therefore, and the law are to be expounded, without a leaning the one way or the other, according to those general principles which usually govern in the construction of fundamental or other laws.

A constitution, from its nature, deals in generals, not in detail. Its framers cannot perceive minute distinctions which arise in the progress of the nation, and therefore confine it to the establishment of broad and general principles.

The judicial department was introduced into the American constitution under impressions, and with views, which are too apparent not to be perceived by all. However true the fact may be, that the tribunals of the states will administer justice as impartially as those of the nation, to parties of every description, it is not less true that the constitution itself either entertains apprehensions on this subject, or views with such indulgence the possible fears and apprehensions of suitors, that it has established national tribunals for the decision of controversies between aliens and a citizen, or between citizens of different states. Aliens, or citizens of different states, are not less susceptible of these

apprehensions, nor can they be supposed to be less the objects of constitutional provision, because they are allowed to sue by a corporate name. That name, indeed, cannot be an alien or a citizen; but the persons whom it represents may be the one or the other; and the controversy is, in fact and in law, between those persons suing in their corporate character, by their corporate name, for a corporate right, and the individual against whom the suit may be instituted. Substantially and essentially, the parties in such a case, where the members of the corporation are aliens, or citizens of a different state from the opposite party, come within the spirit and terms of the jurisdiction conferred by the constitution on the national tribunals.

Such has been the universal understanding on the subject. Repeatedly has this court decided causes between a corporation and an individual without feeling a doubt respecting its jurisdiction. Those decisions are not cited as authority; for they were made without considering this particular point; but they have much weight, as they show that this point neither occurred to the bar or the bench; and that the common understanding of intelligent men is in favor of the right of incorporated aliens, or citizens of a different state from the defendant, to sue in the national courts. It is by a course of acute, metaphysical and abstruse reasoning, which has been most ably employed on this occasion, that this opinion is shaken.

As our ideas of a corporation, its privileges and its disabilities, are derived entirely from the English books, we resort to them for aid, in ascertaining its character. It is defined as a mere creature of the law, invisible, intangible and incorporeal. Yet, when we examine the subject further, we find that corporations have been included within terms of description appropriated to real persons.

The statute of Henry VIII. concerning bridges and highways, enacts, that bridges and highways shall be made and repaired by the "inhabitants of the city, shire, or riding," and that the justices shall have power to tax every "inhabitant of such city," &c., and that the collectors may "distrain every such inhabitant as shall be taxed and refuse payment thereof, in his lands, goods and chattels."

Under this statute those have been construed inhabitants who hold lands within the city where the bridge to be repaired lies, although they reside elsewhere.

Lord Coke says, "every corporation and body politic residing in any county, riding, city, or town corporate, or having lands or tenements in any shire, *que propriis manibus et sumptibus possident et habent,* are said to be inhabitants there, within the purview of this statute."

The tax is not imposed on the person, whether he be a member of the corporation or not, who may happen to reside on the lands; but is imposed on the corporation itself, and, consequently, this ideal existence is considered as an inhabitant, when the general spirit and purpose of the law requires it.

In the case of the *King* v. *Gardner*, reported by Cowper, a corporation was decided, by the Court of King's bench, to come within the description of "occupiers or inhabitants." In that case the poor rates to which the lands of the corporation were declared to be liable, were not assessed to the actual occupant, for there was none, but to the corporation. And the principle established by the case appears to be, that the poor rates on vacant ground belonging to a corporation, may be assessed to the corporation, as being inhabitants or occupiers of that ground. In this case Lord Mansfield notices and overrules an inconsiderate *dictum* of Justice Yates, that a corporation could not be an inhabitant or occupier.

These opinions are not precisely in point; but they serve to show that, for the general purposes and objects of a law, this invisible, incorporeal creature of the law may be considered as having corporeal qualities.

It is true that as far as these cases go they serve to show that the corporation itself, in its incorporeal character, may be considered as an inhabitant or an occupier; and the argument from them would be more strong in favor of considering the corporation itself as endowed for this special purpose with the character of a citizen, than to consider the character of the individiuals who compose it as a subject which the court can inspect, when they use the name of the corporation, for the purpose of asserting their corporate rights. Still the cases show that this technical definition of a corporation does not uniformly circumscribe its capacities, but that courts for legitimate purposes will contemplate it more substantially.

There is a case, however, reported in 12 Mod. which is thought precisely in point. The corporation of London brought a suit against Wood, by their corporate name, in the Mayor's Court. The suit was brought by the mayor and commonalty, and was tried before the mayor and aldermen. The judgment rendered in this cause was brought before the Court of King's bench and reversed, because the court was deprived of its jurisdiction by the character of the individuals who were members of the corporation.

In that case the objection, that a corporation was an invisible, intangible thing, a mere incorporeal legal entity, in which the characters of the individuals who composed it were completely merged, was urged and was considered. The judges unanimously declared that they could look beyond the corporate name, and notice the character of the individual. In the opinions, which were delivered *seriatim*, several cases are put which serve to illustrate the principle and fortify the decision.

The case of *The Mayor and Commonalty* v. *Wood*, is the stronger because it is on the point of jurisdiction. It appears to the court to be a full authority for the case now under consideration. It seems not possible to distinguish them from each other.

If, then, the Congress of the United States had, in terms, enacted that incorporated aliens might sue a citizen, or that the incorporated citizens of one state might sue a citizen of another state, in the federal courts, by its corporate name, this court would not have felt itself justified in declaring that such a law transcended the constitution.

The controversy is substantially between aliens, suing by a corporate name, and a citizen, or between citizens of one state, suing by a corporate name, and those of another state. When these are said to be substantially the parties to the controversy, the court does not mean to liken it to the case of a trustee. A trustee is a real person capable of being a citizen or an alien, who has the whole legal estate in himself. At law, he is the real proprietor, and he represents himself, and sues in his own right. But in this case the corporate name represents persons who are members of the corporation.

If the constitution would authorize Congress to give the courts of the Union jurisdiction in this case, in consequence of the character of the members of the corporation, then the judicial act ought to be construed to give it. For the term citizen ought to be understood as it is used in the constitution, and as it is used in other laws. That is, to describe the real persons who come into court, in this case, under their corporate name.

That corporations composed of citizens are considered by the legislature as citizens, under certain circumstances, is to be strongly inferred from the registering act. It never could be intended that an American registered vessel, abandoned to an insurance company composed of citizens, should lose her character as an American vessel; and yet this would be the consequence of declaring that the members of the corporation were, to every intent and purpose, out of view, and merged in the corporation.

The court feels itself authorized by the case in 12 Mod., on a question of jurisdiction, to look to the character of the individuals who compose the corporation, and they think that the precedents of this court, though they were not decisions on argument, ought not to be absolutely disregarded.

If a corporation may sue in the courts of the Union, the court is of opinion that the averment in this case is sufficient.

Being authorized to sue in their corporate name, they could make the averment, and it must apply to the plaintiffs as individuals, because it could not be true as applied to the corporation.

51

UNITED STATES V. PETERS
5 Cranch 115 (1809)

February 20th, 1809. MARSHALL, Ch. J., delivered the opinion of the court as follows:—With great attention, and with serious concern, the court has considered the return made by the judge for the district of Pennsylvania to the *mandamus* directing him to exercise the sentence pronounced by him in the case of *Gideon Olmstead and others* v. *Rittenhouse's Executrices,* or to show cause for not so doing. The cause shown is an act of the legislature of Pennsylvania, passed subsequent to the rendition of his sentence. This act authorizes and requires the governor to demand, for the use of the state of Pennsylvania, the money which had been decreed to Gideon Olmstead and others; and which was in the hands of the executrices of David Rittenhouse; and in default of payment, to direct the attorney-general to institute a suit for the recovery thereof. This act further authorizes and requires the governor to use any further means he may think necessary for the protection of what it denominates "the just rights of the state," and also to protect the persons and properties of the said executrices of David Rittenhouse, deceased, against any process whatever, issued out of any federal court, in consequence of their obedience to the requisition of the said act.

If the legislatures of the several states may, at will, annul the judgments of the courts of the United States, and destroy the rights acquired under those judgments, the constitution itself becomes a solemn mockery; and the nation is deprived of the means of enforcing its laws by the instrumentality of its own tribunals. So fatal a result must be deprecated by all; and the people of Pennsylvania, not less than the citizens of every other state, must feel a deep interest in resisting principles so destructive of the Union, and in averting consequences so fatal to themselves.

The act in question does not, in terms, assert the universal right of the state to interpose in every case whatever; but assigns, as a motive for its interposition in this particular case, that the sentence, the execution of which it prohibits, was rendered in a cause over which the federal courts have no jurisdiction.

If the ultimate right to determine the jurisdiction of the courts of the Union is placed by the constitution in the several state legislatures, then this act concludes the subject; but if that power necessarily resides in the supreme judicial tribunal of the nation, then the jurisdiction of the district court of Pennsylvania, over the case in which that jurisdiction was exercised, ought to be most deliberately examined; and the act of Pennsylvania, with whatever respect it may be considered, cannot be permitted to prejudice the question.

In the early part of the war between the United States and Great Britain, Gideon Olmstead and others, citizens of Connecticut, who say, they had been carried to Jamaica, as prisoners, were employed as part of the crew of the sloop Active, bound from Jamaica to New York, and laden with a cargo for the use of the British army in that place. On the voyage, they seized the vessel, confined the captain, and sailed for Egg Harbor. In sight of that place, the Active was captured by the Convention, an armed ship belonging to the state of Pennsylvania, brought into port, libelled and condemned as prize to the captors. From this sentence, Gideon Olmstead and others, who claimed the vessel and cargo, appealed to the court of appeals established by congress, by which tribunal, the sentence of condemnation was reversed, the Active and her cargo condemned as prize to the claimants, and process was directed to issue out of the court of admiralty, commanding the marshal of that court to sell the said vessel and cargo, and to pay the net proceeds to the claimants.

The mandate of the appellate court was produced in the inferior court, the judge of which admitted the general jurisdiction of the court established by congress, as an appellate court, but denied its power to control the verdict of a jury which had been rendered in favor of the captors, the officers and crew of the Convention; and therefore, refused obedience to the mandate: but directed the marshal to make the sale, and after deducting charges, to bring the residue of the money into court, subject to its further order.

The claimants then applied to the judges of appeals, for an injunction to prohibit the marshal from paying the money, arising from the sales, into the court of admiralty; which was awarded, and served upon him: in contempt of which, on the 4th of January 1778, he paid the money to the judge, who acknowledged the receipt thereof at the foot of the marshal's return.

On the 1st of May 1779, George Ross, the judge of the court of admiralty, delivered to David Rittenhouse, who was then treasurer of the state of Pennsylvania, the sum of 11,496*l.* 9*s.* 9*d.*, in loan-office certificates; which was the proportion of the prize-money to which that state would have been entitled, had the sentence of the court of admiralty remained in force. On the same day, David Rittenhouse executed a bond of indemnity to George Ross, in which, after reciting that the money was paid to him for the use of the state of Pennsylvania, he binds himself to repay the same, should the said George Ross be thereafter compelled, by due course of law, to pay that sum according to the decree of the court of appeals.

These loan-office certificates were in the name of Matthew Clarkson, who was marshal of the court of admiralty, and were dated the 6th of November 1778. Indents were issued on them to David Rittenhouse, and the whole principal and interest were afterwards funded by him, in his own name, under the act of congress making provision for the debt of the United States.

Among the papers of David Rittenhouse, was a memorandum, made by himself at the foot of a list of the certificates mentioned above, in these words: "Note.—The above certificates will be the property of the state of Pennsylvania, when the state releases me from the bond I gave in 1778, to indemnify George Ross, Esq., judge of the admiralty, for paying the fifty original certificates into the treasury, as the state's share of the prize."

The state did not release David Rittenhouse from the bond mentioned in this memorandum. These certificates remained in the private possession of David Rittenhouse, who drew the interest on them, during his life, and after his death, they remained in possession of his representatives; against whom the libel in this case was filed, for the purpose of carrying into execution the decree of the court of appeals.

While this suit was depending, the state of Pennsylvania forbore to assert its title, and in January 1803, the court decreed in favor of the libellants; soon after which, the legislature passed the act which has been stated.

It is contended, that the federal courts were deprived of jurisdiction in this cause, by that amendment of the constitution, which exempts states from being sued in those courts by individuals. This amendment declares, "that the judicial power of the United States shall not be construed to extend to any suit, in law or equity, commenced or prosecuted against one of the United States by citizens of another state, or by citizens or subjects of any foreign state."

The right of a state to assert, as plaintiff, any interest it may have in a subject, which forms the matter of controversy between individuals, in one of the courts of the United States, is not affected by this amendment; nor can it be so construed as to oust the court of its jurisdiction, should such claim be suggested. The amendment simply provides, that no suit shall be commenced or prosecuted against a state. The state cannot be made a defendant to a suit brought by an individual; but it remains the duty of the courts of the United States to decide all cases brought before them by citizens of one state against citizens of a different state, where a state is not necessarily a defendant. In this case, the suit was not instituted against the state, or its treasurer, but against the executrices of David Rittenhouse, for the proceeds of a vessel condemned in the court of admiralty, which were admitted to be in their possession. If these proceeds had been the actual property of Pennsylvania, however wrongfully acquired, the disclosure of that fact would have presented a case on which it is unnecessary to give an opinion; but it certainly can never be alleged, that a mere suggestion of title in a state, to property in possession of an individual, must arrest the proceedings of the court, and prevent their looking into the suggestion, and examining the validity of the title.

If the suggestion in this case be examined, it is deemed perfectly clear, that no title whatever to the certificates in question was vested in the state of Pennsylvania.

By the highest judicial authority of the nation, it has been long since decided, that the court of appeals erected by congress had full authority to revise and correct the sentences of the courts of admiralty of the several states, in prize causes. That question, therefore, is at rest. Consequently, the decision of the court of appeals in this case annulled the sentence of the court of admiralty, and extinguished the interest of the state of Pennsylvania in the Active and her cargo, which was acquired by that sentence. The full right to that property was immediately vested in the claimants, who might rightfully pursue it, into whosesoever hands it might come. These certificates, in the hands, first, of Matthew Clarkson, the marshal, and afterwards of George Ross, the judge of the court of admiralty, were the absolute property of the claimants. Nor did they change their character, on coming into the possession of David Rittenhouse.

Although Mr. Rittenhouse was treasurer of the state of Pennsylvania, and the bond of indemnity which he executed states the money to have been paid to him for the use of the state of Pennsylvania, it is apparent, that he held them in his own right, until he should be completely indemnified by the state. The evidence to this point is conclusive. The original certificates do not appear to have been deposited in the state treasury, to have been designated in any manner as the property of the state, or to have been delivered over to the successor of David Rittenhouse: they remained in his possession. The indents, issued upon them for interest, were drawn by David Rittenhouse, and preserved with the original certificates. When funded as part of the debt of the United States, they were funded by David Rittenhouse, and the interest was drawn by him. The note made by himself, at the foot of the list, which he preserved, as explanatory of the whole transaction, demonstrates that he held the certificates as security against the bond he had executed to George Ross; and that bond was obligatory, not on the state of Pennsylvania, but on David Rittenhouse, in his private capacity.

These circumstances demonstrate, beyond the possibility of doubt, that the property, which represented the Active and her cargo, was in possession not of the state of Pennsylvania, but of David Rittenhouse, as an individual; after whose death, it passed, like other property, to his representatives.

Since, then, the state of Pennsylvania had neither possession of, nor right to, the property on which the sentence of the district court was pronounced, and since the suit was neither commenced nor prosecuted against that state, there remains no pretext for the allegation, that the case is within that amendment of the constitution which has been cited; and consequently, the state of Pennsylvania can possess no constitutional right to resist the legal process which may be directed in this cause.

It will be readily conceived, that the order which this court is enjoined to make by the high obligations of duty and of law, is not made without extreme regret at the necessity which has induced the application. But it is a solemn duty, and therefore, must be performed. A peremptory *mandamus* must be awarded.

52

HODGSON & THOMPSON v. BOWERBANK
5 Cranch 303 (1809)

Error to the Circuit Court for the district of Maryland. The defendants below were described in the record as "late of the district of Maryland, merchants," but were not stated to be citizens of the state of Maryland. the plaintiffs were described as "aliens and subjects of the king of the united kingdom of Great Britain and Ireland."

Martin contended, that the courts of the United States had not jurisdiction, it not being stated that the defendants were citizens of any state.

C. Lee, contrà.—The judiciary act gives jurisdiction to the circuit courts, in all suits in which an alien is a party. (1 U. S. Stat. 78, § 11.)

MARSHALL, Ch. J.—Turn to the article of the constitution of the United States, for the statute cannot extend the jurisdiction beyond the limits of the constitution.

The words of the constitution were found to be "between a state, or the citizens thereof, and foreign states, citizens or subjects."

THE COURT said, the objection was fatal.

53

OWINGS v. NORWOOD'S LESSEE
5 Cranch 344 (1809)

MARSHALL, C. J. There are only two points in this case.

1. Whether Scarth had such an interest as was protected by the treaty; and,

2. Whether the present case be a case arising under a treaty, within the meaning of the constitution.

This court has no doubt upon either point.

The interest by debt intended to be protected by the treaty, must be an interest holden as a security for money at the time of the treaty; and the debt must still remain due.

The 25th section of the Judiciary Act must be restrained by the constitution, the words of which are, "all cases arising under treaties." The plaintiff in error does not contend that his right grows out of the treaty. Whether it is an obstacle to the plaintiff's recovery, is a question exclusively for the decision of the courts of Maryland.

Harper, on the next day, having suggested to the court that he understood the opinion to be, that this court had no jurisdiction to revise the decisions of the state courts, in cases where the construction of a treaty was drawn in question incidentally, and where the party himself did not claim title under a treaty, was about to make some further observations on those points, when,

MARSHALL, C. J., observed, that *Mr. Harper* had misunderstood the opinion of the court, in that respect. It was not that this court had not jurisdiction if the treaty were drawn in question incidentally.

The reason for inserting that clause in the constitution was, that all persons who have real claims under a treaty should have their causes decided by the national tribunals. It was to avoid the apprehension as well as the danger of state prejudices. The words of the constitution are, "cases arising under treaties." Each treaty stipulates something respecting the citizens of the two nations, and gives them rights. Whenever a right grows out of, or is protected by, a treaty, it is sanctioned against all the laws and judicial decisions of the States; and whoever may have this right, it is to be protected. But if the person's title is not affected by the treaty, if he claims nothing under a treaty, his title cannot be protected by the treaty. If Scarth or his heirs had claimed, it would have been a case arising under a treaty. But neither the title of Scarth, nor of any person claiming under him, can be affected by the decision of this cause.

54

BROWN v. CRIPPIN
4 Hen. & M. 173 (Va. 1809)

Judge TUCKER. The appellant, a citizen of *Pennsylvania,* being sued by the appellees in an action of trespass, in the County Court of *Accomac,* was held to bail in that Court by order of a Justice of that County, founded upon an affidavit made by *Crippin,* one of the plaintiffs in that suit, stating, that *Brown was not a resident of this State,* and was about to depart the same. At the succeeding Court, *Brown* preferred a petition to the Court for the removal of the suit to the next Circuit Court of the *United States,* to be holden for this district, wherein he styles himself a citizen of *Pennsylvania,* and refers to the writ and order of bail, and offered to give security as required by the act of the first Congress, 1 sess. c. 20. s. 12. which the Court refused; first, because it was not shewn to them that the defendant was an alien, or a citizen of any other State; and, secondly, because the defendant was not personally present to execute a bond, conformably to the 12th section of the act of Congress. Afterwards, application was made to the Superior Court of *Accomac* County, to award a *mandamus* to the County Court, commanding them to remove the cause, which was also refused; and from that decision there is an appeal to this Court.

By the act of Congress above mentioned, if a suit be commenced in any State Court against an alien, or by a citizen of the State in which the suit is brought against a citizen of another State, and the matter in dispute, exclusive of costs, exceeds 500 dollars, and the defendant shall, at the time of entering his appearance, file a petition for the removal of the cause into the next Circuit Court of the *United States,* to be held in the District, and offer good and sufficient surety for his entering in such Court, on the first day of its session, copies of the process against him, and also for his there appearing and entering bail in the cause, if special bail was originally requisite therein, it shall then be the duty of the State Court to accept the security, and proceed no further in the cause.

The removal of the cause in such a case is a matter of right which ought not to be refused to any defendant, who makes out his case, and complies with the terms of the law. The order for bail endorsed on the writ, obtained on the application and oath of one of the plaintiffs, and stating that the defendant was not a native of this State, superseded the necessity of any proof of that fact to the Court, on the part of the defendant. The security offered was admitted by the Court to be good and sufficient, and ought to have been accepted. The law does not prescribe that a *bond* shall be taken. A person taken upon a writ of *capias ad respondendum* may be in close custody; and while the superior Courts of this State had jurisdiction over several, and often very remote Counties, it might have been impossible to bring the defendant before the Court during the term, to give bond in the presence of the Court. In such case, the wise provision of the act of Congress would in ninety-nine case out of a hundred be defeated. A stipulation in nature of a recognisance taken in Court, (as is every day's practice in entering special bail in the County Courts,) would have answered every purpose of the law. Both reasons for refusing the prayer of the petition were, therefore, utterly without foundation. And the refusal of the *mandamus* by the superior Court, appears to me to be equally against right. A *mandamus* is a writ of right in every case where it is the proper remedy. Being of opinion that the County Court refused to perform a duty which was enjoined by law, a *mandamus*, at that stage of the cause, was the only remedy. The defendant could neither appeal, nor obtain a writ of error, or of *supersedeas*, until the final decision of the suit, when it might be too late. I do not know that a writ of *certiorari* would lie from the Circuit Court of the *United States* to a County Court, to remove a cause under such circumstances. But of this I have no doubt, that neither the Constitution of the *United States,* nor any act of Congress, does, or can, (so long as the twelfth article of the amendments to the Constitution of the *United States* remains in force,) deprive the superior Courts of this Commonwealth of that control over the proceedings of the inferior Courts, which the laws of this country give to them. I have therefore no doubt of the right of the Superior Court of *Accomac* to grant the *mandamus*, nor that it erred in refusing it. I am therefore of opinion, that the judgment be reversed, and the cause sent back with directions to that Court to award the writ of *mandamus.*

Judge ROANE concurred, as to the judgment agreed to be entered. He said he thought it a very *plain case.*

Judge FLEMING said it was the unanimous opinion of the Court, that the judgment of the Superior Court of Law, for *Accomac* County, be REVERSED.

55

LIVINGSTON V. VAN INGEN

15 Fed. Cas. 697, no. 8,420 (C.C.S.D.N.Y. 1811)

LIVINGSTON, Circuit Justice. The complainants by their bill appear to be proprietors of boats on the Hudson river, propelled by steam, and claim a right to the exclusive navigation of the waters of New York in that way, in virtue of two patents from the United States, and several laws passed by this state. The defendants have built and are using a steam boat on the same river for carrying passengers, and are building another for the same purpose, in violation, as it is alleged, of their rights under these patents and laws. The bill prays that the complainants may be quieted in the possession and enjoyment of these rights;

that the defendants may be restrained by injunction from constructing or using these boats on the waters of the state of New York; and that the rights of the complainants under their patents and the laws of the state may be established. All the parties are citizens of the state of New York, and no action has been brought at law to try the title of the complainants. On the filing of this bill a motion has been made to a judge at his chambers for an injunction to restrain the defendants from the employment of their boat. The argument has been conducted with all the ability which might naturally be expected from the gentlemen concerned, and the importance and novelty of the case.

The application is resisted on two grounds. The defendants contend: 1. That a circuit court of the United States, as a court of equity, between citizens of the same state, has no jurisdiction of this cause. 2. That if it had, this is not a case proper for its interposition in this way.

It will not be denied that the awarding of a writ of injunction of this nature is one of the highest and most important functions which a court of equity can be called upon to exercise. The court is asked to inhibit a party from the full use and enjoyment of his property without any previous trial whatever—when that property is of a perishable nature, and must have been built at a very great expense, and when, if employed, it cannot fail of producing great gains, for the loss of which, however serious or extensive, the owners, if eventually successful in the controversy, will have no remedy against any one; while the plaintiffs, if aggrieved, will be entitled to a threefold recompense for any subtraction or diminution of profits to which they may for some time be exposed. This too, it is expected, will be done without the previous institution of any action at law, and without the opportunity of any other proper mode of trial to decide on the matters which the defendants are authorized by law to allege in their defence. When process of such high import and serious consequences is applied for, it becomes a court, and still more a judge at his chambers, to inquire with more than ordinary circumspection into his powers, and to stay his hand, unless he shall be fully and entirely satisfied of his jurisdiction; that the merits of the complainants are very great, and that they are eminently entitled to the favour of the public, and to every reasonable protection which government can afford, no one will deny. But when we are inquiring not into what ought, but into what has been done, considerations of this kind, however naturally or excusably they may be pressed upon a court, can afford but little aid in coming to a correct decision.

A judge of the supreme court may in vacation allow a writ of injunction in those cases only, where it may be granted by the supreme or a circuit court. That the supreme court, unless on appeal, has the power of awarding this writ is not pretended. The examination therefore has been properly confined to the authority of a circuit court. If the circuit court of this district possesses no jurisdiction over the cause, it follows that the present application must fail. This jurisdiction is denied on the ground, that the parties, being all citizens of the same state, have no right to apply to the equity side of the court for relief by original bill, unless jurisdiction in such case be given by some act of congress. By the federal constitution, the judicial power is vested in one supreme court, and in such inferior courts as congress may from time to time ordain and establish, and extends to all cases in law and equity, arising under the constitution and laws of the United States, and controversies between citizens of different states. A further enumeration of its powers is not necessary for understanding the present question. By the judiciary act [1 Stat. 73], the circuit courts have original cognizance, concurrent with state courts, of all suits of a civil nature at common law or in equity, of a certain value, where the United States are plaintiffs, or an alien is a party; or where the suit is between a citizen of the state where it is brought, and a citizen of another state. By an act passed in 1800 [2 Stat. 37], an action on the case, founded on that, and a former act, is given to a patentee whose rights are invaded, to be prosecuted in the circuit court of the United States, having jurisdiction thereof, for a sum equal to three times the actual damage sustained. But this being a suit in equity, it is asked by what authority it is brought here, unless the parties be citizens of different states: and much has been said of the impropriety of an inferior tribunal extending its jurisdiction to cases not particularly assigned to it.

If these courts be not inferior in the technical sense of the books, which they most certainly are not, they are so in some respects. They are not only so considered by the constitution, but are in fact subordinate to the supreme court, and notwithstanding their high and responsible original powers, which extend to so many and such important cases, of a criminal and civil nature, and by appeal, to admiralty and maritime causes, there can be no doubt that their jurisdiction is special and limited, both in regard to the nature of the cases on which they can decide, and the character of the parties who can come into them. It is as certain, that they are indebted to congress, under the constitution, for their creation, and that instead of extending their powers as the exigencies of suitors may require, or may by themselves be thought reasonable, they have hitherto been regarded as dependent on that body for all the powers they possess. Owing as they do their existence to congress, from them must necessarily flow that portion of the general judicial power which, by the constitution, they have a right to divide among the inferior courts that may be established. Thus constituted and organized, little would it become them to transcend a jurisdiction, which the constitution intended should be limited at the discretion of the legislature, and which congress have circumscribed accordingly. While moving within their legitimate sphere, as marked out by the legislature, they may hope to give satisfaction, and to inspire confidence in the important department of government of which they form a branch. It would seem then enough to say that there being no act of congress conferring on these courts a right in any case to take cognizance of a suit in equity, between citizens of the same state, this court can have no jurisdiction of the present cause, which is between parties of that character. This seemed to be almost conceded, unless by the constitution there was secured to these courts certain

powers which might be called into exercise without waiting for any special authority from congress. To show that this was the case, it was said, that this being a case arising under the laws of the United States and being found in the constitutional enumeration of cases of federal cognizance, it must, whether allotted by congress to a particular tribunal or not, be cognizable by one or other of the courts which may be established. This argument proceeds on a supposition that the whole power of the judiciary must always reside somewhere, so as to be called into operation as occasions may require. If congress had created inferior courts without any designation as to the cases of which they were to take cognizance, it is said they would have concurrent jurisdiction of all cases mentioned in the constitution except of those which were therein exclusively devolved on the supreme court. That this being a case of chancery cognizance, and the district court, not possessing equity power, must, ex necessitate, be triable where such powers exist, or that there will be a failure of justice; and the danger of permitting congress in any way to abridge the objects of cognizance secured by the constitution to the judiciary, and, through them, to the people of the United States, was expatiated on at some length. As congress cannot add to those powers, it should not be admitted for a moment, it was argued, that they possessed the right of subtracting from them, or of permitting them to be dormant, by not legislating sufficiently. Without stopping to inquire whether there be any ground for these apprehensions, or denying any weight to the argument, it will not be deemed disrespectful to the counsel who advanced it, if it is not thought necessary to examine the course of reasoning, from which this conclusion is presumed to follow, because on this point we are not without authority. The supreme court has decided, and after an argument, which, if we except the one to which I have just had the pleasure and honour of attending, has perhaps never been surpassed on any occasion; that if jurisdiction of cases arising under the laws of the United States be not conferred on the circuit courts by an act of congress, they cannot take cognizance of them. The case of the Bank of the United States against Deveaux, is here referred to, which was decided in February term, 1809, a report of which is not yet published.

It was there made one question, whether a right was conferred on the bank to sue in these courts by its act of incorporation, or any other law of congress. It was decided not only that the circuit court derived no jurisdiction over a case arising under the laws of the United States from the judiciary act, that class of cases not being provided for by it, but that from the law which incorporates it, the bank acquired no right to bring an action in those courts, although there were expressions in that act, which it was very strongly insisted on, gave it to them. In support of this decision, if it required any to render it binding, reference might be made to a contemporaneous exposition of the constitution by the great and wise men who composed the legislature that organized the judiciary, and to what appears to have been the understanding of congress from that time to the present day; for whenever it was intended that these courts should take cognizance of a case arising under any law of the United States, such power was expressly delegated to one of the federal courts, congress well knowing that the judiciary act was silent on this point, and not supposing that any such power by the constitution was given to the circuit court. This too may be collected from an act that passed in 1800, which, in terms, gave to the courts then erected, jurisdiction over this class of cases, but which act, being afterwards repealed, although not on account of this clause, left us as before, without any general provision on the subject. If other evidences are wanting that the supreme court has not fallen into so great an error, as it was thought to have done by this decision, it might be collected from the journal of the senate of the United States. There we find that the judiciary act was prepared by a committee consisting of a member from each state, most if not all professional men, and it cannot be believed that, in a law drawn with so much care, and embracing such a variety of provisions, so important an omission was casual. It must have been the result of much reflection, and shows their sense at least, that congress were not bound to clothe the courts which they might create with all the powers which by the constitution they had a right to confer. When it is recollected that three gentlemen of this committee were afterwards judges of the courts of the United States, an allusion to what must have been their opinion when senators, on a point immediately under their consideration, cannot be thought improper. The same principle is recognised by the very laws under which the plaintiffs claim; for the judiciary act not having made any such provision in such a case, unless the parties were citizens of different states, it was thought necessary to establish by those acts the right of a patentee to sue in a circuit court, but at the same time, such right was restricted to its legal forum: as it regards this case then, the legislature is not chargeable with any omission, or with affording a remedy, without a designation of the tribunal which was to administer it, for although by the constitution the judicial power is extended to all cases in law and equity, arising under the laws of the Union, congress may certainly say that the relief which they intended to afford in a particular case shall be at law only. If it had been thought proper to proceed at law in this court, the complainants would probably have found no difficulty on the score of jurisdiction, and it may be added, that if this case be of equity cognizance at all, (which has been strongly controverted and on which no opinion is given,) it is probably so at common law, and in that case congress were not bound, even if they had the right, to give jurisdiction of it to any federal court.

It was further urged in favour of the present jurisdiction, that the supreme court of this state has decided that an action cannot be maintained there, founded on the patent laws of the United States; and that as the court of chancery of the state would give no relief, the parties thus excluded from the federal and state courts, would be without redress, if the decision of the supreme court of the United States were considered as applying to them. It is not for me to say what the chancellor of this state will think his duty, if a similar application be made to him; but if this be a case of equitable jurisdiction at common law, as

it was sometimes alleged to be by the complainant's counsel, no objection is perceived to his taking cognizance of it. But should he think otherwise, there is still another answer to this difficulty, which is that if the parties be remediless it is no fault of the law, which gives them if not a perfect, at least a liberal, and what will probably prove, if they choose to pursue it, a very effectual remedy; for it is not to be believed, as was supposed at the bar, that they will have to bring action after action to establish their right. Let them proceed in only one trial at law, and the defendants will not be hardy or foolish enough to continue on very unequal terms, what will then be settled to be a violation of their patent rights; such a verdict will for ever after keep all intruders at a distance. But if absolutely without remedy elsewhere, it does not follow that this court can help them. A court, constituted like this, is not to reason itself into jurisdiction from considerations of hardship, when a plain and safe rule is prescribed by the supreme court, which is, to examine on all occasions, what powers are committed to it, by the laws of the United States.

Another argument which it may be expected will be noticed, was, that as an action at law under the patent acts may be prosecuted in this court, even between citizens of the same state, there was, necessarily, conferred on it a right to hold jurisdiction of the present bill; for as the court possessed equity powers in virtue of the judiciary act, it was impossible to give it jurisdiction as a court of law, without at the same time calling into exercise its powers as a court of equity. If it becomes necessary in an action at law regularly before it, for either party to appeal to its equity side, in aid or defence of such action, such application might not be improper. But this is not a bill of that kind. It would be the action at law in such case, on which its jurisdiction would attach. But the answer to the argument is, that by the judiciary act no equity powers are given to this court, between citizens of the same state; and it results from the decision which has been cited, that a circuit court must not only confine itself to the cases defined by congress, but that if by a particular act it is authorized to proceed in the given case as a court of law only, a party must come into it on that side, to bring himself within the provisions of it. There being then no law conferring on this court a right to take cognizance as a court of equity of cases of this nature, between citizens of the same state, my opinion is, that this court cannot entertain cognizance of the present bill, and that the plaintiffs therefore can take nothing by their motion. After this decision, it would be superfluous and improper to express any opinion on any other of the important points which were made on the argument of the present question. If the parties were citizens of different states, it is not intended to say that the plaintiffs would or would not be entitled to the equitable relief which they seek.

56

UNITED STATES V. HUDSON & GOODWIN

7 Cranch 32 (1812)

This was a case certified from the Circuit Court for the District of *Connecticut,* in which, upon argument of a general demurrer to an *indictment* for a libel on the President and Congress of the United States, contained in the *Connecticut Courant,* of the 7th of May, 1806, charging them with having in secret voted two millions of dollars as a present to Bonaparte for leave to make a treaty with Spain, the judges of that Court were divided in opinion upon the question, *whether the Circuit Court of the United States had a common law jurisdiction in cases of libel.*

Pinkney, Attorney General, in behalf of the United States, and *Dana* for the Defendants, declined arguing the case.

The Court having taken time to consider, the following opinion was delivered (on the last day of the term, all the judges being present) by JOHNSON, J.

The only question which this case presents is, whether the Circuit Courts of the United States can exercise a common law jurisdiction in criminal cases. We state it thus broadly because a decision on a case of libel will apply to every case in which jurisdiction is not vested in those courts by statute.

Although this question is brought up now for the first time to be decided by this Court, we consider it as having been long since settled in public opinion. In no other case for many years has this jurisdiction been asserted; and the general acquiescence of legal men shews the prevalence of opinion in favor of the negative of the proposition.

The course of reasoning which leads to this conclusion is simple, obvious, and admits of but little illustration. The powers of the general Government are made up of concessions from the several states—whatever is not expressly given to the former, the latter expressly reserve. The judicial power of the United States is a constituent part of those concessions—that power is to be exercised by Courts organized for the purpose, and brought into existence by an effort of the legislative power of the Union. Of all the Courts which the United States may, under their general powers, constitute, one only, the Supreme Court, possesses jurisdiction derived immediately from the Constitution, and of which the legislative power cannot deprive it. All other Courts created by the general Government possess no jurisdiction but what is given them by the power that creates them, and can be vested with none but what the power ceded to the general Government will authorize them to confer.

It is not necessary to inquire whether the general Government, in any and what extent, possesses the power of conferring on its Courts a jurisdiction in cases similar to the present; it is enough that such jurisdiction has not been conferred by any legislative act, if it does not result to those Courts as a consequence of their creation.

And such is the opinion of a majority of this court: For, the power which Congress possess to create Courts of inferior jurisdiction, necessarily implies the power to limit the jurisdiction of those Courts to particular objects; and when a Court is created, and its operations confined to certain specific objects, with what propriety can it assume to itself a jurisdiction—much more extended—in its nature very indefinite—applicable to a great variety of subjects—varying in every State in the Union—and with regard to which there exists no definite criterion of distribution between the district and Circuit Courts of the same district?

The only ground on which it has ever been contended that this jurisdiction could be maintained is, that, upon the formation of any political body, an implied power to preserve its own existence and promote the end and object of its creation, necessarily results to it. But, without examining how far this consideration is applicable to the peculiar character of our constitution, it may be remarked that it is a principle by no means peculiar to the common law. It is coeval, probably, with the first formation of a limited Government; belongs to a system of universal law, and may as well support the assumption of many other powers as those more peculiarly acknowledged by the common law of England.

But if admitted as applicable to the state of things in this country, the consequence would not result from it which is here contended for. If it may communicate certain implied powers to the general Government, it would not follow that the Courts of that Government are vested with jurisdiction over any particular act done by an individual in supposed violation of the peace and dignity of the sovereign power. The legislative authority of the Union must first make an act a crime, affix a punishment to it, and declare the Court that shall have jurisdiction of the offence.

Certain implied powers must necessarily result to our Courts of justice from the nature of their institution. But jurisdiction of crimes against the state is not among those powers. To fine for contempt—imprison for contumacy—inforce the observance of order, &c. are powers which cannot be dispensed with in a Court, because they are necessary to the exercise of all others: and so far our Courts no doubt possess powers not immediately derived from statute; but all exercise of criminal law cases we are of opinion is not within their implied powers.

57

McINTIRE V. WOOD

7 Cranch 504 (1813)

JOHNSON, J., delivered the opinion of the court as follows:—

I am instructed to deliver the opinion of the court in

this case. It comes up on a division of opinion in the circuit court of Ohio, upon a motion for a *mandamus* to the register of the land office, at Marietta, commanding him to grant final certificates of purchase to the plaintiff for lands, to which he supposed himself entitled under the laws of the United States.

This court is of opinion that the circuit court did not possess the power to issue the *mandamus* moved for.

Independent of the particular objections which this case presents from its involving a question of freehold, we are of opinion that the power of the circuit courts to issue the writ of *mandamus*, is confined exclusively to those cases in which it may be necessary to the exercise of their jurisdiction. Had the 11th section of the Judiciary Act covered the whole ground of the constitution, there would be much reason for exercising this power in many cases wherein some ministerial act is necessary to the completion of an individual right arising under laws of the United States, and the 14th section of the same act would sanction the issuing of the writ for such a purpose. But although the judicial power of the United States extends to cases arising under the laws of the United States, the legislature have not thought proper to delegate the exercise of that power to its circuit courts, except in certain specified cases. When questions arise under those laws in the state courts, and the party who claims a right or privilege under them is unsuccessful, an appeal is given to the supreme court, and this provision the legislature has thought sufficient at present for all the political purposes intended to be answered by the clause of the constitution, which relates to this subject.

A case occurred some years since in the circuit court of South Carolina, the notoriety of which may apologize for making an observation upon it here. It was a *mandamus* to a collector to grant a clearance, and unquestionably could not have been issued but upon a supposition inconsistent with the decision in this case. But that *mandamus* was issued upon the voluntary submission of the collector and the district attorney, and in order to extricate themselves from an embarrassment resulting from conflicting duties. *Volenti non fit injuria.*

58

CLARKE V. MOREY
10 Johns. R. 70 (N.Y. 1813)

KENT, Ch. J. delivered the opinion of the court. The second plea states that the plaintiff is an alien, born out of the allegiance of the *United States,* and under the allegiance of the king of the united kingdom of *Great Britain* and *Ireland,* and not naturalized, and that war exists between the *United States* and the said kingdom; and that the plaintiff came into the *United States* and remains here without any letters of safe conduct from the President of the *United States,* or any license to remain here.

This plea is not without precedent in the *English* books; (*Rast. Ent.* 252. b. 605. b. *Denier* v. *Arnaud,* 4 *Mod.* 405, the record of which plea Lord *Kenyon,* in 8 *Term Rep.* 167, says he had examined;) but there are many and weighty reasons why it cannot be supported. To render the plea of alien enemy good, it seems now to be understood to be the law of *England* that the plea must not only aver that the plaintiff was an alien enemy, but that he was adhering to the enemy. The disability is confined to these two cases; 1. Where the right sued for was acquired in actual hostility, as was the case of the ransom bill in *Anthon* v. *Fisher;* (*Doug.* 649, note;) 2. Where the plaintiff, being an alien enemy, was resident in the enemy's country; such was the form of the plea in *George* v. *Powell,* (*Fortesc.* 221,) and in *Le Bret* v. *Papillon;* (4 *East,* 502;) and such was the case with the persons in whose behalf, and for whose benefit the suit was brought upon the policy, in *Brandon* v. *Nesbitt.* (6 *Term Rep.* 23.)

It was considered in the Common Pleas, at *Westminster,* as a settled point, (*Heath,* J., and *Rooke,* J. in *Sparenburgh* v. *Bannatyne,* 1 *Bos. & Pull.* 163,) that an alien enemy under the king's protection, even if he were a prisoner of war, might sue and be sued. This point had long before received a very solemn decision in the case of *Wells* v. *Williams.* (1 *Lord Raym.* 282. 1 *Lutw.* 34. S. C. 1 *Salk.* 46.) It was there decided that if the plaintiff came to *England* before the war, and continued to reside there, by the license and under the protection of the king, he might maintain an action upon his personal contract; and that if even he came to *England* after the breaking out of the war, and continued there under the same protection, he might sue upon his bond or contract; and that the distinction was between such an alien enemy, and one *commorant* in his own country. The plea, in that case, averred that the plaintiff was not only born in *France,* under the allegiance of the *French* king, then being an enemy, but that he came to *England,* without any safe conduct, and the plea was held bad on demurrer. It was considered, that if the plaintiff came to *England* in time of peace, and remained there quietly, it amounted to a license, and that if he came over in time of war, and continued without disturbance, a license would be intended. It is, therefore, not sufficient to state that the plaintiff came here without safe conduct. The plea must set forth, affirmatively, every fact requisite to prove that the plaintiff has no right of action. It is not to be favored by intendment. This was the amount of the decision in *Casseres* v. *Bell;* (8 *Term Rep.* 166;) and one of the judges in that case referred to the decision in *Wells* v. *Williams,* as authority, and so it has uniformly been considered in all the books; and all the former precedents and *dicta* that are repugnant to it may be considered as overruled. Though there is a loose and unsatisfactory note of *Sylvester's Case,* in 7 *Mod.* 150, which was a few years later, and looks somewhat to the contrary; yet it never has been considered as affecting the former decision. Indeed, the law on this subject has undergone a progressive improvement. The doctrine once held in the *English* courts, that an alien's bond became forfeited by the war, (*Year Book,* 19 *Edw.* IV. pl. 6,) would not now be endured. The plea is called in the books an odious plea, and the latter cases concur in the opinion that the ancient severities of war have been greatly and justly softened, by modern usages, the result of commerce and civilization.

In the case before us, we are to take it for granted (for the suit was commenced before the present war) that the plaintiff came to reside here before the war, and no letters of safe conduct were, therefore, requisite, nor any license from the president. The license is implied by law and the usage of nations; if he came here since the war, a license is also implied, and the protection continues until the executive shall think proper to order the plaintiff out of the *United States;* but no such order is stated or averred. This is the evident construction of the act of congress of the 6th *July,* 1798, entitled "An act respecting alien enemies." (*Sess.* 1 cong. 5. c. 73.) Until such order, the law grants permission to the alien to remain, though his sovereign be at war with us. A lawful residence implies protection, and a capacity to sue and be sued. A contrary doctrine would be repugnant to sound policy, no less than to justice and humanity.

The right to sue, in such a case, rests on still broader ground than that of a mere municipal provision, for it has been frequently held that the law of nations is part of the common law. By the law of nations, an alien who comes to reside in a foreign country, is entitled, so long as he conducts himself peaceably, to continue to reside there, under the public protection; and it requires the express will of the sovereign power to order him away. The rigor of the old rules of war no longer exists, as *Bynkershoek* admits, when wars are carried on with the moderation that the influence of commerce inspires. It may be said of commerce, as *Ovid* said of the liberal arts: *Emollit mores, nec sinit esse feros.*

We all recollect the enlightened and humane provision of *Magna Charta* (c. 30) on this subject; and in *France* the ordinance of *Charles* V. as early as 1370, was dictated with the same magnanimity; for it declared that in case of war, foreign merchants had nothing to fear, for they might depart freely with their effects, and if they happened to die in *France,* their goods should descend to their heirs. (*Henault's Abrégé Chron.* tom. 1. 338.) So all the judges of *England* resolved, as early as the time of *Henry* VIII. that if an alien came to *England,* before the declaration of war, neither his person, nor his effects, should be seized in consequence of it. (*Bro.* tit. *Property,* pl. 38. *Jenk. Cent.* 201. *Case* 22.) And it has now become the sense and practice of nations, and may be regarded as the *public law of Europe,* (the anomalous and awful case of the present violent power on the continent excepted,) that the subjects of the enemy, (without confining the rule to merchants,) so long as they are permitted to remain in the country, are to be protected in their persons and property, and to be allowed to sue as well as to be sued. (*Bynk. Quaest. Jur. Pub.* b. 1. c. 7. c. 25. s. 8.) It is even held, that if they are ordered away in consequence of the war, they are still entitled to leave a power of attorney, and to collect their debts by suit. (*Emerigon, Traité des Assurances,* tom. 1. 567.)

Modern treaties have usually made provision for the case of aliens found in the country, at the declaration of war, and have allowed them a reasonable time to collect their effects and remove. *Bynkershoek* gives instances of such treaties, existing above two centuries ago; and for a century past, such a provision has become an established *formula* in the commercial treaties. *Emerigon,* who has examined this subject with the most liberal and enlightened views, considers these treaties as an affirmance of common right, or the public law of *Europe,* and the general rule is so laid down by the later publicists, in conformity with this provision. (*Vattel,* b. 3. c. 4. s. 63. *Le Droit Public de L'Europe, par Mably. Oeuvres,* tom. 6. 334.) Some of these treaties have provided that foreign subjects should be permitted to remain and continue their business, notwithstanding a rupture between the governments, so long as they behave peaceably; (*Treaty of Commerce between Great Britain and France, in 1786, and of Amity and Commerce between Great Britain and the United States, in 1794;*) and where there was no such treaty, the permission has been frequently announced in the very declaration of war. Sir *Michael Foster* (*Discourse of High Treason,* 185, 186) mentions several instances of such declarations; and he says that the aliens were thereby enabled to acquire personal chattels, and to maintain actions for the recovery of their personal rights, in as full a manner as alien friends. The act of congress of *July,* 1798, before alluded to, provides, in cases where there may be no existing treaty, a reasonable time, to be ascertained and declared by the president, to alien enemies resident at the opening of the war, "for the *recovery,* disposal and removal of their goods and effects." This statute may be considered, in this respect, as a true exposition and declaration of the modern law of nations.

The opinion that wars ought not to interfere with the security and collection of debts, has been constantly gaining ground, and the progress of this opinion is worthy of notice, as it will teach us with what equity and liberality, and with what enlarged views of national policy, the question has been treated. A right to confiscate the debts due to the enemy was the rigorous doctrine of the ancient law; but a temporary disability to sue, was all *Grotius* (b. 3. c. 20. s. 16) seemed willing to allow to hostilities. Since his time, continued and successful efforts have been made to strengthen justice, to restrain the intemperance of war, and to promote the intercourse and happiness of mankind. The power to collect debts, notwithstanding the event of war, is not an unusual provision in the conventional law of nations. In the treaty of commerce between *England* and *France,* in 1713, it was provided by the 2d article, that in case of war, the subjects of each power residing in the dominions of the other, should be allowed six months to retire with their property, and in the mean time, should be at full liberty to dispose of the same, "and the subjects on each side were to have and enjoy good and speedy justice, so that during the said space of six months they may be able to recover their goods and effects." So also in the treaty of commerce between *Great Britain* and *Russia,* in 1766, and again in 1797, it was provided, that in case of war, the subjects of each were to be allowed one year to withdraw with their property; and they were also authorized to substitute others to collect their debts for their benefit, "which debts the debtors should be obliged to pay in the same manner as if no such rupture had happened." A similar provision, in substance, was inserted in the treaty between the *United States* and *Russia,* in 1785; and in the treaty of commerce between the *United States* and *Great Britain,* in 1795, the government of each country was prohibited to interfere, either by confiscation or sequestration, with private contracts, and it was expressly declared to be unjust and impolitic, that the debts of individuals should be *impaired* by national differences.

The case before us does not raise the question, nor do we give any opinion in favor of the right of action by aliens who resided in the enemy's country when war was declared, and when the action was commenced. The cases appear to be against such right. But as to aliens who were residents with us when the war broke out, or who have since come to reside here, by a presumed permission, the authorities seem to be decisive. And whether we consider this case in reference to the decisions of the *English* courts, to the act of congress, or to the sense of *European* nations, declared in their treaties, and by their writers on public law, the plea must be overruled; and the plaintiff is entitled to judgment, upon his demurrer.

Judgment for the plaintiff.

59

JACKSON V. ROSE
2 Va. Cas. 34 (1814)

WHITE, J., delivered the opinion of the Court:

This is an action of debt brought by the Plaintiff to recover a penalty inflicted by an Act of Congress to insure the collection of the Revenue of the United States: which penalty, the same Act says, may under circumstances, such as exist in this case, be recovered in a State Court; and the question submitted to the General Court is substantially this: Could Congress Constitutionally give to a State Court, jurisdiction over this case, or can such Court be authorised by an Act of Congress to take cognizance thereof?

The very statement of the question points out its extreme delicacy, and great importance. It involves the great Constitutional rights and powers of the General Government, as well as the rights, Sovereignty, and Independence of the respective State Governments. It calls upon this Court, to mark the limits which separate them from each other, and to make a decision, which may possibly put at issue, upon a great Constitutional point, the Legislature of the United States, and the Supreme Criminal Tribunal of one of the States.

Such a question, involving such consequences, ought to be approached with the utmost circumspection, with the most cool, dispassionate, and impartial investigation, and with a fixed determination, to render such judgment only, as shall be the result of solemn conviction. The Court has not been unmindful of these things: it has approached the subject with those feelings, and with that determination. It has bestowed its best consideration, its deepest reflection

upon it: and after viewing it, in every point of light in which it has been placed by others, or in which the Court has been able to place it, has made up an opinion in which all the Judges present concur, and which it has directed me to pronounce.

But, before that is done, it will be necessary to lay down, and explain, certain principles upon which it is founded. First, it is believed that the Judicial power of any State, or Nation, forms an important part of its Sovereignty, and consists in a right to expound its Laws, to apply them to the various transactions of human affairs as they arise, and to superintend and enforce their execution. And that whosoever is authorised to perform these functions to any extent, has, of necessity, to the same extent, the Judicial power of that State or Nation which authorised him to do so. Secondly, that the Judiciary of one separate and distinct Sovereignty cannot of itself assume, nor can another separate and distinct Sovereignty either authorise, or coerce it to exercise the Judicial powers of such other separate and distinct Sovereignty.

It is indeed true, that the interests of commerce, and the mutual advantages derived to all Nations, by their respectively protecting the rights of property, to the citizens and subjects of each other, whilst residing or trading in their respective territories, have induced civilized Nations generally to permit their Courts to sustain suits brought upon contracts made in foreign countries, and to enforce their execution, according to their true intent and meaning: and, in order to ascertain that, our Courts do permit the Laws of the country where the contract was made, to be proved to the jury, or the Court of Chancery, as the case may be, as facts entering essentially into the substance of the contract. But in doing all this, they do not act by the command, nor under the authority, of the Sovereign of that Nation. Nor are they exercising any portion of its Judicial power. They are only expounding, applying and superintending the execution of the Law of their own State, which authorises that mode of proceeding. And upon the same principle, there can be no doubt but that any contract made, or any civil right arising, under the Laws of the United States, would be enforced in our State Courts, with this additional advantage, that those Laws need not be proved, but would, under the authority of the Constitution, be judicially known to the Judges.

But, though there are the best reasons for permitting our Courts to sustain suits of this description, there is no good reason why one Nation should authorise its Judiciary to carry the Penal Laws of another into execution, and it is believed that no Nation has ever done so, and we have already seen that there is no principle of Universal Law which authorises one Sovereign to empower, or direct the Judiciary of another to do so: such a right can be acquired by compact only: and we shall presently see whether Congress have so acquired it. Without such compact, a fugitive from justice cannot, as a matter of right, be even demanded to be delivered up to the Tribunals of the Nation whose Laws he has violated, much less can he be tried and punished by a foreign tribunal for violating them.

If such a system shall be once adopted, it will introduce a strange kind of Mosaick work into the Judiciary system of Nations. Here, a Code, committing to the flames an Italian for denying the Pope's infallibility: there, the stern Fathers of the Holy Inquisition impaling a poor Turk, because he denies that Mahomet is the Prophet of God: The Judges of Republican Virginia pillorying an Englishman for libelling Royalty, and the Court of King's Bench inflicting the same punishment upon an American for libelling the Government of the United States for the late declaration of war.

Thirdly, that the Government of the United States, although it by no means possesses the entire Sovereignty of this vast Empire, (the great residuum thereof still remaining with the States respectively,) is nevertheless, as to all the purposes for which it was created, and as to all the powers vested therein, unless where it is otherwise provided by the Constitution, completely Sovereign. And that its Sovereignty is an entirely separate and distinct from the Sovereignty of the respective States, as the Sovereignty of one of those States is separate and distinct from the other. So that, (unless as before excepted,) it cannot exercise the powers which belong to the State Governments, nor can any State Government exercise the powers which belong to it: and that there is no one thing to which this principle applies with more strength than to the Revenue of the United States, and things belonging thereto. It being notorious, that a desire to give Congress a complete and entire control over that subject, was the moving principle which called the present Government into existence.

It is admitted, however, that there are some exceptions in the Constitution to this last rule; they are such, however, as prove the rule itself. Thus by the second section of the third Article of the Constitution, among other things, it is declared that the Judicial power of the United States shall extend "to controversies between citizens of different States; between citizens of the same States, claiming lands under the grants of different States." These powers, in the nature of things, belonged to the State Sovereignties, and they were at the adoption of the Constitution, in complete possession of them. Nor could the Courts of the United States, merely as such, by any principle of construction, have claimed them, but there were reasons at that time deemed sufficient to justify the extension of the Judicial power of the United States, and it was extended to them, without, however, taking away the jurisdiction of the State Courts. So that, as respects those matters, the State Courts, and the Courts of the United States have concurrent jurisdiction by compact.

These things being premised, I return to the question: Can Congress, by any Act which it can pass, authorise the State Courts to exercise, or vest in them, any portion of the Judicial power of the United States? more especially that portion of it, which is employed in enforcing its Penal Laws? I shall not stop to prove that the Act in question is, as it respects this case, a Penal Law, or that to enforce the payment of its penalties, in any way or form whatever, would be to explain, apply, and superintend the execution of it. These are self-evident propositions, which would only be obscured by any attempt to elucidate them.

Nor shall I waste much time in considering, whether our Courts can resist an Unconstitutional Law. That question,

as respects our State Laws, has long since been settled in Virginia, and the decisions of her Courts have been acquiesced in by the General Assembly, with that wisdom, and magnanimity which belongs to it. The argument is much stronger as respects the Laws of Congress, the Legislature of a separate and distinct Sovereignty, by whose Laws we are not bound, unless to use the very words of the Constitution, they are "made in pursuance thereof." Were it otherwise; were the State Courts obliged to execute every Law which Congress might pass, without enquiring whether it was, or was not, made in pursuance of the Constitution, it is most manifest that the justly dreaded work of consolidation, would not only be begun, but that in principle it would be completed: and that State Sovereignty, and State Independence would soon cease to exist.

We have seen already that the Government of the United States is, as to the purposes for which it was created, a separate and distinct Sovereignty, having rights, powers, and duties, which it is bound to exercise, and discharge itself, and which it cannot communicate to the States over which it presides, and with which they cannot intermeddle, and that the Judicial power forms a portion, and a most important portion of its Sovereignty. We have seen that there is nothing in Universal Law, or the usage of Nations, which will authorise one Sovereignty to invest its Judicial power, or any part of it, in the Courts of another, or direct them to execute it, more especially that portion of it, which respects its Penal Code.

If then Congress has a right to vest that, or any other portion of the Judicial power of the United States, in the State Courts, it must be in virtue of some compact. But, there is no other instrument from which such a compact can be inferred, but the Constitution of the United States. Let us then see where it has deposited the Judicial power of the General Government; for, where it has placed it, there it must remain.

That instrument does not take the least notice of the State Courts, as respects this subject. But it declares, that "the Judicial power of the United States shall be vested in one Supreme Court, and in such Inferior Courts as Congress may, from time to time, ordain and establish." And by another clause, power is given to Congress "to constitute tribunals inferior to the Supreme Court."

This Judicial power, then, the whole of it, without any exception, is given to this Supreme Court, and those Inferior Courts, to be ordained and established by Congress. It has never yet been contended that Congress can compel, or authorise, the State Courts, or any of them, to perform the functions of this Supreme Court. By what kind of reasoning, then, can it support a claim to exercise such a power with respect to the functions of those Inferior Courts? Did Congress ordain and establish the State Courts? Did it decree their existence? Did it appoint their Judges? Did it institute, did it settle, did it constitute them? Most certainly it has done none of those things. It found them already ordained and established, and finding them so ordained and established, it has, by its Law, directed them to exercise this portion of the Judicial power of the United States.

But, the Judges of these Inferior Courts are to have offices which they are to hold during good behaviour. Now, I take it for granted, that the man who holds an office, is an officer, and an officer, too, of that Government whose business it is the duty of his office to perform. And by the Constitution, "all officers of the United States are to be commissioned by the President," which is not the case with the State Judges.

But, who does the Constitution intend shall decide on the good behaviour of the Judges of those Inferior Courts? Most unquestionably the Senate of the United States, upon impeachment of the House of Representatives. So great an absurdity cannot be supposed, as that the Constitution intended to put the Judicial power of the United States into the hands of Judges, in no way responsible to its Government. Yet no man can pretend that the State Judges can be impeached, and tried by that Government.

Besides, the Constitution of the United States does not provide that the State Judges shall hold their offices during good behaviour. Congress cannot direct that it shall be so, by Law, and in fact some of them are elected for a limited period, and others may be removed by a vote of their State Legislatures: so that if a Law of Congress should be very unpopular in one of those States, the Judges could not execute it, but at the risk of their commissions. Moreover, the Judges of the State Courts are called upon by this Act, to exercise Judicial power which they hold at the will of Congress, and which may be taken from them by the very breath which gave it, and which, it is almost certain, will be taken from them, whenever by a firm and independent exercise of their own judgments, they shall much offend that Honorable Body. So that, under this system, neither the People, nor the Government of the United States would have that security for the uprightness of their Judges which the Constitution contemplates.

But, the Judges of these Inferior Courts are also to receive, for their services, a compensation, which shall not be diminished during their continuance in office, not during the existence of a particular Law, calling for particular services.

From whom are they to receive that compensation? Certainly from the General Government, to which those services are to be rendered. But do the State Judges receive, or are they to receive, any compensation for those services to be rendered to the United States? Every body knows they do not. And we know that if any Judge of this State were to accept of either commission, or compensation, from the General Government, he would by that act vacate his office.

But it is said, that the State Courts do take cognizance of suits brought to enforce contracts made in foreign countries, and that they will take notice of those foreign Laws under the faith of which, such contracts were made, and enforce them agreeably thereto, and that this suit sounds in contract. But, how does it sound in contract? Has the Defendant contracted to pay the amount of this penalty to the Plaintiff? No, it is answered, it is not precisely so; but it is understood to be a principle of Universal Law, that every citizen and subject has entered into an implied contract that he will obey the Laws of his country: that the Laws of his country subject the Defendant to the payment of this penalty, that this suit is founded on that contract, and the State Court has for that reason jurisdiction over it. Indeed! Before we yield our assent, let us see how far this reasoning will carry us. It is sometimes said that an argument which necessarily proves too much, proves nothing. By this same implied contract, every citizen and subject of every Government has agreed to submit his head to the block, or his neck to the cord, whenever the Laws of his country require him to do so. If, therefore, this implied contract will give us jurisdiction over this Penal Law, and justify us in enforcing its sanction, the same principle will give us jurisdiction over the entire Penal Code of every Nation upon earth, which no man will pretend to say we have.

Upon the whole, however painful it may be, and actually it is to us all, to be brought by a sense of duty into conflict with the opinions and Acts of the Legislature of the United States, for which we entertain the highest respect, and the Constitutional Laws of which we feel ourselves bound to obey, and to execute with cheerfulness, when their execution devolves upon us, yet we cannot resist the conviction that this Law is, in this respect, Unconstitutional.

It is the unanimous opinion of this Court, that to assume jurisdiction over this case, would be to exercise a portion of the Judicial power of the United States, which by the Constitution is clearly and distinctly deposited in other hands, and that by doing so, we should prostrate that very instrument which we have taken a solemn oath to support.

The judgment was entered in these words:

"It is the unanimous opinion of the Court, that the State Courts have no right to exercise the Judicial power of the United States, the Constitution having deposited it in other hands, and that to take cognizance of the matter declared for in this case would be to exercise that power. It is therefore decided, that the Law upon the demurrer in the record of the said Case contained, is for the Defendant: which is ordered to be certified."

60

GOUVERNEUR MORRIS TO TIMOTHY PICKERING
22 Dec. 1814
Life 3:322–23

I have received yours of the fifteenth. While I sat in the Convention, my mind was too much occupied by the interests of our country to keep notes of what we had done. Some gentlemen, I was told, passed their evenings in transcribing speeches from shorthand minutes of the day. They can speak positively on matters, of which I have little recollection. My faculties were on the stretch to further our business, remove impediments, obviate objections, and conciliate jarring opinions. All which I can now do is to ask myself what I should do were questions stated anew; for, in all probability, what I should now do would be what I then did, my sentiments and opinions having undergone no essential change in forty years.

Propositions to countenance the issue of paper money, and the consequent violation of contracts, must have met with all the opposition I could make. But, my dear Sir, what can a history of the Constitution avail towards interpreting its provisions. This must be done by comparing the plain import of the words, with the general tenor and object of the instrument. That instrument was written by the fingers, which write this letter. Having rejected redundant and equivocal terms, I believed it to be as clear as our language would permit; excepting, nevertheless, a part of what relates to the judiciary. On that subject, conflicting opinions had been maintained with so much professional astuteness, that it became necessary to select phrases, which expressing my own notions would not alarm others, nor shock their selflove, and to the best of my recollection, this was the only part which passed without cavil.

But, after all, what does it signify, that men should have a written Constitution, containing unequivocal provisions and limitations? The legislative lion will not be entangled in the meshes of a logical net. The legislature will always make the power, which it wishes to exercise, unless it be so organized, as to contain within itself the sufficient check. Attempts to restrain it from outrage, by other means, will only render it more outrageous. The idea of binding legislators by oaths is puerile. Having sworn to exercise the powers granted, according to their true intent and meaning, they will, when they feel a desire to go farther, avoid the shame if not the guilt of perjury, by swearing the true intent and meaning to be, according to their comprehension, that which suits their purpose.

61

AN ACT TO VEST MORE EFFECTUALLY IN THE STATE COURTS AND IN THE DISTRICT COURTS OF THE UNITED STATES JURISDICTION IN THE CASES THEREIN MENTIONED

3 Stat. 244 (1815)

Be it enacted by the Senate and House of Representatives of the United States of America, in Congress assembled, That the respective state or county courts within or next adjoining a collection district established by any act of Congress now in being, or hereafter to be passed for the collection of any direct tax or internal duties of the United States, shall be, and are hereby authorized to take cognisance of all complaints, suits and prosecutions for taxes, duties, fines, penalties and forfeitures arising and payable under any of the acts passed or to be passed as aforesaid, or where bonds are given under the said acts; and the district attorneys of the United States are hereby authorized and directed to appoint by warrant an attorney as their substitute or dep-

uty in all cases where necessary to sue or prosecute for the United States, in any of the said state or county courts within the sphere of whose jurisdiction the said district attorneys do not themselves reside or practise; and the said substitute or deputy shall be sworn or affirmed to the faithful execution of his duty.

SEC. 2. *And be it further enacted,* That the jurisdiction conferred by the foregoing section shall be considered as attaching in the cases therein specified without regard to the amount or sum in controversy, and that it shall be concurrent with the jurisdiction of the district courts of the United States; but may nevertheless be exercised in cases where the fine, penalty, or forfeiture may have been incurred, or the cause of action or complaint have arisen, at a less as well as a greater distance than fifty miles from the nearest place by law established for the holding of a district court of the United States. But in all suits or prosecutions instituted by or on behalf of the United States in any state or county court, the process, proceedings, judgment and execution therein shall not be delayed, suspended or in any way barred or defeated by reason of any law of any state authorizing or directing a stay or suspension of process, proceedings, judgment or execution: *Provided,* That final decrees and judgments in civil actions, passed or rendered in any state court by virtue hereof, may be re-examined in the circuit court of the United States, in the same manner and under the same limitations as are prescribed by the twenty-second section of the act to establish the judicial courts of the United States, passed the twenty-fourth of September, seventeen hundred and eighty-nine.

SEC. 3. *And be it further enacted,* That the state or county courts aforesaid, and the principal or presiding judge of any such court, shall be, and are hereby authorized to exercise all and every power in cases cognisable before them by virtue of this act for the purpose of obtaining a mitigation, or remission of any fine, penalty, or forfeiture, which may be exercised by the judges of the district courts of the United States in cases brought before them by virtue of the law of the United States, passed on the third of March, one thousand seven hundred and ninety-seven, entitled "An act to provide for mitigating or remitting the forfeitures, penalties and disabilities accruing in certain cases therein mentioned," and in the exercise of the authority by this section given to the said state or county courts, or the principal or presiding judge as aforesaid, they shall be governed in every respect by the provisions of the law last mentioned, with this difference only, that instead of notifying the district attorneys of the United States, the said courts, or the presiding judges aforesaid, shall, before exercising said authorities, cause reasonable notice to be given to the substitute or deputy, who may have been appointed to sue or prosecute for the United States, as aforesaid, that he may have an opportunity of showing cause against the mitigation or remission of such fine, penalty or forfeiture.

SEC. 4. *And be it further enacted,* That the district court of the United States shall have cognisance concurrent with the courts and magistrates of the several states, and the circuit courts of the United States, of all suits at common law, where the United States, or any officer thereof, under the authority of any act of Congress, shall sue, although the debt, claim, or other matter in dispute, shall not amount to one hundred dollars.

APPROVED, March 3, 1815.

62

TOWN OF PAWLET V. CLARK
9 Cranch 292 (1815)

March 10th, 1815. (Absent, Todd, J.) STORY, J., delivered the opinion of the court, as follows:—The first question presented in this case is, whether the court has jurisdiction. The plaintiffs claim under a grant from the state of Vermont, and the defendants claim under a grant from the state of New Hampshire, made at the time when the latter state comprehended the whole territory of the former state. The constitution of the United States, among other things, extends the judicial power of the United States to controversies "between citizens of the same state claiming lands under grants of different states." It is argued, that the grant under which the defendants claim is not a grant of a different state, within the meaning of the constitution, because Vermont, at the time of its emanation, was not a distinct government, but was included in the same sovereignty as New Hampshire.

But it seems to us, that there is nothing in this objection. The constitution intended to secure an impartial tribunal for the decision of causes arising from the grants of different states; and it supposed, that a state tribunal might not stand indifferent in a controversy where the claims of its own sovereign were in conflict with those of another sovereign. It had no reference whatsoever to the antecedent situation of the territory, whether included in one sovereignty or another. It simply regarded the fact, whether grants arose under the same or under different states. Now, it is very clear, that although the territory of Vermont was once a part of New Hampshire, yet the state of Vermont, in its sovereign capacity, is not, and never was the same as the state of New Hampshire. The grant of the plaintiffs emanated purely and exclusively from the sovereignty of Vermont; that of the defendants purely and exclusively from the sovereignty of New Hampshire. The sovereign power of New Hampshire remains the same, although it has lost a part of its territory; that of Vermont never existed, until its territory was separated from the jurisdiction of New Hampshire. The circumstance that a part of the territory or population was once under a common sovereign no more makes the states the same, than the circumstance that a part of the members of one corporation constitutes a component part of another corporation, makes the corporation the same. Nor can it be affirmed, in any correct sense, that the grants are of the same state; for the grant of the defendants could not have been made by the state of Vermont, since that state had

not, at that time, any legal existence; and the grant of the plaintiffs could not have been made by New Hampshire, since, at that time, New Hampshire had no jurisdiction or sovereign existence, by the name of Vermont. The case is, therefore, equally within the letter and spirit of the clause of the constitution. It would, indeed, have been a sufficient answer to the objection, that the constitution and laws of the United States, by the admission of Vermont into the Union as a distinct government, had decided that it was a different state from that of New Hampshire.

63

DeLOVIO V. BOIT
7 Fed. Cas. 418, no. 3,776 (C.C.D.Mass. 1815)

STORY, Circuit Justice. This is a libel brought in the district court upon a policy of insurance, alleging it to be a maritime contract, of which that court, as a court of admiralty and maritime jurisdiction, has cognizance. There is a plea to the jurisdiction, and the present question rests solely on the general sufficiency of that plea as a declinatory bar. It has been argued, and now stands for judgment. I shall make no apology for the length of this opinion. The vast importance and novelty of the questions, which are involved in this suit, render it impossible to come to a correct decision without a thorough examination of the whole jurisdiction of the admiralty. I shall, therefore, consider, in the first place, what is the true nature and extent of the ancient jurisdiction of the admiralty; in the next place, how far it has been abridged or altered by statutes, or by common law decisions; and in the last place, what causes are included in the delegation by the constitution to the judicial power of the United States of "all cases of admiralty and maritime jurisdiction."

. . . . .

On the whole, the result of this examination may be summed up in the following propositions. 1. That the jurisdiction of the admiralty, until the statutes of Richard II., extended to all maritime contracts, whether executed at home or abroad, and to all torts, injuries, and offences, on the high seas, and in ports, and havens, as far as the ebb and flow of the tide. 2. That the common law interpretation of these statutes abridges this jurisdiction to things wholly and exclusively done upon the sea. 3. That this interpretation is indefensible, upon principle, and the decisions founded upon it are inconsistent and contradictory. 4. That the interpretation of the same statutes by the admiralty does not abridge any of its ancient jurisdiction, but leaves to it cognizance of all maritime contracts, and all torts, injuries and offences, upon the high sea, and in ports as far the tide ebbs and flows. 5. That this is the true limit, which upon principle would seem to belong to the admiralty; that it is consistent with the language and intent of the statutes; and is supported by analogous reasoning, and public convenience, and a very considerable weight of authority. 6. That under all the circumstances, the courts of law and of admiralty in England are not so tied down by a uniformity of decisions, that they are not at liberty to entertain the question anew, and to settle the doctrines upon their true principles; and that this opinion is supported by some of the best elementary writers in that kingdom.

But whatever may in England be the binding authority of the common law decisions upon this subject, in the United States we are at liberty to re-examine the doctrines, and to construe the jurisdiction of the admiralty upon enlarged and liberal principles. The constitution has delegated to the judicial power of the United States cognizance "of all cases of admiralty and maritime jurisdiction;" and the act of congress (Sept. 24, 1789, c. 20, § 9) has given to the district court "cognizance of all civil causes of admiralty and maritime jurisdiction, including all seizures under laws of impost, navigation or trade, of the United States, where the seizures are made on waters navigable from the sea by vessels of ten or more tons burthen; with their respective districts, as well as upon the high seas."

What is the true interpretation of the clause "all cases of admiralty and maritime jurisdiction?" If we examine the etymology, or received use, of the words "admiralty" and "maritime jurisdiction," we shall find, that they include jurisdiction of all things done upon and relating to the sea, or, in other words, all transactions and proceedings relative to commerce and navigation, and to damages or injuries upon the sea. Cowell, Interpreter, voce "Admiral;" Spel. Gloss. voce "Admiral," sub finem; Godolph. Jur. c. 1; 1 Valin, Comm. 1; Seld. De Dom. Mar. lib. 2, c. 16, p. 160; Stypman, Jus. Marit. par. 1, c. 6, pp. 76, 77; Id. par. 5, c. 1, p. 602; Loccenius, Jus. Marit. lib. 2, c. 2. In all the great maritime nations of Europe, the terms "admiralty jurisdiction" are uniformly applied to the courts exercising jurisdiction over maritime contracts and concerns. We shall find the terms just as familiarly known among the jurists of Scotland, France, Holland and Spain, as of England, and applied to their own courts, possessing substantially the same jurisdiction, as the English admiralty in the reign of Edward the Third. If we pass from the etymology and use of these terms (i. e. "admiralty jurisdiction") in foreign countries, the only expositions of them, that seem to present themselves, are, that they refer, 1. To the jurisdiction of the admiralty as acknowledged in England at the American Revolution; or, 2. At the emigration of our ancestors; or 3. As acknowledged and exercised in the United States at the American Revolution; or, 4. To the ancient and original jurisdiction, inherent in the admiralty of England by virtue of its general organization.

As to the first exposition, it is difficult to perceive upon what ground it can be reasonably maintained, for it would enlarge and limit the jurisdiction by the provisions of statutes, which have been enacted for the government and regulation of the high court of admiralty, and which proprio vigore do not extend to the colonies. It would further involve qualifications of the jurisdiction, which are perfectly arbitrary in themselves, inapplicable to our situation, and contradictory to the commissions and practice of the vice admiralty colonial courts. Even if this exposition were to be adopted, are we to be governed by the doctrines of the common law, or of the admiralty? I am not aware of any superior sanctity in the decisions at common law upon the subject of the jurisdiction of other courts (to which at least they bore no good will), which should entitle them to outweigh the very able and learned decisions of the great civilians of the admiralty. And where could we so properly search for information on this subject, as in the works of those jurists, who have adorned the maritime courts from age to age, and made its jurisdiction the pride and study of their lives?

The second exposition is liable to the same objections; for it is clear, that the statutes of Richard do not extend in terms to the colonies, and it is quite certain, that they were not included in any supposed mischiefs, for they then had no existence. Besides, it is a very material consideration, that, at the emigration of our ancestors, the contest between the courts of common law and the admiralty was at its height; and very soon after (in 1632) it was, by the agreement of the twelve judges, decided in favor of the admiralty. And here again it may be asked, whose doctrines are to be adopted, those of the common law or of the admiralty?

The third exposition requires an examination of the authority and powers of the vice admiralty courts in the United States under the colonial government. In some of the states, and probably in all, the crown established, or reserved to itself the right to establish, admiralty courts; and the nature and the extent of their jurisdictions depended upon the commission of the crown, and upon acts of Parliament conferring additional authorities. The commissions of the crown gave the courts, which were established, a most ample jurisdiction over all maritime contracts, and over torts and injuries, as well in ports as upon the high seas. And acts of parliament enlarged, or rather recognised, this jurisdiction by giving or confirming cognizance of all seizures for contraventions of the revenue laws. The Fabius, 2 C. Rob. Adm. 245. Tested, therefore, by this exposition, the admiralty jurisdiction of the United States would be as large, as its most strenuous advocates ever contended for.

The clause however of the constitution not only confers admiralty jurisdiction, but the word "maritime" is superadded, seemingly ex industria, to remove every latent doubt. "Cases of maritime jurisdiction" must include all maritime contracts, torts and injuries, which are in the understanding of the common law, as well as of the admiralty, "causae civiles et maritimae." In this view there is a peculiar property in the incorporation of the term "maritime" into the constitution. The disputes and discussions, respecting what the admiralty jurisdiction was, could not but be well known to the framers of that instrument. Montgomery v. Henry, 1 Dall. [1 U. S.] 149; Talbot v. Commanders and Owners of Three Brigs, Id. 95. One party sought to limit it by locality; another by the subject matter. It was wise, therefore, to dissipate all question by giving cognizance of all "cases of maritime jurisdiction," or, what is precisely equivalent, of all maritime cases. Upon any other construction, the word "maritime" would be mere tautology; but in this sense it has a peculiar and appropriate force. And Mr. Justice Winchester (speaking with reference to contracts) has very correctly observed, that "neither the judicial act nor the constitution, which it follows, limit the admiralty jurisdiction of the district court in any respect to place. It is bounded only by the nature of the cause, over which it is to decide." Stevens v. The Sandwich [Case No. 13,409]. The language of the constitution will therefore warrant the most liberal interpretation; and it may not be unfit to hold, that it had reference to that maritime jurisdiction, which commercial convenience, public policy, and national rights, have contributed to establish, with slight local differences, over all Europe; that jurisdiction, which, under the name of consular courts, first established itself upon the shores of the Mediterranean, and, from the general equity and simplicity of its proceedings, soon commended itself to all the maritime states; that jurisdiction, in short, which, collecting the wisdom of the civil law, and combining it with the customs and usages of the sea, produced the venerable Consolato del Mare, and still continues in its decisions to regulate the commerce, the intercourse, and the warfare of mankind. Zouch, c. 1, p. 87, etc.; Seld. ad Fletam, c. 8, § 5; Rob. Collect. Marit. 105, note; Le Guidon, c. 3; 1 Emer. 21. Of this great system of maritime law it may be truly said, "Non erit alia lex Romae, alia Athenis, alia nunc, alia posthac; sed et omnes gentes, et omni tempore, una lex et sempiterna et immortalis, continebit." Cic. Frag. de Repub. lib. 3 (Editio Bost. 1817, tom. 17, p. 186).

At all events, there is no solid reason for construing the terms of the constitution in a narrow and limited sense, or for ingrafting upon them the restrictions of English statutes, or decisions at common law founded on those statutes, which were sometimes dictated by jealousy, and sometimes by misapprehension, which are often contradictory, and rarely supported by any consistent principle. The advantages resulting to the commerce and navigation of the United States, from a uniformity of rules and decisions in all maritime questions, authorize us to believe that national policy, as well as juridical logic, require the clause of the constitution to be so construed, as to embrace all maritime contracts, torts and injuries, or, in other words, to embrace all those causes, which originally and inherently belonged to the admiralty, before any statutable restriction. And most cordially do I subscribe to the opinion of the learned Mr. Justice Winchester, in the case already cited (Stevens v. The Sandwich [Case No. 13,409]), "that the statutes of Richard II. have received in England a construction, which must at all times prohibit their extension to this country," and "that no principles can be extracted from the adjudged cases in England, which will explain or support the admiralty jurisdiction, independent of the statutes or the works of jurists, who have written on the general subject." Indeed the doctrine that would extend the statutes of Richard to the present judicial power of the United States seems little short of an absurdity. It is incorporating into the text of the constitution an exception, not only unauthorized by its terms, but wholly inappropriate in phraseology to any other realm than England. We have not as yet any "admirals or their deputies;" we do not refer their jurisdiction to the reign of "the most noble King Edward the Third;" much less would an American citizen dream, that the constitution authorized the admiralty "to arrest ships in the great flotes for the great voyages of the king and of the realm;" and "to have jurisdiction upon the said flotes during the said voyages only," and "saving always to the king all manner of forfeitures and profits thereof coming," and "to the lords, cities and boroughs their liberties and franchises."

There are moreover decisions of the courts of the United States, which completely establish the proposition, that the statutes of Richard, and the common law construction of them, do not attach to this clause of the constitution. We have already seen, that the courts of common law, after these statutes, held, that the admiralty had no jurisdiction of things done within the ebb and flow of the tide, in ports, creeks, and havens. It has, notwithstanding, been repeatedly and solemnly held by the supreme court, that all seizures under laws of impost, navigation and trade, on waters navigable from the sea by vessels of ten or more tons burthen, as well within ports and districts of the United States, as upon the high seas, are causes of admiralty and maritime jurisdiction. U. S. v. La Vengeance, 3 Dall. [3 U. S.] 297; Same v. The Sally, 2 Cranch [6 U. S.] 406; Same v. The Betsey and Charlotte, 4 Cranch [8 U. S.] 443. This limitation, as to the place of seizure, is prescribed by an act of congress (Act Sept. 24, 1789, c. 20, § 9 [1 Stat. 76]), but it is perfectly clear, that congress have no authority to include cases within the admiralty jurisdiction, which the terms of the constitution did not warrant. And the ground is made stronger by the consideration, that the right of trial by jury is preserved by the constitution in all suits at common law, where the value in controversy exceeds twenty dollars; and by the statute, this right is excluded in all cases of admiralty and maritime jurisdiction. It is therefore utterly impossible to reconcile these decisions which in my humble judgment are founded in the most accurate and just conceptions of the admiralty jurisdiction, with the narrow and perplexed doctrines of the common law. The argument then, that attempts to engraft them upon the constitution, is wholly untenable.

On the whole, I am, without the slightest hesitation, ready to pronounce, that the delegation of cognizance of "all civil cases of admiralty and maritime jurisdiction" to the courts of the United States comprehends all maritime contracts, torts, and injuries. The latter branch is necessarily bounded by locality; the former extends over all contracts, (wheresoever they may be made or executed, or whatsoever may be the form of the stipulations,) which relate to the navigation, business or commerce of the sea.

The next inquiry is, what are properly to be deemed "maritime contracts." Happily in this particular there is little room for controversy. All civilians and jurists agree, that in this appellation are included, among other things, charter parties, affreightments, marine hypothecations, contracts for maritime service in the building, repairing, supplying, and navigating ships; contracts between part owners of ships; contracts and quasi contracts respecting averages, contributions and jettisons; and, what is more material to our present purpose, policies of insurance. S. P. Johnson, J., in Croudson v. Leonard, 4 Cranch [8 U. S.]

434; Cleirac, Le Guidon, c. 1, p. 109; Id. c. 3, p. 124; Id. Jurisd. de la Marine, p. 191; 1 Valin, Comm. 112, 120, etc., 127, etc.; 2 Emer. 319; Godolph. 43; Zouch, 90, 92; Eaton, 69, etc., 295, etc.; Malyne, Lex Merc., 303; Id., Collection of Sea Laws, c. 2, p. 47; Consol. del Mare, c. 22; 2 Brown, Adm. c. 4, p. 71; 4 Bl. Comm. 67; Stevens v. The Sandwich [supra]; Targa, Reflex. c. 1. And in point of fact the admiralty courts of other foreign countries have exercised jurisdiction over policies of insurance, as maritime contracts; and a similar claim has been uniformly asserted on the part of the admiralty of England. 2 Boucher, Consol. del Mare, p. 730; 1 Valin, Comm. 120; 2 Emer. 319; Roccus de Assec. note 80; 2 Brown, Adm. 80; Zouch. 92, 102; Molloy, bk. 2, c. 7, § 18. There is no more reason why the admiralty should have cognizance of bottomry instruments, as maritime contracts, than of policies of insurance. Both are executed on land, and both intrinsically respect maritime risks, injuries and losses.

My judgment accordingly is, that policies of insurance are within (though not exclusively within) the admiralty and maritime jurisdiction of the United States. I therefore overrule the plea to the jurisdiction, and assign the respondent to answer peremptorily upon the merits.

In making this decree, I am fully aware, that from its novelty it is likely to be put to the question with more than usual zeal; nor can I pretend to conjecture, how far a superior tribunal may deem it fit to entertain the principles, which I have felt it my solemn duty to avow and support. Whatever may be the event of this judgment, I shall console myself with the memorable words of Lord Nottingham, in the great case of the Duke of Norfolk, 3 Ch. Cas. 52: "I have made several decrees, since I have had the honor to sit in this place, which have been reversed in another place; and I was not ashamed to make them, nor sorry when they were reversed by others."

64

CORPORATION OF NEW ORLEANS v. WINTER

1 Wheat. 91 (1816)

MARSHALL, Ch. J., delivered the opinion of the court, and, after stating the facts, proceeded as follows:

The proceedings of the court, therefore, is arrested *in limine*, by a question respecting its jurisdiction. In the case of Hepburn & Dundas v. Ellzey, this court determined, on mature consideration, that a citizen of the district of Columbia could not maintain a suit in the circuit court of the United States. That opinion is still retained.

It has been attempted to distinguish a *Territory* from the district of Columbia; but the court is of opinion, that this distinction cannot be maintained. They may differ in many respects, but neither of them is a state, in the sense in which that term is used in the constitution. Every reason assigned for the opinion of the court, that a citizen of Co-

lumbia was not capable of suing in the courts of the United States, under the Judiciary Act, is equally applicable to a citizen of a territory. Gabriel Winter, then, being a citizen of the Mississippi Territory, was incapable of maintaining a suit alone in the circuit court of Louisiana. Is his case mended by being associated with others who are capable of suing in that court? In the case of Strawbridge et al. v. Curtis et al., it was decided, that where a joint interest is prosecuted, the jurisdiction cannot be sustained, unless each individual be entitled to claim that jurisdiction. In this case it has been doubted, whether the parties might elect to sue jointly or severally. However this may be, having elected to sue jointly, the court is incapable of distinguishing their case, so far as respects jurisdiction, from one in which they were compelled to unite. The circuit court of Louisiana, therefore, had no jurisdiction of the cause, and their judgment must, on that account, be reversed, and the petition dismissed.

65

MARTIN v. HUNTER'S LESSEE

1 Wheat. 304 (1816)

March 20th, 1816. STORY, J., delivered the opinion of the court.—This is a writ of error from the court of appeals of Virginia, founded upon the refusal of that court to obey the mandate of this court, requiring the judgment rendered in this very cause, at February term 1813, to be carried into due execution. The following is the judgment of the court of appeals rendered on the mandate: "The court is unanimously of opinion, that the appellate power of the supreme court of the United States does not extend to this court, under a sound construction of the constitution of the United States; that so much of the 25th section of the act of congress to establish the judicial courts of the United States, as extends the appellate jurisdiction of the supreme court to this court, is not in pursuance of the constitution of the United States; that the writ of error, in this cause, was improvidently allowed, under the authority of that act; that the proceedings thereon in the supreme court were *coram non judice*, in relation to this court, and that obedience to its mandate be declined by the court."

The questions involved in this judgment are of great importance and delicacy. Perhaps, it is not too much to affirm, that, upon their right decision, rest some of the most solid principles which have hitherto been supposed to sustain and protect the constitution itself. The great respectability, too, of the court whose decisions we are called upon to review, and the entire deference which we entertain for the learning and ability of that court, add much to the difficulty of the task which has so unwelcomely fallen upon us. It is, however, a source of consolation, that we have had the assistance of most able and learned arguments to aid our inquiries; and that the opinion which is now to be pronounced has been weighed with every solicitude to come to a correct result, and matured after solemn deliberation.

Before proceeding to the principal questions, it may not be unfit to dispose of some preliminary considerations which have grown out of the arguments at the bar.

The constitution of the United States was ordained and established, not by the states in their sovereign capacities, but emphatically, as the preamble of the constitution declares, by "the People of the United States." There can be no doubt, that it was competent to the people to invest the general government with all the powers which they might deem proper and necessary; to extend or restrain these powers according to their own good pleasure, and to give them a paramount and supreme authority. As little doubt can there be, that the people had a right to prohibit to the states the exercise of any powers which were, in their judgment, incompatible with the objects of the general compact; to make the powers of the state governments, in given cases, subordinate to those of the nation, or to reserve to themselves those sovereign authorities which they might not choose to delegate to either. The constitution was not, therefore, necessarily carved out of existing state sovereignties, nor a surrender of powers already existing in state institutions, for the powers of the states depend upon their own constitutions; and the people of every state had the right to modify and restrain them, according to their own views of policy or principle. On the other hand, it is perfectly clear, that the sovereign powers vested in the state governments, by their respective constitutions, remained unaltered and unimpaired, except so far as they were granted to the government of the United States. These deductions do not rest upon general reasoning, plain and obvious as they seem to be. They have been positively recognised by one of the articles in amendment of the constitution, which declares, that "the powers not delegated to the United States by the constitution, nor prohibited by it to the states, are reserved to the states respectively, or to the people."

The government, then, of the United States can claim no powers which are not granted to it by the constitution, and the powers actually granted, must be such as are expressly given, or given by necessary implication. On the other hand, this instrument, like every other grant, is to have a reasonable construction, according to the import of its terms; and where a power is expressly given, in general terms, it is not to be restrained to particular cases, unless that construction grow out of the context, expressly, or by necessary implication. The words are to be taken in their natural and obvious sense, and not in a sense unreasonably restricted or enlarged.

The constitution unavoidably deals in general language. It did not suit the purposes of the people, in framing this great charter of our liberties, to provide for minute specifications of its powers, or to declare the means by which those powers should be carried into execution. It was foreseen, that this would be perilous and difficult, if not an impracticable, task. The instrument was not intended to provide merely for the exigencies of a few years, but was to endure through a long lapse of ages, the events of which were locked up in the inscrutable purposes of Providence. It could not be foreseen, what new changes and modifications of power might be indispensable to effectuate the general objects of the charter; and restrictions and specifications, which, at the present, might seem salutary, might, in the end, prove the overthrow of the system itself. Hence, its powers are expressed in general terms, leaving to the legislature, from time to time, to adopt its own means to effectuate legitimate objects, and to mould and model the exercise of its powers, as its own wisdom, and the public interests, should require.

With these principles in view, principles in respect to which no difference of opinion ought to be indulged, let us now proceed to the interpretation of the constitution, so far as regards the great points in controversy.

The third article of the constitution is that which must principally attract our attention. The 1st section declares, "the judicial power of the United States shall be vested in one supreme court, and in such other inferior courts as the congress may, from time to time, ordain and establish." The 2d section declares, that "the judicial power shall extend to all cases in law or equity, arising under this constitution, the laws of the United States, and the treaties made, or which shall be made, under their authority; to all cases affecting ambassadors, other public ministers and consuls; to all cases of admiralty and maritime jurisdiction; to controversies to which the United States shall be a party; to controversies between two or more states; between a state and citizens of another state; between citizens of different states; between citizens of the same state; claiming lands under the grants of different states; and between a state, or the citizens thereof, and foreign states, citizens or subjects." It then proceeds to declare, that "in all cases affecting ambassadors, other public ministers and consuls, and those in which a state shall be a party, the supreme court shall have original jurisdiction. In all the other cases before mentioned, the supreme court shall have appellate jurisdiction, both as to law and fact, with such exceptions, and under such regulations, as the congress shall make."

Such is the language of the article creating and defining the judicial power of the United States. It is the voice of the whole American people, solemnly declared, in establishing one great department of that government which was, in many respects, national, and in all, supreme. It is a part of the very same instrument which was to act, not merely upon individuals, but upon states; and to deprive them altogether of the exercise of some powers of sovereignty, and to restrain and regulate them in the exercise of others.

Let this article be carefully weighed and considered. The language of the article throughout is manifestly designed to be mandatory upon the legislature. Its obligatory force is so imperative, that congress could not, without a violation of its duty, have refused to carry it into operation. The judicial power of the United States *shall* be vested (not *may* be vested) in one supreme court, and in such inferior courts as congress may, from time to time, ordain and establish. Could congress have lawfully refused to create a supreme court, or to vest in it the constitutional jurisdiction? "The judges, both of the supreme and inferior courts, shall hold their offices during good behavior, and shall, at stated times, receive, for their services, a compensation which shall not be diminished during their continuance in office." Could congress create or limit any other tenure of the judicial office? Could they refuse to pay, at stated times, the stipulated salary, or diminish it during the continuance in office? But one answer can be given to these questions: it must be in the negative. The object of the constitution was to establish three great departments of government; the legislative, the executive and the judicial departments. The first was to pass laws, the second, to approve and execute them, and the third, to expound and enforce them. Without the latter, it would be impossible to carry into effect some of the express provisions of the constitution. How, otherwise, could crimes against the United States be tried and punished? How could causes between two states be heard and determined? The judicial power must, therefore, be vested in some court, by congress; and to suppose, that it was not an obligation binding on them, but might, at their pleasure, be omitted or declined, is to suppose, that, under the sanction of the constitution, they might defeat the constitution itself; a construction which would lead to such a result cannot be sound.

The same expression, "shall be vested," occurs in other parts of the constitution, in defining the powers of the other co-ordinate branches of the government. The first article declares that "all legislative powers herein granted shall be vested in a congress of the United States." Will it be contended that the legislative power is not absolutely vested? that the words merely refer to some future act, and mean only that the legislative power may hereafter be vested? The second article declares that "the executive power shall be vested in a president of the United States of America." Could congress vest it in any other person; or, is it to await their good pleasure, whether it is to vest at all? It is apparent, that such a construction, in either case, would be utterly inadmissible. Why, then, is it entitled to a better support, in reference to the judicial department?

If, then, it is a duty of congress to vest the judicial power of the United States, it is a duty to vest the whole judicial power. The language, if imperative as to one part, is imperative as to all. If it were otherwise, this anomaly would exist, that congress might successively refuse to vest the jurisdiction in any one class of cases enumerated in the constitution, and thereby defeat the jurisdiction as to all; for the constitution has not singled out any class on which congress are bound to act in preference to others.

The next consideration is, as to the courts in which the judicial power shall be vested. It is manifest, that a supreme court must be established; but whether it be equally obligatory to establish inferior courts, is a question of some difficulty. If congress may lawfully omit to establish inferior courts, it might follow, that in some of the enumerated cases, the judicial power could nowhere exist. The supreme court can have original jurisdiction in two classes of cases, only, viz., in cases affecting ambassadors, other public ministers and consuls, and in cases in which a state is a party. Congress cannot vest any portion of the judicial power of the United States, except in courts ordained and established by itself; and if in any of the cases enumerated in the constitution, the state courts did not then possess jurisdiction, the appellate jurisdiction of the supreme court (admitting that it could act on state courts) could not reach those cases, and consequently, the injunction of the constitution, that the judicial power "shall be vested," would be disobeyed. It would seem, therefore, to follow, that congress are bound to create some inferior courts, in which to vest all that jurisdiction which, under the constitution, is exclusively vested in the United States, and of which the supreme court cannot take original cognisance. They might establish one or more inferior courts; they might parcel out the jurisdiction among such courts, from time to time, at their own pleasure. But the whole judicial power of the United States should be, at all times, vested, either in an original or appellate form, in some courts created under its authority.

This construction will be fortified by an attentive examination of the second section of the third article. The words are "the judicial power shall extend," &c. Much minute and elaborate criticism has been employed upon these words. It has been argued, that they are equivalent to the words "may extend," and that "extend" means to widen to new cases not before within the scope of the power. For the reasons which have been already stated, we are of opinion, that the words are used in an imperative sense; they import an absolute grant of judicial power. They cannot have a relative signification applicable to powers already granted; for the American people had not made any previous grant. The constitution was for a new government, organized with new substantive powers, and not a mere supplementary charter to a government already existing. The confederation was a compact between states; and its structure and powers were wholly unlike those of the national government. The constitution was an act of the people of the United States to supersede the confederation, and not to be engrafted on it, as a stock through which it was to receive life and nourishment.

If, indeed, the relative signification could be fixed upon the term "extend," it could not (as we shall hereafter see) subserve the purposes of the argument in support of which it has been adduced. This imperative sense of the words "shall extend," is strengthened by the context. It is declared, that "in all cases affecting ambassadors, &c., that the supreme court shall have original jurisdiction." Could congress withhold original jurisdiction in these cases from the supreme court? The clause proceeds—"in all the other cases before mentioned the supreme court shall have appellate jurisdiction, both as to law and fact, with such exceptions, and under such regulations, as the congress shall make." The very exception here shows that the framers of the constitution used the words in an imperative sense. What necessity could there exist for this exception, if the preceding words were not used in that sense? Without such exception, congress would, by the preceding words, have possessed a complete power to regulate the appellate jurisdiction, if the langauge were only equivalent to the words "may have" appellate jurisdiction. It is apparent, then, that the exception was intended as a limitation upon the preceding words, to enable congress to regulate and restrain the appellate power, as the public interests might, from time to time, require.

Other clauses in the constitution might be brought in aid of this construction; but a minute examination of them cannot be necessary, and would occupy too much time. It will be found, that whenever a particular object is to be effected, the language of the constitution is always imperative, and cannot be disregarded, without violating the first principles of public duty. On the other hand, the legislative powers are given in language which implies discretion, as from the nature of legislative power such a discretion must ever be exercised.

It being, then, established, that the language of this clause is imperative, the question is, as to the cases to which it shall apply. The answer is found in the constitution itself. The judicial power shall extend to all the cases enumerated in the constitution. As the mode is not limited, it may extend to all such cases, in any form, in which judicial power may be exercised. It may, therefore, extend to them in the shape of original or appellate jurisdiction, or both; for there is nothing in the nature of the cases which binds to the exercise of the one in preference to the other.

In what cases (if any) is this judicial power exclusive, or exclusive, at the election of congress? It will be observed, that there are two classes of cases enumerated in the constitution, between which a distinction seems to be drawn. The first class includes cases arising under the constitution, laws and treaties of the United States; cases affecting ambassadors, other public ministers and consuls, and cases of admiralty and maritime jurisdiction. In this class, the expression is, and that the judicial power shall extend to all cases; but in the subsequent part of the clause, which embraces all the other cases of national cognisance, and forms the second class, the word "all" is dropped, seemingly *ex industriâ*. Here, the judicial authority is to extend to controversies (not to all controversies) to which the United States shall be a party, &c. From this difference of phraseology, perhaps, a difference of constitutional intention may, with propriety, be inferred. It is hardly to be presumed, that the variation in the language could have been accidental. It must have been the result of some determinate reason; and it is not very difficult to find a reason sufficient to support the apparent change of intention. In respect to the first class, it may well have been the intention of the framers of the constitution imperatively to extend the judicial power, either in an original or appellate form, to *all* cases; and in the latter class, to leave it to congress to qualify the jurisdiction, original or appellate, in such manner as public policy might dictate.

The vital importance of all the cases enumerated in the first class to the national sovereignty, might warrant such a distinction. In the first place, as to cases arising under the constitution, laws and treaties of the United States. Here, the state courts could not ordinarily possess a direct jurisdiction. The jurisdiction over such cases could not exist in the state courts, previous to the adoption of the constitution, and it could not afterwards be directly conferred on them; for the constitution expressly requires the judicial power to be vested in courts ordained and established by the United States. This class of cases would embrace civil as well as criminal jurisdiction, and affect, not only our internal policy, but our foreign relations. It would, therefore, be perilous to restrain it in any manner whatsoever, inasmuch, as it might hazard the national safety. The same remarks may be urged as to cases affecting ambassadors, other public ministers and consuls, who are emphatically placed under the guardianship of the law of nations; and as to cases of admiralty and maritime jurisdiction, the admiralty jurisdiction embraces all questions of prize and salvage, in the correct adjudication of which foreign nations are deeply interested; it embraces also maritime torts, contracts and offences, in which the principles of the law and comity of nations often form an essential inquiry. All these cases, then, enter into the national policy, affect the national rights, and may compromit the national sovereignty. The original or appellate jurisdiction ought not, therefore, to be restrained, but should be commensurate with the mischiefs intended to be remedied, and of course, should extend to all cases whatsoever.

A different policy might well be adopted in reference to the second class of cases; for although it might be fit, that the judicial power should extend to all controversies to which the United States should be a party, yet this power might not have been imperatively given, lest it should imply a right to take cognisance of original suits brought against the United States as defendants in their own courts. It might not have been deemed proper to submit the sovereignty of the United States, against their own will, to judicial cognisance, either to enforce rights or to prevent wrongs; and as to the other cases of the second class, they might well be left to be exercised under the exceptions and regulations which congress might, in their wisdom, choose to apply. It is also worthy of remark, that congress seem, in a good degree, in the establishment of the present judicial system, to have adopted this distinction. In the first class of cases, the jurisdiction is not limited, except by the subject-matter; in second, it is made materially to depend upon the value in controversy.

We do not, however, profess to place any implicit reliance upon the distinction which has here been stated and endeavored to be illustrated. It has the rather been brought into view, in deference to the legislative opinion, which has so long acted upon, and enforced, this distinction. But there is, certainly, vast weight in the argument which has been urged, that the constitution is imperative upon congress to vest all the judicial power of the United States, in the shape of original jurisdiction, in the supreme and inferior courts created under its own authority. At all events, whether the one construction or the other prevail, it is manifest, that the judicial power of the United States is, unavoidably, in some cases, exclusive of all state authority, and in all others, may be made so, at the election of congress. No part of the criminal jurisdiction of the United States can, consistently with the constitution, be delegated to state tribunals. The admiralty and maritime jurisdiction is of the same exclusive cognisance; and it can only be in those cases where, previous to the constitution, state tribunals possessed jurisdiction, independent of national authority, that they can now constitutionally exercise a concurrent jurisdiction. Congress, throughout the judicial act, and particularly in the 9th, 11th and 13th sections, have legislated upon the supposition, that in all the cases to which the judicial powers of the United States extended, they might rightfully vest exclusive jurisdiction in their own courts.

But, even admitting that the language of the constitution is not mandatory, and that congress may constitutionally omit to vest the judicial power in courts of the United States, it cannot be denied, that when it is vested, it may be exercised to the utmost constitutional extent.

This leads us to the consideration of the great question, as to the nature and extent of the appellate jurisdiction of the United States. We have already seen, that appellate jurisdiction is given by the constitution to the supreme court, in all cases where it has not original jurisdiction; subject, however, to such exceptions and regulations as congress may prescribe. It is, therefore, capable of embracing every case enumerated in the constitution, which is not exclusively to be decided by way of original jurisdiction. But the exercise of appellate jurisdiction is far from being limited, by the terms of the constitution, to the supreme court. There can be no doubt, that congress may create a succession of inferior tribunals, in each of which it may vest appellate as well as original jurisdiction. The judicial power is delegated by the constitution, in the most general terms, and may, therefore, be exercised by congress, under every variety of form of appellate or original jurisdiction. And as there is nothing in the constitution which restrains or limits this power, it must, therefore, in all other cases, subsist in the utmost latitude of which, in its own nature, it is susceptible.

As, then, by the terms of the constitution, the appellate jurisdiction is not limited as to the supreme court, and as to this court, it may be exercised in all other cases than those of which it has original cognisance, what is there to restrain its exercise over state tribunals, in the enumerated cases? The appellate power is not limited by the terms of the third article to any particular courts. The words are, "the judicial power (which includes appellate power) shall extend to all cases," &c., and "in all other cases before mentioned the supreme court shall have appellate jurisdiction." It is the case, then, and not the court, that gives the jurisdiction. If the judicial power extends to the case, it will be in vain to search in the letter of the constitution for any qualification as to the tribunal where it depends. It is incumbent, then, upon those who assert such a qualification, to show its existence, by necessary implication. If the text be clear and distinct, no restriction upon its plain and obvious import ought to be admitted, unless the inference be irresistible.

If the constitution meant to limit the appellate jurisdiction to cases pending in the courts of the United States, it would necessarily follow, that the jurisdiction of these courts would, in all the cases enumerated in the constitu-

tion, be exclusive of state tribunals. How, otherwise, could the jurisdiction extend to *all* cases arising under the constitution, laws and treaties of the United States, or to *all* cases of admiralty and maritime jurisdiction? If some of these cases might be entertained by state tribunals, and no appellate jurisdiction as to them should exist, then the appellate power would not extend to *all*, but to *some*, cases. If state tribunals might exercise concurrent jurisdiction over all or some of the other classes of cases in the constitution, without control, then the appellate jurisdiction of the United States might, as to such cases, have no real existence, contrary to the manifest intent of the constitution. Under such circumstances, to give effect to the judicial power, it must be construed to be exclusive; and this not only when the *casus foederis* should arise directly, but when it should arise, incidentally, in cases pending in state courts. This construction would abridge the jurisdiction of such courts far more than has been ever contemplated in any act of congress.

On the other hand, if, as has been contended, a discretion be vested in congress, to establish, or not to establish, inferior courts, at their own pleasure, and congress should not establish such courts, the appellate jurisdiction of the supreme court would have nothing to act upon, unless it could act upon cases pending in the state courts. Under such circumstances, it must be held, that the appellate power would extend to state courts; for the constitution is peremptory, that it shall extend to certain enumerated cases, which cases could exist in no other courts. Any other construction, upon this supposition, would involve this strange contradiction, that a discretionary power, vested in congress, and which they might rightfully omit to exercise, would defeat the absolute injunctions of the constitution in relation to the whole appellate power.

But it is plain, that the framers of the constitution did contemplate that cases within the judicial cognisance of the United States, not only might, but would, arise in the state courts, in the exercise of their ordinary jurisdiction. With this view, the sixth article declares, that "this constitution, and the laws of the United States which shall be made in pursuance thereof, and all treaties made, or which shall be made, under the authority of the United States, shall be the supreme law of the land, and the judges in every state shall be bound thereby, anything in the constitution or laws of any state to the contrary notwithstanding." It is obvious, that this obligation is imperative upon the state judges, in their official, and not merely in their private, capacities. From the very nature of their judicial duties, they would be called upon to pronounce the law applicable to the case in judgment. They were not to decide merely according to the laws or constitution of the state, but according to the constitution, laws and treaties of the United States—"the supreme law of the land."

A moment's consideration will show us the necessity and propriety of this provision, in cases where the jurisdiction of the state courts is unquestionable. Suppose, a contract for the payment of money is made between citizens of the same state, and performance thereof is sought in the courts of that state; no person can doubt, that the jurisdiction completely and exclusively attaches, in the first instance, to such courts. Suppose, at the trial, the defendant sets up in his defence a tender under a state law, making paper-money a good tender, or a state law, impairing the obligation of such contract, which law, if binding, would defeat the suit. The constitution of the United States has declared, that no state shall make any thing but gold or silver coin a tender in payment of debts, or pass a law impairing the obligation of contracts. If congress shall not have passed a law providing for the removal of such a suit to the courts of the United States, must not the state court proceed to hear and determine it? Can a mere plea in defence be, of itself, a bar to further proceedings, so as to prohibit an inquiry into its truth or legal propriety, when no other tribunal exists to whom judicial cognisance of such cases is confided? Suppose, an indictment for a crime, in a state court, and the defendant should allege in his defence, that the crime was created by an *ex post facto* act of the state, must not the state court, in the exercise of a jurisdiction which has already rightfully attached, have a right to pronounce on the validity and sufficiency of the defence? It would be extremely difficult, upon any legal principles, to give a negative answer to these inquiries. Innumerable instances of the same sort might be stated in illustration of the position; and unless the state courts could sustain jurisdiction in such cases, this clause of the sixth article would be without meaning or effect, and public mischiefs, of a most enormous magnitude, would inevitably ensue.

It must, therefore, be conceded, that the constitution not only contemplated, but meant to provide for cases within the scope of the judicial power of the United States, which might yet depend before state tribunals. It was foreseen, that in the exercise of their oridinary jurisdiction, state courts would incidentally take cognisance of cases arising under the constitution, the laws and treaties of the United States. Yet, to all these cases, the judicial power, by the very terms of the constitution, is to extend. It cannot extend, by original jurisdiction, if that was already rightfully and exclusively attached in the state courts, which (as has been already shown) may occur; it must, therefore, extend by appellate jurisdiction, or not at all. It would seem to follow, that the appellate power of the United States must, in such cases, extend to state tribunals; and if, in such cases, there is no reason why it should not equally attach upon all others, within the purview of the constitution.

It has been argued, that such an appellate jurisdiction over state courts is inconsistent with the genius of our governments, and the spirit of the constitution. That the latter was never designed to act upon state sovereignties, but only upon the people, and that if the power exists, it will materially impair the sovereignty of the states, and the independence of their courts. We cannot yield to the force of this reasoning; it assumes principles which we cannot admit, and draws conclusions to which we do not yield our assent.

It is a mistake, that the constitution was not designed to operate upon states, in their corporate capacities. It is crowded with provisions which restrain or annul the sovereignty of the states, in some of the highest branches of their prerogatives. The tenth section of the first article contains a long list of disabilities and prohibitions imposed upon the states. Surely, when such essential portions of state sovereignty are taken away, or prohibited to be exercised, it cannot be correctly asserted, that the constitution does not act upon the states. The language of the constitution is also imperative upon the states, as to the performance of many duties. It is imperative upon the state legislatures, to make laws prescribing the time, places and manner of holding elections for senators and representatives, and for electors of president and vice-president. And in these, as well as some other cases, congress have a right to revise, amend or supersede the laws which may be passed by state legislatures. When, therefore, the states are stripped of some of the highest attributes of sovereignty, and the same are given to the United States; when the legislatures of the states are, in some respects, under the control of congress, and in every case are, under the constitution, bound by the paramount authority of the United States; it is certainly difficult to support the argument, that the appellate power over the decisions of state courts is contrary to the genius of our institutions. The courts of the United States can, without question, revise the proceedings of the executive and legislative authorities of the states, and if they are found to be contrary to the constitution, may declare them to be of no legal validity. Surely, the exercise of the same right over judicial tribunals is not a higher or more dangerous act of sovereign power.

Nor can such a right be deemed to impair the independence of state judges. It is assuming the very ground in controversy, to assert that they possess an absolute independence of the United States. In respect to the powers granted to the United States, they are not independent; they are expressly bound to obedience, by the letter of the constitution; and if they should unintentionally transcend their authority, or misconstrue the constitution, there is no more reason for giving their judgments an absolute and irresistible force, than for giving it to the acts of the other co-ordinate departments of state sovereignty.

The argument urged from the possibility of the abuse of the revising power, is equally unsatisfactory. It is always a doubtful course, to argue against the use or existence of a power, from the possibility of its abuse. It is still more difficult, by such an argument, to ingraft upon a general power, a restriction which is not to be found in the terms in which it is given. From the very nature of things, the absolute right of decision, in the last resort, must rest somewhere—wherever it may be vested, it is susceptible of abuse. In all questions of jurisdiction, the inferior, or appellate court, must pronounce the final judgment; and common sense, as well as legal reasoning, has conferred it upon the latter.

It has been further argued against the existence of this appellate power, that it would form a novelty in our judicial institutions. This is certainly a mistake. In the articles of confederation, an instrument framed with infinitely more deference to state rights and state jealousies, a power was given to congress to establish "courts for revising and determining, finally, appeals in all cases of captures." It is remarkable, that no power was given to entertain original jurisdiction in such cases; and consequently, the appellate power (although not so expressed in terms) was altogether to be exercised in revising the decisions of state tribunals. This was, undoubtedly, so far a surrender of state sovereignty; but it never was supposed to be a power fraught with public danger, or destructive of the independence of state judges. On the contrary, it was supposed to be a power indispensable to the public safety, inasmuch as our national rights might otherwise be compromitted, and our national peace be endangered. Under the present constitution, the prize jurisdiction is confined to the courts of the United States; and a power to revise the decisions of state courts, if they should assert jurisdiction over prize causes, cannot be less important, or less useful, than it was under the confederation.

In this connection, we are led again to the construction of the words of the constitution, "the judicial power shall extend," &c. If, as has been contended at the bar, the term "extend" have a relative signification, and mean to widen an existing power, it will then follow, that, as the confederation gave an appellate power over state tribunals, the constitution enlarged or widened that appellate power to all the other cases in which jurisdiction is given to the courts of the United States. It is not presumed, that the learned counsel would choose to adopt such a conclusion.

It is further argued, that no great public mischief can result from a construction which shall limit the appellate power of the United States to cases in their own courts: first, because state judges are bound by an oath to support the constitution of the United States, and must be presumed to be men of learning and integrity; and secondly, because congress must have an unquestionable right remove all cases within the scope of the judicial power from the state courts to the courts of the United States, at any time before final judgment, though not after final judgment. As to the first reason—admitting that the judges of the state courts are, and always will be, of as much learning, integrity and wisdom, as those of the courts of the United States (which we very cheerfully admit), it does not aid the argument. It is manifest, that the constitution has proceeded upon a theory of its own, and given or withheld powers according to the judgment of the American people, by whom it was adopted. We can only construe its powers, and cannot inquire into the policy or principles which induced the grant of them. The constitution has presumed (whether rightly or wrongly, we do not inquire), that state attachments, state prejudices, state jealousies, and state interests, might sometimes obstruct, or control, or be supposed to obstruct or control, the regular administration of justice. Hence, in controversies between states; between citizens of different states; between citizens claiming grants under different states; between a state and its citizens, or foreigners, and between citizens and foreigners, it enables the parties, under the authority of congress, to have the controversies heard, tried and determined before the national tribunals. No other reason than that which has been stated can be assigned, why some, at least, of those cases should not have been left to the cognisance of the state courts. In respect to the other enumerated cases—the cases arising under the constitution, laws and treaties of the United States, cases affecting ambassadors and other public ministers, and cases of admiralty and maritime jurisdiction—reasons of a higher and more extensive nature, touching the safety, peace and sovereignty of the nation, might well justify a grant of exclusive jurisdiction.

This is not all. A motive of another kind, perfectly compatible with the most sincere respect for state tribunals, might induce the grant of appellate power over their decisions. That motive is the importance, and even necessity of uniformity of decisions throughout the whole United States, upon all subjects within the purview of the constitution. Judges of equal learning and integrity, in different states, might differently interpret the statute, or a treaty of the United States, or even the constitution itself: if there were no revising authority to control these jarring and discordant judgments, and harmonize them into uniformity, the laws, the treaties and the constitution of the United States would be different, in different states, and might, perhaps, never have precisely the same construction, obligation or efficiency, in any two states. The public mischiefs that would attend such a state of things would be truly deplorable; and it cannot be believed, that they could have escaped the enlightened convention which formed the constitution. What, indeed, might then have been only prophecy, has now become fact; and the appellate jurisdiction must continue to be the only adequate remedy for such evils.

There is an additional consideration, which is entitled to great weight. The constitution of the United States was designed for the common and equal benefit of all the people of the United States. The judicial power was granted for the same benign and salutary purposes. It was not to be exercised exclusively for the benefit of parties who might be plaintiffs, and would elect the national *forum*, but also for the protection of defendants who might be entitled to try their rights, or assert their privileges, before the same *forum*. Yet, if the construction contended for be correct, it will follow, that as the plaintiff may always elect the state court, the defendant may be deprived of all the security which the constitution intended in aid of his rights. Such a state of things can, in no respect, be considered as giving equal rights. To obviate this difficulty, we are referred to the power which, it is admitted, congress possesses to remove suits from state courts to the national courts; and this forms the second ground upon which the argument we are considering has been attempted to be sustained.

This power of removal is not to be found in express terms in any part of the constitution; if it be given, it is only given by implication, as a power necessary and proper to carry into effect some express power. The power of removal is certainly not, in strictness of language, an exercise of original jurisdiction; it presupposes an exercise of original jurisdiction to have attached elsewhere. The existence of this power of removal is familiar in courts acting according to the course of the common law, in criminal as well as civil cases, and it is exercised before as well as after judgment. But this is always deemed, in both cases, an exercise of appellate, and not of original jurisdiction. If, then, the right of removal be included in the appellate jurisdiction, it is only because it is one mode of exercising that power, and as congress is not limited by the constitution to any particular mode, or time, of exercising it, it may authorize a removal, either before or after judgment. The time, the process and the manner must be subject to its absolute legislative control. A writ of error is, indeed, but a process which removes the record of one court to the possession of another court, and enables the latter to inspect the proceedings, and give such judgment as its own opinion of the law and justice of the case may warrant. There is nothing in the nature of the process, which forbids it from being applied by the legislature to interlocutory as well as final judgments. And if the right of removal from state courts exist, before judgment, because it is included in the appellate power, it must, for the same reason, exist, after judgment. And if the appellate power, by the constitution, does not include cases pending in state courts, the right of removal, which is but a mode of exercising that power, cannot be applied to them. Precisely the same objections, therefore, exist as to the right of removal before judgment, as after, and both must stand or fall together. Nor, indeed, would the force of the arguments on either side materially vary, if the right of removal were an exercise of original jurisdiction. It would equally trench upon the jurisdiction and independence of state tribunals.

The remedy, too, of removal of suits, would be utterly inadequate to the purposes of the constitution, if it could act only on the parties, and not upon the state courts. In respect to criminal prosecutions, the difficulty seems admitted to be insurmountable; and in respect to civil suits, there would, in many cases, be rights, without corresponding remedies. If state courts should deny the constitutionality of the authority to remove suits from their cognisance, in what manner could they be compelled to relinquish the jurisdiction? In respect to criminal cases, there would at once be an end of all control, and the state decisions would be paramount to the constitution; and though, in civil suits, the courts of the United States might act upon the parties, yet the state courts might act in the same way; and this conflict of jurisdictions would not only jeopardize private rights, but bring into imminent peril the public interests.

On the whole, the court are of opinion, that the appellate power of the United States does extend to cases pending in the state courts; and that the 25th section of the judiciary act, which authorizes the exercise of this jurisdiction in the specified cases, by a writ of error, is supported by the letter and spirit of the constitution. We find no clause in that instrument which limits this power; and we dare not interpose a limitation, where the people have not been disposed to create one.

Strong as this conclusion stands, upon the general language of the constitution, it may still derive support from other sources. It is an historical fact, that this exposition of the constitution, extending its appellate power to state courts, was, previous to its adoption, uniformly and publicly avowed by its friends, and admitted by its enemies, as the basis of their respective reasonings, both in and out of the state conventions. It is an historical fact, that at the time when the judiciary act was submitted to the delibera-

tions of the first congress, composed, as it was, not only of men of great learning and ability, but of men who had acted a principal part in framing, supporting or opposing that constitution, the same exposition was explicitly declared and admitted by the friends and by the opponents of that system. It is an historical fact, that the supreme court of the United States have, from time to time, sustained this appellate jurisdiction, in a great variety of cases, brought from the tribunals of many of the most important states in the Union, and that no state tribunal has ever breathed a judicial doubt on the subject, or declined to obey the mandate of the supreme court, until the present occasion. This weight of contemporaneous exposition by all parties, this acquiescence of enlightened state courts, and these judicial decisions of the supreme court, through so long a period, do, as we think, place the doctrine upon a foundation of authority which cannot be shaken, without delivering over the subject to perpetual and irremediable doubts.

The next question which has been argued, is, whether the case at bar be within the purview of the 25th section of the judiciary act, so that this court may rightfully sustain the present writ of error? This section, stripped of passages unimportant in this inquiry, enacts, in substance, that a final judgment or decree, in any suit in the highest court of law or equity of a state, where is drawn in question the validity of a treaty or statute of, or an authority exercised under, the United States, and the decision is against their validity; or where is drawn in question the validity of a statute of, or an authority exercised under, any state, on the ground of their being repugnant to the constitution, treaties or laws of the United States, and the decision is in favor of such their validity; or of the constitution, or of a treaty or statute of, or commission held under, the United States, and the decision is against the title, right, privilege or exemption specially set up or claimed by either party, under such clause of the said constitution, treaty, statute or commission, may be re-examined, and reversed or affirmed, in the supreme court of the United States, upon a writ of error, in the same manner, and under the same regulations, and the writ shall have the same effect, as if the judgment or decree complained of had been rendered or passed in a circuit court, and the proceeding upon the reversal shall also be the same, except that the supreme court, instead of remanding the cause for a final decision, as before provided, may, at their discretion, if the cause shall have been once remanded before, proceed to a final decision of the same, and award execution. But no other error shall be assigned or regarded as a ground of reversal, in any such case as aforesaid, than such as appears upon the face of the record, and immediately respects the before-mentioned question of validity or construction of the said constitution, treaties, statutes, commissions or authorities in dispute.

That the present writ of error is founded upon a judgment of the court below, which drew in question and denied the validity of a statute of the United States, is incontrovertible, for it is apparent upon the face of the record. That this judgment is final upon the rights of the parties, is equally true; for if well founded, the former judgment of that court was of conclusive authority, and the former judgment of this court utterly void. The decision was, therefore, equivalent to a perpetual stay of proceedings upon the mandate, and a perpetual denial of all the rights acquired under it. The case, then, falls directly within the terms of the act. It is a final judgment in a suit in a state court, denying the validity of a statute of the United States; and unless a distinction can be made between proceedings under a mandate, and proceedings in an original suit, a writ of error is the proper remedy to revise that judgment. In our opinion, no legal distinction exists between the cases.

In causes remanded to the circuit courts, if the mandate be not correctly executed, a writ of error or appeal has always been supposed to be a proper remedy, and has been recognised as such, in the former decisions of this court. The statute gives the same effect to writs of error from the judgments of state courts as of the circuit courts; and in its terms provides for proceedings where the same cause may be a second time brought up on writ of error before the supreme court. There is no limitation or description of the cases to which the second writ of error may be applied; and it ought, therefore, to be co-extensive with the cases which fall within the mischiefs of the statute. It will hardly be denied, that this cause stands in that predicament; and if so, then the appellate jurisdiction of this court has rightfully attached.

But it is contended, that the former judgment of this court was rendered upon a case, not within the purview of this section of the judicial act, and that, as it was pronounced by an incompetent jurisdiction, it was utterly void, and cannot be a sufficient foundation to sustain any subsequent proceedings. To this argument, several answers may be given. In the first place, it is not admitted, that, upon this writ of error, the former record is before us. The error now assigned is not in the former proceedings, but in the judgment rendered upon the mandate issued after the former judgment. The question now litigated is not upon the construction of a treaty, but upon the constitutionality of a statute of the United States, which is clearly within our jurisdiction. In the next place, in ordinary cases, a second writ of error has never been supposed to draw in question the propriety of the first judgment, and it is difficult to perceive how such a proceeding could be sustained, upon principle. A final judgment of this court is supposed to be conclusive upon the rights which it decides, and no statute has provided any process by which this court can revise its own judgments. In several cases which have been formerly adjudged in this court, the same point was argued by counsel, and expressly overruled. It was solemnly held, that a final judgment of this court was conclusive upon the parties, and could not be re-examined.

In this case, however, from motives of a public nature, we are entirely willing to waive all objections, and to go back and re-examine the question of jurisdiction, as it stood upon the record formerly in judgment. We have great confidence, that our jurisdiction will, on a careful examination, stand confirmed, as well upon principle as authority. It will be recollected, that the action was an ejectment for a parcel of land in the Northern Neck, formerly belonging to Lord Fairfax. The original plaintiff claimed the land under a patent granted to him by the state of Virginia, in 1789, under a title supposed to be vested in that state by escheat or forfeiture. The original defendant claimed the land as devisee under the will of Lord Fairfax. The parties agreed to a special statement of facts, in the nature of a special verdict, upon which the district court of Winchester, in 1793, gave a general judgment for the defendant, which judgment was afterwards reversed in 1810, by the court of appeals, and a general judgment was rendered for the plaintiff; and from this last judgment, a writ of error was brought to the supreme court. The statement of facts contained a regular deduction of the title of Lord Fairfax, until his death, in 1781, and also the title of his devisee. It also contained a regular deduction of the title of the plaintiff, under the state of Virginia, and further referred to the treaty of peace of 1783, and to the acts of Virginia respecting the lands of Lord Fairfax, and the supposed escheat or forfeiture thereof, as component parts of the case. No facts disconnected with the titles thus set up by the parties were alleged on either side. It is apparent, from this summary explanation, that the title thus set up by the plaintiff might be open to other objections; but the title of the defendant was perfect and complete, if it was protected by the treaty of 1783. If, therefore, this court had authority to examine into the whole record, and to decide upon the legal validity of the title of the defendant, as well as its application to the treaty of peace, it would be a case within the express purview of the 25th section of the act; for there was nothing in the record upon which the court below could have decided, but upon the title as connected with the treaty; and if the title was otherwise good, its sufficiency must have depended altogether upon its protection under the treaty. Under such circumstances, it was strictly a suit where was drawn in question the construction of a treaty, and the decision was against the title specially set up or claimed by the defendant. It would fall, then, within the very terms of the act.

The objection urged at the bar is, that this court cannot inquire into the title, but simply into the correctness of the construction put upon the treaty by the court of appeals; and that their judgment is not re-examinable here, unless it appear on the face of the record, that some construction was put upon the treaty. If, therefore, that court might have decided the case upon the invalidity of the title (and *non constat*, that they did not), independent of the treaty, there is an end of the appellate jurisdiction of this court. In support of this objection, much stress is laid upon the last clause of the section, which declares, that no other cause shall be regarded as a ground of reversal than such as appears on the face of the record and immediately respects the construction of the treaty, &c., in dispute.

If this be the true construction of the section, it will be wholly inadequate for the purposes which it professes to have in view, and may be evaded at pleasure. But we see no reason for adopting this narrow construction; and there are the strongest reasons against it, founded upon the words as well as the intent of the legislature. What is the case for which the body of the section provides a remedy by writ of error? The answer must be, in the words of the section, a suit where is drawn in question the construction of a treaty, and the decision is against the title set up by the party. It is, therefore, the decision against the title set up, with reference to the treaty, and not the mere abstract construction of the treaty itself, upon which the statute intends to found the appellate jurisdiction. How, indeed, can it be possible to decide, whether a title be within the protection of a treaty, until it is ascertained what that title is, and whether it have a legal validity? From the very necessity of the case, there must be a preliminary inquiry into the existence and structure of the title, before the court can construe the treaty in reference to that title. If the court below should decide, that the title was bad, and therefore, not protected by the treaty, must not this court have a power to decide the title to be good, and therefore, protected by the treaty? Is not the treaty, in both instances, equally construed, and the title of the party, in reference to the treaty, equally ascertained and decided? Nor does the clause relied on in the objection, impugn this construction. It requires, that the error upon which the appellate court is to decide, shall appear on the face of the record, and immediately respect the questions before mentioned in the section. One of the questions is, as to the construction of a treaty, upon a title specially set up by a party, and every error that immediately respects that question must, of course, be within the cognisance of the court. The title set up in this case is apparent upon the face of the record, and immediately respects the decision of that question; any error, therefore, in respect to that title must be re-examinable, or the case could never be presented to the court.

The restraining clause was manifestly intended for a very different purpose. It was foreseen, that the parties might claim under various titles, and might assert various defences, altogether independent of each other. The court might admit or reject evidence applicable to one particular title, and not to all, and in such cases, it was the intention of congress, to limit what would otherwise have unquestionably attached to the court, the right of revising all the points involved in the cause. It, therefore, restrains this right to such errors as respect the questions specified in the section; and in this view, it has an appropriate sense, consistent with the preceding clauses. We are, therefore, satisfied, that, upon principle, the case was rightfully before us, and if the point were perfectly new, we should not hesitate to assert the jurisdiction.

But the point has been already decided by this court upon solemn argument. In *Smith* v. *State of Maryland* (6 Cranch 286), precisely the same objection was taken by counsel, and overruled by the unanimous opinion of the court. That case was, in some respects, stronger than the present; for the court below decided, expressly, that the party had no title, and therefore, the treaty could not operate upon it. This court entered into an examination of that question, and being of the same opinion, affirmed the judgment. There cannot, then, be an authority which could more completely govern the present question.

It has been asserted at the bar, that, in point of fact, the

court of appeals did not decide either upon the treaty, or the title apparent upon the record, but upon a compromise made under an act of the legislature of Virginia. If it be true (as we are informed), that this was a private act, to take effect only upon a certain condition, viz., the execution of a deed of release of certain lands, which was matter *in pais*, it is somewhat difficult to understand, how the court could take judicial cognisance of the act, or of the performance of the condition, unless spread upon the record. At all events, we are bound to consider, that the court did decide upon the facts actually before them. The treaty of peace was not necessary to have been stated, for it was the supreme law of the land, of which all courts must take notice. And at the time of the decision in the court of appeals, and in this court, another treaty had intervened, which attached itself to the title in controversy, and of course, must have been the supreme law to govern the decision, if it should be found applicable to the case. It was in this view that this court did not deem it necessary to rest its former decision upon the treaty of peace, believing that the title of the defendant was, at all events, perfect, under the treaty of 1794.

. . . . .

We have thus gone over all the principal questions in the cause, and we deliver our judgment with entire confidence, that it is consistent with the constitution and laws of the land. We have not thought it incumbent on us to give any opinion upon the question, whether this court have authority to issue a writ of *mandamus* to the court of appeals, to enforce the former judgments, as we did not think it necessarily involved in the decision of this cause.

It is the opinion of the whole court, that the judgment of the court of appeals of Virginia, rendered on the mandate in this cause, be reversed, and the judgment of the district court, held at Winchester, be, and the same is hereby affirmed.

JOHNSON, J.—It will be observed, in this case, that the court disavows all intention to decide on the right to issue compulsory process to the state courts; thus leaving us, in my opinion, where the constitution and laws place us— supreme over persons and cases, so far as our judicial powers extend, but not asserting any compulsory control over the state tribunals. In this view, I acquiesce in their opinion, but not altogether in the reasoning or opinion of my brother who delivered it. Few minds are accustomed to the same habit of thinking, and our conclusions are most satisfactory to ourselves, when arrived at in our own way.

I have another reason for expressing my opinion on this occasion. I view this question as one of the most momentous importance; as one which may affect, in its consequences, the permanence of the American Union. It presents an instance of collision between the judicial powers of the Union and one of the greatest states in the Union, on a point the most delicate and difficult to be adjusted. On the one hand, the general government must cease to exist, whenever it loses the power of protecting itself in the exercise of its constitutional powers. Force, which acts upon the physical powers of man, or judicial process, which addresses itself to his moral principles or his fears, are the only means to which governments can resort in the exercise of their authority. The former is happily unknown to the genius of our constitution, except as far as it shall be sanctioned by the latter; but let the latter be obstructed in its progress, by an opposition which it cannot overcome or put by, and the resort must be to the former, or government is no more.

On the other hand, so firmly am I persuaded that the American people can no longer enjoy the blessings of a free government, whenever the state sovereignties shall be prostrated at the feet of the general government, nor the proud consciousness of equality and security, any longer than the independence of judicial power shall be maintained, consecrated and intangible, that I could borrow the language of a celebrated orator, and exclaim, "I rejoice that Virginia has resisted."

Yet, here, I must claim the privilege of expressing my regret, that the opposition of the high and truly respected tribunal of that state had not been marked with a little more moderation. The only point necessary to be decided in the case then before them was, "Whether they were bound to obey the mandate emanating from this court?" But in the judgment entered on their minutes, they have affirmed that the case was, in this court, *coram non judice*, or, in other words, that this court had not jurisdiction over it. This is assuming a truly alarming latitude of judicial power. Where is it to end? It is an acknowledged principle of, I believe, every court in the world, that not only the decisions, but everything done under the judicial process of courts, not having jurisdiction are, *ipso facto*, void. Are, then, the judgments of this court to be reviewed in every court of the Union? And is every recovery of money, every change of property, that has taken place under our process, to be considered as null, void and tortious?

We pretend not to more infallibility than other courts composed of the same frail materials which compose this. It would be the height of affectation, to close our minds upon the recollection that we have been extracted from the same seminaries in which originated the learned men who preside over the state tribunals. But there is one claim which we can with confidence assert in our own name, upon those tribunals—the profound, uniform and unaffected respect which this court has always exhibited for state decisions, give us strong pretensions to judicial comity. And another claim I may assert, in the name of the American people; in this court, every state in the Union is represented; we are constituted by the voice of the Union, and when decisions take place, which nothing but a spirit to give ground and harmonize can reconcile, ours is the superior claim upon the comity of the state tribunals. It is the nature of the human mind, to press a favorite hypothesis too far, but magnanimity will always be ready to sacrifice the pride of opinion to public welfare.

In the case before us, the collision has been, on our part, wholly unsolicited. The exercise of this appellate jurisdiction over the state decisions has long been acquiesced in, and when the writ of error, in this case, was allowed by the president of the court of appeals of Virginia, we were sanctioned in supposing, that we were to meet with the same acquiescence there. Had that court refused to grant the writ, in the first instance, or had the question of jurisdiction, or, on the mode of exercising jurisdiction, been made here, originally, we should have been put on our guard, and might have so modelled the process of the court, as to strip it of the offensive form of a mandate. In this case, it might have been brought down to what probably the 25th section of the judiciary act meant it should be, to wit, an alternative judgment, either that the state court may finally proceed, at its option, to carry into effect the judgment of this court, or, if it declined doing so, that then this court would proceed itself to execute it. The language, sense and operation of the 25th section on this subject, merit particular attention. In the preceding section, which has relation to causes brought up by writ of error from the circuit courts of the United States, this court is instructed not to issue executions, but to send a special mandate to the circuit court to award execution thereupon. In case of the circuit court's refusal to obey such mandate, there could be no doubt as to the ulterior measures; compulsory process might, unquestionably, be resorted to. Nor, indeed, was there any reason to suppose, that they ever would refuse; and therefore, there is no provision made for authorizing this court to execute its own judgment in cases of that description. But not so, in cases brought up from the state courts; the framers of that law plainly foresaw that the state courts might refuse; and not being willing to leave ground for the implication, that compulsory process must be resorted to, because no special provision was made, they have provided the means, by authorizing this court, in case of reversal of the state decision, to execute its own judgment. In case of reversal only, was this necessary; for, in case of affirmance, this collision could not arise. It is true, that the words of this section are, that this court may, in their discretion, proceed to execute its own judgment. But these words were very properly put in, that it might not be made imperative upon this court to proceed indiscriminately in this way; as it could only be necessary, in case of the refusal of the state courts; and this idea is fully confirmed by the words of the 13th section, which restrict this court in issuing the writ of *mandamus*, so as to confine it expressly to those courts which are constituted by the United States.

In this point of view the legislature is completely vindicated from all intention to violate the independence of the state judiciaries. Nor can this court, with any more correctness, have imputed to it similar intentions. The form of the mandate issued in this case is that known to appellate tribunals, and used in the ordinary cases of writs of error from the courts of the United States. It will, perhaps, not be too much, in such cases to expect of those who are conversant in the forms, fictions and technicality of the law, not to give the process of courts too literal a construction. They should be considered with a view to the ends they are intended to answer, and the law and practice in which they originate. In this view, the mandate was no more than a mode of submitting to that court the option which the 25th section holds out to them.

Had the decision of the court of Virginia been confined to the point of their legal obligation to carry the judgment of this court into effect, I should have thought it unnecessary to make any further observations in this cause. But we are called upon to vindicate our general revising power, and its due exercise in this particular case.

Here, that I may not be charged with arguing upon a hypothetical case, it is necessary to ascertain what the real question is which this court is now called to decide on. In doing this, it is necessary to do what, although, in the abstract, of very questionable propriety, appears to be generally acquiesced in, to wit, to review the case, as it originally came up to this court on the former writ of error. The cause, then, came up upon a case stated between the parties, and under the practice of that state, having the effect of a special verdict. The case stated brings into view the treaty of peace with Great Britain, and then proceeds to present the various laws of Virginia, and the facts upon which the parties found their respective titles. It then presents no particular question, but refers generally to the law arising out of the case. The original decision was obtained prior to the treaty of 1794, but before the case was adjudicated in this court, the treaty of 1794 had been concluded.

The difficulties of the case arise under the construction of the 25th section above alluded to, which, as far as it relates to this case, is in these words: "A final judgment or decree in any suit, in the highest court of law or equity of a state in which a decision in the suit could be had," "where is drawn in question the construction of any clause of the constitution or of a treaty," "and the decision is against the title set up or claimed by either party under such clause, may be re-examined, and reversed or affirmed." "But no other error shall be assigned or regarded as a ground of reversal, in any such case as aforesaid, than such as appears on the face of the record, and immediately respects the before-mentioned questions of validity or construction of the said treaties," &c.

The first point decided under this state of the case was, that the judgment being a part of the record, if that judgment was not such as, upon that case, it ought to have been, it was an error apparent on the face of the record. But it was contended, that the case there stated presented a number of points upon which the decision below may have been founded, and that it did not, therefore, necessarily appear to have been an error immediately respecting a question on the construction of a treaty. But the court held, that as the reference was general to the law arising out of the case, if one question arose, which called for the construction of a treaty, and the decision negatived the right set up under it, this court will reverse that decision, and that it is the duty of the party who would avoid the inconvenience of this principle, so to mould the case as to obviate the ambiguity. And under this point, arises the question, whether this court can inquire into the title of the party, or whether they are so restricted in their judicial powers, as to be confined to decide on the operation of a treaty upon a title previously ascertained to exist.

If there is any one point in the case on which an opinion may be given with confidence, it is this: whether we consider the letter of statute, or the spirit, intent or meaning of the constitution and of the legislature, as expressed in the 25th section, it is equally clear, that the title is the primary object to which the attention of the court is called in every such case. The words are, "and the decision be against the title," so set up, not against the construction of the treaty contended for by the party setting up the title. And how could it be otherwise? The title may exist, notwithstanding the decision of the state courts to the contrary; and in that case, the party is entitled to the benefits intended to be secured by the treaty. The decision to his prejudice may have been the result of those very errors, partialities or defects in state jurisprudence against which the constitution intended to protect the individual. And if the contrary doctrine be assumed, what is the consequence? This court may then be called upon to decide on a mere hypothetical case—to give to construction to a treaty, without first deciding whether there was any interest on which that treaty, whatever be its proper construction, would operate. This difficulty was felt and weighed in the case of *Smith* v. *State of Maryland,* and that decision was founded upon the idea, that this court was not thus restricted.

But another difficulty presented itself: the treaty of 1794 had become the supreme law of the land, since the judgment rendered in the court below. The defendant, who was, at that time, an alien, had now become confirmed in his rights under that treaty. This would have been no objection to the correctness of the original judgment. Were we, then, at liberty to notice that treaty, in rendering the judgment of this court?

Having dissented from the opinion of this court in the original case, on the question of title, this difficulty did not present itself in my way, in the view I then took of the case. But the majority of this court determined, that, as a public law, the treaty was a part of the law of every case depending in this court; that as such, it was not necessary that it should be spread upon the record, and that it was obligatory upon this court, in rendering judgment upon this writ of error, notwithstanding the original judgment may have been otherwise unimpeachable. And to this opinion, I yielded my hearty consent; for it cannot be maintained, that this court is bound to give a judgment, unlawful at the time of rendering it, in consideration that the same judgment would have been lawful, at any prior time. What judgment can now be lawfully rendered between the parties, is the question to which the attention of the court is called. And if the law which sanctioned the original judgment expire, pending an appeal, this court has repeatedly reversed the judgment below, although rendered whilst the law existed. So too, if the plaintiff in error die, pending suit, and his land descend on an alien, it cannot be contended, that this court will maintain the suit, in right of the judgment, in favor of his ancestor, notwithstanding his present disability.

It must here be recollected, that this is an action of ejectment. If the term formally declared upon, expires, pending the action, the court will permit the plaintiff to amend, by extending the term—why? Because, although the right may have been in him at the commencement of the suit, it has ceased, before judgment, and without this amendment, he could not have judgment. But suppose, the suit were really instituted to obtain possession of a leasehold and the lease expire, before judgment, would the court permit the party to amend, in opposition to the right of the case? On the contrary, if the term formally declared on were more extensive than the lease in which the legal title was founded, could they give judgment for more than costs? It must be recollected, that under this judgment, a writ of restitution is the fruit of the law. This, in its very nature, has relation to, and must be founded upon, a present existing right, at the time of judgment. And whatever be the cause which takes this right away, the remedy must, in the reason and nature of things, fall with it.

When all these incidental points are disposed of, we find the question finally reduced to this—does the judicial power of the United States extend to the revision of decisions of state courts, in cases arising under treaties? But in order to generalize the question, and present it in the true form in which it presents itself in this case, we will inquire, whether the constitution sanctions the exercise of a revising power over the decisions of state tribunals in those cases to which the judicial power of the United States extends?

And here it appears to me, that the great difficulty is on the other side. That the real doubt is, whether the state tribunals can constitutionally exercise jurisdiction, in any of the cases to which the judicial power of the United States extends? Some cession of judicial power is contemplated by the third article of the constitution; that which is ceded, can no longer be retained. In one of the circuit courts of the United States, it has been decided (with what correctness I will not say), that the cession of a power to pass an uniform act of bankruptcy, although not acted on by the United States, deprives the states of the power of passing laws to that effect. With regard to the admiralty and maritime jurisdiction, it would be difficult to prove that the states could resume it, if the United States should abolish the courts vested with that jurisdiction; yet, it is blended with the other cases of jurisdiction, in the second section of the third article, and ceded in the same words. But it is contended, that the second section of the third article contains no express cession of jurisdiction; that it only vests a power in congress to assume jurisdiction to the extent therein expressed. And under this head, arose the discussion on the construction proper to be given to that article.

On this part of the case, I shall not pause long. The rules of construction, where the nature of the instrument is ascertained, are familiar to every one. To me, the constitution appears, in every line of it, to be a contract, which, in legal language, may be denominated tripartite. The parties are the people, the states, and the United States. It is returning in a circle, to contend, that it professes to be the exclusive act of the people, for what have the people done, but to form this compact? That the states are recognised as parties to it, is evident, from various passages, and particularly, that in which the United States guaranty to each state a republican form of government.

The security and happiness of the whole was the object, and, to prevent dissension and collision, each surrendered those powers which might make them dangerous to each other. Well aware of the sensitive irritability of sovereign states, where their wills or interests clash, they placed themselves, with regard to each other, on the footing of sovereigns upon the ocean; where power is mutually conceded to act upon the individual, but the national vessel must remain unviolated. And to remove all ground for jealousy and complaint, they relinquish the privilege of being any longer the exclusive arbiters of their own justice, where the rights of others come in question, or the great interests of the whole may be affected by those feelings, partialities or prejudices, which they meant to put down for ever.

Nor shall I enter into a minute discussion on the meaning of the language of this section. I have seldom found much good result from hypercritical severity, in examining the distinct force of words. Language is essentially defective in precision; more so, than those are aware of, who are not in the habit of subjecting it to philological analysis. In the case before us, for instance, a rigid construction might be made, which would annihilate the powers intended to be ceded. The words are, "shall extend to;" now that which extends *to*, does not necessarily include *in*, so that the circle may enlarge, until it reaches the objects that limit it, and yet not take them in. But the plain and obvious sense and meaning of the word *shall*, in this sentence, is in the future sense, and has nothing imperative in it. The language of the framers of the constitution is, "We are about forming a general government—when that government is formed, its powers shall extend," &c. I, therefore, see nothing imperative in this clause, and certainly it would have been very unnecessary to use the word in that sense; for, as there was no controlling power constituted, it would only, if used in an imperative sense, have imposed a moral obligation to act. But the same result arises, from using it in a future sense, and the constitution everywhere assumes, as a postulate, that wherever power is given, it will be used, or at least used, so far as the interests of the American people require it, if not from the natural proneness of man to the exercise of power, at least, from a sense of duty, and the obligation of an oath.

Nor can I see any difference in the effect of the words used in this section, as to the scope of the jurisdiction of the United States courts over the cases of the first and second description, comprised in that section. "Shall extend to controversies," appears to me as comprehensive in effect, as "shall extend to all cases." For, if the judicial power extend "to controversies between citizen and alien," &c., to what controversies of that description, does it not extend? If no case can be pointed out, which is excepted, it then extends to all controversies.

But I will assume the construction as a sound one, that the cession of power to the general government, means no more than that they may assume the exercise of it, whenever they think it advisable. It is clear, that congress have hitherto acted under that impression, and my own opinion is in favor of its correctness. But does it not then follow, that the jurisdiction of the state court, within the range ceded to the general government, is permitted, and may be withdrawn whenever congress think proper to do so? As it is a principle, that every one may renounce a right introduced for his benefit, we will admit, that as congress have not assumed such jurisdiction, the state courts may, constitutionally, exercise jurisdiction in such cases. Yet, surely, the general power to withdraw the exercise of it, includes in it the right to modify, limit and restrain that exercise. "This is my domain, put not your foot upon it, if you do, you are subject to my laws, I have a right to exclude you altogether; I have, then, a right to prescribe the terms of your admission to a participation. As long as you conform to my laws, participate in peace, but I reserve to myself the right of judging how far your acts are conformable to my laws." Analogy, then, to the ordinary exercise of sovereign authority, would sustain the exercise of this controlling or revising power.

But it is argued, that a power to assume jurisdiction to the constitutional extent, does not necessarily carry with it a right to exercise appellate power over the state tribunals. This is a momentous question, and one on which I shall reserve myself uncommitted for each particular case as it shall occur. It is enough, at present, to have shown, that congress have not asserted, and this court has not attempted, to exercise that kind of authority *in personam*, over the state courts, which would place them in the relation of an inferior responsible body, without their own acquiescence. And I have too much confidence in the state tribunals, to believe that a case ever will occur, in which it will be necessary for the general government to assume a controlling power over these tribunals. But is it difficult to suppose a case, which will call loudly for some remedy or restraint? Suppose, a foreign minister, or an officer, acting regularly under authority from the United States, seized to-day, tried to-morrow, and hurried the next day to execution. Such cases may occur, and have occurred, in other countries. The angry, vindictive passions of men have too often made their way into judicial tribunals, and we cannot hope for ever to escape their baleful influence. In the case supposed, there ought to be a power somewhere to restrain or punish, or the Union must be dissolved. At present, the uncontrollable exercise of criminal jurisdiction is most securely confided to the state tribunals. The courts of the United States are vested with no power to scrutinize into the proceedings of the state courts in criminal cases; on the contrary, the general government has, in more than one instance, exhibited their confidence, by a wish to vest them with the execution of their own penal law. And extreme, indeed, I flatter myself, must be the case, in which the general government could ever be induced to assert this right. If ever such a case should occur, it will be time enough to decide upon their constitutional power to do so.

But we know, that by the 3d article of the constitution, judicial power, to a certain extent, is vested in the general government, and that, by the same instrument, power is given to pass all laws necessary to carry into effect the provisions of the constitution. At present, it is only necessary to vindicate the laws which they have passed affecting civil cases pending in state tribunals.

In legislating on this subject, congress, in the true spirit of the constitution, have proposed to secure to every one the full benefit of the constitution, without forcing any one, necessarily, into the courts of the United States. With this view, in one class of cases, they have not taken away absolutely from the state courts all the cases to which their judicial power extends, but left it to the plaintiff to bring his action there, originally, if he choose, or to the defendant, to force the plaintiff into the courts of the United States, where they have jurisdiction, and the former has instituted his suit in the state courts. In this case, they have not made it legal for the defendant to plead to the jurisdiction; the effect of which would be, to put an end to the plaintiff's suit, and oblige him, probably, at great risk or expense, to institute a new action; but the act has given him a right to obtain an order for a removal, on a petition to the state court, upon which the cause, with all its existing advantages, is transferred to the circuit court of the United States. This, I presume, can be subject to no objection; as the legislature has an unquestionable right to make the ground of removal, a ground of plea to the jurisdiction, and the court must then do no more than it is now called upon to do, to wit, give an order or a judgment, or call it what we will, in favor of that defendant. And so far from asserting the inferiority of the state tribunal, this act is rather that of a superior, inasmuch as the circuit court of the United States becomes bound, by that order, to take jurisdiction of the case. This method, so much more unlikely to affect official delicacy than that which is resorted to in the other class of cases, might, perhaps, have been more happily applied to all the cases which the legislature thought it advisable to remove from the state courts. But the other class of cases, in which the present is included, was proposed to be provided for in a different manner. And here, again, the legislature of the Union evince their confidence in the state tribunals; for they do not attempt to give original cognisance to their own circuit courts of such cases, or to remove them by petition and order; but still, believing that their decisions will be generally satisfactory, a writ of error is not given immediately, as a question within the jurisdiction of the United States shall occur, but only in case the decision shall finally, in the court of the last resort, be against the title set up under the constitution, treaty, &c.

In this act, I can see nothing which amounts to an assertion of the inferiority or dependence of the state tribunals. The presiding judge of the state court is himself authorized to issue the writ of error, if he will, and thus give jurisdiction to the supreme court: and if he thinks proper to decline it, no compulsory process is provided by law to oblige him. The party who imagines himself aggrieved is then at liberty to apply to a judge of the United States, who issues the writ of error, which (whatever the form) is, in substance, no more than a mode of compelling the opposite party to appear before this court, and maintain the legality of his judgment obtained before the state tribunal. An exemplification of a record is the common property of every one who chooses to apply and pay for it, and thus the case and the parties are brought before us; and so far is the court itself from being brought under the revising power of this court, that nothing but the case, as presented by the record and pleadings of the parties, is considered, and the opinions of the court are never resorted to, unless for the purpose of assisting this court in forming their own opinions.

The absolute necessity that there was for congress to exercise something of a revising power over cases and parties in the state courts, will appear from this consideration. Suppose, the whole extent of the judicial power of the United States vested in their own courts, yet such a provision would not answer all the ends of the constitution, for two reasons:

1st. Although the plaintiff may, in such case, have the full benefit of the constitution extended to him, yet the defendant would not; as the plaintiff might force him into the court of the state, at his election.

2d. Supposing it possible so to legislate, as to give the courts of the United States original jurisdiction in all cases arising under the constitution, laws, &c., in the words of the 2d section of the 3d article (a point on which I have some doubt, and which in time might, perhaps, under some *quo minus* fiction, or a willing construction, greatly accumulate the jurisdiction of those courts), yet a very large class of cases would remain unprovided for. Incidental questions would often arise, and as a court of competent jurisdiction in the principal case must decide all such questions, whatever laws they arise under, endless might be the diversity of decisions throughout the Union upon the constitution, treaties and laws of the United States; a subject on which the tranquillity of the Union, internally and externally, may materially depend.

I should feel the more hesitation in adopting the opinions which I express in this case, were I not firmly convinced, that they are practical, and may be acted upon, without compromitting the harmony of the Union, or bringing humility upon the state tribunals. God forbid! that the judicial power in these states should ever, for a moment, even in its humblest departments, feel a doubt of its own independence. Whilst adjudicating on a subject which the laws of the country assign finally to the revising power of another tribunal, it can feel no such doubt. An anxiety to do justice is ever relieved, by the knowledge that what we do is not final between the parties. And no sense of dependence can be felt, from the knowledge that the parties, not the court, may be summoned before another tribunal. With this view, by means of laws, avoiding judgments obtained in the state courts in cases over which congress has constitutionally assumed jurisdiction, and inflicting penalties on parties who shall contumaciously persist in infringing the constitutional rights of others—under a liberal extension of the writ of injunction and the *habeas corpus ad subjiciendum*, I flatter myself, that the full extent of the constitutional revising power may be secured to the United States, and the benefits of it to the individual, without ever resorting to compulsory or restrictive process upon the state tribunals; a right which, I repeat again, congress has not asserted, nor has this court asserted, nor does there appear any necessity for asserting.

The remaining points in the case being mere questions of practice, I shall make no remarks upon them.

66

UNITED STATES V. COOLIDGE

1 Wheat. 415 (1816)

This was an indictment in the Circuit Court for the district of Massachusetts, against the defendants, for forcibly rescuing a prize, which had been captured and taken possession of by two American privateers.

The captured vessel was on her way, under the direction of a prizemaster and crew, to the port of Salem, for adjudication. The indictment laid the offence as committed upon the high seas. The question made was, whether the circuit court has jurisdiction over common-law offences against the United States? on which the judges of that court were divided in opinion.

The *Attorney-General* stated, that he had given to this case an anxious attention; as much so, he hoped, as his public duty, under whatever view of it, rendered necessary. That he had also examined the opinion of the court, delivered at February term 1813, in the case of the *United States* v. *Hudson and Goodwin* (7 Cr. 32). That considering the point as decided in that case, whether with or without argument on the part of those who had preceded him as the representative of the government in this court, he desired respectfully to state, without saying more, that it was not his intention to argue it now.

STORY, J.—I do not take the question to be settled by that case.

JOHNSON, J.—I consider it to be settled, by the authority of that case.

WASHINGTON, J.—Whenever counsel can be found ready to argue it, I shall divest myself of all prejudice arising from that case.

LIVINGSTON, J.—I am disposed to hear argument on the point. This case was brought up for that purpose, but until the question is re-argued, the case of the *United States* v. *Hudson and Goodwin* must be taken as law.

March 21st, 1816. JOHNSON, J., delivered the opinion of the court.—Upon the question now before the court, a difference of opinion has existed, and still exists, among the members of the court. We should, therefore, have been willing to have heard the question discussed, upon solemn argument. But the attorney-general has declined to argue the cause; and no counsel appears for the defendant. Under these circumstances, the court would not choose to review their former decision in the case of the *United States* v. *Hudson and Goodwin*, or draw it into doubt. They will, therefore, certify an opinion to the circuit court, in conformity with that decision.

67

COMMONWEALTH V. KOSLOFF

5 Serg. & Rawle 545 (Pa. 1816)

TILGHMAN C. J. The grand inquest for the city and county of *Philadelphia*, having preferred a bill of indictment for a rape, against *Nicholas Kosloff*, Consul General of his Imperial Majesty the Emperor of *Russia*, a motion has been made to quash the indictment for want of jurisdiction in this Court. Two causes are assigned for our want of jurisdiction. 1. That the privilege of immunity from criminal prosecutions, is conferred on Consuls by the Law of Nations. 2. That by the Constitution and Laws of the *United States, exclusive jurisdiction* in all cases affecting Consuls, is vested in the Courts of the *United States.*

1. It is granted, that by the modern law of nations, ambassadors, and other public ministers, are, in general, exempt from criminal prosecutions. Perhaps there are some offences, such as an attempt on the life of the Sovereign with whom they reside, which would warrant their punishment. But in every thing short of an extreme case, it is more conducive to the peace, and more agreeable to the usage of nations, to send them to their own Sovereign, to receive from him the punishment they deserve. It has not been contended, that a Consul is a *public minister*—but it is said, that a Consul General, such as Mr. *Kosloff*, is prohibited from exercising trade and commerce, and entrusted with important concerns from his Sovereign, and so nearly resembles a public minister, that he is entitled to some of his prerogatives, and in particular, to exemption from criminal prosecution. In considering this case, we must exclude from our view, the august personage to whom allusion was made in the argument. Concerning his high character, and the intimacy of the relations to be preserved with him, there is but one voice,—one wish. These considerations would have their deserved weight, in the proper place. But before us there is only a naked question of *right*, in which all nations are equally concerned; for we cannot but see, that that which is granted as the right of one, must be conceded as the right of all. The law of nations is sought for in the usages of nations; in the opinions of approved authors; in treaties; and in the decisions of Judges. With regard to the privileges of Consuls, there is some difference of opinion, among respectable authors. *Wicquefort, Bynkershoek,* and *Martens,* allow to a Consul no privilege, against suits civil or criminal: and the reason they assign, is, that Consuls in no manner represent the person of their Sovereign, but are sent for the purpose of assisting his subjects, particularly in matters of commerce, and sometimes of deciding disputes which may arise between them, by permission of the Government in whose dominions they reside. (See *Wicquef. L'Ambassadeur,* Book I. pa. 65. *Bynk. de foro legatorum.* chap. 10. pa. 113. *Barbeyrac's translation into French. Martens' Summary of the Law of Nations,* book iv. chap. 3. sect. 8.) Opposed to them, is *Vattel,* who, although he does not assert, that a Consul is entitled to the privileges of a public minister in general, is yet of opinion, that from the nature of his functions, "he should be independent of the ordinary criminal justice of the place where he resides, so as not to be molested or imprisoned, unless he himself violates the law of nations by some uncommon crime." *Vatt.* book ii. chap. 2. sect. 34. I am not quite sure what is meant, by *violating the law of nations,* in this passage. Crimes *against the law of nations,* are sometimes understood to be, crimes which *all nations agree to punish.* Such are murder, and rape, among the civilized nations: and if that be the meaning of *Vattel,* his authority would not exempt the Consul from the present prosecution. But what is of more weight than the judgment of authors however respectable, is the opinion and the practice of our own Government, and that of the foreign nations with whom we have had intercourse. We have had treaties with *France, Spain, Great Britain, Holland, Prussia,* and *Sweden,* in all of which the subject of Consuls has been introduced, and in not one of which, have Consuls been protected for suits civil or criminal. I say nothing of our treaties with the *Barbary* powers, because there are special reasons why all nations who send Consuls to them, take care to provide expressly for their personal security. In the treaty with *Great Britain,* made in 1794, Consuls are expressly declared, to be subject to punishment by the law of the country in which they reside. By the consular convention with *France,* in 1788, there is to be full and perfect immunity, concerning the *Chancery and its papers,* but the house of the Consul is to be no asylum for *persons or effects.* And in our other treaties, the most that is stipulated in favour of Consuls is, that they shall respectively enjoy the same prerogatives and favours, that are granted to those of the most favoured nations. These treaties afford a strong proof of the usage of nations—for it cannot be supposed, that they should have omitted to secure Consuls from criminal prosecutions, if it had been thought desirable, or usual, to afford them that protection. But there is not wanting more direct proof of the opinion of our own Government. In the "act for the punishment of certain crimes against the *United States,*" passed *April,* 30, 1790, penalties are inflicted on persons who sue out process from any Court, against an Ambassador or other public minister—but the act is silent as to consuls. And what is directly to the point, the 9th sect. of the "act to establish the *Judicial Courts* of the *United States,*" (passed *September,* 24, 1789,) vests the District Courts with jurisdiction of offences committed by Consuls, in which the punishment does not exceed a fine of 100 dollars, &c. &c. Neither are we left, on this important subject, without the light of judicial decision. Mr. *Ravara,* Consul from *Genoa,* was indicted and convicted for a misdemeanour, in the Circuit Court of the *United States. 2 Dall.* 299. He was defended by able counsel, who contended for his privilege, on the authority of *Vattel.* But the Court decided against him, and it is worthy of remark, that Ch. J. JAY presided, who had been long employed in a diplomatic function of a high grade at the court of *Madrid,* and was one of the ministers of the *United States* who negotiated the treaty which established our Independence, at *Paris.* No person, certainly,

had better opportunities of knowing the usage of nations, or a better capacity for improving these opportunities. From all these considerations, I cannot hesitate in the opinion, that there is nothing in the law of nations, which protects the Consul General of *Russia* from this indictment.

2. A more difficult question remains to be considered— Is the jurisdiction of this Court taken away, by the Constitution and Laws of the *United States?* Before I go into an examination of the Constitution and laws, it may not be improper to say a word or two, respecting the subject in which this question arises. An agent of a foreign Government, accused of a crime committed in the state of *Pennsylvania,* claims, not an exemption from trial, but the right of being tried by a Court of the *United States.* His public relations are, not with the State of *Pennsylvania,* but with the Government of the *United States:* and if the Emperor of *Russia* should suppose that he had cause to complain of our treatment of his officer, he must address himself, not to the Governor of *Pennsylvania,* but to the President of the *United States.* But even where there was a cause of complaint, cases may be easily supposed, in which the President might think it more conducive to the peace of the nation, to send a foreign agent out of the country, to be punished by his own Sovereign, than to inflict punishment on him, by our own laws, here. These considerations are so manifest, that when the people of the *United States* were about to form a Federal Government, through which alone they were to maintain an intercourse with foreign nations, it would have seemed a want of common prudence, not to commit to that Government the management of all affairs respecting the public agents of those nations. Let us now advert to the instrument of our Federal Union, and we shall soon perceive, that the statesmen who framed it, were perfectly aware of the importance of placing all public foreign agents, Consuls included, under the complete superintendance of the Federal Government. It was through the judicial power, that those persons could principally be affected. Accordingly we find it provided, by the 2d sect. of the 3d article of the Constitution, that the judicial power shall extend "to all cases affecting Ambassadors, other public ministers, and Consuls." Words more comprehensive cannot be devised. They include suits of every kind civil, and criminal. This is not denied by the Attorney General of *Pennsylvania,* nor, as I understand, is it denied, that by virtue of this provision, Congress had a right to declare by law, that in no case, civil or criminal, should a State Court have jurisdiction over a Consul. But it is contended, that until Congress does by law declare so, the State Courts have *concurrent* jurisdiction with the Courts of the *United States;* or rather, that in the case before us, the State Courts *alone* have jurisdiction, because, Congress having passed no law defining the crime, or the punishment of rape, the Courts of the *United States* cannot take cognizance of the offence. The Constitution in the 1st section of the 3d article, declares in what Courts the judicial power shall be vested, *viz.* "in one Supreme Court, and in such inferior Courts as the Congress may from time to time ordain and establish."—In the 2d section, it enumerates the different cases to which the judicial power shall

extend, and then goes on to direct the distribution of that power among the different Courts.—"In all cases affecting Ambassadors, other public ministers, and Consuls, and those in which a State shall be a party, the Supreme Court shall have *original* jurisdiction: in all the other cases before mentioned, the Supreme Court shall have *appellate* jurisdiction, both as to law and fact, with such exceptions, and under such restrictions, as the Congress shall make." Thus the judicial power, extending to all cases affecting Consuls, and that portion of it which respects Consuls, being vested in the Supreme Court, it follows, that as soon as the Supreme Court was organized by law, it became immediately vested with original jurisdiction in every case by which a Consul might be affected. But was this an exclusive jurisdiction? The opinion of the Supreme Court, *Marbury* v. *Madison,* 1 *Cranch,* 137, goes far towards establishing the principle of exclusive jurisdiction. The point decided in that case, was, that where the Constitution had vested the Supreme Court with appellate jurisdiction, it was not in the power of Congress to give it original jurisdiction; and the whole scope the argument maintained in the Court's opinion, goes to prove, that where the Constitution had given original jurisdiction, it was not in the power of Congress to give appellate jurisdiction. This will appear from the following extract from that opinion. "If Congress remains at liberty to give this Court appellate jurisdiction, where the Constitution has declared their jurisdiction shall be original, the distribution of jurisdiction made in the Constitution, is form without substance. Affirmative words are often, in their operation, *negative* of other objects than those affirmed, and in this case, a negative or *exclusive* sense must be given to them, or they have no operation at all." "If the solicitude of the Convention, with respect to our peace with foreign powers, induced a provision that the Supreme Court should take original jurisdiction in cases which might be supposed to affect them; yet the clause would have proceeded no further than to provide for such cases, if no further restriction on the power of Congress had been intended. That they should have *appellate* jurisdiction in all *other* cases, with such exceptions as Congress might make, is no restriction, unless the words be deemed exclusive of original jurisdiction." Now taking this to be the construction of the Constitution, all these parts of the "act to establish the Judicial Courts of the *United States,*" which vest jurisdiction in cases affecting Consuls, in the District or Circuit Courts, would be unconstitutional and void. And, if it was intended by the Constitution, that no inferior Court of the *United States* should have jurisdiction, it cannot be supposed that a State Court was to have it, because there is much stronger reason for denying it to the State Courts, than to the inferior Courts of the *United States.* It will be perceived, that this principle shakes the decision in the case of *Ravara,* who was convicted in the Circuit Court, though not that part of the decision which respects the privilege of a Consul. But if the two cases cannot be reconciled, the Circuit Court must give way. Supposing, however, for argument's sake, that the Constitution does not vest the Supreme Court with *exclusive* jurisdiction; let us see whether Congress has not excluded the State Courts by the judiciary act passed 24th

September, 1789. By the 9th section, the District Courts are vested *exclusively of the Courts of the several States*, with cognizance of "all crimes and offences that shall be cognizable under the authority of the *United States*, committed within their respective districts, where no other punishment than whipping, not exceeding thirty stripes, a fine not exceeding 100 dollars, or a term of imprisonment not exceeding six months, is to be inflicted." Consuls are embraced in this jurisdiction, as plainly appears by considering the whole section, and as was declared by this Court, in *Manhardt* v. *Soderstrom*, (1 *Binn.* 138.) Then comes the 11th section; by which the Circuit Courts are vested with *exclusive cognizance* of "all crimes and offences cognizable under the authority of the *United States*, except where the said act otherwise provides, or the laws of the *United States* shall otherwise direct, and concurrent jurisdiction with the District Courts, of the crimes and offences cognizable therein." Does not this exclude the State Courts from jurisdiction in the case of Consuls? The only argument attempted, or that can be devised, in support of the negative, is, that no offence is cognizable in any Court of the *United States*, until Congress has declared it to be an offence, and prescribed the punishment. This is the only consideration which ever had the least weight in my mind. But upon mature reflection, I am unable to deny, that the Courts of the *United States* can take cognizance, when I find it written in the Constitution, *that the Supreme Court shall have jurisdiction in all cases affecting a Consul*. Is he not affected in criminal cases, much more than in civil? How then can I say, that the Supreme Court has no jurisdiction? But how, or by what law is he to be punished, in case of conviction? Shall he be punished by the law of *Pennsylvania*, where the offence was committed, inasmuch as there is no other express law which reaches his case? And it is on account of the *person only* that jurisdiction is given to the Courts of the *United States*. Does the 34th section of the judiciary act apply to the punishment of offences, by which it is enacted, "that the laws of the several States, except where the Constitution, treaties, or statutes of the *United States* shall otherwise require or provide, shall be regarded as rules of decision in trials at common law, in the Courts of the *United States*, in cases where they apply?" May a person convicted in a Court of the *United States*, of a crime of the highest grade, concerning which Congress has made no provision, be punished, according to the opinion of Judge STORY, in *The United States* v. *Coolidge*, 1 *Gallison's Rep.* 488, by fine and imprisonment, on the principles of the common law. Or is the Constitution to be so construed, as to exclude the jurisdiction of all inferior Courts, and yet suffer the authority of the Supreme Court to lie dormant, until called into action by a law which shall form a criminal code on the subject of Consuls? These are questions which may embarrass those who have to answer them, but are not necessary to be answered here. No embarrassment, however, could equal that into which this Court would be thrown, should it determine, that no Court of the *United States* has jurisdiction, in a case which affects a Consul *in every thing short of life*, when the Constitution declares, that the Supreme Court shall have jurisdiction *in all cases affecting him*. Upon full consideration, I am of opinion that the indictment should be quashed, because this Court has no jurisdiction.

BRACKENRIDGE J. concurred in the opinion to quash the indictment, because *exclusive jurisdiction* was vested in the Courts of the *United States*. Concerning the privileges of a Consul he did not think it necessary to give an opinion.

Indictment quashed.

68

MORGAN'S HEIRS V. MORGAN
2 Wheat. 290 (1817)

Mr. Chief Justice MARSHALL delivered the opinion of the court.

In this case two questions respecting the formal proceedings of the circuit court have been made by the counsel for the appellant.

The first is, that one of the complainants in the original suit having settled in the state of Kentucky after this bill was filed, that court could no longer entertain jurisdiction of the cause, and ought to have dismissed the bill.

We are all of opinion that the jurisdiction having once vested, was not devested by the change of residence of either of the parties.

69

WETHERBEE V. JOHNSON
14 Mass. 412 (1817)

PARKER, C. J. An appeal from a judgment of the supreme tribunal of the state to an inferior tribunal of the *United States* would be an anomaly in judicial proceedings; and no such process has ever been supposed to exist, before the passing of the act on which this appeal is claimed, which was during the pendency of this action. But as the act expressly provides such a remedy, for a party supposing himself aggrieved, by a judgment in a suit commenced against him, for any act done by him under color of his office, as inspector or other officer of the customs, we cannot deny him the privilege, if the statute is warranted by the constitution of the *United States*.

Among other things referred, by the constitution of the *United States*, to the judiciary power of the nation, are all cases in law and equity arising under the constitution or laws of the *United States*. If an action be brought by a citizen of any state against another citizen of the *same state*, the courts of the *United States* have not original jurisdiction; but the action must be brought in the state courts. But as the defendant in such suit may, in the act complained of, have been in the execution of some law of the *United States*, Congress may by law provide that the suit shall be removed to the national courts, when the defendant shall make it appear that his case is a proper subject of their jurisdiction, provided he seasonably require it.

Before the statute of March 3, 1815, but two modes existed by which the removal of a cause so circumstanced could be effected. These were both established by the first judiciary act, passed September 24, 1789. The first mode, which is the most convenient and the least exceptionable, was made applicable only to the cases of an alien, or citizen of another state, being defendants. If they are sued in a state court, they may, at the time of entering their appearance, file a petition for the removal of the cause for trial into the Circuit Court; and the court to which the process is returned, upon satisfactory proof that the defendant is an alien or citizen of another state, upon taking sureties for the prosecution of the action in the court to which it is removed, are required to stay all further proceedings. This provision could be easily executed: it saved the jurisdiction of the state court, if the defendant submitted to a trial; and the judgment rendered was left undisturbed.

The same process of removal might have been provided for all other cases of which the state courts have original jurisdiction, and in which questions may arise over which the judicial power of the nation has cognizance according to the constitution, and much doubt and difficulty would have been saved thereby.

But it was thought proper to provide another mode for the exercise of jurisdiction, by the supreme national tribunal, over questions incidentally arising in a state court, which are, by the constitution, subjects of national jurisdiction; and this is to remove the record by writ of error into the Supreme Court of the *United States*. To carry this into effect, some error existing in the record itself must be suggested. So that, unless it appear, by a bill of exceptions or otherwise, that a decision has been made upon some of the questions which are referred by the constitution to the national judiciary, no such process can lie.

Whether this mode of revising judgments of the Supreme Court of a state is justified by the constitution, has been a question of much doubt and argument; and the power claimed by the Supreme Court of the *United States*, under this section of the law, has been denied by the highest court of law in *Virginia*. The justices of that court think that it never was the intention of the constitution of the *United States* to consider the Supreme Courts of the several states as tribunals inferior to the courts of the *United States*; or that a privilege was given to a defendant, who had submitted to the jurisdiction of a state court, taken his trial there, and finally failed in his defence, to harass his adversary, by intercepting the remedy, which he may have obtained at great expense, and carrying his cause to a tribunal whose sessions would be at the seat of the national government, perhaps a thousand miles distant from the place of his residence.

Whether the court of the *United States*, or the court of *Virginia*, are right on this important question, the present case does not call upon us to decide.

In the act under consideration, the removal of a cause upon the petition of the defendant, alleging that the act done was in virtue or under color of his office, as inspector of the customs, is provided for; and it is also provided that either party, after judgment, may remove the cause into the Circuit Court by writ of error. The first of these two modes is similar to the provision respecting aliens, &c., in the first judiciary act. The second substitutes the Circuit Court of the *United States* for the Supreme Court, and provides for a trial of the facts, as well as the law, upon a writ of error—a proceeding before unknown in courts of justice.

But a third mode is also provided in the same act, which is the one under which the appeal in this case is claimed. The sixth section of that act provides that it shall be lawful, in any action pending, or afterwards commenced, before any state court whatever, for any thing done, or omitted to be done, by an inspector or other officer of the customs, for either party to remove and transfer, by appeal, such decision, during the session or term of such court at which the same shall have taken place, from such court to the next Circuit Court of the *United States*, to be held in the district in which such appeal shall be taken in manner aforesaid; and that it shall be competent for either party, within six months from the rendition of judgment in any such cause, by writ of error or other process, to remove the same to the Circuit Court aforesaid; and the Circuit Court shall proceed to try the law and the facts in the same manner as if the suit had been there originally commenced the judgment in such case notwithstanding.

This sweeping clause undoubtedly comprehends the case now before us; so that the only question for us to decide is, whether Congress had authority, by the constitution, to enact it

By this provision, the supreme tribunals of a state are considered, not only as inferior to the Supreme Court of the *United States*, which is not admitted in *Virginia*, but to the Circuit Courts, which are by the constitution and laws expressly made inferior courts of the *United States;* and if it be constitutional, Congress may authorize appeals to the District Court also; and if they should see fit to establish still inferior tribunals, they may provide for an appeal to, or a writ of error from, such courts, however low in the rank of judicial tribunal; giving them authority to reverse and annul the solemn judgments of what are called the supreme tribunals of a state.

This law was passed *flagrante bello*, and, we believe, without a due consideration of the independence of the state courts, and the national judicial power, as established by the constitution of the *United States*. By that constitution, (article 3d, section 1st,) the judicial power of the *United States* is vested in one Supreme Court, and in such inferior courts as Congress may from time to time ordain and establish; and in the second section of the same article, it is provided that, in all cases affecting ambassadors, other public ministers and consuls, and those in which a state shall be a party, the Supreme Court shall have original jurisdiction; and in all other cases, of which they have jurisdiction, it shall be appellate, both as to law and fact, under such regulations as the Congress shall make.

Taking the constitution, in this respect, as it was originally formed and adopted, without reference to the amendments ratified before the first judiciary act was passed, we apprehend its true meaning to be, that none but the Supreme Court of the *United States* could entertain jurisdiction, by way of appeal from the judgments of the state courts, in cases originally cognizable and commenced in those courts; and that any act of Congress, giving such jurisdiction to any inferior court of the *United States*, would have been unconstitutional and void. Indeed, such a power was never supposed to exist; for the consequence would have been universally seen to be a prostration of the dignity, and with that the usefulness, of the state tribunals. The constitution would never have been adopted by any one state, under such a construction.

But even the appellate jurisdiction of the Supreme Court of the *United States*, in the general terms in which it is expressed in the constitution, was thought, by a majority of the states, to be an unnecessary, if not a dangerous, interference with the independence of the state tribunals, and as tending to vex and harass the citizen by a multitude of trials; the last of which would be remote from his place of residence, where it would be difficult, and sometimes impossible, for him to prove facts upon which his cause depended. Besides which, it infringed one of the most ancient and cherished principles of the common law, that the trial of facts should be in the vicinage where they happened.

For these reasons, an amendment was adopted, which is now an article of the constitution, as operative and binding as if it were a part of the original system. This amendment restricts the power, as described in the second section of the third article; and provides that, "In suits at common law, where the value in controversy shall exceed twenty dollars, the right of trial by jury shall be preserved; and no fact tried by a jury shall be otherwise reëxamined in any court of the *United States*, than according to the rules of the common law." Since the adoption of this amendment, the *appellate* power, even of the Supreme Court of the *United States*, can only be exercised over questions of law appearing on record. For the common law knows nothing of a reëxamination of facts once tried by a jury, except in cases of new trial, which can only be granted by the court before which the trial was; no such thing as an appeal being known in that system.

Admitting, then, that the Circuit Court of the *United States* in the district of *Massachusetts* to be superior to the Supreme Judicial Court of *Massachusetts*—which can, however, be only admitted for argument—the constitution of the *United States* has expressly denied it the power of reëxamining a judgment founded on a verdict, by appeal. or in any other way than by writ of error, for some error in law arising on the record.

But the statute of March 3, 1815, provides that, after a trial by jury in the Supreme Court of the state, nay, it may be, after three trials, according to the organization of our state Courts, and the laws regulating them, and all this by the consent of the party against whom final judgment is rendered, he may still appeal to the Circuit Court, where he may have another trial by jury; and if he fails even there, he may be shielded from execution by the will of the judge who sits in the last trial. This is certainly not according to the rules of the common law, and cannot

therefore, by the constitution, be within the power of Congress to establish.

This act of Congress was limited in its operation to one year from the time of its enactment, and it has expired. The defendant's motion was made while it was in force; so that they would be entitled to the privilege it gives, if it were ever binding upon the Court. Since it has expired, and probably will never be revived we should willingly have avoided any discussion of its principles. It was undoubtedly passed under a belief that the necessity of the times required it; but no necessity can justify a judicial tribunal in executing an act which is not authorized by the constitution, when any citizen of the state claims his rights in opposition to it.

70

JAMES MADISON TO JAMES MONROE
27 Dec. 1817
Writings 8:406–7

These considerations remind me of the attempts in the Convention to vest in the Judiciary Dept. a qualified negative on Legislative *bills*. Such a Controul, restricted to Constitutional points, besides giving greater stability & system to the rules of expounding the Instrument, would have precluded the question of a Judiciary annulment of Legislative *Acts*.

71

UNITED STATES V. BEVANS
3 Wheat. 336 (1818)

Mr. Chief Justice MARSHALL delivered the opinion of the court. The question proposed by the circuit court, which will be first considered, is,

Whether the offence charged in this indictment was, according to the statement of facts which accompanies the question, "within the jurisdiction or cognizance of the circuit court of the United States for the district of Massachusetts?"

The indictment appears to be founded on the 8th sec. of the "act for the punishment of certain crimes against the United States." That section gives the courts of the union cognizance of certain offences committed on the high seas, or in any river, haven, basin, or bay, out of the jurisdiction of any particular state.

Whatever may be the constitutional power of congress, it is clear that this power has not been so exercised, in this section of the act, as to confer on its courts jurisdiction over any offence committed in a river, haven, basin or bay, which river, basin or bay is within the jurisdiction of any particular state.

What then is the extent of jurisdiction which a state possesses?

We answer, without hesitation, the jurisdiction of a state is co-extensive with its territory; co-extensive with its legislative power.

The place described is unquestionably within the original territory of Massachusetts. It is then within the jurisdiction of Massachusetts, unless that jurisdiction has been ceded to the United States.

It is contended to have been ceded by that article in the constitution which declares, that "the judicial power shall extend to all cases of admiralty and maritime jurisdiction." The argument is, that the power thus granted is conclusive; and that the murder committed by the prisoner is a case of admiralty and maritime jurisdiction.

Let this be admitted. It proves the power of congress to legislate in the case; not that congress has exercised that power. It has been argued, and the argument in favour of, as well as that against the proposition, deserves great consideration, that courts of common law have concurrent jurisdiction with courts of admiralty, over murder committed in bays which are inclosed parts of the sea; and that for this reason the offence is within the jurisdiction of Massachusetts. But in construing the act of congress, the court believes it to be unnecessary to pursue the investigation which has been so well made at the bar respecting the jurisdiction of these rival Courts.

To bring the offence within the jurisdiction of the courts of the union, it must have been committed in a river, &c. out of the jurisdiction of any state. It is not the offence committed, but the bay in which it is committed, which must be out of the jurisdiction of the state. If, then, it should be true that Massachusetts can take no cognizance of the offence; yet, unless the place itself be out of her jurisdiction, congress has not given cognizance of that offence to its courts. If there be a common jurisdiction, the crime cannot be punished in the courts of the union.

Can the cession of all cases of admiralty and maritime jurisdiction be construed into a cession of the waters on which those cases may arise?

This is a question on which the court is incapable of feeling a doubt. The article which describes the judicial power of the United States is not intended for the cession of territory or of general jurisdiction. It is obviously designed for other purposes. It is in the 8th section of the 2d article, we are to look for cessions of territory and of exclusive jurisdiction. Congress has power to exercise exclusive jurisdiction over this district, and over all places purchased by the consent of the legislature of the state in which the same shall be, for the erection of forts, magazines, arsenals, dock yards, and other needful buildings.

It is observable, that the power of exclusive legislation (which is jurisdiction) is united with cession of territory, which is to be the free act of the states. It is difficult to compare the two sections together, without feeling a conviction, not to be strengthened by any commentary on them, that, in describing the judicial power, the framers of

our constitution had not in view any cession of territory, or, which is essentially the same, of general jurisdiction.

It is not questioned, that whatever may be necessary to the full and unlimited exercise of admiralty and maritime jurisdiction, is in the government of the union. Congress may pass all laws which are necessary and proper for giving the most complete effect to this power. Still, the general jurisdiction over the place, subject to this grant of power, adheres to the territory, as a portion of sovereignty not yet given away. The residuary powers of legislation are still in Massachusetts. Suppose, for example, the power of regulating trade had not been given to the general government. Would this extension of the judicial power to all cases of admiralty and maritime jurisdiction, have devested Massachusetts of the power to regulate the trade of her bay? As the powers of the respective governments now stand, if two citizens of Massachusetts step into shallow water when the tide flows, and fight a duel, are they not within the jurisdiction, and punishable by the laws, of Massachusetts? If these questions must be answered in the affirmative, and we believe they must, then the bay in which this murder was committed, is not out of the jurisdiction of a state, and the circuit court of Massachusetts is not authorized, by the section under consideration, to take cognizance of the murder which has been committed.

It may be deemed within the scope of the question certified to this court, to inquire whether any other part of the act has given cognizance of this murder to the circuit court of Massachusetts?

The third section enacts "that if any person or persons shall, within any fort, arsenal, dock-yard, magazine, or in any other place, or district of country, under the sole and exclusive jurisdiction of the United States, commit the crime of wilful murder, such person or persons, on being thereof convicted, shall suffer death."

Although the bay on which this murder was committed, might not be out of the jurisdiction of Massachusetts, the ship of war on the deck of which it was committed, is, it has been said, "a *place* within the sole and exclusive jurisdiction of the United States," whose courts may consequently take cognizance of the offence.

That a government which possesses the broad power of war; which "may provide and maintain a navy;" which "may make rules for the government and regulation of the land and naval forces," has power to punish an offence committed by a marine, on board a ship of war, wherever that ship may lie, is a proposition never to be questioned in this court. On this section, as on the 8th, the inquiry respects, not the extent of the power of congress but the extent to which that power has been exercised.

The objects with which the word *"place"* is associated, are all, in their nature, fixed and territorial. A fort, an arsenal, a dock-yard, a magazine, are all of this character. When the sentence proceeds with the words, "or in any other place or district of country under the sole and exclusive jurisdiction of the United States," the construction seems irresistible, that, by the words "other place," was intended another place of a similar character with those previously enumerated, and with that which follows. Congress might have omitted, in its enumeration, some similar place within its exclusive jurisdiction, which was not comprehended by any of the terms employed, to which some other name might be given; and therefore, the words "other place," or "district of country," were added; but the context shows the mind of the legislature to have been fixed on territorial objects of a similar character.

This construction is strengthened by the fact that, at the time of passing this law, the United States did not possess a single ship of war. It may, therefore, be reasonably supposed, that a provision for the punishment of crimes in the navy might be postponed until some provision for a navy should be made. While taking this view of the subject, it is not entirely unworthy of remark, that afterwards, when a navy was created, and congress did proceed to make rules for its regulation and government, no jurisdiction is given to the courts of the United States, of any crime committed in a ship of war, wherever it may be stationed. Upon these reasons the court is of opinion, that a murder committed on board a ship of war, lying within the harbour of Boston, is not cognizable in the circuit court for the district of Massachusetts; which opinion is to be certified to the court.

The opinion of the court, on this point, is believed to render it unnecessary to decide the question respecting the jurisdiction of the state court in that case.

72

COOPER V. GALBRAITH
6 Fed. Cas. 472, no. 3,193 (C.C.D.Pa. 1819)

WASHINGTON, Circuit Justice, charged the jury:

The question of jurisdiction is first to be considered. It is composed of law and fact; and as soon as the latter is ascertained, the question is relieved from every difficulty. Citizenship, when spoken of in the constitution in reference to the jurisdiction of the courts of the United States, means nothing more than residence. The citizens of each state, are entitled to all the privileges and immunities of citizens in the several states; but to give jurisdiction to the courts of the United States, the suit must be between citizens residing in different states, or between a citizen and an alien. If a citizen of one state should think proper to change his domicil, and to remove himself and family, if he have one, into another state, with a bona fide intention of abandoning his former place of residence, and to become an inhabitant or resident of the state to which he removes; he becomes, immediately upon such removal, accompanied with such intention, a resident citizen of that state, and may maintain an action in the circuit court of the state which he has abandoned, or in that of any other state, except the one in which he has settled himself. Time, in relation to his new residence, occupation, a sudden removal back to the state he had abandoned, after instituting a suit in the circuit court of that state; and the like; are circumstances which may be relied upon, to show, that his

first removal was not bona fide, or intended to be permanent; but they will not be sufficient to disprove his citizenship in the place of his new domicil, and to exclude him from the jurisdiction of the circuit court for the district in which he had formerly resided; if the jury are satisfied, from the evidence, that his first removal was bona fide, and without an intention of returning. And, if the jury be so satisfied, the jurisdiction will not be ousted, though it should appear, that one of the motives of the plaintiff in removing, or indeed his only motive, was to enable him to bring a suit in a court of the United States, sitting in the state he had removed from. The circumstances to prove a bona fide intention in the lessor of the plaintiff, to change his domicil, are very strong. He was the professor of chemistry, in the College of Carlisle; the salary was small; and it is probable, insufficient to support his family. He spoke to his friends, at different times, of his determination to remove to New Orleans, or to Alabama; and there to prosecute the practice of law. He accordingly resigned his professorship, sold his furniture, broke up his family establishment; and, after spending some time in the family of a friend, as guests, he rented a house for a year, in Camden, and there re-established himself and his family. It was after this step was taken, that he was elected a professor in the university of this city; where he was seen in the forenoon attending to his duties; and in the evening he returned to his family. His occupation in Philadelphia, under these circumstances, is not of itself sufficient to disprove his having been, at the same time, a resident citizen of the state where his family was. In Hylton's Lessee v. Brown [Case No. 6,981], in this court, the case was, that Joseph Griswold, who resided with his family in New-York, came to Philadelphia, with his son, in order to establish him here as a distiller, and to instruct him in that art. He continued here, engaged in that business, for eight or nine months, returning at intervals, during that period, to visit his family; and, after he had completed the business which caused his visit to this city, he returned to his family in New-York, and there remained. The court decided, that the temporary abode of Griswold in Philadelphia, without his family, for a special purpose, with the animo revertendi always continuing, did not make him an inhabitant of this state.

Having thus stated what are the principles of law which must govern this case, the jury will decide, whether, upon the evidence, the removal of the plaintiff to New-Jersey was bona fide, and with intention to become a resident and inhabitant of that state.

73

UNITED STATES V. SCHOONER LITTLE CHARLES
1 Marshall's C.C. 380 (C.C.D.Va. 1819)

The courts of the United States have never doubted their right to proceed under their general powers, as courts of admiralty, where they were not restrained from the use of those powers by statute.

74

COHENS v. VIRGINIA
6 Wheat. 264 (1821)

Mr. Chief Justice MARSHALL delivered the opinion of the Court.

This is a writ of error to a judgment rendered in the Court of Hustings for the borough of Norfolk, as an information for selling lottery tickets, contrary to an act of the Legislature of Virginia. In the State Court, the defendant claimed the protection of an act of Congress. A case was agreed between the parties, which states the act of Assembly on which the prosecution was founded, and the act of Congress on which the defendant relied, and concludes in these words: "If upon this case the Court shall be of opinion that the acts of Congress before mentioned were valid, and, on the true construction of those acts, the lottery tickets sold by the defendants as aforesaid, might lawfully be sold within the State of Virginia, notwithstanding the act or statute of the general assembly of Virginia prohibiting such sale, then judgment to be entered for the defendants; And if the Court should be of opinion that the statute or act of the General Assembly of the State of Virginia, prohibiting such sale, is valid, notwithstanding the said acts of Congress, then judgment to be entered that the defendants are guilty, and that the Commonwealth recover against them one hundred dollars and costs."

Judgment was rendered against the defendants; and the Court in which it was rendered being the highest Court of the State in which the cause was cognizable, the record has been brought into this Court by writ of error.[a]

The defendant in error moves to dismiss this writ, for want of jurisdiction.

In support of this motion, three points have been made, and argued with the ability which the importance of the question merits. These points are—

1st. That a State is a defendant.

2d. That no writ of error lies from this Court to a State Court.

3d. The third point has been presented in different forms by the gentlemen who have argued it. The counsel who opened the cause said, that the want of jurisdiction was shown by the subject matter of the case. The counsel who followed him said, that jurisdiction was not given by the judiciary act. The Court has bestowed all its attention on the arguments of both gentlemen, and supposes that their tendency is to show that this Court has no jurisdic-

[a]The plaintiff in error prayed an appeal from the judgment of the Court of Hustings, but it was refused, on the ground that there was no higher State tribunal which could take cognizance of the case.

tion of the case, or, in other words, has no right to review the judgment of the State Court, because neither the constitution nor any law of the United States has been violated by that judgment.

The questions presented to the Court by the two first points made at the bar are of great magnitude, and may be truly said vitally to affect the Union. They exclude the inquiry whether the constitution and laws of the United States have been violated by the judgment which the plaintiffs in error seek to review; and maintain that, admitting such violation, it is not in the power of the government to apply a corrective. They maintain that the nation does not possess a department capable of restraining peaceably, and by authority of law, any attempts which may be made, by a part, against the legitimate powers of the whole; and that the government is reduced to the alternative of submitting to such attempts, or of resisting them by force. They maintain that the constitution of the United States has provided no tribunal for the final construction of itself, or of the laws or treaties of the nation; but that this power may be exercised in the last resort by the Courts of every State in the Union. That the constitution, laws, and treaties, may receive as many constructions as there are States; and that this is not a mischief, or, if a mischief, is irremediable. These abstract propositions are to be determined; for he who demands decision without permitting inquiry, affirms that the decision he asks does not depend on inquiry.

If such be the constitution, it is the duty of the Court to bow with respectful submission to its provisions. If such be not the constitution, it is equally the duty of this Court to say so; and to perform that task which the American people have assigned to the judicial department.

1st. The first question to be considered is, whether the jurisdiction of this Court is excluded by the character of the parties, one of them being a State, and the other a citizen of that State?

The second section of the third article of the constitution defines the extent of the judicial power of the United States. Jurisdiction is given to the Courts of the Union in two classes of cases. In the first, their jurisdiction depends on the character of the cause, whoever may be the parties. This class comprehends "all cases in law and equity arising under this constitution, the laws of the United States, and treaties made, or which shall be made, under their authority." This clause extends the jurisdiction of the Court to all the cases described, without making in its terms any exception whatever, and without any regard to the condition of the party. If there be any exception, it is to be implied against the express words of the article.

In the second class, the jurisdiction depends entirely on the character of the parties. In this are comprehended "controversies between two or more States, between a State and citizens of another State," "and between a State and foreign States, citizens or subjects." If these be the parties, it is entirely unimportant what may be the subject of controversy. Be it what it may, these parties have a constitutional right to come into the Courts of the Union.

The counsel for the defendant in error have stated that the cases which arise under the constitution must grow out of those provisions which are capable of self-execution; examples of which are to be found in the 2d section of the 4th article, and in the 10th section of the 1st article.

A case which arises under a law of the United States must, we are likewise told, be a right given by some act which becomes necessary to execute the powers given in the constitution, of which the law of naturalization is mentioned as an example.

The use intended to be made of this exposition of the first part of the section, defining the extent of the judicial power, is not clearly understood. If the intention be merely to distinguish cases arising under the constitution, from those arising under a law, for the sake of precision in the application of this argument, these propositions will not be controverted. If it be to maintain that a case arising under the constitution, or a law, must be one in which a party comes into Court to demand something conferred on him by the constitution or a law, we think the construction too narrow. A case in law or equity consists of the right of the one party, as well as of the other, and may truly be said to arise under the constitution or a law of the United States, whenever its correct decision depends on the construction of either. Congress seems to have intended to give its own construction of this part of the constitution in the 25th section of the judiciary act; and we perceive no reason to depart from that construction.

The jurisdiction of the Court, then, being extended by the letter of the constitution to all cases arising under it, or under the laws of the United States, it follows that those who would withdraw any case of this description from that jurisdiction, must sustain the exemption they claim on the spirit and true meaning of the constitution, which spirit and true meaning must be so apparent as to overrule the words which its framers have employed.

The counsel for the defendant in error have undertaken to do this; and have laid down the general proposition, that a sovereign independent State is not suable, except by its own consent.

This general proposition will not be controverted. But its consent is not requisite in each particular case. It may be given in a general law. And if a State has surrendered any portion of its sovereignty, the question whether a liability to suit be a part of this portion, depends on the instrument by which the surrender is made. If, upon a just construction of that instrument, it shall appear that the State has submitted to be sued, then it has parted with this sovereign right of judging in every case on the justice of its own pretensions, and has entrusted that power to a tribunal in whose impartiality it confides.

The American States, as well as the American people, have believed a close and firm Union to be essential to their liberty and to their happiness. They have been taught by experience, that this Union cannot exist without a government for the whole; and they have been taught by the same experience that this government would be a mere shadow, that must disappoint all their hopes, unless invested with large portions of that sovereignty which belongs to independent States. Under the influence of this opinion, and thus instructed by experience, the American people, in the conventions of their respective States, adopted the present constitution.

If it could be doubted, whether from its nature, it were not supreme in all cases where it is empowered to act, that doubt would be removed by the declaration, that "this constitution, and the laws of the United States, which shall be made in pursuance thereof, and all treaties made, or which shall be made, under the authority of the United States, shall be the supreme law of the land; and the judges in every State shall be bound thereby; any thing in the constitution or laws of any State to the contrary notwithstanding."

This is the authoritative language of the American people; and, if gentlemen please, of the American States. It marks, with lines too strong to be mistaken, the characteristic distinction between the government of the Union, and those of the States. The general government, though limited as to its objects, is supreme with respect to those objects. This principle is a part of the constitution; and if there be any who deny its necessity, none can deny its authority.

To this supreme government ample powers are confided; and if it were possible to doubt the great purposes for which they were so confided, the people of the United States have declared, that they are given "in order to form a more perfect union, establish justice, ensure domestic tranquillity, provide for the common defence, promote the general welfare, and secure the blessings of liberty to themselves and their posterity."

With the ample powers confided to this supreme government, for these interesting purposes, are connected many express and important limitations on the sovereignty of the States, which are made for the same purposes. The powers of the Union, on the great subjects of war, peace, and commerce, and on many others, are in themselves limitations of the sovereignty of the States; but in addition to these, the sovereignty of the States is surrendered in many instances where the surrender can only operate to the benefit of the people, and where, perhaps, no other power is conferred on Congress than a conservative power to maintain the principles established in the constitution. The maintenance of these principles in their purity, is certainly among the great duties of the government. One of the instruments by which this duty may be peaceably performed, is the judicial department. It is authorized to decide all cases of every description, arising under the constitution or laws of the United States. From this general grant of jurisdiction, no exception is made of those cases in which a State may be a party. When we consider the situation of the government of the Union and of a State, in relation to each other; the nature of our constitution; the subordination of the State governments to that constitution; the great purpose for which jurisdiction over all cases arising under the constitution and laws of the United States, is confided to the judicial department; are we at liberty to insert in this general grant, an exception of those cases in which a State may be a party? Will the spirit of the constitution justify this attempt to control its words? We think it will not. We think a case arising under the constitution or laws of the United States, is cognizable in the Courts of the Union, whoever may be the parties to that case.

Had any doubt existed with respect to the just construction of this part of the section, that doubt would have been removed by the enumeration of those cases to which the jurisdiction of the federal Courts is extended, in consequence of the character of the parties. In that enumeration, we find "controversies between two or more States, between a State and citizens of another State," "and between a State and foreign States, citizens, or subjects."

One of the express objects, then, for which the judicial department was established, is the decision of controversies between States, and between a State and individuals. The mere circumstance, that a State is a party, gives jurisdiction to the Court. How, then, can it be contended, that the very same instrument, in the very same section, should be so construed, as that this same circumstance should withdraw a case from the jurisdiction of the Court, where the constitution or laws of the United States are supposed to have been violated? The constitution gave to every person having a claim upon a State, a right to submit his case to the Court of the nation. However unimportant his claim might be, however little the community might be interested in its decision, the framers of our constitution thought it necessary for the purposes of justice, to provide a tribunal as superior to influence as possible, in which that claim might be decided. Can it be imagined, that the same persons considered a case involving the constitution of our country and the majesty of the laws, questions in which every American citizen must be deeply interested, as withdrawn from this tribunal, because a State is a party?

While weighing arguments drawn from the nature of government, and from the general spirit of an instrument, and urged for the purpose of narrowing the construction which the words of that instrument seem to require, it is proper to place in the opposite scale those principles, drawn from the same sources, which go to sustain the words in their full operation and natural import. One of these, which has been pressed with great force by the counsel for the plaintiffs in error, is, that the judicial power of every well constituted government must be co-extensive with the legislative, and must be capable of deciding every judicial question which grows out of the constitution and laws.

If any proposition may be considered as a political axiom, this, we think, may be so considered. In reasoning upon it as an abstract question, there would, probably, exist no contrariety of opinion respecting it. Every argument, proving the necessity of the department, proves also the propriety of giving this extent to it. We do not mean to say, that the jurisdiction of the Courts of the Union should be construed to be co-extensive with the legislative, merely because it is fit that it should be so; but we mean to say, that this fitness furnishes an argument in construing the constitution which ought never to be overlooked, and which is most especially entitled to consideration, when we are inquiring, whether the words of the instrument which purport to establish this principle, shall be contracted for the purpose of destroying it.

The mischievous consequences of the construction contended for on the part of Virginia, are also entitled to great consideration. It would prostrate, it has been said,

the government and its laws at the feet of every State in the Union. And would not this be its effect? What power of the government could be executed by its own means, in any State disposed to resist its execution by a course of legislation? The laws must be executed by individuals acting within the several States. If these individuals may be exposed to penalties, and if the Courts of the Union cannot correct the judgments by which these penalties may be enforced, the course of the government may be, at any time, arrested by the will of one of its members. Each member will possess a *veto* on the will of the whole.

The answer which has been given to this argument, does not deny its truth, but insists that confidence is reposed, and may be safely reposed, in the State institutions; and that, if they shall ever become so insane or so wicked as to seek the destruction of the government, they may accomplish their object by refusing to perform the functions assigned to them.

We readily concur with the counsel for the defendant, in the declaration, that the cases which have been put of direct legislative resistance for the purpose of opposing the acknowledged powers of the government, are extreme cases, and in the hope, that they will never occur; but we cannot help believing, that a general conviction of the total incapacity of the government to protect itself and its laws in such cases, would contribute in no inconsiderable degree to their occurrence.

Let it be admitted, that the cases which have been put are extreme and improbable, yet there are gradations of opposition to the laws, far short of those cases, which might have a baneful influence on the affairs of the nation. Different States may entertain different opinions on the true construction of the constitutional powers of Congress. We know, that at one time, the assumption of the debts contracted by the several States, during the war of our revolution, was deemed unconstitutional by some of them. We know, too, that at other times, certain taxes, imposed by Congress, have been pronounced unconsitutional. Other laws have been questioned partially, while they were supported by the great majority of the American people. We have no assurance that we shall be less divided than we have been. States may legislate in conformity to their opinions, and may enforce those opinions by penalties. It would be hazarding too much to assert, that the judicatures of the States will be exempt from the prejudices by which the legislatures and people are influenced, and will constitute perfectly impartial tribunals. In many States the judges are dependent for office and for salary on the will of the legislature. The constitution of the United States furnishes no security against the universal adoption of this principle. When we observe the importance which that constitution attaches to the independence of judges, we are the less inclined to suppose that it can have intended to leave these constitutional questions to tribunals where this independence may not exist, in all cases where a State shall prosecute an individual who claims the protection of an act of Congress. These prosecutions may take place even without a legislative act. A person making a seizure under an act of Congress, may be indicted as a trespasser, if force has been employed, and of this a jury may judge. How extensive may be the mischief if the first decisions in such cases should be final!

These collisions may take place in times of no extraordinary commotion. But a constitution is framed for ages to come, and is designed to approach immortality as nearly as human institutions can approach it. Its course cannot always be tranquil. It is exposed to storms and tempests, and its framers must be unwise statesmen indeed, if they have not provided it, as far as its nature will permit, with the means of self-preservation from the perils it may be destined to encounter. No government ought to be so defective in its organization, as not to contain within itself the means of securing the execution of its own laws against other dangers than those which occur every day. Courts of justice are the means most usually employed; and it is reasonable to expect that a government should repose on its own Courts, rather than on others. There is certainly nothing in the circumstances under which our constitution was formed; nothing in the history of the times, which would justify the opinion that the confidence reposed in the States was so implicit as to leave in them and their tribunals the power of resisting or defeating, in the form of law, the legitimate measures of the Union. The requisitions of Congress, under the confederation, were as constitutionally obligatory as the laws enacted by the present Congress. That they were habitually disregarded, is a fact of universal notoriety. With the knowledge of this fact, and under its full pressure, a convention was assembled to change the system. Is it so improbable that they should confer on the judicial department the power of construing the constitution and laws of the Union in every case, in the last resort, and of preserving them from all violation from every quarter, so far as judicial decisions can preserve them, that this improbability should essentially affect the construction of the new system? We are told, and we are truly told, that the great change which is to give efficacy to the present system, is its ability to act on individuals directly, instead of acting through the instrumentality of State governments. But, ought not this ability, in reason and sound policy, to be applied directly to the protection of individuals employed in the execution of the laws, as well as to their coercion. Your laws reach the individual without the aid of any other power; why may they not protect him from punishment for performing his duty in executing them?

The counsel for Virginia endeavour to obviate the force of these arguments by saying, that the dangers they suggest, if not imaginary, are inevitable; that the constitution can make no provision against them; and that, therefore, in construing that instrument, they ought to be excluded from our consideration. This state of things, they say, cannot arise until there shall be a disposition so hostile to the present political system as to produce a determination to destroy it; and, when that determination shall be produced, its effects will not be restrained by parchment stipulations. The fate of the constitution will not then depend on judicial decisions. But, should no appeal be made to force, the States can put an end to the government by refusing to act. They have only not to elect Senators, and it expires without a struggle.

It is very true that, whenever hostility to the existing system shall become universal, it will be also irresistible. The people made the constitution, and the people can unmake it. It is the creature of their will, and lives only by their will. But this supreme and irresistible power to make or to unmake, resides only in the whole body of the people; not in any sub-division of them. The attempt of any of the parts to exercise it is usurpation, and ought to be repelled by those to whom the people have delegated their power of repelling it.

The acknowledged inability of the government, then, to sustain itself against the public will, and, by force or otherwise, to control the whole nation, is no sound argument in support of its constitutional inability to preserve itself against a section of the nation acting in opposition to the general will.

It is true, that if all the States, or a majority of them, refuse to elect Senators, the legislative powers of the Union will be suspended. But if any one State shall refuse to elect them, the Senate will not, on that account, be the less capable of performing all its functions. The argument founded on this fact would seem rather to prove the subordination of the parts to the whole, than the complete independence of any one of them. The framers of the constitution were, indeed, unable to make any provisions which should protect that instrument against a general combination of the States, or of the people, for its destruction; and, conscious of this inability, they have not made the attempt. But they were able to provide against the operation of measures adopted in any one State, whose tendency might be to arrest the execution of the laws, and this it was the part of true wisdom to attempt. We think they have attempted it.

It has been also urged, as an additional objection to the jurisdiction of the Court, that cases between a State and one of its own citizens, do not come within the general scope of the constitution; and were obviously never intended to be made cognizable in the federal Courts. The State tribunals might be suspected of partiality in cases between itself or its citizens and aliens, or the citizens of another State, but not in proceedings by a State against its own citizens. That jealousy which might exist in the first case, could not exist in the last, and therefore the judicial power is not extended to the last.

This is very true, so far as jurisdiction depends on the character of the parties; and the argument would have great force if urged to prove that this Court could not establish the demand of a citizen upon his State, but is not entitled to the same force when urged to prove that this Court cannot inquire whether the constitution or laws of the United States protect a citizen from a prosecution instituted against him by a State. If jurisdiction depended entirely on the character of the parties, and was not given where the parties have not an original right to come into Court, that part of the 2d section of the 3d article, which extends the judicial power to all cases arising under the constitution and laws of the United States, would be mere surplusage. It is to give jurisdiction where the character of the parties would not give it, that this very important part of the clause was inserted. It may be true, that the partiality of the State tribunals, in ordinary controversies between a State and its citizens, was not apprehended, and therefore the judicial power of the Union was not extended to such cases; but this was not the sole nor the greatest object for which this department was created. A more important, a much more interesting object, was the preservation of the constitution and laws of the United States, so far as they can be preserved by judicial authority; and therefore the jurisdiction of the Courts of the Union was expressly extended to all cases arising under that constitution and those laws. If the constitution or laws may be violated by proceedings instituted by a State against its own citizens, and if that violation may be such as essentially to affect the constitution and the laws, such as to arrest the progress of government in its constitutional course, why should these cases be excepted from that provision which expressly extends the judicial power of the Union to *all* cases arising under the constitution and laws?

After bestowing on this subject the most attentive consideration, the Court can perceive no reason founded on the character of the parties for introducing an exception which the constitution has not made; and we think that the judicial power, as originally given, extends to all cases arising under the constitution or a law of the United States, whoever may be the parties.

It has been also contended, that this jurisdiction, if given, is original, and cannot be exercised in the appellate form.

The words of the constitution are, "in all cases affecting ambassadors, other public ministers, and consuls, and those in which a State shall be a party, the Supreme Court shall have original jurisdiction. In all the other cases before mentioned, the Supreme Court shall have appellate jurisdiction."

This distinction between original and appellate jurisdiction, excludes, we are told, in all cases, the exercise of the one where the other is given.

The constitution gives the Supreme Court original jurisdiction in certain enumerated cases, and gives it appellate jurisdiction in all others. Among those in which jurisdiction must be exercised in the appellate form, are cases arising under the constitution and laws of the United States. These provisions of the constitution are equally obligatory, and are to be equally respected. If a State be a party, the jurisdiction of this Court is original; if the case arise under a constitution or a law, the jurisdiction is appellate. But a case to which a State is a party may arise under the constitution or a law of the United States. What rule is applicable to such a case? What, then, becomes the duty of the Court? Certainly, we think, so to construe the constitution as to give effect to both provisions, as far as it is possible to reconcile them, and not to permit their seeming repugnancy to destroy each other. We must endeavour so to construe them as to preserve the true intent and meaning of the instrument.

In one description of cases, the jurisdiction of the Court is founded entirely on the character of the parties; and the nature of the controversy is not contemplated by the constitution. The character of the parties is every thing, the nature of the case nothing. In the other description of cases, the jurisdiction is founded entirely on the character of the case, and the parties are not contemplated by the constitution. In these, the nature of the case is every thing, the character of the parties nothing. When, then, the constitution declares the jurisdiction, in cases where a State shall be a party, to be original, and in all cases arising under the constitution or a law, to be appellate—the conclusion seems irresistible, that its framers designed to include in the first class those cases in which jurisdiction is given, because a State is a party; and to include in the second, those in which jurisdiction is given, because the case arises under the constitution or a law.

This reasonable construction is rendered necessary by other considerations.

That the constitution or a law of the United States, is involved in a case, and makes a part of it, may appear in the progress of a cause, in which the Courts of the Union, but for that circumstance, would have no jurisdiction, and which of consequence could not originate in the Supreme Court. In such a case, the jurisdiction can be exercised only in its appellate form. To deny its exercise in this form is to deny its existence, and would be to construe a clause, dividing the power of the Supreme Court, in such manner, as in a considerable degree to defeat the power itself. All must perceive, that this construction can be justified only where it is absolutely necessary. We do not think the article under consideration presents that necessity.

It is observable, that in this distributive clause, no negative words are introduced. This observation is not made for the purpose of contending, that the legislature may "apportion the judicial power between the Supreme and inferior Courts according to its will." That would be, as was said by this Court in the case of *Marbury* v. *Madison,* to render the distributive clause "mere surplusage," to make it "form without substance." This cannot, therefore, be the true construction of the article.

But although the absence of negative words will not authorize the legislature to disregard the distribution of the power previously granted, their absence will justify a sound construction of the whole article, so as to give every part its intended effect. It is admitted, that "affirmative words are often, in their operation, negative of other objects than those affirmed;" and that where "a negative or exclusive sense must be given to them, or they have no operation at all," they must receive that negative or exclusive sense. But where they have full operation without it; where it would destroy some of the most important objects for which the power was created; then, we think, affirmative words ought not to be construed negatively.

The constitution declares, that in cases where a State is a party, the Supreme Court shall have original jurisdiction; but does not say that its appellate jurisdiction shall not be exercised in cases where, from their nature, appellate jurisdiction is given, whether a State be or be not a party. It may be conceded, that where the case is of such a nature as to admit of its originating in the Supreme Court, it ought to originate there; but where, from its nature, it cannot originate in that Court, these words ought not to be so construed as to require it. There are many cases in which it would be found extremely difficult, and subversive of the spirit of the constitution, to maintain the construction, that appellate jurisdiction cannot be exercised where one of the parties might sue or be sued in this Court.

The constitution defines the jurisdiction of the Supreme Court, but does not define that of the inferior Courts. Can it be affirmed, that a State might not sue the citizen of another State in a Circuit Court? Should the Circuit Court decide for or against its jurisdiction, should it dismiss the suit, or give judgment against the State, might not its decision be revised in the Supreme Court? The argument is, that it could not; and the very clause which is urged to prove, that the Circuit Court could give no judgment in the case, is also urged to prove, that its judgment is irreversible. A supervising Court, whose peculiar province it is to correct the errors of an inferior Court, has no power to correct a judgment given without jurisdiction, because, in the same case, that supervising Court has original jurisdiction. Had negative words been employed, it would be difficult to give them this construction if they would admit of any other. But, without negative words, this irrational construction can never be maintained.

So, too, in the same clause, the jurisdiction of the Court is declared to be original, "in cases affecting ambassadors, other public ministers, and consuls." There is, perhaps, no part of the article under consideration so much required by national policy as this; unless it be that part which extends the judicial power "to all cases arising under the constitution, laws, and treaties of the United States." It has been generally held, that the State Courts have a concurrent jurisdiction with the federal Courts, in cases to which the judicial power is extended, unless the jurisdiction of the federal Courts be rendered exclusive by the words of the third article. If the words, "to all cases," give exclusive jurisdiction in cases affecting foreign ministers, they may also give exclusive jurisdiction, if such be the will of Congress, in cases arising under the constitution, laws, and treaties of the United States. Now, suppose an individual were to sue a foreign minister in a State Court, and that Court were to maintain its jurisdiction, and render judgment against the minister, could it be contended, that this Court would be incapable of revising such judgment, because the constitution had given it original jurisdiction in the case? If this could be maintained, then a clause inserted for the purpose of excluding the jurisdiction of all other Courts than this, in a particular case, would have the effect of excluding the jurisdiction of this Court in that very case, if the suit were to be brought in another Court, and that Court were to assert jurisdiction. This tribunal, according to the argument which has been urged, could neither revise the judgment of such other Court, nor suspend its proceedings: for a writ of prohibition, or any other similar writ, is in the nature of appellate process.

Foreign consuls frequently assert, in our Prize Courts, the claims of their fellow subjects. These suits are maintained by them as consuls. The appellate power of this Court has been frequently exercised in such cases, and has never been questioned. It would be extremely mischievous to withhold its exercise. Yet the consul is a party on the record. The truth is, that where the words confer only appellate jurisdiction, original jurisdiction is most clearly not given; but where the words admit of appellate jurisdiction, the power to take cognizance of the suit originally, does not necessarily negative the power to decide upon it on an appeal, if it may originate in a different Court.

It is, we think, apparent, that to give this distributive clause the interpretation contended for, to give to its affirmative words a negative operation, in every possible case, would, in some instances, defeat the obvious intention of the article. Such an interpretation would not consist with those rules which, from time immemorial, have guided Courts, in their construction of instruments brought under their consideration. It must, therefore, be discarded. Every part of the article must be taken into view, and that construction adopted which will consist with its words, and promote its general intention. The Court may imply a negative from affirmative words, where the implication promotes, not where it defeats the intention.

If we apply this principle, the correctness of which we believe will not be controverted, to the distributive clause under consideration, the result, we think, would be this: the original jurisdiction of the Supreme Court, in cases where a State is a party, refers to those cases in which, according to the grant of power made in the preceding clause, jurisdiction might be exercised in consequence of the character of the party, and an original suit might be instituted in any of the federal Courts; not to those cases in which an original suit might not be instituted in a federal Court. Of the last description, is every case between a State and its citizens, and, perhaps, every case in which a State is enforcing its penal laws. In such cases, therefore, the Supreme Court cannot take original jurisdiction. In every other case, that is, in every case to which the judicial power extends, and in which original jurisdiction is not expressly given, that judicial power shall be exercised in the appellate, and only in the appellate form. The original jurisdiction of this Court cannot be enlarged, but its appellate jurisdiction may be exercised in every case cognizable under the third article of the constitution, in the federal Courts, in which original jurisdiction cannot be exercised; and the extent of this judicial power is to be measured, not by giving the affirmative words of the distributive clause a negative operation in every possible case, but by giving their true meaning to the words which define its extent.

The counsel for the defendant in error urge, in opposition to this rule of construction, some *dicta* of the Court, in the case of *Marbury* v. *Madison*.

It is a maxim not to be disregarded, that general expressions, in every opinion, are to be taken in connection with the case in which those expressions are used. If they go beyond the case, they may be respected, but ought not to control the judgment in a subsequent suit when the very point is presented for decision. The reason of this maxim is obvious. The question actually before the Court is investigated with care, and considered in its full extent. Other principles which may serve to illustrate it, are considered in their relation to the case decided, but their possible bearing on all other cases is seldom completely investigated.

In the case of *Marbury* v. *Madison,* the single question before the Court, so far as that case can be applied to this, was, whether the legislature could give this Court original jurisdiction in a case in which the constitution had clearly not given it, and in which no doubt respecting the construction of the article could possibly be raised. The Court decided, and we think very properly, that the legislature could not give original jurisdiction in such a case. But, in the reasoning of the Court in support of this decision, some expressions are used which go far beyond it. The counsel for Marbury had insisted on the unlimited discretion of the legislature in the apportionment of the judicial power; and it is against this argument that the reasoning of the Court is directed. They say that, if such had been the intention of the article, "it would certainly have been useless to proceed farther than to define the judicial power, and the tribunals in which it should be vested." The Court says, that such a construction would render the clause, dividing the jurisdiction of the Court into original and appellate, totally useless; that "affirmative words are often, in their operation, negative of other objects than those which are affirmed; and, in this case, (in the case of *Marbury* v. *Madison,*) a negative or exclusive sense must be given to them, or they have no operation at all." "It cannot be presumed," adds the Court, "that any clause in the constitution is intended to be without effect; and, therefore, such a construction is inadmissible, unless the words require it."

The whole reasoning of the Court proceeds upon the idea that the affirmative words of the clause giving one sort of jurisdiction, must imply a negative of any other sort of jurisdiction, because otherwise the words would be totally inoperative, and this reasoning is advanced in a case to which it was strictly applicable. If in that case original jurisdiction could have been exercised, the clause under consideration would have been entirely useless. Having such cases only in its view, the Court lays down a principle which is generally correct, in terms much broader than the decision, and not only much broader than the reasoning with which that decision is supported, but in some instances contradictory to its principle. The reasoning sustains the negative operation of the words in that case, because otherwise the clause would have no meaning whatever, and because such operation was necessary to give effect to the intention of the article. The effort now made is, to apply the conclusion to which the Court was conducted by that reasoning in the particular case, to one in which the words have their full operation when understood affirmatively, and in which the negative, or exclusive sense, is to be so used as to defeat some of the great objects of the article.

To this construction the Court cannot give its assent. The general expressions in the case of *Marbury* v. *Madison* must be understood with the limitations which are given to them in this opinion; limitations which in no degree affect the decision in that case, or the tenor of its reasoning.

The counsel who closed the argument, put several cases for the purpose of illustration, which he supposed to arise under the constitution, and yet to be, apparently, without the jurisdiction of the Court.

Were a State to lay a duty on exports, to collect the money and place it in her treasury, could the citizen who paid it, he asks, maintain a suit in this Court against such State, to recover back the money?

Perhaps not. Without, however, deciding such supposed case, we may say, that it is entirely unlike that under consideration.

The citizen who has paid his money to his State, under a law that is void, is in the same situation with every other person who has paid money by mistake. The law raises an assumpsit to return the money, and it is upon that assumpsit that the action is to be maintained. To refuse to comply with this assumpsit may be no more a violation of the constitution, than to refuse to comply with any other; and as the federal Courts never had jurisdiction over contracts between a State and its citizens, they may have none over this. But let us so vary the supposed case, as to give it a real resemblance to that under consideration. Suppose a citizen to refuse to pay this export duty, and a suit to be instituted for the purpose of compelling him to pay it. He pleads the constitution of the United States in bar of the action, notwithstanding which the Court gives judgment against him. This would be a case arising under the constitution, and would be the very case now before the Court.

We are also asked, if a State should confiscate property secured by a treaty, whether the individual could maintain an action for that property?

If the property confiscated be debts, our own experience informs us that the remedy of the creditor against his debtor remains. If it be land, which is secured by a treaty, and afterwards confiscated by a State, the argument does not assume that this title, thus secured, could be extinguished by an act of confiscation. The injured party, therefore, has his remedy against the occupant of the land for that which the treaty secures to him, not against the State for money which is not secured to him.

The case of a State which pays off its own debts with paper money, no more resembles this than do those to which we have already adverted. The Courts have no jurisdiction over the contract. They cannot enforce it, nor judge of its violation. Let it be that the act discharging the debt is a mere nullity, and that it is still due. Yet the federal Courts have no cognizance of the case. But suppose a State to institute proceedings against an individual, which depended on the validity of an act emitting bills of credit: suppose a State to prosecute one of its citizens for refusing paper money, who should plead the constitution in bar of such prosecution. If his plea should be overruled, and judgment rendered against him, his case would resemble this; and, unless the jurisdiction of this Court might be exercised over it, the constitution would be violated, and the injured party be unable to bring his case before that tribunal to which the people of the United States have assigned all such cases.

It is most true that this Court will not take jurisdiction if it should not: but it is equally true, that it must take jurisdiction if it should. The judiciary cannot, as the legislature may, avoid a measure because it approaches the confines of the constitution. We cannot pass it by because it is doubtful. With whatever doubts, with whatever diffi-culties, a case may be attended, we must decide it, if it be brought before us. We have no more right to decline the exercise of jurisdiction which is given, than to usurp that which is not given. The one or the other would be treason to the constitution. Questions may occur which we would gladly avoid; but we cannot avoid them. All we can do is, to exercise our best judgment, and conscientiously to per-form our duty. In doing this, on the present occasion, we find this tribunal invested with appellate jurisdiction in *all* cases arising under the constitution and laws of the United States. We find no exception to this grant, and we cannot insert one.

To escape the operation of these comprehensive words, the counsel for the defendant has mentioned instances in which the constitution might be violated without giving ju-risdiction to this Court. These words, therefore, however universal in their expression, must, he contends, be limited and controlled in their construction by circumstances. One of these instances is, the grant by a State of a patent of nobility. The Court, he says, cannot annul this grant.

This may be very true; but by no means justifies the in-ference drawn from it. The article does not extend the judicial power to every violation of the constitution which may possibly take place, but to "a case in law or equity," in which a right, under such law, is asserted in a Court of justice. If the question cannot be brought into a Court, then there is no case in law or equity, and no jurisdiction is given by the words of the article. But if, in any contro-versy depending in a Court, the cause should depend on the validity of such a law, that would be a case arising un-der the constitution, to which the judicial power of the United States would extend. The same observation applies to the other instances with which the counsel who opened the cause has illustrated this argument. Although they show that there may be violations of the constitution, of which the Courts can take no cognizance, they do not show that an interpretation more restrictive than the words themselves import ought to be given to this article. They do not show that there can be "a *case* in law or equity," arising under the constitution, to which the judicial power does not extend.

We think, then, that, as the constitution originally stood, the appellate jurisdiction of this Court, in all cases arising under the constitution, laws, or treaties of the United States, was not arrested by the circumstance that a State was a party.

This leads to a consideration of the 11th amendment.

It is in these words: "The judicial power of the United States shall not be construed to extend to any suit in law or equity commenced or prosecuted against one of the United States, by citizens of another State, or by citizens or subjects of any foreign State."

It is a part of our history, that, at the adoption of the constitution, all the States were greatly indebted; and the apprehension that these debts might be prosecuted in the federal Courts, formed a very serious objection to that in-strument. Suits were instituted; and the Court maintained its jurisdiction. The alarm was general; and, to quiet the apprehensions that were so extensively entertained, this amendment was proposed in Congress, and adopted by the State legislatures. That its motive was not to maintain the sovereignty of a State from the degradation supposed to attend a compulsory appearance before the tribunal of the nation, may be inferred from the terms of the amend-ment. It does not comprehend controversies between two or more States, or between a State and a foreign State. The jurisdiction of the Court still extends to these cases: and in these a State may still be sued. We must ascribe the amendment, then, to some other cause than the dignity of a State. There is no difficulty in finding this cause. Those who were inhibited from commencing a suit against a State, or from prosecuting one which might be com-menced before the adoption of the amendment, were per-sons who might probably be its creditors. There was not much reason to fear that foreign or sister States would be creditors to any considerable amount, and there was rea-son to retain the jurisdiction of the Court in those cases, because it might be essential to the preservation of peace. The amendment, therefore, extended to suits commenced or prosecuted by individuals, but not to those brought by States.

The first impression made on the mind by this amend-ment is, that it was intended for those cases, and for those only, in which some demand against a State is made by an individual in the Courts of the Union. If we consider the causes to which it is to be traced, we are conducted to the same conclusion. A general interest might well be felt in leaving to a State the full power of consulting its conve-nience in the adjustment of its debts, or of other claims upon it; but no interest could be felt in so changing the relations between the whole and its parts, as to strip the government of the means of protecting, by the instrumen-tality of its Courts, the constitution and laws from active violation.

The words of the amendment appear to the Court to justify and require this construction. The judicial power is not "to extend to any suit in law or equity commenced or prosecuted against one of the United States by citizens of another State, &c."

What is a suit? We understand it to be the prosecution, or pursuit, of some claim, demand, or request. In law lan-guage, it is the prosecution of some demand in a Court of justice. The remedy for every species of wrong is, says Judge Blackstone, "the being put in possession of that right whereof the party injured is deprived." "The instru-ments whereby this remedy is obtained, are a diversity of suits and actions, which are defined by the Mirror to be 'the lawful demand of one's right.' Or, as Bracton and Fleta express it, in the words of Justinian, *'jus prosequendi in judicio quod alicui debetur.'* " Blackstone then proceeds to describe every species of remedy by suit; and they are all cases where the party suing claims to obtain something to which he has a right.

To commence a suit, is to demand something by the in-stitution of process in a Court of justice; and to prosecute the suit, is, according to the common acceptation of lan-guage, to continue that demand. By a suit commenced by an individual against a State, we should understand pro-cess sued out by that individual against the State, for the purpose of establishing some claim against it by the judgment of a Court; and the prosecution of that suit is its continuance. Whatever may be the stages of its progress, the actor is still the same. Suits had been commenced in the Supreme Court against some of the States before this amendment was introduced into Congress, and others might be commenced before it should be adopted by the State legislatures, and might be depending at the time of its adoption. The object of the amendment was not only to prevent the commencement of future suits, but to arrest the prosecution of those which might be commenced when this article should form a part of the constitution. It therefore embraces both objects; and its meaning is, that the judicial power shall not be construed to extend to any suit which may be commenced, or which, if already commenced, may be prosecuted against a State by the citizen of another State. If a suit, brought in one Court, and carried by legal process to a supervising Court, be a continuation of the same suit, then this suit is not commenced nor prosecuted against a State. It is clearly in its commencement the suit of a State against an individual, which suit is transferred to this Court, not for the purpose of asserting any claim against the State, but for the purpose of asserting a constitutional defence against a claim made by a State.

A writ of error is defined to be, a commission by which the judges of one Court are authorized to examine a record upon which a judgment was given in another Court, and, on such examination, to affirm or reverse the same according to law. If, says my Lord Coke, by the writ of error, the plaintiff may recover, or be restored to any thing, it may be released by the name of an action. In *Bacon's Abridgment, tit. Error,* L. it is laid down, that "where by a writ of error, the plaintiff shall recover, or be restored to any personal thing, as debt, damage, or the like, a release of all actions personal is a good plea; and when land is to be recovered or restored in a writ of error, a release of actions real is a good bar; but where by a writ of error the plaintiff shall not be restored to any personal or real thing, a release of all actions, real or personal, is no bar." And for this we have the authority of Lord Coke, both in his Commentary on *Littleton* and in his *Reports.* A writ of error, then, is in the nature of a suit or action when it is to restore the party who obtains it to the possession of any thing which is withheld from him, not when its operation is entirely defensive.

This rule will apply to writs of error from the Courts of the United States, as well as to those writs in England.

Under the judiciary act, the effect of a writ of error is simply to bring the record into Court, and submit the judgment of the inferior tribunal to re-examination. It does not in any manner act upon the parties; it acts only on the record. It removes the record into the supervising tribunal. Where, then, a State obtains a judgment against an individual, and the Court, rendering such judgment, overrules a defence set up under the constitution or laws of the United States, the transfer of this record into the Supreme Court, for the sole purpose of inquiring whether the judgment violates the constitution or laws of the United States, can, with no propriety, we think, be denom-

inated a suit commenced or prosecuted against the State whose judgment is so far re-examined. Nothing is demanded from the State. No claim against it of any description is asserted or prosecuted. The party is not to be restored to the possession of any thing. Essentially, it is an appeal on a single point; and the defendant who appeals from a judgment rendered against him, is never said to commence or prosecute a suit against the plaintiff who has obtained the judgment. The writ of error is given rather than an appeal, because it is the more usual mode of removing suits at common law; and because, perhaps, it is more technically proper where a single point of law, and not the whole case, is to be re-examined. But an appeal might be given, and might be so regulated as to effect every purpose of a writ of error. The mode of removal is form, and not substance. Whether it be by writ of error or appeal, no claim is asserted, no demand is made by the original defendant; he only asserts the constitutional right to have his defence examined by that tribunal whose province it is to construe the constitution and laws of the Union.

The only part of the proceeding which is in any manner personal, is the citation. And what is the citation? It is simply notice to the opposite party that the record is transferred into another Court, where he may appear, or decline to appear, as his judgment or inclination may determine. As the party who has obtained a judgment is out of Court, and may, therefore, not know that his cause is removed, common justice requires that notice of the fact should be given him. But this notice is not a suit, nor has it the effect of process. If the party does not choose to appear, he cannot be brought into Court, nor is his failure to appear considered as a default. Judgment cannot be given against him for his nonappearance, but the judgment is to be re-examined, and reversed or affirmed, in like manner as if the party had appeared and argued his cause.

The point of view in which this writ of error, with its citation, has been considered uniformly in the Courts of the Union, has been well illustrated by a reference to the course of this Court in suits instituted by the United States. The universally received opinion is, that no suit can be commenced or prosecuted against the United States; that the judiciary act does not authorize such suits. Yet writs of error, accompanied with citations, have uniformly issued for the removal of judgments in favour of the United States into a superior Court, where they have, like those in favour of an individual, been re-examined, and affirmed or reversed. It has never been suggested, that such writ of error was a suit against the United States, and, therefore, not within the jurisdiction of the appellate Court.

It is, then, the opinion of the Court, that the defendant who removes a judgment rendered against him by a State Court into this Court, for the purpose of re-examining the question, whether that judgment be in violation of the constitution or laws of the United States, does not commence or prosecute a suit against the State, whatever may be its opinion where the effect of the writ may be to restore the party to the possession of a thing which he demands.

But should we in this be mistaken, the error does not affect the case now before the Court. If this writ of error be a suit in the sense of the 11th amendment, it is not a suit commenced or prosecuted "by a citizen of another State, or by a citizen or subject of any foreign State." It is not then within the amendment, but is governed entirely by the constitution as originally framed, and we have already seen, that in its origin, the judicial power was extended to all cases arising under the constitution or laws of the United States, without respect to parties.

2d. The second objection to the jurisdiction of the Court is, that its appellate power cannot be exercised, in any case, over the judgment of a State Court.

This objection is sustained chiefly by arguments drawn from the supposed total separation of the judiciary of a State from that of the Union, and their entire independence of each other. The argument considers the federal judiciary as completely foreign to that of a State; and as being no more connected with it in any respect whatever, than the Court of a foreign State. If this hypothesis be just, the argument founded on it is equally so; but if the hypothesis be not supported by the constitution, the argument fails with it.

This hypothesis is not founded on any words in the constitution, which might seem to countenance it, but on the unreasonableness of giving a contrary construction to words which seem to require it; and on the incompatibility of the application of the appellate jurisdiction to the judgments of State Courts, with that constitutional relation which subsists between the government of the Union and the governments of those States which compose it.

Let this unreasonableness, this total incompatibility, be examined.

That the United States form, for many, and for most important purposes, a single nation, has not yet been denied. In war, we are one people. In making peace, we are one people. In all commercial regulations, we are one and the same people. In many other respects, the American people are one; and the government which is alone capable of controling and managing their interests in all these respects, is the government of the Union. It is their government, and in that character they have no other. America has chosen to be, in many respects, and to many purposes, a nation; and for all these purposes, her government is complete; to all these objects, it is competent. The people have declared, that in the exercise of all powers given for these objects, it is supreme. It can, then, in effecting these objects, legitimately control all individuals or governments within the American territory. The constitution and laws of a State, so far as they are repugnant to the constitution and laws of the United States, are absolutely void. These States are constituent parts of the United States. They are members of one great empire—for some purposes sovereign, for some purposes subordinate.

In a government so constituted, is it unreasonable that the judicial power should be competent to give efficacy to the constitutional laws of the legislature? That department can decide on the validity of the constitution or law of a State, if it be repugnant to the constitution or to a law of the United States. Is it unreasonable that it should also be empowered to decide on the judgment of a State tribunal enforcing such unconstitutional law? Is it so very unreasonable as to furnish a justification for controling the words of the constitution?

We think it is not. We think that in a government acknowledgedly supreme, with respect to objects of vital interest to the nation, there is nothing inconsistent with sound reason, nothing incompatible with the nature of government, in making all its departments supreme, so far as respects those objects, and so far as is necessary to their attainment. The exercise of the appellate power over those judgments of the State tribunals which may contravene the constitution or laws of the United States, is, we believe, essential to the attainment of those objects.

The propriety of entrusting the construction of the constitution, and laws made in pursuance thereof, to the judiciary of the Union, has not, we believe, as yet, been drawn into question. It seems to be a corollary from this political axiom, that the federal Courts should either possess exclusive jurisdiction in such cases, or a power to revise the judgment rendered in them, by the State tribunals. If the federal and State Courts have concurrent jurisdiction in all cases arising under the constitution, laws, and treaties of the United States; and if a case of this description brought in a State Court cannot be removed before judgment, nor revised after judgment, then the construction of the constitution, laws, and treaties of the United States, is not confided particularly to their judicial department, but is confided equally to that department and to the State Courts, however they may be constituted. "Thirteen independent Courts," says a very celebrated statesman, (and we have now more than twenty such Courts,) "of final jurisdiction over the same causes, arising upon the same laws, is a hydra in government, from which nothing but contradiction and confusion can proceed."

Dismissing the unpleasant suggestion, that any motives which may not be fairly avowed, or which ought not to exist, can ever influence a State or its Courts, the necessity of uniformity, as well as correctness in expounding the constitution and laws of the United States, would itself suggest the propriety of vesting in some single tribunal the power of deciding, in the last resort, all cases in which they are involved.

We are not restrained, then, by the political relations between the general and State governments, from construing the words of the constitution, defining the judicial power, in their true sense. We are not bound to construe them more restrictively than they naturally import.

They give to the Supreme Court appellate jurisdiction in all cases arising under the constitution, laws, and treaties of the United States. The words are broad enough to comprehend all cases of this description, in whatever Court they may be decided. In expounding them, we may be permitted to take into view those considerations to which Courts have always allowed great weight in the exposition of laws.

The framers of the constitution would naturally examine the state of things existing at the time; and their work sufficiently attests that they did so. All acknowledge that they were convened for the purpose of strengthening the confederation by enlarging the powers of the government, and by giving efficacy to those which it before possessed, but could not exercise. They inform us themselves, in the instrument they presented to the American public, that one of its objects was to form a more perfect union. Under such circumstances, we certainly should not expect to find, in that instrument, a diminution of the powers of the actual government.

Previous to the adoption of the confederation, Congress established Courts which received appeals in prize causes decided in the Courts of the respective States. This power of the government, to establish tribunals for these appeals, was thought consistent with, and was founded on, its political relations with the States. These Courts did exercise appellate jurisdiction over those cases decided in the State Courts, to which the judicial power of the federal government extended.

The confederation gave to Congress the power "of establishing Courts for receiving and determining finally appeals in all cases of captures."

This power was uniformly construed to authorize those Courts to receive appeals from the sentences of State Courts, and to affirm or reverse them. State tribunals are not mentioned; but this clause in the confederation necessarily comprises them. Yet the relation between the general and State governments was much weaker, much more lax, under the confederation than under the present constitution; and the States being much more completely sovereign, their institutions were much more independent.

The Convention which framed the constitution, on turning their attention to the judicial power, found it limited to a few objects, but exercised, with respect to some of those objects, in its appellate form, over the judgments of the State Courts. They extend it, among other objects, to all cases arising under the constitution, laws, and treaties of the United States; and in a subsequent clause declare, that in such cases, the Supreme Court shall exercise appellate jurisdiction. Nothing seems to be given which would justify the withdrawal of a judgment rendered in a State Court, on the constitution, laws, or treaties of the United States, from this appellate jurisdiction.

Great weight has always been attached, and very rightly attached, to contemporaneous exposition. No question, it is believed, has arisen to which this principle applies more unequivocally than to that now under consideration.

The opinion of the *Federalist* has always been considered as of great authority. It is a complete commentary on our constitution; and is appealed to by all parties in the questions to which that instrument has given birth. Its intrinsic merit entitles it to this high rank; and the part two of its authors performed in framing the constitution, put it very much in their power to explain the views with which it was framed. These essays having been published while the constitution was before the nation for adoption or rejection, and having been written in answer to objections founded entirely on the extent of its powers, and on its diminution of State sovereignty, are entitled to the more consideration where they frankly avow that the power objected to is given, and defend it.

In discussing the extent of the judicial power, the *Federalist* says, "Here another question occurs: what relation would subsist between the national and State Courts in these instances of concurrent jurisdiction? I answer, that an appeal would certainly lie from the latter, to the Supreme Court of the United States. The constitution in direct terms gives an appellate jurisdiction to the Supreme Court in all the enumerated cases of federal cognizance in which it is not to have an original one, without a single expression to confine its operation to the inferior federal Courts. The objects of appeal, not the tribunals from which it is to be made, are alone contemplated. From this circumstance, and from the reason of the thing, it ought to be construed to extend to the State tribunals. Either this must be the case, or the local Courts must be excluded from a concurrent jurisdiction in matters of national concern, else the judicial authority of the Union may be eluded at the pleasure of every plaintiff or prosecutor. Neither of these consequences ought, without evident necessity, to be involved; the latter would be entirely inadmissible, as it would defeat some of the most important and avowed purposes of the proposed government, and would essentially embarrass its measures. Nor do I perceive any foundation for such a supposition. Agreeably to the remark already made, the national and State systems are to be regarded as ONE WHOLE. The Courts of the latter will of course be natural auxiliaries to the execution of the laws of the Union, and an appeal from them will as naturally lie to that tribunal which is destined to unite and assimilate the principles of natural justice, and the rules of national decision. The evident aim of the plan of the national convention is, that all the causes of the specified classes shall, for weighty public reasons, receive their original or final determination in the Courts of the Union. To confine, therefore, the general expressions which give appellate jurisdiction to the Supreme Court, to appeals from the subordinate federal Courts, instead of allowing their extension to the State Courts, would be to abridge the latitude of the terms, in subversion of the intent, contrary to every sound rule of interpretation."

A contemporaneous exposition of the constitution, certainly of not less authority than that which has been just cited, is the judiciary act itself. We know that in the Congress which passed that act were many eminent members of the Convention which formed the constitution. Not a single individual, so far as is known, supposed that part of the act which gives the Supreme Court appellate jurisdiction over the judgments of the State Courts in the cases therein specified, to be unauthorized by the constitution.

While on this part of the argument, it may be also material to observe that the uniform decisions of this Court on the point now under consideration, have been assented to, with a single exception, by the Courts of every State in the Union whose judgments have been revised. It has been the unwelcome duty of this tribunal to reverse the judgments of many State Courts in cases in which the strongest State feelings were engaged. Judges, whose talents and character would grace any bench, to whom a disposition to submit to jurisdiction that is usurped, or to surrender their legitimate powers, will certainly not be imputed, have yielded without hesitation to the authority by which their judgments were reversed, while they, perhaps, disapproved the judgment of reversal.

This concurrence of statesmen, of legislators, and of judges, in the same construction of the constitution, may justly inspire some confidence in that construction.

In opposition to it, the counsel who made this point has presented in a great variety of forms, the idea already noticed, that the federal and State Courts must, of necessity, and from the nature of the constitution, be in all things totally distinct and independent of each other. If this Court can correct the errors of the Courts of Virginia, he says it makes them Courts of the United States, or becomes itself a part of the judiciary of Virginia.

But, it has been already shown that neither of these consequences necessarily follows: The American people may certainly give to a national tribunal a supervising power over those judgments of the State Courts, which may conflict with the constitution, laws, or treaties, of the United States, without converting them into federal Courts, or converting the national into a State tribunal. The one Court still derives its authority from the State, the other still derives its authority from the nation.

If it shall be established, he says, that this Court has appellate jurisdiction over the State Courts in all cases enumerated in the 3d article of the constitution, a complete consolidation of the States, so far as respects judicial power is produced.

But, certainly, the mind of the gentleman who urged this argument is too accurate not to perceive that he has carried it too far; that the premises by no means justify the conclusion. "A complete consolidation of the States, so far as respects the judicial power," would authorize the legislature to confer on the federal Courts appellate jurisdiction from the State Courts in all cases whatsoever. The distinction between such a power, and that of giving appellate jurisdiction in a few specified cases in the decision of which the nation takes an interest, is too obvious not to be perceived by all.

This opinion has been already drawn out to too great a length to admit of entering into a particular consideration of the various forms in which the counsel who made this point has, with much ingenuity, presented his argument to the Court. The argument in all its forms is essentially the same. It is founded, not on the words of the constitution, but on its spirit, a spirit extracted, not from the words of the instrument, but from his view of the nature of our Union, and of the great fundamental principles on which the fabric stands.

To this argument, in all its forms, the same answer may be given. Let the nature and objects of our Union be considered; let the great fundamental principles, on which the fabric stands, be examined; and we think the result must be, that there is nothing so extravagantly absurd in giving to the Court of the nation the power of revising the decisions of local tribunals on questions which affect the nation, as to require that words which import this power should be restricted by a forced construction. The question then must depend on the words themselves; and on their construction we shall be the more readily excused for

not adding to the observations already made, because the subject was fully discussed and exhausted in the case of *Martin* v. *Hunter.*

3d. We come now to the third objection, which, though differently stated by the counsel, is substantially the same.

. . . . .

If the 25th section of the judiciary act be inspected, it will at once be perceived that it comprehends expressly the case under consideration.

But it is not upon the letter of the act that the gentleman who stated this point in this form, founds his argument. Both gentlemen concur substantially in their views of this part of the case. They deny that the act of Congress, on which the plaintiff in error relies, is a law of the United States; or, if a law of the United States, is within the second clause of the sixth article.

In the enumeration of the powers of Congress, which is made in the 8th section of the first article, we find that of exercising exclusive legislation over such District as shall become the seat of government. This power, like all others which are specified, is conferred on Congress as the legislature of the Union: for, strip them of that character, and they would not possess it. In no other character can it be exercised. In legislating for the District, they necessarily preserve the character of the legislature of the Union; for, it is in that character alone that the constitution confers on them this power of exclusive legislation. This proposition need not be enforced.

The 2d clause of the 6th article declares, that "This constitution, and the laws of the United States, which shall be made in pursuance thereof, shall be the supreme law of the land."

The clause which gives exclusive jurisdiction is, unquestionably, a part of the constitution, and, as such, binds all the United States. Those who contend that acts of Congress, made in pursuance of this power, do not, like acts made in pursuance of other powers, bind the nation, ought to show some safe and clear rule which shall support this construction, and prove that an act of Congress, clothed in all the forms which attend other legislative acts, and passed in virtue of a power conferred on, and exercised by Congress, as the legislature of the Union, is not a law of the United States, and does not bind them.

One of the gentlemen sought to illustrate his proposition that Congress, when legislating for the District, assumed a distinct character, and was reduced to a mere local legislature, whose laws could possess no obligation out of the ten miles square, by a reference to the complex character of this Court. It is, they say, a Court of common law and a Court of equity. Its character, when sitting as a Court of common law, is as distinct from its character when sitting as a Court of equity, as if the powers belonging to those departments were vested in different tribunals. Though united in the same tribunal, they are never confounded with each other.

Without inquiring how far the union of different characters in one Court, may be applicable, in principle, to the union in Congress of the power of exclusive legislation in some places, and of limited legislation in others, it may be observed, that the forms of proceedings in a Court of law are so totally unlike the forms of proceedings in a Court of equity, that a mere inspection of the record gives decisive information of the character in which the Court sits, and consequently of the extent of its powers. But if the forms of proceedings were precisely the same, and the Court the same, the distinction would disappear.

Since Congress legislates in the same forms, and in the same character, in virtue of powers of equal obligation, conferred in the same instrument, when exercising its exclusive powers of legislation, as well as when exercising those which are limited, we must inquire whether there be any thing in the nature of this exclusive legislation, which necessarily confines the operation of the laws made in virtue of this power to the place with a view to which they are made.

Connected with the power to legislate within this District, is a similar power in forts, arsenals, dock yards, &c. Congress has a right to punish murder in a fort, or other place within its exclusive jurisdiction; but no general right to punish murder committed within any of the States. In the act for the punishment of crimes against the United States, murder committed within a fort, or any other place or district of country, under the sole and exclusive jurisdiction of the United States, is punished with death. Thus Congress legislates in the same act, under its exclusive and its limited powers.

The act proceeds to direct, that the body of the criminal, after execution, may be delivered to a surgeon for dissection, and punishes any person who shall rescue such body during its conveyance from the place of execution to the surgeon to whom it is to be delivered.

Let these actual provisions of the law, or any other provisions which can be made on the subject, be considered with a view to the character in which Congress acts when exercising its powers of exclusive legislation.

If Congress is to be considered merely as a local legislature, invested, as to this object, with powers limited to the fort, or other place, in which the murder may be committed, if its general powers cannot come in aid of these local powers, how can the offence be tried in any other Court than that of the place in which it has been committed? How can the offender be conveyed to, or tried in, any other place? How can he be executed elsewhere? How can his body be conveyed through a country under the jurisdiction of another sovereign, and the individual punished, who, within that jurisdiction, shall rescue the body.

Were any one State of the Union to pass a law for trying a criminal in a Court not created by itself, in a place not within its jurisdiction, and direct the sentence to be executed without its territory, we should all perceive and acknowledge its incompetency to such a course of legislation. If Congress be not equally incompetent, it is because that body unites the powers of local legislation with those which are to operate through the Union, and may use the last in aid of the first; or because the power of exercising exclusive legislation draws after it, as an incident, the power of making that legislation effectual, and the incidental power may be exercised throughout the Union, because the principal power is given to that body as the legislature of the Union.

So, in the same act, a person who, having knowledge of the commission of murder, or other felony, on the high seas, or within any fort, arsenal, dock yard, magazine, or other place, or district of country within the sole and exclusive jurisdiction of the United States, shall conceal the same, &c. he shall be adjudged guilty of misprision of felony, and shall be adjudged to be imprisoned, &c.

It is clear, that Congress cannot punish felonies generally; and, of consequence, cannot punish misprision of felony. It is equally clear, that a State legislature, the State of Maryland for example, cannot punish those who, in another State, conceal a felony committed in Maryland. How, then, is it that Congress, legislating exclusively for a fort, punishes those who, out of that fort, conceal a felony committed within it?

The solution, and the only solution of the difficulty, is, that the power vested in Congress, as the legislature of the United States, to legislate exclusively within any place ceded by a State, carries with it, as an incident, the right to make that power effectual. If a felon escape out of the State in which the act has been committed, the government cannot pursue him into another State, and apprehend him there, but must demand him from the executive power of that other State. If Congress were to be considered merely as the local legislature for the fort or other place in which the offence might be committed, then this principle would apply to them as to other local legislatures, and the felon who should escape out of the fort, or other place, in which the felony may have been committed, could not be apprehended by the marshal, but must be demanded from the executive of the State. But we know that the principle does not apply; and the reason is, that Congress is not a local legislature, but exercises this particular power, like all its other powers, in its high character, as the legislature of the Union. The American people thought it a necessary power, and they conferred it for their own benefit. Being so conferred, it carries with it all those incidental powers which are necessary to its complete and effectual execution.

Whether any particular law be designed to operate without the District or not, depends on the words of that law. If it be designed so to operate, then the question, whether the power so exercised be incidental to the power of exclusive legislation, and be warranted by the constitution, requires a consideration of that instrument. In such cases the constitution and the law must be compared and construed. This is the exercise of jurisdiction. It is the only exercise of it which is allowed in such a case. For the act of Congress directs, that "no other error shall be assigned or regarded as a ground of reversal, in any such case as aforesaid, than such as appears on the face of the record, and immediately respects the before mentioned questions of validity or construction of the said constitution, treaties," &c.

The whole merits of this case, then, consist in the construction of the constitution and the act of Congress. The jurisdiction of the Court, if acknowledged, goes no farther. This we are required to do without the exercise of jurisdiction.

The counsel for the State of Virginia have, in support of this motion, urged many arguments of great weight against the application of the act of Congress to such a case as this; but those arguments go to the construction of the constitution, or of the law, or of both; and seem, therefore, rather calculated to sustain their cause upon its merits, than to prove a failure of jurisdiction in the Court.

After having bestowed upon this question the most deliberate consideration of which we are capable, the Court is unanimously of opinion, that the objections to its jurisdiction are not sustained, and that the motion ought to be overruled.

Motion denied.

75

M'CLUNG v. SILLIMAN
6 Wheat. 598 (1821)

Mr. Justice JOHNSON delivered the opinion of the Court.

This case presents no ordinary group of legal questions. They exhibit a striking specimen of the involutions which ingenuity may cast about legal rights, and an instance of the growing pretensions of some of the State Courts over the exercise of the powers of the general government.

The plaintiff in error, who was also the plaintiff below, supposes himself entitled to a pre-emptive interest in a tract of land in the State of Ohio, and claims of the register of the land office of the United States, the legal acts and documents upon which such rights are initiated. That officer refuses, under the idea, that the right is already legally vested in another; and that he possesses, himself, no power over the subject in controversy. A mandamus is then moved for in the Circuit Court of the United States, and that Court decides, that Congress has vested it with no such controlling power over the acts of the ministerial officers in the given case. The same application is then preferred to the State Court for the county in which the subject in controversy is situated. The State Court sustains its own jurisdiction over the register of the land office, but on a view of the merits of the claim, dismisses the motion.

From both these decisions appeals are made to this Court, in form of a writ of error.

In the case of *M'Intire* v. *Wood*, decided in this Court, in 1813, the mandamus contended for was intended to perfect the same claim, and in point of fact the suit was between the same parties. The influence of that decision on these cases, is resisted, on the ground, that it did not appear in that case, that the controversy was between parties who, under the *description of person*, were entitled to maintain suits in the Courts of the United States; whereas, the averments in the present cases show, that the parties litigant are citizens of different States, and, therefore, competent parties in the Circuit Court. But we think it perfectly clear, from an examination of the decision alluded to, that it was wholly uninfluenced by any considerations drawn from the want of personal attributes of the parties. The case came up on a division of opinion, and the single

question stated is, "whether that Court had power to issue a writ of mandamus to the register of a land office in Ohio, commanding him to issue a final certificate of purchase to the plaintiff for certain lands in the State?"

Both the argument of counsel, and the opinion of the Court, distinctly show, that the power to issue the mandamus in that case, was contended for as incident to the judicial powers of the *United States*. And the reply of the Court is, that though, *argumenti gratia*, it be admitted, that this controlling power over its ministerial officers, would follow from vesting in its Courts the whole judicial power of the United States, the argument fails here, since the legislature has ony made a partial delegation of its judicial powers to the Circuit Courts; that if the inference be admitted as far as the judicial power of the Court actually extends, still, cases arising under the laws of the United States, are not, *per se*, among the cases comprised within the jurisdiction of the *Circuit Court*, under the provisions of the 11th section; jurisdiction being in such cases reserved to the *Supreme Court*, under the 25th section, by way of appeal from the decisions of the State Courts.

There is, then, no just inference to be drawn from the decision in the case of *M'Intire* v. *Wood*, in favour of a case in which the Circuit Courts of the United States are vested with jurisdiction under the 11th section. The idea is in opposition to the express words of the Court, in response to the question stated, which are, "that the Circuit Court did not possess the power to issue the mandamus moved for."

It is now contended, that as the parties to this controversy are competent to sue under the 11th section, being citizens of different States, that this is a case within the provisions of the 14th section, and the Circuit Court was vested with power to issue this writ, under the description of a "writ not specially provided for by statute," but "necessary for the exercise of its jurisdiction." The case certainly does present one of those instances of equivocal language, in which the proposition, though true in the abstract, is in its application to the subject glaringly incorrect. It cannot be denied, that the exercise of this power is necessary to the exercise of jurisdiction in the Court below; but why is it necessary? Not because that Court possesses jurisdiction, but because it does not possess it. It must exercise this power, and compel the emanation of the legal document, or the execution of the legal act by the register of the land office, or the party cannot sue.

The 14th section of the act under consideration, could only have been intended to vest the power now contended for, in cases where the jurisdiction already exists, and not where it is to be courted or acquired, by means of the writ proposed to be sued out. Such was the case brought up from Louisiana, in which the judge refused to proceed to judgment, by which act, the plaintiff must have lost his remedy below, and this Court have been deprived of its appellate control, over the question of right.

The remaining questions bear a striking analogy to that already disposed of.

The State Court having decided in favour of its own jurisdiction over the register, the appellant, so far, had nothing to complain of. It is only where a State Court decides *against* the claim set up under the laws of the United

States, that appellate jurisdiction is given from the State decisions. But in the next step of his progress, he was not equally fortunate. The State Court rejected his application on the merits of his claim, and appear to have decided that an entire section might be divided into fractions, by the river Muskingum, in a legal sense. Of this he now complains, and contends that the decision is contrary to the laws of the United States.

From this state of facts, the following embarrassment arises. The United States officer, the defendant, can have no inducement to contest a jurisdiction that has given judgment in his favour; and the plaintiff in error must sustain its jurisdiction, or relinquish all claim to the relief sought for through its agency. And thus this Court, with its eyes open to the defect in the jurisdiction of the Court below is called upon to take cognizance of the merits of the question, both parties being thus equally interested in sustaining the jurisdiction asserted by that Court.

Let the course which this Court ought to pursue, be tested by consequences. The alternative is to give judgment for or against the plaintiff. If it be given for him, this Court must invoke that Court to issue the writ demanded, or pursuing the alternative given by the 25th section, it must itself proceed to execute the judgment which that Court ought to have given. Or, in other words, to issue the writ of mandamus, in a case to which it is obvious that neither the jurisdiction of that Court, nor this, extends.

No argument can resist such an obvious *deductio in absurdum*.

It is not the first time that this Court has encountered similar difficulties, in its advance to questions brought up from other tribunals. It has avoided them by deciding that it is not bound to encounter phantoms. The party who proposes to avail himself of a defective jurisdiction, has nothing to complain of, if he is left to take the consequences. His antagonist might have had cause to complain—he can have none. And, notwithstanding express evidence of the contrary, this Court feels itself sanctioned, in referring the decision of the State Court, in this case, to the ground on which it ought to have been made, instead of that on which it appears to have been made. The question before an appellate Court is, was the *judgment* correct, not the *ground* on which the judgment professes to proceed.

Whether a State Court generally possesses a power to issue writs of mandamus, or what modifications of its powers may be imposed on it, by the laws which constitute it, it is correctly argued, that this Court cannot be called upon to decide. But when the exercise of that power is extended to officers commissioned by the United States, it is immaterial under what law that authority be asserted, the controlling power of this Court may be asserted on the subject, under the description of an exemption claimed by the officer over whom it is exercised.

It is not easy to conceive on what legal ground a State tribunal can, in any instance, exercise the power of issuing a mandamus to the register of a land office. The United States have not thought proper to delegate that power to their own Courts. But when in the cases of *Marbury* v.

Madison, and that of *M'Intire* v. *Wood*, this Court decided against the exercise of that power, the idea never presented itself to any one, that it was not within the scope of the judicial powers of the United States, although not vested by law, in the Courts of the general Government. And no one will seriously contend, it is presumed, that it is among the reserved powers of the States, because not communicated by law to the Courts of the United States?

There is but one shadow of a ground on which such a power can be contended for, which is, the general rights of legislation which the States possess over the soil within their respective territories? It is not now necessary to consider that power, as to the soil reserved to the United States, in the States respectively. The question in this case is, as to the power of the State Courts, over the officers of the general Government, employed in disposing of that land, under the laws passed for that purpose. And here it is obvious, that he is to be regarded either as an officer of that Government, or as its private agent. In the one capacity or the other, his conduct can only be controlled by the power that created him; since, whatever doubts have from time to time been suggested, as to the supremacy of the United States, in its legislative, judicial, or executive powers, no one has ever contested its supreme right to dispose of its own property in its own way. And when we find it withholding from its own Courts, the exercise of this controlling power over its ministerial officers, employed in the appropriation of its lands, the inference clearly is, that all violations of private right, resulting from the acts of such officers, should be the subject of actions for damages, or to recover the specific property, (according to circumstances) in Courts of competent jurisdiction. That is, that parties should be referred to the ordinary mode of obtaining justice, instead of resorting to the extraordinary and unprecedented mode of trying such questions on a motion for a mandamus.

76

THE SARAH

8 Wheat. 391 (1823)

March 4th, 1823. MARSHALL, Ch. J., delivered the opinion of the court, and after stating the case, proceeded as follows:—By the act constituting the judicial system of the United States, the district courts are courts both of common-law and admiralty jurisdiction. In the trial of all cases of seizure, on land, the court sits as a court of common law. In cases of seizure made on waters navigable by vessels of ten tons burden and upwards, the court sits as a court of admiralty. In all cases at common law, the trial must be by jury. In cases of admiralty and maritime jurisdiction, it has been settled, in the cases of *The Vengeance* (reported in 3 Dallas 297); *The Sally* (in 2 Cranch 406); and *The Betsy and Charlotte* (in 4 Cranch 443); that the trial is to be by the court. Although the two jurisdictions are vested in the same tribunal, they are as distinct from each other as if they were vested in different tribunals, and can no more be blended, than a court of chancery with a court of common law.

The court for the Louisiana district, was sitting as a court of admiralty; and when it was shown, that the seizure was made on land, its jurisdiction ceased. The libel ought to have been dismissed, or amended, by charging that the seizure was made on land. The direction of a jury, in a case where the libel charged a seizure on water, was irregular; and any proceeding of the court, as a court of admiralty, after the fact that the seizure was made on land appeared, would have been a proceeding without jurisdiction. The court felt some disposition to consider this impannelling of a jury, at the instance of the claimants, as amounting to a consent that the libel should stand amended; but, on reflection, that idea was rejected.

If this is considered as a case at common law, it would be necessary to dismiss this appeal, because the judgment could not be brought before this court but by writ of error. If it be considered as a case of admiralty jurisdiction, the sentence ought to be reversed, because it could not be pronounced by a court of admiralty, on a seizure made on land. As the libel charges a seizure on water, it is thought most advisable to reverse all the proceedings to the libel, and to remand the cause to the district court for further proceedings, with directions to permit the libel to be amended.

77

JAMES MADISON TO THOMAS JEFFERSON
27 June 1823
Writings 9:140–43

But after surmounting the difficulty in tracing the boundary between the General & State Govts. the problem remains for maintaining it in practice; particularly in cases of Judicial cognizance. To refer every point of disagreement to the people in Conventions would be a process too tardy, too troublesome, & too expensive; besides its tendency to lessen a salutary veneration for an instrument so often calling for such explanatory interpositions. A paramount or even a definitive Authority in the individual States, would soon make the Constitution & laws different in different States, and thus destroy that equality & uniformity of rights & duties which form the essence of the Compact; to say nothing of the opportunity given to the States individually of involving by their decisions the whole Union in foreign Contests. To leave conflicting decisions to be settled between the Judicial parties could not promise a happy result. The end must be a trial of strength between the Posse headed by the Marshal and the Posse headed by the Sheriff. Nor would the issue be safe if left to a compromise between the two Govts. the case of a disagreement between different Govts. being essentially different from a disagreement between branches of the same Govts. In the latter case neither party being able to consummate its will without the concurrence of the other, there is a necessity on both to consult and to accommodate. Not so, with different Govts. each possessing every branch of power necessary to carry its purpose into compleat effect. It here becomes a question between Independent Nations, with no other *dernier* resort than physical force. Negotiation might indeed in some instances avoid this extremity; but how often would it happen, among so many States, that an unaccommodating spirit in some would render that resource unavailing.

We arrive at the agitated question whether the Judicial Authority of the U.S. be the constitutional resort for determining the line between the federal & State jurisdictions. Believing as I do that the General Convention regarded a provision within the Constitution for deciding in a peaceable & regular mode all cases arising in the course of its operation, as essential to an adequate System of Govt. that it intended the Authority vested in the Judicial Department as a final resort in relation to the States, for cases resulting to it in the exercise of its functions, (the concurrence of the Senate chosen by the State Legislatures, in appointing the Judges, and the oaths & official tenures of these, with the surveillance of public Opinion, being relied on as guarantying their impartiality); and that this intention is expressed by the articles declaring that the federal Constitution & laws shall be the supreme law of the land, and that the Judicial Power of the U. S. shall extend to all cases arising under them: Believing moreover that this was the prevailing view of the subject when the Constitution was adopted & put into execution; that it has so continued thro' the long period which has elapsed; and that even at this time an appeal to a national decision would prove that no general change has taken place: thus believing I have never yielded my original opinion indicated in the "Federalist" No. 39 to the ingenious reasonings of Col: Taylor agst. this construction of the Constitution.

I am not unaware that the Judiciary career has not corresponded with what was anticipated. At one period the Judges perverted the Bench of Justice into a rostrum for partizan harangues. And latterly the Court, by some of its decisions, still more by extrajudicial reasonings & dicta, has manifested a propensity to enlarge the general authority in derogation of the local, and to amplify its own jurisdiction, which has justly incurred the public censure. But the abuse of a trust does not disprove its existence. And if no remedy of the abuse be practicable under the forms of the Constitution, I should prefer a resort to the Nation for an amendment of the Tribunal itself, to continual appeals from its controverted decisions to that Ultimate Arbiter.

78

RUFUS KING TO C. GORE
1 Feb. 1824
Life 6:549–50

The House of R. are now employed in a wide and questionable scheme, of what is called internal improvements; and it seems not unlikely, that the surveys and examinations wh. the bill authorizes, will be approved. The consequence will be the establishment of a construction of the Constitution, that will render the Treasury of the U.S. wholly insecure by exposing the same to the combinations, that will be formed, to apply the same, from time to time, to the local demands of all parts of the country, for the making of Roads, Canals & Bridges. The necessary consequence of the exercise of this power, without check or limitation, must in the end be, to corrupt the public councils, and to endanger those great interests the care of which are confided to the impartiality and integrity of Congress. To survey and explore the route of roads & canals throughout the whole of the U. S. is a useless & unnecessary business; while the ascertainment of the route of particular roads or canals, which it may be desirable & of common benefit to make would be expedient if any power for such purpose be given by the Constitution.

On this subject, I am disposed to doubt, whether a written Constitution, of which we have boasted, can alone define & limit the powers of Govn.; be in fact more precise than a Constitution deposited, & preserved, in rules & maxims like those of the common law, which tho' unwritten are transmitted from age to age, with almost the precision of mathematics or geometry: numbers and diagrams do not change, but such is the imperfection, & uncertainty of language, that words & propositions, which at one time, impart a definite or precise meaning, at another & subsequent time are understood to mean other and different interpretations. Upon this consideration, it may well admit of doubt, whether the written and modern Constitutions of our country are, upon not a few cardinal points, as precise, & incapable of erroneous construction, as the Constitution of England found in the ancient rules and maxims of the unwritten or common Law.

79

OSBORN V. BANK OF THE UNITED STATES
9 Wheat. 738 (1824)

[Marshall, C.J.:] At the close of the argument, a point was suggested, of such vital importance, as to induce the Court to request that it might be particularly spoken to. That point is, the right of the Bank to sue in the Courts of the United States. It has been argued, and ought to be disposed of, before we proceed to the actual exercise of jurisdiction, by deciding on the rights of the parties.

The appellants contest the jurisdiction of the Court on two grounds:

1st. That the act of Congress has not given it.

2d. That, under the constitution, Congress cannot give it.

1. The first part of the objection depends entirely on the language of the act. The words are, that the Bank shall be "made able and capable in law," "to sue and be sued, plead and be impleaded, answer and be answered, defend and be defended, in all State Courts having competent jurisdiction, and in any Circuit Court of the United States."

These words seem to the Court to admit of but one interpretation. They cannot be made plainer by explanation. They give, expressly, the right "to sue and be sued," "in every Circuit Court of the United States," and it would be difficult to substitute other terms which would be more direct and appropriate for the purpose. The argument of the appellants is founded on the opinion of this Court, in *The Bank of the United States v. Deveaux,* (5 Cranch, 85.) In that case it was decided, that the former Bank of the United States was not enabled, by the act which incorporated it, to sue in the federal Courts. The words of the 3d section of that act are, that the Bank may "sue and be sued," &c. "in Courts of record, or any other place whatsoever." The Court was of opinion, that these general words, which are usual in all acts of incorporation, gave only a general capacity to sue, not a particular privilege to sue in the Courts of the United States; and this opinion was strengthened by the circumstance that the 9th rule of the 7th section of the same act, subjects the directors, in case of excess in contracting debt, to be sued in their private capacity, "in any Court of record of the United States, or either of them." The express grant of jurisdiction to the federal Courts, in this case, was considered as having some influence on the construction of the general words of the 3d section, which does not mention those Courts. Whether this decision be right or wrong, it amounts only to a declaration, that a general capacity in the Bank to sue, without mentioning the Courts of the Union, may not give a right to sue in those Courts. To infer from this, that words expressly conferring a right to sue in those Courts, do not give the right, is surely a conclusion which the premises do not warrant.

The act of incorporation, then, confers jurisdiction on the Circuit Courts of the United States, if Congress can confer it.

2. We will now consider the constitutionality of the clause in the act of incorporation, which authorizes the Bank to sue in the federal Courts.

In support of this clause, it is said, that the legislative, executive, and judicial powers, of every well constructed government, are co-extensive with each other; that is, they are potentially co-extensive. The executive department may constitutionally execute every law which the Legislature may constitutionally make, and the judicial department may receive from the Legislature the power of construing every such law. All governments which are not extremely defective in their organization, must possess, within themselves, the means of expounding, as well as enforcing, their own laws. If we examine the constitution of the United States, we find that its framers kept this great political principle in view. The 2d article vests the whole executive power in the President; and the 3d article declares, "that the judicial power shall extend to all cases in law and equity arising under this constitution, the laws of the United States, and treaties made, or which shall be made, under their authority."

This clause enables the judicial department to receive jurisdiction to the full extent of the constitution, laws, and treaties of the United States, when any question respecting them shall assume such a form that the judicial power is capable of acting on it. That power is capable of acting only when the subject is submitted to it by a party who asserts his rights in the form prescribed by law. It then becomes a case, and the constitution declares, that the judicial power shall extend to all cases arising under the constitution, laws, and treaties of the United States.

The suit of *The Bank of the United States v. Osborn and others,* is a case, and the question is, whether it arises under a law of the United States?

The appellants contend, that it does not, because several questions may arise in it, which depend on the general principles of the law, not on any act of Congress.

If this were sufficient to withdraw a case from the jurisdiction of the federal Courts, almost every case, although involving the construction of a law, would be withdrawn; and a clause in the constitution, relating to a subject of vital importance to the government, and expressed in the most comprehensive terms, would be construed to mean almost nothing. There is scarcely any case, every part of which depends on the constitution, laws, or treaties of the United States. The questions, whether the fact alleged as the foundation of the action, be real or fictitious; whether the conduct of the plaintiff has been such as to entitle him to maintain his action; whether his right is barred; whether he has received satisfaction, or has in any manner released his claims, are questions, some or all of which may occur in almost every case; and if their existence be sufficient to arrest the jurisdiction of the Court, words which seem intended to be as extensive as the constitution, laws, and treaties of the Union, which seem designed to give the Courts of the goverment the construction of all its acts, so far as they affect the rights of individuals, would be reduced to almost nothing.

In those cases in which original jurisdiction is given to the Supreme Court, the judicial power of the United States cannot be exercised in its appellate form. In every other case, the power is to be exercised in its original or appellate form, or both, as the wisdom of Congress may direct. With the exception of these cases, in which original jurisdiction is given to this Court, there is none to which the judicial power extends, from which the original jurisdiction of the inferior Courts is excluded by the constitu-

tion. Original jurisdiction, so far as the constitution gives a rule, is co-extensive with the judicial power. We find, in the constitution, no prohibition to its exercise, in every case in which the judicial power can be exercised. It would be a very bold construction to say, that this power could be applied in its appellate form only, to the most important class of cases to which it is applicable.

The constitution establishes the Supreme Court, and defines its jurisdiction. It enumerates cases in which its jurisdiction is original and exclusive; and then defines that which is appellate, but does not insinuate, that in any such case, the power cannot be exercised in its original form by Courts of original jurisdiction. It is not insinuated, that the judicial power, in cases depending on the character of the cause, cannot be exercised in the first instance, in the Courts of the Union, but must first be exercised in the tribunals of the State; tribunals over which the government of the Union has no adequate control, and which may be closed to any claim asserted under a law of the United States.

We perceive, then, no ground on which the proposition can be maintained, that Congress is incapable of giving the Circuit Courts original jurisdiction, in any case to which the appellate jurisdiction extends.

We ask, then, if it can be sufficient to exclude this jurisdiction, that the case involves questions depending on general principles? A cause may depend on several questions of fact and law. Some of these may depend on the construction of a law of the United States; others on principles unconnected with that law. If it be a sufficient foundation for jurisdiction, that the title or right set up by the party, may be defeated by one construction of the constitution or law of the United States, and sustained by the opposite construction, provided the facts necessary to support the action be made out, then all the other questions must be decided as incidental to this, which gives that jurisdiction. Those other questions cannot arrest the proceedings. Under this construction, the judicial power of the Union extends effectively and beneficially to that most important class of cases, which depend on the character of the cause. On the opposite construction, the judicial power never can be extended to a whole case, as expressed by the constitution, but to those parts of cases only which present the particular question involving the construction of the constitution or the law. We say it never can be extended to the whole case, because, if the circumstance that other points are involved in it, shall disable Congress from authorizing the Courts of the Union to take jurisdiction of the original cause, it equally disables Congress from authorizing those Courts to take jurisdiction of the whole cause, on an appeal, and thus will be restricted to a single question in that cause; and words obviously intended to secure to those who claim rights under the constitution, laws, or treaties of the United States, a trial in the federal Courts, will be restricted to the insecure remedy of an appeal upon an insulated point, after it has received that shape which may be given to it by another tribunal, into which he is forced against his will.

We think, then, that when a question to which the judicial power of the Union is extended by the constitution, forms an ingredient of the original cause, it is in the power of Congress to give the Circuit Courts jurisdiction of that cause, although other questions of fact or of law may be involved in it.

The case of the Bank is, we think, a very strong case of this description. The charter of incorporation not only creates it, but gives it every faculty which it possesses. The power to acquire rights of any description, to transact business of any description, to make contracts of any description, to sue on those contracts, is given and measured by its charter, and that charter is a law of the United States. This being can acquire no right, make no contract, bring no suit, which is not authorized by a law of the United States. It is not only itself the mere creature of a law, but all its actions and all its rights are dependant on the same law. Can a being, thus constituted, have a case which does not arise literally, as well as substantially, under the law?

Take the case of a contract, which is put as the strongest against the Bank.

When a Bank sues, the first question which presents itself, and which lies at the foundation of the cause, is, has this legal entity a right to sue? Has it a right to come, not into this Court particularly, but into any Court? This depends on a law of the United States. The next question is, has this being a right to make this particular contract? If this question be decided in the negative, the cause is determined against the plaintiff; and this question, too, depends entirely on a law of the United States. These are important questions, and they exist in every possible case. The right to sue, if decided once, is decided for ever; but the power of Congress was exercised antecedently to the first decision on that right, and if it was constitutional then, it cannot cease to be so, because the particular question is decided. It may be revived at the will of the party, and most probably would be renewed, were the tribunal to be changed. But the question respecting the right to make a particular contract, or to acquire a particular property, or to sue on account of a particular injury, belongs to every particular case, and may be renewed in every case. The question forms an original ingredient in every cause. Whether it be in fact relied on or not, in the defence, it is still a part of the cause, and may be relied on. The right of the plaintiff to sue, cannot depend on the defence which the defendant may choose to set up. His right to sue is anterior to that defence, and must depend on the state of things when the action is brought. The questions which the case involves, then, must determine its character, whether those questions be made in the cause or not.

The appellants say, that the case arises on the contract; but the validity of the contract depends on a law of the United States, and the plaintiff is compelled, in every case, to show its validity. The case arises emphatically under the law. The act of Congress is its foundation. The contract could never have been made, but under the authority of that act. The act itself is the first ingredient in the case, is its origin, is that from which every other part arises. That other questions may also arise, as the execution of the contract, or its performance, cannot change the case, or give

it any other origin than the charter of incorporation. The action still originates in, and is sustained by, that charter.

The clause giving the Bank a right to sue in the Circuit Courts of the United States, stands on the same principle with the acts authorizing officers of the United States who sue in their own names, to sue in the Courts of the United States. The Postmaster General, for example, cannot sue under that part of the constitution which gives jurisdiction to the federal Courts, in consequence of the character of the party, nor is he authorized to sue by the Judiciary Act. He comes into the Courts of the Union under the authority of an act of Congress, the constitutionality of which can only be sustained by the admission that his suit is a case arising under a law of the United States. If it be said, that it is such a case, because a law of the United States authorizes the contract, and authorizes the suit, the same reasons exist with respect to a suit brought by the Bank, That, too, is such a case; because that suit, too, is itself authorized, and is brought on a contract authorized by a law of the United States. It depends absolutely on that law, and cannot exist a moment without its authority.

If it be said, that a suit brought by the Bank may depend in fact altogether on questions unconnected with any law of the United States, it is equally true, with respect to suits brought by the Postmaster General. The plea in bar may be payment, if the suit be brought on a bond, or non-assumpsit, if it be brought on an open account, and no other question may arise than what respects the complete discharge of the demand. Yet the constitutionality of the act authorizing the Postmaster General to sue in the Courts of the United States, has never been drawn into question. It is sustained singly by an act of Congress, standing on that construction of the constitution which asserts the right of the Legislature to give original jurisdiction to the Circuit Courts, in cases arising under a law of the United States.

The clause in the patent law, authorizing suits in the Circuit Courts, stands, we think, on the same principle. Such a suit is a case arising under a law of the United States. Yet the defendant may not, at the trial, question the validity of the patent, or make any point which requires the construction of an act of Congress. He may rest his defence exclusively on the fact, that he has not violated the right of the plaintiff. That this fact becomes the sole question made in the cause, cannot oust the jurisdiction of the Court, or establish the position, that the case does not arise under a law of the United States.

It is said, that a clear distinction exists between the party and the cause; that the party may originate under a law with which the cause has no connexion; and that Congress may, with the same propriety, give a naturalized citizen, who is the mere creature of a law, a right to sue in the Courts of the United States, as give that right to the Bank.

This distinction is not denied; and, if the act of Congress was a simple act of incorporation, and contained nothing more, it might be entitled to great consideration. But the act does not stop with incorporating the Bank: It proceeds to bestow upon the being it has made, all the faculties and capacities which that being possesses. Every act of the Bank grows out of this law, and is tested by it. To use the language of the constitution, every act of the Bank arises out of this law.

A naturalized citizen is indeed made a citizen under an act of Congress, but the act does not proceed to give, to regulate, or to prescribe his capacities. He becomes a member of the society, possessing all the rights of a native citizen, and standing, in the view of the constitution, on the footing of a native. The constitution does not authorize Congress to enlarge or abridge those rights. The simple power of the national Legislature, is to prescribe a uniform rule of naturalization, and the exercise of this power exhausts it, so far as respects the individual. The constitution then takes him up, and, among other rights, extends to him the capacity of suing in the Courts of the United States, precisely under the same circumstances under which a native might sue. He is distinguishable in nothing from a native citizen, except so far as the constitution makes the distinction. The law makes none.

There is, then, no resemblance between the act incorporating the Bank, and the general naturalization law.

Upon the best consideration we have been able to bestow on this subject, we are of opinion, that the clause in the act of incorporation, enabling the Bank to sue in the Courts of the United States, is consistent with the constitution, and to be obeyed in all Courts.

JOHNSON, J., dissenting: . . . In the present instance, I cannot persuade myself, that the constitution sanctions the vesting of the right of action in this Bank, in cases in which the privilege is exclusively personal, or in any case, merely on the ground that a question might *possibly* be raised in it, involving the constitution, or constitutionality of a law, of the United States.

When laws were heretofore passed for raising a revenue by a duty on stamped paper, the tax was quietly acquiesced in, notwithstanding it entrenched so closely on the unquestionable power of the States over the law of contracts; but had the same law which declared void contracts not written upon stamped paper, declared, that every person holding such paper should be entitled to bring his action "in any Circuit Court" of the United States, it is confidently believed that there could have been but one opinion on the constitutionality of such a provision. The whole jurisdiction over contracts, might thus have been taken from the State Courts, and conferred upon those of the United States. Nor would the evil have rested there; by a similar exercise of power, imposing a stamp on deeds generally, jurisdiction over the territory of the State, whoever might be parties, even between citizens of the same State—jurisdiction of suits instituted for the recovery of legacies or distributive portions of intestates' estates—jurisdiction, in fact, over almost every possible case, might be transferred to the Courts of the United States. Wills may be required to be executed on stamped paper; taxes may be, and have been, imposed upon legacies and distributions; and, in all such cases, there is not only a possibility, but a probability, that a question may arise, involving the constitutionality, construction, &c. of a law of the United States. If the circumstance, that the questions which the case involves, are to determine its character, whether those questions be

made in the case or not, then every case here alluded to, may as well be transferred to the jurisdiction of the United States, as those to which this Bank is a party. But still farther, as was justly insisted in argument, there is not a tract of land in the United States, acquired under laws of the United States, whatever be the number of mesne transfers that it may have undergone, over which the jurisdiction of the Courts of the United States might not be extended by Congress, upon the very principle on which the right of suit in this Bank is here maintained. Nor is the case of the alien, put in argument, at all inapplicable. The one acquires its character of individual property, as the other does his political existence, under a law of the United States; and there is not a suit which may be instituted to recover the one, nor an action of ejectment to be brought by the other, in which a right acquired under a law of the United States, does not lie as essentially at the basis of the right of action, as in the suits brought by this Bank. It is no answer to the argument, to say, that the law of the United States is but ancillary to the constitution, as to the alien; for the constitution could do nothing for him without the law: and, whether the question be upon law or constitution, still if the possibility of its arising be a sufficient circumstance to bring it within the jurisdiction of the United States Courts, that possibility exists with regard to every suit affected by alien disabilities; to real actions in time of peace—to all actions in time of war.

I cannot persuade myself, then, that, with these palpable consequences in view, Congress ever could have intended to vest in the Bank of the United States, the right of suit to the extent here claimed. And, notwithstanding the confidence with which this point has been argued, an examination of the terms of the act, and a consideration of them with a view to the context, will be found to leave it by no means a clear case, that such is the legal meaning of the act of incorporation. To be sure, if the act had simply and substantively given the right "to sue and be sued in the Circuit Courts of the United States," there could have been no question made upon the construction of those words. But such is not the fact. The words are, not that the Bank shall be made able and capable in law, to sue, &c., but that it shall, "by a certain name," be made able and capable in law to do the various acts therein enumerated. And these words, under the force of which this suit is instituted, are found in the ordinary incorporating clause of this act, a clause which is well understood to be, and which this Court, in the case of *Deveaux*, has recognised to be, little more than the mere common place or formula of such an act. The name of a corporation is the symbol of its personal existence; a misnomer there is fatal to a suit, (and still more fatal as to other transactions.) By the incorporating clause, a name is given it, and, with that name, a place among created beings; then usually follows an enumeration of the ordinary acts in which it may personate a natural man; and among those acts, the right to sue and be sued, of which the Court, in *Deveaux's* case, very correctly remarks, that it is "a power which if not incident to a corporation, is conferred by every incorporating act, and is not understood to enlarge the jurisdiction of any particular Court, but to give a capacity to the corporation to appear as a corporation in any Court which would by law have cognizance of the cause if brought by individuals." With this qualification, the clause in question will be construed, as an enumeration of incidents, instead of a string of enactments; and such a construction is strongly countenanced by the concluding sentence of the section, for, after running through the whole routine of powers, most of which are unquestionably incidental, and needed no enactment to vest them, it concludes thus: "and generally to do and execute all and singular the acts, matters, and things, which to them it shall and may appertain to do." And, in going over the act, it will be found, that whenever it is contemplated to vest a power not incidental, it is done by a specific provision, made the subject of a distinct clause; such is that power to transact the business of the loan-office of the United States. And, indeed, there is one section of the act, which strikingly exhibits the light in which the law-makers considered the incorporating clause. I mean the tenth; which, notwithstanding that the same clause in the seventh section, which is supposed to confer this sweeping power *to sue,* confers also, in terms equally comprehensive, the power to make laws for the institution, and "to do and execute all and singular the matters and things, which to them it shall and may appertain to do," contains an enactment in the following words: "that they shall have power to appoint such officers, clerks, and servants, under them, for executing the business of the corporation, and to allow them such compensation for their services respectively, as shall be reasonable; and shall be capable of exercising such other powers and authorities for the well governing and ordering the officers of the said corporation, as shall be prescribed by the laws, regulations, and ordinances, of the same;" a section which would have been altogether unnecessary, had the seventh section been considered as enacting, instead of enumerating and limiting. I consider the incorporating clause, then, not as purporting the absolute investment of any power, but as the usual and formal declaration of the extent to which this artificial should personate the natural person, in the transactions incident to ordinary life, or to the peculiar objects of its creation; and, therefore, not vesting the right to sue in the Courts of the United States, but only the right of personating the natural man in the Courts of the United States, as it might, upon general principles, in any other Courts of competent jurisdiction. And this, I say, is consonant to the decision in *Deveaux's* case, and sustained by abundant evidence on the face of the act itself. Indeed, any other view of the effect of the section, converts some of its provisions into absolute nonsense.

It has been argued, and I have no objection to admit, that the phraseology of this act has been varied from that incorporating the former Bank, with a view to meet the decision in *Deveaux's* case. But it is perfectly obvious, that in the prosecution of that design, the purport of *Deveaux's* case has been misapprehended. The Court there decide, that the jurisdiction of the United States depended, (1.) on the character of the cause, (2.) on the character of the parties; that the Judiciary Act confined the jurisdiction of the Circuit Courts to the second class of cases, and the incorporating act contained no words that purported to carry it

further. Whether the legislative power of the United States could extend it as far as is here insisted on, or what words would be adequate to that purpose, the case neither called on the Court to decide, nor has it proposed to decide. If any thing is to be inferred from that decision on those points, it is unfavourable to the sufficiency of the words inserted in the present act. For, the argument of the Court intimates, that where the Legislature propose to give jurisdiction to the Courts of the United States, they do it by a separate provision, as in the case of the action of debt for exceeding the sum authorized to be loaned. And on the words of the incorporating section, it makes this remark, "that it is not understood to enlarge the jurisdiction of any particular Court, but to give a capacity to the corporation to appear as a corporation in any Court, which would by law have cognizance of the cause if brought by individuals. If jurisdiction is given by this clause to the federal Courts, it is equally given to all Courts having original jurisdiction, and for all sums, however small they be." Now, the difference of phraseology between the former act and the present, in the clause in question, is this: the former has these words, "may sue and be sued, &c. in Courts of record or any other place whatsoever;" the present act has substituted these words, "in all State Courts having competent jurisdiction, and in any Circuit Court of the United States." Now, the defect here could not have been the want of adequate words, had the intent appeared to have been, to enlarge the jurisdiction of any particular Court. For, if the Circuit Courts were *Courts of record,* the right of suit given was as full as any other words could have made it. But, as the Court in its own words assigns the ground of its decision, the clause could not have been intended to enlarge the jurisdiction of the State Courts, and therefore could not have been intended to enlarge that of the federal Courts, much less to have extended it to the smallest sum possible. Therefore it concludes, that the clause is one of mere enumeration, containing, as it expresses it, "the powers which, if not incident to a corporation, are conferred by every incorporating act, and are not understood to enlarge," &c. If, then, this variation had in view the object which is attributed to it, the words intended to answer that object have been inserted so unhappily as to neutralize its influence; but, I think it much more consistent with the respect due to the draftsman, who was known to have been an able lawyer, to believe that, with such an object in view, he would have pursued a much more plain and obvious course, and given it a distinct and unequivocal section to itself, or at least have worded it with more marked attention. This opinion is further supported, by considering the absurdities that a contrary opinion would lead to.

A literal translation of the words in question is impossible. Nothing but inconsistencies present themselves, if we attempt to apply it without a reference to the laws and constitution of the United States, forming together the judicial system of the Union. The words are, "may sue and be sued, &c., in any State Court having competent jurisdiction, and in any Circuit Court of the United States." But why should one member of the passage be entitled to an enacting effect, and not the residue? Yet, who will impute to the Legislature or the draftsman, an intention to vest a jurisdiction by these words in a State Court? I do not speak of the positive effect; since the failure of one enactment, because of a want either of power to give or capacity to receive, will not control the effect as to any other enactment. I speak of the intent or understanding of the law-maker; who must have used these words, as applicable to the State Courts, in an enacting sense, if we suppose him to have used them in that sense, as to the Courts of the United States. Yet I should be very unwilling to impute to him, or to the Legislature of the country, ignorance of the fact, that such an enactment, if it was one, could not give a right to sue in the State Courts, if the right did not exist without it. Or, in fact, that such enactment was altogether unnecessary, if the legislative power, which must give effect to such an enactment, was adequate to constitute effectually this body corporate.

But why should this supposed enactment go still farther, and confer the capacity to be sued, as well as to sue, either in the Courts of the one jurisdiction or the other? Did the lawgivers suppose that this corporation would not be subject to suit, without an express enactment for that purpose also? Or was it guilty of the more unaccountable mistake, of supposing that it could confer upon individuals, indiscriminately, this privilege of bringing suits in the Courts of the United States against the Bank? that too, for a cause of action originating, say, in work and labour, or in a special action on the case, or perhaps, ejectment to try title to land mortgaged by a person not having the estate in him, or purchased of a tortious holder for a banking house? I cannot acquiesce in the supposition; and yet, if one is an enactment, and takes effect as such, they are all enactments, for they are uttered *eodem flatu*.

My own conclusion is, that none of them are enactments, but all merely declaratory; or, at most, only enacting, in the words of the Court, in the case of *Deveaux*, that the Bank may, by its corporate name and metaphysical existence, bring suit, or personate the natural man, in the Courts specified, as though it were in fact a natural person; that is, in those cases in which, according to existing laws, suits may be brought in the Courts specified respectively.

Indeed, a more unrestricted sense given to the words of the act, could not be carried into execution; a literal exercise of the right of suit, supposed to be granted, would be impossible. Can the Bank of the United States be sued (in the literal language of the act) "in any Circuit Court of the United States?" in that of Ohio, or Louisiana, for instance? Locality, in this respect, cannot be denied to such an institution; or, at least, it is only incidentally, by distress infinite, or attachment, for instance, that such a suit could be maintained. Nor, on the other hand, could the Bank sue literally in any Circuit Court of the United States. It must, of necessity, be confined to the Circuit Court of that district in which the defendant resides, or is to be found. And thus, at last, we circumscribe these general words, by reference to the judicial system of the United States, as it existed at the time. And why the same restriction should not have been imposed, as to amount, which is imposed as to all other suitors, to wit, 500 dollars and upwards, is to me inscrutable, except on the supposition that this clause was

not intended for any other purpose than that which I have supposed. The United States have suffered no other suitors to institute a suit in its Courts for less than that sum, and it is hard to conceive why the Bank should be permitted to institute a suit to recover, if it will, a single cent. This consideration is expressly drawn into notice by this Court, in the case of *Deveaux,* and if it was entitled to weight then, in fixing the construction of the incorporating section. I see no reason why it should be unnoticed now.

I will dwell no longer on a point, which is in fact secondary and subordinate; for if Congress can vest this jurisdiction, and the people will it, the act may be amended, and the jurisdiction vested. I next proceed to consider, more distinctly, the constitutional question, on the right to vest the jurisdiction to the extent here contended for.

And here I must observe, that I altogether misunderstood the counsel, who argued the cause for the plaintiff in error, if any of them contended against the jurisdiction, on the ground that the cause involved questions depending on general principles. No one can question, that the Court which has jurisdiction of the principal question, must exercise jurisdiction over every question. Neither did I understand them as denying, that if Congress could confer on the Circuit Courts appellate, they could confer original jurisdiction. The argument went to deny the right to assume jurisdiction on a mere hypothesis. It was one of description, identity, definition; they contended, that until a question involving the construction or administration of the laws of the United States did actually arise, the *casus federis* was not presented, on which the constitution authorized the government to take to itself the jurisdiction of the cause. That until such a question actually arose, until such a case was actually presented, *non constat,* but the cause depended upon general principles, exclusively cognizable in the State Courts; that neither the letter nor the spirit of the constitution sanctioned the assumption of jurisdiction on the part of the United States at any previous stage.

And this doctrine has my hearty concurrence in its general application. A very simple case may be stated, to illustrate its bearing on the question of jurisdiction between the two governments. By virtue of treaties with Great Britain, aliens holding lands were exempted from alien disabilities, and made capable of holding, aliening, and transmitting their estates, in common with natives. But why should the claimants of such lands, to all eternity, be vested with the privilege of bringing an original suit in the Courts of the United States? It is true, a question might be made, upon the effect of the treaty, on the rights claimed by or through the alien; but until that question does arise, nay, until a decision against the right takes place, what end has the United States to subserve in claiming jurisdiction of the cause? Such is the present law of the United States, as to all but this one distinguished party; and that law was passed when the doctrines, the views, and ends of the constitution, were, at least, as well understood as they are at present. I attach much importance to the 25th section of the judiciary act, not only as a measure of policy, but as a cotemporaneous exposition of the constitution on this subject; as an exposition of *the words* of the constitution, deduced from a knowledge of its views and policy. The object was, to secure a uniform construction and a steady execution of the laws of the Union. Except as far as this purpose might require, the general government had no interest in stripping the State Courts of their jurisdiction; their policy would rather lead to avoid incumbering themselves with it. Why then should it be vested with jurisdiction in a thousand causes, on a mere possibility of a question arising, which question, at last, does not occur in one of them? Indeed, I cannot perceive how such a reach of jurisdiction can be asserted, without changing the reading of the constitution on this subject altogether. The judicial power extends only to "cases arising," that is, actual, not potential cases. The framers of the constitution knew better, than to trust such a *quo minus* fiction in the hands of any government.

I have never understood any one to question the right of Congress to vest original jurisdiction in its inferior Courts, in cases coming properly within the description of "cases arising under the laws of the United States;" but surely it must first be ascertained, in some proper mode, that the cases are such as the constitution describes. By possibility, a constitutional question may be raised in any conceivable suit that may be instituted; but that would be a very insufficient ground for assuming universal jurisdiction; and yet, that a question has been made, as that, for instance, on the Bank charter, and may again be made, seems still worse, as a ground for extending jurisdiction. For, the folly of raising it again in every suit instituted by the Bank, is too great, to suppose it possible. Yet this supposition, and this alone, would seem to justify vesting the Bank with an unlimited right to sue in the federal Courts. Indeed, I cannot perceive how, with ordinary correctness, a question can be said to be involved in a cause, which only may possibly be made, but which, in fact, is the very last question that there is any probability will be made; or rather, how that can any longer be denominated a question, which has been put out of existence by a solemn decision. The constitution presumes, that the decisions of the supreme tribunal will be acquiesced in; and after disposing of the few questions which the constitution refers to it, all the minor questions belong properly to the State jurisdictions, and never were intended to be taken away in mass.

Efforts have been made to fix the precise sense of the constitution, when it vests jurisdiction in the general government, in "cases arising under the laws of the United States." To me, the question appears susceptible of a very simple solution; that all depends upon the identity of the case supposed; according to which idea, a case may be such in its very existence, or it may become such in its progress. An action may "live, move, and have its being," in a law of the United States; such is that given for the violation of a patent-right, and four or five different actions given by this act of incorporation; particularly that against the President and Directors for over-issuing; in all of which cases the plaintiff must count upon the law itself as the ground of his action. And of the other description, would have been an action of trespass, in this case, had remedy been sought for an actual levy of the tax imposed.

Such was the case of the former Bank against *Deveaux*, and many others that have occurred in this Court, in which the suit, in its form, was such as occur in ordinary cases, but in which the pleadings or evidence raised the question on the law or constitution of the United States. In this class of cases, the occurrence of a question makes the case, and transfers it, as provided for under the twenty-fifth section of the Judiciary Act, to the jurisdiction of the United States. And this appears to me to present the only sound and practical construction of the constitution on this subject; for no other cases does it regard as necessary to place under the control of the general government. It is only when the case exhibits one or the other of these characteristics, that it is acted upon by the constitution. Where no question is raised, there can be no contrariety of construction; and what else had the constitution to guard against? As to cases of the first description, *ex necessitate rei*, the Courts of the United States must be susceptible of original jurisdiction; and as to all other cases, I should hold them, also, susceptible of original jurisdiction, if it were practicable, in the nature of things, to make out the definition of the case, so as to bring it under the constitution judicially, upon an original suit. But until the plaintiff can control the defendant in his pleadings, I see no practical mode of determining when the case does occur, otherwise than by permitting the cause to advance until the case for which the constitution provides shall actually arise. If it never occurs, there can be nothing to complain of; and such are the provisions of the twenty-fifth section. The cause might be transferred to the Circuit Court before an adjudication takes place; but I can perceive no earlier stage at which it can possibly be predicated of such a case, that it is one within the constitution; nor any possible necessity for transferring it then, or until the Court has acted upon it to the prejudice of the claims of the United States. It is not, therefore, because Congress may not vest an *original* jurisdiction, where they can constitutionally vest in the Circuit Courts *appellate* jurisdiction, that I object to this general grant of the right to sue; but, because that the peculiar nature of this jurisdiction is such, as to render it impossible to exercise it in a strictly original form, and because the principle of a possible occurrence of a question as a ground of jurisdiction, is transcending the bounds of the constitution, and placing it on a ground which will admit of an *enormous accession*, if not an *unlimited assumption*, of jurisdiction.

But, dimissing the question of possibility, which, I must think, would embrace every other case as well as those to which this Bank is a party, in what sense can it be predicated of this case, that it is one arising under a law of the United States? It cannot be denied, that jurisdiction of this suit in equity could not be entertained, unless the Court could have had jurisdiction of the action of trespass, which this injunction was intended to anticipate. And, in fact, there is no question, that the Bank here maintains, that the right to sue extends to common trespass, as well as to contracts, or any other cause of action. But suppose trespass in the common form instituted; the declaration is general, and the defendant pleads not guilty, and goes to trial. Where is the feature in such a cause that can give the

Court jurisdiction? What question arises under a law of the United States? or what question that must not be decided exclusively upon the *lex loci,* upon State laws? Take also the case of a contract, and in what sense can it be correctly predicated of that, that in common with every other act of the Bank, it arises out of the law that incorporates it? May it not with equal propriety be asserted, that all the crimes and all the controversies of mankind, arise out of the fiat that called their progenitor into existence? It is not because man was created, that he commits a trespass, or incurs a debt; but because, being indued with certain faculties and propensities, he is led by an appropriate motive to the one action or the other. Sound philosophy attributes effects to their proximate causes. It is but pursuing the grade of creation from one step to another, to deduce the acts of this Bank from State law, or even divine law, with as much correctness as from the law of its immediate creation. Its contracts arise under its own acts, and not under a law of the United States; so far from it, indeed, that their effect, their construction, their limitation, their concoction, are all the creatures of the respective State laws in which they originate. There is a satisfactory illustration of the distinction between contracts which draw their existence from statutes, and those which originate in the acts of man, afforded by this act of incorporation itself. It will be unnecessary to look beyond it. The action of debt before alluded to, given by the ninth clause of the seventh section, against the directors, to any one who will sue, is one of those factitious or statute contracts which exist in, and expire with, the statute that creates it. Not so with the ordinary contracts of the Bank; upon the expiration of the charter, they would be placed in the state of the credits of an intestate before administration; there is no one to sue for them; but the moral obligation would remain, and a Court of equity would enforce it against their debtors, at the suit of the individual stockholders. Nor would this be on the principle of contracts executed under power of attorney; for, the law applicable to principals would govern every question in such causes. All the acts of the corporation are executed *in their own* right, and not in *the right of another.* A personal existence, with all its incidents, is given to them, and it is in right of that existence that they are capable of acting, and do act.

Nor, indeed, in another point of view, is it strictly predicable of this Bank, that its acts arise out of, because its existence is drawn from, a law of the United States. It is because it is *incorporated,* not because incorporated by a *law of the United States,* that it is made capable of exercising certain powers incidentally, and of being vested with others expressly. The same effects would follow, if incorporated by any other competent legislative power. The law of the United States creates the Bank, and the common law, or State law more properly, takes it up and makes it what it is. Who can deny, that in many points the incidents to such an institution may vary in different States, although its existence be derived from the general government? It is the case with the natural alien, when adopted into the national family. His rights, duties, powers, &c., receive always a shade from the *lex loci* of the State in which he fixes his domicil.

If this right to sue could be vested at all in the Bank, it is obvious that it must have been for one or more of three causes: 1. That a law of the United States incorporated it; 2. That a law of the United States vested in it the power to sue; or, 3. That the power to defend itself from trespasses as applicable to this case strictly, or to contract debts as applicable to the Georgia case, was conferred on it by a law of the United States expressly.

The first I have considered. On the second, no one would have the hardihood to contend, that such a grant has any efficacy, unless the suits come within the description of cases arising under a law of the United States, independently of the grant of the right to sue; and it only remains to add a few more remarks on the third ground.

Of the power to repel trespasses, and to enter into contracts, as mere incidents to its creation, I trust I have shown, that neither comes within the description of a case arising under a law of the United States. But where will we find, in the law in question, any express grant of power relative to either? The contracts on which the Georgia case is founded, are declared on as common promissory notes, payable to bearer. Now, as mere incidents, I have no doubt of an action being sustainable in a State Court in both cases. But if an express grant is relied on, as bringing this, or the case of a contract, within the description of "a case arising under a law of the United States," then I look through the law in vain for any express grant, either to make the contract, or repel the trespass. It is true, the sweeping terms with which the incorporating section concludes, import, that "by that name it shall and may be lawful for the Bank to do and execute all and singular the acts, matters, and things, which to them it shall and may appertain to do." But this contains no grant of either, since the inquiry, at last, must be into the incidents of such an institution, and, as incidents, they needed not these words to sustain them; nor could those words give any more force to the right. So that, at last, we are referred to the mere fact of its corporate existence, for the basis of either of the actions, or either of the powers here insisted on, as bringing this cause within the constitutional definition. Having a legal existence as an incorporated banking institution, it has a right to security in its possessions, and to the performance of its contracts; but that right will be precisely the same, if incorporated by a State law, or even, as was held in the case of *Terrett v. Taylor,* if having a common law corporate existence. The common law, or the State law, is referred to by the law of the United States, as the source of these incidents, when it speaks of the acts which are appurtenant to it; and I know of no other law that can define them, or confer them as incidents. Suppose a naturalization act passed, which, after specifying the terms and conditions upon which an alien shall become a citizen, proceeds to declare, "that, as a citizen, he shall lawfully do and execute all and singular the acts, matters, and things, which to 'a citizen,' or 'to him as a citizen,' it shall and may appertain to do," would not these words be a mere nullity? His new existence, and the relations with the society into which he is introduced, that grow out of that connexion, give him the right to defend his property or his existence, (as in this case,) and to enter into and enforce those contracts which, as an alien, he would have been precluded from. He was no more a citizen, without an act of Congress, than this was a Bank. Finally, after the most attentive consideration of this cause, I cannot help thinking, that this idea of taking jurisdiction upon an hypothesis, or even of assuming original, unlimited jurisdiction, of all questions arising under a law of the United States, involves some striking inconsistencies. A Court may take cognizance of a question in a cause, and enter a judgment upon it, and yet not have jurisdiction of the cause itself. Such are all questions of jurisdiction, of which every Court, however limited its jurisdiction, must have cognizance in every cause brought before it. So, also, I see not why, upon the same principle, a law expressly violating the constitution, may not be made the groundwork of a transfer of jurisdiction. Cases may arise, and would arise, under such a law; and if the simple existence, or possibility of such a case, is a sufficient ground of jurisdiction, and that ground sufficient to transfer the whole case to the federal judiciary, the least that can be said of it is, that it was not a case within the mischief intended to be obviated by the constitution. . . .

80

Eakins v. Raub

12 Serg. & Rawle 330 (Pa. 1825)

GIBSON, J. . . . It seems to me there is a plain difference, hitherto unnoticed, between acts that are repugnant to the constitution of the particular state, and acts that are repugnant to the constitution of the *United States;* my opinion being, that the judiciary is bound to execute the former, but not the latter. I shall hereafter attempt to explain this difference, by pointing out the particular provisions in the constitution of the *United States* on which it depends. I am aware, that a right to declare all unconstitutional acts void, without distinction as to either constitution, is generally held as a professional dogma; but, I apprehend rather as a matter of faith than of reason. I admit that I once embraced the same doctrine, but without examination, and I shall therefore state the arguments that impelled me to abandon it, with great respect for those by whom it is still maintained. But I may premise, that it is not a little remarkable, that although the right in question has all along been claimed by the judiciary, no judge has ventured to discuss it, except Chief Justice MARSHALL, (in *Marbury* v. *Madison*, 1 *Cranch*, 176,) and if the argument of a jurist so distinguished for the strength of his ratiocinative powers to be found inconclusive, it may fairly be set down to the weakness of the position which he attempts to defend. *Si Pergama dextra defendi potuit, etiam hac defensa fuisset.* In saying this, I do not overlook the opinion of Judge PATTERSON, in *Vanhorne* v. *Dorrance*, (2 *Dall.* 307,) which abounds with beautiful figures in illustration of his doctrine; but, without intending disrespect, I submit that

metaphorical illustration is one thing and argument another. Now, in questions of this sort, precedents ought to go for absolutely nothing. The constitution is a collection of fundamental laws, not to be departed from in practice nor altered by judicial decision, and in the construction of it, nothing would be so alarming as the doctrine of *communis error*, which offers a ready justification for every usurpation that has not been resisted *in limine*. Instead, therefore, of resting on the fact, that the right in question has universally been assumed by the *American* courts, the judge who asserts it ought to be prepared to maintain it on the principles of the constitution.

I begin, then, by observing that in this country, the powers of the judiciary are divisible into those that are POLITICAL and those that are purely CIVIL. Every power by which one organ of the government is enabled to control another, or to exert an influence over its acts, is a political power. The political powers of the judiciary are *extraordinary* and *adventitious;* such, for instance, as are derived from certain peculiar provisions in the constitution of the *United States,* of which hereafter: and they are derived, by direct grant, from the common fountain of all political power. On the other hand, its civil, are its *ordinary* and *appropriate* powers; being part of its essence, and existing independently of any supposed grant in the constitution. But where the government exists by virtue of a *written* constitution, the judiciary does not necessarily derive from that circumstance, any other than its ordinary and appropriate powers. Our judiciary is constructed on the principles of the common law, which enters so essentially into the composition of our social institutions as to be inseparable from them, and to be in fact, the basis of the whole scheme of our civil and political liberty. In adopting any organ or instrument of the common law, we take it with just such powers and capacities as were incident to it at the common law, except where these are expressly, or by necessary implication, abridged or enlarged in the act of adoption; and, that such act is a written instrument, cannot vary its consequences or construction. In the absence of special provision to the contrary, sheriffs, justices of the peace, and other officers whose offices are established in the constitution, exercise no other powers here, than what similar officers do in *England;* and trial by jury would have been according to the course of the common law, without any declaration to that effect in the constitution. Now, what are the powers of the judiciary at the common law? They are those that necessarily arise out of its immediate business; and they are therefore commensurate only with the judicial execution of the municipal law, or, in other words, with the administration of distributive justice, without extending to any thing of a political cast whatever. Dr. *Paley*, as able a man as ever wrote on those subjects on which he professed to treat, seems to have considered the judiciary as a part of the executive, and judging from its essence, subordinate to the legislature, which he viewed as the depository of the whole sovereignty of the state. With us, although the legislature be the depository of only so much of the sovereignty as the people have thought fit to impart, it is nevertheless sovereign within the limit of its powers, and may relatively claim the same pre-eminence here that it may claim elsewhere. It will be conceded, then that the ordinary and essential powers of the judiciary do not extend to the annulling of an act of the legislature. Nor can the inference be drawn from this, be evaded by saying that in *England* the constitution, resting in principles consecrated by time, and not in an actual written compact, and being subject to alteration by the very act of the legislature, there is consequently no separate and distinct criterion by which the question of constitutionality may be determined; for it does not follow, that because we have such a criterion, the application of it belongs to the judiciary. I take it, therefore, that the power in question does not necessarily arise from the judiciary being established by a written constitution, but that this organ can claim on account of that circumstance, no powers that do not belong to it at the common law; and that, whatever may have been the cause of the limitation of its jurisdiction originally, it can exercise no power of supervision over the legislature, without producing a direct authority for it in the constitution, either in terms or by irresistible implication from the nature of the government: without which the power must be considered as reserved, along with the other ungranted portions of the sovereignty for the immediate use of the people.

The constitution of *Pennsylvania* contains no express grant of political powers to the judiciary. But, to establish a grant by implication, the constitution is said to be a law of superior obligation; and, consequently, that if it were to come into collision with an act of the legislature, the latter would have to give way. This is conceded. But it is a fallacy, to suppose that they can come into collision *before the judiciary*. What is a constitution? It is an act of extraordinary legislation, by which the people establish the structure and mechanism of their governemnt; and in which they prescribe fundamental rules to regulate the motion of the several parts. What is a statute? It is an act of ordinary legislation, by the appropriate organ of the government; the provisions of which are to be executed by the executive or judiciary, or by officers subordinate to them. The constitution, then, contains no practical rules for the administration of *distributive justice*, with which alone the judiciary has to do; these being furnished in acts of ordinary legislation, by that organ of the government, which, in this respect, is exclusively the representative of the people; and it is generally true, that the provisions of a constitution are to be carried into effect immediately by the legislature, and only mediately, if at all, by the judiciary. In what respect is the constitution of *Pennsylvania* inconsistent with this principle? Only, perhaps in one particular provision, to regulate the style of process, and establish an appropriate form of conclusion in criminal prosecutions: in this alone the constitution furnishes a rule for the judiciary, and this the legislature cannot alter, because it cannot alter the constitution. In all other cases, if the act of assembly supposed to be unconstitutional, were laid out of the question, there would remain no rule to determine the point in controversy in the cause, but the statute or common law, as it existed before the act of assembly was passed; and the constitution and act of assembly therefore do not furnish conflicting rules *applicable to the point before*

the court; nor is it at all necessary, that the one or the other of them should give way.

The constitution and the *right* of the legislature to pass the act, may be in collision. But is that a legitimate subject for judicial determination? If it be, the judiciary must be a peculiar organ, to revise the proceedings of the legislature, and to correct its mistakes; and in what part of the constitution are we to look for this proud pre-eminence? Viewing the matter in the opposite direction, what would be thought of an act of assembly in which it should be declared that the Supreme Court had, in a particular case, put a wrong construction on the constitution of the *United States,* and that the judgment should therefore be reversed? It would doubtless be thought a usurpation of judicial power. But it is by no means clear, that to declare a law void which has been enacted according to the forms prescribed in the constitution, is not a usurpation of legislative power. It is an act of sovereignty; and sovereignty and legislative power are said by Sir William *Blackstone* to be convertible te̅ms. It is the business of the judiciary to interpret the laws, not scan the authority of the lawgiver; and without the latter, it cannot take cognizance of a collision between a law and the constitution. So that to affirm that the judiciary has a right to judge of the existence of such collision, is to take for granted the very thing to be proved. And, that a very cogent argument may be made in this way, I am not disposed to deny; for no conclusions are so strong as those that are drawn from the *petitio principii.*

But it has been said to be emphatically the business of the judiciary, to ascertain and pronounce what the law is; and that this necessarily involves a consideration of the constitution. It does so: but how far? If the judiciary will inquire into any thing beside the form of enactment, where shall it stop? There must be some point of limitation to such an inquiry; for no one will pretend, that a judge would be justifiable in calling for the election returns, or scrutinizing the qualifications of those who composed the legislature.

It is next supposed, that as the members of the legislature have no inherent right of legislation, but derive their authority from the people, no law can be valid where authority to pass it, is either simply not given or positively withheld: thus treating the members as the agents of the people, and the constitution as a letter of attorney containing their authority and bounding their sphere of action, and the consequence deduced being, that acts not warranted by the constitution are not the acts of the people, but of those that do them; and that they are therefore *ipso facto* void. The concluding inference is, in military phrase, the key of the position, and if it be tenable, it will decide the controversy; for a law *ipso facto* void, is absolutely a *non entity.* But it is putting the argument on bold ground to say, that a high public functionary shall challenge no more respect than is due to a private individual; and that its acts, although presenting themselves under sanctions derived from a strict observance of the form of enactment prescribed in the constitution, are to be rejected as *ipso facto* void for excess of authority. The constitution is not to be expounded like a deed, but by principles of interpretation much more liberal; as was declared by this court, in *The Farmers and Mechanics' Bank* v. *Smith*, (3 *Serg. & Rawle*, 63.) But, in the case of a public functionary, even according to common law maxims, *omnia presumi debeant rite et solemniter esse acta*. The benefit of this maxim cannot be refused to the legislature by those who advocate the other side, inasmuch as it is the foundation of their own hypothesis; for all respect is demanded for the acts of the judiciary. For instance: let it be supposed that the power to declare a law unconstitutional has been exercised. What is to be done? The legislature must acquiesce, although it may think the construction of the judiciary wrong. But why must it acquiesce? Only because it is bound to pay that respect to every other organ of the government, which it has a right to exact from each of them in turn. This is the argument. But it will not be pretended, that the legislature has not at least an equal right with the judiciary to put a construction on the constitution; nor that either of them is infallible; nor that either ought to be required to surrender its judgment to the other. Suppose, then, they differ in opinion as to the constitutionality of a particular law; if the organ whose business it first is to decide on the subject, is not to have its judgment treated with respect, what shall prevent it from securing the preponderance of its opinion by the strong arm of power? It is in vain to say, the legislature would be the aggressor in this; and that no argument in favour of its authority can be drawn from an abuse of its power. Granting this, yet it is fair to infer, that the framers of the constitution never intended to force the judges either to become martyrs or to flinch from their duty; or to interpose a check that would produce no other effect than an intestine war. Such things have occurred in other states, and would necessarily occur in this, under circumstances of strong excitement in the popular branch. The judges would be legislated out of office, if the majority requisite to a direct removal by impeachment, or the legislative address, could not be had; and this check, instead of producing the salutary effect expected from it, would rend the government in pieces. But suppose that a struggle would not produce consequences so disastrous, still the soundness of any construction which would bring one organ of the government into collision with another, is to be more than suspected; for where collision occurs, it is evident the machine is working in a way the framers of it did not intend. But what I want more immediately to press on the attention, is, the necessity of yielding to the acts of the legislature the same respect that is claimed for the acts of the judiciary. Repugnance to the constitution is not always self evident; for questions involving the consideration of its existence, require for their solution the most vigorous exertion of the higher faculties of the mind, and conflicts will be inevitable, if any branch is to apply the constitution after its own fashion to the acts of all the others. I take it, then, the legislature is entitled to all the deference that is due to the judiciary; that its acts are in no case to be treated as *ipso facto* void, except where they would produce a revolution in the government; and that, to avoid them, requires the act of some tribunal competent under the constitution, (if any such there be,) to pass on their validity. All that remains, therefore, is to inquire whether the judiciary or the people are that tribunal.

Now, as the judiciary is not expressly constituted for that purpose, it must derive whatever authority of the sort it may possess, from the reasonableness and fitness of the thing. But, in theory, all the organs of the government are of equal capacity; or, if not equal, each must be supposed to have superior capacity only for those things which peculiarly belong to it; and, as legislation peculiarly involves the consideration of those limitations which are put on the law-making power, and the interpretation of the laws when made, involves only the construction of the laws themselves, it follows that the construction of the constitution in this particular belongs to the legislature, which ought therefore to be taken to have superior capacity to judge of the constitutionality of its own acts. But suppose all to be of equal capacity in every respect, why should one exercise a controlling power over the rest? That the judiciary is of superior rank, has never been pretended, although it has been said to be co-ordinate. It is not easy, however, to comprehend how the power which gives law to all the rest, can be of no more than equal rank with one which receives it, and is answerable to the former for the observance of its statutes. Legislation is essentially an act of sovereign power; but the execution of the laws by instruments that are governed by prescribed rules and exercise no power of volition, is essentially otherwise. The very definition of law, which is said to be "a rule of civil conduct prescribed by the *supreme* power in the state," shows the intrinsic superiority of the legislature. It may be said, the power of the legislature, also, is limited by prescribed rules. It is so. But it is, nevertheless, the power of the people, and sovereign as far as it extends. It cannot be said, that the judiciary is co-ordinate merely because it is established by the constitution. If that were sufficient, sheriffs, registers of wills, and recorders of deeds, would be so too. Within the pale of their authority, the acts of these officers will have the power of the people for their support; but no one will pretend, they are of equal dignity with the acts of the legislature. Inequality of rank arises not from the manner in which the organ has been constituted, but from its essence and the nature of its functions; and the legislative organ is superior to every other, inasmuch as the power to will and to command, is essentially superior to the power to act and to obey. It does not follow then, that every organ created by special provision in the constitution, is of equal rank. Both the executive, strictly as such, and the judiciary are subordinate; and an act of superior power exercised by an inferior ought, one would think, to rest on something more solid than implication.

It may be alleged, that no such power is claimed, and that the judiciary does no positive act, but merely refuses to be instrumental in giving effect to an unconstitutional law. This is nothing more than a repetition in a different form of the argument,—that an unconstitutional law is *ipso facto* void; for a refusal to act under the law, must be founded on a right in each branch to judge of the acts of all the others, before it is bound to exercise its functions to give those acts effect. No such right is recognised in the different branches of the national government, except the judiciary, (and that, too, on account of the peculiar provisions of the constitution,) for it is now universally held, whatever doubts may have once existed, that congress is bound to provide for carrying a treaty into effect, although it may disapprove of the exercise of the treaty-making power in the particular instance. A government constructed on any other principle, would be in perpetual danger of standing still; for the right to decide on the constitutionality of the laws, would not be peculiar to the judiciary, but would equally reside in the person of every officer whose agency might be necessary to carry them into execution.

Every one knows how seldom men think exactly alike on ordinary subjects; and a government constructed on the principle of assent by all its parts, would be inadequate to the most simple operations. The notion of a complication of counter checks has been carried to an extent in theory, of which the framers of the constitution never dreamt. When the entire sovereignty was separated into its elementary parts, and distributed to the appropriate branches, all things incident to the exercise of its powers were committed to each branch exclusively. The negative which each part of the legislature may exercise, in regard to the acts of the other, was thought sufficient to prevent material infractions of the restraints which were put on the power of the whole; for, had it been intended to interpose the judiciary as an additional barrier, the matter would surely not have been left in doubt. The judges would not have been left to stand on the insecure and ever shifting ground of public opinion as to constructive powers: they would have been placed on the impregnable ground of an express grant. They would not have been compelled to resort to the debates in the convention, or the opinion that was generally entertained at the time. A constitution, or a statute, is supposed to contain the whole will of the body from which it emanated; and I would just as soon resort to the debates in the legislature for the construction of an act of assembly, as to the debates in the convention for the construction of the constitution.

The power is said to be restricted to cases that are free from doubt or difficulty. But the abstract existence of a power cannot depend on the clearness or obscurity of the case in which it is to be exercised; for that is a consideration that cannot present itself, before the question of the existence of the power shall have been determined; and, if its existence be conceded, no considerations of policy arising from the obscurity of the particular case, ought to influence the exercise of it. The judge would have no discretion; but the party submitting the question of constitutionality would have an interest in the decision of it, which could not be postponed to motives of deference for the opinion of the legislature. His rights would depend not on the greatness of the supposed discrepancy with the constitution, but on the existence of any discrepancy at all; and the judge would therefore be bound to decide this question, like every other in respect to which he may be unable to arrive at a perfectly satisfactory conclusion. But he would evade the question instead of deciding it, were he to refuse to decide in accordance with the inclination of his mind. To say, therefore, that the power is to be exercised but in perfectly clear cases, is to betray a doubt of

the propriety of exercising it at all. Were the same caution used in judging of the existence of the power that is inculcated as to the exercise of it, the profession would perhaps arrive at a different conclusion. The grant of a power so extraordinary ought to appear so plain, that he who should run might read. Now, put the constitution into the hands of any man of plain sense, whose mind is free from an impression on the subject, and it will be impossible to persuade him, that the exercise of such a power was ever contemplated by the convention.

But the judges are sworn to support the constitution, and are they not bound by it as the law of the land? In some respects they are. In the very few cases in which the judiciary, and not the legislature, is the immediate organ to execute its provisions, they are bound by it in preference to any act of assembly to the contrary. In such cases, the constitution is a rule to the courts. But what I have in view in this inquiry, is the supposed right of the judiciary, to interfere, in cases where the constitution is to be carried into effect through the instrumentality of the legislature, and where that organ must necessarily first decide on the constitutionality of its own act. The oath to support the constitution is not peculiar to the judges, but is taken indiscriminately by every officer of the government, and is designed rather as a test of the political principles of the man, than to bind the officer in the discharge of his duty: otherwise it were difficult to determine what operation it is to have in the case of a recorder of deeds, for instance, who, in the execution of his office, has nothing to do with the constitution. But granting it to relate to the official conduct of the judge, as well as every other officer, and not to his political principles, still it must be understood in reference to supporting the constitution, *only as far as that may be involved in his official duty;* and, consequently, if his official duty does not comprehend an inquiry into the authority of the legislature, neither does his oath. It is worthy of remark here, that the foundation of every argument in favour of the right of the judiciary, is found at last to be an assumption of the whole ground in dispute. Granting that the object of the oath is to secure a support of the constitution in the discharge of official duty, its terms may be satisfied by restraining it to official duty in the exercise of the *ordinary* judicial powers. Thus, the constitution may furnish a rule of construction, where a particular interpretation of a law would conflict with some constitutional principle; and such interpretation, where it may, is always to be avoided. But the oath was more probably designed to secure the powers of each of the different branches from being usurped by any of the rest; for instance, to prevent the house of representatives from erecting itself into a court of judicature, or the Supreme Court from attempting to control the legislature; and, in this view, the oath furnishes an argument equally plausible *against* the right of the judiciary. But if it require a support of the constitution in any thing beside official duty, it is in fact an oath of allegiance to a particular form of government; and, considered as such, it is not easy to see why it should not be taken by the citizens at large, as well as by the officers of the government. It has never been thought that an officer is under greater restraint as to measures which have for their avowed end a total change of the constitution, than a citizen who has taken no oath at all. The official oath, then, relates only to the official conduct of the officer, and does not prove that he ought to stray from the path of his ordinary business to search for violations of duty in the business of others; nor does it, as supposed, define the powers of the officer.

But do not the judges do a *positive act* in violation of the constitution, when they give effect to an unconstitutional law? Not if the law has been passed according to the forms established in the constitution. The fallacy of the question is, in supposing that the judiciary adopts the acts of the legislature as its own; whereas the enactment of a law and the interpretation of it are not concurrent acts, and as the judiciary is not required to concur in the enactment, neither is it in the breach of the constitution which may be the consequence of the enactment. The fault is imputable to the legislature, and on it the responsibility exclusively rests. In this respect, the judges are in the predicament of jurors who are bound to serve in capital cases, although unable, under any circumstances, to reconcile it to their duty to deprive a human being of life. To one of these, who applied to be discharged from the panel, I once heard it remarked, by an eminent and humane judge, "*You* do not deprive a prisoner of life by finding him guilty of a capital crime: you but pronounce his case to be within the law, and it is therefore those who declare the law, and not you, who deprive him of life."

That every thing addressed to the legislature by way of positive command, is purely directory, will hardly be disputed: it is only to enforce prohibitions that the interposition of judicial authority is thought to be warrantable. But I can see no room for a distinction between the injunctions that are positive and those that are negative: the same authority must enforce both.

But it has been said, that this construction would deprive the citizen of the advantages which are peculiar to a written constitution, by at once declaring the power of the legislature, in practice, to be illimitable. I ask, what are those advantages? The principles of a written constitution are more fixed and certain, and more apparent to the apprehension of the people, than principles which depend on tradition and the vague comprehension of the individuals who compose the nation, and who cannot all be expected to receive the same impressions or entertain the same notions on any given subject. But there is no magic or inherent power in parchment and ink, to command respect and protect principles from violation. In the business of government, a recurrence to first principles answers the end of an observation at sea with a view to correct the dead reckoning; and, for this purpose, a written constitution is an instrument of inestimable value. It is of inestimable value, also, in rendering its principles familiar to the mass of the people; for, after all, there is no effectual guard against legislative usurpation but public opinion, the force of which, in this country, is inconceivably great. Happily this is proved, by experience, to be a sufficient guard against palpable infractions. The constitution of this state has withstood the shocks of strong party excitement for thirty years, during which no act of the legislature has been declared unconstitutional, although the judiciary has constantly asserted a right to do so in clear cases. But it would be absurd to say, that this remarkable observance of the constitution has been produced, not by the responsibility of the legislature to the people, but by an apprehension of control by the judiciary. Once let public opinion be so corrupt as to sanction every misconstruction of the constitution and abuse of power which the temptation of the moment may dictate, and the party which may happen to be predominant, will laugh at the puny efforts of a dependent power to arrest it in its course.

For these reasons, I am of opinion that it rests with the people, in whom full and absolute sovereign power resides to correct abuses in legislation, by instructing their representatives to repeal the obnoxious act. What is wanting to plenary power in the government, is reserved by the people for their own immediate use; and to redress an infringement of their rights in this respect, would seem to be an accessory of the power thus reserved. It might, perhaps, have been better to vest the power in the judiciary; as it might be expected that its habits of deliberation, and the aid derived from the arguments of counsel, would more frequently lead to accurate conclusions. On the other hand, the judiciary is not infallible; and an error by it would admit of no remedy but a more distinct expression of the public will, through the extraordinary medium of a convention; whereas, an error by the legislature admits of a remedy by an exertion of the same will, in the ordinary exercise of the right of suffrage,—a mode better calculated to attain the end, without popular excitement. It may be said, the people would probably not notice an error of their representatives. But they would as probably do so, as notice an error of the judiciary; and, beside, it is a *postulate* in the theory of our government, and the very basis of the superstructure, that the people are wise, virtuous, and competent to manage their own affairs: and if they are not so, in fact, still every question of this sort must be determined according to the principles of the constitution, as it came from the hands of its framers, and the existence of a defect which was not foreseen, would not justify those who administer the government, in applying a corrective in practice, which can be provided only by a convention. Long and uninterrupted usage is entitled to respect; and, although it cannot change an admitted principle of the constitution, it will go far to settle a question of doubtful right. But although this power has all along been claimed by the state judiciary, it has never been exercised. *Austin* v. *The University of Pennsylvania*, (1 *Yeates*, 260,) is the only case even apparently to the contrary; but there the act of assembly had been previously repealed. In *Vanhorne* v. *Dorrance*, decided by the Circuit Court of the *United States* under similar circumstances, the right is peremptorily asserted and examples of monstrous violations of the constitution are put in a strong light by way of example; such as taking away the trial by the jury, the elective franchise, or subverting religious liberty. But any of these would be such a usurpation of the political rights of the citizens, as would work a change in the very structure of the government; or, to speak more properly, it would itself be a revolution, which, to counteract, would justify even insurrection; consequently, a judge might lawfully employ every instrument of official resistance within his reach. By this I mean, that while the citizen should resist with pike and gun, the judge might co-operate with *habeas corpus* and *mandamus*. It would be his duty, as a citizen, to throw himself into the breach, and, if it should be necessary, perish there; but this is far from proving the judiciary to be a *peculiar organ* under the constitution, to prevent legislative encroachment on the powers reserved by the people; and this is all that I contend it is not. Indeed, its absolute inadequacy to the object, is conclusive that it never was intended as such by the framers of the constitution, who must have had in view the probable operation of the government in practice.

But in regard to an act of assembly, which is found to be in collision with the constitution, laws, or treaties of the *United States,* I take the duty of the judiciary to be exactly the reverse. By becoming parties to the federal constitution, the states have agreed to several limitations of their individual sovereignty, to enforce which, it was thought to be absolutely necessary to prevent them from giving effect to laws in violation of those limitations, through the instrumentality of their own judges. Accordingly, it is declared in the fifth article and second section of the federal constitution, that "This constitution, and the laws of the *United States* which shall be made in pursuance thereof, and all treaties made, or which shall be made under the authority of the *United States,* shall be the *supreme* law of the land; and the *judges* in every *state* shall be BOUND thereby; any thing in the *laws* or *constitution* of any *state* to the contrary notwithstanding."

This is an express grant of a political power, and it is conclusive to show that no law of inferior obligation, as every state law must necessarily be, can be executed at the expense of the constitution, laws, or treaties of the *United States.* It may be said, these are to furnish a rule only when there is no state provision on the subject. But, in that view, they could with no propriety be called supreme; for supremacy is a relative term, and cannot be predicated of a thing which exists separately and alone: and this law, which is called supreme, would change its character and become subordinate as soon as it should be found in conflict with a state law. But the judges are to be bound by the federal constitution and laws, notwithstanding any thing in the constitution or laws of the particular state *to the contrary.* If, then, a state were to declare the laws of the *United States* not to be obligatory on her judges, such an act would unquestionably be void; for it will not be pretended, that any member of the union can dispense with the obligation of the federal constitution; and, if it cannot be done directly, and by a general declaratory law, neither can it indirectly, and by by-laws dispensing with it in particular cases. This, therefore, is an express grant of the power, and would be sufficient for the purposes of the argument; but it is not all.

By the third article and second section, appellate jurisdiction of all cases arising under the constitution and laws of the *United States,* is reserved to the federal judiciary, under such regulations as congress may prescribe; and, in execution of this provision, congress has prescribed regulations for removing into the Supreme Court of the *United States,* all causes decided by the highest court of judicature of any state, which involve the construction of the constitution, or of any law or treaty of the *United States.* This is another guard against infraction of the limitations imposed on state sovereignty, and one which is extremely efficient in practice; for reversals of decisions in favour of the constitutionality of acts of assembly, have been frequent on writs of error to the Supreme Court of the *United States.*

Now, a reversal implies that it was not only the right, but the duty of the inferior court to decide otherwise; for where there is but one way of deciding, there can be no error. But what beneficial result would there be produced by the decision of a state court in favour of a state law palpably unconstitutional? The injured party would have the judgment reversed by the court in the last resort, and the cause would come back with a mandate to decide differently, which the state court dare not disobey; so that nothing would eventually be gained by the party claiming under the law of the state, but, on the contrary, he would be burdened with additional costs. I grant, however, that the state judiciary ought not to exercise the power except in cases free from all doubt, because, as a writ of error to the Supreme Court of the *United States* lies to correct an error only in favour of the constitutionality of the state law, an error in deciding against it would be irremediable. Anticipating those who think they perceive in this, exactly what I have censured in those who assume the existence of the same power in respect to laws that are repugnant to the constitution of the state, but restrict the exercise of it to clear cases, I briefly remark that the instances are not parallel; an error in deciding against the validity of the law, being irreparable in the one, and not so in the other.

Unless, then, the respective states are not bound by the engagement, which they have contracted by becoming parties to the constitution of the *United States,* they are precluded from denying either the right or the duty of their judges, to declare their laws void when they are repugnant to that constitution.

The preceding inquiry may perhaps appear foreign to the point immediately before the court; but, as the act of 1815 may be thought repugnant to the constitution of the state, an examination of the powers of the judiciary, became not only proper but necessary.

Then, laying the constitution of the state out of the case, what restriction on state sovereignty is violated by at once repealing any of the saving clauses in the statute of limitations? Those restrictions are contained in the first article and tenth section of the constitution of the *United States;* and, as there is no pretence that a contract has been impaired, none of them can, even by the most strained construction, be supposed to be violated, except that which relates to *ex post facto* laws. But that was held, in *Calder* v. *Bull,* (Dall. 386,) to be applicable only to penal laws. The law in question not only relates to civil rights, but is not even retrospective. It is commonly said, that the statute of limitations *does not run* against any one, who is within the benefit of any clause of the *proviso;* but this is plainly inaccurate. It actually runs,—but ten years from the removal of the disability provided for, are given *in addition* to the original period, and this as a personal privilege in avoidance of the bar, which would otherwise be decisive. If it were actually to begin to run only from the removal of the disability, the party would have twenty-one years from that period. Now, suppose it to be removed at the conclusion of the twentieth year, it will not be pretended that he would still have twenty-one years in addition: yet that consequence would be inevitable, were the statute not to begin to run before. So, where the disability is removed during the first year, the party will not be compelled to make entry with the ensuing ten; for the saving does not come into operation till the period which constitutes a bar in ordinary cases has elapsed: he must, therefore, in such case, make his entry within the original period. Then, by putting in force a limitation which had all along been running against the plaintiffs, the act of 1815 did not operate retrospectively, but deprived them of a prospective exemption, which, having been gratuitous, cannot be said to have originated in contract. I am therefore of opinion that the judgment be affirmed.

81

UNITED STATES V. ORTEGA
11 Wheat. 467 (1826)

March 16th, 1826. WASHINGTON, Justice, delivered the opinion of the court.—The defendant, Juan Gualberto de Ortega, was indicted in the circuit court of the United States for the eastern district of Pennsylvania, for infracting the law of nations, by offering violence to the person of Hilario de Rivas y Salmon, the charge d'affaires of his Catholic Majesty, the King of Spain, in the United States, contrary to the law of nations, and to the act of the congress of the United States in such case provided. The jury having found a verdict of guilty, the defendant moved in arrest of judgment, and assigned for cause, "that the circuit court has not jurisdiction of the matter charged in the indictment, inasmuch as it is a case affecting an ambassador or other public minister." The opinions of the judges of that court upon this point being opposed, the cause comes before this court upon a certificate of such disagreement.

The questions to which the point certified by the court below gives rise, are, first, whether this is a case affecting an ambassador or other public minister, within the meaning of the second section of the third article of the constitution of the United States? If it be, then, the next question would be, whether the jurisdiction of the supreme court in such cases, is not only original, but exclusive of the circuit courts, under the true construction of the above section and article?

The last question need not be decided in the present case, because the court is clearly of opinion, that this is not a case affecting a public minister, within the plain meaning

of the constitution. It is that of a public prosecution, instituted and conducted by and in the name of the United States, for the purpose of vindicating the law of nations, and that of the United States, offended, as the indictment charges, in the person of a public minister, by an assault committed on him by a private individual. It is a case, then, which affects the United States, and the individual whom they seek to punish; but one in which the minister himself, although he was the person injured by the assault, has no concern, either in the event of the prosecution, or in the costs attending it.

It is ordered to be certified to the circuit court for the eastern district of Pennsylvania, that that court has jurisdiction of the matter charged in the indictment, the case not being one which affects an ambassador or other public minister.

82

AMERICAN INSURANCE CO. V. CANTER
1 Pet. 511 (1828)

(See 1.8.9, no. 5)

83

PICQUET V. SWAN
19 Fed. Cas. 609, no. 11,134 (C.C.D.Mass. 1828)

(See Amend. V [due process and taking], no. 23)

84

WILLIAM RAWLE, A VIEW OF THE CONSTITUTION OF THE UNITED STATES 253–73
1829 (2d ed.)

The rules and principles by which the judicial power is to be administered, form the next subject of consideration, and here we have, in the Constitution, the benefit of a text which in some respects is explicit, and in all others, supplies a foundation on which it is apprehended we may securely rest.

The laws of the United States and treaties made under their authority, form the explicit principle of the judiciary power, and in respect to their high obligation no question can arise: but another part of the same sentence leads us into a wider field of inquiry.

The Constitution itself is the supreme law of the land, and *all cases arising under it* are declared to be within the judicial power. To every part of this well-digested work we are bound to give an efficient construction. No words are there used in vain: as a literary composition, the union of precision with brevity constitutes one of its chief ornaments and recommendations. When we find a distinction between cases arising *under the Constitution* and *under laws and treaties,* we are not at liberty to suppose that the former description was introduced without a definite meaning. The other designations are not more plain than this. We understand what is meant by cases arising under laws and under treaties, but something more is evidently meant. We may recollect that in another article of the Constitution, laws made in pursuance thereof, and treaties made under the authority of the United States, are declared to be the supreme law of the land. The subordination of all legislative acts to the Constitution is thereby provided for, and it is inconsistent with the whole frame of its composition to consider any part of it as an useless repetition of words. We are therefore bound to say, that cases may arise under the Constitution which do not arise under the laws, and if this point is conceded or established, we are next to inquire what are those cases.

Of a civil nature nothing can properly be said to *arise* under the Constitution, except contracts to which the United States are parties. Jurisdiction is given to them over controversies in which states and individuals of certain descriptions are concerned, but those cases would exist although the Constitution did not exist. The courts of the United States are, in these respects, merely the organs of justice, and by the first act of congress relative to the judicial establishment it is expressly declared that the laws of the several states, except where the Constitution, treaties, or statutes of the United States shall otherwise require or provide, shall be regarded as rules of decision in trials *at common law,* in courts of the United States, in cases where they apply.

The term, laws of the several states embracing as well their common as their statute laws, there is no difficulty on this subject. It is admitted, that every state in the Union has its peculiar system and rules of decision in cases for which no positive statutes are provided, and of these general rules the United States have the benefit in all cases of contract which may occasion suits on their behalf, either in their own courts or in those of the several states. To their own courts a similar power could not be given by congress unless warranted by the Constitution, but if the Constitution does warrant it, congress may give it. No one has doubted that although no express adoption of this general principle is apparent, it is necessarily contained in the Constitution, in relation to all civil matters.

Contracts obligatory on the party, though merely implied by reason of principles not found in the text of any statute, but originating in universal law, may as well be made by the United States acting through the agency of their executive officers, as by private individuals. No one has doubted that they may be enforced. But it cannot be supposed that in such cases the United States would be obliged to have recourse to the state courts to obtain redress.

In respect to foreigners and citizens of different states, it would be illusory and disgraceful, to hold up to their view a jurisdiction destitute of the necessary means of ex-pounding and deciding their controversies, and therefore inferior in its efficacy to those state tribunals from whose supposed partialities or imperfections, it tendered an asylum.

We cannot therefore otherwise understand the constitutional extension of jurisdiction in the cases described, than as a declaration that whatever relief would be afforded by other judicial tribunals in similar cases, shall be afforded by the courts of the United States, or a strange anomaly would be presented. We may consider it as an inherent and a vital principle in the judicial system, that in all civil cases those rules of decision founded on reason and justice which form the basis of general law, are within the reach and compose parts of the power of our tribunals. And it is apprehended that although the legislature on the creation of inferior tribunals unquestionably possesses the right to distribute the judicial authority among them, it cannot control the constitutional qualities appertaining to such portions of the judicial power as it may vest in any one of those tribunals. Thus it may create a court for the trial of suits to which an alien is a party, or it may wholly omit to institute any such court. By such omission, what may be termed the national promise to provide impartial tribunals, would in this respect remain unexecuted, but whenever it was intended to be redeemed by the erection of a court, the national promise would only be fulfilled by the tribunal being possessed of all the powers necessary to render it efficient.

The act of September 24th, 1789, essentially depends for its validity on the Constitution. Unless the legislature is authorized by the Constitution to declare that the laws of the several states shall be the rules of decision; it is certain that a declaration to that effect would be vain. But the subject may be further pursued.

Legislative expositions of the Constitution, although not binding, are entitled to the greatest respect—and when such laws apply immediately to the *action* of the judicial power, and are fully adopted and uniformly acted upon by the latter, a joint sanction is thus conferred on the construction thereby given to the Constitution. Now the memorable language of this act is, that in trials at *common law,* the laws of the several states shall govern the courts of the United States. But whence do we derive the first position? by what authority do the courts of the United States try causes at common law? Unless the Constitution confers this power they do not possess it—nor does congress profess to *give* it to them, but considers it as already given. The law serves only to modify it, and render it more convenient and practicable.

In another respect, the view here taken, appears to receive some support both from the silence of the act, and from judicial practice.

We find a distinction taken between common law and equity, not only in the section before mentioned, but in that which describes the jurisdiction of the circuit court. "The circuit courts shall have original cognizance concurrent with the courts of the several states, of all suits of a civil nature *at common law* or in equity, when the United States are plaintiffs or petitioners, or an alien is a party, or the suit is between a citizen of the state where the suit is brought and a citizen of another state." In other parts of the same act the distinction is between law, without the prefix *"common,"* and equity. The provision in regard to the laws of the several states is therefore not in words extended to suits in equity. And the course pursued has been to make use of those forms and modes of proceeding adopted in that country from which "we derive our knowledge of the principles of common law and equity." It is observed that in some states no court of chancery exists, and courts of law recognise and enforce in suits at law, all the equitable claims and rights which a court of equity would recognise and enforce; in others such relief is denied, and equitable claims and rights are considered as mere nullities at law. A construction that would adopt the state practice in all its extent would extinguish in some states the exercise of equitable jurisdiction altogether.

Where, for want of a court of equity, rights of an equitable character are enforced in a state court of law, the United States courts will afford relief in the same manner.

But although the forms of proceeding are regulated in this manner under an act of congress, the principles of decision are in nowise modified or regulated by congress. They are therefore to be drawn directly from the Constitution, and the construction given by the supreme court in this respect must be received as decisive, that the word *equity* there introduced means equity as understood in England, and not as it is expounded and practised on in different states. Yet, perhaps in every state having courts of equity, there are variations and peculiarities in the system. Equity is not to be viewed as a pure system of ethics, formed only on the moral sense. Every lawyer knows that it is now a definite science, as closely bound by precedents as the law itself, and its local character would seem to require as much regard from the courts of the United States as the common law of a particular state. It does not appear that this point has yet been directly decided.

We have therefore before us, in all cases at law, a rule so convenient and appropriate, that it would probably have been adopted by the courts, if no act of congress had been passed on the subject, and which would be so justly applicable to cases in equity, that we may consider it likely to be adopted, whenever the necessity shall arise, and in each respect, and however the latter may be settled, we find that in civil cases the judicial power is not confined to positive statutes.

We now proceed to the application of the same principles to cases of a criminal nature. In a matter so important, and on which there has been such a variety of opinions, it seems incumbent distinctly to state the process of reasoning, by which a conclusion apparently differing from that which has influenced so many wise and virtuous members of our community has been attained.

The four following propositions form the basis of this conclusion.

1. On the formation of society, prior to positive laws, certain rules of moral action necessarily arise, the foundation of which is the observance of justice among the members of the society.

2. On the formation of the Constitution of the United States, such rules arose without being expressed: the breach of them constitutes offences against the United States.

3. If no judiciary power had been introduced into the Constitution of the United States, the state courts could have punished those breaches.

4. The creation of such judiciary power was intended to confer jurisdiction over such and other offences, not to negative or destroy it.

1. It was intended by Divine Providence that man should live in a state of society. Reason and reflection were given to him to be used and improved. Social affections were created, as natural impulses to promote their use and improvement, by leading and keeping mankind together. When societies commence, certain rules of action are necessary. Men are not equally honest and virtuous; without some restraint, injustice and violence would soon throw the association, however small, into disorder and confusion. Hence arises at once a law of tacit convention, founded on a few plain principles. It requires no positive law to have it understood, that one shall not, without cause, deprive another of his property, or do injury to his person. When the period arrives for the formation of positive laws, which is after the formation of the original compact, the legislature is employed, not in the discovery that these acts are unlawful, but in the application of punishments to prevent them. In every code we find a distinction between things *mala in se,* things in themselves unlawful; and *mala prohibita,* things which become unlawful from being prohibited by the legislature. But circumstances may delay the formation or the action of a legislative body, or its provisions may be inadequate to the redress of experienced or expected evils. In this interval can no rights to property be acquired or preserved—can no binding contracts be made—are theft, robbery, murder, no crimes? Opinions so monstrous can be entertained by none. On the contrary, the human heart, the universal sense and practice of mankind, the internal consciousness of the Divine will, all concur in pointing out the rules and obligations by which we are bound.

Emphatically termed the law of nature, it is implanted in us by nature itself; it is felt, not learned; it is never misunderstood, and though not always observed, never is forgotten. Cicero in his Treatise *de Legibus,* remarks that law, (and he explains that he speaks of general, not positive law,) is the perfection of reason, seated in nature, commanding what is right, and prohibiting what is wrong. Its beginning is to be traced to times before any law was written, or any express form of government adopted.

This proposition is indeed too plain to be contradicted; and we therefore pass on to the second, which may require a closer examination.

2. We have seen that the Constitution of the United States was the work of the people. It was the formation of a new and peculiar association, having for its objects the attainment or security of many important political rights, which could not otherwise be fully attained or secured; but not embracing in its sphere of action all the political rights to which its members were individually entitled. So far as

related to those other rights, the people were satisfied with other associations, in each of which the law of nature, under the usual appellation of the common law, prevailed. So far as related to the new rights and duties, springing from the new political association, the same tacit compact which is acknowledged to exist in all society, necessarily accompanied this. Nothing short of express negation could exclude it. Every member of society has a direct interest in the prevention or punishment of every act contrary to the well being of that society. Before the Constitution was adopted, every act of such a tendency, having relation to the state association, was punishable by the common law of such state, but when it was adopted, certain actions, whether considered in reference to persons, to particular places, or to the subject itself, were either expressly or by implication withdrawn from the immediate cognizance of the states. The people of the United States did not, however, mean that if those actions amounted to offences they should go unpunished. The right of prosecution and of punishment was not meant to be surrendered. In this instance, the converse of the well known proposition, that whatever is not delegated to the United States is reserved to the people, is the true construction. The people possessed at the moment the full right to the punishment of offences against the law of nature, though they might not be the subject of positive law. They did not surrender this right by adopting the Constitution. An offence against them in a state capacity, became in certain cases an offence against them in relation to the United States. In fact, there is no offence against the United States which is not an offence against the people of the United States. They did not, perhaps we may even say, that without being in some degree guilty of political suicide, they could not cede or relinquish the right to punish such acts. If they had so done, the system itself would soon dissolve. They gave no power to congress to pass any penal laws whatever, except on this basis. Every act declaring a crime and imposing a penalty, rests upon it. It follows that this source of the power of congress must be admitted. It may be attenuated by positive law, but it never can be exhausted, unless we can suppose that positive laws may meet and provide for all the incalculable varieties of human depravity. But in no country has this been found practicable.

In the very terms made use of in the Constitution, it is manifest that a new and distinct class of duties were to arise, which would tend to produce a new and distinct class of offences. The words are, as we have already seen—that the judicial power shall extend to all cases in law and equity arising under this Constitution, the laws of the United States and treaties. No jurisdiction over crimes is given, except as they are included in the antecedent words, cases in law; but it is declared that they shall be tried only by jury. We have thus three divisions of judicial subjects.

I. Cases including crimes arising under the Constitution.

II. Cases including crimes arising under acts of congress.

III. Those arising under treaties.

There may then be crimes arising under the Constitution, on which no act of congress has been passed; but if such an act has been passed, as in all countries positive laws control the common law, the act is punishable under such positive law.

If only the infraction of treaties and acts of congress had been considered as criminal acts, there would have been a manifest impropriety in the introduction of those words *"arising under the Constitution."* But they were certainly used with the intention that they should have the same effect in criminal as in civil cases. The construction we venture to affix, appears to us to render the whole system harmonious, efficient, and complete.

3. Our next position is, that if the Constitution of the United States had been wholly unfurnished with a judicial power, offences of this description could be punished through the medium of the state courts.

In the year 1779, one Cornelius Sweers, a deputy commissary of the United States, was indicted in a court of oyer and terminer then held by the judges of the Supreme Court of Pennsylvania, for forging and altering two receipts given to him by persons of whom he had purchased goods for the use of the United States. The indictment, in compliance with judicial forms, was laid to be against the peace and dignity of the commonwealth of Pennsylvania, with intent to defraud the United States. M'Kean, C. J. after hearing the arguments of counsel, supported the indictment. It is a memorable instance of the power of the common law to accommodate itself to the attainment of substantial justice. Even the articles of confederation did not then exist, but the court recognised the United States as a corporation. It was an offence against the United States, in which the state of Pennsylvania had no other interest than as one of thirteen states. But the prosecution was technically supported as an offence against the state of Pennsylvania. Another important consideration arises from this case. There existed at that time no act of assembly in Pennsylvania which rendered such an action a crime. By the English common law it was not forgery. The court must have proceeded therefore on higher ground. The principles laid down in our second position support their judgment. The soundness of this decision, as well as that in the case of De Long Champs, has never been questioned. We may therefore safely infer, that the state judicatures would, if it were necessary, afford an easy and a certain remedy in all cases of a criminal nature, arising under the Constitution of the Untied States.

4. It only remains to inquire, whether the addition of a judiciary system to the Constitution of the United States diminishes the power of punishing offences arising under it. It is well understood that the motives for annexing a judiciary power were to give force and energy to the government. It was apprehended that less interest in the concerns of the Union, and less uniformity of decision might be found in the state courts; and it was thought expedient that a suitable number of tribunals under the authority of the United States should be dispersed through the country, subject to the revision of superior courts, and finally centering in a common head, the Supreme Court. To these tribunals was imparted the power which the state

courts would, it is presumed, have otherwise continued to exercise, of expounding and enforcing whatever was properly cognizable as an offence against the United States. But it cannot be conceived, that a system intended to strengthen and invigorate the government of the Union, can impair and enfeeble it. It cannot be supposed, that the effect of providing weapons for its defence, is to strip it of its armour. Neither can it be supposed that it was intended to establish a system so incongruous as to confine the United States courts to the trial of offences against positive law, and to rely upon the state courts for relief against acts of another description injurious to the United States; nor yet that the United States, having so strong an interest in being protected against such acts, meant to relinquish and abandon the remedies against them altogether.

In addition to these general grounds, we ought not to omit the peculiar jurisdiction given by the Constitution over districts ceded by states for certain purposes, and also over the territories acquired from the states or from foreign powers. A construction which implies that in *such places* any offence not expressly prohibited by an act of congress may be committed with impunity, cannot be a sound one.

Let us also consider *persons* of a certain description. The Constitution, as we have already seen, gives to the courts of the United States jurisdiction in all cases affecting consuls. Congress, in creating the inferior courts, assigned to them an exclusive jurisdiction in criminal cases over consuls. In 1816, a foreign consul was charged with the commission of an atrocious crime within the state of Pennsylvania, for which an indictment was found against him. He denied the jurisdiction of the state court, and was discharged. He still goes untried, labouring under an unmerited imputation if innocent, and if guilty, unpunished, which, if the doctrine here opposed is correct, is an unavoidable consequence.

Still, however, although these positions may be considered as sound, some serious objections remain for discussion.

1. In the inquiry, whether the courts of the United States possess jurisdiction of a criminal nature in any case not provided for by an act of congress, it has always been supposed that the common law of England was alone to be considered. Chase, J. says, "If the United States can for a moment be supposed to have a common law, it must, I presume, be that of England."

Thus the attention has been confined to a part only of the general question; and if it is understood by courts, that they are only to decide whether the common law of England is in such cases to be the sole rule of decision, it is easy to account for some of the opinions that have been given. Both Chase, J. and Johnson, J. justly observe, that the common law of England has been gradually varied in the different states, and that there exists no uniform rule by which the United States could be governed in respect to it. The latter, with great truth and effect remarks, that if the power implied on the formation of any political body, to preserve its own existence and promote the end and object of its own creation, is applicable to the peculiar

character of our Constitution, (which he declines to examine,) it is a principle by no means peculiar to the common law [of England.] "It is coeval probably with the first formation of a limited government, belongs to a system of universal law, and may as well support the assumption of many other powers, as those peculiarly acknowledged by the common law of England."

We may account for most of the opposition in various parts of the Union from the question having been misunderstood. That the common law of England was kept in view, to a certain extent by the framers of the Constitution, even in criminal cases, and as such adopted by the people, cannot be doubted. The instances are numerous. Impeachment, treason, felony, breach of the peace, habeas corpus, the trial by jury, and many other phrases and appellations, derived from the common law of England, appear both in the original text and the amendments. But this, as justly observed by a learned jurist, was not intended as a source of jurisdiction, but as a rule or mean for its exercise. In this sense alone we are to accept those technical terms, and by no means as evidence that if any common law was intended by the Constitution to be adopted as a rule of action, it was the common law of England.

2. It is plausibly urged, that a system of law which defines crime, without appropriating punishment, possesses no efficacy and does not merit adoption, and it is inquired in what manner are offences against the law of nature to be punished.

The question is not without its intrinsic difficulty, and an answer cannot be attempted without some diffidence, but it is hoped that the following view will be satisfactory.

1. We may lay it down as an axiom, that in every system of law, whether express or implied, crime is held to be liable to punishment of some sort.

The mere sense of guilt, however unhappy it may render the offender, yields no compensation, and affords no security to society.

2. Punishment ought always to bear a just relation to the nature and degree of the offence. Positive law is sometimes arbitrary and unreasonably severe; but the united sense of the community, some of whom may commit, and all of whom may suffer from the commission of crimes, is generally apposite and reasonable. If there is any deviation from the strict measure of punishment, it is generally on the side of humanity.

3. Recurring, as far as we have materials, to the history of ancient law in Europe, for we cannot take Asia or Africa as our guides, we find that although the injured individual, or his nearest friends, were sometimes held to be entitled to take redress into their own hands, and pursue the offender by their own power; a practice so dangerous was gradually overruled, and punishment, rendered the act of the whole, afforded through the medium of the whole, satisfaction proportioned to the offence.

4. In remote times, and in most countries, this satisfaction consisted in the forfeiture of something of value; we have to this effect the authority of *Homer*, Iliad, b. 9, v. 743. "The price of blood discharged, the murderer lives." Of *Tacitus*, in respect to the ancient Germans, "*Luitur etiam*

homicidium certo armentorum ac pecorum numero," &c. homicide is also punished by the forfeiture of a certain number of cattle or sheep; and he adds, that those convicted of other crimes were fined in proportion, a part of which was paid to the prince, and part to him who was wronged, or to his relations. Imprisonment was added either to coerce payment, or as a further punishment.

There was a time, says *Beccaria,* when all punishments were pecuniary. Lord *Kaimes* lays down the same position, and it is a settled principle in the ancient law of England, that where an offence has been committed to which no specific punishment is affixed by statute, it is punishable by fine and imprisonment. Here then we have materials which laborious inquiry would probably increase, for ascertaining the nature of those punishments that by common consent preceded positive law. Their mildness ought not to lead us to reject them. It would be a sorry argument to say, that because a severe punishment cannot be inflicted, the offender shall not be punished at all. Judge Story truly remarks, that it is a *settled principle,* that when an offence exists to which no specific punishment is affixed by statute, it is punishable by fine and imprisonment, but when he adds, that if treason had been left without punishment by an act of congress, the punishment by fine and imprisonment must have attached to it; we must recollect that the power to declare the punishment being expressly given to congress, it seems to be taken out of the general principle that would otherwise be applicable.

On the whole, we arrive at the conclusion, that crimes committed against society have been at all times the subject of punishment of some sort; that independent of positive law, the forfeiture of property, or personal liberty, has been the general, though not perhaps the universal character of punishment; for a difference of manners will always have a strong influence on the extent of punishment, as the people are mild and peaceable, or rugged and ferocious; and that the tribunals of justice in every case within their jurisdiction, are thus provided with a guide, which if found inadequate to the safety of society, may at any time be rendered more effectual by the legislative power.

It has been said, that to give it effect, the common law ought to have been expressly enacted as part of the Constitution. But how could this have been done? Should it have been described as the common law of England? It was not contemplated. The common law of any particular state in the Union? This would have been equally inadmissible. It could have been introduced in no other than some phrases as the following:

"The law of nature, or the just and rational obligations of men in a state of political society, shall be the rule of decision in all cases not otherwise provided for." And surely it would have been deemed a most unnecessary declaration. It has been well observed that the attempt to enumerate the powers necessary and proper to call the general power into effect, would have involved a complete digest of laws on every subject to which the Constitution relates—accommodated not only to the existing state of things, but to all possible changes; for in every new application of a general power, the particular powers, which are the means of attaining the object, must often necessarily vary, although the object remains the same.

In delivering the opinion of the Supreme Court in the United States *v.* Hudson and Goodwin, Judge Johnson observes, that it "is not necessary to inquire whether the general government possesses the power of conferring on its courts a jurisdiction, in cases similar to the present, it is enough that such jurisdiction has not been conferred by any legislative act, if it does not result to these courts as a consequence of their creation." With great deference to an authority so respectable, it is submitted that if the preceding observations are correct, *that* jurisdiction has been expressly given by the act of September 24, 1789, which although repealed by the act of February 13, 1801, was revived by the act of March 8, 1802, and is now in full force. By this act the circuit courts are expressly invested with the cognizance, (the exclusive cognizance says the law,) of all crimes and offences *cognizable under the authority* of the United States, except where the laws of the United States shall otherwise direct. If the offences of which we have been speaking, *arise under the Constitution,* they must be cognizable under the authority of the United States, and are thus rendered cognizable in the circuit courts.

The same learned judge in a subsequent case, when he also delivered the opinion of the Supreme Court, most correctly drew from the Constitution itself, certain principles necessary to support the asserted jurisdiction of a legislative body to punish contempts against itself, which he justly observes involves the interest of the people.

"The interests and dignity of those who created the public functionaries, require the exertion of the powers indispensable to the attainment of the ends of their creation."

The question before the court was only on the jurisdiction of the house. The precise nature of the offence committed, did not appear on the face of the pleadings. It was observed by him, "that we are not to decide that this jurisdiction does not exist, because it is not expressly given. It is true, that such a power, if it exists, must be derived from implication, and the genius and spirit of our institutions are hostile to the exercise of implied powers. Had the faculties of man been competent to the framing of a system in which nothing would have been left to implication, the effort would undoubtedly have been made. But in the whole of our admirable Constitution, there is not a grant of powers, which does not draw after it others not expressed, but vital to their exercise, not substantive and independent, but auxiliary and subordinate."

Now we may be permitted to remark, that the jurisdiction thus raised and supported by necessary implication, could in this case, have operated only on those acts, which, by an implication equally necessary, were to be considered as offences. No act of congress has declared what shall constitute those offences. They must therefore essentially be, what are termed contempts, or breaches of privilege at common law. It was competent for the Supreme Court, (was it not incumbent on them?) to notice that the nonexistence of any legislative provisions on the subject, rendered it impossible to justify an imprisonment by virtue of the speaker's warrant for a non-existing offence. But the observation is, that "the power to institute a prosecution must be dependent on the power to punish. If the house of representatives possessed no power to punish for contempt, the initiatory process issued in the operation of that authority, must have been illegal; there was a want of jurisdiction to justify it." And the omission to take this ground, seems to support the argument excluding the necessity of a statutory provision.

On the same ground we may advert to the exercise of the power of impeachment. In neither of the cases already mentioned, were the acts charged on the parties accused, statutory offences. Yet the doctrine opposed in this work would render the power of impeachment a nullity, in all cases except the two expressly mentioned in the Constitution, treason and bribery; until congress pass laws, declaring what shall constitute the other "high crimes and misdemeanors."

And thus the question seems to be at rest in the contemplation of both *these courts*, for such they must be termed, when acting in those capacities, and both of them are courts from whose decision there is no appeal.

85

JAMES MADISON TO M. L. HURLBERT
May 1830
Writings 9:372

But whatever respect may be thought due to the intention of the Convention, which prepared & proposed the Constitution, as presumptive evidence of the general understanding at the time of the language used, it must be kept in mind that the only authoritative intentions were those of the people of the States, as expressed thro' the Conventions which ratified the Constitution.

That in a Constitution, so new, and so complicated, there should be occasional difficulties & differences in the practical expositions of it, can surprize no one; and this must continue to be the case, as happens to new laws on complex subjects, until a course of practice of sufficient uniformity and duration to carry with it the public sanction shall settle doubtful or contested meanings.

As there are legal rules for interpreting laws, there must be analogous rules for interpreting constns. and among the obvious and just guides applicable to the Constn. of the U. S. may be mentioned—

1. The evils & defects for curing which the Constitution was called for & introduced.

2. The comments prevailing at the time it was adopted.

3. The early, deliberate & continued practice under the Constitution, as preferable to constructions adapted on the spur of occasions, and subject to the vicissitudes of party or personal ascendencies.

86

EX PARTE CRANE
5 Pet. 190 (1831)

MARSHALL, Ch. J., delivered the opinion of the court. . . . A doubt has been suggested, respecting the power of the court to issue this writ. The question was not discussed at the bar, but has been considered by the judges. It is proper that it should be settled, and the opinion of the court announced. We have determined, that the power exists. Without going extensively into this subject, we think it proper to state, briefly, the foundation of our opinion. In England, the writ of *mandamus* is defined to be a command issuing in the king's name, from the court of king's bench, and directed to any person, corporation or inferior court of judicature, within the king's dominions, requiring them to do some particular thing therein specified, which appertains to their office or duty, and which the court of king's bench has previously determined, or at least supposes, to be consonant to right and justice. Blackstone adds, "that it issues to the judges of any inferior court, commanding them to do justice, according to the powers of their office, whenever the same is delayed. For it is the peculiar business of the court of king's bench to superintend all other inferior tribunals, and therein to enforce the due exercise of those judicial or ministerial powers with which the crown or legislature have invested them; and this, not only by restraining their excesses, but also by quickening their negligence, and obviating their denial of justice." 3 Bl. Com. 110.

It is, we think, apparent, that this definition, and this description of the purposes to which it is applicable by the court of king's bench, as supervising the conduct of all inferior tribunals, extends to the case of a refusal by an inferior court to sign a bill of exceptions, when it is an act which "appertains to their office and duty," and which the court of king's bench supposes "to be consonant to right and justice." Yet we do not find a case in which the writ has issued from that court. It has rarely issued from any court; but there are instances of its being sued out of the court of chancery, and its form is given in the register. It is a mandatory writ, commanding the judge to seal it, if the fact alleged be truly stated: "*si ita est.*"

There is some difficulty in accounting for the fact, that no *mandamus* has ever issued from the court of king's bench, directing the justice of an inferior court to sign a bill of exceptions. As the court of chancery was the great *officina brevium* of the kingdom, and the language of the statute of Westm. II. was understood as requiring the king's writ to the justice, the application to that court for the writ might be supposed proper. In 1 Sch. & Lef. 75, the chancellor superseded a writ which had been issued by the cursitor, on application; declaring that it could be granted only by order of the court. He appears, however, to have entertained no doubt of his power to award the writ, on motion. Although the course seems to have been to apply to the chancellor, it has never been determined that a *mandamus* to sign a bill of exceptions may not be granted by the court of king's bench.

It is said by counsel, in argument, in *Bridgman* v. *Holt*, Show. P. C. 122, that by the statute of Westm. II., c. 31, in case the judge refuses, then a writ to command him, which is to issue out of chancery, *quod apponat sigillum suum.* The party grieved by denial, may have a writ upon the statute, commanding the same to be done, &c. "That the law is thus, seems plain, though no precedent can be shown for such a writ: it is only for this reason, because no judge did ever refuse to seal a bill of exceptious; and none was ever refused, because none was ever tendered like this, so artificial and groundless."

The judiciary act, § 13, enacts, that the supreme court shall have power to issue writs of prohibition to the district courts, when proceeding as courts of admiralty and maritime jurisdiction; and writs of *mandamus*, in cases warranted by the principles and usages of law, to any courts appointed, or persons holding offices under the authority of the United States. A *mandamus* to an officer is held to be the exercise of original jurisdiction; but a *mandamus* to an inferior court of the United States, is in the nature of appellate jurisdiction. A bill of exceptions is a mode of placing the law of the case on a record, which is to be brought before this court by a writ of errror.

That a *mandamus* to sign a bill of exceptions is "warranted by the principles and usages of law," is, we think, satisfactorily proved by the fact, that it is given in England by statute; for the writ given by the statute of Westm. II., is so, in fact, and is so termed in the books. The judiciary act speaks of usages of law generally, not merely of common law. In England, it is awarded by the chancellor; but in the United States, it is conferred expressly on this court, which exercises both common law and chancery powers; is invested with appellate power, and exercises extensive control over all the courts of the United States. We cannot perceive a reason, why the single case of a refusal by an inferior court to sign a bill of exceptions, and thus to place the law of the case on the record, should be withdrawn from that general power to issue writs of *mandamus* to inferior courts, which is conferred by statute.

In New York, where a statute exists, similar to that of Westm. II., an application was made to the supreme court for a *mandamus* to an inferior court to amend a bill of exceptions, according to the truth of the case. The court treated the special writ given by the statute as a *mandamus*, and declared, that it was so considered in England; and added, that "though no instance appears of such a writ issuing out of the king's bench, where an inferior court refused to seal a bill of exceptions, there is no case denying to that court the power to award the writ." "It ought to be used, where the law has established no specific remedy, and where in justice and good government there ought to be one." "There is no reason why the awarding of this particular writ does not fall within the jurisdiction of this court, or why it should be exclusively confined to the court

of chancery." In the opinion, then, of the very respectable court, which decided the motion made for a *mandamus*, in *Sikes* v. *Ransom*, 6 Johns. 279, the supreme court of New York possesses the power to issue this writ, in virtue of its general superintendence of inferior tribunals. The judiciary act confers the power expressly on this court. No other tribunal exists by which it can be exercised.

. . . . .

BALDWIN, Justice. *(Dissenting.)*—The common-law definition of a *mandamus*, which is adopted in this court, is, "a command issuing in the king's name, from the court of king's bench, and directed to any person, corporation or inferior court of judicature, within the king's dominion, requiring them to do some particular thing therein specified, which appertains to their office or duty, and which the court of king's bench as previously determined, or, at least, supposes, to be consonant to right and justice." *Marbury* v. *Madison*, 1 Cranch 168.

As the first question which this motion presents is one of the jurisdiction and power of this court to grant the writ prayed for in this case, it will be following the rule established to consider it first (3 Cranch 172; 5 Ibid. 221; 10 Wheat. 20; 1 Cranch 91; 9 Wheat. 816), a rule which never ought to be disregarded, where a question of power arises. Though the question of jurisdiction may not be raised by counsel, it can never escape the attention of the court; for it is one which goes to the foundation of their authority to take judicial cognisance of the case; if they cannot, in the appropriate language of the law, hear and determine it, the cause is *coram non judice*, and every act done is a nullity. If I take this case into judicial consideration, this is an assumption of jurisdiction, that necessarily results from a decision whether this is or, is not a proper case for a *mandamus*, for the court to hear and determine the motion on its merits. Their refusal to grant the motion, is not on the ground that they have not power to consider it, but that, on consideration, they reject it. This is as much an exercise of jurisdiction, as to issue the writ; as, by examining the grounds of the motion, the court assume the power to decide on it, as the justice of the question may seem to require. In my opinion, no new question of jurisdiction ought to be acted on, without an inquiry into the power of this court to grant the motion, or to issue the process. The silent uncontested exercise of jurisdiction may induce the profession to claim it as a right founded on precedent, though the judgment of the court may never have been given on the question of power, or their attention have been drawn to it by the counsel. If, then, process should issue improvidently, and the court should find itself called upon, for the first time, to examine its jurisdiction and power to issue it, when obedience should be refused by the court to which it was directed, and the question, came before us on this return, "the court is unanimously of opinion, that the appellate power of the supreme court of the United States does not extend to this court, under a sound construction of the constitution of the United States; that the writ of *mandamus* in this case was improvidently issued, under the authority of the 25th section of the judiciary act of 1789; that the proceedings thereon in the supreme court were *coram non judice* in relation to this court, and that obedience to its mandate be declined by the court;" this court would find itself in a very unenviable predicament, if, on a careful revision of the constitution and laws, they should be compelled to sanction the open contempt of their process or decree, by an inferior court, to whom an order had been sent from this high tribunal, which it found itself forced to declare null and void. It is hard to say, which would be most fatal to its influence and authority, the example, or the consequences.

The judicial history of this court presents one instance of such a return, on its records, and another, in which the military force of a state was in actual array, in obedience to a law for opposing the execution of a mandate; and a very recent occurence might have furnished a third incident, had not a writ of error abated by the death of the party suing it out. The proceedings which have attended the assertion of the unquestionable jurisdiction of the court over cases which, after having been discussed and considered in all their bearings, have been solemnly decided, afford no uncertain indication of the results to be expected from the exercise of their power, without discussion or inquiry into its existence, and over subjects on which it may, on examination, be found incapable of acting.

When questions of jurisdiction arise, they must be settled by a reference to the constitution and acts of congress. All cases embraced within the judicial power of the government, are capable of being acted upon by the courts of the Union. Those on which the original jurisdiction of this court can be exercised are defined, and cannot be enlarged. 6 Wheat. 395, 396, 399. It has no inherent authority to assume it over any others, and congress are incapable of conferring it by law. 1 Cranch 173. Where the constitution has declared the jurisdiction shall be original, congress cannot give it in its appellate form, and *vice versâ*. *Marbury* v. *Madison*, 1 Cranch 174; 6 Wheat. 399; 9 Ibid. 820, 821. Though the courts of the United States are capable of exercising the whole judicial power, as conferred by the constitution; and though congress are bound to provide by law for its exercise, in all cases to which that judicial power extends; yet it has not been done, and much of it remains dormant for the want of legislation to enable the courts to exercise it, it having been repeatedly and uniformly decided by this court, that legislative provisions are indispensable to give effect to a power, to bring into action the constitutional jurisdiction of the supreme and inferior courts. 5 Cranch 500; 1 Wheat. 337; 6 Ibid. 375, 604; 9 Ibid. 819–21; 12 Ibid. 117–18.

These principles remain unquestioned. They have long been settled, as the judicial exposition of the constitution, on solemn argument and the gravest consideration; and they are binding on all courts and judges. I shall ever be found among the last to oppose my opinion, in opposition to the results of the deliberate judgment of the highest judicial tribunal, when thus formed. They bind my faith, even though the reasons assigned might not carry conviction to my understanding. We must respect the solemn decisions of our predecessors and associates, as we may wish that those who succeed us should respect ours; or the su-

preme law of the land, so far as depends on judicial interpretation, will change with the change of judges. There may be exceptions to this rule. When they do occur, my hope is, that my reasons for a departure will be found in the great principles of the government, which meet with general assent in their adoption, though the most able and upright may differ in their application. But in any cases which have arisen, or may arise, in which the jurisdiction and power of the court over the subject-matter of the parties is not questioned by counsel and deliberately considered by the judges, or should be unnoticed in the opinion of the court, I cannot acknowledge it as an authority, affording a rule for my decision, or a guide to my judgment. Such a decision ought neither to control my reason, or settled conviction of pre-existing rules and principles of law.

These remarks are deemed proper, as there are some cases in which writs of *mandamus* have been issued, under circumstances such as have been referred to, or refused on the merits; but "the question of jurisdiction was not moved, and still remains open," according to the rule laid down by this court in *Durousseau* v. *United States*, 6 Cranch 307, on a question whether a writ of error could issue from the supreme court to the district court of Orleans: and by the Chief Justice, in alluding to the case of the *United States* v. *Simms*, 1 Cranch 252, "no question was made in that case as to the jurisdiction; it passed *sub silentio*, and the court does not consider itself as bound by that case." 6 Cranch 172.

These are the principles on which I shall examine the question of jurisdiction. The first inquiry then will be, has this court, by law, the power to issue a *mandamus* to a circuit court to sign a bill of exceptions, under the 13th and 14th sections of the judiciary act, which have been relied on as authorizing it? So far as this act gives the power to issue a *mandamus* to executive officers, they have solemnly declared the law to be unconstitutional and void, and that the power does not exist. It being considered by the court to be an exercise of original jurisdiction, it remains to inquire, whether it can be issued to any courts appointed under the authority of the United States; and if so, in what cases?

This power is defined, in *Marbury* v. *Madison*, 1 Cranch 175, in these words: "to enable this court, then, to issue a *mandamus*, it must be shown to be an exercise of the appellate jurisdiction, or to be necessary to the exercise of appellate jurisdiction. It is the essential criterion of appellate jurisdiction, that it revises and corrects the proceedings in a cause already instituted, and does not create that cause." In the *United States* v. *Schooner Peggy*, 1 Cranch 110, we are furnished with this as the judicial definition: "it is, in the general, true, that the province of an appellate court is only to inquire whether a judgment when rendered is erroneous or not. That case furnished an exception in these words: "but if subsequent to the judgment, and before the decision of the appellate court, a law intervenes and positively changes the rule which governs, the law must be obeyed, or its obligation be denied." In *McClung* v. *Silliman*, they lay down the same rule: "the question before an appellate court is, was the judgment correct, not the ground on which the judgment professes to proceed." 6 Wheat. 603. Appellate jurisdiction being thus defined, its source can only be found in the constitution which confers it, both as to law and fact, with such exceptions and under such regulations as the congress shall make (1 U. S. Stat. 18), and the judiciary act which makes these exceptions and regulations. The 13th section provides, that the supreme court shall have appellate jurisdiction from the circuit courts, and the courts of the several states in the cases hereafter specially provided for. These are defined in the 22d section, as to the circuit courts, and in the 25th section, as to the state courts. (Ibid. 84, 85.)

This court, from its first organization until this time, have held that this enumeration of the cases in which it had appellate jurisdiction, was an exclusion of all others. 1 Cranch 174–6; 3 Ibid. 172; *United States* v. *Moore*, 6 Ibid. 313–14, 318; 7 Ibid. 32, 44, 287, 108, 110; 6 Wheat. 603; 9 Ibid. 820–21, 19; 12 Ibid. 131–33, 203. The general principle the court have acted on is this: "that they imply a legislative exception from its appellate constitutional power, in the legislative affirmative description of these powers." 6 Cranch 314. But if the appellate jurisidicion of this court is described in general terms, so as to comprehend the case, and there is no exception or regulation which would exclude it from its general provisions (as in *Wilson* v. *Mason*, 1 Cranch 91, which was a writ of error to the district court of Kentucky, on cross-caveats, for the same tract of land), or if it was the obvious intention of the legislature to give the power, and congress have not excepted it, as on the question which arose in the case of *Durousseau* (6 Cranch 312, 318), whether this court could issue a writ of error to the district court of Orleans, they declared it "to be the intent of the legislature to place those courts precisely on the footing of the court of Kentucky in every respect, and to subject their judgments in the same manner to the revision of the supreme court," and therefore, gave the law of 1804 (page 809) a liberal construction. S. P. *Cohens* v. *Virginia*, 6 Wheat. 400.

But where the law of 1803 authorized a writ of error from the circuit to the district court, and omitted to provide one from this court to the circuit court, it was held not to be within its appellate jurisdiction (*United States* v. *Goodwin*, 7 Cranch 108–10), though the law giving this jurisdiction to the supreme court authorized appeals to the supreme court from the circuit court, from all final decrees and judgments rendered, or to be rendered, in any circuit court, or any district court having circuit court jurisdiction, in any cases of equity, or admiralty or maritime jurisdiction, prize or no prize, where the sum in controversy exceeds $2000 (2 U. S. Stat. 244); and the 22d section of the judiciary act authorized it on judgments of the circuit in civil actions, in cases removed there by appeal from the district courts. This too was an action of debt, and the sum in controversy $15,000; but it being on a writ of error from the circuit court, and not an appeal, in the words of the 22d section, this court gave it its liberal construction, which had been settled in the case of *Wiscart* v. *D'Auchy*, cited by Judge WASHINGTON in delivering the opinion of this court in *Goodwin's Case*. "An appeal is a civil-law process, and removes the cause entirely, both as to law and fact, for a review and new trial; a writ of error

is a common-law process, and removes nothing for a re-examination but the law." This statute observes this distinction. 7 Cranch 110–11; 3 Dall., 324.

These seem to me to be the only two cases in which the appellate jurisdiction of the supreme court can be exercised—appeals and writs of error. This corresponds with the definition given by the court itself, as to its own powers, and the strict construction which they have (with the two excepted cases) given to the 22d and 25th sections, which are in their terms confined to final judgments and decrees of circuit and state courts, and these are the only cases, where this court have ever exercised appellate jurisdiction. They have uniformly refused, where the judgment or decree was not final (3 Wheat. 434, 601; 6 Ibid. 603; 12 Ibid. 135), and it cannot well be contended, that a refusal of a circuit court to sign a bill of exceptions, is a final judgment or decree, or that it partakes in any degree of the character of either. The jurisdiction of circuit courts over causes removed from state courts, is considered as appellate. But the time, the process, and the manner must be subject to the absolute legislative control of congress. 12 Wheat. 349. The same may be said of the jurisdiction of this court over causes sent from the circuit court, on a certificate of division; but this is by a special provision of the law of 1802 (2 U. S. Stat. 139), which has been construed with the same strictness as the act of 1789. 6 Wheat. 547; 10 Ibid. 20; 12 Ibid. 132; 6 Ibid. 363, 368.

The writ of *mandamus* contains no order to remove a cause or any proceedings therein to the court issuing it, nor has it that effect. The cause remains in the court below, whether the writ be obeyed or not; the sole object being to compel them to act on the matter themselves, not to remove it for revision. That can only be done by writ of error or appeal. These considerations make it evident, that the issuing a *mandamus* is not only not an exercise of appellate jurisdiction, but wholly different in its nature, object and effect. It was so considered in this court, in the case of *McIntire* v. *Wood*, 7 Cranch 499, 500, in which it was decided, "that the power of the circuit court to issue the writ of *mandamus* is confined exclusively to those cases, in which it may be necessary to the exercise of their jurisdiction;" and that cannot be the exercise of appellate jurisdiction, which, in this case, and in *Marbury* v. *Madison*, the court consider as a case wholly distinct. A *mandamus* being a writ to compel the performance of a ministerial act by a judicial officer, is not, and cannot be a subject-matter for the cognisance of an appellate court, which acts only on the judicial acts, the judgments and the decrees of inferior courts. In the *United States* v. *Lawrence*, 3 Dall. 42, 45, 43, it was unanimously decided, that this court could not issue a *mandamus* to a district judge, acting in a judicial capacity; that they had no power to compel a judge to decide according to any judgment but his own. So, in 1 Cranch 171, where the head of a department acts in a case in which executive discretion is to be exercised, in which he is the mere organ of executive will, it is again repeated, that any application to control in any respect his conduct would be rejected, without hesitation. In *McCluny* v. *Silliman* (2 Wheat. 369), it was determined, that this court had not jurisdiction to issue this writ to the register of a land-office, where it had been refused by the highest court of the state in which it was located; and in the same case, in 6 Wheat. 598, it was distinctly decided, that the power existed neither in the circuit nor supreme court; and all the principles herein stated were re-affirmed and finally settled. If judicial authority is to be respected, it is useless to pursue this branch of the inquiry any further.

I think, then, that the issuing of a *mandamus* by this, or a circuit court, is not an exercise of appellate jurisdiction. There seems to be no judicial opinion in favor of the affirmative of the proposition, and the cases referred to have been decided on the true construction of the 13th section of the judiciary act, which declares, "that the supreme court shall have appellate jurisdiction from the circuit courts of the several states, in cases specially hereinafter provided for." This is a distinct clause, and does not include the power to issue a *mandamus*, as an act of appellate jurisdiction.

The next clause giving this power is, "and shall have power to issue writs of prohibition to the district courts, when proceeding as courts of admiralty and maritime jurisdiction, and writs of *mandamus*, in cases warranted by the principles and usages of law, to any courts appointed, or persons holding office, under the authority of the United States." This is an express declaration of congress, that the power of this court to issue a *mandamus* is not conferred as appellate jurisdiction, in the cases specially provided for in the subsequent part of the law, but only in cases warranted by legal principles and usages, not referring to the constitution and laws of congress, but, as will appear hereafter, to the principles and usages of courts of common law. For it cannot be the sound construction of this section, that the power to issue a *mandamus*, in a case not mentioned in the law, can be raised by implication, in a case not within the express power given in a subsequent clause of the same section.

87

JOSEPH STORY, COMMENTARIES ON THE
CONSTITUTION 3:§§ 1659–75, 1684–90, 1692–94
1833

§ 1659. It has been remarked by the Federalist, in another place, that the jurisdiction of the court of admiralty, as well as of other courts, is a source of frequent and intricate discussions, sufficiently denoting the indeterminate limits, by which it is circumscribed. This remark is equally true in respect to England and America; to the high court of admiralty sitting in the parent country; and to the vice-admiralty courts sitting in the colonies. At different periods, the jurisdiction has been exercised to a very different extent; and in the colonial courts it seems to have had boundaries different from those prescribed to it in England. It has been exercised to a larger extent in Ireland, than in England; and down to this very day it has a most comprehensive reach in Scotland. The jurisdiction claimed by the courts of admiralty, as properly belonging to them, extends to all acts and torts done upon the high seas, and within the ebb and flow of the sea, and to all maritime contracts, that is, to all contracts touching trade, navigation, or business upon the sea, or the waters of the sea within the ebb and flow of the tide. Some part of this jurisdiction has been matter of heated controversy between the courts of common law, and the high court of admiralty in England, with alternate success and defeat. But much of it has been gradually yielded to the latter, in consideration of its public convenience, if not of its paramount necessity. It is not our design to go into a consideration of these vexed questions, or to attempt any general outline of the disputed boundaries. It will be sufficient in this place to present a brief view of that, which is admitted, and is indisputable.

§ 1660. The admiralty and maritime jurisdiction, (and the word, "maritime," was doubtless added to guard against any narrow interpretation of the preceding word, "admiralty,") conferred by the constitution, embraces two great classes of cases; one dependent upon locality, and the other upon the nature of the contract. The first respects acts or injuries done upon the high seas, where all nations claim a common right and common jurisdiction; or acts, or injuries done upon the coast of the sea; or, at farthest, acts and injuries done within the ebb and flow of the tide. The second respects contracts, claims, and services purely maritime, and touching rights and duties appertaining to commerce and navigation. The former is again divisible into two great branches, one embracing captures, and questions of prize arising *jure belli;* the other embracing acts, torts, and injuries strictly of civil cognizance, independent of belligerent operations.

§ 1661. By the law of nations the cognizance of all captures, *jure belli,* or, as it is more familiarly phrased, of all questions of prize, and their incidents, belongs exclusively to the courts of the country, to which the captors belong, and from whom they derive their authority to make the capture. No neutral nation has any right to inquire into, or to decide upon, the validity of such capture, even though it should concern property belonging to its own citizens or subjects, unless its own sovereign or territorial rights are violated; but the sole and exclusive jurisdiction belongs to the courts of the capturing belligerent. And this jurisdiction, by the common consent of nations, is vested exclusively in courts of admiralty, possessing an original, or appellate jurisdiction. The courts of common law are bound to abstain from any decision of questions of this sort, whether they arise directly or indirectly in judgment. The remedy for illegal acts of capture is by the institution of proper prize proceedings in the prize courts of the captors. If justice be there denied, the nation itself becomes responsible to the parties aggrieved; and if every remedy is refused, it then becomes a subject for the consideration of the nation, to which the parties aggrieved belong, which may vindicate their rights, either by a peaceful appeal to negotiation, or a resort to arms.

§ 1662. It is obvious upon the slightest consideration, that cognizance of all questions of prize, made under the authority of the United States, ought to belong exclusively to the national courts. How, otherwise, can the legality of the captures be satisfactorily ascertained, or deliberately vindicated? It seems not only a natural, but a necessary appendage to the power of war, and negotiation with foreign nations. It would otherwise follow, that the peace of the whole nation might be put at hazard at any time by the misconduct of one of its members. It could neither restore upon an illegal capture; nor in many cases afford any adequate redress for the wrong; nor punish the aggressor. It would be powerless and palsied. It could not perform, or compel the performance of the duties required by the law of nations. It would be a sovereign without any solid attribute of sovereignty; and move *in vinculis* only to betray its imbecility. Even under the confederation, the power to decide upon questions of capture and prize was exclusively conferred in the last resort upon the national court of appeals. But like all other powers conferred by that instrument, it was totally disregarded, wherever it interfered with state policy, or with extensive popular interests. We have seen, that the sentences of the national prize court of appeals were treated, as mere nullities; and were incapable of being enforced, until after the establishment of the present constitution. The same reasoning, which conducts us to the conclusion, that the national courts ought to have jurisdiction of this class of admiralty cases, conducts us equally to the conclusion, that, to be effectual for the administration of international justice, it ought to be exclusive. And accordingly it has been constantly held, that this jurisdiction is exclusive in the courts of the United States.

§ 1663. The other branch of admiralty jurisdiction, dependent upon locality, respects civil acts, torts, and injuries done on the sea, or (in certain cases) on waters of the sea, where the tide ebbs and flows, without any claim of exercising the rights of war. Such are cases of assaults, and other personal injuries; cases of collision, or running of ships against each other; cases of spoliation and damage, (as they are technically called,) such as illegal seizures, or depredations upon property; cases of illegal dispossession, or withholding possession from the owners of ships, commonly called possessory suits; cases of seizures under municipal authority for supposed breaches of revenue, or other prohibitory laws; and cases of salvage for meritorious services performed in saving property, whether derelict, or wrecked, or captured, or otherwise in imminent hazard from extraordinary perils.

§ 1664. It is obvious, that this class of cases has, or may have, an intimate relation to the rights and duties of foreigners in navigation and maritime commerce. It may materially affect our intercourse with foreign states; and raise many questions of international law, not merely touching private claims, but national sovereignty, and national reciprocity. Thus, for instance, if a collision should take place at sea between an American and a foreign ship, many important questions of public law might be connected with its just decision; for it is obvious, that it could not be governed by the mere municipal law of either country. So, if a case of recapture, or other salvage service performed to a foreign ship, should occur, it must be decided by the general principles of maritime law, and the doctrines of national reciprocity. Where a recapture is made of a

friendly ship from the hands of its enemy, the general doctrine now established is, to restore it upon salvage, if the foreign country, to which it belongs, adopts a reciprocal rule; or to condemn it to the recaptors, if the like rule is adopted in the foreign country. And in other cases of salvage the doctrines of international and maritime law come into full activity, rather than those of any mere municipal code. There is, therefore, a peculiar fitness in appropriating this class of cases to the national tribunals; since they will be more likely to be there decided upon large and comprehensive principles, and to receive a more uniform adjudication; and thus to become more satisfactory to foreigners.

§ 1665. The remaining class respects contracts, claims, and services purely maritime. Among these are the claims of material-men and others for repairs and outfits of ships belonging to foreign nations, or to other states; bottomry bonds for monies lent to ships in foreign ports to relieve their distresses, and enable them to complete their voyages; surveys of vessels damaged by perils of the seas; pilotage on the high seas; and suits for mariners' wages. These, indeed, often arise in the course of the commerce and navigation of the United States; and seem emphatically to belong, as incidents, to the power to regulate commerce. But they may also affect the commerce and navigation of foreign nations. Repairs may be done, and supplies furnished to foreign ships; money may be lent on foreign bottoms; pilotage and mariners' wages may become due in voyages in foreign employment; and in such cases the general maritime law enables the courts of admiralty to administer a wholesome and prompt justice. Indeed, in many of these cases, as the courts of admiralty entertain suits *in rem*, as well as *in personam*, they are often the only courts, in which an effectual redress can be afforded, especially when it is desirable to enforce a specific maritime lien.

§ 1666. So that we see, that the admiralty jurisdiction naturally connects itself, on the one hand, with our diplomatic relations and duties to foreign nations, and their subjects; and, on the other hand, with the great interests of navigation and commerce, foreign and domestic. There is, then, a peculiar wisdom in giving to the national government a jurisdiction of this sort, which cannot be wielded, except for the general good; and which multiplies the securities for the public peace abroad, and gives to commerce and navigation the most encouraging support at home. It may be added, that, in many of the cases included in these latter classes, the same reasons do not exist, as in cases of prize, for an exclusive jurisdiction; and, therefore, whenever the common law is competent to give a remedy in the state courts, they may retain their accustomed concurrent jurisdiction in the administration of it.

§ 1667. We have been thus far considering the admiralty and maritime jurisdiction in civil cases only. But it also embraces all public offences, committed on the high seas, and in creeks, havens, basins, and bays within the ebb and flow of the tide, at least in such as are out of the body of any county of a state. In these places the jurisdiction of the courts of admiralty over offences is exclusive; for that of the courts of common law is limited to such offences, as are committed within the body of some county. And on the sea coast, there is an alternate, or divided jurisdiction of the courts of common law, and admiralty, in places between high and low water mark; the former having jurisdiction when, and as far as the tide is out, and the latter when, and as far as the tide is in, *usque ad filum aquae*, or to high water mark. This criminal jurisdiction of the admiralty is therefore exclusively vested in the national government; and may be exercised over such crimes and offences, as congress may, from time to time, delegate to the cognisance of the national courts. The propriety of vesting this criminal jurisdiction in the national government depends upon the same reasoning, and is established by the same general considerations, as have been already suggested in regard to civil cases. It is essentially connected with the due regulation, and protection of our commerce and navigation on the high seas, and with our rights and duties in regard to foreign nations, and their subjects, in the exercise of common sovereignty on the ocean. The states, as such, are not known in our intercourse with foreign nations, and not recognised as common sovereigns on the ocean. And if they were permitted to exercise criminal or civil jurisdiction thereon, there would be endless embarrassments, arising from the conflict of their laws, and the most serious dangers of perpetual controversies with foreign nations. In short, the peace of the Union would be constantly put at hazard by acts, over which it had no control; and by assertions of right, which it might wholly disclaim.

§ 1668. The next clause extends the judicial power "to controversies, to which the United States shall be a party." It scarcely seems possible to raise a reasonable doubt, as to the propriety of giving to the national courts jurisdiction of cases, in which the United States are a party. It would be a perfect novelty in the history of national jurisprudence, as well as of public law, that a sovereign had no authority to sue in his own courts. Unless this power were given to the United States, the enforcement of all their rights, powers, contracts, and privileges in their sovereign capacity, would be at the mercy of the states. They must be enforced, if at all, in the state tribunals. And there would not only not be any compulsory power over those courts to perform such functions; but there would not be any means of producing uniformity in their decisions. A sovereign without the means of enforcing civil rights, or compelling the performance, either civilly or criminally, of public duties on the part of the citizens, would be a most extraordinary anomaly. It would prostrate the Union at the feet of the states. It would compel the national government to become a supplicant for justice before the judicature of those, who were by other parts of the constitution placed in subordination to it.

§ 1669. It is observable, that the language used does not confer upon any court cognizance of all controversies, to which the United States shall be a party, so as to justify a suit to be brought against the United States without the consent of congress. And the language was doubtless thus guardedly introduced, for the purpose of avoiding any such conclusion. It is a known maxim, justified by the general sense and practice of mankind, and recognized in the law of nations, that it is inherent in the nature of sovereignty not to be amesnable to the suit of any private person, without its own consent. This exemption is an attribute of sovereignty, belonging to every state in the Union; and was designedly retained by the national governemnt. The inconvenience of subjecting the government to perpetual suits, as a matter of right, at the will of any citizen, for any real or supposed claim or grievance, was deemed far greater, than any positive injury, that could be sustained by any citizen by the delay or refusal of justice. Indeed, it was presumed, that it never would be the interest or inclination of a wise government to withhold justice from any citizen. And the difficulties of guarding itself against fraudulent claims, and embarassing and stale controversies, were believed far to outweigh any mere theoretical advantages, to be derived from any attempt to provide a system for the administration of universal justice.

§ 1670. It may be asked, then, whether the citizens of the United States are wholly destitute of remedy, in case the national government should invade their rights, either by private injustice and injuries, or by public oppression? To this it may be answered, that in a general sense, there is a remedy in both cases. In regard to public oppressions, the whole structure of the government is so organized, as to afford the means of redress, by enabling the people to remove public functionaries, who abuse their trust, and to substitute others more faithful, and more honest, in their stead. If the oppression be in the exercise of powers clearly constitutional, and the people refuse to interfere in this manner, then indeed, the party must submit to the wrong, as beyond the reach of all human power; for how can the people themselves, in their collective capacity, be compelled to do justice, and to vindicate the rights of those, who are subjected to their sovereign control? If the oppression be in the exercise of unconstitutional powers, then the functionaries, who wield them, are amesnable for their injurious acts to the judicial tribunals of the country, at the suit of the oppressed.

§ 1671. As to private injustice and injuries, they may regard either the rights of property, or the rights of contract; for the national government is *per se* incapable of any merely personal wrong, such as an assault and battery, or other personal violence. In regard to property, the remedy for injuries lies against the immediate perpetrators, who may be sued, and cannot shelter themselves under any imagined immunity of the government from due responsibility. If, therefore, any agent of the government shall unjustly invade the property of a citizen under colour of a public authority, he must, like every other violator of the laws, respond in damages. Cases, indeed, may occur, in which he may not always have an adequate redress, without some legislation by congress. As for example, in places ceded to the United States, and over which they have an exclusive jurisdiction, if his real estate is taken without, or against lawful authority. Here he must rely on the justice of congress, or of the executive department. The greatest difficulty arises in regard to the contracts of the national government; for as they cannot be sued without their own consent, and as their agents are not responsible upon any such contracts, when lawfully made, the only redress, which can be obtained, must be by the instrumentality of congress, either in providing (as they may) for suits in the common courts of justice to establish such claims by a general law, or by a special act for the relief of the particular party. In each case, however, the redress depends solely upon the legislative department, and cannot be administered, except through its favour. The remedy is by an appeal to the justice of the nation in that forum, and not in any court of justice, as matter of right.

§ 1672. It has been sometimes thought, that this is a serious defect in the organization of the judicial department of the national government. It is not, however, an objection to the constitution itself; but it lies, if at all, against congress, for not having provided, (as it is clearly within their constitutional authority to do,) an adequate remedy for all private grievances of this sort, in the courts of the United States. In this respect, there is a marked contrast between the actual right and practice of redress in the national government, as well as in most of the state governments, and the right and practice maintained under the British constitution. In England, if any person has, in point of property, a just demand upon the king, he may petition him in his court of chancery (by what is called a petition of right) where the chancellor will administer right, theoretically as a matter of grace, and not upon compulsion; but in fact, as a matter of constitutional duty. No such judicial proceeding is recognised, as existing in any state of this Union, as matter of constitutional right, to enforce any claim, or debt against a state. In the few cases, in which it exists, it is matter of legislative enactment. Congress have never yet acted upon the subject, so as to give judicial redress for any non-fulfilment of contracts by the national government. Cases of the most cruel hardship, and intolerable delay have already occurred, in which meritorious creditors have been reduced to grievous suffering, and sometimes to absolute ruin, by the tardiness of a justice, which has been yielded only after the humble supplications of many years before the legislature. One can scarcely refrain from uniting in the suggestion of a learned commentator, that in this regard the constitutions, both of the national and state governments, stand in need of some reform, to quicken the legislative action in the administration of justice; and, that some mode ought to be provided, by which a pecuniary right against a state, or against the United States, might be ascertained, and established by the judicial sentence of some court; and when so ascertained and established, the payment might be enforced from the national treasury by an absolute appropriation. Surely, it can afford no pleasant source of reflection to an American citizen, proud of his rights and privileges, that in a monarchy the judiciary is clothed with ample powers to give redress to the humblest subject in a matter of private contract, or property against the crown; and, that in a republic there is an utter denial of justice, in such cases, to any citizen through the instrumentality of any judicial process. He may complain; but he cannot compel a hearing. The republic enjoys a despotic sover-

eignty to act, or refuse, as it may please; and is placed beyond the reach of law. The monarch bows to the law, and is compelled to yield his prerogative at the footstool of justice.

§ 1673. . . . This power [to resolve disputes between states] seems to be essential to the preservation of the peace of the Union. "History" (says the Federalist,) gives us a horrid picture of the dissensions and private wars, which distracted and desolated Germany, prior to the institution of the imperial chamber by Maximillian, towards the close of the fifteenth century; and informs us at the same time of the vast influence of that institution, in appeasing the disorders, and establishing the tranquillity of the empire. This was a court invested with authority to decide finally all differences among the members of the Germanic body." But we need not go for illustrations to the history of other countries. Our own has presented, in past times, abundant proofs of the irritating effects resulting from territorial disputes, and interfering claims of boundary between the states. And there are yet controversies of this sort, which have brought on a border warfare, at once dangerous to public repose, and incompatible with the public interests.

§ 1674. Under the confederation, authority was given to the national government, to hear and determine, (in the manner pointed out in the article,) in the last resort, on appeal, all disputes and differences between two or more states concerning boundary, jurisdiction, or any other cause whatsoever. Before the adoption of this instrument, as well as afterwards, very irritating and vexatious controveries existed between several of the states, in respect to soil, jurisdiction, and boundary; and threatened the most serious public mischiefs. Some of these controversies were heard and determined by the court of commissioners, appointed by congress. But, notwithstanding these adjudications, the conflict was maintained in some cases, until after the establishment of the present constitution.

§ 1675. Before the revolution, controversies between the colonies, concerning the extent of their rights of soil, territory, jurisdiction, and boundary, under their respective charters, were heard and determined before the king in council, who exercised original jurisdiction therein, upon the principles of feudal sovereignty. This jurisdiction was often practically asserted, as in the case of the dispute between Massachusetts and New Hampshire, decided by the privy council, in 1679; and in the case of the dispute between New Hampshire and New York, in 1764. Lord Hardwicke recognised this appellate jurisdiction in the most deliberate manner, in the great case of *Penn v. Lord Baltimore*. The same necessity, which gave rise to it in our colonial state, must continue to operate through all future time. Some tribunal, exercising such authority, is essential to prevent an appeal to the sword, and a dissolution of the government. That it ought to be established under the national, rather than under the state, government; or, to speak more properly, that it can be safely established under the former only, would seem to be a position self-evident, and requiring no reasoning to support it. It may justly be presumed, that under the national government in all controversies of this sort, the decision will be impartially made according to the principles of justice; and all the usual and most effectual precautions are taken to secure this impartiality, by confiding it to the highest judicial tribunal.

. . . . .

§ 1684. Next. "Controversies between citizens of different states." Although the necessity of this power may not stand upon grounds quite as strong, as some of the preceding, there are high motives of state policy and public justice, by which it can be clearly vindicated. There are many cases, in which such a power may be indispensable, or in the highest degree expedient, to carry into effect some of the privileges and immunities conferred, and some of the prohibitions upon states expressly declared, in the constitution. For example; it is declared, that the citizens of each state shall be entitled to all the privileges and immunities of citizens of the several states. Suppose an attempt is made to evade, or withhold these privileges and immunities, would it not be right to allow the party aggrieved an opportunity of claiming them, in a contest with a citizen of the state, before a tribunal, at once national and impartial? Suppose a state should pass a tender law, or law impairing the obligation of private contracts, or should in the course of its legislation grant unconstitutional preferences to its own citizens, is it not clear, that the jurisdiction to enforce the obligations of the constitution in such cases ought to be confided to the national tribunals? These cases are not purely imaginary. They have actually occurred; and may again occur, under peculiar circumstances, in the course of state legislation. What was the fact under the confederation? Each state was obliged to acquiesce in the degree of justice, which another state might choose to yield to its citizens. There was not only danger of animosities growing up from this source; but, in point of fact, there did grow up retaliatory legislation, to meet such real or imagined grievances.

§ 1685. Nothing can conduce more to general harmony and confidence among all the states, than a consciousness, that controversies are not exclusively to be decided by the state tribunals; but may, at the election of the party, be brought before the national tribunals. Besides; it cannot escape observation, that the judges in different states hold their offices by a very different tenure. Some hold during good behaviour; some for a term of years; some for a single year; some are irremovable, except upon impeachment; and others may be removed upon address of the legislature. Under such circumstances it cannot but be presumed, that there may arise a course of state policy, or state legislation, exceedingly injurious to the interests of the citizens of other states, both as to real and personal property. It would require an uncommon exercise of candour or credulity to affirm, that in cases of this sort all the state tribunals would be wholly without state prejudice, or state feelings; or, that they would be as earnest in resisting the encroachments of state authority upon the just rights, and interests of the citizens of other states, as a tribunal differently constituted, and wholly independent of state authority. And if justice should be as fairly and as firmly administered in the former, as in the latter, still the mis-

chiefs would be most serious, if the public opinion did not indulge such a belief. Justice, in cases of this sort, should not only be above all reproach, but above all suspicion. The sources of state irritations and state jealousies are sufficiently numerous, without leaving open one so copious and constant, as the belief, or the dread of wrong in the administration of state justice. Besides; if the public confidence should continue to follow the state tribunals, (as in many cases it doubtless will,) the provision will become inert and harmless; for, as the party will have his election of the forum, he will not be inclined to desert the state courts, unless for some sound reason, founded either in the nature of his cause, or in the influence of state prejudices. On the other hand, there can be no real danger of injustice to the other side in the decisions of the national tribunals; because the cause must still be decided upon the true principles of the local law, and not by any foreign jurisprudence. There is another circumstance of no small importance, as a matter of policy; and that is, the tendency of such a power to increase the confidence and credit between the commercial and agricultural states. No man can be insensible to the value, in promoting credit, of the belief of there being a prompt, efficient, and impartial administration of justice in enforcing contracts.

§ 1686. Such are some of the reasons, which are supposed to have influenced the convention in delegating jurisdiction to the courts of the United States in cases between citizens of different states. Probably no part of the judicial power of the Union has been of more practical benefit, or has given more lasting satisfaction to the people. There is not a single state, which has not at some time felt the influence of this conservative power; and the general harmony, which exists between the state courts and the national courts, in the concurrent exercise of their jurisdiction in cases between citizens of different states, demonstrates the utility, as well as the safety of the power. Indeed; it is not improbable, that the existence of the power has operated, as a silent, but irresistible check to undue state legislation; at the same time, that it has cherished a mutual respect and confidence between the state and national courts, as honourable, as it has been beneficent.

§ 1687. The next inquiry growing out of this part of the clause is, who are to be deemed citizens of different states within the meaning of it. Are all persons born within a state to be always deemed citizens of that state, notwithstanding any change of domicil; or does their citizenship change with their change of domicil? The answer to this inquiry is equally plain and satisfactory. The constitution having declared, that the citizens of each state shall be entitled to all privileges and immunities of citizens in the several states, every person, who is a citizen of one state, and removes into another, with the intention of taking up his residence and inhabitancy there, becomes *ipso facto* a citizen of the state, where he resides; and he then ceases to be a citizen of the state, from which he has removed his residence. Of course, when he gives up his new residence or domicil, and returns to his native, or other state residence or domicil, he reacquires the character of the latter. What circumstances shall constitute such a change of residence or domicil, is an inquiry, more properly belonging to a treatise upon public or municipal law, than to commentaries upon constitutional law. In general, however, it may be said, that a removal from one state into another, *animo manendi*, or with a design of becoming an inhabitant, constitutes a change of domicil, and of course a change of citizenship. But a person, who is a native citizen of one state, never ceases to be a citizen thereof, until he has acquired a new citizenship elsewhere. Residence in a foreign country has no operation upon his character, as a citizen, although it may, for purposes of trade and commerce, impress him with the character of the country. To change allegiance is one thing; to change inhabitancy is quite another thing. The right and the power are not coextensive in each case. Every citizen of a state is *ipso facto* a citizen of the United States.

§ 1688. And a person, who is a naturalized citizen of the United States, by a like residence in any state in the Union, becomes *ipso facto* a citizen of that state. So a citizen of a territory of the Union by a like residence acquires the character of the state, where he resides. But a naturalized citizen of the United States, or a citizen of a territory, is not a citizen of a state, entitled to sue in the courts of the United States in virtue of that character, while he resides in any such territory, nor until he has acquired a residence or domicil in the particular state.

§ 1689. A corporation, as such, is not a citizen of a state in the sense of the constitution. But, if all the members of the corporation are citizens, their character will confer jurisdiction; for then it is substantially a suit by citizens suing in their corporate name. And a citizen of a state is entitled to sue, as such, notwithstanding he is a trustee for others, or sues in *autre droit*, as it is technically called; that is, as representative of another. Thus, a citizen may sue, who is a trustee at law, for the benefit of the person entitled to the trust. And an administrator, and executor may sue for the benefit of the estate, which they represent; for in each of these cases it is their personal suit. But if citizens, who are parties to a suit, are merely nominally so; as, for instance, if magistrates are officially required to allow suits to be brought in their names for the use or benefit of a citizen or alien, the latter are deemed the substantial parties entitled to sue.

§ 1690. Next. "Controversies between citizens of the same state, claiming lands under grants of different states." This clause was not in the first draft of the constitution, but was added without any known objection to its propriety. It is the only instance, in which the constitution directly contemplates the cognizance of disputes between citizens of the same state; but certainly not the only one, in which they may indirectly upon constitutional questions have the benefit of the judicial power of the Union. The Federalist has remarked, that the reasonableness of the agency of the national courts in cases, in which the state tribunals cannot be supposed to be impartial, speaks for itself. No man ought certainly to be a judge in his own cause, or in any cause, in respect to which he has the least interest or bias. This principle has no inconsiderable weight in designating the federal courts, as the proper tribunals for the determination of controversies between different states and their citizens. And it ought to have the

same operation in regard to some cases between citizens of the same state. Claims to land under grants of different states, founded upon adverse pretensions of boundary, are of this description. The courts of neither of the granting states could be expected to be unbiassed. The laws may have even prejudged the question; and tied the courts down to decisions in favour of the grants of the state, to which they belonged. And where this has not been done, it would be natural, that the judges, as men, should feel a strong predilection for the claims of their own government. And, at all events, the providing of a tribunal, having no possible interest on the one side, more than the other, would have a most salutary tendency in quieting the jealousies, and disarming the resentments of the state, whose grant should be held invalid. This jurisdiction attaches not only to grants made by different states, which were never united; but also to grants made by different states, which were originally united under one jurisdiction, if made since the separation, although the origin of the title may be traced back to an antecedent period.

. . . . .

§ 1692. In addition to these suggestions, it may be remarked, that it is of great national importance to advance public, as well as private credit, in our intercourse with foreign nations and their subjects. Nothing can be more beneficial in this respect, than to create an impartial tribunal, to which they may have resort upon all occasions, when it may be necessary to ascertain, or enforce their rights. Besides; it is not wholly immaterial, that the law to be administered in cases of foreigners is often very distinct from the mere municipal code of a state, and dependent upon the law merchant, or the more enlarged consideration of international rights and duties, in a case of conflict of the foreign and domestic laws. And it may fairly be presumed, that the national tribunals will, from the nature of their ordinary functions, become better acquainted with the general principles, which regulate subjects of this nature, than other courts, however enlightened, which are rarely required to discuss them.

§ 1693. In regard to controversies between an American and a foreign state, it is obvious, that the suit must, on one side at least, be wholly voluntary. No foreign state can be compelled to become a party, plaintiff or defendant, in any of our tribunals. If, therefore, it chooses to consent to the institution of any suit, it is its consent alone, which can give effect to the jurisdiction of the court. It is certainly desirable to furnish some peaceable mode of appeal in cases, where any controversy may exist between an American and a foreign state, sufficiently important to require the grievance to be redressed by any other mode, than through the instrumentality of negotiations.

§ 1694. The inquiry may here be made, who are to be deemed aliens entitled to sue in the courts of the United States. The general answer is, any person, who is not a citizen of the United States. A foreigner, who is naturalized, is no longer entitled to the character of an alien. And when an alien is the substantial party, it matters not, whether he is a suitor in his own right; or whether he acts, as a trustee, or personal representative; or whether he is compellable by the local law to sue through some official organ. A foreign corporation, established in a foreign country, all of whose members are aliens, is entitled to sue in the same manner, that an alien may personally sue in the courts of the Union. It is not sufficient to vest the jurisdiction, that an alien is a party to the suit, unless the other party be a citizen. British subjects, born before the American revolution, are to be deemed aliens; and may sue American citizens, born before the revolution, as well as those born since that period. The revolution severed the ties of allegiance; and made the inhabitants of each country aliens to each other. In relation to aliens, however, it should be stated, that they have a right to sue only, while peace exists between their country and our own. For if a war breaks out, and they thereby become alien enemies, their right to sue is suspended, until the return of peace.

SEE ALSO:

Mason v. *The Ship Blaleau*, 2 Cranch 240 (1804)
Jennings v. *Carson*, 4 Cranch 2 (1807)
United States v. *Schooner Betsey & Charlotte*, 4 Cranch 443 (1808)
Cheriot v. *Foussat*, 3 Binney 220 (Pa. 1810)
Locke v. *United States*, 7 Cranch 338 (1813)
Brown v. *United States*, 8 Cranch 110 (1814)
The Schooner Adeline, 9 Cranch 244 (1815)
The Samuel, 1 Wheat. 9 (1816)
The Octavia, 1 Wheat. 20 (1816)
United States v. *Hamilton*, 26 Fed. Cas. 93, no. 15,290
   (C.C.D.Mass. 1816)
Slocum v. *Mayberry*, 2 Wheat. 1 (1817)
Gelston v. *Hoyt*, 3 Wheat. 246 (1818)
The Amiable Nancy, 3 Wheat. 546 (1818)
The Margaret, 9 Wheat. 421 (1824)
The Steamboat Thomas Jefferson, 10 Wheat. 428 (1825)
Munro v. *Almeida*, 10 Wheat. 473 (1825)
James Kent, Commentaries 1:331–54 (1826)
Ramsay v. *Allegre*, 12 Wheat. 611 (1827)
The Seneca, 21 Fed. Cas. 1081, no. 12,670 (C.C.E.D.Pa. 1829)
Stearns v. *United States*, 22 Fed. Cas. 1188, no. 13,341 (C.C.D.Vt.
   1830)
Sheppard v. *Taylor*, 5 Pet. 675 (1831)
The Wave, 29 Fed. Cas. 453, no. 17,297 (S.D.N.Y.1831)
Bains v. *The James and Catherine*, 2 Fed. Cas. 410, no. 756
   (C.C.D.Pa. 1832)
Peyroux v. *Howard*, 7 Pet. 324 (1833)

United States as Party

Postmaster General of the United States v. *Early*, 12 Wheat. 136
   (1827)
United States v. *Clarke*, 8 Pet. 436 (1834)

Diversity of Citizenship

Maxfield v. *Levy*, 16 Fed. Cas. 1195, no. 9,321 (C.C.D.Pa. 1797)
Bingham v. *Cabot*, 3 Dall. 382 (1798)
Hope Ins. Co. v. *Boardman*, 5 Cranch 57 (1809)

Browne v. *Strode*, 5 Cranch 303 (1809)
Prentiss v. *Barton's Exec.*, 1 Marshall's C.C. 389 (C.C.D.Va. 1819)
Young v. *Bryan*, 6 Wheat. 146 (1821)
Kitchen v. *Strawbridge*, 14 Fed. Cas. 692, no. 7,854 (C.C.D.Pa.
   1821)
Butler v. *Farnsworth*, 4 Fed. Cas. 902, no. 2,240 (C.C.E.D.Pa.
   1821)
Childress v. *Emory*, 8 Wheat. 642 (1823)
Mullen v. *Torrance*, 9 Wheat. 537 (1824)
Kirkpatrick v. *White*, 14 Fed. Cas. 685, no. 7,850 (C.C.D.Pa. 1826)
Moffat v. *Soley*, 17 Fed. Cas. 559, no. 9,688 (C.C.S.D.N.Y. 1827)
Gassies v. *Ballon*, 6 Pet. 761 (1832)

Land Grants

Colson v. *Lewis*, 2 Wheat. 377 (1817)

Law and Equity

Diggs & Keith v. *Wolcott*, 4 Cranch 179 (1807)

Alienage

King of Spain v. *Oliver*, 14 Fed. Cas. 577, no. 7,814 (C.C.D.Pa.
   1810)
Richard Rush, Judicial Privileges of Foreigners, 1 Oct. 1816,
   1 Ops. Atty. Gen. 192
New Jersey v. *Babcock*, 18 Fed. Cas. 82, no. 10,163 (C.C.D.N.J.
   1823)
Jackson v. *Twentyman*, 2 Pet. 136 (1829)

State Courts

Commonwealth v. *Feely*, 1 Va. Cas. 321 (1813)
United States v. *Lathrop*, 17 Johns. R. 4 (N.Y. 1819)
State v. *Randall*, 2 Aiken 89 (Vt. 1827)
Ely v. *Peck*, 7 Conn. 239 (1828)
William Rawle, A View of the Constitution of the United States
   201–5, 229–32 (2d ed. 1829)

Article 3, Section 2, Clause 2

In all Cases affecting Ambassadors, other public Ministers and Consuls, and those in which a State shall be Party, the supreme Court shall have original Jurisdiction. In all the other Cases before mentioned, the supreme Court shall have appellate Jurisdiction, both as to Law and Fact, with such Exceptions, and under such Regulations as the Congress shall make.

1

FEDERAL FARMER, NO. 15
18 Jan. 1788
Storing 2.8.189, 194

The supreme court, in cases of appeals, shall have jurisdiction both as to law and fact: that is, in all civil causes carried up the supreme court by appeals, the court, or judges, shall try the fact and decide the law. Here an essential principle of the civil law is established, and the most noble and important principle of the common law exploded. To dwell a few minutes on this material point: the supreme court shall have jurisdiction both as to law and fact. What is meant by court? Is the jury included in the term, or is it not? I conceive it is not included: and so the members of convention, I am very sure, understand it. Court, or curia, was a term well understood long before juries existed; the people, and the best writers, in countries where there are no juries, uniformly use the word court, and can only mean by it the judge or judges who determine causes: also, in countries where there are juries we express ourselves in the same manner; we speak of the court of probate, court of chancery, justices court, alderman's court, &c. in which there is no jury. In our supreme courts, common pleas, &c. in which there are jury trials, we uniformly speak of the court and jury, and consider them as distinct. Were it

necessary I might site a multitude of cases from law books to confirm, beyond controversy, this position, that the jury is not included, or a part of the court.

But the supreme court is to have jurisdiction as to law and fact, under such regulations as congress shall make. I confess it is impossible to say how far congress may, with propriety, extend their regulations in this respect. I conceive, however, they cannot by any reasonable construction go so far as to admit the jury, on true common law principles, to try the fact, and give a general verdict. I have repeatedly examined this article: I think the meaning of it is, that the judges in all final questions, as to property and damages, shall have complete jurisdiction, to consider the whole cause, to examine the facts, and on a general view of them, and on principles of equity, as well as law, to give judgment.

. . . . .

By the common law, in Great Britain and America, there is no appeal from the verdict of the jury, as to facts, to any judges whatever—the jurisdiction of the jury is complete and final in this; and only errors in laws are carried up to the house of lords, the special supreme court in Great Britain; or to the special supreme courts in Connecticut, New-York, New-Jersey, &c. Thus the juries are left masters as to facts: but, by the proposed constitution, directly the opposite principle is established. An appeal will lay in all appellate causes from the verdict of the jury, even as to mere facts, to the judges of the supreme court. Thus, in effect, we establish the civil law in this point; for if the jurisdiction of the jury be not final, as to facts, it is of little or no importance.

2

BRUTUS, NO. 14
28 Feb.–6 Mar. 1788
Storing 2.9.168–85

The second paragraph of sect. 2d. art. 3, is in these words: "In all cases affecting ambassadors, other public ministers and consuls, and those in which a state shall be a party, the supreme court shall have original jurisdiction. In all the other cases before mentioned, the supreme court shall have appellate jurisdiction, both as to law and fact, with such exceptions, and under such regulations as the Congress shall make.["]

Although it is proper that the courts of the general government should have cognizance of all matters affecting ambassadors, foreign ministers, and consuls; yet I question much the propriety of giving the supreme court original jurisdiction in all cases of this kind.

Ambassadors, and other public ministers, claim, and are entitled by the law of nations, to certain privileges, and exemptions, both for their persons and their servants.

The meanest servant of an ambassador is exempted by the law of nations from being sued for debt. Should a suit be brought against such an one by a citizen, through inadvertency or want of information, he will be subject to an action in the supreme court. All the officers concerned in issuing or executing the process will be liable to like actions. Thus may a citizen of a state be compelled, at great expence and inconveniency, to defend himself against a suit, brought against him in the supreme court, for inadvertently commencing an action against the most menial servant of an ambassador for a just debt.

The appellate jurisdiction granted to the supreme court, in this paragraph, has justly been considered as one of the most objectionable parts of the constitution: under this power, appeals may be had from the inferior courts to the supreme, in every case to which the judicial power extends, except in the few instances in which the supreme court will have original jurisdiction.

By this article, appeals will lie to the supreme court, in all criminal as well as civil causes. This I know, has been disputed by some; but I presume the point will appear clear to any one, who will attend to the connection of this paragraph with the one that precedes it. In the former, all the cases, to which the power of the judicial shall extend, whether civil or criminal, are enumerated. There is no criminal matter, to which the judicial power of the United States will extend; but such as are included under some one of the cases specified in this section. For this section is intended to define all the cases, of every description, to which the power of the judicial shall reach. But in all these cases it is declared, the supreme court shall have appellate jurisdiction, except in those which affect ambassadors, other public ministers and consuls, and those in which a state shall be a party. If then this section extends the power of the judicial, to criminal cases, it allows appeals in such cases. If the power of the judicial is not extended to criminal matters by this section, I ask, by what part of this system does it appear, that they have any cognizance of them?

I believe it is a new and unusual thing to allow appeals in criminal matters. It is contrary to the sense of our laws, and dangerous to the lives and liberties of the citizen. As our law now stands, a person charged with a crime has a right to a fair and impartial trial by a jury of his country, and their verdict is final. If he is acquitted no other court can call upon him to answer for the same crime. But by this system, a man may have had ever so fair a trial, have been acquitted by ever so respectable a jury of his country; and still the officer of the government who prosecutes, may appeal to the supreme court. The whole matter may have a second hearing. By this means, persons who may have disobliged those who execute the general government, may be subjected to intolerable oppression. They may be kept in long and ruinous confinement, and exposed to heavy and insupportable charges, to procure the attendence of witnesses, and provide the means of their defence, at a great distance from their places of residence.

I can scarcely believe there can be a considerate citizen of the United States, that will approve of this appellate jurisdiction, as extending to criminal cases, if they will give themselves time for reflection.

Whether the appellate jurisdiction as it respects civil matters, will not prove injurious to the rights of the citizens, and destructive of those privileges which have ever been held sacred by Americans, and whether it will not render the administration of justice intolerably burthensome, intricate, and dilatory, will best appear, when we have considered the nature and operation of this power.

It has been the fate of this clause, as it has of most of those, against which unanswerable objections have been offered, to be explained different ways, by the advocates and opponents to the constitution. I confess I do not know what the advocates of the system, would make it mean, for I have not been fortunate enough to see in any publication this clause taken up and considered. It is certain however, they do not admit the explanation which those who oppose the constitution give it, or otherwise they would not so frequently charge them with want of candor, for alledging that it takes away the trial by jury[;] appeals from an inferior to a superior court, as practised in the civil law courts, are well understood. In these courts, the judges determine both on the law and the fact; and appeals are allowed from the inferior to the superior courts, on the whole merits: the superior tribunal will re-examine all the facts as well as the law, and frequently new facts will be introduced, so as many times to render the cause in the court of appeals very different from what it was in the court below.

If the appellate jurisdiction of the supreme court, be understood in the above sense, the term is perfectly intelligible. The meaning then is, that in all the civil causes enumerated, the supreme court shall have authority to re-examine the whole merits of the case, both with respect to the facts and the law which may arise under it, without the intervention of a jury; that this is the sense of this part of the system appears to me clear, from the express words of it, "in all the other cases before mentioned, the supreme court shall have appellate jurisdiction, both as to law and fact, &c." Who are the supreme court? Does it not consist of the judges? and they are to have the same jurisdiction of the fact as they are to have of the law. They will therefore have the same authority to determine the fact as they will have to determine the law, and no room is left for a jury on appeals to the supreme court.

If we understand the appellate jurisdiction in any other way, we shall be left utterly at a loss to give it a meaning; the common law is a stranger to any such jurisdiction: no appeals can lie from any of our common law courts, upon the merits of the case; the only way in which they can go up from an inferior to a superior tribunal is by habeas corpus before a hearing, or by certiorari, or writ of error, after they are determined in the subordinate courts; but in no case, when they are carried up, are the facts re-examined, but they are always taken as established in the inferior courts.

It may still be insisted that this clause does not take away the trial by jury on appeals, but that this may be provided for by the legislature, under that paragraph which authorises them to form regulations and restrictions for the court in the exercise of this power.

The natural meaning of this paragraph seems to be no more than this, that Congress may declare, that certain cases shall not be subject to the appellate jurisdiction, and they may point out the mode in which the court shall proceed in bringing up the causes before them, the manner of their taking evidence to establish the facts, and the method of the courts proceeding. But I presume they cannot take from the court the right of deciding on the fact, any more than they can deprive them of the right of determining on the law, when a cause is once before them; for they have the same jurisdiction as to fact, as they have as to the law. But supposing the Congress may under this clause establish the trial by jury on appeals, it does not seem to me that it will render this article much less exceptionable. An appeal from one court and jury, to another court and jury, is a thing altogether unknown in the laws of our state, and in most of the states in the union. A practice of this kind prevails in the eastern states; actions are there commenced in the inferior courts, and an appeal lies from them on the whole merits to the superior courts: the consequence is well known, very few actions are determined in the lower courts; it is rare that a case of any importance is not carried by appeal to the supreme court, and the jurisdiction of the inferior courts is merely nominal; this has proved so burthensome to the people in Massachusetts, that it was one of the principal causes which excited the insurrection in that state, in the year past; very few sensible and moderate men in that state but what will admit, that the inferior courts are almost entirely useless, and answer very little purpose, save only to accumulate costs against the poor debtors who are already unable to pay their just debts.

But the operation of the appellate power in the supreme judicial of the United States, would work infinitely more mischief than any such power can do in a single state.

The trouble and expence to the parties would be endless and intolerable. No man can say where the supreme court are to hold their sessions, the presumption is, however, that it must be at the seat of the general government: in this case parties must travel many hundred miles, with their witnesses and lawyers, to prosecute or defend a suit; no man of midling fortune, can sustain the expence of such a law suit, and therefore the poorer and midling class of citizens will be under the necessity of submitting to the demands of the rich and the lordly, in cases that will come under the cognizance of this court. If it be said, that to prevent this oppression, the supreme court will set in different parts of the union, it may be replied, that this would only make the oppression somewhat more tolerable, but by no means so much as to give a chance of justice to the poor and midling class. It is utterly impossible that the supreme court can move into so many different parts of the Union, as to make it convenient or even tolerable to attend before them with witnesses to try causes from every part of the United states; if to avoid the expence and inconvenience of calling witnesses from a great distance, to give evidence before the supreme court, the expedient of taking the deposition of witnesses in writing should be adopted, it would not help the matter. It is of great importance in the distribution of justice that witnesses should be examined face to face, that the parties should have the fairest opportunity of cross examining them in order to bring out the whole truth; there is something in the manner in which a witness delivers his testimony which cannot be committed to paper, and which yet very frequently gives a complexion to his evidence, very different from what it would bear if committed to writing, besides the expence of taking written testimony would be enormous; those who are acquainted with the costs that arise in the courts, where all the evidence is taken in writing, well know that they exceed beyond all comparison those of the common law courts, where witnesses are examined viva voce.

The costs accruing in courts generally advance with the grade of the court; thus the charges attending a suit in our common pleas, is much less than those in the supreme court, and these are much lower than those in the court of chancery; indeed the costs in the last mentioned court, are in many cases so exorbitant and the proceedings so dilatory that the suitor had almost as well give up his demand as to prosecute his suit. We have just reason to suppose, that the costs in the supreme general court will exceed either of our courts; the officers of the general court will be more dignified than those of the states, the lawyers of the most ability will practice in them, and the trouble and expence of attending them will be greater. From all these considerations, it appears, that the expence attending suits in the supreme court will be so great, as to put it out of the power of the poor and midling class of citizens to contest a suit in it.

From these remarks it appears, that the administration of justice under the powers of the judicial will be dilatory; that it will be attended with such an heavy expence as to amount to little short of a denial of justice to the poor and middling class of people who in every government stand most in need of the protection of the law; and that the trial by jury, which has so justly been the boast of our fore fathers as well as ourselves is taken away under them.

These extraordinary powers in this court are the more objectionable, because there does not appear the least necessity for them, in order to secure a due and impartial distribution of justice.

The want of ability or integrity, or a disposition to render justice to every suitor, has not been objected against the courts of the respective states; so far as I have been informed, the courts of justice in all the states, have ever been found ready, to administer justice with promptitude and impartiality according to the laws of the land; It is true in some of the states, paper money has been made, and the debtor authorised to discharge his debts with it, at a depreciated value, in orders, tender laws have been passed, obliging the creditor to receive on execution other property than money in discharge of his demand, and in several of the states laws have been made unfavorable to the creditor and tending to render property insecure.

But these evils have not happened from any defect in the judicial departments of the states; the courts indeed are bound to take notice of these laws, and so will the courts of the general government be under obligation to observe the laws made by the general legislature not repugnant to the constitution; but so far have the judicial been from giving undue latitude of construction to laws of this kind, that they have invariably strongly inclined to the other side. All the acts of our legislature, which have been charged with being of this complexion, have uniformly received the strictest construction by the judges, and have been extended to no cases but to such as came within the strict letter of the law. In this way, have our courts, I will not say evaded the law, but so limited it in its operation as to work the least possible injustice: the same thing has taken place in Rhode-Island, which has justly rendered herself infamous, by her tenaciously adhering to her paper money system. The judges there gave a decision, in opposition to the words of the Statute, on this principle, that a construction according to the words of it, would contradict the fundamental maxims of their laws and constitution.

No pretext therefore, can be formed, from the conduct of the judicial courts which will justify giving such powers to the supreme general court, for their decisions have been such as to give just ground of confidence in them, that they will firmly adhere to the principles of rectitude, and there is no necessity of lodging these powers in the courts, in order to guard against the evils justly complained of, on the subject of security of property under this constitution. For it has provided, "that no state shall emit bills of credit, or make any thing but gold and silver coin a tender in payment of debts." It has also declared, that "no state shall pass any law impairing the obligation of contracts."—These prohibitions give the most perfect security against those attacks upon property which I am sorry to say some of the states have but too wantonly made, by passing laws sanctioning fraud in the debtor against his creditor. For "this constitution will be the supreme law of the land, and the judges in every state will be bound thereby; any thing in the constitution and laws of any state to the contrary notwithstanding."

The courts of the respective states might therefore have been securely trusted, with deciding all cases between man and man, whether citizens of the same state or of different states, or between foreigners and citizens, and indeed for ought I see every case that can arise under the constitution or laws of the United States, ought in the first instance to be tried in the court of the state, except those which might arise between states, such as respect ambassadors, or other public ministers, and perhaps such as call in question the claim of lands under grants from different states. The state courts would be under sufficient controul, if writs of error were allowed from the state courts to the supreme court of the union, according to the practice of the courts in England and of this state, on all cases in which the laws of the union are concerned, and perhaps to all cases in which a foreigner is a party.

This method would preserve the good old way of administering justice, would bring justice to every man's door, and preserve the inestimable right of trial by jury. It would be following, as near as our circumstances will admit, the practice of the courts in England, which is almost the only thing I would wish to copy in their government.

But as this system now stands, there is to be as many inferior courts as Congress may see fit to appoint, who are to be authorised to originate and in the first instance to try all the cases falling under the description of this article; there is no security that a trial by jury shall be had in these courts, but the trial here will soon become, as it is in Massachusetts' inferior courts, mere matter of form; for an appeal may be had to the supreme court on the whole merits. This court is to have power to determine in law and in equity, on the law and the fact, and this court is exalted above all other power in the government, subject to no controul, and so fixed as not to be removeable, but upon impeachment, which I shall hereafter shew, is much the same thing as not to be removeable at all.

To obviate the objections made to the judicial power it has been said, that the Congress, in forming the regulations and exceptions which they are authorised to make respecting the appellate jurisdiction, will make provision against all the evils which are apprehended from this article. On this I would remark, that this way of answering the objection made to the power, implies an admission that the power is in itself improper without restraint, and if so, why not restrict it in the first instance.

The just way of investigating any power given to a government, is to examine its operation supposing it to be put in exercise. If upon enquiry, it appears that the power, if exercised, would be prejudicial, it ought not to be given. For to answer objections made to a power given to a government, by saying it will never be exercised, is really admitting that the power ought not to be exercised, and therefore ought not to be granted.

3

A [MARYLAND] FARMER, NO. 6
1 Apr. 1788
Storing 5.1.89

Aristides asserts, "that *the inferior federal* courts, and the *State* courts will have *concurrent original* jurisdiction in all the enumerated cases, *wherein an appeal lies to the supreme federal court,* except only the cases created by, or under the proposed constitution."—By the second section of the third article, "The judicial power is to extend to all cases, in law and equity, arising under the *constitution,* or the LAWS of the United States; and to all controversies between citizens of *different* States, and the citizens of any of the United States, and the citizens, or subjects, of *foreign* States"; and by the eighth section of the first article, "The Congress are invested with *power* to levy and collect taxes, duties, imposts, and excises; and to make such *laws* as shall be necessary and proper for carrying into execution these powers." *Aristides* contends that a *federal* officer, say an excise officer, may be sued by a citizen in a *State* court (I suppose any county court as well as the supreme court) for an abuse of his authority; and with confidence he asserts, "That *no sound lawyer, of a good moral reputation* will maintain the contrary opinion"; and he treats with supercilious contempt the objection of want of remedy in a *State* court, and a trial by jury *for* the citizen *against* a *federal* officer, for an abuse of office, "as a ridiculous bugbear, fit only to alarm minds on which no science has ever dawned." Is it not evident that the jurisdiction in the cases *above-mentioned,* is *expressly* given to the *inferior federal* courts, with an appeal, both as to law and *fact,* to the *supreme federal* court?—Is it not clear that it was intended to keep the *federal* and *State* jurisdictions entirely separate? Were not the *subordinate federal* courts established to protect the continental revenue officers from the *State* jurisdictions?—If an action would lie *against* a *federal* officer in the *State* courts would it not blend and confound the *two* jurisdictions, and that too without any appeal from the *State* courts?—Is not the *supreme federal* court superior to the *State* courts? Is it not superior to the bill of rights, and the constitutions, of the several States?—If the *State* courts have *concurrent jurisdiction* with the *inferior federal* courts, that is, if any suit of which the *latter* has cognizance by the *new* government, may notwithstanding be instituted in the *former,* is it not self-evident that there may be *different* adjudications on the SAME question; and if decided in the *inferior federal* court with an appeal, if decided in a *State* court without any appeal, to the *supreme federal* court? What would be the effect of opposite decisions by two courts having concurrent jurisdiction?—If an action is commenced in a *State* court, *Aristides* thinks, and justly too, that thence there is no appeal to the *supreme federal* court, but only to their own high court of appeals, as heretofore. With confidence he maintains that as the jurisdiction of the *State* courts is *not* taken away by an *express* clause, or *necessary implication,* that they

will still have cognizance of those cases of which jurisdiction is given to the *inferior federal* courts. The *Farmer* believes there is not another lawyer, or Judge, *of sound judgment in the law,* in all America, that entertains a similar opinion.—The *Farmer* is so bold as to hazard his opinion, contrary to that of *Aristides,* that if a citizen of Georgia, or subject of Great-Britain, has any claim against a citizen of Maryland, or if he has any claim against them, that suits in such cases, after the establishment of the *national* government, can only be commenced and prosecuted in the *inferior federal* courts, because the *State* courts are ousted of their jurisdiction of those cases, by *necessary implication,* from the obvious motives for the establishment of the *federal judiciary,* and the evident absurdities that must flow from a *concurrent jurisdiction* in the SAME cases. Is it not absurd to suppose that the *national* government intended that the *State* courts should have jurisdiction to decide on the LAWS of the *United States,* whether consonant or repugnant to the *national constitution;* or whether the *federal* officers abuse their authority?—And yet the grave, the solemn, the didactic *Aristides* asserts, "That every *State* Judge will have a *right* to reject any *act* handed to him as a *law* of the United States, which HE may conceive repugnant to the constitution." How perverted or confused must be the head of that man who can seriously entertain so ridiculous an opinion! He can never claim from his knowledge of the *national,* or any other government to be one of the Judges of the most inferior of the inferior *federal courts—Risum teneatis.* A puisne Judge of a petty State (of Delaware, or Rhode-Island) to have a *right* to declare a LAW of the United States VOID? Will any *sound lawyer,* his moral reputation out of the question, risk his *legal* character so far as to maintain his assertion?—If *Aristides* has not too much pride to be convinced, if he has the candour he professes, or the legal or political knowledge he wishes the world to believe, he would not obstinately continue in error, but confess, how greatly he has misunderstood the *judiciary* system of the *national* government.

4

JAMES IREDELL, NORTH CAROLINA RATIFYING CONVENTION
28 July 1788
Elliot 4:147

. . . an appeal to the Supreme Court will not be allowed but in cases of great importance, where the object may be adequate to the expense. The Supreme Court may possibly be directed to sit alternately in different parts of the Union.

The propriety of having a Supreme Court in every government must be obvious to every man of reflection. There can be no other way of securing the administration of justice uniformly in the several states. There might be, otherwise, as many different adjudications on the same subject as there are states. It is to be hoped that, if this government be established, connections still more intimate than the present will subsist between the different states. The same measure of justice, therefore, as to the objects of their common concern, ought to prevail in all. A man in North Carolina, for instance, if he owed £ 100 here, and was compellable to pay it in good money, ought to have the means of recovering the same sum, if due to him in Rhode Island, and not merely the nominal sum, at about an eighth or tenth part of its intrinsic value. To obviate such a grievance as this, the Constitution has provided a tribunal to administer equal justice to all.

5

ARCHIBALD MACLAINE, NORTH CAROLINA
RATIFYING CONVENTION
29 July 1788
Elliot 4:162

But the gentleman seems to be most tenacious of the judicial power of the states. The honorable gentleman must know, that the doctrine of reservation of power not relinquished, clearly demonstrates that the judicial power of the states is not impaired. He asks, with respect to the trial by jury, "When the cause has gone up to the superior court, and the verdict is set aside, what benefit arises from having had a jury trial in the inferior court?" I would ask the gentleman, "What is the reason, that, on a special verdict or case agreed, the decision is left to the court?" There are a number of cases where juries cannot decide. When a jury finds the fact specially, or when it is agreed upon by the parties, the decision is referred to the court. If the law be against the party, the court decides against him; if the law be for him, the court judges accordingly. He, as well as every gentleman here, must know that, under the Confederation, Congress set aside juries. There was an appeal given to Congress: did Congress determine by a jury? Every party carried his testimony in writing to the judges of appeal, and Congress determined upon it.

The distinction between matters of law and of fact has not been sufficiently understood, or has been intentionally misrepresented. On a demurrer in law, in which the facts are agreed upon by the parties, the law arising thereupon is referred to the court. An inferior court may give an erroneous judgment; an appeal may be had from this court to the Supreme Federal Court, and a right decision had. This is an instance wherein it can have cognizance of matter of law solely. In cases where the existence of facts has been first disputed by one of the parties, and afterwards established as in a special verdict, the consideration of these facts, blended with the law, is left to the court. In such cases, inferior courts may decide contrary to justice and law, and appeals may be had to the Supreme Court. This is an instance wherein it may be said they have jurisdiction both as to law and fact. But where facts only are disputed, and where they are once established by a verdict,

the opinion of the judges of the Supreme Court cannot, I conceive, set aside these facts; for I do not think they have the power so to do by this Constitution.

6

UNITED STATES V. RAVARA
*27 Fed. Cas. 713, nos. 16,122, 16,122a
(C.C.D.Pa. 1793, 1794)*

(See 3.2.1, no. 36)

7

WISCART V. D'AUCHY
3 Dall. 321 (1796)

ELLSWORTH, Chief Justice.—The question, how far a statement of facts by the circuit court is conclusive, having been already argued in another cause, we are prepared to give an opinion upon that point; but will reserve for further consideration, the objection, that the present decree is not such a statement of facts as the law contemplates.

1. If causes of equity or admiralty jurisdiction are removed hither, accompanied with a statement of facts, but without the evidence, it is well; and the statement is conclusive as to all the facts which it contains. This is unanimously the opinion of the court.

2. If such causes are removed, with a statement of the facts, and also with the evidence—still, the statement is conclusive, as to all the facts contained in it. This is the opinion of the court; but not unanimously.

WILSON, Justice.—I consider the rule established by the second proposition to be of such magnitude, that being in the minority on the decision, I am desirous of stating, as briefly as I can, the principles of my dissent.

The decision must, indeed, very materially affect the jurisdiction of all the courts of the United States, particularly of the supreme court, as well as the general administration of justice. It becomes more highly important, as it respects the rights and pretensions of foreign nations, who are usually interested in causes of admiralty and maritime jurisdiction.

It appears, however, that two opinions have been formed on this question—how far those facts involved in the investigation of a cause of admiralty and maritime jurisdiction, that were given in evidence in the circuit court, should also appear in this court, on a writ of error or appeal? For my part, I concur in the opinion, that notwithstanding the provisions of the judicial act, an appeal is the natural and proper mode of removing an admiralty cause; and in that case, there can be no doubt, that all the testimony which was produced in the court below, should also be produced in this court. Such an appeal is expressly sanctioned by the constitution; it may, therefore, clearly, in the first view of the subject, be considered as the most regular process; and as there are not any words in the judicial act, restricting the power of proceeding by appeal, it must be regarded as still permitted and approved. Even, indeed, if a positive restriction existed by law, it would, in my judgment, be superseded by the superior authority of the constitutional provision.

The clauses in the act which more immediately relate to this subject, are the 21st and 22d sections. The material words are these: § 21. "From final decrees in a district court, in causes of admiralty and maritime jurisdiction, where the matter in dispute exceeds the sum or value of $300, exclusive of costs, an appeal shall be allowed to the next circuit court to be held in such district." § 22. "Final decrees and judgments in civil actions in a district court, where the matter in dispute exceeds the sum or value of $50, exclusive of costs, may be re-examined and reversed or affirmed in a circuit court, holden in the same district, upon a writ of error, whereto shall be annexed and returned therewith, at the day and place therein mentioned, an authenticated transcript of the record, and assignment of errors, and prayer for reversal, &c. And upon a like process, may final judgments and decrees in civil actions, and suits in equity, in a circuit court, brought there by original process, or removed there from courts of the several states, or removed there by appeal from a district court, where the matter in dispute exceeds the value of $2000, exclusive of costs, be re-examined and reversed or affirmed in the supreme court, &c."

Though the term "civil causes" is often descriptively applied, in contradistinction to "criminal causes;" yet, it is not uncommon to apply it, likewise, in contradistinction to causes of maritime and admiralty jurisdiction; and if we carefully compare the two sections to which I have referred, I think, the latter distinction will plainly appear to be the genuine object of the legislature. Thus, in the 21st section, provision is made for removing causes of admiralty and maritime jurisdiction, by appeal from the district to the circuit court; and immediately afterwards, in the 22d section, another provision is made for removing final decrees and judgments in civil actions, by writ of error from a district to a circuit court. Here, then, is a direct use of the term "civil actions," in contradistinction to "admiralty causes;" and, pursuing the distinct nature of the respective subjects, with technical precision, we find that an appeal is allowed in admiralty causes; and the remedy by writ of error is strictly confined, in this part of the section, at least, to civil actions.

There would, perhaps, be little difficulty in the case, if the act stopped here. But the 22d section, after mentioning a writ of error, proceeds to declare, that "upon a like process," the final judgments and decrees of the circuit court, in civil actions, and suits at equity, whether originally instituted there, or removed thither, from the state court; or by appeal from the district courts, may be re-examined in the supreme court: and it has been urged, that an admiralty cause is a civil suit, and that such a suit being removed by appeal to the circuit court, can only be finally transferred to this court, by a like process; that is,

by a writ of error. If, however, causes of admiralty jurisdiction are fairly excluded from the first member of the 22d section, that provides for a removal from the district to the circuit court, impartiality and consistency of construction must lead us likewise to exclude them from this member of the section, that provides for a removal from the circuit to the supreme court. By so doing, the two sections of the law can be reconciled; and by so doing, without including admiralty causes, every description of suit may be reasonably satisfied.

But if admiralty causes are not to be removed by writ of error from the circuit court, to which we see they may be transferred from the district court by appeal, it has been asked, how they are to be brought hither for final adjudication? It is true, the act of congress makes no provision on the subject; but it is equally true, that the constitution (which we must suppose to be always in the view of the legislature) had previously declared that in certain enumerated cases, including admiralty and maritime cases, "the supreme court shall have appellate jurisdiction, both as to law and fact, with such exceptions, and under such regulations, as the congress shall make." The appellate jurisdiction, therefore, flowed, as a consequence, from this source; nor had the legislature any occasion to do, what the constitution had already done. The legislature might, indeed, have made exceptions, and introduced regulations upon the subject; but as it has not done so, the case remains upon the strong ground of the constitution, which in general terms, and on general principles, provides and authorizes an appeal; the process that, in its very nature (as I have before remarked), implies a re-examination of the fact, as well as the law.

This construction, upon the whole, presents itself to my mind; not only as the natural result of a candid and connected consideration of the constitution and the act of congress; but as a position in our system of jurisprudence, essential to the security and the dignity of the United States. And if it is of moment to our domestic tranquillity and foreign relations, that causes of admiralty and maritime jurisdiction should, in point of fact as well as of law, have all the authority of the decision of our highest tribunal; and if, at the same time, so far from being prohibited, we find it sanctioned by the supreme law of the land, I think, the jurisdiction ought to be sustained.

ELLSWORTH, Chief Justice.—I will make a few remarks in support of the rule. The constitution, distributing the judicial power of the United States, vests in the supreme court, an original as well as an appellate jurisdiction. The original jurisdiction, however, is confined to cases affecting ambassadors, other public ministers and consuls, and those in which a state shall be a party. In all other cases, only an appellate jurisdiction is given to the court; and even the appellate jurisdiction is, likewise, qualified; inasmuch as it is given "with such exceptions, and under such regulations, as the congress shall make." Here, then, is the ground, and the only ground, on which we can sustain an appeal. If congress has provided no rule to regulate our proceedings, we cannot exercise an appellate jurisdiction; and if the rule is provided, we cannot depart from it. The question, therefore, on the constitutional point of an appellate jurisdiction, is simply, whether congress has established any rule for regulating its exercise?

It is to be considered, then, that the judicial statute of the United States speaks of an appeal and of a writ of error; but it does not confound the terms, nor use them promiscuously. They are to be understood, when used, according to their ordinary acceptation, unless something appears in the act itself, to control, modify or change the fixed and technical sense which they have previously borne. An appeal is a process of civil law origin, and removes a cause entirely; subjecting the fact, as well as the law, to a review and retrial: but a writ of error is a process of common-law origin, and it removes nothing for re-examination, but the law. Does the statute observe this obvious distinction? I think it does. In the 21st section, there is a provision for allowing an appeal in admiralty and maritime causes from the district to the circuit court; but it is declared, that the matter in dispute must exceed the value of $300, or no appeal can be sustained; and yet, in the preceding section, we find, that decrees and judgments in civil actions may be removed by writ of error from the district to the circuit court, though the value of the matter in dispute barely exceeds $50. It is unnecessary, however, to make any remark on this apparent diversity: the only question is, whether the civil actions here spoken of, include causes of admiralty and maritime jurisdiction? Now, the term civil actions would, from its natural import, embrace every species of suit, which is not of a criminal kind; and when it is considered, that the district court has a criminal as well as a civil jurisdiction, it is clear, that the term was used by the legislature, not to distinguish between admiralty causes and other civil actions, but to exclude the idea of removing judgments in criminal prosecutions, from an inferior to a superior tribunal. Besides, the language of the first member of the 22d section seems calculated to obviate every doubt. It is there said, that final *decrees* and judgments in civil actions in a district court may be removed into the circuit court, upon a writ of error; and since there cannot be a *decree* in the district court, in any case, except cases of admiralty and maritime jurisdiction, it follows, of course, that such cases must be intended, and that if they are removed at all, it can only be done by writ of error.

In this way, therefore, the appellate jurisdiction of the circuit court is to be exercised; but it remains to inquire, whether any provision is made for the exercise of the appellate jurisdiction of the supreme court; and I think, there is, by unequivocal words of reference. Thus, the 22d section of the act declares, that "upon a like process," that is, upon a writ of error, final judgments and decrees in civil actions (a description still employed in contradistinction to criminal prosecutions) and suits in equity, in the circuit court, may be here re-examined, and reversed or affirmed. Among the causes liable to be thus brought hither upon a writ of error, are such as had been previously removed into the circuit court, "by appeal from a district court," which can only be causes of admiralty and maritime jurisdiction.

It is observed, that a writ of error is a process more lim-

ited in its effects than an appeal; but whatever may be the operation, if an appellate jurisdiction can only be exercised by this court conformable to such regulations as are made by the congress, and if congress has prescribed a writ of error, and no other mode, by which it can be exercised, still, I say, we are bound to pursue that mode, and can neither make nor adopt another. The law may, indeed, be improper and inconvenient; but it is of more importance, for a judicial determination, to ascertain what the law is, than to speculate upon what it ought to be. If, however, the construction, that a statement of facts by the circuit court is conclusive, would amount to a denial of justice, would be oppressively injurious to individuals, or would be productive of any general mischief, I should then be disposed to resort to any other rational exposition of the law, which would not be attended with these deprecated consequences. But, surely, it cannot be deemed a denial of justice, that a man shall not be permitted to try his cause two or three times over. If he has one opportunity for the trial of all the parts of his case, justice is satisfied; and even if the decision of the circuit court had been made final, no denial of justice could be imputed to our government; much less, can the imputation be fairly made, because the law directs that in cases of appeal, part shall be decided by one tribunal, and part by another; the facts by the court below, and the law by this court. Such a distribution of jurisdiction has long been established in England.

Nor is there anything in the nature of a fact, which renders it impracticable or improper to be ascertained by a judge; and if there were, a fact could never be ascertained in this court, in matters of appeal. If, then, we are competent to ascertain a fact, when assembled here, I can discern no reason why we should not be equally competent to the task, when sitting in the circuit court; nor why it should be supposed, that a judge is more able, or more worthy, to ascertain the facts in a suit in equity (which, indisputably, can only be removed by writ of error), than to ascertain the facts in a cause of admiralty and maritime jurisdiction.

The statute has made a special provision, that the mode of proof, by oral testimony and examination of witnesses, shall be the same in all the courts of the United States, as well in the trial of causes in equity and of admiralty and maritime jurisdiction, as of actions at common law: but it was perceived, that although the personal attendance of witnesses could easily be procured in the district or circuit courts, the difficulty of bringing them from the remotest parts of the Union, to the seat of government, was insurmountable; and therefore, it became necessary, in every description of suits, to make a statement of the facts in the circuit court definitive, upon an appeal to this court.

If, upon the whole, the original constitutional grant of an appellate jurisdiction is to be enforced in the way that has been suggested, then all the testimony must be transmitted, reviewed, re-examined and settled here; great private and public inconvenience would ensue; and it was useless to provide that "the circuit courts should cause the facts on which they found their sentence or decree fully to appear upon the record."

But, upon the construction contained in the rule laid

down by the court, there cannot, in any case, be just cause of complaint, as to the question of fact, since it is ascertained by an impartial and enlightened tribunal; and, as to the question of law, the re-examination in this court is wisely meant, and calculated to preserve unity of principle, in the administration of justice throughout the United States.

On the 12th of August, the Chief Justice delivered the opinion of the court upon the point, whether there was, in this cause, such a statement of facts, as the legislature contemplated?

BY THE COURT.—The decree states, that certain conveyances are fraudulent; and had it stopped with that general declaration, some doubt might reasonably be entertained, whether it was not more properly an inference, than the statement of a fact; since fraud must always principally depend upon the *quo animo*. But the court immediately afterwards proceed to describe the fraud, or *quo animo*, declaring, that "the conveyances were intended to defraud the complainant, and to prevent his obtaining satisfaction for a just demand;" which is not an inference from a fact, but a statement of the fact itself. It is another fact, illustrative of this position, that "the grantee was a party and privy to the fraud."

We are, therefore, of opinion, that the circuit court have sufficiently caused the facts on which they decided, to appear from the pleadings and decree, in conformity to the act of congress.

The decree affirmed.

8

UNITED STATES v. MORE
3 Cranch 159 (1805)

February 13th. The CHIEF JUSTICE suggested a doubt, whether the appellate jurisdiction of this court extends to criminal cases.

February 22d. *Mason,* in support of the appellate jurisdiction of this court in criminal cases.—By the 1st section of the third article of the constitution, the judicial power of the United States is vested in one supreme court, and in such inferior courts as the congress may, from time to time, ordain and establish. By the 2d section, it is extended to all cases in law and equity, arising under the laws of the United States. This is a case in law, arising under the laws of the United States, and is, therefore, within that section.

"In all cases affecting ambassadors, other public ministers and consuls, and those in which a state shall be party, the supreme court shall have original jurisdiction. In all the other cases before mentioned, the supreme court shall have appellate jurisdiction, both as to law and fact, with such exceptions, and under such regulations, as the congress shall make." Congress has made no exception of criminal cases. I understand it to have been said by this court, that it is necessary that congress should have made

a regulation, to enable this court to exercise its appellate jurisdiction. Upon this point, I consider myself bound by the case of *Clarke v. Bazadone.* (1 Cr. 212.) It is clear, then, that this court has the jurisdiction, and the only question is, whether congress has made such a regulation as will enable this court to exercise it.

Such a regulation is contained in the 14th section of the judiciary act of 1789 (1 U. S. Stat. 81), which enacts, "that all the before-mentioned courts of the United States shall have power to issue writs of *scire facias, habeas corpus,* and all other writs, not specially provided for by statute, which may be necessary for the exercise of their respective jurisdictions, and agreeable to the principles and usages of law." The writ of error in a criminal case is a writ not provided for by statute, and necessary for the exercise of the appellate jurisdiction given to the supreme court by the constitution, and agreeable to the principles and usages of law. This court has, therefore, the power to issue it.

There is no reason why the writ of error should be confined to civil cases. A man's life, his liberty and his good name, are as dear to him as his property; and inferior courts are as liable to err in one case as in the other. There is nothing in the nature of the cases which should make a difference; nor is it a novel doctrine, that a writ of error should lie in a criminal case. They have been frequent in that country from which we have drawn almost all our forms of judicial proceedings. It is true, that it is expressly given by the act of congress of 1789, in civil cases only, but it does not thence follow, that it should be denied, in criminal.

MARSHALL, Ch. J.—If congress had erected inferior courts, without saying in what cases a writ of error or appeal should lie from such courts to this, your argument would be irresistible; but when the constitution has given congress power to limit the exercise of our jurisdiction, and to make regulations respecting its exercise; and congress, under that power, has proceeded to erect inferior courts, and has said in what cases a writ of error or appeal shall lie, an exception of all other cases is implied. And this court is as much bound by an implied as an express exception.

Mason.—When legislating over the district of Columbia, congress are bound by no constitution. If they are, they have violated it, by not giving us a republican form of government. The same observation will also apply to Louisiana.

The act of congress which gives a writ of error to the circuit court of this district, differs, in some respects, from that which gives the writ of error to the other courts of the United States. The words of the judiciary act of 1789, § 22, are, "and upon a like process (that is, by a writ of error, citation, &c.), may final judgments and decrees in civil actions, and suits in equity in a circuit court," &c., "be reversed or affirmed in the supreme court." But in the law concerning the district of Columbia, § 8 (2 U. S. Stat. 106), the expressions are, "that any final judgment, order or decree in said court, wherein the matter in dispute, exclusive of costs, shall exceed the value of one hundred dollars, may be re-examined, and reversed or affirmed in the supreme court of the United States, by writ of error or appeal, which shall be prosecuted in the same manner, under the same regulations, and the same proceedings shall be had therein, as is, or shall be, provided in the case of writs of error on judgments, or appeals upon orders or decrees rendered in the circuit court of the United States."

In this section, if the words respecting the value of the matter in dispute were excluded, a writ of error would clearly lie in a criminal case, under the general expression, any final judgment. Then do those words respecting the value, exclude criminal cases? Suppose, the court below had imposed a fine of more than $100, the case would have been within the express words of the act. So it would have been, if a penalty of more than $100 had been imposed by law.

But this court has exercised appellate jurisdiction in a criminal case. *United States* v. *Simms*, 1 Cr. 252.

MARSHALL, Ch. J.—No question was made, in that case, as to the jurisdiction. It passed *sub silentio*, and the court does not consider itself as bound by that case.

Mason.—But the traverser had able counsel, who did not think proper to make the objection.

March 2d, 1805. MARSHALL, Ch. J., delivered the opinion of the court as follows:—This is an indictment against the defendant, for taking fees, under color of his office, as a justice of the peace in the district of Columbia. A doubt has been suggested, respecting the jurisdiction of this court, in appeals or writs of error, from the judgments of the circuit court for that district, in criminal cases; and this question is to be decided, before the court can inquire into the merits of the case.

In support of the jurisdiction of the court, the attorney-general has adverted to the words of the constitution, from which he seemed to argue, that as criminal jurisdiction was exercised by the courts of the United States, under the description of "all cases in law and equity arising under the laws of the United States," and as the appellate jurisdiction of this court was extended to all enumerated cases, other than those which might be brought on originally, "with such exceptions, and under such regulations, as the congress shall make," that the supreme court possessed appellate jurisdiction in criminal, as well as civil cases, over the judgments of every court, whose decisions it would review, unless there should be some exception or regulation make by congress, which should circumscribe the jurisdiction conferred by the constitution.

This argument would be unanswerable, if the supreme court had been created by law, without describing its jurisdiction. The constitution would then have been the only standard by which its powers could be tested, since there would be clearly no congressional regulation or exception on the subject. But as the jurisdiction of the court has been described, it has been regulated by congress, and an affirmative description of its powers must be understood as a regulation, under the constitution, prohibiting the exercise of other powers than those described.

Thus, the appellate jurisdiction of this court, from the judgments of the circuit courts, is described affirmatively: no restrictive words are used. Yet, it has never been sup-

posed, that a decision of a circuit court could be reviewed, unless the matter in dispute should exceed the value of $2000. There are no words in the act, restraining the supreme court from taking cognisance of causes under that sum; their jurisdiction is only limited by the legislative declaration, that they may re-examine the decisions of the circuit court, where the matter in dispute exceeds the value of $2000. This court, therefore, will only review those judgments of the circuit court of Columbia, a power to re-examine which, is expressly given by law.

On examining the act "concerning the district of Columbia," the court is of opinion, that the appellate jurisdiction, granted by that act, is confined to civil cases. The words "matter in dispute," seem appropriated to civil cases, where the subject in contest has a value beyond the sum mentioned in the act. But in criminal cases, the question is the guilt or innocence of the accused. And although he may be fined upwards of $100, yet that is, in the eye of the law, a punishment for the offence committed, and not the particular object of the suit.

The writ of error, therefore, is to be dismissed, this court having no jurisdiction of the case.

9

DUROUSSEAU v. UNITED STATES

6 Cranch 307 (1810)

MARSHALL, Ch. J. delivered the opinion of the court, upon the question of jurisdiction, as follows:

This is the first of several writs of error to sundry judgments rendered by the court of the United States for the territory of Orleans.

The attorney-general having moved to dismiss them, because no writ of error lies from this court to that in any case, or, if in any case, not in such a case as this; the jurisdiction of this court becomes the first subject for consideration.

The act erecting Louisiana into two territories establishes a district court in the territory of Orleans, consisting of one judge who "shall, in all things, have and exercise the same jurisdiction and powers which are, by law, given to, or may be exercised by, the judge of Kentucky district."

On the part of the United States it is contended, that this description of the jurisdiction of the court of New Orleans does not imply a power of revision in this court similar to that which might have been exercised over the judgments of the district court of Kentucky; or, if it does, that a writ of error could not have been sustained to a judgment rendered by the district court of Kentucky, in such a case as this.

On the part of the plaintiffs it is contended, that this court possesses a constitutional power to revise and correct the judgments of inferior courts; or, if not so, that such a power is implied in the act by which the court of Orleans is created, taken in connection with the judicial act; and that a writ of error would lie to a judgment rendered by the court for the district of Kentucky, in such a case as this.

Every question originating in the constitution of the United States claims, and will receive, the most serious consideration of this court.

The third article of that instrument commences with organizing the judicial department. It consists of one supreme court, and of such inferior courts as congress shall, from time to time, ordain and establish. In these courts is vested the judicial power of the United States.

The first clause of the second section enumerates the cases to which that power shall extend.

The second clause of the same section distributes the powers previously described. In some few cases the supreme court possesses original jurisdiction. The constitution then proceeds thus: "In all the other cases before mentioned the supreme court shall have appellate jurisdiction, both as to law and fact, with such exceptions, and under such regulations, as the congress shall make."

It is contended that the words of the constitution vest an appellate jurisdiction in this court, which extends to every case not excepted by congress; and that if the court had been created without any express definition or limitation of its powers, a full and complete appellate jurisdiction would have vested in it, which must have been exercised in all cases whatever.

The force of this argument is perceived and admitted. Had the judicial act created the supreme court, without defining or limiting its jurisdiction, it must have been considered as possessing all the jurisdiction which the constitution assigns to it. The legislature would have exercised the power it possessed of creating a supreme court as ordained by the constitution: and, in omitting to exercise the right of excepting from its constitutional powers, would have necessarily left those powers undiminished. The appellate powers of this court are not given by the judicial act. They are given by the constitution. But they are limited and regulated by the judicial act, and by such other acts as have been passed on the subject.

When the first legislature of the union proceeded to carry the third article of the constitution into effect, they must be understood as intending to execute the power they possessed of making exceptions to the appellate jurisdiction of the supreme court. They have not, indeed, made these exceptions in express terms. They have not declared that the appellate power of the court shall not extend to certain cases; but they have described affirmatively its jurisdiction, and this affirmative description has been understood to imply a negative on the exercise of such appellate power as is not comprehended within it.

The spirit as well as the letter of a statute must be respected, and where the whole context of the law demonstrates a particular intent in the legislature to effect a certain object, some degree of implication may be called in to aid that intent.

It is upon this principle that the court implies a legislative exception from its constitutional appellate power in the legislative affirmative description of those powers.

Thus, a writ of error lies to the judgment of a circuit court, where the matter in controversy exceeds the value of 2,000 dollars. There is no express declaration that it will not lie where the matter in controversy shall be of less value. But the court considers this affirmative description as manifesting the intent of the legislature to except from its appellate jurisdiction all cases decided in the circuits where the matter in controversy is of less value, and implies negative words.

This restriction, however, being implied by the court, and that implication being founded on the manifest intent of the legislature, can be made only where that manifest intent appears. It ought not to be made for the purpose of defeating the intent of the legislature.

Having made these observations on the constitution, the court will proceed to consider the acts on which its jurisdiction, in the present case, depends; and, first, to inquire whether it could take cognisance of this case had the judgment been rendered by the district court of Kentucky.

The ninth section of the judicial act describes the jurisdiction of the district courts.

The tenth section declares that the district court of Kentucky, "besides the jurisdiction aforesaid," shall exercise jurisdiction over all other causes, except appeals and writs of error, which are made cognisable in a circuit court, and shall proceed therein in the same manner as a circuit court: "and writs of error and appeals shall lie from decisions *therein* to a supreme court, in the same causes as from a circuit court to the supreme court, and under the same regulations."

It is contended that this suit, which is an action on a bond conditioned to be void on the relanding of goods within the United States, is one of which the district courts have exclusive jurisdiction, and that a writ of error would not lie to a judgment given in such a case.

This court does not concur with the attorney-general in the opinion that a circuit court has no original jurisdiction in a case of this description. But it is unnecessary to say any thing on this point, because it is deemed clear that a writ of error is given in the case, however this question might be decided.

It would be difficult to conceive an intention in the legislature to discriminate between judgments rendered by the district court of Kentucky, while exercising the powers of a district court, and those rendered by the same court while exercising circuit powers, when it is demonstrated that the legislature makes no distinction in the cases from their nature and character. Causes of which the district courts have exclusive original jurisdiction are carried into the circuit courts, and then become the objects of the appellate jurisdiction of this court. It would be strange if, in a case where the powers of the two courts are united in one court, from whose judgments an appeal lies, causes, of which the district courts have exclusive original jurisdiction, should be excepted from the operation of the appellate power. It would require plain words to establish this construction.

But the court is of opinion that the words import no such meaning. The construction given by the attorney-general to the word "therein," as used in the last instance, in the clause of the tenth section, which has been cited, is too restricted. If, by force of this word, appeals were given only in those causes in which the district court acted as a circuit court exercising its original jurisdiction, the legislature would not have added the words "in the same causes as from a circuit court." This addition, if not an absolute repetition, could only serve to create doubt where no doubt would otherwise exist.

The plain meaning of these words is, that wherever the district court decides a cause which, if decided in a circuit court, either in an original suit, or on an appeal, would be subject to a writ of error from the supreme court, the judgment of the district court shall, in like manner, be subject to a writ of error.

This construction is, if possible, rendered still more obvious by the subsequent part of the same section, which describes the jurisdiction of the district court of Maine in the same terms. Apply the restricted interpretation to the word, "therein," in that instance, and the circuit court of Massachusetts would possess jurisdiction over causes in which the district court of Maine acted as a circuit court; and not over those in which it acted as a district court; a construction which is certainly not to be tolerated.

Had this judgment been rendered by the district court of Kentucky, the jurisdiction of this court would have been perfectly clear.

The remaining question admits of more doubt.

It is said that the words used in the law creating the court of Orleans, describe the jurisdiction and powers of that court, not of this, and that they give no express jurisdiction to this court. Hence it is inferred, with considerable strength of reasoning, that no jurisdiction exists.

If the question depended singly upon the reference made in the law creating the court for the territory of Orleans to the court of Kentucky, the correctness of this reasoning would perhaps be conceded. It would be found difficult to maintain the proposition, that investing the judge of the territory of Orleans with the same jurisdiction and powers which were exercised by the judge of Kentucky, imposed upon that jurisdiction the same restrictions arising from the power of a superior court, as were imposed on the court of Kentucky.

But the question does not depend singly on this reference; it is influenced by other very essential considerations.

Previous to the extension of the circuit system to the western states, district courts were erected in the states of Tennessee and Ohio, and their powers were described in the same terms with those which describe the powers of the court of Orleans. The same reference is made to the district court of Kentucky. Under these laws this court has taken jurisdiction of a cause brought by writ of error from Tennessee. It is true the question was not moved, and, consequently, still remains open. But can it be conceived to have been the intention of the legislature to except, from the appellate jurisdiction of the supreme court, all the causes decided in the western country, except those decided in Kentucky? Can such an intention be thought possible? Ought it to be inferred from ambiguous phrases?

The constitution here becomes all important. The constitution and the laws are to be construed together. It is to be recollected that the appellate powers of the supreme court are defined in the constitution, subject to such exceptions as congress may make. Congress has not expressly made any exceptions; but they are implied from the intent manifested by the affirmative description of its powers. It would be repugnant to every principle of sound construction, to imply an exception against the intent.

This question does not rest on the same principles as if there had been an express exception to the jurisdiction of this court, and its power, in this case, was to be implied from the intent of the legislature. The exception is to be implied from the intent, and there is, consequently, a much more liberal operation to be given to the words by which the courts of the western country have been created.

It is believed to be the true intent of the legislature to place those courts precisely on the footing of the court of Kentucky, in every respect, and to subject their judgments, in the same manner, to the revision of the supreme court. Otherwise the court of Orleans would, in fact, be a supreme court. It would possess greater and less restricted powers than the court of Kentucky, which is, in terms, an inferior court.

10

CHEROKEE NATION v. GEORGIA
5 Pet. 1 (1831)

(See 1.8.3 [Indians], no. 10)

11

JOSEPH STORY, COMMENTARIES ON THE CONSTITUTION 3:§§ 1696–1702, 1748–57, 1762–63, 1767–68
1833

---

§ 1696. The first remark arising out of this clause is, that, as the judicial power of the United States extends to all the cases enumerated in the constitution, it may extend to all such cases in any form, in which judicial power may be exercised. It may, therefore, extend to them in the shape of original, or appellate jurisdiction, or both; for there is nothing in the nature of the cases, which binds to the exercise of the one in preference to the other. But it is clear, from the language of the constitution, that, in one form or the other, it is absolutely obligatory upon congress, to vest all the jurisdiction in the national courts, in that class of cases at least, where it has declared, that it shall extend to *"all cases."*

§ 1697. In the next place, the jurisdiction, which is by the constitution to be exercised by the Supreme Court in an *original* form, is very limited, and extends only to cases affecting ambassadors, and other public ministers, and consuls, and cases, where a state is a party. And congress cannot constitutionally confer on it any other, or further original jurisdiction. This is one of the appropriate illustrations of the rule, that the affirmation of a power in particular cases, excludes it in all others. The clause itself would otherwise be wholly inoperative and nugatory. If it had been intended to leave it to the discretion of congress, to apportion the judicial power between the supreme and inferior courts, according to the will of that body, it would have been useless to have proceeded further, than to define the judicial power, and the tribunals, in which it should be vested. Affirmative words often, in their operation, imply a negative of other objects, than those affirmed; and in this case a negative, or exclusive sense, must be given to the words, or they have no operation at all. If the solicitude of the convention, respecting our peace with foreign powers, might induce a provision to be made, that the Supreme Court should have original jurisdiction in cases, which might be supposed to affect them; yet the clause would have proceeded no further, than to provide for such cases, unless some further restriction upon the powers of congress had been intended. The direction, that the Supreme Court shall have appellate jurisdiction in all cases, with such exceptions, as congress shall make, will be no restriction, unless the words are to be deemed exclusive of original jursidiction. And accordingly, the doctrine is firmly established, that the Supreme Court cannot constitutionally exercise any original jurisdiction, except in the enumerated cases. If congress should confer it, it would be a mere nullity.

§ 1698. But although the Supreme Court cannot exercise original jurisdiction in any cases, except those specially enumerated, it is certainly competent for congress to vest in any inferior courts of the United States original jurisdiction of all other cases, not thus specially assigned to the Supreme Court; for there is nothing in the constitution, which excludes such inferior courts from the exercise of such original jurisdiction. Original jurisdiction, so far as the constitution gives a rule, is co-extensive with the judicial power; and except, so far as the constitution has made any distribution of it among the courts of the United States, it remains to be exercised in an original, or appellate form, or both, as congress may in their wisdom deem fit. Now, the constitution has made no distribution, except of the original and appellate jurisdiction of the Supreme Court. It has no where insinuated, that the inferior tribunals shall have no original jurisdiction. It has no where affirmed, that they shall have appellate jurisdiction. Both are left unrestricted and undefined. Of course, as the judicial power is to be vested in the supreme and inferior courts of the Union, both are under the entire control and regulation of congress.

§ 1699. Indeed, it has been a matter of much question, whether the grant of original jurisdiction to the Supreme Court, in the enumerated cases, ought to be construed to give to that court exclusive original jurisdiction, even of those cases. And it has been contended, that there is nothing in the constitution, which warrants the conclusion, that it was intended to exclude the inferior courts of the Union from a concurrent original jurisdiction. The judiciary act of 1789, (ch. 20, § 11, 13,) has manifestly proceeded upon the supposition, that the jurisdiction was not exclusive;

but, that concurrent original jurisdiction in those cases might be vested by congress in inferior courts. It has been strongly intimated, indeed, by the highest tribunal, on more than one occasion, that the original jurisdiction of the Supreme Court in those cases is exclusive; but the question remains to this hour without any authoritative decision.

§ 1700. Another question of a very different nature is, whether the Supreme Court can exercise appellate jurisdiction in the class of cases, of which original jurisdiction is delegated to it by the constitution; in other words, whether the original jurisdiction excludes the appellate; and so, *e converso*, the latter implies a negative of the former. It has been said, that the very distinction taken in the constitution, between original and appellate jurisdiction, presupposes, that where the one can be exercised, the other cannot. For example, since the original jurisdiction extends to cases, where a state is a party, this is the proper form, in which such cases are to be brought before the Supreme Court; and, therfore, a case, where a state is a party, cannot be brought before the court, in the exercise of its appellate jurisdiction; for the affirmative here, as well as in the cases of original jurisdiction, includes a negative of the cases not enumerated.

§ 1701. If the correctness of this reasoning were admitted, it would establish no more, than that the Supreme Court could not exercise appellate jurisdiction in cases, where a state is a party. But it would by no means establish the doctrine, that the judicial power of the United States did not extend, in an appellate form, to such cases. The exercise of appellate jurisdiction is far from being limited, by the terms of the constitution, to the Supreme Court. There can be no doubt, that congress may create a succession of inferior tribunals, in each of which it may vest appellate, as well as original jurisdiction. This results from the very nature of the delegation of the judicial power in the constitution. It is delegated in the most general terms; and may, therefore, be exercised under the authority of congress, under every variety of form of original and appellate jurisdiction. There is nothing in the instrument, which restrains, or limits the power; and it must, consequently, subsist in the utmost latitude, of which it is in its nature susceptible. The result then would be, that, if the appellate jurisdiction over cases, to which a state is a party, could not, according to the terms of the constitution, be exercised by the Supreme Court, it might be exercised exclusively by an inferior tribunal. The soundness of any reasoning, which would lead us to such a conclusion, may well be questioned.

§ 1702. But the reasoning itself is not well founded. It proceeds upon the ground, that, because the character of the *party* alone, in some instances, entitles the Supreme Court to maintain original jurisdiction, without any reference to the nature of the case, therefore, the character of the *case*, which in other instances is made the very foundation of appellate jurisdiction, cannot attach. Now, that is the very point of controversy. It is not only not admitted, but it is solemnly denied. The argument might just as well, and with quite as much force, be pressed in the opposite direction. It might be said, that the appellate jurisdiction is expressly extended by the constitution to all cases in law and equity, arising under the constitution, laws, and treaties of the United States, and, therefore, in no such cases could the Supreme Court exercise original jurisdiction, even though a state were a party.

. . . . .

§ 1748. It would be difficult, and perhaps not desirable, to lay down any general rules in relation to the cases, in which the judicial power of the courts of the United States is exclusive of the state courts, or in which it may be made so by congress, until they shall be settled by some positive adjudication of the Supreme Court. That there are some cases, in which that power is exclusive, cannot well be doubted; that there are others, in which it may be made so by congress, admits of as little doubt; and that in other cases it is concurrent in the state courts, at least until congress shall have passed some act excluding the concurrent jurisdiction, will scarcely be denied. It seems to be admitted, that the jurisdiction of the courts of the United States is, or at least may be, made exclusive in all cases arising under the constitution, laws, and treaties of the United States; in all cases affecting ambassadors, other public ministers and consuls, in all cases (*in their character exclusive*) of admiralty and maritime jurisdiction; in controversies, to which the United States shall be a party; in controversies between two or more states; in controversies between a state and citizens of another state; and in controversies between a state and foreign states, citizens, or subjects. And it is only in those cases, where, previous to the constitution, state tribunals possessed jurisdiction, independent of national authority, that they can now constitutionally exercise a concurrent jurisdiction. Congress, indeed, in the Judiciary Act of 1789, (ch. 20, § 9, 11, 13,) have manifestly legislated upon the supposition, that, in all cases, to which the judicial power of the United States extends, they might rightfully vest exclusive jurisdiction in their own courts.

§ 1749. It is a far more difficult point, to affirm the right of congress to vest in any state court any part of the judicial power confided by the constitution to the national government. Congress may, indeed, permit the state courts to exercise a concurrent jurisdiction in many cases; but those courts then derive no authority from congress over the subject-matter, but are simply left to the exercise of such jurisdiction, as is conferred on them by the state constitution and laws. There are, indeed, many acts of congress, which permit jurisdiction over the offences therein described, to be exercised by state magistrates and courts; but this (it has been said by a learned judge,) is not, because such permission was considered to be necessary, under the constitution, to vest a concurrent jurisdiction in those tribunals; but because the jurisdiction was exclusively vested in the national courts by the judiciary act; and consequently could not be otherwise executed by the state courts. But, he has added, "for I hold it to be perfectly clear, that congress cannot confer jurisdiction upon any courts, but such as exist under the constitution and laws of the United States; although the state courts may exercise jurisdiction in cases authorized by the laws of the state, and not prohibited by the exclusive jurisdiction of the federal courts." This latter doctrine was positively affirmed by the Supreme Court in *Martin* v. *Hunter;* and indeed seems, upon general principles, indisputable. In that case, the court said, "congress cannot vest any portion of the judicial power of the United States, except in courts, ordained and established by itself."

§ 1750. In regard to jurisdiction over crimes committed against the authority of the United States, it has been held, that no part of this jurisdiction can, consistently with the constitution, be delegated to state tribunals. It is true, that congress has, in various acts, conferred the right to prosecute for offences, penalties, and forfeitures, in the state courts. But the latter have, in many instances, declined the jurisdiction, and asserted its unconstitutionality. And certainly there is, at the present time, a decided preponderance of judicial authority in the state courts against the authority of congress to confer the power.

§ 1751. In the exercise of the jurisdiction confided respectively to the state courts, and those courts of the United States, (where the latter have not appellate jurisdiction,) it is plain, that neither can have any right to interfere with, or control, the operations of the other. It has accordingly been settled, that no state court can issue an injunction upon any judgment in a court of the United States; the latter having an exclusive authority over its own judgments and proceedings. Nor can any state court, or any state legislature, annul the judgments of the courts of the United States, or destroy the rights acquired under them; nor in any manner deprive the Supreme Court of its appellate jurisdiction; nor in any manner interfere with, or control the process (whether mesne or final) of the courts of the United States; nor prescribe the rules or forms of proceeding, nor effect of process, in the courts of the United States; nor issue a mandamus to an officer of the United states, to compel him to perform duties, devolved on him by the laws of the United States. And although writs of *habeas corpus* have been issued by state judges, and state courts, in cases, where the party has been in custody under the authority of process of the courts of the United States, there has been considerable diversity of opinion, whether such an exercise of authority is constitutional; and it yet remains to be decided, whether it can be maintained.

§ 1752. Indeed, in all cases, where the judicial power of the United States is to be exercised, it is for congress alone to furnish the rules of proceeding, to direct the process, to declare the nature and effect of the process, and the mode, in which the judgments, consequent thereon, shall be executed. No state legislature, or state court, can have the slightest right to interfere; and congress are not even capable of delegating the right to them. They may authorize national courts to make general rules and orders, for the purpose of a more convenient exercise of their jurisdiction; but they cannot delegate to any state authority any control over the national courts.

§ 1753. On the other hand the national courts have no authority (in cases not within the appellate jurisdiction of the United States) to issue injunctions to judgments in the state courts; or in any other manner to interfere with their jurisdiction or proceedings.

§ 1754. Having disposed of these points, we may again

recur to the language of the constitution for the purpose of some farther illustrations. The language is, that "the Supreme Court shall have appellate jurisdiction, both as to law and fact, with such exceptions, and under such regulations, as the congress shall make."

§ 1755. In the first place, it may not be without use to ascertain, what is here meant by appellate jurisdiction; and what is the mode, in which it may be exercised. The essential criterion of appellate jurisdiction is, that it revises and corrects the proceedings in a cause already instituted, and does not create that cause. In reference to judicial tribunals, an appellate jurisdiction, therefore, necessarily implies, that the subject matter has been already instituted in, and acted upon, by some other court, whose judgment or proceedings are to be revised. This appellate jurisdiction may be exercised in a variety of forms, and indeed in any form, which the legislature may choose to prescribe; but, still, the substance must exist, before the form can be applied to it. To operate at all, then, under the constitution of the United States, it is not sufficient, that there has been a decision by some officer, or department of the United States; it might be by one clothed with judicial authority, and acting in a judicial capacity. A power, therefore, conferred by congress on the Supreme Court, to issue a mandamus to public officers of the United States generally, is not warranted by the constitution; for it is, in effect, under such circumstances, an exercise of original jurisdiction. But where the object is to revise a judicial proceeding, the mode is wholly immaterial; and a writ of *habeas corpus*, or mandamus, a writ of error, or an appeal, may be used, as the legislature may prescribe.

§ 1756. The most usual modes of exercising appellate jurisdiction, at least those, which are most known in the United States, are by a writ of error, or by an appeal, or by some process of removal of a suit from an inferior tribunal. An appeal is a process of civil law origin, and removes a cause, entirely subjecting the fact, as well as the law, to a review and a re-trial. A writ of error is a process of common law origin; and it removes nothing for re-examination, but the law. The former mode is usually adopted in cases of equity and admiralty jurisdiction; the latter, in suits at common law tried by a jury.

§ 1757. It is observable, that the language of the constitution is, that "the Supreme Court shall have appellate jurisdiction, *both as to law and fact.*" This provision was a subject of no small alarm and misconstruction at the time of the adoption of the constitution, as it was supposed to confer on the Supreme Court, in the exercise of its appellate jurisdiction, the power to review the decision of a jury in mere matters of fact; and thus, in effect, to destroy the validity of their verdict, and to reduce to a mere form the right of a trial by jury in civil cases. The objection was at once seized hold of by the enemies of the constitution; and it was pressed with an urgency and zeal, which were well nigh preventing its ratification. There is certainly some foundation, in the ambiguity of the language, to justify an interpretation, that such a review might constitutionally be within the reach of the appellate power, if congress should choose to carry it to that extreme latitude. But, practically speaking, there was not the slightest danger, that congress

would ever adopt such a course, even if it were within their constitutional authority; since it would be at variance with all the habits, feelings, and institutions of the whole country. At least it might be affirmed, that congress would scarcely take such a step, until the people were prepared to surrender all the great securities of their civil, as well as of their political rights and liberties; and in such an event the retaining of the trial by jury would be a mere mockery. The real object of the provision was to retain the power of reviewing the fact, as well as the law, in cases of admiralty and maritime jurisdiction. And the manner, in which it is expressed, was probably occasioned by the desire to avoid the introduction of the subject of a trial by jury in civil cases, upon which the convention were greatly divided in opinion.

. . . . .

§ 1762. These views, however reasonable they may seem to considerate minds, did not wholly satisfy the popular opinion; and as the objection had a vast influence upon public opinion, and amendments were proposed by various state conventions on this subject, congress at its first session, under the guidance of the friends of the constitution, proposed an amendment, which was ratified by the people, and is now incorporated into the constitution. It is in these words. "In suits at common law, where the value in controversy shall exceed twenty dollars, the right of a trial by jury shall be preserved. And no fact tried by a jury shall be otherwise re-examined in any court of the United States, than according to the rules of the common law." This amendment completely struck down the objection; and has secured the right of a trial by jury, in civil cases, in the fullest latitude of the common law. Like the other amendments, proposed by the same congress, it was coldly received by the enemies of the constitution, and was either disapproved by them, or drew from them a reluctant acquiescence. It weakened the opposition by taking away one of the strongest points of attack upon the constitution. Still it is a most important and valuable amendment; and places upon the high ground of constitutional right the inestimable privilege of a trial by jury in civil cases, a privilege scarcely inferior to that in criminal cases, which is conceded by all to be essential to political and civil liberty.

§ 1763. Upon a very recent occasion the true interpretation and extent of this amendment came before the Supreme Court for decision, in a case from Louisiana, where the question was, whether the Supreme Court could entertain a motion for a new trial, and re-examine the facts tried by a jury, that being the practice under the local law, and there being an act of congress, authorizing the courts of the United States in Louisiana to adopt the local practice, with certain limitations. The Supreme Court held, that no authority was given by the act to re-examine the facts; and if it had been, an opinion was intimated of the most serious doubts of its constitutionality.

. . . . .

§ 1767. The appellate jurisdiction is to be "with such exceptions, and under such regulations, as the congress shall prescribe." But, here, a question is presented upon the construction of the constitution, whether the appellate jurisdiction attaches to the Supreme Court, subject to be withdrawn and modified by congress; or, whether an act of congress is necessary to confer the jurisdiction upon the court. If the former be the true construction, then the entire appellate jurisdiction, if congress should make no exceptions or regulations, would attach *proprio vigore* to the Supreme Court. If the latter, then, notwithstanding the imperative language of the constitution, the Supreme Court is lifeless, until congress have conferred power on it. And if congress may confer power, they may repeal it. So that the whole efficiency of the judicial power is left by the constitution wholly unprotected and inert, if congress shall refrain to act. There is certainly very strong grounds to maintain, that the language of the constitution meant to confer the appellate jurisdiction absolutely on the Supreme Court, independent of any action by congress; and to require this action to divest or regulate it. The language, as to the original jurisdiction of the Supreme Court, admits of no doubt. It confers it wihout any action of congress. Why should not the same language, as to the appellate jurisdiction, have the same interpretation? It leaves the power of congress complete to make exceptions and regulations; but it leaves nothing to their inaction. This construction was asserted in argument at an earlier period of the constitution. It was at that time denied; and it was held by the Supreme Court, that, if congress should provide no rule to regulate the proceedings of the Supreme Court, it could not exercise any appellate jurisdiction. That doctrine, however, has, upon more mature deliberation, been since overturned; and it has been asserted by the Supreme Court, that, if the judicial act (of 1789) had created the Supreme Court, without defining, or limiting its jurisdiction, it must have been considered, as possessing all the jurisdiction, which the constitution assigns to it. The legislature could have exercised the power possessed by it of creating a Supreme Court, as ordained by the constitution; and, in omitting to exercise the right of excepting from its constitutional powers, would have nec-

essarily left those constitutional powers undiminished. The appellate powers of the Supreme Court are not given by the judicial act (of 1789). They are given by the constitution. But they are limited, and regulated by that act, and other acts on the same subject. And where a rule is provided, all persons will agree, that it cannot be departed from.

§ 1768. It should be added, that, while the jurisdiction of the courts of the United States is almost wholly under the control of the regulating power of congress, there are certain incidental powers, which are supposed to attach to them, in common with all other courts, when duly organized, without any positive enactment of the legislature. Such are the power of the courts over their own officers, and the power to protect them and their members from being disturbed in the exercise of their functions.

SEE ALSO:

Generally 3.2.1; Amend. VII
Luther Martin, Letters, no. 4, 19 Mar. 1788, Essays 361–62
Edmund Randolph, Virginia Ratifying Convention,
    10 June 1788, Elliot 3:205
William Lancaster, North Carolina Ratifying Convention,
    30 July 1788, Elliot 4:214
Alexander Contee Hanson, Remarks, 1788, Pamphlets 237–39
United States v. *Ravara*, 2 Dall. 297 (C.C.D.Pa. 1793)
Syndics of Brooks v. *Wayman*, 3 Martin 9 (La. 1813)
Hunter v. *Martin*, 4 Munf. 1 (Va. 1813)
Miller v. *Nicholls*, 4 Wheat. 311 (1819)
Smith v. *Jackson*, 22 Fed. Cas. 575, no. 13,064 (C.C.N.D.N.Y.
    1825)
James Kent, Commentaries 1:292–309 (1826)
Weston v. *City Council of Charleston*, 2 Pet. 449 (1829)
William Rawle, A View of the Constitution of the United States
    241–42, 252 (2d ed. 1829)
Dennie v. *Harris*, 9 Pick. 364 (Mass. 1830)
New York v. *New Jersey*, 5 Pet. 284 (1831)

Article 3, Section 2, Clause 3

The Trial of all Crimes, except in Cases of Impeachment, shall be by Jury; and such Trial shall be held in the State where the said Crimes shall have been committed; but when not committed within any State, the Trial shall be at such Place or Places as the Congress may by Law have directed.

1

DECLARATION OF INDEPENDENCE
4 July 1776

For depriving us in many cases, of the benefits of Trial by Jury:—For transporting us beyond Seas to be tried for pretended offences. . . .

2

JAMES MADISON TO EDMUND RANDOLPH
10 Mar. 1784
Papers 8:4

2. The analogy of the laws throughout the States, and particularly the uniformity of trial by Juries of the vicinage, seem to obviate the capital objections agst. removal to the State where the offence is charged. In the instance of contiguous States a removal of the party accused from one to the other must often be a less grievance, than what happens within the same State when the place of residence & the place where the offence is laid are at distant extremities. The transportation to G. B. seems to have been reprobated on very different grounds: it would have deprived the accused of the privilege of trial by jury *of the vicinage* as well as of the use of his witnesses, and have exposed him to trial in a place where he was not even alledged to have ever made himself obnoxious to it; not to mention the danger of unfairness arising from the circumstances which produced the regulation.

3

RECORDS OF THE FEDERAL CONVENTION

[*2:144, 173; Committee of Detail, IV*]
That Trials for Criml. Offences be in the State where the Offe was comd—by Jury. . . .

. . . . .

Crimes shall be tried in the State, in which they shall be committed; and The Trial of them all Criml Offences,— except in Cases of Impeachment— shall be by Jury.

[2:187; Madison, 6 Aug.]

Sect. 4. The trial of all criminal offences (except in cases of impeachment) shall be in the State where they shall be committed; and shall be by Jury.

[2:433; Mason, 27 Aug.]

The trial of all crimes, except in case of impeachment shall be in the Superior Court of that State where the offence shall have been committed in such manner as the Congress shall by law direct except that the trial shall be by a jury. But when the crime shall not have been committed within any one of the United States the trial shall be at such place and in such manner as Congress shall by law direct, except that such trial shall also be by a jury.

[2:438; Madison, 28 Aug.]

Sect. 4—was so amended nem: con: as to read "The trial of all crimes (except in cases of impeachment) shall be by jury, and such trial shall be held in the State where the said crimes shall have been committed; but when not committed within any State, then the trial shall be at such place or places as the Legislature may direct". The object of this amendment was to provide for trial by jury of offences committed out of any State.

[2:576; Committee of Style]

Sect. 4. The trial of all crimes (except in cases of impeachments) shall be by jury and such trial shall be held in the State where the said crimes shall have been committed; but when not committed within any State then the trial shall be at such place or places as the Legislature may direct.

[2:587; Madison, 12 Sept.]

Mr. Williamson, observed to the House that no provision was yet made for juries in Civil cases and suggested the necessity of it.

Mr. Gorham. It is not possible to discriminate equity cases from those in which juries are proper. The Representatives of the people may be safely trusted in this matter.

Mr. Gerry urged the necessity of Juries to guard agst. corrupt Judges. He proposed that the Committee last appointed should be directed to provide a clause for securing the trial by Juries.

Col: Mason perceived the difficulty mentioned by Mr. Gorham. The jury cases cannot be specified. A general principle laid down on this and some other points would be sufficient. He wished the plan had been prefaced with a Bill of Rights, & would second a Motion if made for the purpose—It would give great quiet to the people; and with the aid of the State declarations, a bill might be prepared in a few hours.

Mr Gerry concurred in the idea & moved for a Committee to prepare a Bill of Rights. Col: Mason 2ded the motion.

Mr. Sherman. was for securing the rights of the people where requisite. The State Declarations of Rights are not repealed by this Constitution; and being in force are sufficient—There are many cases where juries are proper which cannot be discriminated. The Legislature may be safely trusted.

[2:601; Committee of Style]

The trial of all crimes, except in cases of impeachment, shall be by jury; and such trial shall be held in the state where the said crimes shall have been committed; but when not committed within any state, the trial shall be at such place or places as the Congress may by law have directed.

[2:628; Madison, 15 Sept.]

Art III. sect. 2. parag: 3. Mr. Pinkney & Mr. Gerry moved to annex to the end. "And a trial by jury shall be preserved as usual in civil cases."

Mr. Gorham. The constitution of Juries is different in different States and the trial itself is *usual* in different cases in different States,

Mr. King urged the same objections

Genl. Pinkney also. He thought such a clause in the Constitution would be pregnant with embarrassments

The motion was disagreed to nem: con:

[2:635; King, 15 Sept.]

The Judiciary will be a Star Chamber.

[2:640; Mason, 15 Sept.]

There is no declaration of any kind, for preserving the liberty of the press or the trial by jury in civil cases;

4

RICHARD HENRY LEE TO EDMUND RANDOLPH
16 Oct. 1787
Letters 2:454

It is the more unfortunate that this great security of human rights, the trial by jury, should be weakened in this system, as power is unnecessarily given, in the second section of the third article, to call people from their own country, in all cases of controversy about property between citizens of different states and foreigners, to be tried in a distant court where the Congress may sit; for although inferior congressional courts *may*, for the above purpose, be instituted in the different states, yet this is a matter altogether in the pleasure of the new legislature; so that if they please not to institute them, or if they do not regulate the right of appeal, the people will be exposed to endless oppression, and the necessity of submitting to pay unjust demands rather than follow suitors, through great expense, to far distant tribunals, and to be determined upon there, as it may be, without a jury.

5

JAMES WILSON, STATE HOUSE SPEECH
6 Oct. 1787
Pamphlets 157

Another objection that has been fabricated against the new constitution, is expressed in this disingenuous form—"the trial by jury is abolished in civil cases." I must be excused, my fellow citizens, if, upon this point, I take advantage of my professional experience, to detect the futility of the assertion. Let it be remembered, then, that the business of the foederal constitution was not local, but general—not limited to the views and establishments of a single state, but co-extensive with the continent, and comprehending the views and establishments of thirteen independent sovereignties. When, therefore, this subject was in discussion, we were involved in difficulties, which pressed on all sides, and no precedent could be discovered to direct our course. The cases open to a jury, differed in the different states; it was therefore impracticable, on that ground, to have made a general rule. The want of uniformity would have rendered any reference to the practice of the states idle and useless: and it could not, with any propriety, be said, that "the trial by jury shall be as heretofore:" since there has never existed any foederal system of jurisprudence, to which the declaration could relate. Besides, it is not in all cases that the trial by jury is adopted in civil questions: for causes depending in courts of admiralty, such as relate to maritime captures, and such as are agitated in the courts of equity, do not require the intervention of that tribunal. How, then, was the line of discrimination to be drawn? The convention found the task too difficult for them; and they left the business as it stands—in the fullest confidence, that no danger could possibly ensue, since the proceedings of the supreme court are to be regulated by the congress, which is a faithful representation of the people: and the oppression of government is effectually barred, by declaring that in all criminal cases, the trial by jury shall be preserved.

6

FEDERAL FARMER, NO. 2
9 Oct. 1787
Storing 2.8.16

Under one general government alone, there could be but one judiciary, one supreme and a proper number of inferior courts. I think it would be totally impracticable in this case to preserve a due administration of justice, and the real benefits of the jury trial of the vicinage,—there are now supreme courts in each state in the union; and a great number of county and other courts subordinate to each supreme court—most of these supreme and inferior courts are itinerant, and hold their sessions in different parts every year of their respective states, counties and districts—with all these moving courts, our citizens, from the vast extent of the country must travel very considerable distances from home to find the place where justice is administered. I am not for bringing justice so near to individuals as to afford them any temptation to engage in law suits; though I think it one of the greatest benefits in a good government, that each citizen should find a court of justice within a reasonable distance, perhaps, within a day's travel of his home; so that, without great inconveniences and enormous expences, he may have the advantages of his witnesses and jury—it would be impracticable to derive these advantages from one judiciary—the one supreme court at most could only set in the centre of the union, and move once a year into the centre of the eastern and southern extremes of it—and, in this case, each citizen, on an average, would travel 150 or 200 miles to find this court—that, however, inferior courts might be properly placed in the different counties, and districts of the union, the appellate jurisdiction would be intolerable and expensive.

7

FEDERAL FARMER, NO. 3
10 Oct. 1787
Storing 2.8.41

The trial by jury is secured only in those few criminal cases, to which the federal laws will extend—as crimes committed on the seas, against the laws of nations, treason, and counterfeiting the federal securities and coin: But even in these cases, the jury trial of the vicinage is not secured—particularly in the large states, a citizen may be tried for a crime committed in the state, and yet tried in some states 500 miles from the place where it was committed; but the jury trial is not secured at all in civil causes. Though the convention have not established this trial, it is to be hoped that congress, in putting the new system into execution, will do it by a legislative act, in all cases in which it can be done with propriety. Whether the jury trial is not excluded [from] the supreme judicial court, is an important question. By Art. 3. Sect. 2. all cases affecting ambassadors, other public ministers, and consuls, and in those cases in which a state shall be party, the supreme court shall have jurisdiction. In all the other cases before mentioned, the supreme court shall have appellate jurisdiction, both as to *law and fact*, with such exception, and under such regulations, as the congress shall make. By court is understood a court consisting of judges; and the idea of a jury is excluded. This court, or the judges, are to have jurisdiction on appeals, in all the cases enumerated, as to law and fact; the judges are to decide the law and try the fact, and the trial of the fact being assigned to the judges by the constitution, a jury for trying the fact is excluded; however, under the exceptions and powers to make regulations, congress may, perhaps introduce the jury, to try the fact in most necessary cases.

8

A DEMOCRATIC FEDERALIST
17 Oct. 1787
Storing 3.5.5–9

The second and most important objection to the federal plan, which Mr. Wilson pretends to be made *in a disingenuous form*, is the entire *abolition of the trial by jury in civil cases*. It seems to me that Mr. Wilson's pretended answer, is much more *disingenuous* than the objection itself, which I maintain to be strictly founded in fact. He says "that the cases open to trial by jury differing in the different States, it was therefore impracticable to have made a general rule." This answer is extremely futile, because a reference might easily have been made to the *common law of England*, which obtains through every State, and cases in the maritime and civil law courts would of course have been excepted. I must also directly contradict Mr. Wilson when he asserts that there is no trial by jury in the courts of chancery—It cannot be unknown to a man of his high professional learning, that whenever a difference arises about a matter of fact in the courts of equity in America or England, the fact is sent down to the courts of common law to be tried by a jury, and it is what the lawyers call a *feigned issue*. This method will be impracticable under the proposed form of judicial jurisdiction for the United States.

But setting aside the equivocal answers of Mr. Wilson, I have it in my power to prove that under the proposed Federal Constitution, *the trial of facts in civil cases by a jury of the Vicinage* is entirely and effectually abolished, and will be absolutely impracticable. I wish the learned gentleman had explained to us what is meant by the *appellate* jurisdiction as to law and *fact* which is vested in the superior court of the United States? As he has not thought proper to do it, I shall endeavour to explain it to my fellow citizens, regretting at the same time that it has not been done by a man whose abilities are so much superior to mine. The word *appeal*, if I understand it right, in its proper legal signification includes the *fact* as well as the *law*, and precludes every idea of a trial by jury—It is a word of *foreign growth*, and is only known in England and America in those courts which are governed by the civil or ecclesiastical law of the *Romans*. Those courts have always been considered in England as a grievance, and have all been established by the usurpations of the *ecclesiastical* over the *civil* power. It is well known that the courts of chancery in England were formerly entirely in the hands of *ecclesiastics*, who took advantage of the strict forms of the common law, to introduce a foreign mode of jurisprudence under the specious name of *Equity*. Pennsylvania, the freest of the American States has wisely rejected this establishment, and knows not even the name of a court of chancery—And in fact, there can not be any thing more absurd than a distinction between LAW and EQUITY. It might perhaps have suited those barbarous times when the law of England, like almost every other science, was perplexed with quibbles and *Aristotelian* distinctions, but it would be shameful to keep it up in these more enlightened days. At any rate, it seems to me that there is much more *equity* in a trial by jury, than in an appellate jurisdiction from the fact.

An *appeal* therefore is a thing unknown to the common law. Instead of an appeal from facts, it admits of a second, or even third trial by different juries, and mistakes in points of *law*, are rectified by superior courts in the form of a *writ of error*—and to a mere common lawyer, unskilled in the forms of the *civil law* courts, the words *appeal from law and fact*, are mere nonsense, and unintelligible absurdity.

But even supposing that the superior court of the United States had the authority to try facts by *juries of the vicinage*, it would be impossible for them to carry it into execution. It is well known that the supreme courts of the different states, at stated times in every year, go round the different counties of their respective states to try issues of fact, which is called *riding the circuits*. Now, how is it possible that the supreme continental court, which we will suppose to consist at most of five or six judges, can travel at least twice in every year, through the different counties of America, from New Hampshire to Kentuckey and from Kentuckey to Georgia, to try facts by juries of the vicinage. Common sense will not admit of such a supposition. I am therefore right in my assertion, that *trial by jury in civil cases, is, by the proposed constitution entirely done away, and effectually abolished.*

Let us now attend to the consequences of this enormous innovation, and daring encroachment, on the liberties of the citizens. Setting aside the oppression, injustice, and partiality that may take place in the trial of questions of property between man and man, we will attend to one single case, which is well worth our consideration. Let us remember that all cases arising under the new constitution, and all matters between *citizens of different states*, are to be submitted to the new jurisdiction. Suppose therefore, that the military officers of congress, by a wanton abuse of power, imprison the free citizens of America, suppose the excise or revenue officers (as we find in Clayton's Reports, page 44 Ward's case)—that a constable, having a warrant to search for stolen goods, pulled down the clothes of a bed in which there was a woman, and searched under her shift,—suppose, I say, that they commit similar, or greater indignities, in such cases a trial by jury would be our safest resource, heavy damages would at once punish the offender, and deter others from committing the same: but what satisfaction can we expect from a lordly court of justice, always ready to protect the officers of government against the weak and helpless citizen, and who will perhaps sit at the distance of many hundred miles from the place where the outrage was committed?—What refuge shall we then have to shelter us from the iron hand of arbitrary power?—O! my fellow citizens, think of this while it is yet time, and never consent to part with the glorious privilege of trial by jury, but with your lives.

9

CINCINNATUS, NO. 1
1 Nov. 1787
Storing 6.1.7–8

Let us suppose then, that what has happened, may happen again: That a patriotic printer, like Peter Zenger, should incur the resentment of our new rulers, by publishing to the world, transactions which they wish to conceal. If he should be prosecuted, if his judges should be as desirous of punishing him, *at all events,* as the judges were to punish Peter Zenger, what would his innocence or his virtue avail him? This constitution is so admirably framed for tyranny, that, by clear construction, the judges might put the verdict of a jury out of the question. Among the cases in which the court is to have appellate jurisdiction, are—controversies, to which the United States are a party:—In this appellate jurisdiction, the judges are to determine, *both law and fact.* That is, the court is both judge and jury. The attorney general then would have only to move a question of law in the court below, to ground an appeal to the supreme judicature, and the printer would be delivered up to the mercy of his judges. Peter Zenger's case will teach us, what mercy he might expect. Thus, if the president, vice-president, or any officer, or favorite of state, should be censured in print, he might effectually deprive the printer, or author, of his trial by jury, and subject him to something, that will probably very much resemble the Star Chamber of former times. The freedom of the press, the sacred palladium of public liberty, would be pulled down;—all useful knowledge on the conduct of government would be withheld from the people—the press would become subservient to the purposes of bad and arbitrary rulers, and imposition, not information, would be its object.

The printers would do well, to publish the proceedings of the judges, in Peter Zenger's case—they would do well to publish lord Mansfield's conduct in, the King against Woodfall;—that the public mind may be properly warned of the consequences of agreeing to a constitution, which provides no security for the freedom of the press, and leaves it controversial at least—whether in matter of libels against any of our intended rulers; the printer would even have the security of trial by jury. Yet it was the jury only, that saved Zenger, it was a jury only, that saved Woodfall, it can only be a jury that will save any future printer from the fangs of power.

10

CINCINNATUS, NO. 2
8 Nov. 1787
Storing 6.1.13–15

I come now to the consideration of the trial by jury in civil cases. And here you have, indeed, made use of your professional knowledge—But you did not tell the people that your profession was always to advocate one side of a question—to place it in the most favorable, though false, light—to rail where you could not reason—to pervert where you could not refute—and to practice every fallacy on your hearers—to mislead the understanding and pervert judgement. In light of this professional practice, you make a refutable objection of your own, and then triumphantly refute it. The objection you impute to your opponents is—the trial by jury is abolished in civil cases. This you call a disingenuous form—and truly it is very much so on your part and of your own fabrication. The objection in its true form is, that—trial by jury is not secured in civil cases. To this objection, you could not possibly give an answer; you therefore ingenuously coined one to which you could make a plausible reply. We expected, and we had a right to expect, that such an inestimable privilege as this would have been secured—that it would not have been left dependent on the arbitrary exposition of future judges, who, when it may suit the arbitrary views of the ruling powers will explain it away at pleasure. We may expect Tressellians, Jeffree's and Mansfield's here, and if they should not be native with us, they may possibly be imported.

But, if taken even on your own ground it is not so clearly tenable. In point of legal construction, the trial by jury does seem to be taken away in civil cases. It is a law maxim, that the expression of one part is an exclusion of the other. In legal construction therefore, the preservation of trial by jury in criminal, is an exclusion of it in civil cases. Why else should it be mentioned at all? Either it followed of course in both cases, or it depended on being stipulated. If the first, then the stipulation was nugatory—if the latter, then it was in part given up. Therefore, either we must suppose the Convention did a nugatory thing; or that by the express mention of jury in criminal, they meant to exclude it in civil cases. And that they did intend to exclude it, seems the more probable, as in the appeal they have taken special care to render the trial by jury of no effect by expressly making the court judges both of law and fact. And though this is subjected to the future regulation of Congress, yet it would be absurd to suppose, that the regulation meant its annihilation. We must therefore conclude, that in appeals the trial by jury is expressly taken away, and in original process it is by legal implication taken away in all civil cases.

Here then I must repeat—that you ought to have stated

fairly to the people, that the trial by jury was not secured; that they might know what, it was they were to consent to; and if knowing it, they consented, the blame could not fall on you. Before they decide, however, I will take leave to lay before them the opinion of the great and revered Judge Lord Camden, whose authority is, I hope, at least equal to that of Mr. Wilson.—"There is, says he, scarce any matter of challenge allowed to the judge, but several to the jurors and many of them may be removed without any reason alledged." This seems to promise as much impartiality as human nature will admit, and absolute perfection is not attainable, I am afraid, either in judge or jury or any thing else. The trial by [jury in] our country, is in my opinion, the great bulwark of freedom, and for certain, the admiration of all foreign writers and nations. The last writer of any distinguished note, upon the principles of government, the celebrated Montesquieu, is in raptures with this peculiar perfection in the English policy. From juries running riot, if I may [say] so, and acting wildly at particular seasons, I cannot conclude, like some Scottish Doctors of our law and constitutions, that their power should be lessened. This would, to use the words of the wise, learned, and intrepid Lord Chief Justice Vaughan, be—"a strange newfangled conclusion, after a trial so celebrated for so many hundreds of years."

Such are the opinions of Lord Camden and Vaughan, and multitudes of the first names, both English and other foreigners[,] might be cited, who bestow unbounded approbation on this best of all human modes for protecting, life, liberty, and property.

11

THE ADDRESS AND REASONS OF DISSENT OF
THE MINORITY OF THE CONVENTION OF
PENNSYLVANIA TO THEIR CONSTITUENTS
18 Dec. 1787

Storing 3.11.38–41

The judicial power, under the proposed constitution, is founded on the well-known principles of the *civil law*, by which the judge determines both on law and fact, and appeals are allowed from the inferior tribunals to the superior, upon the whole question; so that *facts* as well as *law*, would be re-examined, and even new facts brought forward in the court of appeals; and to use the words of a very eminent Civilian—"The cause is many times another thing before the court or appeals, than what it was at the time of the first sentence."

That this mode of proceeding is the one which must be adopted under this constitution, is evident from the following circumstances:—1st. That the trial by jury, which is the grand characteristic of the common law, is secured by the constitution, only in criminal cases.—2d. That the appeal from both *law* and *fact* is expressly established, which

is utterly inconsistent with the principles of the common law, and trials by jury. The only mode in which an appeal from law and fact can be established, is, by adopting the principles and practice of the civil law; unless the United States should be drawn into the absurdity of calling and swearing juries, merely for the purpose of contradicting their verdicts, which would render juries contemptible and worse than useless.—3d. That the courts to be established would decide on all cases *of law and equity*, which is a well known characteristic of the civil law, and these courts would have conusance not only of the laws of the United States and of treaties, and of cases affecting ambassadors, but of all cases of *admiralty and maritime jurisdiction*, which last are matters belonging exclusively to the civil law, in every nation in Christendom.

Not to enlarge upon the loss of the invaluable right of trial by an unbiassed jury, so dear to every friend of liberty, the monstrous expence and inconveniences of the mode of proceedings to be adopted, are such as will prove intolerable to the people of this country. The lengthy proceedings of the civil law courts in the chancery of England, and in the courts of Scotland and France, are such that few men of moderate fortune can endure the expence of; the poor man must therefore submit to the wealthy. Length of purse will too often prevail against right and justice. For instance, we are told by the learned judge *Blackstone,* that a question only on the property of an ox, of the value of *three* guineas, originating under the civil law proceedings in Scotland, after many interlocutory orders and sentences below, was carried at length from the court of sessions, the highest court in that part of Great Britain, by way of *appeal* to the house of lords, *where* the question of law and fact was finally determined. He adds, that no pique or spirit could in the court of king's bench or common pleas at Westminster, have given continuance to such a cause for a tenth part of the time, nor have cost a twentieth part of the expence. Yet the costs in the courts of king's bench and common pleas in England, are infinitely greater than those which the people of this country have ever experienced. We abhor the idea of losing the transcendant privilege of trial by jury, with the loss of which, it is remarked by the same learned author, that in Sweden, the liberties of the commons were extinguished by an aristocratic senate; and that *trial by jury* and the liberty of the people went out together. At the same time we regret the intolerable delay, the enormous expences and infinite vexation to which the people of this country will be exposed from the voluminous proceedings of the courts of civil law, and especially from the appellate jurisdiction, by means of which a man may be drawn from the utmost boundaries of this extensive country to the seat of the supreme court of the nation to contend, perhaps with a wealthy and powerful adversary. The consequence of this establishment will be an absolute confirmation of the power of aristocratical influence in the courts of justice: for the common people will not be able to contend or struggle against it.

Trial by jury in criminal cases may also be excluded by declaring that the libeller for instance shall be liable to an action of debt for a specified sum; thus evading the common law prosecution by indictment and trial by jury. And the common course of proceeding against a ship for breach of revenue laws by information (which will be classed among civil causes) will at the civil law be within the resort of a court, where no jury intervenes. Besides, the benefit of jury trial, in cases of a criminal nature, which cannot be evaded, will be rendered of little value, by calling the accused to answer far from home; there being no provision that the trial be by a jury of the neighbourhood or country. Thus an inhabitant of Pittsburgh, on a charge of crime committed on the banks of the Ohio, may be obliged to defend himself at the side of the Delaware, and so *vice versa*. To conclude this head: we observe that the judges of the courts of Congress would not be independent, as they are not debarred from holding other offices, during the pleasure of the president and senate, and as they may derive their support in part from fees, alterable by the legislature.

12

LUTHER MARTIN, GENUINE INFORMATION 1788

Storing 2.4.93–94

Thus, Sir, *jury trials*, which have ever been the *boast* of the English constitution, which have been by our several *State constitutions* so *cautiously secured* to us—*jury trials* which have so long been considered the *surest barrier* against *arbitrary power*, and the *palladium* of *liberty*,—with the *loss* of *which* the *loss* of our *freedom* may be dated, are *taken away* by the proposed form of government, not *only* in a *great variety* of questions between *individual* and *individual*, but in *every case* whether *civil* or *criminal* arising *under the laws* of the United States, or the *execution* of those laws.—It is *taken away* in *those very cases* where of *all others* it is *most essential for our liberty*, to have it *sacredly guarded* and *preserved*, in *every case*, whether *civil* or *criminal*, between *government* and *its officers* on the one part, and the *subject* or *citizen* on the other.—Nor was this the effect of inattention, nor did it arise from any real difficulty in establishing and securing jury trials by the proposed constitution, if the convention had wished so to do: but the *same reason* influenced *here* as in the case of the establishment of inferior courts; as they could not trust *State Judges*, so would they not confide in *State juries*.—They alledged that the general government and the State governments would always be at variance; that the citizens of the different States would enter into the views and interests of their respective States, and therefore ought not to be trusted in determining causes in which the general government was any way interested, without giving the general government an opportunity, if it disapproved the verdict of the jury, to appeal, and to have the *facts examined into again* and *decided upon* by *its own judges*, on whom it was thought a reliance might be had by the general government, they being appointed under its authority.

Thus, Sir, in consequence of this *appellate jurisdiction* and its *extension to facts* as well as to law, every *arbitrary act* of the general government, and every *oppression* of all those *variety of officers* appointed under its authority for the *collection* of *taxes, duties, impost, excise,* and other *purposes,* must be *submitted* to by the *individual,* or must be *opposed* with *little prospect* of *success,* and almost *a certain prospect of ruin,* at least in those cases where the *middle* and *common class* of citizens are interested: Since to *avoid* that *oppression,* or to *obtain redress,* the application must be made to one of the courts of the United States—by good fortune should this application be in the *first* instance attended with success, and should damages be recovered equivalent to the injury sustained, an *appeal* lies to the *supreme court,* in which case the citizen must at once give up his cause, or he must attend to it at the distance of perhaps more than a thousand miles from the place of his residence, and must take measures to procure before that court on the appeal all the evidence necessary to support his action, which even if ultimately prosperous must be attended with a *loss of time,* a *neglect of business,* and an *expense* which will be *greater* than the *original grievance,* and *to which* men in *moderate* circumstances would be *utterly unequal.*

13

JAMES IREDELL, MARCUS, ANSWERS TO MR. MASON'S OBJECTIONS TO THE NEW CONSTITUTION 1788

Pamphlets 361–62

In respect to the trial by jury in civil cases, it must be observed it is a mistake to suppose that such a trial takes place in all civil cases now. Even in the common law courts, such a trial is only had where facts are disputed between the parties, and there are even some facts triable by other methods. In the Chancery and Admiralty Courts, in many of the States, I am told they have no juries at all. The States in these particulars differ very much in their practice from each other. A general declaration therefore to preserve the trial by jury in all civil cases would only have produced confusion, so that the courts afterwards in a thousand instances would not have known how to have proceeded.—If they had added, "as heretofore accustomed," that would not have answered the purpose, because there has been no uniform custom about it.—If therefore the Convention had interfered, it must have been by entering into a detail highly unsuitable to a fundamental constitution of government; if they had pleased some States they must have displeased others by innovating upon the modes of administering justice perhaps endeared to them by habit, and agreeable to their settled conviction of propriety. As this was the case it appears to me it was infinitely better, rather than endanger everything by attempting too much, to leave this complicated business of detail to the regulation of the future Legislature, where it can be adjusted coolly and at ease, and upon full and exact information. There is no danger of the trial by jury being rejected, when so justly a favorite of the whole people. The representatives of the people surely can have no interest in making themselves odious, for the mere pleasure of being hated, and when a member of the House of Representatives is only sure of being so for two years, but must continue a citizen all his life, his interest as a citizen, if he is a man of common sense, to say nothing of his being a man of common honesty, must ever be uppermost in his mind. We know the great influence of the monarchy in the British government, and upon what a different tenure the Commons there have their seats in Parliament from that prescribed to our representatives. We know also they have a large standing army. It is in the power of the Parliament, if they dare to exercise it, to abolish the trial by jury altogether. But woe be to the man who should dare to attempt it. It would undoubtedly produce an insurrection, that would hurl every tyrant to the ground who attempted to destroy that great and just favorite of the English nation. We certainly shall be always sure of this guard at least upon any such act of folly or insanity in our representatives. They soon would be taught the consequence of sporting with the feelings of a free people. But when it is evident that such an attempt cannot be rationally apprehended, we have no reason to anticipate unpleasant emotions of that nature. There is indeed little probability that any degree of tyranny which can be figured to the most discolored imagination as likely to arise out of our government, could find an interest in attacking the trial by jury in civil cases;—and in criminal ones, where no such difficulties intervene as in the other, and where there might be supposed temptations to violate the personal security of a citizen, it is sacredly preserved.

14

Federal Farmer, no. 15
18 Jan. 1788
Storing 2.8.190–93

As the trial by jury is provided for in criminal causes, I shall confine my observations to civil causes—and in these, I hold it is the established right of the jury by the common law, and the fundamental laws of this country, to give a general verdict in all cases when they chuse to do it, to decide both as to law and fact, whenever blended together in the issue put to them. Their right to determine as to facts will not be disputed, and their right to give a general verdict has never been disputed, except by a few judges and lawyers, governed by despotic principles. Coke, Hale, Holt, Blackstone, De Lome, and almost every other legal or political writer, who has written on the subject, has uniformly asserted this essential and important right of the jury. Juries in Great-Britain and America have universally practised accordingly. Even Mansfield, with all his wishes

about him, dare not directly avow the contrary. What fully confirms this point is, that there is no instance to be found, where a jury was ever punished for finding a general verdict, when a special one might, with propriety, have been found. The jury trial, especially politically considered, is by far the most important feature in the judicial department in a free country; and the right in question is far the most valuable part, and the last that ought to be yielded, of this trial. Juries are constantly and frequently drawn from the body of the people, and freemen of the country; and by holding the jury's right to return a general verdict in all cases sacred, we secure to the people at large, their just and rightful controul in the judicial department. If the conduct of judges shall be severe and arbitrary, and tend to subvert the laws, and change the forms of government, the jury may check them, by deciding against their opinions and determinations, in similar cases. It is true, the freemen of a country are not always minutely skilled in the laws, but they have common sense in its purity, which seldom or never errs in making and applying laws to the condition of the people, or in determining judicial causes, when stated to them by the parties. The body of the people, principally, bear the burdens of the community; they of right ought to have a controul in its important concerns, both in making and executing the laws, otherwise they may, in a short time, be ruined. Nor is it merely this controul alone we are to attend to: the jury trial brings with it an open and public discussion of all causes, and excludes secret and arbitrary proceedings. This, and the democratic branch in the legislature, as was formerly observed, are the means by which the people are let into the knowledge of public affairs—are enabled to stand as the guardians of each others rights, and to restrain, by regular and legal measures, those who otherwise might infringe upon them. I am not unsupported in my opinion of the value of the trial by jury; not only British and American writers, but De Lome, and the most approved foreign writers, hold it to be the most valuable part of the British constitution, and indisputably the best mode of trial ever invented.

It was merely by the intrigues of the popish clergy, and of the Norman lawyers, that this mode of trial was not used in maritime, ecclesiastical, and military courts, and the civil law proceedings were introduced; and, I believe, it is more from custom and prejudice, than for any substantial reasons, that we do not in all the states establish the jury in our maritime as well as other courts.

In the civil law process the trial by jury is unknown; the consequence is, that a few judges and dependant officers, possess all the power in the judicial department. Instead of the open fair proceedings of the common law, where witnesses are examined in open court, and may be cross examined by the parties concerned—where council is allowed, &c. we see in the civil law process judges alone, who always, long previous to the trial, are known and often corrupted by ministerial influence, or by parties. Judges once influenced, soon become inclined to yield to temptations, and to decree for him who will pay the most for their partiality. It is, therefore, we find in the Roman, and almost all governments, where judges alone possess the judicial powers and try all cases, that bribery has prevailed.

This, as well as the forms of the courts, naturally lead to secret and arbitrary proceedings—to taking evidence secretly—exparte, &c. to perplexing the cause—and to hasty decisions:—but, as to jurors, it is quite impracticable to bribe or influence them by any corrupt means; not only because they are untaught in such affairs, and possess the honest characters of the common freemen of a country; but because it is not, generally, known till the hour the cause comes on for trial, what persons are to form the jury.

But it is said, that no words could be found by which the states could agree to establish the jury-trial in civil causes. I can hardly believe men to be serious, who make observations to this effect. The states have all derived judicial proceedings principally from one source, the British system; from the same common source the American lawyers have almost universally drawn their legal information. All the states have agreed to establish the trial by jury, in civil as well as in criminal causes. The several states, in congress, found no difficulty in establishing it in the Western Territory, in the ordinance passed in July 1787. We find, that the several states in congress, in establishing government in that territory, agreed, that the inhabitants of it, should always be entitled to the benefit of the trial by jury. Thus, in a few words, the jury trial is established in its full extent; and the convention with as much ease, have established the jury trial in criminal cases. In making a constitution, we are substantially to fix principles.—If in one state, damages on default are assessed by a jury, and in another by the judges—if in one state jurors are drawn out of a box, and in another not—if there be other trifling variations, they can be of no importance in the great question. Further, when we examine the particular practices of the states, in little matters in judicial proceedings, I believe we shall find they differ near as much in criminal processes as in civil ones. Another thing worthy of notice in this place—the convention have used the word equity, and agreed to establish a chancery jurisdiction; about the meaning and extent of which, we all know, the several states disagree much more than about jury trials—in adopting the latter, they have very generally pursued the British plan; but as to the former, we see the states have varied, as their fears and opinions dictated.

15

DEBATE IN MASSACHUSETTS RATIFYING CONVENTION
30 Jan. 1788
2 Elliot 109–14

MR. HOLMES. Mr. President, I rise to make some remarks on the paragraph under consideration, which treats of the judiciary power.

It is a maxim universally admitted, that the safety of the subject consists in having a right to a trial as free and impartial as the lot of humanity will admit of. Does the Constitution make provision for such a trial? I think not; for in a criminal process, a person shall not have a right to insist on a trial in the vicinity where the fact was committed, where a jury of the peers would, from their local situation, have an opportunity to form a judgment of the *character* of the person charged with the crime, and also to judge of the *credibility* of the witnesses. There a person must be tried by a jury of strangers; a jury who *may be* interested in his conviction; and where he *may*, by reason of the distance of his residence from the place of trial, be incapable of making such a defence as he is, in justice, entitled to, and which he could avail himself of, if his trial was in the same county where the crime is said to have been committed.

These circumstances, as horrid as they are, are rendered still more dark and gloomy, as there is no provision made in the Constitution to prevent the attorney-general from filing information against any person, whether he is indicted by the grand jury or not; in consequence of which the most innocent person in the commonwealth may be taken by virtue of a warrant issued in consequence of such information, and dragged from his home, his friends, his acquaintance, and confined in prison, until the next session of the court, which has jurisdiction of the crime with which he is charged, (and how frequent those sessions are to be we are not yet informed of,) and after long, tedious, and painful imprisonment, though acquitted on trial, may have no possibility to obtain any kind of satisfaction for the loss of his liberty, the loss of his time, great expenses, and perhaps cruel sufferings.

But what makes the matter still more alarming is, that the mode of criminal process is to be pointed out by Congress, and they have no constitutional check on them, except that the trial is to be by a *jury:* but who this jury is to be, how qualified, where to live, how appointed, or by what rules to regulate their procedure, we are ignorant of as yet: whether they are to live in the county where the trial is; whether they are to be chosen by certain districts, or whether they are to be appointed by the sheriff *ex officio;* whether they are to be for one session of the court only, or for a certain term of time, or for good behavior, or during pleasure, are matters which we are entirely ignorant of as yet.

The mode of trial is altogether indetermined; whether the criminal is to be allowed the benefit of counsel; whether he is to be allowed to meet his accuser face to face; whether he is to be allowed to confront the witnesses, and have the advantage of cross-examination, we are not yet told.

These are matters of by no means small consequence; yet we have not the smallest constitutional security that we shall be allowed the exercise of these privileges, neither is it made certain, in the Constitution, that a person charged with the crime shall have the privilege of appearing before the court or jury which is to try him.

On the whole, when we fully consider this matter, and fully investigate the powers granted, explicitly given, and specially delegated, we shall find Congress possessed of powers enabling them to institute judicatories little less inauspicious than a certain tribunal in Spain, which has long been the disgrace of Christendom: I mean that diabolical institution, the *Inquisition*.

What gives an additional glare of horror to these gloomy circumstances is the consideration, that Congress have to ascertain, point out, and determine, what kind of punishments shall be inflicted on persons convicted of crimes. They are nowhere restrained from inventing the most cruel and unheard-of punishments, and annexing them to crimes; and there is no constitutional check on them, but that *racks* and *gibbets* may be amongst the most mild instruments of their discipline.

There is nothing to prevent Congress from passing laws which shall compel a man, who is accused or suspected of a crime, to furnish evidence against himself, and even from establishing laws which shall order the court to take the charge exhibited against a man for truth, unless he can furnish evidence of his innocence.

I do not pretend to say Congress *will* do this; but, sir, I undertake to say that Congress (according to the powers proposed to be given them by the Constitution) *may* do it; and if they do not, it will be owing *entirely*—I repeat it, it will be owing *entirely*—to the goodness of the men, and not in the *least degree* owing to the goodness of the Constitution.

The framers of our state constitution took particular care to prevent the General Court from authorizing the judicial authority to issue a warrant against a man for a crime, unless his being guilty of the crime was supported by oath or affirmation, prior to the warrant being granted; why it should be esteemed so much more safe to intrust Congress with the power of enacting laws, which it was deemed so unsafe to intrust our state legislature with, I am unable to conceive.

Mr. GORE observed, in reply to Mr. Holmes, that it had been the uniform conduct of those in opposition to the proposed form of government, to determine, in every case where it was possible that the administrators thereof could do wrong, that they would do so, although it were demonstrable that such wrong would be against their own honor and interest, and productive of no advantage to themselves. On this principle alone have they determined that the trial by jury would be taken away in civil cases; when it had been clearly shown, that no words could be adopted, apt to the situation and customs of each state in this particular. Jurors are differently chosen in different states, and in point of qualification the laws of the several states are very diverse; not less so in the causes and disputes which are entitled to trial by jury. What is the result of this? That the laws of Congress may and will be conformable to the local laws in this particular, although the Constitution could not make a universal rule equally applying to the customs and statutes of the different states. Very few governments (certainly not this) can be interested in depriving the people of trial by jury, in questions of *meum et tuum*. In criminal cases alone are they interested to have the trial under their own control; and, in such cases, the Constitution expressly stipulates for trial by jury; but then, says the gentleman from Rochester, (Mr. Holmes,) to the safety of life it is indispensably necessary the trial of crimes should be in the vicinity; and the vicinity is construed to

mean county; this is very incorrect, and gentlemen will see the impropriety, by referring themselves to the different local divisions and districts of the several states. But further, said the gentleman, the idea that the jury coming from the neighborhood, and knowing the character and circumstances of the party in trial, is promotive of justice, on reflection will appear not founded in truth. If the jury judge from any other circumstances but what are part of the cause in question, they are not impartial. The great object is to determine on the real merits of the cause, uninfluenced by any personal considerations; if, therefore, the jury could be perfectly ignorant of the person in trial, a just decision would be more probable. From such motives did the wise Athenians so constitute the famed Areopagus, that, when in judgment, this court should sit at midnight, and in total darkness, that the decision might be on the thing, and not on the person. Further, said the gentleman, it has been said, because the Constitution does not expressly provide for an indictment by grand jury in criminal cases, therefore some officer under this government will be authorized to file informations, and bring any man to jeopardy of his life, and indictment by grand jury will be disused. If gentlemen who pretend such fears will look into the constitution of Massachusetts, they will see that no provision is therein made for an indictment by grand jury, or to oppose the danger of an attorney-general filing informations; yet no difficulty or danger has arisen to the people of this commonwealth from this defect, if gentlemen please to call it so. If gentlemen would be candid, and not consider that, wherever Congress may possibly abuse power, they certainly will, there would be no difficulty in the minds of any in adopting the proposed Constitution.

Mr. DAWES said, he did not see that the right of trial by jury was taken away by the article. The word *court* does not, either by a popular or technical construction, exclude the use of a jury to try facts. When people, in common language, talk of a trial at the *Court* of Common Pleas, or the Supreme Judicial *Court*, do they not include all the branches and members of such court—the *jurors* as well as the judges? They certainly do, whether they mention the jurors expressly or not. Our state legislators have construed the word *court* in the same way; for they have given appeals from a justice of peace to the Court of Common Pleas, and from thence to the Supreme Court, without saying any thing of the jury; but in cases which, almost time out of mind, have been tried without jury, there the jurisdiction is given expressly to the justices of a particular court, as may be instanced by suits upon the absconding act, so called.

Gentlemen have compared the article under consideration to that power which the British claimed, and we resisted, at the revolution; namely, the power of trying the Americans without a jury. But surely there was no parallel in the cases; it was criminal cases in which they attempted to make this abuse of power. Mr. D. mentioned one example of this, which, though young, he well remembered; and that was the case of Nickerson, the pirate, who was tried without a jury, and whose judges were the governors of Massachusetts and of some neighboring provinces, together with Admiral Montague, and some gentlemen of distinction. Although this trial was without a jury, yet, as it was a trial upon the civil law, there was not so much clamor about it as otherwise there might have been; but still it was disagreeable to the people, and was one of the then complaints. But the trial by jury was not attempted to be taken from civil causes. It was no object of power, whether one subject's property was lessened, while another's was increased; nor can it be now an object with the federal legislature. What interest can they have in constituting a judiciary, to proceed in civil causes without a trial by jury? In criminal causes, by the proposed government, there must be a jury. It is asked, Why is not the Constitution as explicit in securing the right of jury in civil as in criminal cases? The answer is, Because it was out of the power of the Convention. The several states differ so widely in their modes of trial, some states using a jury in causes wherein other states employ only their judges, that the Convention have very wisely left it to the federal legislature to make such regulations as shall, as far as possible, accommodate the whole. Thus our own state constitution authorizes the General Court to erect judicatories, but leaves the nature, number, and extent of them, wholly to the discretion of the legislature. The bill of rights, indeed, secures the trial by jury, in civil causes, except in cases where a contrary practice has obtained. Such a clause as this some gentlemen wish were inserted in the proposed Constitution, but such a clause would be abused in that Constitution, as has been clearly stated by the honorable gentleman from Charlestown, (Mr. Gorham,) because the "exception of all cases where a jury have not heretofore been used," would include almost all cases that could be mentioned, when applied to all the states, for they have severally differed in the kinds of causes where they have tried without a jury.

16

GEORGE WASHINGTON TO LAFAYETTE
28 April 1788
Documentary History 4:601–2

For example, there was not a member in the convention, I believe, who had the least objection to what is contended for by the Advocates for a *Bill of Rights* and *Tryal by Jury*. The first, where the people evidently retained every thing which they did not in express terms give up, was considered nugatory as you will find to have been more fully explained by Mr. Wilson and others:—And as to the second, it was only the difficulty of establishing a mode which should not interfere with the fixed modes of any of the States, that induced the Convention to leave it, as a matter of future adjustment.

17

ALEXANDER HAMILTON, FEDERALIST, NO. 83,
558–74
28 May 1788

The objection to the plan of the convention, which has met with most success in this state, and perhaps in several of the other states, is *that* relative to *the want of a constitutional provision* for the trial by jury in civil cases. The disingenuous form in which this objection is usually stated, has been repeatedly adverted to and exposed; but continues to be pursued in all the conversations and writings of the opponents of the plan. The mere silence of the constitution in regard to *civil causes*, is represented as an abolition of the trial by jury; and the declamations to which it has afforded a pretext, are artfully calculated to induce a persuasion that this pretended abolition is complete and universal; extending not only to every species of civil, but even to *criminal causes*. To argue with respect to the latter, would, however, be as vain and fruitless, as to attempt the serious proof of the *existence* of *matter,* or to demonstrate any of those propositions which by their own internal evidence force conviction, when expressed in language adapted to convey their meaning.

With regard to civil causes, subtleties almost too contemptible for refutation, have been adopted to countenance the surmise that a thing, which is only *not provided for,* is entirely *abolished.* Every man of discernment must at once perceive the wide difference between *silence* and *abolition.* But as the inventors of this fallacy have attempted to support it by certain *legal maxims* of interpretation, which they have perverted from their true meaning, it may not be wholly useless to explore the ground they have taken.

The maxims on which they rely are of this nature, "a specification of particulars is an exclusion of generals"; or, "the expression of one thing is the exclusion of another." Hence, say they, as the constitution has established the trial by jury in criminal cases, and is silent in respect to civil, this silence is an implied prohibition of trial by jury in regard to the latter.

The rules of legal interpretation are rules of *common sense,* adopted by the courts in the construction of the laws. The true test therefore, of a just application of them, is its conformity to the source from which they are derived. This being the case, let me ask if it is consistent with reason or common sense to suppose, that a provision obliging the legislative power to commit the trial of criminal causes to juries, is a privation of its right to authorise or permit that mode of trial in other cases? Is it natural to suppose, that a command to do one thing, is a prohibition to the doing of another, which there was a previous power to do, and which is not incompatible with the thing commanded to be done? If such a supposition would be unnatural and unreasonable, it cannot be rational to maintain that an injunction of the trial by jury in certain cases is an interdiction of it in others.

A power to constitute courts, is a power to prescribe the mode of trial; and consequently, if nothing was said in the constitution on the subject of juries, the legislature would be at liberty either to adopt that institution, or to let it alone. This discretion in regard to criminal causes is abridged by the express injunction of trial by jury in all such cases; but it is of course left at large in relation to civil causes, there being a total silence on this head. The specification of an obligation to try all criminal causes in a particular mode, excludes indeed the obligation or necessity of employing the same mode in civil causes, but does not abridge *the power* of the legislature to exercise that mode if it should be thought proper. The pretence therefore, that the national legislature would not be at full liberty to submit all the civil causes of federal cognizance to the determination of juries, is a pretence destitute of all just foundation.

From these observations, this conclusion results, that the trial by jury in civil cases would not be abolished, and that the use attempted to be made of the maxims which have been quoted, is contrary to reason and common sense, and therefore not admissible. Even if these maxims had a precise technical sense, corresponding with the ideas of those who employ them upon the present occasion, which, however, is not the case, they would still be inapplicable to a constitution of government. In relation to such a subject, the natural and obvious sense of its provisions, apart from any technical rules, is the true criterion of construction.

Having now seen that the maxims relied upon will not bear the use made of them, let us endeavour to ascertain their proper use and true meaning. This will be best done by examples. The plan of the convention declares that the power of congress or in other words of the *national legislature*, shall extend to certain enumerated cases. This specification of particulars evidently excludes all pretension to a general legislative authority; because an affirmative grant of special powers would be absurd as well as useless, if a general authority was intended.

In like manner, the judicial authority of the federal judicatures, is declared by the constitution to comprehend certain cases particularly specified. The expression of those cases marks the precise limits beyond which the federal courts cannot extend their jurisdiction; because the objects of their cognizance being enumerated, the specification would be nugatory if it did not exclude all ideas of more extensive authority.

These examples might be sufficient to elucidate the maxims which have been mentioned, and designate the manner in which they should be used. But that there may be no possibility of misapprehension upon this subject I shall add one case more, to demonstrate the proper use of these maxims, and the abuse which has been made of them.

Let us suppose that by the laws of this state, a married woman was incapable of conveying her estate, and that the legislature, considering this as an evil, should enact that she might dispose of her property by deed executed in the presence of a magistrate. In such a case there can be no doubt but the specification would amount to an exclusion of any other mode of conveyance; because the woman having no previous power to alienate her property, the specification determines the particular mode which she is, for that purpose, to avail herself of. But let us further suppose that in a subsequent part of the same act it should be declared that no woman should dispose of any estate of a determinate value without the consent of three of her nearest relations, signified by their signing the deed; could it be inferred from this regulation that a married woman might not procure the approbation of her relations to a deed for conveying property of inferior value? The position is too absurd to merit a refutation, and yet this is precisely the position which those must establish who contend that the trial by juries, in civil cases, is abolished, because it is expressly provided for in cases of a criminal nature.

From these observations it must appear unquestionably true that trial by jury is in no case abolished by the proposed constitution, and it is equally true that in those controversies between individuals in which the great body of the people are likely to be interested, that institution will remain precisely in the same situation in which it is placed by the state constitution, and will be in no degree altered or influenced by the adoption of the plan under consideration. The foundation of this assertion is that the national judiciary will have no cognizance of them, and of course they will remain determinable as heretofore by the state courts only, and in the manner which the state constitutions and laws prescribe. All land causes, except where claims under the grants of different states come into question, and all other controversies between the citizens of the same state, unless where they depend upon positive violations of the articles of union by acts of the state legislatures, will belong exclusively to the jurisdiction of the state tribunals. Add to this that admiralty causes, and almost all those which are of equity jurisdiction are determinable under our own government without the intervention of a jury, and the inference from the whole will be that this institution, as it exists with us at present, cannot possibly be affected to any great extent by the proposed alteration in our system of government.

The friends and adversaries of the plan of the convention, if they agree in nothing else, concur at least in the value they set upon the trial by jury: Or if there is any difference between them, it consists in this; the former regard it as a valuable safeguard to liberty, the latter represent it as the very palladium of free government. For my own part, the more the operation of the institution has fallen under my observation, the more reason I have discovered for holding it in high estimation; and it would be altogether superfluous to examine to what extent it deserves to be esteemed useful or essential in a representative republic, or how much more merit it may be entitled to as a defence against the oppressions of an hereditary monarch, than as a barrier to the tyranny of popular magistrates in a popular government. Discussions of this kind would be more curious than beneficial, as all are satisfied of the utility of the institution, and of its friendly aspect to liberty. But I must acknowledge that I cannot readily discern the inseparable connection between the existence of liberty and the trial by jury in civil cases. Arbitrary impeachments, arbitrary methods of prosecuting pretended offences, and arbitrary punishments upon arbitrary convictions have ever appeared to me to be the great engines of judicial despotism; and these have all relation to criminal proceedings. The trial by jury in criminal cases, aided by the *habeas corpus* act, seems therefore to be alone concerned in the question. And both of these are provided for in the most ample manner in the plan of the convention.

It has been observed, that trial by jury is a safeguard against an oppressive exercise of the power of taxation. This observation deserves to be canvassed.

It is evident that it can have no influence upon the legislature, in regard to the *amount* of the taxes to be laid, to the *objects* upon which they are to be imposed, or to the *rule* by which they are to be apportioned. If it can have any influence therefore, it must be upon the mode of collection, and the conduct of the officers entrusted with the execution of the revenue laws.

As to the mode of collection in this state, under our own constitution, the trial by jury is in most cases out of use. The taxes are usually levied by the more summary proceedings of distress and sale, as in cases of rent. And it is acknowledged on all hands, that this is essential to the efficacy of the revenue laws. The dilatory course of a trial at law to recover the taxes imposed on individuals, would neither suit the exigencies of the public, nor promote the convenience of the citizens. It would often occasion an accumulation of costs, more burthensome than the original sum of the tax to be levied.

And as to the conduct of the officers of the revenue, the provision in favor of trial by jury in criminal cases, will afford the security aimed at. Wilful abuses of a public authority, to the oppression of the subject, and every species of official extortion, are offences against the government; for which, the persons who commit them, may be indicted and punished according to the circumstances of the case.

The excellence of the trial by jury in civil cases, appears to depend on circumstances foreign to the preservation of liberty. The strongest argument in its favour is, that it is a security against corruption. As there is always more time and better opportunity to tamper with a standing body of magistrates than with a jury summoned for the occasion, there is room to suppose, that a corrupt influence would more easily find its way to the former than to the latter. The force of this consideration, is however, diminished by others. The sheriff who is the summoner of ordinary juries, and the clerks of courts who have the nomination of special juries, are themselves standing officers, and acting individually, may be supposed more accessible to the touch of corruption than the judges, who are a collective body. It is not difficult to see that it would be in the power of those officers to select jurors who would serve the purpose of the party as well as a corrupted bench. In the next place, it may fairly be supposed that there would be less difficulty in gaining some of the jurors promiscuously taken from the public mass, than in gaining men who had been chosen by the government for their probity and good character. But making every deduction for these considerations the trial by jury must still be a valuable check upon corruption. It greatly multiplies the impediments to its success. As matters now stand, it would be necessary to corrupt both court and jury; for where the jury have gone evidently wrong, the court will generally grant a new trial, and it would be in most cases of little use to practice upon the jury, unless the court could be likewise gained. Here then is a double security; and it will readily be perceived that this complicated agency tends to preserve the purity of both institutions. By increasing the obstacles to success it discourages attempts to seduce the integrity of either. The temptations to prostitution, which the judges might have to surmount, must certainly be much fewer while the co-operation of a jury is necessary, than they might be if they had themselves the exclusive determination of all causes.

Notwithstanding therefore the doubts I have expressed as to the essentiality of trial by jury, in civil cases, to liberty, I admit that it is in most cases, under proper regulations, an excellent method of determining questions of property; and that on this account alone it would be entitled to a constitutional provision in its favour, if it were possible to fix the limits within which it ought to be comprehended. There is however, in all cases, great difficulty in this; and men not blinded by enthusiasm, must be sensible that in a federal government which is a composition of societies whose ideas and institutions in relation to the matter materially vary from each other, that difficulty must be not a little augmented. For my own part, at every new view I take of the subject, I become more convinced of the reality of the obstacles, which we are authoritatively informed, prevented the insertion of a provision on this head in the plan of the convention.

The great difference between the limits of the jury trial in different states is not generally understood. And as it must have considerable influence on the sentence we ought to pass upon the omission complained of, in regard to this point, an explanation of it is necessary. In this state our judicial establishments resemble more nearly, than in any other, those of Great-Britain. We have courts of common law, courts of probates (analogous in certain matters to the spiritual courts in England) a court of admiralty, and a court of chancery. In the courts of common law only the trial by jury prevails, and this with some exceptions. In all the others a single judge presides and proceeds in general either according to the course of the cannon or civil law, without the aid of a jury.* In New-Jersey there is a court of chancery which proceeds like ours, but neither courts of admiralty, nor of probates, in the sense in which these last are established with us. In that state the courts of common law have the cognizance of those causes, which with us are determinable in the courts of admiralty and of probates, and of course the jury trial is more extensive in

---

*It has been erroneously insinuated, with regard to the court of chancery, that this court generally tries disputed facts by a jury. The truth is, that references to a jury in that court rarely happen, and are in no case necessary, but where the validity of a devise of land comes into question.

New-Jersey than in New-York. In Pennsylvania this is perhaps still more the case, for there is no court of chancery in that state, and its common law courts have equity jurisdiction. It has a court of admiralty, but none of probates, at least on the plan of ours. Delaware has in these respects imitated Pennsylvania. Maryland approaches more nearly to New-York, as does also Virginia, except that the latter has a plurality of chancellors. North-Carolina bears most affinity to Pennsylvania; South-Carolina to Virginia. I believe however that in some of those states which have distinct courts of admiralty, the causes depending in them are triable by juries. In Georgia there are none but common law courts, and an appeal of course lies from the verdict of one jury to another, which is called a special jury, and for which a particular mode of appointment is marked out. In Connecticut they have no distinct courts, either of chancery or of admiralty, and their courts of probates have no jurisdiction of causes. Their common law courts have admiralty, and to a certain extent, equity jurisdiction. In cases of importance their general assembly is the only court of chancery. In Connecticut therefore the trial by jury extends in *practice* further than in any other state yet mentioned. Rhode Island is I believe in this particular pretty much in the situation of Connecticut. Massachusetts and New-Hampshire, in regard to the blending of law, equity and admiralty, jurisdictions are in a similar predicament. In the four eastern states the trial by jury not only stands upon a broader foundation than in the other states, but it is attended with a peculiarity unknown in its full extent to any of them. There is an appeal *of course* from one jury to another till there have been two verdicts out of three on one side.

From this sketch it appears, that there is a material diversity as well in the modification as in the extent of the institution of trial by jury in civil cases in the several states; and from this fact, these obvious reflections flow. First, that no general rule could have been fixed upon by the convention which would have corresponded with the circumstances of all the states; and secondly, that more, or at least as much might have been hazarded, by taking the system of any state for a standard, as by omitting a provision altogether, and leaving the matter as it has been left, to legislative regulations.

The propositions which have been made for supplying the omission, have rather served to illustrate than to obviate the difficulty of the thing. The minority of Pennsylvania have proposed this mode of expression for the purpose—"trial by jury shall be as heretofore"—and this I maintain would be absolutely senseless and nugatory. The United States, in their united or collective capacity, are the OBJECT to which all general provisions in the constitution must necessarily be construed to refer. Now it is evident, that though trial by jury with various limitations is known in each state individually, yet in the United States *as such*, it is at this time altogether unknown, because the present federal government has no judiciary power whatever; and consequently there is no proper antecedent or previous establishment to which the term *heretofore* could relate. It would therefore be destitute of a precise meaning, and inoperative from its uncertainty.

As on the one hand, the form of the provision would not fulfil the intent of its proposers, so on the other, if I apprehend that intent rightly, it would be in itself inexpedient. I presume it to be, that causes in the federal courts should be tried by jury, if in the state where the courts sat, that mode of trial would obtain in a similar case in the state courts—that is to say admiralty causes should be tried in Connecticut by a jury, and in New-York without one. The capricious operation of so dissimilar a method of trial in the same cases, under the same government, is of itself sufficient to indispose every well regulated judgment towards it. Whether the cause should be tried with or without a jury, would depend in a great number of cases, on the accidental situation of the court and parties.

But this is not in my estimation the greatest objection. I feel a deep and deliberate conviction, that there are many cases in which the trial by jury is an ineligible one. I think it so particularly in cases which concern the public peace with foreign nations; that is in most cases where the question turns wholly on the laws of nations. Of this nature among others are all prize causes. Juries cannot be supposed competent to investigations, that require a thorough knowledge of the laws and usages of nations, and they will sometimes be under the influence of impressions which will not suffer them to pay sufficient regard to those considerations of public policy which ought to guide their enquiries. There would of course be always danger that the rights of other nations might be infringed by their decisions, so as to afford occasions of reprisal and war. Though the proper province of juries be to determine matters of fact, yet in most cases legal consequences are complicated with fact in such a manner as to render a separation impracticable.

It will add great weight to this remark in relation to prize causes to mention that the method of determining them has been thought worthy of particular regulation in various treaties between different powers of Europe, and that pursuant to such treaties they are determinable in Great-Britain in the last resort before the king himself in his privy council, where the fact as well as the law undergoes a re-examination. This alone demonstrates the impolicy of inserting a fundamental provision in the constitution which would make the state systems a standard for the national government in the article under consideration, and the danger of incumbering the government with any constitutional provisions, the propriety of which is not indisputable.

My convictions are equally strong that great advantages result from the separation of the equity from the law jurisdiction; and that the causes which belong to the former would be improperly committed to juries. The great and primary use of a court of equity is to give relief *in extraordinary cases*, which are *exceptions** to general rules. To unite the jurisdiction of such cases with the ordinary jurisdiction must have a tendency to unsettle the general rules and to

---

*It is true that the principles by which that relief is governed are now reduced to a regular system, but it is not the less true that they are in the main, applicable to SPECIAL circumstances which form exceptions to general rules.

subject every case that arises to a *special* determination. While the separation of the one from the other has the contrary effect of rendering one a sentinel over the other, and of keeping each within the expedient limits. Besides this the circumstances that constitute cases proper for courts of equity, are in many instances so nice and intricate, that they are incompatible with the genius of trials by jury. They require often such long, deliberate and critical investigation as would be impracticable to men called from their occupations and obliged to decide before they were permitted to return to them. The simplicity and expedition which form the distinguishing characters of this mode of trial require that the matter to be decided should be reduced to some single and obvious point; while the litigations usual in chancery frequently comprehend a long train of minute and independent particulars.

It is true that the separation of the equity from the legal jurisdiction is peculiar to the English system of jurisprudence; which is the model that has been followed in several of the states. But it is equally true, that the trial by jury has been unknown in every case in which they have been united. And the separation is essential to the preservation of that institution in its pristine purity. The nature of a court of equity will readily permit the extension of its jurisdiction to matters of law, but it is not a little to be suspected, that the attempt to extend the jurisdiction of the courts of law to matters of equity will not only be unproductive of the advantages which may be derived from courts of chancery, on the plan upon which they are established in this state, but will tend gradually to change the nature of the courts of law, and to undermine the trial by jury, by introducing questions too complicated for a decision in that mode.

These appear to be conclusive reasons against incorporating the systems of all the states in the formation of the national judiciary; according to what may be conjectured to have been the intent of the Pennsylvania minority. Let us now examine how far the proposition of Massachusetts is calculated to remedy the supposed defect.

It is in this form—"In civil actions between citizens of different states, every issue of fact, arising in *actions at common law*, may be tried by a jury, if the parties, or either of them, request it."

This at best is a proposition confined to one description of causes; and the inference is fair either that the Massachusetts convention considered that as the only class of federal causes, in which the trial by jury would be proper; or that if desirous of a more extensive provision, they found it impracticable to devise one which would properly answer the end. If the first, the omission of a regulation respecting so partial an object, can never be considered as a material imperfection in the system. If the last, it affords a strong corroboration of the extreme difficulty of the thing.

But this is not all: If we advert to the observations already made respecting the courts that subsist in the several states of the union, and the different powers exercised by them, it will appear, that there are no expressions more vague and indeterminate than those which have been employed to characterise *that* species of causes which it is intended shall be entitled to a trial by jury. In this state the boundaries between actions at common law and actions of equitable jurisdiction are ascertained in conformity to the rules which prevail in England upon that subject. In many of the other states, the boundaries are less precise. In some of them, every cause is to be tried in a court of common law, and upon that foundation every action may be considered as an action at common law, to be determined by a jury, if the parties or either of them chuse it. Hence the same irregularity and confusion would be introduced by a compliance with this proposition, that I have already noticed as resulting from the regulation proposed by the Pennsylvania minority. In one state a cause would receive its determination from a jury, if the parties or either of them requested it; but in another state a cause exactly similar to the other must be decided without the intervention of a jury, because the state judicatories varied as to common law jurisdiction.

It is obvious therefore that the Massachusetts proposition, upon this subject, cannot operate as a general regulation until some uniform plan, with respect to the limits of common law and equitable jurisdictions shall be adopted by the different states. To devise a plan of that kind is a task arduous in itself, and which it would require much time and reflection to mature. It would be extremely difficult, if not impossible, to suggest any general regulation that would be acceptable to all the states in the union, or that would perfectly quadrate with the several state institutions.

It may be asked, why could not a reference have been made to the constitution of this state, taking that, which is allowed by me to be a good one, as a standard for the United States? I answer that it is not very probable the other states should entertain the same opinion of our institutions which we do ourselves. It is natural to suppose that they are hitherto more attached to their own, and that each would struggle for the preference. If the plan of taking one state as a model for the whole had been thought of in the convention, it is to be presumed that the adoption of it in that body, would have been rendered difficult by the predilection of each representation in favour of its own government; and it must be uncertain which of the states would have been taken as the model. It has been shewn that many of them would be improper ones. And I leave it to conjecture whether, under all circumstances, it is most likely that New-York or some other state would have been preferred. But admit that a judicious selection could have been effected in the convention, still there would have been great danger of jealousy and disgust in the other states, at the partiality which had been shewn to the institutions of one. The enemies of the plan would have been furnished with a fine pretext for raising a host of local prejudices against it, which perhaps might have hazarded in no inconsiderable degree, its final establishment.

To avoid the embarrassments of a definition of the cases which the trial by jury ought to embrace, it is some times suggested by men of enthusiastic tempers, that a provision might have been inserted for establishing it in all cases whatsoever. For this I believe no precedent is to be found in any member of the union; and the considerations which have been stated in discussing the proposition of the minority of Pennsylvania, must satisfy every sober mind that the establishment of the trial by jury in *all* cases, would have been an unpardonable error in the plan.

In short, the more it is considered, the more arduous will appear the task of fashioning a provision in such a form, as not to express too little to answer the purpose, or too much to be advisable; or which might not have opened other sources of opposition to the great and essential object of introducing a firm national government.

I cannot but persuade myself on the other hand, that the different lights in which the subject has been placed in the course of these observations, will go far towards removing in candid minds, the apprehensions they may have entertained on the point. They have tended to shew that the security of liberty is materially concerned only in the trial by jury in criminal cases, which is provided for in the most ample manner in the plan of the convention; that even in far the greatest proportion of civil cases, and those in which the great body of the community is interested, that mode of trial will remain in its full force, as established in the state constitutions, untouched and unaffected by the plan of the convention: That it is in no case abolished* by that plan; and that there are great if not insurmountable difficulties in the way of making any precise and proper provision for it in a constitution for the United States.

The best judges of the matter will be the least anxious for a constitutional establishment of the trial by jury in civil cases, and will be the most ready to admit that the changes which are continually happening in the affairs of society, may render a different mode of determining questions of property, preferable in many cases, in which that mode of trial now prevails. For my own part, I acknowledge myself to be convinced that even in this state, it might be advantageously extended to some cases to which it does not at present apply, and might as advantageously be abridged in others. It is conceded by all reasonable men, that it ought not to obtain in all cases. The examples of innovations which contract its ancient limits, as well in these states as in Great-Britain, afford a strong presumption that its former extent has been found inconvenient; and give room to suppose that future experience may discover the propriety and utility of other exceptions. I suspect it to be impossible in the nature of the thing, to fix the salutary point at which the operation of the institution ought to stop; and this is with me a strong argument for leaving the matter to the discretion of the legislature.

This is now clearly understood to be the case in Great-Britain, and it is equally so in the state of Connecticut; and yet it may be safely affirmed, that more numerous encroachments have been made upon the trial by jury in this state since the revolution, though provided for by a positive article of our constitution, than has happened in the same time either in Connecticut or Great-Britain. It may

be added that these encroachments have generally originated with the men who endeavour to persuade the people they are the warmest defenders of popular liberty, but who have rarely suffered constitutional obstacles to arrest them in a favourite career. The truth is that the general GENIUS of a government is all that can be substantially relied upon for permanent effects. Particular provisions, though not altogether useless, have far less virtue and efficacy than are commonly ascribed to them; and the want of them will never be with men of sound discernment a decisive objection to any plan which exhibits the leading characters of a good government.

It certainly sounds not a little harsh and extraordinary to affirm that there is no security for liberty in a constitution which expressly establishes the trial by jury in criminal cases, because it does not do it in civil also; while it is a notorious fact that Connecticut, which has been always regarded as the most popular state in the union, can boast of no constitutional provision for either.

18

UNITED STATES V. SHIVE
27 Fed. Cas. 1065, no. 16,278 (C.C.E.D.Pa. 1832)

Before BALDWIN, Circuit Justice, and HOPKINSON, District Judge.

BY THE COURT. The state law giving the defendant a right to challenge peremptorily, does not apply to proceedings in this court; forgery is not a felony at common law, and though the act of congress declares the offence laid in the indictment to be a felony, that does not carry with it a right of peremptory challenge as an incident, and it has never been allowed in this court in a case like the present.

The jury were sworn and the trial had. Among other grounds of defence taken by the counsel of the defendant, he contended that the act of congress chartering the bank which created the offence, was unconstitutional, and that therefore the jury ought to acquit the defendant.

BALDWIN, Circuit Justice, after charging the jury on the law and evidence in the case, proceeded to the objection to the constitutionality of the law.

We could have wished that these would have been the only considerations, which it was our duty to submit to you, but one of the counsel for the defendant has raised another question, on which it is necessary for us to give you our opinion, and that is, whether the act of congress on which this prosecution is founded, is valid or void.

That it has passed through all the forms and branches of legislation, that it has been sanctioned and declared to be the law of the land, by the highest branch of the judicial power; that it is clothed with every sanction and carries with it every obligation known to the constitution, has not been and cannot be denied. If there is law in the land, if

---

*Vide No. LXXXI, in which the supposition of its being abolished by the appellate jurisdiction in matters of fact being vested in the supreme court is examined and refuted.

there is a rule by which courts and juries are bound to administer the criminal justice of the country, it is that which, having been enacted by the legislative authority of the nation, has been solemnly pronounced by the supreme judicial power, to be within the constitutional province of the legislature. Beyond that tribunal, there is no other revision of the acts of congress, that will not end in the prostration of all law and all legitimate government, unless by an amendment to the constitution.

In court of justice, the law of the land is the law of every case, criminal as well as civil, the safety of the public, the rights of individuals do not depend on their opinion of what the law ought to be, but on what it is. The ministers of justice are not the makers of the laws, judges and jurors are, in the words of the defendant's counsel, magistrates to enforce and execute the laws; they are as much bound by them as the criminal they condemn. We sit here by the authority of the law, our duty is prescribed and defined by law, and if we wilfully violate or disregard it, if we sentence a prisoner without a previous law prescribing a punishment, or acquit in opposition to the enacted and established law of the country, we should be the greatest criminals in the nation. We are judges of law, but what is law? Not the opinions of judges and jurors merely, it is the will of the people, expressed through that department of the government, to whom they have confided the law-making power. An act of congress is the exercise of that power conferred by the nation; a judgment of the supreme court affirming its validity and decreeing its binding force, is the constitutional exercise of the judicial power of the nation, confided to that high tribunal. And when a law thus carries with it the imposing authority of the people, the states of this union, and of every department of the government created by the constitution, shall the ministers of justice, its sworn administrators, be the first to trample under their feet the supreme law of the land? Shall we, the creatures of the law, the servants of the constitution, dare to assume the power of abrogating its provisions, disobeying its injunctions, and dispensing with its penalties? The sixth article of the constitution, declares itself and all laws and treaties made pursuant thereto, to be the supreme law of the land, and that all judges shall be bound thereby, notwithstanding any thing in the law or constitution of any state to the contrary.

When the most solemn acts of a sovereign state, in opposition to an act of congress, are thus declared nullities, will a jury assume no moral responsibility by substituting their opinion for the supreme law of the land? If the defendant has violated an act of congress, though not sworn to make it his rule of action, the supreme law declares him a felon. What are you or we if we put ourselves above it? The power to judge of the law as well as the fact in a criminal case, is to ascertain the existence of a law; if you see it in the statute book, you cannot on your oaths say there is no such law, or exercise a power denied to the people of a state by the most solemn constitutional provision, declare the supreme law to be void, because it does not comport with your opinion. Should you assume and exercise this power, your opinion does not become a supreme law, no one is bound by it, other juries will decide for themselves,

and you could not expect that courts would look to your verdict for the construction of the constitution, as to the powers of the legislative or judicial departments of the government; nor that you have the power of declaring what the law is, what acts are criminal, what are innocent, as a rule of action for your fellow citizens or for the court. If juries once exercise this power, we are without a constitution or laws, one jury has the same power as another, you cannot bind those who may take your places, what you declare constitutional to-day, another jury may declare unconstitutional to-morrow. We shall cease to have a government of law, when what is the law, depends on the arbitrary and fluctuating opinions of judges and jurors, instead of the standard of the constitution, expounded by the tribunal to which has been referred all cases arising under the constitution, laws and treaties of the United States.

The counsel of the defendant has referred you to the message of the president, as the true exposition of the constitution in relation to the power of congress to charter the bank. We have no jurisdiction to judge of the propriety of the course of the executive; in the exercise of his constitutional power to prevent the passage of a law, he acts on his responsibility; but the judicial power cannot be exercised on the reasons which have governed the exercise of the veto power. We therefore forbear all remarks upon it. For a similar reason we cannot look to the construction given to the constitution by the executive department as a guide to our judgment; for no appellate or supervisory power over our proceedings, has been confided to that department. We must follow the rule prescribed by the tribunal to whom has been confided the power of expounding the constitution and laws, and of directing our judgment. That tribunal has adjudged this law to be valid, we cannot, and think you will not declare it void.

The jury found the defendant guilty.

19

JOSEPH STORY, COMMENTARIES ON THE CONSTITUTION 3:§§ 1773–75
1833

---

§ 1773. It seems hardly necessary in this place to expatiate upon the antiquity, or importance of the trial by jury in criminal cases. It was from very early times insisted on by our ancestors in the parent country, as the great bulwark of their civil and political liberties, and watched with an unceasing jealousy and solicitude. The right constitutes the fundamental articles of Magna Charta, in which it is declared, *"nullus homo capiatur, nec imprisonetur, aut exulet, aut aliquo modo destruatur, &c.; nisi per legale judicium parium suorum, vel per legem terrae;"* no man shall be arrested, nor imprisoned, nor banished, nor deprived of life, &c. but by the judgment of his peers, or by the law of the land. The judgment of his peers here alluded to, and commonly called in the quaint language of former times a trial *per pais,* or trial by the country, is the trial by a jury, who are called the peers of the party accused, being of the like condition and equality in the state. When our more immediate ancestors removed to America, they brought this great privilege with them, as their birth-right and inheritance, as a part of that admirable common law, which had fenced round, and interposed barriers on every side against the approaches of arbitrary power. It is now incorporated into all our state constitutions, as a fundamental right; and the constitution of the United States would have been justly obnoxious to the most conclusive objection, if it had not recognised, and confirmed it in the most solemn terms.

§ 1774. The great object of a trial by jury in criminal cases is, to guard against a spirit of oppression and tyranny on the part of rulers, and against a spirit of violence and vindictiveness on the part of the people. Indeed, it is often more important to guard against the latter, than the former. The sympathies of all mankind are enlisted against the revenge and fury of a single despot; and every attempt will be made to screen his victims. But how difficult is it to escape from the vengeance of an indignant people, roused into hatred by unfounded calumnies, or stimulated to cruelty by bitter political enmities, or unmeasured jealousies? The appeal for safety can, under such circumstances, scarcely be made by innocence in any other manner, than by the severe control of courts of justice, and by the firm and impartial verdict of a jury sworn to do right, and guided solely by legal evidence and a sense of duty. In such a course there is a double security against the prejudices of judges, who may partake of the wishes and opinions of the government, and against the passions of the multitude, who may demand their victim with a clamorous precipitancy. So long, indeed, as this palladium remains sacred and inviolable, the liberties of a free government cannot wholly fall. But to give it real efficiency, it must be preserved in its purity and dignity; and not, with a view of slight inconveniences, or imaginary burthens, be put into the hands of those, who are incapable of estimating its worth, or are too inert, or too ignorant, or too imbecile, to wield its potent armour. Mr. Justice Blackstone, with the warmth and pride becoming an Englishman living under its blessed protection, has said: "A celebrated French writer, who concludes, that because Rome, Sparta, and Carthage have lost their liberties, therefore those of England in time must perish, should have recollected, that Rome, Sparta, and Carthage, at the time, when their liberties were lost, were strangers to the trial by jury."

§ 1775. It is observable, that the trial of all crimes is not only to be by jury, but to be held in the state, where they are committed. The object of this clause is to secure the party accused from being dragged to a trial in some distant state, away from his friends, and witnesses, and neighbourhood; and thus to be subjected to the verdict of mere strangers, who may feel no common sympathy, or who may even cherish animosities, or prejudices against him. Besides this; a trial in a distant state or territory might subject the party to the most oppressive expenses, or perhaps even to the inability of procuring the proper witnesses to establish his innocence. There is little danger, indeed, that congress would ever exert their power in such an oppressive, and unjustifiable a manner. But upon a subject, so vital to the security of the citizen, it was fit to leave as little as possible to mere discretion. By the common law, the trial of all crimes is required to be in the county, where they are committed. Nay, it originally carried its jealousy still farther, and required, that the jury itself should come from the vicinage of the place, where the crime was alleged to be committed. This was certainly a precaution, which, however justifiable in an early and barbarous state of society, is little commendable in its more advanced stages. It has been justly remarked, that in such cases to summon a jury, labouring under local prejudices, is laying a snare for their consciences; and though they should have virtue and vigour of mind sufficient to keep them upright, the parties will grow suspicious, and indulge other doubts of the impartiality of the trial. It was doubtless by analogy to this rule of the common law, that all criminal trials are required to be in the state, where committed. But as crimes may be committed on the high seas, and elsewhere, out of the territorial jurisdiction of a state, it was indispensable, that, in such cases, congress should be enabled to provide the place of trial.

SEE ALSO:

Generally 3.2.1; 3.2.2; Amends. IV–VIII
James McHenry, Maryland House of Delegates, 29 Nov. 1787, Farrand 3:150
Roger Sherman, Proposals for Constitution, 1787, Farrand 3:616
Charles Pinckney, South Carolina House of Representatives, 16 Jan. 1788, Elliot 3:259–60
Charles Cotesworth Pinckney, South Carolina Ratifying Convention, 18 Jan. 1788, Elliot 4:306–8
Debate in North Carolina Ratifying Convention, 28 July 1788, Elliot 4:143, 144–45, 208
James Wilson, Comparison of Constitutions, Lectures on Law 1791, Works 1:332–33

Article 3, Section 3, Clauses 1 and 2

Treason against the United States, shall consist only in levying War against them, or in adhering to their Enemies, giving them Aid and Comfort. No Person shall be convicted of Treason unless on the Testimony of two Witnesses to the same overt Act, or on Confession in open Court.

The Congress shall have Power to declare the Punishment of Treason, but no Attainder of Treason shall work Corruption of Blood, or Forfeiture except during the Life of the Person attainted.

1

Laws of Maryland at Large
1638
Hurst 71–72

By this Bill the following Offences were to be adjudged Treasons within this Province, *viz.* To compass or conspire the Death of the King, or the Queen his Wife, or of his Son and Heir; or to levy War against his Majesty, or to counterfeit the King's Great or Privy Seal, or his Coin; or to join or adhere to any foreign Prince or State, being a professed Enemy of his Majesty, in any Practice or Attempt against his said Majesty: Or to compass, conspire, or cause the Death of the Lord Proprietary within this Province, or of his Lieut. General for the Time being, (in Absence of his Lordship,) or to join, adhere or confederate with any *Indians,* or any foreign Prince or Governor to the invading of this Province, or disheriting the Lord Proprietary of his Seignory and Dominion therein. All Offences of Treason to be punished by Drawing, Hanging and Quartering of a Man, and Burning of a Woman; the Offender's Blood to be corrupted, and to forfeit all his Lands, Tenements, Goods, &c. to his Lordship. But Punishment of Death to be inflicted on a Lord of a Manor by Beheading.

2

Sir Edward Coke, Third Institute 38
1641

By this act [3 Henry VII] it expressly appeareth by the judgement of the whole Parliament, that besides the confederacy, compassing, conspiracy, or imagination, there must be some other overt act or deed tending thereunto, to make it treason within the statute of *25 E. 3*. And therefore the bare confederacy, compassing, conspiracy, or imaginations by words only, is made felony by this Act. But if the Conspirators do provide any weapon, or other thing, to accomplish their devilish intent, this and the like is an overt act to make it treason.

3

LAWS OF NEW HAVEN COLONY
1656
Hurst 69–70

If any person shall conspire, and attempt any invasion, insurrection, or publick Rebellion against this Jurisdiction, or shall endeavour to surprize, or seize any Plantation, or Town, any Fortification, Platform, or any great Guns, provided for the defence of the Jurisdiction, or any Plantation therein; or shall treacherously and perfidiously attempt the alteration and subversion of the frame of policy, or fundamentall Government laid, and setled for this Jurisdiction, he or they shall be put to death. *Num*. 16. *2 Sam*. 18. *2 Sam*. 20. Or if any person shall consent unto any such mischievous practice, or by the space of foure and twenty houres conceale it, not giving notice thereof to some Magistrate, if there be any Magistrate in the Plantation, or place where he liveth, or if none, to some Deputy for the Jurisdiction, or to the Constable of the place, that the publick safety may be seasonably provided for, he shall be put to death, or severely punished, as the Court of Magistrates weighing all circumstances shall determine.

4

GENERAL LAWS AND LIBERTIES OF
NEW PLIMOUTH COLONY
1671
Hurst 70–71

---

3. Treason against the Person of our Soveraign Lord the King, the State and Common-wealth of England, shall be punished by death.

4. That whosoever shall Conspire and Attempt any Invasion, Insurrection, or Publick Rebellion against this Jurisdiction, or the Surprizal of any Town, Plantation, Fortification or Ammunition, therein provided for the safety thereof, or shall Treacherously and Perfidiously Attempt and Endeavour the Alteration and Subversion of the Fundamental Frame and Constitutions of this Government; every such Person shall be put to Death.

5

CONNECTICUT ACTS AND LAWS
1702
Hurst 72

That if any person or persons, shall compass or imagine the Death of our Soveraign Lord the KING, or of our Lady the QUEEN, or of the Heir apparent to the Crown; or if any person shall leavy War against our Lord the KING, or be adherent to the Kings Enemies, giving them aid, and comfort in the Realm, or elsewhere, and thereof be probably attainted of open deed by His Peers, upon the Testimony of two Lawful and Credible Witnesses upon Oath, brought before the offender face to face, at the time of his arraignment; or voluntary confession of the party arraigned. Or if any person or persons shall counterfeit the Kings Great Seal, or privy Seal, and thereof be duely convicted, as aforesaid, then every such person and persons, so as aforesaid Offending, shall be deemed, declared, and adjudged, to be Traitors, and shall suffer pains of Death, and also lose and forfeit as in cases of High Treason.

And be it further Enacted by the Authority aforesaid, That the Tryal of all, and every person and persons whatsoever, accused, indicted and prosecuted for High Treason, and misprission of such Treason, shall be regulated according to Act of Parliament, made in the Seventh year of His present Majesties Reign, Entituled, *An Act for Regulating of Tryals in Cases of Treason and Misprission of Treason;* and the party so accused, indicted and prosecuted, to be allowed the benefits and priviledges, in and by the said Act granted and declared.

6

SIR MATTHEW HALE, HISTORY OF THE PLEAS
OF THE CROWN
1736 (posthumous)
Emlyn 1:83, 86–87, 115–16, 119, 122

And we need no greater instance of this multiplication of constructive treasons, than the troublesome reign of king *Richard* II. which, tho it were after the limitation of treasons by the statute of *25 E. 3*. yet things were so carried by factions and parties in this king's reign, that this statute was little observed; but as this, or the other party prevailed, so the crimes of high treason were in a manner arbitrarily imposed and adjudged to the disadvantage of that party, that was intended to be suppressed; so that *de facto* that king's reign gives us as various instances of these arbitrary determinations of treasons, and the great inconveniences that arose thereby, as if indeed the statute of *25*

E. 3. had not been made or in force. And tho most of those judgments and declarations were made in parliament; sometimes by the king, lords, and commons; sometimes by the lords, and afterwards affirmed and enacted, as laws; sometimes by a plenipotentiary power committed by acts of parliament to particular lords and others, yet the inconvenience, that grew thereby, and the great uncertainty that happened from the same, was exceedingly pernicious to the king and his kingdom.

. . . . .

Now altho the crime of high treason is the greatest crime against faith, duty, and human society, and brings with it the greatest and most fatal dangers to the government, peace, and happiness of a kingdom, or state, and therefore is deservedly branded with the highest ignominy, and subjected to the greatest penalties, that the law can inflict; yet by these instances, and more of this kind, that might be given, it appears, 1. How necessary it was, that there should be some fixed and settled boundary for this great crime of treason, and of what great importance the statute of *25 E. 3* was, in order to that end. 2. How dangerous it is to depart from the letter of that statute, and to multiply and inhanse crimes into treason by ambiguous and general words, as *accroaching of royal power, subverting of fundamental laws,* and the like; and 3. How dangerous it is by construction and analogy to make treasons, where the letter of the law has not done it: for such a method admits of no limits or bounds, but runs as far as the wit and invention of accusers, and the odiousness and detestation of persons accused will carry men.

. . . . .

Therefore tho this be regularly true, that words alone make not treason or an overt-act, yet it hath these allays and exceptions.

(1.) That words may expound an overt-act to make good an indictment of treason of compassing the king's death, which overt-act possibly of itself may be indifferent and unapplicable to such an intent; and therefore in the indictment of treason may be joined with such an overt-act, to make the same applicable and expositive of such a compassing, as may plainly appear by many of the precedents there cited [in *Pyne's case,* Cro. Car. 125].

(2.) That some words, that are expressly menacing the death or destruction of the king, are a sufficient overt-act to prove that compassing of his death, *M. 9 Car. B. R. Crohagan's case* in *Croke* [Cro. Car. 332], who being an *Irish* priest, *7 Car. 1* at *Lisbon* in *Portugal* used these words, "*I will kill the king* (innuendo dominum *Carolum* regem *Angliae) if I may come unto him,*" and in *Aug. 9 Caroli* he came into *England* for the same purpose. This was proved upon his trial by two witnesses, and for that his traitorous intent and the imagination of his heart was declared by these words, it was held high treason by the course of the common law, and within the express words of the statute of *25 E. 3.* and accordingly he was convicted, and had judgment of high treason; yet it is observable, that there was somewhat of an overt-act joined with it, namely, his coming into *England,* whereby it seems to be within the former consideration, namely, tho the coming into *England* was an act indifferent in itself, as to the point of treason; yet it being

laid in the indictment, that he came to that purpose, and that in a great measure expounded to be so by his minatory words, the words coupled with the act of coming over make his coming over to be probably for that purpose, and accordingly applicable to that end.

. . . . .

If there be an assembling together to consider how they may kill the king, this assembling is an overt-act to make good an indictment of compassing the king's death. This was *Arden's* case [1 Anderson 104], 26 *Eliz.* and accordingly it was ruled *Decem. 14 Caroli* at *Newgate* in the case of *Tonge* and other confederates [Kelyng, 17].

. . . . .

Vide Anderson's Reports Placito 154, which was the case of *Arden* and *Somerville* and others, who conspired the death of queen *Elizabeth,* resolved by all the justices, that a meeting together of these accomplices to consult touching the manner of effecting it was an overt-act to prove it, as well as *Somerville's* buying of a dagger actually to have executed it.

7

SIR MICHAEL FOSTER, DISCOURSE ON HIGH TREASON 183–90, 193–98, 200–201, 205–11, 213, 216–19, 221–24, 226–46, 249–51
1762

Introduction

High Treason being an Offence committed against the Duty of Allegiance, it may be proper before I proceed to the several Species of that Offence which will be the Subject of this Discourse, to consider From whom, and To whom Allegiance is due.

SECT. 1. With regard to Natural-born Subjects there can be no Doubt. They owe Allegiance to the Crown at all Times and in all Places. This is what We call *Natural* Allegiance, in Contradistinction to that which is Local. The Duty of Allegiance, whether Natural or Local, is founded in the Relation the Person standeth in to the Crown, and in the Privileges He deriveth from that Relation. Local Allegiance is founded in the Protection a Foreigner enjoyeth for his Person, his Family or Effects during his Residence here; and it Ceaseth whenever He withdraweth with his Family and Effects. Natural Allegiance is founded in the Relation every Man standeth in to the Crown considered as the Head of that Society whereof He is *born a Member;* and on the peculiar Privileges He deriveth from that Relation, which are with great Propriety called his *Birthright.* This Birthright nothing but his own Demerit can deprive Him of; it is Indefeasible and perpetual. And consequently the Duty of Allegiance which ariseth out of it, and is inseperably Connected with it, is in Consideration of Law likewise Unalienable and Perpetual.

. . . . .

There have been Writers who have carried the Notion of Natural, Perpetual, Unalienable Allegiance much farther than the Subject of this Discourse will lead Me. They say, very truly, that it is due to the Person of the King; and from thence have drawn Consequences, which do not fall within the Compass of the present Inquiry, and shall therefore be passed over. It is undoubtedly due to the Person of the King; but in that respect Natural Allegiance differeth nothing from that we call Local. For Allegiance considered in every Light is alike Due to the Person of the King; and is paid, and in the Nature of Things must constantly be paid, to that Prince who for the time being is in the Actual and Full Possession of the Regal Dignity. The well-known Maxim which the Writers upon our Law have adopted and applied to this Case, *Nemo potest exuere Patriam*, comprehendeth the whole Doctrine of Natural Allegiance, and expresseth My Sense of it.

SECT. 2. An Alien whose Sovereign is in Amity with the Crown of *England*, Residing here and Receiving the Protection of the Law oweth a Local Allegiance to the Crown during the time of his Residence. And if, during that Time He committeth an Offence, which in the Case of a Natural-born Subject would amount to Treason, He may be dealt with as a Traitor. For his Person and Personal Estate are as much under the Protection of the Law as the Natural-born Subject's: and if He is injured in either, He hath the same Remedy at Law for such Injury.

SECT. 3. An Alien whose Sovereign is at Enmity with Us living here under the King's Protection, committing Offences amounting to Treason, may likewise be dealt with as a Traitor. For He oweth a Temporary Local Allegiance, founded on that share of Protection He receiveth.

SECT. 4. And if such Alien seeking the Protection of the Crown having a Family and Effects here should during a War with his Native Country go thither and there Adhere to the King's Enemies *for purposes of Hostility*, He might be dealt with as a Traitor. For He came and settled here under the Protection of the Crown. And though his Person was removed for a time, his Effects and Family continued still under the same Protection. This Rule was laid down by all the Judges assembled at the Queen's Command *Jan.* 12th 1707.

It is to be observed that the Judges in the Resolution last cited laid a considerable Stress on the Queen's Declaration of War against *France* and *Spain;* whereby She took into Her Protection the Persons and Estates of the Subjects of those Crowns residing here and demeaning themselves dutifully, and not Corresponding with the Enemy. King *William* and Queen *Mary* did the same in their Declaration of War against *France,* and so did His present Majesty. These Declarations did in fact put *Frenchmen* residing Here and demeaning themselves dutifully, even in time of War, upon the foot of Aliens coming hither by Licence or Safe-conduct. They enabled Them to acquire Personal Chattles and to maintain Actions for the Recovery of their Personal Rights in as full a manner as Aliens *Amy* may.

. . . . .

SECT. 7. The Case of an Ambassador or His Attendants not being Subjects of *Great Britain* mentioned by Lord *Hale,* doing Acts which in a Subject would amount to High Treason, will as His Lordship observeth, be always governed rather by Prudential Considerations or what are generally called *Reasons of State*, than by any fixed Rules of Law. And as Ambassadors generally Act under Direction and by Orders from their Sovereign, They have seldom been proceeded against further than by Imprisonment, seizing their Papers and sending Them Home in Custody. Which was done in the Case of Count *Gyllenberg* the *Swedish* Minister in the late King's Time.

But whatever Proceedings be against Them for State Crimes, They are to be considered at the worst but as Enemies subject to the Law of Nations; never as Traitors subject to our Municipal Laws, and owing Allegiance to the Crown of *Great Britain*. Unless perhaps in case of Attempts directly and immediately against the Life of the King; in which Case no Orders from their Sovereigns can be presumed, or if in Fact produced, would Justify or Excuse. And therefore I shall not take their Case into Consideration in this place. And for the same Reason I say nothing of the case of Spies taken here in time of War, *actual Hostilities being on foot in the Kingdom at that time,* nor of Prisoners of War.

But for Murder and other Offences of great Enormity, which are against the light of Nature and the Fundamental Laws of All Society, the Persons mentioned in this Section are certainly liable to answer in the ordinary Course of Justice, as other Persons offending in the like manner are. For though They may not be thought to owe Allegiance to the Sovereign, and so incapable of committing High Treason, yet They are to be considered as Members of Society; and consequently bound by that Eternal Universal Law by which All Civil Societies are united and kept together.

SECT. 8. Protection and Allegiance are reciprocal Obligations, and consequently the Allegiance due to the Crown must, as I said before, be paid to Him who is in the Full and Actual Exercise of the Regal Power, and to none Other. I have no occasion to meddle with the Distinction between Kings *de facto* and Kings *de jure*, because the warmest Advocates for that Distinction and for the Principles on which it hath been founded, admit that even a King *de facto* in the Full and Sole Possession of the Crown, is a King within the Statute of Treasons; it is admitted too, that the Throne being Full, any other Person Out of Possession but claiming Title, is no King within the Act, be His Pretensions what they may.

These Principles I think no Lawyer hath ever yet denied. They are founded in Reason, Equity and good Policy.

SECT. 9. A Prince succeeding to the Crown by Descent, or by a *previous Designation of Parliament*, is from the Moment His Title accreweth, a King to all Intents and Purposes within the Statute of Treasons; Antecedent to His own Coronation, or to any Oaths or Engagements taken to Him on the part of the Subject. For as on the one hand, the Solemnity of a Coronation doth not *Confer, but presupposeth* a Right to the Allegiance of the Subject inherent in the Person of the King; so on the other, the Duty of Allegiance doth not flow from any Oaths or Engagements

411

taken on the part of the Subject. For in Both Cases an antecedent Duty is presupposed which is intended to be secured by those Explicit Engagements.

I am however very far from thinking that the Solemnity of a Coronation is to be considered among us meerly as a Royal Ceremony, or as a bare Notification of the Descent of the Crown, as Authors of High Distinction have been pleased to express Themselves. I admit that it is, on the part of the Nation a Publick Solemn Recognition that the Regal Authority, and All the Prerogatives of the Crown are vested in the Person of the King, antecedent to that solemnity. But the Solemnity of a Coronation with us goeth a great deal farther. The Coronation Oath importeth on the part of the King, a Publick Solemn Recognition of the Fundamental Rights of the People; and concludeth with an Engagement under the highest of All Sanctions, that He will Maintain and Defend those Rights; and to the Utmost of His Power make the Laws of the Realm the Rule and Measure of His Conduct.

SECT. 10. The Reader observeth that in the preceding Section I take it for granted that a Title to the Crown may be founded, as well on a Designation by Parliament as on Hereditary Descent. I never entertained a Doubt of this matter, though I am aware that some Lawyers of High Rank have gone upon a contrary Principle. For though the Crown hath, upon Principles of great Wisdom and sound Policy, been in All Ages considered as a Descendable Right, vested in and appropriated to the Royal Line, and hath in Fact continued in that Line ever since the Conquest, yet it is certain that the course of Descent in that Line hath been frequently interrupted by Authority of Parliament.

SECT. 11. Lord Chief Justice *Hale* after mentioning the Cases of *Ed.* 2d and *R.* 2d is pleased to say, that the Former was considered by Parliament *even after His Resignation and Deposition,* as a King against Whom High Treason may be committed. This He groundeth on the Attainders of Those who were concerned in the Murder of Him. But those Attainders seem to Me to have been grounded Singly on a Principle of Law which then prevailed, *that compassing the Death of the Father of the King was High Treason.* And Lord Chief Justice *Coke* accounteth for those Attainders upon this Principle, and upon No other.

. . . . .

Chap. I. Of High Treason in Compassing the King's Death.

The antient Writers in treating of Felonious Homicide considered the Felonious Intention manifested *by plain Facts,* not by bare Words of any kind, in the same light in point of Guilt, as Homicide itself. The Rule was *Voluntas reputatur pro Facto.* And while this Rule prevailed, the Nature of the Offence was expressed by the Term *Compassing* the Death.

This Rule hath been long laid aside as too Rigorous in the Case of Common Persons. But in the Case of the King, Queen, and Prince, the Statute of Treasons hath with great Propriety retained It in it's full Extent and Rigour:

and in describing the Offence hath likewise retained the antient Mode of Expression. "When a Man doth *compass* or *imagine* the Death of our Lord the King, or of our Lady his Queen, or their Eldest Son and Heir, and thereof be [*provablement*] upon sufficient proof Attainted of open Deed by Men of his Condition."

SECT. 1. The Words of the Statute descriptive of the Offence must be strictly pursued in every Indictment for this Species of Treason. It must charge that the Defendant did Traiterously *compass and imagine* &c. and then go on and charge the several Overt-Acts as the Means employed by the Defendant for executing his Traiterous Purposes. For the Compassing is considered as the Treason, the Overt-Acts as the Means made use of to effectuate the Intentions and Imaginations of the Heart. And therefore in the Case of the Regicides, the Indictment Charged that they did Traiterously Compass and Imagine the Death of the King. And the taking off his Head was laid, among others, as an Overt-Act of Compassing: and the Person who was supposed to have given the Stroke was Convicted on the same Indictment.

From what hath been said it followeth, that in every Indictment for this Species of Treason, and indeed for Levying War, or Adhering to the King's Enemies, an Overt-Act must be Alledged and Proved. For the Overt-Act is the Charge to which the Prisoner must apply his Defence. But it is not Necessary that the whole Detail of the Evidence intended to be given should be set forth: the Common Law never required this Exactness, nor doth the Statute of King *William,* which will be considered in it's proper Place, require it. It is sufficient that the Charge be reduced to a reasonable Certainty, so that the Defendant may be apprized of the Nature of it, and prepared to give an Answer to it.

And if divers Overt-Acts are laid and but *one proved* it will be sufficient, and the Verdict must be for the Crown. And therefore, where divers Overt-Acts are laid, and the Indictment in point of Form happeneth to be faulty with regard to some of them, the Court will not Quash it for those Defects. Because that would deprive the Crown of the Opportunity of proving the Overt-Acts that are well laid.

SECT. 2. I said in the last Section, that in the Case of the King, the Statute of Treasons hath with great Propriety retained the Rule, *Voluntas pro facto.* The Principle upon which this is founded is too obvious to need much Enlargement. The King is considered as the Head of the Body Politick, and the Members of that Body are considered as united and kept together by a Political Union with Him and with each other. His Life cannot, in the ordinary Course of Things, be taken away by Treasonable Practices without involving a whole Nation in Blood and Confusion. Consequently every Stroke levelled at His Person is, in the ordinary Course of Things, levelled at the Publick Tranquility. The Law therefore tendereth the Safety of the King with an anxious, and if I may use the Expression, with a Concern bordering *upon Jealousy.* It considereth the wicked Imaginations of the Heart in the same Degree of Guilt as if carried into actual Execution, from the Moment

Measures appear to have been taken to render them Effectual. And therefore, if Conspirators meet and consult how to Kill the King, though they do not then fall upon any Scheme for that Purpose, this is an Overt-Act of Compassing his Death; and so are all Means made use of, be it Advice, Persuasion or Command, to Incite or Incourage others to commit the Fact, or to join in the Attempt. And every Person who but Assenteth to any Overtures for that Purpose will be involved in the same Guilt.

And if a Person be but once Present at a Consultation for such Purposes and Concealeth it, *having had a previous Notice of the Design of the Meeting,* this is an Evidence proper to be left to a Jury of such Assent, though the Party say or do Nothing at such Consultation. The Law is the same if he is Present at more than One such Consultation, and doth not Dissent or make a Discovery. But in the Case of Once falling into the Company of Conspirators, if the Party met them Accidentally or upon some indifferent Occasion, bare Concealment without *Express Assent* will be but Misprision of Treason. The Law was formerly more strict in this Respect; *Si ad tempus dissimulaverit vel* subticuerit, *quasi consentiens & assentiens, erit seductor Domini Regis manifestus.*

SECT. 3. The Care the Law hath taken for the Personal Safety of the King is not confined to Actions or Attempts of the more Flagitious Kind, to Assassination or Poison, or other Attempts directly and immediately aiming at His Life. It is extended to every thing Wilfully and Deliberately done or attempted, whereby His Life may be endangered. And therefore the entring into Measures for Deposing or Imprisoning Him, or to get His Person into the Power of the Conspirators, these Offences are Overt-Acts of Treason within this Branch of the Statute. For Experience hath shewn that between the Prison and the Graves of Princes the distance is very small.

SECT. 4. Offences which are not so Personal as those already mentioned, have been with great Propriety brought within the same Rule; as having a Tendency, though not so immediate, to the same fatal End. And therefore the Entering into Measures in concert with Foreigners or others in order to an Invasion of the Kingdom, or going into a Foreign Country, or even Purposing to go thither to that End *and taking any Steps in order thereto,* these Offences are Overt-Acts of Compassing the King's Death.

. . . . .

The Offence of Inciting Foreigners to invade the Kingdom is a Treason of Signal Enormity. In the lowest Estimation of things and in all Possible Events, it is an Attempt on the part of the Offender to render his Country the Seat of Blood and Desolation. And yet, unless the Powers so incited happen to be actually at War with Us at the Time of such Incitement, the Offence will not fall within any Branch of the Statute of Treasons, except that of Compassing the King's Death. And therefore since it hath a manifest Tendency to endanger the Person of the King, it hath in strict Conformity to the Statute, and to every Principle of substantial Political Justice, been brought within that Species of Treason of Compassing the King's Death. *Ne quid detrimenti Respublica capiat.*

SECT. 5. Lord *Coke* seemeth to have been of Opinion that an Offence falling under one Branch of the Statute cannot be deemed an Overt-Act of a different Species of Treason. I believe Lord *Hale* did once fall into the same Opinion; for in his Summary speaking of Conspiracy to Levy War, He saith, it is no Overt-Act of Compassing the King's Death, *because it relateth to a distinct Treason.* But *Hale* altered His Opinion. And it is every Day's Experience that many Offences falling directly and by Name under other Branches of the Statute, may be brought within this of Compassing the King's Death. Levying War is an Overt-Act of Compassing; and under the Limitations stated in the next Chapter, *Conspiring* to Levy War likewise is an Overt-Act within this Branch. And so is a Treasonable Correspondence with the Enemy, though it falleth more naturally within the Clause of *Adhering to the King's Enemies.* . . .

SECT. 6. How far Words or Writings of a Seditious Nature may be considered as Overt-Acts within this Branch of the Statute hath been the Subject of much Debate. In Mr. *Sidney*'s Case it was said, *Scribere est agere.* This is undoubtedly true under proper Limitations, but it was not applicable to his Case. Writing being a deliberate Act and capable of satisfactory Proof certainly may, under some Circumstances *with Publication* be an Overt-Act of Treason.

. . . . .

SECT. 7. As to meer Words supposed to be Treasonable, they differ widely from Writings in Point of real Malignity and proper Evidence. They are often the Effect of meer Heat of Blood, which in some Natures otherwise well disposed, carrieth the Man beyond the Bounds of Decency or Prudence. They are always liable to great Misconstruction from the Ignorance or Inattention of the Hearers, and too often from a Motive truly Criminal. And therefore I choose to adhere to the Rule which hath been laid down on more Occasions than One since the Revolution, that Loose Words *not relative to any Act or Design* are not Overt-Acts of Treason. But Words of Advice or Persuasion, and all Consultations for the Traiterous Purposes treated of in this Chapter are certainly so. They are uttered in Contemplation of some Traiterous Purpose actually on Foot or Intended, and *in Prosecution* of it.

Lord Chief Justice *Hale* was of Opinion that bare Words are not an Overt-Act of Treason, *Coke* was of the same Opinion. *Hale* hath treated the Subject pretty much at large, and I shall not repeat his Argument. But I must say that I think his Reasons founded on Temporary Acts or Acts since Repealed, which make Speaking the Words therein set forth *Felony or Misdemeanor* are Unanswerable. For if those Words, Seditious to the last Degree, had been deemed Overt-Acts within the Statute of Treasons, the Legislature could not with any sort of Consistency have treated them as Felony or Misdemeanor.

. . . . .

I said at the beginning of this Section that Lord *Coke* was of Opinion that bare Words are not an Overt-Act of Treason. This Opinion He foundeth *singly* upon the Statute of Treasons; for He thought that at Common-Law, Words alone might be an Overt-Act of Compassing the King's

Death. And *Bracton* and the other Authors, who wrote before the Statute, are cited in support of this Opinion. *Bracton* and *Britton* are cited to the same Purpose by *Stanford*.

None of the Authors Either of the Learned Judges hath cited do in express Terms maintain this Doctrine, nor can I collect from what they have said that they at all favoured it. The Word *Machinatus*, used by *Bracton* and *Fleta*, in itself importeth nothing like it. And connected as it is with the other Words *Ausu temerario Machinatus*, it importeth nothing less than something done or attempted against the King's Life.

The Word *Compasser* made use of by *Britton* and the *Mirror* in the Passages cited by *Coke* proveth Nothing: it can prove Nothing in a Question which turneth singly on the true Sense and full Extent of the Word itself.

The Words *Praelocutus fuit Mortem &c.* used by *Bracton* and *Fleta* in setting forth the Substance of an Appeal of Treason, and the Words *Purparler tiel Mort* used by *Britton* for the same Purpose, do in sound come much nearer to the Point. But Sounds will go a very little Way towards fixing the meaning of an Author, unless the Sense and Connection of his Words be attended to. *Bracton* and *Fleta* give us but the Substance of the Appeal, and that very shortly. *Britton* is more full, *Cy face l' encusor son Appeal en cest Manner*, I. *que cy est, Appellat P. que illouques est, de ceo, que come il fuist en tiel certain Lieu, en certain tiel Jour, tiel An, la oya mesme cestuy* I. *purparler tiel Mort ou tiel Treason* [*parenter cestuy P. & un auter tiel par Nosme, & par tiels Aliances. Et que cestuy P. issint le fist & issint purparla felonisment come Felon, & traiterousment come Traytor, cestuy* I. *est prist a prover par son Corps.*] This Precedent plainly importeth a Meeting of the Conspirators and a Consultation between them for the Traiterous Purposes therein mentioned. The Words, *purparler parenter cestuy* P. *& un auter & par tiels Alliances* can mean nothing less. This Passage therefore proveth Nothing with regard to bare Words not relative to Actions; since a Consultation for taking away the King's Life undoubtedly was an Overt-Act at the Common-Law, and is so under the Statute.

The Citations from *Bracton* and *Fleta* will be found to prove as little, if the Words *Praelocutus fuit Mortem* import a Consultation with Others to that Purpose. And that they do so, appeareth highly probable from one of the Pleas which *Fleta* putteth into the Defendant's Mouth, *ad hoc, quod Accusans dicit quòd Praelocutio fuit in praesentiâ talium, respondere poterit, quod nunquam cum* praedictis talibus Colloquium habuit. However, since all those Authors, short and obscure as they are, professedly treat of the same Matter, if *Bracton* and *Fleta* may be explained by *Britton* who did not write long after them, these Passages prove nothing to the Point for which they have been cited.

The Precedent Lord *Coke* fetcheth from the Days of King *Edmund* will receive the same Answer. For it chargeth that the Conspirators, naming them ET AUTERS, met and consulted by what Means to Kill or Imprison the King, and engaged to each other to keep their Treason secret; and to furnish each of them to the utmost of his Power the Means for effecting it.

It may be thought I have taken up too much of the Reader's Time in examining this Opinion of Lord *Coke*, because as I said before, He admitteth that *since the Statute*, Words alone will not make a Man a Traitor. "There must, saith He, be an Overt-Deed; but Words without an Overt-Deed are to be punished in another Degree as an High Misprision." But if it be admitted that bare Words not relative to Actions did at Common-Law amount to an Overt-Deed, I doubt the Words *Open Deed* in the Statute on which this Learned Author relieth have not altered the Case; since the single Question is, what doth or doth not amount to an Open Deed. All the Words descriptive of the Offence "If a Man shall Compass and Imagine and thereof be attainted of Open Deed," are plainly borrowed from the Common-Law: and therefore must bear the same Construction they did at Common-Law, unless there be any thing in the Statute which will necessarily lead us to another.

This hath been urged with some Advantage by a Good modern Writer on the Crown Law, the Best we have except *Hale*, against his Lordship's Construction of the Statute. It is I confess a good Argument *ad Hominem*, but it cannot be carried farther. However, lest it should I thought it would be time not wholly mispent to shew that the Doctrine his Lordship hath advanced upon the Foot of Common-Law, is not supported by any of the Authorities to which He hath appealed.

I have considered the Question touching Words and Writings supposed to be Treasonable the more largely, not only because of the Diversity of Opinions upon it; but likewise for the great Importance of the Point, and the extreme Danger of multiplying Treasons upon slight Occasions.

I cannot conclude this Chapter without putting the Reader in mind of a fine Passage I borrow from the Baron *de Montesquieu*, worthy the Attention of all Persons concerned in the framing of Penal Laws or putting them in Execution, "*Sylla*, saith that excellent Writer, who confounded Tyranny, Anarchy, and Liberty made the *Cornelian* Laws. He seemed to have contrived Regulations meerly with a View to create Crimes. Thus distinguishing an infinite Number of Actions by the Name of Murder, he found Murderers in all Parts. And by a Practice *but too much followed* he laid Snares, sowed Thorns, and opened Precipices, wheresoever the Citizens set their Feet."

Chap. II. Of Levying War and Adhering to the King's Enemies.

Lord Chief Justice *Hale* speaking of such unlawful Assemblies as may amount to a Levying of War within the 25. *E.* 3, taketh a Difference between those Insurrections which have carried the Appearance of an Army formed under Leaders, and provided with Military Weapons and with Drums, Colours, &c. and those other disorderly Tumultuous Assemblies which have been drawn together and conducted to Purposes manifestly Unlawful, but without any of the ordinary Shew and Apparatus of War before mentioned.

I do not think any great Stress can be laid on that Distinction. It is true that in Case of Levying War, the Indictments generally charge that the Defendants were Armed and Arrayed in a Warlike manner; and where the Case would admit of it, the other Circumstances of Swords, Guns, Drums, Colours, &c. have been added. But I think the Merits of the Case have never turned singly on any of those Circumstances.

. . . . .

SECT. 1. The true Criterion therefore in all these Cases is, *Quo Animo* did the Parties Assemble. For if the Assembly be upon Account of some *private* Quarrel, or to take Revenge of *particular* Persons, the Statute of Treasons hath already determined that Point in Favour of the Subject. "If, saith the Statute, any Man ride armed *openly* [So the Word *Descouvert* ought to have been rendered] or secretly with Men of Arms against any Other to Slay or to Rob him, or to take and keep him 'till he make Fine for his Deliverance, it is not the Mind of the King nor his Council that in such Case it shall be judged Treason; but it shall be judged Felony or Trespass according to the Laws of the Land of *old Times used* and according as the Case requireth." Then immediately followeth another Clause which reacheth to the End of the Statute; and provideth that, if in such Case or *other like* the Offence had thentofore been adjudged Treason, whereby the Lands of the Offenders had come to the Crown as Forfeit; the Lords of the Fee should notwithstanding have the Escheat of such Lands, saving to the Crown the Year, Day, and Wast.

I will make a short Observation or two on these Clauses.

1st, The first Clause is evidently declaratory of the Common-Law, it shall be adjudged Felony or Trespass *according to the Law of the Land of old Time used.* The 2d hath a Retrospect to some late Judgments in which the Common Law had not taken Place; and giveth a speedy and effectual Remedy to Lords of the Fee who had suffered by those Judgments.

2dly, The Words of the first Clause descriptive of the Offence, "if any Man ride Armed openly or secretly with Men of Arms" did in the Language of those Times, mean nothing less than the Assembling Bodies of Men, Friends, Tenants or Dependants, armed and arrayed in a Warlike Manner in order to effect some Purpose or other by dint of Numbers and superior Strength. And yet those Assemblies so armed and arrayed, if drawn together for Purposes of a Private Nature, were not deemed Treasonable.

3dly, Though the Statute mentioneth only the Cases of assembling to Kill, Rob or Imprison, yet these, put as they are by Way of Example only, will not exclude others which may be brought within the same Rule. For the Retrospective Clause provideth that "if in such Case *or other like it* hath been Adjudged"—what are the other like Cases? all Cases of the like Private Nature are, I apprehend, within the Reason and Equity of the Act. The Case of the Earls of *Gloucester* and *Hereford*, and many other Cases cited by *Hale*, some before the Statute of Treasons, and others after it, those Assemblies though attended many of them with Bloodshed and with the ordinary Apparatus of War, were not held to be Treasonable Assemblies. For they were not in Construction of Law, raised against the King or His Royal Majesty, but for Purposes of a Private Personal nature.

SECT. 2. Upon the same Principle and within the Reason and Equity of the Statute, Risings to maintain a *Private* Claim of Right, or to destroy *particular* Inclosures, or to remove Nusances which affected or were thought to affect in point *of Interest the Parties Assembled for those Purposes*, or to break Prisons in order to Release *particular* Persons without any other Circumstance of Aggravation, have not been held to amount to Levying War within the Statute.

. . . . .

SECT. 3. But every Insurrection which in Judgment of Law is intended against the Person of the King be it to Dethrone or Imprison Him, or to oblige Him to alter His Measures of Government, or to remove Evil Councellors from about Him, these Risings all amount to Levying War within the Statute; whether attended with the Pomp and Circumstances of Open War or No. And every Conspiracy to Levy War for these Purposes, though not Treason within the Clause of Levying War, is yet an Overt-Act within the other Clause of Compassing the King's Death. For those Purposes cannot be effected by Numbers and open Force without manifest Danger to His Person.

SECT. 4. Insurrections in order to throw down *All* Inclosures, to alter the Established Law or change Religion, to inhance the Price of *All* Labour or to open *All* Prisons, all Risings in order to effect these Innovations of a *Publick and General Concern by an Armed Force,* are in Construction of Law High Treason, within the Clause of Levying War. For though they are not levelled at the Person of the King, they are against *His Royal Majesty.* And besides, they have a direct Tendency to dissolve all the Bonds of Society, and to destroy all Property and all Government too, by Numbers and an Armed Force. Insurrections likewise for redressing *National* Grievances, or for the Expulsion of Foreigners in General, or indeed of any Single Nation living here under the Protection of the King, or for the Reformation of Real or Imaginary Evils *of a Public Nature and in which the Insurgents have no Special Interest,* Risings to effect these Ends by Force and Numbers, are by Construction of Law within the Clause of Levying War. For they are levelled at the King's Crown and Royal Dignity.

. . . . .

SECT. 6. But a bare Conspiracy for effecting a Rising for the Purposes mentioned in the two preceding Sections and in the next, is not an Overt-Act of Compassing the King's Death. Nor will it come under any Species of Treason within the 25. *E.* 3. *unless the Rising be Effected.* And in that Case the Conspirators as well as the Actors will All be equally Guilty. For in High Treason of all Kinds, All the *Participes Criminis* are Principals.

It must be admitted that Conspiracies for these Purposes have been adjudged Treason. But those Judgments were founded on the Temporary Act of 13. *Eliz.* which made Compassing to Levy War, declared by Printing, Writing, or Advised Speaking, High Treason *during the Life of the Queen.*

There was an Act in the 13. *Car.* 2. to the same Purpose on which some Prosecutions were founded; but that Act expired with the Death of the King.

. . . . .

415

SECT. 8. The joining with Rebels in an Act of Rebellion, or with Enemies in Acts of Hostility, will make a Man a Traitor: in the one Case within the Clause of Levying War, in the other within that of Adhering to the King's Enemies. But if this be done for fear of Death, and while the Party is under Actual Force, and He taketh the first Opportunity that offereth to make his Escape, this Fear and Compulsion will excuse Him. It is however incumbent on the Party who maketh Fear and Compulsion his Defence, to shew to the Satisfaction of the Court and Jury that the Compulsion continued during all the Time He staid with the Rebels or Enemies.

I will not say that He is obliged to account for every Day, Week, or Month. That perhaps would be impossible. And therefore if an original Force be proved, and the Prisoner can shew, that He in earnest attempted to escape and was prevented; or that He did get off and was forced back, or that He was narrowly watched, and all Passes guarded; or from other Circumstances, which it is impossible to state with Precision but when proved ought to weigh with a Jury, that an Attempt to escape would have been attended with great Difficulty and Danger; *so that upon the whole He may be presumed to have continued among them against his Will, though not constantly under an Actual Force or Fear of Immediate Death*, these Circumstances and others of the like Tendency proved to the Satisfaction of the Court and Jury, will be sufficient to excuse Him.

But an Apprehension though ever so well grounded, of having Houses Burnt or Estates Wasted or Cattle Destroyed, or of any other Mischief of the like Kind, will not excuse in the Case of Joining and Marching with Rebels or Enemies.

Furnishing Rebels or Enemies with Money, Arms, Ammunition or other Necessaries will *Primâ facie*, make a Man a Traitor. But if Enemies or Rebels come with a Superior Force and Exact Contributions, or live upon the Country at free Quarter, Submission in these Cases is not Criminal. For *flagrante Bello* the *jus Belli* taketh Place, 'tis the only Law then subsisting. And Submission is a Point of the highest Prudence to prevent a greater Publick Evil.

And the bare sending Money or Provisions (except in the Case just excepted) or sending Intelligence to Rebels or Enemies, which in most Cases is the most Effectual Aid that can be given them, will make a Man a Traitor, though the Money or Intelligence should happen to be intercepted. For the Party in sending did all He could: the Treason was compleat *on his Part though it had not the Effect He intended*.

. . . . .

SECT. 9. An Assembly Armed and Arrayed in a Warlike Manner for any Treasonable Purpose is *Bellum Levatum*, though not *Bellum Percussum*. Listing and Marching are sufficient Overt-Acts without coming to a Battle or Action. So Cruising on the King's Subjects under a *French* Commission, *France* being then at War with Us, was held to be Adhering to the King's Enemies, though no Other Act of Hostility was laid or proved.

SECT. 10. Attacking the King's Forces *in Opposition to His Authority* upon a March or in Quarters is Levying War against the King. But if upon a sudden Quarrel, from some Affront given or taken, the Neighbourhood should rise and drive the Forces out of their Quarters, That would be a great Misdemeanor, and if Death should ensue it may be Felony in the Assailants: but it will not be Treason, because there was no Intention against the King's Person or Government.

SECT. 11. Holding a Castle or Fort against the King or His Forces, if *Actual Force be used in order to keep Possession*, is Levying War. But a bare Detainer, as suppose by shutting the Gates against the King or His Forces, without any other Force from within, Lord *Hale* conceiveth will not amount to Treason. But if this be done in *Confederacy with Enemies* or Rebels, that Circumstance will make it Treason; in the One Case under the Clause of Adhering to the King's Enemies, in the Other under that of Levying War. So if a Person having the Custody of a Castle or Fort deliver it up to the Rebels or Enemies, *by Treachery and in Combination with Them*, this is High Treason within the Act; in the former Case 'tis Levying War, in the latter 'tis Adhering to the King's Enemies. But meer Cowardice or Imprudence, though it might subject a Commander in such Case to Death by the Martial Law, will not amount to Treason.

SECT. 12. States in Actual Hostility with Us, though no War be solemnly Declared, are Enemies within the meaning of the Act. And therefore in an Indictment on the Clause of Adhering to the King's Enemies, it is sufficient to Aver that the Prince or State Adhered to *is an Enemy*, without shewing any War Proclaimed. And the Fact, whether War or No, is triable by the Jury; and Publick Notoriety is sufficient Evidence of the Fact. And if the Subject of a Foreign Prince in Amity with Us, invadeth the Kingdom without Commission from his Sovereign, He is an Enemy. And a Subject of *England* adhering to Him is a Traitor within this Clause of the Act.

. . . . .

Chap. III. Touching the Act of the 7. William III. for Regulating Trials in Cases of Treason and Misprision of Treason.

Bishop *Burnet* informeth Us that this Act passed after a long Struggle, contrary to the Hopes and Expectation of the Persons then at the Head of Affairs. "The Design of it," He saith, "seemed to be to make Men as safe in all Treasonable Practices as possible." This is a grievous Imputation on the Persons who forwarded the Bill in either House of Parliament, and might have been spared. But I believe it was the *Language* of Many, and the *Opinion* of Some of the Party with which the Bishop stood connected.

Had the Bill required Two Witnesses to the Same Fact at the Same Time, as his Lordship saith it did, it would indeed have rendered Men very secure in Treasonable Practices: but then it will be difficult to reconcile this to what He saith in a few Lines afterwards. For after setting forth the Substance of some of the Principal Clauses, particularly That relating to Two Witnesses to the Same Fact at the Same Time He addeth, "All these Things were in

416

themselves just and reasonable: and if they had been moved by *other Men* and at *another Time,* they would have met *with little Opposition."*

The Bill did not come to the Royal Assent during the Session it was brought into Parliament. For the Clause which requireth that All the Peers shall be Summoned upon a Trial of a Peer for Treason or Misprision of Treason, a Provision founded in sound Sense and strict Justice, was added by the Lords: and the Bill with that Amendment sent back to the Commons, who disagreed to the Amendment: and so the Bill dropped for that Session.

In a Subsequent Session the Commons sent up their own Bill again, and the Lords added their Clause, which saith the Historian, "was not easily carried; for Those who wished well to the Bill looked on this as a Device to lose it, *as no doubt it was,* and therefore opposed it: but contrary to the Hopes of the Court the Commons were so desirous of the Bill, that when it came down to Them they Agreed to the Clause. And so the Bill passed and had the Royal Assent."

Some Reflections might be made upon the Spirit of Faction which possessed both Sides, in this Competition of Parties, but I forbear. And proceed to offer a few Observations on the several Parts of the Act.

SECT. 1. My first Enquiry will be, What Treasons are within the Act, and How the Law standeth with regard to Those that are Not. By the general Tenor of the Act it extendeth to such High Treasons *only* whereby "any Corruption of Blood may or shall be made to the Offender or his Heirs and to the Misprision of such Treasons."

The First and Second Sections are expresly confined to those Treasons, and the Misprision of them: and All the other Clauses, except those relating to the Trial of Peers, and to the Rejection of Evidence of Overt-Acts not laid in the Indictment, use Words of plain Reference to the Treasons mentioned in the First and Second Sections. And the 13th Section expresly excludeth the Treasons of Counterfeiting His Majesty's Coin, the Great Seal, Privy Seal, Signet, and Sign Manual.

The Case of Petty Treason therefore standeth upon the foot it did before this Act, and so do the Treasons that are expresly excluded. And All the Treasons created by Acts Saving the Corruption of Blood stand likewise on the same foot.

The Statutes Saving the Blood are, 5 *Eliz.* c. 1. S. 10. 11. 12. concerning the Papal Supremacy, 5 *Eliz.* c. 11.—18 *Eliz.* c. 1.—8, 9 *W.* 3. c. 25. and 15, 16 *Geo.* 2. c. 28. touching the Coin. I do not recollect any more of that kind.

. . . . .

SECT. 3. A Question may possibly be made Whether the Benefit of this Act is to be extended to All Treasons working Corruption of Blood created by *Subsequent Acts,* wherein the Benefit of the Act is not saved by Special Provisoe: because the Legislature, which is presumed to do nothing in Vain, hath in some Instances made express Provision for that Purpose. I should not have mentioned this as a Matter of Doubt if Lord *Hale* had not in a similar Case, I mean touching the Extent of the Statutes of *E.* 6,

entertained a Doubt grounded on the same Presumption. For My part, I think the Benefit of the Act ought to be extended to Prosecutions for All manner of High Treasons, *Working Corruption of Blood* and not within the Exceptions, though created by Acts subsequent to it. The Words of the Act take in every possible Case, *"All and Every* Person or Persons that shall be Accused or Indicted for High Treason &c."* the Principles and Views upon which the Legislature proceeded, as they are set forth in the Preamble, will govern every future Case under the like Circumstances. And the known Rules of Construction oblige Us to Construe an Act so beneficial, as Liberally as may be; that is, to extend it as far as the Letter, and especially the visible Scope and Intention of it will warrant Us.

Arguments founded on a general Presumption of the Wisdom and Circumspection of the Legislature always will and ought to have their Weight. It hath been said, and many times with great Propriety, that the making Special Provision in certain Cases by Statute implieth that the Law had not before provided for those Cases; *For the Parliament doth Nothing in Vain.* This is a good general Rule, but it is very well known not to be Universally true. But admitting it was so, yet many valuable Purposes, which Wisdom and a just Concern for the Publick Welfare will suggest, may be answered by an express Provision, not in itself of absolute indispensible Necessity: sometimes for removing Doubts where different Opinions have been entertained; and at other times out of abundant Caution for obviating Doubts that possibly may arise. The Instances of Both kinds are numerous and need not be mentioned in this Place.

. . . . .

SECT. 5. Before I conclude this Enquiry touching the Extent of the Statute, I will just mention the Offences of Importing Money Counterfeit to the similitude of *English* Coin, Counterfeiting Foreign Coin Legitimated by Proclamation, and of Importing such Coin. These Treasons work a Corruption of Blood, and as such are brought within the general Purview of the Act; and do not come within the *Letter* of the Exception, which in the Case of Coin mentions only the Offence of *Counterfeiting* His Majesty's Coin. Whether this Beneficial Law shall be extended to those Treasons, or whether by the Rule of Congruity they shall stand upon the same foot with the Offence of Counterfeiting the Coin of the Kingdom, as in some Cases All Treasons concerning the Coin do; these Questions will be very fit to be considered whenever the Cases shall happen, which probably will not be very soon.

For Prosecutions for the First of those Offences have been very Rare: and for the Others there can be None, as things stand at present, 'till the Crown shall be advised to Legitimate some Species of Foreign Coin. I know of none now Current among Us that is Legitimated, and most probably none will. For if the Offences of Counterfeiting and Diminishing Foreign Coin and of Importing such Counterfeit and Diminished Coin, which are great Evils, and daily growing, were made more Penal than they are at present, I know of no good End that could be answered by Legitimating any Species of it; on the other Hand I foresee great Inconveniences that would attend it.

As to the Treasons which are not within the Act, I shall

be very short in this Place. Petty Treason is intitled to the Benefit of the Acts of the 1st and 5th of *E*. 6. as far as concerns the Point of Evidence; and by 1. 2. *Ph*. and *M*. it is intitled to a Trial according to the due Course and Order of Common-Law. The Treason created by the 1st of *Eliz*. already mentioned standeth in Both these respects upon the same foot.

The other Treasons not comprehended in the general Words or Excepted, relating to the Coin and the Seals &c. are likewise intitled to a Trial according to the due Course and Order of the Common-Law, and to all the Advantages incident to that Method of Trial, which will be hereafter more particularly mentioned.

I now proceed to the Other parts of the Act.

I shall not consider the several Clauses in the Order they stand, but as far as I can, I will range them under the following Heads. What Privileges the Prisoner is intitled to, and What is incumbent on Him *previous* to the Trial, and What *during* the Trial. The Clauses which do not fall under these Heads will be Last considered.

SECT. 6. The Prisoner is to have a Copy of the Whole Indictment, but not of the Witnesses Names, five Days at least before the Trial in order to enable Him to Advise with his Council thereupon, to Plead and make his Defence; His Attorney or Agent or any Person on his behalf requiring the same, and paying reasonable Fees for the Writing thereof, not exceeding 5*s* for the Copy of any One Indictment. *(Sect.* 1.*)*

And if He desireth Council, the Court where He is to be tried or any Judge thereof, shall immediately upon request Assign Him such and so many Council, not exceeding Two, as He shall desire: and such Council shall have free Access to Him at all Seasonable Hours. *(Ibid.)*

He shall likewise have a Copy of the Pannel of the Jurors who are to try Him duly returned by the Sheriff, and delivered to Him Two Days at least before his Trial. And He shall have the like Process to compel his Witnesses to appear at the Trial for Him, as is usually granted to compel Witnesses to appear against Prisoners in the like Case. *(Sect.* 7.*)*

The 7th of the late Queen, whenever it shall fully take Effect, will make some material Alterations in the Law touching Copies of the Indictment and Pannel. And therefore before I conclude some notice shall be taken of it.

At Common-Law no Prisoner in Capital Cases was intitled to a Copy of the Indictment or Pannel, or of Any of the Proceedings against Him. Many Persons, it is true, have upon their Arraignment insisted on a Copy of the Whole Indictment, but it hath been constantly denied. It was denied in the Case of Lord *Preston* and the Two other Gentlemen indicted with Him, by the unanimous opinion of the Judges present, who declared that it never had been granted, though frequently demanded. And Lord *Preston* having said that it was granted to Lord *Russel*, *Holt* told Him that He and some Other of the Judges present who were of Council for that Lord did not advise Him to demand it. "For, saith He, We knew He could not have it by Law." Lord *Preston*, not satisfied with this Answer prayed

that Counsel might be Assigned Him to argue that Point; which the Court unanimously refused, it being, they said, *a Point that would not bear a Debate.*

The Statute of the 46. *E*. 3. which had been formerly insisted upon by Prisoners in the like Case, was much pressed in this. It is not in Print among the Statutes, but an Attested Copy from the Roll was read at the Prisoner's Request, and is printed in the Trial. It plainly relateth to such Records in which the Subject may be Interested, as *Matters of Evidence upon Questions of private Right*. And it Enacteth, "That all Persons shall for the future have free Access to Them, and may have *Exemplifications* of Them whether they make For or Against the king." This was the Opinion of the whole Court.

. . . . .

Though the Act mentioneth only the Copy of the Indictment, yet the Prisoner ought to have a Copy of the *Caption* delivered to Him with the Indictment: for This in many Cases is as necessary to enable Him to conduct himself in Pleading, as the Other. This is now the constant Practice.

But if the Prisoner pleadeth without a Copy of the *Caption*, as some of the Assassines did, He is too late to make that Objection, or indeed any other Objection that turneth upon a Defect in the Copy; for by Pleading, He admitteth that He hath had a Copy *sufficient for the Purposes intended by the Act.*

By the Letter of the Act the Copy is to be delivered five Days before the Trial. But upon the true Construction of it, the Copy after the Bill is Found, for 'till then it is no Indictment, ought to be delivered five Days before the Day of Arraignment, for that is the Prisoner's Time for Pleading. And the five Days must be Exclusive of the Day of Delivery and the Day of Arraignment. So with regard to the Copy of the Pannel, the Two Days must be Exclusive of the Day of Delivery and the Day of Trial. These Points have been long settled, and are now matters of constant Practice.

Though the Words of the Statute are, that the Prisoner shall have a Copy of the Pannel *duly returned by the Sheriff*, yet if the Copy should happen to be delivered before the Return of the Precept, which upon a bare Commission of Oyer and Terminer is commonly made returnable on the Day intended for the Trial, it will be sufficient. For it satisfieth the Words of the Statute and answereth all the Ends of it.

The Little Tract intituled "The Method of Trial of Commoners in Cases of High Treason" published in the Year 1709 by Order of the House of Lords directeth that the Additions of Dwelling-Places and Professions of the Jurors be inserted in the Copy of the Pannel; but the Act doth not require that Exactness, and the Practice is otherwise.

If the Prisoner would avail Himself of any Defect in the Indictment by Miswriting, Mispelling, False or Improper Latin, He must take his Exceptions, *before Evidence given* in Open Court, these are the Words of the Act. *(Sect.* 9.*)*

But though the Act is thus Worded, the Construction of it hath been, that Exceptions grounded on those Mistakes must be taken *before Plea Pleaded*. And in the Cases of Captain *Vaughan* already cited and of one *Sullivan* at the *Old Bayly, October* 1715, and of Mr. *Layer,* the Court refused to hear such Exceptions after Plea. It is true that in *Cranburne's* Case the Court did permit his Council to take those Exceptions after Plea, and in *Rookwood's* after the Jury was Sworn. But it ought to be remembered these were Indulgencies to the Prisoners upon a New Act, and before the Practice was settled to the Contrary, as it now is.

I come now to the Privileges the Prisoner is intitled to during the Time of his Trial.

SECT. 7. He is to have the Assistance of his Council throughout his Trial, to Examine his Witnesses, and to Conduct his whole Defence as well in point of Fact as upon Questions of Law. *(Sect. 1.)*

At Common-Law no Council was allowed upon the Issue of Guilty or Not Guilty in any Capital Case whatsoever, except upon Questions of Law. And then only in Doubtful, not in Plain Cases. I am far from disputing the Propriety of this Rule while it is confined to Felony and the Lower Class of Treasons concerning the Coin and the Seals. I know many things have been thrown out upon this Subject, and Inconveniences some Real some Imaginary, have been suggested by Popular Writers, who seem to have attended singly to those on One side of the Question. But it is impossible in a State of Imperfection to keep clear of all Inconveniences; though Wisdom will always direct Us to the Course which is subject to the Fewest and the Least. And this is the utmost that Human Wisdom can do.

In State-Prosecutions which are the Objects of this Act, and are carried on by the Weight of the Crown and too often in the Spirit of Party, and are generally conducted by Gentlemen of High Rank at the Bar, it is extremely reasonable to allow the Prisoner the Assistance of Council, to the full Extent of the Act. But this the Common-Law did not allow. Accordingly it was refused to every Person concerned in the Assassination-Plot whose Trials came on *after this Act had passed the Royal Assent, but before the Commencement of it.* And in Sir *William Parkins's* Case the very Day before the Act took place, *Holt* said upon the Occasion, *"We must conform to the Law as it is at Present, not to what it will be To-morrow, We are upon our Oaths so to do."* Council as to matters of Fact was likewise denied to Lord *Winton* and to Lord *Lovat,* being in the Case of an Impeachment which is excepted out of the Act. But all the Prisoners I have mentioned had, through the Benignity of the Times, Council to attend Them in Prison previous to their Trials.

Upon the Trial of Issues that do not turn upon the Question of Guilty or Not Guilty but upon Collateral Facts, Prisoners under a Capital Charge whether for Treason or Felony, always were intitled to the full Assistance of Council. *Humphry Stafford* in the 1st of *Hen.* 7. had Council on his Plea of Sanctuary. *Roger Johnson* whose Case is before Reported had Council on the Error in Fact assigned by Him for Reversing his Outlawry, though in a Case concerning the Coin. And so had *John Harvey* and every Prisoner in the like Case with Him upon the Issue taken upon the several matters alledged in the Suggestion filed on the Part of the Crown, pursuant to the Act of the 19th of the King.

SECT. 8. I come now to the Head of Evidence which divideth itself into two Branches. *What Number of Witnesses doth the Act require,* and *What Matters may be given in Evidence.* And though I have postponed the Consideration of this Part of the Act to this Place, yet whatever will be said with regard to Evidence *at the Trial,* must be applied to the Evidence which shall be given *on the Indictment.*

I know a Difference hath been taken in the construction of the Statutes of *E.* 6. and of *Ph.* and *Ma.* between the Indictment and the Trial. But this Distinction is entirely without Foundation even upon the Foot of those Statutes. But the present Act hath not left room for that Distinction. It Enacteth that "no Person shall be *Indicted,* Tried, or Attainted of any Treason whereby any Corruption of Blood may be made to the Offender or his Heirs or of the Misprision of such Treason, but upon the Oaths of Two lawful Witnesses; either Both to the same Overt-Act, or One of them to One and Another to Another Overt-Act of the *same Treason:* unless He shall willingly and without violence in *Open Court* confess the same. Or shall stand Mute, or refuse to Plead, or in Cases of High Treason shall Peremptorily Challenge above the Number of 35 of the Jury." *(Sect. 2.)*

"Provided that any Person being Indicted as aforesaid for any of the said Treasons or Misprisions, may be Outlawed and thereby Attainted. And in Cases of the High Treasons aforesaid where by the Law, after such Outlawry, the Party Outlawed may come in to be Tried, He shall upon such Trial have the Benefit of this Act." *(Sect. 3.)*

"And it further Enacteth and Declareth that if Two or More distinct Treasons of divers Heads or Kinds shall be alledged in One Bill of Indictment, One Witness to One of the said Treasons and Another Witness to Another of the said Treasons shall not be deemed Two Witnesses to the same Treason within the meaning of the Act." *(Sect. 4.)*

It hath been generally agreed, and I think upon just Grounds, (though Lord *Coke* hath advanced a contrary Doctrine) that at Common-Law One Witness was sufficient in the Case of Treason as well as in every Other Capital Case. The only Difficulty hath been upon the Construction of the Statute of *Ph.* and *Ma.* whether that Act hath Repealed the Statutes of *E.* 6. *as far as they make Two Witnesses necessary in All Cases of Treason.*

It may possibly be judged needless at this time to enter far into this Inquiry. But since the Statutes of *E.* 6. plainly extend to Petit Treason and the Act now under Consideration as plainly doth not, it will Not be time altogether mispent to clear up this Point. For Petit Treason standeth in this Respect singly on the foot of the Statutes of *Ed.* 6.

I do not find upon looking over the State Trials that in Crown-Prosecutions any great regard was paid to the Acts of *E.* 6. for near a Century after they were passed; or indeed to the common well-known Rules of Legal Evidence. Though the Authors who wrote in those Days do sometimes speak of the Acts as then in force. In the Case of

William Thomas, when they were undoubtedly in force, they were rendered quite Nugatory by this very extraordinary Resolution, that *One Witness of his own Knowledge, and Another by Hearsay* FROM HIM, though AT THE THIRD OR FOURTH HAND, made Two Witnesses or Accusors within the Acts. And in the Case of Sir *Nicholas Throckmorton* which came to Trial the same Term, no sort of regard was paid to them. For though the Prisoner strongly insisted on the Benefit of them, particularly of That which requireth the Witnesses to be brought face to face upon the Trial, the Council for the Crown went on in the method formerly practised, reading Examinations and Confessions of Persons supposed to be Accomplices, some *Living and Amesneable,* others *lately Hanged for the same Treason.*

In many of the succeeding Trials the Prisoners were told that the Statutes of *Edw.* the 6th *were repealed,* particularly That which required Two Witnesses face to face; That this Law had been found dangerous to the Crown; that Witnesses may be prevailed upon to Unsay in Court what they have Said upon their Examinations; that the Confessions of Persons accusing themselves are the strongest of all Evidence against their Accomplices; That their Partners in Guilt are the *Gens de lour Condition* the Statute of Treasons speaketh of; And that Confessions, though not signed by the Party, are of equal Weight with those that are Signed. This every Man who will do so much Penance as to read over the State Trials during the Reigns of Queen *Eliz.* and King *James,* will find to have been the Doctrine and Practice of the Times. And I do not see that the Case of Sir *Walter Raleigh,* whose Trial having been long since Printed and prefixed to His History hath been more generally Read and Censured than Others, I do not see that That Case, always excepting the extraordinary Behaviour of the King's Attorney, did in point of Hardship differ from Many of the former.

In succeeding Times, when People of all Ranks and Parties had in their Turn been learning Moderation in the School of Adversity, Light began to dawn upon Us. Lord *Coke,* after his Disgrace at Court had given Him Leisure for Cool Reflection, was of Opinion that the Statutes of *Ed.* 6th touching Evidence are Not Repealed by 1. 2. *Ph.* and *Ma.* that Two Witnesses are Still required in Cases of Treason; not barely upon the Indictment, which He Stateth as an Opinion entertained by Some, but also upon the Trial. This as far as I can collect from the Passages I have cited was the Result of all his Searches into this Matter; though He doth not in every Part of the Passage express Himself with that Light and Precision which the Importance of the Subject required.

In the Case of Mr. *Love, Hale* who was Council for Him, insisted that Two Witnesses are necessary upon the Trial in Case of Treason, upon the foot of the Statutes of *Edw.* the 6th *not Repealed,* He saith, *in point of Testimony by the Statute of Ph. and Ma.;* And one of the Council on the side of the Prosecution, who upon the whole argued with Candour, admitted that the Statutes of *E.* 6. are not Repealed by that of *Ph.* and *M.* and that Two Witnesses are still necessary; But insisted, that One Witness to One Overt-Act, and Another to Another Overt-Act of *the same Species of*

Treason are Two sufficient Witnesses within the Acts. This Gentleman was the First I have met with who considered the Point in this Light; in which, as I shall shew presently, it hath been considered ever since the Restoration.

Hale in his Summary is clear that the Statutes of *Ed.* 6. require Two Witnesses to the *Petit Jury* in the Case of Treason. And this, saith He, standeth notwithstanding the Stat. of the 1. 2. *Ph. Ma.* But in his History of the Pleas of the Crown He speaketh more doubtfully. He saith in One place, that it hath been *held by Many* that the Statutes of *E.* 6. are still in Force notwithstanding 1. 2. *Ph. M.* In Another, that Two Witnesses are required *upon the Indictment, not upon the Trial.* In a Third, after having said that it is agreed on all Hands that the Stat. of *Ph.* and *M.* taketh away the *Necessity of Two Witnesses on the Trial,* He proceedeth to consider the Opinion of those who argued that the Trial being the Sole Object of that Statute, it did Not take away the Necessity of Two Witnesses on the Indictment, since the Indictment and Trial are in their Opinion two distinct Things.

He then offereth many strong Reasons founded on great Authority against that Distinction; and sheweth that the Indictment ought to be considered as inseperably incident to the Trial and in truth a Part of it. And concludeth thus, "And thus the Reasons stand on both sides; and though Those seem to be stronger than the Former, yet in a Case of this Moment it is safest to hold That in Practice which hath least Doubt and Danger, especially in Cases of Life." Thus far the Learned Judge appeareth to have been Doubtful *at least,* to say no more. But in another Passage speaking of Informations in Capital Cases taken by Magistrates upon Oath, and in what Cases and under what Restrictions they may be read in Evidence, He saith, "Though Informations upon Oath taken before a Justice of the Peace may make a good Testimony to be read against the Offender *in Case of Felony* where the Witness is not able to Travel, yet in Case of *Treason where Two Witnesses are required* such an Examination is not allowable; for the Statute requireth, that They (if living) be produced upon the Arraignment in the Presence of the Prisoner, to the end He may cross-examine Them." The Statute his Lordship mentioneth can be no other than the 5. 6. *E.* 6. Some other Passages I might have cited from the History of the Pleas of the Crown, where the Learned Author fluctuateth between two opposite Opinions upon this Point, but these are sufficient.

Keiling Reporteth that at a Conference among the Judges preparatory to the Trial of the Regicides, it was agreed that the Law requireth Two Witnesses in the Case of Treason; but that One Witness to One Overt-Act of Compassing (for Compassing the King's Death was the Treason then under Consideration) and Another Witness to Another Act of Compassing, make Two Witnesses of Compassing. He afterwards speaketh very doubtfully upon this Point; and at length saith, that it seemed to Him *that One Witness is sufficient in Treason,* and *that the* 1. 2. *Ph. and M. had Repealed the Statutes of E.* 6.

At Lord *Stafford's* Trial the Necessity of Two Witnesses was treated as a Point beyond all Doubt. But his Lordship insisting that there ought to be Two to *each Overt-Act,* All the Judges present delivered their Opinions *seriatim,* and declared that One Witness to One Overt-Act, and Another to Another Overt-Act of *the same Species of Treason,* are Two sufficient Witnesses within the Statutes: otherwise no Government could be safe if Traitors had but Craft equal to their Villany. From that time the Point hath been settled. And in the succeeding Trials of that Reign and the Next, though many irregular Things were done savouring of the Times, this Rule still kept it's ground. And in all the Trials after the Revolution before the Act of the 7th of King *William* took place, it was strictly observed.

Having given this Short History of the Difficulty which hath been founded on the Statute of *Ph.* and *M.* I will take the Liberty of offering My own Thoughts upon it.

I conceive that the Clause upon which the Doubt arose, "That all Trials for any Treason shall be according to the due *Order and Course of the Common-Law* and not Otherwise," was intended in favour of the Subject, not in the least to his Prejudice. It was founded in the same Principle, and directed to the same Salutary Ends, which the Statute made but the Year before reducing All Treasons to the Standard of the 25. *E.* 3. had in View. By the One, the Subject was secured in his Journey through Life against the numerous Precipices which the Heat and Distemper of Former times had opened in his Way; the Other restored to Him the Benefit of a Trial by a Jury of the proper County, with all the Advantages for Defence peculiar to that method of Trial, where former Statutes had deprived Him of it. This I apprehend was the Sole Intent of this Clause, which will be better explained by what followeth.

By 32. *H.* 8. Treasons committed in *Wales* or where the King's Writ runneth not, were to be Tried in such Shires and by such Commissioners as the King should appoint. By 33d of that King Persons committing Treason, and confessing it and afterwards becoming Lunatick, might be Tried *without being brought to answer,* by the like Special Commission in any County the King should appoint. And by another Act of the same Year, Persons accused of Treason or Misprision committed in *England* or Elsewhere, being Examined by Three of the Privy Council and by Them *vehemently suspected,* might be tried by Special Commission in any County the King should appoint. And by the same Act, the Peremptory Challenge in all Cases of Treason and Misprision was absolutely taken away.

These Acts were derogatory to the *due Course and Order of the Common-Law,* and in many Instances Grievous to the Subject. The Judges have therefore considered them all as Repealed by this General Clause, so far as concerneth Treasons committed in *England* or *Wales.* By this Construction, the Trial by a Jury of the proper County with a Peremptory Challenge of 35, which is with peculiar Propriety called a Trial according *to the due Course and Order of the Common-Law,* is restored.

But the Acts of the 28th and 35th of that Reign for the Trial of Treasons committed on the High Seas or out of the Realm, though they introduced a Method of Trial New in those Cases and Unknown to the Common-Law, have not been held to be Repealed by this Clause; nor is the 33. *H.* 8. Repealed as *far as it concerneth Treason in Foreign Parts.* For these Acts deprive the Subject of no Advantage for Defence to which He was before intitled. On the contrary, instead of a Trial according to the Course and Order of the Civil-Law, they introduced a Trial founded in the Wisdom and Benignity of the Common-Law, with all the Advantages for Defence incident to it; except only in the Point of Locality, which the Nature of the Cases would not admit of.

But the Privilege the Subject is intitled to under the Statutes of *E.* 6. of having the Charge proved by two Lawful Witnesses and those brought face to face at the Trial, a mighty safe-guard against Oppressive Prosecutions, was Never intended to be taken away by this General Clause. Nor in truth did the Legislature apprehend that it could be extended so far.

For by a Subsequent Clause in the same Statute it is Provided "that in all Cases of High Treason concerning Coin Current within the Realm, or for Counterfeiting the King's or Queen's Signet, Privy Seal, Great Seal, or Sign Manual, such manner of Trial and none other shall be observed and kept as heretofore hath been used by the Common-Law of this Realm, any Law, Statute, or other Thing to the contrary Notwithstanding." It will be extremely difficult to account for this Clause, which is admitted on all hands to have taken away the Necessity of Two Witnesses in the Cases touching the Coin and Seals, if the Former Clause had done the same in all Cases of Treason whatsoever; the Latter Clause was certainly inserted to effect something which the Former had not. But I think the next Act maketh the Matter very clear if any Doubt remaineth on this. It Enacteth, that in the Case of Offences therein enumerated touching the Coin the Offenders "may be Indicted, Tried, Convicted, and Attainted by such *like Evidence* and in such Manner and Form as hath been used and accustomed within this Realm, at any time before the First Year of our late Sovereign Lord King *E.* 6." Here the Matter of Evidence, which appeareth to be the only Point then in Contemplation, is plainly expressed and extended by Name to the Indictment as well as the Trial; and the very Time when Two Witnesses first became necessary in Both Cases is pointed out.

If the Legislature did intend by the Former Act to take away the Necessity of Two Witnesses in all Cases of Treason whatsoever, why did it not speak as plainly as it doth in this? And on the other hand, if it was conceived that this was done by the General Words of the Former Act, why is it done in Special Cases in Terms so express by This? The different Penning of Two Clauses in One and the Same Act, and also of Two Acts depending at the same time and probably passed the Royal Assent on the same Day, convinceth Me that the Legislature had in Contemplation two different Objects, distinct in their Nature and Tendency: and accordingly made different Provisions respectively suited to the Nature of Each.

I now return to the Statute of King *William.*

Though it requireth Two Witnesses to each Treason, yet a Collateral Fact not tending to the Proof of the Overt-Acts, may be proved by One. For this Statute confineth itself to the Proof of the Treason, *the Proof of the Overt-Acts.* And the Statutes of *E.* 6, are confined to the Evidence for proving the Prisoner Guilty of the Offences charged on Him, which likewise must be understood of Overt-Acts.

This Difference between the Proof of Overt-Acts and of Collateral Facts, was taken by Lord *Holt* in the Case of Captain *Vaughan*, who insisted and called Witnesses to prove that He was a Subject of *France* born in the Dominions of the *French* King. The Council for the Crown called Witnesses to prove Him born in *Ireland*. And his Council insisting that there was but One credible Witness to that Fact, *Holt* said, "That is no Overt-Act, if there be One Witness to That it is enough; there need not be Two Witnesses to prove Him a Subject, but here are More." His Confession was likewise given in Evidence as to That Fact. But it appearing upon Cross-Examination, to have been made the Night He was taken and when very Drunk, and the Fact of his Birth in *Ireland* being absolutely denied by Him the next Morning upon his Examination taken before a Magistrate, little Regard seems to have been paid to his Confession.

The Case of a Confession made Willingly and without Violence is excepted in this Act and in Both the Statutes of *E.* 6. But there is a Difference in the Wording these Statutes which I have thought did merit Consideration so far as to warrant a Different Construction of them. The Words of this Act are, "unless the Party shall Willingly and without Violence in *Open Court* confess the same." The Words in *Open Court* the Statutes of *E.* 6. have omitted. Those Words seem to have been inserted in order to carry the Necessity of Two Witnesses to the Overt-Acts farther than the Statutes of *E.* 6. were formerly thought to carry it. For the Construction of those Statutes hath been, that a Confession upon an Examination of the Party, *taken out of Court and before a Magistrate or Person having Authority to take such Examination,* proved upon the Trial by Two Witnesses is Evidence of itself sufficient to Convict, without farther Proof of the Overt-Acts. For, say the Books, such Confession *putteth the Case out of the Statute, it satisfieth the Statute:* and by Confession is not meant a Confession before the Judge upon the Prisoner's Arraignment, but upon his Examination before a Magistrate: for, saith *Coke,* the Words, without Violence, mean Willingly *without any Torture,* and the Judge is never present at any Torture, neither upon the Prisoner's Arraignment was ever any Torture offered.

But in the Year 1716. at a Conference among the Judges, preparatory to the Trial of *Francis Francia,* at which the Attorney and Solicitor General *who were to conduct the Prosecution the next Day* lent their Assistance, no Regard seemeth to have been paid to the Authorities I have cited; for it was then agreed that upon the Foot of those Acts of *E.* 6. by Confession is meant only a Confession *upon the Arraignment of the Party,* which it was said *amounteth to a Conviction.*

. . . . .

In truth, with regard to all Collateral Facts not conducing to the Proof of the Overt-Acts, I think We may safely lay it down as a General Rule, that whatever was Evidence at Common-Law is still good Evidence under the Statute; which as I said before is confined to the Proof of the Overt-Acts.

The Reader sees that Opinions have been Various touching the Sufficiency of this Sort of Evidence. But perhaps it may be now too late to controvert the Authority of the Opinion in 1716, warranted as it hath been by later Precedents. All I insist on is that the Rule should never be carried further than that Case warranteth, never further than to a Confession made during the Solemnity of an Examination before a Magistrate, or Person having Authority to take it: when the Party may be presumed to be properly upon his Guard, and apprized of the Danger he standeth in. Which was an Ingredient in the Case of *Francia* and of *Greg* cited in the Argument on *Francia*'s Case. And in all those already cited which came in Judgment before the Statute of King *William.*

For hasty Confessions made to Persons having no Authority to examine, are the Weakest and most Suspicious of All Evidence. Proof may be too easily procured, Words are often Mis-reported, whether through Ignorance, Inattention, or Malice, it mattereth not the Defendant, He is equally affected in either Case; and they are extremely liable to Mis-construction. And withall, this Evidence is not in the Ordinary Course of Things to be Disproved by that Sort of Negative Evidence by which the Proof of plain Facts May be and often is Confronted.

. . . . .

The wording of these Acts touching Confessions, "unless the Party shall willingly and *without Violence* confess the same," suggesteth a Matter which I will just mention. The Common-Law knew of no such Engine of Power as the Rack or Torture to furnish the Crown with Evidence out of the Prisoner's Mouth against Himself or other People. It was, as Lord *Coke* informeth Us, first brought into the Tower by a great Minister in the time of *H.* 6. directly, saith He, *against Law, and cannot be justified by any Usage.* But in fact it was practised, though I believe Sparingly, and never saith King *James,* but in Cases of High Treason, for more than a Century afterwards.

This accounteth extremely well for the inserting the Words, *Without Violence,* in the Statutes of *E.* 6. I cannot so easily account for them in that of King *William.*

SECT. 9. This Act in substance followeth the Rule which had already taken place with regard to the Necessity of Two Witnesses to the same Treason, but it goeth further, and lest the Prisoner should be Surprised or Confounded by a Multiplicity and Variety of Facts which He is to Answer upon the spot, it Enacteth "That no Evidence shall be admitted or given of any Overt-Act that is not expresly laid in the Indictment against any Person or Persons whatsoever." *(Sect.* 8.)

The Sense of this Clause I take to be, that no Overt-Act amounting *to a distinct Independent Charge,* though falling under the same Head of Treason, shall be given in Evidence, unless it be expresly laid in the Indictment; but still, if it amounteth to a direct Proof of any of the Overt-Acts that are laid, it may be given in Evidence of such Overt-Acts.

. . . . .

The Rule of Rejecting all manner of Evidence in Criminal Prosecutions that is Foreign to the Point in Issue, is founded on sound Sense and common Justice. For no Man is bound at the peril of Life or Liberty, Fortune or Reputation, to answer at Once and Unprepared for every Action of his Life. Few even of the Best of Men would choose to be put to it. And had not those concerned in State Prosecutions out of their Zeal for the Publick Service sometimes stepped over this Rule in the Case of Treasons, it would perhaps have been needless to have made an express Provision against it in that Case. Since the Common-Law grounded on the Principles of Natural Justice hath made the like Provision in every Other.

The Clauses in the Act which do not fall under either of the Heads I have spoken to, come now to be considered.

. . . . .

SECT. 11. By the 5th and 6th Sections of the Act no Prosecution shall be for any of the Treasons or Misprisions within the Act, committed in *England, Wales,* or *Berwick* upon *Tweed,* unless the Bill of Indictment be found within Three Years after the Offence committed; save in Cases of Assassination attempted on the Person of the King by Poison or Other ways.

This Limitation is by the Letter of the Act confined to the Southern Parts of *Great Britain,* and before the Union it could not be otherwise. But I conceive that by the general Tenor of the 7. *An.* it is extended to Treasons of the like kind committed in *Scotland:* it was so understood at the time of the Rebellion of 1715; and therefore after all the Proceedings upon the Special Commissions in *England* were over, another Special Commission went into *Scotland* meerly for the finding Bills of Indictment in the proper Counties and Stewarties, in order to prevent the Limitation's taking place.

SECT. 12. I will now consider the Clauses 7. *An.* which I before hinted at. The Eleventh Section of that Act Provideth that "when any Person is indicted for High Treason or Misprision of Treason, a List of the Witnesses that shall be produced at the Trial for proving the said Indictment, and of the Jury, mentioning the Names, Profession and Places of Abode of the said Witnesses and Jurors, shall be given at the same time that the Copy of the Indictment is delivered to the Party Indicted. And that Copies of all Indictments for the Offences aforesaid with such Lists shall be delivered *Ten Days* before the Trial, and in the Presence of Two or More credible Witnesses."

This Provision will, as the Case now stands, take place upon the Death of the Pretender. Whether it may not be proper to postpone the effect of it to the Death of his Sons, upon the same Motive that the Clause in this Act touching the Corruption of Blood upon an Attainder for High Treason hath been postponed to that Event; or indeed, whether it should be suffered to take place at All, must be submitted to better Judgments. But some Objections have occurred to Me which I will mention.

No Provision is made with regard to the Treasons not comprehended within the General Purview of the 7th of King *William* or by Name excepted out of it. The Words of the Act, "Indicted for High Treason or Misprision of Treason" are large enough to take in All manner of High Treasons and Misprision of Treason, and undoubtedly

they will be so understood. For this Act will be considered as One of those which merit a Liberal Construction.

When this Clause shall take place no High Treason or Misprision of Treason, *not even those concerning the Coin,* can possibly be Tried in the Circuit, nor at the *Old Bayly* without great Delay and double Expence. For the Copy of the Indictment cannot be delivered before it is Found by the Grand Jury, They make the Bill preferred to them an Indictment by Finding it. And Ten clear Days exclusive of the Day of Delivery and the Day of Trial, and of intervening *Sundays* which is the present Practice founded on the 7th of King *William,* will carry the Affair much beyond the time allowed for any Assizes or ordinary Gaol Delivery in the Kingdom.

The furnishing the Prisoner with the Names, Professions, and Places of Abode of the Witnesses and Jury so long before the Trial may serve many Bad purposes which are too obvious to be mentioned. One Good purpose and but One it may serve. It giveth the Prisoner an Opportunity of Informing Himself of the Character of the Witnesses and Jury. But this single Advantage will weigh very little in the Scale of Justice or sound Policy, against the Many bad Ends that may be answered by it. However, if it weigheth any thing in the Scale of Justice, the Crown is intitled to the same Opportunity of Sifting the Character of the Prisoner's Witnesses.

Equal Justice is certainly due to the Crown and the Publick. For let it be remembered that the Publick is deeply interested in every Prosecution of this kind that is Well-founded. Or shall we presume that all the Management, all the Practising upon the Hopes or Fears of Witnesses lieth on One side? it is true Power is on the side of the Crown. May it for the sake of the Constitutional Rights of the Subject, always remain where the Wisdom of the Law hath placed it! But in a Government like Ours and in a most Changeable Climate, Power if in Criminal Prosecutions it is but Suspected to Aim at Oppression, generally disarmeth itself. It raiseth and giveth Countenance to a Spirit of Opposition, which falling in with the Pride or Weakness of Some, the false Patriotism of Others, and the Sympathy of All, not to mention Private Attachments and Party Connections, generally turns the Scale to the favourable Side, and frequently against the Justice of the Case.

8

WILLIAM BLACKSTONE, COMMENTARIES
4:74–91, 350–51
1769

The third general division of crimes consists of such, as more especially affect the supreme executive power, or the king and his government; which amount either to a total renunciation of that allegiance, or at the least to a criminal neglect of that duty, which is due from every subject to his sovereign. In a former part of these commentaries we had occasion to mention the nature of allegiance, as the tie or *ligamen* which binds every subject to be true and faithful to his sovereign *liege* lord the king, in return for that protection which is afforded him; and truth and faith to bear of life and limb, and earthly honour; and not to know or hear of any ill intended him, without defending him therefrom. And this allegiance, we may remember, was distinguished into two sorts or species: the one natural and perpetual, which is inherent only in natives of the king's dominions; the other local and temporary, which is incident to aliens also. Every offence therefore more immediately affecting the royal person, his crown, or dignity, is in some degree a breach of this duty of allegiance, whether natural and innate, or local and acquired by residence: and these may be distinguished into four kinds; 1. Treason. 2. Felonies injurious to the king's prerogative. 3. *Praemunire.* 4. Other misprisions and contempts. Of which crimes the first and principal is that of treason.

Treason, *proditio,* in it's very name (which is borrowed from the French) imports a betraying, treachery, or breach of faith. It therefore happens only between allies, saith the mirror: for treason is indeed a general appellation, made use of by the law, to denote not only offences against the king and government, but also that accumulation of guilt which arises whenever a superior reposes a confidence in a subject or inferior, between whom and himself there subsists a natural, a civil, or even a spiritual relation; and the inferior so abuses that confidence, so forgets the obligations of duty, subjection, and allegiance, as to destroy the life of any such his superior or lord. This is looked upon as proceeding from the same principle of treachery in private life, as would have urged him who harbours it to have conspired in public against his liege lord and sovereign: and therefore for a wife to kill her lord or husband, a servant his lord or master, and an ecclesiastic his lord or ordinary; these, being breaches of the lower allegiance, of private and domestic faith, are denominated *petit* treasons. But when disloyalty so rears it's crest, as to attack even majesty itself, it is called by way of eminent distinction *high* treason, *alta proditio;* being equivalent to the *crimen laesae majestatis* of the Romans, as Glanvil denominates it also in our English law.

As this is the highest civil crime, which (considered as a member of the community) any man can possibly commit, it ought therefore to be the most precisely ascertained. For if the crime of high treason be indeterminate, this alone (says the president Montesquieu) is sufficient to make any government degenerate into arbitrary power. And yet, by the antient common law, there was a great latitude left in the breast of the judges, to determine what was treason, or not so: whereby the creatures of tyrannical princes had opportunity to create abundance of constructive treasons; that is, to raise, by forced and arbitrary constructions, offences into the crime and punishment of treason, which never were suspected to be such. Thus the *accroaching,* or attempting to exercise, royal power (a very uncertain charge) was in the 21 Edw. III. held to be treason in a knight of Hertfordshire, who forcibly assaulted and detained one of the king's subjects till he paid him 90*l:* a crime, it must be owned, well deserving of punishment; but which seems to be of a complexion very different from

that of treason. Killing the king's father, or brother, or even his messenger, has also fallen under the same denomination. The latter of which is almost as tyrannical a doctrine as that of the imperial constitution of Arcadius and Honorius, which determines that any attempts or designs against the ministers of the prince shall be treason. But however, to prevent the inconveniences which began to arise in England from this multitude of constructive treasons, the statute 25 Edw. III. c.2. was made; which defines what offences only for the future should be held to be treason: in like manner as the *lex Julia majestatis* among the Romans, promulged by Augustus Caesar, comprehended all the antient laws, that had before been enacted to punish transgressors against the state. This statute must therefore be our text and guide, in order to examine into the several species of high treason. And we shall find that it comprehends all kinds of high treason under seven distinct branches.

I. "When a man doth compass or imagine the death of our lord the king, of our lady his queen, or of their eldest son and heir." Under this description it is held that a queen regnant (such as queen Elizabeth and queen Anne) is within the words of the act, being invested with royal power and entitled to the allegiance of her subjects: but the husband of such a queen is not comprized within these words, and therefore no treason can be committed against him. The king here intended is the king in possession, without any respect to his title: for it is held, that a king *de facto* and not *de jure,* or in other words an usurper that hath got possession of the throne, is a king within the meaning of the statute; as there is a temporary allegiance due to him, for his administration of the government, and temporary protection of the public: and therefore treasons committed against Henry VI were punished under Edward IV, though all the line of Lancaster had been previously declared usurpers by act of parliament. But the most rightful heir of the crown, or king *de jure* and not *de facto,* who hath never had plenary possession of the throne, as was the case of the house of York during the three reigns of the line of Lancaster, is not a king within this statute, against whom treasons may be committed. And a very sensible writer on the crown-law carries the point of possession so far, that he holds, that a king out of possession is so far from having any right to our allegiance, by any other title which he may set up against the king in being, that we are bound by the duty of our allegiance to resist him. A doctrine which he grounds upon the statute 11 Hen. VII. c.1. which is declaratory of the common law, and pronounces all subjects excused from any penalty or forfeiture, which do assist and obey a king *de facto.* But, in truth, this seems to be confounding all notions of right and wrong; and the consequence would be, that when Cromwell had murdered the elder Charles, and usurped the power (though not the name) of king, the people were bound in duty to hinder the son's restoration: and were the king of Poland or Morocco to invade this kingdom, and by any means to get possession of the crown (a term, by the way, of very loose and indistinct signification) the subject would be bound by his allegiance to fight for his natural prince to-day, and by the same duty of allegiance to fight against him to-morrow. The true distinction seems to be, that the statute of Henry the seventh does by no means *command* any opposition to a king *de jure;* but *excuses* the obedience paid to a king *de facto.* When therefore a usurper is in possession, the subject is *excused* and *justified* in obeying and giving him assistance: otherwise, under a usurpation, no man could be safe; if the lawful prince had a right to hang him for obedience to the powers in being, as the usurper would certainly do for disobedience. Nay farther, as the mass of people are imperfect judges of title, of which in all cases possession is *prima facie* evidence, the law compels no man to yield obedience to that prince, whose right is by want of possession rendered uncertain and disputable, till providence shall think fit to interpose in his favour, and decide the ambiguous claim: and therefore, till he is entitled to such allegiance by possession, no treason can be committed against him. Lastly, a king who has resigned his crown, such resignation being admitted and ratified in parliament, is according to sir Matthew Hale no longer the object of treason. And the same reason holds, in case a king abdicates the government; or, by actions subversive of the constitution, virtually renounces the authority which he claims by that very constitution: since, as was formerly observed, when the fact of abdication is once established, and determined by the proper judges, the consequence necessarily follows, that the throne is thereby vacant, and he is no longer king.

Let us next see, what is a *compassing* or *imagining* the death of the king, &c. These are synonymous terms; the word *compass* signifying the purpose or design of the mind or will, and not, as in common speech, the carrying such design to effect. And therefore an accidental stroke, which may mortally wound the sovereign, *per infortunium*, without any traiterous intent, is no treason: as was the case of sir Walter Tyrrel, who, by the command of king William Rufus, shooting at a hart, the arrow glanced against a tree, and killed the king upon the spot. But, as this compassing or imagination is an act of the mind, it cannot possibly fall under any judicial cognizance, unless it be demonstrated by some open, or *overt*, act. And yet the tyrant Dionysius is recorded to have executed a subject, barely for dreaming that he had killed him; which was held for a sufficient proof, that he had thought thereof in his waking hours. But such is not the temper of the English law; and therefore in this, and the three next species of treason, it is necessary that there appear an open or *overt* act of a more full and explicit nature, to convict the traitor upon. The statute expressly requires, that the accused "be thereof upon sufficient proof attainted of some open act by men of his own condition." Thus, to provide weapons or ammunition for the purpose of killing the king, is held to be a palpable overt act of treason in imagining his death. To conspire to imprison the king by force, and move towards it by assembling company, is an overt act of compassing the king's death; for all force, used to the person of the king, in it's consequence may tend to his death, and is a strong presumption of something worse intended than the present force, by such as have so far thrown off their bounden duty to their sovereign: it being an old observation, that there is generally but a short interval between the prisons and the graves of princes. There is no question also, but that taking any measures to render such treasonable purposes effectual, as assembling and consulting on the means to kill the king, is a sufficient overt act of high treason.

How far mere *words,* spoken by an individual, and not relative to any treasonable act or design then in agitation, shall amount to treason, has been formerly matter of doubt. We have two instances, in the reign of Edward the fourth, of persons executed for treasonable words: the one a citizen of London, who said he would make his son heir of the *crown,* being the sign of the house in which he lived; the other a gentleman, whose favourite buck the king killed in hunting, whereupon he wished it, horns and all, in the king's belly. These were esteemed hard cases: and the chief justice Markham rather chose to leave his place than assent to the latter judgment. But now it seems clearly to be agreed, that, by the common law and the statute of Edward III, words spoken amount only to a high misdemesnor, and no treason. For they may be spoken in heat, without any intention, or be mistaken, perverted, or mis-remembered by the hearers; their meaning depends always on their connexion with other words, and things; they may signify differently even according to the tone of voice, with which they are delivered; and sometimes silence itself is more expressive than any discourse. As therefore there can be nothing more equivocal and ambiguous than words, it would indeed be unreasonable to make them amount to high treason. And accordingly in 4 Car. I. on a reference to all the judges, concerning some very atrocious words spoken by one Pyne, they certified to the king, "that though the words were as wicked as might be, yet they were no treason: for, unless it be by some particular statute, no words will be treason." If the words be set down in writing, it argues more deliberate intention; and it has been held that writing is an overt act of treason; for *scribere est agere.* But even in this case the bare words are not the treason, but the deliberate act of writing them. And such writing, though unpublished, has in some arbitrary reigns convicted it's author of treason: particularly in the cases of one Peacham a clergyman, for treasonable passages in a sermon never preached; and of Algernon Sidney, for some papers found in his closet: which, had they been plainly relative to any previous formed design of dethroning or murdering the king, might doubtless have been properly read in evidence as overt acts of that treason, which was specially laid in the indictment. But, being merely speculative, without any intention (so far as appeared) of making any public use of them, the convicting the authors of treason upon such an insufficient foundation has been universally disapproved. Peacham was therefore pardoned: and, though Sidney indeed was executed, yet it was to the general discontent of the nation; and his attainder was afterwards reversed by parliament. There was then no manner of doubt, but that the publication of such a treasonable writing was a sufficient overt act of treason at the common law; though of late even that has been questioned.

2. The second species of treason is, "if a man do violate the king's companion, or the king's eldest daughter un-

married, or the wife of the king's eldest son and heir." By the king's companion is meant his wife; and by violation is understood carnal knowlege, as well without force, as with it: and this is high treason in both parties, if both be consenting; as some of the wives of Henry the eighth by fatal experience evinced. The plain intention of this law is to guard the blood royal from any suspicion of bastardy, whereby the succession to the crown might be rendered dubious: and therefore, when this reason ceases, the law ceases with it; for to violate a queen or princess dowager is held to be no treason: in like manner as, by the feodal law, it was a felony and attended with a forfeiture of the fief, if the vasal vitiated the wife or daughter of his lord; but not so if he only vitiated his widow.

3. The third species of treason is, "if a man do levy war against our lord the king in his realm." And this may be done by taking arms, not only to dethrone the king, but under pretence to reform religion, or the laws, or to remove evil counsellors, or other grievances whether real or pretended. For the law does not, neither can it, permit any private man, or set of men, to interfere forcibly in matters of such high importance; especially as it has established a sufficient power, for these purposes, in the high court of parliament: neither does the constitution justify any private or particular resistance for private or particular grievances; though in cases of national oppression the nation has very justifiably risen as one man, to vindicate the original contract subsisting between the king and his people. To resist the king's forces by defending a castle against them, is a levying of war: and so is an insurrection with an avowed design to pull down *all* inclosures, *all* brothels, and the like; the universality of the design making it a rebellion against the state, an usurpation of the powers of government, and an insolent invasion of the king's authority. But a tumult with a view to pull down a particular house, or lay open a particular enclosure, amounts at most to a riot; this being no general defiance of public government. So, if two subjects quarrel and levy war against each other, it is only a great riot and contempt, and no treason. Thus it happened between the earls of Hereford and Glocester in 20 Edw. I. who raised each a little army, and committed outrages upon each others lands, burning houses, attended with the loss of many lives: yet this was held to be no high treason, but only a great misdemesnor. A bare conspiracy to levy war does not amount to this species of treason; but (if particularly pointed at the person of the king or his government) it falls within the first, or compassing or imagining the king's death.

4. "If a man be adherent to the king's enemies in his realm, giving to them aid and comfort in the realm, or elsewhere," he is also declared guilty of high treason. This must likewise be proved by some overt act, as by giving them intelligence, by sending them provisions, by selling them arms, by treacherously surrendering a fortress, or the like. By enemies are here understood the subjects of foreign powers with whom we are at open war. As to foreign pirates or robbers, who may happen to invade our coasts, without any open hostilities between their nation and our own, and without any commission from any prince or state at enmity with the crown of Great Britain, the giving them any assistance is also clearly treason; either in the light of adhering to the public enemies of the king and kingdom, or else in that of levying war against his majesty. And, most indisputably, the same acts of adherence or aid, which (when applied to foreign enemies) will constitute treason under this branch of the statute, will (when afforded to our own fellow-subjects in actual rebellion at home) amount to high treason under the description of levying war against the king. But to relieve a rebel, fled out of the kingdom, is no treason: for the statute is taken strictly, and a rebel is not an *enemy;* an enemy being always the subject of some foreign prince, and one who owes no allegiance to the crown of England. And if a person be under circumstances of actual force and constraint, through a well-grounded apprehension of injury to his life or person, this fear or compulsion will excuse his even joining with either rebels or enem[i]es *in* the kingdom, provided he leaves them whenever he hath a safe opportunity.

5. "If a man counterfeit the king's great or privy seal," this is also high treason. But if a man takes wax bearing the impression of the great seal off from one patent, and fixes it to another, this is held to be only an abuse of the seal, and not a counterfeiting of it; as was the case of a certain chaplain, who in such manner framed a dispensation for non-residence. But the knavish artifice of a lawyer much exceeded this of the divine. One of the clerks in chancery glewed together two pieces of parchment; on the uppermost of which he wrote a patent, to which he regularly obtained the great seal, the label going through both the skins. He then dissolved the cement; and taking off the written patent, on the blank skin wrote a fresh patent, of a different import from the former, and published it as true. This was held no counterfeiting of the great seal, but only a great misprision; and sir Edward Coke mentions it with some indignation, that the party was living at that day.

6. The sixth species of treason under this statute, is "if a man counterfeit the king's money; and if a man bring false money into the realm counterfeit to the money of England, knowing the money to be false." As to the first branch, counterfeiting the king's money; this is treason, whether the false money be uttered in payment or not. Also if the king's own minters alter the standard or alloy established by law, it is treason. But gold and silver money only are held to be within this statute. With regard likewise to the second branch, importing foreign counterfeit money, in order to utter it here; it is held that uttering it, without importing it, is not within the statute. But of this we shall presently say more.

7. The last species of treason, ascertained by this statute, is "if a man slay the chancellor, treasurer, or the king's justices of the one bench or the other, justices in eyre, or justices of assize, and all other justices assigned to hear and determine, being in their places doing their offices." These high magistrates, as they represent the king's majesty during the execution of their offices, are therefore for the time equally regarded by the law. But this statute extends only to the actual killing of them, and not to wounding, or a bare attempt to kill them. It extends also only to the

officers therein specified; and therefore the barons of the exchequer, as such, are not within the protection of this act.

Thus careful was the legislature, in the reign of Edward the third, to specify and reduce to a certainty the vague notions of treason, that had formerly prevailed in our courts. But the act does not stop here, but goes on. "Because other like cases of treason may happen in time to come, which cannot be thought of nor declared at present, it is accorded, that if any other case supposed to be treason, which is not above specified, doth happen before any judge; the judge shall tarry without going to judgment of the treason, till the cause be shewed and declared before the king and his parliament, whether it ought to be judged treason, or other felony." Sir Matthew Hale is very high in his encomiums on the great wisdom and care of the parliament, in thus keeping judges within the proper bounds and limits of this act, by not suffering them to run out (upon their own opinions) into constructive treasons, though in cases that seem to them to have a like parity of reason; but reserving them to the decision of parliament. This is a great security to the public, the judges, and even this sacred act itself; and leaves a weighty *memento* to judges to be careful, and not overhasty in letting in treasons by construction or interpretation, especially in new cases that have not been resolved and settled. 2. He observes, that as the authoritative decision of these *casus omissi* is reserved to the king and parliament, the most regular way to do it is by a new declarative act: and therefore the opinion of any one or of both houses, though of very respectable weight, is not that solemn declaration referred to by this act, as the only criterion for judging of future treasons.

In consequence of this power, not indeed originally granted by the statute of Edward III, but constitutionally inherent in every subsequent parliament, (which cannot be abridged of any rights by the act of a precedent one) the legislature was extremely liberal in declaring new treasons in the unfortunate reign of king Richard the second: as, particularly, the killing of an embassador was made so; which seems to be founded upon better reason than the multitude of other points, that were then strained up to this high offence: the most arbitrary and absurd of all which was by the statute 21 Ric. II. c. 3. which made the bare purpose and intent of killing or deposing the king, without any overt act to demonstrate it, high treason. And yet so little effect have over-violent laws to prevent any crime, that within two years afterwards this very prince was both deposed and murdered. And, in the first year of his successor's reign, an act was passed, reciting "that no man knew how he ought to behave himself, to do, speak, or say, for doubt of such pains of treason: and therefore it was accorded that in no time to come any treason be judged, otherwise than was ordained by the statute of king Edward the third." This at once swept away the whole load of extravagant treasons introduced in the time of Richard the second.

But afterwards, between the reign of Henry the fourth and queen Mary, and particularly in the bloody reign of Henry the eighth, the spirit of inventing new and strange treasons was revived; among which we may reckon the offences of clipping money; breaking prison or rescue, when the prisoner is committed for treason; burning houses to extort money; stealing cattle by Welchmen; counterfeiting foreign coin; wilful poisoning; execrations against the king; calling him opprobrious names by public writing; counterfeiting the sign manual or signet; refusing to abjure the pope; deflowering, or marrying without the royal licence, any of the king's children, sisters, aunts, nephews, or nieces; bare solicitation of the chastity of the queen or princess, or advances made by themselves; marrying with the king, by a woman not a virgin, without previously discovering to him such her unchaste life; judging or *believing* (manifested by any overt act) the king to have been lawfully married to Anne of Cleve; derogating from the king's royal stile and title; impugning his supremacy; and assembling riotously to the number of twelve, and not dispersing upon proclamation: all which new-fangled treasons were totally abrogated by the statute 1 Mar. c. 1. which once more reduced all treasons to the standard of the statute 25 Edw. III. Since which time, though the legislature has been more cautious in creating new offences of this kind, yet the number is very considerably encreased, as we shall find upon a short review.

These new treasons, created since the statute 1 Mar. c. 1. and not comprehended under the description of statute 25 Edw. III, I shall comprize under three heads. 1. Such as relate to papists. 2. Such as relate to falsifying the coin or other royal signatures. 3. Such as are created for the security of the protestant succession in the house of Hanover.

1. The first species, relating to *papists,* was considered in the preceding chapter, among the penalties incurred by that branch of non-conformists to the national church; wherein we have only to remember that by statute 5 Eliz. c. 1. to defend the pope's jurisdiction in this realm is, for the first time, a heavy misdemesnor; and, if the offence be repeated, it is high treason. Also by statute 27 Eliz. c. 2. if any popish priest, born in the dominions of the crown of England, shall come over hither from beyond the seas; or shall tarry here three days without conforming to the church; he is guilty of high treason. And by statute 3 Jac. I. c. 4. if any natural born subject be withdrawn from his allegiance, and reconciled to the pope or see of Rome, or any other prince or state, both he and all such as procure such reconciliation shall incur the guilt of high treason. These were mentioned under the division before referred to, as spiritual offences, and I now repeat them as temporal ones also: the reason of distinguishing these overt acts of popery from all others, by setting the mark of high treason upon them, being certainly on a civil, and not on a religious, account. For every popish priest of course renounces his allegiance to his temporal sovereign upon taking orders; that being inconsistent with his new engagements of canonical obedience to the pope: and the same may be said of an obstinate defence of his authority here, or a formal reconciliation to the see of Rome, which the statute construes to be a withdrawing from one's natural allegiance; and therefore, besides being reconciled "to the pope," it also adds "or any other prince or state."

2. With regard to treasons relative to the *coin* or other *royal signatures,* we may recollect that the only two offences respecting the coinage, which are made treason by the statute 25 Edw. III. are the actual counterfeiting the gold and silver coin of this kingdom; or the importing such counterfeit money with intent to utter it, knowing it to be false. But these not being found sufficient to restrain the evil practices of coiners and false moneyers, other statutes have been since made for that purpose. The crime itself is made a species of high treason; as being a breach of allegiance, by infringing the king's prerogative, and assuming one of the attributes of the sovereign, to whom alone it belongs to set the value and determination of coin made at home, or to fix the currency of foreign money: and besides, as all money which bears the stamp of the kingdom is sent into the world upon the public faith, as containing metal of a particular weight and standard, whoever falsifies this is an offender against the state, by contributing to render that public faith suspected. And upon the same reasons, by a law of the emperor Constantine, false coiners were declared guilty of high treason, and were condemned to be burned alive: as, by the laws of Athens, all counterfeiters, debasers, and diminishers of the current coin were subjected to capital punishment. However, it must be owned, that this method of reasoning is a little overstrained: counterfeiting or debasing the coin being usually practiced, rather for the sake of private and unlawful lucre, than out of any disaffection to the sovereign. And therefore both this and it's kindred species of treason, that of counterfeiting the seals of the crown or other royal signatures, seem better denominated by the later civilians a branch of the *crimen falsi* or forgery (in which they are followed by Glanvil, Bracton, and Fleta) than by Constantine and our Edward the third, a species of the *crimen laesae majestatis* or high treason. For this confounds the distinction and proportion of offences; and, by affixing the same ideas of guilt upon the man who coins a leaden groat and him who assassinates his sovereign, takes off from that horror which ought to attend the very mention of the crime of high treason, and makes it more familiar to the subject. Before the statute 25 Edw. III. the offence of counterfeiting the coin was held to be only a species of petit treason: but subsequent acts in their new extensions of the offence have followed the example of that, and have made it equally high treason as an endeavour to subvert the government, though not quite equal in it's punishment.

In consequence of the principle thus adopted, the statute 1 Mar. c. 1. having at one blow repealed all intermediate treasons created since the 25 Edw. III. it was thought expedient by statute 1 Mar. st. 2. c. 6. to revive two species thereof; *viz.* 1. That if any person falsely forge or counterfeit any such kind of coin of gold or silver, as is not the proper coin of this realm, but shall be current within this realm by consent of the crown; or, 2. shall falsely forge or counterfeit the sign manual, privy signet, or privy seal; such offences shall be deemed high treason. And by statute 1 & 2 P. & M. c. 11. if any persons do bring into this realm such false or counterfeit foreign money, being cur-

rent here, knowing the same to be false, and shall utter the same in payment, they shall be deemed offenders in high treason. The money referred to in these statutes must be such as is absolutely current here, in all payments, by the king's proclamation; of which there is none at present, Portugal money being only taken by consent, as approaching the nearest to our standard, and falling in well enough with our divisions of money into pounds and shillings: therefore to counterfeit it is no high treason, but another inferior offence. Clipping or defacing the genuine coin was not hitherto included in these statutes; though an offence equally pernicious to trade, and an equal insult upon the prerogative, as well as personal affront to the sovereign; whose very image ought to be had in reverence by all loyal subjects. And therefore, among the Romans, defacing or even melting down the emperor's statues was made treason by the Julian law; together with other offences of the like sort, according to that vague appendix, *"aliudve quid simile si admiserint."* And now, in England, by statute 5 Eliz. c. 11. clipping, washing, rounding, or filing, for wicked gain's sake, any of the money of this realm, or other money suffered to be current here, shall be adjudged high treason; and by statute 18 Eliz. c. 1. the same offence is described in other more general words; *viz.* impairing, diminishing, falsifying, scaling, and lightening; and made liable to the same penalties. By statute 8 & 9 W. III. c. 26. made perpetual by 7 Ann. c. 25. whoever shall knowingly make or mend, or assist in so doing, or shall buy or sell, or have in his possession, any instruments proper only for the coinage of money; or shall convey such instruments out of the king's mint; shall be guilty of high treason: which is by much the severest branch of the coinage law. The statute goes on farther, and enacts, that to mark any coin on the edges with letters, or otherwise, in imitation of those used in the mint; or to colour, gild, or case over any coin resembling the current coin, or even round blanks of base metal; shall be construed high treason. And, lastly, by statute 15 & 16 Geo. II. c. 28. if any person colours or alters any silver current coin of this kingdom, to make it resemble a gold one; or any copper coin, to make it resemble a silver one; this is also high treason: but the offender shall be pardoned, in case he discovers and convicts two other offenders of the same kind.

3. The other new species of high treason is such as is created for the security of the *protestant succession,* over and above such treasons against the king and government as were comprized under the statute 25 Edw. III. For this purpose, after the act of settlement was made, for transferring the crown to the illustrious house of Hanover, it was enacted by statute 13 & 14 W. III. c. 3. that the pretended prince of Wales, who was then thirteen years of age, and had assumed the title of king James III, should be attainted of high treason; and it was made high treason for any of the king's subjects by letters, messages, or otherwise, to hold correspondence with him, or any person employed by him, or to remit any money for his use, knowing the same to be for his service. And by statute 17 Geo. II. c. 39. it is enacted, that if any of the sons of the pretender shall land or attempt to land in this kingdom,

or be found in Great Britain, or Ireland, or any of the dominions belonging to the same, he shall be judged attainted of high treason, and suffer the pains thereof. And to correspond with them, or remit money for their use, is made high treason in the same manner as it was to correspond with the father. By the statute 1 Ann. st. 2. c. 17. if any person shall endeavour to deprive or hinder any person, being the next in succession to the crown according to the limitations of the act of settlement, from succeeding to the crown, and shall maliciously and directly attempt the same by any overt act, such offence shall be high treason. And by statute 6 Ann. c. 7. if any person shall maliciously, advisedly, and directly, by writing or printing, maintain and affirm, that any other person hath any right or title to the crown of this realm, otherwise than according to the act of settlement; or that the kings of this realm with the authority of parliament are not able to make laws and statutes, to bind the crown and the descent thereof; such person shall be guilty of high treason. This offence (or indeed maintaining this doctrine in any wise, that the king and parliament cannot limit the crown) was once before made high treason, by statute 13 Eliz. c. 1. during the life of that princess. And after her decease it continued a high misdemesnor, punishable with forfeiture of goods and chattels, even in the most flourishing aera of indefeasible hereditary right and *jure divino* succession. But it was again raised into high treason, by the statute of Anne before-mentioned, at the time of a projected invasion in favour of the then pretender; and upon this statute one Matthews, a printer, was convicted and executed in 1719, for printing a treasonable pamphlet intitled *vox populi vox Dei.*

Thus much for the crime of treason, or *laesae majestatis,* in all it's branches; which consists, we may observe, originally, in grossly counteracting that allegiance, which is due from the subject by either birth or residence: though, in some instances, the zeal of our legislators to stop the progress of some highly pernicious practices has occasioned them a little to depart from this it's primitive idea. But of this enough has been hinted already: it is now time to pass on from defining the crime to describing it's punishment.

The punishment of high treason in general is very solemn and terrible. 1. That the offender be drawn to the gallows, and not be carried or walk; though usually a sledge or hurdle is allowed, to preserve the offender from the extreme torment of being dragged on the ground or pavement. 2. That he be hanged by the neck, and then cut down alive. 3. That his entrails be taken out, and burned, while he is yet alive. 4. That his head be cut off. 5. That his body be divided into four parts. 6. That his head and quarters be at the king's disposal.

The king may, and often doth, discharge all the punishment, except beheading, especially where any of noble blood are attainted. For, beheading being part of the judgment, that may be executed, though all the rest be omitted by the king's command. But where beheading is no part of the judgment, as in murder or other felonies, it hath been said that the king cannot change the judgment, although at the request of the party, from one species of

death to another. But of this we shall say more hereafter.

In the case of coining, which is a treason of a different complexion from the rest, the punishment is milder for male offenders; being only to be drawn, and hanged by the neck till dead. But in treasons of every kind the punishment of women is the same, and different from that of men. For, as the natural modesty of the sex forbids the exposing and publicly mangling their bodies, their sentence (which is to the full as terrible to sense as the other) is to be drawn to the gallows, and there to be burned alive.

. . . . .

First, in all cases of high treason, petit treason, and misprision of treason, by statutes 1 Edw. VI. c. 12. 5 & 6 Edw. VI. c. 11. and 1 & 2 Ph. & Mar. c. 10. *two* lawful witnesses are required to convict a prisoner; except in cases of coining, and counterfeiting the seals; or unless the party shall willingly and without violence confess the same. By statute 7 W. III. c. 3. in prosecutions for those treasons to which that act extends, the same rule is again enforced, with this addition, that the confession of the prisoner, which shall countervail the necessity of such proof, must be in open court; and it is declared that both witnesses must be to the same overt act of treason, or one to one overt act, and the other to another overt act of the same species of treason, and not of distinct heads or kinds: and no evidence shall be admitted to prove any overt act not expressly laid in the indictment. And therefore in sir John Fenwick's case, in king William's time, where there was but one witness, an act of parliament was made on purpose to attaint him of treason, and he was executed. But in almost every other accusation one positive witness is sufficient. Baron Montesquieu lays it down for a rule, that those laws which condemn a man to death *in any case* on the deposition of a single witness, are fatal to liberty: and he adds this reason, that the witness who affirms, and the accused who denies, makes an equal ballance; there is a necessity therefore to call in a third man .to incline the scale. But this seems to be carrying matters too far: for there are some crimes, in which the very privacy of their nature excludes the possibility of having more than one witness: must these therefore escape unpunished? Neither indeed is the bare denial of the person accused equivalent to the positive oath of a disinterested witness. In cases of indictments for perjury, this doctrine is better founded; and there our law adopts it: for one witness is not allowed to convict a man indicted for perjury; because then there is only one oath against another. In cases of treason also there is the accused's oath of allegiance, to counterpoise the information of a single witness; and that may perhaps be one reason why the law requires a double testimony to convict him: though the principal reason, undoubtedly, is to secure the subject from being sacrificed to fictitious conspiracies, which have been the engines of profligate and crafty politicians in all ages.

9

CONTINENTAL CONGRESS, "COMMITTEE ON SPIES"
(JOHN ADAMS, THOMAS JEFFERSON, JOHN
RUTLEDGE, AND ROBERT LIVINGSTON)
5 June 1776
Adams Works 1:224–25

Resolved, That all persons abiding within any of the United Colonies, and deriving protection from the laws of the same, owe allegiance to the said laws, and are members of such colony; and that all persons passing through, visiting, or make a temporary stay in any of the said colonies, being entitled to the protection of the laws during the time of such passage, visitation or temporary stay, owe, during the same time, allegiance thereto:

That all persons, members of, or owing allegiance to any of the United Colonies, as before described, who shall levy war against any of the said colonies within the same, or be adherent to the king of Great Britain, or others the enemies of the said colonies, or any of them, within the same, giving to him or them aid and comfort, are guilty of treason against such colony:

That it be recommended to the legislatures of the several United Colonies, to pass laws for punishing, in such manner as to them shall seem fit, such persons before described, as shall be provably attainted of open deed, by people of their condition, of any of the treasons before described.

10

JOSEPH HAWLEY TO ELBRIDGE GERRY
17 July 1776
Gerry Life 1:206–8

I have often said that I supposed a declaration of independence would be accompanied with a declaration of high treason: most certainly it must immediately and without the least delay follow it. Can we subsist? Did any state ever subsist without exterminating traitors? I never desire to see high treason extended here further than it is now extended in Britain. But an act of high treason we must have instantly. The colonies have long suffered inexpressibly for want of it. No one thing made the declaration of independence indispensably necessary more than cutting off traitors. It is amazingly wonderful, that having no capital punishment for our intestine enemies, we have not been utterly ruined before now. For God's sake, let us not run such risks a day longer. It appears to me, sir, that high treason ought to be the same in all the United States;— saving to the legislature of each colony or state the right of attainting individuals by act or bill of attainder. The present times show most clearly the wisdom and sound policy of the common law in that doctrine, or part thereof, which consists in attainting by an act of the whole legislature. Our tories (be sure the learned of them) knew very well the absurdity of punishing as high treason any acts or deeds in favour of the government of the king of Great Britain so long as we all allowed him to be king of the colonies. Dear sir, this matter admits of no delay; and when the act declaratory of high treason is passed, the strongest recommendation for a strict execution of it, I humbly conceive, ought to accompany it. Our whole cause is every moment in amazing danger for want of it. The common understanding of the people (like unerring instinct) has long declared this; and from the clear discerning which they have had of it, they have been long in agonies about it: they expect that effectual care will now be taken for the general safety, and that all those who shall be convicted of endeavouring by overt act to destroy the state, shall be cut off from the earth.

11

AN ACT DECLARING WHAT SHALL BE
TREASON, LAWS OF VIRGINIA
1776
Hening 9:168

I. WHEREAS divers opinions may be what case shall be adjudged treason, and what not: *Be it enacted, by the General Assembly of the commonwealth of Virginia,* That if a man do levy war against this commonwealth in the same, or be adherent to the enemies of the commonwealth within the same, giving to them aid and comfort in the commonwealth or elsewhere, and thereof be legally convicted of open deed by the evidence of two sufficient and lawful witnesses, or their own voluntary confession, the cases above rehearsed shall be judged treason, which extendeth to the commonwealth, and the person so convicted shall suffer death without benefit of clergy, and forfeit his lands and chattels to the commonwealth, saving to the widows of such offenders their dower in the lands.

II. *Provided always, and it is enacted,* That no such attainder shall work any corruption of blood.

III. *And it is farther enacted, by the authority aforesaid,* That the governour, or in case of his death, inability, or necessary absence, the counsellor who acts as president, shall in no wise have or exercise a right of granting pardon to any person or persons convicted in manner aforesaid, but may suspend the execution until the meeting of the general assembly, who shall determine whether such person or persons are proper objects of mercy or not, and order accordingly.

12

RESPUBLICA V. CARLISLE
1 Dall. 35 (Pa. 1778)

The Chief Justice delivered the opinion of the court to the following effect:

McKEAN, Chief Justice.—There are three species of treason in Pennsylvania, First. To take a commission or commissions from the king of Great Britain, or any under his authority: 2. To levy war against the state or government thereof: and 3. Knowingly and willingly to aid and assist any enemies at open war against this state, or the United States of America. With respect to this third species of treason, the legislature has further explained the meaning of the words, *aiding and assisting*, to be, "by joining the armies of the enemy, or by enlisting, or procuring or persuading others to enlist, for that purpose; or by furnishing such enemies with arms or ammunition, provision or any other article or articles for their aid or comfort, or by carrying on a traitorous correspondence with them." All these several species of treason are laid in this indictment.

It is here particularly stated, that the defendant took a commission under the king of Great Britain, to watch and guard the gates of the city of Philadelphia; and the offence is certain enough in this description, though, without some *overt* act, it would not be sufficient for a conviction. In order to prove an *overt* act, however, evidence has been offered to show that the prisoner had a power of granting passes into and out of the city, which was at that time in the possession of the enemy. In Fost. 10 *(Berwick's Case)*, a witness deposed, that one Berwick was confined in the room assigned for the rebel officers taken at Carlisle by the duke of Cumberland, and this was deemed a sufficient proof of his holding a commission. The court, on the present occasion, however, are of opinion, that the evidence which is offered, ought to be received, but not as conclusive proof of the defendant's having taken a commission. Nor will the evidence of seizing the salt, or any act of disarming the inhabitants whom the defendant called *rebels,* apply to *this* species of treason; however they may support the allegation, of his having joined the armies of the king of Great Britain.

We think it is sufficient, also, to lay in the indictment, that the defendant sent intelligence to the enemy, without setting forth the particular letter, or its contents; and, though the charge of levying war is not, of itself, sufficient; yet assembling, joining and arraying himself with the forces of the enemy, is a sufficient *overt* act of levying war.

13

RESPUBLICA V. CHAPMAN
1 Dall. 53 (Pa. 1781)

THE CHIEF JUSTICE delivered a learned and circumstantial charge to the jury. After stating the proclamation, the issue, and the evidence, he proceeded as follows:

McKEAN, Chief Justice.—The question that is to be decided on the facts before us, is, whether Samuel Chapman, the prisoner at the bar, ever was a subject of this commonwealth? The reason which has been principally urged to take him out of that description, is that on the 26th day of December, in the year 1776, when he withdrew from Pennsylvania, no government existed to which he could owe allegiance as a subject. I shall, in the first place, consider how far this defence, under the circumstances of the case, would avail the prisoner upon an indictment for high treason.

The Attorney-General has referred to the declaration of Independence, on the 4th of July 1776, when the freedom and sovereignty of the several states were announced to the world; and also, to a resolution of congress recommending the formation of such governments, as were adequate to the exigency of the public affairs. The sister states pursued different modes of complying with this recommendation. The citizens of Connecticut, New Hampshire and Rhode Island, considered themselves in a situation similar to that which occurred in England, on the abdication of James the second; and, wanting only the form of a royal governor, their respective systems of government have still been continued; while the other states adopted temporary expedients, until regular constitutions could be formed, matured and organized.

And here it is contended, that, prior to the constitution under which we now live, the state of Pennsylvania was governed by a council of safety, and committees. But to this, it is answered, that until laws were passed by a competent legislative power, no government could be said to exist; and, as the act of the 28th of January 1779, for the revival of the laws, virtually declares that they were suspended from the 14th May 1776, until the 11th February 1777, it is inferred, that during that period, no allegiance was due, and no treason could be committed.

Although I think this point immaterial to the prisoner, since a government might have existed, and yet not be of such a nature as to affect him, it cannot be denied, that a kind of government, independent of Great Britain, was administered in Pennsylvania, antecedent to the establishment of the present constitution. The powers of sovereignty were then lodged with congress, under whose authority a council of safety had been elected by the people, and were employed, in conjunction with other committees, to conduct the war, and to secure, as far as so imperfect a system could, the rights of life, liberty and property within this state. It is certain, indeed, that a formal compact is not a necessary foundation of government; for, if an individual had assumed the sovereignty, and the people had assented to it, whatever limitations might afterwards have been imposed, still this would have been a legal establishment. No express provision, however, has been at any time made, for defining what should be treason against those temporary bodies; but it may be well enough to observe, that treason is a crime known to the common law.

Afterwards, we find, that a General Convention, elected by the people, met on the 15th day of July 1776, for the express purpose of framing a new government; and during the sessions of this body, its members, collectively, assumed the powers of making ordinances, of appointing members of congress, and of defining high treason, and its punishment. All their proceedings and injunctions, except the ordinance respecting treason, were approved and executed; and the constitution which they eventually agreed upon, was incontrovertibly a dissolution of the government, as far as related to the powers of Great Britain, but not in relation to the powers which had been before exercised by councils and committees.

The Attorney-General has urged that, at least, as soon as the government under the new constitution was formed, which he says was on the 28th of November 1776, the members of council being then chosen, and the legislature actually assembled, the sovereignty of the state was complete, and allegiance followed, by a necessary consequence, without the intervention of any positive law. But the advocates for the prisoner again object, that the government cannot be said to be established, until there is a meeting of all its parts, and that as the executive council never met until the 4th of March 1777, the state was incapable of affording protection, and therefore, was not entitled to allegiance, before that time.

On this occasion, the sentiments of several eminent *civilians* have been read to us; not as authorities binding upon our judgment, but as a means of information derived from the great learning and abilities of the respective writers, and, principally indeed, on account of the intrinsic weight of the reasons by which their doctrines are supported. Locke says, that when the executive is totally dissolved, there can be no treason: for laws are a mere nullity, unless there is a power to execute them. But that is not the case at present in agitation; for before the meeting of council in March 1777, all its members were chosen, and the legislature was completely organized: so that there did antecedently exist a power competent to redress grievances, to afford protection, and generally, to execute the laws; and allegiance being naturally due to such a power, we are of opinion, that from the moment it was created, the crime of high treason might have been committed by any person, who was then a subject of the commonwealth. The act of the 11th of February 1777, expressly authorizes this opinion; for, we find it there said, "That all and every person and persons (except prisoners at war) *now* inhabiting, &c., within the limits of this state; or that shall *voluntarily* come into the same *hereafter* to inhabit, &c., *do* owe, and shall pay allegiance, &c." This, therefore, contradicts the idea, suggested by the advocates for the prisoner, that allegiance was not due until the meeting of the executive council, on the 4th of March ensuing; and, although he cannot be convicted upon that act, yet allegiance being due from the 28th of November 1776, when, as I have already observed the legislature was convened, and the members of council were appointed, treason, which is nothing more than a criminal attempt to destroy the existence of the government, might certainly have been committed, before the different qualities of the crime were defined, and its punishment declared by a positive law. 1 Bl. Com. 46.

Having thus dismissed the preliminary question, whether the prisoner's defence would avail him upon an indictment for high treason, I shall proceed to inquire, if there are any circumstances that take his case out of the general opinion expressed by the court upon that point.

The act for the revival of the laws, passed the 28th of January 1777, was intended, I think, merely to declare, that those laws which were originally enacted under the authority of George the Third, ceased any longer to derive their virtue and validity from that source. But there is great inaccuracy in penning the act; for, though it would seem, by the former part of the second section, to be the sense of the legislature, that from the 14th of May 1776, to the 10th of February 1777, the operation of all the acts of assembly should be suspended; yet, in the close of the same section, obedience to those acts, to the common law, and to so much of the statute law of England, as have *heretofore* been in force in Pennsylvania, is, with some exceptions in point of style and form, expressly enjoined. We may, however, fairly infer from the general tenor of the act, that those who framed it, thought the separation from Great Britain worked a dissolution of all government, and that the force, not only of the acts of assembly, but of the common law and statute law of England, was actually extinguished by that event.

This, therefore, necessarily leads to the consideration of a very important subject. In *civil wars*, every man chooses his party; but generally that side which prevails, arrogates the right of treating those who are vanquished as rebels. The cases which have been produced upon the present controversy, are of an old government being dissolved, and the people assembling in order to form a new one. When such instances occur, the voice of the majority must be conclusive, as to the adoption of the new system; but all the writers agree, that the minority have, individually, an unrestrainable right to remove with their property into another country; that a reasonable time for that purpose ought to be allowed; and, in short, that none are subjects of the adopted government, who have not freely assented to it. What is a reasonable time for departure may, perhaps, be properly left to the determination of a court and jury. But whether a man should be suffered to join a party, or nation, *at open war* with the country he leaves, is a question of singular magnitude. The ground is hitherto untrodden, but there is such apparent injustice in the thing itself, that I am inclined to think, it would amount to an act of treason. Puffendorf, 639.

This is not, however, the situation of the prisoner. Pennsylvania was not a nation at war with another nation; but a country in a state of *civil war*, and there is no precedent in the books to show what might be done in that case; except, indeed, where a prince has subdued the people who took arms against him, before they had formed a regular government, which is, likewise, inapplicable here.

But this difficulty seems to vanish, by having recourse to the opinion of the legislature, in their act of the 11th February 1777; for, when describing from whom allegiance is due, they speak only of persons *then* inhabiting the state, or who should *thereafter* become its inhabitants. Hence, a discrimination is evidently made between those persons, and such as had previously joined the enemy; meaning that this election to adhere to the British government, should not expose the party to any future punishment. It is true, that there are not any negative words to this effect; but, taking the act for the revival of the law also into consideration, we think the design and intention of the legislature sufficiently appears to have been, to allow a choice of his party to every man, until the 11th of February 1777; and that no act savoring of treason, done before that period, should incur the penalties of the law.

This construction, it may be said, is favorable to traitors, and tends to the prejudice of the commonwealth. But we cannot be influenced by observations of a political nature in the exposition of the law; it is our duty to seek for, and to declare, the true intention of the legislature; the policy of that intention, it is their duty to consider. The sentiments which I have now delivered, I always entertained. On the 13th of August 1779, the Executive Council had sixteen or seventeen persons in their power, who, though not attainted, were in circumstances similar to the prisoner's. On that occasion, I was consulted, and gave the same opinion; but with great diffidence, owing to the novelty of the question. Those persons were, accordingly, treated as prisoners of war.

But there is yet another important point to be examined in the case before us. By an act, subsequent to all those which have been mentioned, it is declared, "that all and every person and persons *being subjects or inhabitants of this state,* or those who have real estate in this commonwealth, *who now adhere to,* and knowingly and willingly aid and assist the enemies of this state, or of the United States of America, *by having joined their armies* within this state, or elsewhere, or who hereafter shall do the same, and whom the Supreme Executive Council of this state, by their proclamations, to be issued under the state seal, during the continuance of the war with the king of Great Britain, shall name and require to surrender themselves, by a certain day therein to be mentioned, to some, or one, of the justices of the supreme court, &c., and shall not render themselves accordingly, &c., shall, from and after the day to them to be prefixed by such proclamation, stand and be attainted of high treason to all intents and purposes, &c." Under the authority of this clause, the prisoner was duly required by proclamation to surrender himself; and therefore, his case seems to come properly within the act.

Generally speaking, *ex post facto* laws are unjust and improper; but there may certainly be occasions, when they become necessary for the safety and preservation of the commonwealth; and although no legislature had previously met, yet the assembly that passed this law, if they were impressed with the necessity of the case, had, incontrovertibly, a right to declare any person a traitor who had gone over to the enemy, and still adhered to them. The validity and operation of the law, however, the prisoner is now precluded from controverting, if, at any time before the date of the proclamation, he was a subject of the state of Pennsylvania.

Here, then the matter rests. Had the issue been in the *disjunctive,* the prisoner would clearly have come within the description of an inhabitant of Pennsylvania; but when the word *subject* is annexed, it means a subjection to some sovereign power, and is not barely connected with the idea of territory—it refers to one who owes obedience to the laws, and is entitled to partake of the elections into public office. On this point, therefore, we must again advert to the act of assembly, declaring what shall be treason, which has no retrospect, and to the act for the revival of the laws, which implies a suspension of all the laws from the 14th of May 1776, to the 11th of February 1777. If there were no laws to be obeyed, during that period, the prisoner could not be deemed a subject of the state of Pennsylvania, on the 26th day of September 1776. Whether the legislature meant to include this case, we will not positively determine—it is a new one, and we ought to tread cautiously and securely. But, at all events, it is better to err on the side of mercy, than of strict justice.

The jury found a verdict of *Not guilty.*

14

RESPUBLICA V. WEIDLE
2 Dall. 88 (Pa. 1781)

The court delivered a charge to the following effect:

MCKEAN, Chief Justice.—This indictment charges all the various acts which constitute misprision of treason; and it is the duty of the jury to inquire, whether the evidence supports any one of the charges. It is said, indeed, that the law on which the indictment is founded, is so inaccurately penned, that it cannot be understood, without supplying certain material words; and it is, undoubtedly, true, that although, in a common case, on a mere question of property (as in the case of a will), the rule of construction is according to the sense of the instrument; yet, a law constituting a crime, must be strictly and literally interpreted and pursued. The obscure passage in the act of assembly would be rendered perspicuous and intelligible, without the addition of any words, by expunging the semicolon, and the monosyllable *"or;"* but even that is unnecessary to support the prosecution; since the words spoken tended to excite resistance to the government of this commonwealth, to persuade the audience to return to a dependence upon the crown of Great Britain, and to favor the enemy; which are distinct and substantive charges of misprision of treason.

It is proper to add, that the words must be spoken with a malicious and mischievous intention, in order to render them criminal: a mere loose and idle conversation, without any wickedness of heart, may be indiscreet and reprehensible, but ought not to be construed into misprision of treason. On the other hand, drunkenness is no justification or excuse, for committing the offence; to allow it as such, would open a door for the practice of the greatest enormities with impunity.

Verdict, guilty.

15

RECORDS OF THE FEDERAL CONVENTION

[2:345; Madison, 20 Aug.]

Art: VII sect. 2. concerning Treason which see*

Mr. Madison, thought the definition too narrow. It did not appear to go as far as the Stat. of Edwd. III. He did not see why more latitude might not be left to the Legislature. It wd. be as safe as in the hands of State legislatures; and it was inconvenient to bar a discretion which experience might enlighten, and which might be applied to good purposes as well as be abused.

Mr Mason was for pursuing the Stat: of Edwd. III.

Mr. Govr Morris was for giving to the Union an exclusive right to declare what shd. be treason. In case of a contest between the U– S– and a particular State, the people of the latter must, under the disjunctive terms of the clause, be traitors to one or other authority.

Mr Randolph thought the clause defective in adopting the words "in adhering" only. The British Stat: adds. "giving them aid and comfort" which had a more extensive meaning.

Mr. Elseworth considered the definition as the same in fact with that of the Statute.

Mr. Govr Morris "adhering" does not go so far as "giving aid and Comfort" or the latter words may be restrictive of "adhering". in either case the Statute is not pursued.

Mr Wilson held "giving aid and comfort" to be explanatory, not operative words; and that it was better to omit them—

Mr Dickenson, thought the addition of "giving aid & comfort" unnecessary & improper; being too vague and extending too far— He wished to know what was meant by the "testimony of two witnesses", whether they were to be witnesses to the same overt act or to different overt acts. He thought also that proof of an overt-act ought to be expressed as essential in the case.

Docr Johnson considered "giving aid & comfort" as explanatory of "adhering" & that something should be in-

*Article VII, Sect. 2. "Treason against the United States shall consist only in levying war against the United States, or any of them; and in adhering to the enemies of the United States, or any of them. The Legislature of the United States shall have power to declare the punishment of treason. No person shall be convicted of treason, unless on the testimony of two witnesses. No attainder of treason shall work corruption of bloods nor forfeiture, except during the life of the person attainted."

serted in the definition concerning overt-acts. He contended that Treason could not be both agst. The U. States—and individual States; being an offence agst the Sovereignty which can be but one in the same community—

Mr. Madison remarked that "and" before "in adhering" should be changed into "or" otherwise both offences viz of levying war, & of adhering to the Enemy might be necessary to constitute Treason. He added that as the definition here was of treason against *the U. S.* it would seem that the individual States wd. be left in possession of a concurrent power so far as to define & punish treason particularly agst. themselves; which might involve double punishmt.

It was moved that the whole clause be recommitted which was lost, the votes being equally divided.

N– H– no. Mas– no– Ct no– N– J ay– Pa ay– Del– no– Md. ay. Va. ay– N C– divd S– C–no. Geo– ay.—[Ayes—5; noes—5; divided—1.]

Mr. Wilson & Docr. Johnson moved, that "or any of them" after "United States" be struck out in order to remove the embarrassment: which was agreed to nem. con—

Mr Madison This has not removed the embarrassment. The same Act might be treason agst. the United States as here defined—and agst a particular State according to its laws.

Mr Elseworth— There can be no danger to the Genl authority from this; as the laws of the U. States are to be paramount.

Docr Johnson was still of opinion there could be no Treason agst a particular State. It could not even at present, as the Confederation now stands; the Sovereignty being in the Union; much less can it be under the proposed System.

Col. Mason. The United States will have a qualified sovereignty only. The individual States will retain a part of the Sovereignty. An Act may be treason agst. a particular State which is not so against the U. States. He cited the Rebellion of Bacon in Virginia as an illustration of the doctrine.

Docr. Johnson: That case would amount to Treason agst the Sovereign, the supreme Sovereign, the United States—

Mr. King observed that the controversy relating to Treason might be of less magnitude than was supposed; as the legislature might punish capitally under other names than Treason.

Mr. Govr Morris and Mr Randolph wished to substitute the words of the British Statute and moved to postpone Sect. 2. art VII in order to consider the following substitute—"Whereas it is essential to the preservation of liberty to define precisely and exclusively what shall constitute the crime of Treason, it is therefore ordained, declared & established, that if a man do levy war agst. the U. S. within their territories, or be adherent to the enemies of the U. S. within the said territories, giving them aid and comfort within their territories or elsewhere, and thereof be provably attainted of open deed by the People of his condition, he shall be adjudged guilty of Treason"

On this question

N.H Mas– no. Ct. no. N. J– ay Pa. no. Del. no. Md. no. Va.– ay. N. C. no– S. C. no. Geo– no. [Ayes—2; noes—8.]

It was moved to strike out "agst United States" after "treason" so as to define treason generally—and on this question

Mas. ay—Ct. ay. N—J. ay. Pa ay. Del. ay. Md. ay. Va. no. N. C. no. S. C ay. Geo. ay. [Ayes—8; noes—2.]

It was then moved to insert after "two witnesses" the words "to the same overt act".

Docr Franklin wished this amendment to take place—prosecutions for treason were generally virulent; and perjury too easily made use of against innocence

Mr. Wilson. much may be said on both sides. Treason may sometimes be practised in such a manner, as to render proof extremely difficult—as in a traitorous correspondence with an Enemy.

On the question—as to same overt act

N— H— ay— Mas— ay— Ct. ay. N. J. no— Pa. ay— Del— ay—Md ay. Va no—N. C. no—S. C. ay—Geo—ay— [Ayes—8; noes—3.]

Mr King moved to insert before the word "power" the word "sole", giving the U. States the exclusive right to declare the punishment of Treason.

Mr Broom 2ds. the motion—

Mr Wilson in cases of a general nature, treason can only be agst the U— States. and in such they shd have the sole right to declare the punishment—yet in many cases it may be otherwise. The subject was however intricate and he distrusted his present judgment on it.

Mr King this amendment results from the vote defining treason generally by striking out agst. the U. States; which excludes any treason agst particular States. These may however punish offences as high misdemesnors.

On inserting the word "sole". It passed in the negative

N— H. ay— Mas— ay. Ct no— N. J— no— Pa ay. Del. ay. Md no— Va— no— N— C— no— S. C. ay— Geo— no.—[Ayes—5; noes—6.]

Mr. Wilson. the clause is ambiguous now. "Sole" ought either to have been inserted—or "against the U— S." to be reinstated.

Mr King no line can be drawn between levying war and adhering to enemy—agst the U. States and agst an individual States—Treason agst the latter must be so agst the former.

Mr Sherman, resistance agst. the laws of the U— States as distinguished from resistance agst the laws of a particular State, forms the line—

Mr. Elseworth— the U. S. are sovereign on one side of the line dividing the jurisdictions—the States on the other—each ought to have power to defend their respective Sovereignties.

Mr. Dickenson, war or insurrection agst a member of the Union must be so agst the whole body; but the Constitution should be made clear on this point.

The clause was reconsidered nem. con—& then, Mr. Wilson & Mr. Elseworth moved to reinstate "agst the U. S.". after "Treason"—on which question

N— H— no— Mas. no. Ct. ay— N— J— ay— Pa no— Del. no— Md ay. Va. ay— N. C. ay— S— C. no— Geo. ay—[Ayes—6; noes—5.]

Mr Madison was not satisfied with the footing on which the clause now stood. As treason agst the U— States involves Treason agst. particular States, and vice versa, the same act may be twice tried & punished by the different authorities—Mr Govr Morris viewed the matter in the same lights—

It was moved & 2ded to amend the Sentence to read— "Treason agst. the U. S. shall consist only in levying war against them, or in adhering to their enemies" which was agreed to.

Col— Mason moved to insert the words "giving them aid comfort". as restrictive of "adhering to their Enemies &c"— the latter he thought would be otherwise too indefinite— This motion was agreed to Cont: Del: & Georgia only being in the Negative.

Mr L. Martin—moved to insert after conviction &c—"or on confession in open court"—and on the question, (the negative States thinking the words superfluous) it was agreed to N. H. ay— Mas— no— Ct. ay. N— J. ay— Pa. ay. Del. ay— Md ay— Va ay. N— C— divd S— C. no. Geo— no. [Ayes—7; noes—3; divided—1.]

Art: VII. Sect—2. as amended was then agreed to nem—con.

16

LUTHER MARTIN, GENUINE INFORMATION 1788

Storing 2.4.96–98

By the *principles* of the American revolution, *arbitrary power may* and *ought* to be resisted even by *arms* if necessary— The time may come when it shall be the duty of a *State*, in order to preserve itself from the oppression of the general government, to have recourse to the sword—In which case the proposed form of government declares, that the *State* and every of *its citizens* who *act under its authority* are guilty of a direct act of treason; reducing by this provision the different States to this alternative, that they must *tamely* and *passively yield to despotism*, or *their citizens* must *oppose it* at the *hazard* of the *halter* if unsuccessful—and reducing the citizens of the State which shall take arms, to a situation in which they must be *exposed to punishment*, let them *act as they will*, since if they *obey* the authority of their *State government*, they will be *guilty of treason against the United States*—if they join the *general government* they will be *guilty of treason against their own State*.

To save the citizens of the respective States from this disagreeable dilemma, and to secure them from being punishable as *traitors* to the *United States*, when *acting* expressly in *obedience* to the authority of *their own State*, I wished to have obtained as an amendment to the third section of this article the following clause: "Provided that no act or acts done by *one* or *more* of the States against the United States, or by *any citizen* of any *one* of the United States *under the authority* of *one* or *more* of the *said States*, shall be deemed *treason*, or *punished as such;* but in case of war being levied by one or more of the States against the

United States, the conduct of each party towards the other, and their adherents respectively, shall be regulated by the *laws of war* and of *nations*."

But this provision was not adopted, being too much opposed to the great object of many of the leading members of the convention, which was by all means to *leave the States* at the *mercy* of the *general govenment,* since they could not succeed in their *immediate* and *entire* abolition.

17

JAMES MADISON, FEDERALIST, NO. 43, 290
23 Jan. 1788

As treason may be committed against the United States, the authority of the United States ought to be enabled to punish it. But as new-fangled and artificial treasons, have been the great engines, by which violent factions, the natural offspring of free Governments, have usually wrecked their alternate malignity on each other, the Convention have with great judgment opposed a barrier to this peculiar danger, by inserting a constitutional definition of the crime, fixing the proof necessary for conviction of it, and restraining the congress, even in punishing it, from extending the consequences of guilt beyond the person of its author.

18

AN ACT FOR THE PUNISHMENT OF CERTAIN CRIMES AGAINST THE UNITED STATES
1 Stat. 112 (1790)

SECTION 1. *Be it enacted by the Senate and House of Representatives of the United States of America in Congress assembled,* That if any person or persons, owing allegiance to the United States of America, shall levy war against them, or shall adhere to their enemies, giving them aid and comfort within the United States or elsewhere, and shall be thereof convicted, on confession in open court, or on the testimony of two witnesses to the same overt act of the treason whereof he or they shall stand indicted, such person or persons shall be adjudged guilty of treason against the United States, and shall suffer death.

SEC. 2. *And be it [further] enacted,* That if any person or persons, having knowledge of the commission of any of the treasons aforesaid, shall conceal and not as soon as may be disclose and make known the same to the President of the United States, or some one of the judges thereof, or to the president or governor of a particular state, or some one of the judges or justices thereof, such person or persons on conviction shall be adjudged guilty of misprision of treason, and shall be imprisoned not exceeding seven years, and fined not exceeding one thousand dollars.

19

JAMES WILSON, OF CRIMES IMMEDIATELY AGAINST THE COMMUNITY, LECTURES ON LAW
1791
Works 2:663–69

I have hitherto considered crimes, which wound the community through the sides of individuals: I now come to consider one which directly and immediately aims a stab at the vitals of the community herself. I mean treason against the United States, and against the state of Pennsylvania.

Treason is unquestionably a crime most dangerous to the society, and most repugnant to the first principles of the social compact. It must, however, be observed, that as the crime itself is dangerous and hostile to the state, so the imputation of it has been and may be dangerous and oppressive to the citizens. To the freest governments this observation is by no means inapplicable; as might be shown at large by a deduction, historical and political, which would be both interesting and instructive. But, at present, we have not time for it.

To secure the state, and at the same time to secure the citizens—and, according to our principles, the last is the end, and the first is the means—the law of treason should possess the two following qualities. 1. It should be determinate. 2. It should be stable.

It is the observation of the celebrated Montesquieu, that if the crime of treason be indeterminate, this alone is sufficient to make any government degenerate into arbitrary power. In monarchies, and in republicks, it furnishes an opportunity to unprincipled courtiers, and to demagogues equally unprincipled, to harass the independent citizen, and the faithful subject, by treasons, and by prosecutions for treasons, constructive, capricious, and oppressive.

In point of precision and accuracy with regard to this crime, the common law, it must be owned, was grossly deficient. Its description was uncertain and ambiguous; and its denomination and penalties were wastefully communicated to offences of a different and inferiour kind. To lop off these numerous and dangerous excrescences, and to reduce the law on this important subject to a designated and convenient form, the famous statute of treasons was made in the reign of Edward the third, on the application of the lords and commons. This statute has been in England, except during times remarkably tyrannical or turbulent, the governing rule with regard to treasons ever since. Like a rock, strong by nature, and fortified, as successive occasions required, by the able and the honest assistance of art, it has been impregnable by all the rude and boistrous assaults, which have been made upon it, at different quarters, by ministers and by judges; and as an object of national security, as well as of national pride, it may well be styled the legal Gibraltar of England.

Little of this statute, however, demands our minute attention now; as the great changes in our constitutions have superceded all its monarchical parts. One clause of it, indeed, merits our strictest investigation; because it is transcribed into the constitution of the United States. Another clause in it merits our strongest regard; because it contains and holds forth a principle and an example, worthy of our observance and imitation.

After having enumerated and declared all the different species of treason, which it was thought proper to establish, the statute proceeds in this manner: "and because many other cases of like treason may happen in time to come, which, at present, a man cannot think or declare; it is assented, that if any other case, supposed treason, which is not specified above, happen before any judges, they shall not go to judgment in such case; but shall tarry, till it be shown and declared before the king and his parliament, whether it ought to be judged treason or other felony."

The great and the good Lord Hale observes upon this clause, "the great wisdom and care of the parliament, to keep judges within the bounds and express limits of this statute, and not to suffer them to run out, upon their own opinions, into constructive treasons, though in cases which seem to have a parity of reason"—cases of like treason—"but reserves them to the decision of parliament. This," he justly says, "is a great security as well as direction to judges; and a great safeguard even to this sacred act itself."

It is so. And it was all the safeguard which the parliament, by the constitution, as it is called, of England, could give. It was a safeguard from the arbitrary constructions of courts: it was a shelter from judicial storms: but it was no security against legislative tempests. No parliament, however omnipotent, could bind its successours, possessed of equal omnipotence; and no power, higher than the power of parliament, was then or is yet recognised in the juridical system of England. What was the consequence? In the very next reign, the fluctuating and capricious one of Richard the second, the parliaments were profuse, even to ridicule—if, in such a serious subject, ridicule could find a place—in enacting new, tyrannical, and even contradictory treasons. This they did to such an abominable degree, that, as we are told by the first parliament which met under his successour, "there was no man who knew how he ought to behave himself, to do, speak, or say, for doubt of the pains of such treasons."

In the furious and sanguinary reign of Henry the eighth, the malignant spirit of inventing treasons revived, and was carried to such a height of mad extravagance, that, as we have seen on another occasion, the learned as well as the unlearned, the cautious as well as the unwary, the honest as well as the vicious, were entrapped in the snares. How impotent, as well as cruel and inconsistent, is tyranny in the extreme! His savage rage recoiled, at some times, upon those who were most near to him; at other times, with more justice, upon himself. The beautiful and amiable Boleyn became the victim of that very law, which her husband, in his fit of lustful passion—for the monster was callous to *love*—made for her security. When the enormities of his life and reign were drawing towards their

end, his physicians saw their tyrant in their patient; and they refused to apprize him of his situation, because he had made it treason to predict his death.

Admonished by the history of such times and transactions as these, when legislators are tyrants or tools of tyrants; establishing, under their own control, a power superiour to that of the legislature; and availing themselves of that power, more permanent as well as superiour; the people of the United States have wisely and humanely ordained, that "treason against the United States shall consist only in levying war against them, or in adhering to their enemies, giving them aid and comfort."

In this manner, the citizens of the Union are secured effectually from even legislative tyranny: and in this instance, as in many others, the happiest and most approved example of other times has not only been imitated, but excelled. This single sentence comprehends our whole [law] of national treason; and, as I mentioned before, is transcribed from a part of the statute of Edward the third. By those who proposed the national constitution, this was done, that, in a subject so essentially interesting to each and to all, not a single expression should be introduced, but such as could show in its favour, that it was recommended by the mature experience, and ascertained by the legal interpretation, of numerous revolving centuries.

To the examination, and construction, and well designated force of those expressions, I now solicit your strict attention.

"Treason consists in levying war against the United States." In order to understand this proposition accurately and in all its parts, it may be necessary to give a full and precise answer to all the following questions. 1. What is meant by the expression "levying war?" 2. By whom may the war be levied? 3. Against whom must it be levied?

To each of these questions I mean to give an answer—if possible, a satisfactory answer; but not in the order, in which they are proposed. I begin with the second—by whom may the war spoken of be levied? It is such a war as constitutes treason. The answer then is this: the war must be levied by those who, while they levy it, are at the same time guilty of treason. This throws us back necessarily upon another question—who may commit treason against the United States? To this the answer is—those who owe obedience to their authority. But still another question rises before us—who are they that owe obedience to that authority? I answer—those who receive protection from it. In the monarchy of Great Britain, protection and allegiance are universally acknowledged to be rights and duties reciprocal. The same principle reigns in governments of every kind. I use here the expression *obedience* instead of the expression *allegiance;* because, in England, allegiance is considered as due to the natural, as well as to the moral person of the king; to the man, as well as to the represented authority of the nation. In the United States, the authority of the nation is the sole object on one side. An object strictly corresponding to that, should be the only one required on the other side. The object strictly corresponding to authority is, obedience to that authority. I speak, therefore, with propriety and accuracy unexceptional, when I say, that those who owe obedience to the authority, are such as receive the protection, of the United States.

This close series of investigation has led us to a standard, which is plain and easy, as well as proper and accurate—a standard, which every one can, without the possibility of a mistake, discover by his experience, as well as by his understanding—by what he enjoys, as well as by what he sees. Every one has a monitor within him, which can tell whether he feels protection from the authority of the United States: if he does, to that authority he owes obedience. On the political, as well as on the natural globe, every point must have its antipode. Of obedience the antipode is treason.

I have now shown, by whom the war may be levied. On this subject, a great deal of learning, historical, legal, and political, might be displayed; and changes might easily be rung on the doctrines of natural, and local, and temporary, and perpetual allegiance. I purposely avoid them. The reason is, that so much false is blended with so little genuine intelligence, as to render any discovery you would make an inadequate compensation for your trouble in searching for it. The rights and duties of protection and obedience may, I think, in a much more plain and direct road, be brought home to the bosom and the business of every one.

I now proceed to another question—what is meant by the expression "levying war?" From what has been said in answer to the former question, an answer to this is so far prepared as to inform us, that the term *war* cannot, in this place, mean such a one as is carried on between independent powers. The parties on one side are those who owe obedience. All the curious and extensive learning, therefore, concerning the laws of war as carried on between separate nations, must be thrown out of this question. This is such a war as is levied by those who owe obedience—by citizens; and therefore must be such a war, as, in the nature of things, citizens can levy.

The indictments for this treason generally describe the persons indicted as "arrayed in a warlike manner." As where people are assembled in great numbers, armed with offensive weapons, or weapons of war, if they march thus armed in a body, if they have chosen commanders or officers, if they march with banners displayed, or with drums or trumpets: whether the greatness of their numbers and their continuance together doing these acts may not amount to being arrayed in a warlike manner, deserves consideration. If they have no military arms, nor march or continue together in the posture of war; they may be great rioters, but their conduct does not always amount to a levying of war.

If one, with force and weapons invasive or defensive, hold and defend a castle or fort against the publick power; this is to levy war. So an actual insurrection or rebellion is a levying of war, and by that name must be expressed in the indictment.

But this question will receive a farther illustration from the answer to the third question; because the fact of levying war is often evinced more clearly from the purpose for which, than from the manner in which, the parties assemble. I therefore proceed to examine the last question—

against whom must the war be levied? It must be levied against the United States.

The words of the statute of treasons are, "if any one levy war against the king." I have before observed that, in England, allegiance is considered as due to the natural, as well as to the moral person of the king. This part of the statute of treasons has been always understood as extending to a violation of allegiance in both those points of view—to the levying of war not only against his person, but also against his authority or laws. The levying of war against the United States can, for the reasons already suggested, be considered only in the latter view.

The question now arising is the following—Is such or such a war levied against the United States? This question, as was already intimated, will be best answered by considering the intention with which it was levied. If it is levied on account of some *private* quarrel, or to take revenge of particular persons, it is not a war levied against the United States. A rising to maintain a *private* claim of right; to break prisons for the release of *particular* persons, without any other circumstance of aggravation; or to remove nuisances which affect, or are thought to affect, in point of interest, the parties who assemble—this is not a levying of war against the United States. Insurrections in order to throw down *all* inclosures, to open *all* prisons, to enhance the price of *all* labour, to expel foreigners in general, or those from any single nation living under the protection of government, to alter the established law, or to render it ineffectual—insurrections to accomplish these ends, by numbers and an open and armed force, are a levying of war against the United States.

The line of division between this species of treason and an aggravated riot is sometimes very fine and difficult to be distinguished. In such instances, it is safest and most prudent to consider the case in question as lying on the side of the inferiour crime.

Treason consists in "adhering to the enemies of the United States, giving them aid and comfort." By enemies, are here understood the citizens or subjects of foreign princes or states, with whom the United States are at open war. But the subjects or citizens of such states or princes, in actual hostility, though no war be solemnly declared, are such enemies. The expressions "giving them aid and comfort" are explanatory of what is meant by adherence. To give intelligence to enemies, to send provisions to them, to sell arms to them, treacherously to surrender a fort to them, to cruise in a ship with them against the United States—these are acts of adherence, aid, and comfort.

To join with rebels in a rebellion, or with enemies in acts of hostility, is treason in a citizen, by adhering to those enemies, or levying war with those rebels. But if this be done from apprehension of death, and while the party is under actual force, and he take the first opportunity which offers to make his escape; this fear and compulsion will excuse him.

In England, the punishment of treason is terrible indeed. The criminal is drawn to the gallows, and is not suffered to walk or be carried; though usually a hurdle is allowed to preserve him from the torment of being dragged on the ground. He is hanged by the neck, and is then cut down alive. His entrails are taken out and burned, while he is yet alive. His head is cut off. His body is divided into four parts. His head and quarters are at the disposal of the king.

In the United States and in Pennsylvania, treason is punished in the same manner as other capital crimes.

A traitor is hostile to his country: a pirate is the enemy of mankind—*hostis humani generis.*

Piracy is robbery and depredation on the high seas; and is a crime against the universal law of society. By declaring war against the whole human race, the pirate has laid the whole human race under the necessity of declaring war against him. He has renounced the benefits of society and government: he has abandoned himself to the most savage state of nature. The consequence is, that, by the laws of self defence, every community has a right to inflict upon him that punishment, which, in a state of nature, every individual would be entitled to inflict for any invasion of his person or his personal property.

"If any person," says a law of the United States, "shall commit, upon the high seas, or in any river, haven, basin, or bay, out of the jurisdiction of any particular state, murder or robbery, or any other offence, which, if committed within the body of a county, would, by the laws of the United States, be punished with death; every such offender shall be deemed, taken and adjudged to be a pirate and felon, and being thereof convicted shall suffer death."

By the ancient common law, piracy committed by a subject was deemed a species of treason. According to that law, it consists of such acts of robbery and depredation upon the high seas, as, committed on the land, would amount to a felony there. The law of general society, as well as the law of nations, is a part of the common law.

20

CHARLES LEE, TREASON
21 Aug. 1798
1 Ops. Atty. Gen. 84

(See 1.8.11, no. 9)

21

EX PARTE BOLLMAN & SWARTWOUT
4 Cranch 75 (1807)

MARSHALL, Ch. J. delivered the opinion of the court.

The prisoners having been brought before this court on a writ of *habeas corpus,* and the testimony on which they were committed having been fully examined and attentively considered, the court is now to declare the law upon their case.

This being a mere inquiry, which, without deciding upon guilt, precedes the institution of a prosecution, the question to be determined is, whether the accused shall be discharged or held to trial; and if the latter, in what place they are to be tried, and whether they shall be confined or admitted to bail. "If," says a very learned and accurate commentator, "upon this inquiry it manifestly appears that no such crime has been committed, or that the suspicion entertained of the prisoner was wholly groundless, in such cases only is it lawful totally to discharge him. Otherwise he must either be committed to prison or give bail."

The specific charge brought against the prisoners is treason in levying war against the United States.

As there is no crime which can more excite and agitate the passions of men than treason, no charge demands more from the tribunal before which it is made a deliberate and temperate inquiry. Whether this inquiry be directed to the fact or to the law, none can be more solemn, none more important to the citizen or to the government; none can more affect the safety of both.

To prevent the possibility of those calamities which result from the extension of treason to offences of minor importance, that great fundamental law which defines and limits the various departments of our government has given a rule on the subject both to the legislature and the courts of America, which neither can be permitted to transcend.

"Treason against the United States shall consist only in levying war against them, or in adhering to their enemies, giving them aid and comfort."

To constitute that specific crime for which the prisoners now before the court have been committed, war must be actually levied against the United States. However flagitious may be the crime of conspiring to subvert by force the government of our country, such conspiracy is not treason. To conspire to levy war, and actually to levy war, are distinct offences. The first must be brought into operation by the assemblage of men for a purpose treasonable in itself, or the fact of levying war cannot have been committed. So far has this principle been carried, that, in a case reported by Ventris, and mentioned in some modern treatises on criminal law, it has been determined that the actual enlistment of men to serve against the government does not amount to levying war. It is true that in that case the soldiers enlisted were to serve without the realm, but they were enlisted within it, and if the enlistment for a treasonable purpose could amount to levying war, then war had been actually levied.

It is not the intention of the court to say that no individual can be guilty of this crime who has not appeared in arms against his country. On the contrary, if war be actually levied, that is, if a body of men be actually assembled for the purpose of effecting by force a treasonable purpose, all those who perform any part, however minute, or however remote from the scene of action, and who are actually leagued in the general conspiracy, are to be considered as traitors. But there must be an actual assembling of men for the treasonable purpose, to constitute a levying of war.

Crimes so atrocious as those which have for their object the subversion by violence of those laws and those institutions which have been ordained in order to secure the peace and happiness of society, are not to escape punishment because they have not ripened into treason. The wisdom of the legislature is competent to provide for the case; and the framers of our constitution, who not only defined and limited the crime, but with jealous circumspection attempted to protect their limitation by providing that no person should be convicted of it, unless on the testimony of two witnesses to the same overt act, or on confession in open court, must have conceived it more safe that punishment in such cases should be ordained by general laws, formed upon deliberation, under the influence of no resentments, and without knowing on whom they were to operate, than that it should be inflicted under the influence of those passions which the occasion seldom fails to excite, and which a flexible definition of the crime, or a construction which would render it flexible, might bring into operation. It is therefore more safe as well as more consonant to the principles of our constitution, that the crime of treason should not be extended by construction to doubtful cases; and that crimes not clearly within the constitutional definition, should receive such punishment as the legislature in its wisdom may provide.

To complete the crime of levying war against the United States, there must be an actual assemblage of men for the purpose of executing a treasonable design. In the case now before the court, a design to overturn the government of the United States in New-Orleans by force, would have been unquestionably a design which, if carried into execution, would have been treason, and the assemblage of a body of men for the purpose of carrying it into execution would amount to levying of war against the United States; but no conspiracy for this object, no enlisting of men to effect it, would be an actual levying of war.

In conformity with the principles now laid down, have been the decisions heretofore made by the judges of the United States.

The opinions given by Judge Paterson and Judge Iredell, in cases before them, imply an actual assembling of men, though they rather designed to remark on the purpose to which the force was to be applied than on the nature of the force itself. Their opinions, however, contemplate the actual employment of force.

Judge Chase, in the trial of Fries, was more explicit.

He stated the opinion of the court to be, "that if a body of people conspire and meditate an insurrection to resist or oppose the execution of any statute of the United States by force, they are only guilty of a high misdemeanor; but if they proceed to carry such intention into execution by force, that they are guilty of the treason of levying war; and the *quantum* of the force employed, neither lessens nor increases the crime: whether by one hundred, or one thousand persons, is wholly immaterial." "The court are of opinion," continued Judge Chase, on that occasion, "that a combination or conspiracy to levy war against the United States is not treason, unless combined with an attempt to carry such combination or conspiracy into execution; some actual force or violence must be used in pursuance of such design to levy war; but it is altogether immaterial whether the force used is sufficient to effectuate the object; any

force connected with the intention will constitute the crime of levying war."

The application of these general principles to the particular case before the court will depend on the testimony which has been exhibited against the accused.

The first deposition to be considered is that of General Eaton. This gentleman connects in one statement the purport of numerous conversations held with Colonel Burr throughout the last winter. In the course of these conversations were communicated various criminal projects which seem to have been revolving in the mind of the projector. An expedition against Mexico seems to have been the first and most matured part of his plan, if indeed it did not constitute a distinct and separate plan, upon the success of which other schemes still more culpable, but not yet well digested, might depend. Maps and other information preparatory to its execution, and which would rather indicate that it was the immediate object, had been procured, and for a considerable time in repeated conversations, the whole efforts of Colonel Burr were directed to prove to the witness, who was to have held a high command under him, the practicability of the enterprize, and in explaining to him the means by which it was to be effected.

This deposition exhibits the various schemes of Col. Burr, and its materiality depends on connecting the prisoners at the bar in such of those schemes as were treasonable. For this purpose the affidavit of General Wilkinson, comprehending in its body the substance of a letter from Colonel Burr, has been offered, and was received by the circuit court. To the admission of this testimony great and serious objections have been made. It has been urged that it is a voluntary or rather an extrajudicial affidavit, made before a person not appearing to be a magistrate, and contains the substance only of a letter, of which the original is retained by the person who made the affidavit.

The objection that the affidavit is extrajudicial resolves itself into the question whether one magistrate may commit on an affidavit taken before another magistrate. For if he may, an affidavit made as the foundation of a commitment ceases to be extrajudicial, and the person who makes it would be as liable to a prosecution for perjury as if the warrant of commitment had been issued by the magistrate before whom the affidavit was made.

To decide that an affidavit made before one magistrate would not justify a commitment by another, might in many cases be productive of great inconvenience, and does not appear susceptible of abuse if the verity of the certificate be established. Such an affidavit seems admissible on the principle that before the accused is put upon his trial all the proceeedings are *ex parte*. The court therefore overrule this objection.

That which questions the character of the person who has on this occasion administered the oath is next to be considered.

The certificate from the office of the department of state has been deemed insufficient by the counsel for the prisoners, because the law does not require the appointment of magistrates for the territory of New-Orleans to be certified to that office, because the certificate is in itself informal, and because it does not appear that the magistrate had taken the oath required by the act of congress.

The first of these objections is not supported by the law of the case, and the second may be so readily corrected, that the court has proceeded to consider the subject as if it were corrected, retaining however any final decision, if against the prisoners, until the correction shall be made. With regard to the third, the magistrate must be presumed to have taken the requisite oaths, since he is found acting as a magistrate.

On the admissibility of that part of the affidavit which purports to be as near the substance of the letter from Colonel Burr to General Wilkinson as the latter could interpret it, a division of opinion has taken place in the court. Two judges are of opinion that as such testimony delivered in the presence of the prisoner on his trial would be totally inadmissible, neither can it be considered as a foundation for a commitment. Although in making a commitment the magistrate does not decide on the guilt of the prisoner, yet he does decide on the probable cause, and a long and painful imprisonment may be the consequence of his decision. This probable cause, therefore, ought to be proved by testimony in itself legal, and which, though from the nature of the case it must be *ex parte,* ought in many other respects to be such as a court and jury might hear.

Two judges are of opinion that in this incipient stage of the prosecution an affidavit stating the general purport of a letter may be read, particularly where the person in possession of it is at too great a distance to admit of its being obtained, and that a commitment may be founded on it.

Under this embarassment it was deemed necessary to look into the affidavit for the purpose of discovering whether, if admitted, it contains matter which would justify the commitment of the prisoners at the bar on the charge of treason.

That the letter from Colonel Burr to General Wilkinson relates to a military enterprize meditated by the former, has not been questioned. If this enterprize was against Mexico, it would amount to a high misdemeanor; if against any of the territories of the United States, or if in its progress the subversion of the government of the United States in any of their territories was a mean clearly and necessarily to be employed, if such mean formed a substantive part of the plan, the assemblage of a body of men to effect it would be levying war against the United States.

The letter is in language which furnishes no distinct view of the design of the writer. The co-operation, however, which is stated to have been secured, points strongly to some expedition against the territories of Spain. After making these general statements, the writer becomes rather more explicit, and says, "Burr's plan of operations is to move down rapidly from the falls on the 15th of November with the first 500 or 1,000 men in light boats now constructing for that purpose, to be at Natchez between the 5th and 15th of December, there to meet Wilkinson; then to determine whether it will be expedient in the first instance to seize on or to pass by Baton Rouge. The people of the country to which we are going are pre-

pared to receive us. Their agents now with Burr say that if we will protect their religion, and will not subject them to a foreign power, in three weeks all will be settled."

There is no expression in these sentences which would justify a suspicion that any territory of the United States was the object of the expedition.

For what purpose seize on Baton Rouge; why engage Spain aginst this enterprize, if it was designed against the United States?

"The people of the country to which we are going are prepared to receive us." This language is peculiarly appropriate to a foreign country. It will not be contended that the terms would be inapplicable to a territory of the United States, but other terms would more aptly convey the idea, and Burr seems to consider himself as giving information of which Wilkinson was not possessed. When it is recollected that he was the governor of a territory adjoining that which must have been threatened, if a territory of the United States was threatened, and that he commanded the army, a part of which was stationed in that territory, the probability that the information communicated related to a foreign country, it must be admitted, gains strength.

"The agents now with Burr say, that if we will protect their religion, and will not subject them to a foreign power, in three weeks all will be settled."

This is apparently the language of a people who, from the contemplated change in their political situation, feared for their religion, and feared that they would be made the subjects of a foreign power. That the Mexicans should entertain these apprehensions was natural, and would readily be believed. They were, if the representation made of their dispositions be correct, about to place themselves much in the power of men who professed a different faith from theirs, and who, by making them dependent on England or the United States, would subject them to a foreign power.

That the people of New-Orleans, as a people, if really engaged in the conspiracy, should feel the same apprehensions, and require assurances on the same points, is by no means so obvious.

There certainly is not in the letter delivered to Gen. Wilkinson, so far as that letter is laid before the court, one syllable which has a necessary or a natural reference to an enterprize against any territory of the United States.

That the bearer of this letter must be considered as acquainted with its contents is not to be controverted. The letter and his own declarations evince the fact.

After stating himself to have passed through New-York, and the western states and territories, without insinuating that he had performed on his route any act whatever which was connected with the enterprize, he states their object to be, "to carry an expedition into the Mexican provinces."

This statement may be considered as explanatory of the letter of Col. Burr, if the expressions of that letter could be thought ambiguous.

But there are other declarations made by Mr. Swartwout, which constitute the difficulty of this case. On an inquiry from General Wilkinson, he said, "this territory would be revolutionized where the people were ready to join them, and that there would be some seizing, he supposed, at New-Orleans."

If these words import that the government established by the United States in any of its territories, was to be revolutionized by force, although merely as a step to, or a mean of executing some greater projects, the design was unquestionably treasonable, and any assemblage of men for that purpose would amount to a levying of war. But on the import of the words a difference of opinion exists. Some of the judges suppose they refer to the territory against which the expedition was intended; others to that in which the conversation was held. Some consider the words, if even applicable to a territory of the United States, as alluding to a revolution to be effected by the people, rather than by the party conducted by Col. Burr.

But whether this treasonable intention be really imputable to the plan or not, it is admitted that it must have been carried into execution by an open assemblage of men for that purpose, previous to the arrest of the prisoner, in order to consummate the crime as to him; and a majority of the court is of opinion that the conversation of Mr. Swartwout affords no sufficient proof of such assembling.

The prisoner stated that "Col. Burr, with the support of a powerful association extending from New-York to New-Orleans, was levying an armed body of 7,000 men from the state of New-York and the western states and territories, with a view to carry an expedition to the Mexican territories."

That the association, whatever may be its purpose, is not treason, has been already stated. That levying an army may or may not be treason, and that this depends on the intention with which it is levied, and on the point to which the parties have advanced, has been also stated. The mere enlisting of men, without assembling them, is not levying war. The question then is, whether this evidence proves Col. Burr to have advanced so far in levying an army as actually to have assembled them.

It is argued that since it cannot be necessary that the whole 7,000 men should have assembled, their commencing their march by detachments to the place of rendezvous must be sufficient to constitute the crime.

This position is correct, with some qualification. It cannot be necessary that the whole army should assemble, and that the various parts which are to compose it should have combined. But it is necessary that there should be an actual assemblage, and therefore the evidence should make the fact unequivocal.

The travelling of individuals to the place of rendezvous would perhaps not be sufficient. This would be an equivocal act, and has no warlike appearance. The meeting of particular bodies of men, and their marching from places of partial to a place of general rendezvous would be such an assemblage.

The particular words used by Mr. Swartwout are, that Col. Burr "was levying an armed body of 7,000 men." If the term *levying* in this place imports that they were assembled, then such fact would amount, if the intention be against the United States, to levying war. If it barely im-

ports that he was enlisting or engaging them in his service, the fact would not amount to levying war.

It is thought sufficiently apparent that the latter is the sense in which the term was used. The fact alluded to, if taken in the former sense, is of a nature so to force itself upon the public view, that if the army had then actually assembled, either together or in detachments, some evidence of such assembling would have been laid before the court.

The words used by the prisoner in reference to seizing at New-Orleans, and borrowing perhaps by force from the bank, though indicating a design to rob, and consequently importing a high offence, do not designate the specific crime of levying war against the United States.

It is therefore the opinion of a majority of the court, that in the case of Samuel Swartwout there is not sufficient evidence of his levying war against the United States to justify his commitment on the charge of treason.

Against Erick Bollman there is still less testimony. Nothing has been said by him to support the charge that the enterprize in which he was engaged had any other object than was stated in the letter of Colonel Burr. Against him, therefore, there is no evidence to support a charge of treason.

That both of the prisoners were engaged in a most culpable enterprize against the dominions of a power at peace with the United States, those who admit the affidavit of General Wilkinson cannot doubt. But that no part of this crime was committed in the district of Columbia is apparent. It is therefore the unanimous opinion of the court that they cannot be tried in this district.

The law read on the part of the prosecution is understood to apply only to offences committed on the high seas, or in any river, haven, basin or bay, not within the jurisdiction of any particular state. In those cases there is no court which has particular cognizance of the crime, and therefore the place in which the criminal shall be apprehended, or, if he be apprehended where no court has exclusive jurisdiction, that to which he shall be first brought, is substituted for the place in which the offence was committed.

But in this case, a tribunal for the trial of the offence, wherever it may have been committed, had been provided by congress; and at the place where the prisoners were seized by the authority of the commander in chief, there existed such a tribunal. It would, too, be extremely dangerous to say, that because the prisoners were apprehended, not by a civil magistrate, but by the military power, there could be given by law a right to try the persons so seized in any place which the general might select, and to which he might direct them to be carried.

The act of congress which the prisoners are supposed to have violated, describes as offenders those who begin or set on foot, or provide, or prepare, the means for any military expedition or enterprize to be carried out from thence against the dominions of a foreign prince or state, with whom the United States are at peace.

There is a want of precision in the description of the offence which might produce some difficulty in deciding what cases would come within it. But several other questions arise which a court consisting of four judges finds itself unable to decide, and therefore, as the crime with which the prisoners stand charged has not been committed, the court can only direct them to be discharged. This is done with the less reluctance because the discharge does not acquit them from the offence which there is probable cause for supposing they have committed, and if those whose duty it is to protect the nation, by prosecuting offenders against the laws, shall suppose those who have been charged with treason to be proper objects for punishment, they will, when possessed of less exceptionable testimony, and when able to say at what place the offence has been committed, institute fresh proceedings against them.

22

UNITED STATES V. BURR
25 Fed. Cas. 55, no. 14,693 (C.C.D.Va. 1807)

MARSHALL, Chief Justice, delivered the opinion of the court as follows:

The question now to be decided has been argued in a manner worthy of its importance, and with an earnestness evincing the strong conviction felt by the counsel on each side that the law is with them. A degree of eloquence seldom displayed on any occasion has embellished a solidity of argument and a depth of research by which the court has been greatly aided in forming the opinion it is about to deliver. The testimony adduced on the part of the United States to prove the overt act laid in the indictment having shown, and the attorney for the United States having admitted, that the prisoner was not present when that act, whatever may be its character, was committed, and there being no reason to doubt but that he was at a great distance, and in a different state, it is objected to the testimony offered on the part of the United States to connect him with those who committed the overt act, that such testimony is totally irrelevant, and must, therefore, be rejected. The arguments in support of this motion respect in part the merits of the case as it may be supposed to stand independent of the pleadings, and in part as exhibited by the pleadings.

On the first division of the subject two points are made: 1st. That, conformably to the constitution of the United States, no man can be convicted of treason who was not present when the war was levied. 2d. That if this construction be erroneous, no testimony can be received to charge one man with the overt acts of others until those overt acts as laid in the indictment be proved to the satisfaction of the court. The question which arises on the construction of the constitution, in every point of view in which it can be contemplated, is of infinite moment to the people of this country and to their government, and requires the most temperate and the most deliberate consideration.

"Treason against the United States shall consist only in levying war against them." What is the natural import of the words "levying war?" and who may be said to levy it? Had their first application to treason been made by our constitution they would certainly have admitted of some latitude of construction. Taken most literally, they are, perhaps, of the same import with the words "raising or creating war"; but as those who join after the commencement are equally the objects of punishment, there would probably be a general admission that the term also comprehended making war or carrying on war. In the construction which courts would be required to give these words, it is not improbable that those who should raise, create, make, or carry on war, might be comprehended. The various acts which would be considered as coming within the term would be settled by a course of decisions; and it would be affirming boldly to say that those only who actually constituted a portion of the military force appearing in arms could be considered as levying war. There is no difficulty in affirming that there must be a war or the crime of levying it cannot exist; but there would often be considerable difficulty in affirming that a particular act did or did not involve the person committing it in the guilt and in the fact of levying war. If, for example, an army should be actually raised for the avowed purpose of carrying on open war against the United States and subverting their government, the point must be weighed very deliberately, before a judge would venture to decide that an overt act of levying war had not been committed by a commissary of purchases, who never saw the army, but who, knowing its object, and leaguing himself with the rebels, supplied that army with provisions, or, by a recruiting officer holding a commission in the rebel service, who, though never in camp, executed the particular duty assigned to him.

But the term is not for the first time applied to treason by the constitution of the United States. It is a technical term. It is used in a very old statute of that country whose language is our language, and whose laws form the substratum of our laws. It is scarcely conceivable that the term was not employed by the framers of our constitution in the sense which had been affixed to it by those from whom we borrowed it. So far as the meaning of any terms, particularly terms of art, is completely ascertained, those by whom they are employed must be considered as employing them in that ascertained meaning, unless the contrary be proved by the context. It is, therefore, reasonable to suppose, unless it be incompatible with other expressions of the constitution, that the term "levying war" is used in that instrument in the same sense in which it was understood in England, and in this country, to have been used in the statute of the 25th of Edw. III. from which it was borrowed. It is said that this meaning is to be collected only from adjudged cases. But this position cannot be conceded to the extent in which it is laid down. The superior authority of adjudged cases will never be controverted. But those celebrated elementary writers who have stated the principles of the law, whose statements have received the common approbation of legal men, are not to be disregarded. Principles laid down by such writers as Coke,

Hale, Foster, and Blackstone, are not lightly to be rejected. These books are in the hands of every student. Legal opinions are formed upon them; and those opinions are afterwards carried to the bar, the bench and the legislature. In the exposition of terms, therefore, used in instruments of the present day, the definitions and the dicta of those authors, if not contradicted by adjudications, and if compatible with the words of the statute, are entitled to respect. It is to be regretted that they do not shed as much light on this part of the subject as is to be wished. Coke does not give a complete definition of the term, but puts cases which amount to levying war. "An actual rebellion or insurrection, he says, is a levying of war." In whom? Coke does not say whether in those only who appear in arms, or in all those who take part in the rebellion or insurrection by real open deed. Hale, in treating on the same subject, puts many cases which shall constitute a levying of war, without which no act can amount to treason; but he does not particularize the parts to be performed by the different persons concerned in that war, which shall be sufficient to fix on each the guilt of levying it. Foster says: "The joining with rebels in an act of rebellion, or with enemies in acts of hostility, will make a man a traitor." "Furnishing rebels or enemies with money, arms, ammunition or other necessaries will prima facie make a man a traitor." Foster does not say that he would be a traitor under the words of the statute, independent of the legal rule which attaches the guilt of the principal to an accessory, nor that his treason is occasioned by that rule. In England this discrimination need not be made except for the purpose of framing the indictment; and, therefore, in the English books we do not perceive any effort to make it. Thus, surrendering a castle to rebels, being in confederacy with them, is said by Hale and Foster to be treason under the clause of levying war; but whether it be levying war in fact, or aiding those who levy it, is not said. Upon this point Blackstone is not more satisfactory. Although we find among the commentators upon treason enough to satisfy the inquiry, what is a state of internal war? yet no precise information can be acquired from them which would enable us to decide with clearness whether persons not in arms, but taking part in a rebellion, could be said to levy war, independently of that doctrine which attaches to the accessory the guilt of his principal. If in adjudged cases this question have been taken up and directly decided, the court has not seen those cases. The argument which may be drawn from the form of the indictment, though strong, is not conclusive. In the precedent found in Tremaine, Mary Speake, who was indicted for furnishing provisions to the party of the Duke of Monmouth, is indicted for furnishing provisions to those who were levying war, not for levying war herself. It may correctly be argued that, had this act amounted to levying war, she would have been indicted for levying war; and the furnishing of provisions would have been laid as the overt act. The court felt this when the precedent was produced. But the argument, though strong, is not conclusive, because, in England, the inquiry, whether she had become a traitor by levying war, or by giving aid and comfort to those who were levying war, was unimportant; and because, too, it does not appear from the indictment that she was actually concerned in the rebellion—that she belonged to the rebel party, or was guilty of anything further than a criminal speculation in selling them provisions.

It is not deemed necessary to trace the doctrine, that in treason all are principals, to its source. Its origin is most probably stated correctly by Judge Tucker in a work, the merit of which is with pleasure acknowledged. But if a spurious doctrine have been introduced into the common law, and have for centuries been admitted as genuine, it would require great hardihood in a judge to reject it. Accordingly, we find those of the English jurists who seem to disapprove the principle declaring that it is now too firmly setted to be shaken. It is unnecessary to trace this doctrine to its source for another reason: the terms of the constitution comprise no question respecting principal and accessory, so far as either may be truly and in fact said to levy war. Whether in England a person would be indicted in express terms for levying war or for assisting others in levying war, yet if in correct and legal language he can be said to have levied war, and if it have never been decided that the act would not amount to levying war, his case may, without violent construction, be brought within the letter and the plain meaning of the constitution. In examining these words, the argument which may be drawn from felonies, as, for example, from murder, is not more conclusive. Murder is the single act of killing with malice aforethought. But war is a complex operation, composed of many parts, co-operating with each other. No one man or body of men can perform them all if the war be of any continuance. Although, then, in correct and in law language, he alone is said to have murdered another who has perpetrated the fact of killing, or has been present aiding that fact, it does not follow that he alone can have levied war who has borne arms. All those who perform the various and essential military parts of prosecuting the war, which must be assigned to different persons, may with correctness and accuracy be said to levy war. Taking this view of the subject, it appears to the court that those who perform a part in the prosecution of the war may correctly be said to levy war and to commit treason under the constitution. It will be observed that this opinion does not extend to the case of a person who performs no act in the prosecution of the war—who counsels and advises it—or who, being engaged in the conspiracy, fails to perform his part. Whether such persons may be implicated by the doctrine that whatever would make a man an accessory in felony makes him a principal in treason, or are excluded because that doctrine is inapplicable to the United States, the constitution having declared that treason shall consist only in levying war, and having made the proof of overt acts necessary to conviction, is a question of vast importance, which it would be proper for the supreme court to take a fit occasion to decide, but which an inferior tribunal would not willingly determine unless the case before them should require it.

It may now be proper to notice the opinion of the supreme court in the case of the United States against Bollman and Swartwout. It is said that this opinion, in declaring that those who do not bear arms may yet be guilty of treason, is contrary to law, and is not obligatory because it is extra-judicial and was delivered on a point not argued. This court is therefore required to depart from the principle there laid down. It is true that, in that case, after forming the opinion that no treason could be committed because no treasonable assemblage had taken place, the court might have dispensed with proceeding further in the doctrines of treason. But it is to be remembered that the judges might act separately, and perhaps at the same time on the various prosecutions which might be instituted, and that no appeal lay from their decisions. Opposite judgments on the point would have presented a state of things infinitely to be deplored by all. It was not surprising, then, that they should have made some attempt to settle principles which would probably occur, and which were in some degree connected with the point before them. The court had employed some reasoning to show that without the actual embodying of men war could not be levied. It might have been inferred from this that those only who were so embodied could be guilty of treason. Not only to exclude this inference, but also to affirm the contrary, the court proceeded to observe: "It is not the intention of the court to say that no individual can be guilty of this crime who has not appeared in arms against his country. On the contrary, if war be actually levied, that is, if a body of men be actually assembled for the purpose of effecting by force a treasonable object, all those who perform any part, however minute, or however remote from the scene of action, and who are actually leagued in the general conspiracy, are to be considered as traitors." This court is told that if this opinion be incorrect it ought not to be obeyed, because it was extra-judicial. For myself, I can say that I could not lightly be prevailed on to disobey it, were I even convinced that it was erroneous; but I would certainly use any means which the law placed in my power to carry the question again before the supreme court for reconsideration, in a case in which it would directly occur and be fully argued. The court which gave this opinion was composed of four judges. At the time I thought them unanimous, but I have since had reason to suspect that one of them, whose opinion is entitled to great respect, and whose indisposition prevented his entering into the discussions, on some of those points which were not essential to the decision of the very case under consideration, did not concur in this particular point with his brethren. Had the opinion been unanimous, it would have been given by a majority of the judges. But should the three who were absent concur with that judge who was present, and who perhaps dissents from what was then the opinion of the court, a majority of the judges may overrule this decision. I should, therefore, feel no objection, although I then thought and still think the opinion perfectly correct, to carry the point, if possible, again before the supreme court, if the case should depend upon it. In saying that I still think the opinion perfectly correct, I do not consider myself as going further than the preceding reasoning goes. Some gentlemen have argued as if the supreme court had adopted the whole doctrine of the English books on the subject of accessories to treason. But certainly such is not the fact. Those only who perform a part, and who are leagued in the conspiracy, are declared to be traitors.

To complete the definition both circumstances must concur. They must "perform a part," which will furnish the overt act; and they must be "leagued in conspiracy." The person who comes within this description in the opinon of the court levies war. The present motion, however, does not rest upon this point; for if under this indictment the United States might be let in to prove the part performed by the prisoner, if he did perform any part, the court could not stop the testimony, in its present stage.

2d. The second point involves the character of the overt act which has been given in evidence, and calls upon the court to declare whether that act can amount to levying war. Although the court ought now to avoid any analysis of the testimony which has been offered in this case, provided the decision of the motion should not rest upon it, yet many reasons concur in giving peculiar propriety to a delivery, in the course of these trials, of a detailed opinion on the question, what is levying war? As this question has been argued at great length, it may probably save much trouble to the counsel now to give that opinon.

In opening the case, it was contended by the attorney for the United States, and has since been maintained on the part of the prosecution, that neither arms nor the application of force or violence are indispensably necessary to constitute the fact of levying war. To illustrate these positions, several cases have been stated, many of which would clearly amount to treason. In all of them, except that which was probably intended to be this case, and on which no observation will be made, the object of the assemblage was clearly treasonable. Its character was unequivocal, and was demonstrated by evidence furnished by the assemblage itself. There was no necessity to rely upon information drawn from extrinsic sources, or, in order to understand the fact, to pursue a course of intricate reasoning, and to conjecture motives. A force is supposed to be collected for an avowed treasonable object, in a condition to attempt that object, and to have commenced the attempt by moving towards it. I state these particulars, because although the cases put may establish the doctrine they are intended to support—may prove that the absence of arms, or the failure to apply force to sensible objects by the actual commission of violence on those objects, may be supplied by other circumstances—yet they also serve to show that the mind requires those circumstances to be satisfied that war is levied. Their construction of the opinion of the supreme court is, I think, thus far correct. It is certainly the opinion which was at the time entertained by myself; and which is still entertained. If a rebel army, avowing its hostility to the sovereign power, should front that of the government, should march and countermarch before it, should manoeuvre in its face, and should then disperse from any cause whatever without firing a gun—I confess I could not, without some surprise, hear gentlemen seriously contend that this could not amount to an act of levying war. A case equally strong may be put with respect to the absence of military weapons. If the party be in a condition to execute the purposed treason without the usual implements of war, I can perceive no reason for requiring those implements in order to constitute the crime. It is argued that no adjudged case can be produced

445

from the English books where actual violence has not been committed. Suppose this were true. No adjudged case has, or, it is believed, can be produced from those books in which it has been laid down that war cannot be levied without the actual application of violence to external objects. The silence of the reporters on this point may be readily accounted for. In cases of actual rebellion against the government, the most active and influential leaders are generally most actively engaged in the war; and as the object can never be to extend punishment to extermination, a sufficient number are found among those who have committed actual hostilities to satisfy the avenging arm of justice. In cases of constructive treason, such as pulling down meeting-houses, where the direct and avowed object is not the destruction of the sovereign power, some act of violence might be generally required to give to the crime a sufficient degree of malignity to convert it into treason, to render the guilt of any individual unequivocal. But Vaughan's Case is a case where there was no real application of violence, and where the act was adjudged to be treason. Gentlemen argue that Vaughan was only guilty of adhering to the king's enemies, but they have not the authority of the court for so saying. The judges unquestionably treat the cruising of Vaughan as an overt act of levying war. The opinions of the best elementary writers concur in declaring that where a body of men are assembled for the purpose of making war against the government, and are in a condition to make that war, the assemblage is an act of levying war. These opinions are contradicted by no adjudged case, and are supported by Vaughan's Case. This court is not inclined to controvert them. But although, in this respect, the opinion of the supreme court has not been misunderstood on the part of the prosecution, that opinion seems not to have been fully adverted to in a very essential point in which it is said to have been misconceived by others. The opinion, I am informed, has been construed to mean that any assemblage whatever for a treasonable purpose, whether in force or not in force, whether in a condition to use violence or not in that condition, is a levying of war. It is this construction, which has not, indeed, been expressly advanced at the bar, but which is said to have been adopted elsewhere, that the court deems it necessary to examine.

Independent of authority, trusting only to the dictates of reason, and expounding terms according to their ordinary signification, we should probably all concur in the declaration that war could not be levied without the employment and exhibition of force. War is an appeal from reason to the sword; and he who makes the appeal evidences the fact by the use of the means. His intention to go to war may be proved by words; but the actual going to war is a fact which is to be proved by open deed. The end is to be effected by force; and it would seem that in cases where no declaration is to be made, the state of actual war could only be created by the employment of force, or being in a condition to employ it. But the term, having been adopted by our constitution, must be understood in that sense in which it was universally received in this country when the constitution was framed. The sense in which it was received is to be collected from the most approved authorities of that nation from which we have borrowed the term. Lord Coke says that levying war against the king was treason at the common law. "A compassing or conspiracy to levy war, he adds, is no treason, for there must be a levying of war in fact." He proceeds to state cases of constructive levying war, where the direct design is not to overturn the government, but to effect some general object by force. The terms he employs, in stating these cases, are such as indicate an impression on his mind that actual violence is a necessary ingredient in constituting the fact of levying war. He then proceeds to say: "An actual rebellion or insurrection is a levying of war within this fact." "If any with strength and weapons invasive and defensive doth hold and defend a castle or fort against the king and his power, this is levying of war against the king." These cases are put to illustrate what he denominates "a war in fact." It is not easy to conceive "an actual invasion or insurrection" unconnected with force; nor can "a castle or fort be defended with strength and weapons invasive and defensive" without the employment of actual force. It would seem, then, to have been the opinion of Lord Coke that to levy war there must be an assemblage of men in a condition and with an intention to employ force. He certainly puts no case of a different description. Lord Hale says (1 Hale, P. C. p. 149, pl. 6:) "What shall be said a levying of war is partly a question of fact, for it is not every unlawful or riotous assembly of many persons to do an unlawful act, though de facto they commit the act they intend, that makes a levying of war; for then every riot would be treason, &c.," "but it must be such an assembly as carries with it speciem belli, the appearance of war; as if they ride or march vexillis explicatis, with colors flying, or if they be formed into companies or furnished with military officers, or if they are armed with military weapons, as swords, guns, bills, halberds, pikes, and are so circumstanced that it may be reasonably concluded they are in a posture of war; which circumstances are so various that it is hard to describe them all particularly." "Only the general expressions in all the indictments of this nature that I have seen are more guerrino arraiati," arrayed in warlike manner. He afterwards adds: "If there be a war levied as is above declared, viz, an assembly arrayed in warlike manner, and so in the posture of war for any treasonable attempt, it is bellum levatum but not percussum." It is obvious that Lord Hale supposed an assemblage of men in force, in a military posture, to be necessary to constitute the fact of levying war. The idea, he appears to suggest, that the apparatus of war is necessary, has been very justly combated by an able judge who has written a valuable treatise on the subject of treason; but, it is not recollected that his position, that the assembly should be in a posture of war for any treasonable attempt, has ever been denied. Hawkins (chapter 17, § 23), says "that not only those who rebel against the king, and take up arms to dethrone him, but, also, in many other cases, those who, in a violent and forcible manner, withstand his lawful authority, are said to levy war against him, and therefore those that hold a fort or castle against the king's forces, or keep together armed numbers of men, against the king's express command, have been adjudged to levy war against him." The cases put by Hawkins are all cases of actual force and violence. "Those who rebel against the king, and take up arms to dethrone him." In many other cases those "who, in a violent and forcible manner, withstand his lawful authority." "Those that hold a fort or castle against his forces, or keep together armed numbers of men against his express command." These cases are obviously cases of force and violence. Hawkins next proceeds to describe cases in which war is understood to be levied under the statute, although it was not directly made against the government. This Lord Hale terms an interpretative or constructive levying of war; and it will be perceived that he puts no case in which actual force is dispensed with. "Those also, he says, who make an insurrection in order to redress a public grievance, whether it be a real or pretended one, and of their own authority attempt with force to redress it, are said to levy war against the king, although they have no direct design against his person, inasmuch as they insolently invade his prerogative by attempting to do that by private authority which he, by public justice, ought to do; which manifestly tends to a downright rebellion. As where great numbers by force attempt to remove certain persons from the king," &c. The cases here put by Hawkins, of a constructive levying of war, do in terms require force as a constituent part of the description of the offence.

Judge Foster, in his valuable treatise on Treason, states the opinion which has been quoted from Lord Hale, and differs from that writer so far as the latter might seem to require swords, drums, colors, &c., what he terms the pomp and pageantry of war, as essential circumstances to constitute the fact of levying war. In the Cases of Damaree and Purchase, he says: "The want of those circumstances weighed nothing with the court, although the prisoner's counsel insisted much on that matter." But he adds: "The number of the insurgents supplied the want of military weapons; and they were provided with axes, crows, and other tools of the like nature, proper for the mischief they intended to effect. Furor arma ministrat." It is apparent that Judge Foster here alludes to an assemblage in force, or as Lord Hale terms it, "in a warlike posture;" that is, in a condition to attempt or proceed upon the treason which had been contemplated. The same author afterwards states at large the Cases of Damaree and Purchase from 8 State Trials; and they are cases where the insurgents not only assembled in force, in the posture of war, or in a condition to execute the treasonable design, but they did actually carry it into execution, and did resist the guards who were sent to disperse them. Judge Foster states (section 4) all insurrections to effect certain innovations of a public and general concern, by an armed force, to be, in construction of law, high treason within the clause of levying war. The cases put by Foster of constructive levying of war all contain, as a material ingredient, the actual employment of force. After going through this branch of his subject, he proceeds to state the law in a case of actual levying war: that is, where the war is intended directly against the government. He says (section 9): "An assembly armed and arrayed in a warlike manner for a treasonable purpose is bellum levatum, though not bellum percussum. Listing and marching are sufficient overt acts, without coming to a battle or action. So cruising on the king's subjects under a French commission, France being then at war with us, was held to be adhering to the king's enemies, though no other act of hostility be proved." "An assembly armed and arrayed in a warlike manner for any treasonable purpose" is certainly in a state of force: in a condition to execute the treason for which they assembled. The words, "enlisting and marching," which are overt acts of levying war, do, in the arrangement of the sentence, also imply a state of force; though that state is not expressed in terms; for the succeeding words, which state a particular event as not having happened, prove that event to have been the next circumstance to those which had happened; they are "without coming to a battle or action." "If men be enlisted and march," (that is, if they march prepared for battle or in a condition for action; for marching is a technical term applied to the movement of a military corps,) it is an overt act of levying war, though they do not come to a battle or action. This exposition is rendered the stronger by what seems to be put in the same sentence as a parallel case with respect to adhering to an enemy. It is cruising under a commission from an enemy without committing any other act of hostility. Cruising is the act of sailing in warlike form and in a condition to assail those of whom the cruiser is in quest. This exposition, which seems to be that intended by Judge Foster, is rendered the more certain by a reference to the case in the State Trials from which the extracts are taken. The words used by the chief justice are: "When men form themselves into a body and march rank and file with weapons offensive and defensive, this is levying of war with open force, if the design be public." Mr. Phipps, the counsel for the prisoner, afterwards observed: "Intending to levy war is not treason unless a war be actually levied." To this the chief justice answered: "Is it not actually levying of war if they actually provide arms and levy men, and in a warlike manner set out and cruise and come with a design to destroy our ships?" Mr. Phipps still insisted "it would not be an actual levying of war unless they committed some act of hostility." "Yes, indeed," said the chief justice, "the going on board and being in a posture to attack the king's ships." Mr. Baron Powis added: "But for you to say that because they did not actually fight it is not a levying of war! Is it not plain what they did intend? that they came with that intention? that they came in that posture? that they came armed, and had guns and blunderbusses, and surrounded the ship twice? They came with an armed force; that is strong evidence of the design."

The point insisted on by counsel in the Case of Vaughan, as in this case, was, that war could not be levied without actual fighting. In this the counsel was very properly overruled; but it is apparent that the judges proceeded entirely on the idea that a warlike posture was indispensable to the fact of levying war. Judge Foster proceeds to give other instances of levying war: "Attacking the king's forces in opposition to his authority upon a march or in quarters is levying war." "Holding a castle or fort against the king or his forces, if actual force be used in order to keep possession, is levying war. But a bare detainer, as, suppose, by shutting the gates against the king or his forces, without any other force from within, Lord

Hale conceiveth will not amount to treason." The whole doctrine of Judge Foster on this subject seems to demonstrate a clear opinion that a state of force or violence, a posture of war, must exist to constitute technically as well as really the fact of levying war.

Judge Blackstone seems to concur with his predecessors. Speaking of levying war, he says: "This may be done by taking arms, not only to dethrone the king, but under pretense to reform religion or the laws, or to remove evil counsellors or other grievances, whether real or pretended. For the law does not, neither can it, permit any private man or set of men to interfere forcibly in matters of such high importance." He proceeds to give examples of levying war, which show that he contemplated actual force as a necessary ingredient in the composition of this crime. It would seem, then, from the English authorities, that the words "levying war" have not received a technical different from their natural meaning, so far as respects the character of the assemblage of men which may constitute the fact. It must be a warlike assemblage, carrying the appearance of force, and in a situation to practice hostility.

Several judges of the United States have given opinions at their circuits on the subject, all of which deserve, and will receive the particular attention of this court.

In his charge to the grand jury, when John Fries was indicted in consequence of a forcible opposition to the direct tax, Judge Iredell is understood to have said: "I think I am warranted in saying that if, in the case of the insurgents who may come under your consideration, the intention was to prevent by force of arms the execution of an act of the congress of the United States altogether, any forcible opposition, calculated to carry that intention into effect, was a levying of war against the United States, and, of course, an act of treason." To levy war, then, according to this opinion of Judge Iredell, required the actual exertion of force. Judge Patterson, in his opinions delivered in two different cases, seems not to differ from Judge Iredell. He does not, indeed, precisely state the employment of force as necessary to constitute a levying war, but in giving his opinion, in cases in which force was actually employed, he considers the crime in one case as dependent on the intention; and in the other case he says: "Combining these facts and this design," (that is, combining actual force with a treasonable design,) "the crime is high treason." Judge Peters has also indicated the opinion that force was necessary to constitute the crime of levying war. Judge Chase has been particularly clear and explicit. In an opinion which he appears to have prepared on great consideration, he says: "The court are of opinion that if a body of people conspire and meditate an insurrection to resist or oppose the execution of a statute of the United States by force, they are only guilty of a high misdemeanor; but if they proceed to carry such intention into execution by force, that they are guilty of the treason of levying war; and the quantum of the force employed neither increases nor diminishes the crime; whether by one hundred or one thousand persons is wholly immaterial. The court are of opinion that a combination or conspiracy to levy war against the United States is not treason unless combined with an attempt to carry such combination or conspiracy into exe-

cution; some actual force or violence must be used in pursuance of such design to levy war; but that it is altogether immaterial whether the force used be sufficient to effectuate the object. Any force connected with the intention will constitute the crime of levying of war." In various parts of the opinion delivered by Judge Chase, in the case of Fries, the same sentiments are to be found. It is to be observed that these judges are not content that troops should be assembled in a condition to employ force. According to them some degree of force must have been actually employed. The judges of the United States, then, so far as their opinions have been quoted, seem to have required still more to constitute the fact of levying war than has been required by the English books. Our judges seem to have required the actual exercise of force, the actual employment of some degree of violence. This, however, may be, and probably is, because, in the cases in which their opinions were given, the design not having been to overturn the government, but to resist the execution of a law, such an assemblage as would be sufficient for the purpose would require the actual employment of force to render the object unequivocal.

But it is said all these authorities have been overruled by the decision of the supreme court in the case of U. S. v. Swartwout [4 Cranch (8 U. S.) 75]. If the supreme court have indeed extended the doctrine of treason further than it has heretofore been carried by the judges of England or of this country, their decision would be submitted to. At least this court could go no further than to endeavor again to bring the point directly before them. It would, however, be expected that an opinion which is to overrule all former precedents, and to establish a principle never before recognized, should be expressed in plain and explicit terms. A mere implication ought not to prostrate a principle which seems to have been so well established. Had the intention been entertained to make so material a change in this respect, the court ought to have expressly declared that any assemblage of men whatever, who had formed a treasonable design, whether in force or not, whether in a condition to attempt the design or not, whether attended with warlike appearances or not, constitutes the fact of levying war. Yet no declaration to this amount is made. Not an expression of the kind is to be found in the opinion of the supreme court. The foundation on which this argument rests is the omission of the court to state that the assemblage which constitutes the fact of levying war ought to be in force, and some passages which show that the question respecting the nature of the assemblage was not in the mind of the court when the opinion was drawn; which passages are mingled with others which at least show that there was no intention to depart from the course of the precedents in cases of treason by levying war. Every opinion, to be correctly understood, ought to be considered with a view to the case in which it was delivered. In the case of the United States against Bollman and Swartwout, there was no evidence that even two men had ever met for the purpose of executing the plan in which those persons were charged with having participated. It was, therefore, sufficient for the court to say that unless men were assembled, war could not be levied. That case was decided by this declaration. The court might indeed have defined the species of assemblage which would amount to levying of war; but, as this opinion was not a treatise on treason, but a decision of a particular case, expressions of doubtful import should be construed in reference to the case itself, and the mere omission to state that a particular circumstance was necessary to the consummation of the crime ought not to be construed into a declaration that the circumstance was unimportant. General expressions ought not to be considered as overruling settled principles, without a direct declaration to that effect. After these preliminary observations, the court will proceed to examine the opinion which has occasioned them.

The first expression in it bearing on the present question is, "To constitute that specific crime for which the prisoner now before the court has been committed, war must be actually levied against the United States. However flagitious may be the crime of conspiracy to subvert by force the government of our country, such conspiracy is not treason. To conspire to levy war and actually to levy war are distinct offences. The first must be brought into operation by the assemblage of men for a purpose treasonable in itself, or the fact of levying war cannot have been committed." Although it is not expressly stated that the assemblage of men for the purpose of carrying into operation the treasonable intent which will amount to levying war must be an assemblage in force, yet it is fairly to be inferred from the context; and nothing like dispensing with force appears in this paragraph. The expressions are, "to constitute the crime, war must be actually levied." A conspiracy to levy war is spoken of as "a conspiracy to subvert by force the government of our country." Speaking in general terms of an assemblage of men for this or for any other purpose, a person would naturally be understood as speaking of an assemblage in some degree adapted to the purpose. An assemblage to subvert by force the government of our country, and amounting to a levying of war, should be an assemblage in force. In a subsequent paragraph the court says: "It is not the intention of the court to say that no individual can be guilty of this crime who has not appeared in arms against his country. On the contrary, if war be actually levied, that is, if a body of men be actually assembled in order to effect by force a treasonable purpose, all those who perform any part, however minute, &c., and who are actually leagued in the general conspiracy, are traitors. But there must be an actual assembling of men for the treasonable purpose to constitute a levying of war." The observations made on the preceding paragraph apply to this. "A body of men actually assembled, in order to effect by force a treasonable purpose," must be a body assembled with such appearance of force as would warrant the opinion that they were assembled for the particular purpose. An assemblage to constitute an actual levying of war should be an assemblage with such appearance of force as would justify the opinion that they met for the purpose. This explanation, which is believed to be the natural, certainly not a strained explanation of the words, derives some additional aid from the terms in which the paragraph last quoted commences: "It is not the intention of the court to say that no individual can be guilty of treason who has not appeared in arms against his country." These words seem intended to obviate an inference which might otherwise have been drawn from the preceding paragraph. They indicate that in the mind of the court the assemblage stated in that paragraph was an assemblage in arms; that the individuals who composed it had appeared in arms against their country; that is, in other words, that the assemblage was a military, a warlike assemblage. The succeeding paragraph in the opinion relates to a conspiracy, and serves to show that force and violence were in the mind of the court, and that there was no idea of extending the crime of treason by construction beyond the constitutional definition which had been given of it.

Returning to the case actually before the court, it is said: "A design to overturn the government of the United States in New Orleans by force would have been unquestionably a design which if carried into execution would have been treason; and the assemblage of a body of men for the purpose of carrying it into execution would amount to levying of war against the United States." Now what could reasonably be said to be an assemblage of a body of men for the purpose of overturning the government of the United States in New Orleans by force? Certainly an assemblage in force; an assemblage prepared, and intending to act with force; a military assemblage. The decisions theretofore made by the judges of the United States are, then, declared to be in conformity with the principles laid down by the supreme court. Is this declaration compatible with the idea of departing from those opinions on a point within the contemplation of the court? The opinions of Judge Patterson and Judge Iredell are said "to imply an actual assembling of men, though they rather designed to remark on the purpose to which the force was to be applied than on the nature of the force itself." This observation certainly indicates that the necessity of an assemblage of men was the particular point the court meant to establish, and that the idea of force was never separated from this assemblage.

The opinion of Judge Chase is next quoted with approbation. This opinion in terms requires the employment of force. After stating the verbal communication said to have been made by Mr. Swartwout to General Wilkinson, the court says, "If these words import that the government of New Orleans was to be revolutionized by force, although merely as a step to, or a means of executing some greater projects, the design was unquestionably treasonable; and any assemblage of men for that purpose would amount to a levying of war." The words "any assemblage of men," if construed to affirm that any two or three of the conspirators who might be found together after this plan had been formed would be the act of levying war, would certainly be misconstrued. The sense of the expression, "any assemblage of men," is restricted by the words "for this purpose." Now, could it be in the contemplation of the court that a body of men would assemble for the purpose of revolutionizing New Orleans by force, who should not themselves be in force? After noticing some difference of opinion among the judges respecting the import of the words said to have been used by Mr. Swartwout, the court proceeds to observe: "But whether this treasonable intention be really imputable to the plan or not, it is admitted that it must have been carried into execution by an open assemblage for that purpose, previous to the arrest of the prisoner, in order to consummate the crime as to him." Could the court have conceived "an open assemblage" "for the purpose of overturning the government of New Orleans by force," to be only equivalent to a secret, furtive assemblage without the appearance of force? After quoting the words of Mr. Swartwout, from the affidavit, in which it was stated that Mr. Burr was levying an army of 7,000 men, and observing that the treason to be inferred from these words would depend on the intention with which it was levied, and on the progress which had been made in levying it, the court says: "The question, then, is whether this evidence prove Colonel Burr to have advanced so far in levying an army as actually to have assembled them." Actually to assemble an army of 7,000 men is unquestionably to place those who are so assembled in a state of open force. But as the mode of expression used in this passage might be misconstrued so far as to countenance the opinion that it would be necessary to assemble the whole army in order to constitute the fact of levying war, the court proceeds to say: "It is argued that since it cannot be necessary that the whole 7,000 men should be assembled, their commencing their march by detachments to the place of rendezvous must be sufficient to constitute the crime. This position is correct with some qualification. It cannot be necessary that the whole army should assemble, and that the various parts which are to compose it should have combined. But it is necessary there should be an actual assemblage; and therefore this evidence should make the fact unequivocal. The travelling of individuals to the place of rendezvous would, perhaps, not be sufficient. This would be an equivocal act, and has no warlike appearance. The meeting of particular bodies of men, and their march from places of partial to a place of general rendezvous, would be such an assemblage." The position here stated by the counsel for the prosecution is that the army "commencing its march by detachments to the place of rendezvous (that is, of the army) must be sufficient to constitute the crime." This position is not admitted by the court to be universally correct. It is said to be "correct with some qualification." What is that qualification? "The travelling of individuals to the place of rendezvous (and by this term is not to be understood one individual by himself, but several individuals, either separately or together, but not in military form) would perhaps not be sufficient." Why not sufficient? Because, says the court, "this would be an equivocal act and has no warlike appearance." The act, then, should be unequivocal and should have a warlike appearance. It must exhibit, in the words of Sir Matthew Hale, speciem belli, the appearance of war. This construction is rendered in some measure necessary when we observe that the court is qualifying the position, "that the army commencing their march by detachments to the place of rendezvous must be sufficient to constitute the crime." In qualifying this position they say, "the travelling of individuals would perhaps not be sufficient." Now, a solitary individual travelling to any point, with any intent, could not, without a total disregard of language, be

termed a marching detachment. The court, therefore, must have contemplated several individuals travelling together, and the words being used in reference to the position they intended to qualify, would seem to indicate the distinction between the appearances attending the usual movement of a company of men for civil purposes, and that military movement which might, in correct language, be denominated "marching by detachments." The court then proceeded to say: "The meeting of particular bodies of men, and their marching from places of partial to a place of general rendezvous, would be such an assemblage."

It is obvious from the context that the court must have intended to state a case which would in itself be unequivocal, because it would have a warlike appearance. The case stated is that of distinct bodies of men assembling at different places, and marching from these places of partial to a place of general rendezvous. When this has been done an assemblage is produced which would in itself be unequivocal. But when is it done? What is the assemblage here described? The assemblage formed of the different bodies of partial at a place of general rendezvous. In describing the mode of coming to this assemblage the civil term "travelling" is dropped, and the military term "marching" is employed. If this were intended as a definition of an assemblage which would amount to levying war, the definition requires an assemblage at a place of general rendezvous, composed of bodies of men who had previously assembled at places of partial rendezvous. But this is not intended as a definition; for clearly if there should be no places of partial rendezvous, if troops should embody in the first instance in great force for the purpose of subverting the government by violence, the act would be unequivocal; it would have a warlike appearance; and it would, according to the opinion of the supreme court, properly construed, and according to English authorities, amount to levying war. But this, though not a definition, is put as an example, and surely it may be safely taken as an example. If different bodies of men, in pursuance of a treasonable design, plainly proved, should assemble in warlike appearance at places of partial rendezvous, and should march from those places to a place of general rendezvous, it is difficult to conceive how such a transaction could take place without exhibiting the appearance of war, without an obvious display of force. At any rate, a court in stating generally such a military assemblage as would amount to levying war, and having a case before it in which there was no assemblage whatever, cannot reasonably be understood, in putting such an example, to dispense with those appearances of war which seem to be required by the general current of authorities. Certainly it ought not to be so understood when it says in express terms that "it is more safe as well as more consonant to the principles of our constitution that the crime of treason should not be extended by construction to doubtful cases; and that crimes not clearly within the constitutional definition should receive such punishment as the legislature in its wisdom may provide."

After this analysis of the opinion of the supreme court, it will be observed that the direct question, whether an assemblage of men which might be construed to amount to a levying of war must appear in force or in military form, was not in argument or in fact before the court, and does not appear to have been in terms decided. The opinion seems to have been drawn without particularly adverting to this question; and, therefore, upon a transient view of particular expressions, might inspire the idea that a display of force, that appearances of war, were not necessary ingredients to constitute the fact of levying war. But upon a more intent and more accurate investigation of this opinion, although the terms force and violence are not employed as descriptive of the assemblage, such requisites are declared to be indispensable as can scarcely exist without the appearance of war and the existence of real force. It is said that war must be levied in fact; that the object must be one which is to be effected by force; that the assemblage must be such as to prove that this is its object; that it must not be an equivocal act, without a warlike appearance; that it must be an open assemblage for the purpose of force. In the course of this opinion, decisions are quoted and approved which require the employment of force to constitute the crime. It seems extremely difficult, if not impossible, to reconcile these various declarations with the idea that the supreme court considered a secret, unarmed meeting, although that meeting be of conspirators, and although it met with a treasonable intent, as an actual levying of war. Without saying that the assemblage must be in force or in warlike form, it expresses itself so as to show that this idea was never discarded; and it uses terms which cannot be otherwise satisfied. The opinion of a single judge certainly weighs as nothing if opposed to that of the supreme court; but if he were one of the judges who assisted in framing that opinion, if while the impression under which it was framed was yet fresh upon his mind he delivered an opinion on the same testimony, not contradictory to that which had been given by all the judges together, but showing the sense in which he understood terms that might be differently expounded, it may fairly be said to be in some measure explanatory of the opinion itself. To the judge before whom the charge against the prisoner at the bar was first brought the same testimony was offered with that which had been exhibited before the supreme court; and he was required to give an opinion in almost the same case. Upon this occasion he said "war can only be levied by the employment of actual force. Troops must be embodied, men must be assembled, in order to levy war." Again he observed: "The fact to be proved in this case is an act of public notoriety. It must exist in the view of the world, or it cannot exist at all. The assembling of forces to levy war is a visible transaction; and numbers must witness it." It is not easy to doubt what kind of assemblage was in the mind of the judge who used these expressions; and it is to be recollected that he had just returned from the supreme court, and was speaking on the very facts on which the opinion of that court was delivered. The same judge, in his charge to the grand jury who found this bill, observed: "To constitute the fact of levying war it is not necessary that hostilities shall have actually commenced by engaging the military force of the United States, or that measures of violence against the

government shall have been carried into execution. But levying war is a fact, in the constitution of which force is an indispensable ingredient. Any combination to subvert by force the government of the United States, violently to dismember the Union, to compel a change in the administration, to coerce the repeal or adoption of a general law, is a conspiracy to levy war; and if the conspiracy be carried into effect by the actual employment of force, by the embodying and assembling of men for the purpose of executing the treasonable design which was previously conceived, it amounts to levying of war. It has been held that arms are not essential to levying war, provided the force assembled be sufficient to attain, or, perhaps, to justify attempting the object without them." This paragraph is immediately followed by a reference to the opinion of the supreme court.

It requires no commentary upon these words to show that, in the opinion of the judge who uttered them, an assemblage of men which should constitute the fact of levying war must be an assemblage in force, and that he so understood the opinion of the supreme court. If in that opinion there may be found in some passages a want of precision, and an indefiniteness of expression, which has occasioned it to be differently understood by different persons, that may well be accounted for when it is recollected that in the particular case there was no assemblage whatever. In expounding that opinion the whole should be taken together, and in reference to the particular case in which it was delivered. It is, however, not improbable that the misunderstanding has arisen from this circumstance: The court unquestionably did not consider arms as an indispensable requisite to levying war. An assemblage adapted to the object might be in a condition to effect or to attempt it without them. Nor did the court consider the actual application of the force to the object as at all times an indispensable requisite; for an assemblage might be in a condition to apply force, might be in a state adapted to real war, without having made the actual application of that force. From these positions, which are to be found in the opinion, it may have been inferred, it is thought too hastily, that the nature of the assemblage was unimportant, and that war might be considered as actually levied by any meeting of men, if a criminal intention can be imputed to them by testimony of any kind whatever.

It has been thought proper to discuss this question at large, and to review the opinion of the supreme court, although this court would be more disposed to leave the question of fact, whether an overt act of levying war were committed on Blennerhassett's Island to the jury, under this explanation of the law, and to instruct them that unless the assemblage on Blennerhassett's Island was an assemblage in force, was a military assemblage in a condition to make war, it was not a levying of war, and that they could not construe it into an act of war, than to arrest the further testimony which might be offered to connect the prisoner with that assemblage, or to prove the intention of those who assembled together at that place. This point, however, is not to be understood as decided. It will, perhaps, constitute an essential inquiry in another case.

Before leaving the opinion of the supreme court entirely, on the question of the nature of the assemblage which will constitute an act of levying war, this court cannot forbear to ask, why is an assemblage absolutely required? Is it not to judge in some measure of the end by the proportion which the means bear to the end? Why is it that a single armed individual entering a boat, and sailing down the Ohio for the avowed purpose of attacking New Orleans, could not be said to levy war? Is it not that he is apparently not in a condition to levy war? If this be so, ought not the assemblage to furnish some evidence of its intention and capacity to levy war before it can amount to levying war? And ought not the supreme court, when speaking of an assemblage for the purpose of effecting a treasonable object by force, be understood to indicate an assemblage exhibiting the appearance of force? The definition of the attorney for the United States deserves notice in this respect. It is, "When there is an assemblage of men, convened for the purpose of effecting by force a treasonable object, which force is meant to be employed before the assemblage disperses, this is treason." To read this definition without adverting to the argument, we should infer that the assemblage was itself to effect by force the treasonable object, not to join itself to some other bodies of men and then to effect the object by their combined force. Under this construction, it would be expected the appearance of the assemblage would bear some proportion to the object, and would indicate the intention; at any rate, that it would be an assemblage in force. This construction is most certainly not that which was intended; but it serves to show that general phrases must always be understood in reference to the subject-matter and to the general principles of law.

On that division of the subject which respects the merits of the case connected with the pleadings, two points are also made: 1st. That this indictment, having charged the prisoner with levying war on Blennerhassett's Island, and containing no other overt act, cannot be supported by proof that war was levied at that place by other persons in the absence of the prisoner, even admitting those persons to be connected with him in one common treasonable conspiracy. 2dly. That admitting such an indictment could be supported by such evidence, the previous conviction of some person, who committed the act which is said to amount to levying war, is indispensable to the conviction of a person who advised or procured that act.

As to the first point, the indictment contains two counts, one of which charges that the prisoner, with a number of persons unknown, levied war on Blennerhassett's Island, in the county of Wood, in the district of Virginia; and the other adds the circumstance of their proceeding from that island down the river for the purpose of seizing New Orleans by force. In point of fact, the prisoner was not on Blennerhassett's Island, nor in the county of Wood, nor in the district of Virginia. In considering this point, the court is led first to inquire whether an indictment for levying war must specify an overt act, or would be sufficient if it merely charged the prisoner in general terms with having levied war, omitting the expression of place or circumstance. The place in which a crime was committed is essential to an indictment, were it only to show the jurisdiction

of the court. It is, also, essential for the purpose of enabling the prisoner to make his defence. That at common law an indictment would have been defective which did not mention the place in which the crime was committed can scarcely be doubted. For this, it is sufficient to refer to Hawk. P. C. bk. 2, c. 25, § 84, and Id. chapter 23, § 91. This necessity is rendered the stronger by the constitutional provision that the offender "shall be tried in the state and district wherein the crime shall have been committed," and by the act of congress which requires that twelve petit jurors at least shall be summoned from the county where the offence was committed. A description of the particular manner in which the war was levied seems, also, essential to enable the accused to make his defence. The law does not expect a man to be prepared to defend every act of his life which may be suddenly and without notice alleged against him. In common justice, the particular fact with which he is charged ought to be stated, and stated in such a manner as to afford a reasonable certainty of the nature of the accusation and the circumstances which will be adduced against him. The general doctrine on the subject of indictments is full to this point. Foster (Crown Law, p. 194), speaking of the treason of compassing the king's death, says: "From what has been said, it followeth that in every indictment for this species of treason, and, indeed, for levying war and adhering to the king's enemies, an overt act must be alleged and proved. For the overt act is the charge to which the prisoner must apply his defence." In page 220 Foster repeats this declaration. It is, also, laid down in Hawk. P. C. bk. 8, c. 17, § 29; 1 Hale, P. C. 121; 1 East, P. C. 116, and by the other authorities cited, especially Vaughan's Case. In corroboration of this opinion, it may be observed that treason can only be established by the proof of overt acts, and that by the common law as well as by the statute of 7 Wm. III. those overt acts only which are charged in the indictment can be given in evidence, unless, perhaps, as corroborative testimony after the overt acts are proved. That clause in the constitution, too, which says that in all criminal prosecutions the accused shall enjoy the right "To be informed of the nature and cause of the accusation," is considered as having a direct bearing on this point. It secures to him such information as will enable him to prepare for his defence. It seems, then, to be perfectly clear that it would not be sufficient for an indictment to allege generally that the accused had levied war against the United States. The charge must be more particularly specified by laying what is termed an overt act of levying war. The law relative to an appeal as cited from Stamford, is strongly corroborative of this opinion.

If it be necessary to specify the charge in the indictment, it would seem to follow, irresistibly, that the charge must be proved as laid. All the authorities which require an overt act, require also that this overt act should be proved. The decision in Vaughan's Case is particularly in point. Might it be otherwise, the charge of an overt act would be a mischief instead of an advantage to the accused. It would lead him from the true cause and nature of the accusation, instead of informing him respecting it. But it is contended on the part of the prosecution that, although the accused had never been with the party which assembled at Blennerhassett's Island, and was, at that time, at a great distance, and in a different state, he was yet legally present, and, therefore, may properly be charged in the indictment as being present in fact. It is, therefore, necessary to inquire whether in this case the doctrine of constructive presence can apply. It is conceived by the court to be possible that a person may be concerned in a treasonable conspiracy, and yet be legally as well as actually absent while some one act of the treason is perpetrated. If a rebellion should be so extensive as to spread through every state in the Union, it will scarcely be contended that every individual concerned in it is legally present at every overt act committed in the course of that rebellion. It would be a very violent presumption indeed, too violent to be made without clear authority, to presume that even the chief of the rebel army was legally present at every such overt act. If the main rebel army, with the chief at its head, should be prosecuting war at one extremity of our territory, say in New Hampshire; if this chief should be there captured and sent to the other extremity for the purpose of trial; if his indictment, instead of alleging an overt act which was true in point of fact, should allege that he had assembled some small party which in truth he had not seen, and had levied war by engaging in a skirmish in Georgia at a time when, in reality, he was fighting a battle in New Hampshire; if such evidence would support such an indictment by the fiction that he was legally present, though really absent, all would ask to what purpose are those provisions in the constitution, which direct the place of trial and ordain that the accused shall be informed of the nature and cause of the accusation? But that a man may be legally absent who has counselled or procured a treasonable act is proved by all those books which treat upon the subject, and which concur in declaring that such a person is a principal traitor, not because he was legally present, but because in treason all are principals. Yet the indictment, speaking upon general principles, would charge him according to the truth of the case. Lord Coke says: "If many conspire to levy war, and some of them do levy the same according to the conspiracy, this is high treason in all." Why? because all were legally present when the war was levied? No. "For in treason," continues Lord Coke, "all be principals, and war is levied." In this case the indictment, reasoning from analogy, would not charge that the absent conspirators were present, but would state the truth of the case. If the conspirator had done nothing which amounted to levying of war, and if by our constitution the doctrine that an accessory becomes a principal be not adopted, in consequence of which the conspirator could not be condemned under an indictment stating the truth of the case, it would be going very far to say that this defect, if it be termed one, may be cured by an indictment stating the case untruly.

This doctrine of Lord Coke has been adopted by all subsequent writers, and it is generally laid down in the English books that whatever will make a man an accessory in felony, will make him a principal in treason; but it is nowhere suggested that he is by construction to be considered as present when in point of fact he was absent. Foster has been particularly quoted, and certainly he is precisely in point. "It is well known," says Foster, "that in the language of the law there are no accessories in high treason; all are principals. Every instance of incitement, aid, or protection, which in the case of felony will render a man an accessory before or after the fact, in the case of high treason, whether it be treason at common law or by statute, will make him a principal in treason." The cases of incitement and aid are cases put as examples of a man's becoming a principal in treason, not because he was legally present, but by force of that maxim in the common law, that whatever will render a man an accessory at common law will render him a principal in treason. In other passages the words "command" or "procure" are used to indicate the same state of things; that is, a treasonable assemblage produced by a man who is not himself in that assemblage. In point of law, then, the man who incites, aids, or procures a treasonable act, is not, merely in consequence of that incitement, aid, or procurement, legally present when that act is committed. If it do not result, from the nature of the crime, that all who are concerned in it are legally present at every overt act, then each case depends upon its own circumstances; and to judge how far the circumstances of any case can make him legally present, who is in fact absent, the doctrine of constructive presence must be examined.

Hale in volume 1, p. 615, says: "Regularly no man can be a principal in felony unless he be present." In the same page he says: "An accessory before is he that, being absent at the time of the felony committed, doth yet procure, counsel, or command another to commit a felony." The books are full of passages which state this to be the law. Foster, in showing what acts of concurrence will make a man a principal, says: "He must be present at the perpetration, otherwise he can be no more than an accessory before the fact." These strong distinctions would be idle, at any rate they would be inapplicable to treason, if they were to be entirely lost in the doctrine of constructive presence. Foster adds (page 349): "When the law requireth the presence of the accomplice at the perpetration of the fact in order to render him a principal, it doth not require a strict actual immediate presence, such a presence as would make him an eye or ear witness of what passeth." The terms used by Foster are such as would be employed by a man intending to show the necessity that the absent person should be near at hand, although from the nature of the thing no precise distance could be marked out. An inspection of the cases from which Foster drew this general principle will serve to illustrate it. Hale, P. C. p. 439. In all these cases, put by Hale, the whole party set out together to commit the very fact charged in the indictment; or to commit some other unlawful act, in which they are all to be personally concerned at the same time and place, and are, at the very time when the criminal fact is committed, near enough to give actual personal aid and assistance to the man who perpetrated it. Hale, in page 449, giving the reason for the decision in the case of the Lord Dacre, says: "They all came with an intent to steal the deer; and consequently the law supposes that they came all with the intent to oppose all that should hinder them in that design." The original case says this was their resolution. This opposition would be a personal opposition. This case, even as stated by Hale, would clearly not comprehend any man who entered into the combination, but who, instead of going to the park where the murder was committed, should not set out with the others, should go to a different park, or should even lose his way. In both these cases stated in Hale, P. C. p. 534, the persons actually set out together, and were near enough to assist in the commission of the fact. That in the Case of Pudsey the felony was, as stated by Hale, a different felony from that originally intended, is unimportant in regard to the particular principle now under consideration; so far as respected distance, as respected capacity to assist in case of resistance, it is the same as if the robbery had been that which was originally designed. The case in the original report shows that the felony committed was in fact in pursuance of that originally designed. Foster (page 350) plainly supposes the same particular design, not a general design composed of many particular distinct facts. He supposes them to be co-operating with respect to that particular design. This may be illustrated by a case which is, perhaps, common. Suppose a band of robbers confederated for the general purpose of robbing. They set out together, or in parties, to rob a particular individual; and each performs the part assigned to him. Some ride up to the individual, and demand his purse. Others watch out of sight to intercept those who might be coming to assist the man on whom the robbery is to be committed. If murder or robbery actually take place, all are principals; and all in construction of law are present. But suppose they set out at the same time or at different times, by different roads, to attack and rob different individuals or different companies; to commit distinct acts of robbery. It has never been contended that those who committed one act of robbery, or who failed altogether, were constructively present at the act of those who were associated with them in the common object of robbery, who were to share the plunder, but who did not assist at the particular fact. They do, indeed, belong to the general party; but they are not of the particular party which committed this fact. Foster concludes this subject by observing that "in order to render a person an accomplice and a principal in felony, he must be aiding and abetting at the fact, or ready to afford assistance if necessary:" that is, at the particular fact which is charged. He must be ready to render assistance to those who are committing that fact. He must, as is stated by Hawkins, be ready to give immediate and direct assistance. All the cases to be found in the books go to the same point. Let them be applied to that under consideration.

The whole treason laid in this indictment is the levying of war in Blennerhassett's island; and the whole question to which the inquiry of the court is now directed is whether the prisoner was legally present at that fact. I say this is the whole question; because the prisoner can only be convicted on the overt act laid in the indictment. With respect to this prosecution, it is as if no other overt act existed. If other overt acts can be inquired into, it is for the sole purpose of proving the particular fact charged. It is an evidence of the crime consisting of this particular fact, not as establishing the general crime by a distinct fact. The counsel for the prosecution have charged those engaged in the defence with considering the overt act as treason, whereas it ought to be considered solely as the evidence of the treason; but the counsel for the prosecution seem themselves not to have sufficiently adverted to this clear principle; that though the overt act may not be itself the treason, it is the sole act of that treason which can produce conviction. It is the sole point in issue between the parties. And the only division of that point, if the expression be allowed, which the court is now examining, is the constructive presence of the prisoner at the fact charged.

To return then, to the application of the cases. Had the prisoner set out with the party from Beaver for Blennerhassett's Island, or perhaps had he set out for that place, though not from Beaver, and had arrived in the island, he would have been present at the fact. Had he not arrived in the island, but had taken a position near enough to co-operate with those on the island, to assist them in any act of hostility, or to aid them if attacked, the question whether he was constructively present would be a question compounded of law and fact, which would be decided by the jury, with the aid of the court, so far as respected the law. In this case the accused would have been of the particular party assembled on the island, and would have been associated with them in the particular act of levying war said to have been committed on the island. But if he was not with the party at any time before they reached the island; if he did not join them there, or intend to join them there; if his personal co-operation in the general plan was to be afforded elsewhere, at a great distance, in a different state; if the overt acts of treason to be performed by him were to be distinct overt acts—then he was not of the particular party assembled at Blennerhassett's Island, and was not constructively present, aiding and assisting in the particular act which was there committed. The testimony on this point, so far as it has been delivered, is not equivocal. There is not only no evidence that the accused was of the particular party which assembled on Blennerhassett's Island, but the whole evidence shows he was not of that party. In felony, then, admitting the crime to have been completed on the island, and to have been advised, procured, or commanded by the accused, he would have been incontestably an accessory and not a principal. But in treason, it is said, the law is otherwise, because the theatre of action is more extensive. The reasoning applies in England as strongly as in the United States. While in '15 and '45 the family of Stuart sought to regain the crown they had forfeited, the struggle was for the whole kingdom, yet no man was ever considered as legally present at one place, when actually at another; or as aiding in one transaction while actually employed in another. With the perfect knowledge that the whole nation may be the theatre of action, the English books unite in declaring that he who counsels, procures, or aids treason, is guilty accessorily, and solely in virtue of the common law principle that what will make a man an accessory in felony makes him a principal in treason. So far from considering a man as constructively present at every overt act of the general treason in which he may have been concerned, the whole doctrine of the books limits the proof against him to those particular overt acts of levying war with which he is charged. What would be the effect of a different doctrine? Clearly that which has been stated. If a person levying war in Kentucky may be said to be constructively present and assembled with a party carrying on war in Virginia at a great distance from him, then he is present at every overt act performed anywhere. He may be tried in any state on the continent, where any overt act has been committed. He may be proved to be guilty of an overt act laid in the indictment in which he had no personal participation, by proving that he advised it, or that he committed other acts. This is, perhaps, too extravagant to be in terms maintained. Certainly it cannot be supported by the doctrines of the English law.

The opinion of Judge Patterson in Mitchell's Case has been cited on this point, 2 Dall. [2 U. S.] 348. The indictment is not specially stated, but from the case as reported, it must have been either general for levying war in the county of Allegany, and the overt act must have been the assemblage of men and levying of war in that county, or it must have given a particular detail of the treasonable transactions in that county. The first supposition is the most probable, but let the indictment be in the one form or the other, and the result is the same. The facts of the case are that a large body of men, of whom Mitchell was one, assembled at Braddock's field, in the county of Allegany, for the purpose of committing acts of violence at Pittsburg; that there was also an assemblage at a different time at Couch's fort, at which the prisoner also attended. The general and avowed object of that meeting was to concert measures for resisting the execution of a public law. At Couch's fort the resolution was taken to attack the house of the inspector, and the body there assembled marched to that house and attacked it. It was proved by the competent number of witnesses that he was at Couch's fort armed; that he offered to reconnoitre the house to be attacked; that he marched with the insurgents towards the house; that he was with them after the action attending the body of one of his comrades who was killed in it. One witness swore positively that he was present at the burning of the house; and a second witness swore positively that he was present at the burning of the house; and a second witness said that "it run in his head that he had seen him there." That a doubt should exist in such a case as this is strong evidence of the necessity that the overt act should be unequivocally proved by two witnesses.

But what was the opinion of the judge in this case? Couch's fort and Neville's house being in the same county, the assemblage having been at Couch's fort, and the resolution to attack the house having been there taken, the body having for the avowed purpose moved in execution of that resolution towards the house to be attacked, he inclined to think that the act of marching was in itself levying war. If it was, then the overt act laid in the indictment was consummated by the assemblage at Couch's and the marching from thence; and Mitchell was proved to be guilty by more than two positive witnesses. But without deciding this to be the law, he proceeded to consider the

meeting at Couch's, the immediate marching to Neville's house, and the attack and burning of the house, as one transaction. Mitchell was proved by more than two positive witnesses to have been in that transaction, to have taken an active part in it; and the judge declared it to be unnecessary that all should have been him at the same time and place. But suppose not a single witness had proved Mitchell to have been at Couch's, or on the march, or at Neville's. Suppose he had been at the time notoriously absent in a different state. Can it be believed by any person who observes the caution with which Judge Patterson required the constitutional proof of two witnesses to the same overt act, that he would have said Mitchell was constructively present, and might, on that straining of a legal fiction, be found guilty of treason? Had he delivered such an opinion, what would have been the language of this country respecting it? Had he given this opinion, it would have required all the correctness of his life to strike his name from that bloody list in which the name of Jeffreys is enrolled.

But to estimate the opinion in Mitchell's Case, let its circumstances be transferred to Burr's Case. Suppose the body of men assembled in Blennerhassett's Island had previously met at some other place in the same county; that Burr had been proved to be with them by four witnesses; that the resolution to march to Blennerhassett's Island for a treasonable purpose had been there taken; that he had been seen on the march with them: that one witness had seen him on the island; that another thought he had seen him there; that he had been seen with the party directly after leaving the island; that this indictment had charged the levying of war in Wood county generally—the cases would, then, have been precisely parallel; and the decision would have been the same. In conformity with principle and with authority, then, the prisoner at the bar was neither legally nor actually present at Blennerhassett's Island; and the court is strongly inclined to the opinion that without proving an actual or legal presence by two witnesses, the overt act laid in this indictment cannot be proved.

But this opinion is controverted on two grounds: The first is, that the indictment does not charge the prisoner to have been present. The second, that although he was absent, yet if he caused the assemblage, he may be indicted as being present, and convicted on evidence that he caused the treasonable act. The first position is to be decided by the indictment itself. The court understands the allegation differently from the attorney for the United States. The court understands it to be directly charged that the prisoner did assemble with the multitude, and did march with them. Nothing will more clearly test this construction than putting the case into a shape which it may possibly take. Suppose the law be that the indictment would be defective unless it alleged the presence of the person indicted at the act of treason. If, upon a special verdict, facts should be found which amounted to a levying of war by the accused, and his counsel should insist that he could not be condemned because the indictment was defective in not charging that he was himself one of the assemblage which constituted the treason, or because it alleged the procurement defectively, would the attorney admit this construction of his indictment to be correct? I am persuaded he would not, and that he ought not to make such a concession. If, after a verdict, the indictment ought to be construed to allege that the prisoner was one of the assemblage at Blennerhassett's Island, it ought to be so construed now. But this is unimportant; for if the indictment alleges that the prisoner procured the assemblage, that procurement becomes part of the overt act, and must be proved, as will be shown hereafter. The second position is founded on 1 Hale, P. C. 214, 288, and 1 East P. C. 127.

While I declare that this doctrine contradicts every idea I had ever entertained on the subject of indictments, (since it admits that one case may be stated, and a very different case may be proved,) I will acknowledge that it is countenanced by the authorities adduced in its support. To counsel or advise a treasonable assemblage, and to be one of that assemblage, are certainly distinct acts, and, therefore, ought not to be charged as the same act. The great objection to this mode of proceeding is, that the proof essentially varies from the charge in the character and essence of the offence, and in the testimony by which the accused is to defend himself. These dicta of Lord Hale, therefore, taken in the extent in which they are understood by the counsel for the United States, seem to be repugnant to the declarations we find everywhere that an overt act must be laid, and must be proved. No case is cited by Hale in support of them, and I am strongly inclined to the opinion that had the public received his corrected instead of his original manuscript, they would, if not expunged, have been restrained in their application to cases of a particular description. Laid down generally, and applied universally to all cases of treason, they are repugnant to the principles for which Hale contends, for which all the elementary writers contend, and from which courts have in no case, either directly reported or referred to in the books, ever departed. These principles are, that the indictment must give notice of the offence; that the accused is only bound to answer the particular charge which the indictment contains, and that the overt act laid is that particular charge. Under such circumstances, it is only doing justice to Hale to examine his dicta, and if they admit of being understood in a limited sense, not repugnant to his own doctrines nor to the general principles of law, to understand them in that sense. "If many conspire to counterfeit, or counsel or abet it, and one of them doth the fact upon that couselling or conspiracy, it is treason in all, and they may be all indicted for counterfeiting generally within this statute, for in such case in treason all are principals." This is laid down as applicable singly to the treason of counterfeiting the coin, and is not applied by Hale to other treasons. Had he designed to apply the principle universally he would have stated it as a general proposition; he would have laid it down in treating on other branches of the statute as well as in the chapter respecting the coin; he would have laid it down when treating on indictments generally. But he has done neither. Every sentiment bearing in any manner on this point, which is to be found in Lord Hale while on the doctrine of levying war or on the general doctrine of indictments, militates against the opinion that he

considered the proposition as more extensive than he has declared it to be. No court could be justified in extending the dictum of a judge beyond its terms to cases which he had expressly treated, in which he has not himself applied it, and on which he, as well as others, has delivered opinions which that dictum would overrule. This would be the less justifiable if there should be a clear legal distinction indicated by the very terms in which the judge has expressed himself between the particular case to which alone he has applied the dictum and other cases to which the court is required to extend it. There is this clear legal distinction: "They may," says Judge Hale, "be indicted for counterfeiting generally." But if many conspire to levy war, and some actually levy it, they may not be indicted for levying war generally. The books concur in declaring that they cannot be so indicted. A special overt act of levying war must be laid. This distinction between counterfeiting the coins and that class of treasons among which levying war is placed is taken in the statute of Edward III. That statute requires an overt act of levying war to be laid in the indictment, and does not require an overt act of counterfeiting the coin to be laid. If in a particular case, in which a general indictment is sufficient, it be stated that the crime may be charged generally according to the legal effect of the act, it does not follow that in other cases, where a general indictment would not be sufficient, where an overt act must be laid, that this overt act need not be laid according to the real fact. Hale, then, is to be reconciled to himself and with the general principles of the law only be permitting the limits which he has himself given to his own dictum to remain where he has placed them. In page 238, Hale is speaking generally to the receiver of a traitor, and is stating in what such a receiver partakes of an accessory: 1st. "His indictment must be special of the receipt, and not generally that he did the thing, which may be otherwise in case of one that is procurer, counsellor, or consenter." The words "may be otherwise" do not clearly convey the idea that it is universally otherwise. In all cases of receiver, the indictment must be special on the receipt, and not general. The words "may be otherwise in case of a procurer," &c., signify that it may be otherwise in all treasons, or that it may be otherwise in some treasons. If it may be otherwise in some treasons without contradicting the doctrines of Hale himself as well as of other writers, but cannot be otherwise in all treasons without such contradiction, the fair construction is, that Hale used these words in their restricted sense; that he used them in reference to treasons in which a general indictment would lie, not to treasons where a general indictment would not lie, but an overt act of the treason must be charged. The two passages of Hale thus construed may, perhaps, be law, and may leave him consistent with himself. It appears to the court to be the fair way of construing them.

These observations relative to the passages quoted from Hale apply to that quoted from East, who obviously copies from Hale and relies upon his authority. Upon this point, J. Kelyng, 26, and 1 Hale, P. C. p. 626, have also been relied upon. It is stated in both that if a man be indicted as a principal and acquitted, he cannot afterwards be indicted as an accessory before the fact—whence it is inferred, not without reason, that evidence of accessorial guilt may be received on such an indictment. Yet no case is found in which the question has been made and decided. The objection has never been taken at a trial and overruled nor do the books say it would be overruled. Were such a case produced its application would be questionable. Kelyng says an accessory before the fact is quodam modo in some manner guilty of the fact. The law may not require that the manner should be stated, for in felony it does not require that an overt act should be laid. The indictment, therefore, may be general; but an overt act of levying war must be laid. These cases, then, prove in their utmost extent no more than the cases previously cited from Hale and East. This distinction between indictments which may state the fact generally, and those which must lay it specially, bear some analogy to a general and a special action on the case. In a general action the declaration may lay the assumpsit according to the legal effect of the transaction, but in a special action on the case the declaration must state the material circumstances truly, and they must be proved as stated. This distinction also derives some aid from a passage in Hale (page 625) immediately preceding that which has been cited at the bar. He says: "If A be indicted as principal and B as accessory before or after, and both be acquitted, yet B may be indicted as principal, and the former acquittal as accessory is no bar." The crimes, then, are not the same, and may not indifferently be tried under the same indictment. But why is it that an acquittal as principal may be pleaded in bar to an indictment as accessory, while an acquittal as accessory may not be pleaded in bar to an indictment as principal? If it be answered that the accessorial crime may be given in evidence on an indictment as principal, but that the principal crime may not be given in evidence on an indictment as accessory, the question recurs, on what legal ground does this distinction stand? I can imagine only this: an accessory being quodam modo a principal in indictments where the law does not require the manner to be stated, which need not be special, evidence of accessorial guilt, if the punishment be the same, may possibly be received; but every indictment as accessory must be special. The very allegation that he is an accessory must be a special allegation, and must show how he became an accessory. The charges of this special indictment, therefore, must be proved as laid, and no evidence which proves the crime in a form substantially different can be received. If this be the legal reason for the distinction, it supports the exposition of these dicta which has been given. If it be not the legal reason, I can conceive no other.

But suppose the law to be as is contended by the counsel for the United States. Suppose an indictment charging an individual with personally assembling among others, and thus levying war, may be satisfied with the proof that he caused the assemblage. What effect will this law have upon this case? The guilt of the accused, if there be any guilt, does not consist in the assemblage, for he was not a member of it. The simple fact of assemblage no more affects one absent man than another. His guilt; then, consists in procuring the assemblage, and upon this fact depends his criminality. The proof relative to the character of an as-

semblage must be the same whether a man be present or absent. In the general, to charge any individual with the guilt of an assemblage, the fact of his presence must be proved; it constitutes an essential part of the overt act. If, then, the procurement be substituted in the place of presence, does it not also constitute an essential part of the overt act? Must it not also be proved? Must it not be proved in the same manner that presence must be proved? If in one case the presence of the individual make the guilt of the assemblage his guilt, and in the other case the procurement by the individual make the guilt of the assemblage his guilt, then presence and procurement are equally component parts of the overt act, and equally require two witnesses. Collateral points may, say the books, be proved according to the course of the common law; but is this a collateral point? Is the fact, without which the accused does not participate in the guilt of the assemblage if it was guilty, a collateral point? This cannot be. The presence of the party, where presence is necessary, being a part of the overt act, must be positively proved by two witnesses. No presumptive evidence, no facts from which presence may be conjectured or inferred, will satisfy the constitution and the law. If procurement take the place of presence and become part of the overt act, then no presumptive evidence, no facts from which the procurement may be conjectured or inferred, can satisfy the constitution and the law. The mind is not to be led to the conclusion that the individual was present by a train of conjectures, of inferences, or of reasoning; the fact must be proved by two witnesses. Neither, where procurement supplies the want of presence, is the mind to be conducted to the conclusion that the accused procured the assembly by a train of conjectures or inferences, or of reasoning; the fact itself must be proved by two witnesses, and must have been committed within the district. If it be said that the advising or procurement of treason is a secret transaction, which can scarcely ever be proved in the manner required by this opinion, the answer which will readily suggest itself is, that the difficulty of proving a fact will not justify conviction without proof. Certainly it will not justify conviction without a direct and positive witness in a case where the constitution requires two. The more correct inference from this circumstance would seem to be, that the advising of the fact is not within the constitutional definition of the crime. To advise or procure a treason is in the nature of conspiring or plotting treason, which is not treason in itself. If, then, the doctrines of Kelyng, Hale, and East, be understood in the sense in which they are pressed by the counsel for the prosecution, and are applicable in the United States, the fact that the accused procured the assemblage on Blennerhassett's Island must be proved, not circumstantially, but positively, by two witnesses, to charge him with that assemblage. But there are still other most important considerations which must be well weighed before this doctrine can be applied to the United States.

The 8th [6th] amendment to the constitution has been pressed with great force, and it is impossible not to feel its application to this point. The accused cannot be said to be "informed of the nature and cause of the accusation" unless the indictment give him that notice which may reasonably suggest to him the point on which the accusation turns, so that he may know the course to be pursued in his defence. It is also well worthy of consideration, that this doctrine, so far as it respects treason, is entirely supported by the operation of the common law, which is said to convert the accessory before the fact into the principal, and to make the act of the principal his act. The accessory before the fact is not said to have levied war. He is not said to be guilty under the statute, but the common law attaches to him the guilt of that fact which he has advised or procured; and, as contended, makes it his act. This is the operation of the common law, not the operation of the statute. It is an operation, then, which can only be performed where the common law exists to perform it. It is the creature of the common law, and the creature presupposes its creator. To decide, then, that this doctrine is applicable to the United States would seem to imply the decision that the United States, as a nation, have a common law which creates and defines the punishment of crimes accessorial in their nature. It would imply the further decision that these accessorial crimes are not, in the case of treason, excluded by the definition of treason given in the constitution. I will not pretend that I have not individually an opinion on these points; but it is one which I should give only in a case which absolutely required it, unless I could confer respecting it with the judges of the supreme court.

I have said that this doctrine cannot apply to the United States without implying those decisions respecting the common law which I have stated; because, should it be true, as is contended, that the constitutional definition of treason comprehends him who advises or procures an assemblage that levies war, it would not follow that such adviser or procurer might be charged as having been present at the assemblage. If the adviser or procurer be within the definition of levying war, and, independent of the agency of the common law, do actually levy war, then the advisement or procurement is an overt act of levying war. If it be the overt act on which he is to be convicted, then it must be charged in the indictment; for he can only be convicted on proof of the overt acts which are charged. To render this distinction more intelligible, let it be recollected that, although it should be conceded that since the statute of William and Mary he who advises or procures a treason may, in England, be charged as having committed that treason, by virtue of the common law operation, which is said, so far as respects the indictment, to unite the accessorial to the principal offence and permit them to be charged as one, yet it can never be conceded that he who commits one overt act under the statute of Edward can be charged and convicted on proof of another overt act. If, then, procurement be an overt act of treason under the constitution, no man can be convicted for the procurement under an indictment charging him with actually assembling, whatever may be the doctrine of the common law in the case of an accessorial offender.

It may not be improper in this place again to advert to the opinion of the supreme court, and to show that it contains nothing contrary to the doctrine now laid down. That opinion is, that an individual may be guilty of treason "who has not appeared in arms against his country; that if war be actually levied, that is, if a body of men be actually assembled for the purpose of effecting by force a treasonable object, all those who perform any part, however minute, or however remote from the scene of action, and who are actually leagued in the general conspiracy, are to be considered as traitors." This opinion does not touch the case of a person who advises or procures an assemblage, and does nothing further. The advising, certainly, and perhaps the procuring, is more in the nature of a conspiracy to levy war than of the actual levying of war. According to the opinion, it is not enough to be leagued in the conspiracy, and that war be levied, but it is also necessary to perform a part: that part is the act of levying war. That part, it is true, may be minute, it may not be the actual appearance in arms, and it may be remote from the scene of action, that is, from the place where the army is assembled; but it must be a part, and that part must be performed by a person who is leagued in the conspiracy. This part, however minute or remote, constitutes the overt act of which alone the person who performs it can be convicted. The opinion does not declare that the person who has performed this remote and minute part may be indicted for a part which was, in truth, performed by others, and convicted on their overt acts. it amounts to this and nothing more, that when war is actually levied, not only those who bear arms, but those also who are leagued in the conspiracy, and who perform the various distinct parts which are necessary for the prosecution of war, do, in the sense of the constitution, levy war. It may possibly be the opinion of the supreme court that those who procure a treason and do nothing further are guilty under the constitution. I only say that opinion has not yet been given, still less has it been indicated that he who advises shall be indicted as having performed the fact.

It is, then, the opinion of the court that this indictment can be supported only by testimony which proves the accused to have been actually or constructively present when the assemblage took place on Blennerhassett's Island; or by the admission of the doctrine that he who procures an act may be indicted as having performed that act.

It is further the opinion of the court that there is no testimony whatever which tends to prove that the accused was actually or constructively present when that assemblage did take place; indeed, the contrary is most apparent. With respect to admitting proof of procurement to establish a charge of actual presence, the court is of opinion that if this be admissible in England on an indictment for levying war, which is far from being conceded, it is admissible only by virtue of the operation of the common law upon the statute, and therefore is not admissible in this country unless by virtue of a similar operation—a point far from being established, but on which, for the present, no opinion is given. If, however, this point be established, still the procurement must be proved in the same manner and by the same kind of testimony which would be required to prove actual presence.

The second point in this division of the subject is the necessity of adducing the record of the previous conviction of some one person who committed the fact alleged to be treasonable. This point presupposes the treason of the accused, if any have been committed, to be accessorial in its nature. Its being of this description, according to the British authorities, depends on the presence or absence of the accused at the time the fact was committed. The doctrine on this subject is well understood, has been most copiously explained, and need not be repeated. That there is no evidence of his actual or legal presence is a point already discussed and decided. It is, then, apparent that but for the exception to the general principle which is made in cases of treason, those who assembled at Blennerhassett's Island, if that assemblage were such as to constitute the crime, would be principals, and those who might really have caused that assemblage, although in truth the chief traitors, would in law be accessories. It is a settled principle in the law that the accessory cannot be guilty of a greater offence than his principal. The maxim is "Accessorius sequitur naturam sui principalis"—"The accessory follows the nature of his principal." Hence results the necessity of establishing the guilt of the principal before the accessory can be tried; for the degree of guilt which is incurred by counselling or commanding the commission of a crime depends upon the actual commission of that crime. No man is an accessory to murder unless the fact has been committed. The fact can only be established in a prosecution against the person by whom a crime has been perpetrated. The law supposes a man more capable of defending his own conduct than any other person, and will not tolerate that the guilt of A shall be established in a prosecution against B. Consequently, if the guilt of B depends on the guilt of A, A must be convicted before B can be tried. It would exhibit a monstrous deformity indeed in our system, if B might be executed for being accessory to a murder committed by A, and A should afterwards, upon a full trial, be acquitted of the fact. For this obvious reason, although the punishment of a principal and accessory was originally the same, and although in many instances it is still the same, the accessory could in no case be tried before the conviction of his principal, nor can he yet be tried previous to such conviction, unless he require it, or unless a special provision to that effect be made by statute. If, then, this were a felony, the prisoner at the bar could not be tried until the crime were established by the conviction of the person by whom it was actually perpetrated.

Is the law otherwise in this case, because in treason all are principals? Let this question be answered by reason and by authority. Why is it that in felonies, however atrocious, the trial of the accessory can never precede the conviction of the principal? Not because the one is denominated the principal and the other the accessory; for that would be ground on which a great law principle could never stand. Not because there was, in fact, a difference in the degree of moral guilt; for in the case of murder committed by a hardy villain for a bribe, the person plotting the murder and giving the bribe is, perhaps, of the two, the blacker criminal; and were it otherwise, this would furnish no argument for precedence in trial. What, then, is the reason? It has been already given. The legal guilt of the accessory depends on the guilt of the principal; and the guilt of the principal can only be established in a prosecution against himself. Does not this reason apply in full force to a case of treason? The legal guilt of the person who planned the assemblage on Blennerhassett's Island depends not simply on the criminality of the previous conspiracy, but on the criminality of that assemblage. If those who perpetrated the fact be not traitors, he who advised the fact cannot be a traitor. His guilt, then, in contemplation of law, depends on theirs; and their guilt can only be established in a prosecution against themselves. Whether the adviser of this assemblage be punishable with death as a principal or as an accessory, his liability to punishment depends on the degree of guilt attached to an act which has been perpetrated by others; and which, if it be a criminal act, renders them guilty also. His guilt, therefore, depends on theirs; and their guilt cannot be legally established in a prosecution against him.

The whole reason of the law, then, relative to the principal and accessory, so far as respects the order of trial, seems to apply in full force to a case of treason committed by one body of men in conspiracy with others who are absent. If from reason we pass to authority, we find it laid down by Hale, Foster, and East, in the most explicit terms, that the conviction of some one who has committed the treason must precede the trial of him who has advised or procured it. This position is also maintained by Leach in his notes on Hawkins, and is not, so far as the court has discovered, anywhere contradicted. These authorities have been read and commented on at such length that it cannot be necessary for the court to bring them again into view. It is the less necessary because it is not understood that the law is controverted by the counsel for the United States. It is, however, contended that the prisoner has waived his right to demand the conviction of some one person who was present at the fact, by pleading to his indictment. Had this indictment even charged the prisoner according to the truth of the case, the court would feel some difficulty in deciding that he had, by implication, waived his right to demand a species of testimony essential to his conviction. The court is not prepared to say that the act which is to operate against his rights did not require that it should be performed with a full knowledge of its operation. It would seem consonant to the usual course of proceeding in other respects in criminal cases, that the prisoner should be informed that he had a right to refuse to be tried until some person who committed the act should be convicted; and that he ought not to be considered as waiving the right to demand the record of conviction, unless with the full knowledge of that right he consented to be tried. The court, however, does not decide what the law would be in such a case. It is unnecessary to decide it; because pleading to an indictment, in which a man is charged as having committed an act, cannot be construed to waive a right which he would have possessed had he been charged with having advised the act. No person indicted as a principal can be expected to say, "I am not a principal. I am an accessory. I did not commit, I only advised the act."

The authority of the English cases on this subject depends, in a great measure, on the adoption of the common law doctrine of accessorial treasons. If that doctrine be excluded, this branch of it may not be directly applicable to treasons committed within the United States. If the crime of advising or procuring a levying of war be within the constitutional definition of treason, then he who advises or procures it must be indicted on the very fact; and the question whether the treasonableness of the act may be decided in the first instance in the trial of him who procured it, or must be decided in the trial of one who committed it, will depend upon the reason, as it respects the law of evidence, which produced the British decisions with regard to the trial of principal and accessory, rather than on the positive authority of those decisions. This question is not essential in the present case; because if the crime be within the constitutional definition, it is an overt act of levying war, and, to produce a conviction, ought to have been charged in the indictment.

The law of the case being thus far settled, what ought to be the decision of the court on the present motion? Ought the court to sit and hear testimony which cannot affect the prisoner, or ought the court to arrest that testimony? On this question much has been said—much that may perhaps be ascribed to a misconception of the point really under consideration. The motion has been treated as a motion confessedly made to stop irrelevant testimony; and, in the course of the argument, it has been repeatedly stated, by those who oppose the motion, that irrelevant testimony may and ought to be stopped. That this statement is perfectly correct is one of those fundamental principles in judicial proceedings which is acknowledged by all, and is founded in the absolute necessity of the thing. No person will contend that, in a civil or criminal case, either party is at liberty to introduce what testimony he pleases, legal or illegal, and to consume the whole term in details of facts unconnected with the particular case. Some tribunal, then, must decide on the admissibility of testimony. The parties cannot constitute this tribunal; for they do not agree. The jury cannot constitute it; for the question is whether they shall hear the testimony or not. Who, then, but the court can constitute it? It is of necessity the peculiar province of the court to judge of the admissibility of testimony. If the court admit improper or reject proper testimony, it is an error of judgment; but it is an error committed in the direct exercise of their judicial functions. The present indictment charges the prisoner with levying war against the United States, and alleges an overt act of levying war. That overt act must be proved, according to the mandates of the constitution and of the act of congress, by two witnesses. It is not proved by a single witness. The presence of the accused has been stated to be an essential component part of the overt act in this indictment, unless the common law principle respecting accessories should render it unnecessary; and there is not only no witness who has proved his actual or legal presence, but the fact of his absence is not controverted. The counsel for the prosecution offer to give in evidence subsequent transactions at a different place and in a different state, in order to prove—what? The overt act laid in the indictment? That the prisoner was one of those who assembled at Blennerhassett's Is-

land? No: that is not alleged. It is well known that such testimony is not competent to establish such a fact. The constitution and law require that the fact should be established by two witnesses; not by the establishment of other facts from which the jury might reason to this fact. The testimony, then, is not relevant. If it can be introduced, it is only in the character of corroborative or confirmatory testimony, after the overt act has been proved by two witnesses in such manner that the question of fact ought to be left with the jury. The conclusion that in this state of things no testimony can be admissible is so inevitable that the counsel for the United States could not resist it. I do not understand them to deny that, if the overt act be not proved by two witnesses so as to be submitted to the jury, all other testimony must be irrelevant; because no other testimony can prove the act. Now, an assemblage on Blennerhassett's Island is proved by the requisite number of witnesses; and the court might submit it to the jury whether that assemblage amounted to a levying of war; but the presence of the accused at that assemblage being nowhere alleged except in the indictment, the overt act is not proved by a single witness; and, of consequence, all other testimony must be irrelevant. The only difference between this motion as made, and the motion in the form which the counsel for the United States would admit to be regular, is this: It is now general for the rejection of all testimony. It might be particular with respect to each witness as adduced. But can this be wished, or can it be deemed necessary? If enough be proved to show that the indictment cannot be supported, and that no testimony, unless it be of that description which the attorney for the United States declares himself not to possess, can be relevant, why should a question be taken on each witness? The opinion of this court on the order of testimony has frequently been adverted to as deciding this question against the motion. If a contradiction between the two opinions exist, the court cannot perceive it. It was said that levying war is an act compounded of law and fact, of which the jury, aided by the court, must judge. To that declaration the court still adheres. It was said that if the overt act were not proved by two witnesses, no testimony in its nature corroborative or confirmatory was admissible, or could be relevant. From that declaration there is certainly no departure. It has been asked, in allusion to the present case, if a general commanding an army should detach troops for a distant service, would the men composing that detachment be traitors, and would the commander-in-chief escape punishment? Let the opinion which has been given answer this question. Appearing at the head of an army would, according to this opinion, be an overt act of levying war. Detaching a military corps from it for military purposes might, also, be an overt act of levying war. It is not pretended that he would not be punishable for these acts. It is only said that he may be tried and convicted on his own acts in the state where those acts were committed, not on the acts of others in the state where those others acted.

Much has been said in the course of the argument on points on which the court feels no inclination to comment particularly; but which may, perhaps not improperly, receive some notice. That this court dares not usurp power is most true. That this court dares not shrink from its duty is not less true. No man is desirous of placing himself in a disagreeable situation. No man is desirous of becoming the peculiar subject of calumny. No man might he let the bitter cup pass from him without self-reproach, would drain it to the bottom. But if he have no choice in the case, if there be no alternative presented to him but a dereliction of duty or the opprobrium of those who are denominated the world, he merits the contempt as well as the indignation of his country who can hesitate which to embrace. That gentlemen, in a case the most interesting, in the zeal with which they advocate particular opinions, and under the conviction in some measure produced by that zeal, should, on each side, press their arguments too far, should be impatient at any deliberation in the court, and should suspect or fear the operation of motives to which alone they can ascribe that deliberation, is, perhaps, a frailty incident to human nature; but if any conduct on the part of the court could warrant a sentiment that it would deviate to the one side or the other from the line prescribed by duty and by law, that conduct would be viewed by the judges themselves with an eye of extreme severity, and would long be recollected with deep and serious regret.

The arguments on both sides have been intently and deliberately considered. Those which could not be noticed, since to notice every argument and authority would swell this opinion to a volume, have not been disregarded. The result of the whole is a conviction, as complete as the mind of the court is capable of receiving on a complex subject, that the motion must prevail. No testimony relative to the conduct or declarations of the prisoner elsewhere, and subsequent to the transaction on Blennerhassett's Island, can be admitted; because such testimony, being in its nature merely corroborative and incompetent to prove the overt act in itself, is irrelevant until there be proof of the overt act by two witnesses. This opinion does not comprehend the proof by two witnesses that the meeting on Blennerhassett's Island was procured by the prisoner. On that point the court for the present withholds its opinion for reasons which have been already assigned; and as it is understood from the statements made on the part of the prosecution that no such testimony exists, if there be such let it be offered, and the court will decide upon it.

The jury have now heard the opinion of the court on the law of the case. They will apply that law to the facts, and will find a verdict of guilty or not guilty as their own consciences may direct.

23

UNITED STATES V. HOXIE

26 Fed. Cas. 397, no. 15,407 (C.C.D.Vt. 1808)

LIVINGSTON, Circuit Justice (charging jury). A very solemn and important office now devolves on you, no less than that of deciding whether a fellow citizen has forfeited his life to the laws of his country. It is not often that we are called to the discharge of a more interesting, and at the same time, more painful and delicate duty. It must, however, whenever it occurs, be met with firmness; and, while it is performed with all the humanity and caution due to a party accused, sight must not be lost of those claims which, if a crime has been committed, the public have upon us. The offence charged in the present instance is that of treason. The indictment having been recently read in your hearing, I will not, at this late hour, trouble you with repeating it. To this charge, the prisoner has pleaded not guilty, and for trial has put himself on a jury of his country. Nor will I detain you with a recapitulation of the facts, as they have appeared in evidence, about which there is no dispute, and on which you are now to say, whether the prisoner at the bar be guilty of the crime of treason. But, although there be little, if any, controversy in relation to the facts on which the public prosecutor relies, you will naturally expect some direction from the court, how far, in point of law, they support the charge alleged in the indictment. This direction, with its reasons, the court will now proceed to give you.

Treason, not only holds a conspicuous, and generally the first place in every catalogue of crimes, but is almost universally punished with death. Government is so high a blessing, and its preservation and support are so essential to the welfare of every member of the body politic, that to attempt its subversion, has ever been regarded a most aggravated offence. But, the resentment so naturally enkindled against those who are supposed to aim at the destruction of the only security which we enjoy for life, liberty, and estate, leads us frequently to include, under this high crime, offences greatly inferior in turpitude, much less dangerous in their effects, and in every respect, of a different description and tendency. To prevent, therefore, as far as possible every abuse by the extension of treason to offences, which, in times of public agitation, might, by violent or corrupt constructions, be pretended to belong to it, there was inserted in our national compact, a rule which was to be binding on every department of government. To define and provide punishments for other crimes of federal cognizance, is left to congress; but, with a jealousy on this subject, which a full knowledge of the excesses that had so often been committed in other countries by parties contending for dominion, was well calculated to excite, no other trust was here reposed in the legislature, than that of prescribing in what way treason was to be punished. For its definition, resort was ever to be had to that great fundamental law, which was to be binding at all times; and was not liable to be changed on a sudden emergency, so as to gratify the vengeance, or promote the views of aspiring or designing men. In the constitution we accordingly find this very limited definition of it: "Treason against the United States, shall consist only in levying war against them, or in adhering to their enemies, giving them aid and comfort."

The United States having no public enemy, it is only the first branch of this definition which will require your attention. With all the solicitude which was felt by the framers of our constitution to produce certainty, and to exclude interpretation in a matter so momentous, and with all their circumspection to avoid the use of terms in any degree vague or indefinite, cases have already occurred in this country, and will, no doubt, again arise, in which it will be difficult to say, whether the acts in question amount to a "levying of war," within the meaning of this instrument. Such is the imperfection of language, and so limited human foresight, that it is very difficult, whatever care be employed, always so to describe an offence, as not to leave some doubt of the meaning of the legislature, and still more so, to anticipate every case of a similar nature, which it might have been proper to provide for. To a system of laws so perfect, that Being, who takes in at one view, the past, present, and to come, is alone competent. When doubts, however, arise, as they often must, whether an offence belongs to the class assigned to it in the indictment, their solution in the first instance devolves on the court, whose duty it then is, to give a jury such instructions as it may deem necessary, for their correct understanding of the law.

Having a constitutional regulation on the subject before us, it may be expected by some, that the court will compare with the terms of that instrument alone, the facts which have appeared in proof, and by such test, determine whether the crime of treason has been committed. Were our examination thus restricted, it is impossible a moment's doubt could be harboured of the true character of this transaction. "A levying of war," without having recourse to rules of construction, or artificial reasoning, would seem to be nothing short of the employment, or at least, of the embodying of a military force, armed and arrayed, in a warlike manner, for the purpose of forcibly subverting the government, dismembering the Union, or destroying the legislative functions of congress. These troops should be so armed, and so directed, as to leave no doubt, that the United States, or their government, were the immediate object of their attack.

But, a wider range has been taken at the bar. Not only the constitution, but precedents have been resorted to, to furnish a rule for the present case. The court, so far from feeling a disposition to find fault with this mode of treating the subject, has no objection to adopt it, in its remarks to you. It has already been observed, that, taking the constitution as our guide, not a doubt can be entertained of the prisoner's innocence of treason. Let us see, then, whether the different acts, which in England, or in this country, have been regarded as constituting the crime of "levying war," will make any difference.

In taking notice of precedents, set by British tribunals, the court does not mean to give any opinion on their binding effect in the United States; or discuss a question which has been much agitated—whether, by the use of these terms, it was intended to adopt the technical meaning which they had already received in England: or whether, considering treason as a new offence against a newly created government, the constitution on this point was to be interpreted by itself, without reference to, or with the aid of any common law decisions whatever? These questions

will be left unconsidered—a decision of them now not being thought material. For, if the court does not greatly err, no construction in England, and certainly none in America, has yet carried this doctrine the length to which we are at present expected to go.

In the first place, it is well understood, in both countries, that war must be actually levied, and that no consultation or conspiracy to subvert the government, or laws, however atrocious the offence, can amount to treason. In England, all insurrections to dethrone or imprison the king; or, to force him to change his measures, or to remove evil counsellors; to attack his troops in opposition to his authority; to carry off or destroy his stores provided for defence of the realm, if done conjointly with and in aid of rebels, or enemies, and not only for lucre, or some private, malicious motive; to hold a castle or fort against the king, or his troops, if actual force be used in order to keep possession; to join with rebels freely and voluntarily; to rise for the purpose of throwing down by force all enclosures; alter the established law, or religion; to reduce the general price of victuals; to enhance the price of all labour; to open all prisons; that is, to effect innovations of a public and general concern by an armed force, or for any other purpose which usurps the government in matters of a public and general nature. All these acts have been deemed "a levying of war." So also have insurrections to redress by force national grievances; or to reform real or imaginary evils of a public nature, and in which the insurgents had no special interest; or, by intimidation and violence,—as was the case with Lord George Gordon, who however was acquitted,—to force the repeal of a law. But, when the object of an insurrection if of a local or private nature, not having a direct tendency to destroy all property and all government by numbers and armed force, it will not amount to treason; and, in these, and other cases that occur, the true criterion is, the intention with which the parties assembled.

Having thus brought into one view the principal cases which, in England, have been adjudged to amount to levying of war, the court will now proceed to the trials which have taken place within the United States, for treasons of the same description. In 1794, an insurrection took place in four of the western counties of Pennsylvania, with a view of resisting and preventing, by force, the execution of certain acts of congress imposing a duty on spirits distilled within the United States. In the trial of U. S. v. Mitchel [Case No. 15,788], who was indicted for treason, before a circuit court of the United States, at which Judge Patterson presided, the court held, that "to resist or prevent, by armed force, the execution of a particular act of the United States, is a levying of war against the United States, and, consequently, treason, within the true meaning of the constitution." On the trial of Fries [Case No. 5,126], before the same court, in 1799, for treason, the court (Judge Iredell presiding,) delivered the same opinion, and Fries was convicted. When Fries was again tried,—a new trial having been granted to him,—the same court, then composed of Judge Chase and Judge Peters, delivered the following opinion: "That an insurrection or rising of any body of people within the United States, to attain by force or violence any object of a great public nature, or of public and general or national concern, is a levying of war against the United States." "That any such insurrection to resist or to prevent by force or violence the execution of any statute of the United States, under any pretence of its being unequal, burthensome, oppressive, or unconstitutional, is a levying of war against the United States, within the constitution." Judge Iredell, in a charge to a grand jury, having in view the insurrection in Bucks and Northampton, in the state of Pennsylvania, thus expresses himself: "If the intention be to prevent by force of arms the execution of any act of congress altogether, any forcible opposition calculated to carry that intention into effect, is levying of war against the United States."

The only occasion on which the supreme court of the United States has delivered any opinion on the doctrine of treason was, on the return of a habeas corpus, in the Case of Bollman [4 Cranch (8 U. S.) 75], who had been committed on a charge of that nature. "To constitute this crime," says the court, "war must be actually levied against the United States. However flagitious may be the crime of conspiring to subvert by force the government of our country, such conspiracy is not treason. To conspire to levy war, and actually to levy war, are distinct offences: the first must be brought into operation by the assemblage of men for a purpose treasonable in itself, or the fact of levying war cannot have been committed." "There must," says the court, in another part of its opinion, "be an actual assemblage of men, for the purpose of executing a treasonable design." And again, "It is more safe, as well as more consonant to the principles of our constitution, that the crime of treason should not be extended, by construction, to doubtful cases."

Having now stated the principal decisions abroad and at home, on the subject before us, let us go back to the indictment, and the evidence in support of it, and see if it be possible to bring the prisoner's case within any of those that have been mentioned. The offence laid, stripped of its artificial dress, and technical appearance, is nothing more than the forcible rescuing of a raft from the custody of a military guard placed over it by a collector. It is impossible, to suppress the astonishment which is excited at the attempt which has been made to convince a court and jury of this high criminal jurisdiction, that, between this and levying of war, there is no difference. Can it be seriously thought, that an American jury, with the constitution of the United States as a guide to their interpretation, or even on the cases which have been cited, can be brought, by ingrafting construction on construction, to leave far behind them, English judges and English juries, in their exposition of the crime of treason? Gentlemen, they cannot perceive the tendency of the doctrine which it is now asked of us to sanction. On which of the precedents cited do they rely for our support, or expect us to decide, that an opposition to law, so feeble, so transitory, so free from every traitorous intention, so destitute of every appearance of war, and so evidently calculated for the sole purpose of private gain, was making war against the United States? In what can we discover the treasonable mind, which com-

mon sense, as well as all the authorities tell us, is of the very essence of this offence? Can it be collected from the employment of ten or twelve muskets? Some judges have said, how correctly is here of little moment, that the quantum of force is immaterial. But, when we find it so very small and despicable, it furnishes strong evidence of some intent, very far short of that of measuring their strength with the United States: unless, we can believe, that a force, if it deserve that name, scarcely competent to the reduction of a single family, were meditating hostilities and rebellion against a government, defended by several millions of freemen. But, there is no necessity of any forced interpretation, to arrive at the real intention of these parties. Their conduct shows it to have been of a private nature, and that no further violence was contemplated, than to smuggle a raft which had been seized by the collector, and was then lying at a small distance from a guard, into Canada; for, they forthwith proceeded thither, and having left it a little beyond the line, they returned directly to the United States, not at the head of an army, but peaceably and quietly, each man to his own home, not suspecting that they had a war on their hands, with any power, and least of all with the government of their own country.

Again—Whence is it collected, that their intention was to intimidate congress into a repeal of the embargo laws, or to resist their execution generally? If congress were in session, which was not the case, can gentlemen seriously believe, that means so inadequate would have been employed for purposes which an organized, numerous, and well disciplined army would have found it difficult to accomplish? If you look at the insurrections in 1794, and in 1799, you will be struck with the great difference between the cases which arose out of those occurrences, and the one on which you are now to decide. There is hardly a feature of resemblance; and yet, you are seriously expected to condemn the prisoner, as a traitor, for forcing some lumber from the possession of a collector, because Mitchel, Vigol, and Fries, (who, by the bye, were all pardoned,) were convicted as such, for being concerned in insurrections, which threatened the existence of government, were well calculated to intimidate the legislature, and for a time actually suspended the operation of certain laws which were deemed obnoxious in a large district of country.

It may not be very easy (unless open war and the broad face of rebellion be the criterion,) to fix the exact boundary between treason, and some other offences, which partake, more or less, of an opposition to government. But, difficult as this may be, every one will at once perceive a very wide separation, between regular and numerous assemblages of men, scattered over a large portion of country, under known officers, and in every respect armed and marshalled in military and hostile array, for the avowed purpose, not only of disturbing and arresting the course of public law, in a whole district, by forcibly compelling the officers of government to resign, but by intimidation and violence, of coercing its repeal, and a sudden, transient, weak, unmilitary, and unsystematized resistance, and that in a solitary instance, and for the single object of personal emolument. As obvious is the distinction, between a large armed force, embodied in the heart of our country, with designs inimical to government and the laws, assuming an attitude of defiance, and opposition to any force which might be set against it, and a few dozen men, who, having committed an offence on the very confines of the United States, were in the act of flying to another government, and whose hostility, such as it was, could have no other motive, than that of favouring their escape. These cases cannot be considered as parallel, without destroying, at once, every distinction between trespasses, riots, and treasons. Not an instance can be found in England, during a period of several hundred years, which have elapsed since the statute of treasons, in which an act like the present, was determined to be treason.

Has the prisoner, then, it may be asked, been guilty of no offence? His conduct, no doubt, was highly culpable, and, if the courts of the United States have no common law jurisdiction in criminal cases, as some have thought, the legislature may declare such acts a crime, and assign to it such punishment as may be thought proper. It is not very clear, indeed, that the offence, which is now dignified with the name of treason, is not already provided for, by an act of congress, which punishes the resisting or impeding of any officer of the customs, or any person assisting him, in the execution of his duty, with a fine of four hundred dollars.

By another act, whoever shall knowingly oppose any officer of the United States, in the execution of process, or shall beat or wound him in such service, shall be fined and imprisoned; and, provision is made, by the same law, for the punishment of those who, by force, rescue a prisoner after or before conviction for a capital crime. It may also be remarked, that to kill a sheriff in the discharge of his duty, and who is as much clothed with the authority of law, as the collector or his agents were here, whatever be the number concerned, or the weapons employed, has always been held in England and this country, murder, and not treason.

These laws of congress have been mentioned, and others of a like nature might be referred to, to satisfy you, that the legislature never supposed an act of this kind treason or they would only have declared its punishment; and, although, if it be treason by the constitution, no act of congress can make it otherwise; still, a legislative understanding of that instrument, if not conclusive, is entitled to very respectful attention.

The court, may here again ask, whether it be a greater crime to take from the keeping of one public officer, where no death ensues, a property however valuable, than to force from the custody of another, a person whose life had been declared to be forfeited to the laws of his country; or, to kill a sheriff in the execution of his duty? In all these instances, the laws are opposed, and in the last case, with the aggravation of homicide; but as no traitorous intent exists in either, and no war is made against the United States, neither of them can fall within the meaning of treason.

But as so much stress is laid on the opinions of our own judges, whose attention has been judicially drawn to a consideration of this crime, you will bear with me a little longer, while I show you how very little ground there is for this reliance, and how dangerous a sense you are required to put on these decisions. Nothing will be more easy than to rescue their characters from the reproaches which would adhere to them, if they had really declared, (for such is the language of this prosecution,) that every opposition to a public law, no matter how momentary, how slight, in what shape, or for what purpose, amounted to treason. Not one of them has said any such thing, nor intimated a sentiment of the kind. Judge Patterson and Judge Iredell, who led the way on this occasion, and of whose valuable services death has since deprived their country, were as eminent for their abilities, as venerable for their erudition, and as much admired and beloved for their humanity and virtues, as any men that ever ascended the bench of justice; and it would be a subject of mournful retrospect for them, if such contemplations could now employ their thoughts, that the authorities of their names should be resorted to, for introducing a doctrine which, if here, they would resist with all the energy of talents, and weight of character, for which they were both illustrious. You are already acquainted with the occasions on which these opinions were delivered, and have seen how totally the resemblance fails, between them and the one which has called us together. These opinions have also, in part, been stated to you; but, permit me, now, to read other passages, from them, which apply more directly to the case before us. If a statement of facts like the present, had been submitted to Judge Iredell, and he had been obliged to examine and decide on them, he could not have expressed himself in terms more appropriate, or have delivered an opinion more exactly suited to them, or more in favour of the prisoner, than the one which he gave on the occasion which has been already referred to: after describing what resistance, and with what intent, to a public law, amounted to treason, he proceeds,—"But if the intention is merely to defeat its operation in a particular instance, or through the agency of a particular officer, from some private or personal motive, it does not amount to the crime of treason. The particular motive must be the sole ingredient in the case; for, if combined with a general view, to obstruct an execution of the act, the offence must be deemed treason." The language of Judge Patterson, if not quite as explicit, conveys the same meaning. "The prisoner," says he, meaning Vigol, "went to the house of two different excise officers, in arms, marshalled and arrayed, and at each place committed acts of violence and devastation." "With respect to the intention," he proceeds, "there is not, unhappily, the slightest possibility of doubt. To suppress the office of excise in the fourth survey of Pennsylvania, and particularly, in this instance, to compel the resignation of the officer, so as to render null and void in effect an act of congress, constituted the apparent, the avowed object of the insurrection, and of the outrages, which the prisoner assisted to commit. Combining these facts and these designs, the crime of high treason is consummated in the contemplation of the constitution and law of the United States."

On the trial of Mitchel, the same judge observes: "If the object of the insurrection was, to suppress the excise office, and to prevent the execution of an act of congress, by force and intimidation, the offence, in legal estimation, is high treason. The object was of a general nature and of national concern." But Judge Chase is supposed to have gone further. This is another mistake. As little support can be derived to the prosecution from his opinion, in the Case of Fries. That great and truly profound lawyer, on the fullest consideration, concurred in the judgments which had already been delivered by two of his associates, and expresses himself with all the perspicuity, strength, and precision, for which he is so greatly distinguished. What, in his estimation, constituted treason, has already been seen. You will now hear what he thought of a partial opposition to an act of congress, and for a private or special purpose. On this point he is too explicit to be misunderstood; and yet, that must have been the case, or this prosecution would not have been heard of. "The court," says he (for Mr. Peters, the district judge, whose high judicial reputation adds much to the value of his opinions, concurred with him,) "think, that the assembling bodies of men, armed and arrayed in a warlike manner, for purposes only of a private nature, is not treason, although the judges and peace officers should be insulted and resisted, or even great outrages committed to the persons and property of our citizens."

These learned judges also consider the intention as the only true guide in ascertaining whether certain acts amount to treason, or a less offence, and regard the universality, or generality of the design, as forming an essential ingredient in the composition of this crime. On this point they thus express themselves: "The true criterion to determine whether acts committed are treason, or a less offence, (as a riot,) is the quo animo, the people did assemble. When the intention is universal or general, as to effect some object of a general, public nature, it will be treason, and cannot be considered, construed, or reduced, to a riot. The commission of any number of felonies, riots, or other misdemeanors, cannot alter their nature, so as to make them amount to treason. And, on the other hand, if the intention and acts combined amount to treason, they cannot be sunk down to felony, or riot. The intention with which any acts (as felonies, the destruction of houses, and the like,) are done, will show to what class of crimes the case belongs." If these opinions are understood by the court, and there seems no ambiguity or obscurity in either of them, they all, in express terms, exclude from the rank of treason the facts which compose the present offence; and whatever doubts have been and are yet entertained, by many professional gentlemen of extensive erudition, and exalted integrity, of such parts of these opinions as brought the cases of the insurgents within the constitutional definition of treason, no objection ever has, nor perhaps ever will be, made to the exceptions, which have been so cautiously interwoven into them, for the very purpose of preventing their extension to cases of this kind. Once disregard these exceptions, and render the constitutional rule as flexible or comprehensive as it is now suggested to be, and prosecutions for treason will become as common as indictments for petit larcenies, assaults and batteries, or other misdemeanors. If every opposition to law be treason, for very like this is the language we have heard, as all offences partake in some measure of that quality, who can say how many of them will in time become ranged under the class of treason. Neither you, nor the court, can feel any ambition of leading the way, in setting a precedent so dangerous, or one that will in any degree tend to demolish that barrier which has been raised by the constitution against constructive treasons.

You have been reminded, in the course of this trial, that in criminal cases, a jury has a right to take upon itself the decision of both law and fact. There is no design in the court to dispute this position, or in any degree to encroach on your prerogatives. The trial by jury, whatever doubts may exist as to its excellence in civil actions, has uniformly received, and is most eminently entitled to the highest praise, as a mode of determining between the public and a party accused. It is a subject on which the stores of panegyric have been exhausted. Its perpetuity in this country is secured by the federal constitution, which in this respect, is only a transcript of the provisions which had already found a place in those of the several states. But while you have this right, the court has also its duties to perform. As judges, we are not sent here merely to preside at trials, to preserve order, and to regulate the forms of proceeding; we have a much higher and more important trust committed to us: it is our right and our duty to expound the law to a jury in criminal, as well as civil cases; and although it be not denied, that in public prosecutions, you may decide contrary to such interpretations, it is not too much to say, that it is nevertheless your duty to pay a very respectful consideration to every proposition of law you may receive from the court. Judges have ever been regarded as the proper organs of law; and when it is recollected that they act under the same solemn sanction with yourselves, and have the same interest in a pure administration of justice, it is not probable that any motive can exist, intentionally to deceive you. And who, may it fairly be presumed, generally speaking, will be the best informed on these subjects? Those whose attention has for many years been more or less directed to the jurisprudence of their country, or those whose avocations have left little or no leisure for such inquiries? You are not then, to consider as an intrusion, what it would be a dereliction of duty in a judge to withhold from you; his opinion on the law of every case under consideration. You are already apprized of ours on that, on which you are now to decide. I have the satisfaction to say, that there is no diversity of sentiment between the district judge, with whom I have the honour and pleasure of being associated, and myself. It is the opinion of both of us, that if you believe, which abundantly appears from the testimony, and seems to be conceded on the part of the government, that the prisoner, among others, was hired by the owner of this raft, for the purpose of evading the embargo laws, only in this instance, and for his own private emolument, although it may have been part of the plan to use violence, and force were actually employed against the collector or his agents to accomplish this object, but that this formed no link in a conspiracy to resist or impede the operation of these laws within the district generally as far as their means enabled them, (every attempt to produce proof of which has failed,) then the prisoner is not guilty of the crime of levying war; for then, his case falls most precisely within the exception which has already been read to you from the opinion of Judge Iredell. The intention which all the cases speak of, is not understood by the district attorney and the court in the same sense. He seems to consider, that if the intention be to oppose a law, no matter with what motive, treason is committed; whereas, it is the intention with which such resistance is made, not the opposition itself, that forms the criterion: otherwise, every wilful opposition to a statute, would necessarily be a levying of war. With respect to the prisoner's intention it is made out most satisfactorily, by every witness that has been examined on the part of the public. On this point, there will be, happily for him, no doubt in your minds. There is no testimony of his ever having been before, or since, engaged in a resistance to these or any other laws. The court cannot help thinking that the district attorney must have been greatly deceived in the information which was given to him, of the prisoner's conduct, and that the proofs on trial have fallen very far short of his expectations, or that you would never have been put to the trouble of deciding on this case. But as, notwithstanding the discussion which has taken place, he seems seriously and sincerely to believe treason has been committed, the court has thought it a duty to state to you its opinions, most explicitly, the other way; so that, if any mistake be committed by so great an extension of the crime of treason, neither of us may be chargeable with it; for, "we cannot be too wary," in the language of the great and good Lord Hale, "in multiplying constructive treasons, for we know not where they will end."

The court will now finish its charge. If it has been tedious, you will impute it not to a desire of trespassing unnecessarily on your time, but of guarding you, in a case of very general concern, against those mistakes which the earnestness and eloquence of counsel sometimes produce; and although we might have been content with stating our opinion on the law, in more general terms, we were willing you should know, that it was not merely a speculation of our own, but one which we believe to be sanctioned by the constitution of our country; by decisions in England; by various judgments of our domestic tribunals; and, as far as can be collected from their acts, by the sense of our national legislature.

In addressing you, then, at some length, and with all possible plainness, the court have felt no other motive than a desire to assist you in coming to a correct result on a point which, to the honour of this state, has never before been a subject of public discussion within it.

The whole case, both law and fact, is now committed to you, in the fullest confidence, that you will do justice to your country, the prisoner, and yourselves.

24

PEOPLE V. LYNCH
11 Johns. R. 549 (N.Y. 1814)

Per Curiam. The grounds relied upon for the discharge of the prisoners are, 1st. That the facts charged in the indictment do not amount to the crime of treason against the state of *New-York;* and, 2dly, That the state courts have no jurisdiction of treason against the *United States.*

The indictment, containing several counts which are substantially alike, after setting out a state of war between the *United States* and *Great Britain,* declared and carried on under the authority of the *United States,* alleges, that the prisoners, being citizens of the *state* of *New-York,* and of the *United States of America, as traitors against the people of the state of New-York,* did adhere to, and give aid and comfort to the enemy, by supplying them with provisions of various kinds, on board a public ship of war, upon the high seas. It has been attempted, on the part of the prosecution, to support this indictment under the statute of this state, (1 *N. R. L.* 145.) which declares treason against the people of this state to consist in levying war against the people of this state, within the state, or adhering to the enemies of the people of this state, giving them aid and comfort in this state, or elsewhere. And it has been said, that this act is nugatory, unless it applies to cases like the present; but this by no means follows, for there can be no doubt but such a state of things might exist, as that treason against the people of this state might be committed. This might be, by an open and armed opposition to the laws of the state, or a combination and forcible attempt to overturn or usurp the government. And, indeed, the state, in its political capacity, may, under certain special circumstances; pointed out by the constitution of the *United States,* be engaged in war with a foreign enemy. But no such circumstances are stated in this indictment. *Great Britain* cannot be said to be at war with the state of *New-York,* in its aggregate and political capacity, as an independent government, and, therefore, not an enemy of the state, within the sense and meaning of the statute. The people of this state, as citizens of the *United States,* are at war with *Great Britain,* in consequence of the declaration of war by congress. The state, in its political capacity, is not at war. The subjects of *Great Britain* are the enemies of the *United States of America,* and the citizens thereof, as members of the union, and not of the state of *New-York,* as laid in the indictment.

The alteration in our statute, since the adoption of the constitution of the *United States,* plainly shows the sense of the legislature on this subject. By the act, as it stood in the year 1787, (1 *G. Ed. Laws,* 316.) it was made treason to adhere to, or give aid and comfort to the enemies of the people of the state of *New-York,* or *of the United States of America.* But, in the several revisions of the law, since the adoption of the constitution, the latter words have been omitted, as unnecessary and inapplicable to the situation of the state, as a member of the union. Under the old confederation, there was no judicial power organized, and clothed with authority for the trial and punishment of treason against the *United States of America.* It became necessary, therefore, to provide for it under the judicial powers of the several states; no such necessity, however, exists under our present system. According to this view of the subject, it would seem unnecessary to notice the question of jurisdiction; for, admitting the facts charged against the prisoners to amount to treason against the *United States,* they do not constitute the offence of treason against the people of the state of *New-York,* as charged in the indictment. The offence not being charged as treason against the *United States,* the present indictment cannot be supported, even admitting this court to have jurisdiction. We would barely observe, however, that we think the jurisdiction of the state courts does not extend to the offence of treason against the *United States.* The judicial power of the *United States* extends to all cases arising under the constitution and laws of the *United States.* The declaration of war was by a law of congress; and, in consequence of which, it became criminal in the prisoners to afford aid and comfort to the enemy. And the act establishing the judicial courts of the *United States,* gives to the circuit courts cognizance, exclusive of the courts of the several states, of all crimes and offences cognizable under the authority of the *United States,* except where the laws of the *United States* shall otherwise direct. (1 *Sess.* 1 *Cong.* c. 20. *sec.*11.) In whatever point of view, therefore, the case is considered, we are satisfied that the present indictment cannot be supported. The prisoners must accordingly be discharged.

25

JOSEPH STORY, COMMENTARIES ON THE
CONSTITUTION 3:§§ 1292, 1294–96,
1791–94, 1796
1833

---

§ 1292. The propriety of investing the national government with authority to punish the crime of treason against the United States could never become a question with any persons, who deemed the national government worthy of creation, or preservation. If the power had not been expressly granted, it must have been implied, unless all the powers of the national government might be put at defiance, and prostrated with impunity. Two motives, probably, concurred in introducing it, as an express power. One was, not to leave it open to implication, whether it was to be exclusively punishable with death according to the known rule of the common law, and with the barbarous accompaniments pointed out by it; but to confide the punishment to the discretion of congress. The other was, to impose some limitation upon the nature and extent of the punishment, so that it should not work corruption of blood or forfeiture beyond the life of the offender.

. . . . .

§ 1294. It is well known, that corruption of blood, and forfeiture of the estate of the offender followed, as a necessary consequence at the common law, upon every attainder of treason. By corruption of blood all inheritable qualities are destroyed; so, that an attainted person can neither inherit lands, nor other hereditaments from his ancestors, nor retain those, he is already in possession of, nor transmit them to any heir. And this destruction of all inheritable qualities is so complete, that it obstructs all descents to his posterity, whenever they are obliged to derive a title through him to any estate of a remoter ancestor. So, that if a father commits treason, and is attainted, and suffers death, and then the grandfather dies, his grandson cannot inherit any estate from his grandfather; for he must claim through his father, who could convey to him no inheritable blood. Thus the innocent are made the victims of a guilt, in which they did not, and perhaps could not, participate; and the sin is visited upon remote generations. In addition to this most grievous disability, the person attainted forfeits, by the common law, all his lands, and tenements, and rights of entry, and rights of profits in lands or tenements, which he possesses. And this forfeiture relates back to the time of the treason committed, so as to avoid all intermediate sales and incumbrances; and he also forfeits all his goods and chattels from the time of his conviction.

§ 1295. The reason commonly assigned for these severe punishments, beyond the mere forfeiture of the life of the party attainted, are these: By committing treason the party has broken his original bond of allegiance, and forfeited his social rights. Among these social rights, that of transmitting property to others is deemed one of the chief and most valuable. Moreover, such forfeitures, whereby the posterity of the offender must suffer, as well as himself, will help to restrain a man, not only by the sense of his duty, and dread of personal punishment, but also by his passions and natural affections; and will interest every dependent and relation, he has, to keep him from offending. But this view of the subject is wholly unsatisfactory. It looks only to the offender himself, and is regardless of his innocent posterity. It really operates, as a posthumous punishment upon them; and compels them to bear, not only the disgrace naturally attendant upon such flagitious crimes; but takes from them the common rights and privileges enjoyed by all other citizens, where they are wholly innocent, and however remote they may be in the lineage from the first offender. It surely is enough for society to take the life of the offender, as a just punishment of his crime, without taking from his offspring and relatives that property, which may be the only means of saving them from poverty and ruin. It is bad policy too; for it cuts off all the attachments, which these unfortunate victims might otherwise feel for their own government, and prepares them to engage in any other service, by which their supposed injuries may be redressed, or their hereditary hatred gratified. Upon these and similar grounds, it may be presumed, that the clause was first introduced into the original draft of the constitution; and, after some amendments, it was adopted without any apparent resistance. By the laws since passed by congress, it is declared, that no conviction or judgment, for any capital or other offences, shall work corruption of blood, or any forfeiture of estate. The history of other countries abundantly proves, that one of the strong incentives to prosecute offences, as treason, has been the chance of sharing in the plunder of the victims. Rapacity has been thus stimulated to exert itself in the service of the most corrupt tyranny; and tyranny has been thus furnished with new opportunities of indulging its malignity and revenge; of gratifying its envy of the rich, and good; and of increasing its means to reward favourites, and secure retainers for the worst deeds.

§ 1296. The power of punishing the crime of treason against the United States is exclusive in congress; and the trial of the offence belongs exclusively to the tribunals appointed by them. A state cannot take cognizance, or punish the offence; whatever it may do in relation to the offence of treason, committed exclusively against itself, if indeed any case can, under the constitution, exist, which is not at the same time treason against the United States.

. . . . .

§ 1791. Treason is generally deemed the highest crime, which can be committed in civil society, since its aim is an overthrow of the government, and a public resistance by force of its powers. Its tendency is to create universal danger and alarm; and on this account it is peculiarly odious, and often visited with the deepest public resentment. Even a charge of this nature, made against an individual, is deemed so opprobrious, that, whether just or unjust, it subjects him to suspicion and hatred; and, in times of high political excitement, acts of a very subordinate nature are often, by popular prejudices, as well as by royal resentment, magnified into this ruinous importance. It is, therefore, of very great importance, that its true nature and limits should be exactly ascertained; and Montesquieu was so sensible of it, that he has not scrupled to declare, that if the crime of treason be indeterminate, that alone is sufficient to make any government degenerate into arbitrary power. The history of England itself is full of melancholy instruction on this subject. By the ancient common law it was left very much to discretion to determine, what acts were, and were not, treason; and the judges of those times, holding office at the pleasure of the crown, became but too often instruments in its hands of foul injustice. At the instance of tyrannical princes they had abundant opportunities to create *constructive* treasons; that is, by forced and arbitrary constructions, to raise offences into the guilt and punishment of treason, which were not suspected to be such. The grievance of these constructive treasons was so enormous, and so often weighed down the innocent, and the patriotic, that it was found necessary, as early as the reign of Edward the Third, for parliament to interfere, and arrest it, by declaring and defining all the different branches of treason. This statute has ever since remained the pole star of English jurisprudence upon this subject. And although, upon temporary emergencies, and in arbitrary reigns, since that period, other treasons have been created, the sober sense of the nation has generally abrogated them, or reduced their power within narrow limits.

§ 1792. Nor have republics been exempt from violence and tyranny of a similar character. The Federalist has justly remarked, that newfangled, and artificial treasons have been the great engines, by which violent factions, the natural offspring of free governments, have usually wreaked their alternate malignity on each other.

§ 1793. It was under the influence of these admonitions furnished by history and human experience, that the convention deemed it necessary to interpose an impassable barrier against arbitrary constructions, either by the courts, or by congress, upon the crime of treason. It confines it to two species; first, the levying of war against the United States; and secondly, adhering to their enemies, giving them aid and comfort. In so doing, they have adopted the very words of the Statute of Treason of Edward the Third; and thus by implication, in order to cut off at once all chances of arbitrary constructions, they have recognized the well-settled interpretation of these phrases in the administration of criminal law, which has prevailed for ages.

§ 1794. Fortunately, hitherto but few cases have occurred in the United States, in which it has been necessary for the courts of justice to act upon this important subject. But whenever they have arisen, the judges have uniformly adhered to the established doctrines, even when executive influence has exerted itself with no small zeal to procure convictions.

. . . . .

§ 1796. The other part of the clause, requiring the testimony of two witnesses to the same overt act, or a confession *in open court*, to justify a conviction is founded upon the same reasoning. A like provision exists in British jurisprudence, founded upon the same great policy of protecting men against false testimony, and unguarded confessions, to their utter ruin. It has been well remarked, that confessions are the weakest and most suspicious of all testimony; ever liable to be obtained by artifice, false hopes, promises of favour, or menaces; seldom remembered accurately, or reported with due precision; and incapable, in their nature, of being disproved by other negative evidence. To which it may be added, that it is easy to be forged, and the most difficult to guard against. An unprincipled demagogue, or a corrupt courtier, might otherwise hold the lives of the purest patriots in his hands, without the means of proving the falsity of the charge, if a secret confession, uncorroborated by other evidence, would furnish a sufficient foundation and proof of guilt. And wisely, also, has the constitution declined to suffer the testimony of a single witness, however high, to be sufficient to establish such a crime, which rouses against the victim at once private honour and public hostility. There must, as there should, be a concurrence of two witnesses to the same overt, that is, open act of treason, who are above all reasonable exception.

SEE ALSO:

The Treason Act of 1350, 25 Edw. 3, Stat. 5, c. 2
The Treason Act of 1495, 11 Hen. 7, c. 1
The Treason Act of 1543, 35 Henry 8, c. 2

The Treason Act, 1553, 1 Mary, Stat. 1, c. 1

The Treason Act, 1554, 1 and 2 Philip & Mary, c. 10

The Treason Act of 1695, 7 Wm. 3, c. 3

The Treason Act of 1708, 7 Anne, c. 21

The Treason Act of 1747, 20 Geo. 2, c. 30

The Treason Outlawries (Scotland) Act, 1748, 22 Geo. 2, c. 48

William Blackstone, Commentaries 2:255–56 (1766)

An Act against Treason and Misprision of Treason, 1777, Acts and Resolves of the Province of Massachusetts Bay 5:615

An Act Declaring What Shall Be Treason, 1777, Laws of Pa. 1:435 (1810)

Respublica v. *Molder*, 1 Dall. 33 (Pa. 1778)

Respublica v. *Malin*, 1 Dall. 33 (Pa. 1778)

Respublica v. *Roberts*, 1 Dall. 39 (Pa. 1778)

An Act in Addition to an Act Intitled "An Act against Treason, etc.," 1779, Acts and Resolves of the Province of Massachusetts Bay, 5:921

Respublica v. *McCarty*, 2 Dall. 86 (Pa. 1781)

An Act against Treason and Misprision of Treason, 1784, Laws of Vermont, 1781–84, 238 (1965)

Records of the Federal Convention, Farrand 2:136, 144, 168, 182, 337–39, 351, 571, 601; 4:61

Luther Martin, Maryland House of Representatives, 29 Nov. 1787, Farrand 3:158–59

James Wilson, Pennsylvania Ratifying Convention, 4, 7 Dec. 1787, Elliot 2:469, 487–88

James Wilson, A Charge Delivered to the Grand Jury, May 1791, Works 2:808

Delaware Constitution of 1792, art. 5, sec. 3, Thorpe 1:574

Kentucky Constitution of 1792, art. 8, sec. 1, art. 12, secs. 19–21, Thorpe 3:1272, 1275

James Iredell, Charge to the Grand Jury, C.C.D.Mass., 12 Oct. 1792, Life 2:365–70

James Iredell, Charge of the Grand Jury, C.C.D.Md., 1793, Life 2:391

United States v. *Hamilton*, 3 Dall. 17 (1795)

United States v. *Mitchell*, 26 Fed. Cas. 1277, no. 15,788 (C.C.D.Pa. 1795)

United States v. *Vigol*, 28 Fed. Cas. 376, no. 16,621 (C.C.D.Pa. 1795)

John Taylor, Debate on the Sedition Act, Virginia House of Delegates, Dec. 1798, Sen. Doc. no. 873, 62d Cong., 2d sess. 99–100 (1912)

Case of Fries, 9 Fed. Cas. 826, no. 5,126 (C.C.D.Pa. 1799)

James Iredell, Charge to the Grand Jury, 9 Fed. Cas. 826, no. 5,126 (C.C.D.Pa. 1799)

Case of Fries, 9 Fed. Cas. 924, no. 5,127 (C.C.D.Pa. 1800)

An Act Relative to Treason, 1801, N.Y. Laws in Force, Kent & Radcliff 1:214

St. George Tucker, Blackstone's Commentaries 1:App. 272–73; 5:App. 11–51 (1803)

United States v. *Burr*, 25 Fed. Cas. 2, no. 14,692a (C.C.D.Va. 1807)

United States v. *Burr*, 25 Fed. Cas. 201, no. 14,694a (C.C.D.Va. 1807)

Thomas Jefferson, Seventh Annual Message to Congress, 27 Oct. 1807, Richardson 1:429

Senate, Treason and Other Crimes, 11, 24 Feb. 1808, Annals 17:108–27, 135–49

Rufus King to Timothy Pickering, 16 Feb. 1808, Life 5:73

House of Representatives, Treason and Other Crimes, 2 Mar. 1808, Annals 18:1717–19

United States v. *Pryor*, 27 Fed. Cas. 628, no. 16,096 (C.C.D.Pa. 1814)

John Taylor, An Inquiry into the Principles and Policy of the Government of the United States 473–74 (1814)

United States v. *Hodges*, 26 Fed. Cas. 332, no. 15,374 (C.C.D.Md. 1815)

Alabama Constitution of 1819, art. 6, sec. 2, Thorpe 1:108

William Rawle, A View of the Constitution of the United States 139–46 (2d ed. 1829)

Article 4, Section 1

Full Faith and Credit shall be given in each State to the public Acts, Records, and judicial Proceedings of every other State. And the Congress may by general Laws prescribe the Manner in which such Acts, Records, and Proceedings shall be proved, and the Effect thereof.

1

ARTICLES OF CONFEDERATION, ART. 4, ¶ 3
1 Mar. 1781

Full faith and credit shall be given in each of these states to the records, acts, and judicial proceedings of the courts and magistrates of every other State.

2

JAMES V. ALLEN
1 Dall. 188 (Pa. 1786)

SHIPPEN, President.—This is a motion, in effect, to discharge the defendant from execution, on the ground of his having been confined by a *ca. sa.* for the same debt, in the state of New Jersey, and there discharged as an insolvent debtor, by virtue of an act of assembly of that state: and the question is, whether the discharge of his person from imprisonment there, will entitle him to a like discharge here?

It is contended, that the decisions of even foreign courts of justice, shall have a binding force here; and that in the situation in which we stand with regard to New Jersey, a sister state, we are under an additional obligation to pay respect to the decisions of the courts there, by the terms of the articles of confederation.

The judgment of a foreign court establishing a demand against a defendant, or discharging him from it, according to the laws of that country, would certainly have a binding force here; and not only the decisions of courts, but even the laws of foreign countries, where no suits have been instituted, would, in some cases, be taken notice of here; where such laws are explanatory of the contracts, and appear to have been in the contemplation of the parties, at the time of making them; as if the interest of money should be higher in a foreign country where the contract was made, than in that where the suit was brought, the foreign interest shall be recovered, as being understood to be part of the contract. But it does not follow, that every order of a foreign court with respect to the imprisonment of the defendant's person, or any local laws of that country, with regard to his release from confinement, can have the effect of restraining us from proceeding according to our own laws here. The insolvent law of New Jersey relates not to the substance of the plaintiff's demand, which had already been established, but merely authorizes the court to make an order, on certain terms, for the discharge of the defendant's person from imprisonment; which order has no connection with the merits of the cause, and cannot with any propriety be called the judgment of the court in that action; and the law itself on which the order was founded, is a private act, made for that particular purpose; it is local in its nature, and local in its terms.

Insolvent laws subsist in every state in the Union, and are probably all different from each other; some of them require personal notice to be given to the creditors, others do not, as in the present case; and they have never been considered as binding out of the limits of the state that made them. Even the bankrupt laws of England, while we were the subjects of that country, were never supposed to extend here, so as to exempt the persons of the bankrupts from being arrested.

The articles of confederation, which direct that full faith and credit shall be given in one state to the records, acts and judicial proceedings of the others, will not admit of the construction contended for, otherwise, executions might issue in one state upon the judgments given in another; but seem chiefly intended to oblige each state to receive the records of another as full evidence of such acts and judicial proceedings.

Whatever might have been the effect of an order or judgment of the court of New Jersey, if it had actually discharged the defendant from the plaintiff's *demand*, the present order, as well as the act of assembly on which it is founded, is local in its terms, and goes no further than to discharge him from his imprisonment in the jail of Essex county, in the state of New Jersey; which, if the fullest obedience were paid to it, could not authorize a subsequent discharge from imprisonment, in another jail, in another state.

3

KIBBE V. KIBBE
Kirby 119 (Conn. 1786)

By the Court. It appears by the pleadings, that the defendant was an inhabitant of the state of Connecticut, and was not within the jurisdiction of the Court of Common Pleas for the county of Berkshire, at the time of the pretended service of the writ; therefore, the court had no legal jurisdiction of the cause, and so no action ought to be admitted on said judgment: But full credence ought to be given to judgments of the courts in any of the United States, where both parties are within the jurisdiction of such courts at the time of commencing the suit, and are duly served with the process, and have or might have had a fair trial of the cause; all which, with the original cause of action, ought to appear by the plaintiff's declaration in action of debt on such judgment.

DYER, J., said further,—That the original action was upon a covenant real, and locally annexed where the lands lie; and the judgment being by default, this court never could take cognizance of or examine into the justice of the cause; therefore, cannot enforce the judgment on which this action is brought.

4

RECORDS OF THE FEDERAL CONVENTION

[2:188; Madison, 6 Aug.]

XVI

Full faith shall be given in each State to the acts of the Legislatures, and to the records and judicial proceedings of the Courts and Magistrates of every other State.

[2:445; Journal, 29 Aug.]

It was moved and seconded to commit the following proposition

Whensoever the act of any State, whether legislative executive or judiciary shall be attested and exemplified under the seal thereof, such attestation and exemplification shall be deemed in other State as full proof of the existence of that act—and it's operation shall be binding in every other State, in all cases to which it may relate, and which are within the cognizance and jurisdiction of the State, wherein the said act was done

which passed in the affirmative

It was moved and seconded to commit the following proposition

Full faith ought to be given in each State to the public acts, records, and judicial proceedings of every other State; and the Legislature shall by general laws determine the Proof and effect of such acts, records, and proceedings

which passed in the affirmative

and the foregoing Propositions together with the 16 article were referred to the honorable Mr Rutledge, Mr Randolph, Mr Gorham, Mr Wilson and Mr Johnson

[2:447; Madison, 29 Aug.]

Art: XVI. taken up.

Mr. Williamson moved to substitute in place of it, the words of the Articles of Confederation on the same subject. He did not understand precisely the meaning of the article.

Mr. Wilson & Docr. Johnson supposed the meaning to be that Judgments in one State should be the ground of actions in other States, & that acts of the Legislatures should be included, for the sake of Acts of insolvency &c—

Mr. Pinkney moved to commit art XVI, with the following proposition, "To establish uniform laws upon the subject of bankruptcies, and respecting the damages arising on the protest of foreign bills of exchange"

. . . . .

Mr. Madison was for committing both. He wished the Legislature might be authorized to provide for the *execution* of Judgments in other States, under such regulations as might be expedient—He thought that this might be safely done and was justified by the nature of the Union.

Mr. Randolph said there was no instance of one nation executing judgments of the Courts of another nation. He moved the following proposition.

"Whenever the Act of any State, whether Legislative Executive or Judiciary shall be attested & exemplified under the seal thereof, such attestation and exemplification, shall be deemed in other States as full proof of the existence of that act—and its operation shall be binding in every other State, in all cases to which it may relate, and which are within the cognizance and jurisdiction of the State, wherein the said act was done."

On the question for committing art: XVI with Mr. Pinkney's motion

N. H. no. Mas. no. Ct. ay. N. J. ay. Pa ay. Del. ay. Md. ay. Va. ay. N. C. ay. S. C. ay. Geo. ay. [Ayes—9; noes—2.]

The motion of Mr. Randolph was also committed nem: con:

Mr. Govr. Morris moved to commit also the following proposition on the same subject.

"Full faith ought to be given in each State to the public acts, records, and judicial proceedings of every other State; and the Legislature shall by general laws, determine the proof and effect of such acts, records, and proceedings". and it was committed nem: contrad:

5

JAMES MADISON, FEDERALIST, NO. 42, 287
22 Jan. 1788

The power of prescribing by general laws the manner in which the public acts, records and judicial proceedings of each State shall be proved, and the effect they shall have in other States, is an evident and valuable improvement on the clause relating to this subject in the articles of confederation. The meaning of the latter is extremely indeterminate; and can be of little importance under any interpretation which it will bear. The power here established, may be rendered a very convenient instrument of justice, and be particularly beneficial on the borders of contiguous States, where the effects liable to justice, may be suddenly and secretly translated in any stage of the process, within a foreign jurisdiction.

6

AN ACT TO PRESCRIBE THE MODE IN WHICH THE PUBLIC ACTS, RECORDS AND JUDICIAL PROCEEDINGS IN EACH STATE, SHALL BE AUTHENTICATED SO AS TO TAKE EFFECT IN EVERY OTHER STATE
1 Stat. 122 (1790)

Be it enacted by the Senate and House of Representatives of the United States of America in Congress assembled, That the acts of the legislatures of the several states shall be authenticated by having the seal of their respective states affixed thereto: That the records and judicial proceedings of the courts of any state, shall be proved or admitted in any other court within the United States, by the attestation of the clerk, and the seal of the court annexed, if there be a seal, together with a certificate of the judge, chief justice, or presiding magistrate, as the case may be, that the said attestation is in due form. And the said records and judicial proceedings authenticated as aforesaid, shall have such faith and credit given to them in every court within the United States, as they have by law or usage in the courts of the state from whence the said records are or shall be taken.

APPROVED, May 26, 1790.

7

ARMSTRONG V. CARSON
1 Fed. Cas. 1140, no. 543 (C.C.D.Pa. 1794)

WILSON, Circuit Justice. There can be no difficulty in this case. If the plea would be bad in the courts of New-Jersey, it is bad here: for whatever doubts there might be on the words of the constitution the act of congress effectually removes them; declaring in direct terms, that the record shall have the same effect in this court, as in the court from which it was taken. In the courts of New-Jersey no such plea would be sustained; and, therefore, it is inadmissible in any court sitting in Pennsylvania.

Bradford then proposed settling the interest; but WILSON, Justice, observed, that he had had more than one occasion to object to the court's interposing, in any form, to assess damages. In some states, he said, it had, indeed, grown into a practice; and the courts had in that, and, perhaps, in many other instances, done the business which ought to go to a jury. Lewis referred to a case in the supreme court of the United States, in which this point had been made, tho' not directly, decided: but the judge said, it was not the foundation of the judgment, of the court, and that, in his opinion, a writ of enquiry was the regular mode of proceeding.

It being suggested, however, that the usage in the state

courts was to enter the judgment generally; and that the plaintiff must ascertain the debt, and issue execution at his own peril; that mode was adopted on the present occasion. Judgment for the plaintiff.

8

HITCHCOCK V. AICKEN
1 Caines 460 (N.Y. 1803)

THOMPSON J. The question now submitted to the court is, whether it was competent for the defendant, on the trial to go into evidence as to the merits of the judgment obtained in Vermont; or, in other words, whether this judgment is to be considered as a foreign judgment, and only *prima facie* evidence of the debt?

This case was submitted without argument, and the only point, I conceive, presented for consideration is, whether it was competent for the defendant, on the trial, to open the judgment, and go into an inquiry into the original merits of the action tried in the state of Vermont. I shall assume, in the examination of this question, as points conceded, and which I think, the case will fully authorize me to take for granted, that there was a fair and impartial trial had between these parties in the state of Vermont, and that by the laws and usage of that state, the judgment would be conclusive between the parties there. If such was not the case, it was incumbent on the defendant either to disclose it by pleading, or set it up as a defence, under a general plea. Nothing is here set forth in any way impeaching the justice of this judgment, nor any allegation that it was irregularly or unduly obtained. If I am correct, then, as to the true question presented by the case, and the object of the defendant was to go into an examination of the cause on his part, as if it had never been before tried, I should say it was not competent for him to go into such an examination, but that the judgment was conclusive between the parties. As a general rule on this subject, I should consider judgments in neighboring states *prima facie* evidence of the demand, but liable to be opened and examined in the same manner only as they would be in the state where they were rendered. This I think a plain and simple rule, calculated to promote the ends of justice, and the one necessarily resulting from the political connection between the states; imposed by the constitution and law of the united government relating to this subject. To say that every action of slander, assault and battery, &c. or for a fraud, as was the case before us, and which had been fairly tried, and fully examined in a neighboring state, and judgment rendered, should be again opened, as if no trial had been had, would be manifestly unjust, and tending to oppression. To say that the judgment shall be conclusive between the parties would, in many instances, be giving it a more binding force than it has in the state where rendered; and to put it on the footing of foreign judgments altogether, would be considering that part of

the constitution relative to the records and judicial proceedings of other states as a dead letter: and, besides, to say this judgment is to be considered in the light of a foreign judgment only, might perhaps, leave the question doubtful and unsettled how far it was examinable. In the case of *Walker* v. *Witter*, Doug. Rep. 4, it is decided that a foreign judgment is *prima facie* evidence of the debt, by which I understand the court to mean, that it is not incumbent upon the *plaintiff*, in the first instance, to prove the ground, nature and extent of the demand on which the judgment had been obtained. Thus far, I think, judgments obtained in sister states ought to be considered analogous to foreign judgments; and in the case of *Sinclair* v. *Fraser*, Doug. 5, in note, decided in the House of Lords, on an appeal from the court of sessions in Scotland, the same principle was adopted as to a foreign judgment being *prima facie* evidence of the debt; but the court there said, that it was competent to the *defendant to impeach the justice of it, or to show it to have been irregularly or unduly obtained.* These would appear to be terms sufficiently broad to authorize the opening the judgment in every possible case; for it would be impossible to decide whether injustice had been done by the original judgment, without examining the whole merits of the action. Independent, however, of this consideration, I cannot view the judgment obtained in the state of Vermont in the light of a foreign judgment only, without disregarding the constitution of the United States, and the act of congress, as having no relation to the subject. The 4th article of the constitution declares, "That full faith and credit shall be given in each state to the public acts, records and judicial proceedings of every other state, *and the congress may, by general laws, prescribe the manner in which such acts, records and proceedings shall be proved, and the effect thereof."* This article, I think, manifestly presents two subjects for legislative provision; 1st. To prescribe the manner of proving such acts, records and proceedings; and 2dly. Their effect. In pursuance of this power we find congress, by an act passed 26th May, 1790, (Laws U. S. vol. 1, 159,) after prescribing the mode of proof, declaring, "That the said *records and judicial proceedings,* authenticated as aforesaid, shall have *such faith and credit* given to them, in every court within the United States, as they have by law or usage in the courts of the state from whence the said records, are or shall be taken. The framers of this constitution, doubtless, well understood the light in which foreign judgments were viewed in courts of justice, and must have intended, by this article, to place the states upon a different footing with respect to each other than that on which they stood in relation to foreign nations; had not this been their intention, they would have been silent on the subject. I am aware that the old confederation contained a similar article, (4th article,) declaring that "Full faith and credit shall be given in each of these states to the records, acts and judicial proceedings of the courts and magistrates of every other state." The construction to be given to this article, came, in some measure, under consideration in several of the state courts prior to the adoption of the constitution, but in no case, as far as my researches have extended, under circumstances analogous to the present; and, so far as the cases that I have examined look to the present question, I think we shall find principles recognized which are in perfect unison with those I have adopted. In the case of *James v. Allen*, 1 Dall. 188, decided in Pennsylvania, in the court of *common pleas*, in Philadelphia county, in the year 1786, the question directly before the court was, whether the defendant's *discharge from imprisonment*, by virtue of an insolvent act of the state of New Jersey, would entitle him to a like discharge in Pennsylvania, and the court determined not. But the decision was founded on the nature and terms of the New Jersey insolvent act, saying it was a private act, local in its nature and local in its terms, and went no farther than to discharge him from imprisonment in the *jail of Essex county, in the state of New Jersey*. And the case of *Phelps v. Holker*, 1 Dall. 261, decided in the supreme court of Pennsylvania, in the year 1788, was an action of debt, brought on a judgment obtained in Massachusetts, under their foreign attachment act, and the court decided that it was not *conclusive*, on the ground that it was a proceeding *in rem*, and ought not to be extended farther than the property attached, the act declaring that the judgment and execution in a foreign attachment shall only go against *the goods attached*. The case of *Kibbe v. Kibbe*, Kirby's Rep. 119, decided in the superior court of the state of Connecticut, in the year 1786, was an action of debt upon a judgment obtained in Massachusetts, and the court refused to sustain the action, on the ground that the defendant had not been personally served with process to appear in the original cause. The court saying, *full credence* ought to be given to the judgments of the courts in any of the United States, where both parties are within the jurisdiction of such courts at the time of commencing the suit, and are duly served with the process, and have, or might have had, a fair trial of the cause. Thus, we see, in these cases that the court examined into the law of the state where the proceedings were had, in order to determine their operation and effect. But, as far as any decision in the circuit court of the United States ought to have weight in giving a construction to the constitution and act of congress, we have the question settled in the case of *Armstrong v. Carsons*, 2 Dall. 302, decided in Pennsylvania, in the year 1794. The question before the court was, whether *nil debet* was a good plea to an action of debt on a judgment obtained in the superior court of New Jersey; and *Wilson*, Justice, said *if the plea would be bad in the courts of New Jersey, it is bad here*; for whatever doubts there might be on the words of the constitution, the act of congress effectually removes them, declaring, in direct terms, that the record shall have the same *effect* in this court as in the court from which it was taken. The rule intended by the court to be prescribed here, clearly was the one which would have been adopted by the court in the state where the judgment was rendered. Although the act of congress does not adopt the term *effect*, as stated by the judge, yet, if it means any thing, it means to declare the effect. It says, "The said records and judicial proceedings, authenticated as aforesaid, shall have *such faith and credit* given to them, in every court within the United States, as they have, by law or usage, in the courts of the state from whence the said records are, or shall be taken." If the constitution, instead of saying the

records &c. shall have *full faith and credit* given them, had adopted the precise language of this act, it appears to me there would have been but little doubt but that it would have been considered equivalent to declaring such records to have the like *effect* in every court within the United States as in the courts of the state where rendered. It being a subject within the power of congress to declare the *effect*, I do not see why the act ought not to receive the same construction. If nothing more was intended than to declare the manner of authenticating such records and proceedings, this part of the act is useless; nay, worse it is mischievous, being calculated to mislead. I am the more inclined to think congress intended to declare the effect, because the rule there adopted appears to me to be the only one that could, with propriety, be prescribed, as there was no general and uniform practice in the different states on this subject. If a judgment in the state of Connecticut would not be conclusive there, but only *prima facie* evidence, it would be unreasonable to consider it conclusive here; and if conclusive there between the parties, I can see no substantial reason against considering it so here. When the matter has been once litigated, and the merits fairly tried, it appears to me to be contrary to sound principles, and tending to promote litigation, and against the very genius and spirit of the article of the constitution above referred to, again to open the judgment. I think the rule laid down by the court, in the case of *Kibbe v. Kibbe*, above cited, is founded in justice and good sense, that the judgments of courts, in sister states, ought to receive full credence where both parties were within the jurisdiction of the court at the time of commencing the suit, and were duly served with process, and had, or might have had, a fair trial of the cause. This I take to have been the situation of the case now before us; and, on this ground, I am of opinion, it was not competent for the defendant to go into evidence as to the merits of the original judgment.

I am sensible, that the case of *Armstrong v. Carsons*, 2 Dall. 302, stands in opposition to this doctrine. That was an action of debt in the circuit court of the United States, for the district of Pennsylvania, brought on a judgment obtained in New Jersey, in which the counsel for the defendant yielded the position that the judgment was conclusive; and the court, without a previous discussion, adopted the idea, on the supposition that the act of congress had declared the effect to be conclusive. The presiding judge, in delivering the opinion of the court, states the act as having *expressly declared the effect*. In terms, he was evidently inaccurate, and whatever respect may be due to the decisions of that court, its opinion, in this instance, does not appear to me to be correct, nor to have been founded on a deliberate examination of the subject.

Upon the construction of this article of the constitution, and the act of congress, I am, therefore, of opinion, that the judgments of other states are to be considered in the light of foreign judgments, and, when made the foundation of a suit in our own courts, are not conclusive, but from courtesy, are to be admitted as presumptive evidence only of a title to recover, according to our own laws. To allow them a greater effect might be attended with much inconvenience, and produce an irregular interference of jurisdiction between different states, and, in some cases, enable them to prescribe the law to each other. The consequences cannot easily be foreseen, and might often lead to injustice and individual oppression.

I am of opinion that the verdict be set aside, and a new trial be awarded.

. . . . .

KENT, J. The important question arising in this case is, what is to be the effect in this court, of the judgment in Vermont, according to the constitution and laws of the United States?

The constitution declares that a full faith and credit shall be given in each state, to the public acts, records, and judicial proceedings of every other state, and that congress may, by general laws, prescribe the manner in which such act, records, and proceedings shall be proved, and the effect thereof.

This injunction, that they were to receive *full faith and credit* in every state, made a part also of the articles of confederation; but, under those articles, it seems to have been understood that the question of the *effect* of such records and judicial proceedings was still left open. In the case of *James* v. *Allen,* 1 Dall. 188, in the court of common pleas at Philadelphia, in the year 1786, a question arose on the effect of a discharge under the insolvent law of New Jersey and the construction of this article in the confederation was brought into discussion, and it was contended that a judgment, or other judicial proceedings of another state, was, by this article, rendered unexaminable, and conclusive evidence.

But the court said, that the article would not admit of that construction, and that is was chiefly intended to oblige each state to receive the records of another, as full evidence of such acts and judicial proceedings.

Again, in the case of *Phelps* v. *Holker,* 1 Dall. 261, in the supreme court of Pennsylvania, in April term, 1788, an action of debt was brought upon a judgment in Massachusetts; which judgment was obtained against the defendant by default, and founded on an attachment of a blanket, which was shown to the sheriff as the reputed property of the defendant, and the question was, whether the judgment was conclusive evidence of the debt. It was contended, on one side, that the judgment was, by the articles of confederation, rendered conclusive, and that it made no difference in the case that the judgment was obtained by the process of a foreign attachment. The other side insisted that the articles of confederation provide only that, *in matters of evidence,* mutual faith and credit should be given, and especially, that they ought not to be conclusive when founded on foreign attachment. The court decided, that the defendant was still at liberty to controvert and deny the debt, and that the articles of confederation must not be construed to work such evident injustice as was contained in the doctrine urged by the plaintiff. Another case I shall mention was that of *Kibbe* v. *Kibbe,* Kirby, 119, decided in the superior court of Connecticut, in the year 1786. It was an action of debt on a judgment obtained in Massachusetts by default, and founded on the attachment of a handkerchief, and so, like the preceding case, a proceeding *in rem.* The question came before the court on de-

murrer, and judgment was given for the defendant, on the ground that the court in Massachusetts had no jurisdiction of the cause; but the court admitted that full credence ought to be given to judgments in other states, where both parties were within the jurisdiction of the court, and the defendant duly served with process, and had, or might have had, a fair trial of the cause.

It appears from these decisions, that judgments in other states were not regarded under the confederation as of binding and conclusive effect; and the defendant was admitted to deny the regularity and equity of the proceedings by which the judgment was obtained. This was placing the judgments of the other states on the basis of foreign judgments, which are received only as *prima facie evidence* of the debt; and it lies with the defendant to impeach the justice thereof, or to show them to have been irregularly or unduly granted. *Sinclair* v. *Fraser,* cited in Doug. 5, note, and in Appendix, p. 6, 7, in the case of *Galbraith* and *Neville.*

Such being the received construction of the injunction, that *full faith and credit* was to be given to the judicial proceedings of other states, it remains to see whether the case is altered under the existing constitution of the United States. That constitution, by authorizing congress to prescribe not only the manner in which the acts, records and proceedings of other states shall be proved, but their effect evidently distinguished between giving *full faith and credit,* and the giving effect to the records of another state, and until congress shall have declared by law what that effect shall be, the records of different states are left precisely in the situation they were in under the articles of confederation.

The act of congress of 26th May, 1790, is entitled "An act to prescribe the mode in which the public acts, records, and judicial proceedings in each state shall be authenticated, so as to take effect in every other state." After prescribing the mode of authentication, it declares that the records and judicial proceedings so authenticated, shall have *such faith and credit* given to them in every court within the United States, as they have by law or usage in the courts of the state from whence they are taken. This act leaves the question as to the *effect* of such records precisely where it found it. The articles of confederation, in the first instance and the constitution, in the second, had already declared that such records and proceedings were to receive *full faith and credit;* and this act, without prescribing the effect, defines, or, rather, qualifies, the faith and credit they are to receive. Instead of *full* faith and credit, they are to receive *such* faith and credit. We are bound to give the judgment faith and credit, and this faith and credit was considered by the state courts, while sitting under the government of the articles of confederation, as requiring full assent to the proceedings contained in the record, as matters of evidence and fact, but not as absolutely barring the door against any examination of the regularity of the proceedings, and the justice of the judgment.

I ought here to notice the case of *Armstrong* v. *Executors of Carson,* 2 Dall. 302, as leaning against the conclusions I have drawn. It was an action of debt brought in the circuit court of the United States for Pennsylvania district, on a judgment obtained in the state of New Jersey.

The question was, whether the plea of *nil debet* was good, and the court was of opinion, the plea being bad in New Jersey, was bad there also; for whatever *doubts* there might be on the words of the *constitution*, the act of congress effectually removed them, by declaring, in direct terms, that the record should have the same *effect* in that court as in the court from which it was taken. But the reason given for this opinion, if the report of the case be correct, is clearly founded in mistake.

The act of congress does not declare the record shall have the same *effect*, but only the same *faith and credit*, and there is a manifest and essential difference between the one mode of expression and the other. If, therefore, as the court intimated, there were doubts on the words of the constitution, those doubts, so far from being removed, are rather increased by the law. The language of the constitution is, at least, as cogent and comprehensive, if not more so, than the language of the law.

It is pretty evident that the constitution meant nothing more by full faith and credit, than what respected the evidence of such proceedings; for the words are applied to public acts, as well as to judicial matters; nor ought the act of congress to be carried further than the words will warrant. When we reflect in what manner judgments may, in some instances, be obtained, as in the cases cited, by the attachment of a handkerchief or blanket, it is more favorable to the harmony of the union, and to public justice, that the judgments of the several states should be put on the footing of foreign judgments, than that they should be held absolutely binding and conclusive, or as much so as they may be by the laws of the state which authorized the proceeding; and if we may question the binding force of the proceeding or judgment in one case, we may in another; for, the acts of congress has no exceptions, and must receive a uniform construction. If a debtor be discharged from imprisonment, or from his debts, by the insolvent act of some other state; or if their courts be authorized to grant a stay of suits for a time, are we bound by these acts; for they all are, or may be, judicial proceedings. There are no considerations of national policy that could induce us to suppose the act of congress went the whole length of closing the investigation of the judgment. It would be going further than ever was done in any civilized country, even with respect to its own dominions. Between England and Scotland, England and Wales, (*Walker* v. *Witter*, Doug. 1; *Sinclair* v. *Fraser*, cited in the notes, and *Galbraith* v. *Neville*, 29 Geo. III. cited in the Appendix, p. 5,) or England and its colonial establishments the union is as intimate and as interesting as between the several states; and yet the judgments in Scotland, (Kaims' Equity, vol. 2, 365, 377,) or Wales, or Jamaica, for instance, are held to be foreign judgments. So the court of sessions, in Scotland, consider judgments rendered in England as foreign judgments; that they have no intrinsic authority *extra territorium;* and that in actions upon them, they are to be presumed just till the contrary be proved; and if they are shown to be unjust, or irregular, the suit upon them will not be sustained.

The judgments of other states have been treated in this court in the light of foreign judgments, by admitting the plea of *nil debet* to be the proper plea, instead of the plea of *nul tiel record*. The court had intimated doubts on the question in prior cases; (*Le Conte* v. *Pendleton*, April term 1799, and *Cobbets* ads. *Rush*, January term, 1801;) but in the case of *Post and another* v. *Nerby*, in January term last, they decided that *nul tiel record* was a bad plea; and it follows, pretty conclusively, that if a judgment of another state is not to be treated in the pleadings as a record, it cannot have the same obligatory force. So in the case of *Phelps* v. *Bryant*, Administrator, decided at the last term, we refused to sustain an action on a decree of the superior court of Connecticut, founded on the service of a summons within this state. An act of the legislature had rendered all judgments and decrees, founded on such service, void, as far as respected our own government. But if the decree in that case was of conclusive effect under the constitution and laws of the union, the plea to the merits of that decree, as resulting from the irregular commencement of the suit, would have been bad notwithstanding our statute.

The result of my opinion is, that the judgment in question is to be considered in the light of a foreign judgment, and only *prima facie* evidence of the demand.

Receptum est optima ratione in executione sententiae alibi latae, servari jus loci in quo fit executio, non ubi res judicata est. 2 Huber. 540.

9

TAYLOR V. BRIDEN
8 Johns. R. 172 (N.Y. 1811)

KENT, Ch. J. delivered the opinion of the court. The judgment in *Maryland*, upon which this suit was brought, was rendered against the defendant as an endorsor of a foreign bill of exchange, and he now contends that he was not chargeable, by reason of the want of due notice of the non-acceptance, and of the non-payment of the bill. Whether notice of the non-acceptance of the bill,. without accompanying that notice with the protest for non-acceptance, was competent, under the law of merchants, to charge the party, is a point which we need not now discuss, as the suit in *Maryland* was upon the *protest* for non-payment, as well as for the non-acceptance; and the non-payment, if supported by the requisite notice and proof, was sufficient to sustain the action. It has been urged to the court that there was not due diligence in giving notice of non-payment, and that the question of diligence is open here for investigation, notwithstanding the trial and judgment in the other state. But we are by no means satisfied that such an inquiry ought now to be pursued, after the question has been once fairly litigated and decided. The question of reasonable notice is a compound of law and fact, to be submitted to a jury. (6 *East*, 3. and 14. *in notis*.

1 *Sch.* and *Lefroy*, 461. 1 *Campb.* 248.) The judgment in *Maryland* is presumptive evidence of a just demand; and it was incumbent upon the defendant, if he would obstruct the execution of the judgment here, to show, by positive proof, that it was irregularly or unduly obtained. We do not know the whole amount of the evidence that may have been given upon the trial in *Maryland.* The record contains a deposition, but does not state whether any, or what additional proof was given. To try over again, as of course, every matter of fact which had been duly decided by a competent tribunal, would be disregarding the comity which we justly owe to the courts of other states, and would be carrying the doctrine of re-examination to an oppressive extent. It would be the same as granting a new trial in every case, and upon every question of fact. Suppose a recovery in another state, or in any foreign court, in an action for a *tort*, as for an assault and battery, false imprisonment, slander, &c. and the defendant was duly summoned and appeared, and made his defence, and the trial was conducted orderly and impartially, according to the rules of a civilized jurisprudence, is every such case to be tried again here upon the merits? I much doubt whether the rule can ever go this length. The general language of the books is, that the defendant must *impeach* the judgment, by showing, affirmatively, that it was unjust, by being irregularly or unfairly procured.

In the case of *Hitchcock and Fitch* v. *Aickin*, (1 *Caines*, 460,) this court went no further than to decide the general principle, that a judgment of another state was not conclusive, but was to be placed upon the footing of a foreign judgment under the *English* law. The question then is, how far, and to what extent, do the *English* courts permit foreign judgments to be opened, to let in a re-examination of the merits.

The case of *Sinclair* v. *Fraser*, contains the rule of the *English* courts. It was decided by the House of Lords, on the 4th of *March*, 1771, upon an appeal from the Court of *Sessions* in *Scotland.* (Cited by Mr. *Wedderburne*, the solicitor-general, in the case of the *Duchess of Kingston*, 11 *State Tr.* 222.) A suit was brought upon a judgment in *Jamaica;* and the question was, what should be the effect of the judgment; and the Court of *Sessions* refused to give any effect to it, and held the party bound to prove the ground, the nature and the extent of his demand. But upon appeal to the House of Lords, the judgment of the Court of *Sessions* was reversed, and the rule of law was stated in the judgment of reversal; "that the judgment of the court of *Jamaica* ought to be received, as evidence, *prima facie*, of the debt; and that it lies on the defendant to impeach the *justice* of it, or to show that it was *irregularly* and *unduly* obtained." This decision was cited in *Galbraith* v. *Neville*, (K. B. 25 *Geo.* III. *Doug. Rep.* 3d edit. p. 5. note,) and Mr. Justice *Buller* said, that it had always been considered as establishing the true rule.

In the present case, the defendant has certainly not succeeded in impeaching the judgment. He has, at most, only excited doubts, under the obscure, and, perhaps, very imperfect testimony before us, as to the fact of due diligence in giving notice of the protest for non-payment. And when the party has once litigated his case, before a competent

jurisdiction, and when no fraud or unfairness is pretended, every doubt and every presumption arising on a matter in *pais* ought to be turned against him. We may, with propriety, adopt the observation of Lord *Kenyon*, in the case of *Galbraith* v. *Neville*, as stated in a note to 5 *East*, 475, that "without entering into the question how far a foreign judgment was impeachable, it was, at all events, clear, that it was *prima facie* evidence of the debt, and that no evidence had been adduced to impeach this." The motion on the part of the defendant, for a new trial, is therefore denied.

Motion denied

10

MILLS v. DURYEE
7 Cranch 480 (1813)

STORY, J., delivered the opinion of the Court as follows:

The question in this case is whether *nil debet* is a good plea to an action of debt brought in the Courts of this district on a judgment rendered in a Court of record of the state of New York, one *of the United States.*

The decision of this question depends altogether upon the construction of the constitution and laws of the United States.

By the constitution it is declared that "full faith and credit shall be given in each state to the public acts, records and judicial proceedings of every other state; and the congress may, by general laws, prescribe the manner in which such acts, records and proceedings shall be proved and the effect thereof."

By the act of 26th May, 1790, ch. 11, congress provided for the mode of authenticating the records and judicial proceedings of the state Courts, and then further declared that "the records and judicial proceedings, authenticated as aforesaid, shall have such faith and credit given to them in every Court within the United States, as they have by law or usage in the Courts of the state from whence the said records are or shall be taken."

It is argued, that this act provides only for the admission of such records as evidence, but does not declare the effect of such evidence, when admitted. This argument cannot be supported. The act declares, that the record, duly authenticated, shall have such faith and credit as it has in the state court from whence it is taken. If in such court it has the faith and credit of evidence of the highest nature, viz., record evidence, it must have the same faith and credit in every other court. Congress have therefore declared the effect of the record, by declaring what faith and credit shall be given to it.

It remains only then to inquire, in every case, what is the effect of a judgment in the state where it is rendered? In the present case, the defendant had full notice of the suit, for he was arrested and gave bail, and it is beyond all doubt, that the judgment of the supreme court of New

York was conclusive upon the parties in that state. It must, therefore, be conclusive here also.

But it is said, that admitting that the judgment is conclusive still *nil debet* was a good plea; and *nul tiel record* could not be pleaded, because the record was of another state, and could not be inspected or transmitted by *certiorari.* Whatever may be the validity of the plea of *nil debet,* after verdict, it cannot be sustained in this case. The pleadings in an action are governed by the dignity of the instrument on which it is founded. If it be a record, conclusive between the parties, it cannot be denied but by the plea of *nul tiel record;* and when congress gave the effect of a record to the judgment, it gave all the collateral consequences. There is no difficulty in the proof. It may be proved in the manner prescribed by the act, and such proof is of as high a nature as an inspection, by the court, of its own record, or as an exemplification would be in any other court of the same state. Had this judgment been sued in any other court of New York, there is no doubt that *nil debet* would have been an inadmissible plea. Yet the same objection might be urged, that the record could not be inspected. The law, however, is undoubted, that an exemplification would, in such case, be decisive. The original need not be produced.

Another objection is, that the act cannot have the effect contended for, because it does not enable the courts of another state to issue executions directly on the original judgment. This objection, if it were valid, would equally apply to every other court of the same state where the judgment was rendered. But it has no foundation. The right of a court to issue execution depends upon its own powers and organization. Its judgments may be complete and perfect, and have full effect, independent of the right to issue execution.

The last objection is, that the act does not apply to courts of this district. The words of the act afford a decisive answer, for they extend "to every court within the United States." Were the construction contended for by the plaintiff in error to prevail, that judgments of the state courts ought to be considered *primâ facie* evidence only, this clause in the constitution would be utterly unimportant and illusory. The common law would give such judgments precisely the same effect. It is manifest, however, that the constitution contemplated a power in congress to give a conclusive effect to such judgments. And we can perceive no rational interpretation of the act of congress, unless it declares a judgment conclusive, when a court of the particular state where it is rendered would pronounce the same decision. On the whole, the opinion of a majority of the court is, that the judgment be affirmed, with costs.

JOHNSTON, J. (*dissenting.*)—In this case, I am unfortunate enough to dissent from my brethren. I cannot bring my mind to depart from the canons of the common law, especially, the law of pleading, without the most urgent necessity. In this case, I see none.

A judgment of an independent unconnected jurisdiction is what the law calls a foreign judgment, and it is everywhere acknowledged, that *nil debet* is the proper plea to such a judgment. *Nul tiel record* is the proper plea only

when the judgment derives its origin from the same source of power with the court before which the action on the former judgment is instituted. The former concludes to the country, the latter to the court, and is triable only by inspection.

If a different decision were necessary to give effect to the 1st section 4th article of the constitution, and the act of 26th of May, 1790, I should not hesitate to yield to that necessity. But no such necessity exists; for by receiving the record of the state Court, properly authenticated, as conclusive evidence of the debt, full effect is given to the constitution and the law. And such appears, from the terms made use of by the legislature, to have been their idea of the course to be pursued in the prosecution of the suit upon such a judgment. For *faith* and *credit* are terms strictly applicable to evidence.

I am induced to vary in deciding on this question from an apprehension that receiving the plea of *nul tiel record* may at some future time involve this Court in inextricable difficulty. In the case of Holker and Parker, which we had before us this term, we see an instance in which a judgment for $150,000 was given in Pennsylvania upon an attachment levied on a cask of wine and debt brought on that judgment in the state of Massachusetts. Now if in that action *nul tiel record* must necessarily be pleaded, it would be difficult to find a method by which the enforcing of such judgment could be avoided. Instead of promoting then the object of the constitution by removing all cause for state jealousies, nothing could tend more to enforce them than enforcing such a judgment. There are certain eternal principles of justice which never ought to be dispensed with, and which Courts of justice never can dispense with but when compelled by positive statute. One of those is, that jurisdiction cannot be justly exercised by a state over property not within the reach of its process, or over persons not owing them allegiance or not subjected to their jurisdiction by being found within their limits. But if the states are at liberty to pass the most absurd laws on this subject, and we admit of a course of pleading which puts it out of our power to prevent the execution of judgments obtained under those laws, certainly an effect will be given to that article of the constitution in direct hostility with the object of it.

I will not now undertake to decide, nor does this case require it, how far the Courts of the United States would be bound to carry into effect such judgments; but I am unwilling to be precluded, by a technical nicety, from exercising our judgment at all upon such cases.

11

ELMENDORF v. TAYLOR
10 Wheat. 152 (1825)

Mr. Chief Justice MARSHALL. . . . Were this question now for the first time to be decided, a considerable contrariety of opinion respecting it would prevail in the court; but it will be unnecessary to discuss it, if the point shall appear to be settled in Kentucky. This court has uniformly professed its disposition, in cases depending on the laws of a particular state, to adopt the construction which the courts of the state have given to those laws. This course is founded on the principle, supposed to be universally recognised, that the judicial department of every government, where such department exists, is the appropriate organ for construing the legislative acts of that government. Thus, no court in the universe, which professed to be governed by principle, would, we presume, undertake to say, that the courts of Great Britain, or of France, or of any other nation, had misunderstood their own statutes, and therefore erect itself into a tribunal which should correct such misunderstanding. We receive the construction given by the courts of the nation, as the true sense of the law, and feel ourselves no more at liberty to depart from that construction, than to depart from the words of the statute. On this principle, the construction given by this court to the constitution and laws of the United States is received by all as the true construction; and on the same principle, the construction given by the courts of the several states to the legislative acts of those states, is received as true, unless they come in conflict with the constitution, laws or treaties of the United States. If, then, this question has been settled in Kentucky, we must suppose it to be rightly settled.

12

McCormick v. Sullivant
10 Wheat. 192 (1825)

March 16th, 1825. WASHINGTON, Justice, delivered the opinion of the court, and after stating the case, proceeded as follows:—The question which the plea of Thompson's heirs, and the answer of Winship's heirs, presents, is, whether the general decree of dismissal of the bill in equity, filed by the present plaintiffs in the federal district court of Ohio, against the ancestor of these defendants, under whom they respectively claim title, is a bar of the remedy which is sought to be enforced by the present suit? The reason assigned by the replication, why that decree cannot operate as a bar, is, that the proceedings in that suit do not show that the parties to it, plaintiffs and defendants, were citizens of different states, and that, consequently, the suit was *coram non judice*, and the decree void.

But this reason proceeds upon an incorrect view of the character and jurisdiction of the inferior courts of the United States. They are all of limited jurisdiction; but they are not, on that account, inferior courts, in the technical sense of those words, whose judgments, taken alone, are to be disregarded. If the jurisdiction be not alleged in the proceedings, their judgments and decrees are erroneous, and may, upon a writ of error or appeal, be reversed for that cause. But they are not absolute nullities. This opinion

was strongly intimated, if not decided, by this court, in the case of *Kempe's Lessee* v. *Kennedy* (5 Cranch 185), and was, afterwards, confirmed by the decision made in the case of *Skillern's Executors* v. *May's Executors* (6 Ibid. 267). That suit came before this court upon a writ of error, where the decree of the court below was reversed, and the cause remanded for further proceedings to be had therein. After this, it was discovered by that court, that the jurisdiction was not stated in the proceedings, and the question was made, whether that court could dismiss the suit for that reason? This point, on which the judges were divided, was certified to the supreme court, where it was decided, that the merits of the cause having been finally decided in this court, and its mandate only requiring the execution of its decree, the court below was bound to carry that decree into execution, notwithstanding the jurisdiction of that court was not alleged in the pleadings. Now, it is very clear, that, if the decree had been considered as a nullity, on the ground that jurisdiction was not stated in the proceedings, this court could not have required it to be executed by the inferior court. We are, therefore, of opinion, that the decree of dismissal relied upon in this case, whilst it remains unreversed, is a valid bar of the present suit, as to the above defendants.

13

HALL v. WILLIAMS
6 Pick. 232 (Mass. 1828)

PARKER, C. J. . . . All agree, that until the adoption of the national constitution, the principles of the common law which are applicable in every country to judgments of the tribunals of foreign countries, were applicable to the judgments of the courts of the several States when sought to be enforced by the judiciary power of any State other than that in which they were rendered: that is, they were considered only as *primâ facie* evidence of debt, were to be declared upon, not as records, but as showing a consideration for a promise or debt, and a plea of *nul tiel record* was not a proper plea, but *non assumpsit* or *nil debet*, according to the form of the declaration.

This was definitively settled in England as the true character of foreign judgments, as early as the year 1778, and had long before been the received law of that country. *Walker* v. *Witter*, 1 Doug. 1.

Such was the law, before the revolution, in this and all the colonies and provinces, and so continued until the adoption of the national government, as appears by numerous decisions in the several State courts, which will hereafter be cited to another point; except that by the statute of 14 *Geo.* 3, *c.* 2, in Massachusetts, it was provided that an action of debt might be sustained on judgments of courts of the *neighboring colonies*, (alluding probably to the old league between the then New England provinces,) and that the records of those judgments, attested by the clerk of the courts rendering the same, should be good and sufficient evidence. And the statute of the Commonwealth of 1795, *c.* 61, placed the judgments of courts of all the United States on the same footing on which they were intended to be placed by the constitution of the United States; an act of legislation which was quite unnecessary after the act of Congress of 1790 before referred to. Under these provisions the judgments of sister States are no longer to be considered as mere foreign judgments, to be proved like other facts by testimony to the jury; but are to be treated altogether as domestic judgments in regard to the proof of their existence, and therefore the issue on a plea of *nul tiel record* is to be tried by the court only, so that such a plea concluding to the country is undoubtedly bad, as before stated.

But in regard to the conclusiveness of such judgments to all intents and purposes, there is yet a question of considerable importance, which has been discussed and decided in almost every State in the union in which there are printed reports of their judicial decisions; and the question is presented now by the issue taken on the second and third pleas to this action. The defendants, in answer to the declaration, say that neither of them was served with notice of the suit in which the judgment was rendered, nor appeared or authorized any one to appear for him in the action, and that Fiske was never an inhabitant of, or resident in the State of Georgia. The plaintiffs reply that the defendants are estopped by the record to deny these facts, and the record being set forth on oyer, the defendants demur to the replication of estoppel. If it appeared by the record that the defendants had notice of the suit, or that they appeared in defence, we are inclined to think that it could not be gainsaid; for as we are bound to give full faith and credit to the record, the facts stated in it must be taken to be true, judicially; and if they should be untrue by reason of mistake or otherwise, the aggrieved party must resort to the authorities where the judgment was rendered, for redress, for he could not be allowed to contradict the record by a plea and by an issue to the country thereon. But if the record does not show any service of process, or any appearance in the suit, we think he may be allowed to avoid the effect of the judgment here, by showing that he was not within the jurisdiction of the court which rendered it, for it is manifestly against first principles, that a man should be condemned, either criminally or civilly, without an opportunity to be heard in his defence.

It cannot be pretended, we think, that a citizen of Massachusetts, against whom a judgment may have been rendered in Illinois or Missouri, he never having been within a thousand miles of those States, should be compelled by our courts to execute that judgment, it not appearing by the record that he received any manner of notice that any suit was pending there against him, and being ready to show that he never had any dealings with the party who has obtained the judgment; and yet this must be the consequence, if the doctrine contended for by some is carried to its full length, *viz.* that the record of a judgment is to have exactly the same effect here as it would have in Illinois or Missouri; for in those States, if the process has been served according to their laws, which may be in a

manner quite consistent with an utter ignorance of the suit by the party without the State, the judgment would be binding there until reversed by some proceedings recognised by their laws.

If it be said that a party thus aggrieved may obtain redress by writ of error, or a new trial, in the State where the judgment was rendered, it is a sufficient answer, that never having been within their jurisdiction or amenable to their laws, he shall not be compelled to go from home to a distant State, to protect himself from a judgment, which never, according to universal principles of justice, had any legal operation against him.

The laws of a State do not operate, except upon its own citizens, *extra territorium*; nor does a decree or judgment of its judicial tribunals, except so far as is allowed by comity, or required by the constitution of the United States; and neither of these can be held to sanction so unjust a principle. If the States were merely foreign to each other, we have seen that a judgment in one would not be received in another as a record, but merely as evidence of debt, controvertible by the party sued upon it. By the constitution, such a judgment is to have the same effect it would have in the State where it was rendered; that is, it is to conclude as to every thing over which the court which rendered it had jurisdiction. If the property of a citizen of another State, within its lawful jurisdiction, is condemned by lawful process there, the decree is final and conclusive. If the citizen himself is there and served with process, he is bound to appear and make his defence, or submit to the consequences; but if never there, there is no jurisdiction over his person, and a judgment cannot follow him beyond the territories of the State, and if it does, he may treat it as a nullity, and the courts here will so treat it, when it is made to appear in a legal way that he was never a proper subject of the adjudication. These principles were settled in a most lucid and satisfactory course of reasoning by Chief Justice *Parsons*, in the opinion of the Court delivered by him in the case of *Bissell* v. *Briggs*, 9 Mass. R. 462. This exposition of the constitutional provision respecting the records and judicial proceedings, authenticated as the act of Congress requires, takes a middle ground between the doctrine as held by the Court of this State in the case of *Bartlett* v. *Knight*, 1 Mass. R. 401, and by the court of New York in the case of *Hitchcock et al* v. *Aicken*, 1 Caines's R. 460, in both of which it was held that the constitution and act of Congress had produced no other effect than to establish definitely the mode of authentication, leaving in other respects such judgments entirely upon the footing of foreign judgments according to the principles of the common law. But in the case of *Bissel* v. *Briggs*, the principle settled is, that by virtue of the provision of the constitution and the act of legislation under it, a judgment of another State is rendered in all respects like domestic judgments, when the court where it was recovered had jurisdiction over the subject acted upon and the person against whom it was rendered, leaving open for inquiry in the court where it was sought to be enforced the question of jurisdiction, and taking the obvious distinction between the effect of the judgment upon *property* within the territory, and the *person* who was without it. It was thought that this was carrying the sanctity of judgments of other States as far as was consistent with the safety of the citizen who was not amenable to their laws, and as far as is required by the spirit or letter of the constitution of the United States.

The doctrine thus established here has been approved and adopted by the courts of the great States of Pennsylvania and New York, in both of which before it had been held, that the judgments of the several States were to be treated as foreign judgments. The case of *Borden* v. *Fitch*, 15 Johns. Rep. 121, is full to this point, and was after the publication of the case of *Mills* v. *Duryee*, determined in the Supreme Court of the United States, 7 Cranch, 481, hereafter to be noticed. In this case the opinion of Chief Justice *Parsons* in the case of *Bissell* v. *Briggs* is spoken of as putting the question upon a sound principle; and so also in the case of *Benton* v. *Burgot*, 10 Serg. & Rawle, 242, in Pennsylvania, where the same doctrine is laid down in the opinion of the court delivered by Mr. Justice *Duncan*.

The principle upon which this exception is made to the conclusiveness in every particular, of the judgments of other States, is well expressed by Mr. Justice *Johnson*, of the Supreme Court of the United States, when dissenting from the decision of the court in the case of *Mills* v. *Duryee*. He says it is an eternal principle of justice, "that jurisdiction cannot be justly exercised by a State over property not within the reach of its process, or over persons not owing them allegiance or not subjected to their jurisdiction by being found within their limits."

Indeed, so palpable is this principle, that no doubt could exist in the mind of any lawyer upon the subject, but for the construction supposed to be given to the constitution of the United States, and the act of Congress following it, in the case of *Mills* v. *Duryee*, 7 Cranch, 481, and re-sanctioned in the case of *Hampton* v. *M'Connel*, 3 Wheat. 234, in the brief opinion delivered by Chief Justice *Marshall*. This construction, when first referred to in this Court in the case of the *Commonwealth* v. *Green*, was supposed to have put an end to all questions on this subject, and to have established as the law of the land, that a judgment recovered in one State by a citizen thereof against a citizen of another, was absolute and incontrovertible, and would admit of no inquiry even as to the jurisdiction of the court which rendered it. This Court yielded a painful deference to the decision, without that close examination it would have received if presented to them otherwise than incidentally, and if its bearing had been of importance in the case then before the Court; but the notice taken of the case was merely the expression of an opinion *arguendo*, and not a judicial determination of the question. And as a further reason for not receiving the doctrine implicitly as authority, it may be remarked, that the case to which it was applied was one clearly within the jurisdiction of the court which decided it, so that the point now raised was not brought into question.

This is not the first occasion we have had to regret a too prompt submission to the decision of the Supreme Court of the United States; not however from any diminution of entire respect for that eminent tribunal, but because we have found that further consideration has brought about a qualification of the doctrine which seemed to have been definitively settled, or that some qualifying principle in the case itself has been overlooked by us, in our readiness to yield supremacy to that court on all questions in which by the constitution their judgment is paramount. I allude to the decisions of that court on State insolvent laws, in the case of *Sturges* v. *Crowninshield*, 4 Wheat. 122, the effect of which we understood to be, to overrule the decision of this Court in the case of *Blanchard* v. *Russell*; in consequence of which we dismissed several cases which might have been maintained on the grounds of that decision. We have since learned by the case of *Ogden* v. *Saunders*, 12 Wheat. 213, that there is no decision of the Supreme Court of the United States militating with our decision, and feel ourselves justified in recurring to the principle there decided as the law of this Commonwealth.

The case of *Mills* v. *Duryee* has, as its importance merited, undergone a revision in almost every State court in the Union, of whose decisions we have any printed account; and the opinion has been unanimous, without the dissenting voice, so far as we can learn, of a single judge, that that case, however unqualified it may appear in the report, does not warrant the conclusion, that judgments of State courts are in all respects the same when carried into another State to be enforced, as they are in the State wherein they are rendered, but that in all instances, the jurisdiction of the court rendering the judgment may be inquired into. In truth, all of them sanctioning the principles, and some of them by express reference, which were asserted by this Court in the case of *Bissell* v. *Briggs*, as the only just exposition of the provision in the constitution of the United States in relation to the records and judicial proceedings of States.

In the State of Maine it does not appear that their courts, since the separation, have been called to consider the question.

In New Hampshire there is a most express limitation of the effect of such judgments, similar to the case of *Bissell* v. *Briggs*: the opinion being delivered by *Bell* J., now a senator of that State in Congress, and concurred in by *Woodbury* J., holding the same situation. *Thurber* v. *Blackbourne*, 1 New Hampsh. R. 246.

In Connecticut the same doctrine was held and ably enforced by Chief Justice *Hosmer*, in the opinion of the whole Court as delivered by him. *Aldrich* v. *Kinney*, 4 Connect. R. 380.

In New York and Pennsylvania the cases before cited maintain the same doctrine; also *Shumway* v. *Stillman*, 4 Cowen, 292.

In New Jersey it was decided that the judgment of a State court is conclusive under the constitution and laws of the United States, between the parties, both parties being in court and a defence made or opportunity had to make it, not otherwise. *Curtis* v. *Gibbs*, Pennington, 405.

In Kentucky, if the judgment of a State court be founded on the appearance of the defendant or the actual service of process on his person, the judgment is conclusive, except when it might be impeached in the courts of the State where it is given. But where the defendant did not appear and had constructive notice only, (as by attachment or publication,) it is not conclusive, but may be inquired into and impeached. *Rogers* v. *Coleman*, Hardin, 413. The opinion delivered by Mr. Justice *Trimble*, now of the Supreme Court of the United States, is very full and able, and puts the conclusiveness of the judgment altogether upon the fact of the party's having had an opportunity to defend himself.

With such a cloud of witnesses in favor of the construction given to the clause of the constitution which is in question, by this Court in the case of *Bissell* v. *Briggs*, we may well rest upon that as the true construction, if it is not the most clearly and explicitly overruled by the only tribunal whose authority ought to be submitted to, the Supreme Court of the United States. But notwithstanding all these decisions, many of which are subsequent in point of time to the case of *Mills* v. *Duryee*, and most of them commenting on it, we should be bound to give up the point, if that case settles the question as conclusively as it has been supposed it did.

But all the State judges who have considered that case, are of opinion that it was intended only to embrace judgments where the defendant had been a party to the suit by an actual appearance and defence, or at least by having been duly served with process when within the jurisdiction of the court which gave it; and they formed their opinion upon the following clause in the opinion of Mr. Justice *Story*, viz. "In the present case the defendant had full notice of the suit, for he was arrested and gave bail, and it is beyond all doubt that the judgment of the Supreme Court of New York was conclusive upon the parties in that State." If this is all that was intended to be decided, the case harmonizes with the general course of decisions in the State courts as before cited, and it is in no respect different from the decision of this Court in the case of *Bissell* v. *Briggs*.

In a slight examination of the case made by us when considering the case of *Commonwealth* v. *Green*, we supposed the decision to be more extensive, and felt bound to yield to it in a collateral question not essential to a determination of the cause then before the Court; but having the general question now brought distinctly before us, we fully concur with the numerous learned judges who have given the restricted construction as above stated, to the decision of the case of *Mills* v. *Duryee*.

We therefore are all of opinion, that the record of a judgment of a court of another State is not conclusive evidence, but that to the extent stated in the case of *Bissell* v. *Briggs* it is examinable, in order to ascertain whether the party against whom it is produced was subject to the judicial process on which it is grounded; and that where it appears by the record itself that there was no appearance, and no notice which he was bound to attend to, the judgment against him is a dead letter beyond the territory within which it was pronounced.

14

MORTON V. NAYLOR

1 Hill 439 (S.C. 1833)

O'NEALL, J. These two cases present the same question "whether the Statute of Limitations of this State, is a good plea to an action of debt brought in this State, on a judgment recovered in another State?" Both the decisions of the judges below (GANTT and RICHARDSON) were, that the plea was not good; and with them I concur fully. The difficulties in which the question is involved, seem to me to arise from the footing on which judgments of a sister State have been too often considered: they have been sometimes regarded as precisely analogous to foreign judgments at common law. The Constitution and the Act of Congress have been frequently entirely overlooked. In New York, a long train of decisions placed the judgments of a sister State on the footing of forcing judgments at common law; but in the case of Andrews *v.* Montgomery, 19 J. R. 162, the Court, with Ch. J. Spencer at their head, retraced their steps, and conformed to the decision in Mills *v.* Duryee, 7 Cranch, 481. In this State, our error commenced with the case of Hammond & Hattaway *v.* Smith, 1 Brev. M. S. R. 112. 1 Brev. Dig. 317, (note) that case simply determined that *nil debit* and not *nul tiel* record was the proper plea to an action of debt on a judgment recovered in North Carolina. That decision was made in 1802, by Johnson, Trezvant, Waities, and Grimkie, against the opinions of Bay & Brevard: the opinion of the latter, I think, took the true ground. He said, "the decisions in England, in regard to *foreign* judgments cannot, in my judgment, apply to this case. Foreign judgments are not there considered as *records* to which implicit faith is due; they are considered only as *prima facie* evidence of a debt, and may be examined into. They are regarded in the light of *simple contracts*, and either debt or assumpsit may be maintained on them. 2 Vern. 541. 13 Vin. Ab. 414. Doug. 1. 1 Dall. 261. But surely this is not the footing on which the solemn judgments and judicial proceedings of the Courts of law, of the several States, (united under the same General Government and constituting the *nation*,) are placed, in relation to each other State." JOHNSON, J. who delivered the leading opinion of the majority, placed his decision on a ground which is wholly untenable. He said "upon the usual replication, '*habetur tale recordum*,' the original record ought to be inspected; but this is impossible. *An exemplification of our own judgments is not evidence in such cases*, and, *therefore*, an exemplification of the judgment of a sister State certainly ought not to be." It had escaped the attention of the learned judge, that the common law, on which his judgment was formed, was in the instance which he selected as the reason from which he drew his inference, altered by the Act of 1721, P. L. 117. The preamble to the clause recites that "it may prove inconvenient to have the original records taken out of the respective offices, in order to be produced at the several Courts in this province:" to remedy this evil it was enacted, that an attested copy of any acts or ordinances of the General Assembly of this Province, signed by the Secretary of this Province, and also *attested copies of all records*, signed by the keeper of such records respectively, shall be deemed and allowed *for as good evidence* in the said Courts, as the original could or might have been, if produced to the said Courts." Under this act it is perfectly clear that an attested copy of a judgment obtained in this State, is as good evidence as the original in any State of the pleadings in a cause, and in any one of the different Courts of this State. The question has not been, so far as my knowledge extends, directly made or decided; but in the case of Gage *v.* Sartor, 2 Con. Rep. (by Mill) 247, which was an action of debt on a judgment, the plea was *nul tiel* record, the replication, I presume the usual one, *"habetur tale recordum:"* the proof to support it was an exemplification of a judgment recovered in Laurens District. No objection was taken to the sufficiency of the proof, notwithstanding the learned counsel for the defendant (Mr. CRENSHAW, now one of the judges of Alabama) tasked his ingenuity to the uttermost, for objections arising out of the record, to prevent the plaintiff's recovery. I think I may venture to say, that if the original record, and not the exemplification ought to have been given in evidence, it would hardly have escaped the attention of three such lawyers as Mr. Justice CRENSHAW, my brother JOHNSON, (who was the plaintiff's attorney,) and the late Judge NOTT, who presided at the trial on the circuit.

In a case subsequent to the case of Hammond & Hattaway *v.* Smith, Flournoy *v.* Durkey, decided November, 1808, 3 Brev. M. S. Rep. 192, the action was debt on a judgment recovered in Georgia, the plea *nul tiel* record; the replication averred the existence of such a judgment, and prayed that it might be inspected; the proof was an exemplification of the judgment according to the act of Congress; it was objected to as insufficient, on the ground that the original record ought to have been produced. The presiding judge (Brevard) overruled the objection, and his decision was sustained by the whole court. This decision, it seems to me, in effect reversed that in the case of Hammond & Hattaway *v.* Smith; and from that time to this, the effect of a judgment of a sister State as evidence, has been regarded as an open question.

In Cameron *v.* Wurtz, 4 M'C. 278, it was held, that "in marshalling the assets of an insolvent estate, a judgment recorded in another State, only ranks as a simple contract." That case, however, does not touch the question to be decided in this. The distinction was recognized in that case, that under the constitution of the United States, the judgment, as matter of evidence, was entitled to full faith and credit. The authority of Mills *v.* Duryee, and Hampton *v.* McConnell, was, by the judge who delivered the opinion, supposed not to conflict with the decision then made.

In the case of Miller *v.* Miller, 1 Bail, 242, it was held that an action could not be maintained on a judgment recovered in another State, against a defendant residing in this, who had not been served with process to answer to the action, or who had not appeared to or defended the suit, that decision went on the ground that the judgment

could have no extra territorial operation; and out of the State in which it was recovered, it must, so far as it went to establish a liability on the part of the defendant, be treated as void.

These decisions of this State are all which I have been able to find, which have glanced at the question before us; and they, I think, leave us free to look to the Constitution of the United States and the Act of Congress, for the rule by which this case is to be decided.

The 1st section, 4th art. of the Constitution of the United States, provides that *"full faith and credit* shall be given in each State to the public acts, records and judicial proceedings of every other State. And the Congress may, by general laws, prescribe the manner in which such acts, records and proceedings shall be proved, and *the effect thereof."* The Act of Congress (1790) directs the manner in which "such acts, records and proceedings shall be proved"; and then provides that "the said records and judicial proceedings, authenticated as aforesaid, shall have such faith and credit given to them, in every Court within the United States, as they have *by law or usage, in the Courts of the State from whence the said records are or shall be taken."* 1 Brev. Dig. 317.

After reading the Constitution of the United States and this provision of the Act of Congress, it would seem to be too plain to admit of doubt, that a recovery in another State must, when authenticated as directed by the Act, be regarded for all purposes of evidence in a cause in this State, to have precisely the same effect as if the case was trying in the State where the judgment was recovered. This is giving effect to the words of the Constitution and the Act of Congress. Any other rule would deprive them of it. To say that it was only *prima facie* evidence of a debt by simple contract, is leaving us at common law, and declaring the States to be foreign to each other in a matter where, by their constitution, they have thought proper, in effect, to say "we are one people."

The Constitution of the United States is the declared will of the people of each State, for their own government; and if South Carolina and her co-States had thought proper to declare that the effect of, and the remedy for the enforcement of a judgment, should be the same out of as within the State where it was recovered, we should have no right to say that the common law rule, which the constitution abrogated, should be set up. If this be so, to the extent of the proposition which I have stated, it cannot be doubted that, as the constitution has declared that full *faith and credit* shall be given to the judgment, and authorized Congress to prescribe *"the effect thereof,"* and Congress has prescribed that it shall have such faith and credit given to it in every Court within the United States, as it has by law or usage, in the Courts of the State from whence the said record is, or shall be taken; it must, when given in evidence in a Court of this State, be treated as a record. It does not stand as a foreign judgment at common law; the latter is not regarded as a record, the former is. When authenticated according to the Act of Congress, and received in evidence in a cause, it is as a judgment of record that it is so received, and that we are obliged to regard it; it is conclusive of everything decided by it. The only question which arises under the plea of the Statute of Limitations of this State to an action predicated on such a debt, is presented by reading the Act of Congress—"would such a plea be good in the Courts of the State whence the judgment is?" This question concedes to the judgment, the faith and credit which it would have at home; and this is giving effect to the Act of Congress. It is not pretended that the plea would be good in the State from which the judgment comes; and therefore it cannot be good here.

In coming to this conclusion, it is gratifying to be sustained by the decision of the supreme court. In the case of Mills v. Duryee, 7 Cranch, 481, Judge STORY, who delivered the opinion, speaking of the judgment of another State, said, "if it be a record conclusive between the parties, it cannot be denied, but by the plea of *nul tiel* record; and when Congress gave the *effect of a record to the judgment, it gave all the collateral consequences.* There is no difficulty in the proof. It may be proved in the manner prescribed by the Act, and *such proof is of as high a nature as an inspection by the Court, of its own record, or as an exemplification would be in any other Court of the same State.*"

No evil is to be apprehended from such a decision. The question whether the Court had jurisdiction of the person of the defendant or of the subject matter of the suit, will still remain open to investigation. If the Court pronouncing this judgment, had no jurisdiction of the subject matter, the judgment would be necessarily void; if it had no jurisdiction of the person of the defendant, it could only operate in *rem*, and could not create a debt by judgment against the defendant, to be enforced in another State.

15

JOSEPH STORY, COMMENTARIES ON THE
CONSTITUTION 3:§§ 1298–1307
1833

---

§ 1298. The articles of confederation contained a provision on the same subject. It was, that "full faith and credit shall be given in each of these states to the records, acts, and judicial proceedings of the courts and magistrates of every other state." It has been said, that the meaning of this clause is extremely indeterminate; and that it was of but little importance under any interpretation, which it would bear. The latter remark may admit of much question, and is certainly quite too loose and general in its texture. But there can be no difficulty in affirming, that the authority given to congress, under the constitution, to prescribe the form and effect of the proof is a valuable improvement, and confers additional certainty, as to the true nature and import of the clause. The clause, as reported in the first draft of the constitution, was, "that full faith and credit shall be given in each state to the *acts of the legislature,* and to the records and judicial proceedings of the courts and magistrates of every other state." The amendment was subsequently reported, substantially in the form, in which it now stands, except that the words, in

the introductory clause, were, "Full faith and credit *ought to* be given," (instead of "shall"); and, in the next clause, the *legislature shall,* (instead of, the congress *"may"*); and in the concluding clause, "and the effect, which judgments obtained in one state shall have in another," (instead of, *"and the effect thereof."*) The latter was substituted by the vote of six states against three; the others were adopted without opposition; and the whole clause, as thus amended, passed without any division.

§ 1299. It is well known, that the laws and acts of foreign nations are not judicially taken notice of in any other nation; and that they must be proved, like any other facts, whenever they come into operation or examination in any forensic controversy. The nature and mode of the proof depend upon the municipal law of the country, where the suit is depending; and there are known to be great diversities in the practice of different nations on this subject. Even in England and America the subject, notwithstanding the numerous judicial decisions, which have from time to time been made, is not without its difficulties and embarrassments.

§ 1300. Independent of the question as to *proof,* there is another question, as to the *effect,* which is to be given to foreign judgments, when duly authenticated, in the tribunals of other nations, either as matter to maintain a suit, or to found a defence to a suit. Upon this subject, also, different nations are not entirely agreed in opinion or practice. Most, if not all of them, profess to give some effect to such judgments; but many exceptions are allowed, which either demolish the whole efficiency of the judgment, as such, or leave it open to collateral proofs, which in a great measure impair its validity. To treat suitably of this subject would require a large dissertation, and appropriately belongs to another branch of public law.

§ 1301. The general rule of the common law, recognised both in England and America, is, that foreign judgments are *primâ facie* evidence of the right and matter, which they purport to decide. At least, this may be asserted to be in England the preponderating weight of opinion; and in America it has been held, upon many occasions, though its correctness has been recently questioned, upon principle and authority, with much acuteness.

§ 1302. Before the revolution, the colonies were deemed foreign to each other, as the British colonies are still deemed foreign to the mother country, and, of course, their judgments were deemed foreign judgments within the scope of the foregoing rule. It followed, that the judgments of one colony were deemed re-examinable in another, not only as to the jurisdiction of the court, which pronounced them; but also as to the merits of the controversy, to the extent, in which they were then understood to be re-examinable in England. In some of the colonies, however, laws had been passed, which put judgments in the neighbouring colonies upon a like footing with domestic judgments, as to their conclusiveness, when the court possessed jurisdiction. The reasonable construction of the article of the confederation on this subject is, that it was intended to give the same conclusive effect to judgments of all the states, so as to promote uniformity, as well as certainty, in the rule among them. It is probable, that it did not invariably, and perhaps not generally, receive such a construction; and the amendment in the constitution was, without question, designed to cure the defects in the existing provision.

§ 1302. The clause of the constitution propounds three distinct objects; first, to declare, that full faith and credit shall be given to the records, &c. of every other state; secondly, to prescribe the manner of authenticating them; and thirdly, to prescribe their effect, when so authenticated. The first is declared, and established by the constitution itself, and is to receive no aid, nor is it susceptible of any qualification by congress. The other two are expressly subjected to the legislative power.

§ 1303. Let us then examine, what is the true meaning and interpretation of each section of the clause. "Full faith and credit shall be given in each state to the public acts, records, and judicial proceedings of every other state." The language is positive, and declaratory, leaving nothing to future legislation. "Full faith and credit *shall* be given;" what, then, is meant by full faith and credit? Does it import no more than, that the same faith and credit are to be given to them, which, by the comity of nations, is ordinarily conceded to all foreign judgments? Or is it intended to give them a more conclusive efficiency, approaching to, if not identical with, that of domestic judgments; so that, if the jurisdiction of the court be established, the judgment shall be conclusive, as to the merits? The latter seems to be the true object of the clause; and, indeed, it seems difficult to assign any other adequate motive for the insertion of the clause, both in the confederation and in the constitution. The framers of both instruments must be presumed to have known, that by the general comity of nations, and the long established rules of the common law, both in England and America, foreign judgments were *primâ facie* evidence of their own correctness. They might be impugned for their injustice, or irregularity; but they were admitted to be a good ground of action here, and stood firm, until impeached and overthrown by competent evidence, introduced by the adverse party. It is hardly conceivable, that so much solicitude should have been exhibited to introduce, as between confederated states, much less between states united under the same national government, a clause merely affirmative of an established rule of law, and not denied to the humblest, or most distant foreign nation. It was hardly supposable, that the states would deal less favourably with each other on such a subject, where they could not but have a common interest, than with foreigners. A motive of a higher kind must naturally have directed them to the provision. It must have been, "to form a more perfect Union," and to give to each state a higher security and confidence in the others, by attributing a superior sanctity and conclusiveness to the public acts and judicial proceedings of all. There could be no reasonable objection to such a course. On the other hand, there were many reasons in its favour. The states were united in an indissoluble bond with each other. The commercial and other intercourse with each other would be constant, and infinitely diversified. Credit would be every where given and received; and rights and property would belong to citizens of every state in many other states than that, in which

they resided. Under such circumstances it could scarcely consist with the peace of society, or with the interest and security of individuals, with the public or with private good, that questions and titles, once deliberately tried and decided in one state, should be open to litigation again and again, as often as either of the parties, or their privies, should choose to remove from one jurisdiction to another. It would occasion infinite injustice, after such trial and decision, again to open and re-examine all the merits of the case. It might be done at a distance from the original place of the transaction; after the removal or death of witnesses, or the loss of other testimony; after a long lapse of time, and under circumstances wholly unfavourable to a just understanding of the case.

§ 1304. If it should be said, that the judgment might be unjust upon the merits, or erroneous in point in law, the proper answer is, that if true, that would furnish no ground for interference; for the evils of a new trial would be greater, than it would cure. Every such judgment ought to be presumed to be correct, and founded in justice. And what security is there, that the new judgment, upon the re-examination, would be more just, or more conformable to law, than the first? What state has a right to proclaim, that the judgments of its own courts are better founded in law or in justice, than those of any other state? The evils of introducing a general system of re-examination of the judicial proceedings of other states, whose connexions are so intimate, and whose rights are so interwoven with our own, would far outweigh any supposable benefits from an imagined superior justice in a few cases. Motives of this sort, founded upon an enlarged confidence, and reciprocal duties, might well be presumed to have entered into the minds of the framers of the confederation, and the constitution. They intended to give, not only faith and credit to the public acts, records, and judicial proceedings of each of the states, such as belonged to those of all foreign nations and tribunals; but to give to them *full* faith and credit; that is, to attribute to them positive and absolute verity, so that they cannot be contradicted, or the truth of them be denied, any more than in the state, where they originated.

§ 1305. The next section of the clause is, "And the congress may by general laws prescribe the manner, in which such acts, records, and proceedings shall be proved,—*and the effect thereof.*" It is obvious, that this clause, so far as it authorizes congress to prescribe the mode of authentication, is wholly beside the purpose of the preceding. Whatever may be the faith and credit due to the public acts, records, and proceedings of other states, whether *primâ facie* evidence only, or conclusive evidence; still the mode of establishing them in proof is of very great importance, and upon which a diversity of rules exists in different countries. The object of the present provision is to introduce uniformity in the rules of proof, (which could alone be done by congress.) It is certainly a great improvement upon the parallel article of the confederation. That left it wholly to the states themselves to require any proof of public acts, records, and proceedings, which they might from time to time deem advisable; and where no rule was prescribed, the subject was open to the decision of the judicial tribunals, according to their own views of the local usage and jurisprudence. Many embarrassments must necessarily have grown out of such a state of things. The provision, therefore, comes recommended by every consideration of wisdom and convenience, of public peace, and private security.

§ 1306. But the clause does not stop here. The words added are, "and the effect thereof." Upon the proper interpretation of these words some diversity of opinion has been judicially expressed. Some learned judges have thought, that the word "thereof" had reference to the proof, or authentication; so as to read, "and to prescribe the effect of such proof, or authentication." Others have thought, that it referred to the antecedent words, "acts, records, and proceedings;" so as to read, "and to prescribe the effect of such acts, records, and proceedings." Those, who were of opinion, that the preceding section of the clause made judgments in one state conclusive in all others, naturally adopted the former opinion; for otherwise the power to declare the effect would be wholly senseless; or congress could possess the power to repeal, or vary the full faith and credit given by that section. Those, who were of opinion, that such judgments were not conclusive, but only *primâ facie* evidence, as naturally embraced the other opinion; and supposed, that until congress should, by law, declare what the effect of such judgment should be, they remained only *primâ facie* evidence.

§ 1307. The former seems now to be considered the sounder interpretation. But it is not, practically speaking, of much importance, which interpretation prevails; since each admits the competency of congress to declare the effect of judgments, when duly authenticated; so always, that full faith and credit are given to them; and congress by their legislation have already carried into operation the objects of the clause. The act of 26th of May, 1790, (ch. 11,) after providing for the mode of authenticating the acts, records, and judicial proceedings of the states, has declared, "and the said records and judicial proceedings, authenticated as aforesaid, shall have *such* faith and credit given to them in every court within the United States, as they have by law or usage in the courts of the state, from whence the said records are or shall be taken." It has been settled upon solemn argument, that this enactment does declare the effect of the records, as evidence, when duly authenticated. It gives them the same faith and credit, as they have in the state court, from which they are taken. If in such court they have the faith and credit of the highest nature, that is to say, of *record* evidence, they must have the same faith and credit in every other court. So, that congress have declared the *effect* of the records, by declaring, what degree of faith and credit shall be given to them. If a judgment is conclusive in the state, where it is pronounced, it is equally conclusive every where. If re-examinable there, it is open to the same inquiries in every other state. It is, therefore, put upon the same footing, as a domestic judgment. But this does not prevent an inquiry into the jurisdiction of the court, in which the original judgment was given, to pronounce it; or the right of the state itself to exercise authority over the persons, or the subject matter. The constitution did not mean to confer a new power or jurisdiction; but simply to regulate the effect of the acknowledged jurisdiction over persons and things within the territory.

SEE ALSO:

Walker v. *Witter*, 1 Doug. 1, 99 Eng. Rep. 1, 4–6 (K.B. 1778)
Records of the Federal Convention, Farrand 2:577, 601, 637
Miller v. *Hall*, 1 Dall. 229 (Pa. 1788)
Phelps v. *Holker*, 1 Dall. 261 (Pa. 1788)
Delafield v. *Hand*, 3 Johns. R. 310 (N.Y. 1802)
Bartlet v. *Knight*, 1 Mass. 401 (1805)
Pearsall v. *Dwight*, 2 Mass. 84 (1806)
Rose v. *Himely*, 4 Cranch 241 (1808)
Hudson v. *Guestier*, 4 Cranch 293 (1808)
Green v. *Sarmiento*, 10 Fed. Cas. 1117, no. 5,760 (C.C.D. Pa. 1810)
Robinson v. *Ward*, 8 Johns. R. 86 (N.Y. 1811)
Fenton v. *Garlick*, 8 Johns. R. 194 (N.Y. 1811)
Armroyd v. *Williams*, 1 Fed. Cas. 1132, no. 538 (C.C.D. Pa. 1811), aff'd sub nom. *Williams* v. *Armroyd*, 7 Cranch 423 (1813)
Bissell v. *Briggs*, 9 Mass. 462 (1813)
Hampton v. *M'Connel*, 3 Wheat. 234 (1818)
Jones's Adm. v. *Hook's Adm.*, 2 Rand. 303 (Va. 1824)
Marietta Bank v. *Pindall*, 2 Rand. 465 (Va. 1824)
Raynham v. *Canton*, 3 Pick. 293 (Mass. 1825)
United States v. *Amedy*, 11 Wheat. 392 (1826)
Elliot v. *Peirsol*, 1 Pet. 328 (1828)
Shumway v. *Stillman*, 4 Cowen 292 (N.Y. 1829)
Clarke's Adm. v. *Day*, 2 Leigh. 172 (Va. 1830)
Gulick v. *Loder*, 1 Green 68 (N.J. 1832)
Keene v. *McDonough*, 8 Pet. 308 (1834)
Bank of the United States v. *Donnally*, 8 Pet. 361 (1834)

Article 4, Section 2, Clause 1

The Citizens of each State shall be entitled to all Privileges and Immunities of Citizens in the several States.

---

1. Connecticut Constitutional Ordinance of 1776, sec. 3
2. North Carolina Constitution of 1776, art. 40
3. Vermont Constitution of 1777, ch. 1, art. 17
4. Thomas Jefferson, A Bill Declaring Who Shall Be Deemed Citizens of This Commonwealth, May 1779
5. Articles of Confederation, art. 4, 1 Mar. 1781
6. Records of the Federal Convention
7. *Bayard* v. *Singleton*, 1 N.C. 42 (1787)
8. *Apthorp* v. *Backus*, Kirby 407 (Conn. 1788)
9. James Wilson, Of Man, as a Member of a Confederation, Lectures on Law, 1791
10. *Campbell* v. *Morris*, 3 Harr. & McH. 535 (Md. 1797)
11. St. George Tucker, Blackstone's Commentaries (1803)
12. *Gardner* v. *Ward*, in *Kilham* v. *Ward*, 2 Mass. 236, 244n.a (1806), in 1.8.4 (citizenship), no. 16
13. *Ainslee* v. *Martin*, 9 Mass. 454 (1813)
14. William Eustis, Admission of Missouri, House of Representatives, 12 Dec. 1820
15. Charles Pinckney, Admission of Missouri, House of Representatives, 13 Feb. 1821
16. William Wirt, Rights of Free Negroes in Virginia, 7 Nov. 1821
17. *Douglass* v. *Stephens*, 1 Del. Ch. 465 (1821)
18. *Corfield* v. *Coryell*, 6 Fed. Cas. 546, no. 3,230 (C.C.E.D.Pa. 1823)
19. *Hall* v. *Williams*, 6 Pick. 232 (Mass. 1828), in 4.1, no. 13
20. Joseph Story, Commentaries on the Constitution (1833)
21. *Crandall* v. *State*, 10 Conn. 339 (1834)

1

CONNECTICUT CONSTITUTIONAL ORDINANCE OF 1776, SEC. 3
Poore 1:258

---

3. That all the free Inhabitants of this or any other of the United States of *America,* and Foreigners in Amity with this State, shall enjoy the same Justice and Law within this State, which is general for the State, in all Cases proper for the Cognizance of the Civil Authority and Court of Judicature within the same, and that without Partiality or Delay.

2

NORTH CAROLINA CONSTITUTION OF 1776, ART. 40
Thorpe 5:2793–94

XL. That every foreigner, who comes to settle in this State, having first taken an oath of allegiance to the same, may purchase, or, by other means, acquire, hold, and transfer land, or other real estate; and after one year's residence, shall be deemed a free citizen.

3

VERMONT CONSTITUTION OF 1777, CH. 1, ART. 17
Thorpe 6:3741

XVII. That all people have a natural and inherent right to emigrate from one State to another, that will receive them; or to form a new State in vacant countries, or in such countries as they can purchase, whenever they think that thereby they can promote their own happiness.

4

THOMAS JEFFERSON, A BILL DECLARING WHO SHALL BE DEEMED CITIZENS OF THIS COMMONWEALTH
May 1779
Papers 2:476–78

Be it enacted by the General Assembly, that all white persons born within the territory of this commonwealth and all who have resided therein two years next before the passing of this act, and all who shall hereafter migrate into the same; and shall before any court of record give satisfactory proof by their own oath or affirmation, that they intend to reside therein, and moreover shall give assurance of fidelity to the commonwealth; and all infants wheresoever born, whose father, if living, or otherwise, whose mother was, a citizen at the time of their birth, or who migrate hither, their father, if living, or otherwise their mother becoming a citizen, or who migrate hither without father or mother, shall be deemed citizens of this commonwealth, until they relinquish that character in manner as herein after expressed: And all others not being citizens of any the United States of America, shall be deemed aliens. The clerk of the court shall enter such oath of record, and give the person taking the same a certificate thereof, for which he shall receive the fee of one dollar. And in order to preserve to the citizens of this commonwealth, that natural right, which all men have of relinquishing the country, in which birth, or other accident may have thrown them, and, seeking subsistance and happiness wheresoever they may be able, or may hope to find them: And to declare unequivocally what circumstances shall be deemed evidence of an intention in any citizen to exercise that right, it is enacted and declared, that whensoever any citizen of this commonwealth, shall by word of mouth in the presence of the court of the county, wherein he resides, or of the General Court, or by deed in writing, under his hand and seal, executed in the presence of three witnesses, and by them proved in either of the said courts, openly declare to the same court, that he relinquishes the character of a citizen, and shall depart the commonwealth; or whensoever he shall without such declaration depart the commonwealth and enter into the service of any other state, not in enmity with this, or any other of the United States of America, or do any act whereby he shall become a subject or citizen of such state, such person shall be considered as having exercised his natural right of expatriating himself, and shall be deemed no citizen of this commonwealth from the time of his departure. The free white inhabitants of every of the states, parties to the American confederation, paupers, vagabonds and fugitives from justice excepted, shall be intitled to all rights, privileges, and immunities of free citizens in this commonwealth, and shall have free egress, and regress, to and from the same, and shall enjoy therein, all the privileges of trade, and commerce, subject to the same duties, impositions and restrictions as the citizens of this commonwealth. And if any person guilty of, or charged with treason, felony, or other high misdemeanor, in any of the said states, shall flee from justice and be found in this commonwealth, he shall, upon demand of the Governor, or Executive power of the state, from which he fled, be delivered up to be removed to the state having jurisdiction of his offence. Where any person holding property, within this commonwealth, shall be attainted within any of the said states, parties to the said confederation, of any of those crimes, which by the laws of this commonwealth shall be punishable by forfeiture of such property, the said property shall be disposed of in the same manner as it would have been if the owner thereof had been attainted of the like crime in this commonwealth.

5

ARTICLES OF CONFEDERATION, ART. 4
1 Mar. 1781

ARTICLE IV. The better to secure and perpetuate mutual friendship and intercourse among the people of the different states in this union, the free inhabitants of each of these states, paupers, vagabonds and fugitives from justice excepted, shall be entitled to all privileges and immunities of free citizens in the several states; and the people of each state shall have free ingress and regress to and from any other state, and shall enjoy therein all the privileges of trade and commerce, subject to the same duties, impositions and restrictions as the inhabitants thereof respectively, provided that such restriction shall not extend so far as to prevent the removal of property imported into any state, to any other state, of which the Owner is an inhabitant; provided also that no imposition, duties or restriction shall be laid by any state, on the property of the united states, or either of them.

6

RECORDS OF THE FEDERAL CONVENTION

[2:173; Committee of Detail]

The free Citizens of each State shall be intitled to all Privileges and Immunities of free Citizens in the sevl States.

[2:187; Madison, 6 Aug.]

XIV

The Citizens of each State shall be entitled to all privileges and immunities of citizens in the several States.

[2:437; Madison, 28 Aug.]

On the question to agree to the 14 article as reported it passed in the affirmative [Ayes—9; noes—1; divided—1.]

[2:443; Madison, 28 Aug.]

Art XIV was taken up.

Genl. Pinkney was not satisfied with it. He seemed to wish some provision should be included in favor of property in slaves.

On the question on art: XIV.

N. H. ay. Mas. ay. Ct. ay. N. J. ay— Pa. ay. Del. ay. Md. ay— Va. ay. N— C— ay. S— C. no. Geo. divided [Ayes—9; noes—1; divided—1.]

[2:577; Committee of Style]

The citizens of each State shall be entitled to all privileges and immunities of citizens of the several States.

[2:637; Mason, 15 Sept.]

Section 2nd, Article 4th—The citizens of one State having an estate in another, have not secured to them the right of removing their property as in the 4th Article of the Confederation—amend by adding the following clause: and every citizen having an estate in two or more States shall have a right to remove his property from one State to another.

(not proposed)

7

BAYARD V. SINGLETON
1 N.C. 42 (1787)

They observed that the cause turned chiefly on the point of *alienage* in Mr. Cornell. For this gentleman having from his birth to the time of his death, been always a British subject, and having always lived under the British government, he owed allegiance to the King of Great Britain, and consequently was never a citizen of this, or any other of the United States, nor owed allegiance thereto. For when here, at the time of the transaction aforementioned, he was under the protection of a British flag. That he was therefore, in contemplation of law, as much an *alien,* and at the time of executing the deed, and, from the time of our independence as much an *alien* ENEMY, as if we had been a separate and independent nation, for any number of years or ages before the commencement of the war which was then carried on.

That it is the policy of all Nations and States, that the lands within their government should not be held by foreigners. And therefore it is a general maxim, that the allegiance of a person who holds land ought to be as permanent to the government who holds it, as the tenure of the soil itself.—That therefore by the civil, as well as by the common law of England, *aliens* are incapacitated to hold lands. For that purpose the civil law has made the contracts with *aliens* void. The law of England, which we have adopted, allows them to purchase, but subjects them to forfeiture immediately; and does not allow an *alien* EN-EMY any political rights at all.

That the premises in question, upon these invariable principles of law, could not from the time our government commenced, have been held by Mr. Cornell; because that in consequence of his owing no allegiance to the State, he had no capacity to hold them, and according to the letter of the law of the land, they must have consequently been forfeited to the sovereignty of the State. That the act of confiscation, in which Mr. Cornell was expressly named, and more particularly the act which especially directed the sale of the very premises in question, must have been at least as effectual in vesting them in the State, as any *office found,* according to the practice in England can be, for vesting any forfeited property in the King.

That the circumstances and limited privileges of persons who were sent out of this State under a particular act of our General Assembly, are not applicable to this case. That the case in Vattel, of the majority of the inhabitants of any country deliberately dissolving their old government, and setting up a new one, is neither in reason, nor in the most essential circumstances, anyways similar to this case. That *Calvin's* case reported in Coke, does by no means reach the leading and characteristic circumstances of this case.

8

APTHORP V. BACKUS
Kirby 407 (Conn. 1788)

Law, C. J. and Ellsworth, J.: . . . A state may exclude aliens from acquiring property within it of any kind, as its safety or policy may direct; as England has done, with regard to real property, saving that in favor of commerce, alien merchants may hold leases of houses and stores, and may, for the recovery of their debts, extend lands, and hold them, and upon ouster have an assize. Dyer, 2, 6.—Bac. Abrid. 84.—But it would be against right, that a division of a state or kingdom should work a forfeiture of property, previously acquired under its laws, and that by its own citizens; which is the case here.—The plaintiff's title to the land in question accrued while she was not an alien, nor could she be affected by the disability of an alien, but was as much a citizen of the now state of Connecticut, as any person at present within it, and her descent was cast under its laws;—her title is also secured by the treaty of peace, which stipulates, that there should be no further forfeitures or confiscations, on account of the war, upon either side.

The subsequent statute of this state, declaring aliens incapable of purchasing or holding lands in the state, does not affect the plaintiff's title, otherwise than by recognizing and enforcing it; for it hath a proviso, that the "act shall not be construed to work a forfeiture of any lands which belonged to any subjects of the king of Great Britain before the late war, or to prevent proprietors of such lands from selling and disposing of the same to any inhabitant of any of the United States."—It is not, indeed, expressly said, that the proprietors of such lands may maintain actions for the possession of them, but this is clearly implied; for lands without the possession are of no use; and wherever the law gives or admits a right, it gives or admits also everything incident thereto, as necessary to the enjoyment and exercise of that right:—And besides, they cannot sell their lands till they first get possession of them; for all sales of land in this state, whereof the grantor is dispossessed, except to the person in possession, are, by express statute, void—So that the plaintiff is not barred of her title, or right of action, either at common law, or by statute.

9

James Wilson, Of Man, as a Member of a Confederation, Lectures on Law
1791
Works 1:264–65

When we say, that the government of those states, which unite in the same confederacy, ought to be of the same nature; it is not to be understood, that there should be a precise and exact uniformity in all their particular establishments and laws. It is sufficient that the fundamental principles of their laws and constitutions be consistent and congenial; and that some general rights and privileges should be diffused indiscriminately among them. Among these, the rights and privileges of naturalization hold an important place. Of such consequence was the intercommunication of these rights and privileges in the opinion of my Lord Bacon, that he considered them as the strongest of all bonds to cement and to preserve the union of states. "Let us take a view," says he, "and we shall find, that wheresoever kingdoms and states have been united, and that union incorporated by a bond of mutual naturalization, you shall never observe them afterwards, upon any occasion of trouble or otherwise, to break and sever again." Machiavel, when he inquires concerning the causes, to which Rome was indebted for her splendour and greatness, assigns none of stronger or more extensive operation than this—she easily compounded and incorporated with strangers. This important subject has received a proportioned degree of attention in forming the constitution of the United States. "The citizens of each state shall be entitled to all privileges and immunities of citizens in the several states." In addition to this, the congress have power to "establish a uniform rule of naturalization throughout the United States."

Though a union of laws is, by no means, necessary to a union of states; yet a similarity in their code of *publick* laws is a most desirable object. The publick law is the great sinew of government. The sinews of the different governments, composing the union, should, as far as it can be effected, be equally strong. "In this point," says my Lord Bacon, "the rule holdeth, which was pronounced by an ancient father, touching the diversity of rites in the church; for finding the vesture of the queen in the psalm (who prefigured the church) was of divers colours; and finding again that Christ's coat was without a seam, concludeth well, in veste varietas sit, scissura non sit."

10

Campbell v. Morris
3 Harr. & McH. 535 (Md. 1797)

On the first point it must be observed; that this law makes a distinction between our own citizens and others, in this, that an attachment cannot be obtained against a citizen of *Maryland,* who is out of the state, unless he has absconded from justice, whereas one may be had against a citizen of any other state, who does not reside here; and hence they contend for the defendant that this law is repugnant to the 4th article of the federal constitution, sec. 2. by which it is declared, "That the citizens of each state shall be entitled to all privileges and immunities of citizens in the several states."

The object of the convention in introducing this clause into the constitution, was to invest the citizens of the different states with the general rights of citizenship; that they should not be foreigners, but citizens. To go thus far was essentially necessary to the very existence of a federate government, and in reality was no more than had been provided for by the first confederation in the fourth article.

But it never could have been the intention of the framers of our national government, to melt down the states into one common mass; to put the citizens of each in the exact same situation, and confer on them equal rights: this principle would have been wholly destructive of the state government.

The expressions, however, of the fourth article convey no such idea. It does not declare that "the citizens of each state shall be entitled to all privileges and immunities of the citizens of the several states." Had such been the language of the constitution, it might, with more plausibility, have been contended that this act of assembly was in violation of it; but such are not the expressions of the article; it only says that "The citizens of the several states shall be entitled to all privileges and immunities of citizens in the several states." Thereby designing to give them the rights of citizenship, and not to put all the citizens of the *United States* upon a level; consequently, the injury, as to the effect of a law of any state, will not be whether it makes a discrimination between citizens of the several states; but whether it infringes upon any civil right, which a man as a member of civil society must enjoy. In the present case we must inquire whether the law of 1795, c. 56. takes from *Robert Morris* any of the privileges of a citizen.

It is difficult to conceive how the act of assembly can have such an effect; how the general provisions of the law can do injury or injustice to any man. To be sure, in particular instances, like all general regulations, it may effect injustice.

A man who resides out of the states, would have a complete exemption from his creditors as to his property in this state, if it was not liable to attachment. He cannot be arrested because no process of the state can reach his person. This property, the only fund for the payment of debts, would be protected, if in such instances as this it may not be seized on attachment, or some other process of a similar nature. If resident in any part of *America*, he may be proceeded against in the federal courts, but if out of the *United States*, there would be no remedy.

This act of assembly can never be in violation of a man's civil rights, until it is proved that to make his property liable for the payment of his debts constitutes the violation.

In the present instance the interest of the absent person is abundantly protected by the provisions of the law. A writ must issue at the time of the attachment, to which the defendant may appear and dissolve the attachment; if he neglect to appear, the property is condemned and sold on a *fieri facias;* he has a year to come in after the attachment, and controvert the propriety of the claim. Can a law of this nature be considered as infringing on the rights or privileges of a citizen? If it were so, a knave could secure his property against all the authority of the government.

If the state, at the adoption of the general government, ought to have retained any portion of independent power, it should be that of legislating on the subject of its own jurisprudence, and the manner of proceeding in courts of justice; the goodness or badness of the provisions made on those subjects, is for the legislatures to decide; the execution of the laws only remains for the courts. The obvious necessity of some mode to recover debts from an absent person, has given rise to the different attachment laws of this state. The law of 1715, c. 40. requires the return of *non est,* against a non-resident, before an attachment can be obtained; this will take in our own citizens, provided they reside out of the state. The act of 1795, c. 56. does not authorize an attachment against a citizen of *Maryland,* unless he absconds from justice, but gives remedy against any other person not being a citizen of this state, and not residing therein." This expression affects citizens of other states. In this way has the assembly thought proper to legislate on this subject; they have made the mode of recovery somewhat more dilatory against the citizens of our own state, than against those of other states; still there is no infraction of the privileges and immunities of a citizen, and, of consequence, no violation of the fourth article of the federal constitution.

11

ST. GEORGE TUCKER,
BLACKSTONE'S COMMENTARIES
1:APP. 365
1803

This article, with some variation, formed a part of the confederation: we have in another place supposed, that the states retain the power of admitting aliens to become denizens of the states respectively, notwithstanding the several acts of congress establishing an uniform rule of naturalization. But such denizens, not being properly citizens, would not, I apprehend, be entitled to the benefit of this article in any other state. They would still be regarded as aliens in every state, but in that of which they may be denizens. Consequently, an alien before he is completely naturalized, may be capable of holding lands in one state, but not of holding them in any other.

12

GARDNER V. WARD, IN KILHAM V. WARD
2 Mass. 236, 244n.a (1806)

(See 1.8.4 [citizenship], no. 16)

13

AINSLEE V. MARTIN
9 Mass. 454 (1813)

PARSONS, C. J. Upon the exception to the replication in this case we shall give no opinion, as the sufficiency of the plea to abate the writ seems to be the principal question.

Our statutes recognize alienage and its effects, but have not defined it. We must therefore look to the common law for its definition. By this law, to make a man an alien, he must be born without the allegiance of the commonwealth: although persons may be naturalized or expatriated by statute, or have the privileges of subjects conferred or secured by a national compact.

But it is said, that by this common law definition the demandant is an alien, because born before the declaration of independence.

To this it is answered, that then all the inhabitants, born within the territory of the late province *of Massachusetts Bay*, and who were born before the declaration of independence, are also aliens.

It is therefore necessary to look back and consider the situation and rights of the people of *Massachusetts*, when they renounced all allegiance to the king of *Great Britain*.

The dispute between the colonies and the mother country was founded on the claim made by the *British* parliament to legislate for the colonies in all cases whatever. In that parliament the colonies were not, and it was morally impossible that they should be, effectually represented: and a submission to this claim would have degraded them to the rank of subjects to their fellow subjects in *Great Britain:* at whose will, with the concurrence of the king, they must have holden and enjoyed their dearest rights and privileges. Our ancestors considered it as a right essential to the character of freemen, to be bound by no laws but those to which they, either personally or by their representatives, had assented. This right was recognized as a fundamental principle of the *English* constitution, and was not forfeited or abandoned by them, when they, with the assent of the king, removed to this country. It was acknowledged that they and their posterity owed and were to owe allegiance to him and his successors, as their sovereign, which was the bond of connection between them and their fellow subjects who remained in *England.*

Although in the early stages of the contest the colonies were willing that parliament should exercise the right of external taxation, for the regulation of the general commerce of all the subjects of the king: yet that parliament should lay internal taxes, or have a right to bind the colonies in all cases, were propositions resisted with great unanimity and zeal. This dispute was continued until the revolutionary war commenced; and it was terminated by the colonies renouncing their allegiance to the king.

Until that renunciation, the people of the province of *Massachusetts Bay* considered themselves as constituting a political corporation which possessed exclusively the powers of legislation, which acknowledged the king of *Great Britain* as sovereign, possessing all the rights, privileges and prerogatives of sovereignty; among which was the right of claiming the allegiance of all persons born within the province, as born within the territory of which he was sovereign.

This people, in union with the people of the other colonies, considered the several aggressions of their sovereign on their essential rights, as amounting to an abdication of his sovereignty. The throne was then vacant: but the people, in their political character, did not look after another family to reign; nor did they establish a new dynasty; but assumed to themselves, as a nation, the sovereign power, with all its rights, privileges and prerogatives. Thus the government became a republick, possessing all the rights vested in the former sovereign; among which was the right to the allegiance of all persons born within the territory of the province of *Massachusetts Bay.*

That the people of *Massachusetts* proceeded on these principles, is evident from several considerations.—After the commencement of the war, when there was no governor or lieutenant governor in the province, the chair was deemed to be vacant; and the major part of the council, agreeably to the provisions of the solemn compact made by charter between the king and his people, assumed the executive power.

After the declaration of independence, no act was passed, confirming or establishing the previous laws, or the rights or interests existing under or derived from them; but they were considered as remaining in force, and as having the same effect, so far as they were not necessarily altered or modified by the substitution of the sovereignty of the people. Indeed the people were too wise at that day, to consider the abdication of their former sovereign as a dissolution of the social compact, as the annulling of all their laws, as an extinction of their rights, and as reducing them to a state of nature, without government, or laws, or political rights, until a new social compact could be established.

It was on this principle, that the legislature in the year 1779, by two several acts, the *conspirators' act,* and the *absentee act,* as they were generally called, enacted that certain persons, and certain descriptions of persons were offenders in withdrawing themselves from the country, and joining or assisting the *British* armies before the declaration of independence: and as offenders against the people, inflicted upon them the punishment of expatriation and forfeiture for that offence. The declaring that those persons, most of whom were born within the territories of the province of *Massachusetts Bay,* should be deemed aliens, would be very absurd, unless they were recognized, before and until the passing of those acts, as subjects.

It was therefore then considered as the law of the land, that all persons born within the territories of the government and people, although before the declaration of independence, were born within the allegiance of the same government and people, as the successor of the former sovereign, who had abdicated his throne. And as his successor, the same government and people have succeeded to all the crown lands within the territory, as lawfully appertaining to them. And as the inhabitants of *England,* born in the reign of the second *James,* were considered as born within the allegiance of his successor, *William* the third; because born in the territory, of which he was the sovereign, he having succeeded by parliamentary designation: so all persons, born within the territories of the province of *Massachusetts Bay* during the reign of the late king, are considered as born within the allegiance of the commonwealth of *Massachusetts,* as his lawful successor.

Although soon after the declaration of independence the people assumed, as the name and style of their political corporation, the appellation of "the government and people of the *Massachusetts Bay* in *New England;*" yet when a new form of administering the government was adopted, the name of "the commonwealth of *Massachusetts*" was assumed, not as successor to the government and people, but as a new and more appropriate appellation of the same political corporation, under a new form of administration. And the provision for continuing the former laws and magistrates was adopted from great caution, and not as introducing in fact any new provision, without which we should have had neither laws nor officers.

From the preceding observations it is very clear that the common law, which was in force, had superseded the necessity of defining by statute alienage or allegiance. And from the definitions of alienage and allegiance, the nature and effect of naturalization and of expatriation are manifest. We now have legal princip[le]s, to direct us in pleading alienage.

The plea of alien friend must allege that the supposed alien was born without the allegiance of the commonwealth. To this rule persons expatriated by force of the conspirators' and absentee acts are exceptions. This alienage must be pleaded specially. To the general plea of alien friend, naturalization may be replied, which places the alien upon the same ground as if born a citizen.

The political relations of the commonwealth furnish other replications.—That although born within the allegiance of the king of *England,* and without the allegiance of the commonwealth, they were inhabitants of this state at the ratification of the treaty of peace between the *United*

States and *Great Britain.*—Or that they are citizens of some other of the *United States,* and so by the federal constitution entitled to the privileges of citizens within this state.— Or British subjects may confess and avoid the plea of alienage by bringing themselves within the provisions of the treaty of amity, commerce and navigation made in the year 1794 between the *United States* and *Great Britain.*

This claim of the commonwealth to the allegiance of all persons born within its territories, may subject some persons who, adhering to their former sovereign, and residing within his dominions, are recognized by him as his subjects, to great inconveniences; especially in time of war, when two opposing sovereigns may claim their allegiance. But this inconvenience cannot alter the law of the land. If they return to the country of their birth, they will be protected as subjects. And their situation is not different in law, whatever may be their equitable claims, from the situations of those citizens of the commonwealth, who may be naturalized in the dominions of a foreign prince. The duties of these persons, arising from their allegiance to the country of their birth, remain unchanged and unimpaired by their foreign naturalization. For by the common law no subject can expatriate himself.

Protection and allegiance are reciprocal. The sovereign cannot refuse his protection to any subject, nor discharge him from his allegiance against his consent: and he will remain a subject, unless disfranchised as a punishment for some crime.—So on the other hand, he can never discharge himself from his allegiance to his sovereign, unless the protection, which is due to him from the laws, is unjustly denied him.

We will now consider the record before us. The plea is very properly a plea in abatement. It alleges the demandant to have been born within the allegiance of the king of *Great Britain:* but it admits him to have been born in *Boston,* within the territories of which the commonwealth of *Massachusetts* is now the sovereign. The plea thus far may be pleaded in abatement to every inhabitant of the state, who was living before the fourth of July 1776. It therefore could not avail the tenant. But the plea goes further, and alleges that the demandant, before July 1776, removed into the province of *Canada,* then and now within the dominions of the king of *Great Britain,* and has never returned.

But we are of opinion that his allegiance to that king was founded on his birth within his dominion of the province of *Massachusetts Bay;* and that upon his abdication, that allegiance accrued to the commonwealth, as his lawful successor. The demandant must therefore, in our courts of law, be deemed a subject and not an alien: it not being alleged that he has been expatriated by virtue of any statute or any judgment at law.

The plea is therefore bad: but the interlocutory judgment must be entered, according to the issue in law that is joined, that the replication is good, and that the tenant answer over. For a replication, which might be an insufficient answer to a good plea, may be a sufficient answer to a bad plea.

It may be remarked, that the form and effect of the plea of alien friend, which is pleadable only in real actions, has alone been subject to our deliberation. The case of an alien enemy requires a distinct consideration: but it is not now before us.

14

WILLIAM EUSTIS, ADMISSION OF MISSOURI, HOUSE OF REPRESENTATIVES
12 Dec. 1820
Annals 37:635–38

I am one of those who had hoped that the discussion of this question might have been avoided. But it is upon us, and we must meet and decide it. With gentlemen who have preceded me, I perfectly agree, that the only question to be determined is, whether that article in the constitution of Missouri, making it the duty of the Legislature to provide by law "that free negroes and mulattoes shall not be admitted into that State," is, or is not, repugnant to that clause in the Constitution of the United States, which declares "that the citizens of each State shall be entitled to all the privileges and immunities of citizens in the several States." This question has been fairly met. Those who contend that the article is not repugnant to the Constitution of the United States ground themselves on the position that blacks and mulattoes are not citizens of the United States and have repeatedly referred to the condition of those in Massachusetts to support the assertion. Now, sir, I invite the honorable member from Delaware, who has lately addressed you, with the honorable member from Virginia, who, in his address to the Committee of the Whole, on Friday last, maintained the same position, to go with me and examine the question to its root.

At the commencement of the Revolutionary war, there were found in the Middle and Northern States, many blacks and other people of color, capable of bearing arms; a part of them free, the greater part slaves. The freemen entered our ranks with the whites. The time of those who were slaves was purchased by the States, and they were induced to enter the service in consequence of a law by which, on condition of their serving in the ranks during the war, they were made freemen. In Rhode Island, where their numbers were more considerable, they were formed, under the same considerations, into a regiment commanded by white officers; and it is required, in justice to them, to add, that they discharged their duty with zeal and fidelity. The gallant defence of Red Bank, in which this black regiment bore a part, is among the proofs of their valor.

Among the traits which distinguished this regiment, was their devotion to their officers; when their brave Colonel Greene was afterwards cut down and mortally wounded, the sabres of the enemy reached his body only through the limbs of his faithful guard of blacks, who hovered over him and protected him, every one of whom was killed, and whom he was not ashamed to call his children. The services of this description of men in the navy are also well known. I should not have mentioned either, but for the information of the gentleman from Delaware, whom I understood to say that he did not know that they had served in any considerable numbers.

The war over and peace restored, these men returned to their respective States. And who could have said to them, on their return to civil life after having shed their blood, in common with the whites, in the defence of the liberties of the country, You are not to participate in the rights secured by the struggle, or in the liberty for which you have been fighting? Certainly, no white man in Massachusetts.

The gentleman from Virginia says he must not be told that the term, we the people, in the preamble to the Constitution, means, or includes, Indians, free negroes, mulattoes. If it shall be made to appear that persons of this description, citizens at the time, were parties to, and formed an integral part of that compact, it follows, incontestably, that they are and must be included in it. To justify the inference of gentlemen, the preamble ought to read, We the *white* people. This was impossible; the members of the convention who formed that constitution, from the Middle and Northern States, could never have consented, knowing that there were in those States many thousands of people of color, who had rights under it. They were free— free from their masters? Yes, in the first instance; they also became freemen of the State, and were admitted to all the rights and privileges of white citizens. Was this admission merely nominal? This is answered by the fact that they did enjoy and did exercise the rights of free citizens, and have continued to exercise them, from the peace of 1783 to this day. It has been contended that they are not citizens, because they have been deprived, by a law of Massachusetts, of a part of their civil rights, and in proof, is stated the law forbidding the marriage of a black man with a white woman. The same law, sir, interdicts the marriage of a white man with a black woman. The law, then, applies equally to both, and cannot justify the inference which has been drawn from it. But, if the black man ceased to be a citizen because he had lost this civil right, as contended for by the gentleman from Virginia, the white man also must be determined not to be a citizen, and the State of Missouri would have an equal right to exclude him. Again, sir, the exclusion of the blacks from the ranks of the militia is adduced as another instance of their privation of a civil right. Without dwelling on the well-known fact that militia duty in Massachusetts is a heavy duty, an exemption from which is considered a favor, and that several other descriptions of citizens are also exempted; and admitting that the blacks are interdicted, while others are only exempted from this duty, what is proved by quoting these laws? They prove that they were in the actual enjoyment of these rights, and that a specific law became necessary to deprive them of them. Admitting that the State had a right to pass these laws, and that this description of citizens are curtailed in their exercise of a part of their privileges, what rights are left to them, and what rights do they continue

to enjoy and exercise? We answer, all the broad and essential rights of citizens—the right, in common with the whites, to hold real and personal estate; the right of course to hold and convey land; the right of trial by jury; the right to the writ of habeas corpus; and, in this Government, the all-important right of the elective franchise; and it may be safely affirmed, that, by the laws and constitution of Massachusetts, they were considered as citizens equally with the whites.

It has been justly observed on this subject, by a gentleman on the other side, that facts and practice are better than theory. Here, then, we offer incontrovertible facts, proving, not from theory, but from actual and long continued practice, that black men and mulattoes, in Massachusetts at least, are citizens, having civil and political rights, in common with the whites. If we are asked for evidence of their being in the exercise of these rights, it is answered, that a knowledge of the history and practice of the State for more than forty years past, will show that they have been in the constant exercise of them. To vote in the election of town, county, and State officers, the same qualifications of residence and property are required from them, as from the whites, and, having these qualifications, they have a voice in the election of all State officers. Again, it is particularly affirmed, by the honorable member from Delaware, that this description of persons, whatever right they may have in the several States, have no federal rights, and cannot be considered as citizens of the United States. I had thought, with the honorable member from Pennsylvania, that the question "who were citizens?" was merged and decided by the adoption of the Federal Constitution.

By whom, and for whose use and benefit, was the Constitution formed? By the people, and for the people, inhabiting the several States. Did the Convention who formed it go into the consideration of the character or complexion of the citizens included in the compact? No, sir; they necessarily considered all those as citizens who were acknowledged as such at the time by the constitutions of the States.

Independent of all reasoning, presumption, or theory, we proceed to state facts which prove incontrovertibly their federal rights. I confine my observations to Massachusetts, because the practice in that State is within my own personal knowledge and observation. In that State, sir, the citizens in question constituted, and were in fact an elementary part of the Federal compact. They were as directly represented as the whites, in the initiatory process; and, from their votes, in common with those of the whites, emanated the convention of Massachusetts, by whom the Federal Constitution was received and ratified. Is not this proof? Is it not demonstration that they are entitled to, that they hold and exercise federal rights in common with the other citizens? If a doubt remained, it is answered by another equally important fact. They are also represented, not circuitously and indirectly, but directly, in this House. I very much doubt, sir, if there be a member on this floor from any one district in Massachusetts, whose election does not partake of the votes of these people. In the district which I have the honor to represent, their number, compared with that of the white population, is not great;

but, in an adjoining district, their number of qualified voters have been sufficient, and have actually turned the election of a member of this House.

15

CHARLES PINCKNEY, ADMISSION OF MISSOURI,
HOUSE OF REPRESENTATIVES
13 Feb. 1821
Annals 37:1129, 1134

Mr. Speaker, there are many reasons which make it incumbent on me not to suffer this question, which I consider the final one on the acceptance or rejection of the constitution of Missouri, and her admission into the Union, to pass without presenting my views on the subject to the House. These reasons are, the importance of the question itself, the great interest the State I represent, in part, has in it, and, not among the least, the frequent calls made upon me in this House, and references in the other, as to the true meaning of the second section of the fourth article of the Constitution of the United States, which it appears, from the Journal of the General Convention that formed the Constitution, I first proposed in that body.

. . . . .

I say it is not, in my judgment, unconstitutional, for the following reasons, in which I mean briefly to answer to the call that has been made upon me: It appears by the Journal of the Convention that formed the Constitution of the United States, that I was the only member of that body that ever submitted the plan of a constitution completely drawn in articles and sections; and this having been done at a very early state of their proceedings, the article on which now so much stress is laid, and on the meaning of which the whole of this question is made to turn, and which is in these words: "the citizens of each State shall be entitled to all privileges and immunities in every State," having been made by me, it is supposed I must know, or perfectly recollect, what I meant by it. In answer, I say, that, at the time I drew that constitution, I perfectly knew that there did not then exist such a thing in the Union as a black or colored citizen, nor could I then have conceived it possible such a thing could have ever existed in it; nor, notwithstanding all that has been said on the subject, do I now believe one does exist in it.

16

WILLIAM WIRT, RIGHTS OF FREE NEGROES IN
VIRGINIA
7 Nov. 1821
1 Ops. Atty. Gen. 506

SIR: The question propounded for my opinion on the letter of the collector at Norfolk is, "Whether free persons of color are, in Virginia, citizens of the United States, within the intent and meaning of the acts regulating foreign and coasting trade, so as to be qualified to command vessels?"

I presume that the description, "citizen of the United States," used in the constitution, has the same meaning that it has in the several acts of Congress passed under the authority of the constitution; otherwise there will arise a vagueness and uncertainty in our laws, which will make their execution, if not impracticable, at least extremely difficult and dangerous. Looking to the constitution as the standard of meaning, it seems very manifest that no person is included in the description of citizen of the United States who has not the full rights of a citizen in the State of his residence. Among other proofs of this, it will be sufficient to advert to the constitutional provision, that "the citizens of each State shall be entitled to all the privileges and immunities of citizens in the several States." Now, if a person born and residing in Virginia, but possessing none of the high characteristic privileges of a citizen of the State, is nevertheless a citizen of Virginia in the sense of the constitution, then, on his removal into another State, he acquires all the immunities and privileges of a citizen of that other State, although he possessed none of them in the State of his nativity: a consequence which certainly could not have been in the contemplation of the convention. Again: the only qualification required by the constitution to render a person eligible as President, senator, or representative of the United States, is, that he shall be a "citizen of the United States" of a given age and residence. Free negroes and mulattoes can satisfy the requisitions of age and residence as well as the white man; and if nativity, residence, and allegiance combined, (without the rights and privileges of a white man,) are sufficient to make him a "citizen of the United States" in the sense of the constitution, then free negroes and mulattoes are eligible to those high offices, and may command the purse and sword of the nation.

For these and other reasons, which might easily be multiplied, I am of the opinion that the constitution, by the description of "citizens of the United States," intended those only who enjoyed the full and equal privileges of white citizens in the State of their residence. If this be correct, and if I am right also in the other position—that we must affix the same sense to this description when found in an act of Congress, as it manifestly has in the constitution—then free people of color in Virginia are not citizens of the United States in the sense of our shipping laws, or any other laws, passed under the authority of the federal constitution; for such people have very few of the privileges of the citizens of Virginia.

1. They can vote at no election, although they may be freeholders.

2. They are incapable of any office of trust or profit, civil or military.

3. They are not competent witnesses against a white man in any case, civil or criminal.

4. They are not enrolled in the militia, are incapable of bearing arms, and are forbidden even to have in their possession military weapons, under the penalties of forfeiture and whipping.

5. They are subject to severe corporal punishment for raising their hand against a white man, except in defence against a wanton assault.

6. They are incapable of contracting marriage with a white woman, and the attempt is severely punished.

These are some only of the incapacities which distinguished them from the white citizens of Virginia; but they are, I think, amply sufficient to show that such persons could not have been intended to be embraced by the description "citizens of the United States," in the sense of the constitution and acts of Congress.

The allegiance which the free man of color owes to the State of Virginia, is no evidence of citizenship; for he owes it not in consequence of any oath of allegiance. He is not required or permitted to take any such oath; the allegiance which he owes is that which a sojourning stranger owes—the mere consequence and return for the protection which he receives from the laws.

Besides the general reasons which I have advanced for the exclusion of free negroes and mulattoes in Virginia from the description of "citizens of the United States," under the constitution and laws of the Union, there are special reasons in support of that exclusion with regard to the command of vessels. Under our laws, such persons are not competent witnesses to affect, by their oaths, the life or property of a white man; yet if, by the constitution and laws of the United States, they are citizens competent to the command of vessels, they become clothed with all the duties, powers, and authority of masters of vessels; and, among them, with the competency of affecting by their oaths, protests, &c., the property of white men, insurers, owners, freighters, and of the government itself; of which various instances under our laws, as well as under the maritime law generally, will immediately occur to you. Now, it could never have been the intention of Congress, in requiring that the master of a vessel should be a citizen of the United States, to create a citizen by the assumption of that employment, and clothe the man with rights and privileges of citizenship, which he did not previously possess. The act looked only to those who were previously citizens, and to whom alone it confines the right of entering on the employment.

In addition to these considerations, I may observe, with the collector, that Congress itself has recognised the distinction between citizens of the United States and persons of color, natives of the United States, in several instances; e.g., the 1st section of the act of 3d March, 1813, "for the regulation of seamen on board the public and private ves-

sels of the United States;" and the 3d, 5th, 6th, and 7th sections of the act of March 1, 1817, "concerning the navigation of the United States."

Upon the whole, I am of the opinion that free persons of color in Virginia are not citizens of the United States, within the intent and meaning of the acts regulating foreign and coasting trade, so as to be qualified to command vessels.

17

DOUGLASS V. STEPHENS
1 Del. Ch. 465 (1821)

RIDGELY, CHANCELLOR.—I shall consider this case on the broad question, whether the Constitution of the United States places a citizen of the State of Maryland on an equal footing with a citizen of this State, in the recovery of debts. If it does, the judgment of the Court of Common Pleas must be affirmed; for the Constitution of the United States is the supreme law of the land, and abrogates the laws of every State in the Union inconsistent with it. But if, on the other hand, the term "citizen" is only used in contradistinction to "alien;" and if the Constitution designed to secure to the citizens of other States the mere right of citizenship, that is, that they shall not be deemed aliens, and to confer no other privileges, then the judgment is erroneous, and should be reversed.

Before the Declaration of Independence the colonist of Great Britain in America, and before and since, the subject of the King of England, in every part of the world, could and can acquire, inherit, and hold land in any of his dominions, as fully as an Englishman can in England. This doctrine was carried so far in Calvin's case, that after the union of the crowns of England and Scotland in the person of James I., of England, a Scotchman, born after the Union, was adjudged to be a natural born subject of England, and entitled to the same remedies in the courts of England as an Englishman; and after the conquest of Ireland by Henry II., and the extension of the British laws to that country, those who were born in Ireland were not aliens to the realm of England. Even those who were born in Calais, from the reign of Edward III. until it was lost in Queen Mary's reign, were capable and inheritable to land in England. See Calvin's case, 7 Coke's Rep. 1.

Impressed with these established principles, the people of the United States associated in the year 1774 to resist the oppressive and unconstitutional pretensions of the British King and Parliament. They united and acted in concert, as one people. Far from being aliens to each other, they knew that they were practically, as well as legally, fellow-citizens,—holding lands by purchase and inheritance in the respective governments, and enjoying every right and privilege indiscriminately with the inhabitants, only as the same were curtailed in this State by the Statute under consideration. Indeed, so far was this sentiment of community of interest carried that the people of this State were often represented, in their own Legislature and in Congress, by persons who resided in Pennsylvania. After the Declaration of Independence and the adoption of our State Constitution of 1776, Mr. McKean, though resident in Philadelphia, was a member of our General Assembly; and General Dickinson, of New Jersey, and Mr. ——— of Philadelphia were, at another time, Representatives of this State in the Congress of the United States. Mr. McKean actually signed the Articles of Confederation, on behalf of this State, when he presided in the Supreme Court of Pennsylvania. *2 Del. Laws*, 645: 1 *Dall. Rep.* 32. After the Declaration of Independence, and before the signing of the Articles of Confederation, each State, possibly, had the power to declare the citizens of other States aliens; but such an exercise of power would have been viewed with a most suspicious, unfriendly eye; and would have violated the great principles of our union. The Articles of Confederation, however, sufficiently restrained any such attempt. In the fourth Article it was agreed, the better to secure and perpetuate mutual friendship and intercourse among the people of the several States in this Union, that "the free inhabitants of each of these States,—paupers, vagabonds and fugitives from justice excepted,—shall be entitled to all privileges and immunities of free citizens in the several States; and the people of each State shall have free ingress and regress to and from any other State; and shall enjoy therein all the privileges of trade and commerce, subject to the same duties, impositions, and restrictions as the inhabitants thereof, respectively; *provided,* that such restrictions shall not extend so far as to prevent the removal of property imported into any State to any other State, of which the owner is an inhabitant; *Provided also,* that no imposition of duties or restrictions shall be laid by any State on the property of the United States, or either of them." This Article operated in favor of persons not included within the expression or meaning of the present Constitution, if the words "free inhabitants" were intended, as I presume they were, to include all the inhabitants of a State, except slaves. They comprehended aliens, free negroes, and every possible description of persons, not slaves, with the exception of paupers, vagabonds, and fugitives from justice; and they enlarged the privileges and immunities of such free inhabitants, making them equal to the privileges and immunities of the citizens of a State. Nay, the inhabitants of a State might have been entitled to greater privileges in another State than they could enjoy in their own, and to greater than the mere inhabitants themselves were entitled to in such other State. A State might have qualified the citizenship of its own people, but not the citizenship of the inhabitants of a neighboring State, who chose to visit or reside in such State; and thus no State could have protected itself against any class of persons, however worthless or pernicious they might have been to society, if they were tolerated in a neighboring State. A single State might have poured into other States all its miscreants, merely because they were inhabitants. And, in fine, the population of the United States, in relation to foreigners and all kinds of free persons, would have been subject to the control of any particular State

favorable to the reception of such persons. The present Constitution has wisely corrected this evil, by vesting the right of naturalization exclusively in the United States, and by using the word "citizens" instead of "free inhabitants." There was another objection to this fourth Article of the Confederation. After employing the most comprehensive words, "privileges and immunities," it descended into a detail of some of those privileges and immunities, and weakened the force of those terms by not including in the detail all the privileges and immunities they were designed to protect. Ingress and regress from one State to another, the privileges of trade and commerce, and the removal of property are the only privileges and immunities enumerated, although the words "privileges and immunities" comprehend all the rights, and all the methods of protecting those rights, which belong to a person in a state of civil society,—subject, to be sure, to some restrictions, but to such only as the welfare of society and the general good require.

It is most evident, from a consideration of this Article, that the idea never was entertained that the people of one State could be taken to be aliens in another. The Article was made, the better to secure and perpetuate what then existed. It conferred no new right, but legalized and preserved such as were then fully enjoyed. It is true, that the Legislatures of the several States might have restricted the privileges previously possessed by the citizens of the other States, and they might have violently made the people aliens to each other; but, from the date of the ratification of the confederation, their power in this respect was completely limited; and, without a dissolution of the Confederacy, inhabitancy alone in one State entitled the inhabitants to all privileges and immunities of free citizens in the several States.

Thus stood our Union before the adoption of the present Constitution of the United States. The second section of the fourth Article was designed, if we judge from the words of it and from the whole scope of the Constitution, to restrain to a more definite class of persons the privileges and immunities secured to them, and to extend to the citizens of the several States, in each State, all privileges and immunities of citizens, without implication or construction. The only apparent difficulty in this section arises from the want of a constitutional definition of the word "citizens:" but, by contemplating our manners, the laws enacted before and since the Revolution, the Constitution of the United States and the Statutes of Congress, the meaning of the word "citizen" is as clearly ascertained as any other term or expression which comprehends several attributes or properties.

The word "citizen" imports the same as the word "freeman" in our old Acts of Assembly; and means every white man, who, by birth or naturalization, is or may be qualified to exercise and enjoy, under like circumstances, all the rights which any native born, white inhabitant of the State does or can enjoy. And every white man, born or naturalized in any other State, is such a citizen of such other State as to be entitled, in this State, to all the civil rights of citizenship, and by residence and other qualifications to all the political rights.

When men entered into a State they yielded a part of their absolute rights, or natural liberty, for political or civil liberty, which is no other than natural liberty restrained by human laws, so far as is necessary and expedient for the general advantage of the public. The rights of enjoying and defending life and liberty, of acquiring and protecting reputation and property,—and, in general, of attaining objects suitable to their condition, without injury to another, are the rights of a citizen; and all men by nature have them. See at large *1 Blk. Com. Book I. ch. 1.* But, unless some method had been provided to secure their actual enjoyment, they would be in vain declared, claimed, or asserted. There are, therefore, established certain other subordinate rights of the citizen, which serve principally as barriers to protect and maintain inviolate those great and primary rights. The preservation of these original rights included the preservation of the subordinate rights,—the privileges and immunities which it was intended by the Constitution of this State to preserve to its citizens, and by the Constitution of the United States to preserve, in each State, to the citizens of the other States, for the protection of the primary rights before mentioned.

The right of enjoying and defending life consists in a person's legal and uninterrupted enjoyment of his life, his limbs, his body, his health, and in resisting, even to the commission of homicide, where such resistance is necessary to save one's own life. The right of enjoying and defending life, without the privilege of protecting it by all the means which the law as well as nature, in extreme cases, furnishes, would be illusory to the last degree. Therefore, this privilege belongs to us, and, by the Constitution of the United States, to every other citizen of the United States in common with us.

And so, as to the enjoyment and defence of liberty. To exercise this right every individual entitled to it must have the privilege of locomotion, of changing situation, or removing his person to whatsoever place his inclination may direct, without imprisonment or restraint, unless by due course of law. To secure this right more effectually our constitution (Art. I, Sec. 13,) has declared, that the privilege of *habeas corpus* shall not be suspended, unless when, in cases of rebellion or invasion, the public safety may require it. But, as our Constitution was established for the government of the people of this State, it might be contended that the Legislature may limit its operation to its own citizens, and that the privilege may be withheld from citizens of another State. And, certainly, the argument would be as sound as it is to assert that the Legislature may suspend the privilege of recovering a debt, except on terms of inequality which amount to a prohibition in some instances.

The right of acquiring and protecting reputation and property includes all the privileges incident to such right. Property cannot be acquired and protected without the privilege of applying to courts of justice. No man can be his own arbiter. Our Constitution has declared that all courts shall be open, and every man for an injury done him in his reputation, person, movable or immovable possessions, shall have remedy by due course of law, without sale, denial, or unreasonable delay or expense. This is the assertion of a general right,—the right of all men; and it would be ineffectually declared were not the redress of wrong and the means of enforcing contracts, by which property is acquired, secured and protected. The acquisition of property is effected by contract. A right to property, or the acquisition of property, may be derived either from the act of another or by virtue of some positive institution. When it is derived from another it is generally effected by contract; and it becomes the privilege of every citizen to apply to courts of justice to enforce contracts, or to obtain redress for their violation. It is a privilege which grows out of the right of acquiring property, and is as necessary to its preservation as the air we breathe is to life. Suppose an horse is lent and the borrower refuses to restore him, or suppose an horse to be wrongfully taken, the owner can have remedy by law only. By redressing the injury or wrong the property is protected. So, if an horse is sold, and instead of receiving the price the seller leaves the money in the hands of the purchaser and takes a bond for its payment at a future day, the recovery of this money by a suit at law eventually protects the property. Contract may be traced back to the establishment of exclusive property by civil law; and as contract had its origin in property, so property, or at least property derived from another, now depends on contract. An obligation is a contract, and it is one of the various methods by which property may be acquired; and, therefore, a citizen of another State may claim from the courts of this State the enforcement of his contracts or satisfaction for their breach, precisely as the citizens of this State can; because it is the privilege of a citizen, and is secured to him by the Constitution of the United States. This debt must take its place according to the order of payment prescribed to executors and administrators; otherwise, the creditor will not enjoy in this State all privileges and immunities of citizens; for a common right must be enjoyed by all alike. If his obligation is postponed to a book account, and the obligation of a citizen of the State is preferred to such account, it is certain that he does not,—cannot enjoy all privileges of citizens, where those of this State are entitled to an equality, according to the dignity of their debts. To what purpose are all privileges and immunities reserved to the citizens of each State, if a State can discriminate between its own citizens and the citizens of another State in the privileges of a citizen, and unless the same method to protect their property is allowed to them. If we may cut and carve and limit and restrain other citizens in the exercise of our privileges as citizens, it is evident that they are not entitled to all privileges and immunities of citizens in this State. To recover a debt is a privilege; but unless he can recover it equally, or as fully, as a citizen of this State, something is withheld, and he has not the privilege of a citizen in this State,—unless, indeed, more than the privilege of a citizen is bestowed on our own citizens. On the great question of the suability of States, Chief Justice Jay, in his clear and luminous opinion, in *Chisholm vs. Georgia, 2 Dall. S. C. Repts.* 472, said "the citizens of America are equal as fellow citizens, and as joint tenants in the sovereignty."

The clause in the Constitution is as general as words can make it; and the exception contended for would contradict and do violence not only to this section, but to the leading principles of a free and national Government, one great object of which is to insure justice equally to all. It establishes the faith and credit to be given to the public acts, records and judicial proceedings of each State. It provides for the apprehension of fugitives from justice from one State to another; and it secures to those entitled to the service or labor of another such service or labor, even against the laws or regulations of a State into which such laborer or servant may fly; and, by this section, the rights of every citizen in the United States are protected in each State, by securing to him in the several States all privileges and immunities of citizenship. Thus, the system is completed; and most extraordinary would it be if a difference were made in the recovery of debts. If this 2d section of the 4th Article is to be understood with an exception, it is strange that it was not mentioned. The difficulty is to discover in what instance any privilege or immunity of a citizen of one State may be abridged in another. He may purchase and hold land by any of the several modes by which real estate may be acquired. He may take by descent, where the title is vested in him by the operation of law. He may obtain goods and chattels, in all the forms and varieties peculiar to personal property. He may be an executor, administrator, or witness. He may prosecute every species of suit, both at law and in equity; and, in short, as to every civil right, I know no difference between him and a citizen of the State, unless this Act of Assembly makes one. If this be an exception to the clause of the constitution, and the intention was only to prevent citizens of other States being declared aliens, the Legislature might abolish all the rights, privileges and immunities of the citizens of other States. They might forbid the recovery of debts upon any terms; the privilege of *habeas corpus* might be disallowed them, and they might be subjected to perpetual imprisonment; the descent of land to them might be regulated differently from the descent of land generally; immunity from arrest, in suitors and witnesses during their attendance on courts of justice, might be withdrawn; extraordinary and excessive taxes might be imposed upon the lands of non-residents; and all the ties by which we are united as one people, so far as they depend upon our own internal State government, might be dissolved. Why should the citizens of another State be made aliens as to the recovery of debts, and not to all other purposes? Thus, indirectly, might be done what it cannot be pretended the State could directly do. The only reasonable construction to be given to this clause is that of placing all citizens of the United States on the same footing, and extending to them a perfect equality in their rights, privileges and immunities. If one citizen has a privilege to which others are not entitled, then they are not entitled to all privileges and immunities of citizens in the several States; which is directly contrary to this provision. The Legislature may certainly prescribe different grades for the payment of debts by executors and administrators; and in so doing, no violation will be done to the Constitution of the United States, because all persons having debts of the same grade will rank equally. But a distinction between persons, because one resides in Delaware and the other in Maryland, directly diminishes the privileges of the citizens of Maryland.

Upon the most deliberate consideration of this question, I am of opinion that the citizens of another State—the white citizens I mean—may claim the civil rights, privileges and immunities of citizenship, in the same manner and upon the same terms, that citizens of this State are entitled to them, under similar circumstances. In the payment of debts by an executor or administrator there can be no other distinction than according to the dignity of the debt. A citizen of Maryland may recover a debt due by obligation or bill in preference to a debt due to a citizen of this State on account, because the Constitution of the United States gives him the same privilege which is given to a citizen of this State.

As to political rights, the citizens of this and of other States have equal privileges under like circumstances. If a citizen of Maryland, a white man, of the age of twenty-one years, shall have resided in this State two years next before a general election, and shall have paid a State or county tax, which shall have been assessed at least six months before the election, he is as fully an elector in his proper county as any citizen of the State. And so, with the same qualifications of age, freehold property, residence, inhabitance, he may be elected Representative, Senator or Governor. A citizen of Maryland can, as such, be appointed to no office within a county; but let him become an inhabitant one year, and qualify himself to vote for Representatives, and he will be eligible in the same manner as a citizen of this State. In short, with the same qualifications, and under the like circumstances, every white man who is a citizen of another State is entitled to all the rights, civil and political, and to all privileges and immunities, of citizens of this State.

There is another view that may be taken of the first section of this Act of Assembly. The preference given is not confined to citizens only, but it comprehends the inhabitants generally,—citizens and aliens. It places an alien, if he should be an inhabitant of this State, upon higher ground than any citizen of the United States who does not reside in this State. An alien, who never intends to become a citizen, has a preference given him by this Act. This law was enacted in 1721. In the year 1682, and in 1700, Acts of naturalization were passed; and, according to the provision of those Acts, an alien could not become a freeman—one entitled to the rights, privileges and immunities of natural born subjects—without naturalization. The exclusive right of naturalization is now vested in the Congress of the United States; and no State can give an alien a right or privilege greater than the rights or privileges of citizens of the United States. If this could be done in one instance, it could in all; and in this way the exclusive right of naturalization by Congress would be indirectly impaired. The Act of Assembly under consideration has this effect. It gives privileges to aliens, who are inhabitants of the State, greater than to citizen of other States; and, in this respect, it is repugnant to the Constitution.

Upon the whole, I am of opinion that this first section of the Act of the General Assembly, entitled "An Act directing the priority of payment of debts of persons dying within this government," is in conflict with the Constitution of the United States; and, therefore, is void. The judgment of the Court of Common Pleas should be affirmed.

I confine this opinion entirely to the first section of that Act. It, possibly, may be supposed to have some bearing on the first clause of the second section, which authorizes administrators, appointed out of the State, to recover, upon certain terms, debts due to their intestates; but it is not my intention to express an opinion upon that part of the Act. The clause directing the order of payment of debts by executors and administrators is not in any manner affected by the Constitution of the United States, and stands in full force. This clause is necessarily connected with the present case, and gives to Stephens, the plaintiff below, and to all other citizens of this and of other States, a priority in the recovery of debts due by obligation or bill, over or before accounts of merchants and others. Should any question of this kind arise between a citizen, or an inhabitant, of this State, and an inhabitant, not being a citizen, of another State, it would stand uninfluenced by any opinion I have expressed in this case. I have considered the case between citizens of the State and citizens of another State, and none other.

JOHNS, CHIEF JUSTICE.—The question in this case is, whether the Act of Assembly giving a preference to creditors within the State (1 *Vol. Del. Laws*, 81), contravenes the Constitution of the United States and is incompatible with it.

By the second section of the fourth Article of the Constitution of the United States "the citizens of each State shall be entitled to all the privileges and immunities of citizens in the several States."

The words "privileges and immunities" are nearly synonymous. "Privilege" signifies a peculiar advantage, exemption, immunity. "Immunity" signifies exemption, privilege.

The privileges and immunities to be secured to all citizens of the United States are such only as belong to the citizens of the several States; which includes the whole United States, and must be understood to mean, such privileges as should be common, or the same in every State; and this seems to limit the operation of the clause in the Constitution to federal rules; and to be designed to restrict the powers of Congress as to legislation, so that no privilege or immunity should be granted by it to one citizen of the United States, but such as might be common to all. The language is not that the citizens in any State shall be entitled to all the privileges of citizens in each State. If it was, there would be more plausible ground to say that a citizen of Maryland should have the same privileges and rights in Delaware as a citizen of Delaware is entitled to. But, even supposing the design of this clause of the Constitution to have been to restrict the powers of legislation by the State Legislatures, it cannot be extended so far as that no peculiar advantage can be given by any State to its own citizens, but such as must be extended to all citizens in every State in the Union; because, the privileges secured are not such as are given to citizens in one or more States

by the State laws, but must be such as the citizens in the several States, that is, in *all* the States, are entitled to.

The great object to be attained was to prevent a citizen in one State from being considered an alien in another State—to secure the right to acquire and hold real property. Our situation, antecedent to the formation of the first General Government, in 1778, rendered such a provision necessary; and, accordingly, a similar clause was inserted in the Articles of Confederation then adopted; from which the second Section of the fourth Article of the Constitution of the United States was, probably, taken.

The privileges and immunities, &c., are not enumerated or described; but they are all privileges common in the Union,—which certainly excludes those privileges which belong only to citizens of one or more States, and not to those in every other State. It is more easy to ascertain whether the municipal law of this State giving a preference to State creditors is a law incompatible with the privileges secured by the second section of the fourth Article of the Constitution of the United States, than it is to define all the privileges and immunities which the section was intended to secure to the people of the United States; and this will be sufficient for the purpose of deciding the present case.

By the Constitution of the United States all power, jurisdiction, and rights of sovereignty, not granted by that instrument, or relinquished, are retained by the several States.

Uniformity of laws in the States is contemplated only on two subjects, viz.: bankruptcy and naturalization.

The legislative powers of Congress, defined in the eighth section of the first Article, do not interfere with or abridge the power of the States to make local regulations which are to operate within the State.

The restrictive clauses in the tenth section of the first Article of the Constitution of the United States, limiting the powers of the States, are confined to certain enumerated cases; none of which comprehend the subject of the distribution of the assets of a deceased person's estate among his creditors. The local regulations in the States are variant. In Maryland, I believe, there is no priority given to bond creditors over simple contract creditors. In this State, the former must be paid before the latter. It will not be contended that the second section of the fourth Article of the Constitution of the United States repeals that part of our Act of Assembly which gives a preference to bond creditors. And the effect would be inequitable, to give it such an operation as to repeal another part of the same Act which gives a preference to State creditors; for, then, a Maryland bond creditor might take the whole assets, and exclude simple contract creditors residing in Delaware.

But, it is to be ascertained whether the Act of Assembly is incompatible with the second section of the fourth Article of the Constitution of the United States; and this must depend on the question, whether the right to recover debts out of assets in the hands of an executor or administrator is a privilege intended to be secured by this section.

I am of opinion that the privileges designed to be secured cannot be construed to be any right which a creditor has to recover a debt from the administrator of a deceased person. This must depend on the laws of each State. It is neither a right nor a privilege which, according to the words of the section, the citizens of each State are entitled to in the several States.

There is no rule as to the distribution of assets, which is the same in all the States; nor is this a subject for Congress to legislate on. The rules governing it can only be made by the State Legislatures. If the Maryland creditor has the privilege of commencing and prosecuting a suit for the recovery of his debt, to be regulated by the municipal laws of this State, he enjoys a privilege which this Article intended to secure to him. The *lex loci* must govern as to the distribution of the fund for payment of debts. To recognize the principle on which the incompatibility is attempted to be supported, will abridge the powers of the States to legislate on many subjects not contemplated by the Constitution. The extent of the operation of the principle, in repealing State laws, it will be difficult to ascertain; and it would leave us without a rule in many cases. Laws of a similar nature in some of the States,—such as the laws in Maryland and Massachusetts for payment of debts by tendering property at an appraised value,—have been considered to be still in operation; and this has been sanctioned by Acts of Congress as to debts due to the United States. The attachment laws of Maryland, under which the property of a citizen of a sister State may be seized and sold, have been determined by the Court of Appeals in Maryland to be in force; and it has not been doubted but that our attachment law is yet in force. Our insolvent law, excluding non-residents, is considered to be in operation; and special acts are sometimes passed, to extend it to non-residents. I may refer also to our law of *extent,* and to the Virginia law preventing the sale of land for the payment of debts.

It would be mischievous, and produce much inconvenience, to sanction this new rule as to the settlement of the estates of decedents. Executors and administrators would be involved in difficulties. The practice has been to pay debts within the State in preference to debts due to non-residents, according to the Act of Assembly; and I cannot see that the Act is in conflict with the Constitution of the United States. The policy and liberality of its continuance must rest with the Legislature. We can only say, *Ita lex scripta est.*

18

CORFIELD V. CORYELL
6 Fed. Cas. 546, no. 3,230 (C.C.E.D.Pa. 1823)

WASHINGTON, Circuit Justice. The points reserved present for the consideration of the court, many interesting and difficult questions, which will be examined in the shape of objections made by the plaintiff's counsel to the seizure of the Hiram, and the proceedings of the magistrates of Cumberland county, upon whose sentence the defendant rests his justification of the alleged trespass. These objections are,—

First. That the act of the legislature of New Jersey of the 9th of June 1820, under which this vessel, found engaged in taking oysters in Maurice river cove by means of dredges, was seized, condemned, and sold, is repugnant to the constitution of the United States in the following particulars: 1. To the eighth section of the first article, which grants to congress the power to regulate commerce with foreign nations, and among the several states, and with the Indian tribes. 2. To the second section of the fourth article, which declares, that the citizens of each state shall be entitled to all privileges and immunities of citizens in the several states. 3. To the second section of the third article, which declares, that the judicial power of the United States should extend to all cases of admiralty and maritime jurisdiction.

In case the act should be considered as not being exposed to these constitutional objections, it is then insisted,

Secondly. That the locus in quo was not within the territorial limits of New Jersey. But if it was, then

Thirdly. It was not within the jurisdiction of the magistrates of Cumberland county.

Fourthly. We have to consider the objection made by the defendant's counsel to the form of this action.

The first section of the act of New Jersey declares, that, from and after the 1st of May, till the 1st of September in every year, no person shall rake on any oyster bed in this state, or gather any oysters on any banks or beds within the same, under a penalty of $10. Second section: No person residing in, or out of this state, shall, at any time, dredge for oysters in any of the rivers, bays, or waters of the state, under the penalty of $50. The third section prescribes the manner of proceeding, in cases of violations of the preceding sections. The two next sections have nothing to do with the present case. The sixth section enacts, that it shall not be lawful for any person, who is not, at the time, an actual inhabitant and resident of this state, to gather oysters in any of the rivers, bays, or waters in this state, on board of any vessel, not wholly owned by some person, inhabitant of, or actually residing in this state; and every person so offending, shall forfeit $10, and shall also forfeit the vessel employed in the commission of such offence, with all the oysters, rakes, &c. belonging to the same. The seventh section provides, that it shall be lawful for any person to seize and secure such vessel, and to give information to two justices of the county where such seizure shall be made, who are required to meet for the trial of the said case, and to determine the same; and in case of condemnation, to order the said vessel, &c. to be sold.

The first question then is, whether this act, or either section of it, is repugnant to the power granted to congress to regulate commerce? Commerce with foreign nations, and among the several states, can mean nothing more than intercourse with those nations, and among those states, for purposes of trade, be the object of the trade what it may;

and this intercourse must include all the means by which it can be carried on, whether by the free navigation of the waters of the several states, or by a passage over land through the states, where such passage becomes necessary to the commercial intercourse between the states. It is this intercourse which congress is invested with the power of regulating, and with which no state has a right to interfere. But this power, which comprehends the use of, and passage over the navigable waters of the several states, does by no means impair the right of the state government to legislate upon all subjects of internal police within their territorial limits, which is not forbidden by the constitution of the United States, even although such legislation may indirectly and remotely affect commerce, provided it do not interfere with the regulations of congress upon the same subject. Such are inspection, quarantine, and health laws; laws regulating the internal commerce of the state; laws establishing and regulating turnpike roads, ferries, canals, and the like.

In the case of Gibbons v. Ogden, 9 Wheat. [22 U. S.] 1, which we consider as full authority for the principles above stated, it is said, "that no direct power over these objects is granted to congress, and consequently they remain subject to state legislation. If the legislative power of the Union can reach them, it must be for national purposes; it must be when the power is expressly given for a specified purpose, or is clearly incident to some power which is expressly given." But if the power which congress possesses to regulate commerce does not interfere with that of the state to regulate its internal trade, although the latter may remotely affect external commerce, except where the laws of the state may conflict with those of the general government; much less can that power impair the right of the state governments to legislate, in such manner as in their wisdom may seem best, over the public property of the state, and to regulate the use of the same, where such regulations do not interfere with the free navigation of the waters of the state, for purposes of commercial intercourse, nor with the trade within the state, which the laws of the United States permit to be carried on. The grant to congress to regulate commerce on the navigable waters belonging to the several states, renders those waters the public property of the United States, for all the purposes of navigation and commercial intercourse; subject only to congressional regulation. But this grant contains no cession, either express or implied, of territory, or of public or private property. the jus privatum which a state has in the soil covered by its waters, is totally distinct from the jus publicum with which it is clothed. The former, such as fisheries of all descriptions, remains common to all the citizens of the state to which it belongs, to be used by them according to their necessities, or according to the laws which regulate their use. "Over these," says Vattel (book 1, c. 20, §§ 235, 246), "sovereignty gives a right to the nation to make laws regulating the manner in which the common goods are to be used." "He may make such regulations respecting hunting and fishing, as to seasons, as he may think proper, prohibiting the use of certain nets and other destructive methods." Vattel, bk. 1, c. 20, § 248. The jus publicum consists in the right of all persons to use

the navigable waters of the state for commerce, trade, and intercourse; subject, by the constitution of the United States, to the exclusive regulation of congress. If then the fisheries and oyster beds within the territorial limits of a state are the common property of the citizens of that state, and were not ceded to the United States by the power granted to congress to regulate commerce, it is difficult to perceive how a law of the state regulating the use of this common property, under such penalties and forfeitures as the state legislature may think proper to prescribe, can be said to interfere with the power so granted. The act under consideration forbids the taking of oysters by any persons, whether citizens or not, at unseasonable times, and with destructive instruments; and for breaches of the law, prescribes penalties in some cases, and forfeitures in others. But the free use of the waters of the state for purposes of navigation and commercial intercourse, is interdicted to no person; nor is the slightest restraint imposed upon any to buy and sell, or in any manner to trade within the limits of the state.

It was insisted by the plaintiff's counsel, that, as oysters constituted an article of trade, a law which abridges the right of the citizens of other states to take them, except in particular vessels, amounts to a regulation of the external commerce of the state. But it is a manifest mistake to denominate that a commercial regulation which merely regulates the common property of the citizens of the state, by forbidding it to be taken at improper seasons, or with destructive instruments. The law does not inhibit the buying and selling of oysters after they are lawfully gathered, and have become articles of trade; but it forbids the removal of them from the beds in which they grow, (in which situation they cannot be considered articles of trade,) unless under the regulations which the law prescribes. What are the state inspection laws, but internal restraints upon the buying and selling of certain articles of trade? And yet, the chief justice, speaking of those laws [Gibbons v. Ogden] 9 Wheat. [22 U. S.] 203, observes, that "their object is to improve the quality of articles produced by the labour of a country; to fit them for exportation, or, it may be, for domestic use. They act upon the subject before it becomes an article of foreign commerce, or of commerce among the states, and prepare it for that purpose." Is this not precisely the nature of those laws which prescribe the seasons when, and the manner in which, the taking of oysters is permitted? Paving stones, sand, and many other things, are as clearly articles of trade as oysters; but can it be contended, that the laws of a state, which treat as tort feasors those who shall take them away without the permission of the owner of them, are commercial regulations? We deem it superfluous to pursue this subject further, and close it by stating our opinion to be, that no part of the act under consideration amounts to a regulation of commerce, within the meaning of the eighth section of the first article of the constitution.

2. The next question is, whether this act infringes that section of the constitution which declares that "the citizens of each state shall be entitled to all the privileges and immunities of citizens in the several states?" The inquiry is, what are the privileges and immunities of citizens in the

502

several states?" We feel no hesitation in confining these expressions to those privileges and immunities which are, in their nature, fundamental; which belong, of right, to the citizens of all free governments; and which have, at all times, been enjoyed by the citizens of the several states which compose this Union, from the time of their becoming free, independent, and sovereign. What these fundamental principles are, it would perhaps be more tedious than difficult to enumerate. They may, however, be all comprehended under the following general heads: Protection by the government; the enjoyment of life and liberty, with the right to acquire and possess property of every kind, and to pursue and obtain happiness and safety; subject nevertheless to such restraints as the government may justly prescribe for the general good of the whole. The right of a citizen of one state to pass through, or to reside in any other state, for purposes of trade, agriculture, professional pursuits, or otherwise; to claim the benefit of the writ of habeas corpus; to institute and maintain actions of any kind in the courts of the state; to take, hold and dispose of property, either real or personal; and an exemption from higher taxes or impositions than are paid by the other citizens of the state; may be mentioned as some of the particular privileges and immunities of citizens, which are clearly embraced by the general description of privileges deemed to be fundamental: to which may be added, the elective franchise, as regulated and established by the laws or constitution of the state in which it is to be exercised. These, and many others which might be mentioned, are, strictly speaking, privileges and immunities, and the enjoyment of them by the citizens of each state, in every other state, was manifestly calculated (to use the expressions of the preamble of the corresponding provision in the old articles of confederation) "the better to secure and perpetuate mutual friendship and intercourse among the people of the different states of the Union." But we cannot accede to the proposition which was insisted on by the counsel, that, under this provision of the constitution, the citizens of the several states are permitted to participate in all the rights which belong exclusively to the citizens of any other particular state, merely upon the ground that they are enjoyed by those citizens; much less, that in regulating the use of the common property of the citizens of such state, the legislature is bound to extend to the citizens of all the other states the same advantages as are secured to their own citizens. A several fishery, either as the right to it respects running fish, or such as are stationary, such as oysters, clams, and the like, is as much the property of the individual to whom it belongs, as dry land, or land covered by water; and is equally protected by the laws of the state against the aggressions of others, whether citizens or strangers. Where those private rights do not exist to the exclusion of the common right, that of fishing belongs to all the citizens or subjects of the state. It is the property of all; to be enjoyed by them in subordination to the laws which regulate its use. They may be considered as tenants in common of this property; and they are so exclusively entitled to the use of it, that it cannot be enjoyed by others without the tacit consent, or the express permission of the sovereign who has the power to regulate its use.

This power in the legislature of New Jersey to exclude the citizens of the other states from a participation in the right of taking oysters within the waters of that state, was denied by the plaintiff's counsel, upon principles of public law, independent of the provision of the constitution which we are considering, upon the ground, that they are incapable of being appropriated until they are caught. This argument is unsupported, we think, by authority. Rutherfoth, bk. 1, c. 5, §§ 4, 5, who quotes Grotius as his authority, lays it down, that, although wild beasts, birds, and fishes, which have not been caught, have never in fact been appropriated, so as to separate them from the common stock to which all men are equally entitled, yet where the exclusive right in the water and soil which a person has occasion to use in taking them is vested in others, no other persons can claim the liberty of hunting, fishing, or fowling, on lands, or waters, which are so appropriated. "The sovereign," says Grotius (book 2, c. 2, § 5), "who has dominion over the land, or waters, in which the fish are, may prohibit foreigners (by which expression we understand him to mean others than subjects or citizens of the state) from taking them." That this exclusive right of taking oysters in the waters of New Jersey has never been ceded by that state, in express terms, to the United States, is admitted by the counsel for the plaintiff; and having shown, as we think we have, that this right is a right of property, vested either in certain individuals, or in the state, for the use of the citizens thereof, it would, in our opinion, be going quite too far to construe the grant of privileges and immunities of citizens, as amounting to a grant of a cotenancy in the common property of the state, to the citizens of all the other states. Such a construction would, in many instances, be productive of the most serious public inconvenience and injury, particularly, in regard to those kinds of fish, which, by being exposed to too general use, may be exhausted. The oyster beds belonging to a state may be abundantly sufficient for the use of the citizens of that state, but might be totally exhausted and destroyed if the legislature could not so regulate the use of them as to exclude the citizens of the other states from taking them, except under such limitations and restrictions as the laws may prescribe.

3. It is lastly objected, that this act violates that part of the constitution which extends the judicial power of the United States to all cases of admiralty and maritime jurisdiction. The taking of oysters out of season, and with destructive instruments, such as dredges, is said to be an offence against the ancient ordinances and statutes of the admiralty, and that it is punishable by the admiralty as a misdemeanour. The authority relied upon to establish this doctrine is one of Sir L. Jenkins' charges, to be found in 2 Brown, Civ. & Adm. Law, 475. The amount of the argument is, that, since offences of this kind are cases of admiralty and maritime jurisdiction, the laws of a state upon the same subject, vesting in the state tribunals jurisdiction over them, are repugnant to this grant of jurisdiction to the judiciary of the United States. This argument, we think, cannot be maintained. For although the various misdemeanours enumerated by Sir L. Jenkins in his charges, may have been considered as admiralty offences

at that period, either under the common law, or the ancient ordinances and statutes of the admiralty, it remains yet to be shown that they became such, and were cognizable by the judiciary of the United States, independent of some act of the national legislature to render them so. Many of those offences are already incorporated into the Criminal Code of the United States, and no person, it is presumed, will question the power of congress, by further legislation, to include many other offences to which the jurisdiction of the admiralty in England extended at the period above alluded to. But it is by no means to be conceded that, because offences of the nature we are now considering may rightfully belong to the jurisdiction of the English admiralty, the power of that government to regulate her fisheries being unquestionable, congress has a like power to declare similar acts, or any acts at all, done by individuals in relation to the fisheries within the limits of the respective states, offences against the United States. There are doubtless acts which may be done upon the navigable waters of a state which the government of the United States, and that of the state, have a concurrent power to prohibit, and to punish as offences; such for example as throwing ballast into them, or in any other way impeding the free use and navigation of such rivers. But we hold that the power to regulate the fisheries belonging to the several states, and to punish those who should transgress those regulations, was exclusively vested in the states, respectively, at the time when the present constitution was adopted, and that it was not surrendered to the United States, by the mere grant of admiralty and maritime jurisdiction to the judicial branch of the government. Indeed, this power in the states to regulate the fisheries in their navigable rivers and waters, was not, in direct terms, questioned by the plaintiff's counsel; and yet their argument upon this point, when followed out to its necessary consequences, amounts to a denial of that power.

As to the ancient criminal jurisdiction of the admiralty in cases of misdemeanours generally, committed on the sea, or on waters out of the body of any county; we have very respectable authority for believing that it was not exercised, even if it existed, at the period when the constitution of the United States was formed, and, if so, it would seem to follow that, to the exercise of jurisdiction over such offences, some act of the national legislature to punish them as offences against the United States is necessary. We find from the opinions of learned and eminent counsel who were consulted on the subject, that misdemeanours committed upon the sea had never been construed as being embraced by the statute of 28 Hen. VIII. c. 15, and that the criminal jurisdiction of the admiralty, except as exercised under that statute, had become obsolete, so that, without an act of parliament, they could not be prosecuted at all. 2 Brown, Civ. & Adm. Law, Append. 519–521. If then it could be admitted that congress might legislate upon the subject of fisheries within the limits of the several states, upon the ground of the admiralty and maritime jurisdiction, it would seem to be a conclusive answer to the whole of the argument on this point, that no such legisla-

tion has taken place; and consequently the power of the state governments to pass laws to regulate the fisheries within their respective limits remains as it stood before the constitution was adopted.

Secondly. The next general question to be considered is, whether the boundaries of the state of New Jersey include the place where the Hiram was seized whilst engaged in dredging for oysters? The grant from Charles II. to his brother, the Duke of York, of the territory of which the present state of New Jersey was a part, dated the 12th of March 1663–4, was of all that territory lying between the rivers St. Croix adjoining Nova Scotia, and extending along the sea coast southerly to the east side of Delaware bay, together with all islands, sails, rivers, harbours, marshes, waters, lakes, fishings, huntings and fowlings, and all other royalties, profits, commodities, hereditaments and appurtenances to the same belonging and appertaining, with full power to govern the same. The grant of the Duke of York dated the 24th of June 1664, to Lord Berkeley, and Sir George Carteret, after reciting the above grant, conveys to them all that tract of land lying to the westward of Long Island and Manhattan's Island, bounded on the east, part by the main sea, and part by Hudson's river, "and hath upon the west Delaware bay or river, and extendeth southward," &c. with all rivers, fishings, and all other royalties to the said premises belonging, &c. There is no material difference between these grants as to the boundaries of New Jersey on the westward; and we are of opinion that, although the rule of the law of nations is, that where a nation takes possession of a country separated by a river from another nation, and it does not appear which had the prior possession of the river, they shall each extend to the middle of it; yet, that when the claim to the country is founded, not on discovery and occupancy, but on grant, the boundary on the river must depend upon the just construction of the grant, and the intention of the parties to be discovered from its face. Taking this as the rule, we think the claim of New Jersey under these grants to any part of the bay or river Delaware below low water mark cannot be maintained. The principle here suggested is, we conceive, fully recognized and adopted by the supreme court in the case of Handly's Lessee v. Anthony, 5 Wheat. [18 U. S.] 374. Neither do we conceive that the limits of the state can, by construction, be enlarged in virtue of the grant of all rivers, fishings, and other royalties; which expressions ought, we think, to be confined to rivers, fishings and royalties within the boundaries of the granted premises. This appears to have been the opinion of the crown lawyers, who were consulted more than a century ago respecting the boundaries of New Jersey and Pennsylvania, and this too after hearing counsel upon the question. Their opinion was, that the right to the river Delaware, and the islands therein, still remained in the crown. See Chalmers' Opinions. Notwithstanding this objection to the title of New Jersey, whilst a proprietary government, to any part of the bay and river Delaware, it seems that the proprietaries of West Jersey claimed, if not the whole of the river, a part of it at least below low water mark, as far back as the year 1683, as appears by a resolution of the assembly of that province in that year, "that the proprietary of the province of Pennsylvania should be treated with in reference to the rights and privileges of this province to, or in the river Delaware." By certain concessions of the proprietaries, free holders, and inhabitants of west New Jersey, some time about the year 1767, they granted that all the inhabitants of the province should have liberty of fishing in Delaware river, or on the sea coast. In 1693 a law passed in that province which enacted that all persons not residing within that province or within the province of Pennsylvania, who should kill, or bring on shore, any whale in Delaware bay, or elsewhere within the boundaries of that government, should be liable to a certain penalty. In the year 1771 another act was passed for improving the navigation of the Delaware river, and in 1783 another act was passed which annexed all islands, islets, and dry land in the river Delaware belonging to the state, as low down as the state of Delaware, to such counties as they lay nearest to. And in the same year, the compact was made between the states of New Jersey and Pennsylvania, by which the legislatures of the respective states were authorized to pass laws for regulating and guarding the fisheries in the river Delaware, annexed to their respective shores, and providing that each state should exercise a concurrent jurisdiction on the said river. These acts prove, beyond a doubt, that the proprietaries of west New Jersey, from a very early period, asserted a right to the river Delaware, or to some part thereof, below low water mark, and along its whole length; and since the western boundary of the province, under the grant to the Duke of York, was precisely the same on the bay as on the river, it may fairly be presumed, independent of his grant to the proprietaries in 1680, and the concessions made by them in the year 1676, that this claim was extended to the bay, for the purposes of navigation, fishing, and fowling.

In this state of things the Revolution was commenced, and conducted to a successful issue; when his Britannic majesty, by the treaty of peace, acknowledged the several states to be sovereign and independent, and relinquished all claims, not only to the government, but to the propriety and territorial right of the same. The right of the crown to the bay and river Delaware being thus extinguished, it would seem to follow, that the right claimed by New Jersey in those waters, was thereby confirmed; unless a better title to the same should be found to exist in some other states. Whether the claim of New Jersey extended to the middle of the bay, as we see by the compact with Pennsylvania it did to the middle of the river, is a question which we have no means of solving; but that the proprietors and inhabitants of west New Jersey made use of the bay, both for navigation and fishing, under a claim of title, from a period nearly coeval with the grants of the province, can hardly admit of a doubt. This right, indeed, is expressly granted by the Duke of York to William Penn, and the other proprietaries of west New Jersey by his grant, bearing date the 6th of August 1680. It contains a grant, not only of all bays and rivers to the granted premises belonging, but also the free use of all bays and rivers leading into, or lying between the granted premises, for navigation, fishing, or otherwise. The only objection which could have been opposed to the exercise of those acts of ownership under this grant was, that the duke had himself no title to the bay and river Delaware, under the royal grant to him. But the presumption is, nevertheless, irresistible, that the benefits intended to be bestowed by this grant, and which were confirmed by the other acts of the provincial government before noticed, were considered by the inhabitants of the province as being too valuable not to be enjoyed by them. This use of the bay and river amounted to an appropriation of the water so used (Vattel, bk. 1, c. 22, § 266); and this title became, as has before been observed, indefeasible, by the treaty of peace, except as against some other state having an equally good, or better title. How far this title in New Jersey may be affected by the grants of the Duke of York to William Penn in 1682, of the tract of country which now forms the state of Delaware, it would be improper, in this case to decide. But that the use of the bay for navigation and fishing was claimed and enjoyed by the inhabitants of that province under those grants, is as fairly to be presumed, as that it was so claimed, and used by the inhabitants of New Jersey. And we are strongly inclined to think that, if the right of the former of these states to the bay of Delaware, was founded on no other title than that of appropriation, by having used it for purposes of navigation and fishing; the effect of the Revolution, and of the treaty of peace, was to extend the limits of those states to the middle of the bay, from its mouth upwards. But be the title of the state of Delaware what it may, we are clearly of opinion, that, as between the plaintiff, who asserts, and has certainly shown, no conflicting title in the state of Delaware to the bay, and the state of New Jersey, or those acting under the sanction of her laws, the court is bound to consider that law as a sufficient justification of the proceedings under it, provided the locus in quo was within the body of the county of Cumberland, which is next to be considered.

Thirdly. The third general question then, is, whether admitting the locus in quo to be within the territorial limits of New Jersey, it is within the limits of the county of Cumberland, in which the proceedings complained of took place? The boundaries of this county towards the bay are thus described in the act which created it: "Then bounded by Cape May county to Delaware bay, and then up Delaware bay to the place of beginning." If the opinion of the court upon the last preceding question as to the construction of the original grant from Charles II. to the Duke of York be correct, it would seem to follow that the western boundary of this county extends only to low water mark on Delaware bay; the expressions "to Delaware bay," implying nothing more than to the east side of that bay, which the law extends to low water mark. We mean not, however, to give any decided opinion on this point, because, in the first place, if there be any weight in the above suggestion, (and nothing more is intended,) the legislature of that state can, at any time, should it be deemed necessary, define with greater precision the limits of the county

505

bordering on the bay; and secondly, because we think it unnecessary to decide that point in the present case; being clearly of opinion.

Fourthly. That the objections to this form of action are fatal. It is an action of trespass, brought by the owner of the Hiram, for illegally seizing, taking, and carrying away the said vessel. It appears by the evidence, that, at the time of the alleged trespass, the vessel was in the possession of John Keene, in virtue of a hiring of her to him for a month, by Hand, who had previously hired her of the plaintiff, and that the time for which Keene had hired her, had not expired when the seizure was made. The question is, can the plaintiff, under these circumstances, maintain this action? We hold the law to be clearly settled, that, to enable a person to maintain trespass, or trover, for an injury done to a personal chattel, the plaintiff must have had, at the time the injury was done, either actual, or constructive possession of the thing; as well as the general or qualified property therein. The merely being out of the actual possession is not sufficient to defeat the action, provided he has a right to demand it, because the general property, prima facie, draws to it the possession. But, if the general owner part with the possession to another person, under a contract which entitles such person to an interest in the thing, though for a limited time, the owner cannot be considered as having a constructive possession during that time, and consequently, he cannot maintain an action of trespass for an injury done to it during such possession of the bailee. His only remedy is an action on the case for consequential damages. See 1 Chit. Pl. 166, 167, 150, and the cases there cited. Also, 8 Johns. 337; 7 Johns. 9, 535; 11 Johns. 385. The Hiram then, having been lawfully in possession of Keene, under a contract of hiring for a month, which had not expired at the time the alleged trespass was committed, the action cannot be supported.

Let judgment be entered for the defendant.

19

HALL v. WILLIAMS
6 Pick. 232 (Mass. 1828)

(See 4.1, no. 13)

20

JOSEPH STORY, COMMENTARIES ON THE CONSTITUTION 3:§§ 1799–1800
1833

---

§ 1799. The first is, "The citizens of each state shall be entitled to all privileges and immunities of citizens in the

several states." There was an article upon the same subject in the confederation, which declared, "that the free inhabitants of each of these states, paupers, vagabonds, and fugitives from justice excepted, shall be entitled to all privileges and immunities of free citizens in the several states; and the people of each state shall, in every other, enjoy all the privileges of trade and commerce, subject to the same duties, impositions, and restrictions, as the inhabitants thereof respectively," &c. It was remarked by the Federalist, that there is a strange confusion in this language. Why the terms, *free inhabitants,* are used in one part of the article, *free citizens* in another, and *people* in another; or what is meant by superadding to "all privileges and immunities of free citizens," "all the privileges of trade and commerce," cannot easily be determined. It seems to be a construction, however, scarcely avoidable, that those, who come under the denomination of *free inhabitants* of a state, although not citizens of such state, are entitled, in every other state, to all the privileges of *free citizens* of the latter; that is to greater privileges, than they may be entitled to in their own state. So that it was in the power of a particular state, (to which every other state was bound to submit,) not only to confer the rights of citizenship in other states upon any persons, whom it might admit to such rights within itself, but upon any persons, whom it might allow to become *inhabitants* within its jurisdiction. But even if an exposition could be given to the term, *inhabitants,* which would confine the stipulated privileges to citizens alone, the difficulty would be diminished only, and not removed. The very improper power was, under the confederation, still retained in each state of naturalizing aliens in every other state.

§ 1800. The provision in the constitution avoids all this ambiguity. It is plain and simple in its language; and its object is not easily to be mistaken. Connected with the exclusive power of naturalization in the national government, it puts at rest many of the difficulties, which affected the construction of the article of the confederation. It is obvious, that, if the citizens of each state were to be deemed aliens to each other, they could not take, or hold real estate, or other privileges, except as other aliens. The intention of this clause was to confer on them, if one may so say, a general citizenship; and to communicate all the privileges and immunities, which the citizens of the same state would be entitled to under the like circumstances.

21

CRANDALL v. STATE
10 Conn. 339 (1834)

THIS was an information, filed by the prosecuting attorney for the county of Windham, for a violation of the statute of 1833, regarding the instruction of coloured persons not inhabitants of this state.[1] The information alleged, That at Canterbury, in said county, on the 24th of *September,* 1833, for the purpose of attending and being taught and instructed in a certain school, which before that time had been and then was set up, in said town of Canterbury, for the instruction and education of coloured persons, not inhabitants of this State, *Prudence Crandall,* of said Canterbury, with force and arms, wilfully and knowingly did harbour and board certain coloured persons, to wit, *Ann Eliza Hammond,* and others, whose names are to the attorney aforesaid unknown, and who, when so harboured and boarded, were not inhabitants of any town in this state; all which acts and doings of the said *Prudence Crandall* were done and committed without the consent in writing first obtained of a majority of the civil authority and also of the select-men of said town of Canterbury, where said school was then situated; against the peace of this state, and contrary to the form and effect of the statute law of this state in such case made and provided.

The defendant pleaded *Not guilty;* and on this issue the cause was tried, at Brooklyn, *October* term, 1833, before *Draggett,* Ch. J.

The attorney for the state claimed to have proved that the defendant had harboured and boarded divers colored persons for the purpose of attending the school mentioned in the information; and that such coloured persons were not inhabitants of this state, when so harboured and boarded, but that they belonged to the states of Rhode-Island, Pennsylvania and New-York, and were born in those states respectively, of coloured parents there belonging, and had continued to reside in the places of their birth until the *Spring* of the year 1833, when they came to Canterbury to attend said school, for the purpose of being

instructed in the ordinary branches of school education. Upon these facts being proved, the attorney claimed, that the defendant had incurred the penalty provided by the act; no claim being made that a license had been granted for the school. The defendant claimed, and prayed the court to instruct the jury, that if they should find these facts proved, such coloured persons were to be regarded as citizens of the states where they respectively belonged and that they were entitled to the privileges and immunities secured by the 2nd section of the 4th article of the constitution of the United States; and that said school, for the purpose of acquiring useful knowledge, while the privilege of attending the same school for the same purpose, was allowed to coloured persons belonging to this state, and imposing a penalty for harbouring and boarding coloured persons not belonging to this state, while no such penalty was imposed for harbouring and boarding the coloured inhabitants of this state, was repugnant to the constitution of the United States, and void. The court instructed the jury as follows:

"This is an information filed by the attorney for the state, for an alleged violation of a statute law, passed by the General Assembly, at their last session, relating to inhabitants; the preamble to the act, embracing the reasons for the law.

"It is alleged in this information, that since the 22d day of *August* last, to wit, on the 24th day of *September,* 1833, the defendant has, wilfully and knowingly, harboured and boarded coloured persons not inhabitants of the state, for the purposes mentioned in said act, without having obtained in writing, the consent of the civil authority and the selectment of Canterbury where the school had been set up. As to the facts in this case, there seems to be but little controversy. It has scarcely been denied, that coloured persons have been harboured and boarded, by the defendant, for the objects alleged, within the time set forth in this information. You, gentlemen of the jury, have heard the evidence, and as it is your exclusive business to pass upon these facts, you will say whether or not they are true.

"If these facts are not proved to your satisfaction, then you may dismiss the cause; for in that event, you have no further duty to perform. If, however, you find the *facts* true, then another duty equally important, devolves upon the jury. It is an undeniable proposition, that the jury are judges of both law and fact, in all cases of this nature. It is, however, equally true, that the court is to state *its* opinion to the jury, upon all questions of law, arising in the trial of a criminal cause, and to submit to their consideration, both law and fact, without any direction how to find their verdict.

"The counsel for the defendant, have rested her defence upon a provision of the constitution of the United States, claiming that the statute law of this state, upon which this information is founded, is inconsistent with that provision, and, therefore, void. This is the great question involved in this case: and it is about to be submitted to your consideration.

"It is admitted, that there are no provisions in the constitution of this state, which conflict with this act. It may be

---

[1] The preamble and first section of that act are in the following words: "Whereas, attempts have been made to establish literary institutions in this state, for the instruction of coloured persons belonging to other states and countries, which would tend to the great increase of the coloured population of the state, and thereby to the injury of the people: Therefore,

"Sec. 1. *Be it enacted by the Senate and House of Representatives in General Assembly convened,* That no person shall set up or establish in this state any school, academy, or literary institution, for the instruction or education of coloured persons, who are not inhabitants of this state, nor instruct or teach in any school, academy, or other literary institution whatever in this state, or harbour or board, for the purpose of attending or being taught or instructed in any such school, academy, or literary institution, any coloured person who is not an inhabitant of any town in this state, without the consent in writing, first obtained of a majority of the civil authority, and also of the select-men of the town in which such school, academy, or literary institution is situated; and each and every person who shall knowingly do any act forbidden as aforesaid, or shall be aiding or assisting therein, shall, for the first offence, forfeit and pay to the treasurer of this state, a fine of one hundred dollars, and for the second offence, shall forfeit and pay a fine of two hundred dollars, and so double for every offence of which he or she shall be convicted. And all informing officers are required to make due presentment of all breaches of this act. *Provided,* That nothing in this act shall extend to any district school established in any school society under the laws of this state, or to any school established by any school society under the laws of this state, or to any incorporated academy or incorporated school for instruction in this state."

remarked here, that the constitution of the United States, is above all other law,—it is emphatically the supreme law of the land, and the judges are so to declare it. From the highest court to the lowest, even that of a justice of the peace, all laws, whether made by Congress or state legislatures, are subject to examination, and when brought to the test of the constitution, may be declared utterly void. But in order to do this, the court should first find the law contrary, and plainly contrary, to the constitution. Although this may be done, and done too, by the humblest court, yet it never should be done but upon a full conviction that the law in question is unconstitutional.

"Many things said upon this trial, may be laid out of the case. The consideration of slavery, with all its evils and degrading consequences, may be dismissed with the consideration that it is a degrading evil. The benefits, blessings and advantages of instruction and education, may also cease to claim your attention, except you may well consider that education is a 'fundamental privilege,' for this is the basis of all free government.

"Having read this law, the question comes to us with peculiar force, does it clearly violate the constitution of the United States? The section claimed to have been violated, reads as follows, to wit: Art. 4. sec. 2. 'The citizens of each state shall be entitled to all privileges and immunities of citizens in the several states.' It has been urged, that this section was made to direct, exclusively, the action of the general government, and therefore, can never be applied to state laws. This is not the opinion of the court. The plain and obvious meaning of this provision, is to secure to the *citizens* of all the states, the same privileges as are secured to our own, by our own state laws. Should a citizen of Connecticut purchase a farm in Massachusetts, and the legislature of Massachusetts tax the owner of that farm, four times as much as they would tax a citizen of Massachusetts, because the one resided in Connecticut and the other in Massachusetts; or should a law be passed, by either of those states, that no citizen of the other, should reside or trade in that other, this would, undoubtedly, be an unconstitutional law, and should be so declared.

"The second section was provided as a substitute for the 4th article of the Confederation. That article has also been read, and by comparing them, you can perceive the object intended by the substitute.

"The act in question provides, that coloured persons, who are not inhabitants of this State, shall not be harboured and boarded for the purposes therein mentioned, within this state, without the consent of the civil authority and select-men of the town. We are, then, brought to the great question, are they *citizens* within the provisions of this section of the constitution? The law extends to all persons of colour not inhabitants of this state, whether they live in the state of New-York, or in the West-Indies, or in any other foreign country.

"In deciding this question, I am happy that my opinion can be revised, by the supreme court of this state and of the United States, should you return a verdict against the defendant.

"The persons contemplated in this act are *not citizens* within the obvious meaning of that section of the consti-

tution of the United States, which I have just read. Let me begin, by putting this plain question. Are *Slaves citizens?* At the adoption of the constitution of the United States, every state was a slave state. Massachusetts had begun the work of emancipation within her own borders. And Connecticut, as early as 1784, had also enacted laws making all those free at the age of 25, who might be born within the State, after that time. We all know, that slavery is recognized in that constitution; and it is the duty of this court to take that constitution as it is, for we have sworn to support it. Although the term 'slavery' cannot be found written out in the constitution, yet no one can mistake the object of the 3d section of the 4th article: 'No person held to service or labour in one state, under the laws thereof, escaping into another, shall, in consequence of any law or regulation therein, be discharged from such service or labour, but shall be delivered, upon claim of the party to whom such service or labour may be due.'

"The 2d section of the 1st article, reads as follows:—'Representatives and direct taxes, shall be apportioned among the several states which may be included in this Union, according to their respective numbers, which shall be determined by adding to the whole number of free persons, including those bound to service for a term of years, and excluding *Indians* not taxed, three fifths of *all other persons.*' The 'other persons' are slaves, and they became the basis of representation, by adding them to the white population in that proportion. Then slaves were not considered citizens by the framers of the constitution.

"A *citizen* means a *freeman.* By referring to Dr. *Webster,* one of the most learned men of this or any other country, we have the following definition of the term—'Citizen: 1. A native of a city, or an inhabitant who enjoys the freedom and privileges of the city in which he resides. 2. A townsman, a man of trade, not a gentleman. 3. An inhabitant; a dweller in any city, town or country. 4. In the United States, it means a person, native or naturalized, who has the privilege of exercising the elective franchise, and of purchasing and holding real estate.'

"Are *Indians* citizens? It is admitted in the argument, that they are not; but it is said, they belong to distinct tribes. This cannot be true; because all *Indians* do not belong to a tribe. It may be now added, that by the declared law of New-York, *Indians* are not citizens; and the learned Chancellor *Kent,* says 'they never can be made citizens.' *Indians* were literally natives of our soil; they were born here; and yet they are not citizens.

"The *Mohegans* were once a mighty tribe, powerful and valiant; and who among us ever saw one of them performing military duty, or exercising, with the white men, the privilege of the elective franchise, or holding an office? And what is the reason? I answer, they are not citizens, according to the acceptation of the term in the United States.

"Are *free blacks* citizens? It has been ingeniously said, that vessels may be owned and navigated, by free blacks, and the American flag will protect them; but you will remember, that the statute which makes that provision, is an act of Congress, and not the constitution. Admit, if you please, that Mr. *Cuffee,* a respectable merchant, has owned vessels, and sailed them under the American flag; yet this does not prove him to be such citizen as the constitution contemplates. But that question stands undecided, by any legal tribunal within my knowledge. For the purposes of this case, it is not necessary to determine that question.

"It has been also urged, that as coloured persons may commit treason, they must be considered citizens. Every person born in the United States, as well as every person who may reside here, owes allegiance, of some sort, to the government, because the government affords him protection. Treason against this government, consists in levying war against the government of the United States, or aiding its enemy in time of war. Treason may be committed, by persons who are not entitled to the elective franchise. For if they reside under the protection of the government, it would be treason to levy war against that government, as much as if they were citizens.

"I think Chancellor *Kent*, whose authority it gives me pleasure to quote, determines this question, by fair implication. Had this authority considered free blacks citizens, he had an ample opportunity to say so. But what he has said excludes that idea: In most of the United States, there is a distinction in respect to political privileges, between free white persons and free coloured persons of African blood; and in no part of the country do the latter, in point of fact, participate equally with the whites, in the exercise of civil and political rights. The African race are essentially a degraded caste, of inferior rank and condition in society. Marriages are forbidden between them and whites, in some of the states, and when not absolutely contrary to law, they are revolting, and regarded as an offence against public decorum. By the revised statutes of Illinois, published in 1829, marriages between whites and negroes, or mulattos, are declared void, and the persons so married are liable to be whipped, fined and imprisoned. By an old statute of Massachusetts, of 1705, such marriages were declared void, and are so still. A similar statute provision exists in Virginia and North-Carolina. Such connexions in France and Germany, constitute the degraded state of concubinage, which is known in the civil law. But they are not legal marriages, because the parties want that equality of state or condition, which is essential to the contract.' 2 Kent's Comm. 258.

"I go further back still. When the constitution of the United States was adopted, every state, (Massachusetts excepted,) tolerated slavery. And in some of the states, down to a late period, severe laws have been kept in force regarding slaves. With respect to New-York, at that time, her laws and penalties were severe indeed; and it was not until *July*, 4th, 1827, that this great state was ranked among the free states.

"To my mind, it would be a perversion of terms, and the well known rule of construction, to say, that slaves, free blacks, or Indians, were citizens, within the meaning of that term, as used in the constitution. God forbid that I should add to the degradation of this race of men; but I am bound, by my duty, to say, they are not citizens.

"I have thus shown you that this law is not contrary to the 2d section of the 4th art. of the constitution of the United States; for that embraces only citizens.

"But there is still another consideration. If they were citizens, I am not sure this law would then be unconstitutional. The legislature may *regulate schools*. I am free to say, that education is a fundamental privilege; but this law does not prohibit schools. It places them under the care of the civil authority and select-men; and why is not this a very suitable regulation? I am not sure but the legislature might make a law like this, extending to the white inhabitants of other states, who are unquestionably citizens, placing all schools for them under suitable boards of examination, for the public good; and I can see no objection to the board created by this act.

"What can the legislature of this state do? It can make any law, which any legislature can make, unless it shall violate the constitution of the United States, or the constitution of its own state; and in my opinion, *this* law is not inconsistent with either.

"The jury have nothing to do with the popularity or unpopularity of this or any other law, which may come before them for adjudication. They have nothing to do with its policy or impolicy. Your only enquiry is, whether it is constitutional.

"I may say with truth, that there is no disposition in the judicial tribunals of this state, nor among the people, to nullify the laws of the state, but if constitutional to submit to them, and carry them into full effect, as citizens. If individuals do not like the laws enacted by one legislature, their remedy is at the ballot boxes. It often occurs, on subjects of taxation, that laws are supposed, by some, to be unjust and oppressive. Nearly every session of the Assembly, attempts have been made to alter and change such laws; but as long as they exist, they must have effect.

"You will now take this case into your consideration, and notwithstanding my opinion of the law, you will return your verdict according to law and evidence. I have done my duty, and you will do yours."

The jury returned a verdict against the defendant; and she thereupon filed a motion in arrest of judgment, on two grounds; first, that the superior court had not jurisdiction of the offences charged; and secondly, that the information was insufficient. The court overruled the motion and rendered judgment against the defendant to pay a fine of 100 dollars and costs. The defendant thereupon filed a bill of exceptions to the charge, and a motion in error, containing the following assignment of errors: "That the superior court, in the opinions expressed and intimations given to the jury in the cause, and in deciding that the superior court had jurisdiction of the same, and that said information and the matters therein contained were sufficient, manifestly erred and mistook the law; for that the court should have informed the jury, that said coloured persons were to be regarded as citizens of the states to which they respectively belonged and of the United States, and were entitled to the privileges and immunities secured by the 4th article of the constitution of the United States; and that said law of the state of Connecticut was repugnant to the constitution of the United States and void; and said court should have decided, that it had no jurisdiction of the cause, and that said information was insufficient."

Goddard and *W. W. Ellsworth*, for the plaintiff in error, contended, That the act of the General Assembly, on which this prosecution is founded, is unconstitutional and void. In support of this proposition, they insisted,

1. That the coloured persons mentioned in the information, are *citizens* of their respective states. If they were white, it is conceded they would be. The point turns, then, upon a distinction, in *colour* only. This distinction, as the basis of fundamental rights, is, in the first place, novel. It is not recognized, by the common law of England, or the principles of the British constitution; by our own declaration of independence; or by the constitution of Connecticut.

Secondly, it would be extremely inconvenient, if not impracticable, in its application. Who can tell the proportions and trace the mixtures of blood? What shall be the scale for the ascertainment of citizenship? Shall one half, one quarter, one twentieth, or at the least possible taint of negro blood, be sufficient to take from its possessor the citizen character?

Thirdly, the persons in question are human beings, born in these states, and owe the *same obligation* to the state and to its government as white citizens. In all the writers on public law there is one ancient and universal classification of the people of a country: all who are born within the jurisdiction of a state are natives, and all others are aliens. This classification grows out of the doctrine of natural allegiance, a tie created by birth. All writers agree in the foundation of allegiance, and in its obligations, while it exists; some holding that it can never be thrown off, and some that it may be, under legislative enactments; but all agreeing that while the residence of the citizen continues in the state of his birth, allegiance demands obedience from the citizen and protection from the government. Allegiance is not peculiar to any one government or country; but it is held to exist in every country and every government where there are pretensions to social order and civil institutions. It reaches the man of one complexion as much as that of another: it is the ordinance of the great Parent of all society, fairly inferrible from the nature and necessity of human government. If allegiance is due from our coloured population, its correlative is due from the government, *viz.* protection and equal laws. If allegiance is an ordinance of Heaven, it reaches, and binds, and confers rights upon every man within its range and rightful sway. Here, the free man of colour may take his position, and upon the immutable principles of justice and truth demand his political rights from that government which he is bound to aid and to defend: *he is not a citizen to obey, and an alien to demand protection.* Nor is he of an intermediate class. His relations to society are the same as others; his absolute and relative rights, his rights of person and to things, his acquisitions of property by contract and by inheritance,—and even the soil, which no alien inherits—are the same. So every requisition of the law, in its civil and criminal provisions, reaches him. His legal capabilities and his legal obligations are the same. Every favour or right conferred on the citizens, by general legislation, reaches *him;* every requisition demands *his* obedience. The doctrine of natural allegiance was recognised in *Talbot* v. *Janson,* 3 Dal. 133. *The United States* v. *Williams,* in 1799, before *Ellsworth,* Ch. J. and *Law,* Dist. J. cited 2 Cranch

82. n. *Murray* v. *The Charming Betsey,* 2 Cranch 63. The case of *The Santissima Trinidad,* 7 Wheat. 283. *Jackson* d. *Smith* v. *Goodell,* 20 Johns. Rep. 188.

Fourthly, there is nothing in the constitutions of the native states of these persons, or in the constitution of the United States, depriving them of fundamental rights on the ground of colour. [Here the counsel went into an examination of all the provisions bearing on this subject in the constitution or charter of Rhode-Island, the constitutions of Pennsylvania and New-York, the articles of confederation, the constitution of the United States and the acts of Congress.]

Fifthly, by the free and excellent form of civil government, adopted by the people of this state, and secured by the charter of Charles II., as well as by the constitution of 1818, the privileges of the *habeas corpus* act, which, in Great-Britain, made coloured people *freeman,* are adopted and established as fundamental principles. Stat. Conn. 5. 22. ed. 1808. Const. Conn. art. 1. sec. 1. 5. 14. 16. 17. art. 6.

2. That as *citizens,* the constitution of the United States secures to the persons in question the right of residing in Connecticut, and pursuing the acquisition of knowledge, as people of colour may do, who are settled here.

In the first place, the language of the constitution (art. 4. sec. 2.) is *universal* and *unqualified:* it says, "*every citizen.*"

Secondly, a citizen of another state may come here to *reside,* without being fined, or laid under any peculiar exactions. He must have a right to do what our citizens may do, under like circumstances.

Thirdly he may come here to be *educated.* The right of education is a *fundamental* right. It is the main pillar of our free institutions. *Corfield* v. *Coryell,* 4 Wash. C. C. Rep. 380. 3 Story's Com. 674. 2 Kent's Com. 61.

The law under consideration forbids a citizen of any state to come here to pursue education, as all others may do, because he has not a *legal settlement in the state.* It is a crime to feed him, to teach him or entertain him.

The principal objections against these positions, are, first, that men of colour cannot *vote* in Connecticut; and therefore, they are not citizens of Connecticut.

The first answer to this objection is, that in Pennsylvania and New-York, (as well as in Maine, New-Hampshire, Massachusetts, Vermont, New-Jersey, Delaware, Maryland, North-Carolina and Tennessee,) they *can* vote; and if voting is the criterion of citizenship, they are citizens here.

But secondly, the right of voting is not the criterion of citizenship: the one has no natural or necessary connexion with the other. Cases may exist where persons vote who are not citizens, and where persons are citizens and do not vote. The right of suffrage is nowhere universal and absolute. It is founded in notions of internal police, varying frequently, even in the same government; whereas citizenship grows out of allegiance, which is every where the same, and is unchanging. Persons sometimes vote for one branch of the government only, as was lately the case in New-York. How much of a citizen was such a voter? Formerly, property was a necessary qualification in Connecticut. Were none but persons of property citizens? Suppose a voter in Connecticut should lose his right of suffrage, by reason of criminal conduct, as by law he may do, does he cease to be a citizen? Does he become an *alien*? No female can vote, nor any minor; but are not females and minors citizens?

If voting makes a citizen, what confusion! The same man in one state, is a full citizen; in another, half a citizen; in another a non-descript; in another, an alien. How absurd to create such a distinction in these states!

Again, if voting is the criterion of citizenship, then every person who has been *naturalized*, has a right to vote; for he is a citizen; but every naturalized person has not of course a right to vote. So the widow and children of a person who dies after he has applied for naturalization, but before he has obtained it, are declared citizens; but it is needless to say they cannot vote.

Another objection is, that Indians are not citizens; and hence it is inferred, that these pupils are not. In the first place, these pupils are not Indians. But secondly, Indians have hitherto been treated as members of national tribes, in alliance with the United States, according to treaty stipulations and the intercourse law. They have been held to be without the *practical* jurisdiction of the state. But since Congress has withdrawn its ancient jurisdiction, and the state have extended theirs over these tribes, it is not certain what is the exact political character of an Indian born in these states. Even in New-York, before the late change in our Indian affairs, they were there decided to be *citizens*, by a unanimous opinion of the supreme court, on the ground of the state's having jurisdiction and the Indians owing allegiance. *Jackson* d. *Smith* v. *Goodell*, 20 Johns. Rep. 188. 191, 2, 3.

Again, it is objected, that slaves are not citizens. But these pupils are not slaves. The reason why slaves are not citizens, is, because they are held to be *property*, and not men, and hence have not freedom of choice or action. The reason does not reach these pupils.

It is further objected, that the legislature may, as it has often done, superintend and regulate schools; and that the act in question is only an exercise of that power. The fact asserted here is not true. The power in question is not one of mere supervision and regulation, but it is a power of *exclusion* on the ground of alienage. Such it is in effect; and so it was designed to be. As well might the legislature, in order to raise up a more beautiful or vigorous generation of citizens, prohibit the harbouring or entertaining of any citizen from the other states, who was not six feet high, or had not a well proportioned body, or black eyes, or a clear skin. If this power exists, the legislature may *regulate* every youth at Yale-College, being citizens of other states, out of our borders as *aliens*. If indeed this power exists, such persons can just as well be prohibited all *entrance* into the state, as to be removed, or *regulated* away, after they have come here.

The legislature may, undoubtedly, superintend public schools; for they are instituted by the legislature, and sustained by public money. Nor is it doubted that the legislature may superintend and regulate private schools, as it does trades, professions, taverns, sales at auction, peddling, &c. It may superintend and regulate *all* the pursuits

of the citizens; but then this must be done, by a general and equal law. Mere *birth* in another state cannot be seized upon as ground of distinction and consequent privation. This is not consistent with the paramount authority of the constitution, that "the citizens of each state shall be entitled to all the privileges and immunities of citizens in the several states." Can our legislature say, that no man shall be a lawyer, or physician, or merchant, or mechanic here, who was born in Massachusetts?

But it is asked, may we not keep out of Connecticut paupers and vagabonds; and have not such laws been of long standing? Stat. 281. 2. tit. 51. s. 6. 7. 8. This ancient statute was enacted before the adoption of the articles of confederation or the present constitution of the United States, when this state had a right to exclude the citizens of other states or colonies; for they then stood in no other light than *aliens*. But this law is now contrary to the constitution of the United States, and cannot be sustained. If the 2nd section of the 4th article means any thing, it secures to a citizen of New-York a right to come here, and *remain* here, if he offends against no general law. He cannot be whipped out, nor carried out, of the state, because he has no legal settlement. He may present the shield of the constitution, and, as *Paul* claimed the immunity of a Roman citizen, he may claim the immunity of an American citizen. The legislature may declare, that such an one shall not gain a legal settlement; nor can it be forced to burden the public treasury with the support of a foreign citizen; for the whole matter of settlement and of supporting paupers of any description, is of mere municipal regulation; but it can go no further. Neither the existence of present nor the apprehension of future poverty, can strike out of the constitution the word "citizen;" and a citizen has universal right, title and immunity to a *residence* and other fundamental rights. So the state may guard itself against thieves from without or within, by punishing them for crimes committed in our territory, or by enacting *general* laws of prevention; but it cannot prohibit a citizen of the United States from entering this state and remaining in it, because he has offended elsewhere, or may offend again.

Judson and *C. F. Cleaveland*, for the state, (defendant in error,) after remarking upon the magnitude of the question, as affecting not the town of Canterbury alone, but every town in the state and every state in the Union; as the principles urged by the counsel for the plaintiff in error, if established, would, in their consequences, destroy the government itself and this American nation—blotting out this nation of white men and substituting one from the African race—thus involving the honour of the state, the dignity of the people and the preservation of its name— contended,

1. That the state does possess the power to regulate its own schools, and pursue its own systems of education, in its own chosen way, independently of the question of citizenship. The matter of *education* was never given up to the general government; because the structure, object, and end of that government were of a different character. The government has never attempted any controul over *education*, in any one state in the Union, but only in the district

of *Columbia.* The state governments have uninterruptedly exercised this power; and their capacity to do so will be found much more congenial, than that of the general government. We ought to be satisfied that the state sovereignties maintain their internal police—their domestic arrangements, while the general government moves on in its elevated sphere of action.

It has ever been the policy of this state, to regulate all its *schools, academies,* and *colleges,* and subject them to a strict *visitorial power.* The seeds of morality and virtue are first sown in our schools, and if neglected, the seeds of vice and immorality soon spring up, and would undermine all that we hold dear, even the government itself. If in Connecticut we have any renown, it is because our fathers have watched over the education of youth with becoming solicitude. As early as the year 1717, a statute was passed, by the General Assembly, establishing a *Board of visitors,* such as this act contemplates. Stat. 213, 4. ed. 1750.

This law continued in force until 1795, when the present system was adopted, and a *new Board* was instituted, less burthensome to the people. The law in question goes back to the early policy of the state, and takes the civil authority and select-men, as the proper board under this act. Every *college* and every incorporated academy in this state, have established a board of visitors; and this is not deemed a violation of the constitution. It is essential to good order, and the prosperity of these institutions, that it should be so. It may be presumed, that every state in the Union has exercised the same unquestionable power.

The late President *Dwight,* in his *travels,* has taken pains to collect the laws of Massachusetts, on this subject; and by these laws, it will be seen, that it has equally been the policy of that state to put all her schools, both *public* and *private,* under the superintendence of the *select-men;* and they go so far as not to allow any but *citizens* to instruct their schools.

"If a person who is not a *citizen,* shall keep a school in the commonwealth for one month, he shall be subjected to a fine of 20*l.*"

The legislature of Massachusetts became the guardians of all schools, that such schools may teach the "principles of piety, justice, and *love of country.*"

These are object worthy to be guarded, and are no less so now, than when Dr. *Dwight* wrote, or when the legislature of Massachusetts enacted the laws he had enumerated. This "love of country" ought to remind us, that the states have a great work to do, in regulating and superintending their schools; and as it has never been surrendered under the constitution, we should not, for the mere purpose of indulging the visionary fanatic, now construe it away.

It is incident to all these literary corporations, that students may be admitted or excluded at pleasure. Suppose the corporation of Yale-College should, by solemn vote, prohibit students from South-Carolina, would any constitutional question arise on that prohibition, or could they claim admission, as matter of right under the constitution? The answer is obvious. The corporation has that right of exclusion; and so has the state. Should the trustees of the Plainfield Academy pass an order that in future, no stu-

dent from the state of Rhode-Island should be admitted, is that a violation of the constitution of the United-States? Surely not. The state created these corporations, and could not impart to them power it did not itself possess.

2. That these pupils are not *"citizens"* within the 2nd sect. of the 4th art. of the constitution of the United States, and as such entitled to all the privileges and immunities of citizens of the several states.

In deciding this question, every thing must depend upon the rules of construction, established by the common law. These rules are well understood, and established in ages gone by, they will now be of infinite service in guiding to a correct result.

1st. The *intention* of enacting power is to be sought for.

2d. The whole instrument or *act* must be taken together, so that its parts may be consistent with the whole. And

3d. The period of time when the enactment was made, embracing the language then in use, and the circumstances of the country, enter into the construction of the instrument and indicate its meaning.

In the administration of justice upon a *contract,* a deed or a will, we go back to the period when the contract was made—the condition of the parties at the time when the deed was sealed—and all accompanying circumstances, are taken into the account, to learn the extent of the obligation. In construing a legislative act, of a hundred years standing, the court is not to be governed by the circumstances of the present day. To do so, would be to pervert, and not to construe. With these rules, we come to this question.

What *was* the *intention* of those who framed the constitution? Did they mean to place persons of colour on the footing of equality with themselves, and did they mean to make them *citizens?*

In answering this question, it matters little what may be the opinion of a few madmen or enthusiasts now, but what was the intention of the people of the United States, *at the time* when the constitution was adopted. Any *term,* like the term *inhabitant,* may be used in various senses. That term sometimes means a simple resident, or dweller, but when used in another sense, it means one who may have gained a settlement—one who has removed from another state, and complied with all the requirements of our statute to constitute him a *legal inhabitant.* This is the technical use of that term. So also with the word *citizen.* That term may be used in diverse ways, and convey to the mind diverse meanings. It is quite immaterial how it may have been used in loose debate—in speeches—or in letters; but the question really is, how was it used in the constitution? What was its meaning *then,* and for what purpose was it used there? Before this question can be properly answered, we may be allowed to enquire also, what was then meant by the term *"immunity,"* or *"privilege?"* Privilege then, as now, signified *"any particular benefit, advantage, right or immunity not common to others of the human race."*

"Immunity," as there used, is synonymous with privilege, so that *the* privileges and immunities to be enjoyed by *these citizens,* was something over and above what all the human race could enjoy. We must now advert to the condition of the country, and the circumstances of the human race, then upon the face of this country. The white men and the coloured men composed the grand divisions of the human family. The *white* men then were entitled to particular privileges, above the coloured men: civil and political rights belonged, by the laws of all the states, to the former, but not to the latter. The coloured men were either natives, called Indians, or of African descent, called Negroes. From the Indians this whole country had but recently been conquered; and as in many of the states, they were still very numerous, it cannot even be pretended, that Indians were embraced in the term *citizen*. The African race, as a body, were then *slaves*, and held in bondage, by those who made the constitution. It was then deemed fit and proper to hold slaves. All the states in the Union were slave states, and their laws tolerated slavery. Massachusetts and Connecticut had passed laws that coloured persons born after a certain period should be free at 25, but they still held slaves. And can it be entertained for one moment, that those who framed the constitution should hold one portion of *a race of men* in bondage, while the other portion were made *citizens?* This would be strange inconsistency. Go back to the time when the constitution was made, and enquire after the condition of the country, and take into consideration all its circumstances, and all its difficulties will be out of the way. *Then* it was not immoral to hold slaves. The *best men* bought and sold negroes, without a scruple. This impulse is of modern date; and however creditable to the heart, cannot alter the *constitution.* The immortal *Washington,* who presided at the convention, and who subscribed the instrument, under the laws of Virginia held more than one hundred slaves, as his property, on that day; and he was not thus inconsistent. He never intended to have you say, that the portion of the human race which were held in bondage were slaves, and the residue of that same colour were *citizens.* This position is supported by the fact that in the same article of the constitution, slavery is recognized. The 3d clause of the same section, is as follows: "No *person* held to service or labour, in one state, under the laws thereof, escaping into another, shall, in consequence of any law or regulation therein, be discharged from such service, but shall be delivered up, on claim of the party, to whom such service or labour may be due." Although the term "slave" is not used in this clause, yet its meaning is perfectly obvious. It is as plain to our understandings, as if it had been written, "No slave owned by any person in one state, escaping to any other state, shall, &c." The term "slave," also, would carry with it the inseparable distinction of colour. If *birth* alone gives *citizenship,* why is not this *slave* a *citizen?* Because the terms are contradictory. These slaves are called "persons" in the constitution, and the white men are citizens. So that if we regard at all, the *whole instrument,* as we are bound to do, by the rules of construction, we must reject the use of the term *citizen,* when applied to the coloured race.

The counsel for the plaintiff in error insist, "that the *distinction of colour is novel, inconvenient and impracticable.*" The position thus assumed will embrace Indians, and if we add to this another proposition laid down in the defence, that *birth* and not *colour* constitutes citizenship, the Indians

are surely embraced. Can it be seriously contended, that the constitution does secure to Indians the right of citizens? Practically, it has never been so. When the constitution was adopted, this country had but recently emerged from the Indian wars. These wars were wars of conquest; and the white men had driven the red men from their lands, and acquired a title to those lands, by conquest and by force; and do you believe, that so soon, these conquered individuals would all be made *citizens?* There is another fact, which would repel this idea. In several of the states, when the constitution was adopted, there were more Indians than *white men;* and if citizens, the Indians would have had the supremacy. We need not go abroad for evidence on this point in the case. Connecticut has ever had within its limts numerous Indians, both tribes, and others not belonging to tribes; and whoever saw one of these Indians under our own laws, before or since the revolution, enjoying *one civil* or *political* privilege? If citizenship be a matter of favour, then surely the Indian stands far above the African. This is the Indian's home—it was once his soil, but it has passed into other hands. It is now the white man's country; and the white man is an American citizen.

Chancellor *Kent* adds his high authority to what has been said: "It is the declared law of New-York, that Indians are not citizens, but distinct tribes, being under the protection of government, and consequently, never can be made citizens under the act of Congress." 2 Kent's Com. 72. 2nd ed.

The distinction of colour, so far from being novel, is marked, in numerous ways, in our political system.

The first Congress after the constitution was adopted, was composed of many of those distinguished patriots, who framed the constitution, and from that circumstance would be supposed to know what its spirit was. Some of the earliest work they performed for the country, was to establish by law a uniform rule of naturalization. The first law regarding naturalization was passed by Congress in 1790, and in it this precise and technical language is used: "Any alien, being a *free white person,* may become a *citizen,* by complying with the requisites hereinafter named." In the year 1795, a further regulation was made by law, when the same language is used: "Any *free white* person may become a citizen," &c. In 1798—1802—1813, and 1824, similar laws were passed, on the same subject, and in each of those laws, the same technical language is used. These laws were carrying into effect the constitution itself; and if the constitution in any part of it embraced coloured persons as citizens, then Congress mistook its duty, and early departed from its provisions. Congress have also marked this distinction of colour in the post-office laws. "No person of colour can be engaged in the post-office, or in the transportation of the mail." This is a right open to all but persons of colour. Chancellor *Kent* settles this question beyond cavil: "The act of Congress confines the description of aliens capable of naturalization to 'free white persons.' I presume that this excludes the inhabitants of Africa and their descendants; and it may become a question, to what extent persons of mixed blood, as mulattoes, are excluded, and what shades or degrees of mixture of colour disqualify an alien from application for the benefits of the act of naturalization. Perhaps there might be difficulties as to the copper-coloured natives of America, or the yellow or tawney race of Asiatics, though I should doubt whether any of those were 'white persons,' within the purview of the law." 2 Kent's Com. 72 2nd ed.

Again: "In most of the United States, there is a distinction, in respect to political privileges, between free white persons and free coloured persons of African blood; and in no part of the country do the latter, in point of fact, participate equally with the whites, in the exercise of civil and political rights. The African race are essentially a degraded caste, of inferior rank and condition in society. Marriages are forbidden between them and whites, in some of the states, and when not absolutely contrary to law, they are revolting, and regarded as an offence against public decorum. By the revised statutes of Illinois, published in 1829, marriages between whites and negroes, or mulattoes, are declared void, and the persons so married are liable to be whipped, fined and imprisoned. By an old statute of Massachusetts, of 1705, such marriages were declared void, and are so still. A similar statute provision exists in Virginia and North-Carolina. Such connexions in France and Germany, constitute the degraded state of concubinage, which is known in the civil law. But they are not legal marriages, because the parties want that equality of state or condition, which is essential to the contract." 2 Kent's Com. 258, n. 2nd ed.

This distinguished author was in active life when the constitution was framed, and knows its import, and has emphatically told us, that there ever has been, and still is, this distinction of colour.—To show that this is not "novel," we may refer to the constitutional provisions of many of the states. To begin with the constitution of our own state, we shall find this distinction of colour is kept up throughout that instrument. No person can be elected to the office of governor, lieutenant-governor, or representative, unless he be an *elector,* and none other than *white male citizens* can be made electors. These are the explicit provisions of the constitution of Connecticut, and now one branch of the government is solemnly called on to disregard the distinction of colour!

Let us mark the provisions of the constitutions of other states. In Delaware—in all elections, none but free *white* male citizens can vote. In Maryland—Every free *white* male citizen shall vote. In Virginia—"Every *white* male citizen of the commonwealth, resident therein, shall vote." In South-Carolina "Every free *white* man may vote." In Ohio—"All *white* male inhabitants shall vote." In Louisiana—"Every free *white* male citizen of the United States" shall have right to vote. In Mississippi—"Every free *white* male person shall have right to vote." In Illinois—"All *white* male inhabitants, resident, have right to vote." In Alabama—"Every *white* male person shall vote." Indiana—"Every *white* male citizen of the United States, may vote." Rhode-Island has defined the qualifications of *freemen,* and among these qualifications, a man must be *white,* in order to enjoy the elective franchise. In all these states, constitutional provisions forever cut off the coloured man from the enjoyment of the "immunity" of voting for his rulers.

By the constitution of the state of New-York, a singular disqualification exists. All white men who go into that state, can vote, after a residence of six months, but the coloured man must have resided there three years, and possess, free from incumbrance, real estate to the value of 250 dollars.

But it is said, in relation to coloured persons, that the constitution denominates them citizens: but a simple reading of the article will evince, that this term *there* signifies only the same as *residence.* It is used as synonymous with "inhabitant" and "resident." All these constitutional provisions relate to the right of suffrage. These provisions exclude the black man from the enjoyment of this privilege; and this evidence is so strong that the counsel for the plaintiff in error are obliged to assume the ground, that this *elective franchise* is not an *immunity* or *privilege!*

This is, indeed, the legitimate consequence of the whole argument; but is it true, that the right of suffrage is not a privilege? The whole structure of our government contradicts this proposition. We are distinguished from other nations, by this right of *electing our rulers.* It is the highest privilege which freemen can enjoy; it is an immunity at the very foundation of a republican government. Why was the revolution set in motion? Why was the declaration of independence subscribed by those immortal patriots? Because the people said, that *taxation* and *representation* should go together. This right of suffrage was denied, as a right, and the flames of the revolution burst forth, and taught those who denied the right, that it was one which freemen should enjoy. Take away this right, and American liberty will cease. It is an *immunity* which belongs to these states—one which they never will give up. It belongs to them as citizens, and as it has been denied to the coloured race generally, it is evidence, that that race were not embraced by the framers of the constitution, in the term citizen. Were the aid of a judicial decision needed on this point, it may be found in the opinion of Judge *Washington,* in the case of *Corfield* v. *Coryell,* 4 Wash. C. C. Rep. 371. He says in that case, that "the elective franchise is a fundamental privilege, secured by this article of the constitution." We have, therefore, the authority of Chancellor *Kent* and Judge *Washington,* the laws of congress and the constitutions of the several states in opposition to the extraordinary proposition advanced by the opposing counsel.

There is another part of their argument, which may require an answer. It is claimed, that all such state laws as may authorize the removal of paupers from one state, to that to which they belong, is an infringement of the constitution. A citizen of one state, although a *pauper,* may come here, and it is not in our power to remove him to his home. This doctrine, if true, would overturn half our state legislation. It would put down, as unconstitutional, our statute, which directs that persons coming from another state, may be warned out, and if they refuse, may be removed. It is said, this is an old law, and is now invalid. It will be recollected, that since the adoption of our state constitution, this law has been revised and re-enacted. In 1821, when the late eminent Chief Justice revised the Statutes under the constitution, it did not occur to him, that it was unconstitutional. This is new doctrine, indeed, and would be the result of a constitution wholly novel. Other states have a deep interest in this question. There is not a state in New-England, nor in the Union, but have laws of this character. These laws are made in self-defence—to preserve the state from the overwhelming effects of a bad population and from pauperism. These must all be swept from the statute books, and the state must undo, what it has long been their policy to do. It is truly a startling doctrine, and would sweep into one general vortex all the state sovereignties.

When these states formed a union, it never occurred to the people that all state legislation—all police laws—all pauper laws—and all education laws, were abrogated; and it cannot be apprehended that this court will sanction such claims. The practical construction of the article in question will justify no such decision. There are, indeed, numerous other distinctions made by *state legislation,* between persons who are legal inhabitants of one state, and those coming into that state from another. If the position assumed on the other side be correct, then all these distinctions are invalid, and should be done away. They are infractions of the constitution, according to the claim set up: but according to the practical construction given to the constitution, they are good and wholesome laws. They are laws which never will be altered or repealed, until the state governments are wholly abandoned—until they are merged in the general government. It may be proper to notice some of these distinctions resting not on colour, but on inhabitancy or mere residence. The statute law of this state, (title Inhabitants,) provides that no person not an *inhabitant* of this state, shall be *entertained* or hired, unless he shall give security to the selectment, to save the town from expense. No person shall let any tenement to any such foreigner, unless such bonds of indemnity shall be given. No person shall "bring into this State, any poor and indigent person, under the penalty of sixty-seven dollars." Inhabitants of other states, at the discretion of the civil authority, may be removed from this state, by warrant. Suppose these laws are unconstitutional, then any town in this state may, against the wishes of its inhabitants, be overrun with a bad population, or filled with paupers! This is a result to which the people never can be driven. It is a condition never before contemplated, "novel, inconvenient and impracticable." Among the distinctions of this class, many may be found in the constitutions of the state. In the constitution of Maine, all *students* from other states are prohibited the right of suffrage in the town where the college or seminary is situated. And all officers in the military, naval, or marine service of the United States are likewise prohibited from voting, when from another state, while one who belongs to that state may vote, and all others, with three months residence, may vote. By the same constitution, no person can be a representative unless he shall have resided in the state one year, after he shall be 21; but an inhabitant of the state may vote in one day.

By the constitution of Massachusetts, a citizen of Connecticut removing there, must be a resident of that state five years, before he can be elected a senator. To be elected a representative, and to become an elector of that state, he must have resided therein one year. To be elected governor or lieutenant-governor, he must have resided there seven years. Not so with one who is an inhabitant of that state.

By the constitution of New-Hampshire, a citizen of Connecticut removing there, must reside in that state seven years, before he can be eligible to the office of governor or senator, while there is no such restriction upon the citizens of that state. A similar distinction in the constitution of Vermont may be found, differing only in the length of time.

By the constitution of New-York, a citizen of that state may be elected governor, while a citizen of any other state, going there to reside, must have resided there five years.

By the constitution of Pennsylvania, a person to be a representative, must reside in that state three years next before the election. The governor must have been an inhabitant of that state seven years, and electors must have resided in that state two years; but their own native citizens or inhabitants have no such restrictions placed upon them.

In Delaware, when any person removes there from another state, he cannot enjoy the right of voting, until he has resided in the state two years—he cannot be a senator until he shall have resided there three years—nor governor until he shall have resided there six years. Similar restrictions are imposed, by the constitution of every state in the union; but it is not necessary to detain the court longer with this class of restrictions. They are applied invariably to persons who go from one state to another; and if the position assumed on this defence be correct, then all these constitutions should be remodelled. These provisions are void! There can be no method of escape, except that which has been found, that the elective franchise is not a fundamental privilege!

In relation to these various restrictions, we have a judicial decision of high authority, the case before referred to, of *Corfield* v. *Coryell,* 4 Wash. C. C. Rep. 371. It is in principle exactly similar to the one on trial. The counsel in *that* case, made the same argument that is here made—they urged an infringement of the 4th article; but the learned Judge denied that claim. *Judge Washington* lived when the constitution was adopted—he had imbibed its true spirit; and when called upon to construe its provisions, he gave harmony to the whole, while at the same time he preserves the state governments. His language is emphatic: *"These fundamental rights are secured to the citizens, subject, nevertheless, to such restraints as the government may justly prescribe for the general good of the whole."*

So we may say with equal propriety, and equal force, in this case, that the 'privileges and immunities' of education shall be subject to such restraints as the government may justly prescribe, for the general good of the whole. And who will not say it is for the general good of the whole, to have all schools, academies and colleges, under the superintendence of some board of visiters, that the good ends of education may not be lost? Who will not say, that these states must regulate education, or it never can be regulated? Who will not say, that the whole system of education rests with the states? Who will not say, that a state police, and the whole system of pauper laws, remain with the state governments? Who will say, that Judge *Washington* was wrong in declaring that these fundamental privileges, whatever they may be, must be subject to restraints for the general good of the whole? May we not, under this wise decision, preserve our constitutions—our pauper laws—our police laws, and our school laws? Yes, we may exclude from our state a bad population;—we may provide that pauperism shall not overwhelm the state; and we may provide for its safety, in doing so.

WILLIAMS, J. . . . That question is one of the deepest interest to this community, involving the rights of a large and increasing population, and the correct construction of a clause in the constitution as to the privilege of citizens of the several states in other states, and who compose that class called *citizens*.

When the nature and importance of these questions are considered, the difficulties actually attending the construction of this clause of the constitution, the magnitude of the interests at stake, the excitement which always attends the agitation of questions connected with the interests of one class, and the liberties of another, more particularly at the present time; the jealousies existing on the one hand, and the expectations excited on the other; no desire is felt to agitate the subject unnecessarily. In addition to which, the respect that is due from one branch of the government of this state to another, while it would never deter me from expressing, when necessary, an opinion against the constitutionality of a law, would always lead me to decline an expression on the subject, in a case not requiring such a decision. If then it appears, that the same result must follow if we do not examine at all this constitutional question, which has been argued with so much ability, as if it was decided, for one, I feel no disposition to volunteer an opinion on that subject.

And on examination of this information, it seems to me, that no crime is charged upon this defendant, even if this law is constitutional. . . .

This information charges, that this school was set up in Canterbury, for the purpose of educating these persons of colour, not inhabitants of this state, that they might be instructed and educated; but omits to state, that it was not licensed. This omission is a fatal defect; as in an information on a penal statute, the prosecutor must set forth every fact that is necessary to bring the case within the statute; and every exception within the enacting clause of the act, descriptive of the offence, must be negated.

SEE ALSO:

Generally 1.2.3; 1.8.4 (citizenship); 1.9.1; 4.2.2
Calvin's Case, 7 Co. 1, 3–48 (1608)
An Act to Enable His Majesty's Natural-Born Subjects to Inherit the Estate of Their Ancestors, 11 and 12 Geo. 3, c. 6 (1700)
Vermont Constitution of 1793, ch. 2, Sec. 39, Thorpe 6:3770, 3772
St. George Tucker, Blackstone's Commentaries 3:App. 53–65 (1803)
M'Ilvaine v. *Cox's Lessee,* 4 Cranch 209 (1808)
Dawson's Lessee v. *Godfrey,* 4 Cranch 321 (1808)
Jackson v. *Wright,* 4 Johns. R. 75 (N.Y. 1809)
Jackson v. *Burns,* 3 Binney 75 (Pa. 1810)
Town of Herron v. *Town of Colchester,* 5 Day 169 (Conn. 1811)
Russel v. *Skipwith,* 6 Binney 241 (Pa. 1814)
Orr v. *Hodgson,* 4 Wheat. 453 (1819)
Alabama Constitution of 1819, art. 1, sec. 27, Thorpe 1:98
Blight's Lessee v. *Rochester,* 7 Wheat. 535 (1822)
Jackson v. *White,* 20 Johns. R. 313 (N.Y. 1822)
McCreery v. *Sommerville,* 9 Wheat. 354 (1824)
Gouverneur v. *Robertson,* 11 Wheat. 332 (1826)
Inglis v. *Sailor's Snug Harbor,* 3 Pet. 99 (1830)
Spratt v. *Spratt,* 4 Pet. 393 (1830)
Levy v. *McCartee,* 6 Pet. 102 (1832)

Article 4, Section 2, Clause 2

A Person charged in any State with Treason, Felony, or other Crime, who shall flee from Justice, and be found in another State, shall on Demand of the executive Authority of the State from which he fled, be delivered up, to be removed to the State having Jurisdiction of the Crime.

1

ARTICLES OF CONFEDERATION, ART. 4, ¶ 2
1 Mar. 1781

If any Person guilty of, or charged with treason, felony, or other high misdemeanor in any state, shall flee from Justice, and be found in any of the united states, he shall, upon demand of the Governor or executive power, of the state from which he fled, be delivered up and removed to the state having jurisdiction of his offence.

2

JAMES MADISON TO EDMUND RANDOLPH
10 Mar. 1784
Papers 8:3–4

I have perused with both pleasure and edification your observations on the demand made by the Executive of S. C. of a citizen of this State. If I were to hazard an opinion after yours, it would be that the respect due to the chief magistracy of a confederate State, enforced as it is by the articles of Union, requires an admission of the fact as it has been represented. If the representation be judged incomplete or ambiguous, explanations may certainly be called for; and if on a final view of the charge, Virginia should hold it to be not a casus foederis, she will be at liberty to withhold her citizen, (at least upon that ground) as S. C. will be to appeal to the Tribunal provided for all controversies among the States. Should the Law of S. C. happen to vary from the British Law, the most difficult point of discussion I apprehend will be, whether the terms "Treason &c." are to be referred to those determinate offences so denominated in the latter Code, or to all those to which the policy of the several States may annex the same titles and penalties. Much may be urged I think both in favor of and agst. each of these expositions. The two first of those terms coupled with "breach of the peace" are used in the 5 art: of the Confederation, but in a way that does not clear the ambiguity. The truth perhaps in this as in many other instances, is, that if the Compilers of the text had severally declared their meanings, these would have been as diverse as the comments which will be made upon it.

Wa[i]ving the doctrine of the confederation, my present view of the subject would admit few exceptions to the propriety of surrendering fugitive offenders. My reasons are these: 1. By the express terms of the Union the Citizens of every State are naturalized within all the others, and being entitled to the same privileges, may with the more justice be Subjected to the same penalties. This circumstance materially distinguishes the Citizens of the U. S. from the subjects of other nations not so incorporated. 2. The analogy of the laws throughout the States, and particularly the uniformity of trial by Juries of the vicinage, seem to obviate the capital objections agst. removal to the State where the offence is charged. In the instance of contiguous States a removal of the party accused from one to the other must often be a less grievance, than what happens within the same State when the place of residence & the place where the offence is laid are at distant extremities. The transportation to G. B. seems to have been reprobated on very different grounds: it would have deprived the accused of the privilege of trial by jury *of the vicinage* as well as of the use of his witnesses, and have exposed him to trial in a place where he was not even alledged to have ever made himself obnoxious to it; not to mention the danger of unfairness arising from the circumstances which produced the regulation. 3. Unless Citizens of one State transgressing within the pale of another be given up to be punished by the latter, they cannot be punished at all; and it seems to be a common interest of the States that a few hours or at most a few days should not be sufficient to gain a sanctuary for the authors of the numerous offences below "high misdemeanors." In a word, experience will shew if I mistake not that the relative situation of the U. S. calls for a "Droit Public" much more minute than that comprised in the foederal articles, and which presupposes much greater mutual confidence and amity among the Societies which are to obey it, than the law which has grown out of the transactions & intercourse of jealous & hostile Nations.

3

JAMES MADISON TO THOMAS JEFFERSON
16 Mar. 1784
Papers 8:12

The Executive of S. Carolina, as I am informed by the Attorney have demanded of Virginia the surrender of a citizen of Virga: charged on the affidavit of Jonas Beard Esqr. whom the Executive of S. C. represent to be "a Justice of the peace, a member of the Legislature, and a valuable good man" as follows: that "three days before the 25th. day of Octr. 1783 he (Mr. Beard) was violently assaulted by G. H. during the sitting of the Court of General Sessions, without any provocation thereto given, who beat him (Mr. B) with his fist & switch over the face head and mouth, from which beating he was obliged to keep his room until the said 25th. day of Octr. 1783. and call in the assistance of a physician." Such is the case as collected by Mr. Randolph from the letter of the Executive of S. C. The questions which arise upon it are 1. whether it be a charge of high misdemesnor within the meaning of the 4 art: of Confederation. 2. whether in expounding the terms high misdemesnor the Law of S. Carolina, or the British law as in force in the U S before the Revolution, ought to be the Standard. 3. if it be not a casus foederis what the law of Nations exacts of Virginia? 4. if the law of Nations contains no adequate provision for such occurrences, Whether the intimacy of the Union among the States, the relative position of some, and the common interest of all of them in guarding against impunity for offences which can be punished only by the jurisdiction within which they are committed, do not call for some supplemental regulations on this subject? Mr. R. thinks Virginia not bound to surrender the fugitive untill she be convinced of the fact, by more substantial information, & of its amounting to a high misdemesnor, by inspection of the law of S. C. which & not the British law ought to be the criterion. His reasons are too long to be rehearsed.

4

RECORDS OF THE FEDERAL CONVENTION

[1:245; Madison, 15 June]

9. Resd. that a Citizen of one State committing an offence in another State of the Union, shall be deemed guilty of the same offence as if it had been committed by a Citizen of the State in which the Offence was committed.

[2:174; Committee of Detail]

Any person charged with Treason Felony or high Misdemeanor who shall flee from Justice & be found in any of the U States shall on demd of the executive power of the State from wh. he fled be delivd. up & removed to the State havg Jurisdn of the Offence.—

[2:187; Madison, 6 Aug.]

XV

Any person charged with treason, felony or high misdemeanor in any State, who shall flee from justice, and shall be found in any other State, shall, on demand of the Executive power of the State from which he fled, be delivered up and removed to the State having jurisdiction of the offence.

[2:443; Madison, 28 Aug.]

Art: XV. being taken up. the words "high misdemeanor," were struck out, and "other crime" inserted, in order to comprehend all proper cases: it being doubtful whether "high misdemeanor" had not a technical meaning too limited.

Mr. Butler and Mr Pinkney moved "to require fugitive slaves and servants to be delivered up like criminals."

Mr. Wilson. This would oblige the Executive of the State to do it, at the public expence.

Mr Sherman saw no more propriety in the public seizing and surrendering a slave or servant, than a horse.

Mr. Butler withdrew his proposition in order that some particular provision might be made apart from this article.

Art XV as amended was then agreed to nem: con:

[2:577, 601; Committee of Style]

Any person charged with treason, felony, or other crime in any State, who shall flee from justice, and shall be found in any other State, shall, on demand of the Executive Power of the State from which he fled, be delivered up and removed to the State having jurisdiction of the offence.

. . . . .

A person charged in any state with treason, felony, or other crime, who shall flee from justice, and be found in another state, shall on demand of the executive authority of the state from which he fled be delivered up, and removed to the state having jurisdiction of the crime.

5

CHARLES PINCKNEY, OBSERVATIONS ON THE PLAN OF GOVERNMENT
1787
Farrand 3:112

The 4th article, respecting the extending the rights of the Citizens of each State, throughout the United States; the delivery of fugitives from justice, upon demand, and the giving full faith and credit to the records and proceedings of each, is formed exactly upon the principles of the 4th article of the present Confederation, except with this difference, that the demand of the Executive of a State, for any fugitive, criminal offender, shall be complied with. It is now confined to treason, felony, or other high misdemeanor; but, as there is no good reason for confining it to those crimes, no distinction ought to exist, and a State should always be at liberty to demand a fugitive from its justice, let his crime be what it may.

6

UNITED STATES v. ROBINS
27 Fed. Cas. 825, no. 16,175 (D.S.C. 1799)

(See 6.2, no. 25)

7

STATE v. HOWELL
R. M. Charlton 120 (Ga. 1821)

The prisoner being brought up by the writ of *habeas corpus*, *D'Lyon* moved for his discharge, upon the ground:

1st. That the offence charged was committed, if committed at all, in the State of South Carolina—and that therefore, the prisoner could not be detained, but upon the requisition of the Governor of that State for the prisoner, as a fugitive from justice—and if this objection was overruled, then that the prisoner was entitled to be bailed—to answer to any offence charged to have been committed in the State of Georgia.

On the first ground, I am of the opinion, that a person charged with a felony in another state, and fleeing to this, may upon a principle of comity, which obtains in such cases between sovereign States, be detained for a reasonable period, for the purpose of affording time for an application to the Governor of the State, where the felony is charged to have been committed, to make the demand as stated in the Constitution. Not only the morality and reasonableness of the thing, as involved in the general principle of comity, but the cases referred to by the States' counsel, support the opinion.

2d. As to the application for bail: the prisoner is charged with having in his *possession* a counterfeit Bank Bill, with an intention to pass the same in this State. By the 53d Sect. of the 6th Division of the penal code of this State, that offence is punished by imprisonment at hard labor, for any period of time not exceeding fifteen years. In this high grade of felony, whether the prisoner shall be bailed or not, *rests* in the sound discretion of the Court. The positiveness of the affidavit in this case, and there being no extrinsic circumstances in favor of the prisoner, will not permit me to accede to this branch of the motion, particularly as the proximity of the session of the Superior Court, excludes the idea of any hardship or rigour, in continuing the imprisonment.

It is *ordered*, that the prisoner be remanded and detained in custody, to answer to such bill of indictment as may be preferred against him, at the next Superior Court.

8

JOSEPH STORY, COMMENTARIES ON THE CONSTITUTION 3:§§ 1802–3
1833

§ 1802. It has been often made a question, how far any nation is, by the law of nations, and independent of any treaty stipulations, bound to surrender upon demand fugitives from justice, who, having committed crimes in another country, have fled thither for shelter. Mr. Chancellor Kent considers it clear upon principle, as well as authority, that every state is bound to deny an asylum to criminals, and, upon application and due examination of the case, to surrender the fugitive to the foreign state, where the crime has been committed. Other distinguished judges and jurists have entertained a different opinion. It is not uncommon for treaties to contain mutual stipulations for the surrender of criminals; and the United States have sometimes been a party to such an arrangement.

§ 1803. But, however the point may be, as to foreign nations, it cannot be questioned, that it is of vital importance to the public administration of criminal justice, and the security of the respective states, that criminals, who have committed crimes therein, should not find an asylum in other states; but should be surrendered up for trial and punishment. It is a power most salutary in its general operation, by discouraging crimes, and cutting off the chances of escape from punishment. It will promote harmony and good feelings among the states; and it will increase the general sense of the blessings of the national government. It will, moreover, give strength to a great moral duty, which neighbouring states especially owe to each other, by elevating the policy of the mutual suppression of crimes into a legal obligation. Hitherto it has proved as useful in practice, as it is unexceptionable in its character.

9

CASE OF JOSE FERREIRA DOS SANTOS
2 Marshall's C.C. 493 (C.C.D.Va. 1835)

BARBOUR, J.—Jose Ferreira dos Santos, a Portuguese subject, having been committed for trial before this Court, under a charge of piracy, and the grand jury having found the indictment against him not a true bill, he would be entitled to a discharge from custody, as it regards that accusation. But an application is now made, at the instance of the chargé des affaires of Portugal, that he may be detained, until the government of Portugal shall have time to make a demand on that of the United States, that he may be surrendered to the former, as a fugitive from justice, to be tried there, under a charge of murder; which it is alleged that he has committed in that country. And the question is, whether it is proper, or competent, for this Court to detain him in prison, for the purpose before stated?

The solution of this question depends upon that of two others: 1. Has a nation, whose citizen or subject commits a crime within its own jurisdiction, and is afterwards found within that of another, a right, by the law of nations, upon its demand, to have him delivered up by that other, for the purpose of being tried where the crime was committed? 2. If such right exist, have the judicial officers of the United States, supposing the evidence to be sufficient, any authority to act in relation to it, as auxiliary to the executive department?

As to the first point, as far as I am informed, the subject has not been before any of the federal courts of the Union. The case of Jonathan Robins is not an exception to this remark. He was, indeed, at the request of the then President of the United States, Mr. Adams the elder, delivered up by the district judge of South Carolina, to the British consul, on a charge of murder, committed by him, (Robins,) on board of a British vessel on the high seas.

But, that case depended upon the twenty-seventh article of the treaty with Great Britain, made in the year 1794, by which it was agreed, that fugitives charged with murder, or forgery, committed within the jurisdiction of either, and seeking an asylum within any of the countries of the other, should be reciprocally delivered up, in the manner and upon the terms therein stated.

The question then, in that case, as it relates to this point was, whether the *casus foederis* of this article had occurred; whereas, in this case, there is no treaty stipulation, and the question must, therefore, depend upon the right of the government of Portugal to make the demand, and the consequent obligation of our government to surrender the person charged, independently of any treaty or compact between them.

There have, however, been two decisions upon the subject, made by two distinguished jurists of our country: the one, by Judge Kent, of New York; the other, by Chief Justice Tilghman, of Pennsylvania; the first, asserting the right: see the case in the matter of Daniel Washburn, 4 Johns. Ch. Ca. 106; the other, adopting a different line of reasoning, and arriving in many respects, at different conclusions: see the case of Short v. Deacon, 10 Serg. & Rawle, 126. It becomes necessary, then, to examine the question upon the principles laid down by the writers on public law, with reference to the application made of them in the two cases just cited, to the authoritative declarations of our own government, and generally, to all the bearings and relations of the subject.

Grotius asserts the right to demand, and the consequent obligation to surrender, all persons charged with crimes, who have fled to another country, whether they are citizens or subjects of that country, or foreigners, although, in practice, it is not insisted on, except in crimes against the state, or of a very heinous nature. As to lesser crimes, he says, they are connived at, unless otherwise agreed on, by treaty. In this doctrine, he is followed by Burlamaqui, Heineccius, and Wynne. Vattel, asserts the right and obligation, in case of great crimes; but speaks only as to the *subjects* of the country, on which the demand is made. And his reasoning applies to them only; because it is put upon the principle of the duty of the sovereign to prevent his subjects from doing mischief to other states, and the consequent duty to punish or surrender.

Puffendorf, on the contrary, holds the doctrine, that the obligation to deliver up a criminal, is rather in virtue of some treaty, than in consequence of a common and indispensable obligation. Martens, after stating that a sovereign may punish foreigners who fly to his dominions, after having committed a crime in the dominions of another, as well as those who commit it in his, adds: "but in neither, is he *perfectly obliged* to send them for punishment to their own country, not even supposing them to have been condemned before their escape." He says, also, that according to modern custom, a criminal is frequently sent back to the place where the crime is committed, on the request of a power *who offers to do the like service*, and that we often see instances of this. Ward seems strongly to countenance the idea of Puffendorf.

I have thus given an abbreviated statement of these writers on public law; more detailed views of whose reasoning may be seen by reference to the works themselves, or to quotations from them, in the two cases before cited from New York and Pennsylvania. Thus much was necessary as a basis for my future reasoning. Upon the mere authority of foreign publicists, then, it would appear to be doubtful whether there was, independently of treaty, any obligation, on the part of our government, to surrender to another, a fugitive from justice. To decide the question, let us descend from these principles of abstract writers, and see what has been the practice of Europe in ancient and modern times. Lord Coke, in his 3 Inst. 180, (I quote now from 10 Serg. & Rawle,) after expressing a decided opinion against delivering up fugitives, gives us three instances of a refusal to deliver up; the first, a qualified one; the two others, absolute. Henry VII. of England, demanded of Ferdinand of Spain, the Earl of Suffolk, attainted of high treason by parliament. Ferdinand refused to deliver him, until Henry promised not to put him to death. Henry VIII. of England, demanded of the King of France, Cardinal Pool, being his subject, and attainted of treason; the demand was not complied with. Queen Elizabeth, demanded of Henry IV. of France, Morgan and others of her subjects, who had committed treason against her. He replied, that all kingdoms were free to fugitives, and it was the duty of kings to defend, every one, the liberties of his own kingdom; and, that Elizabeth had, not long before, received Montgomery, the Prince of Condè, and other Frenchmen. Chief Justice Tilghman adds the case of Perkin Warbeck, who had fled to Scotland, and who was refused to be delivered, although demanded by Henry VII. Chancellor Kent, in the case of Washburn, cites some cases in England, as settling the principle, and acting on the practice of surrendering fugitives.

As to Lundy's case, (2 Vent. Rep. 314,) that of the King v. Kimberley, (Strange, 848,) there cited, and the East India Company v. Campbell, (1 Ves. Sr. 247,) Chief Justice Tilghman, in my opinion, gives a satisfactory answer: It is—that the territories where the crime was committed, and to which the criminal fled, were parts of the same empire, and under one common sovereign. The King of England could have no privilege against the King of Ireland, being one and the same person.

He states, indeed, the case of The King v. Hutcheson, (3 Keb. Rep. 785,) who was committed on a charge of a crime committed in Portugal, and refused to be bailed, and who it was said by counsel, (in another case,) was sent to Portugal; and he refers to another, mentioned by Heath, Justice; the crew of a Dutch ship mastered the vessel, and brought her into Deal: and it was a question whether they should be seized and sent to Holland. And it was held, that they might, and the same (he said) had been the law of all civilized nations.

There is no subsequent case cited, and none is known to exist, where the British government has surrendered a fugitive. On the contrary, Mr. Jefferson, in his letter to President Washington, of November 7th, 1791, after speaking on the subject of conventions for the delivery of fugitives, says: "England has no such convention with any nation, and their laws have given no power to their executive, to surrender fugitives of any description; they are, accordingly, constantly refused; and hence, England has been the asylum of the Paolis, the La Mottes, the Calonnes; in short, *of the most atrocious offenders*, as well as of the most innocent victims, who have been able to get there." In corroboration of this, I will state, that but the other day, that is, on the 7th of November last, it was stated in the Intelligencer, that application had been made to the secretary of the home department, (England), for a warrant to arrest Bowen; but it was refused, on the ground that no treaty stipulation required such a course, and without it, it was wholly inadmissible. The case is not stated with particularity. Enough, however, appears, to show that it was not one of the atrocious class, mentioned by Grotius; that, however, is not stated as the reason, but the want of a treaty stipulation. I am not prepared to say, how far the secretary acted upon the principle stated in some of the books, that governments were in the practice of conniving at the lesser offences, or that the demand was not made by our government.

There is, indeed, a case in Canada, in 1829, where a criminal from Vermont was delivered to the authorities of that state, upon a charge of larceny committed there, upon a warrant issued by the governor of the province; he was arrested, and on *habeas corpus*, before the chief justice, it was held lawful; in his opinion, he grounds himself generally upon the authorities and cases before stated, and his decision, therefore, must stand or fall with them. It is worthy of remark, however, that this was a case of simple larceny, and not one of great atrocity, as described by Grotius, and moreover, that the arrest was grounded upon a charge, on oath, of the felony, and not upon a demand by our government; so that it would seem, that the opinion of the government at home, differed from that in the province of Canada. The opinion of European nations on this subject, is manifested by the numerous treaties made by them, containing provision for the mutual surrender of criminals.

In 1 Kent's Comm. p. 37, we are told, that treaties of this kind were made between England and Scotland in 1174, and England and France in 1308, and France and Savoy in 1378. As these were in the comparatively barbarous ages of Europe, let us come down to a period, when civilization had reached a high point. In the letter of Mr. Jefferson, before referred to, dated in 1791, he says: "The delivery of fugitives from one country to another, as practised by several nations, is in consequence of conventions settled between them, defining precisely the cases wherein such deliveries shall take place. I know (says he) that such conventions exist, between France and Spain, France and Sardinia, France and Germany, France and the United Netherlands; between the several sovereigns, constituting the Germanic body, and I believe very generally, between co-terminous states, on the continent of Europe." Why, let me ask, were all these treaties in ancient and modern times? I answer, either because the opinion of Puffendorf was considered right, that without a treaty stipulation, there was no obligation to surrender, or at least, the question was so unsettled, the respective rights and obligations of nations so indeterminate, and the refusal on the part of nations to surrender so frequent, that without treaty, there was no obligation at all, or none of any sort of practical

value; for, what is this imperfect obligation of which the writers speak? It is the right of one to ask, which involves the right of the other to refuse, and as applied to this particular subject, that refusal had become so common, as to be almost the habitual practice, until treaties were formed concerning it. And is not the doctrine of the necessity of treaty stipulation supported, too, by the weightiest reasons?

In the first place, in this way alone, can reciprocity be ensured; in this way alone, can it certainly be ascertained to what crimes the doctrine of surrender is to be applied. Some would apply it to all crimes, some to those against the state, or of deep atrocity. Which are of that character? The New York assembly consider simple larceny, or any crime, punishable in their state prison, as proper to surrender for, and have enacted accordingly. The treaty of 1794, between the United States and Great Britain, confines it to murder and forgery.

Moreover, as to the expense attending the case, in the treaty just cited, it is provided, that the power making the demand shall pay it.

Finally, provision can be made as to the length of time for which a party is to be detained, as is provided in the act of Congress in relation to fugitives from justice, from the several states.

Let us now examine the views of our own government, on this point. Mr. Jefferson, in the letter already referred to, in which he is writing to the President on the subject of a request from the government of South Carolina, that a demand should be made upon the governor of Florida, for the delivery of some fugitives, says: "The laws of the United States, like those of England, receive every fugitive, (that is, as he had just before expressed it, the most atrocious offenders, as well as the most innocent victims,) and no authority has been given to our executives to deliver them up." He states further, that the French government had been anxious to make a convention with us, authorizing them to demand their subjects coming here; that in the Consular Convention, Dr. Franklin agreed to an article, giving to their consuls a right to take and send back captains of vessels, mariners, and *passengers*. Congress refused to ratify it, until the word *passengers* was stricken out. He goes on to say, in fact, however desirable it be, that the perpetrators of crimes, acknowledged to be such by all mankind, should be delivered up to punishment; yet, it is extremely difficult to draw the line between those, and acts rendered criminal by tyrannical laws only: hence, the first step always is, a convention defining the cases where a surrender shall take place.

"If, then, the United States, (he continues), could not deliver up to Governor Quesnada, a fugitive from the laws of his country, we cannot claim, as a right, the delivery of fugitives from us; and it is worthy of consideration, whether the demand proposed to be made in Governor Pinckney's letter, should it be complied with by the other party, might not commit us disagreeably, perhaps dishonourably, in event; for I do not think, that we can take for granted, that the legislature of the United States will establish a convention for the mutual delivery of fugitives; and without a reasonable certainty that they will, I think we ought not to give Governor Quesnada any grounds to expect that, in a similar case, we would re-deliver fugitives from his government."

On the 12th September, 1793, Mr. Jefferson thus writes to Genet, the French minister, in answer to a demand that he had made for the delivery of fugitives:

"The laws of this country take no notice of crimes committed out of their jurisdiction. The most atrocious offender coming within their pale, is received by them as an innocent man; and they have authorized no one to seize or deliver him. The evil of protecting malefactors of every dye, is sensibly felt here, as in other countries; but, until a reformation of the criminal codes of most nations, to deliver fugitives from them, would be, to become their accomplices. The former, therefore, is viewed as the lesser evil." He goes on to say, that unless they come within the consular convention, no person in this country is authorized to deliver them; but on the contrary, they are under the protection of the laws, &c. In the course of the next year, (1794), the British treaty was made; the twenty-seventh article of which, already referred to, provided for this subject.

Thus, as well by the authoritative declarations, as by the acts of our government, the principle has been announced to the world, that the United States acknowledge no obligation to surrender fugitives, except by virtue of some treaty stipulation.

Besides the reasons common to us, with other nations which recommend the justice and utility of this doctrine, we have strong ones arising from the spirit of our institutions, and the provisions of the federal Constitution.

If, for example, we were to take Grotius as our rule, the offence which he emphatically considers as most requiring a surrender, is treason; or, as he expresses it, offences against the state.

Now, let us see what would be the practical effect of this rule? Suppose, that during the late war with Great Britain, a British born subject, who had previously emigrated to the United States, had been found fighting in our ranks, as a soldier, in Canada, and upon his return home, had been demanded by the British government: on their principle of perpetual allegiance, he was still a subject, and had committed treason: upon the principle of Grotius, we must have surrendered him, because he had committed, according to their laws, a crime against the state.

Let us put another case. Suppose that, in the struggle now going on in Texas, an American citizen (of whom we have many) should be found fighting against the authority of Santa Anna, and upon his return home should be demanded. Here, too, according to the rule of Grotius, we must deliver him, because he had committed a crime of state, against the present government *de facto*; and it is a settled principle with us, that we are always to take the present existing government *de facto*, as the one for the time being to be respected as the government. Can any one for a moment suppose, that in either of the cases here put, our government would surrender? Surely not. In the case in Canada, the chief justice says, that cases of this sort cannot be drawn into precedent, because the authority of the state to which the accused has fled, may well be ex-

tended to protect, rather than deliver him up to his accusers, &c.; but is it not apparent, that this is a violation of Grotius's rule? For here is a crime of state committed against the government *de facto*; one which, if successful, is honoured by the name of revolution; if otherwise, is degraded by the epithet of rebellion, and all engaged in it are called traitors.

An attention to some of the provisions of our Constitution, will, I think, fortify this doctrine.

The second clause of the second section of the fourth article provides, that a person charged in any state with treason, felony, or other crime, who shall flee from justice, and be found in another state, shall, on demand of the executive authority of the state from which he fled, be delivered up to be removed to the state having jurisdiction of the crime. The subject of fugitives from justice was thus in the minds of the Convention, and they provided for a delivery of fugitives from the states of the Union. It may, perhaps, be fairly said, that as the Constitution was made for the states, and the people of the states, it had no relation in its nature to foreigners; be it so; but the principle assumed, requires us to deliver up citizens, as well as aliens. In this aspect as to citizens, it was properly within the scope of a constitutional provision; and, according to my view, provision is made in the Constitution, which, although it does not mention it by name, embraces the whole subject, both as to citizens and all others within our jurisdiction, and puts it within the control of a department of the government. It is the clause creating the treaty-making power, and the reasoning stands thus: the Constitution having given to the President and Senate the right to make treaties, without limitation in words, there is no other limitation but their discretion, except that the treaty shall not contravene the Constitution, or invade the rights of other departments.

The various provisions, securing to every person charged with crime, a trial by jury, the right to be confronted by his witnesses, the privilege of not being obliged to be a witness against himself, also, in my opinion, have an important bearing upon this subject. It may be said, that it was intended to apply to crimes against the United States; but, I think, the spirit of them should make the treaty-making power extremely cautious, even as to treaty stipulations, for surrendering our people to a government, where these privileges do not exist; but where there is no treaty, they should, in my opinion, be decisive against a surrender, in the exercise of discretion, even if the law of nations created an imperfect obligation, without a treaty stipulation. I am of opinion, then, that the government of the United States are not under any obligation to deliver the prisoner, in the absence of any treaty stipulation.

The second question is, whether the judicial officers of the United States have any authority to act in relation to it? Perhaps the conclusion at which I have arrived on the first point, might render a discussion of the other unnecessary; but as it was argued, and has been considered, and as I may have fallen into error on the first point, I will very briefly notice it. As a general proposition, the judicial power of a government is created for the purpose of executing *its own laws*. If in deciding, upon a foreign contract, the courts of another country construe it according to the law of the place where made, and intended to be executed; as, for example, to give the interest there allowed, this is not the execution of a foreign law; but of the law of the court, which as to this case, adjudges that as the intention of the parties. As to criminal laws, I believe it is settled every where, that one country will not execute the penal laws of another; not even its revenue laws. So far is this carried in this country, that the courts of one state will not execute the penal laws, either of a sister state, or of the federal government.

The crime charged against the prisoner, is one against the laws of Portugal, not against the United States. Over the crime itself, then, the judicial officers of the United States clearly have no jurisdiction. If they have no jurisdiction over the crime, whence can they derive the authority to arrest the party charged with that crime, and detain him, with a view to a trial therefor, in another and foreign jurisdiction? I do not here enter into the second question discussed in Jonathan Robins' case, whether the duty to be performed there, was a judicial one. That was the case of a treaty. The Constitution extends the jurisdiction of its judiciary, to all cases arising under treaties, &c. That, therefore, is a totally distinct question from this, where there is no treaty, and where a judicial officer is asked to arrest, or, what is the same thing, to detain a person charged with the commission of a crime, not against the government, whose judicial power it is his duty to execute, nor for a trial, in any of the courts of that government, but for one to be had before the tribunals of a foreign country, against whose laws the alleged crime has been committed.

Let us look, for a moment, at the legislation of Congress, upon the subject of arrest in criminal cases. We are authorized to arrest for any crime or offence against the United States, for what purpose? The act of Congress informs us, that it is for trial before such court of the United States, as by that act has cognizance of the offence.

Now, the crime with which this prisoner is charged, is not against the United States, and the arrest or detainer is avowedly asked, not for the purpose of a trial before any court of the United States.

The case of piracy is embraced by the provision of this law; for that is a crime against all nations, and amongst others, against the United States; but, moreover, the Constitution authorizes Congress to define and punish piracy. Congress has defined and provided for its punishment. We are, then, executing a law, made in pursuance of the Constitution, when we take jurisdiction of that offence.

So strict has been the doctrine, as to the judicial officers of one government executing the criminal laws of another, that, although the act of Congress authorizes state magistrates to arrest, for crimes against the United States, yet the general court of Virginia sustained the legality of their warrants, only upon the ground, that it was competent to have authorized private persons to act, and that magistrates are designated as a class of persons by their name of office.

In conclusion I will say, that the counsel who made this application, has presented it in the strongest light, which the principles of public law or the authorities enabled him to do; yet, after the best reflection which I have been able to bestow upon the subject, in the short time which I have had to consider it, I am of opinion, that, without a treaty stipulation, this government is not under any obligation to surrender a fugitive from justice, to another government, for trial; and that, as a judicial officer of the United States, I have no authority whatsoever, either to arrest or detain, with a view to such surrender.

It follows, as a consequence, that the prisoner is entitled to his discharge; and he is discharged accordingly.

SEE ALSO:

An Act to Provide for the Government of the Territory Northwest of the River Ohio, 1 Stat. 50 (1789)
Charles Lee, Extradition, 14 Mar. 1798, 1 Ops. Atty. Gen. 83
Levi Lincoln, Barratry on Private Property in Europe, 29 Oct. 1802, 1 Ops. Atty. Gen. 123
Matter of Washburn, 4 Johns. Ch. 106 (N.Y. 1819)
Short v. Deacon, 10 Serg. & Rawle 125 (Pa. 1823)
Roger B. Taney, Extradition, 16 April 1833, 2 Ops. Atty. Gen. 559

Article 4, Section 2, Clause 3

No Person held to Service or Labour in one State, under the Laws thereof, escaping into another, shall, in Consequence of any Law or Regulation therein, be discharged from such Service or Labour, but shall be delivered up on Claim of the Party to whom such Service or Labour may be due.

1

WILLIAM BLACKSTONE, COMMENTARIES 1:411–13
1765

I. As to the several sorts of servants: I have formerly observed that pure and proper slavery does not, nay cannot, subsist in England; such I mean, whereby an absolute and unlimited power is given to the master over the life and fortune of the slave. And indeed it is repugnant to reason, and the principles of natural law, that such a state should subsist any where. The three origins of the right of slavery assigned by Justinian, are all of them built upon false foundations. As, first, slavery is held to arise *"jure gentium,"* from a state of captivity in war; whence slaves are called *mancipia, quasi manu capti.* The conqueror, say the civilians, had a right to the life of his captive; and, having spared that, has a right to deal with him as he pleases. But it is an untrue position, when taken generally, that, by the law of nature or nations, a man may kill his enemy: he has only a right to kill him, in particular cases; in cases of absolute necessity, for self-defence; and it is plain this absolute necessity did not subsist, since the victor did not actually kill him, but made him prisoner. War is itself justifiable only on principles of self-preservation; and therefore it gives no other right over prisoners, but merely to disable them from doing harm to us, by confining their persons: much less can it give a right to kill, torture, abuse, plunder, or even to enslave, an enemy, when the war is over. Since therefore the right of *making* slaves by captivity, depends on a supposed right of slaughter, that foundation failing, the consequence drawn from it must fail likewise. But, secondly, it is said that slavery may begin *"jure civili;"* when one man sells himself to another. This, if only meant of contracts to serve or work for another, is very just: but when applied to strict slavery, in the sense of the laws of old Rome or modern Barbary, is also impossible. Every sale implies a price, a *quid pro quo*, an equivalent given to the seller in lieu of what he transfers to the buyer: but what equivalent can be given for life, and liberty, both of which (in absolute slavery) are held to be in the master's disposal? His property also, the very price he seems to receive, devolves *ipso facto* to his master, the instant he becomes his slave. In this case therefore the buyer gives nothing, and the seller receives nothing: of what validity then can a sale be, which destroys the very principles upon which all sales are founded? Lastly, we are told, that besides these two ways by which slaves *"fiunt,"* or are acquired, they may also be hereditary: *"servi nascuntur;"* the children of acquired slaves are, *jure naturae*, by a negative kind of birthright, slaves also. But this being built on the two former rights must fall together with them. If neither captivity, nor the sale of oneself, can by the law of nature and reason, reduce the parent to slavery, much less can it reduce the offspring.

Upon these principles the law of England abhors, and will not endure the existence of, slavery within this nation:

so that when an attempt was made to introduce it, by statute 1 Edw. VI. c. 3. which ordained, that all idle vagabonds should be made slaves, and fed upon bread, water, or small drink, and refuse meat; should wear a ring of iron round their necks, arms, or legs; and should be compelled by beating, chaining, or otherwise, to perform the work assigned them, were it never so vile; the spirit of the nation could not brook this condition, even in the most abandoned rogues; and therefore this statute was repealed in two years afterwards. And now it is laid down, that a slave or negro, the instant he lands in England, becomes a freeman; that is, the law will protect him in the enjoyment of his person, his liberty, and his property. Yet, with regard to any right which the master may have acquired, by contract or the like, to the perpetual service of John or Thomas, this will remain exactly in the same state as before: for this is no more than the same state of subjection for life, which every apprentice submits to for the space of seven years, or sometimes for a longer term. Hence too it follows, that the infamous and unchristian practice of withholding baptism from negro servants, lest they should thereby gain their liberty, is totally without foundation, as well as without excuse. The law of England acts upon general and extensive principles: it gives liberty, rightly understood, that is, protection, to a jew, a turk, or a heathen, as well as to those who profess the true religion of Christ; and it will not dissolve a civil contract, either express or implied, between master and servant, on account of the alteration of faith in either of the contracting parties: but the slave is entitled to the same liberty in England before, as after, baptism; and, whatever service the heathen negro owed to his English master, the same is he bound to render when a christian.

2

Sommersett's Case
20 How. St. Tr. 1, 80–82 (K.B. 1771)

Lord *Mansfield.*—On the part of Sommersett, the case which we gave notice should be decided this day, the Court now proceeds to give its opinion. I shall recite the return to the writ of Habeas Corpus, as the ground of our determination; omitting only words of form. The captain of the ship on board of which the negro was taken, makes his return to the writ in terms signifying that there have been, and still are, slaves to a great number in Africa; and that the trade in them is authorized by the laws and opinions of Virginia and Jamaica; that they are goods and chattels; and, as such, saleable and sold. That James Sommersett is a negro of Africa, and long before the return of the king's writ was brought to be sold, and was sold to Charles Steuart, esq. then in Jamaica, and has not been manumitted since; that Mr. Steuart, having occasion to transact business, came over hither, with an intention to return; and brought Sommersett to attend and abide with him, and to carry him back as soon as the business should

be transacted. That such intention has been, and still continues; and that the negro did remain till the time of his departure in the service of his master Mr. Steuart, and quitted it without his consent; and thereupon, before the return of the king's writ, the said Charles Steuart did commit the slave on board the Anne and Mary, to safe custody, to be kept till he should set sail, and then to be taken with him to Jamaica, and there sold as a slave. And this is the cause why he, captain Knowles, who was then and now is, commander of the above vessel, then and now lying in the river of Thames, did the said negro, committed to his custody, detain; and on which he now renders him to the orders of the Court. We pay all due attention to the opinion of sir Philip Yorke, and lord chancellor Talbot, whereby they pledged themselves to the British planters, for all the legal consequences of slaves coming over to this kingdom or being baptized, recognized by lord Hardwicke, sitting as chancellor on the 19th of October, 1749, that trover would lie: that a notion had prevailed, if a negro came over, or became a Christian, he was emancipated, but no ground in law: that he and lord Talbot, when attorney and solicitor-general, were of opinion, that no such claim for freedom was valid; that though the statute of tenures had abolished villeins regardant to a manor, yet he did not conceive but that a man might still become a villein in gross, by confessing himself such in open court. We are so well agreed, that we think there is no occasion of having it argued (as I intimated an intention at first,) before all the judges, as is usual, for obvious reasons, on a return to a Habeas Corpus. The only question before us is, whether the cause on the return is sufficient? If it is, the negro must be remanded; if it is not, he must be discharged. Accordingly, the return states, that the slave departed and refused to serve; whereupon he was kept, to be sold abroad. So high an act of dominion must be recognized by the law of the country where it is used. The power of a master over his slave has been extremely different, in different countries. The state of slavery is of such a nature, that it is incapable of being introduced on any reasons, moral or political, but only by positive law, which preserves its force long after the reasons, occasion, and time itself from whence it was created, is erased from memory. It is so odious, that nothing can be suffered to support it, but positive law. Whatever inconveniences, therefore, may follow from the decision, I cannot say this case is allowed or approved by the law of England; and therefore the black must be discharged.

3

Records of the Federal Convention

[2:443; Madison, 28 Aug.]

Mr. Butler and Mr Pinkney moved "to require fugitive slaves and servants to be delivered up like criminals."

Mr. Wilson. This would oblige the Executive of the State to do it, at the public expence.

Mr Sherman saw no more propriety in the public seizing and surrendering a slave or servant, than a horse.

Mr. Butler withdrew his proposition in order that some particular provision might be made apart from this article.

Art XV as amended was then agreed to nem: con:

[2:446; *Journal, 29 Aug.*]

It was moved and seconded to agree to the following proposition to be inserted after the 15 article

"If any Person bound to service or labor in any of the United States shall escape into another State, He or She shall not be discharged from such service or labor in consequence of any regulations subsisting in the State to which they escape; but shall be delivered up to the person justly claiming their service or labor"

which passed in the affirmative [Ayes—11; noes—0.]

[2:577, 601; *Committee of Style*]

If any Person bound to service or labor in any of the United States shall escape into another State, He or She shall not be discharged from such service or labor in consequence of any regulations subsisting in the State to which they escape; but shall be delivered up to the person justly claiming their service or labor.

. . . . .

No person legally held to service or labour in one state, escaping into another, shall in consequence of regulations subsisting therein be discharged from such service or labor, but shall be delivered up on claim of the party to whom such service or labour may be due.

[2:628; *Madison, 15 Sept.*]

Art. IV. sect 2, parag: 3. the term "legally" was struck out, and "under the laws thereof" inserted after the word "State," in compliance with the wish of some who thought the term legal equivocal, and favoring the idea that slavery was legal in a moral view—

4

DEBATE IN VIRGINIA RATIFYING CONVENTION
15 June 1788

(See 1.9.1, no. 14)

5

JAMES IREDELL, NORTH CAROLINA RATIFYING CONVENTION
29 July 1788
Elliot 4:176

Mr. IREDELL begged leave to explain the reason of this clause. In some of the Northern States they have emancipated all their *slaves*. If any of our slaves, said he, go there,

and remain there a certain time, they would, by the present laws, be entitled to their freedom, so that their masters could not get them again. This would be extremely prejudicial to the inhabitants of the Southern States; and to prevent it, this clause is inserted in the Constitution. Though the word *slave* is not mentioned, this is the meaning of it. The northern delegates, owing to their particular scruples on the subject of slavery, did not choose the word *slave* to be mentioned.

6

AN ACT RESPECTING FUGITIVES FROM JUSTICE, AND PERSONS ESCAPING FROM THE SERVICE OF THEIR MASTERS
1 Stat. 302 (1793)

SEC. 3. *And be it also enacted,* That when a person held to labour in any of the United States, or in either of the territories on the northwest or south of the river Ohio, under the laws thereof, shall escape into any other of the said states or territory, the person to whom such labour or service may be due, his agent or attorney, is hereby empowered to seize or arrest such fugitive from labour, and to take him or her before any judge of the circuit or district courts of the United States, residing or being within the state, or before any magistrate of a county, city or town corporate, wherein such seizure or arrest shall be made, and upon proof to the satisfaction of such judge or magistrate, either by oral testimony or affidavit taken before and certified by a magistrate of any such state or territory, that the person so seized or arrested, doth, under the laws of the state of territory from which he or she fled, owe service or labour to the person claiming him or her, it shall be the duty of such judge or magistrate to give a certificate thereof to such claimant, his agent or attorney, which shall be sufficient warrant for removing the said fugitive from labour, to the state or territory from which he or she fled.

SEC. 4. *And be it further enacted,* That any person who shall knowingly and willingly obstruct or hinder such claimant, his agent or attorney in so seizing or arresting such fugitive from labour, or shall rescue such fugitive from such claimant, his agent or attorney when so arrested pursuant to the authority herein given or declared; or shall harbor or conceal such person after notice that he or she was a fugitive from labour, as aforesaid, shall, for either of the said offences, forfeit and pay the sum of five hundred dollars. Which penalty may be recovered by and for the benefit of such claimant, by action of debt, in any court proper to try the same; saving moreover to the person claiming such labour or service, his right of action for or on account of the said injuries or either of them.

7

MURRAY V. MCCARTY
2 Munf. 393 (Va. 1811)

JUDGE CABELL. The appellant was a slave in Maryland, and was purchased there as such by the appellee, but now claims her freedom under the second section of our act of assembly, passed the 17th of December, 1792, which establishes, as a general rule, "that slaves, which shall hereafter be brought into this commonwealth, and kept therein one whole year, or so long, at different times, as shall amount to one year, shall be free."

It being admitted by the parties that the appellant has been brought into this state since that law took effect, it is obvious that her right to freedom is thereby established, unless the appellee can show that this case comes within some of the exceptions contained in the act of assembly. He relies, for this purpose, on the 4th section, which declares "that nothing in this act contained shall be construed to extend to those who may incline to remove from any of the United States, and become citizens of this, if, within sixty days after such removal, he or she shall take" a certain oath therein prescribed.

But it is evident that the privilege conferred by this clause, of bringing slaves into this commonwealth, can be claimed by those persons only, who, at the time of their removal, were citizens, not of this, but of some other state, and as it is admitted that the appellee was a native of this state, the question arises, whether he had laid aside the character of citizenship thereby acquired, so as to entitle himself to the benefit of this proviso.

Nature has given to all men the right of relinquishing the society in which birth or accident may have thrown them; and of seeking subsistence and happiness elsewhere; and it is believed that this right of emigration, or expatriation, is one of those "inherent rights, of which, when they enter into a state of society, they cannot, by any compact, deprive, or devest their posterity." But, although municipal laws cannot take away or destroy this great right, they may regulate the manner, and prescribe the evidence of its exercise; and, in the absence of the regulations juris positivi, the right must be exercised according to the principles of general law. As we have no act of congress on this subject, and as doubts are entertained whether our act of assembly concerning expatriation is still in force, or, admitting it to be in force, whether it was ever intended to apply to the case of a citizen of Virginia, removing to, and becoming a citizen of, some other of the United States, I shall, in considering M'Carty's citizenship, confine myself to the principles of general or universal law: and I am clearly of opinion, that, even according to those principles, his removal from this state, under the particular circumstances of this case, would not amount to an expatriation. A temporary absence will not devest a man of the character of citizen, or subject of the state, or nation to which he

may belong. There must be a removal with an intention to lay aside that character, and he must actually join himself to some other community. The intention to abandon this state is not proved by any other evidence than the declarations of M'Carty himself; and, although this is one of those cases in which a man's own declarations will be received in his favour, yet, in the present instance, they are contradicted by his own acts, and thereby lose all their weight; for he left his property behind him, and continued to exercise the most important right of a citizen of this state, by voting at the election of the representatives of the people. I do not mean to say that a citizen of this state cannot become a citizen of another state, without carrying his property with him; for, although that would be required according to the principles of general law, it is dispensed with under our particular system, which provides that "citizens of each state shall be entitled to all privileges and immunities of citizens in the several states." I have mentioned the circumstance of his leaving his property, to show, with the aid of other testimony, that he did not intend to cease to be a citizen of this state. But, although the constitution of the United States has wisely given to a citizen of each state the privileges of a citizen of any other state, yet it clearly recognizes the distinction between the character of a citizen of the United States, and of a citizen of any individual state; and also of citizens of different states; and, although a citizen of one state may hold lands in another, yet he cannot interfere in those rights, which, from the very nature of society and of government, belong exclusively to citizens of that state. Such are the rights of election and of representation; for they cannot be imparted to any but citizens, without a subversion of the principles of the social compact. When, therefore, I perceive M'Carty in the exercise of those rights, I am disposed to consider it as rightful, rather than wrongful; which, however, can only be on the idea that he has not relinquished his citizenship. But, admitting him to have intended to abandon this state, he has not executed that intention by attaching himself to another. He made no settlement; he paid no taxes; in fact, he claimed none of the rights, and performed none of the duties, of a citizen of Maryland. He was "a mere sojourner in the land," retaining his character of citizen of Virginia, and, therefore, not entitled to the benefit of a proviso, which, from its very terms, is applicable to those persons only who are not citizens. If mere residence in another state, by a citizen of this state, residence undefined as to object, intention, or duration, shall entitle him, on his return, to bring with him as many slaves as he may think proper, how vain and nugatory is the law which affects to prevent their farther importation.

I wish it to be distinctly understood, that my opinion that M'Carty never ceased to be a citizen of Virginia, and that, therefore, he could not bring his slaves with him on his return, has not been influenced by the circumstance of his having failed to comply with the requisites of our act of assembly concerning expatriation. The view I have taken of the subject has rendered any consideration of that act totally unnecessary. My opinion is founded solely on the impression that, according to the principles of general law, there is not sufficient evidence to prove, 1st. His intention to quit this state; and, 2d. The execution of that intention by his departing out of this commonwealth, and becoming a citizen of Maryland. Had there been sufficient evidence on these points, it might then have become necessary to inquire, whether he ought not, nevertheless, to be considered as a citizen of this state, inasmuch as he had omitted to relinquish that character in the manner prescribed by our act concerning expatriation. But we should have been there met by the previous and important question, whether, as the principal part of that act is taken up in declaring the mode in which aliens may become citizens, the particular part relating to expatriation was not intended to point out the mode in which citizens might become aliens: and if so, whether that act can be made to apply to the case of a citizen of Virginia, who leaves this state and becomes a citizen of some other of the United States; the citizens of the other states, although contradistinguished from citizens of this state, not being aliens with respect to this state, inasmuch as both the articles of confederation, and the constitution of the United States, entitle them to the privileges and immunities of citizens of this state. If arguments drawn from the long and uniform practice of a country are ever allowed to have any influence on a question concerning the construction of its laws, they might here be urged with much force. For, of the innumerable emigrants from Virginia, who have overspread the southern and western states and territories, and filled their highest offices, it is believed that not one has ever deemed it necessary to conform to our act concerning expatriation. Are they still citizens of this state? But we should also have to encounter another previous question. Admitting it to have been the intention of our legislature to give to our act of assembly the most extensive application; does the power to regulate the right of expatriation still belong to the state governments, or does it belong to congress, as incident to the power of naturalization, the power of declaring who shall be citizens? I give no decided opinion upon either of these important questions; but I deem it not improper to state it as my present impression, that, if a citizen of Virginia shall have departed out of this commonwealth with an open and avowed, fair and bona fide intention of quitting it, and of becoming a citizen of some other state, and shall, in fact, have become a citizen thereof, that, from thenceforth, he ceased to be a citizen of Virginia, notwithstanding he may have omitted to comply with the requisites of our expatriation act: and that, should he thereafter be "inclined to remove" from his newly adopted state, and again "become a citizen of this," he will be allowed to bring his slaves with him, "if within sixty days after such removal" he shall take the oath prescribed by law. But as to the particular case now before the court, M'Carty never ceased, on any principle, to be a citizen of Virginia, and had no right to bring slaves into this state. The appellant, Nancy Murray, was, therefore, brought here contrary to law, and having been kept here one whole year, is entitled to her freedom; and the county court ought so to have instructed the jury. I am, consequently, of opinion that both judgments be reversed, and

that the cause be remanded to the county court for a new trial to be had therein, with directions to the court, to instruct the jury accordingly.

JUDGE ROANE. It was decided by the supreme court of the United States, in the case of Scott v. Negro London, (3 Cranch, 324,) that the removal by the master, and the importation of the slave, need not be cotemporaneous and concomitant. I am inclined to concur in that construction of the act in question: but that point is not necessary to be now decided in the view I have taken of the subject.

The next question is, whether the appellee is a person coming within the meaning of the proviso of the act upon this subject. That act declares, that slaves thereafter brought within the commonwealth, and remaining there one whole year, shall be free: to which penalty upon the importer, is added another of a pecuniary nature. The object of the law was, to prohibit the great political evil of introducing more slaves into the commonwealth: but as this prohibition, extended to all possible cases, might be too rigid, and as it was also a favourite policy with the legislature to increase the number of our citizens, the general object of the law was relaxed and given up, in consideration of the latter benefit, in favour of the persons, and under the circumstances, embraced by that proviso. That proviso, however, does not extend to those who are already citizens of this commonwealth. I infer this, 1st. Because that idea is reprobated by the limitation, in the proviso, to those who shall "remove" from any of the United States, "and become citizens of this;" and, 2d. Because, in the latter part of the same proviso, the case of "citizens of this commonwealth" is taken up, and the privilege of importation is confined, as to them, to slaves then owned by them, in any of the United States. This provision defines the extent of the privilege of citizens of this commonwealth in this particular; not only by reason of the imperious words of the first part of the proviso before mentioned, but also from the rule of construction, as applied to the last, that expressio unius est exclusio alterius. This construction results from the express provisions of the act itself; but, were it necessary, we might, in addition, well suppose, that the legislature would discriminate, in this particular, between those who were citizens of this state, (wherever resident,) and those who were not; and considering that the animus revertendi probably existed in the former, (even under any circumstances,) the legislature might well have concluded, that they would not stand in need of such inducements to return to the commonwealth, as those would to remove into it, who had never before been citizens thereof. In the case of Talbot v. Jansen, in the supreme court of the United States, it seems to have been held, that, although an expatriation, under our act, was conclusive evidence of an intention to relinquish the right of citizenship, as to the commonwealth of Virginia, and, by Judge Iredell, (the other judges saying nothing on that point,) was the only evidence of such intention; or, in other words, that a citizen of Virginia cannot expatriate himself therefrom, "in any other manner;" yet that, quoad the United States, a residence in, and even a swearing allegiance to, another country was equivocal; for that a man may, at the same time, enjoy the rights of citizenship in two or more governments, and that, therefore, even under those circumstances, the absent citizen would not be construed to have expatriated himself, or to have renounced forever his intention to return to his country. These considerations entirely justify the omission, by the legislature of Virginia, to extend the invitation in question to her absent citizens also; although, at first view, the reason of the two cases might appear to be the same. The question is therefore narrowed to the single point, whether the appellee had ceased to be a citizen of the commonwealth of Virginia at the time of the importation in question: it is not enough that he was a citizen of any, or every other state in the union if he were then also a citizen of Virginia: I mean a citizen of Virginia in a particular and limited sense, as contradistinguished from the general privilege conferred, by the constitution, upon the citizens of each state in every other state.

That there is both a general and a particular sense in which this relationship of a citizen is contemplated in our country, is evident from the constitution itself, which speaks of "citizens of different states" (inter alia) in the judicial article; from various acts of congress, and judicial decisions on the same subject; and from the consideration, that a contrary idea would savour too much of consolidation, as throwing out of view the particular sovereignties of which the American confederacy is composed. We are told by Judge Paterson, in the aforesaid case of Talbot v. Jansen, and I entirely subscribe to the doctrine, that the situation of America, in this particular, is new, and may produce new and delicate questions; that we have sovereignties moving within sovereignties; that allegiance to a particular state is one thing, and that to the United States is another; that a renunciation of the former allegiance does not draw after it a renunciation of the latter; and that a statute of the United States, on the subject of expatriation, is much wanted. If, under the non-existence of such a statute of the United States, the strong facts of a permanent residence in, and swearing allegiance to, another and a foreign country, were deemed equivocal, in that case, and as not necessarily importing an expatriation from the government of the United States, much less will the weaker and more equivocal facts existing in the case before us, be construed to have that effect, in relation to the commonwealth of Virginia; in which state, also, there being a statute upon the subject of expatriation, a noncompliance with the requisitions thereof will proportionally weaken the inference of an intention to expatriate. The facts stated in the case before us, at most, show only a temporary residence in Maryland, and, at one time, perhaps an intention of permanent residence there; but it is not only agreed that the appellee did not expatriate himself from Virginia, in the manner prescribed by our act, but, also, that he neither purchased permanent property in Maryland, nor took the oath of allegiance to that state. This case, therefore, is infinitely weaker than that of Talbot v. Jansen, in which the party was adjudged to be still a citizen of the United States, and that, independently of the strong additional argument derived from the existence of

our act concerning expatriation, and the noncompliance, with its provisions, on the part of the appellee.

The foregoing ideas, in relation to the connexion between the United States and the several states, go a great way to justify the idea, (upon which the general assembly undoubtedly proceeded, in the case before us,) of a particular and local citizenship to Virginia, and to the other states; by which, as the case may be, an exemption from the penalties of the act will stand or fall.

Whatever the case may be, as to the concurrence of the powers of the two governments, on the subject of the naturalization of aliens, and however the construction, on that subject, is to be adjusted between the respective governments, on the ground of the principles before adopted from the opinion of Judge Paterson, (if not of the whole court,) in the aforesaid case of Talbot v. Jansen; it is clear to me, that the commonwealth of Virginia has never delegated to congress the exclusive power to legislate on the subject of the great natural right of expatriation, as relative to this commonwealth. Those topics of legislative power are entirely distinct and unconnected: the one relates to aliens, the other to citizens; the one to rights to be acquired, the other to rights to be abandoned; the one to a political, the other to a natural right. The power of expatriation, in relation to the commonwealth of Virginia, is one with which congress had certainly nothing to do; it is not granted in the instrument of government; and it is a fundamental principle in our system, that each state retains every power, jurisdiction, and right, which is not delegated to the United States by the constitution, nor prohibited by it to the states. While, therefore, the power of legislating on the subject of expatriation, from the commonwealth of Virginia, has not been given up, and ought not to have been given up, by Virginia, to the United States; and while the legislature of Virginia has not presumed to confer this right upon her own citizens, (it being one of paramount authority, bestowed on us by the God of Nature,) it is but a small boon to ask, for the legislature of Virginia, that she should be permitted to set up a criterion of evidence for her courts, determining when, and when only, this right shall be adjudged to have been asserted!

By the standard of our act, therefore, on this subject, this case is to be tested; and I entirely agree with Judge Iredell in opinion, as aforesaid, that a citizen of Virginia cannot expatriate himself therefrom "in any other manner."

Of this construction the particular citizens of Virginia cannot complain; 1st. Because it is the act of their own government, upon a subject, undoubtedly within its power and jurisdiction; 2d. Because it is beneficial to all the citizens, that this great right should be placed upon a foundation which excludes all possible doubt as to the validity of its exercise, instead of leaving the matter at large, and carving out an infinity of litigation and uncertainty, in this particular; and, 3d. Because the exercise of that right, under the act, is as free as air, and depends upon volition only. As for the citizens of other states, it is not for them to complain, that privileges are denied to the citizens of

Virginia, which are extended to them: privileges, too, which are granted in consideration of benefits conferred by them upon the commonwealth, and which it was not in the power of the other class to confer, they being already citizens of Virginia.

On these grounds, I am of opinion to reverse the judgment of both courts, and render judgment in favour of the appellant, for her freedom.

JUDGE FLEMING. The subject having been nearly exhausted by my brother judges, my opinion in this important case will be concise.

The 2d section of the act, passed the 17th of December, 1792, "to reduce into one the several acts concerning slaves, free negroes and mulattoes," declared in general terms, that "slaves, which should thereafter be brought into this commonwealth, and kept therein one whole year together, or so long, at different times, as should amount to one year, should be free." The 4th section of the same act modified this general regulation by certain provisos, or exceptions. The question then is, has the appellee, M'Carty, brought his case within any of those exceptions? And I am clearly of opinion that he has not.

The case of Scott v. Negro London, 3 Cranch, 324, (which has been cited and much relied on by the counsel for the appellee,) is essentially different from this case; the great point of distinction being that, in that case, the true owner of the slave was a citizen of Maryland who removed into this state, and within sixty days after his removal, took the oath prescribed by law; and it was decided that his rights were not to be affected by the acts of another person, over whom he had no control, and which were done without his knowledge or consent; whereas in this case, the appellee, M'Carty, is, and always has been, a citizen of Virginia, and evidently appears to have endeavoured to evade the provisions of the law.

The judgment, therefore, must be reversed, and entered in favour of the appellant, for her freedom.

8

COMMONWEALTH V. HOLLOWAY
6 Binney 213 (Pa. 1814)

TILGHMAN, C. J. Negro *Lewis,* who is brought before us on this *habeas corpus,* was committed by Alderman *Keppele* as the slave of *Langdon Cheves* esquire, having absconded from his master's service. Mr. *Cheves* is a member of the house of representatives of the *United States,* from the state of *South Carolina,* and has never resided in this state, except as a sojourner. During the recess of congress he remained with his family, in a house which he rented in *Germantown,* in this state. *Lewis* was his slave, and employed as a domestic servant in his family during his stay at *Germantown* for more than six months, between *March* and *December* last. It is contended that in consequence of this residence, *Lewis* acquired his freedom by virtue of the act "for

the gradual abolition of slavery," (passed 1st *March* 1780). The question depends on the 10th section of the act, by which it was enacted, that "no man or woman of any nation or colour, except the negroes or mulattoes which shall be registered as aforesaid, shall at any time hereafter be deemed, adjudged or holden within the territories of this Commonwealth as slaves or servants for life, but as free men or free women, *except the domestic slaves attending upon delegates in congress from the other American states,* foreign ministers and consuls, and persons passing out of the state." Now the last exception in the tenth section, relates to *members of congress,* foreign ministers and consuls; so that the proviso in their favour was considered as still in force. The next position of the counsel for the *habeas corpus* is, that our act is confined to members of congress, *during the time of its session,* allowing a reasonable time for going and returning. The expression of the act is, *delegates in congress;* but I take this to be the same as *delegates to congress,* or in other words members of congress, and that this is the meaning of the law is certain, because, in the proviso in the last part of the same section, *members of congress* are the words used. It is next contended, that whatever may be the literal meaning of the words, the real object of the law was to give to members of congress the benefit of their slaves during the time of their attendance on their public duty *only.* I agree that it is fair to construe the law according to its meaning, provided that meaning is deduced not from conjecture, but from the words of the law; at the same time I am not for adhering to *words,* so far as to produce consequences too absurd or inconvenient, to be supposed to have been intended by the legislature. But I see no absurdity or inconvenience in giving to these words their obvious meaning, which will only confer on members of congress the privilege of being served by their domestics during the time that they remain members, whether congress shall be sitting in this or any other state. On the contrary, I see great inconvenience in reducing the southern members to the necessity of giving up their residence in this state during the recess of congress, or losing the service of their domestics. In the case of Mr. *Cheves,* this inconvenience would be very great indeed, because there was a session of congress between *March* and *December,* his return to *Charleston* by *water* was cut off, and it was impossible to say whether the events of the war might not have induced the president of the *United States* to convene the congress before the month of *December.* We all know that our southern brethren are very jealous of their rights on the subject of slavery, and that their union with the other states could never have been cemented, without yielding to their demands on this point. Nor is it conceivable that the legislature of *Pennsylvania* could have intended to make a law, the probable consequence of which would have been the banishment of the congress from the state. I am therefore of opinion that the true construction of the law, is that which is impressed on the mind by its first reading, that is to say, that the domestic slaves of members of congress who are attending on the family of their masters even during its recess, gain no title to freedom, although they remain in the state more than six months, whether the seat of congress be in *Pennsylvania* or elsewhere. According to this construction the prisoner is to be remanded to the custody of the jailer.

YEATES J. The present case appears to me, to be clearly within the words and spirit of the exception contained in the tenth section of the act of 1st *March* 1780. Mr. *Cheves* is a member of congress, and within the principle for which the privilege was introduced; and a different construction from that contended for on his behalf, would place him upon the footing of a mere sojourner, which is repugnant to the plain terms of the law.

I concur, that *Lewis* be remanded to the jailer,

BRACKENRIDGE J. concurred.

Prisoner remanded.

9

COMMONWEALTH V. HOLLOWAY
2 Serg. & Rawle 305 (Pa. 1816)

TILGHMAN, C. J. The facts in this case are few and undisputed. The mother of *Eliza* was a slave, the property of *James Corse*, of *Maryland*. She absconded from her master, and came to this state, in which, after a residence of about two years, her child, *Eliza*, was born. The question, therefore, is, whether *birth in Pennsylvania* gives freedom to the child of a slave who had absconded from another state, *before she became pregnant*. This question depends upon the law of *Pennsylvania* and the constitution of the *United States*. On the 1st *March*, 1780, the state of *Pennsylvania* passed an act "for the gradual abolition of slavery," by the third section of which, it is enacted, "That, all servitude for life, or slavery of children, in consequence of the slavery of their mothers, in the case of all children born within this state, from and after the passing of this act, shall be utterly taken away, extinguished, and for ever abolished." The fifth section directs the manner in which the owners of slaves should enter them in a public register, and the tenth section declares "That no man, or woman, of any nation, except the negroes or mulattoes who shall be registered, as aforesaid, shall, at any time hereafter, be deemed, adjudged, or holden, within the territories of this Commonwealth, as slaves or servants for life, but as free men and free women, except the domestic slaves attending upon delegates in congress from the other *American* states, foreign ministers, and consuls," and with certain other exceptions, not affecting the present case. Thus far the act is too clear and too positive to admit of a doubt, nor can it be denied that the state of *Pennsylvania* had a right to give freedom to every person within her territory, however impolitic the extreme exercise of that right might have been, considering the situation of some of her sister states. But the situation of those states was neither unthought of nor neglected. Accordingly, we find it provided by the 11th section, "That the said act, or any thing contained in it, should not give any relief or shelter to any absconding or runaway negro or mulatto slave or servant who had ab-

sented himself, or should absent himself from his, or her, owner, master, or mistress, residing in any other state or county, but such owner, master, or mistress, should have like right and aid to demand, claim, and take away his slave or servant, as he might have had in case the said act had not been made." The terms of this proviso do not extend to the *issue* of the absconding slave, nor is there any necessary implication by which it must be extended to issue *begotten* and *born* in *Pennsylvania*. It appears to me, therefore, that, under the act of assembly, this child is entitled to freedom. I desire it, however, to be understood, that it is not intended to intimate any opinion on the case of children of domestic slaves, attending upon members of congress, foreign ministers, or consuls, nor on the case of a child, with which a slave absconding from another state, should be pregnant at the time when she came into this state. All that need to be said at present is, that these cases are distinguishable from the one now decided, and may, perhaps, be found to turn on different principles. But the constitution of the *United States* has been relied on in opposition to the act of assembly, and if there be a repugnancy, there is no doubt but the act of assembly must give way. This constitution was formed upwards of seven years after the passing of the act of assembly. By that time, the operation of the act had been fully experienced by the slave-holding states. It was a subject on which their feelings had been excited, and therefore we must presume that their representatives, in the General Convention of 1787, regarded this important object with vigilant attention. Neither can it be supposed that *Pennsylvania* and the eastern states were inattentive to what had always been deemed, by them, a matter of importance; so that it is a case in which there are peculiar reasons for adhering to the words of the constitution. The subject is introduced in the 2d section of the 4th article, which is expressed as follows: "No person, held to service or labour, in one state, under the laws thereof, *escaping into another*, shall, in consequence of any law or regulation thereof, be discharged from such service or labour, but shall be delivered up on claim of the party to which such service or labour may be due." This is in conformity with the law of *Pennsylvania*. The case of the absconding slave, is provided for, without mention of the issue. I see not upon what ground the constitution can be extended beyond the act of assembly, nor does it appear that, in the opinion of Congress, it can be extended further: for, in the "Act respecting fugitives from justice, and persons escaping from the service of their masters," (passed 12th *February*, 1793,) there is no provision, except in case of persons held to labour in one of the *United States, who shall escape* into another of the said states. I am, therefore, of opinion, that, under the act of assembly of this state, and the constitution of the *United States*, the child *Eliza* was born free.

YEATES, J. The words of the 3d section of the act of the 1st *March*, 1781, are general and comprehensive, and include the cases of all children of slaves who should be born within the state after that day. "They shall not be deemed and considered as servants for life, or slaves." The expressions are strong and imperative, and cannot be got over. Where the meaning of the terms used by the legislature is plain, we are bound to adhere to it, and not to transpose their words, or insert others, unless the result would involve us in palpable absurdity or gross injustice.

Whatever may be our ideas of the rights of slave holders, in our sister states, we cannot deny that it was competent to the legislature to enact a law ascertaining the freedom of the issue of slaves born after the passage of the act, within this state. The only question left to be considered, is, whether there is any thing in the constitution of the *United States*, or in any act of congress, passed in pursuance thereof, which controls or abridges the operation of our state law, in its plain and literal sense. The convention who formed the federal compact, had the whole subject of slavery before them, and we well know the prejudices and jealousies of the southern parts of the union, as to their property in slaves. It was no easy task to reconcile the local interests and discordant prepossessions of the different sections of the *United States;* but the business was accomplished by acts of concession and mutual condescension. The constitution of the *United States,* in art. 4, sect. 2, goes no further than to provide that persons held to service, or labour, in one state, under the laws thereof, escaping into another state, shall not be discharged from such service or labour, but shall be delivered up. And the act of congress, of the 12th *February,* 1793, points out the mode by which fugitive slaves shall be restored to their former masters in another state. It cannot be supposed, for a moment, that the child in question, who was not in existence, when her mother ran away, had escaped, or was a fugitive. Her case, therefore, is not embraced, either by the constitution of the *United States,* or by the act of congress. It irresistibly follows, that negro *Eliza* is not a slave. At the same time, it is to be fully understood, that my opinion goes no further than the case now before us. The children of a female slave, of foreign ministers, or of the members of congress of other states, which may be born amongst us, are not included therein. It will be time enough to decide those particular cases when they shall occur, and come before us for our determination.

GIBSON, J. The case of the relater is embraced by the letter of the third section, and certainly does not fall within any of the exceptions of the tenth section of the act of *March* 1, 1780. By the provisions of either, she is indisputably free. It is not for us to conjecture what provision would have been made, if the present case had presented itself to the consideration of the legislature. An attempt to supply what this Court might consider deficient, would be an assumption of legislative authority. But the 10th section effectually guards against all construction unfavourable to the class of persons intended to be benefited. If, even an equitable construction, in favour of the master, were not precluded, I am far from being satisfied that the present case would be proper for its exercise. The support of the relater has caused him neither trouble nor expense. He was, it is true, deprived of the service of the mother from the time she absconded. But this did not happen in consequence of any act of the relater, and gives him no claim on *her.* Whether his case is to be considered a hard one or not, will depend much on the temper with which the mind may contemplate the positive and artificial rights of the master over the mother on the one hand, on the other, the natural rights of her child.

10

HOUSE OF REPRESENTATIVES, FUGITIVES FROM JUSTICE
30 Jan. 1818
Annals 31:837–40

Mr. ADAMS, of Massachusetts, opposed the bill at much length; on the ground principally that, in guarantying the possession of slave property to those States holding it, the Constitution did not authorize or require the General Government to go as far as this bill proposed, to render the Constitutional provision effectual; that the bill contained provisions dangerous to the liberty and safety of the free people of color in other sections in the Union; and that, in securing the rights of one portion of the community, he could not consent to jeopardise those of another.

Mr. ANDERSON, of Kentucky, spoke some time very earnestly in support of the bill, and in reply to the objections urged by the gentlemen who had at different times opposed it.

Mr. LIVERMORE, of New Hampshire, submitted the reasons for his intention to vote against the bill. He was willing to go to the necessary extent in securing to the owners this species of property, permitted as it was by the Constitution; but the bill contained no sufficient guard to the safety of those colored people who resided in the States where slavery was known only by name. The bill provided that alleged fugitives were not to be identified and proven until they reached the State in which the person seizing them resided; and this would expose the free men of other parts to the hazard of being dragged from one extreme of the country to the other—though this fear was not strengthened by any want of respect for the wisdom and justice of the Southern judiciaries, to which he paid the highest compliment; but the feelings entertained on the subject in the South, he feared, would make less secure the liberty of any colored man carried there, and charged with being a fugitive.

Mr. MASON, of Massachusetts, delivered at length his motives for approving the bill. The Constitution, formed in the spirit of compromise, had guaranteed this kind of property to the Southern States, and as it appeared from the insufficiency of the existing laws, that the proposed bill was necessary to secure this right, he was willing to adopt the measure, as he was always willing to approve any measure to effect what the Constitution sanctioned. The possible abuse of anything was no argument against it, if otherwise expedient, and on this ground he was not prepared to reject the feature of the bill so much opposed. The judicial tribunals of the South, he had no doubt, would decide on the cases as correctly as those of the North, and on this subject perhaps more so, as, he believed, so strong was the feeling on this subject in the latter section of the country, and so great a leaning was there against slavery, that the juries of Massachusetts would, in ninety-nine cases in a hundred, decide in favor of the fugitive. His feelings on this bill were also somewhat interested; as he wished not, by denying just facilities for the recovery of fugitive slaves, to have the town where he lived (Boston) infested, as it would be, without an effectual restraint, with a great portion of the runaways from the South.

Mr. HOLMES, of Massachusetts, followed his colleague in submitting his reasons for approving the bill, and to reconcile the apparent contradiction in a gentleman from his part of the country appearing as the supporter of this bill. His course on this, as on other measures, was based on his duty as a Representative for the whole Union, instead of local interests. This measure, it appeared, was necessary to secure the Constitutional rights of a large portion of the States; and, as to the provision so strongly objected to by some gentlemen, he did not think it competent in Massachusetts to try a question between a Southern master and his slave; it was a kind of question, with which his constituents, to their honor, were not familiar, and he wished them to remain so. He did not believe the freedom of a single man in the North would be endangered by this provision of the bill; the *habeas corpus* would prevent it; and he went into various arguments to prove that the bill was expedient, and free from the evils apprehended by other gentlemen.

Mr. RHEA made some observations in support of the bill, and in reply to the arguments against it. So long as this property was authorized, there could be no doubt of the right of the holder to pursue it, and carry it back without hindrance to the place from whence it escapes. He thanked Heaven, this nation was not chargeable with the odium of introducing this species of property; it was an evil entailed on it; and this bill was in conformity with the principles of the compact which guarantied this property to its holders. There was little danger of persons going from the South to claim free men as their property; such a fear was without foundation. He always felt pain in hearing distinctions made between the slaveholding States and others; nearly all the old original thirteen States had held slaves, and, if circumstances had enabled some of them to get rid of the evil, the only feeling they ought to entertain towards the others, is, compassion that they are not so fortunate.

Mr. STORRS, of New York, entered into a number of arguments in support of the bill. He referred to and reasoned on the words of the Constitution, to show that the bill was consonant to its provisions, and did not exceed the limits within which Congress were authorized to legislate on the subject. He expressed his pleasure at the liberality which had been manifested by some in its discussion, but should like to see a little more displayed by gentlemen from the North, as an evidence they were willing to sacrifice some of their old prejudices to the spirit of harmony and mutual benefit.

Mr. WHITMAN, of Massachusetts, admitted the necessity of some additional regulations on this subject, as the existing law appeared inadequate; but he could not vote for this bill in its present shape. He objected to that provision, which makes it penal in a State officer to refuse his assistance, in executing the act. This feature, if retained, would prevent his voting for the bill, as its penalties would require the State officers either to resign, or perform an act which might be repugnant to their feelings, and render their official stations frequently disagreeable. Furthermore, he did not believe Congress had the right to compel the State officers to perform this duty—they could only authorize it; and, as he believed the bill might be made effectual without this objectionable provision, he hoped it would be recommitted, and receive the necessary modification. In reference to a remark of his colleague, (Mr. MASON) he had no doubt that justice would be administered under this act by the tribunals of Massachusetts, if the duty were devolved on them, as impartially as in any other part of the Union, notwithstanding the prejudices they felt on the subject; yet he did not doubt that exact justice would also be rendered by the tribunals of the South, where prejudices were felt of an opposite character.

Mr. WILLIAMS, of Connecticut, was called up by the remark of Mr. STORRS, and admitted that, if he could not and had not banished all his local prejudices, he ought to have done so. Mr. W. then entered, at large, into an examination of the bill, into his reasons for opposing it unless it was altered in some of its features, and to show that in its present shape it was calculated to excite angry feelings and rouse strong prejudices in those parts of the country where slavery was not tolerated. This effect would be produced by that provision under which a free man of color might be unjustly seized and dragged to a remote part of the country, and his liberty endangered, if not destroyed. In attempting, properly, he admitted, to secure the right of property to one class of citizens, it was unjust that the rights of another class should be put in jeopardy, when, too, as he contended, the danger might be avoided, in one case, without impairing the benefit in the other. Although he wished not to interfere between a slave and his master, yet he argued that the right ought to be tried in the State in which the fugitive should be arrested; and compared the case to that of a runaway apprentice, who could not be seized and carried away by the ex parte testimony of the person claiming him.

The question on the passage of the bill was then taken, and decided in the affirmative—yeas 84, nays 69.

11

WRIGHT V. DEACON
5 Serg. & Rawle 62 (Pa. 1819)

TILGHMAN C. J. This is a matter of considerable importance, and the Court has therefore held it some days under advisement. Whatever may be our private opinions on the subject of slavery, it is well known that our southern brethren would not have consented to become parties to a constitution under which the *United States* have enjoyed so much prosperity, unless their property in slaves had been secured. This constitution has been adopted by the free consent of the citizens of *Pennsylvania*, and it is the duty of every man, whatever may be his office or station, to give it a fair and candid construction. By the 2d sect. of the 4th art. it is provided, "that no person held to service or labour in one state, under the laws thereof, escaping into another, shall, in consequence of any law or regulation therein, be discharged from such service or labour, *but shall be delivered up on claim of the party to whom such service or labour may be due.*" Here is the principle: the fugitive is to be delivered up on *claim* of his master. But it required a law, to regulate the manner in which this principle should be reduced to practice. It was necessary to establish some mode in which the claim should be made, and the fugitive be delivered up. Accordingly it was enacted by the act of Congress "respecting fugitives from justice and persons escaping from the service of their masters," sect. 5. that the person to whom the labour or service of the fugitive was due, his agent or attorney, should be empowered to arrest such fugitive, and carry him before any Judge of the Circuit or District Court of the *United States* residing or being within the state, or before any magistrate of a county, city, or town corporate, wherein such arrest should be made, and upon proof to the satisfaction of the said Judges or magistrate, either by oral testimony, or affidavit taken before and certified by a magistrate of the state or territory from which the said fugitive had fled, that the person so arrested, did, under the law of the said state or territory from which he had fled, owe service or labour to the person claiming him, it should be the duty of the said Judge or magistrate, to give a certificate thereof to such claimant, *which should be sufficient warrant for removal of a fugitive from labour, to the state or territory from which he fled.* It plainly appears from the whole scope and tenor of the constitution and act of Congress, that the fugitive was to be delivered up, on a summary proceeding, without the delay of a formal trial in a court of common law. But, if he had really a right to freedom, that right was not impaired by this proceeding; he was placed just in the situation in which he stood before he fled, and might prosecute his right in the state to which he belonged. Now in the present instance, the proceeding before Judge ARMSTRONG, and the certificate granted by him, are in exact conformity to the act of Congress. That certificate therefore was a legal warrant to remove the plaintiff to the state of *Maryland*. But if this writ of *homine replegiando* is to issue from a state court, what is its effect, but to arrest the warrant of Judge ARMSTRONG, and thus defeat the constitution and law of the *United States?* The constitution and the law say, that the master may remove his slave by virtue of the Judge's certificate: but the state court says, that he shall not remove him. It appears to us, that this is the plain state of the matter, and that the writ has been issued in violation of the constitution of the *United States.* We are, therefore, of opinion, that it should be quashed.

Writ quashed.

12

MISSOURI CONSTITUTION OF 1820,
ART. 3, SECS. 26–28
Thorpe 4:2154

SEC. 26. The general assembly shall not have power to pass laws—

1. For the emancipation of slaves without the consent of their owners; or without paying them, before such emancipation, a full equivalent for such slaves so emancipated; and,

2. To prevent *bona-fide* immigrants to this State, or actual settlers therein, from bringing from any of the United States, or from any of their Territories, such persons as may there be deemed to be slaves, so long as any persons of the same description are allowed to be held as slaves by the laws of this State.

They shall have power to pass laws—

1. To prohibit the introduction into this State of any slaves who may have committed any high crime in any other State or Territory;

2. To prohibit the introduction of any slave for the purpose of speculation, or as an article of trade or merchandise;

3. To prohibit the introduction of any slave, or the offspring of any slave, who heretofore may have been, or who hereafter may be, imported from any foreign country into the United States, or any Territory thereof, in contravention of any existing statute of the United States; and,

4. To permit the owners of slaves to emancipate them, saving the right of creditors, where the person so emancipating will give security that the slave so emancipated shall not become a public charge.

It shall be their duty, as soon as may be, to pass such laws as may be necessary—

1. To prevent free negroes and mulattoes from coming to and settling in this State, under any pretext whatsoever; and,

2. To oblige the owners of slaves to treat them with humanity, and to abstain from all injuries to them extending to life or limb.

SEC. 27. In prosecutions for crimes, slaves shall not be deprived of an impartial trial by jury and a slave convicted of a capital offence shall suffer the same degree of punishment, and no other, that would be inflicted on a free white person for a like offence; and courts of justice, before whom slaves shall be tried, shall assign them counsel for their defence.

SEC. 28. Any person who shall maliciously deprive of life or dismember a slave, shall suffer such punishment as would be inflicted for the like offence if it were committed on a free white person.

13

BUTLER V. DELAPLAINE
7 Serg. & Rawle 378 (Pa. 1821)

DUNCAN, J.—In giving a construction to this lease, we must take into view the subject matter of the contract, the species of property to which it related, and the place in which the right of *Cleland* over the property, was to be exercised. If this were a general hiring of a slave in *Maryland,* to an inhabitant of *Maryland,* it would be difficult to maintain the right of the lessee or bailee to do an act which would extinguish the property itself. There would necessarily be implied an engagement on his part to restore the slaves. The contrary implication would be highly unreasonable. That he had authority to do an act which would put it out of his power to restore, them, would be an instance of folly that cannot be imputed to any one capable of entering into a binding contract. But this was not a general hiring, but a special one. The negroes were demised with the land, for the purpose of cultivating the farm. Though this is a claim of freedom, we are not in favour of liberty to lose sight that this class of people are acknowledged as slaves by the laws of both States. The master has a property in them, and contracts respecting this species of property, are to be construed by the same rules of interpretation, that contracts respecting any other species of property are. We are not at liberty to infer a power of removal, when the contract itself takes away all implication, and states the very purpose for which they were hired, to cultivate this farm of *Norman Bruce,* devised by him to *Cleland.* It follows, that the decision of the Court was correct in stating that the consent of *Cleland* to remove *Charity* into this State, would not entitle her to her freedom. The continuing of a sojourner, must be a single, unbroken one, for six months. There may be cases of a fraudulent shuffling backwards and forwards in *Pennsylvania,* and then into *Maryland,* and then back to *Pennsylvania.* This might be in fraud of the law, and would present a different question; but here there is no evasion—no ground even for suspicion of evasion.

It was well known to the framers of our Acts for the Abolition of slavery, that southern gentlemen, with their families, were in the habit of visiting this State, attended with their domestic slaves, either for pleasure, health, or business; year after year passing the summer months with us, their continuance scarcely ever amounting to six months. If these successive sojournings were to be summed up, it would amount to a prohibition—a denial of the rights of hospitality. The *York* and *Bedford* springs are watering places frequented principally, and in great numbers, by families from *Maryland* and *Virginia,* attended by their domestic slaves. The same families with the same servants return in each season. The construction contended for by the plaintiffs in error, would be an exclusion of the citizens of our sister States from these fountains of health,

unwarranted by any principle of humanity or policy, or the spirit and letter of the law. The retaining a slave for six months by a sojourner, may well be compared to the hiring and service for one year, to obtain a settlement under the poor laws, which must be an entire hiring, and an entire service for the year; or to the period prescribed as a limit to the recovery of real estate where the adverse possession must be continuous, unbroken and uninterrupted. It must be one hiring, and one entire service under the poor laws. It must be continued possession for one interrupted period of twenty-one years under the Limitation Act. And under this law, the retaining must be for one unbroken point of time—one entire six months, and cannot be made up of different points of time joined together.

I cannot agree with the counsel of the plaintiffs in error, that the Court did throw the *onus* of proof of the master's consent, on the slave. All they said, was, if it appeared to the jury from the evidence, that *Charity* was not brought into *Pennsylvania* with the knowledge or connivance of *Norman Bruce,* and no authority was given directly or indirectly by *Bruce* to *Cleland* or *Gilleland,* to bring her into *Pennsylvania,* she continued his slave. The fourth point is nearly the same as the second, for the reasons already stated, that the master's lease to *Cleland,* was no evidence of his leave to *Cleland* to bring her into *Pennsylvania.* It is so far from affording such *prima facie* evidence, of an intention to grant a licence to remove the negroes into *Pennsylvania,* that as clearly as language can exclude such construction, it is here done. It would not be a power necessarily incident to the use of the thing demised, because the slaves are to be used in the cultivation of the farm in *Maryland.* A presumption could not be raised of such intention, because it is against all reason and all probability. It is contended, that every slave brought into this State, and remaining here for six months, unless he is an absconding or runaway slave, became *ipso facto* free, and that whether the party removing him had authority or not, to bring him in. This construction would be a reproach to the framers of the Acts for the abolition of slavery, as it would be an outrage on the property of the citizens of another State, where slavery is tolerated—a confiscation and forfeiture of their rights, without any act done by them in violation of the laws of this State. It would be an invitation and reward offered to strangers who had no right or authority to bring slaves into our State—to overseers, to bring over the gangs of negroes entrusted to their superintendance. Nay, on this principle, if the negro were stolen from *Maryland* and brought into this State, he would become free. The Legislature wisely and humanely desirous to abolish gradually slavery in this State, have cautiously preserved the rights of citizens of other States whose slaves *are introduced* into this State without their knowledge.

The 10th section of the Act of 1st *March,* 1780, provides, that no man or woman, of any nation or colour, except the negroes and mulattoes, who shall be registered, shall be holden within the territories of this Commonwealth as slaves or servants for life, except domestic slaves of delegates to Congress from other States, foreign ministers, &c., and persons passing through and sojourning in this State.

The 11th section provides, that the Act shall not give relief or shelter to any absconding or runaway negro or mulatto slave or servant for life, who has or shall absent himself from his or her owner or master; but he shall have right and aid to demand, claim, and take away his servant or slave, as he might have had in case this Act had not been made, and that all negro and mulatto slaves now owned and heretofore resident in this State, who have absented themselves or been clandestinely carried away, before the passing of this Act, may be registered within five years. Absenting themselves, absconding, being clandestinely carried away, in all these cases, I am of opinion, that the interest of the master is secured; the slave who is removed into this State, without the consent or connivance of the master, may be considered as a slave absenting himself, absconding, or clandestinely carried away; and that such removal under the 4th article, section 2d of the Constitution of the *United States*, would be an escaping into another State; and that under that article, the slave coming into the State, in any other way than by the consent of the owner, whether he comes in as a fugitive or runaway, or is brought in by those who have no authority so to do, cannot be discharged under any law of this State, but must be delivered up on claim of the party to whom his services or labour may be due.

The opinion of the Court was, in all matters on which they were requested to charge the jury entirely correct; and it was left to the jury with the opinion of the Court on the general question of law, with all accuracy, that if they believed that neither *Cleland* nor Mrs. *Gilleland* were the agents of *Norman Bruce*, and that if the removal of *Charity* into the State of *Pennsylvania* was without the consent or approbation of *Bruce* the master, such removal did not entitle the plaintiffs to freedom; and that if no authority directly or indirectly was given by *Bruce* to *Cleland* or *Gilleland* to remove *Charity*, that the verdict should be for the defendant. The judgment is therefore affirmed.

14

JOSEPH STORY, COMMENTARIES ON THE CONSTITUTION 3:§§ 1805–6
1833

---

§ 1805. This clause was introduced into the constitution solely for the benefit of the slave-holding states, to enable them to reclaim their fugitive slaves, who should have escaped into other states, where slavery was not tolerated. The want of such a provision under the confederation was felt, as a grievous inconvenience, by the slave-holding states, since in many states no aid whatsoever would be allowed to the owners; and sometimes indeed they met with open resistance. In fact, it cannot escape the attention of every intelligent reader, that many sacrifices of opinion

and feeling are to be found made by the Eastern and Middle states to the peculiar interests of the south. This forms no just subject of complaint; but it should for ever repress the delusive and mischievous notion, that the south has not at all times had its full share of benefits from the Union.

§ 1806. It is obvious, that these provisions for the arrest and removal of fugitives of both classes contemplate summary ministerial proceedings, and not the ordinary course of judicial investigations, to ascertain, whether the complaint be well founded, or the claim of ownership be established beyond all legal controversy. In case of suspected crimes the guilt or innocence of the party is to be made out at his trial; and not upon the preliminary inquiry, whether he shall be delivered up. All, that would seem in such cases to be necessary, is, that there should be *primâ facie* evidence before the executive authority to satisfy its judgment, that there is probable cause to believe the party guilty, such as upon an ordinary warrant would justify his commitment for trial. And in the cases of fugitive slaves there would seem to be the same necessity of requiring only *primâ facie* proofs of ownership, without putting the party to a formal assertion of his rights by a suit at the common law. Congress appear to have acted upon this opinion; and, accordingly, in the statute upon this subject have authorized summary proceedings before a magistrate, upon which he may grant a warrant for a removal.

15

JACK V. MARTIN
14 Wend. 507 (N.Y. 1835)

By the CHANCELLOR. This cause has been argued in this court upon the assumption, that the decision which is now to be made, necessarily involves the question as to the constitutional right of congress to legislate upon the subject of fugitive slaves and apprentices—or, in the language of the constitution, persons held to service or labor in one state, under the laws thereof, escaping into another; and the decision of the court below is put upon the ground that congress not only has the power to legislate upon the subject, but that their legislation must necessarily be exclusively in relation to this matter; that the law of congress of February 1793 is valid and binding upon the states; under which law any free citizen of this state may be seized as a slave or apprentice who has escaped from servitude, and transported to a distant part of the union, without any trial except a summary examination before a magistrate, who is not even clothed with power to compel the attendance of witnesses upon such investigation; and upon the certificate of such magistrate that he is satisfied that such citizen owes service to the person claiming him under the laws of the state to which he is to be transported. If the decision of this cause turned upon these questions, I am not prepared to say that the congress of the United States had the power, under the constitution, to make the certificate of a state magistrate conclusive evidence of the right of the claimant, to remove a native born citizen of this state to a distant part of the union, so as to deprive him of the benefit of the writ of *habeas corpus* and the right of trial by jury in the state where he is found. In the case of *Martin*, before the circuit court of the United States for the southern district of New-York, to which we were referred on the argument, the fact appears to be assumed that there is no question as to the identity of the individual, whose services are claimed, and that he is in truth a fugitive from the state under whose laws it is alleged that he owes services or labor to the claimant. If these important facts are conceded or judicially established, with the additional fact that the fugitive was actually claimed, and held in servitude in the state from which he fled, whether rightfully or otherwise, previous to his flight, I admit there can be no reasonable objection in principle to the removal of the person whose services were thus claimed, back to the state from which he fled, as the most proper place for the trial and final decision of the question whether the claimant was legally entitled to his services, according to the laws of that state. But suppose, as is frequently the case, that the question to be tried relates merely to the identity of the person claimed as a fugitive slave or apprentice, he insisting that he is a free native born citizen of the state where he is found residing at the time the claim is made, and that he has never been in the state under whose laws his services are claimed—can it for a moment be supposed that the framers of the constitution intended to authorize the transportation of a person thus claimed to a distant part of the union, as a slave, upon a mere summary examination before an inferior state magistrate, who is clothed with no power to compel the attendance of witnesses to ascertain the truth of the allegations of the respective parties? Whatever others may think upon this subject, I must still be permitted to doubt whether the patriots of the revolution who framed the constitution of the United States, and who had incorporated into the declaration of independence, as one of the justifiable causes of separation from our mother country, that the inhabitants of the colonies had been transported beyond seas for trial, could ever have intended to sanction such a principle as to one who was merely *claimed* as a fugitive from servitude in another state.

I am one of those who have been in the habit of believing, that the state legislatures had general powers to pass laws on all subjects, except those in which they were restricted by the constitution of the United States, or their own local constitutions, and that congress had no power to legislate on any subject, except so far as the power was delegated to it by the constitution of the United States. I have looked in vain among the powers delegated to congress by the constitution, for any general authority to that body to legislate on this subject. It certainly is not contained in any express grant of power, and it does not appear to be embraced in the general grant of incidental powers contained in the last clause of the constitution relative to the powers of congress. *Const. art.* 1, § 8, *sub.* 17. The law of the United States respecting fugitives from jus-

tice and fugitive slaves, is not a law to carry into effect any of the powers expressly granted to congress, "or any other power vested by the constitution in the government of the United States, or any department or officer thereof." It appears to be a law to regulate the exercise of the rights secured to the individual states, or the inhabitants thereof, by the second section of the fourth article of the constitution; which section, like the ninth section of the first article, merely imposes a restriction and a duty upon other states and individuals in relation to such rights, but *vests no power* in the federal government, or any department or officer thereof, except the *judicial power* of declaring and enforcing the rights secured by the constitution. The act of February, 1793, conferring ministerial powers upon the state magistrates, and regulating the exercise of the powers of the state executive, is certainly not a law to carry into effect the judicial power of the United States; which judicial power cannot be vested in state officers. If the provisions of the constitution, as to fugitive slaves and fugitives from justice, could not be carried into effect without the actual legislation of congress on the subject, perhaps a power of federal legislation might be implied from the constitution itself; but no such power can be inferred from the mere fact that it may be more convenient that congress should exercise the power, than that it should be exercised by the state legislatures. In these cases of fugitive slaves and fugitives from justice, it is not certain that any legislation whatever is necessary, or was contemplated by the framers of the constitution. The provision as to persons escaping from servitude in one state into another, appears by their journal to have been adopted by a unanimous vote of the convention. At that time the existence of involuntary servitude, or the relation of master and servant, was known to and recognized by the laws of every state in the union except Massachusetts, and the legal right of recaption by the master existed in all, as a part of the customary or common law of the whole confederacy. On the other hand, the common law writ of *homine replegiando*, for the purpose of trying the right of the master to the services of the slave, was well known to the laws of the several states, and was in constant use for that purpose, except so far as it had been superseded by the more summary proceeding by *habeas corpus*, or by local legislation. The object of the framers of the constitution, therefore, was not to provide a new mode by which the master might be enabled to recover the services of his fugitive slave, but merely to restrain the exercise of a power, which the state legislatures respectively would otherwise have possessed, to deprive the master of such pre-existing right of recaption. Under this provision of the constitution, even without any legislation on the subject, the right of the master to claim the fugitive slave is fully secured, so as to give him a valid claim in damages against any one who interferes with the right. *Glen* v. *Hodges*, 9 *Johns. R.* 67. But even if legislation on this subject is actually necessary, in order to secure to the master the full enjoyment of the right of recaption guarantied to him by the constitution, the state legislatures are perfectly competent to pass the necessary laws to carry this provision of the constitution into full effect. The members of the state legislatures, as well as other state officers, both executive and judicial, being bound by oath to support the constitution, it cannot be legally presumed that they will violate their duty in this respect. The constitution of the United States being the paramount law on this subject, the judicial tribunals of the respective states are bound by their oaths to protect the master's constitutional right of recaption, against any improper state legislation, and against the unauthorized acts of individuals, by which such right may be impaired; and the supreme court of the United States, as the tribunal of dernier resort on such a question, is possessed of ample powers to correct any erroneous decision which might be made in the state courts against the right of the master. Upon the fullest examination of the subject, therefore, I find it impossible to bring my mind to the conclusion that the framers of the constitution have authorized the congress of the United States to pass a law by which the certificate of a justice of the peace of the state, shall be made conclusive evidence of the right of the claimant, to remove one who may be a free native born citizen of this state, to a distant part of the union as a slave; and thereby to deprive such person of the benefit of the writ of *habeas corpus,* as well as of his common law suit to try his right of citizenship in the state where the claim is made, and where he is residing at the time of such claim.

Independent, however, of any legislation on the subject, either by the individual states or by congress, if the person whose services are claimed is in fact a fugitive from servitude under the laws of another state, the constitutional provision is imperative, that he shall be delivered up to his master upon claim made; and any state officer or private citizen, who owes allegiance to the United States and has taken the usual oath to support the constitution thereof, cannot, without incurring the moral guilt of perjury, do any act to deprive the master of his right of recaption, where there is no real doubt that the person whose services are claimed is in fact the slave of the claimant. However much, therefore, we may deplore the existence of slavery in any part of the union, as a national as well as a local evil, yet, as the right of the master to reclaim his fugitive slave is secured to him by the federal constitution, no good citizen, whose liberty and property are protected by that constitution, will interfere to prevent this provision from being carried into full effect, according to its spirit and intent; and even where the forms of law are resorted to for the purpose of evading this constitutional provision, or to delay the remedy of the master in obtaining a return of his fugitive slave, it is undoubtedly the right and may become the duty of the court in which any proceedings for that purpose are instituted, to set them aside, if they are not commenced and carried on in good faith, and upon probable grounds for believing that the claim of the master to the services of the supposed slave is invalid.

The constitution of the United States having secured to the master the right of recaption, it is of course a good defence to the present suit, if it is admitted on the record that the plaintiff owed service or labor to the defendant in another state and had escaped from such servitude, without reference to the validity of the act of congress, or of any state legislature on the subject. It therefore becomes necessary to examine the pleadings in this cause, for the purpose of ascertaining whether such is the fact here. In the defendant's first avowry, she distinctly avers that Jack was her slave at New Orleans, owing service to her under the laws of Louisiana, for and during his natural life, and that he escaped from her service there and fled into this state. This was sufficient, under the constitution, to entitle her to judgment for a return of such slave, unless he could deny the truth of these allegations, or show that he was subsequently manumitted, or legally discharged from service. The first answer which he attempts to give to this avowry is, that the defendant is a *resident* of the city of New-York; and his counsel contend that a citizen of this state cannot be the owner of a slave. The second plea is the same as the first, with the exception that the defendant is there alleged to be a *citizen* of New-York; and the third plea merely sets out the removal of the defendant from the state of Louisiana to New-York to reside, while she held and claimed the plaintiff as a slave, under the laws of Louisiana; by which, as the pleader alleges, she became a citizen of this state, and the plaintiff became a freeman. It will be seen that each of these pleas leaves uncontradicted the two material facts stated in the avowry, to wit, that the plaintiff owed service to the defendant under the laws of Louisiana for life, and that while he owed such service, he escaped from such servitude and fled into this state. Independent of the constitutional provision, the state legislature perhaps would have had the power of manumitting any slave belonging to a citizen of this state, in case such slave should flee into the state from another part of the union where slavery was allowed; but the restriction in the constitution, as to the power of the several states to discharge fugitives from servitude, is sufficiently broad to cover such a case; and if a citizen of New-York is authorized to hold slaves, under the laws of another state where they are so held in servitude, the legislature of this state cannot pass a law which will deprive even one of our own citizens of this right to reclaim the fugitive slave who may come to this state without the consent of his master, and to remove him back to the state from which he fled. It stands undenied therefore upon this record, under the first avowry, that the defendant was entitled to the services of the plaintiff, under the guaranty of the federal constitution, and that the judgment of the supreme court was right upon the whole record.

Under the second and third avowries, the fact of slavery was directly put in issue; but inasmuch as each avowry formed a separate and independent defence to the action, the defendant would be entitled to judgment if the first avowry was sustained, although the verdict should be against her upon the issues joined under the other avowries. It would therefore have been a useless expense to have gone down to trial upon these issues, when in no possible event could there have been a judgment in favor of the plaintiff for any thing more than the mere costs of those issues.

The conclusion at which I have arrived in this case, therefore, is, that the judgment of the supreme court should be affirmed, with costs; and that the damages which the defendant in error has sustained by the delay and vexation caused by this writ of error should be awarded to her.

By Senator BISHOP. The decision of this cause involves a principle of some moment, not only as to the rights of the slave-holding states in reclaiming their fugitive slaves, but also as to the permanency of the government under which we live. Divested of all the drapery which is thrown around it by the pleadings and technical objections which have been urged, the question is presented whether the law of the congress of the United States in reference to the apprehension of fugitive slaves, passed at the second session under the constitution, is authorized by any power conferred upon congress by the constitution, and consequently whether the law of this state authorizing a writ *de homine replegiando,* which provides for the arrest of runaway slaves in a manner somewhat different from the law of congress, can be sustained by the state authorities.

The doctrine at this day is too well settled to admit of cavil or doubt, not only by judicial decisions but by the voice of the American people, that the several states have reserved to themselves all the rights and immunities of independent sovereignties, except such powers as are conferred upon congress by the explicit language of the constitution, or are clearly and unequivocally to be implied from it. In arriving at a conclusion upon these points it becomes necessary to inquire what powers have been conferred upon congress by the constitution; and if upon such inquiry it be found that the law of congress in reference to fugitive slaves is recognized by the express or implied powers of the constitution, whether the state law must yield to the law of congress. The fourth article and second section of the constitution of the United States declares, that "no person held to service in one state, under the laws thereof, escaping into another, shall in consequence of any law or regulation therein, be discharged from such service or labor, but shall be delivered up on claim of the party to whom such service or labor may be due." The first article, section eight, and last clause of the constitution, authorizes congress to make all laws which shall be necessary and proper for carrying into execution the foregoing powers and all other powers vested by the constitution in the government of the United States, or in any department or officer thereof; not only giving to congress certain powers there enumerated, but giving authority to legislate upon an infinite variety of subjects which the framers of the constitution evidently anticipated would arise under it when the practical operation of the government was more fully and completely developed. The doctrine laid down in the *Federalist* is, that the constitution, in defining the power of congress, evidently specified those which were matters of immediate and general interest, leaving congress to regulate other matters by law as the exigency of the case might require. Upon the authority of the foregoing clauses of the constitution, congress passed a law at its second session, substantially authorizing the owner of any fugitive slave, his agent or attorney, to seize such slave and take him before a judge of the circuit or district court of the United States within the state, or before any magistrate in the state where such seizure was made, and upon full and satisfac-

tory proof, to be made to such judge or magistrate, that the individual so seized in fact is a slave and owes service to the person claiming him, it becomes the duty of the magistrate to deliver a certificate of such fact to the owner, which shall confer upon him power to remove the slave to the state from which he fled. This law of congress has been universally recognized by all the states in the union as constitutional, and paramount over all state authority, and hundreds of fugitive slaves have been removed under its provisions. I cannot but deem it somewhat singular that it should have been reserved for the superior wisdom of modern days, or perhaps I may venture the intimation, to the zealous efforts for a premature and immediate abolition of slavery, to have discovered that a law which was adopted by our forefathers, practised upon by their descendants, and which has been so benign in its practical effects, is unconstitutional and void. Under the law of congress above referred to, the plaintiff in error was seized, and the requisite proof having been made before the recorder of the city of New-York, a certificate was granted by him, authorizing the removal of the slave to the state of Louisiana, the place from which he fled. A writ *de homine replegiando,* authorized by the laws of this state, which gives the person seized a trial by jury, was resorted to by the plaintiff in error, and hence the decision of this court is sought as to the validity of those laws.

In the case of *Gibbons* v. *Ogden,* 9 *Wheaton,* the supreme court of the United States, in speaking of the powers of congress upon this subject, say: "No direct general power over these objects is granted to congress, and consequently they remain subject to state legislation. If the legislative power of the union can reach them, it must be where the power is expressly given for a special purpose, or is clearly incidental to some power which is expressly given." This case, upon the argument, was relied upon by the counsel for the plaintiff in error, as strongly demonstrating the unconstitutionality of the act of congress. The authority of that position is not questioned, but it does not follow that the principles of that case in any manner militate against positions contended for by the defendant in error. In a subsequent part of the same case, Chief Justice Marshall says that "it is a sound rule of construction in arriving at incidental powers, to take into consideration the motives and objects of the framers of the constitution." The abstract proposition of the justice or injustice of slavery, is wholly irrelevant here, and I apprehend ought not to have the slightest influence upon any member of this court. That is a question upon which all are agreed. Slavery is abhored in all nations where the light of civilization and refinement has penetrated, as repugnant to every principle of justice and humanity, and deserving the condemnation of God and man. These sentiments were adopted by the slave-holding states at the period of the adoption of the constitution, and the same feeling, to a great extent, prevails in those states now. It is not that they advocate the principle of slavery, but they say it is an evil entailed upon them by their ancestors, a remedy for which, without endangering their very existence, has not yet been discovered. In the absence of any precise authority in the constitution in regard to the removal of fugitive slaves, it becomes important to inquire as to the motives of the members of the convention who represented the slave-holding states, and the considerations which were likely to operate most powerfully upon them. There was no subject agitated in the convention which created a more intense and deep interest among the slave-holding states, than that of providing a certain and secure mode of perpetuating the bondage of slaves within their boundaries. Difficulties of the most perplexing and harrassing character, in reference to fugitive slaves, had occurred previous to the adoption of the constitution; and it is absurd to suppose that the members of the convention representing the interests of those states, did not intend carefully to guard against a recurrence of similar evils; and it seems to me to be a fair inference from the proceedings of the convention, that they supposed they had done so effectually by the adoption of the clauses in the constitution above referred to, and that they intended to confer full power upon congress to regulate the whole matter. It is reduced to a moral certainty, that the southern states would never have become members of the union upon any other condition. They knew full well the difficulties which had and would grow out of the subject of slavery. They foresaw, with the spirit of prophecy, that unless some summary mode of reclaiming their fugitive slaves was adopted, all the slaves in the union would soon be emancipated, the owners *nolens volens*. They were fully aware of the unextinguishable prejudices of the north against domestic slavery; they were conscious that the descendants of the pilgrims viewed this species of vassalage with unutterable abhorrence, and that the progress of moral reform, of intelligence and of free principles, would strengthen the prejudices and increase the hostility of the non-slave-holding states. It would seem, therefore, that a portion of the convention had every motive which could possibly actuate men who were determined to protect and secure the enjoyment of their property, to effectually provide in the constitution for the accomplishment of that object: that object was supposed by them to have been effected, and the congress of the United States, which I believe was composed of some of the members of the convention, in the promotion of that object, passed the law which it is now insisted is unconstitutional. The members of the convention from the north and east undoubtedly entertained the same sentiments as the southern members, as to the powers conferred on congress; especially as no doubt was entertained by any member of congress as to the constitutionality of the law in question at the time of its passage. The members of the convention from the non-slave-holding states yielded these positions in the spirit of compromise, which produced the final adoption of the constitution. They regarded the innumerable blessings resulting from our form of government as far outweighing the evils which were to be apprehended from slavery, or from the present mode of arresting fugitive slaves, which it must be confessed is somewhat summary. The proceeding before the magistrate is not, however, I apprehend, as contended on the argument, entirely of an *ex parte* character. The magistrate certainly has the right, and it probably would be his duty to examine any testimony produced on the part of the person alleged to

be a slave, establishing his freedon; and in a late case before the recorder of the city of New-York, witnesses were introduced showing that an individual arrested as a fugitive slave was a freeman, and he was accordingly discharged.

Assuming the constitutionality of the law of congress, the next inquiry which naturally arises is, whether the law of this state, providing a different remedy for the removal of fugitive slaves, is ineffectual and void, or whether it can exist concurrent with the law of the United States. In the case of *Sturges* v. *Crowninshield*, 4 *Wheat*. 122, the supreme court of the United States lay down the doctrine, that "whenever the terms in which a power is granted to congress, or the nature of the power requires that it should be exercised exclusively by congress, the subject is as completely taken from the state legislature as if they had been expressly forbidden to act." It is difficult to conceive of any subject arising under the constitution, where it is more peculiarly proper that congress should have exclusive jurisdiction, than in the mode to be provided for the removal of fugitive slaves; or where the doctrine of the supreme court of the United States more aptly applies, "that when the nature of the power requires that it should be exercised exclusively by congress, state legislation must cease." What is the nature of the power contained in the constitution? The nature and the spirit of it clearly is, as I have attempted to show, to secure to the slave-holding states a perfect control over, and right to remove their fugitive slaves by some summary and effectual process. And how, I would ask, is this object more simply and effectually to be accomplished than by a uniform mode to be established by congress, requiring the same proof and the same proceedings under it in every state in the union? A slaveholder in Louisiana is as familiar with, or can as readily have access to the laws of the United States as to the laws of his own state; he therefore comes prepared with the necessary proof to reclaim his fugitive slave in any part of the union. But if one of his slaves escapes to Vermont and another to New-Hampshire, and the doctrine is to be established that the slave is to be reclaimed according to the laws of those states, the owner leaves his residence wholly ignorant of the requisitions of the laws of those states, and finds on his arrival that his claim to his slave in one state is to be tried by a jury, and in the other by the judges of the county courts; in the one case to be established by the oath of one witness, in the other by the testimony of three witnesses; in short he would be subjected to all the machinery and trammels with which the prejudices and conflicting opinions of different state legislation might invest the whole subject. It is not fair to presume that the owners of slaves, rather than to pass through such an ordeal, would abandon in despair the objects of their pursuit? I think it is, and that legislation by the different state governments would indirectly lead to a total abolition of slavery. Believing, as I do, that the members of the convention anticipated similar results, I cannot arrive at the conclusion that it was ever designed that the state legislatures should exercise any control over the subject; but, on the contrary, that congress should possess exclusive jurisdiction as to the mode of reclaiming fugitive slaves, and that the very nature of the power conferred by the constitution requires, that congress should so exercise it. If these positions are correct, it necessarily follows that the law of this state must yield to the omnipotence of the law of congress.

It was contended on the argument of this cause, with great zeal and earnestness, that under the law of the United States a freeman might be dragged from his family and home into captivity. This is supposing an extreme case, as I believe it is not pretended that any such ever has occurred, or that any complaint of that character has ever been made; at all events, I cannot regard it as a very potent argument. The same position might as well be taken in the case of a fugitive from justice. It might be assumed that he was an innocent man, and was entitled to be tried by a jury of the state where he was arrested, to ascertain whether he had violated the laws of the state from which he fled; whereas the fact is, the executive of this state would feel bound to deliver up the most exalted individual in this state, (however well satisfied he might be of his innocence,) if a requisition was made upon him by the executive of another state. At best, this species of argument is begging the question; for if the law of congress is constitutional, however unjust the law may be, or however severe in its consequences, the defect must be remedied upon the spot of its origin. It must be left to congress to establish a more salutary rule.

A question as to the *residence* of the complainant was raised upon the argument, and it was contended that inasmuch as it is admitted by the pleadings that the defendant in error is a *resident* of the state of New-York, that therefore she is incapable of holding slaves, at least of holding such of them in bondage who have fled to this state. I am well satisfied that the residence of the claimant is wholly immaterial. The only question is, whether the claimant is the owner of the person claimed to be a slave in a state where slavery is tolerated, and from whence the slave fled. A different rule would inevitably lead to the entire emancipation of all the slaves owned by individuals who are now residents of the slave-holding states; for it is easy to perceive that the natural inclinations of the slaves, aided by the untiring efforts now making both in and out of the slave-holding states, to excite them to insurrection, (under the pretence of ameliorating their condition,) would soon induce them to flee from their own state, to the place of residence of their owners. I venture to say that the idea never was entertained, either by the members of the convention who adopted the constitution, or the members of congress who passed the law authorizing the removal of fugitive slaves, that the removal of citizens from a slave-holding state to a free state would operate in this indirect manner as a manumission of their slaves. Several other questions of less importance were discussed upon the argument of this cause, which are worthy of examination; but I shall content myself with stating my acquiescence in the opinion expressed by the supreme court upon those points. I should have been better satisfied with the pleadings, if the statutes of Louisiana tolerating slavery, had been specially referred to; but I am nevertheless inclined to think that the rule requiring the statute of a state or country to be set forth, is not so extensive in its application as to require it in this case. That rule would seem to be confined to cases where a proceeding is predicated directly and particularly upon the effect of such statute. I am however of opinion that the general allegation of the existence of slavery is sufficient in this case.

I cannot refrain, in conclusion, from expressing my full belief, if the doctrine contended for by the plaintiff in error is to be regarded as the established law of the land, and consequently that all the states in the union are to be permitted to legislate upon this subject, requiring as many modes of proceeding in cases of this kind, as there are states, that it will in the end lead indirectly to the abolition of slavery, and that the most fearful consequences in regard to the permanency of our institutions will ensue. I regard this as but the entering wedge to other doctrines which are designed to extirpate slavery; and we may find when it is too late, that the patience of the south, however well founded upon principle, from repeated aggression will become exhausted. These considerations would have no influence with me if I could satisfy myself of the unconstitutionality of the law of congress; but I can never contribute in any manner, either directly or indirectly, to the abolition of slavery, however great an evil it may be, in violation of the constitution and laws of the country, and in violation of the solemn compact which was made by our forefathers at the adoption of the constitution, and which their posterity are bound to preserve inviolate. I am sustained in this view of the case by the whole current of authority, in all the states where the question has been decided. The whole doctrine was investigated in Massachusetts, in a case reported in *Pickering,* and presenting as strong a case as can be imagined. A slave belonging to a person in Virginia fled to the state of Massachusetts; he resided in that state five years, and in the meantime had accumulated a considerable property. It was nevertheless decided, upon solemn argument, that the law of the United States was constitutional; that the slave was not entitled to trial by jury, or by any other mode different from that prescribed by the law of congress; and he was accordingly taken back to Virginia. This was the unanimous opinion of the court. Mr. Justice Thatcher dissented, but not on the ground of the unconstitutionality of the law of congress. The same decision has been made in Pennsylvania, and also by Judge Thompson in a late case in the circuit court of the United States. In addition, if I may be permitted to refer to the decisions of the tribunals of this state, the distinguished and learned individuals who preside over the supreme court of this state and the superior court of the city of New-York, upon mature deliberation, arrived at the same conclusion.

I cannot therefore consent to overturn a doctrine which is founded upon principle, and is sustained by authority; and am accordingly of opinion that the judgment of the supreme court ought to be affirmed.

Upon the question being put, *Shall this judgment be reversed?* the members of the court *unanimously* voted in the negative. Whereupon the judgment of the supreme court was AFFIRMED.

541

SEE ALSO:

Generally 1.9.1; 4.2.2
James Iredell, Marcus, Answers to Mr. Mason's Objections to the
  New Constitution, 1788, Pamphlets 367
St. George Tucker, Blackstone's Commentaries 3:App. 73–97
  (1803)

Levi Lincoln, Rights and Immunities of Public Ministers,
  9 May 1804, 1 Ops. Atty. Gen. 141
Glen v. *Hodges*, 9 Johns. R. 67 (N.Y. 1812)
William Wirt, Restoration of a Danish Slave, 27 Sept. 1822,
  1 Ops. Atty. Gen. 566
Commonweath v. *Griffith*, 2 Pick. 11 (Mass. 1823)
Jack v. *Martin*, 12 Wend. 311 (N.Y. 1834), aff'd 14 Wend. 507,
  q.v. supra.

Article 4, Section 3, Clause 1

New States may be admitted by the Congress into this Union; but no new State shall be formed or erected within the Jurisdiction of any other State; nor any State be formed by the Junction of two or more States, or Parts of States, without the Consent of the Legislatures of the States concerned as well as of the Congress.

1

CONTINENTAL CONGRESS
Oct. 1780
Journals 18:915

Resolved, That the unappropriated lands that may be ceded or relinquished to the United States, by any particular states, pursuant to the recommendation of Congress of the 6 day of September last, shall be disposed of for the common benefit of the United States, and be settled and formed into distinct republican states, which shall become members of the federal union, and have the same rights of sovereignty, freedom and independence, as the other states: that each state which shall be so formed shall contain a suitable extent of territory, not less than one hundred nor more than one hundred and fifty miles square, or as near thereto as circumstances will admit:

That the necessary and reasonable expences which any particular state shall have incurred since the commencement of the present war, in subduing any of the British posts, or in maintaining forts or garrisons within and for the defence, or in acquiring any part of the territory that may be ceded or relinquished to the United States, shall be reimbursed;

That the said lands shall be granted and settled at such

times and under such regulations as shall hereafter be agreed on by the United States in Congress assembled, or any nine or more of them.

2

ARTICLES OF CONFEDERATION, ART. 11
1 Mar. 1781

Article XI. Canada acceding to this confederation, and joining in the measures of the united states, shall be admitted into, and entitled to all the advantages of this union: but no other colony shall be admitted into the same, unless such admission be agreed to by nine states.

3

THOMAS JEFFERSON, REVISED REPORT, PLAN FOR GOVERNMENT OF THE WESTERN TERRITORY
22 Mar. 1784
Papers 6:607–9

The Committee to whom was recommitted the report of a plan for a temporary government of the Western territory have agreed to the following resolutions.

Resolved that so much of the territory ceded or to be ceded by individual states to the United states, as is already purchased or shall be purchased of the Indian iinhabitants and offered for sale by Congress, shall be divided into distinct states, in the following manner, as nearly as such cessions will admit; that is to say, by parallels of latitude, so that each state shall comprehend from South to North two degrees of latitude beginning to count from the completion of thirty one degrees North of the equator; and by meridians of longitude, one of which shall pass thro' the lowest point of the rapids of Ohio, and the other thro' the Western cape of the mouth of the Great Kanhaway. But the territory Eastward of this last meridian, between the Ohio, lake Erie, and Pennsylvania shall be one state whatsoever may be it's comprehension of latitude. That which may lie beyond the completion of the 45th. degree between the said meridians shall make part of the state adjoining it on the South, and that part of the Ohio which is between the same meridians coinciding nearly with the parallel of 39°. shall be substituted so far in lieu of that parallel as a boundary line.

That the settlers on any territory so purchased and offered for sale shall, either on their own petition, or on the order of Congress, receive authority from them with appointments of time and place, for their free males of full age, within the limits of their state to meet together for the purpose of establishing a temporary government, to adopt the constitution and laws of any one of the original states, so that such laws nevertheless shall be subject to alteration by their ordinary legislature; and to erect, subject to a like alteration, counties or townships for the election of members for their legislature.

That such temporary government shall only continue in force in any state until it shall have acquired 20,000 free inhabitants; when giving due proof thereof to Congress, they shall receive from them authority, with appointments of time and place to call a convention of representatives to establish a permanent constitution and government for themselves.

Provided that both the temporary and permanent governments be established on these principles as their basis. 1. That they shall for ever remain a part of this confederacy of the United states of America. 2. That in their persons, property and territory they shall be subject to the government of the United states in Congress assembled, and to the articles of Confederation in all those cases in which the original states shall be so subject. 3. That they shall be subject to pay a part of the federal debts contracted or to be contracted, to be apportioned on them by Congress, according to the same common rule and measure, by which apportionments thereof shall be made on the other states. 4. That their respective governments shall be in republican forms, and shall admit no person to be a citizen who holds any hereditary title. 5. That after the year 1800. of the Christian aera, there shall be neither slavery nor involuntary servitude in any of the said states, otherwise than in punishment of crimes whereof the party shall have been convicted to have been personally guilty.

That whensoever any of the said states shall have, of free inhabitants, as many as shall then be in any one the least numerous of the thirteen original states, such state shall be admitted by it's delegates into the Congress of the United states, on an equal footing with the said original states: provided nine states agree to such admission according to the reservation of the 11th of the articles of Confederation. And in order to adapt the said articles of confederation to the state of Congress when it's numbers shall be thus increased, it shall be proposed to the legislatures of the states originally parties thereto, to require the assent of two thirds of the United states in Congress assembled in all those cases wherein by the said articles the assent of nine states is now required; which being agreed to by them shall be binding on the new states. Until such admission by their delegates into Congress, any of the said states, after the establishment of their temporary government, shall have authority to keep a sitting member in Congress, with a right of debating, but not of voting.

That the preceding articles shall be formed into a charter of compact, shall be duly executed by the president of the United states in Congress assembled, under his hand, and the seal of the United states, shall be promulgated, and shall stand as fundamental constitutions between the thirteen original states and each of the several states now newly described, unalterable but by the joint consent of the United states in Congress assembled, and of the particular state within which such alteration is proposed to be made.

4

RECORDS OF THE FEDERAL CONVENTION

[2:188; Madison, 6 Aug.]

XVII

New States lawfully constituted or established within the limits of the United States may be admitted, by the Legislature, into this Government; but to such admission the consent of two thirds of the members present in each House shall be necessary. If a new State shall arise within the limits of any of the present States, the consent of the Legislatures of such States shall be also necessary to its admission. If the admission be consented to, the new States shall be admitted on the same terms with the original States. But the Legislature may make conditions with the new States, concerning the public debt which shall be then subsisting.

[2:454; Madison, 29 Aug.]

Art: XVII being taken up, Mr. Govr. Morris moved to strike out the two last sentences, to wit "If the admission be consented to, the new States shall be admitted on the same terms with the original States—But the Legislature may make conditions with the new States, concerning the public debt, which shall be then subsisting".—He did not wish to bind down the Legislature to admit Western States on the terms here stated.

Mr Madison opposed the motion, insisting that the Western States neither would nor ought to submit to a Union which degraded them from an equal rank with the other States.

Col. Mason—If it were possible by just means to prevent emigrations to the Western Country, it might be good policy. But go the people will as they find it for their interest, and the best policy is to treat them with that equality which will make them friends not enemies.

Mr Govr Morris. did not mean to discourage the growth of the Western Country. He knew that to be impossible. He did not wish however to throw the power into their hands.

Mr Sherman, was agst. the motion, & for fixing an equality of privileges by the Constitution.

Mr Langdon was in favor of the Motion. he did not know but circumstances might arise which would render it inconvenient to admit new States on terms of equality.

Mr. Williamson was for leaving the Legislature free. The existing *small* States enjoy an equality now, and for that reason are admitted to it in the Senate. This reason is not applicable to new Western States.

On Mr Govr Morris's motion for striking out.

N.H. ay—Mas. ay—Ct ay. N—J. ay. Pa. ay. Del. ay. Md. no Va. no. N—C—ay. S—C—ay. Geo. ay, [Ayes—9; noes—2.]

Mr. L—Martin & Mr Govr. Morris moved to strike out

of art XVII "but to such admission the consent of two thirds of the members present shall be necessary." Before any question was taken on this motion,

Mr Govr. Morris moved the following proposition as a substitute for the XVII art: "New States may be admitted by the Legislature into this Union: but no new State shall be erected within the limits of any of the present States, without the consent of the Legislature of such State, as well as of the Genl. Legislature"

The first part to Union inclusive was agreed to nem: con:

Mr. L—Martin opposed the latter part—Nothing he said would so alarm the limited States as to make the consent of the large States claiming the Western lands, necessary to the establishment of new States within their limits. It is proposed to guarantee the States. Shall Vermont be reduced by force in favor of the States claiming it? Frankland & the Western country of Virginia were in a like situation.

On Mr Govr. Morris's Motion to substitute &c it was agreed to—

N. H. no. Mas. ay. Ct. no. N. J. no. Pa. ay. Del. no Md no. Va. ay. N. C. ay. S. C. ay. Geo. ay. [Ayes—6; noes—5.]

Art: XVII—before the House, as amended.

Mr. Sherman was against it. He thought it unnecessary. The Union cannot dismember a State without its consent.

Mr Langdon thought there was great weight in the argument of Mr. Luther Martin, and that the proposition substituted by Mr. Govr. Morris would excite a dangerous opposition to the plan.

Mr. Govr Morris thought on the contrary that the small States would be pleased with the regulation, as it holds up the idea of dismembering the large States.

Mr. Butler. If new States were to be erected without the consent of the dismembered States, nothing but confusion would ensue. Whenever taxes should press on the people, demagogues would set up their schemes of new States.

Docr. Johnson agreed in general with the ideas of Mr Sherman, but was afraid that as the clause stood, Vermont would be subjected to N—York, contrary to the faith pledged by Congress. He was of opinion that Vermont ought to be compelled to come into the Union.

Mr Langdon said his objections were connected with the case of Vermont. If they are not taken in, & remain exempt from taxes, it would prove of great injury to N. Hampshire and the other neighbouring States

Mr Dickinson hoped the article would not be agreed to. He dwelt on the impropriety of requiring the small States to secure the large ones in their extensive claims of territory.

Mr. Wilson—When the *majority* of a State wish to divide they can do so. The aim of those in opposition to the article, he perceived, was that the Genl. Government should abet the *minority*, & by that means divide a State against its own consent.

Mr Govr. Morris. If the forced division of the States is the object of the new System, and is to be pointed agst one or two States, he expected, the gentleman from these would pretty quickly leave us.

[2:461; Madison, 30 Aug.]

Art XVII resumed for a question on it as amended by Mr. Govr. Morris's substitutes

Mr. Carrol moved to strike out so much of the article as requires the consent of the State to its being divided. He was aware that the object of this prerequisite might be to prevent domestic disturbances, but such was our situation with regard to the Crown lands, and the sentiments of Maryland on that subject, that he perceived we should again be at sea, if no guard was provided for the right of the U. States to the back lands. He suggested that it might be proper to provide that nothing in the Constitution should affect the Right of the U. S. to lands ceded by G. Britain in the Treaty of peace, and proposed a committment to a member from each State. He assured the House that this was a point of a most serious nature. It was desirable above all things that the act of the Convention might be agreed to unanimously. But should this point be disregarded, he believed that all risks would be run by a considerable minority, sooner than give their concurrence.

Mr. L. Martin 2ded. the motion for a committment.

Mr. Rutledge is it to be supposed that the States are to be cut up without their own consent. The case of Vermont will probably be particularly provided for. There could be no room to fear, that Virginia or N—Carolina would call on the U. States to maintain their Government over the Mountains.

Mr. Williamson said that N. Carolina was well disposed to give up her Western lands, but attempts at compulsion was not the policy of the U. S. He was for doing nothing in the constitution in the present case, and for leaving the whole matter in Statu quo.

Mr. Wilson was against the committment. Unanimity was of great importance, but not to be purchased by the majority's yielding to the minority. He should have no objection to leaving the case of New States as heretofore. He knew of nothing that would give greater or juster alarm than the doctrine, that a political society is to be torne asunder without its own consent—

On Mr. Carrol's motion for commitment

N. H. no Mas. no. Ct. no. N. J. ay. Pa. no. Del—ay— Md. ay—Va. no—N—C. no S. C. no. Geo. no. [Ayes—3; noes—8.]

Mr Sherman moved to postpone the substitute for art. XVII agreed to yesterday in order to take up the following amendment "The Legislature shall have power to admit other States into the Union, and new States to be formed by the division or junction of States now in the Union, with the consent of the Legislature of such State" (The first part was meant for the case of Vermont to secure its admission)

On the question, it passed in the Negative

N. H. ay. Mas. ay. Ct. ay. N. J. no. Pa. ay. Del. no. Md. no. Va. no. N. C. no. S. C ay. Geo. no. [Ayes—5; noes—6.]

Docr. Johnson moved to insert the words "hereafter formed or" after the words "shall be" in the substitute for art: XVII, (the more clearly to save Vermont as being already formed into a State, from a dependence on the consent of N. York to her admission.)

The motion was agreed to Del. & Md. only dissenting.

Mr Governr. Morris moved to strike out the word "limits" in the substitute, and insert the word "jurisdiction" (This also was meant to guard the case of Vermont, the jurisdiction of N. York not extending over Vermont which was in the exercise of sovereignty, tho' Vermont was within the asserted limits of New York)

On this question

N—H—ay—Mas— ay. Ct ay— N. J. no. Pa. ay. Del. ay Md. ay. Va ay—N. C. no. S. C. no. Geo. no. [Ayes—7; noes—4.]

Mr. L. Martin, urged the unreasonableness of forcing & guaranteeing the people of Virginia beyond the Mountains, the Western people, of N. Carolina. & of Georgia, & the people of Maine, to continue under the States now governing them, without the consent of those States to their separation. Even if they should become the *majority*, the majority of *Counties*, as in Virginia may still hold fast the dominion over them. Again the majority may place the seat of Government entirely among themselves & for their own conveniency, and still keep the injured parts of the States in subjection, under the guarantee of the Genl. Government agst. domestic violence. He wished Mr Wilson had thought a little sooner of the value of *political* bodies. In the beginning, when the rights of the small States were in question, they were phantoms, ideal beings. Now when the Great States were to be affected, political Societies were of a sacred nature. He repeated and enlarged on the unreasonableness of requiring the small States to guarantee the Western claims of the large ones.—It was said yesterday by Mr Govr Morris, that if the large States were to be split to pieces without their consent, their representatives here would take their leave. If the Small States are to be required to guarantee them in this manner, it will be found that the Representatives of other States will with equal firmness take their leave of the Constitution on the table.

It was moved by Mr. L. Martin to postpone the substituted article, in order to take up the following.

"The Legislature of the U—S—shall have power to erect New States within as well as without the territory claimed by the several States or either of them, and admit the same into the Union: provided that nothing in this constitution shall be construed to affect the claim of the U—S. to vacant lands ceded to them by the late treaty of peace— which passed in the negative: N. J. Del. & Md. only ay.

On the question to agree to Mr. Govr. Morris's substituted article as amended in the words following,

"New States may be admitted by the Legislature into the Union: but no new State shall be hereafter formed or erected within the jurisdiction of any of the present States without the consent of the Legislature of such State as well as of the General Legislature"

N. H. ay. Mas. ay. Ct. ay. N. J—no—Pa. ay. Del. no. Md. no. Va. ay. N—C. ay—S. C—ay. Geo. ay. [Ayes—8; noes—3.]

5

CHARLES PINCKNEY, OBSERVATIONS ON THE PLAN OF GOVERNMENT
1787
Farrand 3:119–20

The article impowering the United States to admit new States into the Confederacy is become indispensable, from the separation of certain districts from the original States, and the increasing population and consequence of the Western Territory. I have also added an article authorizing the United States, upon petition from the majority of the citizens of any State, or Convention authorized for that purpose, and of the Legislature of the State to which they wish to be annexed, or of the States among which they are willing to be divided, to consent to such junction or division, on the terms mentioned in the article.—The inequality of the Federal Members, and the number of small States, is one of the greatest defects of our Union. It is to be hoped this inconvenience will, in time, correct itself; and, that the smaller States, being fatigued with the expence of their State Systems, and mortified at their want of importance, will be inclined to participate in the benefits of the larger, by being annexed to and becoming a part of their Governments. I am informed sentiments of this kind already prevail; and, in order to encourage propositions so generally beneficial, a power should be vested in the Union, to accede to them whenever they are made.

6

LUTHER MARTIN, GENUINE INFORMATION
1788
Storing 2.4.99–107

By the third section of the fourth article, no new State shall be formed or erected within the jurisdiction or any other State, without the consent of the legislature of such State.

There are a number of States which are so circumstanced, with respect to themselves and to the other States, that every principle of justice and sound policy require their dismemberment or division into smaller States.—Massachusetts is divided into two districts, totally separated from each other by the State of New-Hampshire, on the north-east side of which lies the provinces of Main and Sagadohock, more extensive in point of territory, but less populous than old Massachusetts, which lies on the other side of New-Hampshire.: No person can cast their eye on the map of that State but they must in a moment admit, that every argument drawn from convenience, interest, and justice require that the provinces of Main and Saga-

dohock should be erected into a new State, and that they should not be compelled to remain connected with old Massachusetts under all the inconveniences of their situation.

The State of Georgia is larger in extent than the whole island of Great-Britain, extending from its sea coast to the Missisippi, a distance of eight hundred miles or more; its breadth for the most part, about three hundred miles. The States of North-Carolina and Virginia in the same manner reach from the sea coast unto the Missisippi.

The hardship, the inconvenience, and the injustice of compelling the inhabitants of those States who may dwell on the western side of the mountains and along the Ohio and Missisippi rivers to remain connected with the inhabitants of those States respectively, on the atlantic side of the mountains, and subject to the same State governments, would be such, as would in my opinion, justify even recourse to arms, to free themselves from, and to shake off, so ignominous a yoke.

This representation was made in convention, and it was further urged, that the territory of these States were too large, and that the inhabitants thereof would be too much disconnected for a *republican government* to extend to them its benefits, *which* is only suited to a small and compact territory: That a regard also for the peace and safety of the union, ought to excite a desire that those States should become in time divided into separate States, since when their population should become proportioned in any degree to their territory, they would from their strength and power become *dangerous members* of a *federal* government. It was further said, that if the general government was not by its constitution to interfere, the inconvenience would soon remedy itself, for that as the population increased in those States, their legislatures would be obliged to consent to the erection of new States to avoid the evils of a civil war; but as by the proposed constitution the general government is obliged to protect each State against domestic violence, and consequently will be obliged to assist in suppressing such commotions and insurrections as may take place from the struggle to have new States erected, the general government ought to have a power to decide upon the propriety and necessity of establishing or erecting a new State, even without the approbation of the legislature of such States, within whose jurisdiction the new State should be erected, and for this purpose I submitted to the convention the following proposition;—"That on the application of the inhabitants of any district of territory within the limits of any of the States, it shall be lawful for the legislature of the United States, if they shall under all circumstances think it reasonable, to erect the same into a new State, and admit it into the union *without the consent* of the State of which the said district may be a part." And it was said, that we surely might trust the general government with *this power* with *more propriety* than with *many others* with which they were proposed to be entrusted—and that as the general government was bound to suppress all insurrections and commotions which might arise on this subject, it ought to be in the power of the general government to decide upon it, and not in the power of the legislature of a single State, by obstinately and unreasonably opposing the erection of a new State to prevent its taking effect, and thereby extremely to *oppress* that part of its citizens which live remote from, and inconvenient to, the seat of its government, and even to involve the union in war to support its injustice and oppression.—But, upon the vote being taken, Georgia, South-Carolina, North-Carolina, Virginia, Pennsylvania and Massachusetts, were in the *negative.* New-Hampshire, Connecticut, Jersey, Delaware and Maryland, were in the *affirmative.* New-York was absent.

That it was inconsistent with the rights of free and independent States, to have their territory dismembered without their consent, was the principle argument used by the opponents of this proposition. The truth of the objection we readily admitted, but at the same time, insisted that it was not *more inconsistent* with the rights of free and independent States than *that inequality* of *suffrage* and *power* which the *large States* had *extorted* from the *others;* and that if *the smaller States* yielded up *their rights* in *that instance,* they were *entitled* to demand from the States of extensive territory a *surrender* of their rights in *this instance;* and in a particular manner, as it was *equally necessary* for the true interest and happiness of the *citizens* of *their own States,* as of *the Union.* But, Sir, although when the large States demanded *undue* and *improper* sacrifices to be made to their *pride* and *ambition,* they treated the rights of free States with more contempt than ever a British Parliament treated the rights of her colonial establishments, yet when a *reasonable* and *necessary sacrifice* was asked *from them* they spurned the idea with ineffable disdain. They *then perfectly understood* the *full value* and the *sacred obligation* of State rights, and at the least attempt to infringe them *where they were concerned,* they were tremblingly alive and agonized at every pore.

When we reflect how *obstinately* those States contended for that *unjust superiority* of power in the government, which they have *in part* obtained, and for the establishment of this superiority by the constitution. When we reflect that they appeared willing to hazard the existence of the union rather than not to succeed in their unjust attempt—That should their legislatures consent to the erection of new States within their jurisdiction, it would be an immediate sacrifice of that power, to obtain which they appeared disposed to sacrifice every other consideration.

When we further reflect that they *now* have a *motive* for desiring to preserve their territory entire and unbroken, which *they never had before*—the *gratification of their ambition in possessing and exercising superior power over their sister States*—and that this constitution is to give them the *means* to *effect* this desire of *which* they were *formerly destitute*—the *whole force of the United States pledged to them for restraining intestine commotions,* and *preserving to them the obedience and subjection of their citizens,* even in the *extremest part of their territory:*—I say, Sir, when we consider these things, it would be too absurd and improbable to deserve a serious answer, should any person suggest that *these States* mean ever *to give their consent* to the *erection of new States within their territory:* Some of them it is true, have been for some time past *amusing* their inhabitants in those districts that wished to be erected into new States, but should this constitution be adopted, *armed with a sword and halter* to compel their obedience and subjection, they will no longer act with indecision; and the State of Maryland may, and probably will be called upon to assist with her wealth and her blood in subduing the inhabitants of Franklin, Kentucky, Vermont, and the provinces of Main and Sagadohock, and in compelling them to continue in subjection to the States which respectively claim jurisdiction over them.

Let it not be forgotten at the same time, that a great part of the territory of these large and extensive States, which they now hold in possession, and over which they now claim and exercise jurisdiction, were crown lands, unlocated and unsettled when the American revolution took place—Lands which were *acquired* by the *common blood and treasure,* and which *ought* to have been the *common stock,* and for the *common benefit* of the Union. Let it be remembered that the State of Maryland was so deeply sensible of the injustice that these lands should be held by particular States for their own emolument, even at a time when *no superiority* of *authority* or *power* was *annexed to extensive territory,* that in the *midst of the late war* and all the *dangers* which *threatened us, it* withheld for a long time its assent to the articles of confederation for that reason, and when it ratified those articles it entered a *solemn protest* against what it considered so *flagrant injustice:*—But, Sir, the question is not *now* whether those States shall hold that territory unjustly to themselves, but whether by *that act of injustice* they shall *have superiority of power and influence over the other States,* and *have a constitutional right* to *domineer* and *lord it* over them—Nay, more, whether we will *agree* to a *form of government* by which we *pledge* to *those States* the *whole force* of the *union* to *preserve* to them that *extensive territory entire* and *unbroken,* and with *our blood and wealth to assist them,* whenever they please to demand it, to *preserve the inhabitants thereof under their subjection,* for the *purpose* of *encreasing their superiority over us*—of *gratifying their unjust ambition*—in a word, for the *purpose of giving ourselves masters, and of rivetting our chains!*

7

JAMES MADISON, FEDERALIST, NO. 43, 290–91
23 Jan. 1788

In the articles of confederation no provision is found on this important subject. Canada was to be admitted of right on her joining in the measures of the United States; and the other *colonies,* by which were evidently meant, the other British colonies, at the discretion of nine States. The eventual establishment of *new States,* seems to have been overlooked by the compilers of that instrument. We have seen the inconvenience of this omission, and the assumption of power into which Congress have been led by it. With great propriety therefore has the new system supplied the defect. The general precaution that no new States shall be formed without the concurrence of the federal authority and that of the States concerned, is consonant to the principles which ought to govern such transactions. The particular precaution against the erection of new States, by the partition of a State without its consent, quiets the jealousy of the larger States; as that of the smaller is quieted by a like precaution against a junction of States without their consent.

8

THOMAS JEFFERSON, PROPOSED AMENDMENT TO THE CONSTITUTION
July 1803

(See 2.2.2–3, no. 25)

9

THOMAS JEFFERSON TO WILLIAM DUNBAR
17 July 1803

(See 2.2.2–3, no. 26)

10

THOMAS JEFFERSON TO WILSON CARY NICHOLAS
7 Sept. 1803

(See 2.2.2–3, no. 27)

11

RUFUS KING TO TIMOTHY PICKERING
4 Nov. 1803
Life 4:324

Congress may admit new States, but can the Executive by treaty admit them, or, what is equivalent, enter into engagements binding Congress to do so? As by the Louisiana Treaty, the ceded territory must be formed into States, & admitted into the Union, is it understood that Congress can annex any condition to their admission? if not, as Slavery is authorized & exists in Louisiana, and the treaty engages to protect the property of the inhabitants, will not the present inequality, arising from the Representation of Slaves, be increased?

As the provision of the Constitution on this subject may be regarded as one of its greatest blemishes, it would be with reluctance that one could consent to its being extended to the Louisiana States; and provided any act of Congress or of the several states should be deemed requisite to give validity to the stipulation of the treaty on this subject, ought not an effort to be made to limit the Rep-

resentation to the free inhabitants only? Had it been foreseen that we could raise revenue to the extent we have done, from indirect taxes, the Representation of Slaves wd. never have been admitted; but going upon the maxim that taxation and Representation are inseparable, and that the Genl. Govt. must resort to direct taxes, the States in which Slavery does not exist, were injudiciously led to concede to this unreasonable provision of the Constitution.

12

GOUVERNEUR MORRIS TO HENRY W. LIVINGSTON
4 Dec. 1803
Life 3:192

A circumstance, which turned up in conversation yesterday, has led me again to read over your letter of the third of November, and my answer of the twenty-eighth. I perceive now, that I mistook the drift of your inquiry, which is substantially whether the Congress can admit, as a new State, territory, which did not belong to the United States when the Constitution was made. In my opinion they cannot.

I always thought that, when we should acquire Canada and Louisiana it would be proper to govern them as provinces, and allow them no voice in our councils. In wording the third section of the fourth article, I went as far as circumstances would permit to establish the exclusion. Candor obliges me to add my belief, that, had it been more pointedly expressed, a strong opposition would have been made.

13

THOMAS JEFFERSON TO JAMES MADISON
14 July 1804

(See 2.2.2–3, no. 28)

14

JOHN ADAMS TO JOSIAH QUINCY
9 Feb. 1811
Works 9:631–32

But I was about saying a word upon the Constitution. You appear to be fully convinced that the Convention had it not in contemplation to admit any State or States into our confederation, then situated without the limits of the thirteen States. In this point I am not so clear. The Constitution, it is true, must speak for itself, and be interpreted by its own phraseology; yet the history and state of things at the time may be consulted to elucidate the meaning of words, and determine the *bonâ fide* intention of the Convention. Suppose we should admit, for argument's sake, that no member of the Convention foresaw the purchase of Louisiana! It will not follow that many of them did not foresee the necessity of conquering, some time or other, the Floridas and New Orleans, and other territories on this side of the Mississippi. The state of things between this country and Spain in 1787, was such as to render the apprehensions of a war with that power by no means improbable. The boundaries were not settled, the navigation of the river was threatened, and Spain was known to be tampering, and England too.

15

ROBERT W. REID, ADMISSION OF MISSOURI,
HOUSE OF REPRESENTATIVES
1 Feb. 1820
Annals 35:1027–30

I find nothing more to afford even a colorable pretext for the proposed restriction, until we come to these words: "New States may be admitted into the Union." The single word "may" is supposed to be the depository of the power so anxiously sought; and, it is said, if Congress can admit a new State, the Constitution being silent as to the condition to be imposed, the State about to be admitted may be fastened with any condition not specially interdicted by the Constitution itself. This is a *non sequitur*. It is a conclusion most lame and impotent; in direct hostility with the letter as well as the spirit of the Constitution! It is not enough that the Constitution is silent, to authorize the Congress to speak or to act; for Congress is the creature of the Constitution, and must look to it for open, declared, and positive direction. What the Constitution dictates is to be done; what it prohibits is to be avoided; but when it is silent, Congress possesses not authority to direct citizens or States. These must, then, be controlled by their own independent governments. Let it be remembered that the Constitution, being in derogation of State rights, must be construed strictly. This clause of the 3d section of the article, then, only allows to us the power to receive or to reject, without qualification or condition, a State making application to be admitted into the Union.

But there is a condition, without which a State cannot be admitted into the Union; and it is to be found in the 4th section of the 3d article: "The United States shall guaranty to every State in the Union a republican form of government." Now, "guaranty" means, if I at all understand the signification of words, "to undertake that certain stipulations shall be performed." These stipulations can only be found in the constitutions of the States, where they must constitute "a republican form of government." If this be so, then, at the moment a new State is admitted, the same guaranty which applies to the original States extends to her also. She must, consequently, have been in the possession of "a republican form of government" at the time of entering the Union, because it would be preposterous to imagine that to be guarantied of which she was not possessed—that to be secured to her, which, in fact, had no existence. It results, then, that without "a republican form of government" a State cannot come into the Confederacy; and is not the necessity to possess it a *sine qua non*, or condition, without which the new State cannot be admitted? Sir, this condition, being expressed, operates to the exclusion of every other. *"Expressio unius est exclusio alterius,"* is a sound maxim both of common law and common sense.

But, it is objected, slavery is incompatible with that "republican form of government" which the State admitted must possess. We must receive words according to the intention of those who utter them. And we must give construction to the Constitution, by considering all the parts of that instrument together. South Carolina and Georgia were slaveholding States at the time the Constitution was framed and adopted, and yet, in its eye, these were considered to possess republican forms of government. Besides, the right of the citizen to possess slaves is expressly recognised by the instrument of which we speak. I need scarcely advert to the 2d section of the 1st article, wherein the representation is determined; to the permission to import, until a given period, in the 9th section of the 1st article; and to the 2d section of the 2d article, where the relations of master and servant are distinctly asserted. It is evident, then, that a state of domestic slavery was entirely out of view, when the founders of the Confederation determined to "guaranty to the several States a republican form of government."

The Constitution of the United States is plain and simple; it requires no superiority of intellect to comprehend its dictates; it is addressed to every understanding; "he who runs may read." It is, then, a proof of the absence of all authority for the proposed measure, when its advocates, and some, too, of great names, fly from clause to section and from section to article, without fixing "rest for the sole of the foot;" without finding or agreeing upon any one line, phrase, or section, whence this power for which all contend may be brought into existence. And it is perfectly natural that this effect should be produced. A search for the philosopher's stone might as soon be expected to end in certainty.

But it is argued that Congress has ever imposed restrictions upon new States, and no objection has been urged until this moment. If it be true, that only one condition can constitutionally be imposed, it would seem that any other is null and void, and may be thrown off by the State at pleasure. And then this argument, the strength of which is in precedent, cannot avail. Uniformity of decision for hundreds of years cannot make that right which at first was wrong. If it were otherwise, in vain would science and the arts pursue their march towards perfection; in vain the constant progress of truth; in vain the new and bright lights which are daily finding their way to the human mind, like the rays of the distant stars, which, passing onward from the creation of time, are said to be continually reaching our sphere. *Malus usus abolendus est.* When error appears, let her be detected and exposed, and let evil precedents be abolished.

It is true that the old Confederation, by the 6th section of the ordinance of 1787, inhibited slavery in the territory northwest of the Ohio, and that the States of Illinois, Ohio, and Indiana, have been introduced into the Union under this restriction.

Sir, the ordinance of 1787 had an origin perfectly worthy of the end it seems destined to accomplish. It had no authority in the Articles of Confederation, which did not contemplate, with the exception of Canada, the acquisition of territory. It was in contradiction of the resolution of 1780, by which the States were allured to cede their unlocated lands to the General Government, upon the condition that these should constitute several States, to be admitted into the Union upon an equal footing with the original States. It is in fraud of the acts of cession by which the States conveyed territory in faith of the resolution of 1780. And, when recognised by acts of Congress, and applied to the States formed from the territory beyond the Ohio, it is in violation of the Constitution of the United States. So much for the efficacy of the precedent which, although binding here, is not, it would seem, of obligation upon Ohio, Indiana, or Illinois, or, if you impose it, upon Missouri. It is not the force of your legal provisions which attaches the restrictive 6th article of the ordinance to the States I have mentioned. It is the moral sentiment of the inhabitants. Impose it upon Missouri, and she will indignantly throw off the yoke and laugh you to scorn! You will then discover that you have assumed a weapon that you cannot wield—the bow of Ulysses, which all your efforts cannot bend. The open and voluntary exposure of your weakness will make you not only the object of derision at home, but a byword among nations. Can there be a power in Congress to do that which the object of the power may rightfully destroy? Are the rights of Missouri and of the Union in opposition to each other? Can it be possible that Congress has authority to impose a restriction which Missouri, by an alteration of her constitution, may abolish? Sir, the course we are pursuing reminds me of the urchin who, with great care and anxiety, constructs his card edifice, which the slightest touch may demolish, the gentlest breath dissolve.

But let us stand together upon the basis of precedent, and upon that ground you cannot extend this restriction to Missouri. You have imposed it upon the territory beyond the Ohio, but you have never applied it elsewhere. Tennessee, Vermont, Kentucky, Louisiana, Mississippi, and Alabama, have come into the Union without being required to submit to the condition inhibiting slavery; nay, whenever the ordinance of 1787 has been applied to any of these States, the operation of the 6th article has been suspended or destroyed. According, then, to the uniform tenor of the precedent, let the States to be formed of the territory without the boundaries of the territory northwest of Ohio remain unrestricted, and in the enjoyment of the fulness of their rights.

Thus, it appears to me, the power you seek to assume is not to be found in the Constitution, or to be derived from precedents. Shall it, then, without any known process of generation, spring spontaneously from your councils, like the armed Minerva from the brain of Jupiter? The Goddess, sir, although of wisdom, was also the inventress of war—and the power of your creation, although extensive in its dimensions, and ingenious in its organization, may produce the most terrible and deplorable effects. Assure yourselves you have not authority to bind a State coming into the Union with a single hair! If you have, you may rivet a chain upon every limb, a fetter upon every joint. Where, then, I ask, is the independence of your State governments? Do they not fall prostrate, debased, covered with sackcloth and crowned with ashes, before the gigantic power of the Union? They will no longer, sir, resemble planets, moving in order around a solar centre, receiving and imparting lustre. They will dwindle to mere satellites, or, thrown from their orbits, they will wander "like stars condemned, the wrecks of worlds demolished!"

16

JOSEPH STORY, COMMENTARIES ON THE CONSTITUTION 3:§§ 1309–15
1833

---

§ 1309. A clause on this subject was introduced into the original draft of the constitution, varying in some respects from the present, and especially in requiring the consent of two thirds of the members present of both houses to the admission of any new state. After various modifications, attempted or carried, the clause substantially in its present form was agreed to by the vote of eight states against three.

§ 1310. In the articles of confederation no provision is to be found on this important subject. Canada was to be admitted of right, upon her acceding to the measures of the United States. But no other colony (by which was evidently meant no other British colony) was to be admitted, unless by the consent of nine states. The eventual establishment of new states within the limits of the Union seems to have been wholly overlooked by the framers of that instrument. In the progress of the revolution it was not only perceived, that from the acknowledged extent of the territory of several of the states, and its geographical position, it might be expedient to divide it into two states; but a much more interesting question arose, to whom of right belonged the vacant territory appertaining to the crown at the time of the revolution, whether to the states, within whose chartered limits it was situated, or to the Union in its federative capacity. This was a subject of long and ardent controversy, and (as has been already suggested) threatened to disturb the peace, if not to overthrow the government of the Union. It was upon this ground, that several of the states refused to ratify the articles of confederation, insisting upon the right of the confederacy to a portion of the vacant and unpatented territory included within their chartered limits. Some of the states most interested in the vacant and unpatented western territory, at length yielded to the earnest solicitations of congress on this subject. To induce them to make liberal cessions, congress declared, that the ceded territory should be disposed of for the common benefit of the Union, and formed into republican states, with the same rights of sovereignty, freedom, and independence, as the other states; to be of a suitable extent of territory, not less than one hundred, nor more than one hundred and fifty miles square; and that the reasonable expenses incurred by the state, since the commencement of the war, in subduing British posts, or in maintaining and acquiring the territory, should be reimbursed.

§ 1311. Of the power of the general government thus constitutionally to acquire territory under the articles of the confederation, serious doubts were at the time expressed; more serious than, perhaps, upon sober argument, could be justified. It is difficult to conceive, why the common attribute of sovereignty, the power to acquire lands by cession, or by conquest, did not apply to the government of the Union, in common with other sovereignties; unless the declaration, that every power not *expressly* delegated was retained by the states, amounted to (which admitted of some doubt) a constitutional prohibition. Upon more than one occasion it has been boldly pronounced to have been founded in usurpation. . . .

§ 1312. The truth is, that the importance, and even justice of the title to the public lands on the part of the federal government, and the additional security, which it gave to the Union, overcame all scruples of the people, as to its constitutional character. The measure, to which the Federalist alludes in such emphatic terms, is the famous ordinance of congress, of the 13th of July, 1787, which has ever since constituted, in most respects, the model of all our territorial governments; and is equally remarkable for the brevity and exactness of its text, and for its masterly display of the fundamental principles of civil and religious liberty. It begins by providing a scheme for the descent and distributions of estates equally among all the children, and their representatives, or other relatives of the deceased in equal degree, making no distinction between the whole and half blood; and for the mode of disposing of real estate by will, and by conveyances. It then proceeds to provide for the organization of the territorial governments, according to their progress in population, confiding the whole power to a governor and judges in the first instance, subject to the control of congress. As soon as the territory contains five thousand inhabitants, it provides for the establishment of a general legislature, to consist of three branches, a governor, a legislative council, and a house of representatives; with a power to the legislature to appoint a delegate to congress. It then proceeds to state certain fundamental articles of compact between the original states, and the people and states in the territory, which are to remain unalterable, unless by common consent. . . .

§ 1313. It was doubtless with reference principally to this territory, that the article of the constitution, now under consideration, was adopted. The general precaution, that no new states shall be formed without the concur-

rence of the national government, and of the states concerned, is consonant to the principles, which ought to govern all such transactions. The particular precaution against the erection of new states by the partition of a state without its own consent, will quiet the jealousy of the larger states; as that of the smaller will also be quieted by a like precaution against a junction of states without their consent. Under this provision no less than eleven states have, in the space of little more than forty years, been admitted into the Union upon an equality with the original states. And it scarcely requires the spirit of prophecy to foretell, that in a few years the predominance of numbers, of population, and of power will be unequivocally transferred from the old to the new states. May the patriotic wish be for ever true to the fact, *felix prole parens.*

§ 1314. Since the adoption of the constitution large acquisitions of territory have been made by the United States, by the purchase of Louisiana and Florida, and by the cession of Georgia, which have greatly increased the contemplated number of states. The constitutionality of the two former acquisitions, though formerly much questioned, is now considered settled beyond any practical doubt.

§ 1315. At the time, when the preliminary measures were taken for the admission of the state of Missouri into the Union, an attempt was made to include a restriction, prohibiting the introduction of slavery into that state, as a condition of the admission. On that occasion the question was largely discussed, whether congress possessed a constitutional authority to impose such a restriction, upon the ground, that the prescribing of such a condition is inconsistent with the sovereignty of the state to be admitted, and its equality with the other states. The final result of the vote, which authorized the erection of that state, seems to establish the rightful authority of congress to impose such a restriction, although it was not then applied. In the act passed for this purpose, there is an express clause, that in all the territory ceded by France to the United States under the name of Louisiana, which lies north of 36° 30′ N. Lat., not included within the limits of the state of Missouri, slavery and involuntary servitude, otherwise than in the punishment of crimes, whereof the parties shall have been duly convicted, shall be, and is hereby for ever prohibited. An objection of a similar character was taken to the compact between Virginia and Kentucky upon the ground, that it was a restriction upon state sovereignty. But the Supreme Court had no hesitation in overruling it, considering it as opposed by the theory of all free governments, and especially of those, which constitute the American Republics.

SEE ALSO:

David Howell to Jonathan Arnold, 21 Feb. 1784, Staples, Rhode Island in the Continental Congress 1765–1790, 479–81 (1870)

Records of the Federal Convention, Farrand 1:22, 117, 231; 2:147–48, 173, 578, 602

An Act Declaring the Consent of Congress, That a New State Be Formed within the Jurisdiction of the Commonwealth of Virginia, and Admitted into the Union, by the Name of the State of Kentucky, 1 Stat. 189 (1791)

House of Representatives, The Louisiana Treaty, 25 Oct. 1803, Annals 13:432–36, 474

St. George Tucker, Blackstone's Commentaries 1:App. 278–82 (1803)

House of Representatives, Mississippi and Orleans Territory, 28 Dec. 1810, 2, 4, 14–15 Jan. 1811, Annals 22:474–77, 482–85, 493–507, 518–42, 555–76, 577–79

An Act to Enable the People of the Territory of Orleans to Form a Constitutional State Government, 2 Stat. 641 (1811)

An Act for the Admission of Louisiana into the Union, 2 Stat. 701 (1812)

An Act to Enlarge the Limits of the State of Louisiana, 2 Stat. 708 (1812)

House of Representatives, Admission of Missouri, 15 Feb. 1819, Annals 33:1171–72, 1183–86

James Madison to Robert Walsh, 27 Nov. 1819, Farrand 3:438

Senate, Admission of Maine and Missouri, 17, 19–20, 26 Jan. 1820, Annals 35:129–32, 137–38, 139–42, 177–80, 201–4, 211–14, 259–62

House of Representatives, Admission of Missouri, 4, 7 Feb., 13 Dec. 1820, Annals 35:1054–96, 1161–64; 37:644–45

Benjamin F. Butler, Right of the Territories to Become States, 21 Sept. 1835, 2 Ops. Atty. Gen. 726

Article 4, Section 3, Clause 2

The Congress shall have Power to dispose of and make all needful Rules and Regulations respecting the Territory or other Property belonging to the United States; and nothing in this Constitution shall be so construed as to Prejudice any Claims of the United States, or of any particular State.

1. Records of the Federal Convention
2. Levi Lincoln, Governor of the Northwest Territory, 2 Feb. 1802
3. St. George Tucker, Blackstone's Commentaries (1803)
4. *Sere* v. *Pitot*, 2 Cranch 332 (1810)

5. *Johnson & Graham* v. *M'Intosh*, 8 Wheat. 543 (1823), in 1.8.3 (Indians), no. 9
6. James Kent, Commentaries (1826)
7. *American Insurance Co.* v. *Canter*, 1 Pet. 511 (1828), in 1.8.9, no. 5
8. Joseph Story, Commentaries on the Constitution (1833)

1

RECORDS OF THE FEDERAL CONVENTION

[2:321; Journal, 18 Aug.]

The propositions are as follows

To dispose of the unappropriated lands of the United States

[2:458; Journal, 30 Aug.]

It was moved and seconded to agree to the following proposition.

Nothing in this Constitution shall be construed to alter the claims of the United States or of the individual States to the western territory but all such claims may be examined into and decided upon by the supreme Court of the United States

It was moved and seconded to postpone the last proposition in order to take up the following.

The Legislature shall have power to dispose of and make all needful rules and regulations respecting the territory or other property belonging to the United States: and nothing in this Constitution contained shall be so construed as to prejudice any claims either of the United States or of any particular State

It was moved and seconded to add the following clause to the last proposition

"But all such claims may be examined into and decided upon by the Supreme Court of the United States"

which passed in the negative [Ayes—2; noes—8.]

On the question to agree to the following proposition

"The Legislature shall have power to dispose of and make all needful rules and regulations respecting the territory or other property belonging to the United States: and nothing in this Constitution contained shall be so construed as to prejudice any claims either of the United States or of any particular State"

it passed in the affirmative

[2:464; *Madison, 30 Aug.*]

It was moved by Mr. L. Martin to postpone the substituted article, in order to take up the following.

"The Legislature of the U— S— shall have power to erect New States within as well as without the territory claimed by the several States or either of them, and admit the same into the Union: provided that nothing in this constitution shall be construed to affect the claim of the U— S—. to vacant lands ceded to them by the late treaty of peace— which passed in the negative: N. J. Del. & Md. only ay.

On the question to agree to Mr. Govr. Morris's substituted article as amended in the words following,

"New States may be admitted by the Legislature into the Union: but no new State shall be hereafter formed or erected within the jurisdiction of any of the present States without the consent of the Legislature of such State as well as of the General Legislature"

N. H. ay. Mas. ay. Ct. ay. N. J— no— Pa. ay. Del. no. Md. no. Va. ay. N— C. ay— S. C— ay. Geo. ay. [Ayes—8; noes—3.]

Mr. Dickinson moved to add the following clause to the last—

"Nor shall any State be formed by the junction of two or more States or parts thereof, without the consent of the Legislatures of such States, as well as of the Legislature of the U. States". which was agreed to without a count of the Votes.

Mr Carrol moved to add—"Provided nevertheless that nothing in this Constitution shall be construed to affect the claim of the U. S. to vacant lands ceded to them by the Treaty of peace". This he said might be understood as relating to lands not claimed by any particular States. but he had in view also some of the claims of particular States.

Mr. Wilson was agst. the motion. There was nothing in the Constitution affecting one way or the other the claims of the U. S. & it was best to insert nothing, leaving every thing on that litigated subject in statu quo.

Mr. Madison considered the claim of the U. S. as in fact favored by the jurisdiction of the Judicial power of the U— S— over controversies to which they should be parties. He thought it best on the whole to be silent on the subject. He did not view the proviso of Mr. Carrol as dangerous; but to make it neutral and fair, it ought to go farther & declare that the claims of particular States also should not be affected.

Mr. Sherman thought the proviso harmless, especially with the addition suggested by Mr. Madison in favor of the claims of particular States.

Mr. Baldwin did not wish any undue advantage to be given to Georgia. He thought the proviso proper with the addition proposed. It should be remembered that if Georgia has gained much by the Cession in the Treaty of peace, she was in danger during the war, of a Uti possidetis.

Mr. Rutledge thought it wrong to insert a proviso where there was nothing which it could restrain, or on which it could operate.

Mr. Carrol withdrew his motion and moved the following,

"Nothing in this Constitution shall be construed to alter

the claims of the U. S. or of the individual States to the Western territory, but all such claims shall be examined into & decided upon, by the Supreme Court of the U. States."

Mr Govr Morris moved to postpone this in order to take up the following. "The Legislature shall have power to dispose of and make all needful rules and regulations respecting the territory or other property belonging to the U. States; and nothing in this constitution contained, shall be so construed as to prejudice any claims either of the U— S— or of any particular State,"—The postponemt. agd. to nem. con.

Mr. L. Martin moved to amend the proposition of Mr Govr Morris by adding—"But all such claims may be examined into & decided upon by the supreme Court of the U— States".

Mr. Govr. Morris. this is unnecessary, as all suits to which the U. S— are parties— are already to be decided by the Supreme Court.

Mr. L. Martin, it is proper in order to remove all doubts on this point.

Question on Mr. L— Martin's amendatory motion

N— H— no. Mas— no. Ct. no. N. J. ay. Pa. no. Del. no. Md. ay. Va. no—States not farther called the negatives being sufficient & the point given up.

The Motion of Mr. Govr. Morris was then agreed to, Md. alone dissenting.

[2:578, 602; *Committee of Style*]

The Legislature shall have power to dispose of and make all needful rules and regulations respecting the territory or other property belonging to the United States: and nothing in this Constitution contained shall be so construed as to prejudice any claims either of the United States or of any particular State.

. . . . .

The Congress shall have power to dispose of and make all needful rules and regulations respecting the territory or other property belonging to the United States: and nothing in this Constitution shall be so construed as to prejudice any claims of the United States, or of any particular state.

2

LEVI LINCOLN, GOVERNOR OF THE NORTHWEST
TERRITORY
2 Feb. 1802
1 Ops. Atty. Gen. 102

Sir: After the utmost attention which I have been able to pay to the questions respecting the Northwestern Territory, which you did me the honor of submitting to my consideration, there is a difficulty in giving a decisive answer. I can find no grounds or principles for a very confident decision in, or out of, the ordinance for the establishment of that government. Nothing can be collected to aid the inquiry from the acts by which similar governments in other territories have been established, or from the journals of the proceedings of the Assembly and the governor of this Territory, although some of these very questions have been the subjects of zealous debate.

The Territory is as yet considered to be under what is called its temporary government, by the ordinance. That expressly provides that all magistrates and other civil officers shall, during the continuance of the temporary government, be appointed by the *governor*, unless otherwise therein directed. It also ordained that there should be a court appointed, to consist of three judges, who shall have a common-law jurisdiction, and reside in the district; and expressly that Congress should appoint the governor, the secretary, and all military general officers. In the twelfth paragraph of the ordinance, it is said the governor, judges, legislative council, secretary, and such other officers as Congress shall appoint in the district, shall take an oath, &c. In this direction for taking the oath of office, there is a strong implication of the right of Congress, or rather of the President, to appoint these three judges; and I am informed this has been the practice. Independent of this practice, upon the mere construction of the ordinance, I should have hesitated in deciding against the right of the governor to have made even these appointments. The authority of making appointments is expressly given to the governor in all cases in which it is not otherwise directed, and express positive provisions are not usually abridged by implications. As this implication does not necessarily extend beyond the three judges before named, I am inclined to think the governor is justified by the ordinance in his appointment of all other judges and officers.

It is provided by the seventh paragraph of the ordinance, that the governor, previous to the organization of the General Assembly, shall appoint such magistrates, and other civil officers, in each county and township, as he shall *find necessary* for the preservation of the peace and good order in the same; and that, after the General Assembly shall be organized, the powers and duties of magistrates, and other civil officers, shall be regulated and defined by the Assembly. After the formation of the General Assembly, they are to determine what powers and duties are necessary to be exercised in existing counties and townships, and to define and regulate the same, for the preservation of peace and good order: this seems to involve the necessity of their determining what description of magistrates and officers should possess these powers and discharge those duties. They having done this, the governor is to make the appointments. The provision in this paragraph appears to me to amount to this: that, before the General Assembly was organized, the governor was to appoint such officers as he might judge *to be necessary;* afterwards, *such* as the legislature should judge to be necessary.

The eighth paragraph of the ordinance provides, that, for the prevention of crimes, the laws to be adopted or *made* shall have force in all parts of the district; and, for the execution of processes, civil and criminal, that the governor should make proper divisions, and from time to time, as circumstances should require, lay out such parts of the district, in which the Indian title shall have been extinguished, into counties and townships; subject, however, to such alterations as may thereafter be made by the legislature. The authority which the ordinance gives to the legislature is, in general terms, to make laws in all cases for the good government of the district, not repugnant to the principles and articles of the ordinance.

The laying out of counties and towns are usually considered as legislative acts, and, in the present instances, must be considered as appertaining to the legislature, unless, by a proper construction of the ordinance, it is secured to the governor. It being once confessedly vested in him, and, by general terms, implying no limitation in point of time, the authority must be considered as still remaining in him, unless it is taken away expressly, or by some unforeseen change of the subject-matter upon which, or of the circumstances under which, the power is exercised. The civil and criminal processes, the *execution* of which was to be the means of preventing crimes and injuries, and which was to be effected by a division of the described parts of the district into counties and townships, are recognised by the ninth paragraph of the ordinance to be such as should originate under *made* as well as under adopted laws; and if so, it implies a power in the governor to lay out counties and towns, after the General Assembly were sufficiently organized for the making of laws. This construction of the eighth paragraph is in some degree confirmed by the express limitations of the governor's power contained in the fifth and seventh, as there was the same reason for being explicit in the first as in the two last, if the same thing was intended. It to my mind appears to be further confirmed by an express power being given to the legislature to alter such townships and counties as shall have been laid out. On the idea of the authority to lay out counties being vested in the governor, after the formation of a legislature, this was necessary; otherwise, not.

The ordinance provides, that, in case of the death or *removal* from office of a representative, the governor shall issue a writ to the county or township for which he was a member, to elect another in his stead. I perceive no question on the governor's transactions respecting the election of representatives, as returned by the secretary, excepting in reference to Meigs, who is said to have left the Territory. If he had not resigned previous to the issuing of the writ for the election of a representative in his stead, I conceive the writ must be considered as issuing illegally. Knowing that some very respectble gentlemen are decidedly of the opinion that the governor has no right to lay out counties under the ordinance, I have slept many nights on my first impression on the subject; and am still inclined to the opinion I have above expressed, notwithstanding anything I have been able to learn respecting the matter.

3

ST. GEORGE TUCKER,
BLACKSTONE'S COMMENTARIES
1:APP. 283–86
1803

During the revolutionary war, congress recommended to the several states in the union, having claims to waste and unappropriated lands in the western country, a liberal cession to the United States of a portion of their respective claims, for the common benefit of the union. In consequence of which, the state of Virginia ceded to the United States, for the common benefit of the whole confederacy, all the right, title, and claim which the commonwealth had to the territory northwest of the river Ohio, subject to the terms and conditions contained in her several acts of cession, viz. January 2, 1781 . . . Acts of October session, 1783, c. 18, and of December 30, 1788. One of the conditions of the latter act, being, that the said territory should be divided into not more than five, nor less than three states, whose boundaries are therein prescribed, of which we have already had occasion to make mention. It appears by a late document, that the tract of country thus ceded, probably contains about 10,894,447, acres, within the line of the Indian boundary, of which 1,059,120, acres have been either located or set apart for military claims, 575,268, have been sold, or otherwise granted, and about 9,260,089, remained unsold on the first of November, 1801. The acts of 4 Cong. c. 29, and 6 Cong. c. 55, providing for the sale of these lands, contain many wise, and wholesome regulations, the principal of which, are, that they shall be laid out into townships six miles square, by north and south lines, according to the true meridian, and by others crossing them at right angles; that one half of those townships, taking them alternately, shall be subdivided into sections of six hundred and forty acres, which shall be numbered in order; that fair plats of these townships shall be made; that four sections at the center of every township, and every other section upon which a salt spring may be discovered shall be reserved for the use of the United States; that all navigable rivers shall be deemed, and remain public highways; and all lesser streams, and their beds shall become common to the proprietors of the lands on the opposite banks; and that no part of the lands shall be sold for less than two dollars per acre. A former secretary of the treasury estimated the value of these lands at twenty cents per acre, only. Those which have been already sold pursuant to the act of congress, have averaged two dollars and nine cents; or, more than ten times that valuation. The celebrated Doctor Price, in his observations on the importance of the American revolution, recommends the reserving the whole, or a considerable part of these lands, and appropriating a certain sum annually to the clearing unlocated lands, and other improvements thereon; and computes that 100,000*l.* thus expended, with fidelity, would produce a capital of one hundred millions sterling, in about eighty years. This hint is probably worthy of attention to a certain extent: but it might well be questioned, whether, if the measure were adopted as far as he seems to have thought advisable, it might not lay the foundation of so large a revenue, independent of the people, as to be formidable in the hands of any government. To amass immense riches to defray the expences of ambition when occasion may prompt, without seeming to oppress the people, has uniformly been the policy of tyrants. Should such a policy creep into our government, and the sales of land, instead of being appropriated to the discharge of former debts, be converted to a treasure in a bank, those who can at any time command it, may be tempted to apply it to the most nefarious purposes. The improvident alienation of the crown lands in England, has been considered as a circumstance extremely favourable to the liberty of the nation, by rendering the government less independent of the people. The same reason will apply to other governments, whether monarchical or republican: whenever any government becomes independent of the nation all ideas of responsibility are immediately lost: and when responsibility ceases, slavery begins. It is the due restraint, and not the moderation of rulers that constitutes a state of liberty; as the power to oppress, though never exercised, does a state of slavery.

The disposal of the whole of the western lands, at so low a rate as even that now established by congress, as a *minimum*, is a measure of the policy of which, doubts may be entertained. . . . The western territory ought to be regarded as a national stock of wealth. It may be compared to bullion, or coin deposited in the vaults of a bank, which although it produces no present profit, secures the credit of the institution, and is ready to answer any emergency. This supposes the lands, like bullion, to remain always of the same value; but the lands must increase in value at the rate of compound interest, whenever population becomes considerable in those parts of the union. This we see is daily encreasing with great rapidity; and the value of the lands can not fail to keep pace with it. The most fertile spots upon the globe are of no more value than those which are covered by the ocean, so long as they continue remote from population; as the most barren spots are rendered valuable by its progress, and approach. A reserve of one half, or some other considerable proportion of the lands remaining unsold, therefore, seems to be recommended by many prudential considerations.

Other considerable cessions have been made to the United States by other states in the union. The state of Connecticut, made a cession which appears to have been accepted by congress, September 14, 1786. The act of 6 Cong. c. 38, authorises the president of the United States to release the soil of a tract lying west of the west line of Pennsylvania, and extending one hundred and twenty statute miles, westward, and from the completion of the forty-first, to the latitude of the forty-second degree and two minutes, north, which was excepted by the state of Connecticut out of their cession, provided that state shall cede to the United States certain other lands, and relinquish her right of jurisdiction over the territory, the soil of which shall be thus released to that state. . . .

4

SERE V. PITOT
2 Cranch 332 (1810)

MARSHALL, Ch. J. delivered the opinion of the court as follows, viz.

This suit was brought in the court of the United States for the Orleans territory, by the plaintiffs, who are aliens, and syndics or assignees of a trading company composed of citizens of that territory, who have become insolvent. The defendants are citizens of the territory, and have pleaded to the jurisdiction of the court. Their plea was sustained, and the cause now comes on to be heard on a writ of error to that judgment.

. . . . .

Whether the citizens of the territory of Orleans are to be considered as the citizens of a state, within the meaning of the constitution, is a question of some difficulty which would be decided, should one of them sue in any of the circuit courts of the United States. The present inquiry is limited to a suit brought by or against a citizen of the territory, in the district court of Orleans.

The power of governing and of legislating for a territory is the inevitable consequence of the right to acquire and to hold territory. Could this position be contested, the constitution of the United States declares that "congress shall have power to dispose of and make all needful rules and regulations respecting the territory or other property belonging to the United States." Accordingly, we find congress possessing and exercising the absolute and undisputed power of governing and legislating for the territory of Orleans. Congress has given them a legislative, an executive, and a judiciary, with such powers as it has been their will to assign to those departments respectively.

The court possesses the same jurisdiction which was possessed by the court of Kentucky. In the court of Kentucky, a citizen of Kentucky may sue or be sued. But it is said that this privilege is not imparted to a citizen of Orleans, because he is not a citizen of a state. But this objection is founded on the idea that the constitution restrains congress from giving the court of the territory jurisdiction over a case brought by or against a citizen of the territory. This idea is most clearly not to be sustained, and, of consequence, that court must be considered as having such jurisdiction as congress intended to give it.

Let us inquire what would be the jurisdiction of the court, on this restricted construction.

It would have no jurisdiction over a suit brought by or against a citizen of the territory, although an alien, or a citizen of another state might be a party.

It would have no jurisdiction over a suit brought by a citizen of one state, against a citizen of another state, because neither party would be a citizen of the "state" in which the court sat. Of what civil causes, then, between private individuals, would it have jurisdiction? Only of suits between an alien and a citizen of another state who should be found in Orleans. Can this be presumed to have been the intention of the legislature in giving the territory a court possessing the same jurisdiction and power with that of Kentucky.

The principal motive for giving federal courts jurisdiction, is to secure aliens and citizens of other states from local prejudices. Yet all who could be affected by them are, by this construction, excluded from those courts. There could scarcely ever be a civil action between individuals of which the court could take cognisance, and if such a case should arise, it would be one in which no prejudice is to be apprehended.

5

JOHNSON & GRAHAM V. M'INTOSH
8 Wheat. 543 (1823)

(See 1.8.3 [Indians], no. 9)

6

JAMES KENT, COMMENTARIES 1:360–61
1826

It would seem, from these various congressional regulations of the territories belonging to the United States, that congress have supreme power in the government of them, depending on the exercise of their sound discretion. Neither the District of Columbia, nor a territory, is *a state*, within the meaning of the constitution, or entitled to claim the privileges secured to the members of the union. This has been so adjudged by the Supreme Court. Nor will a writ of error or appeal lie from a territorial court to the Supreme Court, unless there be a special statute provision for the purpose. There is such a provision as to Florida, and there is a limited provision of that kind as to Arkansaw and Michigan, extending to cases in which the United States are concerned, and not extending further. If, *therefore*, the government of the United States should carry into execution the project of colonizing the great valley of the Oregan to the west of the Rocky Mountains, it would afford a subject of grave consideration what would be the future civil and political destiny of that country. It would be a long time before it would be populous enough to be created into one or more independent states; and, in the mean time, upon the doctrine taught by the acts of congress, and even by the judicial decisions of the Supreme Court, the colonists would be in a state of the most complete subordination, and as dependent upon the will of congress as the people of this country would have been upon the king and parliament of Great Britain, if they could have sustained their claim to bind us in all cases whatsoever. Such a state of absolute sovereignty on the one hand, and of absolute dependence on the other, is not at all congenial with the free and independent spirit of our native institutions; and the establishment of distant territorial governments, ruled according to will and pleasure, would have a very natural tendency, as all proconsular governments have had, to abuse and oppression.

7

AMERICAN INSURANCE CO. V. CANTER
1 Pet. 511 (1828)

(See 1.8.9, no. 5)

8

JOSEPH STORY, COMMENTARIES ON THE
CONSTITUTION 3:§§ 1317–22
1833

---

§ 1317. The power itself was obviously proper, in order to escape from the constitutional objection already stated to the power of congress over the territory ceded to the United States under the confederation. The clause was not in the original draft of the constitution; but was added by the vote of ten states against one.

§ 1318. As the general government possesses the right to acquire territory, either by conquest, or by treaty, it would seem to follow, as an inevitable consequence, that it possesses the power to govern, what it has so acquired. The territory does not, when so acquired, become entitled to self-government, and it is not subject to the jurisdiction of any state. It must, consequently, be under the dominion and jurisdiction of the Union, or it would be without any government at all. In cases of conquest, the usage of the world is, if a nation is not wholly subdued, to consider the conquered territory, as merely held by military occupation, until its fate shall be determined by a treaty of peace. But during this intermediate period it is exclusively subject to the government of the conqueror. In cases of confirmation or cession by treaty, the acquisition becomes firm and stable; and the ceded territory becomes a part of the nation, to which it is annexed, either on terms stipulated in the treaty, or on such, as its new master shall impose. The relations of the inhabitants with each other do not change; but their relations with their former sovereign are dissolved; and new relations are created between them and their new sovereign. The act transferring the country transfers the allegiance of its inhabitants. But the general laws, not strictly political, remain, as they were, until altered by the new sovereign. If the treaty stipulates, that they shall enjoy the privileges, rights, and immunities of citizens of the United States, the treaty, as a part of the law of the land, becomes obligatory in these respects. Whether the same effects would result from the mere fact of their becoming inhabitants and citizens by the cession, without any express stipulation, may deserve inquiry, if the question should ever occur. But they do not participate in political power; nor can they share in the powers of the general government, until they become a state, and are admitted into the Union, as such. Until that period, the territory remains subject to be governed in such manner, as congress shall direct, under the clause of the constitution now under consideration.

§ 1319. No one has ever doubted the authority of congress to erect territorial governments within the territory of the United States, under the general language of the clause, "to make all needful rules and regulations." Indeed, with the ordinance of 1787 in the very view of the framers, as well as of the people of the states, it is impossible to doubt, that such a power was deemed indispensable to the purposes of the cessions made by the states. So that, notwithstanding the generality of the objection, (already examined,) that congress has no power to erect corporations, and that in the convention the power was refused; we see, that the very power is an incident to that of regulating the territory of the United States; that is, it is an appropriate means of carrying the power into effect. What shall be the form of government established in the territories depends exclusively upon the discretion of congress. Having a right to erect a territorial government, they may confer on it such powers, legislative, judicial, and executive, as they may deem best. They may confer upon it general legislative powers, subject only to the laws and constitution of the United States. If the power to create courts is given to the territorial legislature, those courts are to be deemed strictly territorial; and in no just sense constitutional courts, in which the judicial power conferred by the constitution can be deposited. They are incapable of receiving it. They are legislative courts, created in virtue of the general right of sovereignty in the government, or in virtue of that clause, which enables congress to make all needful rules and regulations respecting the territory of the United States. The power is not confined to the territory of the United States; but extends to "other property belonging to the United States;" so that it may be applied to the due regulation of all other personal and real property rightfully belonging to the United States. And so it has been constantly understood, and acted upon.

§ 1320. As if it were not possible to confer a single power upon the national government, which ought not to be a source of jealousy, the present has not been without objection. It has been suggested, that the sale and disposal of the Western territory may become a source of such immense revenue to the national government, as to make it independent of, and formidable to, the people. To amass immense riches (it has been said) to defray the expenses of ambition, when occasion may prompt, without seeming to oppress the people, has uniformly been the policy of tyrants. Should such a policy creep into our government, and the sales of the public lands, instead of being appropriated to the discharge of the public debt, be converted to a treasure in a bank, those, who, at any time, can command it, may be tempted to apply it to the most nefarious purposes. The improvident alienation of the crown lands in England has been considered, as a circumstance extremely favourable to the liberty of the nation, by rendering the government less independent of the people. The same reason will apply to other governments, whether monarchical or republican.

§ 1321. What a strange representation is this of a republican government, created by, and responsible to, the people in all its departments! What possible analogy can there be between the possession of large revenues in the hands of a monarch, and large revenues in the possession of a government, whose administration is confided to the chosen agents of the people for a short period, and may be dismissed almost at pleasure? If the doctrine be true, which is here inculcated, a republican government is little more than a dream, however its administration may be organized; and the people are not worthy of being trusted with large public revenues, since they cannot provide against corruption, and abuses of them. Poverty alone (it seems) gives a security for fidelity; and the liberties of the people are safe only, when they are pressed into vigilance by the power of taxation. In the view of this doctrine, what is to be thought of the recent purchases of Louisiana and Florida? If there was danger before, how mightily must it be increased by the accession of such a vast extent of territory, and such a vast increase of resources? Hitherto, the experience of the country has justified no alarms on this subject from such a source. On the other hand, the public lands hold out, after the discharge of the national debt, ample revenues to be devoted to the cause of education and sound learning, and to internal improvements, without trenching upon the property, or embarrassing the pursuits of the people by burthensome taxation. The constitutional objection to the appropriation of the other revenues of the government to such objects has not been supposed to apply to an appropriation of the proceeds of the public lands. The cessions of that territory were expressly made for the common benefit of the United States; and therefore constitute a fund, which may be properly devoted to any objects, which are for the common benefit of the Union.

§ 1322. The power of congress over the public territory is clearly exclusive and universal; and their legislation is subject to no control; but is absolute, and unlimited, unless so far as it is affected by stipulations in the cessions, or by the ordinance of 1787, under which any part of it has been settled. But the power of congress to regulate the other national property (unless it has acquired, by cession of the states, exclusive jurisdiction) is not necessarily exclusive in all cases. If the national government own a fort, arsenal, hospital, or lighthouse establishment, not so ceded, the general jurisdiction of the state is not excluded in regard to the site; but, subject to the rightful exercise of the powers of the national government, it remains in full force.

Article 4, Section 4

The United States shall guarantee to every State in this Union a Republican Form of Government, and shall protect each of them against Invasion; and on Application of the Legislature, or of the Executive (when the Legislature cannot be convened) against domestic Violence.

1

VERMONT CONSTITUTION OF 1777, CH. 1, ARTS. 4–8

Thorpe 6:3740

IV. That the people of this State have the sole, exclusive and inherent right of governing and regulating the internal police of the same.

V. That all power being originally inherent in, and consequently, derived from, the people; therefore, all officers of government, whether legislative or executive, are their trustees and servants, and at all times accountable to them.

VI. That government is, or ought to be, instituted for the common benefit, protection, and security of the people, nation or community; and not for the particular emolument or advantage of any single man, family or set of men, who are a part only of that community; and that the community hath an indubitable, unalienable and indefeasible right to reform, alter, or abolish, government, in such manner as shall be, by that community, judged most conducive to the public weal.

VII. That those who are employed in the legislative and executive business of the State, may be restrained from oppression, the people have a right, at such periods as they may think proper, to reduce their public officers to a private station, and supply the vacancies by certain and regular elections.

VIII. That all elections ought to be free; and that all freemen, having a sufficient, evident, common interest with, and attachment to, the community, have a right to elect officers, or be elected into office.

2

JAMES MADISON, VICES OF THE POLITICAL SYSTEM OF THE UNITED STATES
Apr. 1787

Papers 9:350–51

6. want of Guaranty to the States of their Constitutions & laws against internal violence.

6. The confederation is silent on this point and therefore by the second article the hands of the federal authority are tied. According to Republican Theory, Right and power being both vested in the majority, are held to be synonimous. According to fact and experience a minority may in an appeal to force, be an overmatch for the majority. 1. If the minority happen to include all such as possess the skill and habits of military life, & such as possess the great pecuniary resources, one third only may conquer the remaining two thirds. 2. One third of those who participate in the choice of the rulers, may be rendered a majority by the accession of those whose poverty excludes them from a right of suffrage, and who for obvious reasons will be more likely to join the standard of sedition than that of the established Government. 3. Where slavery exists the republican Theory becomes still more fallacious.

3

RECORDS OF THE FEDERAL CONVENTION

[1:22; Madison, 29 May]

11. Resd. that a Republican Government & the territory of each State, except in the instance of a voluntary junction of Government & territory, ought to be guaranteed by the United States to each State

[1:28; Paterson, 29 May]

2. A Guary. by the United States to each State of its Territory, etc.

[1:121; Madison, 5 June]

The 11. propos: *"for guarantying to States Republican Govt. & territory &c,"* being read, Mr. Patterson wished the point of representation could be decided before this clause should be considered, and moved to postpone it: which was not. opposed, and agreed to: Connecticut & S. Carolina only voting agst. it.

[1:202; Madison, 11 June]

Resol: 11. for guarantying Republican Govt. & territory to each State being considered: the words "or partition" were, on motion of Mr. Madison added, after the words "voluntary junction": Mas. N. Y. P. Va. N. C. S. C. G. ay.
Con: N. J. Del. Md. - - - no.

Mr. Read disliked the idea of guarantying territory. It abetted the idea of distinct States wch. would be a perpetual source of discord. There can be no cure for this evil but in doing away States altogether and uniting them all into one great Society.

Alterations having been made in the Resolution, making it read "that a republican Constitution & its existing laws ought to be guaranteed to each State by the U. States" the whole was agreed to nem. con.

[1:206; Yates, 11 June]

The eleventh resolve was then taken into consideration. Mr. Madison moved to add after the word *junctions*, the words, *or separation*.

Mr. Read against the resolve *in toto*. We must put away state governments, and we will then remove all cause of jealousy. The guarantee will confirm the assumed rights of several states to lands which do belong to the confederation.

Mr. Madison moved an amendment, to add to or alter the resolution as follows: *The republican constitutions and the existing laws of each state, to be guaranteed by the United States.*

Mr. Randolph was for the present amendment, because a republican government must be the basis of our national union; and no state in it ought to have it in their power to change its government into a monarchy.—Agreed to

[1:227; *Journal, 13 June*]

Resolved that a republican constitution, and it's existing laws, ought to be guaranteed to each State by the United-States.

[2:47; *Madison, 18 July*]

Resol. 16. "That a Republican Constitution & its existing laws ought to be guaranteid to each State by the U. States."

Mr. Govr. Morris—thought the Resol: very objectionable. He should be very unwilling that such laws as exist in R. Island should be guaranteid.

Mr. Wilson. The object is merely to secure the States agst. dangerous commotions, insurrections and rebellions.

Col. Mason. If the Genl Govt. should have no right to suppress rebellions agst. particular States, it will be in a bad situation indeed. As Rebellions agst. itself originate in & agst. individual States, it must remain a passive Spectator of its own subversion.

Mr. Randolph. The Resoln. has 2. Objects. 1. to secure Republican Government. 2. to suppress domestic commotions. He urged the necessity of both these provisions.

Mr. Madison moved to substitute "that the Constitutional authority of the States shall be guarantied to them respectively agst. domestic as well as foreign violence."

Docr. McClurg seconded the motion.

Mr. Houston was afraid of perpetuating the existing Constitutions of the States. That of Georgia was a very bad one, and he hoped would be revised & amended. It may also be difficult for the Genl. Govt. to decide between contending parties each of which claim the sanction of the Constitution.

Mr. L. Martin was for leaving the States to suppress Rebellions themselves.

Mr. Ghorum thought it strange that a Rebellion should be known to exist in the Empire, and the Genl. Govt. shd. be restrained from interposing to subdue it, At this rate an enterprising Citizen might erect the standard of Monarchy in a particular State, might gather together partizans from all quarters, might extend his views from State to State, and threaten to establish a tyranny over the whole & the Genl. Govt. be compelled to remain an inactive witness of its own destruction. With regard to different parties in a State; as long as they confine their disputes to words they will be harmless to the Genl. Govt. & to each other. If they appeal to the sword it will then be necessary for the Genl. Govt., however difficult it may be to decide on the merits of their contest, to interpose & put an end to it.

Mr. Carrol. Some such provision is essential. Every State ought to wish for it. It has been doubted whether it is a casus federis at present. And no room ought to be left for such a doubt hereafter.

Mr. Randolph moved to add as amendt. to the motion; "and that no State be at liberty to form any other than a Republican Govt." Mr. Madison seconded the motion

Mr. Rutlidge thought it unnecessary to insert any guarantee. No doubt could be entertained but that Congs. had the authority if they had the means to co-operate with any State in subduing a rebellion. It was & would be involved in the nature of the thing.

Mr. Wilson moved as a better expression of the idea, "that a Republican form of Governmt. shall be guarantied to each State & that each State shall be protected agst. foreign & domestic violence.

[2:133, 137, 144, 148, 174; *Committee of Detail*]

Resolved   That a Republican Form of Government shall be guarantied to each State; and that each State shall be protected against foreign and domestic Violence.

. . . . .

25 The said States of N. H. &c guarantee mutually each other and their Rights against all other Powers and against all Rebellions &c.

. . . . .

12. make Laws for calling forth the Aid of the militia, to execute the Laws of the Union to repel Invasion to inforce Treaties suppress internal Comns. . . .

14. To subdue a rebellion in any particular state, on the application of the legislature thereof.

. . . . .

2. The guarantee is
1. to prevent the establishment of any government, not republican
3. to protect each state against internal commotion: and
2. against external invasion.
4. But this guarantee shall not operate in the last Case without an application from the legislature of a state.

. . . . .

The United States shall guaranty to each State a Republican form of Government; and shall protect each State against foreign Invasions, and, on the Application of its Legislature, against domestic Violence.

[2:182, 188; *Madison, 6 Aug.*]

VII

To subdue a rebellion in any State, on the application of its legislature;
To make war;
To raise armies;
To build and equip fleets;
To call forth the aid of the militia, in order to execute the laws of the Union, enforce treaties, suppress insurrections, and repel invasions;

. . . . .

XVIII

The United States shall guaranty to each State a Republican form of Government; and shall protect each State against foreign invasions, and, on the application of its Legislature, against domestic violence.

[2:316; Madison, 17 Aug.]

"To subdue a rebellion in any State, on the application of its legislature"

Mr. Pinkney moved to strike out "on the application of its legislature"

Mr Govr. Morris 2ds.

Mr L– Martin opposed it as giving a dangerous & unnecessary power. The consent of the State ought to precede the introduction of any extraneous force whatever.

Mr. Mercer supported the opposition of Mr. Martin.

Mr Elseworth proposed to add after "legislature" "or Executive".

Mr Govr Morris. The Executive may possibly be at the head of the Rebellion. The Genl Govt. should enforce obedience in all cases where it may be necessary.

Mr. Ellsworth. In many cases The Genl. Govt. ought not to be able to interpose unless called upon. He was willing to vary his motion so as to read, "or without it when the legislature cannot meet."

Mr. Gerry was agst. letting loose the myrmidons of the U. States on a State without its own consent. The States will be the best Judges in such cases. More blood would have been spilt in Massts in the late insurrection, if the Genl. authority had intermeddled.

Mr. Langdon was for striking out as moved by Mr. Pinkney. The apprehension of the national force, will have a salutary effect in preventing insurrections.

Mr Randolph–If the Natl. Legislature is to judge whether the State legislature can or cannot meet, that amendment would make the clause as objectionable as the motion of Mr Pinkney.

Mr. Govr. Morris. We are acting a very strange part. We first form a strong man to protect us, and at the same time wish to tie his hands behind him, The legislature may surely be trusted with such a power to preserve the public tranquillity.

On the motion to add "or without it (application) when the legislature cannot meet"

N. H. ay. Mas. no. Ct ay. Pa. divd. Del. no. Md. no. Va. ay. N–C. divd. S. C. ay. Geo. ay. [Ayes—5; noes—3; divided—2.] so agreed to—

Mr. Madison and Mr. Dickenson moved to insert as explanatory, after "State"—"against the Government thereof" There might be a rebellion agst the U– States.— which was Agreed to nem– con.

[2:466; Madison, 30 Aug.]

Art: XVIII being taken up,—the word "foreign" was struck out. nem: con: as superfluous, being implied in the term "invasion"

Mr. Dickinson moved to strike out "on the application of its Legislature against" He thought it of essential importance to the tranquillity of the U—S. that they should in all cases suppress domestic violence, which may proceed from the State Legislature itself, or from disputes between the two branches where such exist

Mr. Dayton mentioned the Conduct of Rho. Island as shewing the necessity of giving latitude to the power of the U—S. on this subject.

On the question

N. H. no. Mas. no. Ct. no. N. J. ay. Pa. ay. Del. ay— Md. no. Va. no. N. C. no. S. C. no. Geo—no [Ayes—3; noes—8.]

On a question for striking out "domestic violence" and insertg. "insurrections"—it passed in the negative. N. H. no. Mas. no. Ct. no. N. J. ay. Pa. no Del no. Md. no. Va. ay. N. C. ay. S. C. ay. Geo. ay [Ayes—5; noes—6.]

Mr. Dickinson moved to insert the words, "or Executive" after the words "application of its Legislature"—The occasion itself he remarked might hinder the Legislature from meeting.

On this question

N. H. ay. Mas. no. Ct. ay. N. J. ay. Pa. ay. Del. ay. Md divd. Va. no. N. C. ay. S. C. ay. Geo. ay. [Ayes—8; noes—2; divided—1.]

Mr. L—Martin moved to subjoin to the last amendment the words "in the recess of the Legislature" On which question

N. H. no. Mas. no. Ct. no. Pa. no. Del. no. Md. ay. Va. no. N. C. no. S. C. no. Geo—no. [Ayes—1; noes—9.]

On Question on the last clause as amended

N. H. ay. Mas—ay. Ct. ay—N. J. ay—Pa. ay. Del. no. Md. no. Va. ay. N—C— ay— S—C. ay. Geo—ay, [Ayes—9; noes—2.]

[2:578, 602; Committee of Style]

The United States shall guaranty to each State a Republican form of government; and shall protect each State against invasions, and, on the application of its Legislature or Executive, against domestic violence.

. . . . .

Sect. 4. The United States shall guarantee to every state in this union a Republican form of government, and shall protect each of them against invasion; and on application of the legislature or executive, against domestic violence.

4

TENCH COXE, AN EXAMINATION OF THE
CONSTITUTION OF THE UNITED STATES OF AMERICA
Fall 1787
Pamphlets 145–46

The United States guarantee to every state in the union a separate republican form of government. From thence it follows, that any man or body of men, however rich or powerful, who shall make an alteration in the form of government of any state, whereby the powers thereof shall be attempted to be taken out of the hands of the people at large, will stand guilty of high treason; or should a foreign power seduce or over-awe the people of any state, so as to cause them to vest in the families of any ambitious citizens or foreigners the powers of hereditary governors, whether as Kings or Nobles, that such investment of powers would be void in itself, and every person attempting to execute them would also be guilty of treason.

5

WILLIAM SYMMES TO CAPT. PETER OSGOOD, JR.
15 Nov. 1787
Storing 4.5.2

"The United States shall guarrantee to every State a Republican form of government."

Republics are either aristocratical or democratical: and the United States guarranty one of these forms to every State. But I disapprove of any guarranty in the matter. For though it is improbable, that any State will choose to alter the form of its government; yet it ought to be the privilege of every State to do as it will in this affair. If this regulation be admitted, it will be difficult to effect any important changes in State government. For the other States will have nearly as much to do with our government as we ourselves. And what Congress may see in our present constitution, or any future amendments, not strictly republican *in their opinions*, who can tell? Besides it is of no importance to any State how the government of any other State is administered, whether by a single magistrate or two, or by a king.

I therefore presume, that, as this clause meddles too much with the independence of the several States, so also it answers no valuable end to any or to the whole.

6

ALEXANDER HAMILTON, FEDERALIST, NO. 21,
130–32
12 Dec. 1787

(See vol. 1, ch. 5, no. 22)

7

JAMES MADISON, FEDERALIST, NO. 43,
291–95
23 Jan. 1788

In a confederacy founded on republican principles, and composed of republican members, the superintending government ought clearly to possess authority to defend the system against aristocratic or monarchical innovations. The more intimate the nature of such a Union may be, the greater interest have the members in the political institutions of each other; and the greater right to insist that the forms of government under which the compact was entered into, should be *substantially* maintained. But a right implies a remedy; and where else could the remedy be de-

posited, than where it is deposited by the Constitution? Governments of dissimilar principles and forms have been found less adapted to a federal coalition of any sort, than those of a kindred nature. "As the confederate republic of Germany," says Montesquieu, "consists of free cities and petty states subject to different Princes, experience shews us that it is more imperfect than that of Holland and Switzerland." "Greece was undone" he adds, "as soon as the King of Macedon obtained a seat among the Amphyctions." In the latter case, no doubt, the disproportionate force, as well as the monarchical form of the new confederate, had its share of influence on the events. It may possibly be asked what need there could be of such a precaution, and whether it may not become a pretext for alterations in the state governments, without the concurrence of the states themselves. These questions admit of ready answers. If the interposition of the general government should not be needed, the provision for such an event will be a harmless superfluity only in the Constitution. But who can say what experiments may be produced by the caprice of particular states, by the ambition of enterprizing leaders, or by the intrigues and influence of foreign powers? To the second question it may be answered, that if the general government should interpose by virtue of this constitutional authority, it will be of course bound to pursue the authority. But the authority extends no farther than to a guaranty of a republican form of government, which supposes a pre-existing government of the form which is to be guaranteed. As long therefore as the existing republican forms are continued by the States, they are guaranteed by the Federal Constitution. Whenever the states may chuse to substitute other republican forms, they have a right to do so, and to claim the federal guaranty for the latter. The only restriction imposed on them is, that they shall not exchange republican for anti-republican Constitutions; a restriction which it is presumed will hardly be considered as a grievance.

A protection against invasion is due from every society to the parts composing it. The latitude of the expression here used, seems to secure each state not only against foreign hostility, but against ambitious or vindictive enterprizes of its more powerful neighbours. The history both of antient and modern confederacies, proves that the weaker members of the Union ought not to be insensible to the policy of this article.

Protection against domestic violence is added with equal propriety. It has been remarked that even among the Swiss Cantons, which properly speaking are not under one government, provision is made for this object; and the history of that league informs us, that mutual aid is frequently claimed and afforded; and as well by the most democratic, as the other Cantons. A recent and well known event among ourselves, has warned us to be prepared for emergencies of a like nature.

At first view it might seem not to square with the republican theory, to suppose either that a majority have not the right, or that a minority will have the force to subvert a government; and consequently that the foederal interposition can never be required but when it would be improper. But theoretic reasoning in this, as in most other cases, must be qualified by the lessons of practice. Why may not illicit combinations for purposes of violence be formed as well by a majority of a State, especially a small State, as by a majority of a county or a district of the same State; and if the authority of the State ought in the latter case to protect the local magistracy, ought not the foederal authority in the former to support the State authority? Besides, there are certain parts of the State Constitutions which are so interwoven with the Foederal Constitution, that a violent blow cannot be given to the one without communicating the wound to the other. Insurrections in a State will rarely induce a foederal interposition, unless the number concerned in them, bear some proportion to the friends of government. It will be much better that the violence in such cases should be repressed by the Superintending power, than that the majority should be left to maintain their cause by a bloody and obstinate contest. The existence of a right to interpose will generally prevent the necessity of exerting it.

Is it true that force and right are necessarily on the same side in republican governments? May not the minor party possess such a superiority of pecuniary resources, of military talents and experience, or of secret succours from foreign powers, as will render it superior also in an appeal to the sword? May not a more compact and advantageous position turn the scale on the same side against a superior number so situated as to be less capable of a prompt and collected exertion of its strength? Nothing can be more chimerical than to imagine that in a trial of actual force, victory may be calculated by the rules which prevail in a census of the inhabitants, or which determine the event of an election! May it not happen in fine that the minority of CITIZENS may become a majority of PERSONS, by the accession of alien residents, of a casual concourse of adventurers, or of those whom the Constitution of the State has not admitted to the rights of suffrage? I take no notice of an unhappy species of population abounding in some of the States, who during the calm of regular government are sunk below the level of men; but who in the tempestuous scenes of civil violence may emerge into the human character, and give a superiority of strength to any party with which they may associate themselves.

In cases where it may be doubtful on which side justice lies, what better umpires could be desired by two violent factions, flying to arms and tearing a State to pieces, than the representatives of confederate States not heated by the local flame? To the impartiality of Judges they would unite the affection of friends. Happy would it be if such a remedy for its infirmities, could be enjoyed by all free governments; if a project equally effectual could be established for the universal peace of mankind.

Should it be asked what is to be the redress for an insurrection pervading all the States, and comprizing a superiority of the entire force, though not a constitutional right; the answer must be, that such a case, as it would be without the compass of human remedies, so it is fortunately not within the compass of human probability; and that it is a sufficient recommendation of the Foederal Constitution, that it diminishes the risk of a calamity, for which no possible constitution can provide a cure.

Among the advantages of a confederate republic enumerated by Montesquieu, an important one is, "that should a popular insurrection happen in one of the States, the others are able to quell it. Should abuses creep into one part, they are reformed by those that remain sound."

8

JAMES MADISON, VIRGINIA RATIFYING CONVENTION 6 June 1788

Elliot 3:90

But the honorable member sees great danger in the provision concerning the militia. This I conceive to be an additional security to our liberty, without diminishing the power of the states in any considerable degree. It appears to me so highly expedient that I should imagine it would have found advocates even in the warmest friends of the present system. The authority of training the militia, and appointing the officers, is reserved to the states. Congress ought to have the power to establish a uniform discipline throughout the states, and to provide for the execution of the laws, suppress insurrections, and repel invasions: these are the only cases wherein they can interfere with the militia; and the obvious necessity of their having power over them in these cases must convince any reflecting mind. Without uniformity of discipline, military bodies would be incapable of action: without a general controlling power to call forth the strength of the Union to repel invasions, the country might be overrun and conquered by foreign enemies: without such a power to suppress insurrections, our liberties might be destroyed by domestic faction, and domestic tyranny be established.

9

DEBATE IN VIRGINIA RATIFYING CONVENTION 14 June 1788

Elliot 3:417–28

Mr. CORBIN, after a short address to the chair, in which he expressed extreme reluctance to get up, said, that all contentions on this subject might be ended, by adverting to the 4th section of the 4th article, which provides, "that the United States shall guaranty to every state in the Union a republican form of government, and shall protect each of them against invasion, and, on application of the legislature, or of the executive, (when the legislature cannot be convened,) against domestic violence." He thought this section gave the states power to use their own *militia*, and call on Congress for the militia of other states. He observed that our representatives were to return every second year to mingle with their fellow-citizens. He asked, then, how, in the name of God, they would make laws to destroy themselves. The gentleman had told us that nothing could be more humiliating than that the *state governments* could not control the general government. He thought the gentleman might as well have complained that one county could not control the state at large. Mr. Corbin then said that all confederate governments had the care of the national defence, and that Congress ought to have it. Animadverting on Mr. Henry's observations, that the French had been the instruments of their own slavery, that the Germans had enslaved the Germans, and the Spaniards the Spaniards, &c., he asked if those nations knew any thing of representation. The want of this knowledge was the principal cause of their bondage. He concluded by observing that the general government had no power but such as the state government had, and that arguments against the one held against the other.

Mr. GRAYSON, in reply to Mr. Corbin, said he was mistaken when he produced the 4th section of the 4th article, to prove that the state governments had a right to intermeddle with the militia. He was of opinion that a previous application must be made to the federal head, by the legislature when in session, or otherwise by the executive of any state, before they could interfere with the militia. In his opinion, no instance could be adduced where the states could employ the militia; for, in all the cases wherein they could be employed, Congress had the exclusive direction and control of them. Disputes, he observed, had happened in many countries, where this power should be lodged. In England, there was a dispute between the Parliament and King Charles who should have power over the militia. Were this government well organized, he would not object to giving it power over the militia. But as it appeared to him to be without checks, and to tend to the formation of an aristocratic body, he could not agree to it. Thus organized, his imagination did not reach so far as to know where this power should be lodged. He conceived the state governments to be at the mercy of the generality. He wished to be open to conviction, but he could see no case where the states could command the militia. He did not believe that it corresponded with the intentions of those who formed it, and it was altogether without an equilibrium. He humbly apprehended that the power of providing for organizing and disciplining the militia, enabled the government to make laws for regulating them, and inflicting punishments for disobedience, neglect, &c. Whether it would be the spirit of the generality to lay unusual punishments, he knew not; but he thought they had the power, if they thought proper to exercise it. He thought that, if there was a constructive implied power left in the states, yet, as the line was not clearly marked between the two governments, it would create differences. He complained of the uncertainty of the expression, and wished it to be so clearly expressed that the people might see where the states could interfere.

As the exclusive power of arming, organizing, &c., was given to Congress, they might entirely neglect them; or they might be armed in one part of the Union, and totally neglected in another. This he apprehended to be a probable circumstance. In this he might be thought suspicious; but he was justified by what had happened in other countries. He wished to know what attention had been paid to the militia of Scotland and Ireland since the union, and what laws had been made to regulate them. There is, says Mr. Grayson, an excellent militia law in England, and such as I wish to be established by the general government. They have thirty thousand select militia in England. But the militia of Scotland and Ireland are neglected. I see the necessity of the concentration of the forces of the Union. I acknowledge that militia are the best means of quelling insurrections, and that we have an advantage over the English government, for their regular forces answer the purpose. But I object to the want of checks, and a line of discrimination between the state governments and the generality.

Mr. JOHN MARSHALL asked if gentlemen were serious when they asserted that, if the state governments had power to interfere with the militia, it was by implication. If they were, he asked the committee whether the least attention would not show that they were mistaken. The state governments did not derive their powers from the general government; but each government derived its powers from the people, and each was to act according to the powers given it. Would any gentleman deny this? He demanded if powers not given were retained by implication. Could any man say so? Could any man say that this power was not retained by the states, as they had not given it away? For, says he, does not a power remain till it is given away? The state legislatures had power to command and govern their militia before, and have it still, undeniably, unless there be something in this Constitution that takes it away.

For Continental purposes Congress may call forth the militia,—as to suppress insurrections and repel invasions. But the power given to the states by the people is not taken away; for the Constitution does not say so. In the Confederation Congress had this power; but the state legislatures had it also. The power of legislating given them within the ten miles square is exclusive of the states, because it is expressed to be exclusive. The truth is, that when power is given to the general legislature, if it was in the state legislature before, both shall exercise it; unless there be an incompatibility in the exercise by one to that by the other, or negative words precluding the state governments from it. But there are no negative words here. It rests, therefore, with the states. To me it appears, then, unquestionable that the state governments can call forth the militia, in case the Constitution should be adopted, in the same manner as they could have done before its adoption. Gentlemen have said that the states cannot defend themselves without an application to Congress, because Congress can interpose! Does not every man feel a refutation of the argument in his own breast? I will show that there could not be a combination, between those who formed the Constitution, to take away this power. All the restraints intended to be laid on the state governments (besides where an exclusive power is expressly given to Congress) are contained in the 10th section of the 1st article. This power is not included in the restrictions in that section. But what excludes every possibility of doubt, is the

564

last part of it—that "no state shall engage in war, unless actually invaded, or in such imminent danger as will not admit of delay." When invaded, they can engage in war, as also when in imminent danger. This clearly proves that the states can use the militia when they find it necessary. The worthy member last up objects to the Continental government's possessing the power of disciplining the militia, because, though all its branches be derived from the people, he says they will form an aristocratic government, unsafe and unfit to be trusted.

Mr. GRAYSON answered, that he only said it was so constructed as to form a great aristocratic body.

Mr. MARSHALL replied, that he was not certain whether he understood him; but he thought he had said so. He conceived that, as the government was drawn from the people, the feelings and interests of the people would be attended to, and that we should be safe in granting them power to regulate the militia. When the government is drawn from the people, continued Mr. Marshall, and depending on the people for its continuance, oppressive measures will not be attempted, as they will certainly draw on their authors the resentment of those on whom they depend. On this government, thus depending on ourselves for its existence, I will rest my safety, notwithstanding the danger depicted by the honorable gentleman. I cannot help being surprised that the worthy member thought this power so dangerous. What government is able to protect you in time of war? Will any state depend on its own exertions? The consequence of such dependence, and withholding this power from Congress, will be, that state will fall after state, and be a sacrifice to the want of power in the general government. *United we are strong, divided we fall.* Will you prevent the general government from drawing the militia of one state to another, when the consequence would be, that every state must depend on itself? The enemy, possessing the water, can quickly go from one state to another. No state will spare to another its militia, which it conceives necessary for itself. It requires a superintending power, in order to call forth the resources of all to protect all. If this be not done, each state will fall a sacrifice. This system merits the highest applause in this respect. The honorable gentleman said that a general regulation may be made to inflict punishments. Does he imagine that a militia law is to be ingrafted on the scheme of government, so as to render it incapable of being changed? The idea of the worthy member supposes that men renounce their own interests. This would produce general inconveniences throughout the Union, and would be equally opposed by all the states. But the worthy member fears, that in one part of the Union they will be regulated and disciplined, and in another neglected. This danger is enhanced by leaving this power to each state; for some states may attend to their militia, and others may neglect them. If Congress neglect our militia, we can arm them ourselves. Cannot Virginia import arms? Cannot she put them into the hands of her militia-men?

He then concluded by observing, that the power of governing the militia was not vested in the states by implication, because, being possessed of it antecedent to the adoption of the government, and not being divested of it by any grant or restriction in the Constitution, they must necessarily be as fully possessed of it as ever they had been. And it could not be said that the states derived any powers from that system, but retained them, though not acknowledged in any part of it.

Mr. GRAYSON acknowledged that all power was drawn from the people. But he could see none of those checks which ought to characterize a free government. It had not such checks as even the British government had. He thought it so organized as to form an aristocratic body. If we looked at the democratic branch, and the great extent of country, he said, it must be considered, in a great degree, to be an aristocratic representation. As they were elected with craving appetites, and wishing for emoluments, they might unite with the other two branches. They might give reciprocally good offices to one another, and mutually protect each other; for he considered them all as united in interest, and as but one branch. There was no check to prevent such a combination; nor, in cases of concurrent powers, was there a line drawn to prevent interference between the state governments and the generality.

Mr. HENRY still retained his opinion, that the states had no right to call forth the militia to suppress insurrections, &c. But the right interpretation (and such as the nations of the earth had put upon the concession of power) was that, when power was given, it was given exclusively. He appealed to the committee, if power was not confined in the hands of a *few* in almost all countries of the world. He referred to their candor, if the construction of conceded power was not an exclusive concession, in nineteen twentieth parts of the world. The nations which retained their liberty were comparatively few. America would add to the number of the oppressed nations, if she depended on constructive rights and argumentative implication. That the powers given to Congress were exclusively given, was very obvious to him. The rights which the states had must be founded on the restrictions on Congress. He asked, if the doctrine which had been so often circulated, that rights not given were retained, was true, why there were negative clauses to restrain Congress. He told gentlemen that these clauses were sufficient to shake all their implication; for, says he, if Congress had no power but that given to them, why restrict them by negative words? Is not the clear implication this—that, if these restrictions were not inserted, they could have performed what they prohibit?

The worthy member had said that Congress ought to have power to protect all, and had given this system the highest encomium. But he insisted that the power over the militia was concurrent. To obviate the futility of this doctrine, Mr. Henry alleged that it was not reducible to practice. Examine it, says he; reduce it to practice. Suppose an insurrection in Virginia, and suppose there be danger apprehended of an insurrection in another state, from the exercise of the government; or suppose a national war; and there be discontents among the people of this state, that produce, or threaten, an insurrection; suppose Congress, in either case, demands a number of militia,—will they not be obliged to go? Where are your reserved rights, when your militia go to a neighboring state? Which call is to be obeyed, the congressional call, or the call of the state legislature? The call of Congress must be obeyed. I need not remind this committee that the sweeping clause will cause their demands to be submitted to. This clause enables them "to make all laws which shall be necessary and proper to carry into execution all the powers vested by this Constitution in the government of the United States, or in any department or officer thereof." Mr. Chairman, I will turn to another clause, which relates to the same subject, and tends to show the fallacy of their argument.

The 10th section of the 1st article, to which reference was made by the worthy member, militates against himself. It says, that "no state shall engage in war, unless actually invaded." If you give this clause a fair construction, what is the true meaning of it? What does this relate to? Not domestic insurrections, but war. If the country be invaded, a state may go to war, but cannot suppress insurrections. If there should happen an insurrection of slaves, the country cannot be said to be invaded. They cannot, therefore, suppress it without the interposition of Congress. The 4th section of the 4th article expressly directs that, in case of domestic violence, Congress shall protect the states on application of the legislature or executive; and the 8th section of the 1st article gives Congress power to call forth the militia to quell insurrections: there cannot, therefore, be a concurrent power. The state legislatures ought to have power to call forth the efforts of the militia, when necessary. Occasions for calling them out may be urgent, pressing, and instantaneous. The states cannot now call them, let an insurrection be ever so perilous, without an application to Congress. So long a delay may be fatal.

There are three clauses which prove, beyond the possibility of doubt, that Congress, and *Congress only*, can call forth the militia. The clause giving Congress power to call them out to suppress insurrections, &c.; that which restrains a state from engaging in war except when actually invaded; and that which requires Congress to protect the states against domestic violence,—render it impossible that a state can have power to intermeddle with them. Will not Congress find refuge for their actions in these clauses? With respect to the concurrent jurisdiction, it is a political monster of absurdity. We have passed that clause which gives Congress an unlimited authority over the national wealth; and here is an unbounded control over the national strength. Notwithstanding this clear, unequivocal relinquishment of the power of controlling the militia, you say the states retain it, for the very purposes given to Congress. Is it fair to say that you give the power of arming the militia, and at the same time to say you reserve it? This great national government ought not to be left in this condition. If it be, it will terminate in the destruction of our liberties.

Mr. MADISON. Mr. Chairman, let me ask this committee, and the honorable member last up, what we are to understand from this reasoning. The power must be vested in Congress, or in the state governments; or there must be a division or concurrence. He is against division. It is a political monster. He will not give it to Congress for fear of oppression. Is it to be vested in the state governments? If so, where is the provision for general defence? If ever America should be attacked, the states would fall succes-

sively. It will prevent them from giving aid to their sister states; for, as each state will expect to be attacked, and wish to guard against it, each will retain its own militia for its own defence. Where is this power to be deposited, then, unless in the general government, if it be dangerous to the public safety to give it exclusively to the states? If it must be divided, let him show a better manner of doing it than that which is in the Constitution. I cannot agree with the other honorable gentleman, that there is no check. There is a powerful check in that paper. The state governments are to govern the militia when not called forth for general national purposes; and Congress is to govern such part only as may be in the actual service of the Union. Nothing can be more certain and positive than this. It expressly empowers Congress to govern them when in the service of the United States. It is, then, clear that the states govern them when they are not. With respect to suppressing insurrections, I say that those clauses which were mentioned by the honorable gentleman are compatible with a concurrence of the power. By the first, Congress is to call them forth to suppress insurrections, and repel invasions of foreign powers. A concurrence in the former case is necessary, because a whole state may be in insurrection against the Union. What has passed may perhaps justify this apprehension. The safety of the Union and particular states requires that the general govenment should have power to repel foreign invasions. The 4th section of the 4th article is perfectly consistent with the exercise of the power by the states. The words are, "The United States shall guaranty to every state in this Union a republican form of government, and shall protect each of them against invasion, and, on application of the legislature, or of the executive, (when the legislature cannot be convened,) against domestic violence." The word *invasion* here, after power had been given in the former clause to repel invasions, may be thought tautologous, but it has a different meaning from the other. This clause speaks of a particular state. It means that it shall be protected from invasion by other states. A republican government is to be guarantied to each state, and they are to be protected from invasion from other states, as well as from foreign powers; and, on application by the legislature or executive, as the case may be, the militia of the other states are to be called to suppress domestic insurrections. Does this bar the states from calling forth their own militia? No; but it gives them a supplementary security to suppress insurrections and domestic violence.

The other clause runs in these words: "No state shall, without the consent of Congress, lay any duty on tonnage, keep troops or ships of war in time of peace, enter into any agreement or compact with another state, or with a foreign power, or engage in war, unless actually invaded, or in such imminent danger as will not admit of delay." They are restrained from making war, unless invaded, or *in imminent danger*. When in such danger, they are not restrained. I can perceive no competition in these clauses. They cannot be said to be repugnant to a concurrence of the power. If we object to the Constitution in this manner, and consume our time in verbal criticism, we shall never put an end to the business.

Mr. GEORGE MASON. Mr. Chairman, a worthy member

has asked who are the militia, if they be not the *people* of this country, and if we are not to be protected from the fate of the Germans, Prussians, &c., by our representation? I ask, Who are the militia? They consist now of the whole people, except a few public officers. But I cannot say who will be the militia of the future day. If that paper on the table gets no alteration, the militia of the future day may not consist of all classes, high and low, and rich and poor; but they may be confined to the lower and middle classes of the people, granting exclusion to the higher classes of the people. If we should ever see that day, the most ignominious punishments and heavy fines may be expected. Under the present government, all ranks of people are subject to militia duty. Under such a full and equal representation as ours, there can be no ignominious punishment inflicted. But under this national, or rather consolidated government, the case will be different. The representation being so small and inadequate, they will have no fellow-feeling for the people. They may discriminate people in their own predicament, and exempt from duty all the officers and lowest creatures of the national government. If there were a more particular definition of their powers, and a clause exempting the militia from martial law except when in actual service, and from fines and punishments of an unusual nature, then we might expect that the militia would be what they are. But, if this be not the case, we cannot say how long all classes of people will be included in the militia. There will not be the same reason to expect it, because the government will be administered by different people. We know what they are now, but know not how soon they may be altered.

Mr. GEORGE NICHOLAS. Mr. Chairman, I feel apprehensions lest the subject of our debates should be misunderstood. Every one wishes to know the true meaning of the system; but I fear those who hear us will think we are captiously quibbling on words. We have been told, in the course of this business, that the government will operate like a *screw*. Give me leave to say that the exertions of the opposition are like that instrument. They catch at every thing, and take it into their vortex. The worthy member says that this government is defective, because it comes from the people. Its greatest recommendation, with me, is putting the power in the hands of the people. He disapproves of it because it does not say in what particular instances the militia shall be called out to execute the laws. This is a power of the Constitution, and particular instances must be defined by the legislature. But, says the worthy member, those laws which have been read are arguments against the Constitution, because they show that the states are now in possession of the power, and competent to its execution. Would you leave this power in the states, and by that means deprive the general government of a power which will be necessary for its existence? If the state governments find this power necessary; ought not the general government to have a similar power? But, sir, there is no state check in this business. The gentleman near me has shown that there is a very important check.

Another worthy member says there is no power in the states to quell an insurrection of slaves. Have they it now? If they have, does the Constitution take it away? If it does, it must be in one of the three clauses which have been mentioned by the worthy member. The first clause gives the general government power to call them out when necessary. Does this take it away from the states? No. But it gives an additional security; for, besides the power in the state governments to use their own militia, it will be the duty of the general government to aid them with the strength of the Union when called for. No part of this Constitution can show that this power is taken away.

But an argument is drawn from that clause which says "that no state shall engage in war unless actually invaded, or in such imminent danger as will not admit of delay." What does this prohibition amount to? It must be a war with a foreign enemy that the states are prohibited from making; for the exception to the restriction proves it. The restriction includes only offensive hostility, as they are at liberty to engage in war when invaded, or in imminent danger. They are, therefore, not restrained from quelling domestic insurrections, which are totally different from making war with a foreign power. But the great thing to be dreaded is that, during an insurrection, the militia will be called out from the state. This is his kind of argument. Is it possible that, at such a time, the general government would order the militia to be called? It is a groundless objection, to work on gentlemen's apprehensions within these walls. As to the 4th article, it was introduced wholly for the particular aid of the states. A republican form of government is guarantied, and protection is secured against invasion and domestic violence on application. Is not this a guard as strong as possible? Does it not exclude the unnecessary interference of Congress in business of this sort?

The gentleman over the way cannot tell who will be the militia at a future day, and enumerates dangers of select militia. Let me attend to the nature of gentlemen's objections. One objects because there will be select militia; another objects because there will be no select militia; and yet both oppose it on these contradictory principles. If you deny the general·government the power of calling out the militia, there must be a recurrence to a standing army. If you are really jealous of your liberties, confide in Congress.

10

JAMES WILSON, OF MAN IN CONFEDERATION,
LECTURES ON LAW
1791
Works 1:264–65

When we say, that the government of those states, which unite in the same confederacy, ought to be of the same nature; it is not to be understood, that there should be a precise and exact uniformity in all their particular establishments and laws. It is sufficient that the fundamental principles of their laws and constitutions be consistent and congenial; and that some general rights and privileges should be diffused indiscriminately among them. Among these, the rights and privileges of naturalization hold an important place. Of such consequence was the inter-communication of these rights and privileges in the opinion of my Lord Bacon, that he considered them as the strongest of all bonds to cement and to preserve the union of states. "Let us take a view," says he, "and we shall find, that wheresoever kingdoms and states have been united, and that union incorporated by a bond of mutual naturalization, you shall never observe them afterwards, upon any occasion of trouble or otherwise, to break and sever again." Machiavel, when he inquires concerning the causes, to which Rome was indebted for her splendour and greatness, assigns none of stronger or more extensive operation that this—she easily compounded and incorporated with strangers. This important subject has received a proportioned degree of attention in forming the constitution of the United States. "The citizens of each state shall be entitled to all privileges and immunities of citizens in the several states." In addition to this, the congress have power to "establish a uniform rule of naturalization throughout the United States."

Though a union of laws is, by no means, necessary to a union of states; yet a similarity in their code of *publick* laws is a most desirable object. The publick law is the great sinew of government. The sinews of the different governments, composing the union, should, as far as it can be effected, be equally strong. "In this point," says my Lord Bacon, "the rule holdeth, which was pronounced by an ancient father, touching the diversity of rites in the church; for finding the vesture of the queen in the psalm (who prefigured the church) was of divers colours; and finding again that Christ's coat was without a seam, concludeth well, in veste varietas sit, scissura non sit."

11

ST. GEORGE TUCKER,
BLACKSTONE'S COMMENTARIES
1:APP. 366–67
1803

It is an observation of the enlightened Montesquieu, that mankind would have been at length obliged to submit to the government of a single person, if they had not contrived a kind of constitution, by which the internal advantages of a republic might be united with the external force of a monarchy; and this constitution is that of a confederacy of smaller states, to form one large one for their common defence. But these associations ought only to be formed, he tells us, between states whose form of government is not only similar, but also *republican*. The spirit of monarchy is war, and the enlargement of dominion; peace and moderation is the spirit of a republic. These two kinds of government cannot naturally subsist together in a con-

federate republic. Greece, he adds, was undone, as soon as the kings of Macedon obtained a seat among the Amphictions. If the United States wish to preserve themselves from a similar fate, they will consider the guarantee contained in this clause as a corner stone of their liberties.

The possibility of an undue partiality in the federal government in affording it's protection to one part of the union in preference to another, which may be invaded at the same time, seems to be provided against, by that part of this clause which guarantees such protection to each of them. So that every state which may be invaded must be protected by the united force of the confederacy. It may not be amiss further to observe, that every pretext for intermeddling with the domestic concerns of any state, under colour of protecting it against domestic violence is taken away, by that part of the provision which renders an application from the legislative, or executive authority of the state endangered, necessary to be made to the federal government, before it's interference can be at all proper. On the other hand, this article secures an immense acquisition of strength; and additional force to the aid of any of the state governments, in case of an internal rebellion or insurrection against it's authority. . . . The southern states being more peculiarly open to danger from this quarter, ought to be particularly tenacious of a constitution from which they may derive such assistance in the most critical periods.

12

JOHNSON V. DUNCAN
3 Mart. 530 (La. 1815)

MARTIN J. A motion that the Court might proceed in this case, has been resisted on two grounds:

1. That the city and its environs were by general orders of the officer, commanding the military district, put on the 15th of December last, *under strict Martial Law.*

2d. That by the 3d sec. of an act of assembly, approved on the 18th of December last, all proceedings in any civil case are suspended.

I. At the close of the argument, on Monday last, we thought it our duty, lest the smallest delay should countenance the idea, that this Court entertain any doubt on the first ground, instantly to declare *vivâ voce* (although the practice is to deliver our opinions in writing) that the exercise of an authority, vested by law in this Court, could not be suspended by any man.

In any other state but this, in the population of which are many individuals, who not being perfectly acquainted with their rights, may easily be imposed on, it could not be expected that the Judges of this Court should, in complying with the constitutional injunction *in all cases to adduce the reasons on which their judgment is founded*, take up much time to shew that this Court is bound utterly to disregard what is thus called *Martial Law;* if any thing be meant thereby, but the strict enforcing of the rules and articles for the government of the army of the United States, established by Congress or any act of that body relating to military matters, on all individuals belonging to the army or militia in the service of the United States. Yet, we are told that by this proclamation of Martial Law, the officer who issued it has conferred on himself, over all his fellow-citizens, within the space which he has described, a supreme and unlimited power, which being incompatible with the exercise of the functions of civil magistrates, necessarily suspends them.

This bold and novel assertion is said to be supported by the 9th section of the first article of the Constitution of the United States, in which are detailed the limitations of the power of the Legislature of the Union. It is there provided that *the privilege of the writ of Habeas Corpus shall not be suspended, unless, when in cases of invasion or rebellion, the public safety may require it*. We are told that the commander of the military district is the person who is to suspend the writ, and is to do so, whenever *in his judgment* the public safety appears to require it: that, as he may thus paralyse the arm of the justice of his country in the most important case, the protection of the personal liberty of the citizen, it follows that, as he who can do the *more* can do the *less*, he can also suspend all other functions of the civil magistrate, which he does by his proclamation of Martial Law.

This mode of reasoning varies *toto celo* from the decision of the Supreme Court of the United States, in the case of *Swartwout and Bollman*, arrested in this city in 1806 by general Wilkinson. The Court there declared, that the Constitution had exclusively vested in Congress the right of suspending the privilege of the writ of *Habeas Corpus*, and that body was the sole judge of the necessity that called for the suspension. "If, at any time," said the Chief Justice, "the public safety shall require the suspension of the powers vested in the Courts of the United States by this act, (the *Habeas Corpus act*,) it is for the Legislature to say so. This question depends on political considerations, on which the Legislature is to decide: Till the Legislature will be expressed, this Court can only see its duties, and must obey the law." *4 Cranch* 101.

The high authority of this decision seems however to be disregarded; and a contrary opinion is said to have been lately acted upon, to the distress and terror of the good people of this state: it is therefore meet to dispel the clouds which designing men endeavor to cast on this article of the Constitution, that the people should know that their rights, thus defined, are neither doubtful or insecure, but supported on the clearest principles of our laws.

Approaching, therefore, the question, as if I were without the above conclusive authority, I find it provided by the Constitution of this state that "no power of suspending the laws of this state shall be exercised, unless by the Legislature, or under its authority." The proclamation of Martial Law, therefore, if intended to suspend the functions of this Court or its members, is an attempt to exercise powers thus exclusively vested in the Legislature. I therefore cannot hesitate in saying that it is in this respect null and void. If, however, there be aught in the Constitution or laws of the United States that really authorises the commanding officer of a military district to suspend the laws of this state, as that Constitution and these laws are paramount to those of the state, they must regulate the decision of this Court.

This leads me to the examination of the power of suspending the writ of *Habeas Corpus*, and that which it is said to include, of proclaiming Martial Law, as noticed in the Constitution of the United States. As in the whole article cited, no mention is made of the power of any other branch of government but the Legislative, it cannot be said that any of the limitations which it contains extend to any of the other branches. *Iniquum est perimi de pacto id de quo cogitatum non est*. If, therefore, this suspending power exist in the executive (under whose authority it has been endeavoured to exercise it) it exists without any limitation, then the president possesses without a limitation a power which the Legislature cannot exercise without a limitation. Thus he possesses a greater power *alone* than the house of representatives, the senate and himself *jointly*.

Again, the power of repealing a law and that of suspending it (which is a partial repeal) are Legislative powers. For *eodem modo quo quid constituitur, eodem modo destruitur*. As every Legislative power, that may be exercised under the Constitution of the United States, is exclusively vested in Congress, all others are retained by the people of the several states.

In England, at the time of the invasion of the pretender, assisted by the forces of hostile nations, the *Habeas Corpus* act was indeed suspended, but the executive did not thus of itself stretch its own authority, the precaution was deliberated upon and taken by the representatives of the people. *Delolme* 409. And there the power is safely lodged without the danger of its being abused. Parliament may repeal the law on which the safety of the people depends; but it is not their own caprices and arbitrary humours, but the caprices and arbitrary humours of other men which they will have gratified, when they shall have thus overthrown the columns of public liberty. *Id.* 275.

If it be said that the laws of war, being the laws of the United States, authorise the proclamation of Martial Law, I answer that in peace or in war no law can be enacted but by the Legislative power. In England, from whence the American jurist derives his principles in this respect, "Martial Law cannot be used without the authority of parliament," *5 Comyns* 229. The authority of the monarch himself is insufficient. In the case of *Grant* vs. *Sir C. Gould, H. Hen. Bl.* 69, which was on a prohibition (applied for in the Court of Common Pleas) to the defendant as judge advocate of a Court Martial to prevent the execution of the sentence of that military tribunal, the counsel, who resisted the motion, said it was not to be disputed that Martial Law can only be exercised in England; so far as it is authorised by the mutiny act and the articles of war, all which are established by parliament, or its authority, and the Court declared it totally inaccurate to state any other Martial Law, as having any place whatever within the realm of England. In that country, and in these states, by Martial Law is understood the jurisprudence of these cases, which are decided by military judges or Courts Martial. When Martial Law is established, and prevails in any country, said lord Loughborough, in the case cited, it is totally of a different nature from that which is inaccurately called Martial Law (because the decisions are by a Court Martial) but which bears no affinity to that which was formerly attempted to be exercised in this kingdom, *which was contrary to the Constitution* and which has been for a century totally exploded. When Martial Law prevails, continues the judge, the authority under which it is exercised claims jurisdiction over all *military* persons in *all* circumstances: even their *debts* are subject to inquiry by military authority, every species of offence committed by any person *who appertains to the army* is tried, not by a civil judicature, but by the judicature of the corps or regiment to which he belongs.

This is Martial law as defined by Hale and Blackstone, and which the Court declared not to exist in England. Yet, it is confined to *military* persons. Here it is contended, and the Court must admit, if we sustain the objection, that it extends to *all* persons, that it dissolves for a while the government of the state.

Yet, according to our laws, all military courts are under a constant subordination to the ordinary courts of law. Officers who have abused their powers though only in regard to their own soldiers, are liable to prosecution in a Court of law, and compelled to make satisfaction. Even any flagrant abuse of authority by members of a Court Martial, when sitting to judge their own people, and determine in cases entirely of a military kind, makes them liable to the animadversion of the Civil Judge, *Delolme*, 447, *Jacob's Law Dict. Verbo Court Martial*. How preposterous then the idea that a military commander may, by his own authority, destroy the tribunal established by law as the asylum of those oppressed by military despotism!

. . . . .

DERBIGNY, J. On the first question, that which concerns the effect which the publication of the *Martial Law* has produced, with respect to the civil authorities, we might well have omitted giving a written opinion, now that the return of peace has re-established the empire of the laws; but, having declared, on the day on which the discussion of this subject took place, that the powers vested in us by law could not be suspended by any but legislative authority, it is proper that we should give some explanation of the reasons on which that declaration was founded.

I will, therefore, examine how *Martial Law* ought to be understood among us, and how far it introduces an alteration in the ordinary course of government.

To have a correct idea of *Martial Law* in a free country, examples must not be sought in the arbitrary conduct of absolute governments. The monarch, who unites in his hands all the powers, may delegate to his generals an authority unbounded as his own. But in a republic where the constitution has fixed the extent and limits of every branch of government in time of war, as well as of peace, there can exist nothing vague, uncertain or arbitrary in the exercise of any authority.

The Constitution of the United States, in which every thing necessary to the general and individual security has been foreseen, does not provide, that in times of public danger, the executive power shall reign to the exclusion of

all others. It does not trust into the hands of a dictator the reins of the government. The framers of that charter were too well aware of the hazards to which they would have exposed the fate of the republic by such a provision; and had they done it, the states would have rejected a constitution stained with a clause so threatening to their liberties. In the mean time, conscious of the necessity of removing all impediments to the exercise of the executive power, in cases of rebellion or invasion, they have permitted Congress to suspend the privilege of the writ of *Habeas Corpus* in those circumstances, if the public safety should require it. Thus far, and no farther, goes the Constitution. Congress, has not hitherto thought it necessary to authorize that suspension. Should the case ever happen, it is to be supposed that it would be accompanied with such restrictions, as would prevent any wanton abuse of power. "In England (says the author of a justly celebrated work on the Constitution of that country) at the time of the invasion of the pretender, assisted by the forces of hostile nations, the *Habeas Corpus* act was indeed suspended; but the executive power did not thus of itself stretch its own authority; the precaution was deliberated upon, and taken by the representatives of the people; and the detaining of individuals in consequence of the suspension of the act was limited to a fixed time. Notwithstanding the just fears of internal and hidden enemies, which the circumstances of the times might raise, the deviation from the former course of the law was carried no further than the single point we have mentioned. Persons detained by order of the government were to be dealt with in the same manner as those arrested at the suit of private individuals: the proceedings against them were to be carried on no otherwise than in a public place; they were to be tried by their peers, and have all the usual legal means of defence allowed to them, such as calling of witnesses, peremptory challenge of jurors, &c." and can it be asserted that while British subjects are thus secured against oppression in the worst of times, American citizens are left at the mercy of the will of an individual, who may, in certain cases, *the necessity of which is to be judged of by himself*, assume a supreme, overbearing, unbounded power! The idea is not only repugnant to the principles of any free government, but subversive of the very foundations of our own.

Under the constitution and laws of the United States, the President has a right to call, or cause to be called into the service of the United States, even the whole militia of any part of the union, in case of invasion. This power, exercised here by his delegate, has placed all the citizens subject to militia duty under military authority and military law. *That* I conceive to be the extent of the *Martial Law*, beyond which, all is usurpation of power. In that state of things the course of judicial proceedings is certainly much shackled, but the judicial authority exists, and ought to be exercised whenever it is practicable. Even where circumstances have made it necessary to suspend the privilege of the writ of *Habeas Corpus*, and such suspension has been pronounced by the competent authority, there is no reason why the administration of justice generally should be stopped. For, because the citizens are deprived temporarily of the protection of the tribunals as to the safety of their persons, it does by no means follow that they cannot have recourse to them in all other cases.

The proclamation of the *Martial Law*, therefore, cannot have had any other effect than that of placing under military authority all the citizens subject to militia service. It is in that sense alone that the vague expression of *Martial Law* ought to be understood among us. To give it any larger extent would be trampling upon the constitution and laws of our country.

But the counsel for the appellant, to support his assertion that in the circumstances then existing, the Court could not administer justice, went further and said, that the city of New-Orleans had become a camp, since it had pleased the General of the seventh military district to declare it so, and that within the precincts of a camp there can exist no other authority than that of the commanding officer. If the premises were true, the consequence would certainly follow. But the abuse of words cannot change the situation of things. A camp is a space of ground occupied by an army for their temporary habitation while, they keep the field. That space has limits: it does not extend beyond the ground actually occupied by the army. The camp of the American army during the invasion of our territory by the British, was placed at the distance of four miles below the city. During that time the city might be considered as a besieged place, having an entrenched camp in front. But the transformation of the city itself into a camp by the mere declaration of the General, is no more to be conceived, than would the transformation of a camp into a city by the same means.

It is therefore our opinion that the authority of courts of justice has not been suspended *of right* by the proclamation of the *Martial Law*, nor by the declaration of the general of the seventh military district that the city of New-Orleans was a camp; and we now repeat what we declared when the subject was discussed, "that the powers vested in us by law can be suspended by none but legislative authority."

. . . . .

The doctrine established, in the first part of the opinion of the Court, in the above case, is corroborated by the decision of the District Court of the United States for the Louisiana District, in the case of *United States* vs. *Jackson*, in which the defendant, having acted in opposition to it, was fined $1000. In *Lamb's case*, Judge Bay, of South Carolina, recognised the definition of Martial Law, given by this Court, expressing himself thus: "If by Martial Law is to be understood that dreadful system, the *law of arms*, which in former times was exercised by the King of England and his Lieutenants when *his word was the law*, and his *will the power*, by which it was *exercised*, I have no hesitation in saying that such a monster could not exist in this land of liberty and freedom. The political atmosphere of America would destroy it in embryo. It was against such a tyrannical monster that we triumphed in our revolutionary conflict. Our fathers sealed the conquest by their blood, and their posterity will never permit it to tarnish our soil by its unhallowed feet, or harrow up the feelings of our gallant sons, by its ghastly appearance. All our civil institutions forbid it and the manly hearts of our contrymen are steeled against it. But, if by this military code are to be understood the rules and regulations for the government of our men in arms, when marshalled in defence of our country's rights and honor, then I am bound to say, there is nothing unconstitutional in such a system." *Car. Law Rep.* 330.

13

WILLIAM RAWLE, A VIEW OF THE CONSTITUTION OF THE UNITED STATES 295–304, 305–7
1829 (2d ed.)

The Union is an association of the people of republics; its preservation is calculated to depend on the preservation of those republics. The people of each pledge themselves to preserve that form of government in all. Thus each becomes responsible to the rest, that no other form of government shall prevail in it, and all are bound to preserve it in every one.

But the mere compact, without the power to enforce it, would be of little value. Now this power can be no where so properly lodged, as in the Union itself. Hence, the term guarantee, indicates that the United States are authorized to oppose, and if possible, prevent every state in the Union from relinquishing the republican form of government, and as auxiliary means, they are expressly authorized and required to employ their force on the application of the constituted authorities of each state, "*to repress domestic violence.*" If a faction should attempt to subvert the government of a state for the purpose of destroying its republican form, the paternal power of the Union could thus be called forth to subdue it.

Yet it is not to be understood, that its interposition would be justifiable, if the people of a state should determine to retire from the Union, whether they adopted another or retained the same form of government, or if they should, with the express intention of seceding, expunge the representative system from their code, and thereby incapacitate themselves from concurring according to the mode now prescribed, in the choice of certain public officers of the United States.

The principle of representation, although certainly the wisest and best, is not essential to the being of a republic, but to continue a member of the Union, it must be preserved, and therefore the guarantee must be so construed. It depends on the state itself to retain or abolish the principle of representation, because it depends on itself whether it will continue a member of the Union. To deny this right would be inconsistent with the principle on which all our political systems are founded, which is, that the people have in all cases, a right to determine how they will be governed.

This right must be considered as an ingredient in the original composition of the general government, which, though not expressed, was mutually understood, and the doctrine heretofore presented to the reader in regard to the indefeasible nature of personal allegiance, is so far qualified in respect to allegiance to the United States. It was observed, that it was competent for a state to make a compact with its citizens, that the reciprocal obligations of protection and allegiance might cease on certain events; and it was further observed, that allegiance would necessarily cease on the dissolution of the society to which it was due.

The states, then, may wholly withdraw from the Union, but while they continue, they must retain the character of representative republics. Governments of dissimilar forms and principles cannot long maintain a binding coalition. "Greece," says Montesquieu, "was undone as soon as the king of Macedon obtained a seat in the amphyctionic council." It is probable, however, that the disproportionate force as well as the monarchical form of the new confederate had its share of influence in the event. But whether the historical fact supports the theory or not, the principle in respect to ourselves is unquestionable.

We have associated as republics. Possessing the power to form monarchies, republics were preferred and instituted. The history of the ancient, and the state of the present world, are before us. Of modern republics, Venice, Florence, the United Provinces, Genoa, all but Switzerland have disappeared. They have sunk beneath the power of monarchy, impatient at beholding the existence of any other form than its own. An injured province of Turkey, recalling to its mind the illustrious deeds of its ancestors, has ventured to resist its oppressors, and with a revival of the name of Greece, a hope is entertained of the permanent institution of another republic. But monarchy stands by with a jealous aspect, and fearful lest its own power should be endangered by the revival of the maxim, that sovereignty can ever reside in the people, affects a cold neutrality, with the probable anticipation that it will conduce to barbarian success. Yet that gallant country, it is trusted, will persevere. An enlightened people, disciplined through necessity, and emboldened even by the gloom of its prospects, may accomplish what it would not dare to hope.

This abstract principle, this aversion to the extension of republican freedom, is now invigorated and enforced by an alliance avowedly for the purpose of overpowering all efforts to relieve mankind from their shackles. It is essentially and professedly the exaltation of monarchies over republics, and even over every alteration in the forms of monarchy, tending to acknowledge or secure the rights of the people. The existence of such a combination warrants and requires that in some part of the civilized world, the republican system should be able to defend itself. But this would be imperfectly done, by the erection of separate, independent, though contiguous governments. They must be collected into a body, strong in proportion to the firmness of its union; respected and feared in proportion to its strength. The principle on which alone the Union is rendered valuable, and which alone can continue it, is the preservation of the republican form.

In what manner this guaranty shall be effectuated is not explained, and it presents a question of considerable nicety and importance.

Not a word in the Constitution is intended to be inoperative, and one so significant as the present was not lightly inserted. The United States are therefore bound to carry it into effect whenever the occasion arises, and finding as we do, in the same clause, the engagement to protect each state against domestic violence, which can only be by the arms of the Union, we are assisted in a due construction of the means of enforcing the guaranty. If the majority of the people of a state deliberately and peaceably resolve to relinquish the republican form of government, they cease to be members of the Union. If a faction, an inferior number, make such an effort, and endeavour to enforce it by violence, the case provided for will have arisen, and the Union is bound to employ its power to prevent it.

The power and duty of the United States to interfere with the particular concerns of a state are not, however, limited to the violent efforts of a party to alter its constitution. If from any other motives, or under any other pretexts, the internal peace and order of the state are disturbed, and its own powers are insufficient to suppress the commotion, it becomes the duty of its proper government to apply to the Union for protection. This is founded on the sound principle that those in whom the force of the Union is vested, in diminution of the power formerly possessed by the state, are bound to exercise it for the good of the whole, and upon the obvious and direct interest that the whole possesses in the peace and tranquillity of every part. At the same time it is properly provided, in order that such interference may not wantonly or arbitrarily take place; that it shall only be on the request of the state authorities: otherwise the self-government of the state might be encroached upon at the pleasure of the Union, and a small state might fear or feel the effects of a combination of larger states against it under colour of constitutional authority; but it is manifest, that in every part of this excellent system, there has been the utmost care to avoid encroachments on the internal powers of the different states, whenever the general good did not imperiously require it.

No form of application for this assistance is pointed out, nor has been provided by any act of congress, but the natural course would be to apply to the president, or officer for the time being, exercising his functions. No occasional act of the legislature of the United States seems to be necessary, where the duty of the president is pointed out by the Constitution, and great injury might be sustained, if the power was not promptly exercised.

In the instance of foreign invasion, the duty of immediate and unsolicited protection is obvious, but the generic term *invasion*, which is used without any qualification, may require a broader construction.

If among the improbable events of future times, we shall see a state forgetful of its obligation to refer its controversies with another state to the judicial power of the Union, endeavour by force to redress its real or imaginary wrongs, and actually invade the other state, we shall perceive a case in which the supreme power of the Union may justly interfere: perhaps we may say is bound to do so.

The invaded state, instead of relying merely on its own strength for defence, and instead of gratifying its revenge by retaliation, may prudently call for and gratefully receive the strong arm of the Union to repel the invasion, and reduce the combatants to the equal level of suitors in the high tribunal provided for them. In this course, the political estimation of neither state could receive any degradation. The decision of the controversy would only be regulated by the purest principles of justice, and the party really injured, would be certain of having the decree in its favour carried into effect.

It rests with the Union, and not with the states separately or individually, to increase the number of its members. The admission of another state can only take place on its own application. We have already seen, that in the formation of colonies under the denomination of territories, the habit has been, to assure to them their formation into states when the population should become sufficiently large. On that event, the inhabitants acquire a right to assemble and form a constitution for themselves, and the United States are considered as bound to admit the new state into the Union, provided its form of government be that of a representative republic. This is the only check or control possessed by the United States in this respect.

If a measure so improbable should occur in the colony, as the adoption of a monarchical government, it could not be received into the Union, although it assumed the appellation of a state, but the guaranty of which we have spoken, would not literally apply—the guaranty is intended to secure republican institutions to states, and does not in terms extend to colonies. As soon, however, as a state is formed out of a colony, and admitted into the Union, it becomes the common concern to enforce the continuance of the republican form. There can be no doubt, however, that the new state may decline to apply for admission into the Union, but it does not seem equally clear, that if its form of government coincided with the rules already mentioned, its admission could be refused. The inhabitants emigrate from the United States, and foreigners are permitted to settle, under the express or implied compact, that when the proper time arrives, they shall become members of the great national community, without being left to an exposed and unassisted independence, or compelled to throw themselves into the arms of a foreign power. It would seem, however, that the constitution adopted, ought to be submitted to the consideration of congress, but it would not be necessary that this measure should take place at the time of its formation, and it would be sufficient if it were presented and approved at the time of its admission. The practice of congress has not, however, corresponded with these positions, no previous approbation of the constitution has been deemed necessary.

It must also be conceded, that the people of the new state retain the same power to alter their constitution, that is enjoyed by the people of the older states, and provided such alterations are not carried so far as to extinguish the republican principle, their admission is not affected.

The secession of a state from the Union depends on the will of the people of such state. The people alone as we have already seen, hold the power to alter their constitution. The Constitution of the United States is to a certain extent, incorporated into the constitutions of the several states by the act of the people. The state legislatures have only to perform certain organical operations in respect to it. To withdraw from the Union comes not within the general scope of their delegated authority. There must be an express provision to that effect inserted in the state constitutions. This is not at present the case with any of them, and it would perhaps be impolitic to confide it to them. A matter so momentous, ought not to be entrusted to those who would have it in their power to exercise it lightly and precipitately upon sudden dissatisfaction, or causeless jealousy, perhaps against the interests and the wishes of a majority of their constituents.

But in any manner by which a secession is to take place, nothing is more certain than that the act should be deliberate, clear, and unequivocal. The perspicuity and solemnity of the original obligation require correspondent qualities in its dissolution. The powers of the general government cannot be defeated or impaired by an ambiguous or implied secession on the part of the state, although a secession may perhaps be conditional. The people of the state may have some reasons to complain in respect to acts of the general government, they may in such cases invest some of their own officers with the power of negotiation, and may declare an absolute secession in case of their failure. Still, however, the secession must in such case be distinctly and peremptorily declared to take place on that event, and in such case—as in the case of an unconditional secession,—the previous ligament with the Union, would be legitimately and fairly destroyed. But in either case the people is the only moving power.

A suggestion relative to this part of the subject has appeared in print, which the author conceives to require notice.

It has been laid down that if all the states, or a majority of them, refuse to elect senators, the legislative powers of the Union will be suspended.

Of the first of these supposed cases there can be no doubt. If one of the necessary branches of legislation is wholly withdrawn, there can be no further legislation, but if a part, although the greater part of either branch should be withdrawn it would not affect the power of those who remained.

In no part of the Constitution is a specific number of states required for a legislative act. Under the articles of confederation the concurrence of nine states was requisite for many purposes. If five states had withdrawn from that Union, it would have been dissolved. In the present Constitution there is no specification of numbers after the first formation. It was foreseen that there would be a natural tendency to increase the number of states with the increase of population then anticipated and now so fully verified. It was also known, though it was not avowed, that a state might withdraw itself. The number would therefore be variable.

· · · · ·

To withdraw from the Union is a solemn, serious act. Whenever it may appear expedient to the people of a state, it must be manifested in a direct and unequivocal manner. If it is ever done indirectly, the people must refuse to elect representatives, as well as to suffer their legislature to re-appoint senators. The senator whose time had not yet expired, must be forbidden to continue in the exercise of his functions.

But without plain, decisive measures of this nature, proceeding from the only legitimate source, the people, the United States cannot consider their legislative powers over such states suspended, nor their executive or judicial powers any way impaired, and they would not be obliged to desist from the collection of revenue within such state.

As to the remaining states among themselves, there is no opening for a doubt.

Secessions may reduce the number to the smallest integer admitting combination. They would remain united under the same principles and regulations among themselves that now apply to the whole. For a state cannot be compelled by other states to withdraw from the Union, and therefore, if two or more determine to remain united, although all the others desert them, nothing can be discovered in the Constitution to prevent it.

The consequences of an absolute secession cannot be mistaken, and they would be serious and afflicting.

The seceding state, whatever might be its relative magnitude, would speedily and distinctly feel the loss of the aid and countenance of the Union. The Union losing a proportion of the national revenue, would be entitled to demand from it a proportion of the national debt. It would be entitled to treat the inhabitants and the commerce of the separated state, as appertaining to a foreign country. In public treaties already made, whether commercial or political, it could claim no participation, while foreign powers would unwillingly calculate, and slowly transfer to it, any portion of the respect and confidence borne towards the United States.

Evils more alarming may readily be perceived. The destruction of the common band would be unavoidably attended with more serious consequences than the mere disunion of the parts.

Separation would produce jealousies and discord, which in time would ripen into mutual hostilities, and while our country would be weakened by internal war, foreign enemies would be encouraged to invade with the flattering prospect of subduing in detail, those whom, collectively, they would dread to encounter.

Such in ancient times was the fate of Greece, broken into numerous independent republics. Rome, which pursued a contrary policy, and absorbed all her territorial acquisitions in one great body, attained irresistible power.

But it may be objected, that Rome also has fallen. It is true; and such is the history of man. Natural life and political existence alike give way at the appointed measure of time, and the birth, decay, and extinction of empires only serve to prove the tenuity and illusion of the deepest schemes of the statesman, and the most elaborate theories of the philosopher. Yet it is always our duty to inquire into, and establish those plans and forms of civil association most conducive to present happiness and long duration: the rest we must leave to Divine Providence, which hitherto has so graciously smiled on the United States of America.

We may contemplate a dissolution of the Union in another light, more disinterested but not less dignified, and consider whether we are not only bound to ourselves but to the world in general, anxiously and faithfully to preserve it.

The first example which has been exhibited of a perfect self-government, successful beyond the warmest hopes of its authors, ought never to be withdrawn while the means of preserving it remain.

If in other countries, and particularly in Europe, a systematic subversion of the political rights of man shall gradually overpower all rational freedom, and endanger all political happiness, the failure of our example should not be held up as a discouragement to the legitimate opposition of the sufferers; if, on the other hand, an emancipated people should seek a model on which to frame their own structure; our Constitution, as permanent in its duration as it is sound and splendid in its principles, should remain to be their guide.

In every aspect therefore which this great subject presents, we feel the deepest impression of a sacred obligation to preserve the union of our country; we feel our glory, our safety, and our happiness, involved in it; we unite the interests of those who coldly calculate advantages with those who glow with what is little short of filial affection; and we must resist the attempt of its own citizens to destroy it, with the same feelings that we should avert the dagger of the parricide.

14

JOSEPH STORY, COMMENTARIES ON THE CONSTITUTION 3:§§ 1808, 1819
1833

§ 1808. The want of a provison of this nature was felt, as a capital defect in the plan of the confederation, as it might in its consequences endanger, if not overthrow, the Union. Without a guaranty, the assistance to be derived from the national government in repelling domestic dangers, which might threaten the existence of the state constitutions, could not be demanded, as a right, from the national government. Usurpation might raise its standard, and trample upon the liberties of the people, while the national government could legally do nothing more, than behold the encroachments with indignation and regret. A successful faction might erect a tyranny on the ruins of order and law; while no succour could be constitutionally afforded by the Union to the friends and supporters of the government. But this is not all. The destruction of the national government itself, or of neighbouring states, might result from a successful rebellion in a single state. Who can determine, what would have been the issue, if the insurrection in Massachusetts, in 1787, had been successful, and the malecontents had been headed by a Caesar or a Cromwell? If a despotic or monarchical government were established in one state, it would bring on the ruin of the whole republic. Montesquieu has acutely remarked, that confederated governments should be formed only between states, whose form of government is not only similar, but also republican.

. . . . .

§ 1819. It may not be amiss further to observe, (in the language of another commentator,) that every pretext for intermeddling with the domestic concerns of any state, under colour of protecting it against domestic violence, is taken away by that part of the provision, which renders an application from the legislature, or executive authority of the state endangered necessary to be made to the general government, before its interference can be at all proper.

On the other hand, this article becomes an immense acquisition of strength, and additional force to the aid of any state government, in case of an internal rebellion, or insurrection against its authority. The southern states, being more peculiarly open to danger from this quarter, ought (he adds) to be particularly tenacious of a constitution, from which they may derive such assistance in the most critical periods.

SEE ALSO:

Generally vol. 1, ch. 4; 1.8.15; 1.8.16
David Howell to Jonathan Arnold, 21 Feb. 1784, Staples, Rhode Island in the Continental Congress 1765–90, 479–81 (1870)
Northwest Ordinance, 13 July 1787, Tansill 47–54
Timothy Fuller, Admission of Missouri, House of Representatives, 15 Feb. 1819, Annals 33:1180–83

Article 5

The Congress, whenever two thirds of both Houses shall deem it necessary, shall propose Amendments to this Constitution, or, on the Application of the Legislatures of two thirds of the several States, shall call a Convention for proposing Amendments, which, in either Case, shall be valid to all Intents and Purposes, as Part of this Constitution, when ratified by the Legislatures of three fourths of the several States, or by Conventions in three fourths thereof, as the one or the other Mode of Ratification may be proposed by the Congress; Provided that no Amendment which may be made prior to the Year One thousand eight hundred and eight shall in any Manner affect the first and fourth Clauses in the Ninth Section of the first Article; and that no State, without its Consent, shall be deprived of it's equal Suffrage in the Senate.

1

VERMONT CONSTITUTION OF 1786, CH. 2, ART. 40
Thorpe 6:3760–61

XL. In order that the freedom of this Commonwealth may be preserved inviolate forever, there shall be chosen by ballot, by the freemen of this State, on the last Wednesday in March, in the year one thousand seven hundred and eighty-five, and on the last Wednesday in March in every seven years thereafter, thirteen persons, who shall be chosen in the same manner the Council is chosen, except that they shall not be out of the Council or General Assembly, to be called the Council of Censors; who shall meet together on the first Wednesday of June next ensuing their election, the majority of whom shall be a quorum in every case, except as to calling a convention, in which two-thirds of the whole number elected shall agree: and whose duty it shall be to inquire whether the Constitution has been preserved inviolate in every part, during the last septenary (including the year of their service;) and whether the legislative and executive branches of government have performed their duty, as guardians of the people, or assumed to themselves, or exercised other or greater powers than they are entitled to by the Constitution: they are also to inquire, whether the public taxes have been justly laid and collected in all parts of this Commonwealth—in what manner the public monies have been disposed of—and whether the laws have been duly executed. For these purposes, they shall have power to send for persons, papers, and records; they shall have authority to pass public censures—to order impeachments—and to recommend to the Legislature the repealing such laws as appear to them to have been enacted contrary to the principles of the Constitution; these powers they shall continue to have, for, and during the space of one year from the day of their election, and no longer. The said Council of Censors shall also have power to call a Convention, to meet within two years after their sitting, if there appears to them an absolute necessity of amending any article of this Constitution which may be defective—explaining such as may be thought not clearly expressed—and of adding such as are necessary for the preservation of the rights and happiness of the people; but the articles to be amended, and the amendments proposed and such articles as are proposed to be added or abolished, shall be promulgated at least six months before the day appointed for the election of such Convention, for the previous consideration of the people, that they may have an opportunity of instructing their delegates on the subject.

2

RECORDS OF THE FEDERAL CONVENTION

[1:22; Madison, 29 May]

13. Resd. that provision ought to be made for the amendment of the Articles of Union whensoever it shall seem necessary, and that the assent of the National Legislature ought not to be required thereto.

[1:121; Madison, 5 June]

propos: 13. "that provision ought to be made for hereafter amending the system now to be established, without requiring the assent of the Natl. Legislature." being taken up.

Mr. Pinkney doubted the propriety or necessity of it.

Mr. Gerry favored it. The novelty & difficulty of the experiment requires periodical revision. The prospect of such a revision would also give intermediate stability to the Govt. Nothing had yet happened in the States where this provision existed to proves its impropriety.—The Proposition was postponed for further consideration: the votes being. Mas: Con. N. Y. Pa. Del. Ma. N. C.—ay Virga. S. C. Geo: no

[1:202; Madison, 11 June]

Resolution 13. for amending the national Constitution hereafter without consent of Natl. Legislature being considered, several members did not see the necessity of the Resolution at all, nor the propriety of making the consent of the Natl. Legisl. unnecessary.

Col. Mason urged the necessity of such a provision. The plan now to be formed will certainly be defective, as the Confederation has been found on trial to be. Amendments therefore will be necessary, and it will be better to provide for them, in an easy, regular and Constitutional way than to trust to chance and violence. It would be improper to require the consent of the Natl. Legislature, because they may abuse their power, and refuse their consent on that very account. The opportunity for such an abuse, may be the fault of the Constitution calling for amendmt.

Mr. Randolph enforced these arguments.

The words, "without requiring the consent of the Natl. Legislature" were postponed. The other provision in the clause passed nem. con.

[2:159; Committee of Detail, VIII]

This Constitution ought to be amended whenever such Amendment shall become necessary; and on the Application of the Legislatures of two thirds of the States in the Union, the Legislature of the United States shall call a Convention for that Purpose.

[2:188; Madison, 6 Aug.]

XIX

On the application of the Legislatures of two thirds of the States in the Union, for an amendment of this Constitution, the Legislature of the United States shall call a Convention for that purpose.

[2:461; *Journal, 30 Aug.*]

On the question to agree to the 19 article as reported it passed in the affirmative

[2:461; *Madison, 30 Aug.*]

Mr. Govr. Morris suggested that the Legislature should be left at liberty to call a Convention, whenever they please.

The art: was agreed to nem: con:

[2:557; *Madison, 10 Sept.*]

Mr Gerry moved to reconsider art XIX. viz, "On the application of the Legislatures of two thirds of the States in the Union, for an amendment of this Constitution, the Legislature of the U. S. shall call a Convention for that purpose." (see Aug. 6)

This Constitution he said is to be paramount to the State Constitutions. It follows, hence, from this article that two thirds of the States may obtain a Convention, a majority of which can bind the Union to innovations that may subvert the State-Constitutions altogether. He asked whether this was a situation proper to be run into—

Mr. Hamilton 2ded. the motion, but he said with a different view from Mr. Gerry—He did not object to the consequences stated by Mr. Gerry—There was no greater evil in subjecting the people of the U. S. to the major voice than the people of a particular State—It had been wished by many and was much to have been desired that an easier mode for introducing amendments had been provided by the articles of Confederation. It was equally desirable now that an easy mode should be established for supplying defects which will probably appear in the new System. The mode proposed was not adequate. The State Legislatures will not apply for alterations but with a view to increase their own powers—The National Legislature will be the first to perceive and will be most sensible to the necessity of amendments, and ought also to be empowered, whenever two thirds of each branch should concur to call a Convention—There could be no danger in giving this power, as the people would finally decide in the case.

Mr Madison remarked on the vagueness of the terms, "call a Convention for the purpose." as sufficient reason for reconsidering the article. How was a Convention to be formed? by what rule decide? what the force of its acts?

On the motion of Mr. Gerry to reconsider

N. H. divd. Mas. ay—Ct. ay. N. J.—no. Pa ay. Del. ay. Md. ay. Va. ay. N—C. ay. S. C. ay. Geo. ay. [Ayes—9; noes—1; divided—1.]

Mr. Sherman moved to add to the article "or the Legislature may propose amendments to the several States for their approbation, but no amendments shall be binding until consented to by the several States"

Mr. Gerry 2ded. the motion

Mr. Wilson moved to insert "two thirds of" before the words "several States"—on which amendment to the motion of Mr. Sherman

N. H. ay. Mas. no Ct. no. N. J. no Pa. ay—Del—ay Md. ay. Va. ay. N. C. no. S. C. no. Geo. no. [Ayes—5; noes—6.]

Mr. Wilson then moved to insert "three fourths of" before "the several Sts" which was agreed to nem: con:

Mr. Madison moved to postpone the consideration of the amended proposition in order to take up the following,

"The Legislature of the U—S—whenever two thirds of both Houses shall deem necessary, or on the application of two thirds of the Legislatures of the several States, shall propose amendments to this Constitution, which shall be valid to all intents and purposes as part thereof, when the same shall have been ratified by three fourths at least of the Legislatures of the several States, or by Conventions in three fourths thereof, as one or the other mode of ratification may be proposed by the Legislature of the U. S:"

Mr. Hamilton 2ded. the motion.

Mr. Rutlidge said he never could agree to give a power by which the articles relating to slaves might be altered by the States not interested in that property and prejudiced against it. In order to obviate this objection, these words were added to the proposition: "provided that no amendments which may be made prior to the year 1808. shall in any manner affect the 4 & 5 sections of the VII article"—The postponement being agreed to,

On the question On the proposition of Mr. Madison & Mr. Hamilton as amended

N. H. divd. Mas. ay. Ct. ay. N. J. ay. Pa. ay. Del. no. Md. ay. Va ay. N. C. ay S. C. ay. Geo. ay. [Ayes—9; noes—1; divided—1.]

[2:629; *Madison, 15 Sept.*]

Art—V. "The Congress, whenever two thirds of both Houses shall deem necessary, or on the application of two thirds of the Legislatures of the several States shall propose amendments to this Constitution, which shall be valid to all intents and purposes as part thereof, when the same shall have been ratified by three fourths at least of the Legislatures of the several States, or by Conventions in three fourths thereof, as the one or the other mode of ratification may be proposed by the Congress: Provided that no amendment which may be made prior to the year 1808 shall in any manner affect the 1 & 4 clauses in the 9. section of article I."

Mr. Sherman expressed his fears that three fourths of the States might be brought to do things fatal to particular States, as abolishing them altogether or depriving them of their equality in the Senate. He thought it reasonable that the proviso in favor of the States importing slaves should be extended so as to provide that no State should be affected in its internal police, or deprived of its equality in the Senate.

Col: Mason thought the plan of amending the Constitution exceptionable & dangerous. As the proposing of amendments is in both the modes to depend, in the first immediately, and in the second, ultimately, on Congress, no amendments of the proper kind would ever be obtained by the people, if the Government should become oppressive, as he verily believed would be the case.

Mr. Govr. Morris & Mr. Gerry moved to amend the article so as to require a Convention on application of ⅔ of the Sts

Mr Madison did not see why Congress would not be as much bound to propose amendments applied for by two thirds of the States as to call a call a Convention on the like application. He saw no objection however against providing for a Convention for the purpose of amendments, except only that difficulties might arise as to the form, the quorum &c. which in Constitutional regulations ought to be as much as possible avoided.

The motion of Mr. Govr Morris and Mr. Gerry was agreed to nem: con (see: the first part of the article as finally past)

Mr Sherman moved to strike out of art. V. after "legislatures" the words "of three fourths" and so after the word "Conventions" leaving future Conventions to act in this matter, like the present Conventions according to circumstances.

On this motion

N—H—divd. Mas—ay—Ct ay. N—J. ay—Pa no. Del—no. Md no. Va no. N. C. no. S—C. no. Geo—no. [Ayes—3; noes—7; divided—1.]

Mr Gerry moved to strike out the words "or by Conventions in three fourths thereof"

On this motion

N—H—no. Mas. no—Ct. ay. N—J. no. Pa no—Del—no. Md no. Va. no. N—C. no S. C. no—Geo—no. [Ayes—1; noes—10.]

M—Sherman moved according to his idea above expressed to annex to the end of the article a further proviso "that no State shall without its consent be affected in its internal police, or deprived of its equal suffrage in the Senate",

Mr. Madison. Begin with these special provisos, and every State will insist on them, for their boundaries, exports &c.

On the motion of Mr. Sherman

N. H—no. Mas. no. Ct ay. N. J. ay—Pa no. Del—ay. Md. no. Va. no N. C. no. S. C. no. Geo. no. [Ayes—3; noes—8.]

Mr. Sherman then moved to strike out art V altogether Mr Brearley 2ded. the motion, on which

N. H. no. Mas. no. Ct. ay. N. J. ay. Pa. no. Del. divd. Md. no. Va. no. N. C. no. S. C. no. Geo. no [Ayes—2; noes—8; divided—1.]

Mr. Govr Morris moved to annex a further proviso— "that no State, without its consent shall be deprived of its equal suffrage in the Senate"

This motion being dictated by the circulating murmurs of the small States was agreed to without debate, no one opposing it, or on the question, saying no.

3

CHARLES PINCKNEY, OBSERVATIONS ON THE PLAN OF GOVERNMENT
1787
Farrand 3:120–21

The 16th article proposes to declare, that if it should hereafter appear necessary to the United States to recommend the Grant of any additional Powers, that the assent of a given number of the States shall be sufficient to invest them and bind the Union as fully as if they had been confirmed by the Legislatures of all the States. The principles of this, and the article which provides for the future alteration of the Constitution by its being first agreed to in Congress, and ratified by a certain proportion of the Legislatures, are precisely the same; they both go to destroy that unanimity which upon these occasions the present System has unfortunately made necessary—the propriety of this alteration has been so frequently suggested, that I shall only observe that it is to this unanimous consent, the depressed situation of the Union is undoubtedly owing. Had the measures recommended by Congress and assented to, some of them by eleven and others by twelve of the States, been carried into execution, how different would have been the complexion of Public Affairs? To this weak, this absurd part of the Government, may all our distresses be fairly attributed.

If the States were equal in size and importance, a majority of the Legislatures might be sufficient for the grant of any new Powers; but disproportioned as they are and must continue for a time; a larger number may now in prudence be required—but I trust no Government will ever again be adopted in this Country, whose Alteration cannot be effected but by the assent of all its Members. The hazardous situation the United Netherlands are frequently placed in on this account, as well as our own mortifying experience, are sufficient to warn us from a danger which has already nearly proved fatal. It is difficult to form a Government so perfect as to render alterations unnecessary; we must expect and provide for them:—But difficult as the forming a perfect Government would be, it is scarcely more so, than to induce Thirteen separate Legislatures, to think and act alike upon one subject—the alterations that nine think necessary, ought not to be impeded by four—a minority so inconsiderable should be obliged to yield. Upon this principle the present articles are formed, and are in my judgment so obviously proper, that I think it unnecessary to remark farther upon them.

4

EDMUND RANDOLPH TO SPEAKER OF VIRGINIA HOUSE OF DELEGATES
10 Oct. 1787

(See 7, no. 4)

5

FEDERAL FARMER, NO. 4
12 Oct. 1787
Storing 2.8.58

It may also be worthy our examination, how far the provision for amending this plan, when it shall be adopted, is of any importance. No measures can be taken towards amendments, unless two-thirds of the congress, or two-thirds of the legislatures of the several states shall agree.—While power is in the hands of the people, or democratic part of the community, more especially as at present, it is easy, according to the general course of human affairs, for the few influential men in the community, to obtain conventions, alterations in government, and to persuade the common people they may change for the better, and to get from them a part of the power: But when power is once transferred from the many to the few, all changes become extremely difficult; the government, in this case, being beneficial to the few, they will be exceedingly artful and adroit in preventing any measures which may lead to a change; and nothing will produce it, but great exertions and severe struggles on the part of the common people. Every man of reflection must see, that the change now proposed, is a transfer of power from the many to the few, and the probability is, the artful and ever active aristocracy, will prevent all peaceable measures for changes, unless when they shall discover some favourable moment to increase their own influence. I am sensible, thousands of men in the United States, are disposed to adopt the proposed constitution, though they perceive it to be essentially defective, under an idea that amendments of it, may be obtained when necessary. This is a pernicious idea, it argues a servility of character totally unfit for the support of free government; it is very repugnant to that perpetual jealousy respecting liberty, so absolutely necessary in all free states, spoken of by Mr. Dickinson.—However, if our countrymen are so soon changed, and the language of 1774, is become odious to them, it will be in vain to use the language of freedom, or to attempt to rouse them to free enquiries: But I shall never believe this is the case with them, whatever present appearances may be, till I shall have very strong evidence indeed of it.

6

JAMES MADISON, FEDERALIST, NO. 43, 296
23 Jan. 1788

That useful alterations will be suggested by experience, could not but be foreseen. It was requisite therefore that a mode for introducing them should be provided. The mode preferred by the Convention seems to be stamped with every mark of propriety. It guards equally against that extreme facility which would render the Constitution too mutable; and that extreme difficulty which might perpetuate its discovered faults. It moreover equally enables the general and the state governments to originate the amendment of errors as they may be pointed out by the experience on one side or on the other. The exception in favour of the equality of suffrage in the Senate was probably meant as a palladium to the residuary sovereignty of the States, implied and secured by that principle of representation in one branch of the Legislature; and was probably insisted on by the States particularly attached to that equality. The other exception must have been admitted on the same considerations which produced the privilege defended by it.

7

DEBATE IN MASSACHUSETTS RATIFYING CONVENTION
30 Jan. 1788
Elliot 2:116–17

The Hon. Mr. KING observed, that he believed gentlemen had not, in their objections to the Constitution, recollected that this article was a part of it; for many of the arguments of gentlemen were founded on the idea of future amendments being impracticable. The honorable gentleman observed on the superior excellence of the proposed Constitution in this particular, and called upon gentlemen to produce an instance, in any other national constitution, where the people had so fair an opportunity to correct any abuse which might take place in the future administration of the government under it.

Dr. JARVIS. Mr. President, I cannot suffer the present article to be passed, without rising to express my entire and perfect approbation of it. Whatever may have been my private opinion of any other part, or whatever faults or imperfections I have remarked, or fancied I have seen, in any other instance, here, sir, I have found complete satisfaction: this has been a resting place, on which I have reposed myself in the fullest security, whenever a doubt has occurred, in considering any other passage in the proposed Constitution. The honorable gentleman last speaking has called upon those persons who are opposed to our receiving the present system, to show another government, in which such a wise precaution has been taken to secure to the people the right of making such alterations and amendments, in a peaceable way, as experience shall have proved to be necessary. Allow me to say, sir, as far as the narrow limits of my own information extend, I know of no such example. In other countries, sir,—unhappily for mankind,—the history of their respective revolutions has been written in blood; and it is in this only that any great or important change in our political situation has been effected, without public commotions. When we shall have adopted the Constitution before us, we shall have in this article an adequate provision for all the purposes of political reformation. If, in the course of its operation, this government shall appear to be too severe, here are the means by which this severity may be assuaged and corrected. If, on the other hand, it shall become too languid in its movements, here, again, we have a method designated, by which a new portion of health and spirit may be infused into the Constitution.

There is, sir, another view, which I have long since taken of this subject, which has produced the fullest conviction, in my own mind, in favor of our receiving the government which we have now in contemplation. Should it be rejected, I beg gentlemen would observe, that a concurrence of all the states must be had before a new convention can be called to form another Constitution; but the present article provides, upon nine states' concurring in any alteration or amendment to be proposed either by Congress or any future convention, that this situation shall be a part of the Constitution, equally powerful and obligatory with any other part. If it be alleged that this union is not likely to happen, will it be more likely that a union of a greater number of concurring sentiments may be had, as must be, in case we reject the Constitution in hopes of a better? But that this is practicable, we may safely appeal to the history of this country as a proof, in the last twenty years. We have united against the British; we have united in calling the late federal Convention; and we may certainly unite again in such alterations as in reason shall appear to be important for the peace and happiness of America.

In the constitution of this state, the article providing for alterations is limited in its operation to a given time; but in the present Constitution, the article is perfectly at large, unconfined to any period, and may admit of measures being taken in any moment after it is adopted. In this point it has undoubtedly the advantage. I shall not sit down, sir, without repeating, that, as it is clearly more difficult for twelve states to agree to another convention, than for nine to unite in favor of amendments, so it is certainly better to receive the present Constitution, in the hope of its being amended, than it would be to reject it altogether, with, perhaps, the vain expectation of obtaining another more agreeable than the present. I see no fallacy in the argument, Mr. President; but, if there is, permit me to call upon any gentleman to point it out, in order that it may be corrected; for, at present, it seems to me of such force as to give me entire satisfaction.

8

JAMES MADISON, FEDERALIST, NO. 49, 338–43
2 Feb. 1788

(See vol. 1, ch. 2, no. 19)

9

DEBATE IN VIRGINIA RATIFYING CONVENTION
5–6 June 1788
Elliot 3:49–51, 55–56, 88–89, 101–2

[*5 June*]

[Mr. PATRICK HENRY:] The way to amendment is, in my conception, shut. Let us consider this plain, easy way. "The Congress, whenever two thirds of both houses shall deem it necessary, shall propose amendments to this Constitution, or on the application of the legislatures of two thirds of the several states, shall call a Convention for proposing amendments, which, in either case, shall be valid to all intents and purposes, as part of this Constitution, when ratified by the legislatures of three fourths of the several states, or by the Conventions in three fourths thereof, as the one or the other mode of ratification may be proposed by the Congress. Provided, that no amendment which may be made prior to the year 1808, shall in any manner affect the 1st and 4th clauses in the 9th section of the 1st article; and that no state, without its consent, shall be deprived of its equal suffrage in the Senate."

Hence it appears that three fourths of the states must ultimately agree to any amendments that may be necessary. Let us consider the consequence of this. However uncharitable it may appear, yet I must tell my opinion—that the most unworthy characters may get into power, and prevent the introduction of amendments. Let us suppose—for the case is supposable, possible, and probable—that you happen to deal those powers to unworthy hands; will they relinquish powers already in their possession, or agree to amendments? Two thirds of the Congress, or of the state legislatures, are necessary even to propose amendments. If one third of these be unworthy men, they may prevent the application for amendments; but what is destructive and mischievous, is, that three fourths of the state legislatures, or of the state conventions, must concur in the amendments when proposed! In such numerous bodies, there must necessarily be some designing, bad men. To suppose that so large a number as three fourths of the states will concur, is to suppose that they will possess genius, intelligence, and integrity, approaching to miraculous. It would indeed be miraculous that they should concur in the same amendments, or even in such as would bear some likeness to one another; for four of the smallest states, that do not collectively contain one tenth part of the population of the United States, may obstruct the most salutary and necessary amendments. Nay, in these four states, six tenths of the people may reject these amendments; and suppose that amendments shall be opposed to amendments, which is highly probable,—is it possible that three fourths can ever agree to the same amendments? A bare majority in these four small states may hinder the adoption of amendments; so that we may fairly and justly conclude that one twentieth part of the American people may prevent the removal of the most grievous inconveniences and oppression, by refusing to accede to amendments. A trifling minority may reject the most salutary amendments. Is this an easy mode of securing the public liberty? It is, sir, a most fearful situation, when the most contemptible minority can prevent the alteration of the most oppressive government; for it may, in many respects, prove to be such. Is this the spirit of republicanism?

What, sir, is the genius of democracy? Let me read that clause of the bill of rights of Virginia which relates to this: 3d clause:—that government is, or ought to be, instituted for the common benefit, protection, and security of the people, nation, or community. Of all the various modes and forms of government, that is best, which is capable of producing the greatest degree of happiness and safety, and is most effectually secured against the danger of maladministration; and that whenever any government shall be found inadequate, or contrary to those purposes, a majority of the community hath an indubitable, unalienable, and indefeasible right to reform, alter, or abolish it, in such manner as shall be judged most conducive to the public weal.

This, sir, is the language of democracy—that a majority of the community have a right to alter government when found to be oppressive. But how different is the genius of your new Constitution from this! How different from the sentiments of freemen, that a contemptible minority can prevent the good of the majority! If, then, gentlemen, standing on this ground, are come to that point, that they are willing to bind themselves and their posterity to be oppressed, I am amazed and inexpressibly astonished. If this be the opinion of the majority, I must submit; but to me, sir, it appears perilous and destructive. I cannot help thinking so. Perhaps it may be the result of my age. These may be feelings natural to a man of my years, when the American spirit has left him, and his mental powers, like the members of the body, are decayed. If, sir, amendments are left to the twentieth, or tenth part of the people of America, your liberty is gone forever. We have heard that there is a great deal of bribery practised in the House of Commons, in England, and that many of the members raise themselves to preferments by selling the rights of the whole of the people. But, sir, the tenth part of that body cannot continue oppressions on the rest of the people. English liberty is, in this case, on a firmer foundation than American liberty. It will be easily contrived to procure the opposition of one tenth of the people to any alteration, however judicious. The honorable gentleman who presides told us that, to prevent abuses in our government, we will assemble in Convention, recall our delegated powers, and punish our servants for abusing the trust reposed in them. O sir, we should have fine times, indeed, if, to punish tyrants, it were only sufficient to assemble the people! Your arms, wherewith you could defend yourselves, are gone; and you have no longer an aristocratical, no longer a democratical spirit. Did you ever read of any revolution in a nation, brought about by the punishment of those in power, inflicted by those who had no power at all? You read of a riot act in a country which is called one of the freest in the world, where a few neighbors cannot assemble without the risk of being shot by a hired soldiery, the engines of despotism. We may see such an act in America.

. . . . .

[Mr. HENRY:] Will the great rights of the people be secured by this government? Suppose it should prove oppressive, how can it be altered? Our bill of rights declares, "that a majority of the community hath an indubitable, unalienable, and indefeasible right to reform, alter, or abolish it, in such manner as shall be judged most conducive to the public weal."

I have just proved that one tenth, or less, of the people of America—a most despicable minority—may prevent this reform or alteration. Suppose the people of Virginia should wish to alter their government; can a majority of them do it? No; because they are connected with other men, or, in other words, consolidated with other states. When the people of Virginia, at a future day, shall wish to alter their government, though they should be unanimous in this desire, yet they may be prevented therefrom by a despicable minority at the extremity of the United States. The founders of your own Constitution made your government changeable: but the power of changing it is gone from you. Whither is it gone? It is placed in the same hands that hold the rights of twelve other states; and those who hold those rights have right and power to keep them. It is not the particular government of Virginia: one of the leading features of that government is, that a majority can alter it, when necessary for the public good. This government is not a Virginian, but an American government. Is it not, therefore, a consolidated government? The sixth clause of your bill of rights tells you, "that elections of members to serve as representatives of the people in Assembly ought to be free, and that all men having sufficient evidence of permanent common interest with, and attachment to, the community, have the right of suffrage, and cannot be *taxed*, or deprived of their property for public uses, without their own consent, or that of their representatives so elected, nor bound by any law to which they have not in like manner assented for the public good." But what does this Constitution say? The clause under consideration gives an unlimited and unbounded power of taxation. Suppose every delegate from Virginia opposes a law laying a tax; what will it avail? They are opposed by a majority; eleven members can destroy their efforts: those feeble ten cannot prevent the passing the most oppressive tax law; so that, in direct opposition to the spirit and express language of your declaration of rights, you are taxed, not by your own consent, but by people who have no connection with you.

[6 June]

[Mr. MADISON:] He complains of this Constitution, because it requires the consent of at least three fourths of the states to introduce amendments which shall be necessary for the happiness of the people. The assent of so many he urges as too great an obstacle to the admission of salutary amendments, which, he strongly insists, ought to be at the will of a bare majority. We hear this argument, at the very moment we are called upon to assign reasons for proposing a constitution which puts it in the power of nine states to abolish the present inadequate, unsafe, and pernicious Confederation! In the first case, he asserts that a majority ought to have the power of altering the government, when found to be inadequate to the security of public happiness. In the last case, he affirms that even three fourths of the community have not a right to alter a government which experience has proved to be subversive of national felicity! nay, that the most necessary and urgent alterations cannot be made without the absolute unanimity of all the states! Does not the thirteenth article of the Confederation expressly require that no alteration shall be made without the unanimous consent of all the states? Could any thing in theory be more perniciously improvident and injudicious than this submission of the will of the majority to the most trifling minority? Have not experience and practice actually manifested this theoretical inconvenience to be extremely impolitic? Let me mention one fact, which I conceive must carry conviction to the mind of any one: the smallest state in the Union has obstructed every attempt to reform the government; that little member has repeatedly disobeyed and counteracted the general authority; nay, has even supplied the enemies of its country with provisions. Twelve states had agreed to certain improvements which were proposed, being thought absolutely necessary to preserve the existence of the general government; but as these improvements, though really indispensable, could not, by the Confederation, be introduced into it without the consent of every state, the refractory dissent of that little state prevented their adoption. The inconveniences resulting from this requisition, of unanimous concurrence in alterations in the Confederation, must be known to every member in this Convention; it is therefore needless to remind them of them. Is it not self-evident that a trifling minority ought not to bind the majority? Would not foreign influence be exerted with facility over a small minority? Would the honorable gentleman agree to continue the most radical defects in the old system, because the petty state of Rhode Island would not agree to remove them?

. . . . .

[Mr. NICHOLAS:] The worthy member has exclaimed, with uncommon vehemence, against the mode provided for securing amendments. He thinks amendments can never be obtained, because so great a number is required to concur. Had it rested solely with Congress, there might have been danger. The committee will see that there is another mode provided, besides that which originates with Congress. On the application of the legislatures of two thirds of the several states, a convention is to be called to propose amendments, which shall be a part of the Constitution when ratified by the legislatures of three fourths of the several states, or by conventions in three fourths thereof. It is natural to conclude that those states who will apply for calling the convention will concur in the ratification of the proposed amendments.

There are strong and cogent reasons operating on my mind, that the amendments, which shall be agreed to by those states, will be sooner ratified by the rest than any other that can be proposed. The conventions which shall be so called will have their deliberations confined to a few points; no local interest to divert their attention; nothing but the necessary alterations. They will have many advantages over the last Convention. No experiments to devise; the general and fundamental regulations being already laid down.

10

DEBATE IN NORTH CAROLINA RATIFYING CONVENTION
29 July 1788
Elliot 4:176–78

Mr. IREDELL. Mr. Chairman, this is a very important clause. In every other constitution of government that I have ever heard or read of, no provision is made for necessary amendments. The misfortune attending most constitutions which have been deliberately formed, has been, that those who formed them thought their wisdom equal to all possible contingencies, and that there could be no error in what they did. The gentlemen who framed this Constitution thought with much more diffidence of their capacities; and, undoubtedly, without a provision for amendment it would have been more justly liable to objection, and the characters of its framers would have appeared much less meritorious. This, indeed, is one of the greatest beauties of the system, and should strongly recommend it to every candid mind. The Constitution of any government which cannot be regularly amended when its defects are experienced, reduces the people to this dilemma—they must either submit to its oppressions, or bring about amendments, more or less, by a civil war. Happy this, the country we live in! The Constitution before us, if it be adopted, can be altered with as much regularity, and as little confusion, as any act of Assembly; not, indeed, quite so easily, which would be extremely impolitic; but it is a most happy circumstance, that there is a remedy in the system itself for its own fallibility, so that alterations can without difficulty be made, agreeable to the general sense of the people. Let us attend to the manner in which amendments may be made. The proposition for amendments may arise from Congress itself, when two thirds of both houses shall deem it necessary. If they should not, and yet amendments be generally wished for by the people, two thirds of the legislatures of the different states may require a general convention for the purpose, in which case Congress are under the necessity of convening one. Any amendments which either Congress shall propose, or which shall be proposed by such general convention, are afterwards to be submitted to the legislatures of the different states, or conventions called for that purpose, as Congress shall think proper, and, upon the ratification of three fourths of the states, will become a part of the Constitution. By referring this business to the legislatures, expense would be saved; and in general, it may be presumed, they would speak the genuine sense of the people. It may, however, on some occasions, be better to consult an immediate delegation for that special purpose. This is therefore left discretionary. It is highly probable that amendments agreed to in either of these methods would be conducive to the public welfare, when so large a majority of the states consented to them. And in one of these modes, amendments that are now wished for may, in a short time, be made to this Constitution by the states adopting it.

It is, however, to be observed, that the 1st and 4th clauses in the 9th section of the 1st article are protected from any alteration till the year 1808; and in order that no consolidation should take place, it is provided that no state shall, by any amendment or alteration, be ever deprived of an equal suffrage in the Senate without its own consent. The first two prohibitions are with respect to the census, (according to which direct taxes are imposed,) and with respect to the importation of slaves. As to the first, it must be observed, that there is a material difference between the Northern and Southern States. The Northern States have been much longer settled, and are much fuller of people, than the Southern, but have not land in equal proportion, nor scarcely any slaves. The subject of this article was regulated with great difficulty, and by a spirit of concession which it would not be prudent to disturb for a good many years. In twenty years, there will probably be a great alteration, and then the subject may be reconsidered with less difficulty and greater coolness. In the mean time, the compromise was upon the best footing that could be obtained. A compromise likewise took place in regard to the importation of slaves. It is probable that all the members reprobated this inhuman traffic; but those of South Carolina and Georgia would not consent to an immediate prohibition of it—one reason of which was, that, during the last war, they lost a vast number of negroes, which loss they wish to supply. In the mean time, it is left to the states to admit or prohibit the importation, and Congress may impose a limited duty upon it.

Mr. BASS observed, that it was plain that the introduction of amendments depended altogether on Congress.

Mr. IREDELL replied, that it was very evident that it did not depend on the will of Congress; for that the legislatures of two thirds of the states were authorized to make application for calling a convention to propose amendments, and, on such application, it is provided that Congress *shall* call such convention, so that they will have no option.

11

ST. GEORGE TUCKER,
BLACKSTONE'S COMMENTARIES
1:APP. 371–72
1803

11. Lastly; the fifth article provides the mode by which future amendments to the constitution may be proposed, discussed, and carried into effect, without hazarding a dissolution of the confederacy, or suspending the operations of the existing government. And this may be effected in two different modes: the first on recommendation from congress, whenever two thirds of both houses shall concur in the expediency of any amendment. The second, which secures to the states an influence in case congress should neglect to recommend such amendments, provides, that congress shall, on application from the legislatures of two thirds of the states, call a convention for proposing amendments; which in either case shall be valid to all intents and purposes as part of the constitution, when ratified by the legislatures of three fourths of the several states, or by conventions in three fourths thereof, as the one or the other mode, of the ratification may be proposed by the congress. Both of these provisions appear excellent. Of the utility and practicability of the former, we have already had most satisfactory experience. The latter will probably never be resorted to, unless the federal government should betray symptoms of corruption, which may render it expedient for the states to exert themselves in order to the application of some radical and effectual remedy. Nor can we too much applaud a constitution, which thus provides a safe, and peaceable remedy for its own defects, as they may from time to time be discovered. A change of government in other countries is almost always attended with convulsions which threaten its entire dissolution; and with scenes of horror, which deter mankind from any attempt to correct abuses, or remove oppressions until they have become altogether intolerable. In America we may reasonably hope, that neither of these evils need be apprehended; nor is there any reason to fear that this provision in the constitution will produce any degree of instability in the government; the mode both of originating and of ratifying amendments, in either mode which the constitution directs, must necessarily be attended with such obstacles, and delays, as must prove a sufficient bar against light, or frequent innovations. And as a further security against them, the same article further provides, that no amendment which may be made, prior to the year one thousand eight hundred and eight, shall, in any manner, affect those clauses of the ninth section of the first article, which relate to the migration or importation of such persons as the states may think proper to allow; and to the manner in which direct taxes shall be laid: and that no state, without its consent shall be deprived of its equal suffrage in the senate.

12

JOSEPH STORY, COMMENTARIES ON THE
CONSTITUTION 3:§§ 1821–24
1833

§ 1821. Upon this subject, little need be said to persuade us, at once, of its utility and importance. It is obvious, that no human government can ever be perfect; and that it is impossible to foresee, or guard against all the exigencies, which may, in different ages, require different adaptations and modifications of powers to suit the various necessities of the people. A government, forever changing and changeable, is, indeed, in a state bordering upon anarchy and confusion. A government, which, in its own organization, provides no means of change, but assumes to be fixed and unalterable, must, after a while, become wholly unsuited to the circumstances of the nation; and it will either degenerate into a despotism, or by the pressure of its inequalities bring on a revolution. It is wise, therefore, in every government, and especially in a republic, to provide means for altering, and improving the fabric of government, as time and experience, or the new phases of human affairs, may render proper, to promote the happiness and safety of the people. The great principle to be sought is to make the changes practicable, but not too easy; to secure due deliberation, and caution; and to follow experience, rather than to open a way for experiments, suggested by mere speculation or theory.

§ 1822. In regard to the constitution of the United States, it is confessedly a new experiment in the history of nations. Its framers were not bold or rash enough to believe, or to pronounce it to be perfect. They made use of the best lights, which they possessed, to form and adjust its parts, and mould its materials. But they knew, that time might develope many defects in its arrangements, and many deficiencies in its powers. They desired, that it might be open to improvement; and under the guidance of the sober judgment and enlightened skill of the country, to be perpetually approaching nearer and nearer to perfection. It was obvious, too, that the means of amendment might avert, or at least have a tendency to avert, the most serious perils, to which confederated republics are liable, and by which all have hitherto been shipwrecked. They knew, that the besetting sin of republics is a restlessness of temperament, and a spirit of discontent at slight evils. They knew the pride and jealousy of state power in confederacies; and they wished to disarm them of their potency, by providing a safe means to break the force, if not wholly to ward off the blows, which would, from time to time, under the garb of patriotism, or a love of the people, be aimed at the constitution. They believed, that the power of amendment was, if one may so say, the safety valve to let off all temporary effervescences and excitements; and the real effective instrument to control and adjust the movements of the machinery, when out of order, or in danger of self-destruction.

§ 1823. Upon the propriety of the power, in some form, there will probably be little controversy. The only question is, whether it is so arranged, as to accomplish its objects in the safest mode; safest for the stability of the government; and safest for the rights and liberties of the people.

§ 1824. Two modes are pointed out, the one at the instance of the government itself, through the instrumentality of congress; the other, at the instance of the states, through the instrumentality of a convention. Congress, whenever two thirds of each house shall concur in the expediency of an amendment, may propose it for adoption. The legislatures of two thirds of the states may require a convention to be called, for the purpose of proposing amendments. In each case, three fourths of the states, either through their legislatures, or conventions, called for the purpose, must concur in every amendment, before it becomes a part of the constitution. That this mode of obtaining amendments is practicable, is abundantly demonstrated by our past experience in the only mode hitherto found necessary, that of amendments proposed by congress. In this mode twelve amendments have already been incorporated into the constitution. The guards, too, against the too hasty exercise of the power, under temporary discontents or excitements, are apparently sufficient. Two thirds of congress, or of the legislatures of the states, must concur in proposing, or requiring amendments to be proposed; and three fourths of the states must ratify them. Time is thus allowed, and ample time, for deliberation, both in proposing and ratifying amendments. They cannot be carried by surprise, or intrigue, or artifice. Indeed, years may elapse before a deliberate judgment may be passed upon them, unless some pressing emergency calls for instant action. An amendment, which has the deliberate judgment of two-thirds of congress, and of three fourths of the states, can scarcely be deemed unsuited to the prosperity, or security of the republic. It must combine as much wisdom and experience in its favour, as ordinarily can belong to the management of any human concerns. In England the supreme power of the nation resides in parliament; and, in a legal sense, it is so omnipotent, that it has authority to change the whole structure of the constitution, without resort to any confirmation of the people. There is, indeed, little danger, that it will so do, as long as the people are fairly represented in it. But still it does, theoretically speaking, possess the power; and it has actually exercised it so far, as to change the succession to the crown, and mould to its will some portions of the internal structure of the constitution.

SEE ALSO:

Generally 1.9.1; 1.9.4; Bill of Rights
Records of the Federal Convention, Farrand 1:237; 2:84, 136, 148, 555–56, 578, 602
House of Representatives, Amendments to the Constitution, 5 May 1789, Annals 1:248–51
Kentucky Constitution of 1792, Thorpe 3:1273–74
George Mason, Account of Proceedings in Convention, 30 Sept. 1792, Farrand 3:367–68
Kentucky Constitution of 1799, art. 9, sec. 1, Thorpe 3:1288
Senate, Amendments to the Constitution, 12 April 1808, Annals 17:332–58

Article 6, Clause 1

All Debts contracted and Engagements entered into, before the Adoption of this Constitution, shall be as valid against the United States under this Constitution as under the Confederation.

1

ARTICLES OF CONFEDERATION, ART. 12
1 Mar. 1781

ARTICLE XII. All bills of credit emitted, monies borrowed and debts contracted by, or under the authority of congress, before the assembling of the united states, in pursuance of the present confederation, shall be deemed and considered as a charge against the united states, for payment and satisfaction whereof the said united states, and the public faith are hereby solemnly pledged.

2

RECORDS OF THE FEDERAL CONVENTION

[2:6; Madison, 14 July]

[Mr. King:] The Genl. Governt. can never wish to intrude on the State Governts. There could be no temptation. None had been pointed out. In order to prevent the interference of measures which seemed most likely to happen, he would have no objection to throwing all the State debts into the federal debt, making one aggregate debt of about 70,000,000, of dollars, and leaving it to be discharged by the Genl. Govt.

[2:47; Madison, 18 July]

Mr. Wilson did not entirely approve of the manner in which the clause relating to the engagements of Congs. was expressed; but he thought some provision on the subject would be proper in order to prevent any suspicion that the obligations of the Confederacy might be dissolved along with the Governt. under which they were contracted.

[2:322; Journal, 18 Aug.]

To secure the payment of the public debt.

To secure all Creditors, under the new Constitution, from a violation of the public faith. when pledged by the authority of the Legislature

[2:355; Madison, 21 Aug.]

Governour Livingston, from the Committee of Eleven to whom was referred the propositions respecting the debts of the several States, and also the Militia, entered on the 18th. inst: delivered the following report:

"The Legislature of the U. S. shall have power to fulfil the engagements which have been entered into by Congress, and to discharge as well the debts of the U– S: as the debts incurred by the several States during the late war, for the common defence and general welfare"

. . . . .

Mr. Gerry considered giving the power only, without adopting the obligation, as destroying the security now enjoyed by the public creditors of the U—States. He enlarged on the merit of this class of citizens, and the solemn faith which had been pledged under the existing Confederation. If their situation should be changed as here proposed great opposition would be excited agst. the plan— He urged also that as the States had made different degrees of exertion to sink their respective debts, those who had done most would be alarmed, if they were now to be saddled with a share of the debts of States which had done least.

Mr. Sherman. It means neither more nor less than the confederation as it relates to this subject.

Mr Elseworth moved that the Report delivered in by Govr. Livingston should lie on the table. Agreed to nem. con.

[2:377; Madison, 22 Aug.]

. . . the first clause containing the words "The Legislature of the U. S. *shall have power* to fulfil the engagements which have been entered into by Congress" being under consideration,

Mr. Elsworth argued that they were unnecessary. The

U—S—heretofore entered into Engagements by Congs who were their Agents. They will hereafter be bound to fulfil them by their new agents.

Mr Randolph thought such a provision necessary; for though the U. States will be bound, the new Govt will have no authority in the case unless it be given to them.

Mr. Madison thought it necessary to give the authority in order to prevent misconstruction. He mentioned the attempts made by the Debtors to British subjects to shew that contracts under the old Government, were dissolved by the Revolution which destroyed the political identity of the Society.

Mr Gerry thought it essential that some explicit provision should be made on this subject, so that no pretext might remain for getting rid of the public engagements.

Mr. Govr. Morris moved by way of amendment to substitute—"The Legislature *shall* discharge the debts & fulfil the engagements of the U. States".

It was moved to vary the amendment by striking out "discharge the debts" & to insert "liquidate the claims", which being negatived,

The amendment moved by Mr. Govr. Morris was agreed to all the States being in the affirmative.

[2:392; Madison, 23 Aug.]

The 1st sect. of art: VII being so amended as to read "The Legislature *shall* fulfil the engagements and discharge the debts of the U. S, & shall have the power to lay & collect taxes duties imposts & excises", was agreed to

Mr. Butler expressed his dissatisfaction lest it should compel payment as well to the Blood-suckers who had speculated on the distresses of others, as to those who had fought & bled for their country. He would be ready he said tomorrow to vote for a discrimination between those classes of people, and gave notice that he should move for a reconsideration.

[2:400; Madison, 24 Aug.]

Mr. Butler, according to notice, moved that clause 1st. sect. 1. of art VII, as to the discharge of debts, be reconsidered tomorrow—He dwelt on the division of opinion concerning the domestic debts, and the different pretensions of the different classes of holders. Genl. Pinkney 2ded. him.

Mr. Randolph wished for a reconsideration in order to better the expression, and to provide for the case of the State debts as is done by Congress.

On the question for reconsidering

N—H. no. Mas: ay. Cont. ay N. J. ay. Pena. absent. Del. ay—Md. no. Va. ay—N. C. absent, S. C. ay. Geo. ay. [Ayes—7; noes—2; absent—2.]—and tomorrow assigned for the reconsideration.

[2:412; Madison, 25 Aug.]

The 1st. clause of 1 sect. of art: VII being reconsidered

Col. Mason objected to the term, "*shall*"—fullfil the engagements & discharge the debts &c as too strong. It may be impossible to comply with it. The Creditors should be kept in the same plight. They will in one respect be necessarily and properly in a better. The Government will be more able to pay them. The use of the term *shall* will beget speculations and increase the pestilent practice of stock-jobbing. There was a great distinction between original creditors & those who purchased fraudulently of the ignorant and distressed. He did not mean to include those who have bought Stock in open market. He was sensible of the difficulty of drawing the line in this case, but He did not wish to preclude the attempt. Even fair purchasers, at 4, 5, 6, 8 for 1 did not stand on the same footing with the first Holders, supposing them not to be blameable. The interest they receive even in paper is equal to their purchase money. What he particularly wished was to leave the door open for buying up the securities, which he thought would be precluded by the term "shall" as requiring *nominal payment*, & which was not inconsistent with his ideas of public faith. He was afraid also the word "*shall*," might extend to all the old continental paper.

Mr Langdon wished to do no more than leave the Creditors in statu quo.

Mr. Gerry said that for himself he had no interest in the question being not possessed of more of the securities than would, by the interest, pay his taxes. He would observe however that as the public had received the value of the literal amount, they ought to pay that value to some body. The frauds on *the soldiers* ought to have been foreseen. These poor & ignorant people could not but part with their securities. There are other creditors who will part with any thing rather than be cheated of the capital of their advances. The interest of the States he observed was different on this point, some having more, others less than their proportion of the paper. Hence the idea of a scale for reducing its value had arisen. If the public faith would admit, of which he was not clear, he would not object to a revision of the debt so far as to compel restitution to the ignorant & distressed, who have been defrauded. As to Stock-jobbers he saw no reason for the censures thrown on them—They keep up the value of the paper. Without them there would be no market.

Mr. Butler said he meant neither to increase nor diminish the security of the Creditors.

Mr. Randolph moved to postpone the clause in favor of the following "All debts contracted & engagements entered into, by or under the authority of Congs. shall be as valid agst the U. States under this constitution as under the Confederation"

Docr Johnson. The debts are debts of the U—S—of the great Body of America. Changing the Government cannot change the obligation of the U—S—which devolves of course on the New Government. Nothing was in his opinion necessary to be said. If any thing, it should be a mere declaration as moved by Mr. Randolph.

Mr. Govr. Morris, said he never had become a public Creditor that he might urge with more propriety the compliance with public faith. He had always done so and always would, and preferr'd the term "*shall*" as the most explicit. As to *buying up* the debt, the term "*shall*" was not inconsistent with it, if provision be first made for paying the interest: if not, such an expedient was a mere evasion. He was content to say nothing as the New Government would be bound of course—but would prefer the clause with the term "*shall*", because it would create many friends to the plan.

On Mr. Randolph's Motion

N—H—ay—Mas. ay. Ct ay—N. J. ay—Pa. no Del. ay—Maryd. ay Va. ay—N. C.—ay—S. C. ay Geo. ay—[Ayes—10; noes—1.]

Mr. Sherman thought it necessary to connect with the clause for laying taxes duties &c an express provision for the object of the old debts &c—and moved to add to the 1st. clause of 1st. sect—of art VII "for the payment of said debts and for the defraying the expences that shall be incurred for the common defence and general welfare".

The proposition, as being unnecessary was disagreed to, Connecticut alone, being in the affirmative.

3

JAMES MADISON, FEDERALIST, NO. 43, 295–96
23 Jan. 1788

This can only be considered as a declaratory proposition; and may have been inserted, among other reasons, for the satisfaction of the foreign creditors of the United States, who cannot be strangers to the pretended doctrine that a change in the political form of civil society, has the magical effect of dissolving its moral obligations.

Among the lesser criticisms which have been exercised on the Constitution, it has been remarked that the validity of engagements ought to have been asserted in favour of the United States, as well as against them; and in the spirit which usually characterizes little critics, the omission has been transformed and magnified into a plot against the national rights. The authors of this discovery may be told, what few others need be informed of, that as engagements are in their nature reciprocal, an assertion of their validity on one side necessarily involves a validity on the other side; and that as the article is merely declaratory, the establishment of the principle in one case is sufficient for every case. They may be further told that every Constitution must limit its precautions to dangers that are not altogether imaginary; and that no real danger can exist that the government would DARE, with or even without this Constitutional declaration before it, to remit the debts justly due to the public, on the pretext here condemned.

4

ELBRIDGE GERRY, PUBLIC CREDIT, HOUSE
OF REPRESENTATIVES
25 Feb. 1790
Annals 2:1360–61

Gentlemen have said, that it never was in contemplation to assume the State debts. When the present Constitution was under consideration in the General Convention, a proposition was brought forward, that the General Government should assume and provide for the State debts, as well as the debts of the Union. It was opposed on this ground, that it did not extend to the repayment of that part which the States had sunk, as well as that which remained unpaid; had it not been for this objection, I believe that the very provision which gentlemen say was never expected, would have been incorporated in the Constitution itself. If I recollect rightly, it was also contended, in Convention, that the proposition would be useless, as Congress were authorized, under other parts of the Constitution, to make full provision on this head. From this circumstance, gentlemen will see that the assumption of the State debts was in contemplation from the very commencement of the new Government.

5

ALEXANDER HAMILTON TO EDWARD CARRINGTON
26 May 1792
Papers 11:428

As to the third point, the question of an assumption of the State debts by the United States was in discussion when the convention that framed the present government was sitting at Philadelphia, and in a long conversation which I had with Mr. Madison in an afternoon's walk, I well remember that we were perfectly agreed in the expediency and propriety of such a measure; though we were both of opinion that it would be more advisable to make it a measure of administration than an article of Constitution, from the impolicy of multiplying obstacles to its reception on collateral details.

SEE ALSO:

Records of the Federal Convention, Farrand 2:571, 603

Oliver Ellsworth to Elbridge Gerry, The Landholder, no. 8, 24 Dec. 1787, Essays 174–75

Elbridge Gerry to a Landholder, no. 1, 5 Jan. 1788, Essays 127–28

Luther Martin, Defense of Elbridge Gerry, 18 Jan. 1788, Essays 341–42

Oliver Ellsworth to Luther Martin, The Landholder, no. 10, 29 Feb. 1788, Essays 187–89

James Madison to Edmund Randolph, 10 Apr. 1788, Papers 11:18

Elbridge Gerry, Reply to a Landholder, no. 2, 30 Apr. 1788, Essays 131

House of Representatives, Public Credit, 15, 17 Feb. 1790, Annals 2:1205–10, 1214–15, 1249–50

James Madison to Andrew Stevenson, 17 Nov. 1830, Letters 4:123–25

Joseph Story, Commentaries on the Constitution 3:§§ 1827–29 (1833)

Article 6, Clause 2

This Constitution, and the Laws of the United States which shall be made in Pursuance thereof; and all Treaties made, or which shall be made, under the Authority of the United States, shall be the supreme Law of the Land; and the Judges in every State shall be bound thereby, any Thing in the Constitution or Laws of any State to the Contrary notwithstanding.

1

ARTICLES OF CONFEDERATION, ART. 13
1 Mar. 1781

ARTICLE XIII. Every state shall abide by the determinations of the united states in congress assembled, on all questions which by this confederation are submitted to them. And the Articles of this confederation shall be inviolably observed by every state, and the union shall be perpetual; nor shall any alteration at any time hereafter be made in any of them; unless such alteration be agreed to in a congress of the united states, and be afterwards confirmed by the legislatures of every state.

2

CONTINENTAL CONGRESS
21 Mar. 1787
Journals 32:124–25

Congress unanimously agreed to the following resolutions.

Resolved That the legislatures of the several States cannot of right pass any act or acts for interpreting, explaining or construing a national treaty or any part or clause of it; nor for restraining, limiting or in any manner impeding, retarding or counteracting the operation and execution of the same for that on being constitutionally made ratified and published they become in virtue of the confederation part of the law of the land and are not only independent of the will and power of such legislatures but also binding and obligatory on them.

Resolved That all such acts or parts of Acts as may be now existing in any of the States repugnant to the treaty of Peace ought to be forthwith repealed, as well to prevent their continuing to be regarded as violations of that treaty as to avoid the disagreeable necessity there might otherwise be of raising and discussing questions touching their validity and Obligation.

Resolved That it be recommended to the several States to make such repeal rather by describing than reciting the said acts and for that purpose to pass an Act declaring in general terms that all such acts and parts of acts repugnant to the treaty of peace between the United States and his britannic Majesty or any article thereof shall be and thereby are repealed and that the courts of law and equity in all causes and questions cognizable by them respectively and arising from or touching the said treaty shall decide and adjudge according to the true intent and meaning of the same, any thing in the said acts or parts of acts to the contrary thereof in any wise notwithstanding.

3

JOHN JAY, CONTINENTAL CONGRESS
13 Apr. 1787
Journals 32:177–84

The Secretary for foreign Affairs having in pursuance of an order of Congress reported the draught of a letter to the States to accompany the resolutions passed the 21st day of March 1787, the same was taken into consideration, and Unanimously agreed to, as follows,

SIR: Our Secretary for foreign Affairs has transmitted to You copies of a letter to him from our Minister at the Court of London of the 4th day of March 1786, and of the papers mentioned to have been enclosed with it.

We have deliberately and dispassionately examined and considered the several facts and matters urged by Britain as infractions of the treaty of peace on the part of America, and we regret that in some of the States too little attention appears to have been paid to the public faith pledged by that treaty. Not only the obvious dictates of religion, morality and national honor, but also the first principles of good policy, demand a candid and punctual compliance with engagements constitutionally and fairly made. Our national constitution having committed to us the management of the national concerns with foreign States and powers, it is our duty to take care that all the rights which they ought to enjoy within our Jurisdiction by the laws of nations and the faith of treaties remain inviolate. And it is also our duty to provide that the essential interests and peace of the whole confederacy be not impaired or endangered by deviations from the line of public faith into which any of its members may from whatever cause be unadvisedly drawn. Let it be remembered that the thirteen Independent Sovereign States have by express delegation of power, formed and vested in us a general though limited Sovereignty for the general and national purposes specified in the Confederation. In this Sovereignty they cannot severally participate (except by their Delegates) nor with it have concurrent Jurisdiction, for the 9th Article of the confederation most expressly conveys to us the sole and exclusive right and power of determining on war and peace, and of entering into treaties and alliances &c. When therefore a treaty is constitutionally made ratified and published by us, it immediately becomes binding on the whole nation and superadded to the laws of the land, without the intervention of State Legislatures. Treaties derive their obligation from being compacts between the Sovereign of this, and the Sovereign of another Nation, whereas laws or statutes derive their force from being the Acts of a Legislature competent to the passing of them. Hence it is clear that Treaties must be implicitly received and observed by every Member of the Nation; for as State Legislatures are not competent to the making of such compacts or treaties, so neither are they competent in that capacity, authoritatively to decide on, or ascertain the construction and sense of them. When doubts arise respecting the construction of State laws, it is not unusual nor improper for the State Legislatures by explanatory or declaratory Acts to remove those doubts; but the case between laws and compacts or treaties is in this widely different; for when doubts arise respecting the sense and meaning of a treaty they are so far from being cognizable by a State Legislature that the United States in Congress Assembled have no Authority to settle and determine them; For as the Legislature only which constitutionally passes a law has power to revise and amend it, so the sovereigns only who are parties to the treaty have power, by mutual consent and posterior Articles to correct or explain it.

In cases between Individuals, all doubts respecting the meaning of a treaty, like all doubts respecting the meaning of a law, are in the first instance mere judicial questions, and are to be heard and decided in the Courts of Justice having cognizance of the causes in which they arise; and whose duty it is to determine them according to the rules and maxims established by the laws of Nations for the interpretation of treaties. From these principles it follows of necessary consequence, that no individual State has a right by legislative Acts to decide and point out the sense in which their particular Citizens and Courts shall understand this or that Article of a treaty.

It is evident that a contrary doctrine would not only militate against the common and established maxims and Ideas relative to this subject, but would prove no less inconvenient in practice, than it is irrational in theory; for in that case the same Article of the same treaty might by law be made to mean one thing in New Hampshire, another thing in New York, and neither the one nor the other of them in Georgia.

How far such legislative Acts would be valid and obligatory even within the limits of the State passing them, is a question which we hope never to have occasion to discuss. Certain however it is that such Acts cannot bind either of the contracting Sovereigns, and consequently cannot be obligatory on their respective Nations.

But if treaties and every Article in them be (as they are and ought to be) binding on the whole Nation, if individual States have no right to accept some Articles and reject others, and if the impropriety of State Acts to interpret and decide the sense and construction of them be apparent; still more manifest must be the impropriety of State Acts to controul, delay or modify the operation and execution of these national compacts.

When it is considered that the several States Assembled by their Delegates in Congress have express power to form treaties, surely the treaties so formed are not afterwards to be subject to such alterations as this or that State Legislature may think expedient to make, and that too without the consent of either of the parties to it—that is, in the present case, without the consent of all the United States, who collectively are parties to this treaty on the one side, and his britannic Majesty on the other. Were the Legislatures to possess and to exercise such power, we should soon be involved as a Nation in Anarchy and confusion at home, and in disputes which would probably terminate in

hostilities and War with the Nations with whom we may have formed treaties. Instances would then be frequent of treaties fully executed in one State, and only partly executed in another and of the same Article being executed in one manner in one State, and in a different manner, or not at all in another State. History furnishes no precedent of such liberties taken with treaties under form of Law in any nation. Contracts between Nations, like contracts between Individuals, should be faithfully executed even though the sword in the one case, and the law in the other did not compel it, honest nations like honest Men require no constraint to do Justice; and tho impunity and the necessity of Affairs may sometimes afford temptations to pare down contracts to the Measure of convenience, yet it is never done but at the expence of that esteem, and confidence, and credit which are of infinitely more worth than all the momentary advantages which such expedients can extort.

But although contracting Nations cannot like individuals avail themselves of Courts of Justice to compel performance of contracts, yet an appeal to Heaven and to Arms, is always in their power and often in their Inclination.

But it is their duty to take care that they never lead their people to make and support such Appeals, unless the sincerity and propriety of their conduct affords them good reason to rely with confidence on the Justice and protection of Heaven.

Thus much we think it useful to observe in order to explain the principles on which we have unanimously come to the following resolution, (viz) "*Resolved*, That the Legislatures of the several States cannot of right pass any Act or Acts for interpreting, explaining or construing a national treaty or any part or clause of it, nor for restraining, limiting or in any manner impeding, retarding, or counteracting the operation and execution of the same; for that on being constitutionally made, ratified and published they become in virtue of the confederation part of the Law of the Land, and are not only independent of the will and power of such Legislatures, but also binding and obligatory on them."

As the treaty of peace so far as it respects the matters and things provided for in it, is a Law to the United States, which cannot by all or any of them be altered or changed, all State Acts establishing provisions relative to the same objects, which are incompatible with it, must in every point of view be improper. Such acts do nevertheless exist, but we do not think it necessary either to enumerate them particularly, or to make them severally the subjects of discussion. It appears to us sufficient to observe and insist, that the treaty ought to have free course in its operation and execution, and that all obstacles interposed by State Acts be removed. We mean to act with the most scrupulous regard to Justice and candour towards Great Britain, and with an equal degree of delicacy, moderation and decision towards the States who have given occasion to these discussions.

For these reasons we have in general terms

Resolved, That all such Acts or parts of Acts, as may be now existing in any of the States repugnant to the treaty of peace ought to be forthwith repealed, as well to prevent their continuing to be regarded as violations of that treaty as to avoid the disagreeable necessity there might otherwise be of raising and discussing questions touching their validity and obligation.

Although this resolution applies strictly only to such of the States as have passed the exceptionable Acts alluded to, yet to obviate all future disputes and questions as well as to remove those which now exist, we think it best that every State without exception should pass a law on the Subject. We have therefore "*Resolved,* That it be recommended to the several States to make such repeal rather by describing than reciting the said Acts, and for that purpose to pass an Act, declaring in general terms, that all such Acts and parts of Acts repugnant to the treaty of peace between the United States, and his Britannic Majesty, or any Article thereof, shall be and thereby are repealed; And that the Courts of Law and Equity in all causes and Questions cognizable by them respectively, and arising from or touching the said Treaty, shall decide and adjudge according to the true intent and meaning of the same, any thing in the said Acts or parts of Acts to the contrary thereof in any wise notwithstanding."

Such Laws would answer every purpose and be easily formed, the more they were of the like tenor throughout the States the better. They might each recite that, Whereas certain laws or Statutes made and passed in some of the United States, are regarded and complained of as repugnant to the Treaty of peace with Great Britain, by reason whereof not only the good faith of the United States, pledged by that treaty has been drawn into Question, but their essential Interests under that treaty greatly affected. And Whereas Justice to Great Britain as well as regard to the honor and Interests of the United States require, that the said treaty be faithfully executed, and that all obstacles thereto, and particularly such as do or may be construed to proceed from the Laws of this State, be effectually removed, therefore,

Be it enacted by   and it is hereby enacted by the Authority of the same, that such of the Acts or parts of Acts of the Legislature of this State, as are repugnant to the treaty of peace between the United States, and his britannic Majesty, or any Article thereof, shall be and hereby are repealed. And further that the Courts of Law and Equity within this State be and they hereby are directed and required, in all causes and questions cognizable by them respectively, and arising from or touching the said treaty, to decide and adjudge according to the tenor, true intent and meaning of the same anything in the said Acts or parts of Acts to the contrary thereof in any wise notwithstanding.

Such a general Law would we think be preferable to one that should minutely enumerate the Acts and clauses intended to be repealed; because omissions might accidentally be made in the enumeration, or Questions might arise and perhaps not be satisfactorily determined respecting particular Acts or clauses, about which contrary opinions may be entertained. By repealing in general terms all Acts and clauses repugnant to the treaty, the business will be turned over to its proper Department, viz, the Judicial, and the Courts of Law will find no difficulty in deciding whether any particular Act or clause is or is not contrary to the treaty. Besides when it is considered that the Judges in general are Men of Character and Learning, and feel as well as know the obligations of Office and the value of reputation, there is no reason to doubt that their conduct and Judgments relative to these as well as other Judicial matters will be wise and upright.

Be please, Sir, to lay this letter before the Legislature of Your State without delay. We flatter ourselves they will concur with us in opinion, that candour and Justice are as necessary to true policy, as they are to sound Morality, and that the most honorable way of delivering ourselves from the embarrassment of mistakes is fairly to correct them. It certainly is time that all doubts respecting the public faith be removed, and that all questions and differences between us and Great Britain be amicably and finally settled. The States are informed of the reasons why his britannic Majesty still continues to occupy the frontier Posts, which by the treaty he agreed to evacuate; and we have the strongest assurances that an exact compliance with the treaty on our part, shall be followed by a punctual performance of it on the part of Great Britain.

It is important that the several Legislatures should as soon as possible take these matters into consideration; and we request the favor of You to transmit to us an authenticated copy of such Acts and proceedings of the Legislature of Your State, as may take place on the Subject, and in pursuance of this letter.

4

ALEXANDER HAMILTON, REMARKS ON ACT REPEALING LAWS INCONSISTENT WITH TREATY OF PEACE, NEW YORK ASSEMBLY
17 Apr. 1787
Papers 4:150–52

Mr. Hamilton in a very animated and powerful speech, expressed great uneasiness that any opposition should be made to this bill, particularly as this state was individually interested therein. He felt greater regret from a conviction in his own mind, on this occasion, that the bill should be objected to, as there was not a single law in existence in this state, in direct contravention of the treaty of peace. He urged the committee to consent to the passing of the bill, from the consideration, that the state of New-York was the only state to gain any thing by a strict adherence to the treaty. There was no other state in the union that had so much to expect from it. The restoration of the western posts, was an object of more than £100,000 per annum. Great Britain, he said, held those posts on the plea that the United States have not fulfilled the treaty. And which we have strong assurances, she will relinquish, on the fulfillment of our engagements with her. But how far Great Britain might be sincere in her declaration, was unknown. Indeed, he doubted it himself. But while he doubted the sincerity of Great Britain, he could not but be of opinion that it was the duty of this state to enact a law for the repeal of all laws which may be against the said treaty, as by doing away all exceptions, she would be reduced to a crisis. She would be obliged to shew to the world, whether she was in earnest or not; and whether she will sacrifice her honor and reputation to her interest. With respect to the bill as it was drafted in conformity to the recommendation of Congress; he viewed it as a wise, and a salutary measure; one calculated to meet the approbation of the different states, and most likely to answer the end proposed. Were it possible to examine an intricate maze of laws, and to determine which of them, or what parts of laws were opposed to the treaty, it still might not have the intended effect, as different parties would have the judging of this matter. What one should say was a law not inconsistent with the peace, another might say was so, and there would be no end, no decision of the business. Even some of the states might view laws in a different manner. The only way to comply with the treaty, was to make a general and unexceptionable repeal. Congress with an eye to this, had proposed a general law, from which the one before them was a copy. He thought it must be obvious to every member of the committee, that as there was no law in direct opposition to the treaty, no difficulty could arise from passing the bill.

Some gentlemen, he observed, were apprehensive that this bill would restore the confiscated estates, &c. This he did not admit. However, if they were so disposed they might add a proviso to prevent it. He had wrote one, which any of the gentlemen might move for if they thought it necessary; in his opinion it was not.

The treaty only provided that no future confiscations should take place; and that Congress should *earnestly recommend* a restoration of property. But there was nothing obligatory in this.

If this state should not come into the measure, would it not be a very good plea for the other states to favor their own citizens, and say why should we do this, when New-York, the most interested of any of the states, refuses to adopt it; and shall we suffer this imputation when, in fact, we have no laws in existence that militate against the treaty. He stated the great disadvantages that our merchants experienced from the western posts being in the hands of the British, and asked if it was good policy to let them remain so.

It had been said that the judges would have too much power; this was misapprehended. He stated the powers of the judges with great clearness and precision. He insisted that their powers would be the same, whether this law was passed or not. For, that as all treaties were known by the constitution as the laws of the land, so must the judges act on the same, any law to the contrary notwithstanding.

Cicero, the great Roman Orator and lawyer, lays it down as a rule, that when two laws clash, that which relates to the most important matters ought to be preferred. If this rule prevails, who can doubt what would be the conduct of the judges, should any laws exist inconsistent with the treaty of peace: But it would be impolitic to leave them to the dilemma, either of infringing the treaty to enforce the particular laws of the state, or to explain away the laws of the state to give effect to the treaty.

He declared that the full operation of the bill, would be no more than merely to declare the treaty the law of the land. And that the judges viewing it as such, shall do away all laws that may appear in direct contravention of it. Treaties were known constitutionally, to be the law of the land, and why be afraid to leave the interpretation of those laws, to the judges; the constitution knows them as the interpreters of the law. He asked if there was any member of the committee that would be willing to see the first treaty of peace ever made by this country violated. This he did not believe, he could not think that any member on that floor harboured such sentiments.

He was in hopes the committee would agree with him in sentiment, and give a proof of their attachment to our national engagements by passing the bill, which would do away every exception of the British Court.

5

RECORDS OF THE FEDERAL CONVENTION

[1:21; Madison, 29 May]
6. Resolved . . . that the National Legislature ought to be empowered . . . to negative all laws passed by the several States, contravening in the opinion of the National Legislature the articles of Union; . . .

[1:54; Madison, 31 May]
The other clauses giving powers necessary to preserve harmony among the States to negative all State laws contravening in the opinion of the Nat Leg the articles of Union down to the last clause, (the words "or any treaties subsisting under the authority of the Union", being added after the words "contravening &c. the articles of the Union"; on motion of Dr. Franklin) were agreed to witht. debate or dissent.

[1:164; Madison, 8 June]
On a reconsideration of the clause giving the Natl. Legislature a negative on such laws of the States as might be contrary to the articles of Union, or Treaties with foreign nations,

Mr. Pinkney moved "that the National Legislature shd. have authority to negative all Laws which they shd. judge to be improper". He urged that such a universality of the power was indispensably necessary to render it effectual; that the States must be kept in due subordination to the nation; that if the States were left to act of themselves in any case, it wd. be impossible to defend the national prerogatives, however extensive they might be on paper; that the acts of Congress had been defeated by this means; nor had foreign treaties escaped repeated violations; that this universal negative was in fact the corner stone of an efficient national Govt.; that under the British Govt. the negative of the Crown had been found beneficial, and the

States are more one nation now, than the *Colonies* were then.

Mr. Madison seconded the motion. He could not but regard an indefinite power to negative legislative acts of the States as absolutely necessary to a perfect system. Experience had evinced a constant tendency in the States to encroach on the federal authority; to violate national Treaties, to infringe the rights & interests of each other; to oppress the weaker party within their respective jurisdictions. A negative was the mildest expedient that could be devised for preventing these mischiefs. The existence of such a check would prevent attempts to commit them. Should no such precaution be engrafted, the only remedy wd. lie in an appeal to coercion. Was such a remedy elegible? was it practicable? Could the national resources, if exerted to the utmost enforce a national decree agst. Massts. abetted perhaps by several of her neighbours? It wd. not be possible. A small proportion of the Community in a compact situation, acting on the defensive, and at one of its extremities might at any time bid defiance to the National authority. Any Govt. for the U. States formed on the supposed practicability of using force agst. the unconstitutional proceedings of the States, wd. prove as visionary & fallacious as the Govt. of Congs. The negative wd. render the use of force unnecessary. The States cd. of themselves then pass no operative act, any more than one branch of a Legislature where there are two branches, can proceed without the other. But in order to give the negative this efficacy, it must extend to all cases. A discrimination wd. only be a fresh source of contention between the two authorities. In a word, to recur to the illustrations borrowed from the planetary System, This prerogative of the General Govt. is the great pervading principle that must controul the centrifugal tendency of the States; which, without it, will continually fly out of their proper orbits and destroy the order & harmony of the political system.

Mr. Williamson was agst. giving a power that might restrain the States from regulating their internal police.

Mr. Gerry cd. not see the extent of such a power, and was agst. every power that was not necessary. He thought a remonstrance agst. unreasonable acts of the States wd. reclaim them. If it shd. not force might be resorted to. He had no objection to authorize a negative to paper money and similar measures. When the confederation was depending before Congress, Massachusetts was then for inserting the power of emitting paper money amg. the exclusive powers of Congress. He observed that the proposed negative wd. extend to the regulations of the militia, a matter on which the existence of a State might depend. The Natl. Legislature with such a power may enslave the States. Such an idea as this will never be acceded to. It has never been suggested or conceived among the people. No speculative projector, and there are eno' of that character among us, in politics as well as in other things, has in any pamphlet or newspaper thrown out the idea. The States too have different interests and are ignorant of each other's interests. The negative therefore will be abused, New States too having separate views from the old States will never come into the Union, They may even be under some foreign influence; are they in such case to participate in the negative on the will of the other States?

Mr. Sherman thought the cases in which the negative ought to be exercised, might be defined. He wished the point might not be decided till a trial at least shd. be made for that purpose

Mr. Wilson would not say what modifications of the proposed power might be practicable or expedient. But however novel it might appear the principal of it when viewed with a close & steady eye, is right. There is no instance in which the laws say that the individuals shd. be bound in one case, & at liberty to judge whether he will obey or disobey in another. The cases are parallel, Abuses of the power over the individual person may happen as well as over the individual States. Federal liberty is to States, what civil liberty, is to private individuals. And States are not more unwilling to purchase it, by the necessary concession of their political sovereignty, tha[n] the savage is to purchase Civil liberty by the surrender of the personal sovereignty. which he enjoys in a State of nature. A definition of the cases in which the Negative should be exercised, is impracticable. A discretion must be left on one side or the other? Will it not be most safely lodged on the side of the Natl. Govt.?—Among the first sentiments expressed in the first Congs. one was that Virga. is no more. That Massts. is no [more], that Pa. is no more &c. We are now one nation of brethren. We must bury all local interests & distinctions. This language continued for some time. The tables at length began to turn. No sooner were the State Govts. formed than their jealousy & ambition began to display themselves. Each endeavoured to cut a slice from the common loaf, to add to its own morsel, till at length the confederation became frittered down to the impotent condition in which it now stands. Review the progress of the articles of Confederation thro' Congress & compare the first & last draught of it. To correct its vices is the business of this convention. One of its vices is the want of an effectual controul in the whole over its parts. What danger is there that the whole will unnecessarily sacrifice a part? But reverse the case, and leave the whole at the mercy of each part, and will not the general interest be continually sacrificed to local interests?

Mr. Dickenson deemed it impossible to draw a line between the cases proper & improper for the exercise of the negative. We must take our choice of two things. We must either subject the States to the danger of being injured by the power of the Natl. Govt. or the latter to the danger of being injured by that of the States. He thought the danger greater from the States. To leave the power doubtful, would be opening another spring of discord, and he was for shutting as many of them as possible.

Mr. Bedford. In answer to his colleagues question, where wd. be the danger to the States from this power, would refer him to the smallness of his own State which may be injured at pleasure without redress. It was meant he found to strip the small States of their equal right of suffrage. In this case Delaware would have about 1/90 for its share in the General Councils, whilst Pa. & Va. would possess 1/3 of the whole. Is there no difference of interests, no rivalship of commerce, of manufactures? Will not these large States crush the small ones whenever they stand in the way of their ambitions or interested views. This shows the impossibility of adopting such a system as that on the table, or any other founded on a change in the prinple of representation. And after all, if a State does not obey the law of the new System, must not force be resorted to as the only ultimate remedy, in this as in any other system. It seems as if Pa. & Va. by the conduct of their deputies wished to provide a system in which they would have an enormous & monstrous influence. Besides, How can it be thought that the proposed negative can be exercised? are the laws of the States to be suspended in the most urgent cases until they can be sent seven or eight hundred miles, and undergo the deliberations of a body who may be incapable of Judging of them? Is the National Legislature too to sit continually in order to revise the laws of the States?

Mr. Madison observed that the difficulties which had been started were worthy of attention and ought to be answered before the question was put. The case of laws of urgent necessity must be provided for by some emanation of the power from the Natl. Govt. into each State so far as to give a temporary assent at least. This was the practice in Royal Colonies before the Revolution and would not have been inconvenient; if the supreme power of negativing had been faithful to the American interest, and had possessed the necessary information. He supposed that the negative might be very properly lodged in the senate alone, and that the more numerous & expensive branch therefore might not be obliged to sit constantly.—He asked Mr. B. what would be the consequence to the small States of a dissolution of the Union wch. seemed likely to happen if no effectual substitute was made for the defective System existing, and he did not conceive any effectual system could be substituted on any other basis than that of a proportional suffrage? If the large States possessed the Avarice & ambition with which they were charged, would the small ones in their neighbourhood, be more secure when all controul of a Genl. Govt. was withdrawn.

Mr. Butler was vehement agst. the Negative in the proposed extent, as cutting off all hope of equal justice to the distant States. The people there would not he was sure give it a hearing.

On the question for extending the negative power to all cases as proposd. by (Mr. P. & Mr. M——) Mas. ay. Cont. no. N. Y. no. N. J. no. Pa. ay. Del. divd. Mr. Reed & Mr. Dickenson ay. Mr. Bedford & Mr. Basset no. Maryd. no. Va. ay. Mr. R. Mr. Mason no. Mr. Blair, Docr. Mc. Cg. Mr. M. ay. Genl. W. not consulted. N. C. no. S. C. no Geo. no. [Ayes—3; noes—7; divided—1.]

[1:169; Yates, 8 June]

Mr. Pinkney moved, *That the national legislature shall have the power of negativing all laws to be passed by the state legislatures which they may judge improper*, in the room of the clause as it stood reported.

He grounds his motion on the necessity of one supreme controlling power, and he considers this as the *corner-stone* of the present system; and hence the necessity of retrenching the state authorities in order to preserve the good government of the national council.

Mr. Williamson against the motion. The national legislature ought to possess the power of negativing such laws only as will encroach on the national government.

Mr. Madison wished that the line of jurisprudence could be drawn—he would be for it—but upon reflection he finds it impossible, and therefore he is for the amendment. If the clause remains without the amendment it is inefficient—The judges of the state must give the state laws their operation, although the law abridges the rights of the national government—how is it to be repealed? By the power who made it? How shall you compel them? By force? To prevent this disagreeable expedient, the power of negativing is absolutely necessary—this is the only attractive principle which will retain its centrifugal force, and without this the planets will fly from their orbits.

Mr. Gerry supposes that this power ought to extend to all laws already made; but the preferable mode would be to designate the powers of the national legislature, to which the negative ought to apply—he has no objection to restrain the laws which may be made for issuing paper money. Upon the whole he does not choose on this important trust, *to take a leap in the dark*.

Mr. Pinkney supposes that the proposed amendment had no retrospect to the state laws already made. The adoption of the new government must operate as a complete repeal of all the constitutions and state laws, as far as they are inconsistent with the new government.

Mr. Wilson supposes the surrender of the rights of a federal government to be a surrender of sovereignty. True, we may define some of the rights, but when we come near the line it cannot be found. One general excepting clause must therefore apply to the whole. In the beginning of our troubles, congress themselves were as one state—dissentions or state interests were not known—they gradually crept in after the formation of the constitution, and each took to himself a slice. The original draft of confederation was drawn on the first ideas, and the draft concluded on how different!

Mr. Bedford was against the motion, and states the proportion of the intended representation of the number 90: Delaware 1—Pennsylvania and Virginia one third. On this computation where is the weight of the small states when the interest of the one is in competition with the other on trade, manufactures and agriculture? When he sees this mode of government so strongly advocated by the members of the great states, he must suppose it a question of *interest*.

Mr. Madison confesses it is not without its difficulties on many accounts—some may be removed, others modified, and some are unavoidable. May not this power be vested in the senatorial branch? they will probably be always sitting. Take the question on the other ground, who is to determine the line when drawn in doubtful cases? The state legislatures cannot, for they will be partial in support of their own powers—no tribunal can be found. It is impossible that the articles of confederation can be amended—they are too tottering to be invigorated—nothing but the present system, or something like it, can restore the peace and harmony of the country.

The question put on Mr. Pinkney's motion—7 states

against it—Delaware divided—Virginia, Pennsylvania and Massachusetts for it.

[1:245; Madison, 15 June]

6. Resd. that all Acts of the U. States in Congs. made by virtue & in pursuance of the powers hereby & by the articles of confederation vested in them, and all Treaties made & ratified under the authority of the U. States shall be the supreme law of the respective States so far forth as those Acts or Treaties shall relate to the said States or their Citizens, and that the Judiciary of the several States shall be bound thereby in their decisions, any thing in the respective laws of the Individual States to the contrary notwithstanding; and that if any State, or any body of men in any State shall oppose or prevent ye. carrying into execution such acts or treaties, the federal Executive shall be authorized to call forth ye power of the Confederated States, or so much thereof as may be necessary to enforce and compel an obedience to such Acts, or an Observance of such Treaties.

[1:250, 256; Madison, 16 June]

[Mr. Lansing] The States will never feel a sufficient confidence in a general Government to give it a negative on their laws. The Scheme is itself totally novel. There is no parallel to it to be found. The authority of Congress is familiar to the people, and an augmentation of the powers of Congress will be readily approved by them.

. . . . .

[Mr. Randolph] There are but two modes, by which the end of a Genl. Govt. can be attained: the 1st. is by coercion as proposed by Mr. Ps. plan. 2. by real legislation as propd. by the other plan. Coercion he pronounced to be *impracticable, expensive, cruel to individuals*. It tended also to habituate the instruments of it to shed the blood & riot in the spoils of their fellow Citizens, and consequently trained them up for the service of Ambition. We must resort therefore to a national *Legislation over individuals*, for which Congs. are unfit. To vest such power in them, would be blending the Legislative with the Executive, contrary to the recd. maxim on this subject: If the Union of these powers heretofore in Congs. has been safe, it has been owing to the general impotency of that body. Congs. are moreover not elected by the people, but by the Legislatures who retain even a power of recall. They have therefore no will of their own, they are a mere diplomatic body, and are always obsequious to the views of the States, who are always encroaching on the authority of the U. States. A provision for harmony among the States, as in trade, naturalization &c.—for crushing rebellion whenever it may rear its crest—and for certain other general benefits, must be made. The powers for these purposes, can never be given to a body, inadequate as Congress are in point of representation, elected in the mode in which they are, and possessing no more confidence than they do: for notwithstanding what has been said to the contrary, his own experience satisfied him that a rooted distrust of Congress pretty generally prevailed. A Natl. Govt. alone, properly constituted, will answer the purpose; and he begged it to be considered that the present is the last moment for establishing one. After this select experiment, the people will yield to despair.

[1:293; Madison, 18 June]

X All laws of the particular States contrary to the Constitution or laws of the United States to be utterly void; and the better to prevent such laws being passed, the Governour or president of each state shall be appointed by the General Government and shall have a negative upon the laws about to be passed in the State of which he is Governour or President

[1:318; Madison, 19 June]

[Mr. Madison] The plan of Mr. Paterson, not giving even a negative on the Acts of the States, left them as much at liberty as ever to execute their unrighteous projects agst. each other.

. . . . .

5. Will it secure a good internal legislation & administration to the particular States? In developing the evils which vitiate the political system of the U. S. it is proper to take into view those which prevail within the States individually as well as those which affect them collectively: Since the former indirectly affect the whole; and there is great reason to believe that the pressure of them had a full share in the motives which produced the present Convention. Under this head he enumerated and animadverted on 1. the multiplicity of the laws passed by the several States. 2. the mutability of their laws. 3. the injustice of them. 4. the impotence of them: observing that Mr. Patterson's plan contained no remedy for this dreadful class of evils, and could not therefore be received as an adequate provision for the exigencies of the Community.

[1:438; Madison, 27 June]

[Mr. L. Martin] . . . , that the States, particularly the smaller, would never allow a negative to be exercised over their laws: that no State in ratifying the Confederation had objected to the equality of votes; that the complaints at present run not agst. this equality but the want of power; . . .

[1:447; Madison, 28 June]

[Mr. Madison]. The negative on the State laws proposed, will make it an essential branch of the State Legislatures & of course will require that it should be exercised by a body established on like principles with the other branches of those Legislatures.-

[2:27; Madison, 17 July]

The next.—"To negative all laws passed by the several States contravening in the opinion of the Nat: Legislature the articles of Union, or any treaties subsisting under the authority of ye Union"

Mr. Govr. Morris opposed this power as likely to be terrible to the States, and not necessary, if sufficient Legislative authority should be given to the Genl. Government.

Mr. Sherman thought it unnecessary, as the Courts of the States would not consider as valid any law contravening the Authority of the Union, and which the legislature would wish to be negatived.

Mr. L. Martin considered the power as improper & inadmissable. Shall all the laws of the States be sent up to the Genl. Legislature before they shall be permitted to operate?

Mr. Madison, considered the negative on the laws of the States as essential to the efficacy & security of the Genl. Govt. The necessity of a general Govt. proceeds from the propensity of the States to pursue their particular interests in opposition to the general interest. This propensity will continue to disturb the system, unless effectually controuled. Nothing short of a negative on their laws will controul it. They can pass laws which will accomplish their injurious objects before they can be repealed by the Genl Legislre. or be set aside by the National Tribunals. Confidence can not be put in the State Tribunals as guardians of the National authority and interests. In all the States these are more or less dependt. on the Legislatures. In Georgia they are appointed annually by the Legislature. In R. Island the Judges who refused to execute an unconstitutional law were displaced, and others substituted, by the Legislature who would be willing instruments of the wicked & arbitrary plans of their masters. A power of negativing the improper laws of the States is at once the most mild & certain means of preserving the harmony of the system. Its utility is sufficiently displayed in the British System. Nothing could maintain the harmony & subordination of the various parts of the empire, but the prerogative by which the Crown, stifles in the birth every Act of every part tending to discord or encroachment. It is true the prerogative is sometimes misapplied thro' ignorance or a partiality to one particular part of ye. empire: but we have not the same reason to fear such misapplications in our System. As to the sending all laws up to the Natl. Legisl: that might be rendered unnecessary by some emanation of the power into the States, so far at least, as to give a temporary effect to laws of immediate necessity.

Mr. Govr. Morris was more & more opposed to the negative. The proposal of it would disgust all the States. A law that ought to be negatived will be set aside in the Judiciary departmt. and if that security should fail; may be repealed by a Nationl. law.

Mr. Sherman. Such a power involves a wrong principle, to wit, that a law of a State contrary to the articles of the Union, would if not negatived, be valid & operative.

Mr. Pinkney urged the necessity of the Negative.

On the question for agreeing to the power of negativing laws of States &c." it passed in the negative.

Mas. ay. Ct. no. N. J. no. Pa. no. Del. no. Md. no. Va. ay. N. C. ay. S. C. no. Geo. no. [Ayes—3; noes—7.]

Mr. Luther Martin moved the following resolution "that the Legislative acts of the U. S. made by virtue & in pursuance of the articles of Union, and all treaties made & ratified under the authority of the U. S. shall be the supreme law of the respective States, as far as those acts or treaties shall relate to the said States, or their Citizens and inhabitants—& that the Judiciaries of the several States shall be bound thereby in their decisions, any thing in the respective laws of the individual States to the contrary notwithstanding" which was agreed to nem: con:.

[2:389; Madison, 23 Aug.]

Mr. Rutlidge moved to amend Art: VIII to read as follows,

"This Constitution & the laws of the U. S. made in pursuance thereof, and all Treaties made under the authority of the U. S. shall be the supreme law of the several States and of their citizens and inhabitants; and the Judges in the several States shall be bound thereby in their decisions, any thing in the Constitutions or laws of the several States, to the contrary nothwithstanding"—

which was agreed to, nem: contrad:

. . . . .

Mr C—Pinkney moved to add as an additional power to be vested in the Legislature of the U. S. "To negative all laws passed by the several States interfering in the opinion of the Legislature with the General interests and harmony of the Union;" provided that two thirds of the members of each House assent to the same" This principle he observed had formerly been agreed to. He considered the precaution as essentially necessary: The objection drawn from the predominance of the large States had been removed by the equality established in the Senate—Mr. Broome 2ded. the proposition.

Mr. Sherman thought it unnecessary; the laws of the General Government being Supreme & paramount to the State laws according to the plan, as it now stands.

Mr. Madison proposed that it should be committed—He had been from the beginning a friend to the principle; but thought the modification might be made better.

Mr. Mason wished to know how the power was to be exercised. Are all laws whatever to be brought up? Is no road nor bridge to be established without the Sanction of the General Legislature? Is this to sit constantly in order to receive & revise the State Laws? He did not mean by these remarks to condemn the expedient, but he was apprehensive that great objections would lie agst. it.

Mr. Williamson thought it unnecessary, & having been already decided, a revival of the question was a waste of time.

Mr. Wilson considered this as the key-stone wanted to compleat the wide arch of Government we are raising. The power of self-defence had been urged as necessary for the State Governments—It was equally necessary for the General Government. The firmness of Judges is not of itself sufficient Something further is requisite—It will be better to prevent the passage of an improper law, than to declare it void when passed.

Mr. Rutlidge. If nothing else, this alone would damn and ought to damn the Constitution. Will any State ever agree to be bound hand & foot in this manner. It is worse than making mere corporations of them whose bye laws would not be subject to this shackle.

Mr Elseworth observed that the power contended for wd. require either that all laws of the State Legislatures should previously to their taking effect be transmitted to the Genl Legislature, or be repealable by the Latter; or that the State Executives should be appointed by the Genl Government, and have a controul over the State laws. If the last was meditated let it be declared.

Mr. Pinkney declared that he thought the State Executives ought to be so appointed with such a controul. & that it would be so provided if another Convention should take place.

Mr Governr. Morris did not see the utility or practicability of the proposition of Mr. Pinkney, but wished it to be referred to the consideration of a Committee.

Mr Langdon was in favor of the proposition. He considered it as resolvable into the question whether the extent of the National Constitution was to be judged of by the Genl or the State Governments.

On the question for commitment, it passed in the negative.

N—H. ay. Masts: no. Cont. no N. J. no. Pa. ay. Del: ay. Md. ay. Va. ay. N. C. no. S. C. no. Geo. no. [Ayes—5; noes—6.]

6

CHARLES PINCKNEY, OBSERVATIONS ON THE PLAN OF GOVERNMENT
1787

Farrand 3:119

In every Confederacy of States, formed for their general benefit and security, there ought to be a power to oblige the parties to furnish their respective quotas without the possibility of neglect or evasion;—there is no such clause in the present Confederation, and it is therefore *without this indispensable security*. Experience justifies me in asserting that we may detail as minutely as we can, the duties of the States, but unless they are assured that these duties will be required and enforced, the details will be regarded as nugatory. No Government has more severely felt the want of a coercive Power than the United States; for want of it the principles of the Confederation have been neglected with impunity in the hour of the most pressing necessity, and at the imminent hazard of its existence: Nor are we to expect they will be more attentive in future. Unless there is a compelling principle in the Confederacy, there must be an injustice in its tendency; It will expose an unequal proportion of the strength and resources of some of the States, to the hazard of war in defence of the rest—the first principles of Justice direct that this danger should be provided against—many of the States have certainly shewn a disposition to evade a performance of their Federal Duties, and throw the burden of Government upon their neighbors. It is against this shameful evasion in the delinquent, this forced assumption in the more attentive, I wish to provide, and they ought to be guarded against by every means in our power. Unless this power of coercion is infused, and exercised when necessary, the States will most assuredly neglect their duties. The consequence is either a dissolution of the Union, or an unreasonable sacrifice by those who are disposed to support and maintain it.

7

EDMUND RANDOLPH, SUGGESTIONS FOR THE CONCILIATION OF THE SMALL STATES
10 July 1787

Documentary History 5:438

---

4. That altho' every negative given to the law of a particular State shall prevent its operation, any State may appeal to the national Judiciary against a negative; and that such negative if adjudged to be contrary to the power granted by the articles of the Union, shall be void

5. that any individual conceiving himself injured or oppressed by the partiality or injustice of a law of any particular State may resort to the National Judiciary, who may adjudge such law to be void, if found contrary to the principles of equity and justice.

8

JAMES McCLURG TO JAMES MADISON
22 Aug. 1787

Documentary History 4:264

I have still some hope that I shall hear from you of ye reinstatement of ye *Negative*—as it is certainly ye only mean by which the several Legislatures can be restrain'd from disturbing ye order & harmony of ye whole, & ye Governmt. render'd properly *national*, & *one*. I should suppose yt some of its former opponents must by this time have seen ye necessity of advocating it, if they wish to support their own principles.

9

FEDERAL FARMER, NO. 4
12 Oct. 1787

Storing 2.8.46–48

There are certain rights which we have always held sacred in the United States, and recognized in all our constitutions, and which, by the adoption of the new constitution in its present form, will be left unsecured. By article 6, the proposed constitution, and the laws of the United States, which shall be made in pursuance thereof; and all treaties made, or which shall be made under the authority of the United States, shall be the supreme law of the land; and the judges in every state shall be bound thereby; any thing in the constitution or laws of any state to the contrary not-withstanding.

It is to be observed that when the people shall adopt the proposed constitution it will be their last and supreme act; it will be adopted not by the people of New-Hampshire, Massachusetts, etc. but by the people of the United States; and wherever this constitution, or any part of it, shall be incompatible with the ancient customs, rights, the laws or the constitutions heretofore established in the United States, it will entirely abolish them and do them away: And not only this, but the laws of the United States which shall be made in pursuance of the federal constitution will be also supreme laws, and wherever they shall be incompatible with those customs, rights, laws or constitutions heretofore established, they will also entirely abolish them and do them away.

By the article before recited, treaties also made under the authority of the United States, shall be the supreme law: It is not said that these treaties shall be made in pursuance of the constitution—nor are there any constitutional bounds set to those who shall make them: The president and two thirds of the senate will be empowered to make treaties indefinitely, and when these treaties shall be made, they will also abolish all laws and state constitutions incompatible with them. This power in the president and senate is absolute, and the judges will be bound to allow full force to whatever rule, article or thing the president and senate shall establish by treaty, whether it be practicable to set any bounds to those who make treaties, I am not able to say: if not, it proves that this power ought to be more safely lodged.

10

AN OLD WHIG, NO. 2
Fall 1787
Storing 3.3.13

Where then is the restraint? How are Congress bound down to the powers expressly given? what is reserved or can be reserved?

Yet even this is not all—as if it were determined that no doubt should remain, by the sixth article of the constitution it is declared that, "this constitution, and the laws of the United States which shall be made in pursuance thereof; and all treaties made, or which shall be made, under the authority of the United States, shall be the supreme law of the land, and the judges in every state shall be bound thereby, *any thing in the constitutions or laws of any state to the contrary notwithstanding.*" The Congress are therefore vested with the supreme legislative power, without controul. In giving such immense, such unlimited powers, was there no necessity of a bill of rights to secure to the people their liberties? Is it not evident that we are left wholly dependent on the wisdom and virtue of the men who shall from time to time be the members of Con-

gress? and who shall be able to say seven years hence, the members of Congress will be wise and good men, or of the contrary character.

11

JAMES MADISON TO THOMAS JEFFERSON
24 Oct. 1787

(See vol. 1, ch. 17, no. 22)

12

ALEXANDER HAMILTON, FEDERALIST, NO. 15,
90–98
1 Dec. 1787

(See vol. 1, ch. 5, no. 21)

13

ALEXANDER HAMILTON, FEDERALIST, NO. 27,
171–75
25 Dec. 1787

It has been urged in different shapes that a constitution of the kind proposed by the Convention, cannot operate without the aid of a military force to execute its laws. This however, like most other things that have been alledged on that side, rests on mere general assertion; unsupported by any precise or intelligible designation of the reasons upon which it is founded. As far as I have been able to divine the latent meaning of the objectors, it seems to originate in a pre-supposition that the people will be disinclined to the exercise of foederal authority in any matter of an internal nature. Waving any exception that might be taken to the inaccuracy or inexplicitness of the distinction between internal and external, let us enquire what ground there is to presuppose that disinclination in the people? Unless we presume, at the same time, that the powers of the General Government will be worse administered than those of the State governments, there seems to be no room for the presumption of ill-will, disaffection or opposition in the people. I believe it may be laid down as a general rule, that their confidence in and obedience to a government, will commonly be proportioned to the goodness or badness of its administration. It must be admitted that there are exceptions to this rule; but these exceptions depend so entirely on accidental causes, that they cannot be considered as having any relation to the intrinsic merits or demerits of a constitution. These can only be judged of by general principles and maxims.

Various reasons have been suggested in the course of these papers, to induce a probability that the General Government will be better administered than the particular governments: The principal of which reasons are that the extension of the spheres of election will present a greater option, or latitude of choice to the people, that through the medium of the State Legislatures, which are select bodies of men, and who are to appoint the members of the national Senate,—there is reason to expect that this branch will generally be composed with peculiar care and judgment: That these circumstances promise greater knowledge and more extensive information in the national councils: And that they will be less apt to be tainted by the spirit of faction, and more out of the reach of those occasional ill humors or temporary prejudices and propensities, which in smaller societies frequently contaminate the public councils, beget injustice and oppression of a part of the community, and engender schemes, which though they gratify a momentary inclination or desire, terminate in general distress, dissatisfaction and disgust. Several additional reasons of considerable force, to fortify that probability, will occur when we come to survey with a more critic[al] eye, the interior structure of the edifice, which we are invited to erect. It will be sufficient here to remark, that until satisfactory reasons can be assigned to justify an opinion, that the foederal government is likely to be administered in such a manner as to render it odious or contemptible to the people, there can be no reasonable foundation for the supposition, that the laws of the Union will meet with any greater obstruction from them, or will stand in need of any other methods to enforce their execution, than the laws of the particular members.

The hope of impunity is a strong incitement to sedition—the dread of punishment—a proportionately strong discouragement to it. Will not the government of the Union, which, if possessed of a due degree of power, can call to its aid the collective resources of the whole confederacy, be more likely to repress the *former* sentiment, and to inspire the *latter*, than that of a single State, which can only command the resources within itself? A turbulent faction in a State may easily suppose itself able to contend with the friends to the government in that State; but it can hardly be so infatuated as to imagine itself a match for the combined efforts of the Union. If this reflection be just, there is less danger of resistance from irregular combinations of individuals, to the authority of the confederacy, than to that of a single member.

I will in this place hazard an observation which will not be the less just, because to some it may appear new; which is, that the more the operations of the national authority are intermingled in the ordinary exercise of government; the more the citizens are accustomed to meet with it in the common occurrences of their political life; the more it is familiarised to their sight and to their feelings; the further it enters into those objects which touch the most sensible cords, and put in motion the most active springs of the human heart; the greater will be the probability that it will conciliate the respect and attachment of the community. Man is very much a creature of habit. A thing that rarely strikes his senses will generally have but little influence upon his mind. A government continually at a distance and out of sight, can hardly be expected to interest the sensations of the people. The inference is, that the authority of the Union, and the affections of the citizens towards it, will be strengthened rather than weakened by its extension to what are called matters of internal concern; and will have less occasion to recur to force in proportion to the familiarity and comprehensiveness of its agency. The more it circulates through those channels and currents, in which the passions of mankind naturally flow, the less will it require the aid of the violent and perilous expedients of compulsion.

One thing at all events, must be evident, that a government like the one proposed, would bid much fairer to avoid the necessity of using force, than that species of league contended for by most of its opponents; the authority of which should only operate upon the States in their political or collective capacities. It has been shewn, that in such a confederacy, there can be no sanction for the laws but force; that frequent delinquencies in the members, are the natural offspring of the very frame of the government; and that as often as these happen they can only be redressed, if at all, by war and violence.

14

ALEXANDER HAMILTON, FEDERALIST, NO. 33,
207–8
2 Jan. 1788

But it is said, that the laws of the Union are to be the *supreme law* of the land. But what inference can be drawn from this or what would they amount to, if they were not to be supreme? It is evident they would amount to nothing. A LAW by the very meaning of the term includes supremacy. It is a rule which those to whom it is prescribed are bound to observe. This results from every political association. If individuals enter into a state of society the laws of that society must be the supreme regulator of their conduct. If a number of political societies enter into a larger political society, the laws which the latter may enact, pursuant to the powers entrusted to it by its constitution, must necessarily be supreme over those societies, and the individuals of whom they are composed. It would otherwise be a mere treaty, dependent on the good faith of the parties, and not a government; which is only another word for POLITICAL POWER AND SUPREMACY. But it will not follow from this doctrine that acts of the larger society which are *not pursuant* to its constitutional powers but which are invasions of the residuary authorities of the smaller societies will become the supreme law of the land. These will be merely acts of usurpation and will deserve to be treated as such. Hence we perceive that the clause which declares the supremacy of the laws of the Union, like the one we have just before considered, only declares a truth, which flows immediately and necessarily from the institution of a Foederal Government. It will not, I presume, have escaped observation that it *expressly* confines this supremacy to laws made *pursuant to the Constitution;* which I mention merely as an instance of caution in the Convention; since that limitation would have been to be understood though it had not been expressed.

Though a law therefore for laying a tax for the use of the United States would be supreme in its nature, and could not legally be opposed or controuled; yet a law for abrogating or preventing the collection of a tax laid by the authority of a State (unless upon imports and exports) would not be the supreme law of the land, but an usurpation of power not granted by the constitution. As far as an improper accumulation of taxes on the same object might tend to render the collection difficult or precarious, this would be a mutual inconvenience not arising from a superiority or defect of power on either side, but from an injudicious exercise of power by one or the other, in a manner equally disadvantageous to both. It is to be hoped and presumed however that mutual interest would dictate a concert in this respect which would avoid any material inconvenience. The inference from the whole is—that the individual States would, under the proposed constitution, retain an independent and uncontroulable authority to raise revenue to any extent of which they may stand in need by every kind of taxation except duties on imports and exports. It will be shewn in the next paper that this CONCURRENT JURISDICTION in the article of taxation was the only admissible substitute for an intire subordination, in respect to this branch of power, of the State authority to that of the Union.

15

DEBATE IN SOUTH CAROLINA HOUSE OF REPRESENTATIVES
16–17 Jan. 1788

(See 2.2.2–3, no. 6)

16

JAMES MADISON, FEDERALIST, NO. 44, 306
25 Jan. 1788

The indiscreet zeal of the adversaries to the Constitution, has betrayed them into an attack on this part of it also, without which it would have been evidently and radically defective. To be fully sensible of this we need only suppose for a moment, that the supremacy of the State Constitutions had been left compleat by a saving clause in their favor.

In the first place, as these Constitutions invest the State Legislatures with absolute sovereignty, in all cases not excepted by the existing articles of confederation, all the authorities contained in the proposed Constitution, so far as they exceed those enumerated in the confederation, would have been annulled, and the new Congress would have

been reduced to the same impotent condition with their predecessors.

In the next place, as the Constitutions of some of the States do not even expressly and fully recognize the existing powers of the confederacy, an express saving of the supremacy of the former, would in such States have brought into question, every power contained in the proposed Constitution.

In the third place, as the Constitutions of the States differ much from each other, it might happen that a treaty or national law of great and equal importance to the States, would interfere with some and not with other Constitutions, and would consequently be valid in some of the States at the same time that it would have no effect in others.

In fine, the world would have seen for the first time, a system of government founded on an inversion of the fundamental principles of all government; it would have seen the authority of the whole society every where subordinate to the authority of the parts; it would have seen a monster in which the head was under the direction of the members.

17

IMPARTIAL EXAMINER, NO. 1
20 Feb. 1788
Storing 5.14.4

Suffer me, then, in the first place to advert to a part of the sixth article in this constitution. It may, perhaps, appear somewhat irregular, to begin with this article, since it is almost the last proposed: yet, if it be considered that this at once defines the extent of Congressional authority, and indisputably fixes its supremacy, every idea of impropriety on this head will probably vanish. The clause alluded to contains the following words, "This constitution, and the laws of the United States, which shall be made in pursuance thereof, and all treaties made, or which shall be made, under the authority of the United States, shall be the supreme law of the land; and the judges in every state shall be bound thereby; any thing in the constitution or laws of any state to the contrary, notwithstanding." If this constitution should be adopted, here the sovereignty of America is ascertained and fixed in the foederal body at the same time that it abolishes the present independent sovereignty of each state. Because this government being general, and not confined to any particular part of the continent; but pervading every state and establishing its authority equally in all, its superiority will consequently be recognized in each; and all other powers can operate only in a secondary subordinate degree. For the idea of two sovereignties existing within the same community is a perfect solecism. If they be supposed equal, their operation must be commensurate, and like two mechanical powers of equal *momenta* counteracting each other;—there the force of the one will be destroyed by the force of the other: and so there will be no efficiency in either. If one be greater than the other, they will be similar to two unequal bodies in motion with a given degree of velocity, and impinging each other from opposite points;—the motion of the lesser in this case will necessarily be destroyed by that of the greater: and so there will be efficiency only in the greater. But what need is there for a mathematical deduction to shew the impropriety of two such distinct coexisting sovereignties? The natural understanding of all mankind perceives the apparent absurdity arising from such a supposition: since, if the word means any thing at all, it must mean that *supreme power*, which must reside somewhere in [a] state; or, in other terms, it is the united powers of each individual member of the state collected and consolidated into *one body*. This collection, this union, this supremacy of power can, therefore, exist only in one body. This is obvious to every man: and it has been very properly suggested that under the proposed constitution each state will dwindle into "the insignificance of a town corporate." This certainly will be their utmost consequence; and, as such, they will have no authority to make laws, even for their own private government any farther than the permissive indulgence of Congress may grant them leave.

18

GEORGE MASON, VIRGINIA RATIFYING CONVENTION
11 June 1788
Papers 3:1062–63

Let us advert to the 6th article. It expressly declares that, "This Constitution and the laws of the United States, which shall be made in pursuance thereof; and all treaties made, or which shall be made under the authority of the United States, shall be the supreme law of the land, and the judges in every state shall be bound thereby, any thing in the constitution or laws of any state to the contrary notwithstanding." Now, sir, if the laws and constitution of the general government, as expressly said, be paramount to those of any state, are not those rights with which we were afraid to trust our own citizens annuled and given up to the general government? The bill of rights is a part of our own constitution. The judges are obliged to take notice of the laws of the general government, consequently the rights secured by our bill of rights are given up. If they are not given up, where are they secured? By implication? Let gentlemen shew that they are secured in a plain, direct, unequivocal manner. It is not in their power. Then where is the security? Where is the barrier drawn between the government and the rights of the citizens, as secured in our own state government? These rights are given up in that paper, but I trust this convention will never give them up, but will take pains to secure them to the latest posterity. If a check be necessary in our own state govern-

ment, it is much more so in a government where our representatives are to be at the distance of 1000 miles from us without any responsibility.

19

DEBATE IN NORTH CAROLINA
RATIFYING CONVENTION
29–30 July 1788
Elliot 4:178–91, 215

Mr. IREDELL. This clause is supposed to give too much power, when, in fact, it only provides for the execution of those powers which are already given in the foregoing articles. What does it say? That "this Constitution, and the laws of the United States which shall be made in pursuance thereof, and all treaties made, or which shall be made, under the authority of the United States, shall be the supreme law of the land; and the judges in every state shall be bound thereby, any thing in the constitution or laws of any state to the contrary notwithstanding." What is the meaning of this, but that, as we have given power, we will support the execution of it? We should act like children, to give power and deny the legality of executing it. It is saying no more than that, when we adopt the government, we will maintain and obey it; in the same manner as if the Constitution of this state had said that, when a law is passed in conformity to it, we must obey that law. Would this be objected to? Then, when the Congress passes a law consistent with the Constitution, it is to be binding on the people. If Congress, under pretence of executing one power, should, in fact, usurp another, they will violate the Constitution. I presume, therefore, that this explanation, which appears to me the plainest in the world, will be entirely satisfactory to the committee.

Mr. BLOODWORTH. Mr. Chairman, I confess his explanation is not satisfactory to me. I wish the gentleman had gone farther. I readily agree that it is giving them no more power than to execute their laws. But how far does this go? It appears to me to sweep off all the constitutions of the states. It is a total repeal of every act and constitution of the states. The judges are sworn to uphold it. It will produce an abolition of the state governments. Its sovereignty absolutely annihilates them.

Mr. IREDELL. Mr. Chairman, every power delegated to Congress is to be executed by laws made for that purpose. It is necessary to particularize the powers intended to be given, in the Constitution, as having no existence before; but, after having enumerated what we give up, it follows, of course, that whatever is done, by virtue of that authority, is legal without any new authority or power. The question, then, under this clause, will always be, whether Congress has exceeded its authority. If it has not exceeded it, we must obey, otherwise not. This Constitution, when adopted, will become a part of our state Constitution; and the latter must yield to the former only in those cases where power is given by it. It is not to yield to it in any other case whatever. For instance, there is nothing in the Constitution of this state establishing the authority of a federal court. Yet the federal court, when established, will be as constitutional as the superior court is now under our Constitution. It appears to me merely a general clause, the amount of which is that, when they pass an act, if it be in the execution of a power given by the Constitution, it shall be binding on the people, otherwise not. As to the sufficiency or extent of the power, that is another consideration, and has been discussed before.

Mr. BLOODWORTH. This clause will be the destruction of every law which will come in competition with the laws of the United States. Those laws and regulations which have been, or shall be, made in this state, must be destroyed by it, if they come in competition with the powers of Congress. Is it not necessary to define the extent of its operation? Is not the force of our tender-laws destroyed by it? The worthy gentleman from Wilmington has endeavored to obviate the objection as to the Constitution's destroying the credit of our paper money, and paying debts in coin, but unsatisfactorily to me. A man assigns, by legal action, a bond to a man in another state; could that bond be paid by money? I know it is very easy to be wrong. I am conscious of being frequently so. I endeavor to be open to conviction. This clause seems to me too general, and I think its extent ought to be limited and defined. I should suppose every reasonable man would think some amendments to it were necessary.

Mr. MACLAINE. Mr. Chairman, that it will destroy the state sovereignty is a very popular argument. I beg leave to have the attention of the committee. Government is formed for the happiness and prosperity of the people at large. The powers given it are for their own good. We have found, by several years' experience, that government, taken by itself nominally, without adequate power, is not sufficient to promote their prosperity. Sufficient powers must be given to it. The powers to be given the general government are proposed to be withdrawn from the authority of the state governments, in order to protect and secure the Union at large. This proposal is made to the people. No man will deny their authority to delegate powers and recall them, in all free countries. But, says the gentleman last up, the construction of the Constitution is in the power of Congress, and it will destroy the sovereignty of the state governments. It may be justly said that it diminishes the power of the state legislatures, and the diminution is necessary to the safety and prosperity of the people; but it may be fairly said that the members of the general government,—the President, senators, and representatives,—whom we send thither, by our free suffrages, to consult our common interest, will not wish to destroy the state governments, because the existence of the general government will depend on that of the state governments.

But what is the sovereignty, and who is Congress? One branch, the people at large; and the other branch, the states by their representatives. Do people fear the delegation of power to themselves—to their own representatives?

But he objects that the laws of the Union are to be the supreme laws of the land. Is it not proper that their laws should be the laws of the land, and paramount to those of any particular state?—or is it proper that the laws of any particular state should control the laws of the United States? Shall a part control the whole? To permit the local laws of any state to control the laws of the Union, would be to give the general government no powers at all. If the judges are not to be bound by it, the powers of Congress will be nugatory. This is self-evident and plain. Bring it home to every understanding; it is so clear it will force itself upon it. The worthy gentleman says, in contradiction to what I have observed, that the clause which restrains the states from emitting paper money, &c., will operate upon the present circulating paper money, and that gold and silver must pay paper contracts. The clause cannot possibly have a retrospective view. It cannot affect the existing currency in any manner, except to enhance its value by the prohibition of future emissions. It is contrary to the universal principles of jurisprudence, that a law or constitution should have a retrospective operation, unless it be expressly provided that it shall. Does he deny the power of the legislature to fix a scale of depreciation as a criterion to regulate contracts made for depreciated money? As to the question he has put, of an assigned bond, I answer that it can be paid with paper money. For this reason, the assignee can be in no better situation than the assignor. If it be regularly transferred, it will appear what person had the bond originally, and the present possessor can recover nothing but what the original holder of it could. Another reason which may be urged is, that the federal courts could have no cognizance of such a suit. Those courts have no jurisdiction in cases of debt between the citizens of the same state. The assignor being a citizen of the same state with the debtor, and assigning it to a citizen of another state, to avoid the intent of the Constitution, the assignee can derive no advantage from the assignment, except what the assignor had a right to; and consequently the gentleman's objection falls to the ground.

Every gentleman must see the necessity for the laws of the Union to be paramount to those of the separate states, and that the powers given by this Constitution must be executed. What, shall we ratify a government and then say it shall not operate? This would be the same as not to ratify. As to the amendments, the best characters in the country, and those whom I most highly esteem, wish for amendments. Some parts of it are not organized to my wish. But I apprehend no danger from the structure of the government. One gentleman (Mr. Bass) said he thought it neither necessary nor proper. For my part, I think it essential to our very existence as a nation, and our happiness and prosperity as a free people. The men who composed it were men of great abilities and various minds. They carried their knowledge with them. It is the result, not only of great wisdom and mutual reflection, but of "mutual deference and concession." It has trifling faults, but they are not dangerous. Yet at the same time I declare that, if gentlemen propose amendments, if they be not such as would destroy the government entirely, there is not a single member here more willing to agree to them than myself.

Mr. DAVIE. Mr. Chairman: permit me, sir, to make a few observations on the operation of the clause so often mentioned. This Constitution, as to the powers therein granted, is constantly to be the supreme law of the land. Every power ceded by it must be executed, without being counteracted by the laws or constitutions of the individual states. Gentlemen should distinguish that it is not the supreme law in the exercise of a power not granted. It can be supreme only in cases consistent with the powers specially granted, and not in usurpations. If you grant any power to the federal government, the laws made in pursuance of that power must be supreme, and uncontrolled in their operation. This consequence is involved in the very nature and necessity of the thing. The only rational inquiry is, whether those powers are necessary, and whether they are properly granted. To say that you have vested the federal government with power to legislate for the Union, and then deny the supremacy of the laws, is a solecism in terms. With respect to its operation on our own paper money, I believe that a little consideration will satisfy every man that it cannot have the effect asserted by the gentleman from New Hanover. The Federal Convention knew that several states had large sums of paper money in circulation, and that it was an interesting property, and they were sensible that those states would never consent to its immediate destruction, or ratify any system that would have that operation. The mischief already done could not be repaired: all that could be done was, to form some limitation to this great political evil. As the paper money had become private property, and the object of numberless contracts, it could not be destroyed or intermeddled with in that situation, although its baneful tendency was obvious and undeniable. It was, however, effecting an important object to put bounds to this growing mischief. If the states had been compelled to sink the paper money instantly, the remedy might be worse than the disease. As we could not put an immediate end to it, we were content with prohibiting its future increase, looking forward to its entire extinguishment when the states that had an emission circulating should be able to call it in by a gradual redemption.

In Pennsylvania, their paper money was not a tender in discharge of private contracts. In South Carolina, their bills became eventually a tender; and in Rhode Island, New York, New Jersey, and North Carolina, the paper money was made a legal tender in all cases whatsoever. The other states were sensible that the destruction of the circulating paper would be a violation of the rights of private property, and that such a measure would render the accession of those states to the system absolutely impracticable. The injustice and pernicious tendency of this disgraceful policy were viewed with great indignation by the states which adhered to the principles of justice. In Rhode Island, the paper money had depreciated to eight for one, and a hundred per cent. with us. The people of Massachusetts and Connecticut had been great sufferers by the dishonesty of Rhode Island, and similar complaints existed against this state. This clause became in some measure a preliminary with the gentlemen who represented the other states. "You have," said they, "by your iniquitous laws and paper emissions shamefully defrauded our citizens. The Confederation prevented our compelling you to do them justice; but before we confederate with you again, you must not only agree to be honest, but put it out of your power to be otherwise." Sir, a member from Rhode Island itself could not have set his face against such language. The clause was, I believe, unanimously assented to: it has only a future aspect, and can by no means have a retrospective operation; and I trust the principles upon which the Convention proceeded will meet the approbation of every honest man.

Mr. CABARRUS. Mr. Chairman, I contend that the clause which prohibits the states from emitting bills of credit will not affect our present paper money. The clause has no retrospective view. This Constitution declares, in the most positive terms, that no *ex post facto* law shall be passed by the general government. Were this clause to operate retrospectively, it would clearly be *ex post facto*, and repugnant to the express provision of the Constitution. How, then, in the name of God, can the Constitution take our paper money away? If we have contracted for a sum of money, we ought to pay according to the nature of our contract. Every honest man will pay in specie who engaged to pay it. But if we have contracted for a sum of paper money, it must be clear to every man in this committee, that we shall pay in paper money. This is a Constitution for the *future* government of the United States. It does not look back. Every gentleman must be satisfied, on the least reflection, that our paper money will not be destroyed. To say that it will be destroyed, is a popular argument, but not founded in fact, in my opinion. I had my doubts, but on consideration, I am satisfied.

Mr. BLOODWORTH. Mr. Chairman, I beg leave to ask if the payment of sums now due be *ex post facto*. Will it be an *ex post facto* law to compel the payment of money now due in silver coin? If suit be brought in the federal court against one of our citizens, for a sum of money, will paper money be received to satisfy the judgment? I inquire for information; my mind is not yet satisfied. It has been said that we are to send our own gentlemen to represent us, and that there is not the least doubt they will put that construction on it which will be most agreeable to the people they represent. But it behoves us to consider whether they can do so if they would, when they mix with the body of Congress. The Northern States are much more populous than the Southern ones. To the north of the Susquehannah there are thirty-six representatives, and to the south of it only twenty-nine. They will always outvote us. Sir, we ought to be particular in adopting a Constitution which may destroy our currency, when it is to be the supreme law of the land, and prohibits the emission of paper money. I am not, for my own part, for giving an indefinite power. Gentlemen of the best abilities differ in the construction of the Constitution. The members of Congress will differ too. Human nature is fallible. I am not for throwing ourselves out of the Union; but we ought to be cautious by proposing amendments. The majority in several great adopting states was very trifling. Several of them have proposed amendments, but not in the mode most satisfactory to my mind. I hope this Convention never will adopt it till the amendments are actually obtained.

Mr. IREDELL. Mr. Chairman, with respect to this clause, it cannot have the operation contended for. There is nothing in the Constitution which affects our present paper money. It prohibits, for the future, the emitting of any, but it does not interfere with the paper money now actually in circulation in several states. There is an express clause which protects it. It provides that there shall be no *ex post facto* law. This would be *ex post facto*, if the construction contended for were right, as has been observed by another gentleman. If a suit were brought against a man in the federal court, and execution should go against his property, I apprehend he would, under this Constitution, have a right to pay our paper money, there being nothing in the Constitution taking away the validity of it. Every individual in the United States will keep his eye watchfully over those who administer the general government, and no usurpation of power will be acquiesced in. The possibility of usurping powers ought not to be objected against it. Abuse may happen in any government. The only resource against usurpation is the inherent right of the people to prevent its exercise. This is the case in all free governments in the world. The people will resist if the government usurp powers not delegated to it. We must run the risk of abuse. We must take care to give no more power than is necessary; but, having given that, we must submit to the possible dangers arising from it.

With respect to the great weight of the Northern States, it will not, on a candid examination, appear so great as the gentleman supposes. At present, the regulation of our representation is merely temporary. Whether greater or less, it will hereafter depend on actual population. The extent of this state is very great, almost equal to that of any state in the Union; and our population will probably be in proportion. To the north of Pennsylvania, there are twenty-seven votes. To the south of Pennsylvania, there are thirty votes, leaving Pennsylvania out. Pennsylvania has eight votes. In the division of what is called the northern and southern interests, Pennsylvania does not appear to be decidedly in either scale. Though there may be a combination of the Northern States, it is not certain that the interests of Pennsylvania will coincide with theirs. If, at any time, she join us, we shall have thirty-eight against twenty-seven. Should she be against us, they will have only thirty-five to thirty. There are two states to the northward, who have, in some respect, a similarity of interests with ourselves. What is the situation of New Jersey? It is, in one respect, similar to ours. Most of the goods they use come through New York, and they pay for the benefit of New York, as we pay for that of Virginia. It is so with Connecticut; so that, in every question between importing and non-importing states, we may expect that two of the Northern States would probably join with North Carolina. It is impossible to destroy altogether this idea of separate interests. But the difference between the states does not appear to me so great as the gentleman imagines; and I

beg leave to say, that, in proportion to the increase of population, the Southern States will have greater weight than the Northern, as they have such large quantities of land still uncultivated, which is not so much the case to the north. If we should suffer a small temporary inconvenience, we shall be compensated for it by having the weight of population in our favor in future.

Mr. BLOODWORTH. Mr. Chairman, when I was in Congress, the southern and northern interests divided at Susquehannah. I believe it is so now. The advantage to be gained by future population is no argument at all. Do we gain any thing when the other states have an equality of members in the Senate, notwithstanding the increase of members in the House of Representatives? This is no consequence at all. I am sorry to mention it, but I can produce an instance which will prove the facility of misconstruction. [Here Mr. Bloodworth cited an instance which took place in Congress with respect to the Indian trade, which, not having been distinctly heard, is omitted.]

They may trample on the rights of the people of North Carolina if there be not sufficient guards and checks. I only mentioned this to show that there may be misconstructions, and that, in so important a case as a constitution, every thing ought to be clear and intelligible, and no ground left for disputes.

Mr. CALDWELL. Mr. Chairman, it is very evident that there is a great necessity for perspicuity. In the sweeping clause, there are words which are not plain and evident. It says that "this Constitution, and the laws of the United States which shall be made in pursuance thereof, &c., shall be the supreme law of the land." The word *pursuance* is equivocal and ambiguous; a plainer word would be better. They may pursue bad as well as good measures, and therefore the word is improper; it authorizes bad measures. Another thing is remarkable,—that gentlemen, as an answer to every improper part of it, tell us that every thing is to be done by our own representatives, who are to be good men. There is no security that they will be so, or continue to be so. Should they be virtuous when elected, the laws of Congress will be unalterable. These laws must be annihilated by the same body which made them. It appears to me that the laws which they make cannot be altered without calling a convention. [Mr. Caldwell added some reasons for this opinion, but spoke too low to be heard.]

Gov. JOHNSTON. Mr. Chairman, I knew that many gentlemen in this Convention were not perfectly satisfied with every article of this Constitution; but I did not expect that so many would object to this clause. The Constitution must be the supreme law of the land; otherwise, it would be in the power of any one state to counteract the other states, and withdraw itself from the Union. The laws made in pursuance thereof by Congress ought to be the supreme law of the land; otherwise, any one state might repeal the laws of the Union at large. Without this clause, the whole Constitution would be a piece of blank paper. Every treaty should be the supreme law of the land; without this, any one state might involve the whole Union in war. The worthy member who was last up has started an objection which I cannot answer. I do not know a word in the English language so good as the word *pursuance,* to express the idea meant and intended by the Constitution. Can any one understand the sentence any other way than this? When Congress makes a law in virtue of their constitutional authority, it will be an actual law. I do not know a more expressive or a better way of representing the idea by words. Every law consistent with the Constitution will have been made in pursuance of the powers granted by it. Every usurpation or law repugnant to it cannot have been made in pursuance of its powers. The latter will be nugatory and void. I am at a loss to know what he means by saying the laws of the Union will be unalterable. Are laws as immutable as constitutions? Can any thing be more absurd than assimilating the one to the other? The idea is not warranted by the Constitution, nor consistent with reason.

Mr. J. M'DOWALL wished to know how the taxes are to be paid which Congress were to lay in this state. He asked if paper money would discharge them. He calculated that the taxes would be higher, and did not know how they could be discharged; for, says he, every man is to pay so much more, and the poor man has not the money locked up in his chest. He was of opinion that our laws could be repealed entirely by those of Congress.

Mr. MACLAINE. Mr. Chairman, taxes must be paid in gold or silver coin, and not in imaginary money. As to the subject of taxation, it has been the opinion of many intelligent men that there will be no taxes laid immediately, or, if any, that they will be very inconsiderable. There will be no occasion for it, as proper regulations will raise very large sums of money. We know that Congress will have sufficient power to make such regulations. The moment that the Constitution is established, Congress will have credit with foreign nations. Our situation being known, they can borrow any sum. It will be better for them to raise any money they want at present by borrowing than by taxation. It is well known that in this country gold and silver vanish when paper money is made. When we adopt, if ever, gold and silver will again appear in circulation. People will not let their hard money go, because they know that paper money cannot repay it. After the war, we had more money in gold and silver, in circulation, than we have nominal money now. Suppose Congress wished to raise a million of money more than the imposts. Suppose they borrow it. They can easily borrow it in Europe at four per cent. The interest of that sum will be but £40,000. So that the people, instead of having the whole £1,000,000 to pay, will have but £40,000 to pay, which will hardly be felt. The proportion of £40,000 for this state would be a trifle. In seven years' time, the people would be able, by only being obliged to pay the interest annually, to save money, and pay the whole principal, perhaps, afterwards, without much difficulty. Congress will not lay a single tax when it is not to the advantage of the people at large. The western lands will also be a considerable fund. The sale of them will aid the revenue greatly, and we have reason to believe the impost will be productive.

Mr. J. M'DOWALL. Mr. Chairman, instead of reasons and authorities to convince me, assertions are made. Many respectable gentlemen are satisfied that the taxes will be higher. By what authority does the gentleman say that the impost will be productive, when our trade is come to nothing? Sir, borrowing money is detrimental and ruinous to nations. The interest is lost money. We have been obliged to borrow money to pay interest! We have no way of paying additional and extraordinary sums. The people cannot stand them. I should be extremely sorry to live under a government which the people could not understand, and which it would require the greatest abilities to understand. It ought to be plain and easy to the meanest capacity. What would be the consequence of ambiguity? It may raise animosity and revolutions, and involve us in bloodshed. It becomes us to be extremely cautious.

Mr. MACLAINE. Mr. Chairman, I would ask the gentleman what is the state of our trade. I do not pretend to a very great knowledge in trade, but I know something of it. If our trade be in a low situation, it must be the effect of our present weak government. I really believe that Congress will be able to raise almost what sums they please by the impost. I know it will, though the gentleman may call it assertion. I am not unacquainted with the territory or resources of this country. The resources, under proper regulations, are very great. In the course of a few years, we can raise money without borrowing a single shilling. It is not disgraceful to borrow money. The richest nations have recurred to loans on some emergencies. I believe, as much as I do in my existence, that Congress will have it in their power to borrow money if our government be such as people can depend upon. They have been able to borrow now under the present feeble system. If so, can there be any doubt of their being able to do it under a respectable government?

Mr. M'DOWALL replied, that our trade was on a contemptible footing; that it was come almost to nothing, and lower in North Carolina than any where; that therefore little could be expected from the impost.

Mr. J. GALLOWAY. Mr. Chairman, I should make no objection to this clause were the powers granted by the Constitution sufficiently defined; for I am clearly of opinion that it is absolutely necessary for every government, and especially for a general government, that its laws should be the supreme law of the land. But I hope the gentlemen of the committee will advert to the 10th section of the 1st article. This is a negative which the Constitution of our own state does not impose upon us. I wish the committee to attend to that part of it which provides that no state shall pass any law which will impair the obligation of contracts. Our public securities are at a low ebb, and have been so for many years. We well know that this country has taken those securities as specie. This hangs over our heads as a contract. There is a million and a half in circulation at least. That clause of the Constitution may compel us to make good the nominal value of these securities. I trust this country never will leave it to the hands of the general government to redeem the securities which they have already given. Should this be the case, the consequence will be, that they will be purchased by speculators, when the citizens will part with them, perhaps for a very trifling consideration. Those speculators will look at the Constitution, and see that they will be paid in gold and silver. They will buy them at a half-crown in the pound, and get the full nominal value for them in gold and silver. I therefore wish the committee to consider whether North Carolina can redeem those securities in the manner most agreeable to her citizens, and justifiable to the world, if this Constitution be adopted.

Mr. DAVIE. Mr. Chairman, I believe neither the 10th section, cited by the gentleman, nor any other part of the Constitution, has vested the general government with power to interfere with the public securities of any state. I will venture to say that the last thing which the general government will attempt to do will be this. They have nothing to do with it. The clause refers merely to contracts between individuals. That section is the best in the Constitution. It is founded on the strongest principles of justice. It is a section, in short, which I thought would have endeared the Constitution to this country. When the worthy gentleman comes to consider, he will find that the general government cannot possibly interfere with such securities. How can it? It has no negative clause to that effect. Where is there a negative clause, operating negatively on the states themselves? It cannot operate retrospectively, for this would be repugnant to its own express provisions. It will be left to ourselves to redeem them as we please. We wished we could put it on the shoulders of Congress, but could not. Securities may be higher, but never less. I conceive, sir, that this is a very plain case, and that it must appear perfectly clear to the committee that the gentleman's alarms are groundless.

. . . . .

Mr. LANCASTER: . . . Treaties are to be the supreme law of the land. This has been sufficiently discussed: it must be amended some way or other. If the Constitution be adopted, it ought to be the supreme law of the land, and a perpetual rule for the governors and governed. But if treaties are to be the supreme law of the land, it may repeal the laws of different states, and render nugatory our bill of rights.

20

JAMES MADISON TO EDMUND PENDLETON
2 Jan. 1791
Papers 13:342–44

"Your first quere is, are the words of the Treaty 'there shall be no legal impediment to the bona fide recovery of debts on either side' a law of repeal, or a covenant that a law of repeal shall be passed?"—As Treaties are declared to be the supreme *law* of the land, I should suppose that the *words* of the *treaty* are to be taken for the *words* of the *law*, unless the stipulation be expressly or necessarily executory, which does not in this instance appear to be the case.

"Was not the contrary the sense of the Congress who made the Treaty, when they called on the States to repeal the several laws containing such impediments?"—As well as I recollect, the Act of Congress on that occasion, supposed the impediments to be repealed by the Treaty, and recommended a repeal by the States, merely as declaratory and in order to obviate doubts and discussions. Perhaps too, on a supposition that a legal repeal might have been necessary previous to the new Constitution, it may be rendered unnecessary by the terms of this instrument above quoted, which seem to give a *legal* force to the Treaty.

"Admitting the treaty to be a law of repeal, what is the extent of it? Does it repeal all acts of limitation, & such as regulate the modes of proving debts?"—This question probably involves several very nice points, and requires a more critical knowledge of the State of the American laws, the course of legal proceedings, and the circumstances of the British debts, than I possess. Under this disadvantage, I am afraid to say more than that the probable intention of the parties, and the expression, "bona fide recovery of debts" seem to plead for a liberal & even favorable interpretation of the article. Unless there be very strong and clear objections, such an interpretation would seem to require, that the debts should be viewed as in the State, in which the original obstacles to their recovery, found them; so far at least as the nature of the case will permit.

"What is meant by the *supreme law* as applied to treaties? Is it like those of the Medes & Persians unalterable? or may not the contracting powers annul it by consent? or a breach on one side discharge the other from an obligation to perform its part?"—Treaties as I understand the Constitution are made *supreme* over the constitutions and laws of the particular States, and, like a subsequent law of the U. S., over pre-existing laws of the U. S. provided however that the Treaty be within the prerogative of making Treaties, which no doubt has certain limits.

That the contracting powers can annul the Treaty, cannot I presume, be questioned; the same authority precisely being exercised in annulling as in making a Treaty.

That a breach on one side (even of a single article, each being considered as a condition of every other article) discharges the other, is as little questionable; but with this reservation, that the other side is at liberty to take advantage or not of the breach, as dissolving the Treaty. Hence I infer that the Treaty with G. B, which has not been annulled by mutual consent, must be regarded as in full force, by all on whom its execution in the U. S. depends, until it shall be declared by the party to whom a right has accrued by the breach of the other party to declare, that advantage is taken of the breach, & the Treaty is annulled accordingly. In case it should be adviseable to take advantage of the adverse breach a question may perhaps be started, whether the power vested by the Constitution with respect to Treaties in the President & Senate, makes them the competent Judges, or whether as the Treaty is a law the whole Legislature are to judge of its annulment—or whether, in case the President & Senate be competent in ordinary Treaties, the Legislative authority be requisite to annul a *Treaty of peace*, as being equipollent to a Declaration of war, to which that authority alone, by our Constitution, is competent.

21

WARE V. HYLTON
3 Dall. 199 (1796)

CHASE, Justice.—The defendants in error, on the 7th day of July 1774, passed their penal bond to Farrel & Jones, for the payment of 2976*l.* 11*s.* 6*d.* of good British money; but the condition of the bond, of the time of payment, does not appear on the record. On the 20th October 1777, the legislature of the commonwealth of Virginia passed a law to sequester British property. In the 3d section of the law, it was enacted, "that it should be lawful for any citizen of Virginia, owing money to a subject of Great Britain, to pay the same, or any part thereof, from time to time, as he should think fit, into the loan-office, taking thereout a certificate for the same, in the name of the creditor, with an indorsement, under the hand of the commissioner of the said office, expressing the name of the payer; and shall deliver such certificate to the governor and the council, whose receipt shall discharge him from so much of the debt. And the governor and the council shall, in like manner, lay before the general assembly, once in every year, an account of these certificates, specifying the names of the persons by, and for whom they were paid; and shall see to the safe-keeping of the same; subject to the future directions of the legislature: provided, that the governor and the council may make such allowance, as they shall think reasonable, out of the interest of the money so paid into the loan-office, to the wives and children, residing in the state, of such creditor." On the 26th of April 1780, the defendants in error paid into the loan-office of Virginia, part of their debt, to wit, $3,111⅑, equal to 933*l.* 14*s.* 0*d.* Virginia currency; and obtained a certificate from the commissioners of the loan-office, and a receipt from the governor and the council of Virginia, agreeable to the above in part recited law.

The defendants in error being sued on the above bond, in the circuit court of Virginia, pleaded the above law, and the payment above stated, in bar of so much of the plaintiff's debt. The plaintiff, to avoid this bar, replied the fourth article of the definitive treaty of peace between Great Britain and the United States, of the 3d of September 1783. To this replication, there was a general demurrer and joinder. The circuit court allowed the demurrer, and the plaintiff brought the present writ of error.

. . . . .

From these observations, and the authority of Bynkershoek, Lee, Burlamaque and Rutherforth, I conclude, that Virginia had a right, as a sovereign and independent nation, to confiscate any British property within its territory, unless she had before delegated that power to congress, which Mr. Lewis contended she had done. The proof of the allegation that Virginia had transferred this authority to congress, lies on those who make it; because if she had

parted with such power, it must be conceded, that she once rightfully possessed it.

It has been inquired, what powers congress possessed from the first meeting in September 1774, until the ratification of the articles of confederation, on the 1st of March 1781? It appears to me, that the powers of congress, during that whole period, were derived from the people they represented, expressly given, through the medium of their state conventions, or state legislatures; or that after they were exercised, they were impliedly ratified by the acquiescence and obedience of the people. After the confederacy was completed, the powers of congress rested on the authority of the state legislatures, and the implied ratifications of the people; and was a government over governments. The powers of congress originated from necessity, and arose out of, and were only limited by events; or, in other words, they were revolutionary in their very nature. Their extent depended on the exigencies and necessities of public affairs. It was absolutely and indispensably necessary that congress should possess the power of conducting the war against Great Britain, and therefore, if not expressly given by all (as it was by some of the states), I do not hesitate to say, that congress did rightfully possess such power. The authority to make war, of necessity, implies the power to make peace; or the war must be perpetual. I entertain this general idea, that the several states retained all internal sovereignty; and that congress properly possessed the great rights of external sovereignty: among other, the right to make treaties of commerce and alliance; as with France, on the 6th of February 1778. In deciding on the powers of congress, and of the several states, before the confederation, I see but one safe rule, namely, that all the powers actually exercised by congress, before that period, were rightfully exercised, on the presumption not to be controverted, that they were so authorized by the people they represented, by an express or implied grant; and that all the powers exercised by the state conventions or state legislatures were also rightfully exercised, on the same presumption of authority from the people. That congress did not possess all the powers of war is self-evident, from this consideration alone, that she never attempted to lay any kind of tax on the people of the United States, but relied altogether on the state legislatures to impose taxes, to raise money to carry on the war, and to sink the emissions of all the paper money issued by congress. It was expressly provided, in the 8th article of the confederation, that "all charges of war (and all other expenses for the common defence and general welfare), and allowed by congress, shall be defrayed out of a common treasury, to be supplied by the several states in proportion to the value of the land in each state; and the taxes for paying the said proportion, shall be levied by the legislatures of the several states." In every free country, the power of laying taxes is considered a legislative power over the property and persons of the citizens; and this power the people of the United States granted to their state legislatures, and they neither could, nor did, transfer it to congress; but on the contrary, they expressly stipulated that it should remain with them. It is an incontrovertible fact, that congress never attempted to confiscate any kind of British property, within the United States (except what their army or vessels of war captured), and thence I conclude that congress did not conceive the power was vested in them. Some of the states did exercise this power, and thence, I infer, they possessed it. On the 23d of March, 3d of April, and 24th of July 1776, congress confiscated British property taken on the high seas.

The second point made by the counsel for the plaintiff in error was, "if the legislature of Virginia had a right to confiscate British debts, yet she did not exercise that right by the act of the 20th October 1777." If this objection is well founded, the plaintiff in error must have judgment for the money covered by the plea of that law, and the payment under it. The preamble recites, that the public faith, and the law and the usage of nations require, that debts incurred, during the connection with Great Britain, should not be confiscated. No language can possibly be stronger to express the opinion of the legislature of Virginia, that British debts ought not to be confiscated, and if the words, or effect and operation, of the enacting clause are ambiguous or doubtful, such construction should be made as not to extend the provisions in the enacting clause, beyond the intention of the legislature, so clearly expressed in the preamble; but if the words in the enacting clause, in their nature, import and common understanding, are not ambiguous, but plain and clear, and their operation and effect certain, there is no room for construction. It is not an uncommon case, for a legislature, in a preamble, to declare their intention to provide for certain cases, or to punish certain offences, and in enacting clauses to include other cases, and other offences. But I believe very few instances can be found, in which the legislature declared, that a thing ought not to be done, and afterwards did the very thing they reprobated. There can be no doubt, that strong words in the enacting part of a law may extend beyond the preamble. If the preamble is contradicted by the enacting clause, as to the intention of the legislature, it must prevail, on the principle, that the legislature changed their intention.

I am of opinion, that the law of the 20th of October 1777, and the payment in virtue thereof, amounts either to a confiscation or extinguishment of so much of the debt as was paid into the loan-office of Virginia. 1st. The law makes it lawful for a citizen of Virginia, indebted to a subject of Great Britain, to pay the whole, or any part of his debt, into the loan-office of that commonwealth. 2d. It directs the debtor to take a certificate of his payment, and to deliver it to the governor and the council; and it declares that the receipt of the governor and the council for the certificate shall discharge him (the debtor) from so much of the debt as he paid into the loan-office. 3d. It enacts that the certificate shall be subject to the future direction of the legislature. And 4th, it provides, that the governor and council may make such allowance, as they shall think reasonable, out of the interest of the money paid, to the wives and children, residing within the state, of such creditor. The payment by the debtor into the loan-office is made a lawful act. The public receive the money, and they discharge the debtor, and they make the certificate (which

is the evidence of the payment) subject to their direction; and they benevolently appropriate part of the money paid, to wit, the interest of the debt, to such of the family of the creditor as may live within the state. All these acts are plainly a legislative interposition between the creditor and debtor; which annilates the right of the creditor; and is an exercise of the right of ownership over the money; for the giving part to the family of the creditor, under the restriction of being residents of the state, or to a stranger, can make no difference. The government of Virginia had precisely the same right to dispose of the whole as of part of the debt. Whether all these acts amount to a confiscation of the debt, or not, may be disputed, according to the different ideas entertained of the proper meaning of the word confiscation. I am inclined to think, that all these acts, collectively considered, are substantially a confiscation of the debt. The verb confiscate is derived from the Latin *con*, with, and *fiscus*, a basket, or hamper, in which the emperor's treasure was formerly kept. The meaning of the word to confiscate is, to transfer property from private to public use; or to forfeit property to the prince or state. In the language of Mr. Lee (page 118), the debt was taken hold of; and this he considers as confiscation. But if, strictly speaking, the debt was not confiscated, yet it certainly was extinguished, as between the creditor and debtor; the debt was legally paid, and of consequence extinguished. The state interfered and received the debt, and discharged the debtor from his creditor; and not from the state, as suggested. The debtor owed nothing to the state of Virginia, but she had a right to take the debt, or not, at her pleasure. To say, that the discharge was from the state, and not from the debtor, implies that the debtor was under some obligation or duty to pay the state what he owed his British creditor. If the debtor was to remain charged to his creditor, notwithstanding his payment; not one farthing would have been paid into the loan-office. Such a construction, therefore, is too violent, and not to be admitted. If Virginia had confiscated British debts, and received the debt in question, and said nothing more, the debtor would have been discharged by the operation of the law. In the present case, there is an express discharge, on payment, certificate and receipt.

It appears to me, that the plea, by the defendant, of the act of assembly, and the payment agreeable to its provisions, which is admitted, is a bar to the plaintiff's action, for so much of his debt as he paid into the loan-office; unless the plea is avoided or destroyed, by the plaintiff's replication of the fourth article of the definitive treaty of peace between Great Britain and the United States, on the 3d of September 1783.

The question then may be stated thus: whether the 4th article of the said treaty nullifies the law of Virginia, passed on the 20th of October 1777; destroys the payment made under it; and revives the debt, and gives a right of recovery thereof, against the original debtor?

It was doubted by one of the counsel for the defendants in error (Mr. Marshall), whether congress had a power to make a treaty, that could operate to annul a legislative act of any of the states, and to destroy rights acquired by, or vested in individuals, in virtue of such acts. Another of the defendant's counsel (Mr. Campbell) expressly, and with great zeal, denied that congress possessed such power. But a few remarks will be necessary to show the inadmissibility of this objection to the power of congress.

1st. The legislatures of all the states have often exercised the power of taking the property of its citizens for the use of the public, but they uniformly compensated the proprietors. The principle to maintain this right is for the public good, and to that the interest of individuals must yield. The instances are many; and among them are lands taken for forts, magazines or arsenals; or for public roads or canals; or to erect towns.

2d. The legislatures of all the states have often exercised the power of divesting rights vested; and even of impairing, and in some instances, of almost annihilating the obligation of contracts, as by tender laws, which made an offer to pay, and a refusal to receive, paper money, for a specie debt, an extinguishment, to the amount tendered.

3d. If the legislature of Virginia could, by a law, annul any former law; I apprehend, that the effect would be to destroy all rights acquired under the law so nullified.

4th. If the legislature of Virginia could not, by ordinary acts of legislation, do these things, yet, possessing the supreme sovereign power of the state, she certainly could do them, by a treaty of peace; if she had not parted with the power of making such treaty. If Virginia had such power, before she delegated it to congress, it follows, that afterwards, that body possessed it. Whether Virginia parted with the power of making treaties of peace, will be seen by a perusal of the 9th article of the confederation (ratified by all the states, on the first of March 1781), in which it was declared, "that the United States in congress assembled, shall have the sole and exclusive right and power of determining on peace or war, except in the two cases mentioned in the 6th article; and of entering into treaties and alliances, with a proviso, when made, respecting commerce." This grant has no restriction, nor is there any limitation on the power in any part of the confederation. A right to make peace, necessarily includes the power of determining on what terms peace shall be made. A power to make treaties must, of necessity, imply a power to decide the terms on which they shall be made: a war between two nations can only be concluded by treaty.

Surely, the sacrificing public or private property, to obtain peace, cannot be the cases in which a treaty would be void. Vatt. lib. 2, c. 12, § 160, 161, p. 173; lib. 6, c. 2, § 2. It seems to me, that treaties made by congress, according to the confederation, were superior to the laws of the states; because the confederation made them obligatory on all the states. They were so declared by congress on the 13th of April 1787; were so admitted by the legislatures and executives of most of the states; and were so decided by the judiciary of the general government, and by the judiciaries of some of the state governments.

If doubts could exist, before the establishment of the present national government, they must be entirely removed by the 6th article of the constitution, which provides "That all treaties made, or which shall be made, under the authority of the United States, shall be the supreme law of the land; and the judges in every state shall be bound thereby, anything in the constitution or laws of any state to the contrary notwithstanding." There can be no limitation on the power of the people of the United States. By their authority, the state constitutions were made, and by their authority the constitution of the United States was established; and they had the power to change or abolish the state constitutions, or to make them yield to the general government, and to treaties made by their authority. A treaty cannot be the supreme law of the land, that is, of all the United States, if any act of a state legislature can stand in its way. If the constitution of a state (which is the fundamental law of the state, and paramount to its legislature) must give way to a treaty, and fall before it; can it be questioned, whether the less power, an act of the state legislature, must not be prostrate? It is the declared will of the people of the United States, that every treaty made by the authority of the United States, shall be superior to the constitution and laws of any individual state; and their will alone is to decide. If a law of a state, contrary to a treaty, is not void, but voidable only, by a repeal, or nullification by a state legislature, this certain consequence follows, that the will of a small part of the United States may control or defeat the will of the whole. The people of America have been pleased to declare, that all treaties made before the establishment of the national constitution, or laws of any of the states, contrary to a treaty, shall be disregarded.

Four things are apparent, on a view of this 6th article of the national constitution. 1st. That it is retrospective, and is to be considered in the same light as if the constitution had been established before the making of the treaty of 1783. 2d. That the constitution or laws of any of the states, so far as either of them shall be found contrary to that treaty, are, by force of the said article, prostrated before the treaty. 3d. That, consequently, the treaty of 1783 has superior power to the legislature of any state, because no legislature of any state has any kind of power over the constitution, which was its creator. 4th. That it is the declared duty of the state judges to determine any constitution or laws of any state, contrary to that treaty (or any other), made under the authority of the United States, null and void. National or federal judges are bound by duty and oath to the same conduct.

The argument, that congress had not power to make the 4th article of the treaty of peace, if its intent and operation was to annul the laws of any of the states, and to destroy vested rights (which the plaintiff's counsel contended to be the object and effect of the 4th article), was unnecessary, but on the supposition that this court possess a power to decide whether this article of the treaty is within the authority delegated to that body, by the articles of confederation. Whether this court constitutionally possess such a power, is not necessary now to determine, because I am fully satisfied, that congress were invested with the authority to make the stipulation in the 4th article. If the court possess a power to declare treaties void, I shall never exercise it, but in a very clear case indeed. One further remark will show how very circumspect the court ought to be, before they would decide against the right of congress to make the stipulation objected to. If congress had no power (under the confederation) to make the 4th article of the treaty, and for want of power, that article is void, would it not be in the option of the crown of Great Britain to say, whether the other articles in the same treaty shall be obligatory on the British nation?

. . . . .

II. The article in the constitution concerning treaties I have always considered, and do now consider, was in consequence of the conflict of opinions I have mentioned on the subject of the treaty in question. It was found, in this instance, as in many others, that when thirteen different legislatures were necessary to act in unison on many occasions, it was in vain to expect that they would always agree to act as congress might think it their duty to require. Requisitions formerly were made binding in point of moral obligation (so far as the amount of money was concerned, of which congress was the constitutional judge), but the right and the power being separated, it was found often impracticable to make them act in conjunction. To obviate this difficulty, which every one knows had been the means of greatly distressing the Union, and injuring its public credit, a power was given to the representatives of the whole Union to raise taxes, by their own authority, for the good of the whole. Similar embarrassments had been found about the treaty: this was binding in moral obligation, but could not be constitutionally carried into effect (at least in the opinion of many), so far as acts of legislation then in being constituted an impediment, but by a repeal. The extreme inconveniencies felt from such a system dictated the remedy which the constitution has now provided, "that all treaties made or which shall be made under the authority of the United States, shall be the supreme law of the land; and that the judges in every state shall be bound thereby, anything in the constitution or laws of any state to the contrary notwithstanding." Under this constitution, therefore, so far as a treaty constitutionally is binding, upon principles of moral obligation, it is also, by the vigor of its own authority, to be executed in fact. It would not otherwise be the supreme law, in the new sense provided for, and it was so before, in a moral sense.

The provision extends to subsisting as well as to future treaties. I consider, therefore, that when this constitution was ratified, the case as to the treaty in question stood upon the same footing, as if every act constituting an impediment to a creditor's recovery had been expressly repealed, and any further act passed, which the public obligation had before required, if a repeal alone would not have been sufficient.

22

KENTUCKY RESOLUTIONS
10 Nov. 1798, 14 Nov. 1799

(See Amend. I [speech and press], no. 18)

23

JAMES MADISON, VIRGINIA RESOLUTIONS
21 Dec. 1798

(See Amend. I [speech and press], no. 19)

24

JOHN MARSHALL, REPORT OF THE MINORITY ON THE VIRGINIA RESOLUTIONS
22 Jan. 1799

J. House of Delegates (Va.) 6:93–95 (1798–99)

(See Amend. I [speech and press], no. 20)

25

UNITED STATES V. ROBINS
27 Fed. Cas. 825, no. 16,175 (D.S.C. 1799)

BEE, District Judge. The question on which I am now to give a decision, is grounded on a habeas corpus to bring the prisoner before me; and on motion by counsel on behalf of the consul of his Britannic majesty, the officer authorized by treaty to make the requisition, that the prisoner, charged with murder committed within the jurisdiction of Great Britain, shall be delivered up to justice, in virtue of the 27th article of the treaty of amity and commerce between the United States and Great Britain, signed the 19th of November, 1794.

Objections have been made by counsel on behalf of the prisoner to this motion, on a variety of grounds; and this case has been very fully argued on both sides. Two papers have been produced on behalf of the prisoner: one, a certificate from a notary public at New York, dated 20th of May, 1795, that Jonathan Robbins, a mariner, had that day deposed on oath before him, that he, the said Jonathan Robbins, was a citizen of the United States, and a native of Connecticut; the other is an affidavit of the prisoner, made in open court, that he is a native of Connecticut: and that about two years ago he was pressed from the brig Betsy of New York, on board the British frigate Hermione, and was detained there against his will, until the vessel was captured by the crew, and carried into a Spanish port, and that he gave no assistance. The motion before me has been opposed on a variety of grounds. It is contended, that it is a question of magnitude whether a citizen of the United States shall be tried by a jury of his own country, or in a foreign one: that the 27th article of the treaty, on which this motion is founded, is contrary to the constitution of the United States, and is therefore void; that the treaty can only relate to foreigners: that the fact in this case being committed on the high seas, the courts of the United States have competent jurisdiction: that a grand jury ought to make inquest, before a party shall be sent away for trial. It was also contended that this would strike at the root of the liberties of the people: that the constitution secured the right of trial by jury to the citizens; and that treaties and laws altering that, were of subordinate authority; and of course void: that the treaty making power may be abused; and it could never give authority to seize a person and send him away for trial. It was also contended, that this is not an offence within the contemplation of the treaty: the word "jurisdiction," means "territorial jurisdiction"; and that the act must be confined to offences committed within the territory of either; that the sending a person in confinement to be tried in a foreign country, is a punishment not to be inflicted on a citizen: that the treaty is a head without a body, legs or arms: that the affidavits do not come up to the point, and are not sufficient to prevent the party being entitled to bail.

These were the points on which the objections to this motion were argued. In the course of the arguments, warm and pathetic appeals to the passions were made on some of the old grounds of opposition to the treaty, which I endeavoured to check, because, as this treaty has been ratified agreeably to the express provisions of the constitution, and is therein declared to be the supreme law of the land, and I am religiously and solemnly bound by the oath I have taken to administer justice according to the constitution and laws, it is not in my power, nor is it my inclination, ever to deviate therefrom. If we attend to the constitution, and the amendments which are now part of it, we shall find, that all the provisions there made respecting criminal prosecutions, and trials for crimes by a jury, are expressly limited to crimes committed within a state or district of the United States. Indeed, reason and common sense point out that it should be so: for, what control can the laws of one nation have over offences committed in the territories of another? It must be remembered, also, that in the 27th article of the amendments, where it is provided that no person shall be held to answer for a capital offence, unless on a presentment by a grand jury, an exception is made to cases arising in the land or sea service, or even in the militia when in actual service, in time of war or public danger. This shows unequivocally, that trials by jury may be dispensed with, even for crimes committed within the United States; and those observations are at once an answer to all the arguments founded on the right to trials by jury, they being expressly limited to crimes committed within the United States, and even then with some exceptions.

The objections made to the treaty's being contrary to the constitution, have been so often and so fully argued and refuted, that I was in hopes no time would have been occupied on that subject, more especially as that treaty has been recognized by the legislature of the United States and is now in full operation. It is remarkable, that in the midst of all the warmth against the treaty, at its first publication, the 27th article was one of the few that was never excepted to; and I believe this is the first instance in which it had been held up as dangerous to liberty. The crime of murder is justly reprobated in all countries; and in commercial ones the crime of forgery is so dangerous to trade and commerce, that provision has been made in various treaties for delivering up fugitives from justice for these offences; and many instances may be produced of criminals sent back to be tried where the fact was perpetrated. What says the 27th article of the treaty now under consideration? In the first place it is founded on reciprocity: in the next, it is general to all persons, who, being charged with murder or forgery, whether citizens, subjects, or foreigners. It is for the furtherance of justice, because the culprits would otherwise escape punishment; no prosecution would lie against them in a foreign country; and if it did, it would be difficult to procure evidence to convict or acquit. This clause is founded on the same principle with that part of the constitution which declares, that the trial for a crime shall be held in the state where it shall be committed; and the act of congress to prevent fugitives from justice escaping punishment, declares, that they shall be delivered up when demanded, to be tried where they committed the offence, either on a bill found, or an affidavit charging them with the offence. The principle, then, being the same, and the one being expressly founded on the constitution and laws of the United States, no solid objection can lie against this clause of the treaty. Nor does it make any difference, whether the offence is committed by a citizen, or another person. This will obviate the objection made by the counsel on that head. And I cannot but take this occasion to observe, that the two papers produced by the prisoner, are only affidavits of his own, or a certificate founded on an affidavit, which are not evidence; and if they were, prove little or nothing. It is somewhat remarkable, that a man of the name of Jonathan Robbins, with the paper produced in his possession, should continue on board a British frigate for a length of time, under another name, and acting as a warrant officer, which impressed men are not likely to be entrusted with, and that he should afterwards take the name of Nathan Robbins, and lay in jail here five or six months, without the circumstance being made known until now.

All the arguments against delivering up the prisoner seem to imply that he was to be punished without a trial; the contrary of which is the fact: we know that no man can be punished by the laws of Great Britain without a trial. If he is innocent, he will be acquitted: if otherwise, he must suffer. This would be the case here, under similar circumstances.

The objection most relied on against this motion, is to the word jurisdiction, in the 27th article of the treaty, and that the crime being committed on the high seas, the courts of the United States have a concurrent jurisdiction. There is no doubt that the circuit courts of the United States have a concurrent jurisdiction, and this arises under the general law of nations; and if the 27th clause of the treaty in question had not expressly declared the right to demand, and the obligation to deliver over, the prisoner must have been tried here. With respect to the meaning of the word "jurisdiction," I think the case quoted from Vatt. Law Nat. bk. 1, c. 19, § 216, is conclusive, and this is corroborated by Ruth. Inst. bk. 2, c. 9, as to the jurisdiction over the men on board the vessels; and the clause itself seems to have contemplated this, because the word "jurisdiction" is used distinctly from countries in the next line; and this shows, that territorial jurisdiction, as contended for, cannot apply to the present case.

When application was first made, I thought this a matter for the executive interference, because the act of congress respecting fugitives from justice, from one state to another, refers it altogether to the executive of the states; but as the law and the treaty are silent upon the subject, recurrence must be had to the general powers vested in the judiciary by law and the constitution, the 3d article of which declares the judicial power shall extend to treaties, by express words. The judiciary have in two instances in this state, where no provisions were expressly stipulated, granted injunctions to suspend the sale of prizes under existing treaties. If it were otherwise, there would be a failure of justice.

I have carefully reviewed the arguments advanced by the counsel for the prisoner. I have looked into the constitution, the treaty, the laws, and the cases quoted: and upon a full investigation of them all, I am of opinion, that from the affidavits filed with the clerk of the court, there is sufficient evidence of criminality to justify the apprehension and commitment of the prisoner for trial, for murder committed on board a ship of war belonging to his Brittanic majesty, on the high seas: that requisition having been made by the British consul, the officer authorized to make the same, in virtue of the 27th article of the treaty of amity and commerce between the United States and Great Britain, I am bound by the express words of that clause of the treaty, to deliver him up to justice. And I do therefore order and command the marshal, in whose custody the prisoner now is, to deliver the body of the said Nathan Robbins, alias Thomas Nash, to the British consul, or such person or persons as he shall appoint to receive him.

Contemporary Comments

[JOHN MARSHALL] "I observe in a late paper of the Examiner, several strictures on the case of Robbins, who was delivered to the British consul at Charleston, under the 27th article of the treaty of amity and commerce between Great Britain and America, censuring the measure in general, but reprobating the conduct of the president in a particular manner. These strictures, calculated to exasperate the public mind, would probably lose their effect upon a fair explanation of the nature of the business, and therefore I have thought it worth while, for the sake of removing unjust impressions, and satisfying the minds of those who really wish for information relative to the necessary mode of proceeding in cases of that kind, to endeavour to make a just representation of the matter, as far as I am able to understand the case from the mutilated publications which we have seen of it. As to the opinion of the learned judge upon the case, I shall not enter into any arguments in support of it, because they would be useless and unnecessary, as the reasoning contained in his own excellent speech upon the subject is perfectly correct, and must be convincing to every unprejudiced mind. I shall therefore confine myself to that part of the case which re-

spects the president's letter only: which I am induced to do, not because I think it needs any justification with candid men, who know the nature of such proceedings, but because I wish to prevent the effects which are intended to be produced from it upon the minds of those who do not possess the kind of information necessary to enable them to judge impartially on the subject. The case, from the publication which I have seen, I suppose to be this. The British government, having discovered that Robbins was in Charleston, applied to the judge for a warrant to secure him until application could be made to government for him. The warrant was granted, and an application, with the evidences of the charge, were laid before the president, who, being satisfied that it was a case within the treaty, directed the judge, as he was arrested under his warrant, to deliver him up, and the single question is, whether this proceeding in the present case was regular. By the treaty of amity made when the two nations neither did nor could contemplate this, or the case of any other individual, it is mutually stipulated that fugitives from justice who have been guilty of murder or forgery in one of the nations, and have taken shelter in the territories of the other, shall be delivered up to the injured government. Those stipulations are reciprocal, and America, whenever a case shall happen, will have the same right to demand a fugitive of Great Britain that the latter had to demand Robbins of the United States. Nor can either nation refuse, for the words are positive. They are: 'It is further agreed, that his majesty and the United States, on mutual requisitions by their respective ministers or officers authorized to make the same, will deliver up to justice all persons who, being charged of murder or forgery committed within the jurisdiction of either, shall seek an asylum within any of the countries of the other, provided that this shall only be done on such evidence of criminality as, according to the laws of the place where the fugitive or persons charged shall be found, would justify his apprehension and commitment for trial, if the offence had there been committed. The expense of such apprehension and delivery shall be borne and defrayed by those who make the requisition and receive the fugitive.' These words contain an absolute engagement to deliver such characters up, and neither nation can refuse or neglect it without a violation of the treaty. It is, therefore, a certain fact, that Great Britain, by the express words of the treaty, had a right to demand Robbins in the present case, who was accused of murder, one of the enumerated offences for which fugitives were to be delivered up. There must, therefore, have been some mode of carrying the provision of the treaty in this respect into execution, or else the articles would be nugatory; and it would be absurd to suppose the parties meant to stipulate for a thing which could not be performed. The question then is, what mode should be pursued when a requisition of this kind is made, and what proceedings should take place in order to comply with it. The treaty has not pointed out any mode, and therefore we must recur to principles and the nature of things in order to discover it. As nations do not communicate with each other but through the channel of their government, the natural, the obvious, and the proper mode, is an application on the part of the government (requiring the fugitive) to the executive of the nation to which he has fled, to secure and cause him to be delivered up. (1) Because the government being the only channel of communication between the nations, the British government, in cases of this kind, has nothing to do with the detail and internal regulations of ours, nor we with theirs. For as the governments have respectively undertaken to do the thing which is required, the injured nation is not concerned any further with the business than merely to exhibit the proofs and call on the other for the performance of the treaty; and the nation called on must attend to the details and internal regulations themselves. (2) Because the government to which the fugitive has fled ought to be informed why an inhabitant is forced away from its territories; and therefore a removal of any person therefrom, without an application to the chief magistrate, would not only be dangerous to the personal safety of individuals, but would be an indignity and an affront which ought not to be offered. (3) Because, without such an application, the injured nation could not complain of an infraction of the treaty on the part of the other government in not delivering up the fugitive. For it would be an irresistible argument to such a complaint, that no application was ever made to the government itself. Nor would it strengthen the complaint, that an application was made to some inferior authority; because an application to subordinate officers who do not represent the general national concerns, would not only be improper on account of the inconvenient practices it might introduce (for by that means a man might be carried off without government having an opportunity of protecting him), but, in case the requisition were not complied with, could not be a just ground of reproach to the government itself, which was never informed of the application. (4) Because, it is manifest from what has been said, as well as from the very nature of things, that government must have a right to decide whether a fugitive should be delivered up or not. For it is a mere question of state, and all questions relative to the affairs of the nation emphatically belong to the government to decide upon. Therefore, in case of a requisition for a fugitive by the United States from Great Britain, the application would be to the executive, and not to the judiciary, or any other inferior department of the government. It follows, therefore, that an application to the government itself is essential; and accordingly, in the case under consideration, such an application was actually made. But surely the business was not to rest there. Some further steps were necessary, or else the application would have been to no purpose.

"The government, as we have already seen, was bound by engagement to cause delivery to be made; and therefore the president was under the necessity of taking some order in the business which might produce the object of the application. For, having been informed that the man was under confinement, upon the charge on which the application was made, until the determination of government upon the subject could be known, he was bound to give some directions in the business, so that the prisoner might either be liberated or delivered up, and those directions could only be given in writing. If the president had said to the British ambassador: 'You must apply to the judge under whose warrant he was arrested, and he will deliver the prisoner to you,' the obvious answer would have been, 'Sir, I cannot do so without your warrant. If I apply to your judge, I shall certainly be told again as I was told before, that he cannot interfere in a business of state without the knowledge of government; and it will be in vain for me to tell him that I have your instructions upon the subject, unless I am able to produce some evidence of them.' It follows, therefore, that the president was bound to give some written instructions upon the subject; because no other would, or ought to have been credited by the judge.

"The only question then is, whether the letter of the secretary of state contained the proper instructions or not? If I am right in my position that the application, in all such cases, should be made to the executive, and that the executive has a right to decide whether the requisition should be complied with or not; it follows necessarily, that when information was given to the judge that application had been made, it ought to have been accompanied with some expression of the will of government upon the subject. For it would have been ridiculous in the president to have ordered a letter to be written to the judge, informing him that an application had been made, without informing him also what government had resolved to do in the business; because that would have left the judge exactly where he was; and he would have been at liberty to have considered it as a mere private letter from one gentleman to another, and not as an official document, on which he was bound to act. So that, if under that impression he had resolved to have taken no steps in the business, he not only would have stood excused himself, but the British government would have had just cause to complain that our conduct was illusory, and that the stipulations of that treaty were evaded. But, if it be admitted that any declaration of the president was necessary upon the subject, more eligible terms than those used by the secretary of state, even according to the garbled publication which we have of them, could not have been chosen. For they are the usual phrases all over the United States, from the governor down to the county court magistrate. There is not a mandate of any kind in use amongst us, which does not contain the word 'require'; and it will surely be admitted that the word 'advise' is at least as harmless as the words 'command' and 'at your peril,' which are to be found in the warrant of every superior to his inferior officer throughout the United States. Let me now, then, ask any candid man, if the inference drawn by the Examiner from this letter, namely, that the president had endeavoured to influence the opinion of a judge, in a matter depending before him, be a correct one? On the contrary, it is manifest from what has been said, that the matter never was, nor could be regularly before the judge, until he had received this letter, which was the ground and foundation on which he was to proceed. Until then he had no authority to act definitely upon the question; and so the judge evidently appears to have considered it himself. For it was handed to the counsel on both sides, plainly as the authority on which he proceeded. Otherwise, he would not have shown it at all, or else he would have done it in a very different manner. It was, therefore, a mere official paper, and not a letter which was intended to be intruded upon the judge, in order to influence his determination in a matter depending before him. It was itself the very process, if I may use the expression, which brought the case before the judge.

"Perhaps it will be said that the judge himself has denied the authority of the executive; and there is a passage in his speech which looks that way. But this is a part of the opinion of the judge which seems liable to be questioned; and I strongly suspect it is not truly stated in the public prints, or else it comes to this, that the judge was of opinion that everything relative to treaties was to be transacted by the judges and not by the executive; a position which he certainly did not mean to maintain, and, therefore, the passage alluded to ought to be understood with some qualification.

"Perhaps the following solution may reconcile his opinion with the doctrine I have been contending for: The judge probably meant to say, that he once thought it a question which exclusively belonged to the executive, and therefore, that he, as a judge, could not in any manner be required to aid in the execution of the treaty. But finding, by recurrence to the constitution, that the judicial power extended to treaties, he was then satisfied that the judges might be called on, where circumstances rendered it proper, to take the necessary steps, in order to have the treaty carried into effect, as by issuing a warrant to secure the fugitive, until the determination of government could be known, and after that was promulgated, giving the necessary orders for carrying the determination into effect. With this qualification, the opinion of the judge was correct, and I therefore incline to think that he ought to be so understood in the passage under consideration. Upon the whole, the president appears to have done no more than his duty. For suppose it had been said that the British government had applied to the president for a fugitive from justice under the treaty, and that the latter, instead of ordering him to be delivered up, had refused or neglected to do it, without assigning any reason for it. How could the president have justified his conduct in that case? And might it not then have been said with propriety, that he had neglected his duty and omitted to execute one of the supreme laws of the land, which he was bound to observe and have carried into effect? In short, if some men would use but half the industry in examining into the real motives of the president's conduct upon any occasion, that they do in finding out reasons to reproach him, they would soon be convinced that, in no instance of his administration, has he either encroached upon the duty of others, or omitted to perform his own." 1 Hall. Jour. Jur. 28.

[CHARLES PINCKNEY] "To the Citizens of the United States: As congress must by law provide, at their next session, for any similar cases which may occur under the British treaty, and as it is of general importance to the citizens of the United States, the following examination of the case of Jonathan Robbins, lately decided in the district court of South Carolina, is with deference submitted to their consideration: Fellow Citizens—As I believe you have not been much troubled with my remarks on any subject, I hope you will more readily excuse the favour I now ask, in requesting your attention to the present. I am induced to make them, because the question is of very great public consequence, and involves the dearest and most valuable rights of every man in the United States. It reaches all situations, as well the elevated and opulent as the most indigent. It affects the knowledge and independence of our judicials in the most important manner; and as I know it has excited the sensibility of the people, and must be so far made the subject of inquiry in congress as to enable them to provide for similar cases; I have supposed some examination of it may be necessary, in that spirit of deference and delicacy in which all such inquiries should be conducted. I shall not go into a definition of the principles of a free government, and the blessings its citizens ought to expect; because few of our own, even amongst the most illiterate, are ignorant of the nature of a representative government, the right of suffrage, and the inestimable privilege of the trial by jury, in all cases in which their characters, lives or property are concerned. To a people so informed, it is scarcely necessary to remark, that to men of feeling the value of character, of honorable fame, is dearer than life or property, or even the most tender connections: that to all men, whether of the nicest honour or otherwise, the love of life is dearer than that of property, and that they would readily sacrifice the one to preserve the other. Hence it follows, that those privileges which guard the character and lives of our citizens are viewed with a more jealous eye, and will be asserted with more firmness and promptitude, than even those which protect their properties, vigilant as they are with respect to these. A number of our citizens, therefore, believing that the inestimable privileges secured to them by the constitution and laws of the United States, have been affected in the case of Jonathan Robbins, that it is one which may if established as a precedent, reach some valuable inhabitants of this country, and to the intent that these privileges should be more carefully guarded by a positive law in future, the following remarks are submitted, with a view to bring this business more fully before the public than it has hitherto been. The following is the statement of the case, with the accompanying affidavits: It appears, however, by the result, that these affidavits, and the question whether the prisoner was an American, and an impressed seaman or not, were, in the opinion of the court, altogether immaterial: the court would have felt itself bound to deliver up any respectable citizen of the United States, if claimed under the circumstances of the prisoner. It appears by the preceding statement, that the judge, under the circumstances of this case, would feel himself obliged to deliver up any respectable citizen of the 'United States.' I do not mention this because he used the words 'respectable citizen'; but I do it to show, that this is a question which seriously concerns every part of the community, and that no citizen whose business may oblige him to go to other countries, is hereafter safe from such demands. It will not depend upon him to say he is not a mariner, or to show proofs or certificates to the contrary. It will depend upon the force with which he is attacked, and the temper or violence of the officer who directs it. Instances, it is said, have lately occurred where not only the seamen but the passengers have been impressed, who, although declaring they were not seamen, were still impressed as such, and obliged to perform their duties. No production of papers, no entreaties availed them: they were compelled to submit. Had these men been enterprising, or an opportunity offered, and they had possessed themselves of their oppressors, and brought them into port: or had they, in the attempt to regain their freedom, been obliged to destroy them, while the world would have applauded the act, the judge must, from the decision, have delivered them to a similar demand; neither influence, fortune, or friends could have saved them. However superior in these, in political privileges they were only equal to the unknown and friendless Robbins. A consistent and inflexible magistrate must view them with the same impartial eye: he must give to them the same construction of the law or constitution; he could not vary them without the immediate loss of character. An enlightened people, therefore, will as attentively, nay, they ought more carefully to guard them in the person of a poor and unprotected than a rich or considerable man. The latter will always find powerful friends to support and protect his privileges; while the rights of the former may in silence and with impunity be unattended to merely because he is unknown, and has not an advocate to assert them. This would probably have been the case in the present instance, had not some gentlemen voluntarily offered themselves to examine and discuss its consequences. The public are obliged to them: it is an excellent example, I hope it will be followed upon every occasion, and that it will make us infinitely more vigilant of our rights than ever. We must never forget that in this country the poor and the rich, the humble and the influential, are entitled to equal privileges; that we ought to consider a violation of the rights of the most indigent and unprotected man, as an injury to the whole; while we have a pen to guide, or a voice to lift, they should constantly be exerted against the exercise of tyranny or oppression, by whatever nation committed or to whomsoever the violence may be done.

"I now proceed to examine the case and the nature of the evidence, on which Mr. Bee determined to deliver Jonathan Robbins to the demand of the British minister. I believe it is the first instance which has occurred, of a demand under the British treaty in the United States; certainly, in this state. The law respecting the delivery of fugitives from justice was silent on the delivery of fugitives to foreign powers, therefore the judge conceived himself not only authorized but bound to interfere. By his own statement it appears to have been entirely a new case, in which I should suppose he had considerable discretion, and was not bound by any particular legislative act to deliver on a mere affidavit or any 'trivial surmise or hearsay evidence.' It was his duty to have maturely considered what were the legal import and meaning of the words, 'charged with murder and forgery,' and how far, according to the laws of this country, there was such evidence of criminality as would justify the sending any man, claiming to be a citizen, and not disproved as such, from his country, to be tried by a foreign tribunal, and most probably by a court martial. The judge's auditors must have been surprised when they heard him say 'that no man can be punished by the laws of Great Britain without a trial; if he is innocent, he will be acquitted; if guilty, he must be punished.' This observation was by no means applicable to the present case: the true question before the court was, whether Jonathan Robbins, producing a notarial certificate of being a citizen of the United States, and asserting that he was impressed by violence into the British service, was, from the nature of the affidavits before him, to be torn from his country and connexions, and deprived of all the rights of citizenship, and sent to be tried by a foreign tribunal, acting without a jury, in the most summary manner, and by martial law. I do not pretend to equal legal knowledge with the judge: but I have sometimes attended to points of this kind; and as far as I am able to form, am clearly of opinion that the prisoner, not having been disproved to be a citizen of the United States, there was not such evidence before the court as justified the judge in giving so important an order, as to surrender him to the demand of the British consul.

. . . . .

"I now come to the policy of the measure in the United States. More than any other nation, except Great Britain, ought the privileges of our seamen to be vigilantly attended to—they are the instrument of our commerce, and to them their country must look up as the true means of becoming an important naval power—of having the ability to protect and guard their rights, and to insure to its citizens the blessings of peace: they are more exposed to the attacks and insolence of powerful and overbearing nations than any other class of our citizens, and are therefore more entitled to the care and attention of our public guardians. Possessing as the United States do, bulky products, every day increasing, and to export which great quantities of shipping and numbers of seamen are necessary, to what portion of their citizens can they look with more anxiety than to them? Numerous as they may become within these ten years, who knows to what extent the parental and fostering hand of government may increase them within the like succeeding period? But to effect this we must value and cherish them. We must recollect that they are not our men, but citizens—that they do not, the moment they become impressed by a superior foreign force, lose their rights or become lost to their country. Can it be supposed, because they are seamen, they have no families, no tender connexions, no comforts to endear their homes to them? Rough and boisterous as is the element they traverse, and laborious as are their lives, among none of our citizens are to be found more true independence and generosity, or more ardent attachment to their country. If, then, they have those passions, that impatience of insult, that invincible thirst for revenge, which indignities like impressment and tyranny never fail to provoke, are they to be punished for using opportunities to exercise them? Are they to submit to the manacle and the lash, without a murmur, because they fear their country, however possessing the means, may not have the inclination to protect them? If so, adieu to your commerce and your navy! Your seamen will fly to other governments more

615

sensible of their value, and more disposed to assert and maintain their rights.

"I will here take notice of the letter which the judge was said to have received from the secretary of state, mentioning, that 'the president advises and requests the delivery of the prisoner,' because it has made some noise, and I do not view it in the same light with others. I believe that neither of them meant to influence the opinion of the judge—that they supposed it was a mere matter of course—that there was no doubt as to the identity or country of the prisoner; and they probably never heard of his claim of citizenship; that they were anxious, on the part of this government, faithfully to execute the treaty, and that the letter to the judge had another intent. This I really believe to be the case; but the noise it has made will show the extreme impropriety of the higher executive officers of our government ever touching, in the most distant manner, on any subjects that may come before the judicial. However innocent the intention, as I think it was in this instance, it is very apt to give rise to unfavourable opinions;—and none more dangerous to a community can be entertained, than that of a wish of the executive to influence the judicial. It weakens the confidence of the public in both; and lessens the respect it is their wish to show them. The present instance will probably operate to advantage; because it is to be supposed that after this our secretaries will be careful to avoid ever writing to a judge on any subject that may possibly come before him. In one thing I perfectly agree with Mr. Bee; and that is, in his avoiding to question the constitutionality of the treaty, although I think it constitutional. On no subject am I more convinced, than that it is an unsafe and dangerous doctrine in a republic, ever to suppose that a judge ought to possess the right of questioning or deciding upon the constitutionality of treaties, laws, or any act of the legislature. It is placing the opinion of an individual, or of two or three, above that of both branches of congress, a doctrine which is not warranted by the constitution, and will not, I hope, long have many advocates in this country.

"I shall here conclude my remarks on this case. They are made in that spirit of deference and respect, which is intended to avoid giving offence, while it examines with candour the subject under discussion. My earnest wish is to draw the attention of congress to the amendment of the act, and to prove to them the necessity of providing in future against the delivery of any fugitives, unless a bill is found against them by a grand jury: to guard them against entering into any articles on this subject in other treaties, unless they assent to it; and particularly to warn them against ever forming any agreements respecting fugitives from justice, except with nations whose citizens possess the right of trial by jury, and are willing to reciprocate so indispensable a provision.

"A South Carolina Planter.
"Charleston, August 3d, 1799."

26

JAMES MADISON, REPORT ON THE VIRGINIA
RESOLUTIONS
Jan. 1800

(See Amend. I [speech and press], no. 24)

27

UNITED STATES v. SCHOONER PEGGY
1 Cranch 103 (1801)

The Chief Justice [Marshall] delivered the opinion of the court.

. . . . .

The constitution of the United States declares a treaty to be the supreme law of the land. Of consequence, its obligation on the courts of the United States must be admitted. It is certainly true that the execution of a contract between nations is to be demanded from, and, in the general, superintended by the executive of each nation; and, therefore, whatever the decision of this court may be relative to the rights of parties litigating before it, the claim upon the nation, if unsatisfied, may still be asserted. But yet where a treaty is the law of the land, and as such affects the rights of parties litigating in court, that treaty as much binds those rights, and is as much to be regarded by the court, as an act of congress; and although restoration may be an executive, when viewed as a substantive act, independent of, and unconnected with, other circumstances, yet to condemn a vessel, the restoration of which is directed by a law of the land, would be a direct infraction of that law, and, of consequence, improper.

It is in the general truth that the province of an appellate court is only to inquire whether a judgment, when rendered, was erroneous or not. But if subsequent to the judgment and before the decision of the appellate court a law intervenes and positively changes the rule which governs, the law must be obeyed, or its obligation denied. If the law be constitutional, and of that no doubt in the present case has been expressed, I know of no court which can contest its obligation. It is true that in mere private cases between individuals, a court will and ought to struggle hard against a construction which will, by a retrospective operation, affect the rights of parties, but in great national concerns where individual rights, acquired by war, are sacrificed for national purposes, the contract making the sacrifice ought always to receive a construction conforming to its manifest import; and if the nation has given up the vested rights of its citizens, it is not for the court but for the government to consider whether it be a case proper for compensation. In such a case the court must decide according to existing laws, and if it be necessary to set aside a judgment rightful, when rendered, but which cannot be affirmed but in violation of law, the judgment must be set aside.

28

ST. GEORGE TUCKER,
BLACKSTONE'S COMMENTARIES
1:APP. 369–70
1803

It may seem very extraordinary, that a people jealous of their liberty, and not insensible of the allurements of power, should have entrusted the federal government with such extensive authority as this article conveys: controlling not only the acts of their ordinary legislatures, but their very constitutions, also.

The most satisfactory answer seems to be, that the powers entrusted to the federal government being all positive, enumerated, defined, and limited to particular objects; and those objects such as relate more immediately to the intercourse with foreign nations, or the relation in respect to war or peace, in which we may stand with them; there can, in these respects, be little room for collision, or interference between the states, whose jurisdiction may be regarded as confided to their own domestic concerns, and the United States, who have no right to interfere, or exercise a power in any case not delegated to them, or absolutely necessary to the execution of some delegated power. That, as this control cannot possibly extend beyond those objects to which the federal government is competent, under the constitution, and under the declaration contained in the twelfth article, so neither ought the laws, or even the constitution of any state to impede the operation of the federal government in any case within the limits of it's constitutional powers. That a law limited to such objects as may be authorised by the constitution, would, under the true construction of this clause, be the suprerme law of the land; but a law not limited to those objects, or not made pursuant to the constitution, would not be the supreme law of the land, but an act of usurpation, and consequently void. A further answer seems also to be, that without this provision the constitution could not have taken effect in those states where the articles of confederation were sanctioned by the constitution; nor could it be supposed that the constitution of the United States would possess any stability so long as it was liable to be affected by any future change in the constitution of any of the states. Other reasons are assigned by the Federalist, for which I shall refer the student to that work.

29

JOHN BRECKENRIDGE, MUNICIPAL AUTHORITY
TO IMPOSE TAXES
28 Apr. 1806
1 Ops. Atty Gen. 157

I am of opinion that there rests no power in the city council, nor in any department of the government of Orleans, to tax the property of the United States within that territory. I believe the exercise of such power has never been before attempted in any part of the United States, and I think the general government ought not to admit the principle. Laying the tax will be harmless, for I see no means by which the payment of it can be enforced.

30

HARRISON V. STERRY
5 Cranch 289 (1809)

(See 1.8.4 [bankruptcy], no. 5)

31

McKIM V. VOORHIES
7 Cranch 279 (1812)

All the Judges being present,

TODD, J. stated the opinion of the Court to be, that the State Court had no jurisdiction to enjoin a judgment of the Circuit Court of the United States; and that the Court below should be ordered to issue the writ of *habere facias*.

32

FAIRFAX'S DEVISEE V. HUNTER'S LESSEE
7 Cranch 603 (1813)

STORY, J., delivered the opinion of the court.

The first question is, whether Lord Fairfax was proprietor of, and seized of the soil of the waste and unappropriated lands in the northern neck, by virtue of the royal grants, 2 Charles, 2 and 4 James 2, or whether he had mere seignoral rights therein as lord paramount, disconnected from all interest in the land, except of sale or alienation.

The royal charter expressly conveys all that entire tract, territory, and parcel of land, situate, &c., together with the rivers, islands, woods, timber, &c., mines, quarries of stone, and coal, &c., to the grantees and their heirs and assigns, to their only use and behoof, and to no other use, intent, or purpose whatsoever.

It is difficult to conceive terms more explicit than these to vest a title and interest in the soil itself. The land is given, and the exclusive use thereof, and if the union of the title and the exclusive use do not constitute the *dominium directum* and *utile*, the complete and absolute dominion in property, it will not be easy to fix on any thing which shall constitute such dominion.

The ground of the objection would seem to have been, that the royal charter had declared that the grantees should hold of the king as tenants in *capite*, and that it proceeded to declare that the grantees and their heirs and assigns should have power "freely and without molestation of the king, to give, grant, or by any ways or means sell or alien all and singular the granted premises, and every part and parcel thereof, to any person or persons being willing to contract for and buy the same," which words were to be considered as restrictive or explanatory of the preceding words of the charter, and as confining the rights granted to the mere authority to sell or alien.

But it is very clear that this clause imposes no restriction or explanation of the general terms of the grant. As the grantees held as tenants in *capite* of the king, they could not sell or alien without the royal license, and if they did, it was in ancient strictness an absolute forfeiture of the land. 2 Ins. 66; and after the statute 1 Edw. 3, ch. 12, though the forfeiture did not attach, yet a reasonable fine was to be paid to the king upon the alienation. 2 Ins. 67; Staundf. Prer. 27; 2 Bl. Com. 72. It was not until ten years after the first charter, (12 Ch. 2, ch. 24,) that all fines for alienations and tenures of the king in *capite* were abolished, 2 Bl. Com. 77. So that the object of this clause was manifestly to give the royal assent to alienations without the claim of any fine therefor.

We are therefore satisfied that, by virtue of the charter, and the intermediate grants, Lord Fairfax, at the time of his death, had the absolute property of the soil of the land in controversy, and the acts of ownership exercised by him over the whole waste and unappropriated lands, as stated in the case, vested in him a complete seizin and possession thereof. Even if there had been no acts of ownership proved, we should have been of opinion that as there was no adverse possession, and the land was waste and unappropriated, the legal seizin must be, upon principle, considered as passing with the title.

On this point, we have the satisfaction to find that our view of the title of Lord Fairfax seems incidentally confirmed by the opinion of the court of appeals, of Virginia, in Picket v. Dowdell, 2 Wash. 106; Johnson v. Buffington, 2 Wash. 116; and Curry v. Burns, 2 Wash. 121.

The next question is as to the nature and character of the title which Denny Fairfax took by the will of Lord Fairfax, he being, at the time of the death of Lord Fairfax, an alien enemy.

It is clear, by the common law, that an alien can take lands by purchase, though not by descent; or in other words, he cannot take by the act of law, but he may by the act of the party. This principle has been settled in the year books, and has been uniformly recognized as sound law from that time. 11 Hen. 4, 26; 14 Hen. 4, 20; Co. Litt. 2 b. Nor is there any distinction, whether the purchase be by grant or by devise. In either case, the estate vests in the alien. Pow. Dev. 316, &c.; Park. Rep. 144; Co. Litt. 2 b.; not for his own benefit, but for the benefit of the State; or in the language of the ancient law, the alien has the capacity to take, but not to hold lands, and they may be seized into the hands of the sovereign. 11 H. 4, 26; 14 H. 4, 20. But until the lands are so seized, the alien has complete dominion over the same. He is a good tenant of the freehold in a *precipe* on a common recovery. 4 Leon, 84; Goldsb. 102; 10 Mod. 128. And may convey the same to a purchaser. Sheafe v. O'Neile, 1 Mass. Rep. 256. Though Co. Litt. 52, b., seems to the contrary, yet it must probably mean that he can convey a defeasible estate only, which an office found will divest. It seems, indeed, to have been held that an alien cannot maintain a real action for the recovery of lands. Co. Litt. 129, b.; Thel. Dig. ch. 6; Dyer 2, b.; but it does not then follow that he may not defend, in a real action, his title to the lands against all persons but the sovereign.

We do not find that in respect to these general rights and disabilities, there is any admitted difference between alien friends and alien enemies. During the war, the property of alien enemies is subject to confiscation *jure belli*, and their civil capacity to sue is suspended. Dyer 2, b.; Brandon v. Nesbitt, 6 T. R. 23; 3 Bos. and Pull. 113; 5 Rob. 102. But as to capacity to purchase, no case has been cited in which it has been denied; and in The Attorney-General v. Wheedon and Shales, Park. Rep. 267, it was adjudged that a bequest to an alien enemy was good, and, after a peace, might be enforced. Indeed, the common law in these particulars seems to coincide with the *Jus Gentium*. Bynk. Quest. Pub. Jur., ch. 7; Vattel, b. 2, ch. 8, § 112, 114; Grot. lib. 2, ch. 6, § 16.

It has not been attempted to place the title of Denny Fairfax upon the ground of his being an *antenatus*, born under a common allegiance before the American revolution, and this has been abandoned upon good reason; for whatever doubts may have been formerly entertained, it is now settled that a British subject born before, cannot, since the Revolution, take lands by descent in the United States. 4 Cranch, 321, Dawson's Lessee v. Godfrey.

But it has been argued, that although D. Fairfax had capacity to take the lands as devisee, yet he took to the use of the commonwealth only, and had, therefore, but a momentary seizin; that in fact he was but a mere trustee of the estate at will of the commonwealth, and that by operation of law, immediately upon the death of the testator, Lord Fairfax, the title vested in the commonwealth, and left but a mere naked possession in the devisee.

If we are right in the position, that the capacity of an alien enemy does not differ in this respect from an alien friend, it will not be easy to maintain this argument. It is incontrovertibly settled upon the fullest authority, that the title acquired by an alien by purchase, is not devested until office found. The principle is founded upon the ground, that as the freehold is in the alien, and he is tenant to the lord of whom the lands are holden, it cannot be devested out of him but by some notorious act by which it may appear that the freehold is in another; 1 Bac. Abr. Alien C. p. 133. Now an office of entitling is necessary to give this notoriety, and fix the title in the sovereign. So it was adjudged in Page's case, 5 Co. 22, and has been uniformly recognized; Park. Rep. 267; Park. 144; Hob. 231; Bro. Denizen, pl. 17; Co. Litt. 2 b.; and the reason of the difference, why, when alien dies, the sovereign is seized without office found, is because otherwise the freehold would be in abeyance, as an alien cannot have any inheritable blood. Nay even after office found, the king is not adjudged in possession, unless the possession were then vacant; for if the possession were then in another, the king must enter or seize by his officer before the possession in deed shall be adjudged in him; 14 H. 7, 21; 15 H. 7, 6, 20; Staundf. Prerog. Reg. ch. 18, p. 54; 4 Co. 58, a.; and if we were to yield to the authority of Staundford, (Prer. Reg. ch. 18, p. 56,) that in the case of alien enemy, the king "*ratione guerrae*," might seize without office found, yet the same learned authority assures us, "that the king must seize in those cases, ere he can have an interest in the lands, because they be penal towards the party;" 4 Co. 58, b.; and until the king be in possession by office found, he cannot grant lands which are forfeited by alienage; Staundf. Pre. Reg. ch. 18, f. 54; Stat. 18 Hen. 6, ch. 6.

To apply these principles to the present case, Denny Fairfax had a complete, though defeasible title, by virtue of the devise, and as the possession was either vacant or not adverse, of course the law united a seizin to his title in the lands in controversy; and this title could only be devested by an inquest of office, perfected by an entry and seizure where the possession was not vacant. And no grant by the commonwealth, according to the common law, could be valid, until the title was, by such means, fixed in the commonwealth. It is admitted that no entry or seizure was made by the commonwealth "*ratione guerrae*" during the war. It is also admitted, that no inquest of office was ever made pursuant to the acts on this subject at any time. And it would seem therefore to follow, upon common law reasoning, that the grant to the lessor of the original plaintiff, by the public patent of 30th April, 1789, issued improvidently and erroneously, and passed nothing. And if this be true, and there be no act of Virginia altering the common law, it is quite immaterial what is the validity of the title of the original defendant as against the commonwealth; for the plaintiff must recover by the strength of his own title, and not by the weakness of that of his adversary.

But it is contended, first, That the common law as to inquests of office and seizure, so far as the same respects the lands in controversy is completely dispensed with by statutes of the commonwealth, so as to make the grant to the original plaintiff in 1789 complete and perfect; and secondly, and further, if it be not so, yet as the devisee died pending the suit, the freehold was thereby cast upon

the commonwealth without an inquest, and thus arises a retroactive confirmation of the title of the original plaintiff, of which he may now avail himself. As to the first point, we will not say that it was not competent for the legislature, (supposing no treaty in the way,) by a special act to have vested the land in the commonwealth without an inquest of office for the cause of alienage. But such an effect ought not, upon principles of public policy, to be presumed upon light grounds; that an inquest of office should be made in cases of alienage, is a useful and important restraint upon public proceedings. No part of the United States seems to have been more aware of its importance, or more cautious to guard against its abolition than the commonwealth of Virginia. It prevents individuals from being harassed by numerous suits introduced by litigious grantees. It enables the owner to contest the question of alienage directly by a traverse of the office. It affords an opportunity for the public to know the nature, the value, and the extent of its acquisitions *pro defectu haeredis;* and above all it operates as a salutary suppression of that corrupt influence which the avarice of speculation might otherwise urge upon the legislature. The common law, therefore, ought not to be deemed to be repealed, unless the language of a statute be clear and explicit for this purpose.

Let us now consider the several acts which have been referred to in the argument, from which we think it will abundantly appear that, during the war, the lands in controversy were never, by any public law, vested in the commonwealth. We dismiss, at once, the act of 1777, c. 9, and of 1779, c. 14, as they are restrained to estates held by British subjects at the times of their respective enactments, and do not extend to estates subsequently acquired.

The next act is that of 1782, c. 8; the 24th section, after reciting that "since the death of the late proprietor of the Northern Neck, there is reason to suppose that the said proprietorship hath descended upon alien enemies," enacts, that persons holding lands in said Neck, shall retain sequestered in their hands, all quitrents which were then due, until the right of descent should be more fully ascertained; and that all quitrents, thereafter to become due, shall be paid into the public treasury, and the parties exonerated from the future claim of the proprietor. Admitting that this section as to the quitrents, was equivalent to an inquest of office; it cannot be extended, by construction, to include the waste lands of the proprietor. Neither the words, nor the intention, of the legislature would authorize such a construction. But it may well be doubted if, even as to the quitrents, the provision is not to be considered as a sequestration *jure belli*, rather than a seizure for alienage, for it proceeds on the ground that the property had descended, not upon aliens, but alien enemies. So far as the treaty of peace might be deemed material in the case, this distinction would deserve consideration.

The next is the act of 1782, c. 33, which, after reciting that "the death of Lord Fairfax may occasion great inconvenience to those who may incline to make entries for vacant lands in the Northern Neck, proceeds (sec. 3,) to enact, that all entries made with the surveyors, &c., and returned to the office formerly kept by Lord Fairfax, shall be held as good and valid as those heretofore made under his direction, "until some mode shall be taken up and adopted by the general assembly, concerning the territory of the Northern Neck." This act, so far from containing in itself any provision for vesting all the vacant lands of Lord Fairfax in the commonwealth, expressly reserves, to a future time, all decisions as to the disposal of the territory. It suffers rights and titles to be acquired exactly in the same manner, and with the same conditions, which Lord Fairfax had by permanent regulations prescribed in his office. No other acts were passed on the subject during the war.

We are now led to consider the act of 1785, ch. 47, which has presented some difficulty, if it stand unaffected by the treaty of peace. The 4th section, after a recital "that since the death of the late proprietor, no mode hath been adopted to enable those who had before his death made entries within the said district according to an act, &c. (act 1782, c. 33,) to obtain titles to the same," enacts that in all cases of such entries, grants shall be issued by the commonwealth to the parties in the same manner, as by law is directed in cases of other unappropriated lands. The 5th section than declares that the unappropriated lands within the Northern Neck should be subject to the same regulations, and be granted in the same manner, and *caveats* should be proceeded upon, tried, and determined, as is by law directed, in cases of other unappropriated lands belonging to the commonwealth. The 6th section extinguishes for the future all quitrents.

The patent of the original plaintiff issued pursuant to the 5th section of this act.

It has been argued, that the act of 1785 amounts to a legislative appropriation of all the lands in controversy. That it must be considered as completely devesting the title of Denny Fairfax for the cause of alienage, and vesting it in the commonwealth. After the most mature reflection, we cannot subscribe to the argument. In acts of sovereignty so highly penal, it is against the ordinary rule to enlarge, by implication and inference, the extent of the language employed. It would be to declare purposes which the legislature have not chosen to avow, and to create vested estates, when the common law would pronounce a contrary sentence, and the guardians of the public interests have not expressed an intention to abrogate that law. If the legislature have proceeded upon the supposition that the lands were already vested in the commonwealth, we do not perceive how it helps the case. If the legislature, upon a mistake of facts, proceed to grant defective titles, we know of no rule of law which requires a court to declare, in penal cases, that to be actually done which ought previously to have been done. Perhaps as to grants under the 4th section upon entries under the act of 1782, c. 33, it might not be too much to hold, that such grants conveyed no more than the title of the commonwealth, exactly in the same state as the commonwealth itself held it, namely, an inchoate right, to be reduced into possession and consummated by a suit in the nature, or with the effect, of an inquest of office. But we give no opinion on this point, because the patent of the original plaintiff mani-

festly issued under the succeeding section, and upon a construction, which we give to this section, it issued improvidently and passed no title whatever. That construction is, that the unappropriated lands in the Northern Neck should be granted in the same manner as the other lands of the commonwealth, when the title of the commonwealth was perfected by possession. It seems to us difficult to contend, that the legislature meant to grant mere titles and rights of entry, of the commonwealth, to lands in the same manner as it did lands of which the commonwealth was in actual possession and seizin. It would be selling suits and controversies through the whole country, and enacting a general statute in favor of maintenance, an offence which the common law has denounced with extraordinary severity. Consistent, therefore, with the manifest intention of the legislature, grants were to issue for lands in the Northern Neck, precisely in the same manner as for lands in other parts of the State, and under the same limitation, namely, that the commonwealth should have, at the time of the grant, a complete title and seizin.

We are the more confirmed in this construction by the act concerning escheators, (act 1779, c. 45,) which regulates the manner of proceeding in cases of escheat, and was by a subsequent act, (act 1785, c. 53,) expressly extended to the countries in the Northern Neck. This act of 1779, expressly prohibits the granting of any lands, seized into the hands of the commonwealth upon office found, till the lapse of twelve months after the return of the inquisition and verdict into the office of the general court, and afterwards authorizes the proper escheator to proceed to sell in case no claim should be filed, within that time, and substantiated against the commonwealth. It is apparent, from this act, that it was not the intention of the legislature to dispose of lands, accruing by escheat, in the same manner as lands to which the commonwealth already possessed a perfect title. It has not been denied that the regulations of this act were designed to apply as well to titles accruing upon purchases by aliens, which are not in strictness, escheats, as upon forfeitures for other causes; and, but for the act of 1785, c. 47, we do not perceive but that the vacant lands, held by the devisee of Lord Fairfax, in the Northern Neck, would have been completely within the act regulating proceedings upon escheats.

The real fact appears to have been, that the legislature supposed that the commonwealth were in actual seizin and possession of the vacant lands of Lord Fairfax, either upon the principle that an alien enemy could not take by devise, or the belief that the acts of 1782, c. 8, and c. 33, had already vested the property in the commonwealth. In either case it was a mistake which surely ought not to be pressed to the injury of third persons.

But if the construction, which we have suggested, be incorrect, we think that, at all events, the title of Hunter, under the grant of 1789, cannot be considered as more extensive than the title of the commonwealth, namely, a title inchoate and imperfect; to be consummated by an actual entry under an inquest of office, or its equivalent, a suit and judgment at law by the grantee.

This view of the acts of Virginia, renders it wholly unnecessary to consider a point, which has been very elaborately argued at the bar, whether the treaty of peace, which declares "that no future confiscations shall be made," protects from forfeiture, under the municipal laws respecting alienage, estates held by British subjects at the time of the ratification of that treaty. For we are well satisfied that the treaty of 1794 completely protects and confirms the title of Denny Fairfax, even admitting that the treaty of peace left him wholly unprovided for.

The ninth article is in these words: "It is agreed that British subjects who now hold lands in the territories of the United States, and American citizens who now hold lands in the dominions of his majesty, shall continue to hold them according to the nature and tenure of their respective estates and titles therein; and may grant, sell, or devise the same to whom they please in like manner as if they were natives, and that neither they nor their heirs or assigns shall, so far as respects the said lands and the legal remedies incident thereto, be considered as aliens."

Now, we cannot yield to the argument that Denny Fairfax had no title, but a mere naked possession or trust estate. In our judgment, by virtue of the devise to him, he held a fee simple in his own right. At the time of the commencement of this suit, in 1791, he was in complete possession and seizin of the land. That possession and seizin continued up to and after the treaty of 1794, which being the supreme law of the land, confirmed the title to him, his heirs and assigns, and protected him from any forfeiture by reason of alienage.

It was once in the power of the commonwealth of Virginia, by an inquest of office or its equivalent, to have vested the estate completely in itself or its grantee. But it has not so done, and its own inchoate title (and of course the derivative title, if any, of its grantee) has by the operation of the treaty become ineffectual and void.

It becomes unnecessary to consider the argument as to the effect of the death of Denny Fairfax pending the suit, because, admitting it to be correctly applied in general, the treaty of 1794 completely avoids it. The heirs of Denny Fairfax were made capable in law to take from him by descent, and the freehold was not, therefore, on his death, cast upon the commonwealth.

On the whole, the court are of opinion that the judgment of the court of appeals of Virginia ought to be reversed, and that the judgment of the district court of Winchester be affirmed, with costs, &c.

JOHNSON, J. After the maturest investigation of this case that circumstances would permit me to make, I am obliged to dissent from the opinion of the majority of my brethren.

The material questions are—

1st. Whether an alien can take lands as a devisee, and if he can,

2d. Whether an inquest of office was indispensably necessary to devest him of his interest for the benefit of the State?

3d. Whether the disability of the devisee was not cured by the treaty of peace, or the treaty of 1794.

With regard to the treaty of peace, it is very clear to me that that does not affect the case. The words of the fourth article are: "There shall be no future confiscations made, nor any prosecution commenced against any person or persons for or by reason of the part which he or they may have taken in the present war."

Now should we admit, as has been strongly insisted, that to escheat is to confiscate, it would still remain to show that this was "a confiscation on account of the part taken by the devisee in the war of the Revolution." But the disability of an alien to hold real estate is the result of a general principle of the common law, and was in no wise attached to the individual on account of his conduct in the revolutionary struggle. The alien who had taken part with this country, and fought the battles of the States, may have been affected by it no less than he who fought against us, and the member of any other community in the world may as well have been the object of its application as the subject of Great Britain. The object evidently was to secure the individual from legal punishment—not to cure a legal disability existing in him.

With regard to the bearing of the treaty of 1794 on the interests of the parties, the only difficulty arises from the vague signification of the words, "now holding," made use of in the article which relates to this subject. But in conformity with the liberal spirit in which national contracts ought to be construed, I am satisfied to consider that treaty as extending to all cases, "of a rightful possession or legal title, defeasible only on the ground of alien disability, and existing at the date of that treaty."

What, then, were the rights of the devisee in this case? and were they in existence at the date of this treaty?

Whoever looks into the learning on the capacity of an alien to take lands as devisee, will find it involved in some difficulties. There is no decided case, that I know of, upon the subject. And the opinions of learned men upon it, when compared, will be found to have been expressed with doubt, or scarcely reconcilable to each other. The general rule is, that an alien may take by purchase, but cannot hold. Yet so fragile or flimsy is the right he acquires, that, if tortiously dispossessed, no one contends that he can maintain an action against the evictor. To assert that he has a right, and yet admit that he has no remedy, appears to me rather paradoxical. Yet all admit that the bailiff of the king cannot enter on an alien purchaser until office found. But where a freehold is cast upon the alien by act of law, as by descent, dower, curtesy, &c., it is admitted that no inquest of office is necessary to vest the estate in the king, and he may enter immediately. Whether an alien devisee is to be considered as a purchaser, according to the meaning of that term, as applied to an alien, or whether his estate is to be considered as one of those which are cast on him by operation of law, is an alternative, either branch of which may be laid hold of with some confidence. Chief Baron Gilbert asserts, without reservation, that a devise to an alien is void. (Gilbert on Devises, p. 15.) But Mr. Powell maintains that he takes under it as a purchaser. (Powell on Devises, 317.) In support of Gilbert's opinion, it might be urged that a devise takes effect under statute, and in that view the interest may be said to be cast on the alien by operation of law. Yet I have no hesitation in deciding in favor of the doctrine, as laid down by Powell. Not on the words of Lord Hardwicke, as quoted from Knight and Du Plessis; for the judge there expressly declines giving an opinion; but from a reference to the principle upon which the doctrine is certainly founded.

The only unexceptionable reason that can be assigned, why an alien can take by deed, though he cannot hold, is, that otherwise the proprietor would be restricted in his choice of an alienee; or in other words, in his right of alienation. And to declare such a conveyance null and void would be attended with this absurdity, that the estate would still remain in the alienor in opposition to his own will and contract. It would, therefore, seem that the law on this subject would be more satisfactorily expressed by asserting that an alien is a competent party to a contract, so that a conveyance, executed to him, shall divest the feoffer or donor, in order that it may escheat. The tendency of this doctrine to favor the royal prerogative of escheat, would no doubt secure to it a welcome reception, yet it is not too much to pronounce it reasonable in the abstract. This reason is as applicable to the case of a devise as of a contract, and in the technical application of the term purchaser, a devisee is included. But it is contended, that the grant to Lord Fairfax was a grant or cession of sovereign power, and, as such, was assumed by the State when it declared itself independent. Upon considering, as well the acts of the State, with regard to this property, as the acts of Lord Fairfax himself, there is reason to think that both acted under this impression. But to decide on this question, we must look into the deed of cession, and upon its construction the decision of this court must depend. And here, in every part of it, we find it divested of the chief attributes of sovereignty, not a power legislative, judicial, or executive given, and the words such as are adapted to convey an interest, but no jurisdiction. Some few royal prerogatives, it is true, are expressly conveyed, and these unquestionably must have accrued to the State upon the assertion of independence. But the interest in the soil remained to the grantee. So far, therefore, I feel no difficulty about sustaining the claim of the devisee. But did this interest remain in him at the time of the treaty of 1794?

I am of opinion it did not. The interest acquired under the devise was a mere *scintilla juris*, and that *scintilla* was extinguished by the grant of the State vesting this tract in the plaintiff in error. I will not say what would have been the effect of a more general grant. But this grant emanated under a law expressly relating to the lands of Lord Fairfax, authorizing them to be entered, surveyed, and granted. The only objection that can be set up to the validity of this grant is, that it was not preceded by an inquest of office. And the question then will be, whether it was not competent for the State to assert its rights over the alien's property, by any other means than an inquest of office. I am of opinion that it was. That the mere executive of the State could not have done it, I will readily admit; but what was there to restrict the supreme legislative power from dispensing with the inquest of office? In the case of Smith *v.* The State of Maryland, (6 Cranch, 286,) this court sustained a specific confiscation of lands under a law of the State, where there was neither conviction nor inquest of office. And in Great Britain, in the case of treason, an in-

quest of office is expressly dispensed with by the statute 33 H. VIII. c. 30. So that there is nothing mystical, nor any thing of indispensable obligation, in this inquest of office. It is, in Great Britain, a salutary restraint upon the exercise of arbitrary power by the crown, and affords the subject a simple and decent mode of contesting the claim of his sovereign; but the legislative power of that country certainly may assert, and has asserted, the right of dispensing with it, and I see no reason why it was not competent for the legislature of the State of Virginia to do the same.

Several collateral questions have arisen, in this case, on which, as I do not differ materially from my brethren, I will only express my opinion in the briefest manner.

I am of opinion that, whenever the case, made out in the pleadings, does not, in law, sanction the judgment which has been given upon it, the error sufficiently appears upon the record to bring the case within the 25th section of the Judiciary Act.

I am also of opinion that, whenever a case is brought up to this court under that section, the title of the parties litigant must necessarily be inquired into, and that such an inquiry must, in the nature of things, precede the consideration, how far the law, treaty, and so forth, is applicable to it; otherwise, an appeal to this court would be worse than nugatory.

And that, in ejectment at least, if not in every possible case, the decision of this court must conform to the state of rights of the parties at the time of its own judgment: so that a treaty, although ratified subsequent to the decision of the court appealed from, becomes a part of the law of the case and must control our decision.

33

UNITED STATES v. HART
26 Fed. Cas. 193, no. 15,316 (C.C.D.Pa. 1817)

WASHINGTON, Circuit Justice. It is unnecessary at this time to enter into an examination of the objections made to the constitutionality of this law, and to the jurisdiction of this court, as the defendant may have the full benefit of them on a motion in arrest of judgment, if the verdict should be against him, and there should be any thing in the objections. I shall merely observe for the present, that by passing them over, it is not to be understood that the court means, in any respect, to countenance them. If the ordinance of the city is in collision with the act of congress, there can be no question but that the former must give way. The constitution of the United States, and the laws made in pursuance thereof, are declared by the constitution to be the supreme law of the land; and the judges both of the federal and state courts, are bound thereby, any thing in the constitution or laws of any state, to the contrary notwithstanding. But, there is in truth no collision between this ordinance and the act of congress on which this indictment is founded. If the mail carrier should violate the ordinance, the act of congress does not shelter him from the penalty imposed by the ordinance. But the ordinance does not authorise any officer to stop the mail, and consequently he cannot justify his having done it, under that ordinance. The defendant's counsel have then resorted to the common law, which authorises a constable, without a warrant, to prevent a breach of the peace; and it is contended, that for any person to drive through a populous city, at such a rate as to endanger the lives or the safety of the inhabitants, amounts to a breach of the peace.

This view of the subject presents two questions. First, was the mail carrier in the act of breaking the peace, at the time when he was stopped by the defendant; and if he was, then, secondly, would this fact excuse him under a fair interpretation of the law under consideration. As to the first question the court is of opinion that driving a carriage through a crowded or populous street, at such a rate or in such a manner as to endanger the safety of the inhabitants, is an indictable offence at common law, and amounts to a breach of the peace. But, whether in the two cases stated in this indictment, the mail carrier so conducted himself as to come within this principle, is a question proper for the jury to decide. If they decide this fact affirmatively, then upon the principles of the common law, the constable was authorised without a warrant, to prevent the peace from being broken. The second question will depend upon the fair construction of the act of congress, and we are of opinion that it ought not to be so construed as to shield the carrier against this preventive remedy, because a temporary stoppage of the mail may be the consequence. Suppose the officer had a warrant against a felon who had placed himself in the stage, or that the driver should commit murder in the street in the presence of an officer, and then place himself on the box; could it be contended, that the sanctity of the mail would extend to protect those persons against arrest, because a temporary stoppage of the mail would be the consequence? We think not. It could not be said in any of these cases, that the act amounted to a wilful stoppage of the mail.

Verdict not guilty.

34

McCULLOCH v. MARYLAND
4 Wheat. 316 (1819)

[D. WEBSTER, for the plaintiff in error] . . . 2. The second question is, whether, if the bank be constitutionally created, the state governments have power to tax it? The people of the United States have seen fit to divide sovereignty, and to establish a complex system. They have conferred certain powers on the state governments, and certain other powers on the national government. As it was easy to foresee that question must arise between these governments thus constituted, it became of great moment to determine, upon what principle these questions should be decided, and who should decide them. The constitution, therefore, declares, that the constitution itself, and the laws passed in pursuance of its provisions, shall be the supreme law of the land, and shall control all state legislation and state constitutions, which may be incompatible therewith; and it confides to this court the ultimate power of deciding all questions arising under the constitution and laws of the United States. The laws of the United States, then, made in pursuance of the constitution, are to be the supreme law of the land, anything in the laws of any state to the contrary notwithstanding. The only inquiry, therefore, in this case is, whether the law of the state of Maryland imposing this tax be consistent with the free operation of the law establishing the bank, and the full enjoyment of the privileges conferred by it? If it be not, then it is void; if it be, then it may be valid. Upon the supposition, that the bank is constitutionally created, this is the only question; and this question seems answered, as soon as it is stated. If the states may tax the bank, to what extent shall they tax it, and where shall they stop? An unlimited power to tax involves, necessarily, a power to destroy; because there is a limit beyond which no institution and no property can bear taxation. A question of constitutional power can hardly be made to depend on a question of more or less. If the states may tax, they have no limit but their discretion; and the bank, therefore, must depend on the discretion of the state governments for its existence. This consequence is inevitable. The object in laying this tax, may have been revenue to the state. In the next case, the object may be to expel the bank from the state; but how is this object to be ascertained, or who is to judge of the motives of legislative acts? The government of the United States has itself a great pecuniary interest in this corporation. Can the states tax this property? Under the confederation, when the national government, not having the power of direct legislation, could not protect its own property by its own laws, it was expressly stipulated, that "no impositions, duties or restrictions should be laid by any state on the property of the United States." Is it supposed, that property of the United States is now subject to the power of the state governments, in a greater degree than under the confederation? If this power of taxation be admitted, what is to be its limit? The United States have, and must have, property locally existing in all the states; and may the states impose on this property, whether real or personal, such taxes as they please? Can they tax proceedings in the federal courts? If so, they can expel those judicatures from the states. As Maryland has undertaken to impose a stamp-tax on the notes of this bank, what hinders her from imposing a stamp-tax also on permits, clearances, registers and all other documents connected with imposts and navigation? If, by one, she can suspend the operations of the bank, by the other, she can equally well shut up the custom-house. The law of Maryland, in question, makes a requisition. The sum called for is not assessed on property, nor deducted from profits or income. It is a direct imposition on the power, privilege or franchise of the corporation. The act purports, also, to restrain the circulation of the paper of the bank to bills of certain descriptions. It narrows and abridges the powers of the bank in a manner which, it would seem, even congress could not do. This law of Maryland cannot be sustained, but upon principles and reasoning which would subject every important measure of the national government to the revision and control of the state legislatures. By the charter, the bank is authorized to issue bills of any denomination above five dollars. The act of Maryland purports to restrain and limit their powers in this respect. The charter, as well as the laws of the United States, makes it the duty of all collectors and receivers to receive the notes of the bank in payment of all debts due the government. The act of Maryland makes it penal, both on the person paying and the person receiving such bills, until stamped by the authority of Maryland. This is a direct interference with the revenue. The legislature of Maryland might, with as much propriety, tax treasury-notes. This is either an attempt to expel the bank from the state; or it is an attempt to raise a revenue for state purposes, by an imposition on property and franchises holden under the national government, and created by that government, for purposes connected with its own administration. In either view, there cannot be a clearer case of interference. The bank cannot exist, nor can any bank established by congress exist, if this right to tax it exists in the state governments. One or the other must be surrendered; and a surrender on the part of the government of the United States would be a giving up of those fundamental and essential powers without which the government cannot be maintained. A bank may not be, and is not, absolutely essential to the existence and preservation of the government. But it is essential to the existence and preservation of the government, that congress should be able to exercise its constitutional powers, at its own discretion, without being subject to the control of state legislation. The question is not, whether a bank be necessary or useful, but whether congress may not constitutionally judge of that necessity or utility; and whether, having so judged and decided, and having adopted measures to carry its decision into effect, the state governments may interfere with that decision, and defeat the operation of its measures. Nothing can be plainer than that, if the law of congress, establishing the bank, be a constitutional act, it must have its full and complete effects. Its operation cannot be either defeated or impeded by acts of state legislation. To hold otherwise, would be to declare, that congress can only exercise its constitutional powers, subject to the controlling discretion, and under the sufferance, of the state governments.

. . . . .

[L. MARTIN, Attorney General of Maryland] . . . 2. But admitting that congress has a right to incorporate a banking company, as one of the means necessary and proper to execute the specific powers of the national government; we insist, that the respective states have the right to tax the property of that corporation, within their territory; that the United States cannot, by such an act of incorporation, withdraw any part of the property within the state from the grasp of taxation. It is not necessary for us to contend, that any part of the public property of the United States, its munitions of war, its ships and treasure, are subject to state taxation. But if the United States hold shares in the stock of a private banking company, or any other trading company, their property is not exempt from taxation, in common with the other capital stock of the company; still less, can it communicate to the shares belonging to private stockholders, an immunity from local taxation. The right of taxation by the state, is co-extensive with all private property within the state. The interest of the United States in this bank is private property, though belonging to public persons. It is held by the government, as an undivided interest with private stockholders. It is employed in the same trade, subject to the same fluctuations of value, and liable to the same contingencies of profit and loss. The shares belonging to the United States, or of any other stockholders, are not subjected to direct taxation by the law of Maryland. The tax imposed, is a stamp tax upon the notes issued by a banking-house within the state of Maryland. Because the United States happen to be partially interested, either as dormant or active partners, in that house, is no reason why the state should refrain from laying a tax which they have, otherwise, a constitutional right to impose, any more than if they were to become interested in any other house of trade, which should issue its notes, or bills of exchange, liable to a stamp duty, by a law of the state. But it is said, that a right to tax, in this case, implies a right to destroy; that it is impossible to draw the line of discrimination between a tax fairly laid for the purposes of revenue, and one imposed for the purpose of prohibition. We answer, that the same objection would equally apply to the right of congress to tax the state banks; since the same difficulty of discriminating occurs in the exercise of that right. The whole of this subject of taxation is full of difficulties, which the convention found it impossible to solve, in a manner entirely satisfactory. The first attempt was to divide the subjects of taxation between the state and the national government. This being found impracticable or inconvenient, the state governments surrendered altogether their right to tax imports and exports, and tonnage; giving the authority to tax all other subjects to congress, but reserving to the states a concurrent right to tax the same subjects to an unlimited extent. This was one of the anomalies of the government, the evils of which must be endured, or mitigated by discretion and mutual forbearance. The debates in the state conventions show that the power of state taxation was understood to be absolutely unlimited, except as to imports and tonnage duties. The states would not have adopted the constitution, upon any other understanding. As to the judicial proceedings, and the custom-house papers of the United States, they are not property, by their very nature; they are not the subjects of taxation; they are the proper instruments of national sovereignty, essential to the exercise of its powers, and in legal contemplation altogether extra-territorial as to state authority.

. . . . .

[MARSHALL, C.J.] . . . It being the opinion of the court, that the act incorporating the bank is constitutional; and that the power of establishing a branch in the state of Maryland might be properly exercised by the bank itself, we proceed to inquire—

2. Whether the state of Maryland may, without violating the constitution, tax that branch? That the power of taxation is one of vital importance; that it is retained by the states; that it is not abridged by the grant of a similar power to the government of the Union; that it is to be concurrently exercised by the two governments—are truths which have never been denied. But such is the paramount character of the constitution, that its capacity to withdraw any subject from the action of even this power, is admitted. The states are expressly forbidden to lay any duties on imports or exports, except what may be absolutely necessary for executing their inspection laws. If the obligation of this prohibition must be conceded—if it may restrain a state from the exercise of its taxing power on imports and exports—the same paramount character would seem to restrain, as it certainly may restrain, a state from such other exercise of this power, as is in its nature incompatible with, and repugnant to, the constitutional laws of the Union. A law, absolutely repugnant to another, as entirely repeals that other as if express terms of repeal were used.

On this ground, the counsel for the bank place its claim to be exempted from the power of a state to tax its operations. There is no express provision for the case, but the claim has been sustained on a principle which so entirely pervades the constitution, is so intermixed with the materials which compose it, so interwoven with its web, so blended with its texture, as to be incapable of being separated from it, without rending it into shreds. This great principle is, that the constitution and the laws made in pursuance thereof are supreme; that they control the constitution and laws of the respective states, and cannot be controlled by them. From this, which may be almost termed an axiom, other propositions are deduced as corollaries, on the truth or error of which, and on their application to this case, the cause has been supposed to depend. These are, 1st. That a power to create implies a power to preserve: 2d. That a power to destroy, if wielded by a different hand, is hostile to, and incompatible with these powers to create and to preserve: 3d. That where this repugnancy exists, that authority which is supreme must control, not yield to that over which it is supreme.

These propositions, as abstract truths, would, perhaps, never be controverted. Their application to this case, however, has been denied; and both in maintaining the affirmative and the negative, a splendor of eloquence, and strength of argument, seldom, if ever, surpassed, have been displayed.

The power of congress to create, and of course, to continue, the bank, was the subject of the preceding part of this opinion; and is no longer to be considered as questionable. That the power of taxing it by the states may be exercised so as to destroy it, is too obvious to be denied. But taxation is said to be an absolute power, which acknowledges no other limits than those expressly prescribed in the constitution, and like sovereign power of every

other description, is intrusted to the discretion of those who use it. But the very terms of this argument admit, that the sovereignty of the state, in the article of taxation itself, is subordinate to, and may be controlled by the constitution of the United States. How far it has been controlled by that instrument, must be a question of construction. In making this construction, no principle, not declared, can be admissible, which would defeat the legitimate operations of a supreme government. It is of the very essence of supremacy, to remove all obstacles to its action within its own sphere, and so to modify every power vested in subordinate governments, as to exempt its own operations from their own influence. This effect need not be stated in terms. It is so involved in the declaration of supremacy, so necessarily implied in it, that the expression of it could not make it more certain. We must, therefore, keep it in view, while construing the constitution.

The argument on the part of the state of Maryland, is, not that the states may directly resist a law of congress, but that they may exercise their acknowledged powers upon it, and that the constitution leaves them this right, in the confidence that they will not abuse it. Before we proceed to examine this argument, and to subject it to test of the constitution, we must be permitted to bestow a few considerations on the nature and extent of this original right of taxation, which is acknowledged to remain with the states. It is admitted, that the power of taxing the people and their property, is essential to the very existence of government, and may be legitimately exercised on the objects to which it is applicable, to the utmost extent to which the government may choose to carry it. The only security against the abuse of this power, is found in the structure of the government itself. In imposing a tax, the legislature acts upon its constituents. This is, in general, a sufficient security against erroneous and oppressive taxation.

The people of a state, therefore, give to their government a right of taxing themselves and their property, and as the exigencies of government cannot be limited, they prescribe no limits to the exercise of this right, resting confidently on the interest of the legislator, and on the influence of the constituent over their representative, to guard them against its abuse. But the means employed by the government of the Union have no such security, nor is the right of a state to tax them sustained by the same theory. Those means are not given by the people of a particular state, not given by the constituents of the legislature, which claim the right to tax them, but by the people of all the states. They are given by all, for the benefit of all—and upon theory, should be subjected to that government only which belongs to all.

It may be objected to this definition, that the power of taxation is not confined to the people and property of a state. It may be exercised upon every object brought within its jurisdiction. This is true. But to what source do we trace this right? It is obvious, that it is an incident of sovereignty, and is co-extensive with that to which it is an incident. All subjects over which the sovereign power of a state extends, are objects of taxation; but those over which it does not extend, are, upon the soundest principles, exempt from taxation. This proposition may almost be pronounced self-evident.

The sovereignty of a state extends to everything which exists by its own authority, or is introduced by its permission; but does it extend to those means which are employed by congress to carry into execution powers conferred on that body by the people of the United States? We think it demonstrable, that it does not. Those powers are not given by the people of a single state. They are given by the people of the United States, to a government whose laws, made in pursuance of the constitution, are declared to be supreme. Consequently, the people of a single state cannot confer a sovereignty which will extend over them.

If we measure the power of taxation residing in a state, by the extent of sovereignty which the people of a single state possess, and can confer on its government, we have an intelligible standard, applicable to every case to which the power may be applied. We have a principle which leaves the power of taxing the people and property of a state unimpaired; which leaves to a state the command of all its resources, and which places beyond its reach, all those powers which are conferred by the people of the United States on the government of the Union, and all those means which are given for the purpose of carrying those powers into execution. We have a principle which is safe for the states, and safe for the Union. We are relieved, as we ought to be, from clashing sovereignty; from interfering powers; from a repugnancy between a right in one government to pull down, what there is an acknowledged right in another to build up; from the incompatibility of a right in one government to destroy, what there is a right in another to preserve. We are not driven to the perplexing inquiry, so unfit for the judicial department, what degree of taxation is the legitimate use, and what degree may amount to the abuse of the power. The attempt to use it on the means employed by the government of the Union, in pursuance of the constitution, is itself an abuse, because it is the usurpation of a power which the people of a single state cannot give. We find, then, on just theory, a total failure of this original right to tax the means employed by the government of the Union, for the execution of its powers. The right never existed, and the question whether it has been surrendered, cannot arise.

But, waiving this theory for the present, let us resume the inquiry, whether this power can be exercised by the respective states, consistently with a fair construction of the constitution? That the power to tax involves the power to destroy; that the power to destroy may defeat and render useless the power to create; that there is a plain repugnance in conferring on one government a power to control the constitutional measures of another, which other, with respect to those very measures, is declared to be supreme over that which exerts the control, are propositions not to be denied. But all inconsistencies are to be reconciled by the magic of the word *confidence*. Taxation, it is said, does not necessarily and unavoidably destroy. To carry it to the excess of destruction, would be an abuse, to presume which, would banish that confidence which is essential to all government. But is this a case of confidence? Would the

people of any one state trust those of another with a power to control the most insignificant operations of their state government? We know they would not. Why, then, should we suppose, that the people of any one state should be willing to trust those of another with a power to control the operations of a government to which they have confided their most important and most valuable interests? In the legislature of the Union alone, are all represented. The legislature of the Union alone, therefore, can be trusted by the people with the power of controlling measures which concern all, in the confidence that it will not be abused. This, then, is not a case of confidence, and we must consider it is as it really is.

If we apply the principle for which the state of Maryland contends, to the constitution, generally, we shall find it capable of changing totally the character of that instrument. We shall find it capable of arresting all the measures of the government, and of prostrating it at the foot of the states. The American people have declared their constitution and the laws made in pursuance thereof, to be supreme; but this principle would transfer the supremacy, in fact, to the states. If the states may tax one instrument, employed by the government in the execution of its powers, they may tax any and every other instrument. They may tax the mail; they may tax the mint; they may tax patent-rights; they may tax the papers of the custom-house; they may tax judicial process; they may tax all the means employed by the government, to an excess which would defeat all the ends of government. This was not intended by the American people. They did not design to make their government dependent on the states.

Gentlemen say, they do not claim the right to extend state taxation to these objects. They limit their pretensions to property. But on what principle, is this distinction made? Those who make it have furnished no reason for it, and the principle for which they contend denies it. They contend, that the power of taxation has no other limit than is found in the 10th section of the 1st article of the constitution; that, with respect to everything else, the power of the states is supreme, and admits of no control. If this be true, the distinction between property and other subjects to which the power of taxation is applicable, is merely arbitrary, and can never be sustained. This is not all. If the controlling power of the states be established; if their supremacy as to taxation be acknowledged; what is to restrain their exercising control in any shape they may please to give it? Their sovereignty is not confined to taxation; that is not the only mode in which it might be displayed. The question is, in truth, a question of supremacy; and if the right of the states to tax the means employed by the general government be conceded, the declaration that the constitution, and the laws made in pursuance thereof, shall be the supreme law of the land, is empty and unmeaning declamation.

In the course of the argument, the Federalist has been quoted; and the opinions expressed by the authors of that work have been justly supposed to be entitled to great respect in expounding the constitution. No tribute can be paid to them which exceeds their merit; but in applying their opinions to the cases which may arise in the progress of our government, a right to judge of their correctness must be retained; and to understand the argument, we must examine the proposition it maintains, and the objections against which it is directed. The subject of those numbers, from which passages have been cited, is the unlimited power of taxation which is vested in the general government. The objection to this unlimited power, which the argument seeks to remove, is stated with fulness and clearness. It is, "that an indefinite power of taxation in the latter (the government of the Union) might, and probably would, in time, deprive the former (the government of the states) of the means of providing for their own necessities; and would subject them entirely to the mercy of the national legislature. As the laws of the Union are to become the supreme law of the land; as it is to have power to pass all laws that may be necessary for carrying into execution the authorities with which it is proposed to vest it; the national government might, at any time, abolish the taxes imposed for state objects, upon the pretence of an interference with its own. It might allege a necessity for doing this, in order to give efficacy to the national revenues; and thus, all the resources of taxation might, by degrees, become the subjects of federal monopoly, to the entire exclusion and destruction of the state governments."

The objections to the constitution which are noticed in these numbers, were to the undefined power of the government to tax, not to the incidental privilege of exempting its own measures from state taxation. The consequences apprehended from this undefined power were, that it would absorb all the objects of taxation, "to the exclusion and destruction of the state governments." The arguments of the Federalist are intended to prove the fallacy of these apprehensions; not to prove that the government was incapable of executing any of its powers, without exposing the means it employed to the embarrassments of state taxation. Arguments urged against these objections, and these apprehensions, are to be understood as relating to the points they mean to prove. Had the authors of those excellent essays been asked, whether they contended for that construction of the constitution, which would place within the reach of the states those measures which the government might adopt for the execution of its powers; no man, who has read their instructive pages, will hesitate to admit, that their answer must have been in the negative.

It has also been insisted, that, as the power of taxation in the general and state governments is acknowledged to be concurrent, every argument which would sustain the right of the general government to tax banks chartered by the states, will equally sustain the right of the states to tax banks chartered by the general government. But the two cases are not on the same reason. The people of all the states have created the general government, and have conferred upon it the general power of taxation. The people of all the states, and the states themselves, are represented in congress, and, by their representatives, exercise this power. When they tax the chartered institutions of the states, they tax their constituents; and these taxes must be uniform. But when a state taxes the operations of the government of the United States, it acts upon institutions created, not by their own constituents, but by people over

whom they claim no control. It acts upon the measures of a government created by others as well as themselves, for the benefit of others in common with themselves. The difference is that which always exists, and always must exist, between the action of the whole on a part, and the action of a part on the whole—between the laws of a government declared to be supreme, and those of a government which, when in opposition to those laws, is not supreme.

But if the full application of this argument could be admitted, it might bring into question the right of congress to tax the state banks, and could not prove the rights of the states to tax the Bank of the United States.

The court has bestowed on this subject its most deliberate consideration. The result is a conviction that the states have no power, by taxation or otherwise, to retard, impede, burden, or in any manner control, the operations of the constitutional laws enacted by congress to carry into execution the powers vested in the general government. This is, we think, the unavoidable consequence of that supremacy which the constitution has declared. We are unanimously of opinion, that the law passed by the legislature of Maryland, imposing a tax on the Bank of the United States, is unconstitutional and void.

This opinion does not deprive the states of any resources which they originally possessed. It does not extend to a tax paid by the real property of the bank, in common with the other real property within the state, nor to a tax imposed on the interest which the citizens of Maryland may hold in this institution, in common with other property of the same description throughout the state. But this is a tax on the operations of the bank, and is, consequently, a tax on the operation of an instrument employed by the government of the Union to carry its powers into execution. Such a tax must be unconstitutional.

35

COHENS v. VIRGINIA
6 Wheat. 264 (1821)

(See 3.2.1, no. 74)

36

UNITED STATES v. HOAR
26 Fed. Cas. 329, no. 15,373 (C.C.D.Mass. 1821)

STORY, Circuit Justice. The only point, which has been argued here, is, whether the United States are barred of their suit by the statutes of limitations of Massachusetts above pleaded. It has not been denied, and indeed is too plain for argument, that the statutes of limitations of Massachusetts cannot proprio vigore bind or bar the suits of the national government in the national courts. If such an effect can be attributed to them, it can only be by reason of some extension of them for this purpose, by the national legislature. And it is contended, that such is the effect of the 34th section of the judiciary act of 1789, c. 20 [1 Stat. 92]. That section declares, "that the laws of the several states, except where the constitution, treaties, or statutes of the United States shall otherwise require or provide, shall be regarded as rules of decision in trials at common law in the courts of the United States, in cases where they apply." The whole stress of the argument, therefore, turns upon the question, whether this is a case, where the laws of the state do apply. Now, I think, it may be laid down as a safe proposition, that no statute of limitations has been held to apply to actions brought by the crown, unless there has been an express provision including it. For it is said, that, where a statute is general, and thereby any prerogative, right, title, or interest is divested or taken from the king, in such case the king shall not be bound, unless the statute is made by express words to extend to him. Bac. Abr. "Prerogative," E. 5. And, accordingly, it was ruled in the Case of Magdalen College, 11 Cooke, 68, 74b, 1 Rolle, 151, that "the king has a prerogative, quod nullum tempus occurrit regi, and, therefore, the general acts of limitation, or of plenarty, shall not extend to him." And the same doctrine is maintained in the most respectable authorities. Plowd. 244, 3 Inst. 188; Bac. Abr. "Prerogative," E. 5, p. 561; Com. Dig. Pr. D 86; Temps. G. 11; Bro. St. Lim. 67. It is true, that Bracton lays down a different doctrine as to certain crown lands, for he says (Bract. lib. 2, c. 5, § 7): "Sunt etiam aliae res quae pertinent ad coronam, quae non sunt ita sacrae, quin transferri possunt, sicut sunt fundi, terrae et tenementa et hujus modi, per quae corona regis roboratur et in quibus currit tempus contra regem, sicut contra quamlibet privatum personam." And Staunford, citing this passage, says, this is as much as to say, that if the king had right to any such lands or tenements, and had surceased his time, so long, that it exceeded the time of limitation in a suit of right, he had lost then his right forever. Staunf. Pr. 42b. And in Britton's time the same rule prevailed, for he declared, that as to lands not held as appurtenant to the crown, the prescription in a suit of right shall run against the king, as against other people. Britton, De Droit Le Roy, c. 18, p. 29. As to lands and other things held jure coronae, it is manifest, as well from Bracton as from Britton, that the rule governed, quod nullum tempus occurrit regi. Bract. lib. 3, c. 3, p. 103; Britton, c. 18, p. 29. But however this distinction may anciently have been, it is clear from the authorities, that the rule, excepting the crown from the operation of the statutes of limitation, has for several centuries universally prevailed; and a recent statute (9 Geo. III, c. 16) was the first that expressly limited the right to recover any estate or hereditaments. The true reason, indeed, why the law has determined, that there can be no negligence or laches imputed to the crown, and, therefore, no delay should bar its right, though sometimes asserted to be, because the king is always busied for the public good, and, therefore, has not leisure to assert his right within the times limited to subjects (1 Bl. Comm. 247), is to be found in the great public policy of preserving the public rights, revenues, and property from injury and loss, by the negligence of public officers. And though this is sometimes called a prerogative right, it is in fact nothing more than a reservation, or exception, introduced for the public benefit, and equally applicable to all governments. We find accordingly, in our own state, the doctrine is well settled, that no laches can be imputed to the government, and against it no time runs, so as to bar its rights (Inhabitants of Stoughton v. Baker, 4 Mass. 528); so, that it is clear, that the statutes of limitations pleaded in this case would be no bar to a suit brought to enforce any right of the state in its own courts.

But, independently of any doctrine founded on the notion of prerogative, the same construction of statutes of this sort ought to prevail, founded upon the legislative intention. Where the government is not expressly or by necessary implication included, it ought to be clear from the nature of the mischiefs to be redressed, or the language used, that the government itself was in contemplation of the legislature, before a court of law would be authorized to put such an interpretation upon any statute. In general, acts of the legislature are meant to regulate and direct the acts and rights of citizens; and in most cases the reasoning applicable to them applies with very different, and often contrary force to the government itself. It appears to me, therefore, to be a safe rule founded in the principles of the common law, that the general words of a statute ought not to include the government, or affect its rights, unless that construction be clear and indisputable upon the text of the act.

It has not been contended in argument, that the judiciary act of 1789, in the section under consideration, meant to enlarge the construction of the statutes of Massachusetts. It is most manifest, that the terms give the same efficacy, and none other, to these statutes in the federal, that they have proprio vigore in the state, courts. And yet, unless this doctrine of enlargement can be maintained, it is difficult to perceive upon what ground the case of the defendant can be supported. The statutes of Massachusetts could not originally have contemplated suits by the United States, not because, they were in substance enacted, before the federal constitution was adopted, on which I lay no stress; but because it was not within the legitimate exercise of the powers of the state legislature. It is not to be presumed, that a state legislature mean to transcend their constitutional powers; and, therefore, however general the words may be, they are always restrained to persons and things, over which the jurisdiction of the state may be rightfully exerted. And if a construction could ever be justified, which should include the United States, at the same time, that it excluded the state, it is not to be presumed, that congress could intend to sanction an usurpation of power by a state to regulate and control the rights of the United States. In the language of the act of 1789, it would not be a case, where the laws of the state could apply. The mischiefs, too, of such a construction, would be very great. The public rights, revenue, and property would be subject to the arbitrary limitations of the states; and the limitations are so various in these states, that the government would hold their rights by a very different tenure in each. I am of opinion, therefore, that the first and second pleas of the defendant are bad in point of law, and, that judgment ought to be for the plaintiffs.

As to the third set of pleadings, it is impossible to sustain the replication as a good answer to the plea of plene administravit, for it neither denies nor avoids the matter of that plea. If the United States meant to deny that matter, it is surprising, that the usual and technical replication was not made; and if it meant to admit the truth and justice of that plea, the true course was to have admitted the same in terms, and prayed judgment of assets quando acciderint. But here, the replication does neither. It asserts, that there are assets of the deceased, not saying in the hands of the administrator, sufficient to pay all his debts, and yet does not take issue upon the point of plene administravit. It is a perfectly anomalous and incongruous pleading, and is bad in substance as well as in form.

The only remaining question, is, whether the plea of plene administravit generally is good in this case. It is suggested at the bar, that under the peculiar system of laws of Massachusetts, this plea, however good at common law, is not sustainable. By these laws the rights of creditors of a deceased debtor are equal, and no one has a priority over another, but all are to be paid pari passu, excepting debts to the United States, to the commonwealth, and for charges of the last sickness and funeral of the deceased, which have a priority, where the estate is insolvent. Jewett v. Jewett, 5 Mass. 275; Act Cong. March 3, 1797, c. 74, § 5; [1 Story's Laws, 465; 1 Stat. 515, c. 20]; Fisher v. Blight, 2 Cranch [6 U. S.] 358. It is supposed, therefore, that in cases of insolvency, the administrator is bound to pursue the statute provided for such cases, and can avail himself only of the special plene administravit growing out of the provisions of that statute. If the estate be in fact insolvent, the administrator cannot lawfully prefer one creditor to another in the payment of debts; and if he pays one creditor in full to the injury of the others, it will be a wasteful administration, and at his own peril. While a single creditor remains unpaid, if the assets are exhausted, the administrator is guilty of waste. Such, as I understand it, is the drift of the argument.

Now, in the first place, it does not appear to me, that upon principle any special plea of plene administravit is necessary, where the assets have been in fact paid according to the directions of the statute of insolvency; for if the assets are rightfully applied, the mode is matter of evidence and not of pleading. A special plene administravit can only be necessary, where the administrator either admits assets to a limited extent, or he sets up a right of retainer for the payment of other debts, to which they are legally appropriated, or he has paid debts of an inferior nature, without notice of the plaintiff's claim. And so is the doctrine of the common law according to the better authorities. Hickey v. Hayter, 6 Term R. 384; Toll. Ex'rs, bk. 3, c. 2, § 2, pp. 267, 282; Parker v. Atfield, Salk. 311; Toll. Ex'rs, bk. 3, c. 3, p. 208; Id. bk. 3, c. 5, p. 367; 1 Saund. 333, note 6, 334, note 8; 3 Bac. Abr. "Executors and Administrators," L. pp. 77, 82. In the next place, it seems to me, that there may be cases, where the estate may be insolvent, and yet the administrator would not be bound to

procure a commission, and proceed under the statute of insolvency. If, for example, the assets were less than the privileged or priority debts, a commission of insolvency would be utterly useless to the other creditors; and surely the law would not force the administrator to nugatory acts. In such a case it seems to me, that a general plene administravit would be good, if the administrator had in fact applied the assets in discharge of such debts. If he had not so applied them, then he might specially plead these debts and no assets ultra. Other cases may be put of an analogous nature; and unless some stubborn authority could be shewn, founded in our local jurisprudence (and none such has been produced), I should not be bold enough to overrule, what I consider a most salutary doctrine of the common law. Judgments, bonds, and some other debts at the common law are privileged debts, and are entitled to a priority of payment. And yet, if the administrator have no notice either actual or constructive of such privileged debts, he will be justified in paying debts of an inferior nature, provided a reasonable time has elapsed after the decease of the intestate. Com. Dig., "Administration," C. 2; 3 Bac. Abr. "Executors and Administrators," L. p. 82, and Guillim's note; Sawyer v. Mercer, 1 Term R. 690; Toll. Ex'rs, bk. 3, c. 2, pp. 292, 293; Britton v. Batthurst, 3 Lev. 114. And in principle there cannot be any just distinction, whether such payment be voluntary or compulsive. Toll. Ex'rs, bk. 3, c. 2, p. 293. But in such case, if he be afterwards sued for such privileged debt, he cannot plead plene administravit generally, but is bound to aver, that he had fully administered before notice of such debt. Sawyer v. Mercer, 1 Term R. 690; Toll. Ex'rs, bk. 3, c. 2, p. 293. Now it is precisely in this view, that the plea of the defendant is defective. The debt of the United States is a privileged debt, and the plea should have shown, that the assets were exhausted before knowledge of this debt. It seems to me, therefore, that the plea must be adjudged bad.

In point of fact, it is admitted at the bar, and by the pleadings, that Col. Tuttle's estate is solvent; but the administrator has, in consequence of the lapse of time, and in pursuance of the general principles of law, distributed the surplus assets after the payment of all known debts among the heirs. Whether such a distribution, either voluntary or under a probate decree, would protect him from a suit by the United States, need not now be decided. If it would not, the United States might well have taken issue on the plene administravit; if it would, it ought to have been specially pleaded. Judgment for United States.

37

JAMES MADISON TO THOMAS JEFFERSON
27 June 1823
Writings 9:142

Believing as I do that the General Convention regarded a provision within the Constitution for deciding in a peaceable & regular mode all cases arising in the course of its operation, as essential to an adequate System of Govt. that it intended the Authority vested in the Judicial Department as a final resort in relation to the States, for cases resulting to it in the exercise of its functions, (the concurrence of the Senate chosen by the State Legislatures, in appointing the Judges, and the oaths & official tenures of these, with the surveillance of public Opinion, being relied on as guarantying their impartiality); and that this intention is expressed by the articles declaring that the federal Constitution & laws shall be the supreme law of the land, and that the Judicial Power of the U. S. shall extend to all cases arising under them: Believing moreover that this was the prevailing view of the subject when the Constitution was adopted & put into execution; that it has so continued thro' the long period which has elapsed; and that even at this time an appeal to a national decision would prove that no general change has taken place: thus believing I have never yielded my original opinion indicated in the "Federalist" No. 39 to the ingenious reasonings of Col: Taylor agst. this construction of the Constitution.

38

WILLIAM WIRT, RIGHT TO TAX GOVERNMENT PROPERTY
8 Sept. 1823

(See 1.8.17, no. 20)

39

GIBBONS V. OGDEN
9 Wheat. 1 (1824)

(See 1.8.3 [commerce], no. 16)

40

AMERICAN INSURANCE CO. V. CANTER
1 Pet. 511 (1828)

(See 1.8.9, no. 5)

41

ANDREW JACKSON, VETO MESSAGE
10 July 1832

(See 1.8.18, no. 20)

42

JOSEPH STORY, COMMENTARIES ON THE CONSTITUTION 3:§§ 1831–33, 1835–36
1833

---

§ 1831. The propriety of this clause would seem to result from the very nature of the constitution. If it was to establish a national government, that government ought, to the extent of its powers and rights, to be supreme. It would be a perfect solecism to affirm, that a national government should exist with certain powers; and yet, that in the exercise of those powers it should not be supreme. What other inference could have been drawn, than of their supremacy, if the constitution had been totally silent? And surely a positive affirmance of that, which is necessarily implied, cannot in a case of such vital importance be deemed unimportant. The very circumstance, that a question might be made, would irresistibly lead to the conclusion, that it ought not to be left to inference. A law, by the very meaning of the term, includes supremacy. It is a rule, which those, to whom it is prescribed, are bound to observe. This results from every political association. If individuals enter into a state of society, the laws of that society must be the supreme regulator of their conduct. If a number of political societies enter into a larger political society, the laws, which the latter may enact, pursuant to the powers entrusted to it by its constitution, must necessarily be supreme over those societies, and the individuals, of whom they are composed. It would otherwise be a mere treaty, dependent upon the good faith of the parties, and not a government, which is only another name for political power and supremacy. But it will not follow, that acts of the larger society, which are not pursuant to its constitutional powers, but which are invasions of the residuary authorities of the smaller societies, will become the supreme law of the land. They will be merely acts of usurpation, and will deserve to be treated as such. Hence we perceive, that the above clause only declares a truth, which flows immediately and necessarily from the institution of a national government. It will be observed, that the supremacy of the laws is attached to those only, which are made in pursuance of the constitution; a caution very proper in itself, but in fact the limitation would have arisen by irresistible implication, if it had not been expressed.

§ 1832. In regard to treaties, there is equal reason, why they should be held, when made, to be the supreme law of the land. It is to be considered, that treaties constitute solemn compacts of binding obligation among nations; and unless they are scrupulously obeyed, and enforced, no foreign nation would consent to negotiate with us; or if it did, any want of strict fidelity on our part in the discharge of the treaty stipulations would be visited by reprisals, or war. It is, therefore, indispensable, that they should have the obligation and force of a law, that they may be executed by the judicial power, and be obeyed like other laws. This will not prevent them from being cancelled or abrogated by the nation upon grave and suitable occasions; for it will not be disputed, that they are subject to the legislative power, and may be repealed, like other laws, at its pleasure; or they may be varied by new treaties. Still, while they do subsist, they ought to have a positive binding efficacy as laws upon all the states, and all the citizens of the states. The peace of the nation, and its good faith, and moral dignity, indispensably require, that all state laws should be subjected to their supremacy. The difference between considering them as laws, and considering them as executory, or executed contracts, is exceedingly important in the actual administration of public justice. If they are supreme laws, courts of justice will enforce them directly in all cases, to which they can be judicially applied, in opposition to all state laws, as we all know was done in the case of the British debts secured by the treaty of 1783, after the constitution was adopted. If they are deemed but solemn compacts, promissory in their nature and obligation, courts of justice may be embarrassed in enforcing them, and may be compelled to leave the redress to be administered through other departments of the government. It is notorious, that treaty stipulations (especially those of the treaty of peace of 1783) were grossly disregarded by the states under the confederation. They were deemed by the states, not as laws, but like requisitions, of mere moral obligation, and dependent upon the good will of the states for their execution. Congress, indeed, remonstrated against this construction, as unfounded in principle and justice. But their voice was not heard. Power and right were separated; the argument was all on one side; but the power was on the other. It was probably to obviate this very difficulty, that this clause was inserted in the constitution; and it would redound to the immortal honour of its authors, if it had done no more, than thus to bring treaties within the sanctuary of justice, as laws of supreme obligation. There are, indeed, still cases, in which courts of justice can administer no effectual redress; as when the terms of a stipulation import a contract, when either of the parties engages to perform a particular act the treaty addresses itself to the political, and not to the judicial, department; and the legislature must execute the contract, before it can become a rule for the courts.

§ 1833. It is melancholy to reflect, that, conclusive as this view of the subject is in favour of the supremacy clause, it was assailed with great vehemence and zeal by the adversaries of the constitution; and especially the concluding clause, which declared the supremacy, "any thing in the constitution or laws of any state to the contrary notwithstanding." And yet this very clause was but an expression of the necessary meaning of the former clause, introduced from abundant caution, to make its obligation more strongly felt by the state judges. The very circumstance, that any objection was made, demonstrated the utility, nay the necessity of the clause, since it removed every pretence, under which ingenuity could, by its miserable subterfuges, escape from the controlling power of the constitution.

. . . . .

§ 1835. At an early period of the government a question arose, how far a treaty could embrace commercial regulations, so as to be obligatory upon the nation, and upon congress. It was debated with great zeal and ability in the house of representatives. On the one hand it was contended, that a treaty might be made respecting commerce, as well as upon any other subject; that it was a contract between the two nations, which, when made by the president, by and with the consent of the senate, was binding upon the nation; and that a refusal of the house of representatives to carry it into effect was breaking the treaty, and violating the faith of the nation. On the other hand, it was contended, that the power to make treaties, if applicable to every object, conflicted with powers, which were vested exclusively in congress; that either the treaty making power must be limited in its operation, so as not to touch objects committed by the constitution to congress; or the assent and co-operation of the house of representatives must be required to give validity to any compact, so far as it might comprehend these objects: that congress was invested with the exclusive power to regulate commerce; that therefore, a treaty of commerce required the assent and co-operation of the house of representatives; that in every case, where a treaty required an appropriation of money, or an act of congress to carry it into effect, it was not in this respect obligatory, till congress had agreed to carry it into effect; and, that they were at free liberty to make, or withhold such appropriation, or act, without being chargeable with violating the treaty, or breaking the faith of the nation. In the result, the house of representatives adopted a resolution declaring, that the house of representatives do not claim any agency in making treaties; but when a treaty stipulates regulations on any of the subjects submitted to the power of congress, it must depend for its execution, as to such stipulations, on a law or laws to be passed by congress; and that it is the constitutional right and duty of the house of representatives, in all such cases, to deliberate on the expediency or inexpediency of carrying such treaty into effect, and to determine and act thereon, as in their judgment may be most conducive to the public good. It is well known, that the president and the senate, on that occasion, adopted a different doctrine, maintaining, that a treaty once ratified became the law of the land, and congress were constitutionally bound to carry it into effect. At the distance of twenty years, the same question was again presented for the consideration of both houses, upon a bill to carry into effect a clause in the treaty of 1815 with Great Britain, abolishing discriminating duties; and, upon that occasion, it was most ably debated. The result was, that a declaratory clause was adopted, instead of a mere enacting clause, so that the binding obligation of treaties was affirmatively settled.

§ 1836. From this supremacy of the constitution and laws and treaties of the United States, within their constitutional scope, arises the duty of courts of justice to declare any unconstitutional law passed by congress or by a state legislature void. So, in like manner, the same duty arises, whenever any other department of the national or state governments exceeds its constitutional functions. But the judiciary of the United States has no general jurisdiction to declare acts of the several states void, unless they are repugnant to the constitution of the United States, notwithstanding they are repugnant to the state constitution. Such a power belongs to it only, when it sits to administer the local law of a state, and acts exactly, as a state tribunal is bound to act. But upon this subject it seems unnecessary to dwell, since the right of all courts, state as well as national, to declare unconstitutional laws void, seems settled beyond the reach of judicial controversy.

43

JAMES MADISON, NOTES ON NULLIFICATION 1835–36

Writings 9:606–7

A political system which does not contain an effective provision for a peaceable decision of all controversies arising within itself, would be a Govt. in name only. Such a provision is obviously essential; and it is equally obvious that it cannot be either peaceable or effective by making every part an authoritative umpire. The final appeal in such cases must be to the authority of the whole, not to that of the parts separately and independently. This was the view taken of the subject, whilst the Constitution was under the consideration of the people. It was this view of it which dictated the clause declaring that the Constitution & laws of the U. S. should be the supreme law of the Land, anything in the constn or laws of any of the States to the contrary notwithstanding.

SEE ALSO:

Generally vol. 1, chs. 5, 8

James Madison, Vices of the Political System, Apr. 1787, Papers 9:348–51

Records of the Federal Convention, Farrand 1:171–73, 243; 2:132, 144, 169, 183, 409, 572, 589, 603, 639

Vox Populi, no. 3, 19 Nov. 1787, Storing 4.4.35–40

Oliver Ellsworth, Connecticut Ratifying Convention, 7 Jan. 1788, Farrand 3:240–41

Oliver Ellsworth, Reply to a Landholder, no. 10, 29 Feb. 1788, Essays 184

Luther Martin, Letter, no. 4, 21 Mar. 1788, Essays 360–61

Alexander Hamilton, New York Ratifying Convention, 28 June 1788, Elliot 2:326

Hamilton v. *Eaton*, 11 Fed. Cas. 336, no. 5,980 (C.C.D.N.C. 1792)

Henfield's Case, 11 Fed. Cas. 1099, no. 6,360 (C.C.D.Pa. 1793)

William Bradford, Suits against Foreigners, 26 July 1794, 1 Ops. Atty. Gen. 50

Charles Lee, Treaty with Great Britain, 3 Jan. 1798, 1 Ops. Atty. Gen. 82

Levi Lincoln, Restoration under Treaty with France, 17, 25 June 1802, 1 Ops. Atty. Gen. 114, 119

Levi Lincoln, Claims under Treaty with France, 15 Nov. 1803, 1 Ops. Atty. Gen. 136

United States v. *Nicholls*, 4 Yeates 251 (Pa. 1805)

John Breckenridge, Treaty with Great Britain—Duties, Tonnage, etc., 22 Mar. 1806, 1 Ops. Atty. Gen. 155

United States v. *Bright*, 24 Fed. Cas. 1232, no. 14,647 (C.C.D.Pa. 1809)

The Ann, 1 Fed. Cas. 926, no. 397 (C.C.D.Mass. 1812)

Fisher v. *Harnden*, 9 Fed. Cas. 129, no. 4,819 (C.C.D.N.Y. 1812), rev'd 1 Wheat. 300

John Marshall, On Extradition of Thomas Nash, House of Representatives, 5 Wheat. App. 3 (1820)

Mills v. *Martin*, 19 Johns R. 7 (N.Y. 1821)

Hughes v. *Edwards*, 9 Wheat. 489 (1824)

William Wirt, Validity of the South Carolina Police Bill, 8 May 1824, 1 Ops. Atty. Gen. 659

James Kent, Commentaries 1:382–87, 398–402 (1826)

Foster v. *Neilson*, 2 Pet. 253 (1829)

James Madison to N.P. Trist, Dec. 1831, Documentary History 5:375–76

James Madison to W.C. Rives, 21 Oct. 1833, Documentary History 5:393–95

Joseph Story, Commentaries on the Constitution 3:§§ 1400–1401, 1403 (1833)

Article 6, Clause 3

The Senators and Representatives before mentioned, and the Members of the several State Legislatures, and all executive and judicial Officers, both of the United States and of the several States, shall be bound by Oath or Affirmation, to support this Constitution; but no religious Test shall ever be required as a Qualification to any Office or public Trust under the United States.

1

AN ACT FOR THE WELL-GOVERNING AND
REGULATING OF CORPORATIONS
13 Chas. 2, st. 2, cl. 1, sec. 3 (1661)

"I, A.B. do declare and believe that it is not lawful upon any pretence whatsoever, to take arms against the King; and that I do abhor that traitorous position of taking arms by his authority against his person, or against those that are commissioned by him. . . ."

2

DELAWARE CONSTITUTION OF 1776, ART. 22
Thorpe 1:566

ART. 22. Every person who shall be chosen a member of either house, or appointed to any office or place of trust, before taking his seat, or entering upon the execution of his office, shall take the following oath, or affirmation, if conscientiously scrupulous of taking an oath, to wit:

"I, A B, will bear true allegiance to the Delaware State, submit to its constitution and laws, and do no act wittingly whereby the freedom thereof may be prejudiced."

And also make and subscribe the following declaration, to wit:

"I, A B, do profess faith in God the Father, and in Jesus Christ His only Son, and in the Holy Ghost, one God, blessed for evermore; and I do acknowledge the holy scriptures of the Old and New Testament to be given by divine inspiration."

And all officers shall also take an oath of office.

3

VERMONT CONSTITUTION OF 1777, CH. 2, SEC. 9
Thorpe 6:3743

SECTION IX. A quorum of the house of representatives shall consist of two-thirds of the whole number of members elected; and having met and chosen their speaker, shall, each of them, before they proceed to business, take and subscribe, as well the oath of fidelity and allegiance herein after directed, as the following oath or affirmation, viz.

I _____ _____ do solemnly swear, by the ever living God, (or, I do solemnly affirm in the presence of Almighty God) that as a member of this assembly, I will not propose or assent to any bill, vote, or resolution, which shall appear to me injurious to the people; nor do or consent to any act or thing whatever, that shall have a tendency to lessen or abridge their rights and privileges, as declared in the Constitution of this State; but will, in all things, conduct myself as a faithful, honest representative and guardian of the people, according to the best of my judgment and abilities.

And each member, before he takes his seat, shall make and subscribe the following declaration, viz.

I do believe in one God, the Creator and Governor of the universe, the rewarder of the good and punisher of the wicked. And I do acknowledge the scriptures of the old and new testament to be given by divine inspiration, and own and profess the protestant religion.

And no further or other religious test shall ever, hereafter, be required of any civil officer or magistrate in this State.

4

MASSACHUSETTS CONSTITUTION OF 1780, ARTICLES OF AMENDMENTS, ARTS. 6–7
Thorpe 3:1912–13

ART. VI. Instead of the oath of allegiance prescribed by the constitution, the following oath shall be taken and subscribed by every person chosen or appointed to any office, civil or military, under the government of this commonwealth, before he shall enter on the duties of his office, to wit:—

"I, A. B., do solemnly swear, that I will bear true faith and allegiance to the Commonwealth of Massachusetts, and will support the constitution thereof. So help me, GOD."

Provided, That when any person shall be of the denomination called Quakers, and shall decline taking said oath, he shall make his affirmation in the foregoing form, omitting the word "swear" and inserting, instead thereof, the word "affirm," and omitting the words "So help me, God," and subjoining, instead thereof, the words, "This I do under the pains and penalities of perjury."

ART. VII. No oath, declaration, or subscription, excepting the oath prescribed in the preceding article, and the oath of office, shall be required of the governor, lieutenant-governor, councillors, senators, or representatives, to qualify them to perform the duties of their respective offices.

[Editors' note.—These amendments of 9 Apr. 1821 ought to be compared to the original language of pt. 2, chap. 6, art. 1 of the Massachusetts Constitution of 1780. See vol. 1, ch. 1, no. 6.]

5

BENJAMIN FRANKLIN TO RICHARD PRICE
9 Oct. 1780
Writings 8:153–54

I am fully of your Opinion respecting religious Tests; but, tho' the People of Massachusetts have not in their new Constitution kept quite clear of them, yet, if we consider what that People were 100 Years ago, we must allow they have gone great Lengths in Liberality of Sentiment on religious Subjects; and we may hope for greater Degrees of Perfection, when their Constitution, some years hence, shall be revised. If Christian Preachers had continued to teach as Christ and his Apostles did, without Salaries, and as the Quakers now do, I imagine Tests would never have existed; for I think they were invented, not so much to secure Religion itself, as the Emoluments of it. When a Religion is good, I conceive that it will support itself; and, when it cannot support itself, and God does not take care to support, so that its Professors are oblig'd to call for the help of the Civil Power, it is a sign, I apprehend, of its being a bad one. But I shall be out of my Depth, if I wade any deeper in Theology, and I will not trouble you with Politicks, nor with News which are almost as uncertain; but conclude with a heartfelt Wish to embrace you once more, and enjoy your sweet Society in Peace, among our honest, worthy, ingenious Friends at the *London.*

6

PETITION OF THE PHILADELPHIA SYNAGOGUE TO
COUNCIL OF CENSORS OF PENNSYLVANIA
23 Dec. 1783
Stokes 1:287–89

To the honourable the COUNCIL of CENSORS, assembled agreeable to the Constitution of the State of Pennsylvania. The Memorial of Rabbi Ger. Seixas of the Synagogue of the Jews at Philadelphia, Simon Nathan their Parnass or President, Asher Myers, Bernard Gratz and Haym Salomon the Mahamad, or Associates of their council in behalf of themselves and their brethren Jews, residing in Pennsylvania,

Most respectfully showeth,

That by the tenth section of the Frame of Government of this Commonwealth, it is ordered that each member of the general assembly of representatives of the freemen of Pennsylvania, before he takes his seat, shall make and subscribe a declaration, which ends in these words, "I do acknowledge the Scriptures of the old and new Testament to be given by divine inspiration," to which is added an assurance, that "no further or other religious test shall ever hereafter be required of any civil officer or magistrate in this state."

Your memorialists beg leave to observe, that this clause seems to limit the civil rights of your citizens to one very special article of the creed; whereas by the second paragraph of the declaration of the rights of the inhabitants, it is asserted without any other limitation than the professing the existence of God, in plain words, "that no man who acknowledges the being of a God can be justly deprived or abridged of any civil rights as a citizen on account of his religious sentiments." But certainly this religious test deprives the Jews of the most eminent rights of freemen, solemnly ascertained to all men who are not professed Atheists.

May it please your Honors,

Although the Jews in Pennsylvania are but few in number, yet liberty of the people in one country, and the declaration of the government thereof, that these liberties are the rights of the people, may prove a powerful attractive to men, who live under restraints in another country. Holland and England have made valuable acquisitions of men, who for their religious sentiments, were distressed in their own countries.—And if Jews in Europe or elsewhere, should incline to transport themselves to America, and would, for reason of some certain advantage of the soil, climate, or the trade of Pennsylvania, rather become inhabitants thereof, than of any other State; yet the disability of Jews to take seat among the representatives of the people, as worded by the said religious test, might determine their free choice to go to New York, or to any other of the United States of America, where there is no such like restraint laid upon the nation and religion of the Jews, as in Pennsylvania.—Your memorialists cannot say that the Jews are particularly fond of being representatives of the people in assembly or civil officers and magistrates in the State; but with great submission they apprehend that a clause in the constitution, which disables them to be elected by their fellow citizens to represent them in assembly, is a stigma upon their nation and religion, and it is inconsonant with the second paragraph of the said bill of rights; otherwise Jews are as fond of liberty as their religious societies can be, and it must create in them a displeasure, when they perceive that for their professed dissent to doctrine, which is inconsistent with their religious sentiments, they should be excluded from the most important and honourable part of the rights of a free citizen.

Your memorialists beg further leave to represent, that in the religious books of the Jews, which are or may be in every man's hands, there are no such doctrines or principles established as are inconsistent with the safety and happiness of the people of Pennsylvania, and that the conduct and behaviour of the Jews in this and the neighbouring States, has always tallied with the great design of the Revolution; that the Jews of Charlestown, New York, New-Port and other posts, occupied by the British troops, have distinguishedly suffered for their attachment to the Revolution principles; and their brethren at St. Eustatius, for the same cause, experienced the most severe resentments of the British commanders. The Jews of Pennsylvania in proportion to the number of their members, can count with any religious society whatsoever, the Whigs among either of them; they have served some of them in the Continental army; some went out in the militia to fight the common enemy; all of them have cheerfully contributed to the support of the militia, and of the government of this State; they have no inconsiderable property in lands and tenements, but particularly in the way of trade, some more, some less, for which they pay taxes; they have, upon every plan formed for public utility, been forward to contribute as much as their circumstances would admit of; and as a nation or a religious society, they stand unimpeached of any matter whatsoever, against the safety and happiness of the people.

And your memorialists humbly pray, that if your honours, from any consideration than the subject of this address, should think proper to call a convention for revising the constitution, you would be pleased to recommend this to the notice of that convention.

7

BENJAMIN RUSH TO EDWARD HAND
10 Nov. 1784
Letters 1:340

The fragments of the Republican party met at the city tavern after their defeat, and agreed to recommend it to their friends throughout the state to set on foot petitions *indirectly* among the nonjurors for a revision of the test law. The Republicans must appear in this maneuver as little as possible. It is most probable the petitions will have no effect upon the present Assembly. But their refusal will serve to show their inconsistency, to rouse and irritate the sons and friends of the nonjurors, and above all to fix the dye of their infamy in such a manner that neither time nor repentance will ever be able to wipe it away.

8

BENJAMIN RUSH TO RICHARD PRICE
15 Oct. 1785, 22 Apr. 1786
Letters 1:371, 385–86

[*15 Oct. 1785*]

I took the liberty of publishing, with your name, your excellent letter on the test law of Pennsylvania. It has already had a great effect on the minds of many people, and I doubt not will contribute more than anything to repeal that law. Dr. Franklin, who has succeeded Mr. Dickinson as our governor, has expressed his surprise at the continuance of such a law since the peace, and we hope will add the weight of his name to yours to remove such a stain from the American Revolution.

[*22 Apr. 1786*]

I am very happy in being able to inform you that the test law was so far repealed a few weeks ago in Pennsylvania as to confer equal privileges upon every citizen of the state. The success of the friends of humanity in this business should encourage them to persevere in their attempts to enlighten and reform the world. Your letter to me upon the subject of that unjust law was the instrument that cut its last sinew.

9

NOAH WEBSTER, ON TEST LAWS, OATHS OF ALLEGIANCE AND ABJURATION, AND PARTIAL EXCLUSIONS FROM OFFICE
Mar. 1787
Collection 151–53

To change the current of opinion, is a most difficult task, and the attempt is often ridiculed. For this reason, I expect the following remarks will be passed over with a slight reading, and all attention to them cease with a hum.

The revisal of the test law has at length passed by a respectable majority of the Representativs of this State. This is a prelude to wiser measures; people are just awaking from delusion. The time will come (and may the day be near!) when all test laws, oaths of allegiance, abjuration,

and partial exclusions from civil offices, will be proscribed from this land of freedom.

Americans! what was the origin of these discriminations? What is their use?

They originated in savage ignorance, and they are the instruments of slavery. Emperors and generals, who wished to attach their subjects to their persons and government; who wished to exercise despotic sway over them or prosecute villainous wars, (for mankind have always been butchering each other) found the solemnity of oaths had an excellent effect on poor superstitious soldiers and vassals; oracles, demons, eclipses; all the terrifying phenomena of nature, have at times had remarkable effects in securing the obedience of men to tyrants. Oaths of fealty, and farcical ceremonies of homage, were very necessary to rivet the chains of feudal vassals; for the whole system of European tenures was erected on usurpation, and is supported solely by ignorance, superstition, artifice, or military force. Oaths of allegiance may possibly be still necessary in Europe, where there are so many contending powers contiguous to each other: But what is their use in America? To secure fidelity to the State, it will be answered. But where is the danger of defection? Will the inhabitants join the British in Nova Scotia or Canada? Will they rebel? Will they join the savages, and overthrow the State? No; all these are visionary dangers. My countrymen, if a State has any thing to fear from its inhabitants, the constitution or the laws must be wrong. Danger cannot possibly arise from any other cause.

Permit me to offer a few ideas to your minds; and let them be the subject of more than one hour's reflection.

An oath creates no new obligation. A witness, who swears to tell the whole truth, is under no new obligation to tell the whole truth. An oath reminds him of his duty; he swears to do as he ought to do; that is, he adds an express promise to an implied one. A moral obligation is not capable of addition or diminution.

When a man steps his foot into a State, he becomes subject to its general laws. When he joins it as a member, he is subject to all its laws. The act of entering into society, binds him to submit to its laws, and to promote its interest. Every man, who lives under a government, is under allegiance to that government. Ten thousand oaths do not increase the obligation upon him to be a faithful subject.

But, it will be asked, how shall we distinguish between the friends and enemies of the government? I answer, by annihilating all distinctions. A good constitution, and good laws, make good subjects. I challenge the history of mankind to produce an instance of bad subjects under a good government. The test law in Pensylvania has produced more disorder, by making enemies in this State, than have cursed all the union besides. During the war, every thing gave way to force; but the feelings and principles of war ought to be forgotten in peace.

Abjuration! a badge of folly, borrowed from the dark ages of bigotry. If the government of Pensylvania is better than that of Great Britain, the subjects will prefer it, and abjuration is perfectly nugatory. If not, the subject will have his partialities in spite of any solemn renunciation of a foreign power.

But what right has even the Legislature to deprive any class of citizens of the benefits and emoluments of civil government? If any men have forfeited their lives or estates, they are no longer subjects; they ought to be banished or hung. If not, no law ought to exclude them from civil emoluments. If any have committed public crimes, they are punishable; if any have been guilty, and have not been detected, the oath, as it now stands, obliges them to confess their guilt. To take the oath, is an implicit acknowlegement of innocence; to refuse it, is an implicit confession that the person has aided and abetted the enemy. This is rank despotism. The inquisition can do no more than force confession from the accused.

I pray God to enlighten the minds of the Americans. I wish they would shake off every badge of tyranny. Americans!—The best way to make men honest, is to let them enjoy equal rights and privileges; never suspect a set of men will be rogues, and make laws proclaiming that suspicion. Leave force to govern the wretched vassals of European nabobs, and reconcile subjects to your own constitutions by their excellent nature and beneficial effects. No man will commence enemy to a government which givs him as many privileges as his neighbors enjoy.

10

Records of the Federal Convention

[1:22; Madison, 29 May]

14. Resd. that the Legislative Executive & Jucidiary powers within the several States ought to be bound by oath to support the articles of Union

[1:28; Paterson, 29 May]

5. That the leg. ex. and judy. Officers should be bound by Oath to observe the Union.

[1:122; Madison, 5 June]

propos. 14. *"requiring oath from the State officers to support national Govt."* was postponed after a short uninteresting conversation; the votes, Con. N. Jersey. Md. Virg: S. C. Geo. ay

N. Y. Pa. Del. N. C. . . . no

Massachusetts. . . . divided

[1:194; Journal, 11 June]

It was then moved and seconded to agree to the 14 resolution submitted by Mr Randolph namely

"Resolved that the legislative, executive, and judiciary powers within the several States ought to be bound by oath to support the articles of union"

It was then moved by Mr Martin seconded by   to strike out the words "within the several States"

and on the question to strike out.

it passed in the negative [Ayes—4; noes—7.]

It was then moved and seconded to agree to the 14th resolution as submitted by Mr. Randolph

And on the question to agree to the same.

it passed in the affirmative [Ayes—6; noes—5.]

[1:203; Madison, 11 June]

Resolution 14. requiring oaths from the members of the State Govts. to observe the Natl. Constitution & laws, being considered.

Mr. Sharman opposed it as unnecessarily intruding into the State jurisdictions.

Mr. Randolph considered it as necessary to prevent that competition between the National Constitution & laws & those of the particular States, which had already been felt. The officers of the States are already under oath to the States. To preserve a due impartiality they ought to be equally bound to the Natl. Govt. The Natl. authority needs every support we can give it. The Executive & Judiciary of the States, notwithstanding their nominal independence on the State Legislatures are in fact, so dependent on them, that unless they be brought under some tie to the Natl. system, they will always lean too much to the State systems, whenever a contest arises between the two.

Mr. Gerry did not like the clause. He thought there was as much reason for requiring an oath of fidelity to the States, from Natl. officers, as vice. versa.

Mr. Luther Martin moved to strike out the words requiring such an oath from the State Officers viz "within the several States." observing that if the new oath should be contrary to that already taken by them it would be improper; if coincident the oaths already taken will be sufficient.

On the question for striking out as proposed by Mr. L. Martin

Massts. no. Cont. ay. N. Y. no. N. J. ay. Pa. no. Del. ay. Md. ay. Va. no. N. C. no. S. C. no. Geo. no. [Ayes—4; noes—7.]

Question on whole Resolution as proposed by Mr. Randolph;

Massts. ay. Cont. no. N. Y. no. N. J. no. Pa. ay. Del. no. Md. no. Va. ay. N. C. ay. S. C. ay. Geo. ay. [Ayes—6; noes—5.]

[1:207; Yates, 11 June]

Mr. Williamson. This resolve will be unnecessary, as the union will become the law of the land.

Governor Randolph. He supposes it to be absolutely necessary. Not a state government, but its officers will infringe on the rights of the national government. If the state judges are not sworn to the observance of the new government, will they not judicially determine in favor of their state laws? We are erecting a supreme national government; ought it not to be supported, and can we give it too many sinews?

Mr. Gerry rather supposes that the national legislators ought to be sworn to preserve the state constitutions, as they will run the greatest risk to be annihilated—and therefore moved it.

For Mr. Gerry's amendment, 7 ayes, 4 noes.

Main question then put on the clause or resolve—6 ayes, 5 noes. New-York in the negative.

[1:227; *Journal, 13 June*]

Resolved that the Legislative, Executive, and judiciary powers within the several States ought to be bound by oath to support the articles of union

[2:84; *Journal, 23 June*]

It was moved and seconded to add after the word "States" in the 18 resolution, the words "and of the national government"

which passed in the affirmative

On the question to agree to the 18th resolution as amended namely

"That the legislative, Executive, and Judiciary Powers within the several States, and of the national Government, ought to be bound by oath to support the articles of union"

[2:87; *Madison, 23 July*]

Resoln. 18. "requiring the Legis: Execut: & Judy. of the States to be bound by oath to support the articles of Union". taken into consideration.

Mr. Williamson suggests that a reciprocal oath should be required from the National officers, to support the Governments of the States.

Mr. Gerry moved to insert as an amendmt. that the oath of the Officers of the National Government also should extend to the support of the Natl. Govt. which was agreed to nem. con.

Mr. Wilson said he was never fond of oaths, considering them as a left handed security only. A good Govt. did not need them. and a bad one could not or ought not to be supported. He was afraid they might too much trammel the Members of the Existing Govt in case future alterations should be necessary; and prove an obstacle to Resol: 17. just agd. to.

Mr. Ghorum did not know that oaths would be of much use; but could see no inconsistency between them and the 17. Resol: or any regular amendt. of the Constitution. The oath could only require fidelity to the existing Constitution. A constitutional alteration of the Constitution, could never be regarded as a breach of the Constitution, or of any oath to support it.

Mr Gerry thought with Mr. Ghorum there could be no shadow of inconsistency in the case. Nor could he see any other harm that could result from the Resolution. On the other side he thought one good effect would be produced by it. Hitherto the officers of the two Governments had considered them as distinct from, not as parts of the General System, & had in all cases of interference given a preference to the State Govts. The proposed oaths will cure that error.—

The Resoln. (18). was agreed to nem. con.—

[2:461; *Journal, 30 Aug.*]

It was moved or seconded to add the words "or affirmation" after the word "oath" 20 article

which passed in the affirmative.

On the question to agree to the 20 article as amended it passed in the affirmative [Ayes—8; noes—1; divided—2.]

It was moved and seconded to add the following clause to the 20 Article.

"But no religious test shall ever be required as a qualification to any office or public trust under the authority of the United States"

which passed unan: in the affirmative

[2:468; *Madison, 30 Aug.*]

Art: XX. taken up—"or affirmation" was added after "oath."

Mr. Pinkney. moved to add to the art:—"but no religious test shall ever be required as a qualification to any office or public trust under the authority of the U. States"

Mr. Sherman thought it unnecessary, the prevailing liberality being a sufficient security agst. such tests.

Mr. Govr. Morris & Genl. Pinkney approved the motion,

The motion was agreed to nem: con: and then the whole Article, N— C. only no—& Md. divided.

11

Jonas Phillips to President and Members of the Convention
7 Sept. 1787
Documentary History 1:281–83

With leave and submission I address myself To those in whome there is wisdom understanding and knowledge. they are the honourable personages appointed and Made overseers of a part of the terrestrial globe of the Earth, Namely the 13 united states of america in Convention Assembled, the Lord preserve them amen—

I the subscriber being one of the people called Jews of the City of Philadelphia, a people scattered and despersed among all nations do behold with Concern that among the laws in the Constitution of Pennsylvania their is a Clause Sect. 10 to viz—I do believe in one God the Creature and governour of the universe the Rewarder of the good and the punisher of the wicked—and I do acknowledge the scriptures of the old and New testament to be given by a devine inspiration—to swear and believe that the new testament was given by devine inspiration is absolutely against the religious principle of a Jew. and is against his Conscience to take any such oath—By the above law a Jew is deprived of holding any publick office or place of Goverment which is a Contridectory to the bill of Right Sect 2. viz

That all men have a natural and unalienable Right To worship almighty God according to the dectates of their own Conscience and understanding, and that no man aught or of Right can be Compelled to attend any Relegious Worship or Erect or support any place of worship or Maintain any minister contrary to or against his own free will and Consent nor Can any man who acknowledges the being of a God be Justly deprived or abridged of any Civil Right as a Citizen on account of his Religious sentiments or peculiar mode of Religious Worship, and that no authority Can or aught to be vested in or assumed by any power what ever that shall in any Case interfere or in any manner Controul the Right of Conscience in the free Exercise of Religious Worship—

It is well known among all the Citizens of the 13 united States that the Jews have been true and faithful whigs, and during the late Contest with England they have been foremost in aiding and assisting the States with their lifes and fortunes, they have supported the Cause, have bravely faught and bleed for liberty which they Can not Enjoy—Therefore if the honourable Convention shall in ther Wisdom think fit and alter the said oath and leave out the words to viz—and I do acknowleedge the scripture of the new testement to be given by devine inspiration then the Israeletes will think them self happy to live under a goverment where all Relegious societys are on an Eaquel footing—I solecet this favour for my self my Childreen and posterity and for the benefit of all the Isrealetes through the 13 united States of america

My prayers is unto the Lord. May the people of this States Rise up as a great and young lion, May they prevail against their Enemies, May the degrees of honour of his Excellencey the president of the Convention George Washington, be Extollet and Raise up. May Every one speak of his glorious Exploits. May God prolong his days among us in this land of Liberty—May he lead the armies against his Enemys as he has done hereuntofore—May God Extend peace unto the united States—May they get up to the highest Prosperetys—May God Extend peace to them and their seed after them so long as the Sun and moon Endureth—and may the almighty God of our father Abraham Isaac and Jacob endue this Noble Assembly with wisdom Judgement and unamity in their Councells, and may they have the Satisfaction to see that their present toil and labour for the wellfair of the united States may be approved of, Through all the world and perticular by the united States of america is the ardent prayer of Sires

12

TENCH COXE, AN EXAMINATION OF THE CONSTITUTION
Fall 1787

Pamphlets 146

No religious test is ever to be required of any officer or servant of the United States. The people may employ any wise or good citizen in the execution of the various duties of the government. In Italy, Spain, and Portugal, no protestant can hold a public trust. In England every Presbyterian, and other person not of their established church, is incapable of holding an office. No such impious deprivation of the rights of men can take place under the new foederal constitution. The convention has the honour of proposing the first public act, by which any nation has ever

divested itself of a power, every exercise of which is a trespass on the Majesty of Heaven.

No qualification in monied or landed property is required by the proposed plan; nor does it admit any preference from the preposterous distinctions of birth and rank. The office of the President, a Senator, and a Representative, and every other place of power or profit, are therefore open to the whole body of the people. Any wise, informed and upright man, be his property what it may, can exercise the trusts and powers of the state, provided he possesses the moral, religious and political virtues which are necessary to secure the confidence of his fellow citizens.

13

JAMES MADISON TO EDMUND PENDLETON
28 Oct. 1787

Papers 10:223

Is not a religious test as far as it is necessary, or would operate, involved in the oath itself? If the person swearing believes in the supreme Being who is invoked, and in the penal consequences of offending him, either in this or a future world or both, he will be under the same restraint from perjury as if he had previously subscribed a test requiring this belief. If the person in question be an unbeliever in these points and would notwithstanding take the oath, a previous test could have no effect. He would subscribe it as he would take the oath, without any principle that could be affected by either.

14

OLIVER ELLSWORTH, LANDHOLDER, NO. 7
17 Dec. 1787

Essays 168–71

Some very worthy persons, who have not had great advantages for information, have objected against that clause in the constitution which provides, that no religious test shall ever be required as a qualification to any office or public trust under the United States. They have been afraid that this clause is unfavorable to religion. But my countrymen, the sole purpose and effect of it is to exclude persecution, and to secure to you the important right of religious liberty. We are almost the only people in the world, who have a full enjoyment of this important right of human nature. In our country every man has a right to worship God in that way which is most agreeable to his conscience. If he be a good and peaceable person he is liable to no penalties or incapacities on account of his religious sentiments; or in other words, he is no subject to persecution.

But in other parts of the world, it has been, and still is, far different. Systems of religious error have been adopted, in times of ignorance. It has been the interest of tyrannical kings, popes, and prelates, to maintain these errors. When the clouds of ignorance began to vanish, and the people grew more enlightened, there was no other way to keep them in error, but to prohibit their altering their religious opinions by severe persecuting laws. In this way persecution became general throughout Europe. It was the universal opinion that one religion must be established by law; and that all who differed in their religious opinions, must suffer the vengeance of persecution. In pursuance of this opinion, when popery was abolished in England, and the Church of England was established in its stead, severe penalities were inflicted upon all who dissented from the established church. In the time of the civil wars, in the reign of Charles I., the presbyterians got the upper hand, and inflicted legal penalties upon all who differed from them in their sentiments respecting religious doctrines and discipline. When Charles II, was restored, the Church of England was likewise restored, and the presbyterians and other dissenters were laid under legal penalties and incapacities. It was in this reign, that a religious test was established as a qualification for office; that is, a law was made requiring all officers civil and military (among other things) to receive the Sacrament of the Lord's Supper, according to the usage of the Church of England, written [within?] six months after their admission to office under the penalty of 500£ and disability to hold the office. And by another statute of the same reign, no person was capable of being elected to any office relating to the government of any city or corporation, unless, within a twelvemonth before, he had received the sacrament according to the rites of the Church of England. The pretence for making these severe laws, by which all but churchmen were made incapable of any office civil or military, was to exclude the papists; but the real design was to exclude the protestant dissenters. From this account of test-laws, there arises an unfavorable presumption against them. But if we consider the nature of them and the effects which they are calculated to produce, we shall find that they are useless, tyrannical, and peculiarly unfit for the people of this country.

A religious test is an act to be done, or profession to be made, relating to religion (such as partaking of the sacrament according to certain rites and forms, or declaring one's belief of certain doctrines,) for the purpose of determining whether his religious opinions are such, that he is admissable to a publick office. A test in favour of any one denomination of Christians would be to the last degree absurd in the United States. If it were in favour of either congregationalists, presbyterians, episcopalions, baptists, or quakers, it would incapacitate more than three-fourths of the American citizens for any publick office; and thus degrade them from the rank of freemen. There need no argument to prove that the majority of our citizens would never submit to this indignity.

If any test-act were to be made, perhaps the least exceptionable would be one, requiring all persons appointed to office to declare at the time of their admission, their belief in the being of a God, and in the divine authority of the scriptures. In favour of such a test, it may be said, that one who believes these great truths, will not be so likely to violate his obligations to his country, as one who disbelieves them; we may have greater confidence in his integrity. But I answer: His making a declaration of such a belief is no security at all. For suppose him to be an unprincipled man, who believes neither the word nor the being of God; and to be governed merely by selfish motives; how easy is it for him to dissemble! how easy is it for him to make a public declaration of his belief in the creed which the law prescribes; and excuse himself by calling it a mere formality. This is the case with the test-laws and creeds in England. The most abandoned characters partake of the sacrament, in order to qualify themselves for public employments. The clergy are obliged by law to administer the ordinance unto them, and thus prostitute the most sacred office of religion, for it is a civil right in the party to receive the sacrament. In that country, subscribing to the thirty-nine articles is a test for administration into holy orders. And it is a fact, that many of the clergy do this, when at the same time they totally disbelieve several of the doctrines contained in them. In short, test-laws are utterly ineffectual: they are no security at all; because men of loose principles will, by an external compliance, evade them. If they exclude any persons, it will be honest men, men of principle, who will rather suffer an injury, than act contrary to the dictates of their consciences. If we mean to have those appointed to public offices, who are sincere friends to religion, we, the people who appoint them, must take care to choose such characters; and not rely upon such cob-web barriers as test-laws are.

But to come to the true principle by which this question ought to be determined: The business of a civil government is to protect the citizen in his rights, to defend the community from hostile powers, and to promote the general welfare. Civil government has no business to meddle with the private opinions of the people. If I demean myself as a good citizen, I am accountable, not to man, but to God, for the religious opinions which I embrace, and the manner in which I worship the supreme being. If such had been the universal sentiments of mankind, and they had acted accordingly, persecution, the bane of truth and nurse of error, with her bloody axe and flaming hand, would never have turned so great a part of the world into a field of blood.

But while I assert the rights of religious liberty, I would not deny that the civil power has a right, in some cases, to interfere in matters of religion. It has a right to prohibit and punish gross immoralities and impieties; because the open practice of these is of evil example and detriment. For this reason, I heartily approve of our laws against drunkenness, profane swearing, blasphemy, and professed atheism. But in this state, we have never thought it expedient to adopt a test-law; and yet I sincerely believe we have as great a proportion of religion and morality, as they have in England, where every person who holds a public office, must either be a saint by law, or a hypocrite by practice. A test-law is the parent of hypocrisy, and the offspring of error and the spirit of persecution. Legislatures have no right to set up an inquisition, and examine into the private opinions of men. Test-laws are useless and ineffectual, unjust and tyrannical; therefore the Convention have done wisely in excluding this engine of persecution, and providing that no religious test shall ever be required.

15

ALEXANDER HAMILTON, FEDERALIST, NO. 27,
174–75
25 Dec. 1787

The plan reported by the Convention, by extending the authority of the foederal head to the individual citizens of the several States, will enable the government to employ the ordinary magistracy of each in the execution of its laws. It is easy to perceive that this will tend to destroy, in the common apprehension, all distinction between the sources from which they might proceed; and will give the Foederal Government the same advantage for securing a due obedience to its authority, which is enjoyed by the government of each State; in addition to the influence on public opinion, which will result from the important consideration of its having power to call to its assistance and support the resources of the whole Union. It merits particular attention in this place, that the laws of the confederacy, as to the *enumerated* and *legitimate* objects of its jurisdiction, will become the SUPREME LAW of the land; to the observance of which, all officers legislative, executive and judicial in each State, will be bound by the sanctity of an oath. Thus the Legislatures, Courts and Magistrates of the respective members will be incorporated into the operations of the national government, *as far as its just and constitutional authority extends;* and will be rendered auxiliary to the enforcement of its laws. Any man, who will pursue by his own reflections the consequences of this situation, will perceive that there is good ground to calculate upon a regular and peaceable execution of the laws of the Union; if its powers are administered with a common share of prudence. If we will arbitrarily suppose the contrary, we may deduce any inferences we please from the supposition; for it is certainly possible, by an injudicious exercise of the authorities of the best government, that ever was or ever can be instituted, to provoke and precipitate the people into the wildest excesses. But though the adversaries of the proposed constitution should presume that the national rulers would be insensible to the motives of public good, or to the obligations of duty; I would still ask them, how the interests of ambition, or the views of encroachment, can be promoted by such a conduct?

16

"WILLIAM PENN," NO. 2
3 Jan. 1788
Storing 3.12.18–19

These facts will no doubt afford an interesting page in the history of the contradictions of the human mind. Unfortunately, they do not stand single, and this is not the only instance that we find in the constitutions of the different states, of a general principle being expressly declared as a part of the natural rights of the citizens, and afterwards being as expressly contradicted in the practice. Thus we find it declared in every one of our bills of rights, "that there shall be a perfect liberty of conscience, and that no sect shall ever be entitled to a preference over the others." Yet in Massachusetts and Maryland, all the officers of government, and in Pennsylvania the members of the legislature, are to be of the Christian religion; in New-Jersey, North-Carolina, and Georgia, the protestant, and in Delaware, the trinitarian sects, have an exclusive right to public employments; and in South-Carolina the constitution goes so far as to declare the creed of the established church. Virginia and New-York are the only states where there is a perfect liberty of conscience. I cannot say any thing as to Connecticut and Rhode-Island, as their constitutions are silent on the subject, and I have not been informed of their practice.

Whether these religious restrictions are right or wrong it is not my intention, nor is it my object to examine in the course of these disquisitions—I only meant to shew, that in laying down a political system it is safer to rely on principles than upon precedents, because the former are fixed and immutable, while the latter vary with men, places, times and circumstances.

17

OLIVER WOLCOTT, CONNECTICUT RATIFYING
CONVENTION
9 Jan. 1788
Elliot 2:202

I do not see the necessity of such a *test* as some gentlemen wish for. The Constitution enjoins an oath upon all the officers of the United States. This is a direct appeal to that God who is the avenger of perjury. Such an appeal to him is a full acknowledgment of his being and providence. An acknowledgment of these great truths is all that the gentleman contends for. For myself, I should be content either with or without that clause in the Constitution which excludes test laws. Knowledge and liberty are so prevalent in this country, that I do not believe that the United States would ever be disposed to establish one religious sect, and lay all others under legal disabilities. But as we know not what may take place hereafter, and any such test would be exceedingly injurious to the rights of free citizens, I cannot think it altogether superfluous to have added a clause, which secures us from the possibility of such oppression. I shall only add, that I give my assent to this Constitution, and am happy to see the states in a fair way to adopt a Constitution which will protect their rights and promote their welfare.

18

LUTHER MARTIN, GENUINE INFORMATION
1788
Storing 2.4.108

The part of the system, which provides that *no religious test* shall ever be required as a qualification to any office or public trust under the United States, was adopted by a great majority of the convention, and without much debate,—however, there were some members *so unfashionable* as to think that a *belief of the existence of a Deity*, and of a *state of future rewards and punishments* would be some security for the good conduct of our rulers, and that in a Christian country it would be at *least decent* to hold out some distinction between the professors of Christianity and downright infidelity or paganism.

19

JAMES MADISON, FEDERALIST, NO. 44, 307
25 Jan. 1788

It has been asked, why it was thought necessary, that the State magistracy should be bound to support the Foederal Constitution, and unnecessary, that a like oath should be imposed on the officers of the United States in favor of the State Constitutions?

Several reasons might be assigned for the distinction. I content myself with one which is obvious & conclusive. The members of the Foederal Government will have no agency in carrying the State Constitutions into effect. The members and officers of the State Governments, on the contrary, will have an essential agency in giving effect to the Foederal Constitution. The election of the President and Senate, will depend in all cases, on the Legislatures of the several States. And the election of the House of Representatives, will equally depend on the same authority in the first instance; and will probably, for ever be conducted by the officers and according to the laws of the States.

20

DEBATE IN MASSACHUSETTS RATIFYING CONVENTION
30 Jan. 1788
Elliot 2:117–19, 120

[Dr. JARVIS.] In the conversation on Thursday, on the sixth article, which provides that "no religious test shall ever be required as a qualification to any office," &c., several gentlemen urged that it was a departure from the principles of our forefathers, who came here for the preservation of their religion; and that it would admit deists, atheists, &c., into the general government; and, people being apt to imitate the examples of the court, these principles would be disseminated, and, of course, a corruption of morals ensue. Gentlemen on the other side applauded the liberality of the clause, and represented, in striking colors, the impropriety, and almost impiety, of the requisition of a test, as practised in Great Britain and elsewhere. In this conversation, the following is the substance of the observations of the

Rev. Mr. SHUTE. Mr. President, to object to the latter part of the paragraph under consideration, which excludes a religious test, is, I am sensible, very popular; for the most of men, somehow, are rigidly tenacious of their own sentiments in religion, and disposed to impose them upon others as the *standard* of truth. If, in my sentiments upon the point in view, I should differ from some in this honorable body, I only wish from them the exercise of that candor, with which true religion is adapted to inspire the honest and well-disposed mind.

To establish a religious test as a qualification for offices in the proposed federal Constitution, it appears to me, sir, would be attended with injurious consequences to some individuals, and with no advantage to the *whole*.

By the injurious consequences to individuals, I mean, that some, who, in every other respect, are qualified to fill some important post in government, will be excluded by their not being able to stand the religious test; which I take to be a privation of part of their civil rights.

Nor is there to me any conceivable advantage, sir, that would result to the whole from such a test. Unprincipled and dishonest men will not hesitate to subscribe to *any thing* that may open the way for their advancement, and put them into a situation the better to execute their base and iniquitous designs. Honest men alone, therefore, however well qualified to serve the public, would be excluded by it, and their country be deprived of the benefit of their abilities.

In this great and extensive empire, there is, and will be, a great variety of sentiments in religion among its inhabitants. Upon the plan of a religious test, the question, I think, must be, Who shall be excluded from national trusts? Whatever answer bigotry may suggest, the dictates of candor and equity, I conceive, will be, *None*.

Far from limiting my charity and confidence to men of my own denomination in religion, I suppose, and I believe, sir, that there are worthy characters among men of every denomination—among the Quakers, the Baptists, the Church of England, the Papists; and even among those who have no other guide, in the way to virtue and heaven, than the dictates of natural religion.

I must therefore think, sir, that the proposed plan of government, in this particular, is wisely constructed; that, as all have an equal claim to the blessings of the government under which they live, and which they support, so none should be excluded from them for being of any particular denomination in religion.

The presumption is, that the eyes of the people will be upon the faithful in the land; and, from a regard to their own safety, they will choose for their rulers men of known abilities, of known probity, of good moral characters. The apostle Peter tells us that God is no respecter of persons, but, in every nation, he that feareth him, and worketh righteousness, is *acceptable* to him. And I know of no reason why men of such a character, in a community of whatever denomination in religion, *caeteris paribus*, with other suitable qualifications, should not be *acceptable* to the people, and why they may not be employed by them with safety and advantage in the important offices of government. The exclusion of a religious test in the proposed Constitution, therefore, clearly appears to me, sir, to be in favor of its adoption.

Col. JONES (of Bristol) thought, that the rulers ought to believe in God or Christ, and that, however a test may be prostituted in England, yet he thought, if our public men were to be of those who had a good standing in the church, it would be happy for the United States, and that a person could not be a good man without being a good Christian.

. . . . .

Col. JONES said, that one of his principal objections was, the omission of a religious test.

Rev. Mr. PAYSON. Mr. President, after what has been observed, relating to a religious test, by gentlemen of acknowledged abilities, I did not expect that it would again be mentioned, as an objection to the proposed Constitution, that such a test was not required as a qualification for office. Such were the abilities and integrity of the gentlemen who constructed the Constitution, as not to admit of the presumption, that they would have betrayed so much vanity as to attempt to erect bulwarks and barriers to the throne of God. Relying on the candor of this Convention, I shall take the liberty to express my sentiments on the nature of a religious test, and shall endeavor to do it in such propositions as will meet the approbation of every mind.

The great object of religion being God supreme, and the seat of religion in man being the heart or conscience, *i. e.*, the reason God has given us, employed on our moral actions, in their most important consequences, as related to the tribunal of God, hence I infer that God alone is the God of the conscience, and, consequently, attempts to erect human tribunals for the consciences of men are impious encroachments upon the prerogatives of God. Upon these principles, had there been a religious test as a qualification for office, it would, in my opinion, have been a great blemish upon the instrument.

21

WILLIAM WILLIAMS, LETTER
11 Feb. 1788
Essays 207–9

Since the Federal Constitution has had so calm, dispassionate and so happy an issue, in the late worthy Convention of this State; I did not expect any members of that hon. body to be challenged in a News-paper, and especially by name, and by anonymous writers, on account of their opinion, or decently expressing their sentiments relative to the great subject then under consideration, or any part of it. Nor do I yet see the propriety, or happy issue of such a proceeding. However as a gentleman in your Paper feels uneasy, that every sentiment contained in his publications, (tho' in general they are well written) is not received with perfect acquiescence and submission, I will endeavour to satisfy him, or the candid reader, by the same channel, that I am not so reprehensible as he supposes, in the matter refer'd to. When the clause in the 6th article, which provides that "no religious test should ever be required as a qualification to any office or trust, &c." came under consideration, I observed I should have chose that sentence and anything relating to a religious test, had been totally omitted rather than stand as it did, but still more wished something of the kind should have been inserted, but with a reverse sense, so far as to require an explicit acknowledgment of the being of a God, his perfections and his providence, and to have been prefixed to, and stand as, the first introductory words of the Constitution, in the following or similar terms, viz. *We the people of the United States, in a firm belief of the being and perfections of the one living and true God, the creator and supreme Governour of the world, in his universal providence and the authority of his laws; that he will require of all moral agents an account of their conduct; that all rightful powers among men are ordained of, and mediately derived from God; therefore in a dependence on his blessing and acknowledgment of his efficient protection in establishing our Independence, whereby it is become necessary to agree upon and settle a Constitution of federal government for ourselves,* and in order to form a more perfect union &c., as it is expressed in the present introduction, do ordain &c., and instead of none, that no other religious test should ever be required &c., and that supposing, but not granting, this would *be no security at all*, that it would make hypocrites, &c. yet this would not be a sufficient reason against it; as it would be a public declaration against, and disapprobation of men, who did not, even with sincerity, make such a profession, and they must be left to the searcher of hearts; that it would however, be the voice of the great body of the people, and an acknowledgment proper and highly becoming them to express on this great and only occasion, and according to the course of Providence, one mean of obtaining blessings from the most high. But that since it was not, and so difficult and dubious to get inserted, I would not wish to make it a capital objection; that I had no more idea of a religious test, which should restrain offices to any particular sect, class, or denomination of men or Christians in the long list of diversity, than to regulate their bestowments by the stature or dress of the candidate, nor did I believe one sensible catholic man in the state wished for such a limitation; and that therefore the News-Paper observations, and reasonings (I named no author) against a test, in favour of any one denomination of Christians, and the sacrilegious injunctions of the test laws of England &c., combatted objections which did not exist, and *was building up a man of straw and knocking him down again.* These are the same and only ideas and sentiments I endeavoured to communicate on that subject, tho' perhaps not precisely in the same terms; as I had not written, nor preconceived them, except the proposed test, and whether there is any reason in them or not, I submit to the public.

I freely confess such a test and acknowledgment would have given me great additional satisfaction; and I conceive the arguments against it, on the score of hypocrisy, would apply with equal force against requiring an oath from any officer of the united or individual states; and with little abatement, to any oath in any case whatever; but divine and human wisdom, with universal experience, have approved and established them as useful, and a security to mankind.

I thought it was my duty to make the observations, in this behalf, which I did, and to bear my testimony for God; and that it was also my duty to say *the Constitution,* with this, and some other faults of another kind, was yet too wise and too necessary to be rejected.

22

JAMES MADISON TO EDMUND RANDOLPH
10 Apr. 1788
Papers 11:19

As to the religious test, I should conceive that it can imply at most nothing more than that without that exception, a power would have been given to impose an oath involving a religious test as a qualification for office. The constitution of necessary offices being given to the Congress, the proper qualifications seem to be evidently involved. I think too there are several other satisfactory points of view in which the exception might be placed.

23

PROPOSED AMENDMENT, SOUTH CAROLINA
RATIFYING CONVENTION
23 May 1788
Dumbauld 180

Resolved that the third section of the Sixth Article ought to be amended by inserting the word *"other"* between the words *"no"* and *"religious"*

24

EDMUND RANDOLPH, VIRGINIA RATIFYING
CONVENTION
10 June 1788
Elliot 3:204–5

Freedom of religion is said to be in danger. I will candidly say, I once thought that it was, and felt great repugnance to the constitution for that reason. I am willing to acknowledge my apprehensions removed—and I will inform you by what process of reasoning I did remove them. The constitution provides, that "the senators and representatives before mentioned, and the members of the several state legislatures, and all executive and judicial officers, both of the United States and of the several states, shall be bound by oath, or affirmation, to support this constitution; but no religious test shall ever be required as a qualification to any office or public trust under the United States." It has been said, that if the exclusion of the religious test were an exception from the general power of congress, the power over religion would remain. I inform those who are of this opinion, that no power is given expressly to congress over religion. The senators and representatives, members of the state legislatures, and executive and judicial officers, are bound by oath, or affirmation, to support this constitution. This only binds them to support it in the exercise of the powers constitutionally given it. The exclusion of religious tests is an exception from this general provision, with respect to oaths, or affirmations. Although officers, &c. are to swear that they will support this constitution, yet they are not bound to support one mode of worship, or to adhere to one particular sect. It puts all sects on the same footing. A man of abilities and character, of any sect whatever, may be admitted to any office or public trust under the United States. I am a friend to a variety of sects, because they keep one another in order. How many different sects are we composed of throughout the United States? How many different sects will be in congress? We cannot enumerate the sects that may be in congress. And there are so many now in the United States that they will prevent the establishment of any one sect in prejudice to the rest, and will forever oppose all attempts to infringe religious liberty. If such an attempt be made, will not the alarm be sounded throughout America? If congress be as wicked as we are foretold they will, they would not run the risk of exciting the resentment of all, or most of the religious sects in America.

25

PROPOSED AMENDMENT, NEW YORK RATIFYING
CONVENTION
26 July 1788
Dumbauld 198

That the Senators and Representatives and all Executive Judicial Officers of the United States shall be bound by Oath or Affirmation not to infringe or violate the Constitutions or Rights of the respective States.

26

WILLIAM LANCASTER, NORTH CAROLINA
RATIFYING CONVENTION
30 July 1788
Elliot 4:215

As to a religious test, had the article which excludes it provided none but what had been in the states heretofore, I would not have objected to it. It would secure religion. Religious liberty ought to be provided for. I acquiesce with the gentleman, who spoke, on this point, my sentiments better than I could have done myself. For my part, in reviewing the qualifications necessary for a President, I did not suppose that the pope could occupy the President's chair. But let us remember that we form a government for millions not yet in existence. I have not the art of divination. In the course of four or five hundred years, I do not know how it will work. This is most certain, that Papists may occupy that chair, and Mahometans may take it. I see nothing against it. There is a disqualification, I believe, in every state in the Union—it ought to be so in this system. It is said that all power not given is retained. I find they thought proper to insert negative clauses in the Constitution, restraining the general government from the exercise of certain powers. These were unnecessary if the doctrine be true, that every thing not given is retained. From the insertion of these we may conclude the doctrine to be fallacious.

27

JOSEPH STORY, COMMENTARIES ON THE
CONSTITUTION 3:§§ 1838–43
1833

§ 1838. That all those, who are entrusted with the execution of the powers of the national government, should be bound by some solemn obligation to the due execution of the trusts reposed in them, and to support the constitution, would seem to be a proposition too clear to render any reasoning necessary in support of it. It results from the plain right of society to require some guaranty from every officer, that he will be conscientious in the discharge of his duty. Oaths have a solemn obligation upon the minds of all reflecting men, and especially upon those, who feel a deep sense of accountability to a Supreme being. If, in the ordinary administration of justice in cases of private rights, or personal claims, oaths are required of those, who try, as well as of those, who give testimony, to guard against malice, falsehood, and evasion, surely like guards ought to be interposed in the administration of high public trusts, and especially in such, as may concern the welfare and safety of the whole community. But there are known denominations of men, who are conscientiously scrupulous of taking oaths (among which is that pure and distinguished sect of Christians, commonly called Friends, or Quakers,) and therefore, to prevent any unjustifiable exclusion from office, the constitution has permitted a solemn affirmation to be made instead of an oath, and as its equivalent.

§ 1839. But it may not appear to all persons quite so clear, why the officers of the state governments should be equally bound to take a like oath, or affirmation; and it has been even suggested, that there is no more reason to require that, than to require, that all of the United States officers should take an oath or affirmation to support the state constitutions. A moment's reflection will show sufficient reasons for the requisition of it in the one case, and the omission of it in the other. The members and officers of the national government have no agency in carrying into effect the state constitutions. The members and officers of the state governments have an essential agency in giving effect to the national constitution. The election of the president and the senate will depend, in all cases, upon the legislatures of the several states; and, in many cases, the election of the house of representatives may be affected by their agency. The judges of the state courts will frequently be called upon to decide upon the constitution, and laws, and treaties of the United States; and upon rights and claims growing out of them. Decisions ought to be, as far as possible, uniform; and uniformity of obligation will greatly tend to such a result. The executive authority of the several states may be often called upon to exert powers, or allow rights, given by the constitution, as in filling vacancies in the senate, during the recess of the legislature; in issuing writs of election to fill vacancies in the house of representatives; in officering the militia, and giving effect to laws for calling them; and in the surrender of fugitives from justice. These, and many other functions, devolving on the state authorities, render it highly important, that they should be under a solemn obligation to obey the constitution. In common sense, there can be no well-founded objection to it. There may be serious evils growing out of an opposite course. One of the objections, taken to the articles of confederation, by an enlightened state, (New-Jersey,) was, that no oath was required of members of congress, previous to their admission to their seats in congress. The laws and usages of all civilized nations, (said that state,) evince the propriety of an oath on such occasions; and the more solemn and important the deposit, the more strong and explicit ought the obligation to be.

§ 1840. As soon as the constitution went into operation, congress passed an act, prescribing the time and manner of taking the oath, or affirmation, thus required, as well by officers of the several states, as of the United States. On that occasion, some scruple seems to have been entertained, by a few members, of the constitutional authority of congress to pass such an act. But it was approved without much opposition. At this day, the point would be generally deemed beyond the reach of any reasonable doubt.

§ 1841. The remaining part of the clause declares, that "no religious test shall ever be required, as a qualification to any office or public trust, under the United States." This clause is not introduced merely for the purpose of satisfying the scruples of many respectable persons, who feel an invincible repugnance to any religious test, or affirmation. It had a higher object; to cut off for ever every pretence of any alliance between church and state in the national government. The framers of the constitution were fully sensible of the dangers from this source, marked out in the history of other ages and countries; and not wholly unknown to our own. They knew, that bigotry was unceasingly vigilant in its stratagems, to secure to itself an exclusive ascendancy over the human mind; and that intolerance was ever ready to arm itself with all the terrors of the civil power to exterminate those, who doubted its dogmas, or resisted its infallibility. The Catholic and the Protestant had alternately waged the most ferocious and unrelenting warfare on each other; and Protestantism itself, at the very moment, that it was proclaiming the right of private judgment, prescribed boundaries to that right, beyond which if any one dared to pass, he must seal his rashness with the blood of martyrdom. The history of the parent country, too, could not fail to instruct them in the uses, and the abuses of religious tests. They there found the pains and penalties of non-conformity written in no equivocal language, and enforced with a stern and vindictive jealousy. One hardly knows, how to repress the sentiments of strong indignation, in reading the cool vindication of the laws of England on this subject, (now, happily, for the most part abolished by recent enactments,) by Mr. Justice Blackstone, a man, in many respects distinguished for habitual moderation, and a deep sense of justice. "The second species," says he "of non-conformists, are those, who offend through a mistaken or perverse zeal. Such were esteemed by our laws, enacted since the time of the reformation, to be papists, and protestant dissenters; both of which were supposed to be equally schismatics in not communicating with the national church; with this difference, that the papists divided from it upon material, though erroneous, reasons; but many of the dissenters, upon matters of indifference, or, in other words, upon no reason at all. Yet certainly our ancestors were mistaken in their plans of compulsion and intolerance. The sin of schism, as such, is by no means the object of temporal coercion and punishment. If, through weakness of intellect, through misdirected piety, through perverseness and acerbity of temper, or, (which is often the case,) through a prospect of secular advantage in herding with a party, men quarrel with the ecclesiastical establishment, the civil magistrate has nothing to do with it; unless their tenets and practice are such, as threaten ruin or disturbance to the state. He is bound, indeed, to protect the established church; and, if this can be better effected, by admitting none but its genuine members to offices of trust and emolument, he is certainly at liberty so to do; the disposal of offices being matter of favour and discretion. But, this point being once secured, all persecution for diversity of opinions, however ridiculous or absurd they may be, is contrary to every principle of sound policy and civil freedom. The names and subordination of the clergy, the posture of devotion, the materials and colour of the minister's garment, the joining in a known, or an unknown form of prayer, and other matters of the same kind, must be left to the option of every man's private judgment."

§ 1842. And again: "As to papists, what has been said of the protestant dissenters would hold equally strong for a general toleration of them; provided their separation was founded only upon difference of opinion in religion, and their principles did not also extend to a subversion of the civil government. If once they could be brought to renounce the supremacy of the pope, they might quietly enjoy their seven sacraments, their purgatory, and auricular confession; their worship of reliques and images; nay even their transubstantiation. But while they acknowledge a foreign power, superior to the sovereignty of the kingdom, they cannot complain, if the laws of that kingdom will not treat them upon the footing of good subjects."

§ 1843. Of the English laws respecting papists, Montesquieu observes, that they are so rigorous, though not professedly of the sanguinary kind, that they do all the hurt, that can possibly be done in cold blood. To this just rebuke, (after citing it, and admitting its truth,) Mr. Justice Blackstone has no better reply to make, than that these laws are seldom exerted to their utmost rigour; and, indeed, if they were, it would be very difficult to excuse them. The meanest apologist of the worst enormities of a Roman emperor could not have shadowed out a defence more servile, or more unworthy of the dignity and spirit of a freeman. With one quotation more from the same authority, exemplifying the nature and objects of the English test laws, this subject may be dismissed. "In order the better to secure the established church against perils from nonconformists of all denominations, infidels, Turks, Jews, heretics, papists, and sectaries, there are, however, two bulwarks erected, called the corporation and test-acts. By the former of which, no person can be legally elected to any office relating to the government of any city or corporation, unless, within a twelvemonth before, he has received the sacrament of the Lord's supper according to the rights of the church of England; and he is also enjoined to take the oaths of allegiance and supremacy, at the same time, that he takes the oath of office; or, in default of either of these requisites, such election shall be void. The other, called the test-act, directs all officers, civil and military, to take the oaths, and make the declaration against transubstantiation, in any of the king's courts at Westminster, or at the quarter sessions, within six calendar months after their admission; and also within the same time to receive the sacrament of the Lord's supper, according to the usage of the church of England, in some public church immediately after divine service and sermon; and to deliver into court a certificate thereof signed by the minister and church-warden, and also to prove the same by two credible witnesses, upon forfeiture of 500*l*, and disability to hold the said office. And of much the same nature with these is the statute 7 Jac. I. c. 2., which permits no persons to be naturalized, or restored in blood, but such as undergo a like test; which test, having been removed in 1753, in favour of the Jews, was the next session of parliament restored again with some precipitation." It is easy to foresee, that without some prohibition of religious tests, a successful sect, in our country, might, by once possessing power, pass test-laws, which would secure to themselves a monopoly of all the offices of trust and profit, under the national government.

SEE ALSO:

Generally Amend. I (religion)
Records of the Federal Convention, Farrand 2:133, 146, 148, 159–60, 174, 188, 579, 603
A Friend to the Rights of the People, 8 Feb. 1788, Storing 4.23.3
David, 7 Mar. 1788, Storing 4.24.2–6
Archibald Maclaine, North Carolina Ratifying Convention, 28 July 1788, Elliot 4:140
House of Representatives, Manner of Taking Certain Oaths, 6 May 1789, Annals 1:266–71
St. George Tucker, Blackstone's Commentaries 1:App. 369–70 (1803)
Arkansas Constitution of 1836, art. 7, sec. 2, Thorpe 1:284

Article 7

The Ratification of the Conventions of nine States, shall be sufficient for the Establishment of this Constitution between the States so ratifying the Same.

1. Resolution of Congress, 21 Feb. 1787
2. Records of the Federal Convention
3. Benjamin Franklin to the Federal Convention, 17 Sept. 1787
4. Edmund Randolph to Speaker of Virginia House of Delegates, 10 Oct. 1787
5. Luther Martin, Maryland House of Delegates, 29 Nov. 1787
6. William Short to James Madison, 21 Dec. 1787
7. Luther Martin, Genuine Information, 1788
8. George Washington to Edmund Randolph, 8 Jan. 1788
9. Samuel, 10 Jan. 1788
10. James Madison, Federalist, no. 43, 23 Jan. 1788
11. Federal Farmer, no. 18, 25 Jan. 1788
12. Thomas Jefferson to Alexander Donald, 7 Feb. 1788
13. Edmund Randolph, Virginia Ratifying Convention, 4 June 1788
14. Debate in Virginia Ratifying Convention, 12, 24–25 June 1788
15. Act of Continental Congress Putting Constitution into Effect, 13 Sept. 1788
16. *Owings* v. *Speed*, 5 Wheat. 419 (1820)

1

RESOLUTION OF CONGRESS
21 Feb. 1787
Documentary History 4:78

Resolved that in the opinion of Congress it is expedient that on the second Monday in May next a Convention of delegates who shall have been appointed by the several states be held at Philadelphia for the sole and express purpose of revising the Articles of Confederation and reporting to Congress and the several legislatures such alterations and provisions therein as shall when agreed to in Congress and confirmed by the states render the federal constitution adequate to the exigencies of Government & the preservation of the Union.

2

RECORDS OF THE FEDERAL CONVENTION

[1:22; Madison, 29 May]

15. Resd. that the amendments which shall be offered to the Confederation, by the Convention ought at a proper time, or times, after the approbation of Congress to be submitted to an assembly or assemblies of Representatives, recommended by the several Legislatures to be expressly chosen by the people, to consider & decide thereon.

[1:122; Madison, 5 June]

propos. 15. for "*recommending conventions under appointment* of the people *to ratify the new Constitution &c.*" being taken up.

Mr. Sherman thought such a popular ratification unnecessary. the articles of Confederation providing for changes and alterations with the assent of Congs. and ratification of State Legislatures.

Mr. Madison thought this provision essential. The articles of Confedn. themselves were defective in this respect, resting in many of the States on the Legislative sanction only. Hence in conflicts between acts of the States, and of Congs. especially where the former are of posterior date, and the decision is to be made by State Tribunals, an uncertainty must necessarily prevail, or rather perhaps a certain decision in favor of the State authority. He suggested also that as far as the articles of Union were to be considered as a Treaty only of a particular sort, among the Governments of Independent States, the doctrine might be set up that a breach of any one article, by any of the parties, absolved the other parties from the whole obligation. For these reasons as well as others he thought it indispensable that the new Constitution should be ratified in the most

unexceptionable form, and by the supreme authority of the people themselves.

Mr. Gerry. Observed that in the Eastern States the Confedn. had been sanctioned by the people themselves. He seemed afraid of referring the new system to them. The people in that quarter have at this time the wildest ideas of Government in the world. They were for abolishing the Senate in Massts. and giving all the other powers of Govt. to the other branch of the Legislature.

Mr. King supposed the last article of ye Confedn. Rendered the legislature competent to the ratification. The people of the Southern States where the federal articles had been ratified by the Legislatures only, had since *impliedly* given their sanction to it. He thought notwithstanding that there might be policy in varying the mode. A Convention being a single house, the adoption may more easily be carried thro' it. than thro' the Legislatures where there are several branches. The Legislatures also being to lose power, will be most likely to raise objections. The people having already parted with the necessary powers it is immaterial to them, by which Government they are possessed, provided they be well employed.

Mr. Wilson took this occasion to lead the Committee by a train of observations to the idea of not suffering a disposition in the plurality of States to confederate anew on better principles, to be defeated by the inconsiderate or selfish opposition of a few States. He hoped the provision for ratifying would be put on such a footing as to admit of such a partial union, with a door open for the accession of the rest.—

Mr. Pinkney hoped that in the case the experiment should not unanimously take place nine States might be authorized to unite under the same Governmt.

[1:126; Yates, 5 June]

The 15th or last resolve, *That the amendment which shall be offered to the confederation, ought at a proper time or times after the approbation of congress to be submitted to an assembly or assemblies of representatives, recommended by the several legislatures, to be expressly chosen by the people, to consider and decide thereon,* was taken into consideration.

Mr. Madison endeavored to enforce the necessity of this resolve—because the new national constitution ought to have the highest source of authority, at least paramount to the powers of the respective constitutions of the states—points out the mischiefs that have arisen in the old confederation, which depends upon no higher authority than the confirmation of an ordinary act of a legislature—Instances the law operation of treaties, when contravened by any antecedent acts of a particular state.

Mr. King supposes, that as the p[e]ople have tacitly agreed to a federal government, that therefore the legislature in every state have a right to confirm any alterations or amendments in it—a convention in each state to approve of a new government he supposes however the most eligible.

Mr. Wilson is of opinion, that the people by a convention are the only power that can ratify the proposed system of the new government.

It is possible that not all the states, nay, that not even a majority, will immediately come into the measure; but such as do ratify it will be immediately bound by it, and others as they may from time to time accede to it.

Question put for postponement of this resolve. 7 states for postponment—3 against it.

[1:128; Pierce, 5 June]

Mr. Butler was of opinion that the alteration of the confederation ought not to be confirmed by the different Legislatures because they have sworn to support the Government under which they act, and therefore that Deputies should be chosen by the People for the purpose of ratifying it.

Mr. King thought that the Convention would be under the necessity of referring the amendments to the different Legislatures, because one of the Articles of the confederation expressly made it necessary.

As the word perpetual in the Articles of confederation gave occasion for several Members to insist upon the main principles of the confederacy, i e that the several States should meet in the general Council on a footing of compleat equality each claiming the right of sovereignty, Mr. Butler observed that the word perpetual in the confederation meant only the constant existence of our Union, and not the particular words which compose the Articles of the union.

Some general discussions came on.—

[1:179; Madison, 9 June]

[Mr. Paterson] It has been said that if a Natl. Govt. is to be formed so as to operate on the people and not on the States, the representatives ought to be drawn from the people. But why so? May not a Legislature filled by the State Legislatures operate on the people who chuse the State Legislatures? or may not a practicable coercion be found. He admitted that there was none such in the existing System. He was attached strongly to the plan of the existing confederacy, in which the people chuse their Legislative representatives; and the Legislatures their federal representatives. No other amendments were wanting than to mark the orbits of the States with due precision, and provide for the use of coercion, which was the great point. He alluded to the hint thrown out heretofore by Mr. Wilson of the necessity to which the large States might be reduced of confederating among themselves, by a refusal of the others to concur. Let them unite if they please, but let them remember that they have no authority to compel the others to unite. N. Jersey will never confederate on the plan before the Committee. She would be swallowed up. He had rather submit to a monarch, to a despot, than to such a fate. He would not only oppose the plan here but on his return home do everything in his power to defeat it there

[1:214; Madison, 12 June]

The Question taken on Resolution 15, to wit, referring the new system to the people of the States for ratification it passed in the affirmative: Massts. ay. Cont. no. N.Y. no.

N. J. no. Pa. ay Del. divd. Md. divd. Va. ay. N. C. ay. S. C. ay. Geo. ay. [Ayes—6; noes—3; divided—2.]

[1:237; Madison, 13 June]

19. Resd. that the amendments which shall be offered to the confederation by the convention ought at a proper time or times after the approbation of Congs. to be submitted to an Assembly or Assemblies recommended by the several Legislatures to be expressly chosen by the people to consider and decide thereon.

[1:250; Madison, 16 June]

Mr. Patterson. said as he had on a former occasion given his sentiments on the plan proposed by Mr. R. he would now avoiding repetition as much as possible give his reasons in favor of that proposed by himself. He preferred it because it accorded 1. with the powers of the Convention. 2 with the sentiments of the people. If the confederacy was radically wrong, let us return to our States, and obtain larger powers, not assume them of ourselves. I came here not to speak my own sentiments, but the sentiments of those who sent me. Our object is not such a Governmt. as may be best in itself, but such a one as our Constituents have authorized us to prepare, and as they will approve. If we argue the matter on the supposition that no Confederacy at present exists, it can not be denied that all the States stand on the footing of equal sovereignty. All therefore must concur before any can be bound. If a proportional representation be right, why do we not vote so here? If we argue on the fact that a federal compact actually exists, and consult the articles of it we still find an equal Sovereignty to be the basis of it. He reads the 5th. art: of Confederation giving each State a vote—& the 13th. declaring that no alteration shall be made without unanimous consent. This is the nature of all treaties. What is unanimously done, must be unanimously undone. It was observed (by Mr. Wilson) that the larger State[s] gave up the point, not because it was right, but because the circumstances of the moment urged the concession. Be it so. Are they for that reason at liberty to take it back. Can the donor resume his gift Without the consent of the donee. This doctrine may be convenient, but it is a doctrine that will sacrifice the lesser States. The large States acceded readily to the confederacy. It was the small ones that came in reluctantly and slowly. N. Jersey & Maryland were the two last, the former objecting to the want of power in Congress over trade: both of them to the want of power to appropriate the vacant territory to the benefit of the whole. If the sovereignty of the States is to be maintained, the Representatives must be drawn immediately from the States, not from the people: and we have no power to vary the idea of equal sovereignty. The only expedient that will cure the difficulty, is that of throwing the States into Hotchpot. To say that this is impracticable, will not make it so. Let it be tried, and we shall see whether the Citizens of Massts. Pena. & Va. accede to it. It will be objected that Coercion will be impracticable. But will it be more so in one plan than the other? Its efficacy will depend on the quantum of power collected, not on its being drawn from the States, or from the individuals; and according to his plan it may be exerted on individuals as well as according that of Mr. R. a distinct executive & Judiciary also were equally provided by this plan.

. . . . .

[Mr. Wilson] . . . 13. finally ye ratification is in this to be by the people themselves—in that by the legislative authorities according to the 13 art: of Confederation.

With regard to the *power of the Convention*, he conceived himself authorized to *conclude nothing*, but to be at liberty to *propose any thing*. In this particular he felt himself perfectly indifferent to the two plans.

With *regard to the sentiments of the people*, he conceived it difficult to know precisely what they are. Those of the particular circle in which one moved, were commonly mistaken for the general voice. He could not persuade himself that the State Govts. & sovereignties were so much the idols of the people, nor a Natl. Govt. so obnoxious to them, as some supposed. Why sd. a Natl. Govt. be unpopular? Has it less dignity? will each Citizen enjoy under it less liberty or protection? Will a Citizen of *Delaware* be degraded by becoming a Citizen of the *United States*? Where do the people look at present for relief from the evils of which they complain? Is it from an internal reform of their Govt.? No. Sir, It is from the Natl. Councils that relief is expected. For these reasons he did not fear, that the people would not follow us into a national Govt. and it will be a further recommendation of Mr. R.'s plan that it is to be submitted to *them* and not to the *Legislatures*, for ratification.

[1:314; Madison, 19 June]

Mr. Madison. Much stress had been laid by some gentlemen on the want of power in the Convention to propose any other than a *federal* plan. To what had been answered by others, he would only add, that neither of the characteristics attached to a *federal* plan would support this objection. One characteristic, was that in a *federal* Government, the power was exercised not on the people individually; but on the people *collectively*, on the *States*. Yet in some instances as in piracies, captures &c. the existing Confederacy, and in many instances, the amendments to it proposed by Mr. Patterson must operate immediately on individuals. The other characteristic was, that a *federal* Govt. derived its appointments not immediately from the people, but from the States which they respectively composed. Here too were facts on the other side. In two of the States, Connect. and Rh. Island, the delegates to Congs. were chosen, not by the Legislatures, but by the people at large; and the plan of Mr. P. intended no change in this particular.

It had been alledged (by Mr. Patterson) that the Confederation having been formed by unanimous consent, could be dissolved by unanimous Consent only Does this doctrine result from the nature of compacts? does it arise from any particular stipulation in the articles of Confederation? If we consider the federal union as analogous to the fundamental compact by which individuals compose one Society, and which must in its theoretic ori-

gin at least, have been the unanimous act of the component members, it cannot be said that no dissolution of the compact can be effected without unanimous consent. a breach of the fundamental principles of the compact by a part of the Society would certainly absolve the other part from their obligations to it. If the breach of *any* article by *any* of the parties, does not set the others at liberty, it is because, the contrary is *implied* in the compact itself, and particularly by that law of it, which gives an indefinite authority to the majority to bind the whole in all cases. This latter circumstance shews that we are not to consider the federal Union as analogous to the social compact of individuals: for if it were so, a Majority would have a right to bind the rest, and even to form a new Constitution for the whole, which the Gentn: from N. Jersey would be among the last to admit. If we consider the federal union as analogous not to the social compacts among individual men: but to the conventions among individual States. What is the doctrine resulting from these conventions? Clearly, according to the Expositors of the law of Nations, that a breach of any one article, by any one party, leaves all the other parties at liberty, to consider the whole convention as dissolved, unless they choose rather to compel the delinquent party to repair the breach. In some treaties indeed it is expressly stipulated that a violation of particular articles shall not have this consequence, and even that particular articles shall remain in force during war, which in general is understood to dissolve all subsisting Treaties. But are there any exceptions of this sort to the Articles of confederation? So far from it that there is not even an express stipulation that force shall be used to compell an offending member of the Union to discharge its duty. He observed that the violations of the federal articles had been numerous & notorious. Among the most notorious was an Act of N. Jersey herself; by which she *expressly refused* to comply with a constitutional requisition of Congs.—and yielded no farther to the expostulations of their deputies, than barely to rescind her vote of refusal without passing any positive act of compliance. He did not wish to draw any rigid inferences from these observations. He thought it proper however that the true nature of the existing confederacy should be investigated, and he was not anxious to strengthen the foundations on which it now stands

[1:335; Madison, 20 June]

Mr. Elseworth 2ded. by Mr. Gorham moves to alter it so as to run "that the Government of the United States ought to consist of a supreme legislative, Executive and Judiciary". This alteration he said would drop the word *national*, and retain the proper title "the United States." He could not admit the doctrine that a breach of any of the federal articles could dissolve the whole. It would be highly dangerous not to consider the Confederation as still subsisting. He wished also the plan of the Convention to go forth as an amendment to the articles of Confederation, since under this idea the authority of the Legislatures could ratify it. If they are unwilling, the people will be so too. If the plan goes forth to the people for ratification several succeeding Conventions within the States would be unavoidable. He did not like these conventions. They were better fitted to pull down than to build up Constitutions.

[2:88; Madison, 23 July]

Resol: 19. referring the new Constitution to Assemblies to be chosen by the people for the express purpose of ratifying it" was next taken into consideration.

Mr. Elseworth moved that it be referred to the Legislatures of the States for ratification. Mr. Patterson 2ded. the motion.

Col. Mason considered a reference of the plan to the authority of the people as one of the most important and essential of the Resolutions. The Legislatures have no power to ratify it. They are the mere creatures of the State Constitutions, and cannot be greater than their creators. And he knew of no power in any of the Constitutions, he knew there was no power in some of them, that could be competent to this object. Whither then must we resort? To the people with whom all power remains that has not been given up in the Constitutions derived from them. It was of great moment he observed that this doctrine should be cherished as the basis of free Government. Another strong reason was that admitting the Legislatures to have a competent authority, it would be wrong to refer the plan to them, because succeeding Legislatures having equal authority could undo the acts of their predecessors; and the National Govt. would stand in each State on the weak and tottering foundation of an Act of Assembly. There was a remaining consideration of some weight. In some of the States the Govts. were not derived from the clear & undisputed authority of the people. This was the case in Virginia. Some of the best & wisest citizens considered the Constitution as established by an assumed authority. A National Constitution derived from such a source would be exposed to the severest criticisms.

Mr. Randolph. One idea has pervaded all our proceedings, to wit, that opposition as well from the States as from individuals, will be made to the System to be proposed. Will it not then be highly imprudent, to furnish any unnecessary pretext by the mode of ratifying it. Added to other objections agst. a ratification by Legislative authority only, it may be remarked that there have been instances in which the authority of the Common law has been set up in particular States agst. that of the Confederation which has had no higher sanction than Legislative ratification.— Whose opposition will be most likely to be excited agst. the System? That of the local demogagues who will be degraded by it from the importance they now hold. These will spare no efforts to impede that progress in the popular mind which will be necessary to the adoption of the plan, and which every member will find to have taken place in his own, if he will compare his present opinions with those brought with him into the Convention. It is of great importance therefore that the consideration of this subject should be transferred from the Legislatures where this class of men, have their full influence to a field in which their efforts can be less mischievous. It is moreover worthy of consideration that some of the States are averse

to any change in their Constitution, and will not take the requisite steps, unless expressly called upon to refer the question to the people.

Mr. Gerry. The arguments of Col. Mason & Mr. Randolph prove too much, they prove an unconstitutionality in the present federal system & even in some of the State Govts. Inferences drawn from such a source must be inadmissable. Both the State Govts. & the federal Govt. have been too long acquiesced in, to be now shaken. He considered the Confederation to be paramount to any State Constitution. The last article of it authorizing alterations must consequently be so as well as the others, and everything done in pursuance of the article must have the same high authority with the article.—Great confusion he was confident would result from a recurrence to the people. They would never agree on any thing. He could not see any ground to suppose that the people will do what their rulers will not. The rulers will either conform to, or influence the sense of the people.

Mr. Ghorum was agst. referring the plan to the Legislatures. 1. Men chosen by the people for the particular purpose, will discuss the subject more candidly than members of the Legislature who are to lose the power which is to be given up to the Genl. Govt. 2. Some of the Legislatures are composed of several branches. It will consequently be more difficult in these cases to get the plan through the Legislatures, than thro' a Convention. 3. in the States many of the ablest men are excluded from the Legislatures, but may be elected into a Convention. Among these may be ranked many of the Clergy who are generally friends to good Government. Their services were found to be valuable in the formation & establishment of the Constitution of Massachts. 4. the Legislatures will be interrupted with a variety of little business. by artfully pressing which, designing men will find means to delay from year to year, if not to frustrate altogether the national system. 5—If the last art: of the Confederation is to be pursued the unanimous concurrence of the States will be necessary. But will any one say. that all the States are to suffer themselves to be ruined, if Rho. Island should persist in her opposition to general measures. Some other States might also tread in her steps. The present advantage which N. York seems to be so much attached to, of taxing her neighbours by the regulation of her trade, makes it very probable, that she will be of the number. It would therefore deserve serious consideration whether provision ought not to be made for giving effect to the System without waiting for the unanimous concurrence of the States.

Mr. Elseworth. If there be any Legislatures who should find themselves incompetent to the ratification, he should be content to let them advise with their constituents and pursue such a mode as wd be competent. He thought more was to be expected from the Legislatures than from the people. The prevailing wish of the people in the Eastern States is to get rid of the public debt; and the idea of strengthening the Natl. Govt. carries with it that of strengthening the public debt. It was said by Col. Mason 1. that the Legislatures have no authority in this case. 2.

that their successors having equal authority could rescind their acts. As to the 2d. point he could not admit it to be well founded. An Act to which the States by their Legislatures, make themselves parties, becomes a compact from which no one of the parties can recede of itself. As to the 1st. point, he observed that a new sett of ideas seemed to have crept in since the articles of Confederation were established. Conventions of the people, or with power derived expressly from the people, were not then thought of. The Legislatures were considered as competent. Their ratification has been acquiesced in without complaint. To whom have Congs. applied on subsequent occasions for further powers? To the Legislatures; not to the people. The fact is that we exist at present, and we need not enquire how, as a federal Society, united by a charter one article of which is that alterations therein may be made by the Legislative authority of the States. It has been said that if the confederation is to be observed, the States must *unanimously* concur in the proposed innovations. He would answer that if such were the urgency & necessity of our situation as to warrant a new compact among a part of the States, founded on the consent of the people; the same pleas would be equally valid in favor of a partial compact, founded on the consent of the Legislatures.

Mr. Williamson thought the Resoln. (19) so expressed as that it might be submitted either to the Legislatures or to Conventions recommended by the Legislatures. He observed that some Legislatures were evidently unauthorized to ratify the system. He thought too that Conventions were to be preferred as more likely to be composed of the ablest men in the States.

Mr. Govr. Morris considered the inference of Mr. Elseworth from the plea of necessity as applied to the establishment of a new System on ye. consent of the people of a part of the States, in favor of a like establishnt. on the consent of a part of the Legislatures as a non sequitur. If the Confederation is to be pursued no alteration can be made without the unanimous consent of the Legislatures: Legislative alterations not conformable to the federal compact, would clearly not be valid. The Judges would consider them as null & void. Whereas in case of an appeal to the people of the U. S., the supreme authority, the federal compact may be altered by a *majority of them*; in like manner as the Constitution of a particular State may be altered by a majority of the people of the State. The amendmt. moved by Mr. Elseworth erroneously supposes that we are proceeding on the basis of the Confederation. This Convention is unknown to the Confederation.

Mr. King thought with Mr. Elseworth that the Legislatures had a competent authority, the acquiescence of the people of America in the Confederation, being equivalent to a formal ratification by the people. He thought with Mr. E—also that the plea of necessity was as valid in the one case as in the other. At the same time he preferred a reference to the authority of the people expressly delegated to Conventions, as the most certain means of obviating all disputes & doubts concerning the legitimacy of the new Constitution; as well as the most likely means of drawing forth the best men in the States to decide on it. He remarked that among other objections made in the State of

N. York to granting powers to Congs. one had been that such powers as would operate within the State, could not be reconciled to the Constitution; and therefore were not grantible by the Legislative authority. He considered it as of some consequence also to get rid of the scruples which some members of the States Legislatures might derive from their oaths to support & maintain the existing Constitutions.

Mr. Madison thought it clear that the Legislatures were incompetent to the proposed changes. These changes would make essential inroads on the State Constitutions, and it would be a novel & dangerous doctrine that a Legislature could change the constitution under which it held its existence. There might indeed be some Constitutions within the Union, which had given, a power to the Legislature to concur in alterations of the federal Compact. But there were certainly some which had not; and in the case of these, a ratification must of necessity be obtained from the people. He considered the difference between a system founded on the Legislatures only, and one founded on the people, to be the true difference between a *league* or *treaty*, and a *Constitution*. The former in point of *moral obligation* might be as inviolable as the latter. In point of *political operation*, there were two important distinctions in favor of the latter. 1. A law violating a treaty ratified by a preexisting law, might be respected by the Judges as a law, though an unwise or perfidious one. A law violating a constitution established by the people themselves, would be considered by the Judges as null & void. 2. The doctrine laid down by the law of Nations in the case of treaties is that a breach of any one article by any of the parties, frees the other parties from their engagements. In the case of a union of people under one Constitution, the nature of the pact has always been understood to exclude such an interpretation. Comparing the two modes in point of expediency he thought all the considerations which recommended this Convention in preference to Congress for proposing the reform were in favor of State Conventions in preference to the Legislatures for examining and adopting it.

On question on Mr. Elseworth's motion to refer the plan to the Legislatures of the States

N. H. no. Mas. no. Ct. ay. Pa. no- Del. ay- Md. ay. Va. no. N- C- no. S. C.- no. Geo. no. [Ayes—3; noes—7.]

Mr. Govr. Morris moved that the reference of the plan be made to one general Convention, chosen & authorized by the people to consider, *amend*, & establish the same.— Not seconded.

On question for agreeing to Resolution 19, touching the mode of Ratification as reported from the Committee of the Whole; viz, to refer the Constn. after the approbation of Congs. to assemblies chosen by the people:

N. H. ay. Mas- ay. Ct. ay. Pa. ay. Del. no. Md. ay. Va. ay. N. C. ay. S. C. ay. Geo. ay. [Ayes—9; noes—1.]

[2:133, 136, 148, 149, 160; *Committee of Detail*]
Resolved That the Amendments which shall be offered to the Confederation by the Convention ought at a proper Time or Times, after the Approbation of Congress, to be submitted to an Assembly or Assemblies of Representatives, recommended by

the several Legislatures, to be expressly chosen by the People to consider and decide thereon.

· · · · ·

23. The assent of the Legislature of   States shall be sufficient to invest future additional Powers in U.S. in C. ass. and shall bind the whole Confederacy.

· · · · ·

4. The ratification of the reform is—After the approbation of Congress—to be made
>by a special convention in each State
>recommended by the assembly
>to be chosen for the express purpose
>of considering and approving or rejecting
>it in toto:
>and this recommendation may be used from time to time

· · · · ·

Addenda
1. The assent of the Conventions of   states shall give operation to this constitution
2. Each assenting state shall notify its assent to congress: who shall publish a day for its commencement, not exceeding After such publication, or with the assent of the major part of the assenting states after the expiration of   days from the giving of the assent of the ninth state,
>1. each legislature shall direct the choice of representatives, according to the seventh article and provide for their support:
>2. each legislature shall also choose senators; and provide for their support
>3. they shall meet at the Place & on the day assigned by congress,
>4. They shall as soon as may be after meeting elect the executive: and proceed to execute this constitution.

· · · · ·

Resolved, That the Constitution proposed by this Convention, to the People of the United States for their approbation be laid before the United States in Congress assembled for their Agreement and Recommendation and be afterwards submitted to a Convention chosen in each State under the Recommendation of its Legislature, in order to receive the Ratification of such Convention.

[2:189; Madison, 6 Aug.]

The ratifications of the Conventions of   States shall be sufficient for organizing this Constitution.

XXII

This Constitution shall be laid before the United States in Congress assembled, for their approbation; and it is the opinion of this Convention, that it should be afterwards submitted to a Convention chosen, under the recommendation of its legislature, in order to receive the ratification of such Convention.

XXIII

To introduce this government, it is the opinion of this Convention, that each assenting Convention should notify its assent and ratification to the United States in Congress assembled; that Congress, after receiving the assent and ratification of the Conventions of   States, should appoint and publish a day, as early as may be, and appoint a place for commencing proceedings under this Constitution; that after such publication, the Legislatures of the several States should elect members of the Senate, and direct the election of members of the House of Representatives; and that the members of the Legislature should meet at the time and place assigned by Congress, and should, as soon as may be, after their meeting, choose the President of the United States, and proceed to execute this Constitution."

[2:211; McHenry, 7 Aug.]

I now begged his particular attention to my last proposition. By the XXII article we were called upon to agree that the system should be submitted to a convention chosen in each State under the recommendation of its legislature. And that a less number of conventions than the whole agreeing to the system should be sufficient to organise the constitution.

We had taken an oath to support our constitution and frame of government. We had been empowered by a legislature legally constituted to revise the confederation and fit it for the *exigencies of government,* and *preservation of the union.* Could we do this business in a manner contrary to our constitution? I feared (This was said first I *thought*— then I *feared*) we could not. If we relinquished any of the rights or powers of our government to the U.S. of America, we could no otherwise agree to that relinquishment than in the mode our constitution prescribed for making changes or alterations in it.

Mr. Carrol said he had felt his doubts respecting the propriety of this article as it respected Maryland; but he hoped we should be able to get over this difficulty.

Mr. Jenifer now came in to whom Mr. Carroll repeated what we had said upon my propositions and our determinations. Mr. Jenifer agreed to act in unison with us but seemed to have vague ideas of the mischiefs of the system as it stood in the report.

I wished to impress him with the necessity to support us, and touched upon some popular points.

[2:468; Madison, 30 Aug.]

Art: XXI. taken up. viz: "The ratifications of the Conventions of   States shall be sufficient for organizing this Constitution."

Mr. Wilson proposed to fill the blank with "seven" that being a majority of the whole number & sufficient for the commencement of the plan.

Mr. Carrol moved to postpone the article in order to take up the Report of the Committee of Eleven . . . —and on the question

N. H—no. Mas—no. Ct. no. N. J. ay. Pa. no. Del. ay. Md. ay. Va. no. N. C. no. S. C. no. Geo. no. [Ayes—3; noes—8.]

Mr. Govr. Morris thought the blank ought to be filled in a twofold way, so as to provide for the event of the ratifying States being contiguous which would render a smaller number sufficient, and the event of their being dispersed, which wd require a greater number for the introduction of the Government.

Mr. Sherman. observed that the States being now confederated by articles which require unanimity in changes, he thought the ratification in this case of ten States at least ought to be made necessary.

Mr. Randolph was for filling the blank with "Nine" that being a respectable majority of the whole, and being a number made familiar by the constitution of the existing Congress.

Mr Wilson mentioned "eight" as preferable.

Mr. Dickinson asked whether the concurrence of Congress is to be essential to the establishment of the system, whether the refusing States in the Confederacy could be deserted—and whether Congress could concur in contravening the system under which they acted?

Mr. Madison. remarked that if the blank should be filled with "seven" eight, or "nine"—the Constitution as it stands might be put in force over the whole body of the people. tho' less than a majority of them should ratify it.

Mr. Wilson. As the Constitution stands, the States only which ratify can be bound. We must he said in this case go to the original powers of Society, The House on fire must be extinguished, without a scrupulous regard to ordinary rights.

Mr. Butler was in favor of "nine". He revolted at the idea, that one or two States should restrain the rest from consulting their safety.

Mr. Carrol moved to fill the blank with "the thirteen". unanimity being necessary to dissolve the existing confederacy which had been unanimously established.

Mr King thought this amendt. necessary, otherwise as the Constitution now stands it will operate on the whole though ratified by a part only.

[2:475; Madison, 31 Aug.]

Mr. King moved to add to the end of art: XXI the words "between the said States" so as to confine the operation of the Govt. to the States ratifying it.

On the question

N. H. ay. Mas. ay. Ct. ay. N—J—ay. Pa. ay. Md. no. Virga. ay. N. C. ay. S. C. ay. Geo. ay. [Ayes—9; noes—1.]

Mr. Madison proposed to fill the blank in the article with "Any seven or more States entitled to thirty three members at least in the House of Representatives according to the allotment made in the 3 Sect: of art: 4." This he said would require the concurrence of a majority of both the States and people.

Mr. Sherman doubted the propriety of authorizing less than all the States to execute the Constitution, considering the nature of the existing Confederation. Perhaps all the States may concur, and on that supposition it is needless to hold out a breach of faith.

Mr. Clymer and Mr. Carrol moved to postpone the consideration of Art: XXI in order to take up the Reports of Committees not yet acted on— On this question, the States were equally divided. N. H. ay. Mas. no. Ct. divd. N. J— no. Pa. ay— Del—ay. Md. ay. Va. no. N. C no. S. C. no. G. ay. [Ayes—5; noes—5; divided—1.]

Mr Govr. Morris moved to strike out "Conventions of

the" after "ratifications". leaving the States to pursue their own modes of ratification.

Mr. Carrol mentioned the mode of altering the Constitution of Maryland pointed out therein, and that no other mode could be pursued in that State.

Mr. King thought that striking out "Conventions". as the requisite mode was equivalent to giving up the business altogether. Conventions alone, which will avoid all the obstacles from the complicated formation of the Legislatures, will succeed, and if not positively required by the plan, its enemies will oppose that mode.

Mr. Govr. Morris said he meant to facilitate the adoption of the plan, by leaving the modes approved by the several State Constitutions to be followed.

Mr. Madison considered it best to require Conventions; Among other reasons, for this, that the powers given to the Genl. Govt. being taken from the State Govts the Legislatures would be more disinclined than conventions composed in part at least of other men; and if disinclined, they could devise modes apparently promoting, but really. thwarting the ratification. The difficulty in Maryland was no greater than in other States, where no mode of change was pointed out by the Constitution, and all officers were under oath to support it. The people were in fact, the fountain of all power, and by resorting to them, all difficulties were got over. They could alter constitutions as they pleased. It was a principle in the Bills of rights, that first principles might be resorted to.

Mr. McHenry said that the officers of Govt. in Maryland were under oath to support the mode of alteration prescribed by the Constitution.

Mr Ghorum urged the expediency of "Conventions" also Mr. Pinkney, for reasons, formerly urged on a discussion of this question.

Mr. L. Martin insisted on a reference to the State Legislatures. He urged the danger of commotions from a resort to the people & to first principles in which the Governments might be on one side & the people on the other. He was apprehensive of no such consequences however in Maryland, whether the Legislature or the people should be appealed to. Both of them would be generally against the Constitution. He repeated also the peculiarity in the Maryland Constitution.

Mr. King observed that the Constitution of Massachusetts was made unalterable till the year 1790, yet this was no difficulty with him. The State must have contemplated a recurrence to first principles before they sent deputies to this Convention.

Mr. Sherman moved to postpone art. XXI. & to take up art: XXII on which question,

N. H. no. Mas. no. Ct. ay—N. J. no—P. ay—Del—ay— Md ay. Va. ay. N. C. no S. C. no—Geo—no—[Ayes—5; noes—6.]

On Mr Govr. Morris's motion to strike out "Conventions of the," it was negatived.

N. H. no. Mas. no. Ct. ay. N. J. no. Pa ay. Del. no. Md. ay—Va no—S—C no—Geo. ay. [Ayes—4; noes—6.]

On filling the blank in Art: XXI with "thirteen" moved by Mr. Carrol, & L. Martin

N. H. no. Mas. no. Ct. no.—All no—except Maryland.

Mr. Sherman & Mr. Dayton moved to fill the blank with "ten"

Mr. Wilson supported the motion of Mr. Madison, requiring a majority both of the people and of States.

Mr Clymer was also in favor of it.

Col: Mason was for preserving ideas familiar to the people. Nine States had been required in all great cases under the Confederation & that number was on that account preferable

On the question for "ten"

N. H. no. Mas. no. Ct ay. N.J—ay. Pa. no. Del—no. Md. ay. Va. no. N. C. no. S. C. no. Geo. ay. [Ayes—4; noes—7.]

On question for "nine"

N—H. ay. Mas. ay. Ct. ay—N—J. ay. Pa. ay—Del. ay. Md. ay—Va. no. N. C. no. S. C. no. Geo—ay, [Ayes—8; noes—3.]

Art: XXI. as amended was then agreed to by all the States, Maryland excepted, & Mr. Jenifer being, ay—

Art. XXII taken up, to wit, "This Constitution shall be laid before the U—S. in Congs. assembled for their approbation; and it is the opinion of this Convention that it should be afterwards submitted to a Convention chosen, in each State under the recommendation of its Legislature, in order to receive the ratification of such Convention"

Mr. Govr. Morris & Mr. Pinkney moved to strike out the words "for their approbation" On this question

N. H. ay. Mas. no. Ct. ay. N—J. ay. Pa. ay. Del. ay. Md. no Va. ay. N. C—ay. S. C—ay. Geo. no. [Ayes—8; noes—3.]

Mr Govr. Morris & Mr. Pinkney then moved to amend the art: so as to read

"This Constitution shall be laid before the U. S. in Congress assembled; and it is the opinion of this Convention that it should afterwards be submitted to a Convention chosen in each State, in order to receive the ratification of such Convention: to which end the several Legislatures ought to provide for the calling Conventions within their respective States as speedily as circumstances will permit".—Mr. Govr. Morris said his object was to impress in stronger terms the necessity of calling Conventions in order to prevent enemies to the plan, from giving it the go by. When it first appears, with the sanction of this Convention, the people will be favorable to it. By degrees the State officers, & those interested in the State Govts will intrigue & turn the popular current against it.

Mr. L—Martin believed Mr. Morris to be right, that after a while the people would be agst. it. but for a different reason from that alledged. He believed they would not ratify it unless hurried into it by surprize.

Mr. Gerry enlarged on the idea of Mr. L. Martin in which he concurred, represented the system as full of vices, and dwelt on the impropriety of destroying the existing Confederation, without the unanimous Consent of the parties to it:

Question on Mr Govr. Morris's and Mr. Pinckney's motion

N. H—ay. Mas. ay. Ct no. N—J. no. Pa. ay. Del—ay. Md. no. Va no. N—C—no—S—C. no. Geo. no—[Ayes—4; noes—7.]

Mr. Gerry moved to postpone art: XXII.

Col: Mason 2ded. the motion, declaring that he would sooner chop off his right hand than put it to the Constitution as it now stands. He wished to see some points not yet decided brought to a decision, before being compelled to give a final opinion on this article. Should these points be improperly settled, his wish would then be to bring the whole subject before another general Convention.

Mr. Govr Morris was ready for a postponement. He had long wished for another Convention, that will have the firmness to provide a vigorous Government, which we are afraid to do.

Mr. Randolph stated his idea to be, in case the final form of the Constitution should not permit him to accede to it, that the State Conventions should be at liberty to propose amendments to be submitted to another General Convention which may reject or incorporate them, as shall be judged proper.

On the question for postponing

N. H. no. Mas. no. Ct no. N. J—ay—Pa. no. Del. no. Md ay—Va. no. N. C. ay. S—C. no. Geo. no. [Ayes—3; noes—8.]

On the question on Art: XXII

N. H. ay. Mas. ay. Ct. ay. N. J. ay. Pa. ay—Del. ay. Md. no. Va ay. N—C. ay. S—C. ay. Geo. ay. [Ayes—10; noes—1.]

Art: XXIII being taken up. as far the words "assigned by Congress" inclusive, was agreed to nem: con: the blank having been first filled with the word "nine" as of course.

On a motion for postponing the residue of the clause, concerning the choice of the President &c,

N. H. no. Mas. ay. Ct. no. N—J. no. Pa. no. Del. no. Md. no. Va. no. N. C. ay. S—C. no. Geo. no. [Ayes—4; noes—7.]

Mr. Govr. Morris then moved to strike out the words "choose the President of the U. S. and"—this point, of choosing the President not being yet finally determined, & on this question

N—H—no. Mas. ay. Ct. ay. N. J. ay. Pa. ay. Del. ay. Md. divd. Va. ay. N—C. ay—S. C. ay—Geo. ay [Ayes—9; noes—1; divided—1.]

[2:559; Madison, 10 Sept.]

Mr. Gerry moved to reconsider art: XXI & XXII from the latter of which "for the approbation of Congs." had been struck out. He objected to proceeding to change the Government without the approbation of Congress as being improper and giving just umbrage to that body. He repeated his objections also to an annulment of the confederation with so little scruple or formality.

Mr. Hamilton concurred with Mr. Gerry as to the indecorum of not requiring the approbation of Congress. He considered this as a necessary ingredient in the transaction. He thought it wrong also to allow nine States as provided by art XXI. to institute a new Government on the ruins of the existing one. He wd propose as a better modification of the two articles (XXI & XXII) that the plan should be sent to Congress in order that the same if approved by them, may be communicated to the State Legislatures, to the end that they may refer it to State Conventions; each Legislature declaring that if the convention of the State should think the plan ought to take effect among nine ratifying States, the same shd take effect accordingly.

Mr. Gorham—Some States will say that nine States shall

be sufficient to establish the plan—others will require unanimity for the purpose—And the different and conditional ratifications will defeat the plan altogether.

Mr. Hamilton—No Convention convinced of the necessity of the plan will refuse to give it effect on the adoption by nine States. He thought this mode less exceptionable than the one proposed in the article, and would attain the same end,

Mr Fitzimmons remarked that the words "for their approbation" had been struck out in order to save Congress from the necessity of an Act inconsistent with the Articles of Confederation under which they held their authority.

Mr. Randolph declared if no change should be made in this part of the plan, he should be obliged to dissent from the whole of it. He had from the beginning he said been convinced that radical changes in the system of the Union were necessary. Under this conviction he had brought forward a set of republican propositions as the basis and outline of a reform. These Republican propositions had however, much to his regret been widely, and in his opinion, irreconcileably departed from—In this state of things it was his idea and he accordingly meant to propose, that the State Conventions shd. be at liberty to offer amendments to the plan,—and that these should be submitted to a second General Convention, with full power to settle the Constitution finally—He did not expect to succeed in this proposition, but the discharge of his duty in making the attempt, would give quiet to his own mind.

Mr. Wilson was against a reconsideration for any of the purposes which had been mentioned.

Mr King thought it would be more respectful to Congress to submit the plan generally to them; than in such a form as expressly and necessarily to require their approbation or disapprobation. The assent of nine States he considered as sufficient; and that it was more proper to make this a part of the Constitution itself, than to provide for it by a supplemental or distinct recommendation.

Mr. Gerry urged the indecency and pernicious tendency of dissolving in so slight a manner, the solemn obligations of the articles of confederation. If nine out of thirteen can dissolve the compact, Six out of nine will be just as able to dissolve the new one hereafter.

Mr. Sherman was in favor of Mr. King's idea of submitting the plan generally to Congress. He thought nine States ought to be made sufficient: but that it would be best to make it a separate act and in some such form as that intimated by Col: Hamilton, than to make it a particular article of the Constitution.

On the question for reconsidering the two articles. XXI & XXII—

N. H. divd. Mas. no Ct. ay. N. J. ay. Pa. no Del. ay. Md. ay—Va. ay. N. C. ay. S. C. no. Geo. ay. [Ayes—7; noes—3; divided—1.]

Mr. Hamilton then moved to postpone art XXI in order to take up the following, containing the ideas he had above expressed. viz

Resolved that the foregoing plan of a Constitution be transmitted to the U. S. in Congress assembled, in order that if the same shall be agreed to by them, it may be communicated to the Legislatures of the several States, to the end that they may provide for its final ratification by referring the same to the Consideration of a Convention of Deputies in each State to be chosen by the people thereof, and that it be recommended to the said Legislatures in their respective acts for organizing such convention to declare, that if the said Convention shall approve of the said Constitution, such approbation shall be binding and conclusive upon the State, and further that if the said Convention should be of opinion that the same upon the assent of any nine States thereto, ought to take effect between the States so assenting, such opinion shall thereupon be also binding upon such State, and the said Constitution shall take effect between the States assenting thereto"

Mr. Gerry 2ded. the motion.

Mr. Wilson. This motion being seconded, it is necessary now to speak freely He expressed in strong terms his disapprobation of the expedient proposed, particularly the suspending the plan of the Convention on the approbation of Congress. He declared it to be worse than folly to rely on the concurrence of the Rhode Island members of Congs. in the plan. Maryland had voted on this floor; for requiring the unanimous assent of the 13 States to the proposed change in the federal System. N—York has not been represented for a long time past in the Convention. Many individual deputies from other States have spoken much against the plan. Under these circumstances Can it be safe to make the assent of Congress necessary. After spending four or five months in the laborious & arduous task of forming a Government for our Country, we are ourselves at the close throwing insuperable obstacles in the way of its success.

Mr. Clymer thought that the mode proposed by Mr. Hamilton would fetter & embarrass Congs. as much as the original one, since it equally involved a breach of the articles of Confederation.

Mr. King concurred with Mr. Clymer. If Congress can accede to one mode, they can to the other. If the approbation of Congress be made necessary, and they should not approve, the State Legislatures will not propose the plan to Conventions; or if the States themselves are to provide that nine States shall suffice to establish the System, that provision will be omitted, every thing will go into confusion, and all our labor be lost.

Mr. Rutlidge viewed the matter in the same light with Mr. King

On the question to postpone in order to take up Col: Hamiltons motion

N. H—no. Mas. no. Ct. ay. N. J. no. Pa no. Del. no. Md. no. Va. no. N—C. no. S. C. no. Geo. no. [Ayes—1; noes—10.]

A Question being then taken on the article XXI. It was agreed to, unanimously.

Col: Hamilton withdrew the remainder of the motion to postpone art XXII, observing that his purpose was defeated by the vote just given;

Mr. Williamson & Mr. Gerry moved to re-instate the words "for the approbation of Congress" in art: XXII. which was disagreed to nem: con:

[2:579, 603; Committee of Style]

XXI.

The ratification of the Conventions of nine States shall be sufficient for organising this Constitution between the said States.

XXII.

This Constitution shall be laid before the United States in Congress assembled, and it is the opinion of this Convention that it should be afterwards submitted to a Convention chosen in each State, under the recommendation of its Legislature, in order to receive the ratification of such Convention.

XXIII.

To introduce this government, it is the opinion of this Convention, that each assenting Convention should notify its assent and ratification to the United States in Congress assembled; that Congress, after receiving the assent and ratification of the Conventions of nine States, should appoint and publish a day, as early as may be, and appoint a place for commencing proceedings under this Constitution; that after such publication, the Legislatures of the several States should elect Members of the Senate, and direct the election of Members of the House of Representatives; and that the Members of the Legislature should meet at the time and place assigned by Congress and should, as soon as may be, after their meeting, proceed to execute this Constitution.

That it be an instruction to the Committee to prepare an address to the People to accompany the present constitution, and to be laid with the same before the United States in Congress.

. . . . .

VII.

The ratification of the conventions of nine States, shall be sufficient for the establishment of this constitution between the States so ratifying the same.

[2:631; Madison, 15 Sept.]

Mr. Randolph animadverting on the indefinite and dangerous power given by the Constitution to Congress, expressing the pain he felt at differing from the body of the Convention, on the close of the great & awful subject of their labours, and anxiously wishing for some accommodating expedient which would relieve him from his embarrassments, made a motion importing "that amendments to the plan might be offered by the State Conventions, which should be submitted to and finally decided on by another general Convention" Should this proposition be disregarded, it would he said be impossible for him to put his name to the instrument. Whether he should oppose it afterwards he would not then decide but he would not deprive himself of the freedom to do so in his own State, if that course should be prescribed by his final judgment—

Col: Mason 2ded. & followed Mr. Randolph in animadversions on the dangerous power and structure of the Government, concluding that it would end either in monarchy, or a tyrannical aristocracy; which, he was in doubt. but one or other, he was sure. This Constitution had been formed without the knowledge or idea of the people. A second Convention will know more of the sense of the people, and be able to provide a system more consonant to it. It was improper to say to the people, take this or nothing. As the Constitution now stands, he could neither give it his support or vote in Virginia; and he could not sign here what he could not support there. With the expedient of another Convention as proposed, he could sign.

Mr. Pinkney. These declarations from members so respectable at the close of this important scene, give a peculiar solemnity to the present moment. He descanted on the consequences of calling forth the deliberations & amendments of the different States on the subject of Government at large. Nothing but confusion & contrariety could spring from the experiment. The States will never agree in their plans—And the Deputies to a second Convention coming together under the discordant impressions of their Constituents, will never agree. Conventions are serious things, and ought not to be repeated—He was not without objections as well as others to the plan. He objected to the contemptible weakness & dependence of the Executive. He objected to the power of a majority only of Congs over Commerce. But apprehending the danger of a general confusion, and an ultimate decision by the Sword, he should give the plan his support.

3

BENJAMIN FRANKLIN TO THE FEDERAL CONVENTION
17 Sept. 1787
Farrand 2:641–43

The engrossed Constitution being read,

Docr. Franklin rose with a speech in his hand, which he had reduced to writing for his own conveniency, and which Mr. Wilson read in the words following.

Mr. President

I confess that there are several parts of this constitution which I do not at present approve, but I am not sure I shall never approve them: For having lived long, I have experienced many instances of being obliged by better information or fuller consideration, to change opinions even on important subjects, which I once thought right, but found to be otherwise. It is therefore that the older I grow, the more apt I am to doubt my own judgment, and to pay more respect to the judgment of others. Most men indeed as well as most sects in Religion, think themselves in possession of all truth, and that whereever others differ from them it is so far error. Steele, a Protestant in a Dedication tells the Pope, that the only difference between our Churches in their opinions of the certainty of their doctrines is, the Church of Rome is infallible and the Church of England is never in the wrong. But though many private persons think almost as highly of their own infallibility as of that of their sect, few express it so naturally as a certain french lady, who in a dispute with her sister, said "I don't know how it happens, Sister but I meet with no body but myself, that's always in the right"—*Il n'y a que moi qui a toujours raison.*"

In these sentiments, Sir, I agree to this Constitution with all its faults, if they are such; because I think a general Government necessary for us, and there is no form of Government but what may be a blessing to the people if well administered, and believe farther that this is likely to be well administered for a course of years, and can only end in Despotism, as other forms have done before it, when the people shall become so corrupted as to need despotic Government, being incapable of any other. I doubt too whether any other Convention we can obtain may be able to make a better Constitution. For when you assemble a number of men to have the advantage of their joint wisdom, you inevitably assemble with those men, all their prejudices, their passions, their errors of opinion, their local interests, and their selfish views. From such an Assembly can a perfect production be expected? It therefore astonishes me, Sir, to find this system approaching so near to perfection as it does; and I think it will astonish our enemies, who are waiting with confidence to hear that our councils are confounded like those of the Builders of Babel; and that our States are on the point of separation, only to meet hereafter for the purpose of cutting one another's throats. Thus I consent, Sir, to this Constitution because I expect no better, and because I am not sure, that it is not the best. The opinions I have had of its errors, I sacrifice to the public good—I have never whispered a syllable of them abroad—Within these walls they were born, and here they shall die—If every one of us in returning to our Constituents were to report the objections he has had to it, and endeavor to gain partizans in support of them, we might prevent its being generally received, and thereby lose all the salutary effects & great advantages resulting naturally in our favor among foreign Nations as well as among ourselves, from our real or apparent unanimity. Much of the strength & efficiency of any Government in procuring and securing happiness to the people, depends. on opinion, on the general opinion of the goodness of the Government, as well as well as of the wisdom and integrity of its Governors. I hope therefore that for our own sakes as a part of the people, and for the sake of posterity, we shall act heartily and unanimously in recommending this Constitution (if approved by Congress & confirmed by the Conventions) wherever our influence may extend, and turn our future thoughts & endeavors to the means of having it well administered.

On the whole, Sir, I cannot help expressing a wish that every member of the Convention who may still have objections to it, would with me, on this occasion doubt a little of his own infallibility—and to make manifest our unanimity, put his name to this instrument."—He then moved that the Constitution be signed by the members and offered the following as a convenient form viz. "Done in Convention, by the unanimous consent of *the States* present the 17th. of Sepr. &c—In Witness whereof we have hereunto subscribed our names."

4

EDMUND RANDOLPH TO SPEAKER OF VIRGINIA HOUSE OF DELEGATES
10 Oct. 1787
Pamphlets 272–74

It would have been a peculiar pleasure to me to have ascertained before I left Virginia, the temper and genius of my fellow citizens, considered relatively to a government, so substantially differing from the confederation as that which is now submitted. But this was, for many obvious reasons, impossible; and I was thereby deprived of what I thought the necessary guides.

I saw, however, that the confederation was tottering from its own weakness, and that the sitting of a convention was a signal of its total insufficiency. I was therefore ready to assent to a scheme of government, which was proposed, and which went beyond the limits of the confederation, believing, that without being too extensive it would have preserved our tranquility, until that temper and that genius should be collected.

But when the plan which is now before the general assembly, was on its passage through the convention, I moved, that the State conventions should be at liberty to amend, and that a second general convention should be holden, to discuss the amendments, which should be suggested by them. This motion was in some measure justified by the manner in which the confederation was forwarded originally, by congress to the State legislatures, in many of which amendments were proposed, and those amendments were afterwards examined in congress. Such a motion was doubly expedient here, as the delegation of so much power was sought for. But it was negatived. I then expressed my unwillingness to sign. My reasons were the following:

1. It is said in the resolutions which accompany the constitution, that it is to be submitted to a convention of delegates chosen in each State by the people thereof, for their assent and ratification. The meaning of these terms is allowed universally to be, that the convention must either adopt the constitution in the whole, or reject it in the whole, and is positively forbidden to amend, if therefore, I had signed, I should have felt myself bound to be silent as to amendments, and to endeavor to support the constitution without the correction of a letter. With this consequence before my eyes, and with a determination to attempt an amendment, I was taught by a regard for consistency not to sign.

2. My opinion always was, and still is, that every citizen of America, let the crisis be what it may, ought to have a full opportunity to propose, through his representatives, any amendment which in his apprehension, tends to the public welfare. By signing, I should have contradicted this sentiment.

3. A constitution ought to have the hearts of the people on its side. But if at a future day it should be burdensome

after having been adopted in the whole, and they should insinuate that it was in some measure forced upon them, by being confined to the single alternative of taking or rejecting it altogether, under my impressions, and with my opinions, I should not be able to justify myself had I signed.

4. I was always satisfied, as I have now experienced, that this great subject would be placed in new lights and attitudes by the criticism of the world, and that no man can assure himself how a constitution will work for a course of years, until at least he shall have heard the observations of the people at large. I also fear more from inaccuracies in a constitution, than from gross errors in any other composition; because our dearest interests are to be regulated by it; and power, if loosely given, especially where it will be interpreted with great latitude, may bring sorrow in its execution. Had I signed with these ideas, I should have virtually shut my ears against the information which I ardently desired.

5. I was afraid that if the constitution was to be submitted to the people, to be wholly adopted or wholly rejected by them, they would not only reject it, but bid a lasting farewell to the union. This formidable event I wished to avert, by keeping myself free to propose amendments, and thus, if possible, to remove the obstacles to an effectual government. But it will be asked, whether all these arguments, were not . . . well weighed in convention. They were, sir, with great candor. Nay, when I called to mind the respectability of those, with whom I was associated, I almost lost confidence in these principles. On other occasions, I should cheerfully have yielded to a majority; on this the fate of thousands yet unborn, enjoined me not to yield until I was convinced.

Again, may I be asked, why the mode pointed out in the constitution for its amendment, may not be a sufficient security against its imperfections, without now arresting it in its progress? My answers are—1. That it is better to amend, while we have the constitution in our power, while the passions of designing men are not yet enlisted, and while a bare majority of the States may amend than to wait for the uncertain assent of three fourths of the States. 2. That a bad feature in government, becomes more and more fixed every day. 3. That frequent changes of a constitution, even if practicable, ought not to be wished, but avoided as much as possible. And 4. That in the present case, it may be questionable, whether, after the particular advantages of its operation shall be discerned, three fourths of the States can be induced to amend.

5

LUTHER MARTIN, MARYLAND HOUSE OF DELEGATES
29 Nov. 1787
Farrand 3:159

The ratification of this Constitution is so repugnant to the Terms on which we are all bound to amend and alter the former, that it became a matter of surprise to many that the proposition could meet with any countanance or support. Our present Constitution expressly directs that all the States must agree before it can be dissolved; but on the other hand it was contended that a Majority ought to govern—That a dissolution of the Federal Government did not dissolve the State Constitutions which were paramount the Confederacy. That the Federal Government being formed out of the State Governments the People at large have no power to interfere in the *Federal Constitution* Nor has the *State* or *Federal* Government any power to confirm a new Institution. That this Government if ratified and Established will be *immediately* from the *People*, paramount the *Federal Constitution* and operate as a dissolution of it.

6

WILLIAM SHORT TO JAMES MADISON
21 Dec. 1787
Madison Papers 10:342

On the statement which you gave me Sir, of the advocates & opponents to the new Constitution in Virginia, it seems impossible that it should pass in that State. Should it have the same fate in Rhode-Island, N. York & Maryland, we shall see the ill consequences of a clause which alarmed me from the beginning; I mean the adoption of the new constitution by nine States. The dissenting States being thus dispersed seem to have the quality only of separating the assenting States without the power of uniting themselves. I think the adoption by nine & the refusal by four of the States is the worst possible situation to which the new plan can give birth; & it seems probable that that will be the situation. Would it not have been better to have fixed on the number eleven or twelve instead of nine? In that case the plan would have been either refused altogether or adopted by such a commanding majority as would almost necessarily have brought in the others in the end. There is one thing however which may be opposed to all the arguments that may be adduced in opposition to the new plan; & that is that the members who composed the convention must have had a fuller & better view of the ground & must have considered it more attentively than those who object to it. They must have seen certainly a variety of difficulties which their debates must have presented in full view & which are hidden perhaps from the most penetrating observation under other circumstances. Particularly to us at this distance, I am sure it is impossible to form a proper opinion on the subject. There is only one reflexion wch. occurs to me in which I have any confidence of being right: & that is that the Members of the convention would not have proposed so desperate a remedy if the evil had not appeared to them equally desperate. I am afraid the case will not be mended by the Patient's refusing to take the violent dose prescribed.

7

LUTHER MARTIN, GENUINE INFORMATION
1788
Storing 2.4.110–14

It was attempted to obtain a resolve that if seven States, whose votes in the first branch should amount to a majority of the representation in that branch, concurred in the adoption of the system, it should be sufficient, and this attempt was supported on the principle, that a majority ought to govern the minority;—but to this it was objected, that although it was true, after a constitution and form of government is agreed on, in every act done under and consistent with that constitution and form of government, the act of the majority, unless otherwise agreed in the constitution, should bind the minority, yet it was directly the *reverse* in *originally forming* a constitution, or *dissolving it*— That in originally forming a constitution, it was necessary that *every individual* should agree to it to become bound thereby—and that when *once adopted* it could not be *dissolved* by consent, unless with the consent of *every individual* who was party to the original agreement—That in forming our original federal government *every member* of that government, that is each State, expressly consented to it; that it is a *part* of the *compact* made and entered into in the *most solemn manner*, that there should be no *dissolution* or *alteration* of that federal government without the consent of *every State*, the members of, and parties to the original compact; that therefore *no alteration* could be made by a consent of a *part* of these States, or by the consent of the *inhabitants* of a *part of the States*, which could either *release* the States so consenting, from the obligation they are under to the other States, or which could in any manner become *obligatory* upon those States that should not ratify such alterations. Satisfied of the *truth* of these positions, and not holding ourselves at liberty to *violate* the *compact*, which this state had *solemnly entered into* with the others, by *altering* it in a *different* manner from that which by the same compact is provided and stipulated, a number of the members and among those the *delegation* of *this State* opposed the ratification of this system in *any other manner* than by the *unanimous consent* and agreement of all the States.

By our original articles of confederation any alterations proposed, are in the first place to be *approved* by Congress.—Accordingly as the resolutions were originally adopted by the convention, and as they were reported by the committee of detail, it was proposed that this system should be laid before Congress *for their approbation;* but, Sir, the warm advocates of this system fearing it would not meet with the approbation of Congress, and determined, even though Congress and the respective State legislatures should disapprove the same, to force it upon them, if possible, through the intervention of the people at large, moved to strike out the words "for their approbation" and succeeded in their motion; to which, it being directly in violation of the mode prescribed by the articles of confederation for the alteration of our federal government, a part of the convention, and myself in the number, thought it a duty to give a decided negative.

Agreeable to the articles of confederation entered into in the most *solemn manner*, and for the *observance* of which the States *pledged* themselves to each other, and called upon the *Supreme Being* as a *witness* and *avenger* between them, *no alterations* are to be made in those articles unless after they are approved by Congress, they are agreed to and ratified by the *legislature* of *every* State; but by the resolve of the convention this constitution is not to be ratified by the legislatures of the respective States, but is to be submitted to conventions chosen by the people, and if ratified by them is to be binding.

This resolve was opposed among others by the delegation of Maryland;—your delegates were of opinion, that as the form of government proposed was, if adopted, most essentially to *alter* the *constitution* of *this State*, and as our constitution had pointed out a mode by which, and by which *only*, alterations were to be made therein, a convention of the people could not be called to agree to and ratify the said form of government without a *direct violation* of our constitution, which it is the duty of every individual in this State to protect and support;—In this opinion all your delegates who were attending were unanimous; I, Sir, opposed it also upon a more extensive ground, as being directly *contrary* to the mode of altering our federal government *established* in our original compact, and as such being a *direct violation* of the mutual faith plighted by the States to each other, I gave it my negative.

I also was of opinion, that the States considered as States, in their political capacity, are the members of a federal government; that the States in their political capacity, or as Sovereignties, are entitled, and *only entitled* originally to agree upon the form of, and submit themselves to, a federal government, and afterwards by mutual consent to dissolve or alter it—That every thing which relates to the formation, the dissolution or the alteration of a *federal government* over States equally free, sovereign and independent is the *peculiar* province of the *States* in their *sovereign* or *political* capacity, in the same manner as what relates to forming alliance or treaties of peace, amity or commerce, and that the people at large in their individual capacity, have no more right to interfere in the one case than in the other: That according to these principles we originally acted in forming our confederation; it was the States as

States, by their representatives in Congress, that formed the articles of confederation; it was the States as States, by their legislatures, ratified those articles, and it was there established and provided that the States as States, that is by their legislatures, should agree to any alterations that should hereafter be proposed in the federal government, before they should be binding—and any alterations agreed to in any other manner cannot release the States from the obligation they are under to each other by virtue of the original articles of confederation. The people of the different States never made any objection to the manner the articles of confederation were formed or ratified, or to the mode by which alterations were to be made in that government—with the rights of their respective States they wished not to interfere—Nor do I believe the people in their individual capacity, would ever have expected or desired to have been appealed to on the present occasion, in violation of the rights of their respective States, if the favourers of the proposed constitution, imagining they had a better chance of forcing it to be adopted by a *hasty* appeal to the people at large, who could not be so good judges of the dangerous consequence, had not insisted upon this mode—nor do these positions in the least interfere with the principle, that all power originates from the people, because when once the people have *exercised their power* in *establishing* and *forming* themselves into a *State government*, it never devolves *back* to them, nor have they a *right* to *resume* or *again to exercise that power* until such events takes place as will amount to a *dissolution* of their *State government*:—And it is an established principle that a dissolution or alteration of a *federal* government doth not dissolve the *State* governments which compose it. It was also my opinion, that upon *principles of sound policy*, the agreement or disagreement to the proposed system ought to have been by the State legislatures, in which case, let the event have been what it would, there would have been but little prospects of the *public peace* being *disturbed* thereby—Whereas the attempt to force down this system, although Congress and the respective State legislatures should disapprove, by appealing to the people, and to procure its establishment in a manner totally unconstitutional, has a tendency to set the *State governments* and their *subjects* at *variance* with each other—to *lessen* the *obligations* of *government*—to *weaken* the *bands* of *society*—to introduce *anarchy* and *confusion*—And to *light* the *torch* of *discord* and *civil war* throughout this continent. All these considerations weighed with me most forcibly against giving my assent to the mode by which it is resolved this system is to be ratified, and were urged by me in opposition to the measure.

8

GEORGE WASHINGTON TO EDMUND RANDOLPH
8 Jan. 1788
Writings 29:357–58

The various passions and medium by which men are influenced are concomitants of fallibility—engrafted into our nature for the purposes of unerring wisdom; but had I entertained a latent hope (at the time you moved to have the Constitution submitted to a second Convention) that a more perfect form would be agreed to, in a word that any Constitution would be adopted under the impressions and instructions of the members, the publications, which have taken place since would have eradicated every form of it. . . .

To my Judgment, it is more clear than ever, that an attempt to amend the Constitution which is submitted, would be productive of more heat and greater confusion than can well be conceived. There are some things in the new form, I will readily acknowledge, wch. never did, and I am persuaded never will, obtain my *cordial* approbation; but I then did conceive, and do now most firmly believe, that, in the aggregate, it is the best Constitution that can be obtained at this Epocha, and that this, or a dissolution of the Union awaits our choice, and are the only alternatives before us. Thus believing, I had not, nor have I now any hesitation in deciding on which to lean.

I pray your forgiveness for the expression of these sentiments. In acknowledging the receipt of your Letter on this subject, it was hardly to be avoided, although I am well disposed to let the matter rest entirely on its own merits, and mens minds to their own workings.

9

SAMUEL
10 Jan. 1788
Storing 4.14.9

Again, I find in the last acts of the Constitution, that it is an open professed resolution, to break a solemn covenant, made by the several States, in the confederation *of the United States of America*. Which having named the States, in the 3d, article, says "the said States hereby severally enter into a firm league of friendship, with each other, for their common defence, &c."—Then going on to describe this *firm league*, till it comes to the last Art. it concludes, "And the articles of this Confederation, shall be inviolably observed by every State; and the Union shall be perpetual; nor shall any alteration at any time hereafter be made in any of them; unless such alteration be agreed to, in Congress of the United States, and be after-wards confirmed by the Legislatures of every State." But this new Constitution, does not appear to be agreed to by Congress, neither is it a Confederation of the States; but professedly of the people, as in the very first words of it; and concludes, that the ratification of the conventions of nine States, shall be sufficient for the establishment of this Constitution, between the States so ratifying the same." This is expressly repugnant to the Confederation, the sacred national covenant we are under; and to set up a schism in the nation. This is not proposed to be done by the same contracting parties. For that was a covenant of union between the States. This is to be by the people of the States, to throw off all their allegiance to the federal Constitution of the nation, and the covenant Constitutions of the several States; And if the conventions in nine States will adopt it, then to seperate, and set up this in violation of all covenant obligations, of the most solemn important kind and consequence.

10

JAMES MADISON, FEDERALIST, NO. 43, 296–98
23 Jan. 1788

This article speaks for itself. The express authority of the people alone could give due validity to the Constitution. To have required the unanimous ratification of the thirteen States, would have subjected the essential interests of the whole to the caprice or corruption of a single member. It would have marked a want of foresight in the Convention, which our own experience would have rendered inexcusable.

Two questions of a very delicate nature present themselves on this occasion. 1. On what principle the confederation, which stands in the solemn form of a compact among the States, can be superceded without the unanimous consent of the parties to it? 2. What relation is to subsist between the nine or more States ratifying the Constitution, and the remaining few who do not become parties to it.

The first question is answered at once by recurring to the absolute necessity of the case; to the great principle of self-preservation; to the transcendent law of nature and of nature's God, which declares that the safety and happiness of society are the objects at which all political institutions aim, and to which all such institutions must be sacrificed. PERHAPS also an answer may be found without searching beyond the principles of the compact itself. It has been heretofore noted among the defects of the Confederation, that in many of the States, it had received no higher sanction than a mere legislative ratification. The principle of reciprocality seems to require, that its obligation on the other States should be reduced to the same standard. A compact between independent sovereigns, founded on ordinary acts of legislative authority, can pretend to no higher validity than a league or treaty between the parties.

It is an established doctrine on the subject of treaties, that all the articles are mutually conditions of each other; that a breach of any one article is a breach of the whole treaty; and that a breach committed by either of the parties absolves the others; and authorises them, if they please, to pronounce the treaty violated and void. Should it unhappily be necessary to appeal to these delicate truths for a justification for dispensing with the consent of particular States to a dissolution of the federal pact, will not the complaining parties find it a difficult task to answer the MULTIPLIED and IMPORTANT infractions with which they may be confronted? The time has been when it was incumbent on us all to veil the ideas which this paragraph exhibits. The scene is now changed, and with it, the part which the same motives dictate.

The second question is not less delicate; and the flattering prospect of its being merely hypothetical, forbids an over-curious discussion of it. It is one of those cases which must be left to provide for itself. In general it may be observed, that although no political relation can subsist between the assenting and dissenting States, yet the moral relations will remain uncancelled. The claims of justice, both on one side and on the other, will be in force, and must be fulfilled; the rights of humanity must in all cases be duly and mutually respected; whilst considerations of a common interest, and above all the remembrance of the endearing scenes which are past, and the anticipation of a speedy triumph over the obstacles to re-union, will, it is hoped, not urge in vain MODERATION on one side, and PRUDENCE on the other.

11

FEDERAL FARMER, NO. 18
25 Jan. 1788
Storing 2.8.229

The states all agreed about seven years ago, that the confederation should remain unaltered, unless every state should agree to alterations: but we now see it agreed by the convention, and four states, that the old confederacy shall be destroyed, and a new one, of nine states, be erected, if nine only shall come in. Had we agreed, that a majority should alter the confederation, a majority's agreeing would have bound the rest: but now we must break the old league, unless all the states agree to alter, or not proceed with adopting the constitution. Whether the adoption by nine states will not produce a nearly equal and dangerous division of the people for and against the constitution—whether the circumstances of the country were such as to justify the hazarding a probability of such a situation, I shall not undertake to determine. I shall leave it to be determined hereafter, whether nine states, under a new federal compact, can claim the benefits of any treaties made with a confederation of thirteen, under a distinct compact and form of existence—whether the new confederacy can recover debts due to the old confederacy, or the arrears of taxes due from the states excluded.

12

THOMAS JEFFERSON TO ALEXANDER DONALD
7 Feb. 1788
Papers 12:571

I wish with all my soul that the nine first Conventions may accept the new Constitution, because this will secure to us the good it contains, which I think great and important. But I equally wish that the four latest conventions, whichever they be, may refuse to accede to it till a declaration of rights be annexed. This would probably command the offer of such a declaration, and thus give to the whole fabric, perhaps as much perfection as any one of that kind ever had. By a declaration of rights I mean one which shall stipulate freedom of religion, freedom of the press, freedom of commerce against monopolies, trial by juries in all cases, no suspensions of the habeas corpus, no standing armies. These are fetters against doing evil which no honest government should decline.

13

EDMUND RANDOLPH, VIRGINIA RATIFYING
CONVENTION
4 June 1788
Elliot 3:28

He also objects because nine states are sufficient to put the government in motion. What number of states ought we to have said? Ought we to have required the concurrence of all the thirteen? Rhode Island—in rebellion against integrity—Rhode Island plundered all the world by her paper money; and, notorious for her uniform opposition to every federal duty, would then have it in her power to defeat the Union; and may we not judge with absolute certainty, from her past conduct, that she would do so? Therefore, to have required the ratification of all the thirteen states would have been tantamount to returning without having done any thing. What other number would have been proper? Twelve? The same spirit that has actuated me in the whole progress of the business, would have prevented me from leaving it in the power of any one state to dissolve the Union; for would it not be lamentable that nothing could be done, for the defection of one state? A majority of the whole would have been too few. Nine states therefore seem to be a most proper number.

14

DEBATE IN VIRGINIA RATIFYING CONVENTION
12, 24–25 June 1788
Elliot 3:303–5, 314–18, 616–22, 629–31, 637–40

[*12 June*]

[Mr. PENDLETON:] Permit me to deliver a few sentiments on the great and important subject of previous and subsequent amendments. When I sat down to read that paper, I did not read it with an expectation that it was perfect, and that no man would object to it. I had learned, sir, that an expectation of such perfection in any institute devised by *man*, was as vain as the search for the philosopher's stone. I discovered objections—I thought I saw there some sown seeds of disunion—not in the immediate operation of the government, but which *might* happen in some future time. I wish amendments to remove these. But these remote possible errors may be eradicated by the amendatory clause in the Constitution. I see no danger in making the experiment, since the system itself points out an easy mode of removing any errors which shall have been experienced. In this view, then, I think we may safely trust in the government. With respect to the eight states who have already acceded to it, do gentlemen believe that, should we propose amendments as the *sine qua non* of our adoption, they would listen to our proposals? I conceive, sir, that they would not retract. They would tell us—*No, gentlemen, we cannot accept of your conditions. You put yourselves upon the ground of opposition. Your amendments are dictated by local considerations. We, in our adoption, have been influenced by considerations of general utility to the Union. We cannot abandon principles, like these, to gratify you.* Thus, sir, by previous amendments, we present a hostile countenance. If, on the contrary, we imitate the conduct of those states, our language will be conciliatory and friendly. Gentlemen, we put ourselves on the same ground that you are on. We are not actuated by local considerations, but by such as affect the people of America in general. This conduct will give our amendments full weight.

I was surprised when I heard introduced the opinion of a gentleman (Mr. Jefferson) whom I highly respect. I know the great abilities of that gentleman. Providence has, for the good of mankind, accompanied those extensive abilities with a disposition to make use of them for the good of his fellow-beings; and I wish, with all my heart, that he was here to assist us on this interesting occasion. As to his letter, impressed as I am with the force of his authority, I think it was improper to introduce it on this occasion. The opinion of a private individual, however enlightened, ought not to influence our decision. But, admitting that this opinion ought to be conclusive with us, it strikes me in a different manner from the honorable gentleman. I have seen the letter in which this gentleman has written his opinion upon this subject. It appears that he is possessed of that Constitution, and has in his mind the idea of amending it—he has in his mind the very question, of subsequent or previous amendments, which is now under consideration. His sentiments on this subject are as follows: "I wish, with all my soul, that the nine first conventions may accept the new Constitution, because it will secure to us the good it contains, which I think great and important. I wish the four latest, whichever they be, may refuse to accede to it till amendments are secured." He then enumerates the amendments which he wishes to be secured, and adds, "We must take care, however, that neither this nor any other objection to the form, produce a schism in our Union. That would be an incurable evil; because friends falling out never cordially reunite." Are these sentiments in favor of those who wish to prevent its adoption by previous amendments? He wishes the first nine states to adopt it. What are his reasons? Because he thinks it will secure to us the good it contains, which he thinks *great* and *important*; and he wishes the other four may refuse it, because he thinks it may tend to obtain necessary amendments. But he would not wish that a schism should take place in the Union on any consideration. If, then, we are to be influenced by his opinion at all, we shall ratify it, and secure thereby the good it contains. The Constitution points out a plain and ordinary method of reform, without any disturbance or convulsions whatever. I therefore think that we ought to ratify it, in order to secure the Union, and trust to this method for removing those inconveniences which experience shall point out.

. . . . .

[Mr. HENRY] The honorable gentleman has endeavored to explain the opinion of Mr. Jefferson, our common friend, into an advice to adopt this new government. What are his sentiments? He wishes nine states to adopt, and that four states may be found somewhere to reject it. Now, sir, I say, if we pursue his advice, what are we to do? To prefer form to substance? For, give me leave to ask, what is the substantial part of his counsel? It is, sir, that four states should *reject*. They tell us that, from the most authentic accounts, New Hampshire will adopt it. When I denied this, gentlemen said they were absolutely certain of it. Where, then, will four states be found to reject, if we adopt it? If we do, the counsel of this enlightened and worthy countryman of ours will be thrown away; and for what? He wishes to secure amendments and a bill of rights, if I am not mistaken. I speak from the best information, and if wrong, I beg to be put right. His amendments go to that despised thing, called *a bill of rights*, and all the rights which are dear to human nature—trial by jury, the liberty of religion and the press, &c. Do not gentlemen see that, if we adopt, under the idea of following Mr. Jefferson's opinion, we amuse ourselves with the shadow, while the substance is given away? If Virginia be for adoption, what states will be left, of sufficient respectability and importance to secure amendments by their rejection? As to North Carolina, it is a *poor, despised place*. Its dissent will not have influence to introduce any amendments. Where is the American spirit of liberty? Where will you find attachment to the rights of mankind, when Massachusetts, the great northern state, Pennsylvania, the

great middle state, and Virginia, the great southern state, shall have adopted this government? Where will you find magnanimity enough to reject it? Should the remaining states have this magnanimity, they will not have sufficient weight to have the government altered. This state has weight and importance. Her example will have powerful influence—her rejection will procure amendments. Shall we, by our adoption, hazard the loss of amendments? Shall we forsake that importance and respectability which our station in America commands, in hopes that relief will come from an obscure part of the Union? I hope my countrymen will spurn at the idea.

The necessity of amendments is universally admitted. It is a word which is reëchoed from every part of the continent. A majority of those who hear me think amendments are necessary. Policy tells us they are necessary. Reason, self-preservation, and every idea of propriety, powerfully urge us to secure the dearest rights of human nature. Shall we, in direct violation of these principles, rest this security upon the uncertainty of its being obtained by a few states, more weak and less respectable than ourselves, and whose virtue and magnanimity may be overborne by the example of so many adopting states? *Poor* Rhode Island, and North Carolina, and even New York, surrounded with federal walls on every side, may not be magnanimous enough to reject; and if they do reject it, they will have but little influence to obtain amendments. I ask, if amendments be necessary, from whence can they be so properly proposed as from this state? The example of Virginia is a powerful thing, particularly with respect to North Carolina, whose supplies must come *through* Virginia. Every possible opportunity of procuring amendments is gone, our power and political salvation are gone, if we ratify unconditionally. The important right of making treaties is upon the most dangerous foundation. The President, and a few senators, possess it in the most unlimited manner, without any real responsibility, if, from sinister views, they should think proper to abuse it; for they may keep all their measures in the most profound secrecy, as long as they please. Were we not told that war was the case wherein secrecy was the most necessary? But, by the paper on your table, their secrecy is not limited to this case only. It is as unlimited and unbounded as their powers. Under the abominable veil of political secrecy and contrivance, your most valuable rights may be sacrificed by a most corrupt faction, without having the satisfaction of knowing who injured you. They are bound by honor and conscience to act with integrity, but they are under no constitutional restraint. The navigation of the Mississippi, which is of so much importance to the happiness of the people of this country, may be lost by the operation of that paper. There are seven states now decidedly opposed to this navigation. If it be of the highest consequence to know who they are who shall have voted its relinquishment, the federal veil of secrecy will prevent that discovery. We may labor under the magnitude of our miseries without knowing or being able to punish those who produced them. I did not wish that transactions relative to treaties should, when unfinished, be exposed; but it should be known, after they were concluded, who had advised them to be made, in order to secure some degree of certainty that the public interest shall be consulted in their formation.

We are told that all powers not given are reserved. I am sorry to bring forth hackneyed observations. But, sir, important truths lose nothing of their validity or weight, by frequency of repetition. The English history is frequently recurred to by gentlemen. Let us advert to the conduct of the people of that country. The people of England lived without a declaration of rights till the war in the time of Charles I. That king made usurpations upon the rights of the people. Those rights were, in a great measure, before that time undefined. Power and privilege then depended on implication and logical discussion. Though the declaration of rights was obtained from that king, his usurpations cost him his life. The limits between the liberty of the people, and the prerogative of the king, were still not clearly defined.

The rights of the people continued to be violated till the Stuart family was banished, in the year 1688. The people of England magnanimously defended their rights, banished the tyrant, and prescribed to William, Prince of Orange, by the bill of rights, on what terms he should reign; and this bill of rights put an end to all construction and implication. Before this, sir, the situation of the public liberty of England was dreadful. For upwards of a century, the nation was involved in every kind of calamity, till the bill of rights put an end to all, by defining the rights of the people, and limiting the king's prerogative. Give me leave to add (if I can add any thing to so splendid an example) the conduct of the American people. They, sir, thought a bill of rights necessary. It is alleged that several states, in the formation of their government, omitted a bill of rights. To this I answer, that they had the substance of a bill of rights contained in their constitutions, which is the same thing. I believe that Connecticut has preserved it, by her Constitution, her royal charter, which clearly defines and secures the great rights of mankind—secures to us the great, important rights of humanity; and I care not in what form it is done.

Of what advantage is it to the American Congress to take away this great and general security? I ask, Of what advantage is it to the public, or to Congress, to drag an unhappy debtor, not for the sake of justice, but to gratify the malice of the plaintiff, with his witnesses, to the federal court, from a great distance? What was the principle that actuated the Convention in proposing to put such dangerous powers in the hands of any one? Why is the trial by jury taken away? All the learned arguments that have been used on this occasion do not prove that it is secured. Even the advocates for the plan do not all concur in the certainty of its security. Wherefore is religious liberty not secured? One honorable gentleman, who favors adoption, said that he had had his fears on the subject. If I can well recollect, he informed us that he was perfectly satisfied, by the powers of reasoning, (with which he is so happily endowed,) that those fears were not well grounded. There is many a religious man who knows nothing of argumentative reasoning; there are many of our most worthy citizens who cannot go through all the labyrinths of syllogistic, argumentative deductions, when they think that the rights of conscience are invaded. This sacred right ought not to depend on constructive, logical reasoning.

When we see men of such talents and learning compelled to use their utmost abilities to convince themselves that there is no danger, is it not sufficient to make us tremble? Is it not sufficient to fill the minds of the ignorant part of men with fear? If gentlemen believe that the apprehensions of men will be quieted, they are mistaken, since our best-informed men are in doubt with respect to the security of our rights. Those who are not so well informed will spurn at the government. When our common citizens, who are not possessed with such extensive knowledge and abilities, are called upon to change their bill of rights (which, in plain, unequivocal terms, secures their most valuable rights and privileges) for construction and implication, will they implicitly acquiesce? Our declaration of rights tells us that "all men are by nature free and independent," &c. [Here Mr. Henry read the declaration of rights.] Will they exchange these rights for logical reasons? If you had a thousand acres of land dependent on this, would you be satisfied with logical construction? Would you depend upon a title of so disputable a nature? The present opinions of individuals will be buried in entire oblivion when those rights will be thought of. That sacred and lovely thing, religion, ought not to rest on the ingenuity of logical deduction. Holy religion, sir, will be prostituted to the lowest purposes of human policy. What has been more productive of mischief among mankind than religious disputes? Then here, sir, is a foundation for such disputes, when it requires learning and logical deduction to perceive that religious liberty is secure.

[24 June]

Mr. MADISON. Mr. Chairman, nothing has excited more admiration in the world than the manner in which free governments have been established in America; for it was the first instance, from the creation of the world to the American revolution, that free inhabitants have been seen deliberating on a form of government, and selecting such of their citizens as possessed their confidence, to determine upon and give effect to it. But why has this excited so much wonder and applause? Because it is of so much magnitude, and because it is liable to be frustrated by so many accidents. If it has excited so much wonder that the United States have, in the middle of war and confusion, formed free systems of government, how much more astonishment and admiration will be excited, should they be able, peaceably, freely, and satisfactorily, to establish one general government, when there is such a diversity of opinions and interests—when not cemented or stimulated by any common danger! How vast must be the difficulty of concentrating, in one government, the interests, and conciliating the opinions, of so many different, heterogeneous bodies!

How have the confederacies of ancient and modern times been formed? As far as ancient history describes the former to us, they were brought about by the wisdom of some eminent sage. How was the imperfect union of the Swiss cantons formed? By danger. How was the confederacy of the United Netherlands formed? By the same. They are surrounded by dangers. By these, and one influential character, they were stimulated to unite. How was the Germanic system formed? By danger, in some degree, but principally by the overruling influence of individuals.

When we consider this government, we ought to make great allowances. We must calculate the impossibility that every state should be gratified in its wishes, and much less that every individual should receive this gratification. It has never been denied, by the friends of the paper on the table, that it has defects; but they do not think that it contains any real danger. They conceive that they will, in all probability, be removed, when experience will show it to be necessary. I beg that gentlemen, in deliberating on this subject, would consider the alternative. Either nine states shall have ratified it, or they will not. If nine states will adopt it, can it be reasonably presumed, or required, that nine states, having freely and fully considered the subject, and come to an affirmative decision, will, upon the demand of a single state, agree that they acted wrong, and could not see its defects—tread back the steps which they have taken, and come forward, and reduce it to uncertainty whether a general system shall be adopted or not? Virginia has always heretofore spoken the language of respect to the other states, and she has always been attended to. Will it be that language to call on a great majority of the states to acknowledge that they have done wrong? Is it the language of confidence to say that we do not believe that amendments for the preservation of the common liberty, and general interests, of the states, will be consented to by them? This is the language neither of confidence nor respect. Virginia, when she speaks respectfully, will be as much attended to as she has hitherto been when speaking this language.

It is a most awful thing that depends on our decision—no less than whether the thirteen states shall unite freely, peaceably, and unanimously, for security of their common happiness and liberty, or whether every thing is to be put in confusion and disorder. Are we to embark in this dangerous enterprise, uniting various opinions to contrary interests, with the vain hope of coming to an amicable concurrence?

It is worthy of our consideration that those who prepared the paper on the table found difficulties not to be described in its formation: mutual deference and concession were absolutely necessary. Had they been inflexibly tenacious of their individual opinions, they would never have concurred. Under what circumstances was it formed? When no party was formed, or particular proposition made, and men's minds were calm and dispassionate. Yet, under these circumstances, it was difficult, extremely difficult, to agree to any general system.

Suppose eight states only should ratify, and Virginia should propose certain alterations, as the previous condition of her accession. If they should be disposed to accede to her proposition, which is the most favorable conclusion, the difficulty attending it will be immense. Every state which has decided it, must take up the subject again. They

must not only have the mortification of acknowledging that they had done wrong, but the difficulty of having a reconsideration of it among the people, and appointing new conventions to deliberate upon it. They must attend to *all* the amendments, which may be dictated by as great a diversity of political opinions as there are local attachments. When brought together in one assembly, they must go through, and accede to, every one of the amendments. The gentlemen who, within this house, have thought proper to propose previous amendments, have brought no less than forty amendments, a bill of rights which contains twenty amendments, and twenty other alterations, some of which are improper and inadmissible. Will not every state think herself equally entitled to propose as many amendments? And suppose them to be contradictory! I leave it to this Convention whether it be probable that they can agree, or agree to any thing but the plan on the table; or whether greater difficulties will not be encountered than were experienced in the progress of the formation of the Constitution.

I have said that there was a great contrariety of opinions among the gentlemen in the opposition. It has been heard in every stage of their opposition. I can see, from their amendments, that very great sacrifices have been made by some of them. Some gentlemen think that it contains too much state influence; others, that it is a complete consolidation; and a variety of other things. Some of them think that the equality in the Senate is not a defect; others, that it is the bane of all good government. I might, if there were time, show a variety of other cases where their opinions are contradictory. If there be this contrariety of opinions in this house, what contrariety may not be expected, when we take into view thirteen conventions equally or more numerous! Besides, it is notorious, from the debates which have been published, that there is no sort of uniformity in the grounds of the opposition.

The state of New York has been adduced. Many in that state are opposed to it from local views. The two who opposed it in the general Convention from that state are in the state Convention. Every step of this system was opposed by those two gentlemen. They were unwilling to part with the old Confederation. Can it be presumed, then, sir, that gentlemen in this state, who admit the necessity of changing, should ever be able to unite in sentiments with those who are totally averse to any change?

I have revolved this question in my mind with as much serious attention, and called to my aid as much information, as I could, yet I can see no reason for the apprehensions of gentlemen; but I think that the most happy effects for this country would result from adoption, and if Virginia will agree to ratify this system, I shall look upon it as one of the most fortunate events that ever happened for human nature. I cannot, therefore, without the most excruciating apprehensions, see a possibility of losing its blessings. It gives me infinite pain to reflect that all the earnest endeavors of the warmest friends of their country to introduce a system promotive of our happiness, may be blasted by a rejection, for which I think, with my honorable friend, that previous amendments are but another name. The gentlemen in opposition seem to insist on those amendments, as if they were all necessary for the liberty and happiness of the people. Were I to hazard an opinion on the subject, I would declare it infinitely more safe, in its present form, than it would be after introducing into it that long train of alterations which they call amendments.

With respect to the proposition of the honorable gentleman to my left, (Mr. Wythe,) gentlemen apprehend that, by enumerating three rights, it implied there were no more. The observations made by a gentleman lately up, on that subject, correspond precisely with my opinion. That resolution declares that the powers granted by the proposed Constitution are the gift of the people, and may be resumed by them when perverted to their oppression, and every power not granted thereby remains with the people, and at their will. It adds, likewise, that no right, of any denomination, can be cancelled, abridged, restrained, or modified, by the general government, or any of its officers, except in those instances in which power is given by the Constitution for these purposes. There cannot be a more positive and unequivocal declaration of the principle of the adoption—that every thing not granted is reserved. This is obviously and self-evidently the case, without the declaration. Can the general government exercise any power not delegated? If an enumeration be made of our rights, will it not be implied that every thing omitted is given to the general government? Has not the honorable gentleman himself admitted that an imperfect enumeration is dangerous? Does the Constitution say that they shall not alter the law of descents, or do those things which would subvert the whole system of the state laws? If it did, what was not excepted would be granted. Does it follow, from the omission of such restrictions, that they can exercise powers not delegated? The reverse of the proposition holds. The delegation alone warrants the exercise of any power.

With respect to *the amendments* proposed by the honorable gentleman, it ought to be considered how far they are good. As far as they are palpably and insuperably objectionable, they ought to be opposed. One amendment he proposes is, that any army which shall be necessary shall be raised by the consent of two thirds of the states. I most devoutly wish that there may never be an occasion for having a single regiment. There can be no harm in declaring that standing armies, in time of peace, are dangerous to liberty, and ought to be avoided, as far as it may be consistent with the protection of the community. But when we come to say that the national security shall depend, not on a majority of the people of America, but that it may be frustrated by less than one third of the people of America, I ask if this be a safe or proper mode. What parts of the United States are most likely to stand in need of this protection? The weak parts, which are the Southern States. Will it be safe to leave the United States at the mercy of one third of the states—a number which may comprise a very small proportion of the American people? They may all be in that part of America which is least exposed to danger. As far as a remote situation from danger would render exertions for public defence less active, so far the Southern States would be endangered.

The regulation of *commerce*, he further proposed, should depend on two thirds of both houses. I wish I could recollect the history of this matter; but I cannot call it to mind with sufficient exactness. But I well recollect the reasoning of some gentlemen on that subject. It was said, and I believe with truth, that every part of America does not stand in equal need of security. It was observed that the Northern States were most competent to their own safety. Was it reasonable, asked they, that they should bind themselves to the defence of the Southern States, and still be left at the mercy of the minority for commercial advantages? Should it be in the power of the minority to deprive them of this and other advantages, when they were bound to defend the whole Union, it might be a disadvantage for them to confederate.

These were his arguments. This policy of guarding against political inconveniences, by enabling a small part of the community to oppose the government, and subjecting the majority to a small minority, is fallacious. In some cases it may be good; in others it may be fatal. In all cases, it puts it in the power of the minority to decide a question which concerns the majority.

I was struck with surprise when I heard him express himself alarmed with respect to the emancipation of slaves. Let me ask, if they should even attempt it, if it will not be a usurpation of power. There is no power to warrant it, in that paper. If there be, I know it not. But why should it be done? Says the honorable gentleman, for the general welfare: it will infuse strength into our system. Can any member of this committee suppose that it will increase our strength? Can any one believe that the American councils will come into a measure which will strip them of their property, and discourage and alienate the affections of five thirteenths of the Union? Why was nothing of this sort aimed at before? I believe such an idea never entered into any American breast, nor do I believe it ever will enter into the heads of those gentlemen who substitute unsupported suspicions for reasons.

I am persuaded that the gentlemen who contend for previous amendments are not aware of the dangers which must result. Virginia, after having made opposition, will be obliged to recede from it. Might not the nine states say, with a great deal of propriety, "It is not proper, decent, or right, in you, to demand that we should reverse what we have done. Do as we have done; place confidence in us, as we have done in one another; and then we shall freely, fairly, and dispassionately consider and investigate your propositions, and endeavor to gratify your wishes. But if you do not do this, it is more reasonable that you should yield to us than we to you. You cannot exist without us; you must be a member of the Union."

The case of Maryland, instanced by the gentleman, does not hold. She would not agree to confederate, because the other states would not assent to her claims of the western lands. Was she gratified? No; she put herself like the rest. Nor has she since been gratified. The lands are in the common stock of the Union.

As far as his amendments are not objectionable, or unsafe, so far they may be subsequently recommended—not because they are necessary, but because they can produce no possible danger, and may gratify some gentlemen's wishes. But I never can consent to his previous amendments, because they are pregnant with dreadful dangers.

[25 *June*]

Mr. MADISON. Mr. Chairman, I should not have risen at all, were it not for what the honorable gentleman said. If there be any suspicions that, if the ratification be made, the friends of the system will withdraw their concurrence, and much more, their persons, it shall never be with my approbation. Permit me to remark that, if he has given us a true state of the disposition of the several members of the Union, there is no doubt they will agree to the same amendments after adoption. If we propose the conditional amendments, I entreat gentlemen to consider the distance to which they throw the ultimate settlement, and the extreme risk of perpetual disunion. They cannot but see how easy it will be to obtain subsequent amendments. They can be proposed when the legislatures of two thirds of the states shall make application for that purpose; and the legislatures of three fourths of the states, or conventions in the same, can fix the amendments so proposed. If there be an equal zeal in every state, can there be a doubt that they will concur in reasonable amendments? If, on the other hand, we call on the states to rescind what they have done, and confess that they have done wrong, and to consider the subject again, it will produce such unnecessary delays, and is pregnant with such infinite dangers, that I cannot contemplate it without horror. There are uncertainty and confusion on the one hand, and order, tranquillity, and certainty, on the other. Let us not hesitate to elect the latter alternative. Let us join with cordiality in those alterations we think proper. There is no friend to the Constitution but who will concur in that mode.

Mr. MONROE, after an exordium which could not be heard, remarking that the question now before the committee was, whether previous or subsequent amendments were the most prudent, strongly supported the former. He could not conceive that a conditional ratification would, in the most remote degree, endanger the Union; for that it was as clearly the interest of the adopting states to be united with Virginia, as it could be her interest to be in union with them. He demanded if they would arm the states against one another, and make themselves enemies of those who were respectable and powerful from their situation and numbers. He had no doubt that they would, in preference to such a desperate and violent measure, come forward and make a proposition to the other states, so far as it would be consistent with the general interest. Adopt it now, unconditionally, says he, and it will never be amended, not even when experience shall have proved its defects. An alteration will be a diminution of their power, and there will be great exertions made to prevent it. I have no dread that they will immediately infringe the dearest rights of the people, but that the operation of the government will be oppressive in process of time. Shall we not pursue the dictates of common sense, and the example of all free and wise nations, and insist on amendments with manly fortitude?

It is urged that there is an impossibility of getting previous amendments, and that a variety of circumstances concur to render it impracticable. This argument appears to me fallacious, and as a specious evasion. The same cause which has hitherto produced a spirit of unanimity, and a predilection for the Union, will hereafter produce the same effects.

How did *the federal Convention* meet? From the beginning of time, in any age or country, did ever men meet under so loose, uncurbed a commission? There was nothing to restrain them but their characters and reputation. They could not organize a system without defects. This cannot, then, be perfect. Is it not presumable that by subsequent attempts we shall make it more complete and perfect?

What are the great objections now made? Are they local? What are the amendments brought forth by my friends? Do they not contemplate the great interests of the people, and of the Union at large? I am satisfied, from what we have seen of the disposition of the other states, that, instead of disunion and national confusion, there will be harmony and perfect concord. Disunion is more to be apprehended from the adoption of a system reprobated by some, and allowed by all to be defective. The arguments of gentlemen have no weight on my mind. It is unnecessary to enter into the refutation of them. My honorable friends have done it highly to my satisfaction. Permit me only to observe, with respect to those amendments, that they are harmless. Do they change a feature of the Constitution? They secure our rights without altering a single feature. I trust, therefore, that gentlemen will concur with them.

. . . . .

Mr. TYLER. Mr. Chairman, I should have been satisfied with giving my vote on the question to-day; but, as I wish to hand down to posterity my opposition to this system, I conceive it to be my duty to declare the principles on which I disapprove it, and the cause of my opposition. I have seriously considered the subject in my mind, and when I consider the effects which may happen to this country from its adoption, I tremble at it. My opposition to it arose first from general principles, independent of any local consideration. But when I find that the Constitution is expressed in indefinite terms, in terms which the gentlemen who composed it do not all concur in the meaning of,—I say that, when it is thus liable to objections and different constructions, I find no rest in my mind. Those clauses which answer different constructions will be used to serve particular purposes. If the able members who composed it cannot agree on the construction of it, shall I be thought rash or wrong to pass censure on its ambiguity?

The worthy member last up has brought us to a degrading situation—that we have no right to propose amendments. I should have expected such language had we already adopted a Constitution which will preclude us from this advantage. If we propose to them to reconsider what they have done, and not rescind it, will it be dictating to them? I do not undertake to say that our amendments will bind other states: I hope no gentleman will be so weak as to say so. But no gentleman on the other side will deny our right of proposing amendments. Wherefore is it called dictatorial? It is not my wish that they should rescind but so much as will secure our peace and liberty. We wish to propose such amendments to the sister states as will reconcile all the states. Will gentlemen think this will dissolve the Union?

Among all the chimeras adduced on this occasion, we are intimidated with the fear of being attacked by the petty princes of Europe. The little predatory nations of Europe are to cross the Atlantic and fall upon us; and to avoid this, we must adopt this government, with all its defects. Are we to be frightened into its adoption?

The gentleman has objected to previous amendments, because the people did not know them. Have they seen their subsequent amendments?

[Here Mr. Innes rose, and explained the difference—that previous amendments would be binding on the people, though they had never seen them, and should have no opportunity of considering them before they should operate; but that subsequent amendments, being only recommendatory in their nature, could be reviewed by the people before they would become a part of the system; and, if they disapproved of them, they might direct their delegates in Congress to alter and modify them.]

Mr. TYLER then proceeded: I have seen their subsequent amendments, and, although they hold out something like the thing we wish, yet they have not entered pointedly and substantially into it. What have they said about direct taxation? They have said nothing on this subject. Is there any limitation of, or restriction on, the federal judicial power? I think not. So that gentlemen hold out the idea of amendments which will not alter one dangerous part of it. It contains many dangerous articles. No gentleman here can give such a construction of it as will give general satisfaction. Shall we be told that we shall be attacked by the Algerines, and that disunion will take place, unless we adopt it? Such language as this I did not expect here. Little did I think that matters would come to this, when we separated from the mother country. There, sir, every man is amenable to punishment. There is far less responsibility in this government. British tyranny would have been more tolerable. By our present government, every man is secure in his person, and the enjoyment of his property. There is no man who is not liable to be punished for misdeeds. I ask, What is it that disturbs men whose liberty is in the highest zenith? Human nature will always be the same. Men never were, nor ever will, be satisfied with their happiness.

They tell you that one letter's alteration will destroy it. I say that it is very far from being perfect. I ask, if it were put in immediate operation, whether the people could bear it—whether two bodies can tax the same species of property. The idea of two omnipotent powers is inconsistent. The natural tendency must be, either a revolt, or the destruction of the state governments, and a consolidation of them all into one general system. If we are to be consolidated, let it be on better grounds. So long as climate

will have effect on men, so long will the different climates of the United States render us different. Therefore a consolidation is contrary to our nature, and can only be supported by an arbitrary government.

Previous and subsequent amendments are now the only dispute; and when gentlemen say that there is a greater probability of obtaining the one than the other, they accompany their assertions with no kind of argument. What is the reason that amendments cannot be got after ratification? Because we have granted power. Because the amendments you propose will diminish their power, and undo some clauses in that paper. This argument proves to me that they cannot be serious. It has been plainly proved to you that it is impracticable. Local advantages are given up, as well as the regulation of trade. When it is the case, will the little states agree to an alteration? When gentlemen insist on this, without producing any argument, they will find no credulity in me. Another convention ought to be had, whether the amendments be previous or subsequent. They say another convention is dangerous. How is this proved? It is only their assertion. Gentlemen tell us we shall be ruined without adoption. Is this reasonable? It does not appear so to me.

15

ACT OF CONTINENTAL CONGRESS PUTTING CONSTITUTION INTO EFFECT
13 Sept. 1788
Elliot 1:332–33

The ratification of New Hampshire, being the ninth in order, was received by Congress on the 2d of July, 1788. The following is an extract from the Journal of that day:—

UNITED STATES IN CONGRESS ASSEMBLED.

WEDNESDAY, *July* 2, 1788.

The state of New Hampshire having ratified this Constitution, transmitted to them by the act of the 28th of September last, and transmitted to Congress their ratification, and the same being read, the president reminded Congress that this was the ninth ratification transmitted and laid before them; whereupon,—

On motion of Mr. Clarke, seconded by Mr. Edwards,—

Ordered, That the ratifications of the Constitution of the United States, transmitted to Congress, be referred to a committee to examine the same, and report an act to Congress for putting the said Constitution into operation, in pursuance of the resolutions of the late Federal Convention.

On the question to agree to this order, the yeas and nays being required by Mr. Yates:—

New Hampshire,...	Mr. Gilman, ...Ay. Mr. Wingate, ...Ay.	} Ay.
Massachusetts, ..	Mr. Dane, ...Ay. Mr. Otis,............Ay.	} Ay.
Rhode Island,...	Mr. Arnold,............. Mr. Hazard,............	} Excused.
Connecticut, ...	Mr. Huntington,....Ay. Mr. Edwards,.......Ay.	} Ay.
New York,......	Mr. L'Hommedieu, Ay. Mr. Yates, ...No.	} Divided.
New Jersey,.....	Mr. Clarke,........Ay. Mr. Elmer,.........Ay. Mr. Dayton, ...Ay.	} Ay.
Pennsylvania,...	Mr. Bingham, ...Ay. Mr. Read,..........Ay.	} Ay.
Maryland,......	Mr. Contee,........Ay.	
Virginia, ...	Mr. Griffin,........Ay. Mr. Carrington, ...Ay. Mr. Brown,........Ay.	} Ay.
South Carolina,.....	Mr. Huger, ...Ay. Mr. Parker,........Ay. Mr. Tucker, ...Ay.	} Ay.
Georgia,........	Mr. Few,...........Ay. Mr. Baldwin, ...Ay.	} Ay.

So it passed in the affirmative.

On the 14th of July, 1788, the committee reported an act for putting the Constitution into operation, which was debated until the 13th of September of the same year, when the following resolution was adopted:—

"Whereas the Convention assembled in Philadelphia, pursuant to the resolution of Congress of the 21st of February, 1787, did, on the 17th of September, in the same year, report to the United States in Congress assembled a Constitution for the people of the United States; whereupon Congress, on the 28th of the same September, did resolve, unanimously 'That the said report, with the resolutions and letter accompanying the same, be transmitted to the several legislatures, in order to be submitted to a convention of delegates, chosen in each state by the people thereof, in conformity to the resolves of the Convention made and provided in that case;' and whereas the Constitution so reported by the Convention, and by Congress transmitted to the several legislatures, has been ratified in the manner therein declared to be sufficient for the establishment of the same, and such ratifications, duly authenticated, have been received by Congress, and are filed in the office of the secretary; therefore,—

"*Resolved*, That the first Wednesday in January next be the day for appointing electors in the several states which, before the said day, shall have ratified the said Constitution; that the first Wednesday in February next be the day for the electors to assemble in their respective states, and vote for a President: and that the first Wednesday in March next be the time, and the present seat of Congress the place, for commencing proceedings under the said Constitution."

The elections of the several states were held conformably to the above resolution. On Wednesday the 4th of March, 1789, proceedings commenced under the Constitution; and on the 30th of April, of the same year, GEORGE WASHINGTON, elected by the unanimous suffrage of the electors, was inaugurated as President of the United States.

16

OWINGS V. SPEED
5 Wheat. 419 (1820)

Mr. Chief Justice MARSHALL delivered the opinion of the Court. This was an ejectment brought by the plaintiff in the Circuit Court of the United States, for the District of Kentucky, to recover a lot of ground lying in Bardstown.

. . . . .

Before we determine on the construction of the Constitution in relation to a question of this description, it is necessary to inquire whether the provisions of that instrument apply to any acts of the State legislatures which were of the date with that which it is now proposed to consider.

This act was passed in the session of 1788. Did the Constitution of the United States then operate upon it?

In September, 1787, after completing the great work in which they had been engaged, the Convention resolved that the Constitution should be laid before the Congress of the United States, to be submitted by that body to Conventions of the several States, to be convened by their respective legislatures; and expressed the opinion, that as soon as it should be ratified by the Conventions of nine States, Congress should fix a day on which electors should be appointed by the States, a day on which the electors should assemble to vote for President and Vice President, "and the time and place for commencing proceedings under this Constitution."

The Conventions of nine States having adopted the Constitution, Congress, in September or October, 1788, passed a resolution in conformity with the opinions expressed by the Convention, and appointed the first Wednesday in March of the ensuing year as the day, and the then seat of Congress as the place, "for commencing proceedings under the Constitution."

Both Governments could not be understood to exist at the same time. The new Government did not commence until the old Government expired. It is apparent that the Government did not commence on the Constitution being ratified by the ninth State; for these ratifications were to be reported to Congress, whose continuing existence was recognised by the Convention, and who were requested to continue to exercise their powers for the purpose of bringing the new government into operation. In fact, Congress did continue to act as a government until it dissolved on the first of November, by the successive disappearance of its members. It existed potentially until the 2d of March, the day preceding that on which the members of the new Congress were directed to assemble.

The resolution of the Convention might originally have suggested a doubt, whether the Government could be in operation for every purpose before the choice of a President; but this doubt has been long solved, and were it otherwise, its discussion would be useless, since it is apparent that its operation did not commence before the first Wednesday in March, 1789, before which time Virginia had passed the act which is alleged to violate the Constitution.

SEE ALSO:

Generally Bill of Rights
R. D. Spaight to James Iredell, 12 Aug. 1787, Farrand 3:68
An Old Whig, no. 8, Feb. 1788, Storing 3.3.50
Luther Martin, Letter, no. 4, 21 Mar. 1788, Essays 362–63
North Carolina Ratification of Constitution, 1 Aug. 1788, 21 Nov. 1789, Elliot 1:331–32, 333
Rhode Island Ratification of Constitution, 29 May 1790, Elliot 1:334–37
Vermont Ratification of Constitution, 10 Jan. 1791, Elliot 1:337–38

Constitution of the United States and the First Twelve Amendments

We the People of the United States, in Order to form a more perfect Union, establish Justice, insure domestic Tranquility, provide for the common defence, promote the general Welfare, and secure the Blessings of Liberty to ourselves and our Posterity, do ordain and establish this Constitution for the United States of America.

Article. I.

SECTION 1. All legislative Powers herein granted shall be vested in a Congress of the United States, which shall consist of a Senate and House of Representatives.

SECTION 2. The House of Representatives shall be composed of Members chosen every second Year by the People of the several States, and the Electors in each State shall have the Qualifications requisite for Electors of the most numerous Branch of the State Legislature.

No person shall be a Representative who shall not have attained to the Age of twenty five Years, and been seven Years a Citizen of the United States, and who shall not, when elected, be an Inhabitant of that State in which he shall be chosen.

Representatives and direct Taxes shall be apportioned among the several States which may be included within this Union, according to their respective Numbers, which shall be determined by adding to the whole Number of free Persons, including those bound to Service for a Term of Years, and excluding Indians not taxed, three fifths of all other Persons. The actual Enumeration shall be made within three Years after the first Meeting of the Congress of the United States, and within every subsequent Term of ten Years, in such Manner as they shall by Law direct. The Number of Representatives shall not exceed one for every thirty Thousand, but each State shall have at Least one Representative; and until such enumeration shall be made, the State of New Hampshire shall be entitled to chuse three, Massachusetts eight, Rhode-Island and Providence Plantations one, Connecticut five, New-York six, New Jersey four, Pennsylvania eight, Delaware one, Maryland six, Virginia ten, North Carolina five, South Carolina five, and Georgia three.

When vacancies happen in the Representation from any State, the Executive Authority thereof shall issue Writs of Election to fill such Vacancies.

The House of Representatives shall chuse their Speaker and other Officers; and shall have the sole Power of Impeachment.

SECTION 3. The Senate of the United States shall be composed of two Senators from each State, chosen by the Legislature thereof, for six Years; and each Senator shall have one Vote.

Immediately after they shall be assembled in Consequence of the first Election, they shall be divided as equally as may be into three Classes. The Seats of the Senators of the first Class shall be vacated at the Expiration of the second Year, of the second Class at the Expiration of the fourth Year, and of the third Class at the Expiration of the sixth Year, so that one third may be chosen every second Year; and if Vacancies happen by Resignation, or otherwise, during the Recess of the Legislature of any State, the Executive thereof may make temporary Appointments until the next Meeting of the Legislature, which shall then fill such Vacancies.

No Person shall be a Senator who shall not have attained to the Age of thirty Years, and been nine Years a Citizen of the United States, and who shall not, when elected, be an Inhabitant of that State for which he shall be chosen.

The Vice President of the United States shall be President of the Senate, but shall have no Vote, unless they be equally divided.

The Senate shall chuse their other Officers, and also a President pro tempore, in the Absence of the Vice President, or when he shall exercise the Office of President of the United States.

The Senate shall have the sole Power to try all Impeachments. When sitting for that Purpose, they shall be on Oath or Affirmation. When the President of the United States is tried, the Chief Justice shall preside: And no Person shall be convicted without the Concurrence of two thirds of the Members present.

Judgment in Cases of Impeachment shall not extend further than to removal from Office, and disqualification to hold and enjoy any Office of honor, Trust or Profit under the United States: but the Party convicted shall nevertheless be liable and subject to Indictment, Trial, Judgment and Punishment, according to Law.

SECTION 4. The Times, Places and Manner of holding Elections for Senators and Representatives, shall be prescribed in each State by the Legislature thereof; but the Congress may at any time by Law make or alter such Regulations, except as to the Places of chusing Senators.

The Congress shall assemble at least once in every Year, and such Meeting shall be on the first Monday in December, unless they shall by Law appoint a different Day.

SECTION 5. Each House shall be the Judge of the Elections, Returns and Qualifications of its own Members, and a Majority of each shall constitute a Quorum to do Business; but a smaller Number may adjourn from day to day, and may be authorized to compel the Attendance of absent Members, in such Manner, and under such Penalties as each House may provide.

Each House may determine the Rules of its Proceedings, punish its Members for disorderly Behaviour, and, with the Concurrence of two thirds, expel a Member.

Each House shall keep a Journal of its Proceedings, and from time to time publish the same, excepting such Parts as may in their Judgment require Secrecy; and the Yeas and Nays of the Members of either House on any question shall, at the Desire of one fifth of those Present, be entered on the Journal.

Neither House, during the Session of Congress, shall, without the Consent of the other, adjourn for more than three days, nor to any other Place than that in which the two Houses shall be sitting.

SECTION 6. The Senators and Representatives shall receive a Compensation for their Services, to be ascertained by Law, and paid out of the Treasury of the United States. They shall in all Cases, except Treason, Felony and Breach of the Peace, be privileged from Arrest during their Attendance at the Session of their respective Houses, and in going to and returning from the same; and for any Speech or Debate in either House, they shall not be questioned in any other Place.

No Senator or Representative shall, during the Time for which he was elected, be appointed to any civil Office under the Authority of the United States, which shall have been created, or the Emoluments whereof shall have been encreased during such time; and no Person holding any Office under the United States, shall be a Member of either House during his Continuance in Office.

SECTION 7. All Bills for raising Revenue shall originate in the House of Representatives; but the Senate may propose or concur with Amendments as on other Bills.

Every Bill which shall have passed the House of Representatives and the Senate, shall, before it become a Law, be presented to the President of the United States; If he approve he shall sign it, but if not he shall return it, with his Objections to that House in which it shall have originated, who shall enter the Objections at large on their Journal, and proceed to reconsider it. If after such Reconsideration two thirds of that House shall agree to pass the Bill, it shall be sent, together with the Objections, to the other House, by which it shall likewise be reconsidered, and if approved by two thirds of that House, it shall become a Law. But in all such Cases the Votes of both Houses shall be determined by yeas and Nays, and the Names of the Persons voting for and against the Bill shall be entered on the Journal of each House respectively. If any Bill shall not be returned by the President within ten days (Sundays excepted) after it shall have been presented to him, the Same shall be a Law, in like Manner as if he had signed it, unless the Congress by their Adjournment prevent its Return in which Case it shall not be a Law.

Every Order, Resolution, or Vote to which the Concurrence of the Senate and House of Representatives may be

necessary (except on a question of Adjournment) shall be presented to the President of the United States; and before the Same shall take Effect, shall be approved by him, or being disapproved by him, shall be repassed by two thirds of the Senate and House of Representatives, according to the Rules and Limitations prescribed in the Case of a Bill.

SECTION 8. The Congress shall have Power To lay and collect Taxes, Duties, Imposts and Excises, to pay the Debts and provide for the common Defence and general Welfare of the United States; but all Duties, Imposts and Excises shall be uniform throughout the United States;

To borrow Money on the credit of the United States;

To regulate Commerce with foreign Nations, and among the several States, and with the Indian Tribes;

To establish an uniform Rule of Naturalization, and uniform Laws on the subject of Bankruptcies throughout the United States;

To coin Money, regulate the Value thereof, and of foreign Coin, and fix the Standard of Weights and Measures;

To provide for the Punishment of counterfeiting the Securities and current Coin of the United States;

To establish Post Offices and post Roads;

To promote the progress of Science and useful Arts, by securing for limited Times to Authors and Inventors the exclusive Right to their respective Writings and Discoveries;

To constitute Tribunals inferior to the supreme Court;

To define and punish Piracies and Felonies committed on the high Seas, and Offences against the Law of Nations;

To declare War, grant Letters of Marque and Reprisal, and make Rules concerning Captures on Land and Water;

To raise and support Armies, but no Appropriation of Money to that Use shall be for a longer Term than two Years;

To provide and maintain a Navy;

To make Rules for the Government and Regulation of the land and naval Forces;

To provide for calling forth the Militia to execute the Laws of the Union, suppress Insurrections and repel Invasions;

To provide for organizing, arming, and disciplining, the Militia, and for governing such Part of them as may be employed in the Service of the United States, reserving to the States respectively, the Appointment of the Officers, and the Authority of training the Militia according to the discipline prescribed by Congress;

To exercise exclusive Legislation in all Cases whatsoever, over such District (not exceeding ten Miles square) as may, by Cession of particular States, and the Acceptance of Congress, become the Seat of the Government of the United States, and to exercise like Authority over all Places purchased by the Consent of the Legislature of the State in which the Same shall be, for the Erection of Forts, Magazines, Arsenals, dock-Yards, and other needful Buildings;—And

To make all Laws which shall be necessary and proper for carrying into Execution the foregoing Powers, and all other Powers vested by this Constitution in the Government of the United States, or in any Department or Officer thereof.

SECTION 9. The Migration or Importation of such Persons as any of the States now existing shall think proper to admit, shall not be prohibited by the Congress prior to the Year one thousand eight hundred and eight, but a Tax or duty may be imposed on such Importation, not exceeding ten dollars for each Person.

The Privilege of the Writ of Habeas Corpus shall not be suspended, unless when in Cases of Rebellion or Invasion the public Safety may require it.

No Bill of Attainder or ex post facto Law shall be passed.

No Capitation, or other direct, Tax shall be laid, unless in Proportion to the Census or Enumeration herein before directed to be taken.

No Tax or Duty shall be laid on Articles exported from any State.

No Preference shall be given by any Regulation of Commerce or Revenue to the Ports of one State over those of another: nor shall Vessels bound to, or from, one State, be obliged to enter, clear, or pay Duties in another.

No Money shall be drawn from the Treasury, but in Consequence of Appropriations made by Law; and a regular Statement and Account of the Receipts and Expenditures of all public Money shall be published from time to time.

No Title of Nobility shall be granted by the United States: And no Person holding any Office of Profit or Trust under them, shall, without the Consent of the Congress, accept of any present, Emolument, Office, or Title, of any kind whatever, from any King, Prince, or foreign State.

SECTION 10. No State shall enter into any Treaty, Alliance, or Confederation; grant Letters of Marque and Reprisal; coin Money; emit Bills of Credit; make any Thing but gold and silver Coin a Tender in Payment of Debts; pass any Bill of Attainder, ex post facto Law, or Law impairing the Obligation of Contracts, or grant any Title of Nobility.

No State shall, without the Consent of the Congress, lay any Imposts or Duties on Imports or Exports, except what may be absolutely necessary for executing it's inspection Laws: and the net Produce of all Duties and Imposts, laid by any State on Imports or Exports, shall be for the Use of the Treasury of the United States; and all such Laws shall be subject to the Revision and Controul of the Congress.

No State shall, without the Consent of Congress, lay any Duty of Tonnage, keep Troops, or Ships of War in time of Peace, enter into any Agreement or Compact with another State, or with a foreign Power, or engage in War, unless actually invaded, or in such imminent Danger as will not admit of delay.

Article. II.

SECTION 1. The executive Power shall be vested in a President of the United States of America. He shall hold his Office during the Term of four Years, and, together with the Vice President, chosen for the same Term, be elected as follows

Each State shall appoint, in such Manner as the Legislature thereof may direct, a Number of Electors, equal to the whole Number of Senators and Representatives to which the State may be entitled in the Congress: but no Senator or Representative, or Person holding an Office of Trust or Profit under the United States, shall be appointed an Elector.

The Electors shall meet in their respective States, and vote by Ballot for two Persons, of whom one at least shall not be an Inhabitant of the same State with themselves. And they shall make a List of all the Persons voted for, and of the Number of Votes for each; which List they shall sign and certify, and transmit sealed to the Seat of the Government of the United States, directed to the President of the Senate. The President of the Senate shall, in the Presence of the Senate and House of Representatives, open all the Certificates, and the Votes shall then be counted. The Person having the greatest Number of Votes shall be the President, if such Number be a Majority of the whole Number of Electors appointed; and if there be more than one who have such Majority, and have an equal Number of Votes, then the House of Representatives shall immediately chuse by Ballot one of them for President; and if no Person have a Majority, then from the five highest on the List the said House shall in like Manner chuse the President. But in chusing the President, the Votes shall be taken by States, the Representation from each State having one Vote; A quorum for this Purpose shall consist of a Member or Members from two thirds of the States, and a Majority of all the States shall be necessary to a Choice. In every Case, after the Choice of the President, the Person having the greatest Number of Votes of the Electors shall be the Vice President. But if there should remain two or more who have equal Votes, the Senate shall chuse from them by Ballot the Vice President.

The Congress may determine the Time of chusing the Electors, and the Day on which they shall give their Votes; which Day shall be the same throughout the United States.

No Person except a natural born Citizen, or a Citizen of the United States, at the time of the Adoption of this Constitution, shall be eligible to the Office of President; neither shall any Person be eligible to that Office who shall not have attained to the Age of thirty five Years, and been fourteen Years a Resident within the United States.

In Case of the Removal of the President from Office, or of his Death, Resignation, or Inability to discharge the Powers and Duties of the said Office, the Same shall devolve on the Vice President, and the Congress may by Law provide for the Case of Removal, Death, Resignation or Inability, both of the President and Vice President, declaring what Officer shall then act as President, and such Officer shall act accordingly, until the Disability be removed, or a President shall be elected.

The President shall, at stated Times, receive for his Services, a Compensation, which shall neither be increased nor diminished during the Period for which he shall have been elected, and he shall not receive within that Period any other Emolument from the United States, or any of them.

Before he enter on the Execution of his Office, he shall take the following Oath or Affirmation:—"I do solemnly swear (or affirm) that I will faithfully execute the Office of President of the United States, and will to the best of my Ability, preserve, protect and defend the Constitution of the United States."

SECTION 2. The President shall be Commander in Chief of the Army and Navy of the United States, and of the Militia of the several States, when called into the actual Service of the United States; he may require the Opinion, in writing, of the principal Officer in each of the executive Departments, upon any Subject relating to the Duties of their respective Offices, and he shall have Power to grant Reprieves and Pardons for Offences against the United States, except in Cases of Impeachment.

He shall have Power, by and with the Advice and Consent of the Senate, to make Treaties, provided two thirds of the Senators present concur; and he shall nominate, and by and with the Advice and Consent of the Senate, shall appoint Ambassadors, other public Ministers and Consuls, Judges of the supreme Court, and all other Officers of the United States, whose Appointments are not herein otherwise provided for, and which shall be established by Law: but the Congress may by Law vest the Appointment of such inferior Officers, as they think proper, in the President alone, in the Courts of Law, or in the Heads of Departments.

The President shall have Power to fill up all Vacancies that may happen during the Recess of the Senate, by granting Commissions which shall expire at the End of their next Session.

SECTION 3. He shall from time to time give to the Congress Information of the State of the Union, and recommend to their Consideration such Measures as he shall judge necessary and expedient; he may, on extraordinary Occasions, convene both Houses, or either of them, and in Case of Disagreement between them, with Respect to the Time of Adjournment, he may adjourn them to such Time as he shall think proper; he shall receive Ambassadors and other public Ministers; he shall take Care that the Laws be faithfully executed, and shall Commission all the Officers of the United States.

SECTION 4. The President, Vice President and all civil Officers of the United States, shall be removed from Office on Impeachment for, and Conviction of, Treason, Bribery, or other high Crimes and Misdemeanors.

Article. III.

SECTION 1. The judicial Power of the United States, shall be vested in one supreme Court, and in such inferior Courts as the Congress may from time to time ordain and establish. The Judges, both of the supreme and inferior Courts, shall hold their Offices during good Behaviour, and shall, at stated Times, receive for their Services, a Compensation, which shall not be diminished during their Continuance in Office.

SECTION 2. The judicial Power shall extend to all Cases, in Law and Equity, arising under this Constitution, the Laws of the United States, and Treaties made, or which shall be made, under their Authority;—to all Cases affecting Ambassadors, other public Ministers and Consuls;—to all Cases of admiralty and maritime Jurisdiction;—to Controversies to which the United States shall be a Party;—to Controversies between two or more States;—between a State and Citizens of another State;—between Citizens of different States,—between Citizens of the same State claiming Lands under Grants of different States, and between a State, or the Citizens thereof, and foreign States, Citizens or Subjects.

In all Cases affecting Ambassadors, other public Ministers and Consuls, and those in which a State shall be Party, the supreme Court shall have original Jurisdiction. In all the other Cases before mentioned, the supreme Court shall have appellate Jurisdiction, both as to Law and Fact, with such Exceptions, and under such Regulations as the Congress shall make.

The Trial of all Crimes, except in Cases of Impeachment, shall be by Jury; and such Trial shall be held in the State where the said Crimes shall have been committed; but when not committed within any State, the Trial shall be at such Place or Places as the Congress may by Law have directed.

SECTION 3. Treason against the United States, shall consist only in levying War against them, or in adhering to their Enemies, giving them Aid and Comfort. No Person shall be convicted of Treason unless on the Testimony of two Witnesses to the same overt Act, or on Confession in open Court.

The Congress shall have Power to declare the Punishment of Treason, but no Attainder of Treason shall work Corruption of Blood, or Forfeiture except during the Life of the Person attainted.

Article. IV.

SECTION 1. Full Faith and Credit shall be given in each State to the public Acts, Records, and judicial Proceedings of every other State. And the Congress may by general Laws prescribe the Manner in which such Acts, Records and Proceedings shall be proved, and the Effect thereof.

SECTION 2. The Citizens of each State shall be entitled to all Privileges and Immunities of Citizens in the several States.

A Person charged in any State with Treason, Felony, or other Crime, who shall flee from Justice, and be found in another State, shall on Demand of the executive Authority of the State from which he fled, be delivered up, to be removed to the State having Jurisdiction of the Crime.

No Person held to Service or Labour in one State, under the Laws thereof, escaping into another, shall, in Consequence of any Law or Regulation therein, be discharged from such Service or Labour, but shall be delivered up on

Claim of the Party to whom such Service or Labour may be due.

SECTION 3. New States may be admitted by the Congress into this Union; but no new State shall be formed or erected within the Jurisdiction of any other State; nor any State be formed by the Junction of two or more States, or Parts of States, without the Consent of the Legislatures of the States concerned as well as of the Congress.

The Congress shall have Power to dispose of and make all needful Rules and Regulations respecting the Territory or other Property belonging to the United States; and nothing in this Constitution shall be so construed as to Prejudice any Claims of the United States, or of any particular State.

SECTION 4. The United States shall guarantee to every State in this Union a Republican Form of Government, and shall protect each of them against Invasion; and on Application of the Legislature, or of the Executive (when the Legislature cannot be convened) against domestic Violence.

Article. V.

The Congress, whenever two thirds of both Houses shall deem it necessary, shall propose Amendments to this Constitution, or, on the Application of the Legislatures of two thirds of the several States, shall call a Convention for proposing Amendments, which, in either Case, shall be valid to all Intents and Purposes, as Part of this Constitution, when ratified by the Legislatures of three fourths of the several States, or by Conventions in three fourths thereof, as the one or the other Mode of Ratification may be proposed by the Congress; Provided that no Amendment which may be made prior to the Year One thousand eight hundred and eight shall in any Manner affect the first and fourth Clauses in the Ninth Section of the first Article; and that no State, without its Consent, shall be deprived of it's equal Suffrage in the Senate.

Article. VI.

All Debts contracted and Engagements entered into, before the Adoption of this Constitution, shall be as valid against the United States under this Constitution, as under the Confederation.

This Constitution, and the Laws of the United States which shall be made in Pursuance thereof; and all Treaties made, or which shall be made, under the Authority of the United States, shall be the supreme Law of the Land; and the Judges in every State shall be bound thereby, any Thing in the Constitution or Laws of any State to the Contrary notwithstanding.

The Senators and Representatives before mentioned, and the Members of the several State Legislatures, and all executive and judicial Officers, both of the United States and of the several States, shall be bound by Oath or Affirmation, to support this Constitution; but no religious Test shall ever be required as a Qualification to any Office or public Trust under the United States.

Article. VII.

The Ratification of the Conventions of nine States, shall be sufficient for the Establishment of this Constitution between the States so ratifying the Same.

> The Word, "the," being interlined between the seventh and eighth Lines of the first Page, The Word "Thirty" being partly written on an Erazure in the fifteenth Line of the first Page, The Words "is tried" being interlined between the thirty second and thirty third Lines of the first Page and the Word "the" being interlined between the forty third and forty fourth Lines of the second Page. Attest WILLIAM JACKSON Secretary

done in Convention by the Unanimous Consent of the States present the Seventeenth Day of September in the Year of our Lord one thousand seven hundred and Eighty seven and of the Independance of the United States of America the Twelfth In witness whereof We have hereunto subscribed our Names,

Go: WASHINGTON—Presidt. and deputy from Virginia

New Hampshire	John Langdon Nicholas Gilman
Massachusetts	Nathaniel Gorham Rufus King
Connecticut	Wm. Saml. Johnson Roger Sherman
New York	Alexander Hamilton
New Jersey	Wil: Livingston David Brearley. Wm. Paterson. Jona: Dayton
Pensylvania	B Franklin Thomas Mifflin Robt Morris Geo. Clymer Thos. FitzSimons Jared Ingersoll James Wilson Gouv Morris
Delaware	Geo: Read Gunning Bedford jun John Dickinson Richard Bassett Jaco: Broom
Maryland	James McHenry Dan of St Thos. Jenifer Danl Carroll
Virginia	John Blair— James Madison Jr.
North Carolina	Wm. Blount Richd. Dobbs Spaight. Hu Williamson
South Carolina	J. Rutledge Charles Cotesworth Pinckney Charles Pinckney Pierce Butler.
Georgia	William Few Abr Baldwin

Amendments to the Constitution

Article I

Congress shall make no law respecting an establishment of religion, or prohibiting the free exercise thereof; or abridging the freedom of speech, or of the press; or the right of the people peaceably to assemble, and to petition the Government for a redress of grievances.

Article II

A well regulated Militia, being necessary to the security of a free State, the right of the people to keep and bear Arms, shall not be infringed.

Article III

No Soldier shall, in time of peace be quartered in any house, without the consent of the Owner, nor in time of war, but in a manner to be prescribed by law.

Article IV

The right of the people to be secure in their persons, houses, papers, and effects, against unreasonable searches and seizures, shall not be violated, and no Warrants shall issue, but upon probable cause, supported by Oath or affirmation, and particularly describing the place to be searched, and the persons or things to be seized.

Article V

No person shall be held to answer for a capital, or otherwise infamous crime, unless on a presentment or indictment of a Grand Jury, except in cases arising in the land or naval forces, or in the Militia, when in actual service in time of War or public danger; nor shall any person be subject for the same offence to be twice put in jeopardy of life or limb; nor shall be compelled in any criminal case to be a witness against himself, nor be deprived of life, liberty, or property, without due process of law; nor shall private property be taken for public use, without just compensation.

Article VI

In all criminal prosecutions, the accused shall enjoy the right to a speedy and public trial, by an impartial jury of the State and district wherein the crime shall have been committed, which district shall have been previously ascertained by law, and to be informed of the nature and cause of the accusation; to be confronted with the witnesses against him; to have compulsory process for obtaining witnesses in his favor, and to have the Assistance of Counsel for his defence.

Article VII

In Suits at common law, where the value in controversy shall exceed twenty dollars, the right of trial by jury shall be preserved, and no fact tried by a jury, shall be otherwise re-examined in any Court of the United States, than according to the rules of the common law.

Article VIII

Excessive bail shall not be required, nor excessive fines imposed, nor cruel and unusual punishments inflicted.

Article IX

The enumeration in the Constitution, of certain rights, shall not be construed to deny or disparage others retained by the people.

Article X

The powers not delegated to the United States by the Constitution, nor prohibited by it to the States, are reserved to the States respectively, or to the people.

Article XI

The Judicial power of the United States shall not be construed to extend to any suit in law or equity, commenced or prosecuted against one of the United States by Citizens of another State, or by Citizens or Subjects of any Foreign State.

Article XII

The Electors shall meet in their respective states, and vote by ballot for President and Vice-President, one of whom, at least, shall not be an inhabitant of the same state with themselves; they shall name in their ballots the person voted for as President, and in distinct ballots the person voted for as Vice-President, and they shall make distinct lists of all persons voted for as President, and of all persons voted for as Vice-President, and of the number of votes for each, which lists they shall sign and certify, and transmit sealed to the seat of the government of the United States, directed to the President of the Senate;— The President of the Senate shall, in the presence of the Senate and House of Representatives, open all the certificates and the votes shall then be counted;—The person having the greatest number of votes for President, shall be the President, if such number be a majority of the whole number of Electors appointed; and if no person have such majority, then from the persons having the highest numbers not exceeding three on the list of those voted for as President, the House of Representatives shall choose immediately, by ballot, the President. But in choosing the President, the votes shall be taken by states, the representation from each state having one vote; a quorum for this purpose shall consist of a member or members from two-thirds of the states, and a majority of all the states shall be necessary to a choice. And if the House of Representatives shall not choose a President whenever the right of choice shall devolve upon them, before the fourth day of March next following, then the Vice-President shall act as President, as in the case of the death or other constitutional disability of the President. The person having the greatest number of votes as Vice-President, shall be the Vice-President, if such number be a majority of the whole number of Electors appointed, and if no person have a majority, then from the two highest numbers on the list, the Senate shall choose the Vice-President; a quorum for the purpose shall consist of two-thirds of the whole number of Senators, and a majority of the whole number shall be necessary to a choice. But no person constitutionally ineligible to the office of President shall be eligible to that of Vice-President of the United States.

Short Titles Used

Documentary citations given in short-title forms as "Life," "Papers," "Works," etc., are to be understood as referring to editions of the author of that particular document. Exceptions are clearly noted.

John Adams, Diary *Diary and Autobiography of John Adams.* Edited by L. H. Butterfield et al. 4 vols. Cambridge: Belknap Press of Harvard University Press, 1961.

John Adams, Papers *Papers of John Adams.* Edited by Robert J. Taylor et al. Cambridge: Belknap Press of Harvard University Press, 1977–.

John Adams, Works *The Works of John Adams.* Edited by Charles Francis Adams. 10 vols. Boston: Little, Brown & Co., 1850–56.

See also: Butterfield; Cappon; Warren-Adams Letters

J. Q. Adams, Writings *Writings of John Quincy Adams.* Edited by Worthington Chauncey Ford. 7 vols. New York: Macmillan Co., 1913–17. ,

Samuel Adams, Writings *The Writings of Samuel Adams.* Edited by Harry Alonzo Cushing. 4 vols. New York: G. P. Putnam's Sons, 1904–8.

American Archives *American Archives.* Edited by M. St. Clair Clarke and Peter Force. 4th ser., 6 vols. Washington, D.C., 1837–46. 5th ser., 3 vols. Washington, D.C., 1848–53.

American Colonial Documents Jensen, Merrill, ed. *American Colonial Documents to 1776.* English Historical Documents, edited by David C. Douglas, vol. 9. New York: Oxford University Press, 1969.

Annals *Annals of Congress. The Debates and Proceedings in the Congress of the United States.* "History of Congress." 42 vols. Washington, D.C.: Gales & Seaton, 1834–56.

Bailyn Bailyn, Bernard, ed. *Pamphlets of the American Revolution, 1750–1776.* Vol. 1, *1750–1765.* Cambridge: Belknap Press of Harvard University Press, 1965.

Blackstone, Commentaries Blackstone, William. *Commentaries on the Laws of England: A Facsimile of the First Edition of 1765–1769.* Chicago: University of Chicago Press, 1979.

Boyd Boyd, Julian P., ed. *Fundamental Laws and Constitutions of New Jersey, 1664–1964.* New Jersey Historical Series, vol. 17. Princeton: D. Van Nostrand Co., Inc., 1964.

Bradford, Of Plymouth Plantation Bradford, William. *Of Plymouth Plantation, 1620–1647.* Edited by Samuel Eliot Morison. New York: Modern Library, 1967.

Burgh [Burgh, James.] *Political Disquisitions: or, An Enquiry into Public Errors, Defects, and Abuses. . . .* 3 vols. London, 1774–75.

Burke, Works *The Works of the Right Honourable Edmund Burke.* 6 vols. London: Henry G. Bohn, 1854–56.

Burnett Burnett, Edmund C., ed. *Letters of Members of the Continental Congress.* 8 vols. Washington: Carnegie Institution of Washington, 1921–36.

Butterfield Adams, Abigail Smith. *The Book of Abigail and John: Selected Letters of the Adams Family, 1762–1784.* Edited by L. H. Butterfield et al. Cambridge: Harvard University Press, 1975.

Cannon *The Letters of Junius.* Edited by John Cannon. Oxford: At the Clarendon Press, 1978.

Cappon *The Adams-Jefferson Letters: The Complete Correspondence between Thomas Jefferson and Abigail and John Adams.* Edited by Lester J. Cappon. 2 vols. Chapel Hill: University of North Carolina Press for the Institute of Early American History and Culture, Williamsburg, Virginia, 1959.

Chase Chase, Frederick. *A History of Dartmouth College and the Town of Hanover New Hampshire.* Edited by John K. Lord. 2 vols. Cambridge: John Wilson & Son, 1891.

Colonial Records *The Colonial Records of North Carolina.* Edited by William L. Saunders. 10 vols. Raleigh: Josephus Daniels, 1886–90.

Crèvecoeur Crèvecoeur, J. Hector St. John. *Letters from an American Farmer.* New York: Albert & Charles Boni, 1925.

Documentary History *Documentary History of the Constitution of the United States of America, 1786–1870.* 5 vols. Washington, D.C.: Department of State, 1901–5.

Dumbauld Dumbauld, Edward. *The Bill of Rights and What It Means Today.* Norman: University of Oklahoma Press, 1957.

Early History *Early History of the University of Virginia, as Contained in the Letters of Thomas Jefferson and Joseph C. Cabell, Hitherto Unpublished. . . .* Richmond: J. W. Randolph, 1856.

Elliot Elliot, Jonathan, ed. *The Debates in the Several State Conventions on the Adoption of the Federal Constitution as Recommended by the General Convention at Philadelphia in 1787. . . .* 5 vols. 2d ed. 1888. Reprint. New York: Burt Franklin, n.d.

Emlyn Hale, Sir Matthew. *Historia Placitorum Coronae. The History of the Pleas of the Crown.* Edited by Sollom Emlyn. 2 vols. London, 1736. Reprint. Classical English Law Texts. London: Professional Books, Ltd., 1971.

Essays Ford, Paul Leicester, ed. *Essays on the Constitution of the United States, Published during Its Discussion by the People, 1787–1788.* Brooklyn: Historical Printing Club, 1892.

Farrand Farrand, Max, ed. *The Records of the Federal Convention of 1787.* Rev. ed. 4 vols. New Haven and London: Yale University Press, 1937.

Federalist Hamilton, Alexander; Madison, James; and Jay, John. *The Federalist.* Edited by Jacob E. Cooke. Middletown, Conn.: Wesleyan University Press, 1961.

Foster Foster, Sir Michael. *A Report of Some Proceedings on the Commission . . . for the Trial of the Rebels in the Year 1746 . . . , and of Other Crown Cases.* London, 1762. Reprint. Classical English Law Texts. Abingdon, England: Professional Books, Ltd., 1982.

Four Letters on Interesting Subjects *Four Letters on Interesting Subjects.* Philadelphia: 1776. Evans 14759.

Franklin, Papers *The Papers of Benjamin Franklin.* Edited by Leonard W. Labaree et al. New Haven: Yale University Press, 1959–.

Franklin, Writings *The Writings of Benjamin Franklin.* Edited by Albert Henry Smyth. 10 vols. New York: Macmillan Co., 1905–7.

Gerry, Life Austin, James T. *The Life of Elbridge Gerry. With Contemporary Letters.* 2 vols. Boston, 1828–29.

Gray Hale, Sir Matthew. *The History of the Common Law of England.* Edited by Charles M. Gray. Classics of British Historical Literature. Chicago: University of Chicago Press, 1971.

Gwyn Gwyn, W. B. *The Meaning of the Separation of Powers: An Analysis of the Doctrine from Its Origin to the Adoption of the United States Constitution.* Tulane Studies in Political Science, vol. 9. New Orleans: Tulane University, 1965.

Hamilton, Papers *The Papers of Alexander Hamilton.* Edited by Harold C. Syrett et al. 26 vols. New York and London: Columbia University Press, 1961–79.

See also: Federalist

Handlin Handlin, Oscar, and Handlin, Mary, eds. *The Popular Sources of Political Authority: Documents on the Massachusetts Constitution of 1780.* Cambridge: Belknap Press of Harvard University Press, 1966.

Harrington *The Political Writings of James Harrington: Representative Selections.* Edited by Charles Blitzer. New York: Liberal Arts Press, 1955.

History of Congress *History of Congress; Exhibiting a Classification of the Proceedings of the Senate, and the House of Representatives, from March 4, 1789, to March 3, 1793. . . .* Philadelphia: Lea & Blanchard, 1843.

Hume Hume, David. *Essays Moral, Political and Literary.* 1742, 1752.

Hurst Hurst, James Willard. *The Law of Treason in the United States: Collected Essays.* Westport, Conn.: Greenwood Publishing Corp., 1971.

Iredell, Life *Life and Correspondence of James Iredell.* Edited by Griffith J. McRee. 2 vols. New York: D. Appleton & Co., 1857.

Iredell, Papers *The Papers of James Iredell.* Edited by Don Higginbotham. Raleigh: North Carolina Division of Archives and History, 1976–.

Jacobson Trenchard, John, and Gordon, Thomas. *Cato's Letters.* In *The English Libertarian Heritage,* edited by David L. Jacobson. American Heritage Series. Indianapolis: Bobbs-Merrill, 1965.

Jamestown, The Three Charters of the Virginia Company of London *The Three Charters of the Virginia Company of London.* Jamestown 350th Anniversary Historical Booklet, no. 4. 1957

Jay, Correspondence *The Correspondence and Public Papers of John Jay.* Edited by Henry P. Johnston. 4 vols. New York and London: G. P. Putnam's Sons, 1890–93.

Jay, Unpublished Papers *John Jay: Unpublished Papers.* Edited by Richard B. Morris et al. New York: Harper & Row, 1975–.

See also: Federalist

Jefferson, Notes on the State of Virginia Jefferson, Thomas. *Notes on the State of Virginia.* Edited by William Peden. Chapel Hill: University of North Carolina Press for the Institute of Early American History and Culture, Williamsburg, Virginia, 1954.

Jefferson, Papers *The Papers of Thomas Jefferson.* Edited by Julian P. Boyd et al. Princeton: Princeton University Press, 1950–.

Jefferson, Works *The Works of Thomas Jefferson.* Collected and edited by Paul Leicester Ford. Federal Edition. 12 vols. New York and London: G. P. Putnam's Sons, 1904–5.

Jefferson, Writings *The Writings of Thomas Jefferson.* Edited by Andrew A. Lipscomb and Albert Ellery Bergh. 20 vols. Washington: Thomas Jefferson Memorial Association, 1905.

Jensen *The Documentary History of the Ratification of the Constitution.* Edited by Merrill Jensen et al. Madison: State Historical Society of Wisconsin, 1976–.

Journals *Journals of the Continental Congress, 1774–1789.* Edited by Worthington C. Ford et al. 34 vols. Washington, D.C.: Government Printing Office, 1904–37.

Kent Kent, James. *Commentaries on American Law.* 4 vols. New York, 1826–30.

King, Life *The Life and Correspondence of Rufus King.* Edited by Charles R. King. 6 vols. New York: G. P. Putnam's Sons, 1894–1900.

Land Eddis, William. *Letters from America.* Edited by Aubrey C. Land. Cambridge: Belknap Press of Harvard University Press, 1969.

Leake Leake, Isaac Q. *Memoir of the Life and Times of General John Lamb.* Albany, N.Y., 1857.

Lee, Letters *The Letters of Richard Henry Lee.* Edited by James Curtis Ballagh. 2 vols. New York: Macmillan Co., 1911–14.

Lincoln, Collected Works *The Collected Works of Abraham Lincoln.* Edited by Roy P. Basler et al. 8 vols. New Brunswick, N.J.: Rutgers University Press, 1953.

Locke, Second Treatise Locke, John. *Two Treatises of Government.* Edited by Peter Laslett. New York: Mentor Books, New American Library, 1965.

See also: Montuori

Machiavelli Machiavelli, Niccolò. *Discourses on the First Ten Books of Titus Livius.* Translated by Christian E. Detmold. New York: Modern Library, 1940.

McMaster McMaster, John Bach, and Stone, Frederick D., eds. *Pennsylvania and the Federal Constitution, 1787–1788.* Lancaster: Published for the Subscribers by the Historical Society of Pennsylvania, 1888.

Madison, Letters *Letters and Other Writings of James Madison.* Published by order of Congress. 4 vols. Philadelphia: J. B. Lippincott & Co., 1865.

Madison, Papers *The Papers of James Madison.* Edited by William T. Hutchinson et al. Chicago and London: University of Chicago Press, 1962–77 (vols. 1–10); Charlottesville: University Press of Virginia, 1977– (vols. 11–).

Madison, W. & M. Q. Fleet, Elizabeth. "Madison's 'Detached Memoranda.'" *William and Mary Quarterly*, 3d ser., 3 (1946): 534–68.

Madison, Writings *The Writings of James Madison.* Edited by Gaillard Hunt. 9 vols. New York: G. P. Putnam's Sons, 1900–1910.

See also: Federalist

Marshall, Life Beveridge, Albert J. *The Life of John Marshall.* 4 vols. Boston: Houghton Mifflin Co., 1916–19.

Marshall, Papers *The Papers of John Marshall.* Edited by Herbert A. Johnson et al. Chapel Hill: University of North Carolina Press, in association with the Institute of Early American History and Culture, Williamsburg, Virginia, 1974–.

Maryland Archives *Archives of Maryland: Proceedings and Acts of the General Assembly of Maryland.* Edited by William Hand Browne. Vol. 1. Baltimore: Maryland Historical Society, 1883.

Mason, Papers *The Papers of George Mason, 1725–1792.* Edited by Robert A. Rutland. 3 vols. Chapel Hill: University of North Carolina Press, 1970.

Meade Meade, Robert Douthat. *Patrick Henry: Patriot in the Making.* Philadelphia: J. B. Lippincott Co., 1957.

MHS Collections *Collections of the Massachusetts Historical Society.*

Monroe, Writings *The Writings of James Monroe.* Edited by Stanislaus Murray Hamilton. 7 vols. New York and London: G. P. Putnam's Sons, 1898–1903.

Montesquieu *The Spirit of Laws.* 1748. Translated by Thomas Nugent, 1750.

Montuori Locke, John. *A Letter concerning Toleration.* Latin and English texts revised and edited by Mario Montuori. The Hague: Martinus Nijhoff, 1963.

Gouverneur Morris, Amerikastudien Adams, Willi Paul. "'The Spirit of Commerce Requires that Property be Sacred': Gouverneur Morris and the American Revolution." *Amerikastudien* 21 (1976): 309–31.

Gouverneur Morris, Life *The Life of Gouverneur Morris, with Selections from His Correspondence and Miscellaneous Papers.* Edited by Jared Sparks. 3 vols. Boston, 1832.

Robert Morris, Papers *The Papers of Robert Morris, 1781–1784.* Edited by E. James Ferguson et al. Pittsburgh: University of Pittsburgh Press, 1973–.

New England Federalism Adams, Henry, ed. *Documents Relating to New-England Federalism.* Boston: Little, Brown & Co., 1877.

Niles Niles, Hezekiah, *Principles and Acts of the Revolution in America.* Centennial Offering. New York: A. S. Barnes & Co., 1876.

Old Family Letters Biddle, Alexander. *Old Family Letters.* Ser. A. Philadelphia: J. B. Lippincott Co., 1892.

Otis, Political Writings "Some Political Writings of James Otis." Collected by Charles F. Mullett. *University of Missouri Studies* 4 (1929): 257–432.

Paine, Life *The Life and Works of Thomas Paine.* Edited by William M. Van der Weyde. Patriots' Edition. 10 vols. New Rochelle, N.Y.: Thomas Paine National Historical Association, 1925.

Pamphlets Ford, Paul Leicester, ed. *Pamphlets on the Constitution of the United States, Published during Its Discussion by the People, 1787–1788.* Brooklyn, 1888. Reprint. New York: De Capo Press, 1968.

Penn, Select Works *The Select Works of William Penn.* 5 vols. 3d ed. London, 1782.

Pickering, Life Upham, Charles W. *The Life of Timothy Pickering.* 2 vols. Boston: Little, Brown & Co., 1873.

Pinkney Wheaton, Henry. *Some Account of the Life, Writings, and Speeches of William Pinkney.* Baltimore: E. J. Coale, 1826.

Randolph, History of Virginia Randolph, Edmund. *History of Virginia.* Edited by Arthur H. Shaffer. Charlottesville: University Press of Virginia for the Virginia Historical Society, 1970.

Rawle Rawle, William. *A View of the Constitution of the United States of America.* 2d ed. Philadelphia, 1829. Reprint. New York: Da Capo Press, 1970.

Read, Life Read, William Thompson. *Life and Correspondence of George Read.* Philadelphia: J. B. Lippincott & Co., 1870.

Records of the Federal Convention. *See* Farrand

Remonstrance and Petition, W. & M. Q. Schmidt, F. T., and Wilhelm, B. R. "Early Proslavery Petitions in Virginia." *William and Mary Quarterly*, 3d ser., 30 (1973): 133–46.

Richardson Richardson, James D., comp. *A Compilation of the Messages and Papers of the Presidents, 1789–1897.* 10 vols. Washington, D.C.: Government Printing Office, 1896–99.

Robertson Robertson, C. Grant, ed. *Select Statutes, Cases and Documents to Illustrate English Constitutional History, 1660–1832.* 4th ed., rev. London: Methuen & Co., Ltd., 1923.

Rush, Letters *Letters of Benjamin Rush.* Edited by L. H. Butterfield. 2 vols. Memoirs of the American Philosophical Society, vol. 30, parts 1 and 2. Princeton: Princeton University Press, for the American Philosophical Society, 1951.

Rush, Selected Writings *The Selected Writings of Benjamin Rush.* Edited by Dagobert D. Runes. New York: Philosophical Library, 1947.

Scribner *Revolutionary Virginia: The Road to Independence.* Vol 6, *The Time for Decision, 1776: A Documentary Record,* edited by Robert L. Scribner and Brent Tarter. Charlottesville: University Press of Virginia for the Virginia Independence Bicentennial Commission, 1981.

Sidney, Works *The Works of Algernon Sydney. A New Edition.* London, 1772.

Sources *Sources of Our Liberties.* Edited by Richard L. Perry under the general supervision of John C. Cooper. [Chicago:] American Bar Foundation, 1952.

State Trials *State Trials of the United States during the Administrations of Washington and Adams.* Edited by Francis Wharton. Philadelphia: Carey & Hart, 1849.

Stokes Stokes, Anton Phelps, ed. *Church and State in the United States.* 3 vols. New York: Harper & Bros., 1950.

Storing Storing, Herbert J., ed. *The Complete Anti-Federalist.* 7 vols. Chicago: University of Chicago Press, 1981.

Story Story, Joseph. *Commentaries on the Constitution of the United States.* 3 vols. Boston, 1833.

Tansill *Documents Illustrative of the Formation of the Union of the American States.* Edited by Charles C. Tansill. 69th Cong., 1st sess. House Doc. No. 398. Washington, D.C.: Government Printing Office, 1927.

Taylor Taylor, Robert J., ed. *Massachusetts, Colony to Commonwealth: Documents on the Formation of Its Constitution, 1775–1780.* Chapel Hill: University of North Carolina Press for the Institute of Early American History and Culture, Williamsburg, Virginia, 1961.

Thorpe Thorpe, Francis Newton, ed. *The Federal and State Constitutions, Colonial Charters, and Other Organic Laws of the States, Territories, and Colonies Now or Heretofore Forming the United States of America.* 7 vols. Washington, D.C.: Government Printing Office, 1909.

Tucker, Blackstone's Commentaries Tucker, St. George. *Blackstone's Commentaries: With Notes of Reference to the Constitution and Laws of the Federal Government of the United States and of the Commonwealth of Virginia.* 5 vols. Philadelphia, 1803. Reprint. South Hackensack, N.J.: Rothman Reprints, 1969.

Walker, U. Pa. L. Rev. Radin, Max. "The Doctrine of the Separation of Powers in Seventeenth Century Controversies." *University of Pennsylvania Law Review* 86 (1938): 842–66.

Warren, Life Frothingham, Richard. *Life and Times of Joseph Warren.* Boston: Little, Brown & Co., 1865.

Warren-Adams Letters *Warren-Adams Letters, Being Chiefly a Correspondence among John Adams, Samuel Adams, and James Warren.* Vol. 2, 1778–1814. Collections of the Massachusetts Historical Society, vol. 73. [Boston:] Massachusetts Historical Society, 1925.

Washington, Writings *The Writings of George Washington from the Original Manuscript Sources, 1745–1799.* Edited by John C. Fitzpatrick. 39 vols. Washington, D.C.: Government Printing Office, 1931–44.

Webster, Collection Webster, Noah. *A Collection of Essays and Fugitiv Writings on Moral, Historical, Political and Literary Subjects.* Boston, 1790. Reprint. Delmar, N.Y.: Scholars' Facsimiles & Reprints, 1977.

Webster, Political Papers Webster, Noah. *A Collection of Papers on Political, Literary and Moral Subjects.* New York, 1843. Reprint. New York: Burt Franklin, 1968.

Wharton Wharton, Francis, ed. *The Revolutionary Diplomatic Correspondence of the United States.* 6 vols. Washington, D.C.: Government Printing Office, 1889.

Wilson, Works *The Works of James Wilson.* Edited by Robert Green McCloskey. 2 vols. Cambridge: Belknap Press of Harvard University Press, 1967.

Winthrop Winthrop, John. *The History of New England from 1630 to 1649.* Edited by James Savage. 2 vols. Boston: Little, Brown & Co., 1853.

Woodhouse Woodhouse, A. S. P., ed. *Puritanism and Liberty, Being the Army Debates (1647–9) from the Clarke Manuscripts with Supplementary Documents.* 2d ed. London: J. M. Dent & Sons Ltd., 1951.

Index of Constitutional Provisions

Table of Cases

Index of Authors and Documents

References are to chapter or to constitutional section, and to document number. References to volume 1 are by chapter and document number (e.g., ch. 15, no. 23); references to constitutional provisions in volumes 2–4 are by article, section, clause, and document number (e.g., 1.8.8, no. 12); and references to volume 5 are by Amendment and document number (e.g., Amend. I [religion], no. 66). In the case of documents whose several clauses are ranged under a large number of headings (e.g., the Bill of Rights of 1689, the Massachusetts Constitution of 1780, and the like), reference is made only to appearances of the complete text.